State, Economy, and Society in Western Europe 1815 – 1975
Volume II

State, Economy, and Society in Western Europe 1815 – 1975

A Data Handbook in two Volumes

Peter Flora

Franz Kraus and Winfried Pfenning

Volume II

The Growth of Industrial Societies and
Capitalist Economies

Campus Verlag · Frankfurt
Macmillan Press · London
St. James Press · Chicago

1987

International Standard Book Numbers:

Campus Verlag, Vol. 1   3-593-33138-1
              Vol. 2   3-593-33139-X

Macmillan Press, Vol. 1   0-333-35943-7
                Vol. 2   0-333-35944-5

St. James Press, Vol. 1   0-912289-00-7
                Vol. 2   0-912289-06-6

VOLUME II

The Growth of Industrial Societies and Capitalist Economies

VOLUME I

The Growth of Mass Democracies and Welfare States

PREFACE

Tempus fugit. When I finished the preface to the first volume of our handbook in 1982, it was summer and I was still living in Florence. The magic of Tuscany may have deluded my mind. I thought that we would be able to finish the second volume within a year. We were not. It is now almost Christmas in the winter of 1985. I am surviving in Mannheim, and Tuscany's magic has long since disappeared in the cisalpine clouds. Is there a convincing explanation for this delay which caused our publisher so much despair? There is none, at least I can't find one, or there are too many.

Among the many reason, the most important was the decision by Franz Kraus and Winfried Pfenning to establish a completely new data collection on the structural change of the labour force, based on more than a hundred population and occupational census. This great endeavour was only the last step in raising their former status of near slavery in the first volume to full authorship in the second. However, their merits go far beyond this.

Franz Kraus was also responsible for the two chapters on the growth, origin and use of national product, which he finished more than five years ago. Furthermore, and this will be his *opus magnum*, he has created a unique collection of historical data on income distribution drawn from tax statistics. The chapter in this volume contains only a part of this collection. An analysis of the whole data set will be published in 1986 as a separate study within the series 'European Social Science Studies' at Campus Verlag.

Winfried Pfenning was responsible for the chapter on labour disputes (which he finished), as well as the chapter on trade unions (which he did not finish). He deserted academia for commercial market research in the summer of 1985, I can't blame him. A completion of his chapter on trade union development would have held up the publication of the second volume for at least another six months. Therefore, we decided to drop it. This is unfortunate, not only for reasons of substance, but also for reasons of symmetry. The second volume now has only nine chapters instead of ten.

However, one must do Winfried Pfenning justice. He was responsible for the computerization of our data sets and laid the basis of the machine-readable documentations. For three years this work was funded by the Stiftung Volkswagenwerk. Once again, I take the opportunity to thank the foundation for its manifold support of our projects. I also extend my thanks to the students who assisted Winfried Pfenning when he worked at the Zentralarchiv in Cologne: Sofia Bengel, Irene Bolz, Hannelore Burmann, Annekatrin Gehring, Rolf Knepperges and Sabine Rest.

The first four chapters have a long and confusing history. Parts of them were finished successively in Mannheim (1973–76), Cologne (1976–79), Florence and Cologne (1979–82) and again in Mannheim (1982–85). All those who have made contributions to the earlier phases have been credited in the preface to the first volume. Here I should mention again Kurt Seebohm who has contributed much to the data collection on population and family movements. And I should also again thank the central archive of the ICPSR at Ann Arbor for helping us in the computerization of our complex tables on population structure, a work which was largely completed in Cologne (1979–82).

In the last years in Mannheim, a whole battalion of students has worked on the completion of the chapters on urbanization and housing, the labour force and labour disputes. I would like to thank Bernhard Ebbinghaus, Katrin Behagel, Reinhard Goehrtz, Thomas Huber, Uwe Keil, Klaus Mayer, Klaus Overhoff, Elmar Rieger, Michael Schönemann, and Siegbert Sussek (who also made the graphs). I am most indebted to the two Ursulas who typed most of the tables, Ursula Nocentini at the European University Institute and Ursula Rossi at the University of Mannheim. Last not least, I wish to thank Margaret Herden for her attempt to split unreadable German sentences into more comprehensible English phrases.

Let me finish with a sigh of relief and an oath: NEVER AGAIN!

Peter Flora

Mannheim, Christmas 1985

The two volumes of the handbook

The structure and contents of the first volume of this historical data handbook are closely related to Stein Rokkan's macro-model of Europe in which he tried to develop a systematic account of the major variations among the European nation-states. Of the four phases of political development which he distinguished, *the growth of mass democracies and welfare states* form the core of the first volume. Due to limitations of available data, the other two processes of state formation and nation-building, which in the European context predated the institutionalization of political and social rights, are dealt with to a far lesser extent.

That political development in Europe would lead to a system of nation-states was not evident at the beginning. If one follows Charles Tilly (1975), then the nation-state represented only one of five possible paths of development in the thirteenth century; the others being the persistence of feudalism, the evolution of an embracive trading network, and the creation of a political or a theocratic empire.

Today, we know of course that the nation-state finally triumphed: a relatively centralized political system with a consolidated territory, differentiated political structures and a monopoly of the legitimate use of force. It triumphed for several reasons. Most important were probably the political fragmentation of Europe and the openness of her periphery, but also early capitalism, the growth of cities, commerce and manufacturing, which offered the resources for centre building and state formation.

It took some time, howerver, to triumph; at least until his sixteenth century when the Hapsburgh failed to consolidate their empire. According to Wallerstein (1974), this failure was an essential precondition for the emergence of a capitalist world-economy which none of the emerging nation-states could control.

A world-economy, in Wallerstein's understanding, is one of two types of world-system which he defines in terms of a relatively closed division of labour and plurality of cultural systems. In contrast to a politically unified world-empire, a world-economy embraces several political systems. In a capitalist world-economy, production is predominantly oriented towards market exchange, and profit becomes the driving force in quantitative expansion and qualitative improvement. It is furthermore characterized by labour becoming a 'commodity', i.e. by the extension of a labour market, in contrast to a system in which the owners are mainly small farmers and artisans.

What one today calls modernization, started in Europe in the context of an international system of nation-states and a capitalist world-economy. This framework has shaped the European development, and with Europe's expansion it has left its imprint on other world regions. Thus the nation-state, although hardly achieved anywhere, is still the predominant model of political development. And the position of the newly independent states in the international division of labour — a structure of dependence and inequality — sets limits to the options open for national development.

At the same time, however, we have learned today that there are more paths to modernity, more ways to build industrial and urban societies, than those suggested by European experience. 'Capitalist development' or even 'capitalist-democratic development' is only one form of modernization, and history has certainly not yet exhausted the combinatorics of modern institutions. Beyond the variations in basic political and economic institutions, however, all modern or modernizing societies share many fundamental characteristics. This combination of uniformity and variety is expressed by the title of the second volume of the handbook *'The growth of industrial societies and capitalist economies'*.

When Tocqueville wanted to know more about the future of France he went to study American democracy. When Marx wished to understand more about the future of Germany he began to study English industrial capitalism. They could do this only because both of them had concepts of a *general* development, different as these were. But Tocqueville was a little more prudent. Not only was he aware of the unique features of American democracy, he also conceived of alternative developments of democracy, pluralistic and totalitarian as we would call them today. Marx, on the other hand, cared less about the unique features of English capitalism, and he did not conceive of forms of non-bourgeois or even non-capitalist industrialization.

Marx' reliance on England as exemplifying capitalism made him underestimate the role of the state in capitalist development. His conception of capitalism as a general and necessary stage of development gave him no reason to distinguish between 'capitalism' and 'industrialism'. Marx was primarily interested in the class character of capitalist societies, based on the institutions of private property and wage labour; and he was interested in the logic of capitalist development, as shown in the process of capital accumulation and endemic crises of overproduction. From this point of view 'industrialism' is important only insofar as the existence of a capitalist society presupposes a high level of industrialization.

The reverse, however, does not hold true. For this we should not blame Marx too much, because at the time when he was writing there was no example of non-capitalist industrialization. Even after the Russian Revolution and the accelerated industrialization of Russia in the 1930s, it took a long time until a clear distinction was drawn, first perhaps by Raymond Aron in his famous lectures on the industrial society of 1955 (1962). For Aron 'industrial society' is the general type of modern society, and he distinguishes subtypes by the form of ownership of the means of production and by the basic allocation mechanism. Accordingly, predominantly private ownership, wage labour and the division between employers and employees, profit orientation as crucial momentum, and decentralized allocation via the market, are the essential characteristics of 'capitalist societies'. To these Aron adds the openness of the national economy vis-a-vis the world economy with the resulting pressures of adaptation, the decisive influence of consumer decisions on the distribution of resources, and the existence of free trade unions.

These capitalist societies share, however, certain features with other industrial societies. Aron emphasizes above all the accumulation of capital and the concentration of the workforce, the high level of economic rationality, the extended division of labour within enterprises, and the separation of family and workplace. He also mentions the expansion of formal education, the importance of science and technology, the bureaucratization of production, the increase of dependent labour, and the regulation of work and work life. In this sense 'industrialization' has a standardizing impact on the social structure of modern societies, although differences in class structures and other aspects clearly persist. This limited convergence with respect to social structure, however, does not in Aron's view imply a convergence in politics, of democracy and dictatorship.

After Aron, and mainly under the influence of American sociology, the concepts of industrial society' and 'industrialization' were largely replaced by 'modern society' and 'modernization'. This was necessary, although it has not contributed much to the clarification of concepts. It was necessary, because the broad changes which European societies underwent for more than two hundred years and which other societies undergo today, cannot merely be interpreted as preconditions, implications or consequences of industrialization in a stricter sense. It has created conceptual confusion, because for a long time the uniformities of the modernization process were overstressed. This led to a neglect of the alternative paths to modernity which spring from differences in inherited institutions as well as from changing external conditions.

The vital revolution and demographic transition

The secular increase of Europe's population from the second quarter of the eigtheenth century was a revolution, but not a completely new phenomenon. In fact it represented the third major upswing in European population history, the first extending from the middle of the eleventh to the end of the thirteenth century, and the second from the middle of the fifteenth to the end of the sixteenth century. The third upswing was initially caused by a release from the population constraints associated with war and epidemic, and by considerable improvements in agricultural production and commerce.

Although population increase predated the Industrial Revolution in a stricter sense, it was this later process which transformed the third upswing into the Vital Revolution. This time the upward movement not only started from a higher level, but it was able to maintain, and for some time even to increase its momentum. Unlike the previous upswings, population growth was not terminated or reversed by catastrophes but was eventually slowed down by a change of the basic 'generative structure'.

The demographic revolution was broadly synchronized with the spread of industrialization and the shift from rural to urban life. In the nineteenth century improvements in the quality of food, shelter, clothing, water supply and sanitation gradually brought about a reduction in death rates, this reduction being accelerated after 1900 when modern medical science began more systematically to contain infectious disease and reduce infant mortality. This decline in death rates outweighed the usually later decline in birth rates, giving rise to a population surge which culminated in the period from the late nineteenth century to World War I.

In most instances fertility had already begun to decline in the nineteenth century and showed an irregular but generally downward trend from the turn of the century. Upsurges in birth rates after 1918, in the late 1930s, and after 1945 did little more than compensate in some measure for birth deficits associated with war and depression. For the first time, during the depression of the 1930s net reproduction rates (which measure the future reproduction of the population on the basis of the current rates of fertility and mortality) fell below the level of 1.00. After World War II, however, there was a widespread increase of birth rates, and it was not until the 1960s that they started to decline again, bringing net reproduction rates to even lower levels.

Europe's demographic development has formed the empirical basis for a generalized 'theory of demographic transition' which essentially states:

1. Pre-industrial societies are characterized by high levels both of fertility and mortality. Because of high fertility populations are young and because of high mortality population increase is small. Fertility generally is higher than mortality, but population growth is frequently checked by catastrophic mortality. This is due to the extreme vulnerability of pre-industrial societies to calamities of all sorts which makes epidemics in particular a regulatory device.
2. Fully industrialized and urbanized societies instead are characterized by low levels both of fertility and mortality. Because of low fertility populations are old and population increase is small or even negative. Due to the higher adaptive capacities of these societies mortality fluctuates only moderately whereas fertility is more volatile.
3. The demographic transition from high to low levels of fertility and mortality is characterized by a time-lag between the decline of mortality and the decline of fertility. This produces a high rate of natural population increase as a transient phenomenon. The reason for this time-lag is assumed to be that industrialization has a more immediate impact on mortality whereas a decline of fertility requires far more complex changes in social structure which ultimately are also produced by the process of modernization.

In terms of this simplified model one can specify some features of the demographic transition which are peculiar to Europe in comparison to the late-comers among the modernizing countries: a much slower and more gradual decline of mortality because of the later impact of modern medicine; a generally lower fertility because of a specific 'European marriage pattern'; as a consequence, a comparatively lower natural increase of population with demographic pressures further eased by the exceptional opportunity of intercontinental migration (between 1846 and 1932, according to Carr-Saunders (1936), more than 50 million Europeans emigrated overseas).

The first and last features speak for themselves, but the second needs some explanation. There is a distinctively (North-Western) European marriage pattern which can be traced back to the seventeenth century and which existed up to World War II. Its distinctive marks are (a) an advanced age at marriage and (b) a high proportion of people who never married (Hajnal 1965). This pattern was related to a specific household system in which the great majority of households were nuclear-family households which did not contain relatives, but which included life-cycle servants (i.e. young women and men who lived in the household of their masters).

Malthus thought that late marriage in Europe resulted in lower birth rates, as one of the 'positive' or 'negative' checks which would appear when population transcends its 'optimum size' and approaches a certain 'ceiling'. His model of development was formulated in terms of fixed land and population growth. Whereas the 'passion between the sexes' makes population grow in 'geometrical progression', food supply only increases 'arithmetically'. With the supply of free land exhausted, the law of diminishing returns leads to a decline in labour's marginal product. This means a fall in living standards which in turn produces the above checks to population growth.

Ironically, Malthus, bound to traditional Europe, developed his gloomy futurology at a time when the technological process was beginning to invalidate the law of dimishing returns by constantly raising labour's productivity. Thus, by contrast with Malthus' theory of stagnation, Kuznets (1966), the great pioneer in the development of historical national accounting systems, regards population and economic growth as being closely related. He understands modern economic growth as a sustained increase in per capita or per worker product, most often accompanied by an increase in population and usually by sweeping structural changes.

The urban and industrial revolutions

Modern economic growth, according to Kuznets, is characterized by rates of increase in per capita product which range from less than 15 to about 30 percent per decade. Assuming a rate of population growth of about 10 percent per decade, this means an enormous growth of total output ranging from 20 to close to 50 percent per decade.

Sustained economic growth of these proportions was only made possible by the Industrial Revolution, the most dramatic of all revolutions in world history. In a narrow sense, the Industrial Revolution was a process by which societies accuired control over vast sources of inanimate energy. But such a definition does not do justice to the complex economic, social, political and cultural implications of this phenomenon. Kuznets therefore stresses that the rate of increase in per capita product was not primarily due to quantity of input, but to improvements in quality, i.e. increases in useful knowledge and better institutional arrangements for its utilization. Furthermore, the growth in efficiency was not only rapid but also pervasive. This means that the industrial revolution was preceded and accompanied by an agricultural revolution and by a striking increase in the capacity of transportation and communication.

The Industrial Revolution occurred in England because of a specific constellation of historical circumstances, and from England it soon spread to the rest of Europe. By 1850 is had penetrated into Belgium, France, Germany, and Switzerland; by 1900 it had extended to Northern Italy and Scandinavia. Until the entry of Japan in the late nineteenth century, followed by the U.S.S.R. in the 1930s, modern economic growth was concentrated in the European countries and their offshoots overseas. In these countries per capita incomes were well above the average even before industrialization.

The Industrial Revolution gave Europe a tremendous advantage over the rest of the world, founding its world-wide predominance in the nineteenth century. But even within Europe, the different timing of industrialization or of the economic take-off as W. W. Rostow has called it, meant great inequalities in the rate of aggregate growth which often cumulated in marked shifts in relative economic and political power among the European nations.

Beyond the creation of new inequalities between countries, however, modern economic growth in general strengthened the interdependence between nations, in terms of the international flow of men, goods and capital. This is especially true for the period from the second quarter of the nineteenth century up to 1914. World War I radically changed these international flows. International migration has never resumed pre-1914 levels, whereas the flow of goods and capital did, but only after World War II.

Internally, modern economic growth produced a basic transformation of social structure. Two broad changes were especially important: the marked and rapid changes in industry, status and occupational structures of the labour force; and the great increase of mobility in its various forms, the occupational shifts within and between generations and the considerable migration within countries, urbanization being the most important form.

Urbanization is not the same as urban growth. Cities have a history of almost ten thousand years which is closely related to the creation of large political structures, the growth of great religious cults, and the expansion of trade. Urbanization, on the other hand, is a much more recent phenomenon. In its simplest ecological meaning it is an increase in the proportion of the total population of an area which is living in cities. Before the Industrial Revolution there was no country with much more than a tenth of its population living in cities, and few cities had more than a million people. Up to the mid-nineteenth century no society could be described as predominantly urbanized.

It is a curious fact that urbanized societies arose in a region, North-West Europe, which had not given rise to the major cities of the past. However, this region has given birth from the tenth and twelfth centuries onwards to a unique form of city. The cities of Medieval and Renaissance Europe had something essentially different from towns in other world regions. They were autonomous organisms, clearly separated from the surrounding countryside, the core of new social and political structures, of a new culture and a new economy.

At a certain point, however, these cities, founded on guilds and corporations, became an obstacle for an inter-urban restructuring of economic life. Thus, the current wave of urbanization started much later, around 1700, with the emergence of national states and the extension of the capitalist world economy. It developed into a truly revolutionary process through its connection with the later industrialization.

Industrial urbanization differs from other forms of urbanization not only in terms of pace, scale and thoroughness, but also in quality. It does not produce a city structure as a specific social form. The city instead tends to loose its different structural and cultural characteristics: it tends to coincide with global society. This is mainly due to the technological implications of the increasing division of labour. These have centralizing as well as decentralizing consequences, leading to urban concentration as well as geographical diffusion.

Modern urbanization thus is best understood in terms of its connection with economic growth. As Kingsley Davis (1974) has put it, urbanization is a finite cycle through which nations go in their transition from agrarian to industrial society and which can be represented by a curve in the shape of an attenuated S. However, even if this curve is similar for all modernizing countries, in comparison to the latecomers, urbanization in Europe had at least two specific marks: its pace was much slower and its connection with industrialization much closer.

Until the nineteenth century, Europe was agricultural and rural. Within a century it became industrial and urban. This long-term transformation is often described in terms of a sequence of different types of societies: a traditional society in which agrarian work predominates, an industrial society characterized by manufacturing, a post-industrial society in which service work prevails. Clark and Fisher were the first to analyze this development in terms of a sectoral change of the labour force. Somewhat later Jean Fourastié (1963) tried to incorporate these changes into a broader concept of a transitional period between a stable 'primary civilization' of the past and a stable 'tertiary civilization' of the future.

It is technological progress which destroys the traditional balance. It increases the productivity of capital and labour, but these productivity gains vary among economic sectors (being high in the 'secondary', medium in the 'primary', and low in the 'tertiary' sector). Because the elasticity of demand also varies among sectors (being low in the 'primary', medium in the 'secondary', and high in the 'tertiary' sector), intersectoral differences in productivity increases lead to a change in the structure of demand, and thus to a change in the structure of production, and ultimately to a change in the structure of employment.

Given these intersectoral differences, technological progress, according to Fourastié, produces the following:

— a steady decline of employment in the primary sector, essentially agriculture, in form of an inverted attenuated S, from almost 80 percent to maybe less than 5 percent;
— a steady increase of employment in the tertiary sector, basically all varieties of services, in a kind of mirror-image of the decline of agricultural employment;
— a transient increase in industrial employment, starting slowly, then accelerating in the 'expansion period' up to a maximum of say 50 percent, after which it begins to decline again, flattening out at the end at a much lower level.

The transitional period therefore is marked by the rise of industry to predominance, and by its subsequent relative decline. For Fourastié, this is a period of economic, political and social instability. The traditional crises of agricultural underproduction are replaced by crises of industrial overproduction with recurrent mass unemployment. The rapid and thorough changes in the structure of the labour force generate anomie, lead to a mobilization of large population groups, and create political conflicts and crises.

In a recent work, however, Hartmut Kaelble (1983) has shown that a pronounced period of industrial society can only be found in Europe. The modernization of advanced non-European societies was characterized instead by a direct transition from an agrarian to a service society. Only in Europe was industrial work the most dynamic sector of employment from the nineteenth century until recently, and even now the move towards a service society seems to be less marked than abroad. The explanation which Kaelble offers for this

— once more — unique European development lies, above all, in the high exportation of manufactured goods from Europe to the world market and in the labour intensive industrialization of Europe. The longstanding predominance of a large and homogeneous industrial working class has certainly contributed a great deal to the interpretation of European modernization as the emergence of class society.

The rise and subsidence of class society

One can define class in such a generic way that the term applies to all societies in human history which have surpassed the subsistence level and have a certain division of labour. In these societies the control of the means of production may be crucial in the structuring of social inequality. It seems more useful, however, to interpret class society as a modern phenomenon which emerged in Europe from the ruins of feudalism. The extension of markets in general and of the labour market in particular, was a precondition for the emergence of class society. Capitalism had to destroy the legally sanctioned differentiation between estates, the feudal bonds and personalized ties of fealty, and the relatively self-sufficient character of local communities.

In this perspective, class society is something essentially different from estate society. It is founded upon the differentiation of two institutional spheres, commerce and industry on the one hand and the state on the other, thus breaking up the old fusion of economic and political power. Classes are defined as large-scale (national or even international) groupings of nominally free persons who have a common relation to the means of production, and occupy a similar position in the division of labour and market exchange. They do not necessarily have a sense of identity, a common class consciousness or class organization.

Our understanding of the long-term change of class structures has been shaped again and again by the arguments of, with, and about Marx. This is not the place to repeat — yet again — his basic ideas. In one way he had a very clear view of the future development, namely that capitalism would lead to a concentration of productive capital in the hands of fewer people and that the share of dependent work would steadily increase. In another way, however, he was rather misled, namely that in the long run capitalist development would produce a much more simpified class structure and an increasingly clear-cut and overt class conflict. The contrary is true: today, the class structure is more complex than ever, and class conflict has become more diffuse and simultaneously more institutionalized.

In order to overcome sterile disputes about the existence of class society, Anthony Giddens (1973) has suggested that we speak about types and levels of class structuration, an idea derived from Weber's class analysis. For Weber a class structure is a specific form of social inequality in which life chances are essentially determined by market position. In this sense market position is class position. There can be a great variety of different market positions and therefore a plurality of classes, the two most important dimensions being property (ownership classes) and qualification (acquisition classes). The whole spectrum of classes may be more or less structured, according to Weber, depending on the extent of inter-class mobility. Class structuring will also depend, Giddens adds, on the typical division of labour and the authority structure in enterprises as well as on differentiations in the sphere of consumption.

The complexity of this concept emphasizes the difficulties involved in a systematic empirical analysis of the long-term change of class structuration in the process of industrialization. Especially as regards the distribution of property, social mobility, work and authority relationships in enterprises or consumption patterns, one has to rely mainly on case studies which never give a complete picture.

To some extent this is also true for the distribution of educational and vocational qualifications among the population, although in this case one can use — at least indirectly — the available information on the evolution of the national education systems. There can be little doubt that the extension of secondary and higher education has changed the form and extent of class structuration: by the upgrading of market capacities — in the form of 'human capital' — of broader population groups on the one hand, and by creating greater differences among the employed labour force on the other.

In principle, both tendencies must be reflected in the distribution of income, strengthening the middle income strata and differentiating income from dependent work. We certainly do not know enough about long-term changes in income inequality at the national level, as our information is dependent upon the — relatively late — introduction of national income taxation. Some broad trends, however, seem to be confirmed by existing studies (Kraus 1981). Changes in the top income strata seem to have been decisive for the trend in overall income inequality. The relative decline of top incomes appears to have been a general development, starting perhaps in the late nineteenth century and being most evident during both world wars. It is probable that all other income groups have gained to some extent from this relative decline, but the middle groups seem to have profited the most.

European societies have become less class structured because market positions seem to be more differentiated and market capacities more continuously distributed. They are also less class structured in the sense that today individual life chances are less determined by market position. Material welfare is much less dependent on market income. Direct and indirect taxes, transfer payments, and the provision of public services have clearly reduced the importance of wages and assets in determining economic status.

It is not unlikely that the initial phase of European industrialization was marked by an increasing class structuration (Kaelble 1983). But since the turn of the century this — real or presumed — trend has been reversed. The long-term process of class de-structuration has been paralled by an increasing organization and institutionalization of class conflict. In a very broad sense, this refers to the evolution of mass democracies which has frequently been interpreted as an institutionalization of class conflict, leading to the creation of welfare states. In a stricter sense, however, it refers to the establishment of trade unions and recognized forms of collective bargaining.

The trade unions, the second major pillar of the working class movement, developed throughout Europe as a product of the industrial revolution. However, the countries responded in very different ways to this general development. Reinhard Bendix (1964) has distinguished three broad types of policies. The Scandinavian and Swiss type can be characterized as a modernization of the traditional organization of crafts, allowing for a high degree of continuity and a low degree of repression. The absolutist type instead represented a major break with the traditions of liberty as a corporate privilege, leading to the repression of all sorts of associations. In the liberal type exemplified by England, workingmen's associations were also suppressed, but the right of association was preserved in other respects. Thus, the political and institutional frame work of trade union development greatly varied across Europe.

Trade unions were first organized by highly qualified groups in certain crafts with remnants of a 'guild spirit'. The raison d'être of these craft unions was not only to organize strike support, but also to provide social security on a mutual benefit basis and to monopolize qualified labour. The first national craft unions were established in the last third of the nineteenth century, and this process was largely concluded on the eve of World War I. The foundation of national trade union federations started at about the same time, culminating around the turn of the century.

The formation of industrial unions according to the principle of 'one establishment — one union' was a basic goal of national trade union federations everywhere, but the success with which the unions pursued this goal has greatly varied. To some extent, these variations are explained by differences in the early development of craft unions. This explains at least the major differences between the United Kingdom, Ireland and Scandinavia, where craft unionism still predominates, and the other countries where industrial unions were formed to a large extent. Some of the variations are also explained by later developments which have weakened the industry principle and furthered organization along status lines. The general change in the occupational structure, brought on by the growth of public and private bureaucracies and the emergence of new professions, has led to the formation of white-collar organizations in all countries, some dating back to the end of World War I. But again there are great variations in the form and the degree of the unionization of white-collar employees and civil servants.

Finally, one must also take into account the varying impact of rival political unionism on the structure of the trade union systems. Political cleavages were especially strong in the Catholic countries and the Protestant countries with a strong Catholic minority. Only in Austria and Germany, the cleavage between Catholic and socialist trade unions has been overcome. It persists in Belgium, France, Italy, the Netherlands and Swizerland, where unification attempts have largely failed. In several countries, the structure is further complicated by the varying splits between socialist and communist trade unions.

Differences in the organization of labour are closely tied to variatons in strike patterns. Over the last hundred years the form and frequency of strikes has profoundly changed. According to Edward Shorter and Charles Tilly (1974) three great changes have occurred in virtually all Western European countries:

— secular increase in the rate of conflict during the last quarter of the nineteenth century and the first quarter of the twentieth century, followed by a large-scale decline during the 1920s and the Depression;
— a secular decrease in the duration of conflict starting around the Great Depression, and continuing after the Second World War;
— an increase in participation in strikes, sometimes beginning during the Great Depression, sometimes beginning just after the Second World War.

The user of this handbook will be able to check these statements on the basis of the data given in the concluding chapter of the second volume. They will not be able, unfortunately, to analyse the relationships between changes in labour disputes and the development of the trade unions. The chapter on trade unions is missing for reasons explained in the preface.

The other chapters are structured according to the outline given in this introduction. The second volume starts with two chapters in Part VI both of which are related to the demographic transition. They are followed in Part VII by two chapters on the process of urbanization and the changing housing conditions. The two chapters of Part VIII then give the essential data on economic growth, i.e. on the growth of the national product, its changing origin and use. These are followed again in Part IX by two chapters on the most important concomitants of economic growth, a changing division of labour and a changing economic inequality.

References

Raymond Aron, *Dix-huit Leçons sur la Société Industrielle*. Paris, Gallimard, 1962.

Reinhard Bendix, *Nation-Building and Citizenship*. New York, Wiley, 1964.

A. M. Carr-Saunders, *World Population: Past Growth and Present Trends*. Oxford, Oxford University Press, 1936.

Kingsley Davis, 'The urbanization of the human population', pp. 160—177 in: Charles Tilly (ed.), *An Urban World*. Boston, Little, Brown and Company, 1974.

Jean Fourastié, *Le Grand Espoir du XXe Siècle*. Paris, Gallimard, 1963.

Anthony Giddens, *The Class Structure of the Advanced Societies*. London, Hutchinson, 1973.

J. Hajnal, 'The European marriage pattern in perspective', pp. 101—143 in: D. V. Glass and D. E. C. Eversley (eds), *Population in History, Essays in Historical Demography*. London, Edward Arnold, 1965.

Hartmut Kaelble, 'Was Prometheus most unbound in Europe?', *Journal of European History*, 14, 1985.

Franz Kraus, 'The historical development of income inequality in Western Europe and the United States', pp. 187—236 in: Peter Flora and Arnold J. Heidenheimer (eds), *The Development of Welfare States in Europe and America*. New Brunswick and London, Transaction Books, 1981.

Simon Kuznets, *Modern Economic Growth. Rate, Structure, and Spread*. New Haven and London, Yale University Press, 1966.

Edward Shorter and Charles Tilly, *Strikes in France 1830—1968*. Cambridge, Cambridge University Press, 1974.

Charles Tilly (ed.), *The Formation of National States in Western Europe*. Princeton, Princeton University Press, 1975.

Immanuel Wallerstein, *The Modern World-System. Capitalist Agriculture and the Origins of the European World-Economy in the Sixteenth Century*. New York, Academic Press, 1974.

VI

Population and Families

Chapter 1

POPULATION GROWTH

An analysis of the structure and change of larger populations requires that demographic data are collected in two ways. The first is a population census which is held at regular intervals, and the second is a continually operating vital registration system. In most European countries, these two instruments were developed in the nineteenth century, and in some countries they go back as far as the eighteenth century. Prior to this period one has to rely on more irregular and limited population counts, parish registers, or more indirect sources.

The earlier (e.g. Roman) 'censuses' were only partial population counts (heads of families, or that part of the population liable to taxation or military service), and must be supplemented by estimates of the non-enumerated portion of the total population. The first modern counts of total population were carried out in Renaissance Italy and Spain. Other European countries were relatively late in following suit: Norway in 1664 and 1701, Bohemia in 1702, Iceland in 1703, Austria in 1754, and Denmark in 1769. Sweden was the first country to institute a regular system of census taking in 1749. These, however, were not direct censuses but enumerations on the basis of population registers established at the same time. In 1790 the United States was the first to begin with a series of direct decennial censuses. Great Britain followed in 1801, and most European countries had adopted the practice by the mid-nineteenth century (see the following table).

The information recorded about each individual in a census varies from country to country and has been greatly extended over time. Only part of this collected information has been utilized for our handbook: Chapter 1 of this second volume presents data on the age and sex distribution of the population; chapter 2 on the civil status of the population by age and sex; and chapter 7 on the economically active population by industrial sector and occupational status. In the first volume of the handbook we presented census figures on total population and its distribution by nationality (chapter 1), and by religion, language, and literacy (chapter 2). Unless otherwise noted, these figures always refer to the *total resident population*.

The second main source of demographic data is the vital registration system, which normally includes marriages in addition to births and deaths. Here one must distinguish between ecclesiastical and civil registration. In some areas, parish registers kept by religious officials go back as far as the fourteenth century. In general, the recording of vital events received a strong impetus from the Reformation and Counter-Reformation with the attempt to register religious affiliation. The transformation of ecclesiastical into civil registration first took place in Northern Europe in the mid-eighteenth century. In most European countries civil registration started in the first half of the nineteenth century. In general, these civil registers (although not always beyond suspicion), are more reliable than their ecclesiastical predecessors.

A vital registration system allows us to study population change. Simple population change is divided into 'natural' changes (births and deaths), and 'mechanical' changes (emigration and immigration). The difference between births and deaths, commonly expressed per head of population, is called the natural increase (or decrease) of population. The well-known theory of demographic transition is formulated in terms of these three variables: the birth rate, the death rate, and the rate of natural increase of population. Chapter 1 therefore begins with a series of fifteen graphs which visualize the respective form of demographic transition for thirteen countries (the United Kingdom being subdivided into England and Wales, Scotland, and Ireland/Northern Ireland).

The statistics for these graphs are contained in the subsequent tables, in alphabetical order of countries. The three rates, expressed per thousand population, are based on the absolute figures of births, deaths and total population given there. In general, birth and death statistics are somewhat more reliable than total population figures. They are normally good for countries and periods with a need for birth and death certificates. Unless otherwise noted, total population figures refer to the *mid-year population*. Population figures (whether mid- or end-year) are usually calculated on the basis of the preceding population census, birth and

Dates of Population Censuses

Netherlands	Norway	Sweden	Switzerland	England and Wales	Scotland	Ireland/ Northern I.
	1- 2-1801	31-12-1800		10- 3-1801	10- 3-1801	
		31-12-1805				
		31-12-1810		27- 5-1811	17- 5-1811	
	30- 4-1815	31-12-1815				
		31-12-1820		28- 5-1821	28- 5-1821	28- 5-1821
	27-11-1825	31-12-1825				
1- 1-1830		31-12-1830		30- 5-1831	29- 5-1831	29- 5-1831
	29-11-1835	31-12-1835				
			1- 2-1837			
1- 1-1840		31-12-1840		7- 6-1841	7- 6-1841	7- 6-1841
	31-12-1845	31-12-1845				
19-11-1849		31-12-1850	18/23- 3-1850	31- 3-1851	31- 3-1851	30- 3-1851
	31-12-1855	31-12-1855				
31-12-1859		31-12-1860	10-12-1860	8- 4-1861	8- 4-1861	8- 4-1861
	31-12-1865					
1-12-1869		31-12-1870	1-12-1870	3- 4-1871	3- 4-1871	3- 4-1871
	31-12-1875					
31-12-1879		31-12-1880	1-12-1880	4- 4-1881	4- 4-1881	4- 4-1881
31-12-1889	31-12-1890	31-12-1890	1-12-1890	6- 4-1891	5- 4-1891	6- 4-1891
31-12-1899	3-12-1900	31-12-1900	1-12-1900	1- 4-1901	31- 3-1901	2- 4-1901
31-12-1909	1-12-1910	31-12-1910	1-12-1910	2- 4-1911	2- 4-1911	2- 4-1911
31-12-1920	1-12-1920	31-12-1920	1-12-1920	19- 6-1921	19- 6-1921	
						18- 4-1926
31-12-1930	1-12-1930	31-12-1930	1-12-1930	26- 4-1931	26- 4-1931	
		31-12-1935				26- 2-1937
		31-12-1940	1-12-1941			
	3-12-1946	31-12-1945				
31- 5-1947						
	1-12-1950	31-12-1950	1-12-1950	8- 4-1951	8- 4-1951	8- 4-1951
31- 5-1960	1-11-1960	1-11-1960	1-12-1960	23- 4-1961	23- 4-1961	23- 4-1961
		1-11-1965				9-10-1966
28- 2-1971	1-11-1970	1-11-1970	1-12-1970	25- 4-1971	25- 4-1971	25- 4-1971
		1-11-1975				

Austria	Belgium	Denmark	Finland	France	Germany	Ireland	Italy
		1- 2-1801	31-12-1800	1-1801			
			31-12-1805	1-1806			
			31-12-1810				
1- 1-1818			31-12-1815				
1- 1-1821			31-12-1820	8-1821		28- 5-1821	
1- 1-1824			31-12-1825				
1- 1-1827							
1- 1-1830			31-12-1830	5/6-1831		29- 5-1831	
1- 1-1834		18- 2-1834	31-12-1835	5/6-1836	12-1834		
1- 1-1837					12-1837		
1- 1-1840		1- 2-1840	31-12-1840	5/6-1841	12-1840	7- 6-1841	
1- 1-1843					12-1843		
1- 1-1846	15-10-1846	1- 2-1845	31-12-1845	6-1846	12-1846		
31-10-1850		1- 2-1850	31-12-1850	4/5-1851	12-1849	30- 3-1851	
					12-1852		
	31-12-1856	1- 2-1855	31-12-1855	5/6-1856	12-1855		
31-12-1857					12-1858		
		1- 2-1860	31-12-1860	5/6-1861	12-1861	8- 4-1861	31-12-1861
	31-12-1866		31-12-1865	4/5-1866	12-1864		
					12-1867		
31-12-1869		1- 2-1870	31-12-1870	6-1872	1-12-1871	3- 4-1871	31-12-1871
	31-12-1876		31-12-1875	11-12-1876	1-12-1875		
31-12-1880	31-12-1880	1- 2-1880	31-12-1880	18-12-1881	1-12-1880	4- 4-1881	31-12-1881
				30- 5-1886	1-12-1885		
31-12-1890	31-12-1890	1- 2-1890	31-12-1890	12- 4-1891	1-12-1890	6- 4-1891	
				29- 3-1896	2-12-1895		
31-12-1900	31-12-1900	1- 2-1901	31-12-1900	24- 3-1901	1-12-1900	2- 4-1901	9- 2-1901
		1- 2-1906		4- 3-1906	1-12-1905		
31-12-1910	31-12-1910	1- 2-1911	31-12-1910	5- 3-1911	1-12-1910	2- 4-1911	10- 6-1911
		1- 2-1916					
31- 1-1920	31-12-1920	1- 2-1921	31-12-1920	6- 3-1921			1-12-1921
7- 3-1923		5-11-1925		7- 3-1926	16- 6-1925	18- 4-1926	
	31-11-1930	5-11-1930	31-12-1930	8- 3-1931			21- 4-1931
22- 3-1934		5-11-1935		8- 3-1936	16- 6-1933	27- 4-1936	21- 4-1936
17- 5-1939		5-11-1940	31-12-1940		17- 5-1939	16-11-1941	
		15- 6-1945		10- 3-1946	29-10-1946		
10-1948	31-12-1947						
1- 6-1951		7-11-1950	31-12-1950		13- 9-1950	8- 4-1951	4-11-1951
		1-10-1955		10- 5-1954		8- 4-1956	
21- 3-1961	31-12-1961	26- 9-1960	31-12-1960	7- 3-1962	6- 6-1961	9- 4-1961	15-10-1961
		27- 9-1965				17- 4-1966	
12- 5-1971	31-10-1970	9-11-1970	31-12-1970	1- 3-1968	27- 5-1970	18- 4-1971	24-10-1971
				1- 3-1975			

death statistics, and estimates of net migration (numbers of immigrants less emigrants). In some countries changes of address are registered, but normally under-registration is high and migration figures are far more unreliable than birth and death statistics. Official population figures are usually corrected on the basis of new population censuses retrospectively for the whole preceding inter-census period. These figures have been used here unless othewise noted. In any case, errors in total population figures are of minor importance for birth and death *rates*, and consequently, for the rate of natural increase of population.

This is not true, however, for the population growth rate (defined here as the difference of total population in the years i and i—1, divided by the population in the year i—1, and multiplied by 1,000). It is obvious that errors in population estimates greatly influence this rate, as they do with respect to the net migration rate (here simply defined as the difference between the population growth rate and the rate of natural increase of population). The rates of both population growth and net migration should therefore be studied over a period of several years, and preferably for an entire intercensus period. Any interpretation of the net migration rates must furthermore take into account that the population growth rate refers to the change of *mid-year* population and the natural increase of population to the *calendar year*.

No attempt has been made to utilize statistics on emigration and immigration as these are generally rather unreliable and incomplete. More reliable statistics are only available for one prominent aspect of migration, the intercontinental emigration from Europe from the early nineteenth century until the 1930s. These can be found in A.M. Carr-Saunders' famous study (World Population: Past Growth and Present Trends, Oxford University Press, 1936), and are not reproduced here.

The calculation of crude birth and death rates is, of course, only a first and very simple step in describing the 'natural' change of population. For a more detailed analysis of the changes of fertility and mortality, these rates must be differentiated according to age, sex, marital status and other available criteria. More detailed fertility rates are given in chapter 2, in the form of a 'general marital fertility rate' (defined as the ratio of total legitimate births to total married female population aged 15—44 years), and the corresponding 'general non-marital fertility rate' (defined as the ratio of total illegitimate births to total non-married female population of the same age).

With respect to mortality, however, additional information is provided in chapter 1. The tables which contain the crude death rates also give infant mortality rates (defined as the ratio of total deaths under one year of age to total live births). Infant mortality statistics suffer from under-registration, at least in earlier times, and from varying delimitation between still-births and infant deaths. Thus, in order to improve international and intertemporal comparisons, the foetal death rate (defined as the ratio of total children who are still-born or who die within a specified period after birth to total live births) has been added, in separate form and aggregated with the infant mortality rate.

The infant mortality rate is of course only one, although the most prominent, age-specific death rate. A more complete picture of the development of mortality requires the establishment of population life tables which are based on a complete set of mortality rates (i.e. the probability of dying within a year after reaching a particular age). These life tables are used to calculate age-specific life expectancy — always assuming stable mortality patterns. These data are presented here after the tables with the time-series, first in the form of four comparative graphs and second in tabular form. Whereas the graphs illustrate the prolongation of life expectancy at birth for men and women in a comparison of all countries, the tables give life expectancy at various ages for each single country.

The changes in mortality as well as fertility have greatly transformed the age structure of the European populations. Therefore, the chapter concludes with a set of tables and graphs with data on the age distribution of total population, male and female population. For comparative reasons, these data are presented as relative and not as absolute figures.

The demographic transition

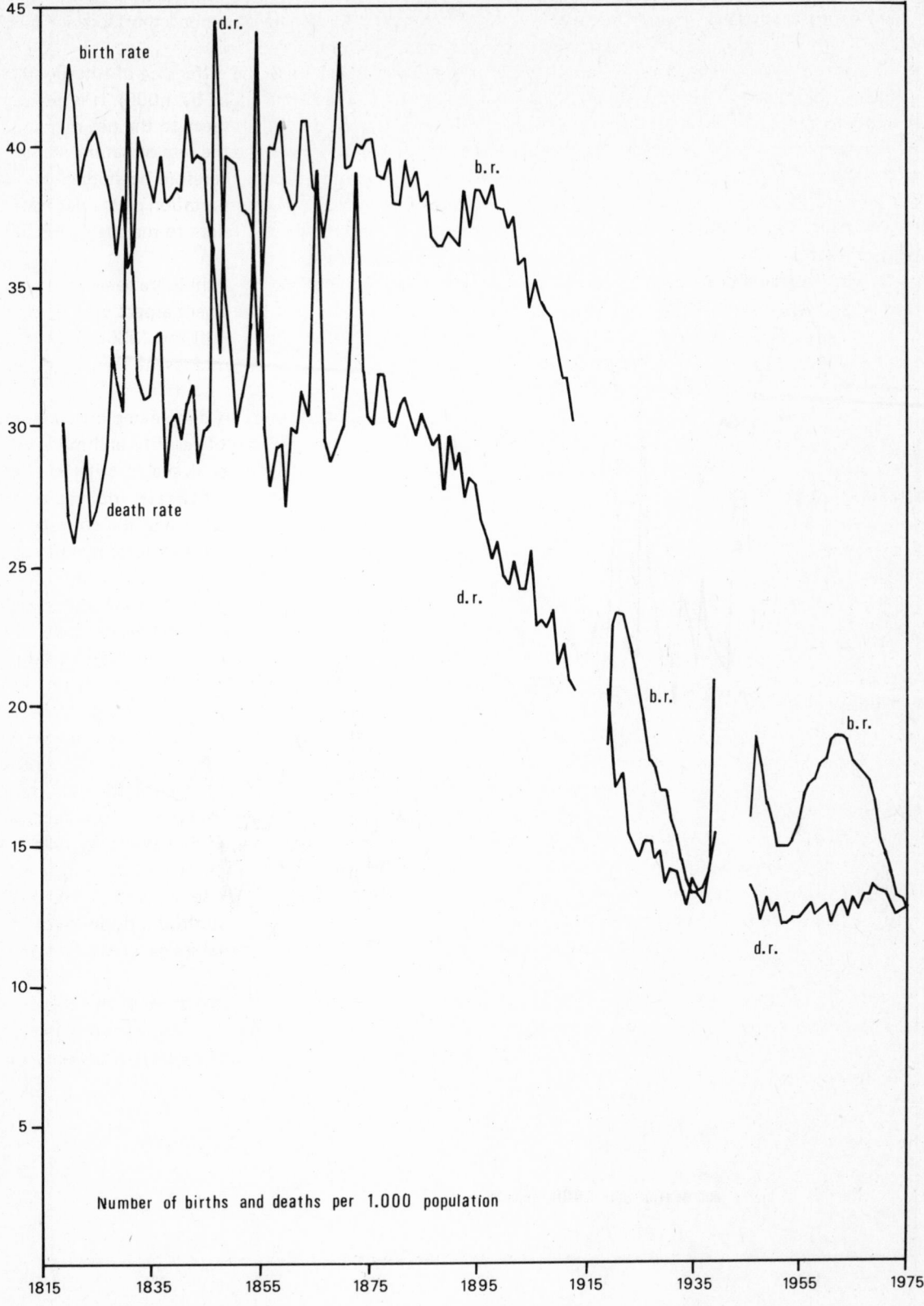

Number of births and deaths per 1.000 population

Belgium

The demographic transition

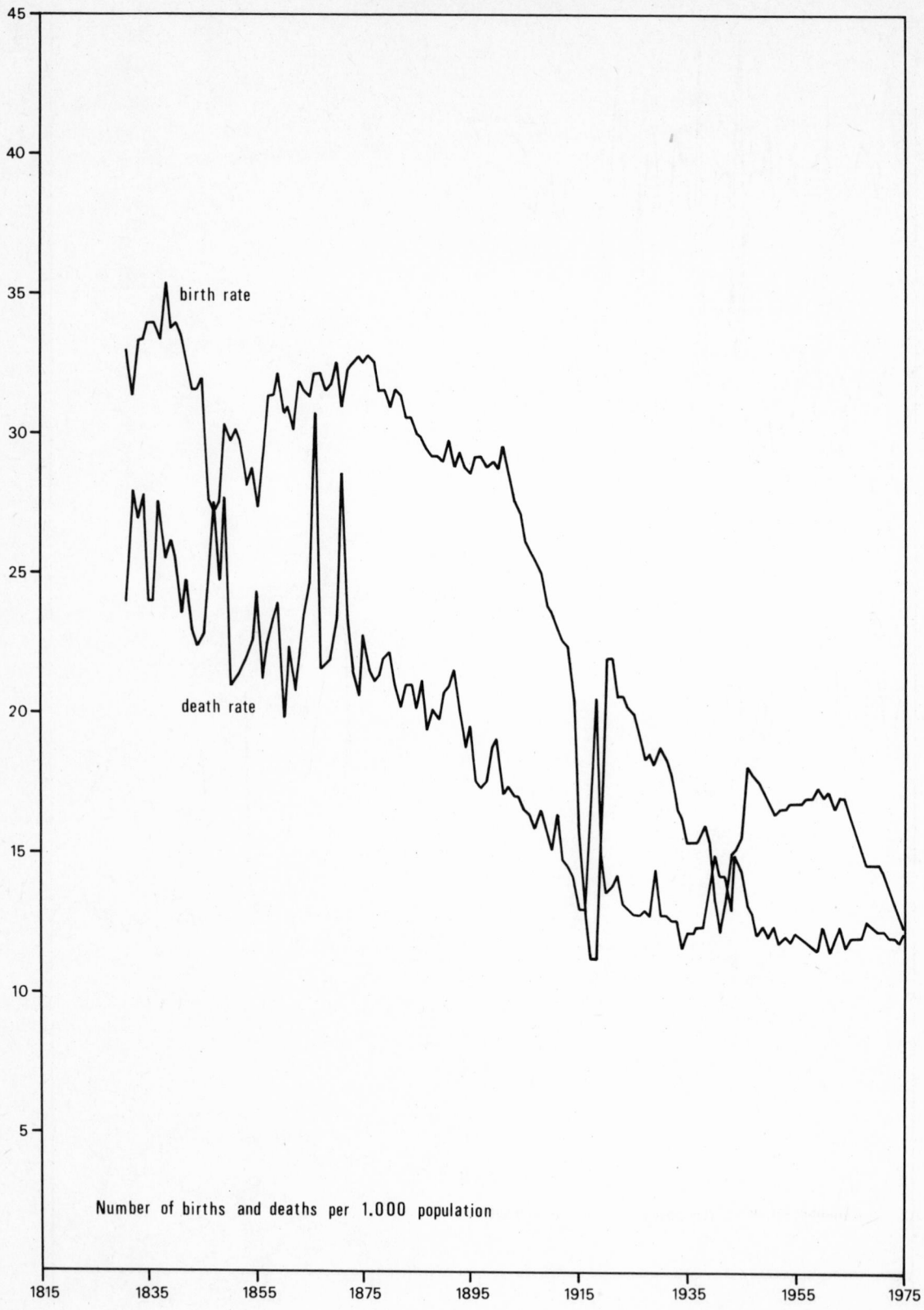

birth rate

death rate

Number of births and deaths per 1.000 population

22

Denmark

The demographic transition

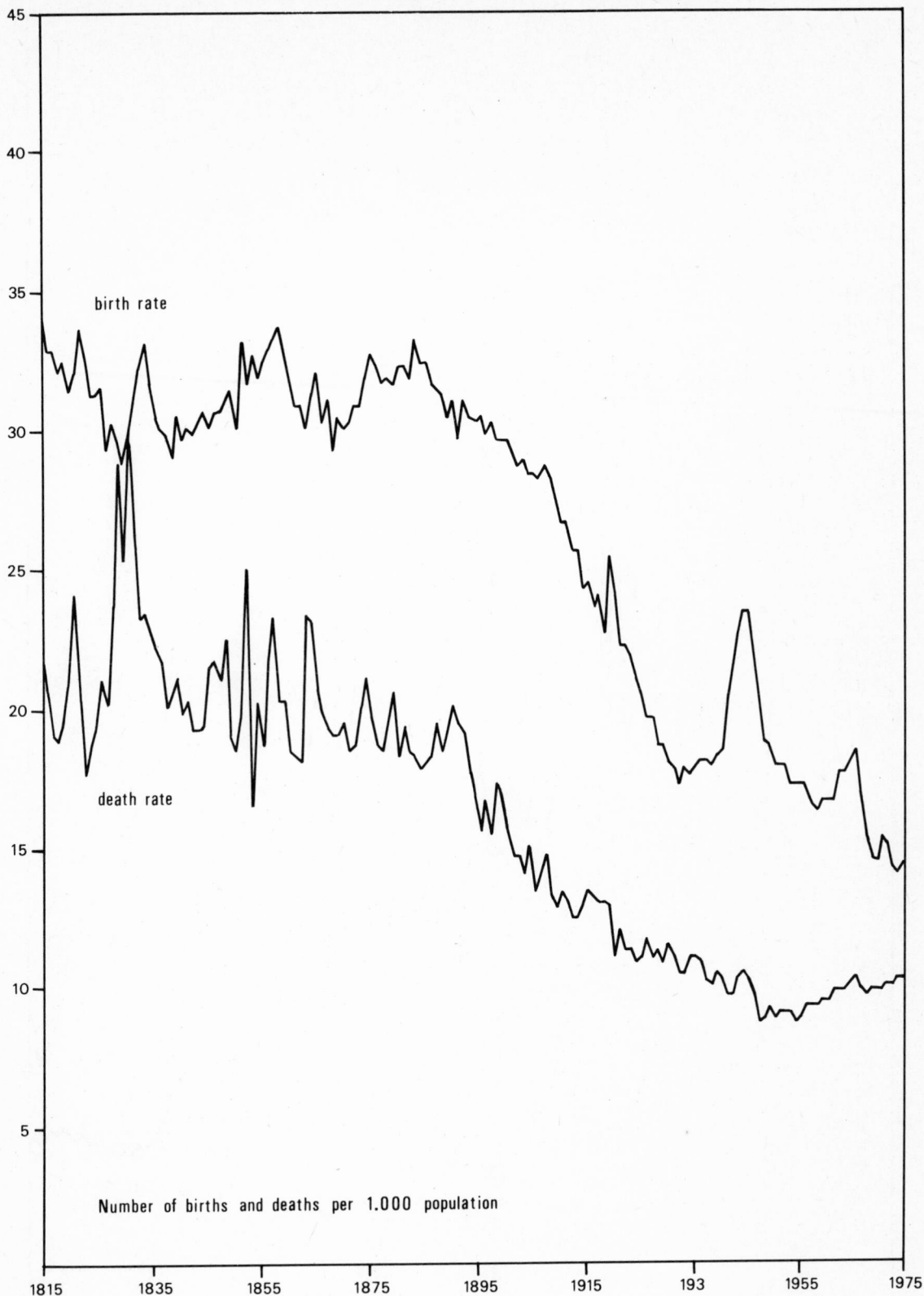

birth rate

death rate

Number of births and deaths per 1.000 population

Finland

The demographic transition

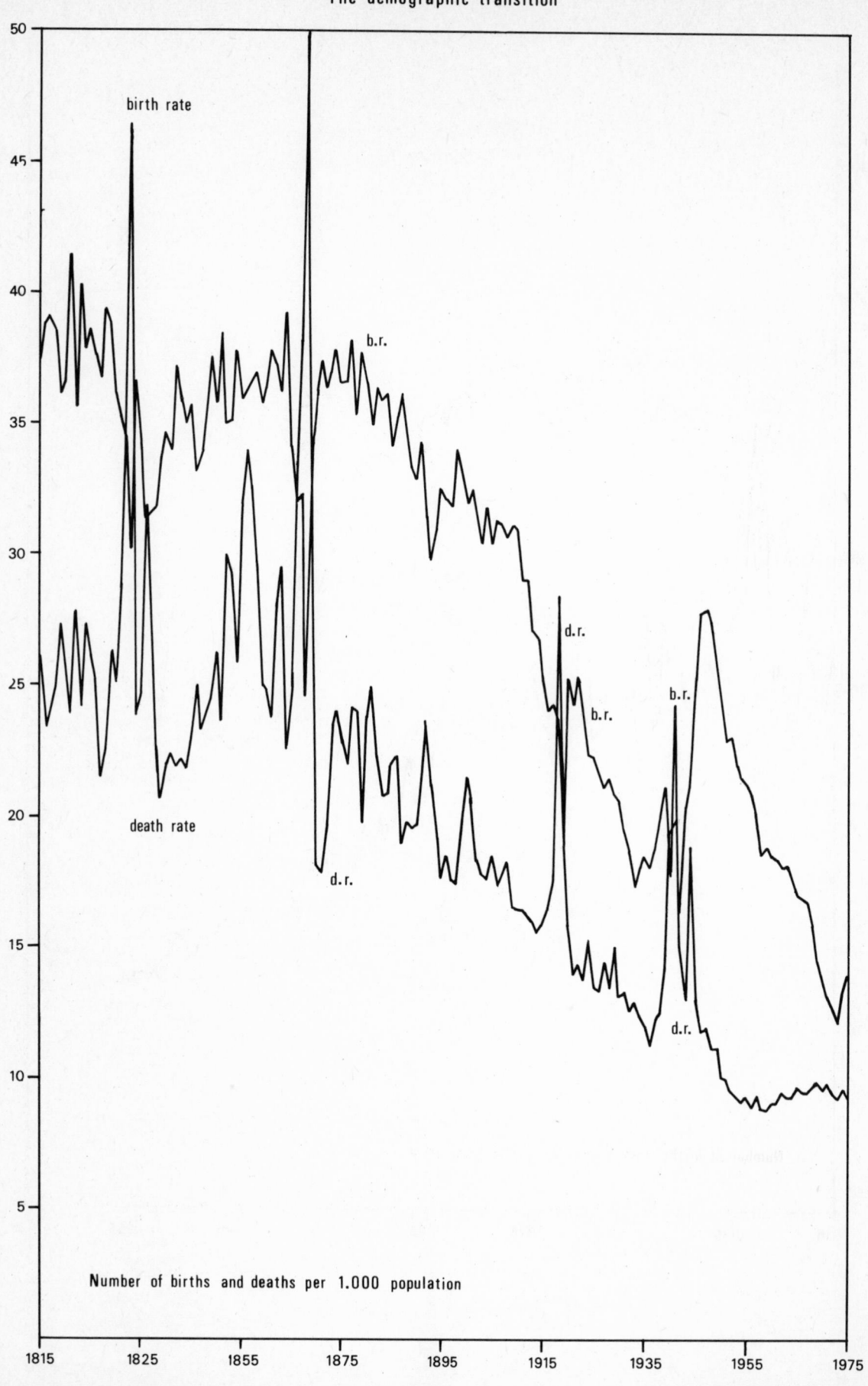

birth rate

b.r.

death rate

d.r.

d.r.

b.r.

d.r.

b.r.

d.r.

Number of births and deaths per 1.000 population

1815   1825   1855   1875   1895   1915   1935   1955   1975

24

F r a n c e

The demographic transition

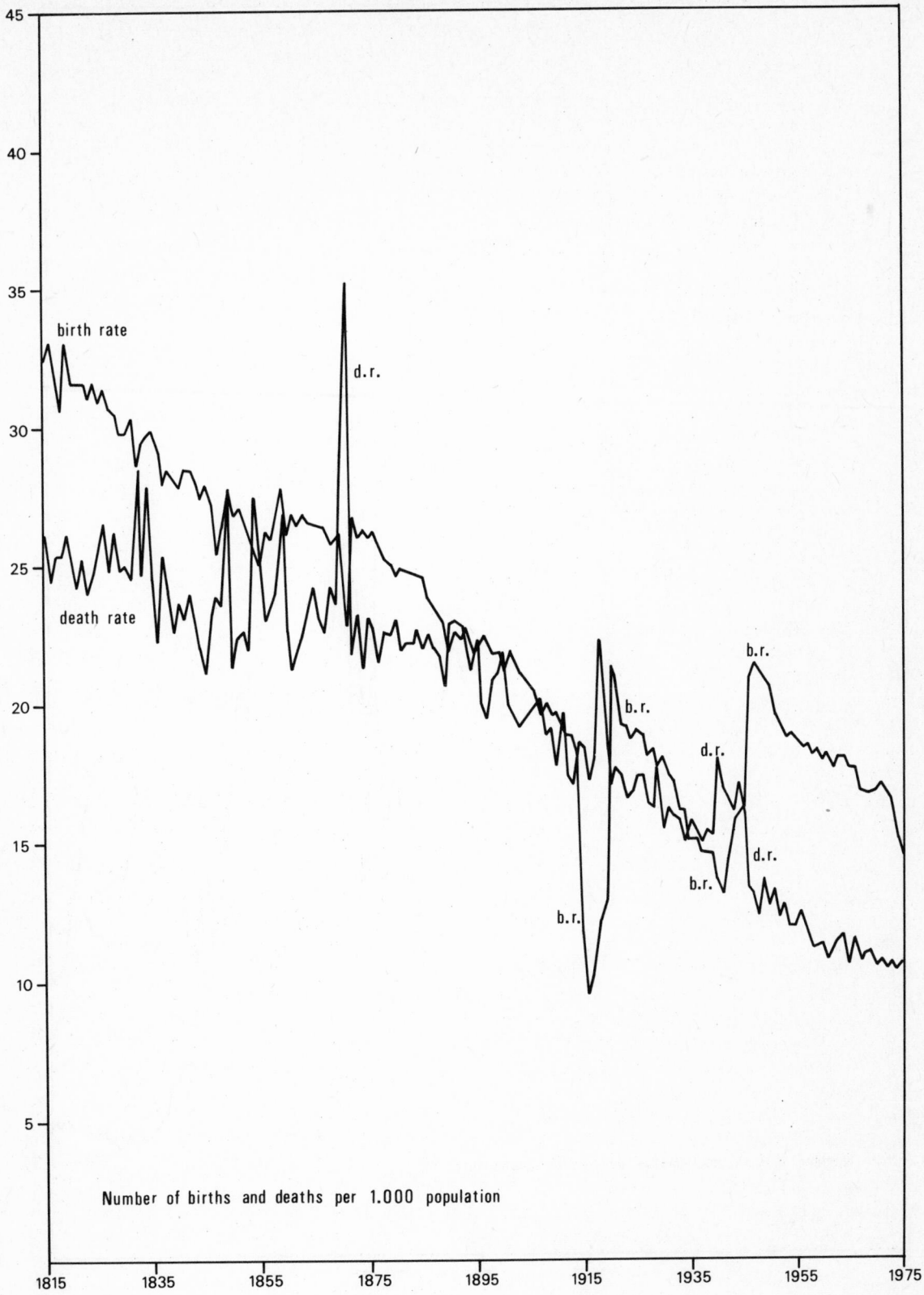

Number of births and deaths per 1.000 population

Germany

The demographic transition

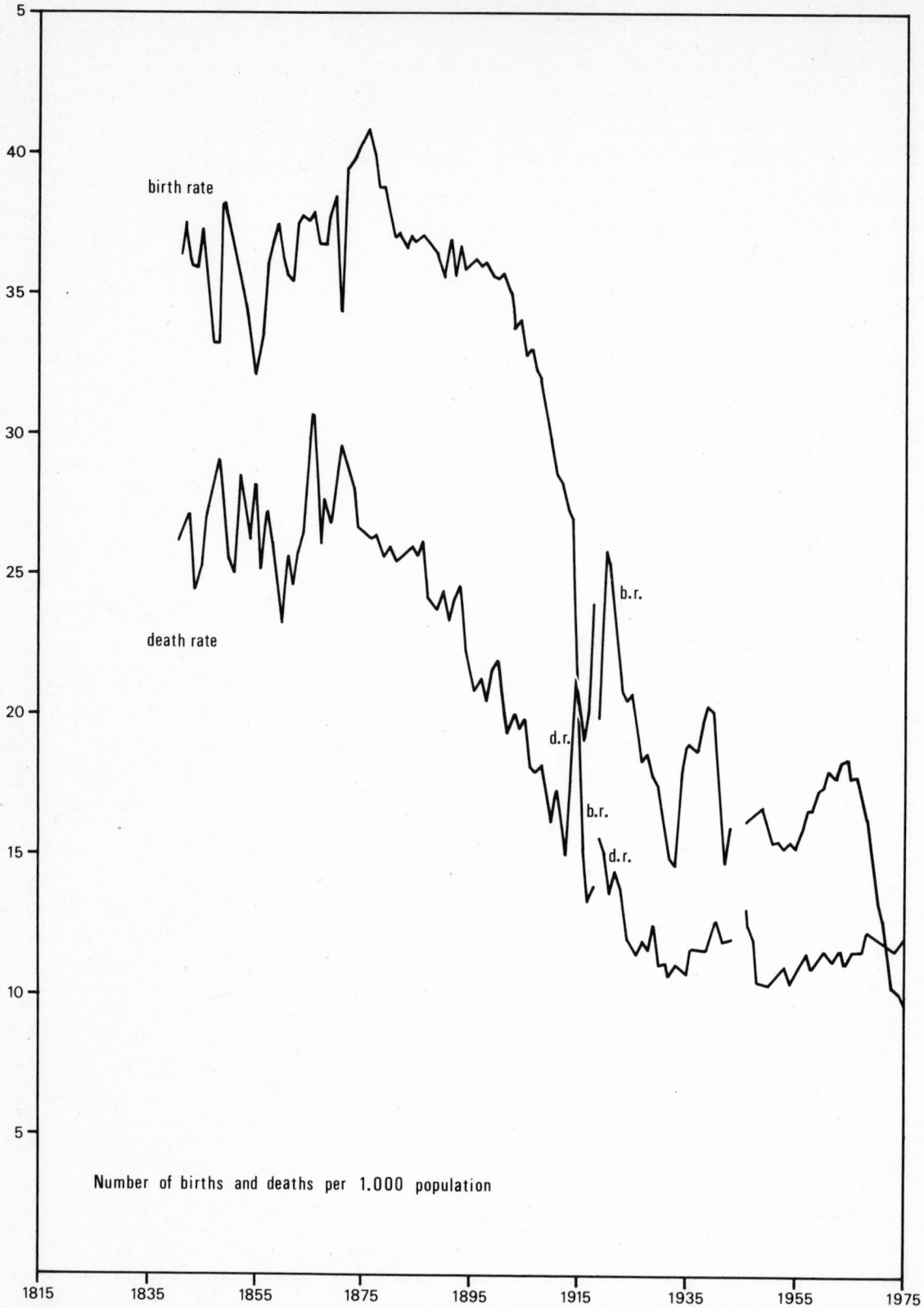

birth rate

death rate

b.r.

d.r.

b.r.

d.r.

Number of births and deaths per 1.000 population

Ireland

The demographic transition

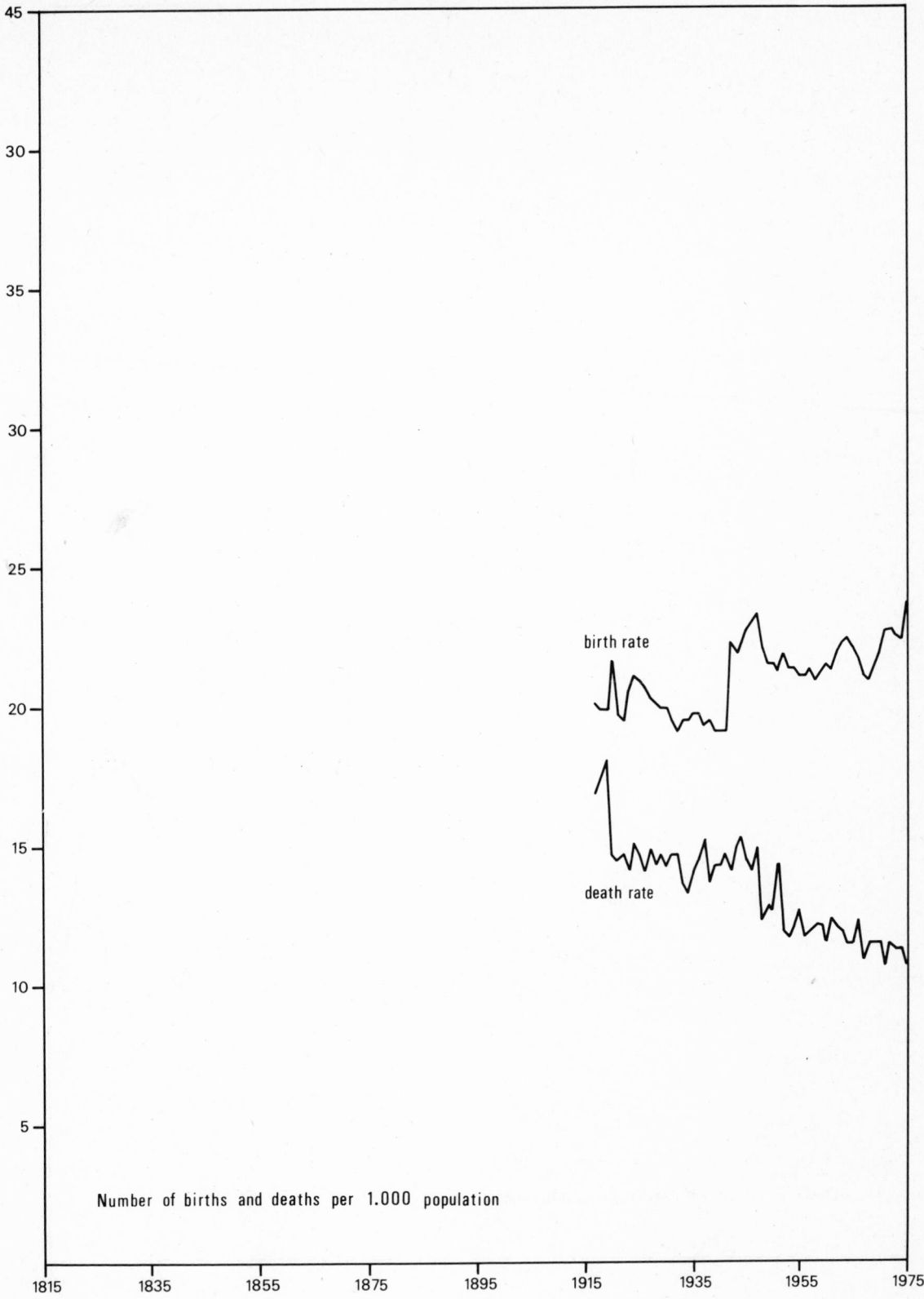

Number of births and deaths per 1.000 population

birth rate

death rate

Italy

The demographic transition

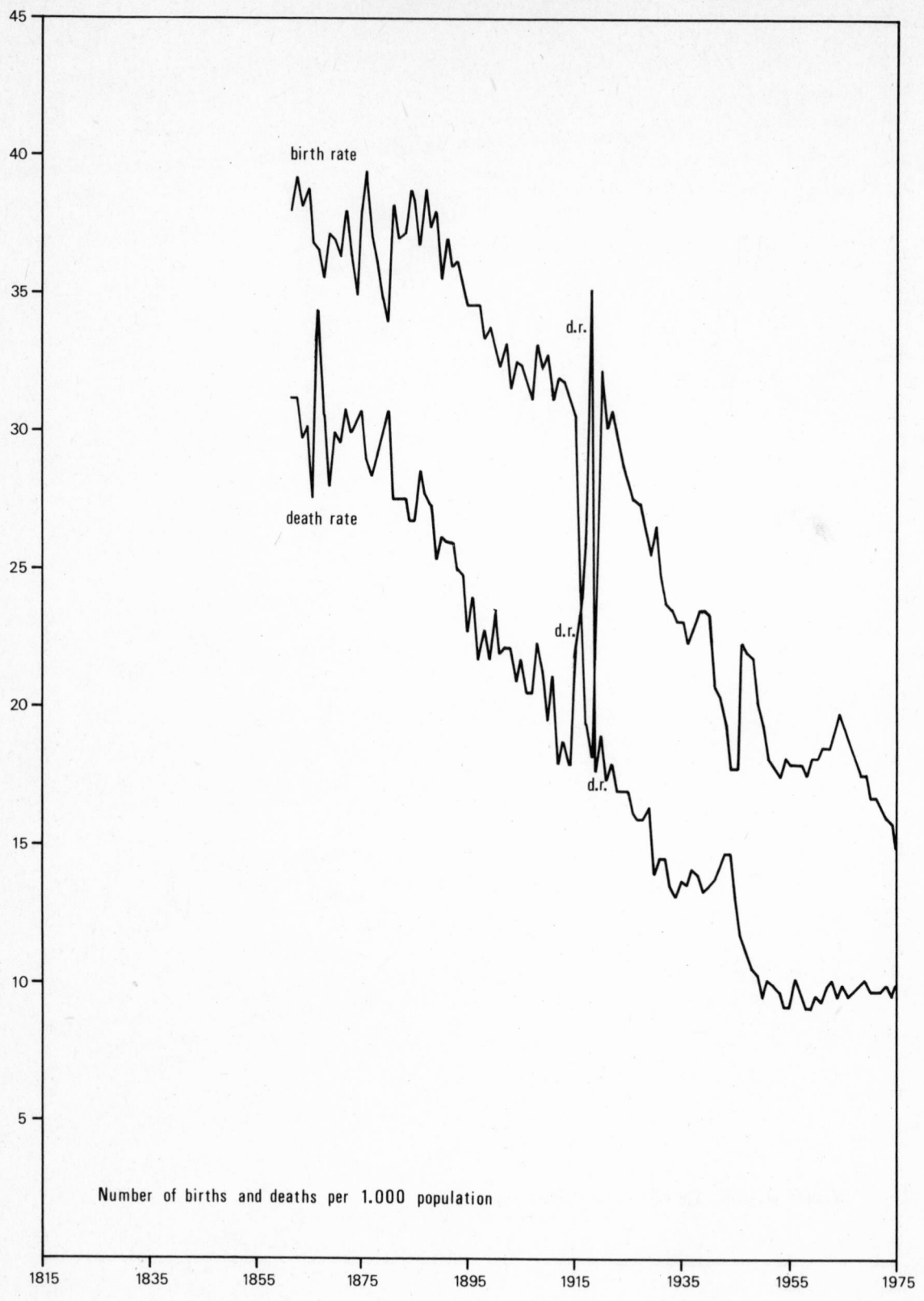

birth rate

death rate

d.r.

d.r.

d.r.

Number of births and deaths per 1.000 population

Netherlands

The demographic transition

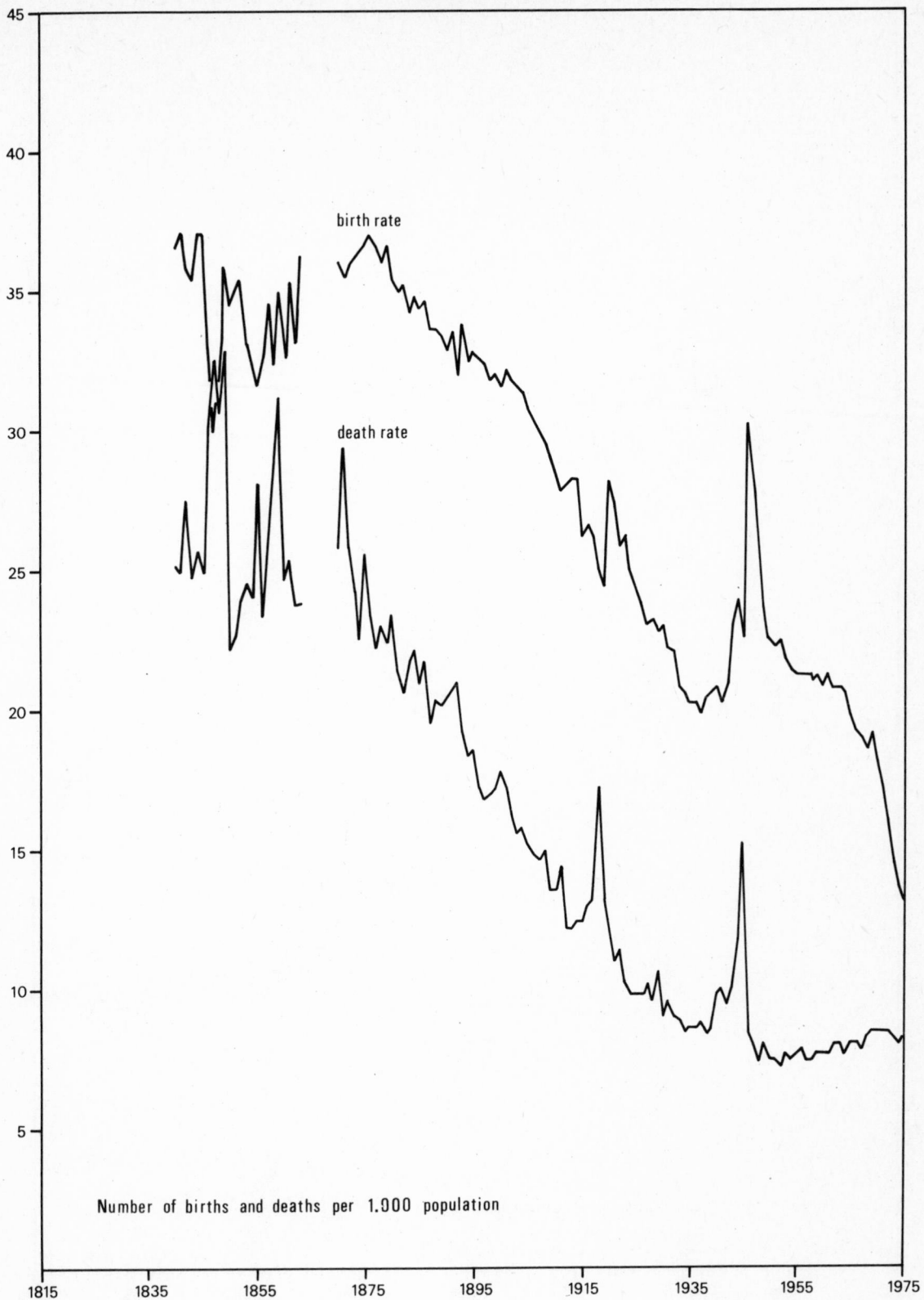

birth rate

death rate

Number of births and deaths per 1.000 population

Norway

The demographic transition

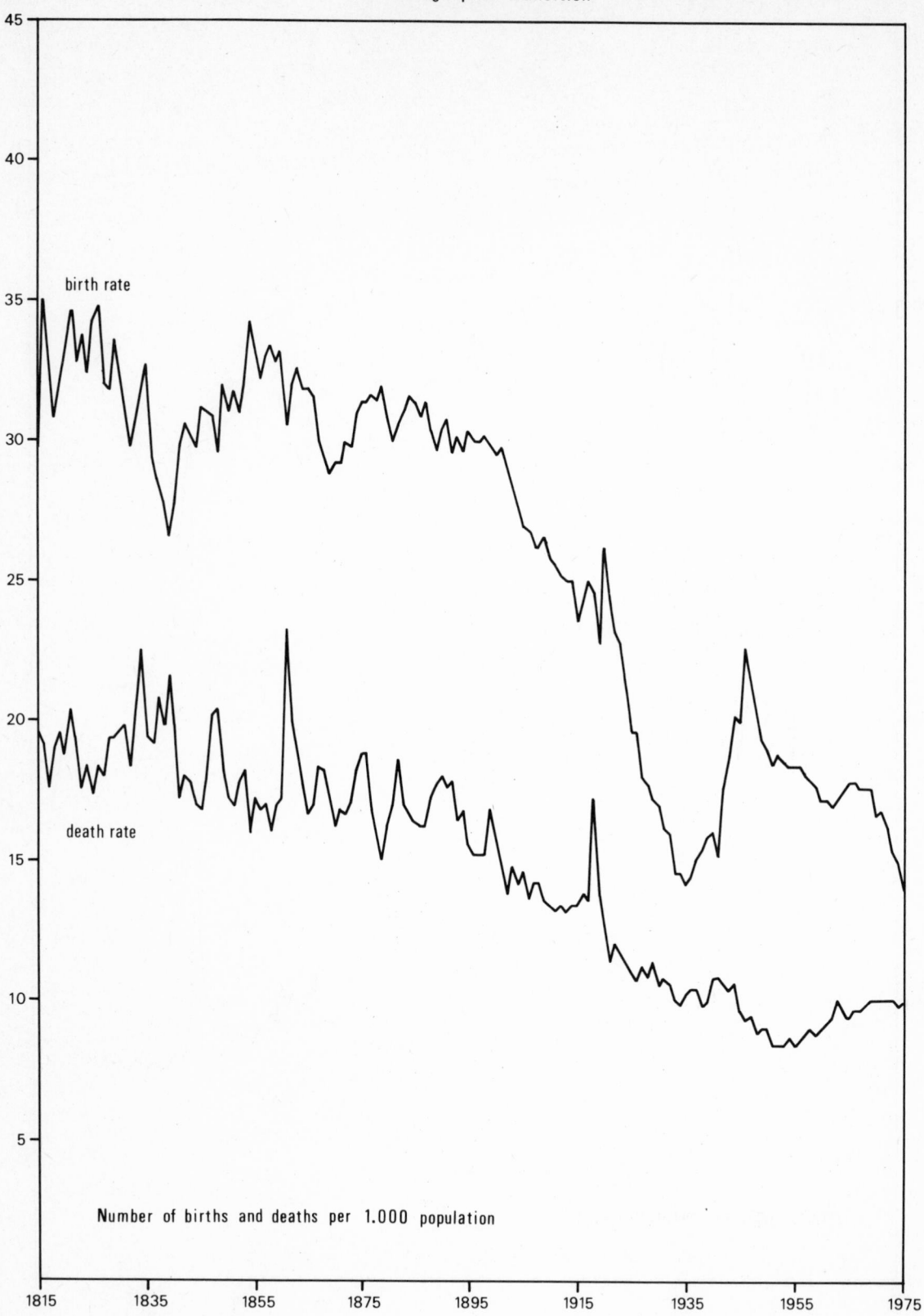

birth rate

death rate

Number of births and deaths per 1.000 population

Sweden

The demographic transition

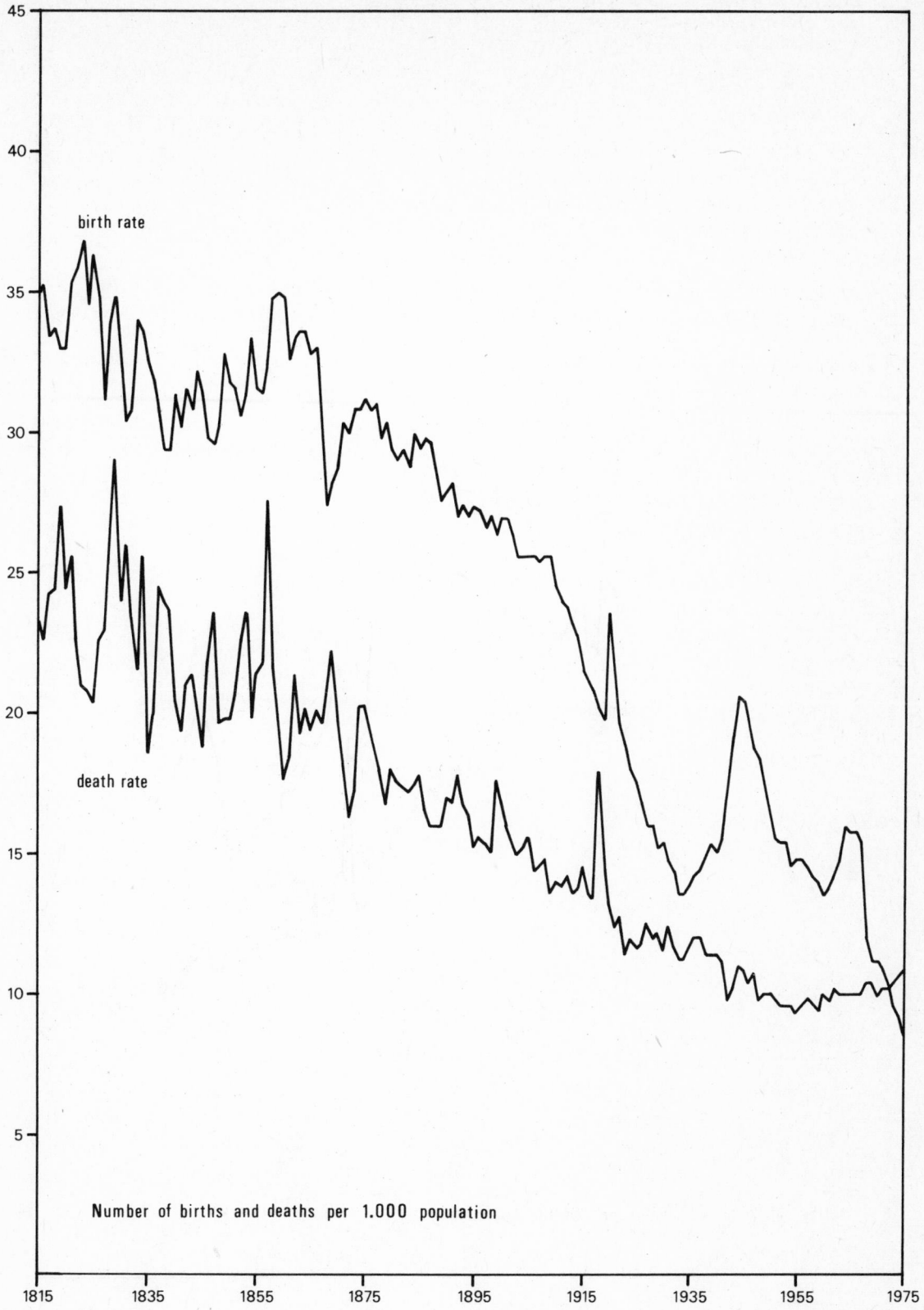

birth rate

death rate

Number of births and deaths per 1.000 population

Switzerland

The demographic transition

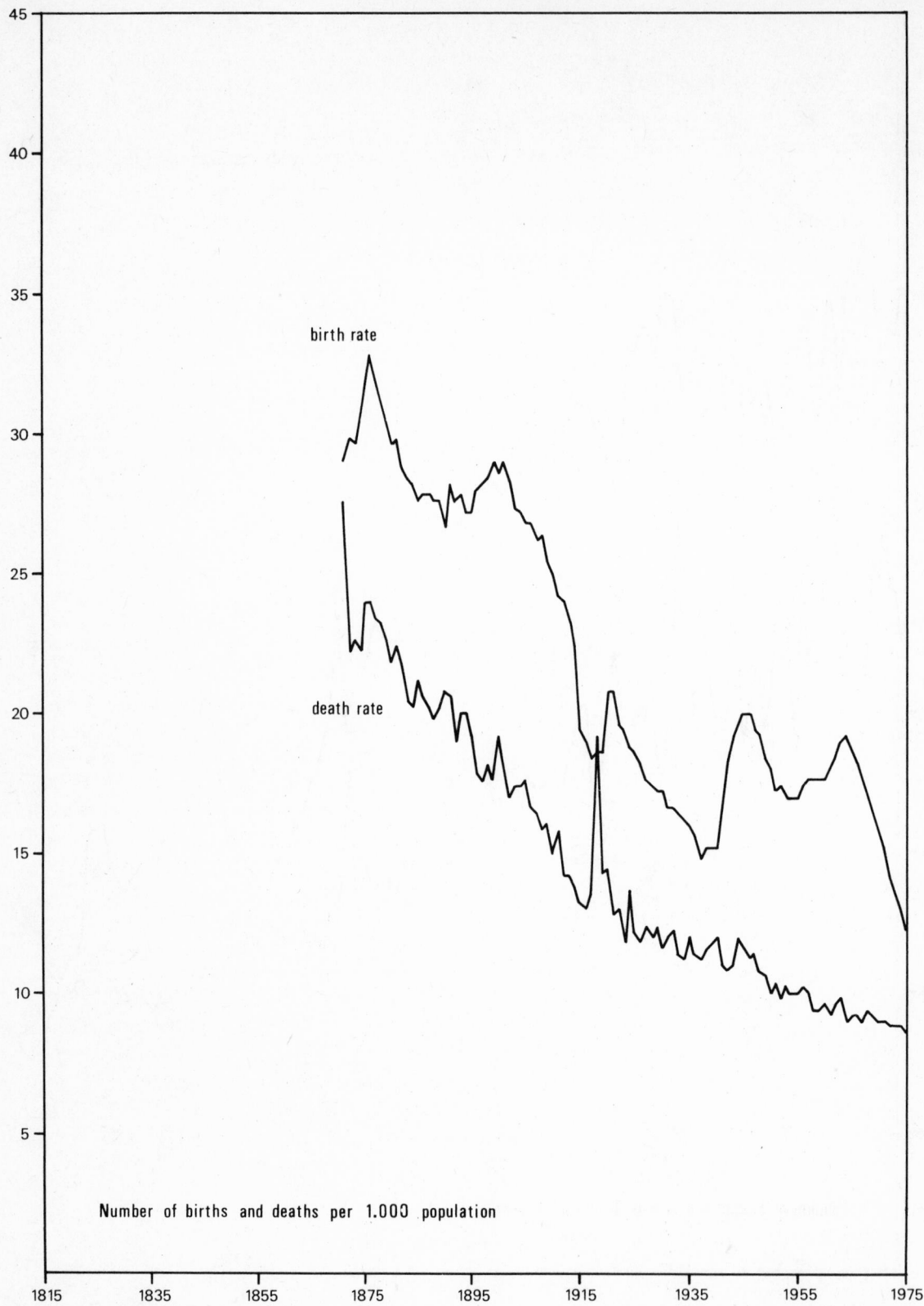

birth rate

death rate

Number of births and deaths per 1.000 population

32

England and Wales

The demographic transition

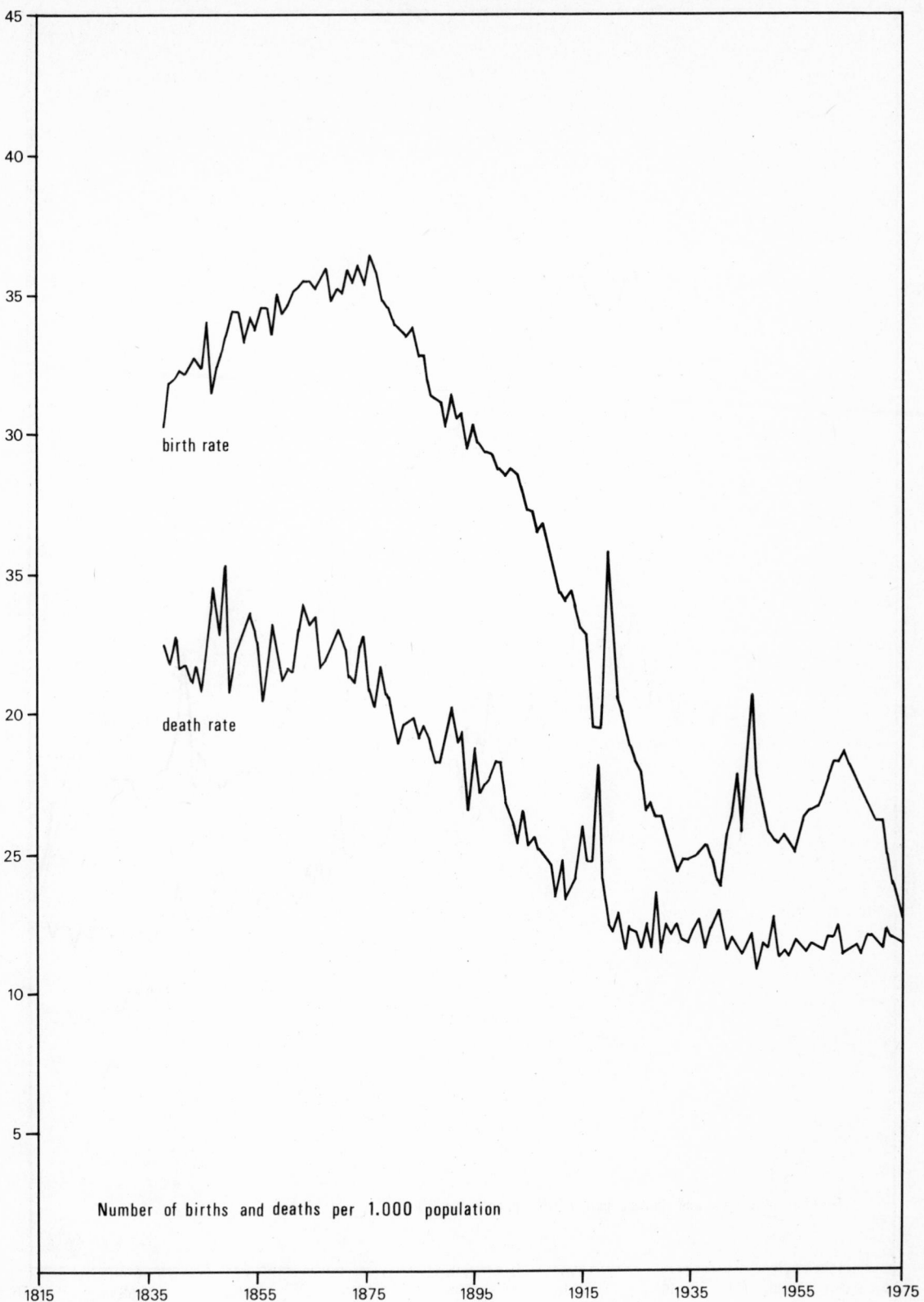

Number of births and deaths per 1.000 population

33

Scotland

The demographic transition

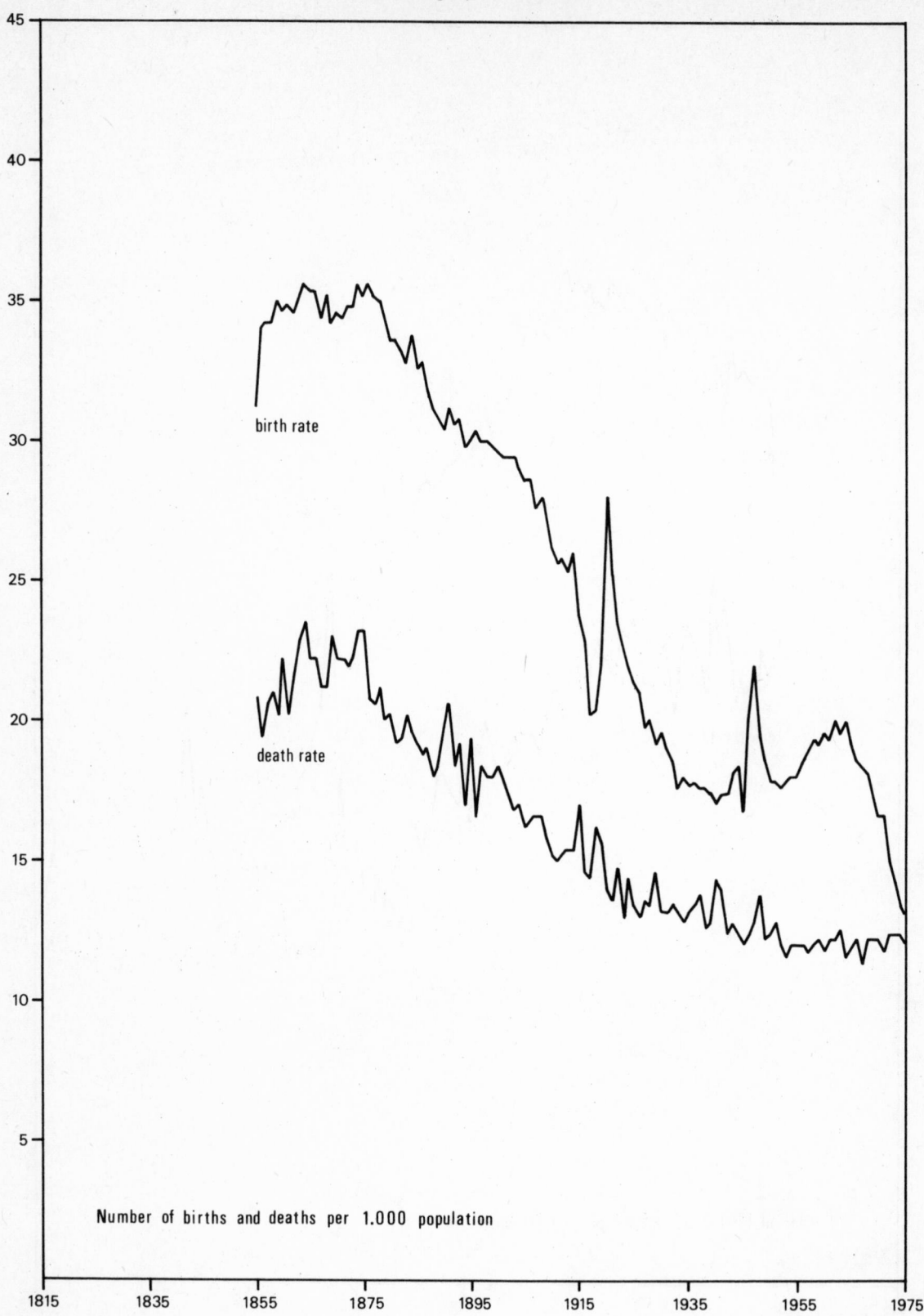

birth rate

death rate

Number of births and deaths per 1.000 population

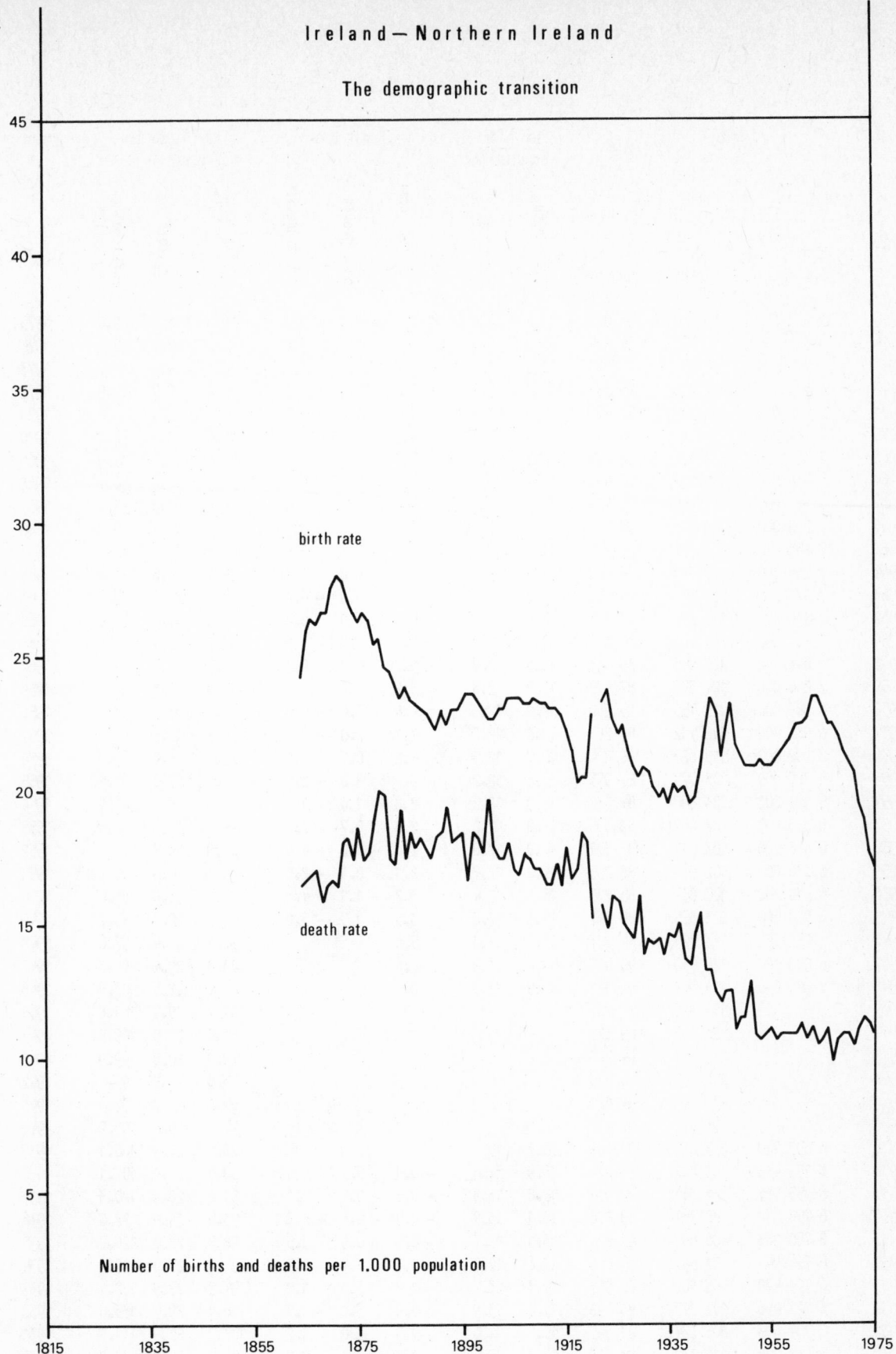

Ireland—Northern Ireland

The demographic transition

birth rate

death rate

Number of births and deaths per 1.000 population

35

Population Growth

Year	Totals			Per 1.000 population		Rates			Per 1.000 live births			Year
	Midyear Population a)	Live Births	Deaths b)	birth rate	death rate	natural incr.	pop. growth	net migration	infant mort.	stillbirths	infant mort. and stillb.	
1975	7 520 000	93 757	96 041	12.5	12.8	- 0.3	- 1.7	- 1.4	20.5	8.4	29.0	1975
1974	7 533 000	97 430	94 324	12.9	12.5	0.4	1.1	0.6	23.5	8.5	32.0	1974
1973	7 525 000	98 041	92 768	13.0	12.3	0.7	4.0	3.3	23.8	8.9	32.7	1973
1972	7 495 000	104 033	95 323	13.9	12.7	1.2	5.2	4.0	25.2	9.7	34.9	1972
1971	7 456 000	108 510	97 334	14.6	13.1	1.5	4.0	2.5	26.1	9.7	35.8	1971
1970	7 426 000	112 301	98 819	15.1	13.3	1.8	4.4	2.6	25.9	10.2	36.1	1970
1969	7 393 000	121 377	98 715	16.4	13.4	3.1	4.5	1.4	25.4	10.4	35.9	1969
1968	7 360 000	126 115	96 014	17.1	13.0	4.1	5.0	0.9	25.5	10.9	36.4	1968
1967	7 323 000	127 404	95 438	17.4	13.0	4.4	4.5	0.1	26.4	11.0	37.4	1967
1966	7 290 000	128 577	91 440	17.6	12.5	5.1	4.8	- 0.3	28.1	11.4	39.5	1966
1965	7 255 000	129 924	94 273	17.9	13.0	4.9	5.5	0.6	28.3	12.0	40.3	1965
1964	7 215 000	133 841	89 081	18.6	12.3	6.2	6.0	- 0.2	29.2	12.6	41.8	1964
1963	7 172 000	134 809	91 579	18.8	12.8	6.0	5.9	- 0.2	31.3	13.5	44.7	1963
1962	7 130 000	133 253	90 854	18.7	12.7	5.9	6.0	0.1	32.8	13.8	46.6	1962
1961	7 087 000	131 563	85 673	18.6	12.1	6.5	5.5	- 1.0	32.7	13.4	46.1	1961
1960	7 048 000	125 945	89 603	17.9	12.7	5.2	4.8	- 0.3	37.5	15.2	52.7	1960
1959	7 014 000	124 377	87 970	17.7	12.5	5.2	3.8	- 1.3	39.8	15.6	55.4	1959
1958	6 987 000	119 755	85 980	17.1	12.3	4.8	3.0	- 1.8	40.7	16.5	57.2	1958
1957	6 966 000	118 712	89 298	17.0	12.8	4.2	2.0	- 2.2	44.2	17.5	61.7	1957
1956	6 952 000	115 827	86 824	16.7	12.5	4.2	0.7	- 3.5	43.3	18.0	61.3	1956
1955	6 947 000	108 575	84 995	15.6	12.2	3.4	1.0	- 2.4	45.6	17.8	63.4	1955
1954	6 940 000	103 895	84 632	15.0	12.2	2.8	1.0	- 1.8	48.3	18.7	67.1	1954
1953	6 933 000	102 867	83 399	14.8	12.0	2.8	0.7	- 2.1	49.9	18.6	68.5	1953
1952	6 928 000	103 012	83 372	14.8	12.0	2.8	- 1.2	- 4.0	51.9	20.3	72.2	1952
1951	6 936 000	102 764	88 253	14.8	12.7	2.1	0.1	- 2.0	61.3	20.9	82.2	1951
1950	6 935 100	107 854	85 710	15.6	12.4	3.2	- 1.1	- 4.3	66.1	22.0	88.0	1950
1949	6 942 500	113 375	89 247	16.3	12.9	3.5	- 1.5	- 5.0	75.2	20.4	95.7	1949
1948	6 952 744	123 221	84 213	17.7	12.1	5.6			76.2	21.4	97.6	1948
1947	6 920 107	128 953	90 027	18.6	13.0	5.6			78.3	21.4	99.8	1947
1946	7 000 000	111 302	94 077	15.9	13.4	2.5			81.4	22.5	103.9	1946
1945		101 369	173 767						161.7	19.9	181.6	1945
1944		126 938	109 622						87.8	22.0	109.8	1944
1943		122 443	94 269						79.1	20.8	99.9	1943
1942		116 172	90 510						73.6	21.5	95.1	1942
1941		135 398	94 121						69.8	22.7	92.5	1941
1940		145 926	99 475						74.2	25.6	99.9	1940
1939	6 652 720	137 825	101 709	20.7	15.3				73.1	27.0	100.1	1939
1938	6 753 413	93 812	94 755	13.9	14.0	- 0.1	- 0.3	- 0.1	80.1	27.0	107.1	1938
1937	6 755 337	86 351	90 035	12.8	13.3	- 0.5	- 0.4	0.1	91.9	28.3	120.3	1937
1936	6 758 198	88 264	89 078	13.1	13.2	- 0.1	- 0.4	- 0.3	93.1	29.0	122.0	1936
1935	6 760 963	88 689	92 524	13.1	13.7	- 0.6	0.9	1.5	98.7	28.0	126.7	1935
1934	6 754 949	91 567	85 685	13.6	12.7	0.9	1.4	0.5	91.6	27.5	119.1	1934
1933	6 745 479	96 369	88 977	14.3	13.2	1.1	3.0	1.9	94.2	27.9	122.1	1933
1932	6 725 056	102 277	93 599	15.2	13.9	1.3	3.0	1.7	106.1	29.4	135.6	1932
1931	6 704 633	106 324	93 895	15.9	14.0	1.9	3.0	1.2	103.2	27.9	131.1	1931
1930	6 684 210	112 230	90 315	16.8	13.5	3.3	3.1	- 0.2	104.2	29.0	133.2	1930
1929	6 663 787	112 047	97 300	16.8	14.6	2.2	3.1	0.9	111.9	29.1	140.9	1929
1928	6 643 364	116 729	95 959	17.6	14.4	3.1	3.1	- 0.1	118.0	30.3	148.3	1928
1927	6 622 941	118 668	99 080	17.9	15.0	3.0	3.1	0.1	126.3	31.0	157.3	1927

Austria

Population Growth

Year	Totals			Per 1.000 population		Rates			Per 1.000 live births			Year
	Midyear Population a)	Live Births	Deaths	birth rate	death rate	natural incr.	pop. growth	net migration	infant mort.	stillbirths	infant mort. and stillb.	
1926	6 602 518	127 250	98 905	19.3	15.0	4.3	3.1	- 1.2	124.3	30.7	155.0	1926
1925	6 582 095	135 841	94 988	20.6	14.4	6.2	3.1	- 3.1	119.2	30.4	149.6	1925
1924	6 561 672	142 141	98 055	21.7	14.9	6.7	2.8	- 3.9	127.0	33.3	160.3	1924
1923	6 543 325	146 885	99 924	22.4	15.3	7.2	2.4	- 4.8	140.6	33.2	173.8	1923
1922	6 527 708	150 958	113 467	23.1	17.4	5.7	3.7	- 2.0	156.4	31.4	187.8	1922
1921	6 503 567	151 138	110 451	23.2	17.0	6.3	7.5	1.2	153.8			1921
1920	6 454 800	146 644	122 775	22.7	19.0	3.7	5.5	1.8	156.8	32.0	188.8	1920
1919	6 419 563	118 518	130 658	18.5	20.4	- 1.9			156.4	30.9	187.3	1919

a) Calculated average population, with the following exceptions: 1939 (population census of May 17); 1946 and 1947 (population estimates of July 21 and June 22, on the basis of ration-cards issued); 1948 (population enumeration of October 10); 1951 (population census of June 1); 1953 (population enumeration of October 10).
b) Excluding military losses in World War II.

Austria

Population Growth

Year	Totals			Per 1.000 population		Rates			Per 1.000 live births			Year
	Midyear Population	Live Births	Deaths	birth rate	deat rate	natural incr.	pop. growth	net migration	infant mort.	stillbirths	infant mort. and stillb.	
1913	28 847 478	864 763	589 919	30.0	20.4	9.5	7.5	− 2.1	189.8	25.5	215.3	1913
1912	28 632 299	903 407	592 426	31.6	20.7	10.9	7.4	− 3.5	181.5	24.7	206.2	1912
1911	28 420 412	898 702	628 305	31.6	22.1	9.5	7.8	− 1.7	207.5	24.8	232.3	1911
1910	28 197 552	923 545	602 046	32.8	21.4	11.4	8.5	− 2.9	188.7	25.2	213.9	1910
1909	27 956 890	941 239	646 122	33.7	23.1	10.6	8.4	− 2.1	208.6	25.3	233.9	1909
1908	27 720 731	941 375	627 771	34.0	22.6	11.3	8.8	− 2.5	199.3	25.7	225.0	1908
1907	27 476 680	942 169	629 913	34.3	22.9	11.4	9.4	− 2.0	208.6	26.3	234.9	1907
1906	27 218 896	961 258	619 063	35.3	22.7	12.6	8.1	− 4.5	202.0	27.0	229.0	1906
1905	26 999 548	921 764	684 537	34.1	25.4	8.8	7.7	− 1.1	231.0	26.3	257.3	1905
1904	26 792 018	961 430	642 333	35.9	24.0	11.9	9.0	− 2.9	209.7	27.0	236.7	1904
1903	26 550 998	943 953	638 092	35.6	24.0	11.5	9.2	− 2.3	214.7	27.6	242.3	1903
1902	26 306 168	984 240	656 400	37.4	25.0	12.5	9.7	− 2.7	215.9	27.0	242.9	1902
1901	26 049 896	961 501	631 377	36.9	24.2	12.7	10.0	− 2.6	209.0	28.6	237.6	1901
1900	25 788 469	967 939	658 680	37.5	25.5	12.0	10.2	− 1.8	230.6	28.5	259.1	1900
1899	25 526 512	960 205	658 269	37.6	25.8	11.8	9.8	− 2.0	218.6	29.4	248.0	1899
1898	25 275 262	923 241	635 115	36.5	25.1	11.4	9.9	− 1.5	224.3	29.0	253.3	1898
1897	25 025 487	944 764	646 019	37.8	25.8	11.9	10.0	− 1.9	228.3	28.4	256.7	1897
1896	24 774 187	948 619	657 011	38.3	26.5	11.8	9.3	− 2.5	229.5	29.2	258.7	1896
1895	24 543 614	941 184	682 899	38.3	27.8	10.5	7.9	− 2.6	235.1	29.2	264.3	1895
1894	24 349 532	901 398	682 805	37.0	28.0	9.0	8.1	− 0.9	251.2	30.3	281.6	1894
1893	24 152 635	923 470	660 081	38.2	27.3	10.9	7.3	− 3.6	232.0	29.9	261.9	1893
1892	23 976 437	871 278	693 421	36.3	28.9	7.4	7.0	− 0.4	259.3	29.9	289.2	1892
1891	23 808 612	919 503	673 315	38.6	28.3	10.3	7.4	− 3.0	243.0	29.9	272.9	1891
1890	23 632 863	868 935	696 342	36.8	29.5	7.3	8.1	0.8	259.2	29.3	288.5	1890
1889	23 442 500	898 350	646 787	38.3	27.6	10.7	8.8	− 2.0	236.3	29.3	265.6	1889
1888	23 237 368	889 901	686 573	38.3	29.5	8.8	8.1	− 0.7	248.8	29.0	277.8	1888
1887	23 050 000	889 478	672 302	38.6	29.2	9.4	8.0	− 1.4	244.1	29.3	273.4	1887
1886	22 864 800	876 063	678 458	38.3	29.7	8.6	7.1	− 1.6	249.6	28.5	278.1	1886
1885	22 702 894	860 663	689 493	37.9	30.4	7.5	7.4	− 0.1	255.3	28.5	283.8	1885
1884	22 533 947	878 321	666 523	39.0	29.6	9.4	7.7	− 1.7	247.1	27.8	275.0	1884
1883	22 360 000	858 832	677 337	38.4	30.3	8.1	7.3	− 0.8	252.9	27.7	280.6	1883
1882	22 196 053	873 522	686 951	39.4	30.9	8.4	6.7	− 1.7	255.9	27.4	283.3	1882
1881	22 046 750	833 476	676 515	37.8	30.7	7.1	6.8	− 0.3	250.0	26.9	276.9	1881
1880	21 897 631	827 980	654 258	37.8	29.9	7.9	8.4	0.5	249.9	26.6	276.5	1880
1879	21 713 750	855 593	652 491	39.4	30.0	9.4	7.9	− 1.4	239.7	26.2	265.9	1879
1878	21 542 000	833 251	683 661	38.7	31.7	6.9	6.8	− 0.2	251.6	25.8	277.4	1878
1877	21 396 000	830 776	677 748	38.8	31.7	7.2	8.5	1.3	258.3	25.2	283.6	1877
1876	21 214 523	853 436	634 363	40.2	29.9	10.3	9.8	− 0.5	246.9	24.8	271.7	1876
1875	21 005 714	842 303	634 088	40.1	30.2	9.9	8.7	− 1.2	243.2	24.4	267.5	1875
1874	20 823 333	829 709	662 929	39.8	31.8	8.0	4.2	− 3.8		24.1		1874
1873	20 736 428	828 030	811 150	39.9	39.1	0.8	3.4	2.6	290.4	24.4	314.7	1873
1872	20 665 952	810 147	677 022	39.2	32.8	6.4	7.5	1.0	270.4	23.6	294.0	1872
1871	20 511 666	801 515	616 729	39.1	30.1	9.0	9.3	0.3	255.5	24.1	279.6	1871

Year	Totals			Per 1.000 population			Rates		Per 1.000 live births c)			Year
	Midyear Population a)	Live Births b)	Deaths b)	birth rate	death rate	natural incr.	pop. growth a)	net migration a)	infant mort.	stillbirths	infant mort. and stillb.	
1870	20 320 000	888 281	598 581	43.7	29.5	14.3	10.3	- 4.0				1870
1869	20 110 909	795 360	583 995	39.5	29.0	10.5						1869
1868	19 949 214	758 591	571 558	38.0	28.6	9.4			254.7	21.0	275.7	1868
1867	19 787 522	726 538	580 055	36.7	29.3	7.4						1867
1866	19 625 830	746 507	804 338	38.1	41.0	- 2.9						1866
1865	19 464 138	746 445	598 863	38.4	38.0	7.6						1865
1864	19 302 446	789 827	585 142	40.9	30.2	10.6	8.5	- 0.1				1864
1863	19 140 754	781 505	576 481	40.8	30.1	10.7			258.5	21.0	279.5	1863
1862	18 979 062	726 474	562 792	38.3	29.7	8.6						1862
1861	18 817 370	708 209	563 402	37.6	29.9	7.7						1861
1860	18 655 678	715 606	502 809	38.4	27.0	11.4						1860
1859	18 493 986	753 880	540 475	40.7	29.2	11.5						1859
1858	18 332 294	729 666	532 920	39.8	29.1	10.7			242.8	21.0	263.8	1858
1857	18 191 663	725 334	503 915	39.9	27.7	12.2						1857
1856	18 093 156	653 172	541 887	36.1	29.9	6.2						1856
1855	17 994 649	577 177	787 649	32.1	43.8	-11.7						1855
1854	17 896 142	654 267	622 695	36.6	34.8	1.8	5.5	1.3				1854
1853	17 797 635	665 994	570 885	37.4	32.1	5.3			254.3	19.0	273.3	1853
1852	17 699 128	667 761	550 839	37.7	31.1	6.6						1852
1851	17 600 621	690 861	525 856	39.3	29.9	9.4						1851
1850	17 540 362	691 873	575 468	39.4	32.8	6.6						1850
1849	17 556 594	695 429	609 568	39.6	34.7	4.9						1849
1848	17 572 826	571 778	721 927	32.5	41.0	- 8.5	- 0.9	- 1.3	262.1	14.0	276.1	1848
1847	17 589 058	635 342	782 144	36.1	44.4	- 8.3						1847
1846	17 605 290	654 050	526 392	37.2	29.9	7.3						1846
1845	17 523 376	691 756	520 623	39.5	29.7	9.8	10.4	0.8				1845
1844	17 343 318	687 288	495 741	39.6	28.6	11.0						1844
1843	17 163 260	674 451	539 014	39.3	31.4	7.9			246.6	13.0	259.6	1843
1842	16 990 213	699 399	522 093	41.1	30.7	10.4						1842
1841	16 824 175	644 065	495 966	38.3	29.5	8.8	9.8	0.7				1841
1840	16 658 137	642 003	505 938	38.5	30.4	8.2						1840
1839	16 493 106	626 012	493 877	38.0	30.0	8.0						1839
1838	16 329 082	618 357	460 489	37.9	28.2	9.7	10.0	2.0	242.9	12.0	254.9	1838
1837	16 165 058	640 732	536 594	39.6	33.2	6.4						1837
1836	16 021 532	606 378	530 279	37.9	33.1	4.8						1836
1835	15 898 500	613 040	493 335	38.5	31.0	7.5	7.8	0.9				1835
1834	15 775 468	620 493	488 079	39.3	30.9	8.4						1834
1833	15 698 224	632 034	497 165	40.3	31.7	8.6			254.9	11.0	264.9	1833
1832	15 666 772	570 677	555 332	36.4	35.4	1.0	2.0	- 0.6				1832
1831	15 635 320	556 457	660 136	35.6	42.2	- 6.6						1831
1830	15 603 868	593 753	474 312	38.1	30.4	7.7						1830
1829	15 512 012	560 441	487 629	36.1	31.4	4.7						1829
1828	15 359 752	578 697	503 677	37.7	32.8	4.9	9.9	3.5				1828
1827	15 207 492	587 827	440 769	38.7	29.0	9.7						1827
1826	15 029 259	595 942	415 818	39.7	27.7	12.0						1826
1825	14 825 055	598 227	398 309	40.4	26.9	13.5	13.8	0.7				1825
1824	14 620 851	586 397	386 508	40.1	26.4	13.7						1824

Austria

Population Growth

| Year | Totals | | | Per 1.000 population | | Rates | | | Per 1.000 live births | | | Year |
	Midyear Population a)	Live Births b)	Deaths b)	birth rate	death rate	natural incr.	pop. growth a)	net mirgration a)	infant mort.	stillbirths	infant mort. and stillb.	
1823	14 426 346	572 163	415 706	39.6	28.8	10.8						1823
1822	14 241 544	550 154	387 769	38.6	27.2	11.4	13.0	0.3				1822
1821	14 056 742	582 983	361 587	41.5	25.7	15.8						1821
1820	13 867 068	594 846	368 659	42.9	26.6	16.3	14.1	- 0.8				1820
1819	13 672 501	604 956	409 149	44.2	29.9	14.3						1819
1818	13 477 934											

a) For the period 1818 to 1869 midyear population figures are estimated on the basis of figures given by population enumerations and censuses in January 1818, 1821, 1824, 1827, 1830, 1834, 1837, 1840, 1843, 1946, in October 1850 and 1857, and in December 1869. Therefore, population growth rates and net migration rates are only presented as average annual rates between these years.

b) From 1819 to 1855 the annual figures of live births and of deaths refer to the period from November 1 of the preceding year to October 31 of the respective year (e.g.: 1819 = 1 Nov. 1818 – 31 Oct. 1819).

c) For the period 1831 to 1870 figures on infant mortality and stillbirths have only been available as five-year-averages.

Year	Totals			Per 1.000 population		Rates			Per 1.000 live births			Year
	Midyear a) Population	Live Births	Deaths	birth rate	death rate	natural incr.	pop. growth	net migration	infant mort.	stillbirths	infant mort. and stillb.	
1975	9 800 700	119 273	119 273	12.2	12.2	0.0	2.9	2.9	14.7	9.6	24.4	1975
1974	9 772 419	123 155	116 039	12.6	11.9	0.7	3.1	2.4	17.4	9.5	27.0	1974
1973	9 741 720	129 425	118 313	13.3	12.1	1.1	3.1	2.0	17.7	10.8	28.5	1973
1972	9 711 114	134 437	116 743	13.8	12.0	1.8	3.9	2.1	19.1	10.9	30.0	1972
1971	9 673 161	139 104	118 853	14.4	12.3	2.1	1.8	-0.3	20.7	11.4	32.1	1971
1970	9 655 549	141 119	118 888	14.6	12.3	2.3	1.0	-1.3	21.3	11.5	32.7	1970
1969	9 646 032	140 834	119 375	14.6	12.4	2.2	2.8	0.6	21.4	12.3	33.7	1969
1968	9 618 755	141 242	121 275	14.7	12.6	2.1	3.9	1.9	21.8	12.2	34.1	1968
1967	9 580 990	145 899	114 509	15.2	12.0	3.3	5.6	2.3	23.0	12.7	35.7	1967
1966	9 527 807	150 636	114 557	15.8	12.0	3.8	6.7	2.9	24.8	13.4	38.2	1966
1965	9 463 667	154 856	114 507	16.4	12.1	4.3	9.0	4.8	23.8	13.8	37.6	1965
1964	9 378 113	160 371	109 342	17.1	11.7	5.4	9.4	4.0	25.4	14.6	40.0	1964
1963	9 289 770	158 196	115 618	17.0	12.4	4.6	5.3	0.8	27.4	14.2	41.5	1963
1962	9 240 071	154 338	111 545	16.7	12.1	4.6	3.3	-1.3	27.7	14.8	42.4	1962
1961	9 209 235	158 431	106 259	17.2	11.5	5.7	2.7	-2.9	28.1	14.9	43.0	1961
1960	9 153 489	155 520	113 106	17.0	12.4	4.6	5.4	0.8	31.0	15.3	46.3	1960
1959	9 103 729	158 237	103 513	17.4	11.4	6.0	5.6	-0.4	30.4	15.4	45.7	1959
1958	9 052 706	155 048	105 746	17.1	11.7	5.4	7.0	1.6	31.3	16.3	47.6	1958
1957	8 989 110	152 871	107 236	17.0	11.9	5.1	7.3	2.2	35.9	16.4	52.3	1957
1956	8 923 844	150 210	108 016	16.8	12.1	4.7	6.2	1.5	39.4	17.0	56.4	1956
1955	8 868 475	149 195	108 316	16.8	12.2	4.6	5.5	0.9	40.7	18.4	59.2	1955
1954	8 819 379	148 538	104 795	16.8	11.9	5.0	4.7	-0.3	41.4	18.5	59.8	1954
1953	8 777 873	146 125	106 024	16.6	12.1	4.6	5.4	0.8	41.9	20.1	62.0	1953
1952	8 730 405	146 064	103 624	16.7	11.9	4.9	6.0	1.1	44.8	20.6	65.5	1952
1951	8 678 386	142 314	107 688	16.4	12.4	4.0	4.5	0.5	50.0	21.9	72.0	1951
1950	8 639 368	145 672	104 039	16.9	12.0	4.8	3.0	-1.9	53.4	23.4	76.9	1950
1949	8 613 847	147 854	106 704	17.2	12.4	4.8	6.6	1.8	57.2	24.4	81.6	1949
1948	8 557 403	150 416	103 576	17.6	12.1	5.5	12.5	7.0	59.1	26.2	85.3	1948
1947	8 450 360	150 227	108 136	17.8	12.8	5.0	9.9	4.9	68.8	26.9	95.7	1947
1946	8 366 530	152 962	110 413	18.3	13.2	5.1	3.2	-1.8	74.8	27.3	102.1	1946
1945	8 339 405	130 526	121 155	15.7	14.5	1.1	5.9	4.7	99.6	25.6	125.2	1945
1944	8 290 569	127 122	124 861	15.3	15.1	0.3	6.0	5.7	82.6	25.4	108.0	1944
1943 b)	8 241 194	123 349	107 767	15.0	13.1	1.9	-0.6	-2.5	74.5	25.2	99.7	1943
1942 b)	8 246 459	108 603	117 291	13.2	14.2	-1.1	-3.6	-2.5	83.9	25.5	109.4	1942
1941 b)	8 276 033	100 616	118 670	12.2	14.3	-2.2	-8.4	-6.2	91.6	27.3	118.9	1941
1940 b)	8 345 475	112 497	125 083	13.5	15.0	-1.5	-5.5	-4.0	93.2	28.7	121.9	1940
1939	8 391 404	130 019	110 393	15.5	13.2	2.3	2.1	-0.3	82.4	30.1	112.5	1939
1938	8 373 876	133 610	104 684	16.0	12.5	3.5	3.3	-0.1	81.3	30.8	112.1	1938
1937	8 346 089	128 696	104 163	15.4	12.5	2.9	3.7	0.7	82.8	31.1	113.8	1937
1936	8 315 449	127 751	101 595	15.4	12.2	3.1	3.3	0.2	86.1	32.3	118.3	1936
1935	8 287 746	128 432	102 132	15.5	12.3	3.2	3.1	0.0	84.6	32.6	117.2	1935
1934	8 261 751	133 514	96 851	16.2	11.7	4.4	3.8	-0.7	82.5	34.0	116.4	1934
1933	8 230 699	136 757	104 640	16.6	12.7	3.9	5.4	1.5	92.0	34.2	126.2	1933
1932	8 186 317	145 835	104 221	17.8	12.7	5.1	7.4	2.3	93.6	33.3	126.9	1932
1931	8 125 594	149 657	103 773	18.4	12.8	5.6	6.1	0.4	89.3	33.8	123.1	1931
1930	8 076 096	152 530	103 397	18.9	12.8	6.1	5.5	-0.6	99.5	33.7	133.3	1930
1929	8 031 729	147 311	115 901	18.3	14.4	3.9	8.0	4.1	110.5	34.5	144.9	1929
1928	7 967 673	148 071	102 270	18.6	12.8	5.7	8.1	2.3	94.1	35.0	129.1	1928
1927	7 903 339	146 296	103 007	18.5	13.0	5.5	7.6	2.1	98.4	34.9	133.3	1927

Belgium

Population Growth

Year	Totals			Per 1.000 population		Rates			Per 1.000 live births			Year
	Midyear Population	Live Births	Deaths	birth rate	death rate	natural incr.	pop. growth	net migration	infant mort.	stillbirths	infant mort. and stillb.	
1926	7 843 239	151 009	101 018	19.3	12.9	6.4	12.1	5.7	103.8	35.6	139.4	1926
1925	7 748 175	155 330	99 569	20.0	12.9	7.2	13.2	6.0	99.7	36.2	135.9	1925
1924	7 645 647	154 083	99 653	20.2	13.0	7.1	9.5	2.4	94.5	39.4	134.0	1924
1923	7 573 194	156 600	100 084	20.7	13.2	7.5	8.2	0.8	99.7	40.8	140.5	1923
1922	7 510 851	154 781	106 615	20.6	14.2	6.4	8.9	2.5	113.8	42.7	156.5	1922
1921	7 443 851	164 603	102 908	22.1	13.8	8.3			122.1	42.3	164.4	1921
1920	7 491 298	164 950	102 505	22.0	13.7	8.3			110.2	41.1	151.2	1920
1919	7 566 302	123 314	113 732	16.3	15.0	1.3			103.0	46.8	149.8	1919
1918 c)	7 598 815	85 056	157 340	11.2	20.7	-9.5			133.8			1918
1917 c)	7 667 336	86 675	124 824	11.3	16.3	-5.0			140.1			1917
1916 c)	7 700 907	99 360	101 044	12.9	13.1	-0.2	-0.2	-2.9	116.3			1916
1915 c)	7 696 845	124 291	100 674	16.1	13.1	3.1			125.1			1915
1914 c)	7 661 625	156 389	108 720	20.4	14.2	6.2			130.0			1914
1913	7 605 072	171 099	111 227	22.5	14.6	7.9			129.9	45.8	175.7	1913
1912	7 530 899	171 187	112 378	22.7	14.9	7.8			119.9	45.5	165.4	1912
1911	7 457 098	171 802	122 843	23.0	16.5	6.6			166.5	44.0	210.5	1911
1910	7 437 844	176 413	112 826	23.7	15.2	8.5			134.0	45.4	179.4	1910
1909	7 419 174	176 431	117 571	23.8	15.8	7.9			137.6	46.9	184.4	1909
1908	7 352 003	183 834	121 964	25.0	16.6	8.4			147.2	46.6	193.7	1908
1907	7 278 092	185 138	115 347	25.4	15.8	9.6			132.5	44.9	177.3	1907
1906	7 199 585	186 271	118 884	25.9	16.5	9.4	10.4	0.6	153.1	45.7	198.8	1906
1905	7 117 729	187 437	118 343	26.3	16.6	9.7			146.2	45.8	192.1	1905
1904	7 030 065	191 721	119 506	27.3	17.0	10.3			151.7	44.9	196.6	1904
1903	6 940 649	192 301	118 675	27.7	17.1	10.6			154.9	44.6	199.4	1903
1902	6 848 039	195 871	119 330	28.6	17.4	11.2			143.9	45.8	189.7	1902
1901	6 746 774	200 077	116 077	29.7	17.2	12.5			142.2	46.3	188.5	1901
1900	6 719 040	193 789	129 046	28.8	19.2	9.6			171.6	46.4	218.0	1900
1899	6 707 132	194 268	126 963	29.0	18.9	10.0			166.6	45.8	212.5	1899
1898	6 628 163	190 921	117 457	28.8	17.7	11.1			159.8	46.6	206.4	1898
1897	6 541 240	190 987	113 586	29.2	17.4	11.8			148.7	45.9	194.6	1897
1896	6 453 335	188 533	113 748	29.2	17.6	11.6			142.2	48.7	190.9	1896
1895	6 376 371	183 015	125 148	28.7	19.6	9.1	9.8	0.0	172.1	47.1	219.2	1895
1894	6 302 115	181 466	118 213	28.8	18.8	10.0			151.9	47.2	199.1	1894
1893	6 228 814	183 062	125 530	29.4	20.2	9.2			164.9	47.2	212.0	1893
1892	6 165 900	177 485	133 693	28.8	21.7	7.1			168.9	47.9	216.7	1892
1891	6 102 883	181 917	128 786	29.8	21.1	8.7			162.4	47.2	209.5	1891
1890	6 081 560	176 595	126 545	29.0	20.8	8.2			166.4	46.6	213.0	1890
1889	6 061 921	177 542	119 726	29.3	19.8	9.5			159.6	47.4	207.0	1889
1888	6 002 393	175 586	121 097	29.3	20.2	9.1			165.3	48.0	213.3	1888
1887	5 942 359	175 466	115 296	29.5	19.4	10.1			145.3	49.7	194.9	1887
1886	5 881 627	175 091	124 905	29.8	21.2	8.5	9.5	-0.1	178.4	49.3	227.8	1886
1885	5 819 118	175 043	117 775	30.1	20.2	9.8			149.8	48.7	198.5	1885
1884	5 752 883	176 721	121 070	30.7	21.0	9.7			168.4	47.2	215.6	1884
1883	5 688 002	174 484	119 196	30.7	21.0	9.7			154.5	47.8	202.3	1883
1882	5 620 522	176 345	114 298	31.4	20.3	11.0			151.3	48.0	199.3	1882
1881	5 552 928	175 411	117 007	31.6	21.1	10.5			154.7	46.8	201.5	1881

Population Growth

Year	Totals			Per 1.000 population		Rates			Per 1.000 live births			Year
	Midyear Population	Live Births	Deaths	birth rate	death rate	natural incr.	pop. growth	net migration	infant mort.	stillbirths	infant mort. and stillb.	
1880	5 528 432	171 864	123 323	31.1	22.3	8.8			186.5	46.9	233.5	1880
1879	5 506 897	174 641	121 060	31.7	22.0	9.7				46.6		1879
1878	5 444 835	172 730	117 271	31.7	21.5	10.2			160.9	44.7	205.6	1878
1877	5 374 458	175 077	114 269	32.6	21.3	11.3			130.8	46.0	176.8	1877
1876	5 369 562	176 915	116 787	32.9	21.7	11.2			138.6	44.8	183.4	1876
1875	5 369 786	175 552	122 480	32.7	22.8	9.9			158.4	44.1	202.5	1875
1874	5 295 214	173 978	109 595	32.9	20.7	12.2	9.6	- 0.1	136.9	44.5	181.5	1874
1873	5 214 416	170 708	112 873	32.7	21.6	11.1			142.2	45.6	187.8	1873
1872	5 144 359	167 377	120 129	32.5	23.4	9.2			145.1	45.2	190.3	1872
1871	5 100 753	158 760	145 746	31.1	28.6	2.6			173.4	45.7	219.0	1871
1870	5 054 581	164 572	118 359	32.6	23.4	9.1			145.4	46.0	191.4	1870
1869	4 991 490	158 687	109 607	31.8	22.0	9.8			106.5	47.0	153.5	1869
1868	4 929 719	156 134	107 556	31.7	21.8	9.9			141.6	47.9	189.5	1868
1867	4 862 814	157 149	105 576	32.3	21.7	10.6			127.5	47.6	175.1	1867
1866	4 906 092	158 010	151 116	32.2	30.8	1.4			164.4	50.3	214.7	1866
1865	4 962 461	156 323	122 341	31.5	24.7	6.8			189.1	48.6	237.8	1865
1864	4 916 796	155 872	115 948	31.7	23.6	8.1			165.1	50.1	215.2	1864
1863	4 864 794	155 564	107 959	32.0	22.2	9.8			157.2	48.3	205.5	1863
1862	4 809 411	145 568	100 124	30.3	20.8	9.4	6.4	-1.6	150.4	47.3	197.8	1862
1861	4 757 126	147 253	106 381	31.0	22.4	8.6			163.6	47.3	210.9	1861
1860	4 701 611	144 668	92 871	30.8	19.8	11.0			138.7	48.2	186.9	1860
1859	4 647 212	149 812	111 650	32.2	24.0	8.2			171.8	49.9	221.7	1859
1858	4 600 217	145 074	107 910	31.5	23.5	8.1			164.0	48.7	212.7	1858
1857	4 553 349	143 291	103 458	31.5	22.7	8.7			168.4	47.6	215.9	1857
1856	4 568 264	134 187	97 395	29.4	21.3	8.1			148.3	45.7	194.0	1856
1855	4 596 081	125 955	112 716	27.4	24.5	2.9			168.3	45.2	213.5	1855
1854	4 566 802	131 837	103 266	28.9	22.6	6.3			150.2	45.8	195.9	1854
1853	4 532 434	127 728	100 333	28.2	22.1	6.0			145.3	46.1	191.5	1853
1852	4 494 811	134 397	95 971	29.9	21.4	8.5	4.3	-1.2	148.4	47.9	196.4	1852
1851	4 449 733	134 248	94 699	30.2	21.3	8.9			147.6	47.5	195.0	1851
1850	4 403 222	131 416	92 820	29.8	21.1	8.8			140.8	48.1	188.9	1850
1849	4 369 665	133 105	121 462	30.5	27.8	2.7			147.4	46.5	193.9	1849
1848	4 348 769	120 383	108 287	27.7	24.9	2.8			141.4	45.2	186.6	1848
1847	4 337 748	118 106	120 168	27.2	27.7	-0.5			156.6	42.7	199.3	1847
1846	4 317 805	119 610	107 835	27.7	25.0	2.7			175.2	43.3	218.5	1846
1845	4 278 494	137 012	97 783	32.0	22.9	9.2			144.7	43.8	188.5	1845
1844	4 236 145	133 976	94 911	31.6	22.4	9.2			138.4	43.9	182.3	1844
1843	4 193 285	132 911	97 055	31.7	23.1	8.6			148.6	43.3	191.9	1843
1842	4 155 544	135 027	103 068	32.5	24.8	7.7			159.9	40.5	200.4	1842
1841	4 105 501	138 135	97 108	33.6	23.7	10.0			151.9	40.0	192.0	1841
1840	4 053 626	138 144	103 902	34.1	25.6	8.4						1840
1839 d)	4 015 638	136 022	105 448	33.9	26.3	7.6						1839

Population Growth

Year	Totals			Per 1.000 population			Rates		Per 1.000 live births			Year
	Midyear Population	Live Births	Deaths	birth rate	death rate	natural incr.	pop. growth	net migration	infant mort.	stillbirths	infant mort. and stillb.	
1838	4 295 560	152 170	109 950	35.4	25.6	9.8						1838
1837	4 257 887	142 648	118 142	33.5	27.7	5.8						1837
1836	4 225 706	144 198	101 231	34.1	24.0	10.2						1836
1835	4 202 850	142 917	101 143	34.0	24.1	9.9						1835
1834	4 173 313	139 762	116 573	33.5	27.9	5.6						1834
1833	4 126 167	137 792	111 302	33.4	27.0	6.4						1833
1832	4 096 074	129 070	114 910	31.5	28.1	3.5						1832
1831	4 083 033	135 050	98 088	33.1	24.0	9.1						1831
1830		131 676	104 229									1830

a) Midyear population figures have been calculated on the basis of population figures at the end of the year. At least up to 1920, the system of population registration was unreliable, and population census figures were used to correct the figures. This procedure produced breaks in the years following the censuses which makes the calculation of annual population growth rates and net migration rates based on the midyear population meaningless. Therefore, from 1846 to 1920, population census figures (see Volume I) have been used to calculate these rates.

b) Excluding 41 municipalities under direct German administration.

c) Excluding 50 municipalities.

d) On April 19, 1839 parts of the Belgian provinces of Limbourg and Luxembourg were ceded to the Netherlands. The 1839 midyear population has been estimated using population figures for these two provinces.

Year	Total population		
	Belgium	Limbourg	Luxembourg
1.1.1838	4 273 176	292 087	323 951
1.1.1839	4 317 944	295 112	327 885
1.1.1840	4 028 677	168 681	172 473

Population Growth

Year	Totals			Per 1.000 population		Rates			Per 1.000 live birth			Year
	Midyear Population	Live Births	Deaths	birth rate	death rate	natural incr.	pop. growth	net migration	infant mort.	stillbirths	infant mort. and stillb.	
1975	5 060 000	72 071	50 895	14.2	10.1	4.2	3.0	- 1.2	10.4	6.7	17.1	1975
1974	5 045 000	71 327	51 637	14.1	10.2	3.9	4.6	0.7	10.7	6.2	16.9	1974
1973	5 022 000	71 895	50 526	14.3	10.1	4.3	6.0	1.7		7.3		1973
1972	4 992 000	75 505	50 445	15.1	10.1	5.0	5.8	0.8	12.2	7.6	19.8	1972
1971	4 963 000	75 359	48 858	15.2	9.8	5.3	6.9	1.5	13.5	8.0	21.5	1971
1970	4 929 000	70 802	48 233	14.4	9.8	4.6	7.7	3.1	14.2	8.8	23.0	1970
1969	4 891 000	71 298	47 943	14.6	9.8	4.8	4.9	0.1	14.8	8.9	23.8	1969
1968	4 867 000	74 543	47 290	15.3	9.7	5.6	5.8	0.2	16.4	8.2	24.6	1968
1967	4 839 000	81 410	47 836	16.8	9.9	6.9	8.7	1.8	15.8	10.7	26.6	1967
1966	4 797 000	88 332	49 344	18.4	10.3	8.1	8.1	0.0	17.6	8.1	25.7	1966
1965	4 758 000	85 796	47 884	18.0	10.1	8.0	8.0	0.0	18.7	10.6	29.3	1965
1964	4 720 000	83 356	46 811	17.7	9.9	7.7	7.6	- 0.1	18.7	11.3	30.0	1964
1963	4 684 000	82 413	45 773	17.6	9.8	7.8	7.9	0.1	19.1	11.5	30.6	1963
1962	4 647 000	77 808	45 334	16.7	9.8	7.0	8.0	1.0	20.1	12.0	32.1	1962
1961	4 610 000	76 439	43 310	16.6	9.4	7.2	6.3	- 0.9	21.8	12.7	34.5	1961
1960	4 581 000	76 077	43 681	16.6	9.5	7.1	7.4	0.4	21.5	12.6	34.1	1960
1959	4 547 000	73 928	42 159	16.3	9.3	7.0	7.0	0.1	22.5	14.8	37.3	1959
1958	4 515 000	74 681	41 560	16.5	9.2	7.3	6.0	- 1.4	22.4	15.7	38.1	1958
1957	4 488 000	75 264	41 730	16.8	9.3	7.5	4.9	- 2.6	23.4	15.5	38.9	1957
1956	4 466 000	76 725	39 588	17.2	8.9	8.3	6.0	- 2.3	24.9	17.8	42.7	1956
1955	4 439 000	76 845	38 789	17.3	8.7	8.6	7.4	- 1.1	27.5	18.2	45.7	1955
1954	4 406 000	76 365	39 885	17.3	9.1	8.3	8.4	0.1	29.5	19.6	49.1	1954
1953	4 369 000	78 261	39 350	17.9	9.0	8.9	8.0	- 0.9	30.0	19.3	49.3	1953
1952	4 334 000	76 943	39 173	17.8	9.0	8.7	6.9	- 1.8	35.4	19.5	54.9	1952
1951	4 304 000	76 559	37 960	17.8	8.8	9.0	7.7	- 1.3	31.7	18.6	50.3	1951
1950	4 271 000	79 558	39 300	18.6	9.2	9.4	9.6	0.2	31.0	17.2	48.2	1950
1949	4 230 000	79 919	37 793	18.9	8.9	10.0	9.5	- 0.5	38.2	17.1	55.3	1949
1948	4 190 000	84 938	35 981	20.3	8.6	11.7	10.5	- 1.2	39.0	18.2	57.2	1946
1947	4 146 000	91 714	40 043	22.1	9.7	12.5	10.9	- 1.6	45.7	17.8	63.5	1947
1946	4 101 000	96 111	42 013	23.4	10.2	13.2	13.7	0.5	51.4	19.1	70.4	1946
1945	4 045 000	95 062	42 298	23.5	10.5	13.0	11.6	- 1.4	56.0	19.8	75.8	1945
1944	3 998 000	90 641	41 087	22.7	10.3	12.4	12.3	- 0.1	54.7	20.0	74.7	1944
1943	3 949 000	84 319	37 982	21.4	9.6	11.7	11.6	- 0.1	50.9	21.7	72.7	1943
1942	3 903 000	79 545	37 527	20.4	9.6	10.8	10.2	- 0.5	53.3	21.3	74.7	1942
1941	3 863 000	71 306	39 756	18.5	10.3	8.2	8.0	- 0.1	61.1	23.6	84.7	1941
1940	3 832 000	70 121	39 730	18.3	10.4	7.9	7.0	- 0.9	56.2	25.9	82.1	1940
1939	3 805 000	67 914	38 535	17.8	10.1	7.7	7.4	- 0.4	65.2	26.9	92.1	1939
1938	3 777 000	68 463	39 056	18.1	10.3	7.8	7.4	- 0.4	66.2	25.8	91.9	1938
1937	3 749 000	67 440	40 442	18.0	10.8	7.2	7.2	0.0	73.4	26.1	99.5	1937
1936	3 722 000	66 418	40 919	17.8	11.0	6.9	7.3	0.4	75.9	26.5	102.4	1936
1935	3 695 000	65 223	40 816	17.7	11.0	6.6	7.8	1.2	79.5	25.8	105.3	1935
1934	3 666 000	65 116	38 050	17.8	10.4	7.4	9.0	1.6	64.4	23.3	87.7	1934
1933	3 633 000	62 780	38 287	17.3	10.5	6.7	8.3	1.5	67.5	23.4	90.9	1933
1932	3 603 000	64 650	39 701	17.9	11.0	6.9	9.4	2.5	72.0	20.7	92.7	1932
1931	3 569 000	64 266	40 578	18.0	11.4	6.6	7.6	0.9	81.4	22.1	103.5	1931
1930	3 542 000	66 303	38 174	18.7	10.8	7.9	6.8	- 1.2	80.0	21.0	100.9	1930
1929	3 518 000	65 297	39 684	18.6	11.2	7.3	6.0	- 1.4	82.9	21.4	104.3	1929
1928	3 497 000	68 516	38 484	19.6	11.0	8.6	6.3	- 2.3	80.8	20.8	101.7	1928
1927	3 475 000	68 024	40 190	19.6	11.6	8.0	6.6	- 1.4	83.2	20.7	103.9	1927

Denmark

Population Growth

Year	Totals			Per 1.000 population		Rates			Per 1.000 live birth			Year
	Midyear Population	Live Births	Deaths	birth rate	death rate	natural incr.	pop. growth	net migration	infant mort.	stillbirths	infant mort. and stillb.	
1926	3 452 000	70 734	38 093	20.5	11.0	9.5	7.8	- 1.6	84.4	20.4	104.8	1926
1925	3 425 000	71 897	37 083	21.0	10.8	10.2	10.5	0.3	79.9	24.2	104.0	1925
1924	3 389 000	73 836	38 091	21.8	11.2	10.5	10.9	0.4	84.5	24.4	108.9	1924
1923	3 352 000	74 827	37 903	22.3	11.3	11.0	10.1	- 0.9	82.9	24.5	107.4	1923
1922	3 318 000	73 886	39 451	22.3	11.9	10.4	10.5	0.2	84.1	24.6	108.6	1922
1921 a)	3 283 000	78 815	36 215	24.0	11.0	13.0			77.0	25.4	102.4	1921
1920	3 079 000	78 230	39 841	25.4	12.9	12.5	12.3	- 0.1	90.7	25.5	116.2	1920
1919	3 041 000	68 722	39 590	22.6	13.0	9.6	11.5	1.9	91.6	25.0	116.6	1919
1918	3 006 000	72 505	39 038	24.1	13.0	11.1	11.3	0.2	96.6	26.0	122.5	1918
1917	2 972 000	70 306	39 224	23.7	13.2	10.5	12.1	1.7	101.6	25.4	127.0	1917
1916	2 936 000	71 559	39 265	24.4	13.4	11.0	11.9	0.9	99.0	25.1	124.1	1916
1915	2 901 000	70 192	37 174	24.2	12.8	11.4	12.1	0.7		25.3		1915
1914	2 866 000	73 294	35 921	25.6	12.5	13.0	11.5	- 1.5		23.6		1914
1913	2 833 000	72 475	35 364	25.6	12.5	13.1	10.9	- 2.2		23.9		1913
1912	2 802 000	74 659	36 486	26.6	13.0	13.6	11.4	- 2.2	93.2	23.5	116.7	1912
1911	2 770 000	73 933	37 236	26.7	13.4	13.2	11.9	- 1.3	105.8	23.7	129.5	1911
1910	2 737 000	75 297	35 184	27.5	12.9	14.7	12.8	- 1.9	102.2	23.7	125.9	1910
1909	2 702 000	76 301	35 837	28.2	13.3	15.0	12.6	- 2.4	97.7	23.8	121.5	1909
1908	2 668 000	76 233	39 072	28.6	14.6	13.9	12.4	- 1.6	123.2	24.2	147.4	1908
1907	2 635 000	74 324	37 275	28.2	14.1	14.1	12.1	- 1.9	108.4	24.6	133.0	1907
1906	2 603 000	74 217	35 231	28.5	13.5	15.0	11.1	- 3.8	113.7	23.1	136.9	1906
1905	2 574 000	73 082	38 598	28.4	15.0	13.4	10.9	- 2.5	121.0	24.4	145.4	1905
1904	2 546 000	73 691	35 903	28.9	14.1	14.8	8.2	- 6.6	111.5	24.0	135.5	1904
1903	2 525 000	72 348	36 945	28.7	14.6	14.0	12.3	- 1.7	115.9	24.1	140.0	1903
1902	2 494 000	72 795	36 404	29.2	14.6	14.6	12.4	- 2.2	113.9	24.2	138.1	1902
1901	2 463 000	73 211	38 786	29.7	15.7	14.0	12.6	- 1.4	134.3	24.8	159.1	1901
1900	2 432 000	72 129	40 891	29.7	16.8	12.8	11.9	- 0.9	128.4	24.2	152.6	1900
1899	2 403 000	71 355	41 477	29.7	17.3	12.4	13.3	0.9	154.3	24.8	179.2	1899
1898	2 371 000	71 670	36 671	30.2	15.5	14.8	13.9	- 0.8	122.9	25.7	148.6	1898
1897	2 338 000	69 576	38 744	29.8	16.6	13.2	13.7	0.5	129.4	25.9	155.3	1897
1896	2 306 000	70 271	36 090	30.5	15.7	14.8	13.0	- 1.8	125.6	24.5	150.1	1896
1895	2 276 000	68 871	38 573	30.3	16.9	13.3	12.3	- 1.0	136.5	25.0	161.5	1895
1894	2 248 000	68 300	39 508	30.4	17.6	12.8	9.8	- 3.0	134.2	24.6	158.8	1894
1893	2 226 000	68 530	42 295	30.8	19.0	11.8	7.2	- 4.6	149.5	25.5	175.1	1893
1892	2 210 000	65 468	43 079	29.6	19.5	10.1	6.8	- 3.3	139.9	25.9	165.7	1892
1891	2 195 000	67 937	43 954	31.0	20.0	10.9	7.3	- 3.6	134.2	25.4	159.6	1891
1890	2 179 000	66 376	41 377	30.5	19.0	11.5	8.3	- 3.2	132.7	26.1	158.9	1890
1889	2 161 000	67 385	40 004	31.2	18.5	12.7	8.3	- 4.3	140.6	27.5	168.1	1889
1888	2 143 000	67 427	41 868	31.5	19.5	11.9	8.9	- 3.1	138.9	26.6	165.5	1888
1887	2 124 000	67 417	38 645	31.7	18.2	13.5	10.4	- 3.2	131.2	29.7	160.8	1887
1886	2 102 000	68 062	38 076	32.4	18.1	14.3	12.4	- 1.9	135.6	28.9	164.5	1886
1885	2 076 000	67 464	37 000	32.5	17.8	14.7	12.0	- 2.6	121.8	30.4	152.2	1885
1884	2 051 000	68 340	37 597	33.3	18.3	15.0	10.7	- 4.3	136.9	28.3	165.1	1884
1883	2 029 000	64 474	37 403	31.8	18.4	13.3	7.9	- 5.5	138.1	29.8	167.9	1883
1882	2 013 000	65 070	38 738	32.3	19.2	13.1	8.9	- 4.1	150.8	29.3	180.2	1882
1881	1 995 000	64 145	36 471	32.2	18.3	13.9	9.5	- 4.3	120.8	31.1	151.9	1881
1880	1 976 000	62 612	40 237	31.7	20.4	11.3	8.1	- 3.2	150.8	30.6	181.4	1880
1879	1 960 000	62 455	38 531	31.9	19.7	12.2	10.2	- 2.0	130.5	30.5	161.1	1879
1878	1 940 000	61 290	35 792	31.6	18.4	13.1	11.9	- 1.3	137.9	30.2	168.1	1878

Denmark

Population Growth

Year	Totals			Per 1.000 population		Rates			Per 1.000 live births			Year
	Midyear Population	Live Births	Deaths	birth rate	death rate	natural incr.	pop. growth	net migration	infant mort.	stillbirths	infant mort. and stillb.	
1877	1 917 000	61 844	35 806	32.3	18.7	13.6	12.0	− 1.6	129.9	31.2	161.0	1877
1876	1 894 000	61 788	37 365	32.6	19.7	12.9	10.6	− 2.3	143.7	35.3	179.0	1876
1875	1 874 000	59 749	39 423	31.9	21.0	10.8	9.6	− 1.2	154.3	34.2	188.4	1875
1874	1 856 000	57 278	37 046	30.9	20.0	10.9	9.7	− 1.2	145.0	35.7	180.8	1874
1873	1 838 000	56 571	34 250	30.8	18.6	12.1	9.2	− 2.9	126.1	36.1	162.2	1873
1872	1 821 000	55 221	33 433	30.3	18.4	12.0	7.7	− 4.3	131.0	37.2	168.2	1872
1871	1 807 000	54 396	35 075	30.1	19.4	10.7	7.7	− 2.9	129.0	37.0	165.9	1871
1870	1 793 000	54 420	34 091	30.4	19.0	11.3	8.9	− 2.4	130.9	37.7	168.6	1870
1869	1 777 000	52 109	33 781	29.3	19.0	10.3	10.1	− 0.2	125.4	37.4	162.7	1869
1868	1 759 000	54 490	33 816	31.0	19.2	11.8	10.2	− 1.5	144.8	37.7	182.5	1868
1867	1 741 000	52 700	34 553	30.3	19.8	10.4	10.3	− 0.1	134.1	39.1	173.2	1867
1866	1 723 000	55 141	35 707	32.0	20.7	11.3	8.7	− 2.6	126.1	40.1	166.2	1866
1865	1 708 000	53 218	39 266	31.2	23.0	8.2	11.7	3.5	144.9	41.6	186.6	1865
1864	1 688 000	50 797	39 100	30.1	23.2	6.9	9.5	2.5	154.9	41.1	196.0	1864
1863	1 672 000	51 701	30 333	30.9	18.1	12.8	12.6	− 0.2	125.4	43.3	168.7	1863
1862	1 651 000	50 942	30 200	30.9	18.3	12.6	12.1	− 0.4	131.0	40.6	171.6	1862
1861	1 631 000	51 616	29 947	31.6	18.4	13.3	12.3	− 1.0	126.3	41.3	167.6	1861
1860	1 611 000	52 536	32 524	32.6	20.2	12.4	13.0	0.6	135.6	43.0	178.7	1860
1859	1 590 000	53 361	32 268	33.6	20.3	13.3	12.6	− 0.7	133.0	45.6	178.6	1859
1858	1 570 000	52 115	36 388	33.2	23.2	10.0	11.5	1.4	142.0	44.4	186.4	1858
1857	1 552 000	51 054	33 768	32.9	21.8	11.1	13.5	2.4	147.9	45.5	193.4	1857
1856	1 531 000	49 553	28 662	32.4	18.7	13.6	13.7	0.1	122.5	46.2	168.7	1856
1855	1 510 000	48 168	30 157	31.9	20.0	11.9	13.2	1.3	126.1	48.2	174.3	1855
1854	1 490 000	48 725	24 439	32.7	16.4	16.3	10.7	− 5.6	120.7	47.0	167.7	1854
1853	1 474 000	46 614	36 797	31.6	25.0	6.7	10.2	3.5	153.2	48.1	201.3	1853
1852	1 459 000	48 390	28 550	33.2	19.6	13.6	12.3	− 1.3	136.7	46.9	183.6	1852
1851	1 441 000	43 338	26 570	30.1	18.4	11.6	11.8	0.2	135.3	46.6	181.9	1851
1850	1 424 000	44 768	27 231	31.4	19.1	12.3	10.5	− 1.8	126.8	47.2	174.0	1850
1849	1 409 000	43 645	31 512	31.0	22.4	8.6	9.2	0.6	144.7	45.6	190.3	1849
1848	1 396 000	42 747	29 423	30.6	21.1	9.5	9.3	− 0.2	144.6	45.8	190.4	1848
1847	1 383 000	42 291	30 018	30.6	21.7	8.6	8.7	− 0.2	153.1	44.0	197.1	1847
1846	1 371 000	41 225	29 474	30.1	21.5	8.6	9.5	0.9	170.7	43.1	213.8	1846
1845	1 358 000	41 601	26 400	30.6	19.4	11.2	11.0	− 0.1	138.9	43.8	182.7	1845
1844	1 343 000	40 746	25 971	30.3	19.3	11.0	11.9	0.9	131.1	45.2	176.3	1844
1843	1 327 000	39 551	25 590	29.8	19.3	10.5	9.0	− 1.5	129.2	46.4	175.6	1843
1842	1 315 000	39 534	26 503	30.1	20.2	9.9	9.9	0.0	141.5	44.5	186.0	1842
1841	1 302 000	38 718	25 813	29.7	19.8	9.9	10.0	0.1	141.8	47.6	189.4	1841
1840	1 289 000	39 210	27 055	30.4	21.0	9.4	7.8	− 1.7	141.2	46.5	187.7	1840
1839	1 279 000	37 051	26 234	29.0	20.5	8.5	8.6	0.1	147.1	45.1	192.2	1839
1838	1 268 000	37 763	25 375	29.8	20.0	9.8	7.9	− 1.9	126.8	46.2	173.0	1838
1837	1 258 000	37 755	27 336	30.0	21.7	8.3	7.2	− 1.1	142.1	45.8	187.9	1837
1836	1 249 000	38 050	27 864	30.5	22.3	8.2	7.2	− 0.9	161.7	44.7	206.4	1836
1835	1 240 000	39 301	28 439	31.7	22.9	8.8	8.1	− 0.7	151.7	44.0	195.7	1835
1834	1 230 000	40 644	28 941	33.0	23.5	9.5	8.9	− 0.6		43.8		1834
1833	1 219 000	39 327	28 357	32.3	23.3	9.0	5.7	− 3.3		45.2		1833
1832	1 212 000	32 765	31 839	27.0	26.3	0.8	0.8	0.1		44.4		1832
1831	1 211 000	35 997	36 480	29.7	30.1	− 0.4	1.7	2.1		46.1		1831
1830	1 209 000	34 969	30 595	28.9	25.3	3.6	2.5	− 1.1		43.1		1830
1829	1 206 000	35 742	34 721	29.6	28.8	0.8	4.1	3.3		42.0		1829

Denmark

Population Growth

Year	T o t a l s			Per 1.000 population		R a t e s			Per 1.000 live births			Year
	Midyear Population	Live Births	Deaths	birth rate	death rate	natural incr.	pop. growth	net migration	infant mort.	stillbirths	infant mort. and stillb.	
1828	1 201 000	36 344	28 295	30.3	23.6	6.7	7.5	0.8		42.6		1828
1827	1 192 000	34 813	23 886	29.2	20.0	9.2	10.1	0.9		40.7		1827
1826	1 180 000	37 062	24 939	31.4	21.1	10.3	11.9	1.6		40.0		1826
1825	1 166 000	36 451	22 429	31.3	19.2	12.0	12.0	0.0		39.3		1825
1824	1 152 000	36 072	21 392	31.3	18.6	12.7	13.9	1.1		37.0		1824
1823	1 136 000	37 021	20 058	32.6	17.7	14.9	14.1	- 0.8		40.0		1823
1822	1 120 000	37 786	22 751	33.7	20.3	13.4	10.7	- 2.7		37.3		1822
1821	1 108 000	35 536	26 642	32.1	24.0	8.0	9.9	1.9		35.7		1821
1820	1 097 000	34 551	22 902	31.5	20.9	10.6	12.8	2.1		36.7		1820
1819	1 083 000	35 196	21 099	32.5	19.5	13.0	12.9	- 0.1		35.0		1819
1818	1 069 000	34 311	20 174	32.1	18.9	13.2	13.1	- 0.1		36.7		1818
1817	1 055 000	34 610	20 048	32.8	19.0	13.8	13.3	- 0.5		35.4		1817
1816	1 041 000	34 286	21 508	32.9	20.7	12.3	12.5	0.2		35.7		1816
1815	1 028 000	35 028	22 251	34.1	21.6	12.4	9.7	- 2.7		35.3		1815

a) Territorial change

48

Finland

Population Growth

Year	Totals			Per 1.000 population		Rates			Per 1.000 live births			Year
	Midyear Population a)	Live Births	Deaths	birth rate	death rate	natural incr.	pop. growth	net migration	infant mort.	stillbirths	infant mort. and stillb.	
1975	4 711 400	65 719	43 828	13.9	9.3	4.6	4.4	- 0.2	9.6	5.8	15.3	1975
1974	4 690 600	62 472	44 674	13.3	9.5	3.8	5.2	1.4	11.0	7.4	18.5	1974
1973	4 666 100	56 787	43 418	12.2	9.3	2.9	5.7	2.8	10.6	7.4	18.1	1973
1972	4 639 700	58 864	43 958	12.7	9.5	3.2	5.9	2.7	12.0	8.7	20.8	1972
1971	4 612 100	61 067	45 876	13.2	9.9	3.3	1.3	- 2.0	12.7	7.7	20.4	1971
1970	4 606 300	64 559	44 119	14.0	9.6	4.4	- 3.8	- 8.2	13.2	8.0	21.3	1970
1969	4 623 800	67 450	45 966	14.6	9.9	4.6	- 0.6	- 5.2	14.3	9.3	23.5	1969
1968	4 626 500	73 654	45 013	15.9	9.7	6.2	4.5	- 1.7	14.4	9.9	24.4	1968
1967	4 605 700	77 289	43 790	16.8	9.5	7.3	5.4	- 1.9	14.8	10.7	25.5	1967
1966	4 580 900	77 697	43 548	17.0	9.5	7.5	3.8	- 3.7	15.0	11.2	26.2	1966
1965	4 563 700	77 885	44 473	17.1	9.7	7.3	3.3	- 4.0	17.6	12.5	30.1	1965
1964	4 548 500	80 428	42 512	17.7	9.3	8.3	5.6	- 2.7	17.0	12.3	29.4	1964
1963	4 523 000	82 251	42 010	18.2	9.3	8.9	7.0	- 1.9	18.2	12.6	30.7	1963
1962	4 491 400	81 454	42 889	18.1	9.5	8.6	6.8	- 1.8	20.5	13.4	33.9	1962
1961	4 461 000	81 996	40 616	18.4	9.1	9.3	7.0	- 2.2	20.8	14.3	35.1	1961
1960	4 429 600	82 129	39 797	18.5	9.0	9.6	8.0	- 1.5	21.0	15.3	36.4	1960
1959	4 394 000	83 253	38 827	18.9	8.8	10.1	8.0	- 2.1	23.6	16.2	39.8	1959
1958	4 359 000	81 148	38 833	18.6	8.9	9.7	8.0	- 1.7	24.5	17.2	41.7	1958
1957	4 324 000	86 985	40 741	20.1	9.4	10.7	9.8	- 0.9	27.9	17.4	45.3	1957
1956	4 281 700	88 896	38 713	20.8	9.0	11.7	10.9	- 0.8	25.7	18.6	44.3	1956
1955	4 234 900	89 740	39 573	21.2	9.3	11.8	11.3	- 0.5	29.7	18.2	47.9	1955
1954	4 186 900	89 845	37 988	21.5	9.1	12.4	11.3	- 1.1	30.6	18.0	48.6	1954
1953	4 139 400	90 866	39 925	22.0	9.6	12.3	11.8	- 0.5	34.2	17.9	52.1	1953
1952	4 090 500	94 314	39 024	23.1	9.5	13.5	10.6	- 3.0	31.8	19.2	51.0	1952
1951	4 047 300	93 063	40 386	23.0	10.0	13.0	9.5	- 3.5	35.4	18.4	53.8	1951
1950	4 008 900	98 065	40 681	24.5	10.1	14.3	11.5	- 2.8	43.5	18.9	62.4	1950
1949	3 962 900	103 515	44 501	26.1	11.2	14.9	12.9	- 1.9	48.3	17.6	65.9	1949
1948	3 911 600	107 759	43 668	27.5	11.2	16.4	13.4	- 3.0	51.9	18.0	69.6	1948
1947	3 859 200	108 168	46 053	28.0	11.9	16.1	13.8	- 2.3	58.5	19.5	78.0	1947
1946	3 806 000	106 075	44 748	27.9	11.8	16.1	12.6	- 3.5	56.2	19.6	75.8	1946
1945	3 758 000	95 758	49 046	25.5	13.1	12.4	6.2	- 6.3	63.2	21.5	84.7	1945
1944	3 734 800	79 446	70 570	21.3	18.9	2.4	3.8	1.4	68.6	20.7	89.3	1944
1943	3 720 700	76 112	49 634	20.5	13.3	7.1	3.3	- 3.8	61.1	21.3	82.4	1943
1942	3 708 300	61 672	56 141	16.6	15.1	1.5	1.8	0.3	67.3	22.6	89.9	1942
1941	3 701 700	89 565	73 334	24.2	19.8	4.4	1.1	- 3.3	59.2	21.4	80.6	1941
1940 b)	3 697 700	65 849	71 846	17.8	19.4	- 1.6	3.2	4.8	88.3	21.0	109.3	1940
1939 b)	3 685 900	78 164	52 614	21.2	14.3	6.9			69.7	22.0	91.7	1939
1938	3 819 208	76 695	47 901	20.1	12.5	7.5	- 0.4	- 8.0	67.8	24.7	92.5	1938
1937	3 820 913	72 319	47 150	18.9	12.3	6.6	6.3	- 0.3	68.6	24.2	92.8	1937
1936	3 797 004	68 895	42 723	18.1	11.3	6.9	5.9	- 0.9	65.9	25.8	91.8	1936
1935	3 774 435	69 942	45 370	18.5	12.0	6.5	6.4	- 0.1	66.8	26.4	93.1	1935
1934	3 750 279	67 713	46 318	18.1	12.4	5.7	5.5	- 0.2	73.0	27.6	100.6	1934
1933	3 729 643	65 047	47 960	17.4	12.9	4.6	5.5	0.9	75.7	26.2	101.8	1933
1932	3 709 129	69 352	46 700	18.7	12.6	6.1	7.2	1.1	70.9	26.9	97.8	1932
1931	3 682 286	71 866	48 968	19.5	13.3	6.2	7.5	1.3	74.8	28.5	103.3	1931
1930	3 654 581	75 236	48 240	20.6	13.2	7.4	6.6	- 0.8	75.1	27.7	102.8	1930
1929	3 630 520	76 011	54 489	20.9	15.0	5.9	7.4	1.4	97.6	26.7	124.3	1929
1928	3 603 805	77 523	48 713	21.5	13.5	8.0	7.7	- 0.3	84.0	25.2	109.2	1928
1927	3 576 125	75 611	51 727	21.1	14.5	6.7	8.1	1.4	97.1	27.6	124.7	1927

Finland

Population Growth

Year	Totals			Per 1.000 population		Rates			Per 1.000 live births			Year
	Midyear a) Population	Live Births	Deaths	birth rate	death rate	natural incr.	pop. growth	net migration	infant mort.	stillbirths	infant mort. and stillb.	
1926	3 547 207	76 875	47 526	21.7	13.4	8.3	9.1	0.9	85.6	28.6	114.2	1926
1925	3 514 797	78 260	47 493	22.3	13.5	8.8	8.4	- 0.4	85.0	26.7	111.7	1925
1924	3 485 424	78 057	53 442	22.4	15.3	7.1	8.9	1.8	106.9	26.9	133.8	1924
1923	3 454 561	81 961	47 556	23.7	13.8	10.0	9.9	0.0	92.4	27.4	119.8	1923
1922	3 420 263	80 140	49 180	23.4	14.4	9.1	10.6	1.5	99.2	27.6	126.8	1922
1921	3 384 147	82 165	47 361	24.3	14.0	10.3	10.4	0.2	94.6	27.3	121.9	1921
1920	3 348 792	84 714	53 304	25.3	15.9	9.4	5.3	- 4.1	96.7	26.1	122.8	1920
1919	3 331 201	63 896	62 932	19.2	18.9	0.3	- 1.9	- 2.2	134.6	26.0	160.6	1919
1918	3 337 643	79 494	95 102	23.8	28.5	- 4.7	0.9	5.6	115.2	25.2	140.4	1918
1917	3 334 511	81 046	58 863	24.3	17.7	6.7	7.0	0.3	118.2	26.8	145.0	1917
1916	3 311 323	79 653	54 577	24.1	16.5	7.6	8.3	0.7	110.1	26.7	136.8	1916
1915	3 283 795	83 206	52 205	25.3	15.9	9.4	10.4	0.9	110.5	26.5	137.0	1915
1914	3 249 741	87 577	50 690	26.9	15.6	11.4	11.2	- 0.2	104.2	26.3	130.5	1914
1913	3 213 500	87 250	51 876	27.2	16.1	11.0	11.9	0.9	112.8	25.3	138.1	1913
1912	3 175 387	92 275	51 645	29.1	16.3	12.8	12.7	- 0.1	108.6	25.4	134.0	1912
1911	3 135 074	91 238	51 648	29.1	16.5	12.6	13.4	0.7	113.9	26.2	140.0	1911
1910	3 093 219	92 984	51 007	30.1	16.5	13.6	14.8	1.3	117.7	25.6	143.3	1910
1909	3 047 343	95 005	50 577	31.2	16.6	14.6	14.3	- 0.3	111.0	26.1	137.1	1909
1908	3 003 758	92 146	55 305	30.7	18.4	12.3	13.6	1.3	125.1	24.6	149.7	1908
1907	2 962 937	92 457	53 028	31.2	17.9	13.3	14.4	1.1	112.0	23.6	135.6	1907
1906	2 920 255	91 401	50 857	31.3	17.4	13.9	13.6	- 0.3	119.4	25.3	144.7	1906
1905	2 880 522	87 841	52 773	30.5	18.3	12.2	13.6	1.4	134.6	25.0	159.6	1905
1904	2 841 303	90 253	50 227	31.8	17.7	14.1	13.8	- 0.2	119.8	25.2	145.0	1904
1903	2 801 968	85 120	49 992	30.4	17.8	12.5	13.2	0.7	127.3	25.3	152.6	1903
1902	2 764 971	87 082	50 999	31.5	18.4	13.1	12.9	- 0.2	129.0	26.7	155.7	1902
1901	2 729 419	88 637	56 225	32.5	20.6	11.9	11.7	- 0.2	144.5	25.9	170.4	1901
1900	2 697 490	86 339	57 915	32.0	21.5	10.5	12.5	1.9	153.1	26.5	179.6	1900
1899	2 663 871	88 358	53 042	33.2	19.9	13.3	15.5	2.2	136.9	27.3	164.2	1899
1898	2 622 679	89 106	45 751	34.0	17.4	16.5	16.0	- 0.6	128.4	27.0	155.4	1898
1897	2 580 820	82 330	45 233	31.9	17.5	14.4	14.4	0.1	133.1	27.2	160.3	1897
1896	2 543 583	81 656	47 061	32.1	18.5	13.6	14.6	1.0	142.8	27.3	170.1	1896
1895	2 506 452	81 783	44 482	32.6	17.7	14.9	13.6	- 1.3	129.0	27.2	156.2	1895
1894	2 472 341	76 206	47 467	30.8	19.2	11.6	10.8	- 0.8	139.9	27.7	167.6	1894
1893	2 445 668	73 030	51 902	29.9	21.2	8.6	9.0	0.4	142.7	29.0	171.7	1893
1892	2 423 580	76 433	57 486	31.5	23.7	7.8	11.0	3.2	169.6	27.5	197.1	1892
1891	2 396 814	82 120	50 715	34.3	21.2	13.1	13.7	0.6	144.7	27.4	172.1	1891
1890	2 363 921	77 860	46 479	32.9	19.7	13.3	14.0	0.7	141.7	27.4	169.1	1890
1889	2 330 940	77 881	45 679	33.4	19.6	13.8	14.9	1.1	142.4	29.3	171.7	1889
1888	2 296 159	80 172	45 417	34.9	19.8	15.1	16.5	1.3	146.3	29.5	175.8	1888
1887	2 258 356	81 724	42 875	36.2	19.0	17.2	15.4	- 1.8	131.8	29.1	160.9	1887
1886	2 223 545	78 576	49 514	35.3	22.3	13.1	13.0	0.0	157.1	28.0	185.1	1886
1885	2 194 532	75 129	48 261	34.2	22.0	12.2	14.2	1.9	162.3	28.8	191.0	1885
1884	2 163 471	78 147	45 204	36.1	20.9	15.2	15.5	0.3	148.2	29.0	177.1	1884
1883	2 129 848	76 378	44 291	35.9	20.8	15.1	15.0	- 0.1	148.7	28.4	177.1	1883
1882	2 097 972	76 053	46 821	36.3	22.3	13.9	12.5	- 1.4	163.8	28.8	192.6	1882
1881	2 071 712	72 436	51 744	35.0	25.0	10.0	12.1	2.1	186.3	28.1	214.4	1881
1880	2 046 726	74 784	48 857	36.5	23.9	12.7	16.2	3.5	166.9	28.9	195.8	1880
1879	2 013 621	76 150	39 468	37.8	19.6	18.2	15.2	- 3.0	138.4	28.7	167.2	1879
1878	1 983 002	70 275	47 739	35.4	24.1	11.4	13.1	1.7	189.6	29.4	219.0	1878

Finland

Population Growth

Year	Totals			Per 1.000 population		Rates			Per 1.000 live births			Year
	Midyear a) Population	Live Births	Deaths	birth rate	death rate	natural incr.	pop. growth	net migration	infant mort.	stillbirths	infant mort. and stillb.	
1877	1 957 041	74 831	47 458	38.2	24.2	14.0	15.0	1.0	160.5	26.6	187.2	1877
1876	1 927 651	70 759	42 451	36.7	22.0	14.7	14.7	0.0	162.6	29.4	192.0	1876
1875	1 899 382	69 521	43 458	36.6	22.9	13.7	13.9	0.1	170.8	29.9	200.7	1875
1874	1 873 046	70 808	45 225	37.8	24.1	13.7	13.7	0.1	180.8	30.3	211.1	1874
1873	1 847 293	68 422	43 525	37.0	23.6	13.5	15.2	1.7	183.9	29.7	213.6	1873
1872	1 819 228	66 189	35 888	36.4	19.7	16.7	18.1	1.4	173.4	30.2	203.6	1872
1871	1 786 307	66 567	31 958	37.3	17.9	19.4	18.0	- 1.4	141.1	29.1	170.2	1871
1870	1 754 164	63 748	31 841	36.3	18.2	18.2	11.8	- 6.4	136.6	29.9	166.5	1870
1869	1 733 549	58 395	43 675	33.7	25.2	8.5	−24.4	−32.9	140.8	30.0	170.8	1869
1868	1 775 838	43 757	137 720	24.6	77.6	−52.9	−31.0	21.9	391.7	43.1	434.8	1868
1867	1 830 822	59 164	69 774	32.3	38.1	- 5.8	- 5.2	0.6	223.4	35.0	258.4	1867
1866	1 840 375	58 853	61 894	32.0	33.6	- 1.7	2.9	4.5	217.6	33.3	250.9	1866
1865	1 835 113	62 780	45 743	34.2	24.9	9.3	12.5	3.2		29.7		1865
1864	1 812 201	71 307	40 975	39.3	22.6	16.7	11.3	- 5.5		26.9		1864
1863	1 791 807	64 988	52 984	36.3	29.6	6.7	7.5	0.8		27.9		1863
1862	1 778 418	66 328	50 005	37.3	28.1	9.2	11.1	1.9		27.4		1862
1861	1 758 684	66 534	41 845	37.8	23.8	14.0	12.7	- 1.3		28.5		1861
1860	1 736 341	63 183	43 113	36.4	24.8	11.6	11.5	- 0.1				1860
1859	1 716 365	61 454	42 969	35.8	25.0	10.8	9.2	- 1.6				1859
1858	1 700 610	62 670	50 440	36.9	29.7	7.2	4.0	- 3.2				1858
1857	1 693 865	55 610	55 143	32.8	32.6	0.3	1.7	1.4				1857
1856	1 690 994	61 319	57 438	36.3	34.0	2.3	2.3	0.0				1856
1855	1 687 096	60 370	53 998	35.8	32.0	3.8	5.8	2.0				1855
1854	1 677 339	62 949	43 498	37.5	25.9	11.6	6.8	- 4.8				1854
1853	1 665 990	58 398	48 844	35.1	29.3	5.7	3.5	- 2.3				1853
1852	1 660 200	58 069	49 736	35.0	30.0	5.0	7.8	2.8				1852
1851	1 647 262	62 955	39 107	38.2	23.7	14.5	11.2	- 3.3				1851
1850	1 628 883	58 269	42 913	35.8	26.3	9.4	11.6	2.1				1850
1849	1 610 065	60 320	39 456	37.5	24.5	13.0	13.2	0.2				1849
1848	1 588 857	58 021	37 885	36.5	23.8	12.7	12.0	- 0.6				1848
1847	1 569 743	53 211	36 531	33.9	23.3	10.6	9.8	- 0.8				1847
1846	1 554 387	51 604	38 984	33.2	25.1	8.1	10.8	2.7				1846
1845	1 537 633	54 884	35 259	35.7	22.9	12.8	13.2	0.5				1845
1844	1 517 276	53 124	33 147	35.0	21.8	13.2	13.6	0.5				1844
1843	1 496 573	53 597	33 278	35.8	22.2	13.6	14.7	1.1				1843
1842	1 474 603	54 806	32 296	37.2	21.9	15.3	13.7	- 1.5				1842
1841	1 454 348	49 440	32 550	34.0	22.4	11.6	12.1	0.5				1841
1840	1 436 715	49 794	31 717	34.7	22.1	12.6	12.6	0.0				1840
1839	1 418 624	47 804	29 190	33.7	20.6	13.1	11.0	- 2.1				1839
1838	1 403 042	44 652	31 593	31.8	22.5	9.3	6.1	- 3.2				1838
1837	1 394 503	44 080	39 553	31.6	28.4	3.2	1.0	- 2.2				1837
1836	1 393 047	43 290	44 397	31.1	31.9	- 0.8	4.5	5.3				1836
1835	1 386 784	47 525	34 245	34.3	24.7	9.6	11.5	1.9				1835
1834	1 370 833	50 238	32 825	36.6	23.9	12.7	- 1.3	−14.0				1834
1833	1 372 644	41 492	63 738	30.2	46.4	−16.2	- 7.3	8.9				1833
1832	1 382 683	47 696	46 737	34.5	33.8	0.7	4.1	3.4				1832
1831	1 376 989	48 531	39 312	35.2	28.5	6.7	17.9	11.2				1831
1830	1 352 352	48 964	33 968	36.2	25.1	11.1	20.8	9.7				1830
1829	1 324 203	51 202	34 804	38.7	26.3	12.4	14.5	2.2				1829

Finland

Population Growth

Year	Totals			Per 1.000 population		Rates			Per 1.000 live birth			Year
	Midyear Population a)	Live Births	Deaths	birth rate	death rate	natural incr.	pop. growth	net migration	infant mort.	stillbirths	infant mort. and stillb.	
1828	1 304 955	51 262	29 466	39.3	22.6	16.7	15.7	- 1.0				1828
1827	1 284 438	47 142	27 606	36.7	21.5	15.2	13.6	- 1.6				1827
1826	1 266 947	47 675	31 927	37.6	25.2	12.4	12.4	0.0				1826
1825	1 251 176	48 120	32 619	38.5	26.1	12.4	11.7	- 0.6				1825
1824	1 236 484	46 762	33 742	37.8	27.3	10.5	13.5	3.0				1824
1823	1 219 748	49 168	29 578	40.3	24.2	16.1	12.2	- 3.8				1823
1822	1 204 823	42 898	33 535	35.6	27.8	7.8	13.4	5.6				1822
1821	1 188 732	49 165	27 241	41.4	22.9	18.4	15.7	- 2.8				1821
1820	1 170 097	42 789	29 606	36.6	25.3	11.3	11.5	0.2				1820
1819	1 156 651	41 747	31 468	36.1	27.2	8.9	12.7	3.8				1819
1818	1 141 990	43 918	28 304	38.5	24.8	13.7	15.7	2.1				1818
1817	1 124 015	43 863	26 956	39.0	24.0	15.0	16.6	1.6				1817
1816	1 105 331	42 863	25 829	38.8	23.4	15.4	12.0	- 3.4				1816
1815	1 092 093	40 898	28 370	37.4	26.0	11.5	8.1	- 3.4				1815

a) 1815-1890: average population calculated on the basis of figures for endyear population; 1891-1975: midyear population

b) Territorial change

P o p u l a t i o n   G r o w t h

Year	Totals			Per 1.000 population		Rates			Per 1.000 live births			Year
	Midyear[a] Population (in 1.000)	Live[b] Births	Deaths[c]	birth rate	death rate	natural incr.	pop. growth	net migration	infant mort.	stillbirths[b]	infant mort. and stillb.	
1975	52 748	743 200	558 600	14.1	10.6	3.5	7.7	4.2	11.3	13.6	24.9	1975
1974	52 340	799 600	550 500	15.3	10.5	4.8	4.0	−0.8	12.3	14.3	26.5	1974
1973	52 131	854 900	556 500	16.4	10.7	5.7	8.2	2.5	12.8	15.0	27.7	1973
1972	51 703	875 100	547 500	16.9	10.6	6.3	8.8	2.4	13.4	15.3	28.7	1972
1971	51 249	878 000	551 500	17.1	10.8	6.4	9.4	3.0	14.2	16.1	30.3	1971
1970	50 768	847 800	539 700	16.7	10.6	6.1	8.9	2.9	15.1	16.6	31.7	1970
1969	50 315	839 500	570 600	16.7	11.3	5.3	8.0	2.6	16.4	17.5	33.9	1969
1968	49 914	832 800	550 500	16.7	11.0	5.7	7.3	1.7	16.9	17.9	34.8	1968
1967	49 548	837 500	539 900	16.9	10.9	6.0	7.8	1.7	17.2	18.6	35.8	1967
1966	49 164	860 200	525 500	17.5	10.7	6.8	8.3	1.5	18.0	19.1	37.1	1966
1965	48 758	862 300	560 300	17.7	11.5	6.2	7.1	0.9	18.1	19.4	37.5	1965
1964	48 410	874 200	516 500	18.1	10.7	7.4	11.6	4.2	19.3	19.9	39.2	1964
1963	47 850	865 300	554 300	18.1	11.6	6.5	17.8	11.3	21.5	20.5	42.0	1963
1962	47 000	828 900	537 700	17.6	11.4	6.2	17.9	11.7	21.7	20.6	42.3	1962
1961	46 160	835 200	496 900	18.1	10.8	7.3	10.4	3.1	21.7	20.6	42.3	1961
1960	45 680	816 300	517 400	17.9	11.3	6.5	9.6	3.1	23.3	21.7	45.0	1960
1959	45 240	825 600	505 500	18.2	11.2	7.1	9.9	2.9	25.2	21.0	46.1	1959
1958	44 790	808 600	496 900	18.1	11.1	7.0	10.7	3.8	27.1	21.9	49.0	1958
1957	44 310	812 600	528 200	18.3	11.9	6.4	10.6	4.2	29.0	22.6	51.7	1957
1956	43 840	803 100	541 900	18.3	12.4	6.0	9.4	3.4	31.6	22.3	53.9	1956
1955	43 430	802 300	522 700	18.5	12.0	6.4	8.5	2.1	34.3	22.1	56.3	1955
1954	43 060	807 200	515 300	18.8	12.0	6.8	7.2	0.4	36.5	22.3	58.8	1954
1953	42 750	801 100	553 400	18.7	12.9	5.8	6.8	1.0	37.7	23.1	60.8	1953
1952	42 460	818 500	521 100	19.3	12.3	7.0	7.1	0.1	40.8	23.0	63.8	1952
1951	42 160	822 800	561 900	19.5	13.3	6.2	7.8	1.6	46.2	24.4	70.6	1951
1950	41 830	858 100	530 300	20.5	12.7	7.8	8.4	0.5	47.4	24.6	72.0	1950
1949	41 480	868 600	569 600	20.9	13.7	7.2	8.9	1.7	55.8	23.9	79.8	1949
1948	41 110	867 100	509 500	21.1	12.4	8.7	19.2	10.5	51.9	24.2	76.1	1948
1947	40 320	867 000	534 000	21.5	13.2	8.3	0.7	− 7.5	66.9	26.5	93.4	1947
1946[d]	40 290	840 200	542 200	20.9	13.5	7.4			67.8	28.1	95.9	1946
1945[d]	39 700	643 000	641 000	16.2	16.1	0.1			108.9	27.7	136.5	1945
1944[d]	38 900	627 000	664 000	16.1	17.1	−1.0			77.7	27.0	104.6	1944
1943[d]	39 000	613 000	624 000	15.7	16.0	−0.3			75.4	25.6	101.0	1943
1942[d]	39 400	573 000	654 000	14.5	16.6	−2.1			71.0	27.1	98.1	1942
1941[d]	39 600	520 000	673 000	13.1	17.0	−3.9			72.7	29.8	102.5	1941
1940[d]	41 000	559 000	738 000	13.6	18.0	−4.4			90.5	32.2	122.7	1940
1939	41 900	612 400	642 500	14.6	15.3	−0.7	− 1.4	− 0.7	63.5	35.8	99.3	1939
1938	41 960	612 200	647 500	14.6	15.4	−0.8	− 0.7	1.6	65.5	36.1	101.6	1938
1937	41 930	618 100	629 500	14.7	15.0	−0.3	− 0.5	− 0.7	65.4	34.3	99.7	1937
1936	41 910	630 800	642 300	15.1	15.3	−0.3	− 0.7	− 0.4	66.9	34.6	101.5	1936
1935	41 940	640 500	658 400	15.3	15.7	−0.4	− 0.2	0.2	68.9	34.2	103.0	1935
1934	41 950	677 900	634 100	16.2	15.1	1.0	1.4	0.4	69.5	34.4	103.9	1934
1933	41 890	678 700	660 400	16.2	15.8	0.4	0.7	0.3	74.8	35.1	109.9	1933
1932	41 860	722 400	659 800	17.3	15.8	1.5	0.0	− 1.5	77.0	35.2	112.1	1932
1931	41 860	733 900	679 100	17.5	16.2	1.3	6.0	4.7	75.9	35.0	110.9	1931
1930	41 610	750 000	648 900	18.0	15.6	2.4	9.1	6.7	78.1	34.7	112.8	1930
1929	41 230	730 100	738 700	17.7	17.9	−0.2	4.4	4.6	96.0	34.8	130.8	1929
1928	41 050	749 300	674 000	18.3	16.4	1.8	2.7	0.8	91.6	35.6	127.2	1928
1927	40 940	743 800	675 500	18.2	16.5	1.7	1.7	0.0	83.4	35.5	118.8	1927

Population Growth

Year	Totals			Per 1.000 population		Rates			Per 1.000 live births			Year
	Midyear Population (in 1.000) a)	Live Births b)	Deaths c)	birth rate	death rate	natural incr.	pop. growth	net migration	infant mort.	stillbirths b)	infant mort. and stillb.	
1926	40 870	767 500	712 800	18.8	17.4	1.3	6.4	5.0	96.6	36.6	133.6	1926
1925	40 610	770 100	707 800	19.0	17.4	1.5	7.4	5.9	88.9	37.7	126.6	1925
1924	40 310	753 500	678 900	18.7	16.8	1.9	10.7	8.8	84.8	38.4	123.2	1924
1923	39 880	761 300	665 700	19.1	16.7	2.4	11.5	9.1	96.3	40.5	136.7	1923
1922	39 420	759 700	687 700	19.3	17.4	1.8	4.6	2.7	86.6	42.0	128.6	1922
1921	39 240	811 800	693 100	20.7	17.7	3.0	6.1	3.1	116.9	42.7	159.6	1921
1920	39 000	833 500	671 600	21.4	17.2	4.2	7.7	3.5	99.2	42.5	141.7	1920
1919 e)	38 700	503 600	736 500	13.0	19.0	-6.0	-1.3	4.7	122.5	50.6	173.2	1919
1918 e)	38 750	470 000	865 000	12.1	22.3	-10.2			140.4	46.8	187.2	1918
1917 e)	39 500	410 000	710 000	10.4	18.0	-7.6			126.8	48.8	175.6	1917
1916 e)	40 100	382 000	695 000	9.5	17.3	-7.8			125.7	49.7	175.4	1916
1915 e)	40 700	480 000	745 000	11.8	18.3	-6.5			143.8	43.8	187.5	1915
1914 e)	41 700	753 000	770 000	18.1	18.5	-0.4			112.9	43.8	156.7	1914
1913	39 770	746 000	702 200	18.8	17.1	1.1	2.5	1.4	112.5	46.5	159.0	1913
1912	39 670	750 400	692 400	18.9	17.4	1.5	1.3	-0.2	104.5	46.2	150.7	1912
1911	39 620	742 400	775 400	18.7	19.6	-0.8	2.0	2.2	157.1	45.9	203.0	1911
1910	39 540	774 400	703 000	19.6	17.8	1.8	2.8	1.0	110.5	46.5	157.0	1910
1909	39 430	769 600	755 000	19.5	19.1	0.4	1.5	1.2	117.7	46.9	164.6	1909
1908	39 370	792 200	744 100	20.1	18.9	1.2	2.5	1.3	127.4	47.3	174.7	1908
1907	39 270	772 700	791 800	19.7	20.2	-0.5	0.0	0.5	131.2	47.6	178.9	1907
1906	39 270	806 800	780 200	20.5	19.9	0.7	1.3	0.6	143.5	46.2	198.8	1906
1905	39 220	807 300	770 200	20.6	19.6	0.9	0.8	-0.2	135.8	46.9	182.7	1905
1904	39 190	818 200	761 200	20.9	19.4	1.5	1.8	0.3	144.2	47.3	191.5	1904
1903	39 120	826 700	753 600	21.1	19.3	1.9	1.8	-0.1	137.1	47.3	184.3	1903
1902	39 050	845 400	761 400	21.6	19.5	2.2	1.8	-0.4	135.2	47.6	182.8	1902
1901	38 980	857 300	784 900	22.0	20.1	1.9	1.0	-0.8	142.0	47.5	189.4	1901
1900	38 940	827 300	853 300	21.2	21.9	-0.7	1.3	2.0	160.8	47.4	208.1	1900
1899	38 890	847 600	816 200	21.8	21.0	0.8	1.8	1.0	163.2	47.1	210.2	1899
1898	38 820	843 900	810 100	21.7	20.9	0.9	3.1	2.2	168.9	47.2	216.0	1898
1897	38 700	859 100	751 000	22.2	19.4	2.8	3.9	1.1	152.0	49.1	201.1	1897
1896	38 550	865 600	771 900	22.5	20.0	2.4	2.3	-0.1	147.5	49.2	196.7	1896
1895	38 460	834 200	852 000	21.7	22.2	-0.5	1.0	1.5	178.6	49.9	228.5	1895
1894	38 420	855 400	815 600	22.3	21.2	1.0	1.0	0.0	157.8	49.1	206.9	1894
1893	38 380	874 700	867 500	22.8	22.6	0.2	0.5	0.3	172.9	48.5	221.3	1893
1892	38 360	855 800	875 900	22.3	22.8	-0.5	0.3	0.8	181.8	49.0	230.8	1982
1891	38 350	866 400	876 900	22.6	22.9	-0.3	-0.8	-0.5	160.7	49.1	209.7	1891
1890	38 380	838 100	876 500	21.8	22.8	-1.0	0.3	1.3	176.1	48.3	224.4	1890
1889	38 370	880 500	794 900	22.9	20.7	2.2	2.1	-0.1	155.4	48.3	203.6	1889
1888	38 290	882 600	837 900	23.1	21.9	1.2	0.8	-0.4	165.2	47.7	212.9	1888
1887	38 360	899 300	842 800	23.5	22.0	1.5	0.8	-0.7	161.1	47.7	208.8	1887
1886	38 230	912 800	860 200	23.9	22.5	1.4	3.1	1.8	173.4	47.8	221.2	1886
1885	38 110	924 600	836 900	24.3	22.0	2.3	2.6	0.3	161.6	47.6	209.2	1885
1884	38 010	937 800	858 800	24.7	22.6	2.1	3.9	1.9	176.9	48.3	225.2	1884
1883	37 860	937 900	841 100	24.8	22.2	2.6	3.4	0.9	165.0	46.6	211.6	1883
1882	37 730	935 600	838 500	24.8	22.2	2.6	3.7	1.1	165.0	47.5	212.5	1882
1881	37 590	937 100	828 800	24.9	22.0	2.9	3.7	0.8	165.5	46.7	212.3	1881
1880	37 450	920 200	858 200	24.6	22.9	1.7	3.5	1.8	180.1	45.3	225.4	1880
1879	37 320	936 500	839 900	25.1	22.5	2.6	3.8	1.2	157.7	46.9	204.6	1879

Year	Totals			Per 1.000 population		Rates			Per 1.000 live births			Year
	Midyear a) Population (in 1.000)	Live b) Births	Deaths c)	birth rate	death rate	natural incr.	pop. growth	net migration	infant mort.	stillbirths b)	infant mort. and stillb.	
1878	37 180	937 300	839 200	25.2	22.6	2.6	4.8	2.2	169.7	46.2	215.9	1878
1877	37 000	944 600	802 000	25.5	21.7	3.9	4.6	0.7	158.4	45.9	204.3	1877
1876	36 830	966 700	834 100	26.2	22.6	3.6	4.6	1.0	165.3	46.2	211.5	1876
1875	36 660	951 000	845 100	25.9	23.1	2.9	4.6	1.7	169.9	46.1	216.0	1875
1874	36 490	954 700	781 700	26.2	21.4	4.7	4.1	- 0.6	158.3	46.7	205.0	1874
1873	36 340	946 400	844 600	26.0	23.2	2.8	5.5	2.7	179.1	47.0	226.1	1873
1872	36 140	966 000	793 100	26.7	21.9	4.8	- 1.4	- 6.2	152.0	45.5	197.5	1872
1871 f)	36 190	826 100	1 271 000	22.8	35.1	-12.3			237.6	48.8	286.4	1871
1870	38 440	995 900	1 090 800	25.9	28.4	- 2.5	1.3	3.8	201.4	47.9	249.3	1870
1869	38 390	999 800	905 700	26.0	23.6	2.5	1.6	-0.9	176.2	47.8	224.0	1869
1868	38 330	984 100	922 000	25.7	24.1	1.6	2.6	1.0	192.0	47.0	239.0	1868
1867	38 230	1 003 800	866 900	26.3	22.7	3.6	3.9	0.3	171.5	46.6	218.2	1867
1866	38 080	1 006 300	884 600	26.4	23.2	3.2	1.6	- 1.6	161.9	47.4	209.3	1866
1865	38 020	1 005 800	921 900	26.5	24.2	2.2	4.2	2.0	191.0	46.7	237.7	1865
1864	37 860	1 005 900	860 300	26.6	22.7	3.8	4.0	0.1	173.9	46.3	220.2	1864
1863	37 710	1 012 800	846 900	26.9	22.5	4.4	5.0	0.6	178.9	44.9	223.8	1863
1862	37 520	995 200	813 000	26.5	21.7	4.9	3.5	- 1.4	163.1	45.1	208.2	1862
1861 f)	37 390	1 005 100	866 600	26.9	23.2	3.7			189.4	44.8	234.2	1861
1860	36 510	956 900	781 600	26.2	21.4	4.8	0.3	- 4.5	152.7	46.3	199.0	1860
1859	36 500	1 017 900	979 300	27.9	26.8	1.1	4.4	3.3	211.7	45.7	257.4	1859
1858	36 340	969 300	874 200	26.7	24.1	2.6	1.1	- 1.5	175.6	45.2	220.8	1858
1857	36 300	940 700	858 800	25.9	23.7	2.3	3.0	0.8	185.4	44.5	229.9	1857
1856	36 190	952 100	837 100	26.3	23.1	3.2	3.0	- 0.1	167.2	42.9	210.1	1856
1855	36 080	902 300	937 900	25.0	26.0	- 1.0	- 4.2	- 3.2	175.9	42.1	218.0	1855
1854	36 230	923 500	992 800	25.5	27.4	- 1.9	4.4	6.3	180.2	43.1	223.3	1854
1853	36 070	937 000	795 600	26.0	22.1	3.9	3.3	- 0.6	150.3	41.2	191.5	1853
1852	35 950	965 000	810 700	26.8	22.6	4.3	4.2	- 0.1	162.5	38.8	201.2	1852
1851	35 800	971 300	799 100	27.1	22.3	4.8	4.7	- 0.1	161.8	38.7	200.6	1851
1850	35 630	954 200	761 600	26.8	21.4	5.4	2.2	- 3.2	147.0	38.9	185.9	1850
1849	35 550	985 800	973 500	27.7	27.4	0.3	0.8	0.5	170.2	37.8	208.1	1849
1848	35 520	940 200	836 700	26.5	23.6	2.9	1.4	- 1.5	157.9	36.5	194.4	1848
1847	35 470	901 900	849 100	25.4	23.9	1.5	2.0	0.5	162.7	36.6	199.2	1847
1846	35 400	965 900	820 900	27.3	23.2	4.1	6.8	2.7	171.4	35.7	207.2	1846
1845	35 160	982 500	742 000	27.9	21.1	6.8	7.4	0.6	143.3	35.0	178.3	1845
1844	34 900	959 500	768 000	27.5	22.0	5.5	6.9	1.4	154.8	35.6	190.4	1844
1843	34 660	978 400	799 000	28.2	23.1	5.2	6.1	0.9	156.9	33.6	190.5	1843
1842	34 450	983 000	825 900	28.5	24.0	4.6	6.4	1.8	166.2	32.6	198.8	1842
1841	34 230	976 800	794 900	28.5	23.2	5.3	4.4	- 0.9	156.5	32.5	189.0	1841
1840	34 080	952 400	809 000	27.9	23.7	4.2	4.1	- 0.1	162.2	32.3	194.6	1840
1839	33 940	958 200	771 900	28.2	22.7	5.5	4.4	- 1.1	159.9			1839
1838	33 790	963 100	817 500	28.5	24.2	4.3	3.0	- 1.3	168.5			1838
1837	33 690	943 700	853 100	28.0	25.3	2.7	4.5	1.8	170.5			1837
1836	33 540	979 700	747 700	29.2	22.3	6.9	8.3	1.4	168.9			1836
1835	33 260	993 800	816 400	29.9	24.5	5.3	5.7	0.4	174.8			1835
1834	33 070	986 500	918 000	29.8	27.8	2.1	5.4	3.4	208.4			1834
1833	32 890	970 200	812 500	29.5	24.7	4.8	4.9	0.1	173.0			1833
1832	32 730	937 400	933 800	28.6	28.5	0.1	4.9	4.8	185.3			1832
1831	32 570	986 800	800 400	30.3	24.6	5.7	6.1	0.4	174.3			1831

France

Population Growth

Year	Totals			Per 1.000 population		Rates			Per 1.000 live births			Year
	Midyear[a]) Population (in 1.000)	Live[b]) Births	Deaths[c])	birth rate	death rate	natural incr.	pop. growth	net migration	infant mort.	stillbirths	infant mort. and stillb.	
1830	32 370	968 000	808 400	29.9	25.0	4.9	2.8	- 2.2	181.4			1830
1829	32 280	965 500	802 600	29.9	24.9	5.0	8.7	3.6	176.0			1829
1828	32 000	976 900	837 500	30.5	26.2	4.4	6.3	1.9	188.4			1828
1827	31 800	980 100	791 600	30.8	24.9	5.9	6.3	0.4	181.2			1827
1826	31 600	992 300	837 600	31.4	26.5	4.9	6.0	1.1	193.5			1826
1825	31 410	973 500	800 100	31.0	25.5	5.5	8.9	3.4	198.0			1825
1824	31 130	984 200	764 100	31.6	24.5	7.1	6.1	- 1.0	190.7			1824
1823	30 940	963 300	743 500	31.1	24.0	7.1	7.8	0.7	183.6			1823
1822	30 700	972 600	777 000	31.7	25.3	6.4	8.1	1.8	197.7			1822
1821	30 450	965 400	741 300	31.7	24.3	7.4	6.6	- 0.8	184.6			1821
1820	30 250	960 000	769 300	31.7	25.4	6.3	6.3	0.0	186.0			1820
1819	30 060	987 600	786 000	32.9	26.1	6.7	6.0	- 0.7	185.0			1819
1818	29 880	914 600	755 500	30.6	25.3	5.3	6.0	0.7	183.2			1818
1817	29 700	944 500	750 600	31.8	25.3	6.5	7.4	0.9	180.9			1817
1816	29 480	968 900	723 700	32.9	24.5	8.3	3.4	- 4.9	176.8			1816
1815	29 380	953 100	762 900	32.4	26.0	6.5	1.4	- 5.1	190.2			1815

a) Population figures are based on the census population (but including those persons not counted under the census due to temporary absence from the country), the number of births, deaths and migrations. They refer to the following territory: 1815-1860: 538,000 sq.km, 1861-1870: 551,000 sq.km, 1871-1913: 536,000 sq.km, 1914-1975: 551,000 sq.km.

b) Children born alive who die prior to being registered (i.e. up until three days after birth) are counted as still-births. The number of live births thus only refers to the number of declared births and the number of still-births includes children born alive but dying prior to registration.

c) The number of deaths excludes children born alive but dying prior to registration.

d) Figures are official estimates based on statistics for 86/87 departments and available information for the other departments. The number of deaths does not include civil or military deaths due to war accidents (ca. 600,000 persons in the period 1939-1945).

e) Present territory. Figures are official estimates based on statistics for 77 departments. The number of deaths excludes military losses (ca. 360,000 in 1914, 320,000 in 1915, 270,000 in 1916, 145,000 in 1917, and 250,000 in 1918).

f) Territorial change.

Year	Totals			Per 1.000 population		Rates			Per 1.000 live births			Year
	Midyear Population a)	Live Births	Deaths	birth rate	death rate	natural incr.	pop. growth	net migration	infant mort.	stillbirths	infant mort. and stillb.	
1975	61 829	600 512	749 260	9.7	12.1	− 2.4	− 3.6	− 1.2	19.8	7.8	27.6	1975
1974	62 054	626 373	727 511	10.1	11.7	− 1.6	1.3	2.9	21.1	8.6	29.7	1974
1973	61 976	635 633	731 028	10.3	11.8	− 1.5	4.9	6.4	22.9	8.9	31.9	1973
1972	61 672	701 214	731 264	11.4	11.9	− 0.5	6.0	6.5	22.7	9.4	32.0	1972
1971	61 302	778 526	730 670	12.7	11.9	0.8	10.6	9.8	23.3	9.9	33.2	1971
1970	60 651	810 808	734 843	13.4	12.1	1.3	9.6	8.4	23.6	10.3	33.9	1970
1969	60 067	903 456	744 360	15.0	12.4	2.6	9.4	6.8	23.4	10.7	34.2	1969
1968	59 500	969 825	734 048	16.3	12.3	4.0	3.6	− 0.4	22.8	11.0	33.8	1968
1967	59 286	1 019 459	687 349	17.2	11.6	5.6	2.3	− 3.3	22.9	11.2	34.1	1967
1966	59 148	1 050 345	686 321	17.8	11.6	6.2	8.9	2.8	23.6	11.6	35.2	1966
1965	58 619	1 044 328	677 628	17.8	11.6	6.3	11.1	4.8	23.9	12.4	36.2	1965
1964	57 971	1 065 437	644 128	18.4	11.1	7.3	6.3	− 1.0	25.3	12.8	38.0	1964
1963	57 389	1 054 123	673 128	18.4	11.7	6.6	10.1	3.5	27.0	13.3	40.3	1963
1962	56 837	1 018 552	644 819	17.9	11.4	6.6	9.7	3.1	29.3	14.1	43.4	1962
1961	56 175	1 012 687	627 561	18.0	11.2	6.9	11.8	4.9	31.7	14.5	46.2	1961
1960	55 433	968 629	642 962	17.5	11.6	5.9	13.4	7.5	33.8	15.5	49.3	1960
1959	54 876	951 942	605 504	17.4	11.0	6.3	11.8	5.5	34.3	15.7	50.0	1959
1958	54 292	904 465	597 305	16.7	11.0	5.7	11.9	6.2	36.0	16.7	52.7	1958
1957	53 656	892 228	615 016	16.6	11.5	5.2	12.2	7.0	36.4	17.8	54.2	1957
1956	53 008	855 887	599 413	16.2	11.3	5.0	12.0	7.0	38.7	18.8	57.5	1956
1955	52 382	820 128	581 872	15.7	11.1	4.6	9.7	5.1	41.8	20.2	62.0	1955
1954	51 880	816 028	555 459	15.7	10.7	5.0	10.3	5.3	43.1	20.6	63.7	1954
1953	51 350	796 096	578 027	15.5	11.3	4.2	9.7	5.5	46.6	20.7	67.2	1953
1952	50 859	799 080	545 963	15.7	10.7	5.0	6.6	1.6	48.3	21.5	69.8	1952
1951	50 528	795 608	543 897	15.8	10.8	5.0	8.8	3.8	53.3	22.4	75.6	1951
1950	50 173	812 835	528 747	16.2	10.5	5.7	19.8	14.1	55.7	22.3	78.0	1950
1949	49 198	832 803	517 194	16.9	10.5	6.4	19.6	13.2	59.0	22.5	81.4	1949
1948	48 251	806 074	515 092	16.7	10.7	6.0	26.8	20.8				1948
1947	46 992	781 421	574 628	16.6	12.2	4.4	17.4	13.0				1947
1946	46 190	732 998	588 331	15.9	12.7	3.1						1946
1943 b)	70 411	1 124 718	853 246 c)	16.0	12.1	3.9						1943
1942 b)	70 834	1 055 915	847 861 c)	14.9	12.0	2.9						1942
1941 b)	70 244	1 308 232	844 435 c)	18.6	12.0	6.6						1941
1940 b)	69 838	1 402 258	885 591 c)	20.1	12.7	7.4						1940
1939 b)	69 314	1 413 230	854 348 c)	20.4	12.3	8.1						1939
1938 b)	68 424	1 348 534	799 220	19.7	11.7	8.0	8.7	0.6	59.8	23.5	83.3	1938
1937	67 831	1 277 046	794 367	18.8	11.7	7.1	7.1	0.0	64.4	24.7	89.1	1937
1936	67 349	1 278 583	795 793	19.0	11.8	7.2	7.1	− 0.1	66.2	26.2	92.3	1936
1935 d)	66 871	1 263 976	792 018	18.9	11.8	7.1			68.6	26.2	94.7	1935
1934	65 595	1 182 789	716 957	18.0	10.9	7.1	5.7	− 1.4	65.8	27.5	93.3	1934
1933	65 218	956 971	729 499	14.7	11.2	3.5	4.7	1.2	76.6	29.7	106.3	1933
1932	64 911	978 210	699 620	15.1	10.8	4.3	4.3	0.0	79.2	30.6	109.8	1932
1931	64 631	1 031 770	725 816	16.0	11.2	4.7	5.2	0.5	83.0	31.5	114.5	1931
1930	64 294	1 127 450	710 850	17.5	11.1	6.5	5.2	− 1.2	84.6	32.3	116.9	1930
1929	63 957	1 147 458	805 962	17.9	12.6	5.3	5.3	0.0	96.4	32.0	128.4	1929
1928	63 618	1 182 815	739 520	18.6	11.6	7.0	5.8	− 1.2	89.3	32.5	121.8	1928
1927	63 252	1 161 719	757 020	18.4	12.0	6.4	6.1	− 0.3	97.0	33.4	130.5	1927

Year	Totals			Per 1.000 population		Rates			Per 1.000 live births			Year
	Midyear Population	Live Births	Deaths	birth rate	death rate	natural incr.	pop.growth	net migration	infant mort.	stillbirths	infant mort. and stillb.	
1926	62 866	1 227 900	734 359	19.5	11.7	7.9	7.2	- 0.6	101.6	34.2	135.9	1926
1925	62 411	1 292 499	744 691	20.7	11.9	8.8	7.3	- 1.4	105.2	33.9	139.1	1925
1924	61 953	1 270 820	759 075	20.5	12.3	8.3	6.1	- 2.2	108.6	33.7	142.3	1924
1923 d)	61 577	1 297 449	857 898	21.1	13.9	7.1	6.4	- 0.8	131.8	32.9	164.7	1923
1922 d)	61 185	1 404 215	880 626	23.0	14.4	8.6			129.7	33.2	163.0	1922
1921 d)	62 473	1 581 130	869 555	25.3	13.9	11.4	10.9	- 0.5	132.1	32.2	164.3	1921
1920 d)	61 794	1 599 287	932 929	25.9	15.1	10.8			131.1	32.7	163.8	1920
1919	62 897	1 260 500	978 380	20.0	15.6	4.5			120.8	30.9	151.6	1919
1918	66 811	926 813	1 606 475	13.9	24.0	-10.2	- 8.3	1.8		31.8		1918
1917	67 368	912 109	1 345 424	13.5	20.0	- 6.4	- 5.2	1.3		30.5		1917
1916	67 715	1 029 484	1 298 054	15.2	19.2	- 4.0	- 2.5	1.5		31.9		1916
1915	67 883	1 382 546	1 450 420	20.4	21.4	- 1.0	1.4	2.4		31.1		1915
1914	67 790	1 818 596	1 291 310	26.8	19.0	7.8	12.0	4.2	163.5	30.7	194.2	1914
1913	66 978	1 838 750	1 004 950	27.5	15.0	12.4	12.4	0.0	150.8	30.4	181.1	1913
1912	66 146	1 869 636	1 029 749	28.3	15.6	12.7	11.9	- 0.8	147.4	30.1	177.5	1912
1911	65 359	1 870 729	1 130 784	28.6	17.3	11.3	12.1	0.8	192.2	30.1	222.3	1911
1910	64 568	1 924 778	1 045 665	29.8	16.2	13.6	13.2	- 0.4	161.8	30.2	192.0	1910
1909	63 717	1 978 278	1 094 217	31.0	17.2	13.9	13.4	- 0.5	169.6	30.4	199.9	1909
1908	62 863	2 015 052	1 135 490	32.1	18.1	14.0	13.5	- 0.5	178.2	30.6	208.7	1908
1907	62 013	1 999 933	1 117 309	32.3	18.0	14.2	13.9	- 0.4	175.5	30.5	206.0	1907
1906	61 153	2 022 477	1 112 202	33.1	18.2	14.9	13.7	- 1.2	185.2	30.8	216.0	1906
1905	60 314	1 987 153	1 194 314	32.9	19.8	13.1	13.9	0.8	205.3	30.8	236.2	1905
1904	59 475	2 025 847	1 163 183	34.1	19.6	14.5	14.2	- 0.3	196.4	31.3	227.7	1904
1903	58 629	1 983 078	1 170 905	33.8	20.0	13.9	14.7	0.8	204.0	31.8	235.8	1903
1902	57 767	2 024 735	1 122 492	35.1	19.4	15.6	15.5	- 0.2	183.1	31.9	215.1	1902
1901	56 874	2 032 313	1 174 489	35.7	20.7	15.1	14.6	- 0.5	206.8	32.2	239.0	1901
1900	56 046	1 996 139	1 236 382	35.6	22.1	13.6	14.2	0.7	223.1	32.3	255.4	1900
1899	55 248	1 980 304	1 185 197	35.8	21.5	14.4	15.2	0.8	210.8	32.8	243.6	1899
1898	54 406	1 964 731	1 117 860	36.1	20.5	15.6	15.4	- 0.2	205.6	33.2	238.8	1898
1897	53 569	1 926 690	1 142 056	36.0	21.3	14.6	15.2	0.6	215.9	33.4	249.3	1897
1896	52 753	1 914 749	1 098 966	36.3	20.8	15.5	14.3	- 1.2	196.4	33.9	230.3	1896
1895	52 001	1 877 278	1 151 488	36.1	22.1	14.0	12.7	- 1.2	223.8	34.3	258.1	1895
1894	51 339	1 841 205	1 144 331	35.9	22.3	13.6	10.9	- 2.6	207.3	34.3	241.6	1894
1893	50 778	1 865 715	1 248 201	36.7	24.6	12.2	9.8	- 2.3	218.1	33.5	251.6	1893
1892	50 279	1 795 971	1 211 402	35.7	24.1	11.6	10.2	- 1.4	224.8	34.0	258.8	1892
1891	49 767	1 840 172	1 164 421	37.0	23.4	13.6	10.6	- 3.0	213.7	34.2	247.9	1891
1890	49 239	1 759 253	1 199 006	35.7	24.4	11.4	14.8	3.4	220.8	34.7	255.5	1890
1889	48 512	1 772 570	1 153 087	36.5	23.8	12.8	10.1	- 2.6	220.3	37.2	257.5	1889
1888	48 020	1 761 407	1 142 826	36.7	23.8	12.9	10.0	- 2.9	213.2	38.0	251.2	1888
1887	47 540	1 757 079	1 151 924	37.0	24.2	12.7	9.2	- 3.5	215.6	39.0	254.6	1887
1886	47 103	1 746 133	1 233 737	37.1	26.2	10.9	8.4	- 2.4	239.6	39.2	278.8	1886
1885	46 705	1 729 927	1 199 742	37.0	25.7	11.4	7.9	- 3.4	220.4	39.7	260.1	1885
1884	46 335	1 725 583	1 203 500	37.2	26.0	11.3	6.9	- 4.3	228.8	39.6	268.4	1884
1883	46 014	1 683 699	1 190 002	36.6	25.9	10.7	6.5	- 4.3	225.2	39.3	264.5	1883
1882	45 717	1 702 348	1 176 853	37.2	25.7	11.5	6.4	- 5.1	222.1	39.4	261.5	1882
1881	45 426	1 682 149	1 156 391	37.0	25.5	11.6	7.3	- 4.2	218.0	39.6	257.6	1881
1880	45 093	1 696 175	1 173 205	37.6	26.0	11.6	10.1	- 1.5		40.0		1880

Germany

Population Growth

Year	Totals			Per 1.000 population		Rates			Per 1.000 live births			Year
	Midyear Population	Live Births	Deaths	birth rate	death rate	natural incr.	pop. growth	net migration	infant mort.	stillbirths	infant mort. and stillb.	
1879	44 639	1 735 871	1 143 773	38.9	25.6	13.3	11.5	– 1.8		40.8		1879
1878	44 127	1 714 433	1 157 960	38.9	26.2	12.6	11.8	– 0.8		41.2		1878
1877	43 608	1 744 659	1 152 023	40.0	26.4	13.6	12.6	– 1.0		40.8		1877
1876	43 057	1 761 046	1 134 452	40.9	26.3	14.6	12.7	– 1.8		41.8		1876
1875	42 510	1 724 412	1 172 393	40.6	27.6	13.0	12.4	– 0.6		43.0		1875
1874	41 983	1 683 440	1 122 396	40.1	26.7	13.4	10.7	– 2.6		41.3		1874
1873	41 532	1 648 117	1 174 293	39.7	28.3	11.4	8.4	– 3.1		40.8		1873
1872	41 185	1 626 037	1 194 732	39.5	29.0	10.5	4.6	– 5.9		40.7		1872
1871	40 995	1 414 248	1 212 869	34.5	29.6	4.9	4.7	– 0.3		41.9		1871
1870	40 804	1 569 206	1 117 875	38.5	27.4	11.1	7.6	– 3.4		42.3		1870
1869	40 493	1 529 387	1 089 503	37.8	26.9	10.9	6.7	– 4.2		42.4		1869
1868	40 223	1 481 727	1 110 620	36.8	27.6	9.2	4.8	– 4.5		42.1		1868
1867	40 031	1 471 747	1 045 534	36.8	26.1	10.6	6.6	– 4.0		41.5		1867
1866	39 765	1 505 287	1 217 591	37.9	30.6	7.2	5.5	– 1.7		42.4		1866
1865	39 545	1 488 620	1 091 419	37.6	27.6	10.0	9.1	– 1.0		42.3		1865
1864	39 187	1 481 778	1 027 756	37.8	26.2	11.6	10.8	– 0.8		42.6		1864
1863	38 763	1 454 340	996 193	37.5	25.7	11.8	10.4	– 1.4		42.7		1863
1862	38 360	1 358 896	945 530	35.4	24.6	10.8	9.4	– 1.4		43.0		1862
1861	38 001	1 357 355	972 989	35.7	25.6	10.1	10.3	0.2		42.9		1861
1860	37 609	1 367 012	873 364	36.3	23.2	13.1	11.2	– 1.9		43.7		1860
1859	37 188	1 393 339	956 924	37.5	25.7	11.7	9.7	– 2.1		43.9		1859
1858	36 828	1 354 817	985 176	36.8	26.8	10.0	8.3	– 1.8		43.7		1858
1857	36 524	1 315 034	991 753	36.0	27.2	8.9	7.3	– 1.5		42.1		1857
1856	36 257	1 215 390	913 913	33.5	25.2	8.3	3.3	– 5.0		41.0		1856
1855	36 136	1 162 945	1 016 284	32.2	28.1	4.1	0.1	– 4.0		41.0		1855
1854	36 096	1 226 769	972 726	33.2	26.3	6.9	2.3	– 4.6		41.1		1854
1853	35 989	1 244 192	978 650	34.6	27.2	7.4	3.6	– 3.7		41.4		1853
1852	35 858	1 271 446	1 018 138	35.5	28.4	7.1	6.6	– 0.4		41.6		1852
1851	35 620	1 306 877	889 601	36.7	25.0	11.7	8.9	– 2.8		41.9		1851
1850	35 303	1 311 724	903 521	37.2	25.6	11.6	8.5	– 3.1				1850
1849	35 004	1 333 379	947 476	38.1	27.1	11.0	4.7	– 6.3				1849
1848	34 839	1 160 533	1 011 954	33.3	29.0	4.3	1.6	– 2.7				1848
1847	34 784	1 156 820	983 981	33.3	28.3	5.0	5.0	0.0				1847
1846	34 610	1 244 369	939 436	36.0	27.1	8.8	9.4	0.6				1846
1845	34 284	1 278 286	867 729	37.3	25.3	12.0	10.6	– 1.4				1845
1844	33 922	1 216 429	830 345	35.9	24.5	11.4	9.3	– 2.0				1844
1843	33 605	1 209 762	905 608	36.0	26.9	9.1	9.1	0.1				1843
1842	33 298	1 251 102	902 529	37.6	27.1	10.5	9.6	– 0.9				1842
1841	32 979	1 201 517	864 075	36.4	26.2	10.2						1841

a) Average resident population; 1841-1870: territory as of 1871-1937: territory of respective period; 1938-1943: territory as of December 12, 1937; 1946-1975: present territory, including West Berlin and Saare; 1946-1975: population registration figures corrected on the basis of the 1956, 1961 and 1970 censuses.

b) Territory as of December 12, 1937.

c) 1939-1943: excluding military losses.

d) Territorial change.

Ireland

Population Growth

Year	Totals			Per 1.000 population		Rates			Per 1.000 live births			Year
	Midyear Population a)	Live Births	Deaths	birth rate	death rate	natural incr.	pop. growth	net migration	infant mort.	stillbirths	infant mort. and stillb.	
1975	3 127 000	67 178	33 173	21.5	10.6	10.9	11.8	1.0	17.5	11.4	28.9	1975
1974	3 090 000	68 907	34 921	22.3	11.3	11.0	12.6	1.6	17.8	12.4	30.2	1974
1973	3 051 000	68 713	34 192	22.5	11.2	11.3	12.1	0.8	18.0	11.9	29.9	1973
1972	3 014 000	68 527	34 381	22.7	11.4	11.3	11.9	0.6	18.0	13.0	31.0	1972
1971	2 978 000	67 551	31 890	22.7	10.7	12.0	9.4	-2.6	18.0	12.9	30.9	1971
1970	2 950 000	64 382	33 686	21.8	11.4	10.4	8.1	-2.3	19.5	13.8	33.3	1970
1969	2 926 000	62 912	33 734	21.5	11.5	10.0	4.4	-5.5	20.6	14.0	34.6	1969
1968	2 913 000	61 004	33 157	20.9	11.4	9.6	4.5	-5.1	21.0	15.1	36.1	1968
1967	2 900 000	61 307	31 400	21.1	10.8	10.3	5.5	-4.8	24.4	16.0	40.4	1967
1966	2 884 000	62 215	35 113	21.6	12.2	9.4	2.8	-6.6	25.0	15.8	40.8	1966
1965	2 876 000	63 525	33 022	22.1	11.5	10.6	4.2	-6.4	25.0			1965
1964	2 864 000	64 072	32 630	22.4	11.4	11.0	4.9	-6.1	25.0			1964
1963	2 850 000	63 246	33 795	22.2	11.9	10.3	7.0	-3.3	27.0			1963
1962	2 830 000	61 782	33 838	21.8	12.0	9.9	4.2	-5.6	27.0			1962
1961	2 818 000	59 825	34 763	21.2	12.3	8.9	-5.0	-13.9	29.0			1961
1960	2 832 000	60 735	32 660	21.4	11.5	9.9	-4.9	-14.9	29.3			1960
1959	2 846 000	60 188	34 243	21.1	12.0	9.1	-2.5	-11.6	32.0			1959
1958	2 853 000	59 510	34 248	20.9	12.0	8.9	-11.2	-20.1	35.4			1958
1957	2 885 000	61 242	34 311	21.2	11.9	9.3	-4.5	-13.8	33.1			1957
1956	2 898 000	60 740	33 910	21.0	11.7	9.3	-7.9	-17.2	35.6			1956
1955	2 921 000	61 622	36 761	21.1	12.6	8.5	-6.8	-15.4	36.7			1955
1954	2 941 000	62 534	35 535	21.3	12.1	9.2	-2.7	-11.9	37.8			1954
1953	2 949 000	62 558	34 591	21.2	11.7	9.5	-1.4	-10.8	39.7			1953
1952	2 953 000	64 631	35 105	21.9	11.9	10.0	-2.7	-12.7	41.4			1952
1951	2 961 000	62 878	42 382	21.2	14.3	6.9	-2.7	-9.6	45.7			1951
1950	2 969 000	63 565	37 741	21.4	12.7	8.7	-4.0	-12.7	46.0			1950
1949	2 981 000	64 153	38 062	21.5	12.8	8.8	-1.3	-10.1	53.2			1949
1948	2 985 000	65 930	36 357	22.1	12.2	9.9	3.7	-6.2	50.3			1948
1947	2 974 000	68 978	44 061	23.2	14.8	8.4	5.7	-2.7	68.0			1947
1946	2 957 000	67 922	41 457	23.0	14.0	8.9	1.7	-7.3	64.6			1946
1945	2 952 000	66 861	42 762	22.6	14.5	8.2	2.7	-5.5	70.9			1945
1944	2 944 000	65 425	45 128	22.2	15.3	6.9	-0.7	-7.6	79.5			1944
1943	2 946 000	64 375	43 494	21.9	14.8	7.1	-5.8	-12.9	82.6			1943
1942	2 963 000	66 117	41 640	22.3	14.1	8.3	-10.1	-18.4	69.4			1942
1941	2 993 000	56 780	43 797	19.0	14.6	4.3	11.7	7.4	73.5			1941
1940	2 958 000	56 594	41 885	19.1	14.2	5.0	8.1	3.1	66.4			1940
1939	2 934 000	56 070	41 717	19.1	14.2	4.9	-1.0	-5.9	65.8			1939
1938	2 937 000	56 925	40 041	19.4	13.6	5.7	-3.7	-9.5	66.7			1938
1937	2 948 000	56 488	45 086	19.2	15.3	3.9	-6.4	-10.3	73.0			1937
1936	2 967 000	58 115	42 586	19.6	14.4	5.2	-1.3	-6.6	74.2			1936
1935	2 971 000	58 266	41 543	19.6	14.0	5.6	0.0	-5.6	68.4			1935
1934	2 971 000	57 897	39 083	19.5	13.2	6.3	3.0	-3.3	63.3			1934
1933	2 962 000	57 364	40 539	19.4	13.7	5.7	4.4	-1.3	65.2			1933
1932	2 949 000	56 240	42 984	19.1	14.6	4.5	5.4	0.9	72.2			1932
1931	2 933 000	57 086	42 947	19.5	14.6	4.8	2.0	-2.8	68.9			1931
1930	2 927 000	58 353	41 702	19.9	14.2	5.7	-3.4	-9.1	68.0			1930
1929	2 937 000	58 280	42 991	19.8	14.6	5.2	-2.4	-7.6	70.4			1929
1928	2 944 000	59 176	41 792	20.1	14.2	5.9	-4.4	-10.3	67.9			1928
1927	2 957 000	60 054	43 677	20.3	14.8	5.5	-4.7	-10.3	70.8			1927

Ireland

Population Growth

Year	Totals			Per 1.000 population		Rates			Per 1.000 live births			Year
	Midyear Population a)	Live Births	Deaths	birth rate	death rate	natural incr.	pop. growth	net migration	infant mort.	stillbirths	infant mort. and stillb.	
1926	2 971 000	61 176	41 740	20.6	14.0	6.5	-4.7	-11.3	74.4			1926
1925	2 985 000	62 069	43 650	20.8	14.6	6.2	-6.7	-12.9	67.9			1925
1924	3 005 000	63 402	45 180	21.1	15.0	6.1	-3.0	-9.1	71.7			1924
1923	3 014 000	61 690	42 217	20.5	14.0	6.5	-2.7	-9.1	66.4			1923
1922	3 022 000	58 849	44 547	19.5	14.7	4.7	-23.9	-28.6	68.9			1922
1921	3 096 000	61 010	44 537	19.7	14.4	5.3	-2.3	-7.6	72.6			1921
1920	3 103 000	67 015	45 521	21.6	14.7	6.9	0.3	-6.6	77.5			1920
1919	3 102 000	61 829	55 776	19.9	18.0	2.0	11.6	9.7	84.4			1919
1918	3 066 000	61 092	53 682	19.9	17.5	2.4	0.3	-2.1	80.2			1918
1917	3 065 000	61 421	51 713	20.0	16.9	3.2	-1.0	-4.1	84.1			1917
1916	3 068 000						0.0					1916
1915	3 068 000						-7.8					1915
1914	3 092 000						-3.6					1914
1913	3 103 000						-5.5					1913
1912	3 120 000						-3.8					1912
1911	3 132 000						-2.2					1911
1910	3 139 000											1910

a) 1910-1975: territory of the Republic of Ireland.

Italy

Population Growth[a]

Year	Totals			Per 1.000 population		Rates			Per 1.000 live births			Year
	Midyear[b] Population (in 1.000)	Live Births	Deaths	birth rate	death rate	natural incr.	pop. growth	net migration	infant mort.	stillbirths	infant mort. and stillb.	
1975	54 930	827 520	550 552	15.1	10.0	5.0	5.9	0.9	20.7	11.1	31.8	1975
1974	54 606	868 882	532 052	15.9	9.7	6.2	6.1	- 0.1	22.9	12.3	35.2	1974
1973	54 271	874 546	547 487	16.1	10.1	6.0	6.3	0.3	26.2	13.4	39.6	1973
1972	53 931	888 203	533 824	16.5	9.9	6.6	6.4	- 0.2	27.0	14.0	41.0	1972
1971	53 584	906 182	522 654	16.9	9.8	7.2	6.7	- 0.5	28.5	14.8	43.3	1971
1970	53 226	900 070	519 338	16.9	9.8	7.2	6.9	- 0.3	29.2	15.6	44.8	1970
1969	52 856	934 278	536 924	17.7	10.2	7.5	6.6	- 0.9	30.3	16.3	46.6	1969
1968	52 506	930 172	532 571	17.7	10.1	7.6	6.8	- 0.8	32.7	17.5	50.2	1968
1967	52 150	948 772	510 122	18.2	9.8	8.4	7.4	- 1.0	33.2	18.3	51.5	1967
1966	51 764	979 940	496 281	18.9	9.6	9.3	7.5	- 1.8	34.7	19.7	54.4	1966
1965	51 374	990 458	518 008	19.3	10.1	9.2	8.2	- 1.0	36.0	20.2	56.2	1965
1964	50 952	1 016 120	490 050	19.9	9.6	10.3	8.3	- 2.0	36.1	21.2	57.3	1964
1963	50 530	960 336	516 377	19.0	10.2	8.8	6.7	- 2.1	40.1	22.4	62.5	1963
1962	50 190	937 257	509 174	18.7	10.1	8.5	5.7	- 2.8	41.8	23.4	65.2	1962
1961	49 902	929 657	468 455	18.6	9.4	9.2	5.2	- 4.0	40.7	23.8	64.5	1961
1960	49 642	910 192	480 932	18.3	9.7	8.6	5.8	- 2.9	43.9	25.1	69.0	1960
1959	49 356	901 017	454 740	18.3	9.2	9.0	6.4	- 2.7	45.4	25.9	71.3	1959
1958	49 041	870 468	457 690	17.7	9.3	8.4	6.1	- 2.3	59.7	26.6	86.3	1958
1957	48 743	878 906	484 190	18.0	9.9	8.1	5.6	- 2.5	50.0	27.9	78.1	1957
1956	48 469	873 608	497 550	18.0	10.3	7.8	5.5	- 2.2	48.8	28.0	76.7	1956
1955	48 200	869 333	446 689	18.0	9.3	8.8	6.2	- 2.5	50.9	29.2	80.1	1955
1954	47 899	870 689	441 897	18.2	9.2	9.0	6.1	- 2.8	53.0	30.2	83.2	1954
1953	47 604	839 478	472 711	17.6	9.9	7.7	5.5	- 2.3	58.5	30.5	88.9	1953
1952	47 345	844 447	474 526	17.8	10.0	7.8	5.3	- 2.5	63.5	31.7	95.2	1952
1951	47 092	860 998[c]	481 911	18.3	10.2	8.1	6.8	- 1.2	66.6	31.9	98.6	1951
1950	46 769	908 622[c]	452 088	19.4	9.7	9.8	7.9	- 1.9	63.8	33.3	97.1	1950
1949[e]	46 399	937 146[c]	482 097	20.2	10.4	9.8	7.5	- 2.3	74.0	32.9	106.9	1949
1948[e]	46 050	1 005 851[c]	486 392	21.8	10.6	11.3			72.2	33.8	106.0	1948
1947	46 392	1 011 490[c]	520 897	22.0	11.3	10.7	7.4	- 3.3	84.2	32.2	116.5	1947
1946	46 048	1 036 098[c]	544 973	22.5	11.8	10.7	6.2	- 4.5	86.8	30.5	117.3	1946
1945	45 762	815 678[c]	609 956[d]	17.8	13.3	4.5	3.4		103.1	31.8	134.8	1945
1944	45 606	814 746[c]	679 837[d]	17.9	14.9	3.0	2.5		103.2	28.0	131.2	1944
1943	45 490	882 105[c]	675 612[d]	19.4	14.9	4.5	3.9		115.1	29.4	144.4	1943
1942	45 311	926 063	643 607[d]	20.4	14.2	6.2	6.3		112.4	28.9	141.4	1942
1941	45 026	937 546	621 735[d]	20.8	13.8	7.0	8.7		115.2	29.6	144.8	1941
1940	44 634	1 046 479	606 907[d]	23.4	13.6	9.8	10.9		102.7	30.8	133.4	1940
1939	44 148	1 040 213	590 530	23.6	13.4	10.2	10.2	0.1	97.0	32.4	129.3	1939
1938	43 695	1 037 180	612 229	23.7	14.0	9.7	8.1	- 1.6	106.3	33.0	139.2	1938
1937	43 341	991 867	615 420	22.9	14.2	8.7	7.4	- 1.3	108.8	32.9	141.6	1937
1936	43 020	962 686	589 636	22.4	13.7	8.7	7.6	- 1.1	100.4	33.5	133.9	1936
1935	42 693	996 708	593 953	23.3	13.9	9.4	8.0	- 1.4	101.2	34.0	135.2	1935
1934	42 352	992 966	563 339	23.4	13.3	10.1	8.2	- 2.0	98.7	34.6	133.3	1934
1933	42 005	995 979	574 113	23.7	13.7	10.0	7.8	- 2.2	100.1	35.4	135.6	1933
1932	41 677	990 995	610 646	23.8	14.7	9.1	8.1	- 1.0	110.5	35.2	145.6	1932
1931	41 339	1 026 197	609 405	24.8	14.7	10.1	9.3	- 0.8	112.9	35.5	148.4	1931
1930	40 956	1 092 678	576 751	26.7	14.1	12.6	8.5	- 4.1	105.5	36.5	142.0	1930
1929	40 607	1 037 700	667 223	25.6	16.4	9.1	8.0	- 1.1	124.8	36.8	161.6	1929
1928	40 281	1 072 316	645 654	26.6	16.0	10.6	8.8	- 1.8	120.3	37.1	157.3	1928
1927	39 926	1 093 772	639 843	27.4	16.0	11.4	8.4	- 3.0	120.2	38.3	158.5	1927

Italy

Population Growth[a]

Year	Totals			Per 1.000 population		Rates			Per 1.000 live births			Year
	Midyear[b] Population (in 1.000)	Live Births	Deaths	birth rate	death rate	natural incr.	pop. growth	net migration	infant mort.	stillbirths	infant mort. and stillb.	
1926	39 590	1 094 666	680 274	27.7	17.2	10.5	8.2	– 2.2	126.5	40.6	167.1	1926
1925	39 265	1 108 565	669 695	28.2	17.1	11.2	8.6	– 2.6	119.4	43.9	163.2	1925
1924	38 927	1 124 650	663 077	28.9	17.0	11.9	9.1	– 2.7	126.2	43.8	170.0	1924
1923	38 571	1 155 157	654 827	29.9	17.0	13.0	9.7	– 3.3	127.5	45.1	172.5	1923
1922[e]	38 196	1 175 834	690 054	30.8	18.1	12.7			126.5	46.2	172.7	1922
1921[e]	36 189	1 118 344	642 234	30.2	17.4	12.6	8.0	– 4.9	129.3	48.1	177.4	1921
1920	35 900	1 158 041	681 749	32.3	19.0	13.3	5.1	– 8.2	126.7	45.2	171.9	1920
1919	35 717	770 620	676 329	21.6	18.9	2.6	– 5.8	– 8.4	129.1	47.3	176.5	1919
1918	35 922	655 353	1 268 290	18.2	35.3	– 17.1	– 11.7	6.6	191.8	50.5	242.4	1918
1917	36 343	713 732	948 710	19.5	26.1	– 6.6	– 3.8	2.8	158.2	43.1	201.3	1917
1916	36 481	881 626	854 703	24.2	23.4	0.7	5.8	5.1	166.3	42.2	208.6	1916
1915	36 271	1 109 183	809 703	30.6	22.3	8.3	15.7	7.4	146.8	42.6	189.4	1915
1914	35 701	1 114 091	643 355	31.2	18.0	13.2	9.8	– 3.4	130.3	42.7	173.1	1914
1913	35 351	1 122 482	663 966	31.8	18.8	13.0	3.0	– 10.0	138.2	41.8	180.0	1913
1912	35 246	1 133 985	635 788	32.2	18.0	14.1	6.1	– 8.1	128.0	41.9	169.9	1912
1911	35 033	1 093 545	742 811	31.2	21.2	10.0	8.0	– 2.0	156.7	43.4	200.1	1911
1910	34 751	1 144 410	682 459	32.9	19.6	13.3	8.5	– 4.8	140.0	44.0	184.0	1910
1909	34 455	1 115 831	738 460	32.4	21.4	11.0	7.5	– 3.5	157.0	45.1	202.1	1909
1908	34 198	1 138 813	770 054	33.3	22.5	10.8	7.2	– 3.6	147.9	45.2	193.0	1908
1907	33 952	1 062 333	700 333	31.3	20.6	10.7	6.9	– 3.8	155.9	45.2	201.1	1907
1906	33 718	1 070 978	696 875	31.8	20.7	11.1	6.8	– 4.3	160.9	45.0	205.8	1906
1905	33 489	1 084 518	730 340	32.4	21.8	10.6	7.5	– 3.1	166.2	45.6	211.8	1905
1904	33 237	1 085 431	698 604	32.7	21.0	11.6	7.0	– 4.6	161.1	45.3	206.3	1904
1903	33 004	1 042 090	736 311	31.6	22.3	9.3	6.6	– 2.7	171.9	44.8	216.7	1903
1902	32 787	1 093 074	727 181	33.3	22.2	11.2	7.2	– 3.9	171.8	44.5	216.4	1902
1901	32 550	1 057 763	715 036	32.5	22.0	10.5	5.3	– 5.2	166.3	43.7	210.0	1901
1900	32 377	1 067 376	768 917	33.0	23.7	9.2	5.0	– 4.2	174.1	42.8	216.9	1900
1899	32 216	1 088 558	703 393	33.8	21.8	12.0	5.7	– 6.2	154.6	42.2	196.7	1899
1898	32 031	1 070 074	732 265	33.4	22.9	10.5	6.4	– 4.1	171.4	42.1	213.6	1898
1897	31 826	1 101 848	695 602	34.6	21.9	12.8	6.8	– 5.9	164.1	42.8	206.9	1897
1896	31 609	1 095 505	758 129	34.7	24.0	10.7	5.6	– 5.1	177.2	42.3	219.5	1896
1895	31 432	1 092 102	783 813	34.7	24.9	9.8	5.9	– 3.9	188.2	42.0	230.2	1895
1894	31 245	1 102 935	776 372	35.3	24.8	10.5	6.9	– 3.6		41.9		1894
1893	31 030	1 126 296	776 713	36.3	25.0	11.3	6.7	– 4.6		41.1		1893
1892	30 823	1 110 573	802 779	36.0	26.0	10.0	6.6	– 3.4	186.1	40.3	226.4	1892
1891	30 621	1 132 139	795 327	37.0	26.0	11.0	6.5	– 4.5	183.8	39.2	223.0	1891
1890	30 422	1 083 103	795 911	35.6	26.2	9.4	7.7	– 1.7	198.3	38.9	237.2	1890
1889	30 188	1 149 197	768 068	38.1	25.4	12.6	7.8	– 4.8	184.3	38.2	222.6	1889
1888	29 951	1 119 563	820 431	37.4	27.4	10.0	7.2	– 2.8	199.7	37.5	237.2	1888
1887	29 736	1 152 906	828 992	38.8	27.9	10.9	6.9	– 4.0	193.4	36.9	230.3	1887
1886	29 532	1 086 960	844 603	36.8	28.6	8.2	7.3	– 0.9	200.1	36.1	236.2	1886
1885	29 315	1 125 970	787 217	38.4	26.9	11.6	9.4	– 2.1	193.7	34.9	228.6	1885
1884	29 039	1 130 741	780 361	38.9	26.9	12.0	8.6	– 3.4	185.9	33.8	219.7	1884
1883	28 788	1 071 452	794 196	37.2	27.6	9.6	7.6	– 2.1	198.4	34.7	233.2	1883
1882	28 570	1 061 094	787 326	37.1	27.6	9.6	8.1	– 1.4	205.7	33.3	239.0	1882
1881	28 337	1 081 125	784 181	38.2	27.7	10.5	5.1	– 5.4	192.2	32.6	224.8	1881
1880	28 194	957 900	869 992	34.0	30.9	3.1	4.0	0.9	225.0	31.7	256.7	1880
1879	28 081	1 064 153	836 682	37.9	29.8	8.1	6.2	– 1.9	206.8	31.6	238.4	1879
1878	27 906	1 012 475	813 550	36.3	29.2	7.1	6.7	– 0.4	204.8	30.9	235.7	1878

Italy

Population Growth [a]

Year	Totals			Per 1.000 population		Rates			Per 1.000 live births			Year
	Midyear [b] Population (in 1.000)	Live Births	Deaths	birth rate	death rate	natural incr.	pop. growth	net migration	infant mort.	stillbirths	infant mort. and stillb.	
1877	27 718	1 029 037	787 817	37.1	28.4	8.7	8.4	− 0.3	208.1	30.5	238.6	1877
1876	27 486	1 083 721	796 420	39.4	29.0	10.5	7.6	− 2.9	203.1	30.5	233.6	1876
1875	27 278	1 035 377	843 161	38.0	30.9	7.0	4.7	− 2.3	215.5	28.8	244.3	1875
1874	27 149	951 658	827 253	35.1	30.5	4.6	4.3	− 0.3	223.7	28.4	252.0	1874
1873	27 032	985 188	813 973	36.4	30.1	6.3	5.5	− 0.8	214.1	28.8	242.8	1873
1872 [e]	26 882	1 020 682	827 498	38.0	30.8	7.2			223.2	28.9	252.2	1872
1871 [e]	25 877	960 020	778 798	36.5	29.6	6.9	6.7	− 0.2	227.2	27.6	254.9	1871
1870	25 703	951 495	773 169	37.0	30.1	6.9	7.9	1.0	230.2	25.9	256.1	1870
1869	25 500	952 134	713 832	37.3	28.0	9.3	6.9	− 2.4	215.2	24.8	240.0	1869
1868	25 324	900 416	777 224	35.6	30.7	4.9	3.5	− 1.4	238.0	23.7	261.7	1868
1867 [e]	25 236	927 396	866 865	36.7	34.4	2.4			223.4	24.2	247.6	1867
1866	22 496	876 917	657 452	36.8	27.6	9.2	8.5	− 0.7	209.3	26.8	236.1	1866
1865	22 304	865 387	672 897	38.8	30.2	8.6	7.7	− 0.9	226.1	15.7	241.8	1865
1864	22 132	845 454	659 063	38.2	29.8	8.4	7.1	− 1.3	228.5	16.8	245.3	1864
1863	21 974	862 360	686 777	39.2	31.3	8.0	6.2	− 1.8	231.6	22.0	253.6	1863
1862	21 838	833 054	681 212	38.1	31.2	7.0						1862

a) All figures refer to the present population in the respective territory.

b) 1862-1961: mean population calculated on the basis of end-year population figures; 1962-1975: mean population calculated on the basis of the 1961 end-year population and the annual figures of births, deaths and net migration.

c) Postwar territory, excluding Trieste.

d) Excluding deaths in war zones and deaths of military personnel abroad.

e) Territorial change.

Population Growth

Year	Totals			Per 1.000 population		Rates			Per 1.000 live births			Year
	Midyear Population	Live Births	Deaths	birth rate	death rate	natural incr.	pop. growth	net migration	infant mort.	stillbirths	infant mort. and stillb.	
1975	13 666 335	177 876	113 737	13.0	8.3	4.7	8.9	4.2	10.6	7.7	18.4	1975
1974	13 545 056	185 982	109 250	13.7	8.1	5.7	7.8	2.1	11.3	8.9	20.2	1974
1973	13 439 321	194 993	110 682	14.5	8.2	6.3	8.2	2.0	11.5	9.1	20.7	1973
1972	13 328 593	214 133	113 576	16.1	8.5	7.5	10.1	2.5	11.7	9.3	21.0	1972
1971	13 194 496	227 180	110 243	17.2	8.4	8.9	11.8	3.0	12.1	10.3	22.4	1971
1970	13 038 525	238 912	109 619	18.3	8.4	9.9	12.3	2.4	12.7	10.8	23.6	1970
1969	12 877 983	247 588	107 615	19.2	8.4	10.9	11.5	0.6	13.2	11.1	24.3	1969
1968	12 729 720	237 112	104 989	18.6	8.2	10.4	10.8	0.4	13.6	11.4	25.0	1968
1967	12 592 813	238 678	99 792	19.0	7.9	11.0	10.8	-0.2	13.4	11.9	25.3	1967
1966	12 456 251	239 611	100 516	19.2	8.1	11.2	13.0	1.8	14.7	13.1	27.8	1966
1965	12 294 732	245 216	98 026	19.9	8.0	12.0	13.6	1.7	14.4	13.3	27.7	1965
1964	12 127 120	250 914	93 437	20.7	7.7	13.0	13.3	0.3	14.8	13.6	28.4	1964
1963	11 965 966	249 879	95 734	20.9	8.0	12.9	13.4	0.5	15.8	14.5	30.3	1963
1962	11 805 689	246 150	93 969	20.9	8.0	12.9	14.1	1.3	17.0	14.8	31.8	1962
1961	11 638 712	247 009	87 923	21.2	7.6	13.7	13.1	-0.6	15.4	15.1	30.5	1961
1960	11 486 631	238 789	87 486	20.8	7.6	13.2	12.1	-1.1	16.5	15.2	31.7	1960
1959	11 347 639	242 198	85 752	21.3	7.6	13.8	14.2	0.4	16.8	16.0	32.8	1959
1958	11 186 875	236 543	84 175	21.1	7.5	13.6	14.3	0.7	17.2	17.0	34.3	1958
1957	11 026 383	233 608	82 677	21.2	7.5	13.7	12.4	-1.3	17.2	17.2	34.4	1957
1956	10 889 351	231 204	84 521	21.2	7.8	13.5	12.7	-0.8	19.0	17.2	36.2	1956
1955	10 750 842	228 878	81 364	21.3	7.6	13.7	12.6	-1.1	20.2	17.3	37.5	1955
1954	10 615 380	227 845	79 295	21.5	7.5	14.0	11.5	-2.5	21.2	17.7	38.9	1954
1953	10 493 184	228 609	80 551	21.8	7.7	14.1	10.6	-3.5	22.1	17.7	39.8	1953
1952	10 381 987	232 596	75 986	22.4	7.3	15.1	11.3	-3.8	22.4	18.5	41.0	1952
1951	10 264 311	228 631	77 194	22.3	7.5	14.8	14.7	-0.1	25.1	18.6	43.7	1951
1950	10 113 527	229 369	75 580	22.7	7.5	15.2	15.6	0.4	25.2	19.7	44.9	1950
1949	9 955 594	236 177	81 077	23.7	8.1	15.6	15.6	0.0	26.8	19.7	46.5	1949
1948	9 800 153	247 923	72 459	25.3	7.4	17.9	17.4	-0.5	29.3	19.3	48.5	1948
1947	9 629 275	267 348	77 646	27.8	8.1	19.7	21.4	1.7	33.5	20.5	54.0	1947
1946	9 423 480	284 456	80 151	30.2	8.5	21.7	17.1	-4.6	38.7	20.6	59.3	1946
1945	9 262 298	209 607	141 398	22.6	15.3	7.4	9.5	2.1	79.7	19.6	99.2	1945
1944	9 174 432	219 946	108 087	24.0	11.8	12.2	7.9	-4.3	46.3	18.8	65.2	1944
1943	9 102 410	209 379	91 438	23.0	10.0	13.0	6.6	-6.3	40.1	18.8	58.9	1943
1942	9 041 989	189 975	86 040	21.0	9.5	11.5	8.5	-3.0	39.5	19.7	59.2	1942
1941	8 965 484	181 959	89 716	20.3	10.0	10.3	9.7	-0.6	43.6	21.7	65.3	1941
1940	8 878 611	184 846	87 722	20.8	9.9	10.9	11.0	0.0	39.1	25.7	64.9	1940
1939	8 781 273	180 917	75 841	20.6	8.6	12.0	11.1	-0.9	33.7	25.4	59.1	1939
1938	8 684 082	178 422	74 043	20.5	8.5	12.0	9.9	-2.1	36.5	25.3	61.8	1938
1937	8 598 258	170 220	75 516	19.8	8.8	11.0	9.6	-1.4	38.1	25.8	63.9	1937
1936	8 515 713	171 675	73 923	20.2	8.7	11.5	9.7	-1.8	38.9	25.7	64.6	1936
1935	8 433 266	170 425	73 660	20.2	8.7	11.5	10.9	-0.6	40.0	25.8	65.8	1935
1934	8 341 208	172 214	70 164	20.6	8.4	12.2	12.5	0.3	42.6	25.7	68.3	1934
1933	8 236 891	171 289	72 096	20.8	8.8	12.0	13.9	1.8	43.9	25.7	69.6	1933
1932	8 122 482	178 525	73 059	22.0	9.0	13.0	15.3	2.3	46.3	25.9	72.2	1932
1931	7 998 568	177 387	77 048	22.2	9.6	12.5	14.3	1.8	49.6	25.6	75.2	1931
1930	7 883 870	182 310	71 682	23.1	9.1	14.0	13.0	-1.0	50.9	25.2	76.1	1930
1929	7 781 376	177 216	83 224	22.8	10.7	12.1	13.3	1.2	59.0	25.3	84.4	1929
1928	7 678 187	179 028	73 816	23.3	9.6	13.7	13.3	-0.4	52.6	25.8	78.4	1928

Population Growth

Year	Totals			Per 1.000 population		Rates			Per 1.000 live births			Year
	Midyear Population	Live Births	Deaths	birth rate	death rate	natural incr.	pop. growth	net migration	infant mort.	stillbirths	infant mort. and stillb.	
1927	7 576 272	175 098	77 614	23.1	10.2	12.9	13.8	1.0	58.7	26.6	85.3	1927
1926	7 471 512	177 498	73 357	23.8	9.8	13.9	14.2	0.2	61.1	25.5	86.6	1926
1925	7 365 732	178 545	72 121	24.2	9.8	14.4	13.8	- 0.6	58.4	26.1	84.5	1925
1924	7 263 893	182 430	71 167	25.1	9.8	15.3	15.7	0.4	60.6	26.7	87.3	1924
1923	7 149 847	187 512	72 809	26.2	10.2	16.0	16.5	0.4	56.4	28.5	84.8	1923
1922	7 032 179	181 886	80 381	25.9	11.4	14.4	15.8	1.3	67.3	39.6	106.9	1922
1921	6 921 288	189 546	77 002	27.4	11.1	16.3	14.6	- 1.7	76.2	38.8	114.9	1921
1920	6 820 389	192 987	81 525	28.3	12.0	16.3	10.0	- 6.3	72.8	38.9	111.7	1920
1919	6 752 144	164 447	89 646	24.4	13.3	11.1	7.0	- 4.0	84.1	36.0	120.1	1919
1918	6 704 612	167 636	115 440	25.0	17.2	7.8	13.7	6.0	92.8	39.3	132.1	1918
1917	6 612 434	173 112	87 273	26.2	13.2	13.0	20.0	7.0	87.1	39.2	126.3	1917
1916	6 480 142	172 572	84 024	26.6	13.0	13.7	17.9	4.3	84.5	40.0	124.5	1916
1915	6 363 953	167 426	79 613	26.3	12.5	13.8	17.7	3.9	86.8	39.6	126.3	1915
1914	6 251 189	176 831	77 739	28.3	12.4	15.9	17.0	1.2	94.8	39.0	133.8	1914
1913	6 144 636	173 541	75 867	28.2	12.3	15.9	14.7	- 1.2	91.4	38.7	130.1	1913
1912	6 054 487	170 269	74 647	28.1	12.3	15.8	13.0	- 2.8	87.0	39.0	126.0	1912
1911	5 975 660	166 527	86 786	27.9	14.5	13.3	12.8	- 0.5	137.2	39.9	177.1	1911
1910	5 898 957	168 894	79 984	28.6	13.6	15.1	6.3	- 8.8	107.9	40.5	148.4	1910
1909	5 861 813	170 766	80 283	29.1	13.7	15.4	12.9	- 2.5	99.1	41.1	140.3	1909
1908	5 786 232	171 861	86 936	29.7	15.0	14.7	13.2	- 1.5	124.8	40.8	165.6	1908
1907	5 709 748	171 506	83 350	30.0	14.6	15.4	13.6	- 1.8	111.9	41.8	153.7	1907
1906	5 631 821	170 952	83 259	30.4	14.8	15.6	14.4	- 1.1	127.1	41.4	168.5	1906
1905	5 550 535	170 767	85 016	30.8	15.3	15.4	14.5	- 1.0	130.9	42.0	172.9	1905
1904	5 470 301	171 495	87 091	31.4	15.9	15.4	14.8	- 0.6	136.9	42.5	179.4	1904
1903	5 389 082	170 108	83 933	31.6	15.6	16.0	15.6	- 0.4	135.1	42.4	177.5	1903
1902	5 305 207	168 728	86 248	31.8	16.3	15.5	15.8	0.3	129.9	42.5	172.4	1902
1901	5 221 180	168 380	89 967	32.2	17.2	15.0	15.2	0.2	149.3	43.3	192.6	1901
1900	5 141 633	162 611	92 043	31.6	17.9	13.7	10.2	- 3.6	155.2	44.8	200.1	1900
1899	5 089 380	163 289	87 319	32.1	17.2	14.9	9.8	- 5.1	148.5	44.7	193.2	1899
1898	5 039 418	160 765	85 813	31.9	17.0	14.9	14.5	- 0.4	156.2	44.9	201.2	1898
1897	4 966 431	161 441	83 856	32.5	16.9	15.6	14.6	- 1.0	148.3	45.7	194.0	1897
1896	4 894 055	160 247	84 291	32.7	17.2	15.5	13.6	- 1.9	147.7	47.0	194.7	1896
1895	4 827 549	158 130	90 007	32.8	18.6	14.1	13.1	- 1.0	166.6	48.1	214.7	1895
1894	4 764 279	154 722	87 970	32.5	18.5	14.0	13.2	- 0.8	152.4	47.8	200.2	1894
1893	4 701 243	159 005	90 372	33.8	19.2	14.6	11.8	- 2.8	163.7	47.4	211.1	1893
1892	4 645 660	148 714	97 530	32.0	21.0	11.0	11.3	- 0.3	173.9	49.1	223.0	1892
1891	4 593 155	154 687	94 844	33.7	20.6	13.0	12.0	- 1.0	169.4	47.6	217.0	1891
1890	4 537 990	149 329	93 246	32.9	20.5	12.4	6.5	- 5.9	171.4	49.4	220.8	1890
1889	4 508 674	150 529	91 135	33.4	20.2	13.2	6.7	- 6.5	176.6	49.4	226.0	1889
1888	4 478 401	151 094	91 241	33.7	20.4	13.4	12.8	- 5.0	173.2	51.4	224.7	1888
1887	4 420 864	149 157	87 093	33.7	19.7	14.0	13.0	- 1.0	162.5	52.0	214.5	1887
1886	4 363 434	150 851	95 239	34.6	21.8	12.7	12.9	0.2	191.7	51.8	243.4	1886
1885	4 307 142	148 028	90 304	34.4	21.0	13.4	12.9	- 0.5	169.4	52.6	222.1	1885
1884	4 251 669	148 480	94 413	34.9	22.2	12.7	12.4	- 0.3	193.7	51.2	244.9	1884
1883	4 199 018	144 102	91 656	34.3	21.8	12.5	13.2	0.7	186.7	53.3	240.0	1883
1882	4 143 524	146 454	85 950	35.3	20.7	14.6	13.6	- 1.0	174.6	50.8	225.5	1882
1881	4 087 334	142 969	87 726	35.0	21.5	13.5	9.4	- 4.1	181.9	54.0	235.9	1881
1880	4 048 801	143 855	95 282	35.5	23.5	12.0	9.7	- 2.3	217.6	52.3	269.9	1880

Netherlands

Population Growth

Year	Totals			Per 1.000 population		Rates			Per 1.000 live births			Year
	Midyear Population	Live Births	Deaths	birth rate	death rate	natural incr.	pop. growth	net migration	infant mort.	stillbirths	infant mort. and stillb.	
1879	4 009 448	147 014	90 024	36.7	22.5	14.2	14.0	-0.2	181.6	54.9	236.5	1879
1878	3 953 339	142 746	90 739	36.1	23.0	13.2	14.7	1.6	197.1	54.3	251.3	1878
1877	3 895 124	142 618	86 289	36.6	22.2	14.5	14.8	0.3	188.3	52.4	240.7	1877
1876	3 837 491	142 210	90 187	37.1	23.5	13.6	12.8	-0.8	200.9	53.5	254.4	1876
1875	3 788 395	138 469	96 834	36.6	25.6	11.0	12.3	1.4		55.2		1875
1874	3 741 632	136 072	85 069	36.4	22.7	13.6	12.4	-1.3		55.9		1874
1873	3 695 331	133 796	89 287	36.2	24.2	12.0	10.7	-1.4		55.0		1873
1872	3 655 969	131 664	94 594	36.0	25.9	10.1	7.7	-2.4		55.5		1872
1871	3 627 801	128 305	106 974	35.4	29.5	5.9	7.3	1.5		56.9		1871
1870	3 601 146	129 997	93 066	36.1	25.8	10.3				53.9		1870
1869												1869
1868												1868
1867												1867
1866												1866
1865												1865
1864												1864
1863	3 431 887	124 758	82 064	36.3	23.9	12.4	11.9	-0.5	184.4	54.6	239.0	1863
1862	3 391 691	112 768	80 822	33.2	23.8	9.4	11.0	1.6	192.7	53.9	246.6	1862
1861	3 354 731	118 687	85 133	35.4	25.4	10.0	9.6	-0.4	195.5	53.4	248.9	1861
1860	3 322 778	108 850	82 545	32.7	24.8	7.9	5.0	2.9	186.3	54.1	240.4	1860
1859	3 306 252	115 569	103 067	35.0	31.2	3.8	4.1	-0.3	227.4	56.4	283.8	1859
1858	3 292 793	106 846	91 925	32.4	27.9	4.5	7.9	3.4	211.6	56.6	268.2	1858
1857	3 267 058	113 426	87 625	34.7	26.8	7.9	10.0	2.1	211.7	53.4	265.1	1857
1856	3 234 576	106 008	76 145	32.8	23.5	9.2	8.8	-0.4	179.3	52.3	231.6	1856
1855	3 206 297	101 815	90 202	31.7	28.1	3.6	8.5	4.9	201.4	52.8	254.2	1855
1854	3 179 289	104 244	76 475	32.8	24.1	8.7	10.7	2.0	182.7	51.0	233.7	1854
1853	3 145 593	104 297	77 315	33.2	24.6	8.6	13.5	4.9	190.3	52.9	243.2	1853
1852	3 103 835	110 067	74 609	35.5	24.0	11.4	15.9	4.5	201.5	51.6	253.1	1852
1851	3 055 293	107 369	69 390	35.1	22.7	12.4	3.8	-8.6	179.2	52.8	232.0	1851
1850	3 043 732	105 338	67 619	34.6	22.2	12.4	-3.9	-16.3	168.5	53.0	221.5	1850
1849	3 055 559	109 932	100 937	36.0	33.0	2.9	1.1	1.6	160.8	49.9	210.7	1849
1848	3 052 106	96 617	93 874	31.7	30.8	0.9	-1.1	-2.0	170.5	49.0	219.4	1848
1847	3 055 377	91 670	99 458	30.0	32.6	-2.6	-0.5	2.1				1847
1846	3 056 949	100 702	91 930	32.9	30.1	2.9	6.8	3.9				1846
1845	3 036 283	109 324	75 638	36.0	24.9	11.1	10.7	-0.4				1845
1844	3 004 223	108 598	77 523	36.1	25.8	10.3	10.5	0.2				1844
1843	2 972 995	105 350	73 615	35.4	24.8	10.7	9.8	-0.9				1843
1842	2 944 115	105 629	80 934	35.9	27.5	8.4	10.9	2.5				1842
1841	2 912 333	108 326	72 762	37.2	25.0	12.2	12.3	0.1				1841
1840	2 877 083	105 698	72 636	36.7	25.2	11.5						1840

Population Growth

Year	Totals			Per 1.000 population		Rates			Per 1.000 live births			Year
	Midyear a) Population	Live Births	Deaths	birth rate	death rate	natural incr.	pop. growth	net migration	infant mort.	stillbirths	infant mort. and stillb.	
1975	4 007 313	56 345	40 061	14.1	10.0	4.1	5.5	1.4	11.1	8.1	19.2	1975
1974	3 985 258	59 603	39 464	15.0	9.9	5.1	6.2	1.1	10.4	8.8	19.2	1974
1973	3 960 613	61 208	39 958	15.5	10.1	5.4	7.0	1.6	11.9	9.4	21.3	1973
1972	3 933 004	64 260	39 375	16.3	10.0	6.3	7.6	1.3	11.8	9.6	21.4	1972
1971	3 903 039	65 550	38 981	16.8	10.0	6.8	6.6	- 0.2	12.8	9.5	22.3	1971
1970	3 877 386	64 551	38 723	16.6	10.0	6.7	6.8	0.1	12.7	10.8	23.5	1970
1969	3 850 977	67 746	38 994	17.6	10.1	7.5	8.3	0.8	13.8	11.2	25.0	1969
1968	3 818 983	67 350	37 668	17.6	9.9	7.8	8.9	1.1	13.7	11.2	24.9	1968
1967	3 785 000	66 779	36 216	17.6	9.6	8.1	8.5	0.4	14.8	11.0	25.8	1967
1966	3 752 749	67 061	36 010	17.9	9.6	8.3	7.9	- 0.4	14.6	12.1	26.7	1966
1965	3 723 153	66 277	35 371	17.8	9.5	8.3	7.7	- 0.6	16.8	11.0	27.8	1965
1964	3 694 339	65 570	35 171	17.7	9.5	8.2	7.5	- 0.7	16.4	12.2	28.6	1964
1963	3 666 540	63 290	36 850	17.3	10.1	7.2	7.5	0.3	16.9	12.7	29.6	1963
1962	3 638 919	62 254	34 318	17.1	9.4	7.7	8.0	0.3	17.7	13.8	31.5	1962
1961	3 609 800	62 555	33 313	17.3	9.2	8.1	7.9	- 0.2	17.9	13.2	31.0	1961
1960	3 581 239	61 880	32 543	17.3	9.1	8.2	7.9	- 0.3	18.9	14.1	33.0	1960
1959	3 552 854	63 005	31 761	17.7	8.9	8.8	8.4	- 0.4	18.7	13.3	32.0	1959
1958	3 522 993	62 985	31 645	17.9	9.0	8.9	8.8	- 0.1	20.0	14.5	34.5	1958
1957	3 491 938	63 063	30 560	18.1	8.8	9.3	9.1	- 0.2	20.5	14.9	35.4	1957
1956	3 459 992	64 171	29 981	18.5	8.7	9.9	9.4	- 0.5	21.2	15.4	36.6	1956
1955	3 427 409	63 552	29 099	18.5	8.5	10.1	9.7	- 0.4	20.6	15.2	35.8	1955
1954	3 394 246	62 739	29 158	18.5	8.6	9.9	9.8	- 0.1	21.4	14.6	36.0	1954
1953	3 360 888	62 985	28 412	18.7	8.5	10.3	9.9	- 0.4	22.0	15.7	37.8	1953
1952	3 327 728	62 543	28 417	18.8	8.5	10.3	9.6	- 0.7	23.7	15.5	39.2	1952
1951	3 295 871	60 571	27 736	18.4	8.4	10.0	9.3	- 0.6	25.7	16.4	42.1	1951
1950	3 265 126	62 410	29 699	19.1	9.1	10.0	9.5	- 0.6	28.2	16.4	44.6	1950
1949	3 234 228	63 052	29 082	19.5	9.0	10.5	10.3	- 0.2	27.7	16.7	44.4	1949
1948	3 201 013	65 618	28 375	20.5	8.9	11.6	11.2	- 0.4	29.6	18.0	47.5	1948
1947	3 165 011	67 625	29 894	21.4	9.4	11.9	12.0	0.1	34.6	18.7	53.3	1947
1946	3 126 883	70 727	29 220	22.6	9.3	13.3	11.4	- 1.9	34.6	19.2	53.8	1946
1945	3 091 181	61 814	30 030	20.0	9.7	10.3	10.0	- 0.3	36.4	20.3	56.7	1945
1944	3 060 216	62 241	32 652	20.3	10.7	9.7	9.1	- 0.6	36.7	20.0	56.7	1944
1943	3 032 430	57 281	31 623	18.9	10.4	8.5	7.8	- 0.7	35.4	21.1	56.5	1943
1942	3 008 883	53 225	32 062	17.7	10.7	7.0	6.2	- 0.8	35.9	20.6	56.5	1942
1941	2 990 234	45 773	32 209	15.3	10.8	4.5	5.7	1.2	43.0	21.1	64.0	1941
1940	2 973 067	47 943	32 045	16.1	10.8	5.3	6.3	0.9	38.7	22.5	61.2	1940
1939	2 954 415	46 603	29 870	15.8	10.1	5.7	6.3	0.6	37.2	22.4	59.7	1939
1938	2 935 803	45 319	29 211	15.4	9.9	5.5	5.8	0.3	37.3	22.7	60.1	1938
1937	2 918 742	43 808	30 217	15.0	10.4	4.7	5.2	0.6	42.0	22.9	64.9	1937
1936	2 903 519	42 240	30 100	14.5	10.4	4.2	4.9	0.7	42.0	25.1	67.1	1936
1935	2 889 211	41 321	29 747	14.3	10.3	4.0	5.2	1.2	44.2	25.0	69.2	1935
1934	2 874 206	41 833	28 340	14.6	9.9	4.7	5.5	0.8	39.3	24.0	63.4	1934
1933	2 858 343	42 114	28 943	14.7	10.1	4.6	5.9	1.3	47.6	26.4	74.0	1933
1932	2 841 529	45 451	30 102	16.0	10.6	5.4	6.2	0.8	46.8	25.1	71.9	1932
1931	2 823 882	45 989	30 674	16.3	10.9	5.4	5.8	0.4	46.3	26.9	73.2	1931
1930	2 807 438	47 844	29 616	17.0	10.5	6.5	4.4	- 2.1	45.6	26.6	72.3	1930
1929	2 795 105	48 372	32 023	17.3	11.5	5.8	3.7	- 2.1	54.4	26.7	81.1	1929
1928	2 784 675	49 881	30 301	17.9	10.9	7.0	3.5	- 3.5	49.0	26.1	75.0	1928
1927	2 774 864	50 175	31 141	18.1	11.2	6.9	4.2	- 2.6	50.7	24.4	75.1	1927

Population Growth

Year	Totals			Per 1.000 population		Rates			Per 1.000 live births			Year
	Midyear[a) Population	Live Births	Deaths	birth rate	death rate	natural incr.	pop. growth	net migration	infant mort.	stillbirths	infant mort. and stillb.	
1926	2 763 106	54 163	29 933	19.6	10.8	8.8	5.9	- 2.9	47.9	23.2	71.1	1926
1925	2 746 815	54 066	30 481	19.7	11.1	8.6	6.6	- 2.0	50.2	25.1	75.3	1925
1924	2 728 764	58 021	30 850	21.3	11.3	10.0	5.7	- 4.2	50.0	24.6	74.7	1924
1923	2 713 116	61 731	31 543	22.8	11.6	11.1	6.7	- 4.4	49.5	20.8	70.3	1923
1922	2 694 840	62 908	32 484	23.3	12.1	11.3	10.0	- 1.3	54.5	20.8	75.3	1922
1921	2 667 868	64 610	30 698	24.2	11.5	12.7	12.4	- 0.3	53.8	18.1	71.9	1921
1920	2 634 664	69 326	33 634	26.3	12.8	13.5	12.1	- 1.5	57.5	20.6	78.1	1920
1919	2 602 869	59 486	35 821	22.9	13.8	9.1	9.7	0.6	61.7	23.3	85.0	1919
1918	2 577 729	63 486	44 218	24.6	17.2	7.5	10.5	3.1	62.9	23.8	86.8	1918
1917	2 550 543	63 969	34 699	25.1	13.6	11.5	11.1	- 0.4	64.0	22.7	86.7	1917
1916	2 522 178	61 120	34 910	24.2	13.8	10.4	9.7	- 0.7	64.0	23.8	87.7	1916
1915	2 497 766	58 975	33 425	23.6	13.4	10.2	10.1	- 0.1	67.3	23.2	90.5	1915
1914	2 472 419	62 111	33 280	25.1	13.5	11.7	10.3	- 1.3	67.6	22.1	89.7	1914
1913	2 446 874	61 294	32 442	25.0	13.3	11.8	9.7	- 2.1	64.3	22.3	86.6	1913
1912	2 423 184	61 409	32 663	25.3	13.5	11.9	9.2	- 2.6	67.2	23.2	90.4	1912
1911	2 400 796	61 727	31 691	25.7	13.2	12.5	7.1	- 5.4	64.5	22.8	87.4	1911
1910	2 383 677	61 486	32 207	25.8	13.5	12.3	6.8	- 5.5	67.2	22.9	90.1	1910
1909	2 367 494	63 324	32 111	26.7	13.6	13.2	9.3	- 3.9	69.5	22.9	92.4	1909
1908	2 345 564	61 686	33 366	26.3	14.2	12.1	7.1	- 5.0	75.0	23.2	98.2	1908
1907	2 328 962	61 302	33 345	26.3	14.3	12.0	4.2	- 7.8	65.8	23.0	88.8	1907
1906	2 319 191	62 091	31 668	26.8	13.7	13.1	4.6	- 8.5	69.1	23.1	92.2	1906
1905	2 308 572	62 601	34 050	27.1	14.7	12.4	4.8	- 7.6	81.5	23.3	104.8	1905
1904	2 297 494	64 143	32 895	27.9	14.3	13.6	4.2	- 9.4	74.8	24.6	99.4	1904
1903	2 287 768	65 470	33 847	28.6	14.8	13.8	5.4	- 8.5	77.9	25.0	102.9	1903
1902	2 275 485	66 494	31 670	29.2	13.9	15.3	9.0	- 6.3	73.8	24.0	97.8	1902
1901	2 254 911	67 303	33 821	29.8	15.0	14.8	10.8	- 4.0	91.1	25.5	116.6	1901
1900	2 230 483	66 299	35 345	29.7	15.8	13.9	11.8	- 2.0	90.4	24.4	114.8	1900
1899	2 204 083	65 968	36 935	29.9	16.8	13.2	13.7	0.6	106.7	25.6	132.3	1899
1898	2 173 807	65 926	33 228	30.3	15.3	15.0	14.8	- 0.3	89.4	24.1	113.6	1898
1897	2 141 721	64 333	32 873	30.0	15.3	14.7	14.0	- 0.7	95.6	24.7	120.3	1897
1896	2 111 678	63 254	32 101	30.0	15.2	14.8	13.5	- 1.2	96.5	25.8	122.3	1896
1895	2 083 088	63 318	32 582	30.4	15.6	14.8	12.7	- 2.1	95.5	25.8	121.3	1895
1894	2 056 657	60 889	34 754	29.6	16.9	12.7	9.2	- 3.5	103.0	28.2	131.2	1894
1893	2 037 797	61 823	33 537	30.3	16.5	13.9	5.8	- 8.1	89.1	29.8	118.9	1893
1892	2 026 016	59 933	36 218	29.6	17.9	11.7	6.7	- 5.0	103.8	28.5	132.3	1892
1891	2 012 503	61 901	35 621	30.8	17.7	13.1	7.7	- 5.3	96.9	28.3	125.2	1891
1890	1 996 929	60 747	35 961	30.4	18.0	12.4	6.3	- 6.1	97.2	27.3	124.5	1890
1889	1 984 295	58 811	35 235	29.6	17.8	11.9	3.9	- 8.0	110.0	27.5	137.5	1889
1888	1 976 615	60 052	34 126	30.4	17.3	13.1	3.4	- 9.7	97.3	26.4	123.6	1888
1887	1 969 807	61 827	31 904	31.4	16.2	15.2	5.8	- 9.4	87.5	27.8	115.3	1887
1886	1 958 323	60 466	31 844	30.9	16.3	14.6	7.4	- 7.3	90.6	29.2	119.8	1886
1885	1 943 916	61 231	31 985	31.5	16.5	15.0	7.6	- 7.4	93.1	30.1	123.2	1885
1884	1 929 058	61 019	32 071	31.6	16.6	15.0	5.0	-10.0	96.3	29.3	125.6	1884
1883	1 919 317	59 440	32 545	31.0	17.0	14.0	- 0.2	-14.2	96.6	30.8	127.4	1883
1882	1 919 767	58 762	35 786	30.6	18.6	12.0	- 1.7	-13.6	111.0	31.6	142.6	1882
1881	1 922 948	57 778	32 716	30.0	17.0	13.0	2.0	-11.0	96.6	34.4	131.0	1881
1880	1 919 075	59 315	31 065	30.9	16.2	14.7	8.8	- 5.9	95.3	34.9	130.1	1880
1879	1 902 126	61 106	28 730	32.1	15.1	17.0	13.3	- 3.7	91.7	35.6	127.3	1879
1878	1 876 835	59 066	29 950	31.5	16.0	15.5	13.5	- 2.1	103.1	34.9	138.1	1878

Norway

Population Growth

Year	Totals			Per 1.000 population		Rates			Per 1.000 live births			Year
	Midyear a) Population	Live Births	Deaths	birth rate	death rate	natural incr.	pop. growth	net migration	infant mort.	stillbirths	infant mort. and stillb.	
1877	1 851 571	58 717	31 252	31.7	16.9	14.8	12.3	− 2.6	107.2	34.8	142.0	1877
1876	1 828 856	57 699	34 485	31.5	18.9	12.7	14.1	1.4	108.1	38.4	146.5	1876
1875	1 803 129	56 856	33 871	31.5	18.8	12.7	11.1	− 1.7	114.9	37.1	152.1	1875
1874	1 783 129	55 259	32 705	31.0	18.3	12.6	9.1	− 3.5	112.7	37.3	150.0	1874
1873	1 766 840	52 749	29 979	29.9	17.0	12.9	6.6	− 6.2	105.9	38.9	144.7	1873
1872	1 755 092	52 592	29 257	30.0	16.7	13.3	5.8	− 7.5	102.5	39.2	141.7	1872
1871	1 744 936	51 163	29 453	29.3	16.9	12.4	5.5	− 7.0	98.7	39.9	138.6	1871
1870	1 735 425	50 618	28 171	29.2	16.2	12.9	3.6	− 9.4	100.7	36.8	137.5	1870
1869	1 729 235	49 985	29 656	28.9	17.1	11.8	3.1	− 8.6	111.4	38.5	149.9	1869
1868	1 723 810	50 872	31 568	29.5	18.3	11.2	4.5	− 6.7	126.1	38.0	164.1	1868
1867	1 716 112	51 607	31 693	30.1	18.5	11.6	5.4	− 6.2	121.8	38.2	160.0	1867
1866	1 706 911	54 166	29 106	31.7	17.1	14.7	9.8	− 4.9	107.6	36.4	144.0	1866
1865	1 690 134	53 939	28 066	31.9	16.6	15.3	12.9	− 2.4	103.2	41.3	144.5	1865
1864	1 668 254	53 158	29 692	31.9	17.8	14.1	13.1	− 1.0	100.7	41.6	142.3	1864
1863	1 646 433	53 905	31 076	32.7	18.9	13.9	11.8	− 2.1	105.7	39.7	145.4	1863
1862	1 626 986	52 190	32 502	32.1	20.0	12.1	8.1	− 4.0	109.8	41.8	151.6	1862
1861	1 613 878	49 546	37 493	30.7	23.2	7.5	11.0	3.6	113.2	43.0	156.2	1861
1860	1 596 089	53 074	27 398	33.3	17.2	16.1	16.5	0.4	102.0	44.1	146.0	1860
1859	1 569 801	54 556	26 738	34.8	17.0	17.7	16.9	− 0.8	104.3	41.6	145.9	1859
1858	1 543 195	51 671	24 796	33.5	16.1	17.4	14.5	− 2.9	102.4	43.5	145.8	1858
1857	1 520 744	50 198	26 017	33.0	17.1	15.9	13.2	− 2.7	100.3	42.6	142.9	1857
1856	1 500 612	48 311	25 357	32.2	16.9	15.3	14.6	− 0.7	97.1	45.8	142.9	1856
1855	1 478 722	49 438	25 362	33.4	17.2	16.3	14.7	− 1.6	102.5	43.0	145.5	1855
1854	1 457 020	49 896	23 362	34.2	16.0	18.2	11.8	− 6.4	97.2	43.7	140.9	1854
1853	1 439 755	46 039	26 391	32.0	18.3	13.6	9.9	− 3.7	102.5	43.4	145.9	1853
1852	1 425 472	44 219	25 565	31.0	17.9	13.1	11.6	− 1.5	118.6	42.3	160.9	1852
1851	1 408 903	44 899	24 092	31.9	17.1	14.8	12.0	− 2.7	107.8	42.7	150.4	1851
1850	1 391 941	43 082	23 971	31.0	17.2	13.7	11.0	− 2.7	102.0	43.5	145.5	1850
1849	1 376 619	44 113	25 226	32.0	18.3	13.7	9.6	− 4.1	99.4	41.9	141.3	1849
1848	1 363 383	40 554	27 916	29.7	20.5	9.3	8.8	− 0.4	120.5	42.1	162.6	1848
1847	1 351 331	41 610	27 489	30.8	20.3	10.4	10.8	0.4	119.5	41.1	160.6	1847
1846	1 336 727	41 528	23 887	31.1	17.9	13.2	13.1	− 0.1	117.8	41.0	158.7	1846
1845	1 319 184	41 200	22 303	31.2	16.9	14.3	13.2	− 1.1	117.6	41.2	158.9	1845
1844	1 301 772	38 973	22 297	29.9	17.1	12.8	12.0	− 0.8	117.2	41.2	158.4	1844
1843	1 286 192	38 800	23 069	30.2	17.9	12.2	12.1	− 0.1	117.5	39.1	156.6	1843
1842	1 270 597	39 056	22 847	30.7	18.0	12.8	12.7	0.0	122.9	40.8	163.8	1842
1841	1 254 404	37 372	21 649	29.8	17.3	12.5	10.6	− 2.0	115.4	41.0	156.3	1841
1840	1 241 140	34 548	24 593	27.8	19.8	8.0	6.9	− 1.2	138.6	40.4	179.0	1840
1839	1 232 621	32 881	26 652	26.7	21.6	5.1	6.9	1.8	158.0	40.4	198.4	1839
1838	1 224 163	33 985	24 348	27.8	19.9	7.9	8.4	0.5	134.6	39.0	173.7	1838
1837	1 213 908	34 842	25 218	28.7	20.8	7.9	9.5	1.5	134.8	40.0	174.8	1837
1836	1 202 404	35 367	23 134	29.4	19.2	10.2	11.9	1.7	134.0	36.1	170.1	1836
1835	1 188 130	38 780	23 151	32.6	19.5	13.2	11.3	− 1.9		35.3		1835
1834	1 174 761	37 240	26 356	31.7	22.4	9.3	9.9	0.6		36.5		1834
1833	1 163 178	35 718	23 656	30.7	20.3	10.4	10.9	0.6		37.6		1833
1832	1 150 463	34 400	21 254	29.9	18.5	11.4	11.3	− 0.1		36.2		1832
1831	1 137 417	35 225	22 502	31.0	19.8	11.2	12.0	0.8		31.5		1831
1830	1 123 733	36 307	22 161	32.3	19.7	12.6	13.7	1.1		31.4		1830
1829	1 108 360	37 280	21 457	33.6	19.4	14.3	13.6	− 0.7		31.2		1829

Population Growth

Year	Totals			Per 1.000 population		Rates			Per 1.000 live births			Year
	Midyear a) Population	Live Births	Deaths	birth rate	death rate	natural incr.	pop. growth	net migration	infant mort.	stillbirths	infant mort. and stillb.	
1828	1 093 287	34 767	21 217	31.8	19.4	12.4	13.5	1.1		32.4		1828
1827	1 078 551	34 538	19 391	32.0	18.0	14.0	15.4	1.4		33.8		1827
1826	1 061 892	37 006	19 606	34.8	18.5	16.4	16.7	0.3		30.7		1826
1825	1 044 173	35 856	18 201	34.3	17.4	16.9	15.4	- 1.6		30.8		1825
1824	1 028 142	33 388	18 981	32.5	18.5	14.0	15.0	1.0		27.0		1824
1823	1 012 730	34 375	17 958	33.9	17.7	16.2	14.7	- 1.5		30.9		1823
1822	997 797	32 869	19 421	32.9	19.5	13.5	13.8	0.3		31.2		1822
1821	984 054	34 166	20 127	34.7	20.5	14.3	14.2	0.0		30.8		1821
1820	970 050	32 309	18 340	33.3	18.9	14.4	13.2	- 1.2		31.6		1820
1819	957 226	30 537	18 859	31.9	19.7	12.2	11.9	- 0.3		29.7		1819
1818	945 844	29 102	18 016	30.8	19.0	11.7	13.2	1.4		30.2		1818
1817	933 395	30 300	16 487	32.5	17.7	14.8	15.2	0.4		30.4		1817
1816	919 242	32 259	17 767	35.1	19.3	15.8	12.9	- 2.8		28.4		1816
1815	907 347	27 153	17 855	29.9	19.7	10.2	5.8	- 4.5		27.3		1815

a) mean population

Sweden

Population Growth

Year	Totals			Per 1.000 population		Rates			Per 1.000 live births			Year
	Midyear Population	Live Births	Deaths	birth rate	death rate	natural incr.	pop. migration	net migration	infant mort.	stillbirths	infant mort. and stillb.	
1975	8 192 566	70 089	88 208	8.6	10.8	− 2.2	3.9	6.1	12.8	8.6	21.4	1975
1974	8 160 560	75 423	86 316	9.2	10.6	− 1.3	2.9	4.2	13.9	9.7	23.6	1974
1973	8 136 774	78 549	85 640	9.7	10.5	− 0.9	1.8	2.7	13.8	10.0	23.8	1973
1972	8 122 293	84 131	84 056	10.4	10.3	0.0	3.0	2.9	14.4	9.1	23.5	1972
1971	8 098 328	89 703	82 717	11.1	10.2	0.9	6.9	6.0	14.2	10.1	24.2	1971
1970	8 042 803	89 895	80 026	11.2	10.0	1.2	9.3	8.1	13.5	10.3	23.8	1970
1969	7 968 018	90 105	83 352	11.3	10.5	0.8	7.0	6.2	14.0	9.7	23.7	1969
1968	7 912 217	95 196	82 476	12.0	10.4	1.6	5.6	4.0	15.5	10.8	26.3	1968
1967	7 867 931	121 360	79 783	15.4	10.1	5.3	7.6	2.4	12.9	9.5	22.4	1967
1966	7 807 797	123 354	78 440	15.8	10.0	5.8	9.5	3.7	12.6	10.0	22.6	1966
1965	7 733 853	122 806	78 194	15.9	10.1	5.8	9.4	3.6	13.3	10.3	23.7	1965
1964	7 661 354	122 664	76 661	16.0	10.0	6.0	7.4	1.4	14.2	11.3	25.6	1964
1963	7 604 328	112 903	76 460	14.8	10.1	4.8	5.6	0.8	15.4	12.1	27.5	1963
1962	7 561 588	107 284	76 791	14.2	10.2	4.0	5.5	1.5	15.4	12.6	28.0	1962
1961	7 519 998	104 501	73 555	13.9	9.8	4.1	5.3	1.2	15.8	12.8	28.6	1961
1960	7 480 359	102 219	75 093	13.7	10.0	3.6	4.6	0.9	16.6	13.9	30.5	1960
1959	7 446 249	104 743	70 889	14.1	9.5	4.5	5.0	0.4	16.6	15.0	31.7	1959
1958	7 409 144	105 502	71 065	14.2	9.6	4.6	6.1	1.5	15.9	15.9	31.8	1958
1957	7 363 802	107 168	73 132	14.6	9.9	4.6	6.7	2.1	17.8	15.9	33.6	1957
1956	7 314 552	107 960	70 205	14.8	9.6	5.2	7.1	2.0	17.3	17.0	34.3	1956
1955	7 262 388	107 305	68 634	14.8	9.5	5.3	6.7	1.4	17.4	17.0	34.4	1955
1954	7 213 490	105 096	69 030	14.6	9.6	5.0	5.8	0.8	18.7	17.2	35.9	1954
1953	7 171 461	110 144	69 553	15.4	9.7	5.7	6.5	0.9	18.7	18.2	37.0	1953
1952	7 124 673	110 192	68 270	15.5	9.6	5.9	7.3	1.4	20.0	18.6	38.7	1952
1951	7 072 830	110 168	69 799	15.6	9.9	5.7	8.3	2.6	21.6	19.6	41.2	1951
1950	7 014 005	115 414	70 296	16.5	10.0	6.4	8.3	1.9	21.0	20.3	41.3	1950
1949	6 955 535	121 272	69 537	17.4	10.0	7.4	10.4	2.9	23.3	20.5	43.8	1949
1948	6 883 467	126 683	67 693	18.4	9.8	8.6	11.7	3.1	23.2	19.8	43.0	1948
1947	6 802 865	128 779	73 579	18.9	10.8	8.1	12.4	4.3	25.4	21.6	47.0	1947
1946	6 718 717	132 597	70 635	19.7	10.5	9.2	12.4	3.2	26.5			1946
1945	6 635 549	135 373	71 901	20.4	10.8	9.6	11.4	1.8	29.9	24.6	54.5	1945
1944	6 560 088	134 991	72 284	20.6	11.0	9.6	10.6	1.0	31.1	23.6	54.7	1944
1943	6 490 514	125 392	66 105	19.3	10.2	9.1	9.0	− 0.2	28.9	22.3	51.3	1943
1942	6 432 337	113 961	63 741	17.7	9.9	7.8	6.7	− 1.1	29.3	22.9	52.2	1942
1941	6 388 953	99 727	71 910	15.6	11.3	4.4	5.1	0.7	37.0	25.1	62.1	1941
1940	6 356 368	95 778	72 748	15.1	11.4	3.6	4.8	1.2	39.2	29.4	68.7	1940
1939	6 325 759	97 380	72 876	15.4	11.5	3.9	4.5	0.6	39.5	28.0	67.5	1939
1938	6 297 468	93 946	72 693	14.9	11.5	3.4	3.4	0.1	42.5	28.5	71.0	1938
1937	6 275 805	90 373	75 392	14.4	12.0	2.4	2.7	0.3	45.2	29.6	74.7	1937
1936	6 258 697	88 938	74 836	14.2	12.0	2.3	2.7	0.4	43.4	28.3	71.7	1936
1935	6 241 798	85 906	72 813	13.8	11.7	2.1	3.1	1.0	45.9	27.6	73.4	1935
1934	6 222 328	85 092	69 921	13.7	11.2	2.4	3.4	1.0	47.2	27.7	74.9	1934
1933	6 200 965	85 020	69 607	13.7	11.2	2.5	4.0	1.5	49.5	27.4	76.9	1933
1932	6 176 405	89 779	71 459	14.5	11.6	3.0	3.9	0.9	50.7	27.9	78.6	1932
1931	6 152 319	91 074	77 121	14.8	12.5	2.3	3.4	1.2	56.6	28.9	85.6	1931
1930	6 131 135	94 220	71 790	15.4	11.7	3.7	3.0	− 0.6	54.7	27.6	82.4	1930
1929	6 112 635	92 861	74 538	15.2	12.2	3.0	2.6	− 0.4	58.5	27.3	85.8	1929
1928	6 096 557	97 868	73 267	16.1	12.0	4.0	2.5	− 1.5	58.8	27.1	85.9	1928
1927	6 081 146	97 994	77 219	16.1	12.7	3.4	2.8	− 0.6	59.8	26.1	85.8	1927

Population Growth

Year	Totals			Per 1.000 population		Rates			Per 1.000 live births			Year
	Midyear Population	Live Births	Deaths	birth rate	death rate	natural incr.	pop. growth	net migration	infant mort.	stillbirths	infant mort. and stillb.	
1926	6 063 965	102 007	71 344	16.8	11.8	5.1	3.2	- 1.9	56.0	26.1	82.1	1926
1925	6 044 840	106 292	70 918	17.6	11.7	5.9	4.0	- 1.9	55.7	24.5	80.2	1925
1924	6 020 939	109 055	72 001	18.1	12.0	6.2	4.0	- 2.1	60.3	25.4	85.7	1924
1923	5 996 640	113 435	68 424	18.9	11.4	7.5	4.3	- 3.2	56.2	25.1	81.3	1923
1922	5 970 918	116 946	76 343	19.6	12.8	6.8	7.0	0.2	62.5	24.9	87.4	1922
1921	5 929 403	127 723	73 536	21.5	12.4	9.1	9.0	- 0.1	64.0	25.1	89.1	1921
1920	5 875 763	138 753	78 128	23.6	13.3	10.3	7.7	- 2.6	63.3	23.2	86.5	1920
1919	5 830 444	115 193	84 289	19.8	14.5	5.3	4.0	- 1.3	69.6	23.1	92.8	1919
1918	5 807 349	117 955	104 591	20.3	18.0	2.3	4.8	2.5	64.6	24.4	89.0	1918
1917	5 779 207	120 855	77 385	20.9	13.4	7.5	7.6	0.1	64.5	23.3	87.8	1917
1916	5 735 153	121 679	77 771	21.2	13.6	7.7	6.8	- 0.9	69.7	25.4	95.1	1916
1915	5 696 174	122 997	83 587	21.6	14.7	6.9	6.5	- 0.4	75.8	25.2	100.9	1915
1914	5 659 095	129 458	78 311	22.9	13.8	9.0	6.7	- 2.4	72.9	24.7	97.6	1914
1913	5 621 388	130 200	76 724	23.2	13.6	9.5	6.8	- 2.7	69.7	24.7	94.4	1913
1912	5 582 996	132 868	79 241	23.8	14.2	9.6	7.3	- 2.3	70.9	25.0	95.9	1912
1911	5 542 101	132 977	76 462	24.0	13.8	10.2	7.7	- 2.5	72.0	25.3	97.3	1911
1910	5 499 422	135 625	77 212	24.7	14.0	10.6	8.4	- 2.2	75.1	24.7	99.9	1910
1909	5 453 021	139 505	74 538	25.6	13.7	11.9	9.1	- 2.9	72.2	25.0	97.1	1909
1908	5 403 657	138 874	80 568	25.7	14.9	10.8	8.6	- 2.2	85.4	24.7	110.2	1908
1907	5 357 384	136 793	78 149	25.5	14.6	10.9	7.7	- 3.2	76.8	25.9	102.7	1907
1906	5 315 970	136 620	76 366	25.7	14.4	11.3	7.2	- 4.2	81.0	25.2	106.3	1906
1905	5 277 848	135 409	82 443	25.7	15.6	10.0	7.0	- 3.1	88.3	25.2	113.5	1905
1904	5 241 051	134 952	80 152	25.7	15.3	10.5	5.9	- 4.5	84.4	26.2	110.5	1904
1903	5 210 022	133 896	78 610	25.7	15.1	10.6	4.4	- 6.2	92.8	25.7	118.5	1903
1902	5 186 990	137 364	79 722	26.5	15.4	11.1	6.0	- 5.1	86.4	25.6	111.9	1902
1901	5 155 835	139 370	82 772	27.0	16.1	11.0	7.6	- 3.4	102.9	26.0	129.0	1901
1900	5 116 722	138 139	86 146	27.0	16.8	10.2	7.1	- 3.0	98.5	25.9	124.4	1900
1899	5 080 160	133 882	89 678	26.4	17.7	8.7	8.6	- 0.1	111.7	26.5	138.1	1899
1898	5 036 275	136 523	75 949	27.1	15.1	12.0	10.0	- 2.1	90.8	27.1	117.8	1898
1897	4 986 100	132 999	76 558	26.7	15.4	11.3	9.1	- 2.3	98.6	27.9	126.4	1897
1896	4 940 914	134 308	77 259	27.2	15.6	11.5	9.0	- 2.5	103.3	26.2	129.6	1896
1895	4 896 221	134 599	74 368	27.5	15.2	12.3	9.7	- 2.6	94.7	26.3	121.0	1895
1894	4 848 667	131 409	79 444	27.1	16.4	10.7	6.8	- 3.9	100.9	26.3	127.2	1894
1893	4 815 508	131 729	81 027	27.4	16.8	10.5	2.2	- 8.3	101.2	26.1	127.3	1893
1892	4 804 808	129 622	85 894	27.0	17.9	9.1	2.3	- 6.8	109.2	25.9	135.1	1892
1891	4 793 866	135 516	80 603	28.3	16.8	11.5	3.0	- 8.5	107.9	26.2	134.2	1891
1890	4 779 695	133 597	81 824	28.0	17.1	10.8	3.8	- 7.0	103.1	26.6	129.7	1890
1889	4 761 333	132 069	76 124	27.7	16.0	11.7	4.1	- 7.6	107.2	26.6	133.9	1889
1888	4 741 579	136 451	75 831	28.8	16.0	12.8	3.3	- 9.5	100.3	27.6	127.9	1888
1887	4 726 045	140 169	76 227	29.7	16.1	13.5	5.5	- 8.0	103.1	27.5	130.6	1887
1886	4 699 979	139 882	78 045	29.8	16.6	13.2	7.7	- 5.4	111.2	28.3	139.5	1886
1885	4 663 609	137 308	82 781	29.4	17.8	11.7	8.5	- 3.2	114.3	29.2	143.5	1885
1884	4 624 022	138 745	81 077	30.0	17.5	12.5	7.1	- 5.4	113.2	27.7	140.8	1884
1883	4 591 350	132 875	79 478	28.9	17.3	11.6	3.4	- 8.2	115.7	28.0	143.7	1883
1882	4 575 680	134 300	79 406	29.4	17.4	12.0	1.5	-10.5	124.6	28.0	152.6	1882
1881	4 568 955	132 804	80 800	29.1	17.7	11.4	- 0.7	-12.1	112.7	29.2	142.0	1881
1880	4 572 285	134 262	82 753	29.4	18.1	11.3	3.7	- 7.6	120.7	30.1	150.8	1880
1879	4 555 382	139 043	77 152	30.5	16.9	13.6	10.4	- 3.2	111.2	30.2	141.4	1879
1878	4 508 203	134 464	81 418	29.8	18.1	11.8	11.3	- 0.4	134.2	29.2	163.3	1878

Population Growth

Year	Totals			Per 1.000 population		Rates			Per 1.000 live births			Year
	Midyear Population	Live Births	Deaths	birth rate	death rate	natural incr.	pop. growth	net migration	infant mort.	stillbirths	infant mort. and stillb.	
1877	4 457 127	138 476	83 175	31.1	18.7	12.4	11.4	− 1.0	125.5	30.3	155.8	1877
1876	4 406 502	135 890	86 334	30.8	19.6	11.2	10.0	− 1.2	140.2	32.0	172.2	1876
1875	4 362 425	135 958	88 439	31.2	20.3	10.9	9.8	− 1.1	149.0	32.1	181.0	1875
1874	4 319 766	133 249	87 760	30.8	20.3	10.5	10.6	0.0	146.7	34.4	181.1	1874
1873	4 274 192	131 643	73 525	30.8	17.2	13.6	11.0	− 2.6	128.8	32.6	161.4	1873
1872	4 227 295	126 983	68 802	30.0	16.3	13.8	9.7	− 4.1	128.3	32.6	160.9	1872
1871	4 186 351	127 333	72 046	30.4	17.2	13.2	5.4	− 7.8	113.7	34.4	148.1	1871
1870	4 163 641	119 838	82 449	28.8	19.8	9.0	− 0.5	− 9.5	131.9	33.4	165.3	1870
1869	4 165 919	117 677	92 775	28.2	22.3	6.0	− 4.4	−10.4	145.8	33.5	179.2	1869
1868	4 184 381	114 955	87 807	27.5	21.0	6.5	1.5	− 5.0	168.3	33.9	202.2	1868
1867	4 178 179	128 832	82 072	30.8	19.6	11.2	9.8	− 1.4	140.1	33.4	173.5	1867
1866	4 137 409	136 989	82 666	33.1	20.0	13.1	11.0	− 2.2	126.9	34.4	161.3	1866
1865	4 092 101	134 281	79 216	32.8	19.4	13.5	11.2	− 2.3	135.1	33.5	168.5	1865
1864	4 046 313	136 004	81 937	33.6	20.2	13.4	12.9	− 0.5	136.7	34.1	170.8	1864
1863	3 994 232	134 279	77 227	33.6	19.3	14.3	13.2	− 1.1	132.6	35.4	168.0	1863
1862	3 941 619	131 584	84 350	33.4	21.4	12.0	13.5	1.5	139.3	34.2	173.5	1862
1861	3 888 534	126 634	71 829	32.6	18.5	14.1	16.7	2.6	137.3	32.6	169.8	1861
1860	3 823 732	133 162	67 502	34.8	17.7	17.2	16.4	− 0.8	123.8	32.6	156.3	1860
1859	3 760 987	131 605	75 720	35.0	20.1	14.9	13.3	− 1.5	143.1	35.2	178.4	1859
1858	3 710 921	129 039	80 498	34.8	21.7	13.1	8.3	− 4.8	142.7	32.8	175.5	1858
1857	3 680 295	119 349	101 491	32.4	27.6	4.9	6.3	1.5	165.4	33.6	199.0	1857
1856	3 656 999	115 082	79 618	31.5	21.8	9.7	8.9	− 0.8	144.7	33.4	178.1	1856
1855	3 624 568	115 072	77 734	31.7	21.4	10.3	10.7	0.4	144.9	34.1	179.0	1855
1854	3 585 720	120 107	70 846	33.5	19.8	13.7	9.4	− 4.3	126.2	33.2	159.4	1854
1853	3 551 863	111 407	84 047	31.4	23.7	7.7	6.6	− 1.1	161.0	32.6	193.7	1853
1852	3 528 528	108 305	80 090	30.7	22.7	8.0	8.2	0.2	162.5	32.3	194.8	1852
1851	3 499 594	111 065	72 506	31.7	20.7	11.0	10.8	− 0.3	152.1	33.7	185.8	1851
1850	3 461 914	110 399	68 514	31.9	19.8	12.1	12.3	0.2	146.2			1850
1849	3 419 370	112 304	67 842	32.8	19.8	13.0	11.6	− 1.4	141.7			1849
1848	3 379 763	102 524	66 513	30.3	19.7	10.7	8.1	− 2.6	141.0			1848
1847	3 352 499	99 179	79 405	29.6	23.7	5.9	6.8	0.9	173.2			1847
1846	3 329 732	99 703	72 683	29.9	21.8	8.1	10.2	2.1	163.1			1846
1845	3 295 835	103 660	62 074	31.5	18.8	12.6	12.1	− 0.5	148.6			1845
1844	3 255 883	104 693	66 009	32.2	20.3	11.9	10.5	− 1.4	140.8			1844
1843	3 221 704	99 154	69 115	30.8	21.5	9.3	9.9	0.5	159.4			1843
1842	3 189 968	100 976	67 177	31.7	21.1	10.6	10.6	0.0	161.8			1842
1841	3 156 024	95 734	61 279	30.3	19.4	10.9	10.6	0.3	159.2			1841
1840	3 122 673	98 160	63 555	31.4	20.4	11.1	7.8	− 3.3	145.6			1840
1839	3 098 360	91 363	72 988	29.5	23.6	5.9	4.9	− 1.0	164.2			1839
1838	3 083 223	90 565	74 309	29.4	24.1	5.3	5.0	− 0.3	175.9			1838
1837	3 067 770	94 616	75 611	30.8	24.6	6.2	8.3	2.1	194.9			1837
1836	3 042 398	96 857	60 763	31.8	20.0	11.9	12.5	0.7	152.6			1836
1835	3 004 247	98 144	55 738	32.7	18.6	14.1	11.0	− 3.1	142.5			1835
1834	2 971 098	100 231	76 294	33.7	25.7	8.1	10.1	2.1	173.5			1834
1833	2 940 971	100 309	63 947	34.1	21.7	12.4	9.9	− 2.5	159.4			1833
1832	2 911 920	89 862	68 078	30.9	23.4	7.5	6.0	− 1.5	166.0			1832
1831	2 894 561	88 253	75 274	30.5	26.0	4.5	6.5	2.1	198.3			1831
1830	2 875 607	94 626	69 251	32.9	24.1	8.8	7.2	− 1.6	180.5			1830
1829	2 854 960	99 488	82 719	34.8	29.0	5.9	6.2	0.3	194.0			1829

Sweden

Population Growth

Year	Totals			Per 1.000 population		Rates			Per 1.000 live births			Year
	Midyear Population	Live Births	Deaths	birth rate	death rate	natural incr.	pop. migration	net migration	infant mort.	stillbirths	infant mort. and stillb.	
1828	2 837 254	95 354	75 860	33.6	26.7	6.9	7.4	0.5	170.3			1828
1827	2 816 323	88 138	64 920	31.3	23.1	8.2	10.0	1.8	160.6			1827
1826	2 788 089	97 125	63 027	34.8	22.6	12.2	14.0	1.8	171.6			1826
1825	2 749 065	100 315	56 465	36.5	20.5	16.0	15.0	- 1.0	154.0			1825
1824	2 707 954	93 577	56 256	34.6	20.8	13.8	14.9	1.1	155.8			1824
1823	2 667 673	98 259	56 067	36.8	21.0	15.8	14.6	- 1.2	147.5			1823
1822	2 628 592	94 309	59 390	35.9	22.6	13.3	11.7	- 1.6	162.4			1822
1821	2 597 780	92 072	66 416	35.4	25.6	9.9	9.4	- 0.4	175.6			1821
1820	2 573 235	84 841	62 930	33.0	24.5	8.5	7.4	- 1.1	163.4			1820
1819	2 554 096	84 250	69 881	33.0	27.4	5.6	7.9	2.3	183.1			1819
1818	2 533 927	85 714	61 745	33.8	24.4	9.5	9.7	0.2	168.7			1818
1817	2 509 463	83 821	60 863	33.4	24.3	9.1	11.2	2.1	178.8			1817
1816	2 481 275	87 644	56 225	35.3	22.7	12.7	11.9	- 0.7	183.5			1816
1815	2 451 653	85 239	57 829	34.8	23.6	11.2	8.4	- 2.8	169.9			1815

Population Growth

Year	Totals			Per 1.000 population		Rates			Per 1.000 live births			Year
	Midyear Population	Live Births	Deaths	birth rate	death rate	natural incr.	pop. growth	net migration	infant mort.	stillbirths	infant mort. and stillb.	
1975	6 405 000	78 464	55 924	12.3	8.7	3.5	- 5.9	- 9.4	10.7	7.2	18.0	1975
1974	6 442 800	84 507	56 403	13.1	8.8	4.4	1.8	- 2.5	12.5	7.1	19.6	1974
1973	6 431 000	87 518	56 990	13.6	8.9	4.7	7.2	2.4	13.2	7.6	20.8	1973
1972	6 385 000	91 342	56 489	14.3	8.8	5.5	9.6	4.1	13.3	8.7	22.0	1972
1971	6 324 000	96 261	57 856	15.2	9.1	6.1	9.0	2.9	14.4	8.6	23.0	1971
1970	6 267 000	99 216	57 091	15.8	9.1	6.7	8.8	2.1	15.1	8.9	24.0	1970
1969	6 212 000	102 520	58 002	16.5	9.3	7.2	12.9	5.7	15.4	9.4	24.7	1969
1968	6 132 000	105 130	57 374	17.1	9.4	7.8	11.3	3.5	16.1	10.2	26.2	1968
1967	6 063 000	107 417	55 142	17.7	9.1	8.6	11.1	2.4	17.5	10.0	27.4	1967
1966	5 996 000	109 738	55 804	18.3	9.3	9.0	8.8	- 0.2	17.1	10.0	27.1	1966
1965	5 943 000	111 835	55 547	18.8	9.3	9.5	11.6	2.1	10.2	10.6	20.7	1965
1964	5 874 000	112 890	53 609	19.2	9.1	10.1	17.7	7.6	19.0	11.3	30.3	1964
1963	5 770 000	109 993	56 989	19.1	9.9	9.2	19.1	9.9	20.5	11.4	31.9	1963
1962	5 660 000	104 322	55 125	18.4	9.7	8.7	29.0	20.3	21.2	12.2	33.4	1962
1961	5 496 000	99 238	51 004	18.1	9.3	8.8	24.4	15.6	21.0	12.0	33.0	1961
1960	5 362 000	94 372	52 094	17.6	9.7	7.9	19.2	11.3	21.1	11.5	32.7	1960
1959	5 259 000	92 973	50 077	17.7	9.5	8.2	11.4	3.3	22.2	12.0	34.2	1959
1958	5 199 000	91 421	49 281	17.6	9.5	8.1	14.0	5.9	22.2	12.6	34.8	1958
1957	5 126 000	90 823	51 066	17.7	10.0	7.8	15.8	8.0	22.9	14.3	37.2	1957
1956	5 045 000	87 912	51 573	17.4	10.2	7.2	12.9	5.7	25.8	13.7	39.5	1956
1955	4 980 000	85 331	50 366	17.1	10.1	7.0	10.2	3.2	26.5	14.5	41.0	1955
1954	4 929 000	83 741	49 113	17.0	10.0	7.0	10.3	3.3	27.2	15.6	42.8	1954
1953	4 878 000	83 029	49 684	17.0	10.2	6.8	12.9	6.1	29.8	15.3	45.1	1953
1952	4 815 000	83 549	47 624	17.4	9.9	7.5	13.7	6.2	29.1	15.3	44.5	1952
1951	4 749 000	81 903	49 952	17.2	10.5	6.7	11.6	4.9	30.1	16.0	46.2	1951
1950	4 694 000	84 776	47 372	18.1	10.1	8.0	11.5	3.5	31.2	17.1	48.2	1950
1949	4 640 000	85 308	49 497	18.4	10.7	7.7	12.5	4.8	34.3	16.9	51.2	1949
1948	4 582 000	87 763	49 679	19.2	10.8	8.3	12.7	4.3	35.9	17.3	53.2	1948
1947	4 524 000	87 724	51 384	19.4	11.4	8.0	12.6	4.6	39.3	16.2	55.6	1947
1946	4 467 000	89 126	50 276	20.0	11.3	8.7	12.3	3.6	39.2	15.8	55.1	1946
1945	4 412 000	88 522	51 086	20.1	11.6	8.5	10.9	2.4	40.7	16.3	57.1	1945
1944	4 364 000	85 627	52 336	19.6	12.0	7.6	9.4	1.8	42.2	16.7	58.9	1944
1943	4 323 000	83 049	47 409	19.2	11.0	8.2	8.6	0.3	39.8	16.8	56.6	1943
1942	4 286 000	78 875	46 928	18.4	10.9	7.5	7.5	0.1	38.3	16.8	55.1	1942
1941	4 253 700	71 926	47 336	16.9	11.1	5.8	6.4	0.6	41.1	18.9	60.0	1941
1940	4 226 400	64 115	50 759	15.2	12.0	3.2	4.9	1.8	46.2	20.9	67.1	1940
1939	4 205 600	63 837	49 484	15.2	11.8	3.4	3.3	- 0.1	42.6	22.2	64.8	1939
1938	4 191 800	63 790	48 576	15.2	11.6	3.6	2.9	- 0.8	42.8	21.4	64.2	1938
1937	4 179 800	62 480	47 274	14.9	11.3	3.6	2.8	- 0.8	46.7	20.9	67.6	1937
1936	4 168 000	64 966	47 650	15.6	11.4	4.2	3.1	- 1.1	46.5	22.1	68.6	1936
1935	4 155 200	66 378	50 233	16.0	12.1	3.9	3.7	- 0.2	47.9	22.3	70.2	1935
1934	4 140 000	67 277	46 806	16.3	11.3	4.9	4.4	- 0.6	45.7	22.0	67.7	1934
1933	4 121 900	67 509	47 181	16.4	11.4	4.9	4.8	- 0.2	47.8	23.6	71.4	1933
1932	4 102 200	68 650	49 911	16.7	12.2	4.6	5.5	0.9	51.0	23.5	74.4	1932
1931	4 079 700	68 249	49 414	16.7	12.1	4.6	6.9	2.3	49.4	23.5	72.9	1931
1930	4 051 400	69 855	46 939	17.2	11.6	5.7	7.4	1.7	50.8	24.3	75.1	1930
1929	4 021 500	69 006	50 438	17.2	12.5	4.6	8.3	3.7	52.1	24.8	76.9	1929
1928	3 988 200	69 594	48 063	17.4	12.1	5.4	8.1	2.7	53.6	25.0	78.6	1928

Year	Totals			Per 1.000 population		Rates			Per 1.000 live births			Year
	Midyear Population	Live Births	Deaths	birth rate	death rate	natural incr.	pop. growth	net migration	infant mort.	stillbirths	infant mort. and stillb.	
1927	3 955 900	69 533	49 202	17.6	12.4	5.1	6.1	0.9	56.8	25.2	82.0	1927
1926	3 931 900	72 118	46 452	18.3	11.8	6.5	5.6	0.9	56.5	25.6	82.1	1926
1925	3 909 700	72 570	47 877	18.6	12.2	6.3	3.6	- 2.7	58.4	26.7	85.1	1925
1924	3 895 500	73 508	48 988	18.9	12.6	6.3	3.1	- 3.2	62.0	28.0	90.0	1924
1923	3 883 300	75 551	45 983	19.5	11.8	7.6	2.4	- 5.2	60.5	28.4	88.9	1923
1922	3 873 900	76 290	50 292	19.7	13.0	6.7	- 0.5	- 7.2	69.6	29.4	99.1	1922
1921	3 875 800	80 808	49 518	20.8	12.8	8.1	- 0.3	- 8.4	74.0	29.3	103.3	1921
1920	3 876 900	81 190	55 992	20.9	14.4	6.5	2.0	- 4.5	83.7	30.0	113.7	1920
1919	3 869 200	72 125	54 932	18.6	14.2	4.4	- 2.7	- 7.1	82.4	28.8	111.3	1919
1918	3 879 600	72 658	75 034	18.7	19.3	- 0.6	- 2.0	- 1.4	88.2	30.6	118.8	1918
1917	3 887 500	72 065	53 306	18.5	13.7	4.8	1.2	- 3.6	79.2	28.6	107.7	1917
1916	3 882 900	73 660	50 623	19.0	13.0	5.9	0.0	- 5.9	78.5	30.2	108.7	1916
1915	3 882 800	75 545	51 524	19.5	13.3	6.2	- 3.7	- 9.9	90.0	31.6	121.6	1915
1914	3 897 300	87 330	53 629	22.4	13.8	8.6	8.5	- 0.1	91.5	32.0	123.5	1914
1913	3 864 000	89 757	55 427	23.2	14.3	8.9	11.6	2.8	96.0	31.7	127.7	1913
1912	3 819 000	92 196	54 102	24.1	14.2	10.0	11.3	1.3	93.8	32.3	126.1	1912
1911	3 775 900	91 320	59 619	24.2	15.8	8.4	10.9	2.5	123.4	31.4	154.8	1911
1910	3 734 800	93 514	56 498	25.0	15.1	9.9	11.8	1.9	105.0	33.7	138.7	1910
1909	3 690 700	94 112	59 416	25.5	16.1	9.4	11.7	2.3	114.9	33.8	148.7	1909
1908	3 647 400	96 245	57 697	26.4	15.8	10.6	11.9	1.3	107.6	33.5	141.0	1908
1907	3 604 000	94 508	59 252	26.2	16.4	9.8	12.2	2.5	121.0	33.7	154.8	1907
1906	3 559 900	95 595	59 204	26.9	16.6	10.2	12.4	2.2	126.7	35.3	162.0	1906
1905	3 515 800	94 653	61 800	26.9	17.6	9.3	12.5	3.1	128.8	36.0	164.8	1905
1904	3 471 900	94 867	60 857	27.3	17.5	9.8	12.6	2.8	140.1	36.2	176.3	1904
1903	3 428 000	93 824	59 626	27.4	17.4	10.0	12.8	2.8	133.3	35.1	168.4	1903
1902	3 384 200	96 481	57 702	28.5	17.1	11.5	12.9	1.4	131.7	36.4	168.1	1902
1901	3 340 600	97 028	60 018	29.0	18.0	11.1	12.2	1.1	137.2	37.2	174.4	1901
1900	3 299 900	94 316	63 606	28.6	19.3	9.3	11.3	2.0	149.7	35.8	185.5	1900
1899	3 262 700	94 472	57 591	29.0	17.7	11.3	11.4	0.1	136.5	36.2	172.7	1899
1898	3 225 500	91 793	58 914	28.5	18.3	10.2	11.5	1.3	155.0	36.9	191.9	1898
1897	3 188 300	90 078	56 399	28.3	17.7	10.6	11.7	1.1	141.1	36.5	177.6	1897
1896	3 151 100	88 428	56 096	28.1	17.8	10.3	11.8	1.5	132.3	36.7	169.0	1896
1895	3 113 900	84 973	59 747	27.3	19.2	8.1	11.9	3.8	159.2	37.8	196.9	1895
1894	3 076 700	84 142	61 885	27.3	20.1	7.2	12.1	4.9	152.7	37.7	190.4	1894
1893	3 039 500	84 897	61 059	27.9	20.1	7.8	12.2	4.4	151.6	37.7	189.4	1893
1892	3 002 300	83 125	57 178	27.7	19.0	8.6	12.4	3.7	149.7	37.8	187.5	1892
1891	2 965 100	83 596	61 183	28.2	20.6	7.6	4.9	- 2.7	162.9	37.4	200.2	1891
1890	2 950 600	78 548	61 805	26.6	20.9	5.7	3.7	- 2.0	156.9	39.1	196.1	1890
1889	2 939 700	81 176	59 715	27.6	20.3	7.3	3.7	- 3.6	159.1	38.2	197.3	1889
1888	2 928 800	81 098	58 229	27.7	19.9	7.8	3.7	- 4.1	153.0	41.3	194.3	1888
1887	2 917 900	81 287	58 939	27.9	20.2	7.7	3.7	- 3.9	162.1	41.5	203.6	1887
1886	2 907 000	80 763	60 061	27.8	20.7	7.1	3.7	- 3.4	164.3	41.8	206.2	1886
1885	2 896 100	80 349	61 548	27.7	21.3	6.5	3.8	- 2.7	173.0	40.2	213.2	1885
1884	2 885 200	81 571	58 301	28.3	20.2	8.1	3.8	- 4.3	160.8	39.5	200.3	1884
1883	2 874 300	81 974	58 733	28.5	20.4	8.1	3.8	- 4.3	163.9	39.3	203.2	1883
1882	2 863 400	82 689	62 849	28.9	21.9	6.9	3.8	- 3.1	172.0	39.9	211.9	1882
1881	2 852 500	85 142	63 979	29.8	22.4	7.4	4.8	- 2.6	186.9	39.5	226.4	1881
1880	2 838 700	84 165	62 223	29.6	21.9	7.7	6.2	- 1.5	179.9	38.6	218.5	1880

Switzerland

Population Growth

Year	Totals			Per 1.000 population			Rates			Per 1.000 live births			Year
	Midyear Population	Live Births	Deaths	birth rate	death rate	natural incr.	pop. growth	net migration	infant mort.	stillbirths	infant mort. and stillb.	
1879	2 821 000	86 180	63 651	30.5	22.6	8.0	6.3	− 1.7	180.9	40.8	221.7	1879
1878	2 803 300	87 833	65 311	31.3	23.3	8.0	6.3	− 1.7	191.3	40.9	232.2	1878
1877	2 785 600	89 244	65 353	32.0	23.5	8.6	6.4	− 2.2	191.3	40.5	231.8	1877
1876	2 767 900	90 786	66 819	32.8	24.1	8.7	6.4	− 2.3	197.2	42.0	239.1	1876
1875	2 750 300	87 579	66 113	31.8	24.0	7.8	6.4	− 1.4	196.8	48.3	245.1	1875
1874	2 732 600	83 051	60 845	30.4	22.3	8.1	6.5	− 1.6	189.3	46.6	235.9	1874
1873	2 714 900	80 572	61 676	29.7	22.7	7.0	6.5	− 0.4	200.2	48.7	248.9	1873
1872	2 697 200	80 329	59 758	29.8	22.2	7.6	6.6	− 1.1	183.4	49.6	233.0	1872
1871	2 679 500	77 633	74 002	29.0	27.6	1.4			221.7	51.5	273.2	1871

England and Wales

Population Growth

Year	Totals Midyear a) Population (in 1.000)	Totals Live Births	Totals Deaths	Per 1.000 population birth rate	Per 1.000 population death rate	Rates natural incr.	Rates pop. growth	Rates net migration	Per 1.000 live birth infant mort.	Per 1.000 live birth stillbirths	Per 1.000 live birth infant mort. and stillb.	Year
1975	49 199	603 000	582 841	12.3	11.8	0.4	0.0	- 0.5	15.7	1o.0	25.7	1975
1974	49 201	640 000	585 292	13.0	11.9	1.1	0.5	- 0.6	16.3	1o.9	27.3	1974
1973	49 175	676 000	587 478	13.7	11.9	1.8	2.8	1.0	16.9	11.8	28.7	1973
1972	49 038	725 000	591 889	14.8	12.1	2.7	3.8	1.0	17.2	12.4	29.7	1972
1971	48 854	783 000	567 262	16.0	11.6	4.4	3.6	- 0.9	17.5	12.6	3o.2	1971
1970	48 680	784 000	575 194	16.1	11.8	4.3	2.9	- 1.4	18.2	13.2	31.4	1970
1969	48 540	798 000	579 378	16.4	11.9	4.5	4.0	- 0.5	18.0	13.4	31.4	1969
1968	48 346	819 000	576 754	16.9	11.9	5.0	4.8	- 0.2	18.3	14.5	32.8	1968
1967	48 113	832 000	542 516	17.3	11.3	6.0	6.0	0.0	18.3	15.1	33.4	1967
1966	47 824	850 000	555 673	17.8	11.6	6.2	6.0	0.2	19.0	15.6	34.6	1966
1965	47 540	863 000	549 000	18.2	11.6	6.6	6.8	- 0.2	19.0	16.0	35.0	1965
1964	47 219	876 000	535 000	18.6	11.3	7.2	5.6	1.2	19.9	16.6	36.5	1964
1963	46 901	854 000	572 000	18.2	12.2	6.0	6.8	0.8	21.1	17.6	38.7	1963
1962	46 640	839 000	557 000	18.0	11.9	6.0	9.6	3.6	21.7	18.4	40.1	1962
1961	46 196	811 000	552 000	17.6	12.0	5.6	9.2	3.6	21.4	19.4	40.8	1961
1960	45 775	785 000	526 000	17.1	11.5	5.7	8.5	2.8	21.8	20.2	42.0	1960
1959	45 386	749 000	528 000	16.5	11.6	4.9	6.1	1.2	22.2	21.2	43.4	1959
1958	45 109	741 000	527 000	16.4	11.7	4.7	4.5	- 0.3	22.5	22.0	44.5	1958
1957	44 907	723 000	514 000	16.1	11.4	4.7	5.3	0.7	23.1	23.0	46.1	1957
1956	44 667	700 000	521 000	15.7	11.7	4.0	5.1	1.1	23.6	23.4	47.1	1956
1955	44 441	668 000	519 000	15.0	11.7	3.4	3.8	0.4	24.9	23.7	48.6	1955
1954	44 274	674 000	502 000	15.2	11.3	3.9	3.7	- 0.2	25.5	24.0	49.5	1954
1953	44 109	684 000	503 000	15.5	11.4	4.1	3.5	- 0.6	26.8	22.9	49.7	1953
1952	43 955	674 000	498 000	15.3	11.3	4.0	3.2	- 0.8	27.5	23.2	50.7	1952
1951	43 815	678 000	550 000	15.5	12.6	2.9			29.8	23.6	53.4	1951
1950	44 020 b)	697 000	510 000	15.8	11.6	4.2	5.3	1.1	29.9	23.1	52.9	1950
1949	43 785 b)	731 000	511 000 c)	16.7	11.7	5.0	6.5		32.7	23.2	55.9	1949
1948	43 502 b)	775 000	470 000 c)	17.8	10.8	7.0	10.4		34.5	23.7	58.3	1948
1947	43 050 b)	881 000	518 000 c)	20.5	12.0	8.4	8.1		41.8	24.7	66.6	1947
1946	42 700 b)	821 000	492 000 c)	19.2	11.5	7.7	1.5		40.9	27.9	68.8	1946
1945	42 636 b)	680 000	488 000 c)	15.9	11.4	4.5	0.4		47.0	28.4	75.4	1945
1944	42 449 b)	751 000	492 000 c)	17.7	11.6	6.1	4.5		44.5	28.4	72.9	1944
1943	42 259 b)	684 000	501 000 c)	16.2	11.9	4.3	8.6		48.9	31.1	80.0	1943
1942	41 897 b)	652 000	480 000 c)	15.6	11.5	4.1	3.6		49.5	34.3	83.8	1942
1941	41 748 b)	579 000	535 000 c)	13.9	12.8	1.1	- 2.7		59.7	36.1	95.7	1941
1940	41 862 b)	590 000	581 000 c)	14.1	13.9	0.2	9.6		57.4	38.6	96.1	1940
1939	41 460	614 000	500 000 c)	14.8	12.1	2.7	5.9	3.2	50.8	39.6	90.4	1939
1938	41 215	621 000	479 000	15.1	11.6	3.4	4.5	1.0	52.7	39.8	92.5	1938
1937	41 031	611 000	510 000	14.9	12.4	2.5	4.7	2.2	57.6	40.6	98.2	1937
1936	40 839	605 000	495 000	14.8	12.1	2.7	4.8	2.1	58.6	41.4	100.0	1936
1935	40 645	599 000	477 000	14.7	11.7	3.0	4.4	1.4	56.9	42.5	99.4	1935
1934	40 467	598 000	477 000	14.8	11.8	3.0	2.9	- 0.1	58.6	42.2	100.7	1934
1933	40 350	580 000	497 000	14.4	12.3	2.1	3.7	1.6	63.7	43.2	107.0	1933
1932	40 201	614 000	484 000	15.3	12.0	3.2	5.3	2.1	65.0	43.1	108.1	1932
1931	39 988	632 000	492 000	15.8	12.3	3.5	4.7	1.2	65.9	42.6	108.5	1931
1930	39 801	649 000	455 000	16.3	11.4	4.9	5.0	0.2	72.0	42.5	114.4	1930
1929	39 600	644 000	533 000	16.3	13.5	2.8	3.0	0.2	86.8	41.7	128.5	1929
1928	39 483	660 000	461 000	16.7	11.7	5.0	5.0	- 0.1	77.7	41.8	119.5	1928
1927	39 286	654 000	485 000	16.6	12.3	4.3	4.4	0.1	82.9			1927

Year	Totals			Per 1.000 population		Rates			Per 1.000 live births			Year
	Midyear Population	Live Births	Deaths	birth rate	death rate	natural incr.	pop. growth	net migration	infant mort.	stillbirths	infant mort. and stillb.	
1926	39 114	695 000	454 000	17.8	11.6	6.2	4.6	− 1.6	70			1926
1925	38 935	711 000	473 000	18.3	12.1	6.1	3.6	− 2.5	75			1925
1924	38 795	730 000	474 000	18.8	12.2	6.6	8.9	2.3	75			1924
1923	38 449	758 000	445 000	19.7	11.6	8.1	6.3	− 1.8	69			1923
1922	38 205	780 000	487 000	20.4	12.7	7.7	7.1	− 0.5	77			1922
1921	37 932	849 000	458 000	22.4	12.1	10.3			83			1921
1920	37 247d)	958 000	466 000	25.7	12.5	13.2			80			1920
1919	35 427d)	692 000	504 000	19.5	14.2	5.3			89			1919
1918	34 024d)	663 000	612 000	19.5	18.0	1.5			97			1918
1917	34 197d)	668 000	499 000	19.5	14.6	4.9			96			1917
1916	34 642d)	786 000	508 000	22.7	14.7	8.0			91			1916
1915	35 284d)	815 000	562 000	23.1	15.9	7.2			110			1915
1914	36 967	879 000	516 000	23.8	14.0	9.8	10.6	0.8	105			1914
1913	36 574	882 000	505 000	24.1	13.8	10.3	6.8	− 3.6	108			1913
1912	36 327	873 000	487 000	24.0	13.4	10.6	5.3	− 5.4	95			1912
1911	36 136	881 000	528 000	24.4	14.6	9.8	9.5	− 0.2	130			1911
1910	35 792	897 000	483 000	25.1	13.5	11.6	10.3	− 1.3	105			1910
1909	35 424	914 000	518 000	25.8	14.6	11.2	10.3	− 0.9	109			1909
1908	35 059	940 000	521 000	26.8	14.9	12.0	10.3	− 1.7	120			1908
1907	34 699	918 000	524 000	26.5	15.1	11.4	10.3	− 1.1	118			1907
1906	34 342	935 000	531 000	27.2	15.5	11.8	10.3	− 1.5	132			1906
1905	33 989	929 000	520 000	27.3	15.3	12.0	10.3	− 1.7	128			1905
1904	33 639	945 000	550 000	28.1	16.4	11.7	10.3	− 1.5	145			1904
1903	33 293	948 000	514 000	28.5	15.4	13.0	11.4	− 1.7	132			1903
1902	32 915	941 000	535 000	28.6	16.3	12.3	9.2	− 3.1	133			1902
1901	32 612	930 000	552 000	28.5	16.9	11.6	11.1	− 0.5	151			1901
1900	32 249	927 000	588 000	28.7	18.2	10.5	11.4	0.9	154			1900
1899	31 881	929 000	581 000	29.1	18.2	10.9	11.4	0.5	163			1899
1898	31 518	923 000	552 000	29.3	17.5	11.8	11.4	− 0.3	160			1898
1897	31 158	922 000	541 000	29.6	17.4	12.2	11.4	− 0.8	156			1897
1896	30 803	915 000	527 000	29.7	17.1	12.6	11.4	− 1.2	148			1896
1895	30 451	922 000	569 000	30.3	18.7	11.6	11.4	− 0.2	161			1895
1894	30 104	890 000	499 000	29.6	16.6	13.0	11.4	− 1.6	137			1894
1893	29 761	915 000	570 000	30.7	19.2	11.6	11.4	− 0.2	159			1893
1892	29 421	898 000	560 000	30.5	19.0	11.5	11.4	− 0.1	148			1892
1891	29 086	914 000	587 000	31.4	20.2	11.2	11.1	− 0.2	149			1891
1890	28 764	870 000	562 000	30.2	19.5	10.7	11.0	0.3	151			1890
1889	28 448	886 000	518 000	31.1	18.2	12.9	11.0	− 2.0	144			1889
1888	28 136	880 000	511 000	31.3	18.2	13.1	11.0	− 2.1	136			1888
1887	27 827	886 000	531 000	31.8	19.1	12.8	11.0	− 1.8	145			1887
1886	27 522	904 000	537 000	32.8	19.5	13.3	11.0	− 2.4	149			1886
1885	27 220	894 000	522 000	32.8	19.2	13.7	10.9	− 2.7	138			1885
1884	26 922	907 000	531 000	33.7	19.7	14.0	11.0	− 3.0	147			1884
1883	26 627	891 000	523 000	33.5	19.6	13.8	11.0	− 2.8	137			1883
1882	26 334	889 000	517 000	33.8	19.6	14.1	10.9	− 3.2	141			1882
1881	26 046	884 000	492 000	33.9	18.9	15.1	12.7	− 2.3	130			1881
1880	25 714	882 000	528 000	34.3	20.5	13.8	13.3	− 0.4	153			1880
1879	25 371	880 000	526 000	34.7	20.7	14.0	13.3	− 0.6	135			1879
1878	25 033	892 000	540 000	35.6	21.6	14.1	13.3	− 0.8	152			1878

| Year | Totals | | | Per 1.000 population | | Rates | | | Per 1.000 live births | | | Year |
	Midyear Population (in 1.000)	Live Births	Deaths	birth rate	death rate	natural incr.	pop. growth	net migration	infant mort.	stillbirths	infant mort. and stillb.	
1877	24 700	888 000	501 000	36.0	20.3	15.7	13.4	− 2.3	136			1877
1876	24 370	888 000	510 000	36.4	20.9	15.5	13.0	− 2.5	146			1876
1875	24 054	851 000	546 000	35.4	22.7	12.7	13.7	1.0	158			1875
1874	23 724	855 000	526 000	36.0	22.2	13.9	13.3	− 0.5	151			1874
1873	23 408	830 000	493 000	35.5	21.1	14.4	13.3	− 1.1	149			1873
1872	23 096	826 000	492 000	35.8	21.3	14.5	13.3	− 1.2	150			1872
1871	22 789	797 000	515 000	35.0	22.6	12.4	12.6	0.3	158			1871
1870	22 501	793 000	516 000	35.2	22.9	12.3	12.4	0.0	160			1870
1869	22 223	773 000	495 000	34.8	22.3	12.5	12.3	− 0.2	156			1869
1868	21 949	787 000	481 000	35.9	21.9	13.9	12.4	− 1.5	155			1868
1867	21 677	768 000	471 000	35.4	21.7	13.7	12.3	− 1.4	153			1867
1866	21 410	754 000	500 000	35.2	23.4	11.9	12.4	0.5	160			1866
1865	21 145	748 000	491 000	35.4	23.2	12.2	12.3	0.2	160			1865
1864	20 884	740 000	496 000	35.4	23.8	11.7	12.4	0.7	153			1864
1863	20 626	727 000	474 000	35.2	23.0	12.3	12.4	0.1	149			1863
1862	20 371	713 000	437 000	35.0	21.5	13.5	12.4	− 1.2	142			1862
1861	20 119	696 000	435 000	34.6	21.6	13.0	10.8	− 2.2	153			1861
1860	19 902	684 000	422 000	34.4	21.2	13.2	10.8	− 2.4	148			1860
1859	19 687	690 000	441 000	35.0	22.4	12.6	11.0	− 1.7	153			1859
1858	19 471	655 000	449 000	33.6	23.1	10.6	11.0	0.5	151			1858
1857	19 256	663 000	419 000	34.4	21.8	12.7	11.1	− 1.6	156			1857
1856	19 042	657 000	391 000	34.5	20.5	14.0	11.2	− 2.8	143			1856
1855	18 829	635 000	426 000	33.7	22.6	11.1	11.3	0.2	153			1855
1854	18 616	634 000	437 000	34.1	23.5	10.6	11.4	0.8	157			1854
1853	18 404	612 000	421 000	33.3	22.9	10.4	11.5	1.1	159			1853
1852	18 193	624 000	407 000	34.3	22.4	11.9	11.5	− 0.4	158			1852
1851	17 983	616 000	396 000	34.3	22.0	12.2	11.7	− 0.6	153			1851
1850	17 773	593 000	369 000	33.4	20.8	12.6	11.8	− 0.8	162			1850
1849	17 564	578 000	441 000	32.9	25.1	7.8	11.8	4.0	160			1849
1848	17 357	563 000	398 000	32.4	22.9	9.5	11.9	2.4	153			1848
1847	17 150	540 000	419 000	31.5	24.4	7.1	12.0	5.0	164			1847
1846	16 944	573 000	390 000	33.8	23.0	10.8	12.1	1.3	164			1846
1845	16 739	544 000	350 000	32.5	20.9	11.6	12.2	0.6	142			1845
1844	16 535	541 000	357 000	32.7	21.6	11.1	12.3	1.1	148			1844
1843	16 332	527 000	347 000	32.3	21.2	11.0	12.4	1.3	150			1843
1842	16 130	518 000	350 000	32.1	21.7	10.4	12.5	2.0	152			1842
1841	15 929	512 000	344 000	32.1	21.6	10.5	12.4	1.9	145			1841
1840	15 731	502 000	359 000	31.9	22.8	9.1	13.8	4.7	154			1840
1839	15 514	493 000	339 000	31.8	21.9	9.9	14.6	4.6	151			1839
1838	15 288	464 000	343 000	30.4	22.4	7.9	12.0	4.1				1838
1837	15 104						11.7					1837
1836	14 928						13.7					1836
1835	14 724						13.9					1835
1834	14 520						13.2					1834
1833	14 328						11.4					1833
1832	14 165						12.1					1832
1831	13 994						13.5					1831
1830	13 805						13.0					1830
1829	13 625						13.0					1829

Population Growth

Year	Totals			Per 1.000 population			Rates		Per 1.000 live births			Year
	Midyear Population (in 1.000)	Live Births	Deaths	birth rate	death rate	natural incr.	pop. growth	net migration	infant mort.	stillbirths	infant mort. and stillb.	
1828	13 438						14.2					1828
1827	13 247						13.1					1827
1826	13 074						13.1					1826
1825	12 903						14.1					1825
1824	12 721						15.1					1824
1823	12 529						16.7					1823
1822	12 320						17.4					1822
1821	12 106						16.8					1821
1820	11 903						15.1					1820
1819	11 723						14.3					1819
1818	11 555						15.3					1818
1817	11 378						16.0					1817
1816	11 196						17.1					1816
1815	11 004						16.7					1815

a) Estimated midyear home population.

b) Total population, i.e. including members of H.M. Forces overseas.

c) From 3 September 1939 to 31 December 1949, for males, and from 1 June 1941 to 31 December 1949, for females, mortality rates are based upon civilian deaths only; but, as in other years, the number of deaths include those of non-civilians registered in the United Kingdom.

d) Figures are for civilians only

Population Growth

Year	Totals			Per 1.000 population		Rates			Per 1.000 live births			Year
	Midyear Population a)	Live Births	Deaths	birth rate	death rate	natural incr.	pop. growth	net migration	infant mort.	stillbirths	infant mort. and stillb.	
1975	5 206 000	67 900	63 125	13.0	12.1	0.9	- 2.1	- 3.0	17.2	11.3	28.5	1975
1974	5 217 000	70 100	64 740	13.4	12.4	1.0	1.0	- 0.1	18.9	12.1	31.0	1974
1973	5 212 000	74 400	64 545	14.3	12.4	1.9	0.4	- 1.5	19.0	11.7	30.7	1973
1972	5 210 000	78 600	65 017	15.1	12.5	2.6	- 1.3	- 4.0	18.8	13.4	32.2	1972
1971	5 217 000	86 700	61 614	16.6	11.8	4.8	0.6	- 4.2	19.9	13.3	33.2	1971
1970	5 214 000	87 300	63 640	16.7	12.2	4.5	1.0	- 3.6	19.6	14.1	33.8	1970
1969	5 209 000	90 300	63 821	17.3	12.3	5.1	1.7	- 3.4	21.1	14.2	35.3	1969
1968	5 200 000	94 800	63 311	18.2	12.2	6.1	0.4	- 5.7	20.8	15.0	35.8	1968
1967	5 198 000	96 200	59 523	18.5	11.5	7.1	- 0.6	- 7.6	21.0	16.0	37.1	1967
1966	5 201 000	96 500	63 689	18.6	12.2	6.3	- 0.2	- 6.1	23.2	16.5	39.7	1966
1965	5 210 000	100 700	62 900	19.3	12.1	7.2	- 0.2	- 7.0	23.1	18.2	41.3	1965
1964	5 209 000	104 400	61 100	20.0	11.7	8.3	0.8	- 7.5	24.0	18.2	42.2	1964
1963	5 205 000	102 700	65 500	19.7	12.6	7.1	1.5	- 5.6	25.6	19.4	45.0	1963
1962	5 197 000	104 300	63 200	20.1	12.2	7.9	2.5	- 5.4	26.5	20.3	46.9	1962
1961	5 184 000	101 200	63 900	19.5	12.3	7.2	1.4	- 5.8	25.8	21.2	47.1	1961
1960	5 177 000	101 300	61 800	19.6	11.9	7.6	2.9	- 4.7	26.4	22.2	48.6	1960
1959	5 162 000	99 300	63 100	19.2	12.2	7.0	4.1	- 2.9	28.4	22.7	51.0	1959
1958	5 141 000	99 500	62 100	19.4	12.1	7.3	3.1	- 4.2	27.7	23.4	51.1	1958
1957	5 125 000	98 000	61 100	19.1	11.9	7.2	1.0	- 6.2	28.6	24.3	52.9	1957
1956	5 120 000	95 300	61 800	18.6	12.1	6.5	1.6	- 5.0	28.6	24.4	53.1	1956
1955	5 112 000	92 500	61 600	18.1	12.1	6.0	1.6	- 4.5	30.4	25.2	55.6	1955
1954	5 104 000	92 300	61 400	18.1	12.0	6.1	1.0	- 5.1	31.0	26.0	57.0	1954
1953	5 099 000	90 900	58 900	17.8	11.6	6.3	- 0.4	- 6.7	30.8	25.4	56.2	1953
1952	5 101 000	90 400	61 500	17.7	12.1	5.7	- 0.2	- 5.9	35.2	26.9	62.1	1952
1951	5 102 000	90 600	65 800	17.8	12.9	4.9			37.4	27.4	64.8	1951
1950	5 168 000 b)	92 500	64 000	17.9	12.4	5.5	2.3	- 3.2	38.6	27.6	66.2	1950
1949	5 156 000 b)	95 700	63 500 c)	18.6	12.3	6.2	1.2		41.4	27.9	69.2	1949
1948	5 150 000 b)	100 300	60 900 c)	19.5	11.8	7.7	5.8		44.7	29.6	74.3	1948
1947	5 120 000 b)	113 100	66 200 c)	22.1	12.9	9.2	- 9.2		55.8	31.5	87.3	1947
1946	5 167 000 b)	104 400	64 600 c)	20.2	12.5	7.7	- 3.9		53.8	33.4	87.2	1946
1945	5 187 000 b)	86 900	62 700 c)	16.8	12.1	4.7	- 4.4		56.3	33.9	90.2	1945
1944	5 210 000 b)	95 900	64 900 c)	18.4	12.5	6.0	4.0		65.0	33.6	98.6	1944
1943	5 189 000 b)	94 700	66 700 c)	18.3	12.9	5.4	2.9		65.2	36.9	102.1	1943
1942	5 174 000 b)	90 700	64 900 c)	17.5	12.5	5.0	2.7		69.3	39.7	109.0	1942
1941	5 160 000 b)	89 700	72 600 c)	17.4	14.1	3.3	18.4		82.8	41.2	124.0	1941
1940	5 065 000 b)	86 400	72 700 c)	17.1	14.4	2.7			78.3	44.0	122.3	1940
1939	5 007 000	86 900	64 400 c)	17.4	12.9	4.5	2.8		68.5	44.1	112.6	1939
1938	4 993 000	88 600	62 900	17.7	12.6	5.1	3.2	- 1.9	69.6			1938
1937	4 977 000	87 800	69 000	17.6	13.9	3.8	2.2	- 1.6	80.3			1937
1936	4 966 000	88 900	66 800	17.9	13.5	4.5	2.6	- 1.8	82.3			1936
1935	4 953 000	87 900	65 300	17.7	13.2	4.6	3.8	- 0.7	76.8			1935
1934	4 934 000	88 800	63 700	18.0	12.9	5.1	4.5	- 0.6	77.7			1934
1933	4 912 000	86 500	64 900	17.6	13.2	4.4	5.9	1.5	81.1			1933
1932	4 883 000	91 000	66 000	18.6	13.5	5.1	8.2	3.1	86.2			1932
1931	4 843 000	92 200	64 200	19.0	13.3	5.8	3.1	- 2.7	81.8			1931
1930	4 828 000	94 500	64 200	19.6	13.3	6.3	- 0.8	- 7.1	83.1			1930
1929	4 832 000	92 900	70 900	19.2	14.7	4.6	- 3.3	- 7.9	86.8			1929
1928	4 848 000	96 800	65 300	20.0	13.5	6.5	- 1.0	- 7.5	85.7			1928
1927	4 853 000	96 700	65 800	19.9	13.6	6.4	- 2.3	- 8.6	88.7			1927

Population Growth

Year	Totals			Per 1.000 population		Rates			Per 1.000 live births			Year
	Midyear Population	Live Births	Deaths	birth rate	death rate	natural incr.	pop. growth	net migration	infant mort.	stillbirths	infant mort. and stillb.	
1926	4 864 000	102 400	63 800	21.1	13.1	7.9	- 0.6	- 8.6	83			1926
1925	4 867 000	104 100	65 500	21.4	13.5	7.9	1.0	- 6.9	91			1925
1924	4 862 000	106 900	70 400	22.0	14.5	7.5	- 5.3	-12.9	98			1924
1923	4 888 000	111 900	63 300	22.9	13.0	9.9	- 2.0	-12.0	80			1923
1922	4 898 000	115 100	72 900	23.5	14.9	8.6	3.3	- 5.3	101			1922
1921	4 882 000	123 200	66 200	25.2	13.6	11.7	3.7	- 8.0	90			1921
1920	4 864 000	136 500	68 100	28.1	14.0	14.1	9.0	- 5.0	92			1920
1919	4 820 000	106 300	75 100	22.1	15.6	6.5	1.7	- 4.8	102			1919
1918	4 812 000	98 600	78 300	20.5	16.3	4.2	0.4	- 3.8	100			1918
1917	4 810 000	97 400	69 500	20.2	14.4	5.8	3.1	- 2.7	107			1917
1916	4 795 000	109 900	70 600	22.9	14.7	8.2	5.0	- 3.2	97			1916
1915	4 771 000	114 200	81 600	23.9	17.1	6.8	5.0	- 1.8	126			1915
1914	4 747 000	123 900	73 600	26.1	15.5	10.6	4.0	- 6.6	111			1914
1913	4 728 000	120 500	73 100	25.5	15.5	10.0	- 2.7	-12.8	110			1913
1912	4 741 000	122 800	72 400	25.9	15.3	10.6	- 2.1	-12.7	105			1912
1911	4 751 000	121 900	71 700	25.7	15.1	10.6	2.5	- 0.8	112			1911
1910	4 739 000	124 100	72 200	26.2	15.2	11.0	6.3	- 4.6	108			1910
1909	4 709 000	128 700	74 600	27.3	15.8	11.5	6.2	- 5.3	108			1909
1908	4 680 000	131 400	77 900	28.1	16.6	11.4	6.4	- 5.0	121			1908
1907	4 650 000	128 800	77 300	27.7	16.6	11.1	6.2	- 4.8	110			1907
1906	4 621 000	132 000	75 600	28.6	16.4	12.2	6.1	- 6.1	115			1906
1905	4 593 000	131 400	74 500	28.6	16.2	12.4	6.3	- 6.1	116			1905
1904	4 564 000	132 600	78 000	29.1	17.1	12.0	6.1	- 5.8	123			1904
1903	4 536 000	133 500	76 000	29.4	16.8	12.7	6.4	- 6.3	118			1903
1902	4 507 000	132 300	78 000	29.4	17.3	12.0	6.2	- 5.8	113			1902
1901	4 479 000	132 200	80 100	29.5	17.9	11.6	9.4	- 2.3	129			1901
1900	4 437 000	131 400	82 300	29.6	18.5	11.1	10.4	- 0.7	128			1900
1899	4 391 000	130 700	79 600	29.8	18.1	11.6	10.5	- 1.2	131			1899
1898	4 345 000	130 900	78 400	30.1	18.0	12.1	10.6	- 1.5	134			1898
1897	4 299 000	128 900	79 100	30.0	18.4	11.6	10.5	- 1.1	138			1897
1896	4 254 000	129 200	70 700	30.4	16.6	13.8	10.3	- 3.4	115			1896
1895	4 210 000	126 500	81 900	30.0	19.5	10.6	10.5	- 0.1	133			1895
1894	4 166 000	124 400	71 200	29.9	17.1	12.8	10.6	- 2.2	117			1894
1893	4 122 000	127 100	79 700	30.8	19.3	11.5	10.4	- 1.1	136			1893
1892	4 079 000	125 000	75 600	30.6	18.5	12.1	10.5	- 1.6	117			1892
1891	4 036 000	126 000	83 600	31.2	20.7	10.5	8.2	- 2.3	128			1891
1890	4 003 000	121 500	79 000	30.4	19.7	10.6	7.5	- 3.1	131			1890
1889	3 973 000	122 800	73 200	30.9	18.4	12.5	7.3	- 5.2	121			1889
1888	3 944 000	123 300	71 200	31.3	18.1	13.2	7.6	- 5.6	113			1888
1887	3 914 000	124 400	74 500	31.8	19.0	12.7	7.4	- 5.3	122			1887
1886	3 885 000	127 900	73 600	32.9	18.9	14.0	7.5	- 6.5	116			1886
1885	3 856 000	126 100	74 600	32.7	19.3	13.4	7.5	- 5.8	121			1885
1884	3 827 000	129 200	75 200	33.8	19.6	14.1	7.3	- 6.8	118			1884
1883	3 799 000	124 500	76 900	32.8	20.2	12.5	7.4	- 5.2	119			1883
1882	3 771 000	126 200	73 000	33.5	19.4	14.1	7.4	- 6.7	118			1882
1881	3 743 000	126 200	72 300	33.7	19.3	14.4	9.9	- 4.5	113			1881
1880	3 706 000	124 600	75 200	33.6	20.3	13.3	10.5	- 2.8	125			1880
1879	3 667 000	125 700	73 400	34.3	20.0	14.3	10.6	- 3.6	108			1879
1878	3 628 000	126 800	76 800	35.0	21.2	13.8	10.5	- 3.3	123			1878

Scotland

Population Growth

Year	Totals			Per 1.000 population		Rates			Per 1.000 live births			Year
	Midyear Population	Live Births	Deaths	birth rate	death rate	natural incr.	pop.growth	net migration	infant mort.	stillbirths	infant mort. and stillb.	
1877	3 590 000	126 800	74 000	35.3	20.6	14.7	10.6	− 4.1	115			1877
1876	3 552 000	126 500	74 100	35.6	20.9	14.8	10.4	− 4.3	121			1876
1875	3 515 000	123 600	81 700	35.2	23.2	11.9	10.5	− 1.4	132			1875
1874	3 478 000	123 700	80 700	35.6	23.2	12.4	10.6	− 1.7	125			1874
1873	3 441 000	119 700	76 900	34.8	22.3	12.4	10.5	− 2.0	125			1873
1872	3 405 000	118 800	75 300	34.9	22.1	12.8	10.6	− 2.2	124			1872
1871	3 369 000	116 100	74 700	34.5	22.2	12.3	9.5	− 2.8	130			1871
1870	3 337 000	115 400	74 200	34.6	22.2	12.3	9.3	− 3.1	123			1870
1869	3 306 000	113 400	75 900	34.3	23.0	11.3	9.4	− 2.0	129			1869
1868	3 275 000	115 500	69 500	35.3	21.2	14.0	9.2	− 4.9	118			1868
1867	3 245 000	114 000	69 100	35.1	21.3	13.8	9.2	− 4.6	119			1867
1866	3 215 000	113 700	71 400	35.4	22.2	13.2	9.3	− 3.8	122			1866
1865	3 185 000	113 100	70 900	35.5	22.3	13.2	9.1	− 4.1	125			1865
1864	3 156 000	112 300	74 400	35.6	23.6	12.0	9.2	− 2.8	126			1864
1863	3 127 000	109 300	71 500	35.0	22.9	12.1	9.3	− 2.8	120			1863
1862	3 098 000	107 100	67 200	34.6	21.7	12.9	9.4	− 3.5	117			1862
1861	3 069 000	107 000	62 400	34.9	20.3	14.5	4.6	−10.0	111			1861
1860	3 055 000	105 600	68 200	34.6	22.3	12.2	4.3	− 8.0	127			1860
1859	3 042 000	106 500	61 700	35.0	20.3	14.7	4.6	−10.1	108			1859
1858	3 028 000	104 000	63 600	34.3	21.0	13.3	5.3	− 8.1	121			1858
1857	3 012 000	103 400	61 900	34.3	20.6	13.8	5.3	− 8.5	118			1857
1856	2 996 000	101 800	58 500	34.0	19.5	14.5	6.0	− 8.4	118			1856
1855	2 978 000	93 300	62 000	31.3	20.8	10.5	6.4	− 4.1	125			1855
1854	2 959 000						6.8					1854
1853	2 939 000						7.1					1853
1852	2 918 000						7.5					1852
1851	2 896 000						7.9					1851
1850	2 873 000						8.4					1850
1849	2 849 000						9.1					1849
1848	2 823 000						9.2					1848
1847	2 797 000						9.7					1847
1846	2 770 000						10.1					1846
1845	2 742 000						10.6					1845
1844	2 713 000						10.7					1844
1843	2 684 000						11.5					1843
1842	2 653 000						11.7					1842
1841	2 622 000						8.0					1841
1840	2 601 000						10.4					1840
1839	2 574 000						10.1					1839
1838	2 548 000						9.8					1838
1837	2 523 000						10.3					1837
1836	2 497 000						10.0					1836
1835	2 472 000						10.1					1835
1834	2 447 000						10.2					1834
1833	2 422 000						9.9					1833
1832	2 398 000						10.0					1832
1831	2 374 000						12.2					1831
1830	2 345 000						12.4					1830
1829	2 316 000						12.1					1829

Population Growth

Year	Totals			Per 1.000 population		Rates			Per 1.000 live births			Year
	Midyear Population	Births	Deaths	birth rate	death rate	natural incr.	pop. growth	net migration	infant mort.	stillbirths	infant mort. and stillb.	
1828	2 288 000						12.7					1828
1827	2 259 000						11.5					1827
1826	2 233 000						12.5					1826
1825	2 205 000						11.8					1825
1824	2 179 000						10.6					1824
1823	2 156 000						13.9					1823
1822	2 126 000						12.2					1822
1821	2 100 000						13.8					1821
1820	2 071 000						14.0					1820
1819	2 042 000						13.7					1819
1818	2 014 000						13.9					1818
1817	1 986 000						13.6					1817
1816	1 959 000						13.3					1816
1815	1 933 000						14.5					1815

a) Estimated midyear home population.
b) Total population, i.e. including members of H.M. Forces overseas.
c) From 3 September 1939 to 31 December 1949, for males, and from 1 June 1941 to 31 December 1949, for females, mortality rates are based upon civilian deaths only; but, as in other years, the number of deaths include those of non-civilians registered in the United Kingdom.

Year	Totals			Per 1.000 population		Rates			Per 1.000 live births			Year
	Midyear Population	Live Births	Deaths	birth rate	death rate	natural incr.	pop. growth	net migration	infant mort.	stillbirths	infant mort. and stillb.	
1975	1 537 000	26 100	16 511	17.0	10.7	6.2	- 6.5	-12.7	20.9	13.8	34.7	1975
1974	1 547 000	27 200	17 327	17.6	11.2	6.4	0.0	- 6.4	20.9	13.3	34.2	1974
1973	1 547 000	29 200	17 669	18.9	11.4	7.5	1.3	- 6.2	20.5	14.5	35.0	1973
1972	1 545 000	30 000	17 032	19.4	11.0	8.4	4.5	- 3.9	22.7	14.5	37.2	1972
1971	1 538 000	31 800	16 202	20.7	10.5	10.1	7.2	- 3.0	22.9	14.5	37.4	1971
1970	1 527 000	32 100	16 551	21.0	10.8	10.2	8.5	- 1.7	24.4	15.5	39.9	1970
1969	1 514 000	32 400	16 338	21.4	10.8	10.6	7.3	- 3.3	24.0	16.3	40.3	1969
1968	1 503 000	33 200	15 933	22.1	10.6	11.5	9.3	- 2.2	23.5	17.8	41.3	1968
1967	1 489 000	33 400	14 671	22.4	9.9	12.6	8.7	- 3.8	25.5	16.6	42.1	1967
1966	1 476 000	33 200	16 441	22.5	11.1	11.4	4.7	- 6.6	25.0	19.5	44.5	1966
1965	1 469 000	33 900	15 600	23.1	10.6	12.5	7.5	- 5.0	26.4	19.8	46.2	1965
1964	1 458 000	34 300	15 300	23.5	10.5	13.0	8.2	- 4.8	27.0	19.9	46.9	1964
1963	1 446 000	33 400	15 900	23.1	11.0	12.1	7.6	- 4.5	26.5	22.9	49.4	1963
1962	1 435 000	32 600	15 200	22.7	10.6	12.1	5.6	- 6.6	27.5	22.8	50.3	1962
1961	1 427 000	31 900	16 100	22.4	11.3	11.1	4.9	- 6.2	27			1961
1960	1 420 000	32 000	15 300	22.5	10.8	11.8	8.5	- 3.3	27			1960
1959	1 408 000	30 800	15 400	21.9	10.9	10.9	4.3	- 6.7	28			1959
1958	1 402 000	30 300	15 100	21.6	10.8	10.8	2.1	- 8.7	28			1958
1957	1 399 000	30 100	15 200	21.5	10.9	10.7	1.4	- 9.2	29			1957
1956	1 397 000	29 500	14 800	21.1	10.6	10.5	2.1	- 8.4	29			1956
1955	1 394 000	29 000	15 400	20.8	11.0	9.8	5.0	- 4.7	32			1955
1954	1 387 000	28 800	15 100	20.8	10.9	9.9	2.2	- 7.7	33			1954
1953	1 384 000	29 000	14 800	21.0	10.7	10.3	6.5	- 3.8	38			1953
1952	1 375 000	28 800	14 800	20.9	10.8	10.2	1.5	- 8.7	39			1952
1951	1 373 000	28 500	17 600	20.8	12.8	7.9	- 2.9	-10.9	41			1951
1950	1 377 000	28 800	15 800	20.9	11.5	9.4	4.4	- 5.1	41			1950
1949	1 371 000	29 100	15 600	21.2	11.4	9.8	6.6	- 3.3	45			1949
1948	1 362 000	29 500	15 100	21.7	11.1	10.6	8.8	- 1.8	46			1948
1947	1 350 000	31 300	16 900	23.2	12.5	10.7	0.0	-10.7	53			1947
1946	1 350 000	30 100	16 700	22.3	12.4	9.9	- 6.7	-16.6	54			1946
1945	1 359 000	29 000	16 400	21.3	12.1	9.3	1.5	- 7.8	68			1945
1944	1 357 000	30 900	17 000	22.8	12.5	10.2	11.8	1.5	67			1944
1943	1 341 000	31 500	17 700	23.5	13.2	10.3	8.9	- 1.3	78			1943
1942	1 329 000	29 600	17 500	22.3	13.2	9.1	15.8	6.7	76			1942
1941	1 308 000	26 900	20 100	20.6	15.4	5.2	6.9	1.7	77			1941
1940	1 299 000	25 400	19 000	19.6	14.6	4.9	3.1	- 1.8	86			1940
1939	1 295 000	25 200	17 500	19.5	13.5	5.9	6.9	1.0	71			1939
1938	1 286 000	25 700	17 600	20.0	13.7	6.3	3.9	- 2.4	75			1938
1937	1 281 000	25 400	19 300	19.8	15.1	4.8	3.9	- 0.9	78			1937
1936	1 276 000	25 900	18 400	20.3	14.4	5.9	3.9	- 2.0	77			1936
1935	1 271 000	24 700	18 600	19.4	14.6	4.8	4.7	- 0.1	86			1935
1934	1 265 000	25 400	17 500	20.1	13.8	6.2	5.5	- 0.7	70			1934
1933	1 258 000	24 600	18 200	19.6	14.5	5.1	5.6	0.5	80			1933
1932	1 251 000	25 100	17 800	20.1	14.2	5.8	6.4	0.6	83			1932
1931	1 243 000	25 700	18 000	20.7	14.5	6.2	4.8	- 1.4	73			1931
1930	1 237 000	25 900	17 200	20.9	13.9	7.0	2.4	- 9.5	68			1930
1929	1 240 000	25 400	19 900	20.5	16.0	4.4	- 5.6	-10.1	86			1929
1928	1 247 000	26 000	18 000	20.9	14.4	6.4	- 2.4	- 8.8	78			1928
1927	1 250 000	26 700	18 200	21.4	14.6	6.8	- 3.2	-10.0	78			1927

Population Growth

Year	Totals			Per 1.000 population		Rates			Per 1.000 live births			Year
	Midyear Population	Live Births	Deaths	birth rate	death rate	natural incr.	pop. growth	net migration	infant mort.	stillbirths	infant mort. and stillb.	
1926	1 254 000	28 200	18 900	22.5	15.1	7.4	− 2.4	− 9.8	85			1926
1925	1 257 000	27 700	19 800	22.0	15.8	6.3	− 0.8	− 7.1	86			1925
1924	1 258 000	28 500	20 300	22.7	16.1	6.5	− 0.8	− 7.3	85			1924
1923	1 259 000	30 100	18 700	23.9	14.9	9.1	− 7.9	−17.0	77			1923
1922	1 269 000	29 500	19 800	23.2	15.6	7.6			77			1922

Ireland

Year	Midyear Population	Live Births	Deaths	birth rate	death rate	natural incr.	pop. growth	net migration	infant mort.	stillbirths	infant mort. and stillb.	Year
1920	4 361 000	99 500	66 500	22.8	15.2	7.6	2.1	− 5.5	83			1920
1919	4 352 000	89 300	78 600	20.5	18.1	2.5	16.5	14.1	88			1919
1918	4 280 000	87 300	78 700	20.4	18.4	2.0	1.6	− 0.4	86			1918
1917	4 273 000	86 400	72 700	20.2	17.0	3.2	0.0	− 3.2	88			1917
1916	4 273 000	91 400	71 400	21.4	16.7	4.2	− 1.2	− 5.9	83			1916
1915	4 278 000	95 600	76 100	22.3	17.8	4.6	−13.1	−17.6	92			1915
1914	4 334 000	98 800	71 300	22.8	16.5	6.3	− 2.8	− 9.1	87			1914
1913	4 346 000	100 100	74 700	23.0	17.2	5.8	− 5.1	−10.9	97			1913
1912	4 368 000	101 000	72 200	23.1	16.5	6.6	− 3.0	− 9.6	86			1912
1911	4 381 000	101 800	72 500	23.2	16.5	6.7	− 0.9	− 7.6	94			1911
1910	4 385 000	102 000	74 900	23.3	17.1	6.2	− 0.5	− 6.6	95			1910
1909	4 387 000	102 800	75 000	23.4	17.1	6.3	0.5	− 5.9	92			1909
1908	4 385 000	102 000	76 900	23.3	17.5	5.7	− 0.7	− 6.4	97			1908
1907	4 388 000	101 700	77 300	23.2	17.6	5.6	− 2.3	− 7.8	92			1907
1906	4 398 000	103 500	74 400	23.5	16.9	6.6	− 0.2	− 6.8	93			1906
1905	4 399 000	102 800	75 100	23.4	17.1	6.3	− 2.0	− 8.3	95			1905
1904	4 408 000	103 800	79 500	23.5	18.0	5.5	− 2.3	− 7.8	100			1904
1903	4 418 000	101 800	77 400	23.0	17.5	5.5	− 3.8	− 9.4	96			1903
1902	4 435 000	101 900	77 700	23.0	17.5	5.5	− 2.7	− 8.2	100			1902
1901	4 447 000	101 000	79 100	22.7	17.8	4.9	− 4.9	− 9.9	101			1901
1900	4 469 000	101 500	87 700	22.7	19.6	3.1	− 7.4	−10.5	109			1900
1899	4 502 000	103 900	79 700	23.1	17.7	5.4	− 3.6	− 8.9	108			1899
1898	4 518 000	105 500	82 400	23.4	18.2	5.1	− 2.7	− 7.8	110			1898
1897	4 530 000	106 700	83 900	23.6	18.5	5.0	− 2.6	− 7.7	109			1897
1896	4 542 000	107 600	75 700	23.7	16.7	7.0	− 4.0	−11.0	95			1896
1895	4 560 000	106 100	84 400	23.3	18.5	4.8	− 6.4	−11.1	104			1895
1894	4 589 000	105 400	83 600	23.0	18.2	4.8	− 3.9	− 8.7	102			1894
1893	4 607 000	106 100	82 800	23.0	18.0	5.1	− 5.9	−10.9	102			1893
1892	4 634 000	104 200	90 000	22.5	19.4	3.1	− 9.9	−13.0	105			1892
1891	4 680 000	108 100	86 000	23.1	18.4	4.7	− 8.1	−12.8	95			1891
1890	4 718 000	105 300	85 800	22.3	18.2	4.1	− 8.3	−12.4	95			1890
1889	4 757 000	107 800	82 900	22.7	17.4	5.2	− 9.2	−14.5	94			1889
1888	4 801 000	109 600	85 900	22.8	17.9	4.9	−11.7	−16.6	97			1888
1887	4 857 000	112 400	88 600	23.1	18.2	4.9	−10.1	−15.0	95			1887
1886	4 906 000	113 900	87 300	23.2	17.8	5.4	− 6.7	−12.1	94			1886
1885	4 939 000	116 000	90 700	23.5	18.4	5.1	− 7.3	−12.4	95			1885
1884	4 975 000	118 900	87 200	23.9	17.5	6.4	− 9.8	−16.2	92			1884
1883	5 024 000	118 200	96 300	23.5	19.2	4.4	−15.3	−19.7	98			1883
1882	5 101 000	122 600	88 500	24.0	17.3	6.7	− 8.8	−15.5	95			1882

Ireland

Population Growth

Year	Totals			Per 1.000 population		Rates			Per 1.000 live births			Year
	Midyear Population	Live Births	Deaths	birth rate	death rate	natural incr.	pop. growth	net migration	infant mort.	stillbirths	infant mort. and stillb.	
1881	5 146 000	125 800	90 100	24.4	17.5	6.9	−11.1	−18.0	91			1881
1880	5 203 000	128 100	102 900	24.6	19.8	4.8	−12.1	−17.0	112			1880
1879	5 266 000	135 100	105 100	25.7	20.0	5.7	− 3.0	− 8.8	101			1879
1878	5 282 000	134 100	99 600	25.4	18.9	6.5	− 0.8	− 7.3	97			1878
1877	5 286 000	139 700	93 600	26.4	17.7	8.7	1.5	− 7.2	92			1877
1876	5 278 000	140 500	92 300	26.6	17.5	9.1	− 0.2	− 9.3	94			1876
1875	5 279 000	138 300	98 100	26.2	18.6	7.6	− 3.8	−11.4	95			1875
1874	5 299 000	141 300	92 000	26.7	17.4	9.3	− 5.5	−14.8	94			1874
1873	5 328 000	144 400	97 600	27.1	18.3	8.8	− 8.4	−17.2	96			1873
1872	5 373 000	149 300	97 300	27.8	18.1	9.7	− 4.7	−14.3	97			1872
1871	5 398 000	151 400	88 300	28.0	16.4	11.7	− 3.9	−15.6	91			1871
1870	5 419 000	149 800	90 500	27.6	16.7	10.9	− 5.5	−16.5	95			1870
1869	5 449 000	145 700	89 600	26.7	16.4	10.3	− 3.1	−13.4	93			1869
1868	5 466 000	146 100	86 200	26.7	15.8	11.0	− 3.8	−14.8	95			1868
1867	5 487 000	144 400	93 500	26.3	17.0	9.3	− 6.6	−15.8	97			1867
1866	5 523 000	146 100	93 000	26.5	16.8	9.6	−13.0	−22.7	94			1866
1865	5 595 000	145 000	93 100	25.9	16.6	9.3	− 8.2	−17.5	98			1865
1864	5 641 000	136 400	93 100	24.2	16.5	7.7	−13.7	−21.3	98			1864
1863	5 718 000						−10.1					1863
1862	5 776 000						− 2.1					1862
1861	5 788 000						− 5.7					1861
1860	5 821 000						− 7.0					1860
1859	5 862 000						− 4.9					1859
1858	5 891 000						− 4.8					1858
1857	5 919 000						− 9.1					1857
1856	5 973 000						− 7.0					1856
1855	6 015 000						−11.3					1855
1854	6 083 000						−19.1					1854
1853	6 199 000						−22.3					1853
1852	6 337 000						−27.9					1852
1851	6 514 000						−55.9					1851
1850	6 878 000						−55.0					1850
1849	7 256 000						−52.9					1849
1848	7 640 000						−50.4					1848
1847	8 025 000						−32.8					1847
1846	8 288 000						− 0.8					1846
1845	8 295 000						2.2					1845
1844	8 277 000						4.5					1844
1843	8 240 000						2.3					1843
1842	8 221 000						2.6					1842
1841	8 200 000						5.4					1841
1840	8 156 000						5.5					1840
1839	8 111 000						5.3					1839
1838	8 068 000						5.5					1838
1837	8 024 000						5.4					1837
1836	7 981 000						5.4					1836
1835	7 938 000						5.4					1835
1834	7 895 000						5.4					1834
1833	7 852 000						5.3					1833

Ireland

Population Growth

Year	Totals			Per 1.000 population		Rates			Per 1.000 live births			Year
	Midyear Population	Live Births	Deaths	birth rate	death rate	natural incr.	pop. growth	net migration	infant mort.	stillbirths	infant mort. and stillb.	
1832	7 810 000						5.5					1832
1831	7 767 000						13.1					1831
1830	7 665 000						13.2					1830
1829	7 564 000						13.2					1829
1828	7 464 000						13.1					1828
1827	7 366 000						13.2					1827
1826	7 269 000						13.2					1826
1825	7 173 000						13.2					1825
1824	7 078 000						13.1					1824
1823	6 985 000						13.2					1823
1822	6 893 000						13.2					1822
1821	6 802 000						13.2					1821
1820	6 712 000						13.1					1820
1819	6 624 000						13.3					1819
1818	6 536 000						13.2					1818
1817	6 450 000						13.2					1817
1816	6 365 000						13.2					1816
1815	6 281 000						13.2					1815

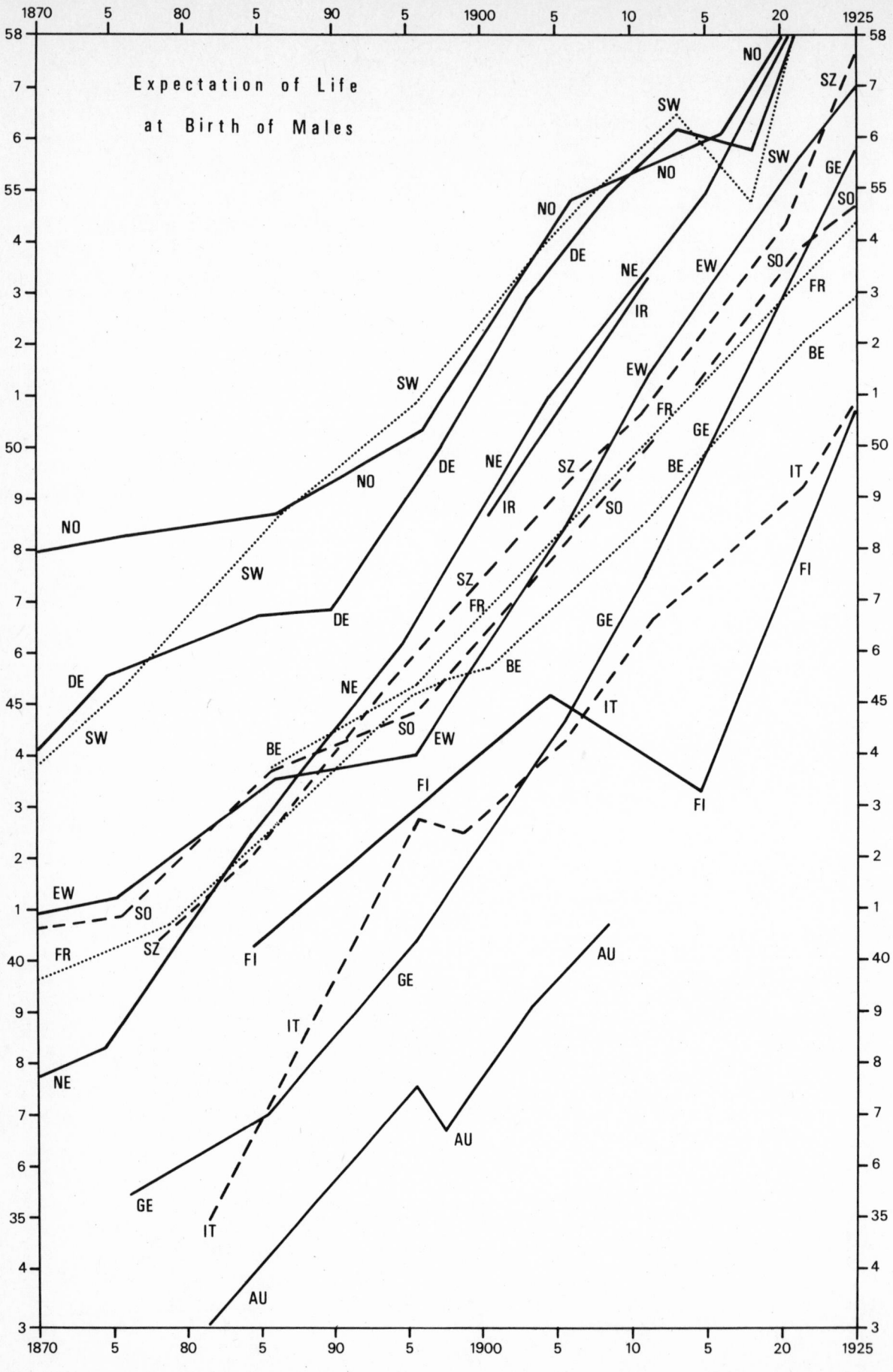

Expectation of Life
at Birth of Males

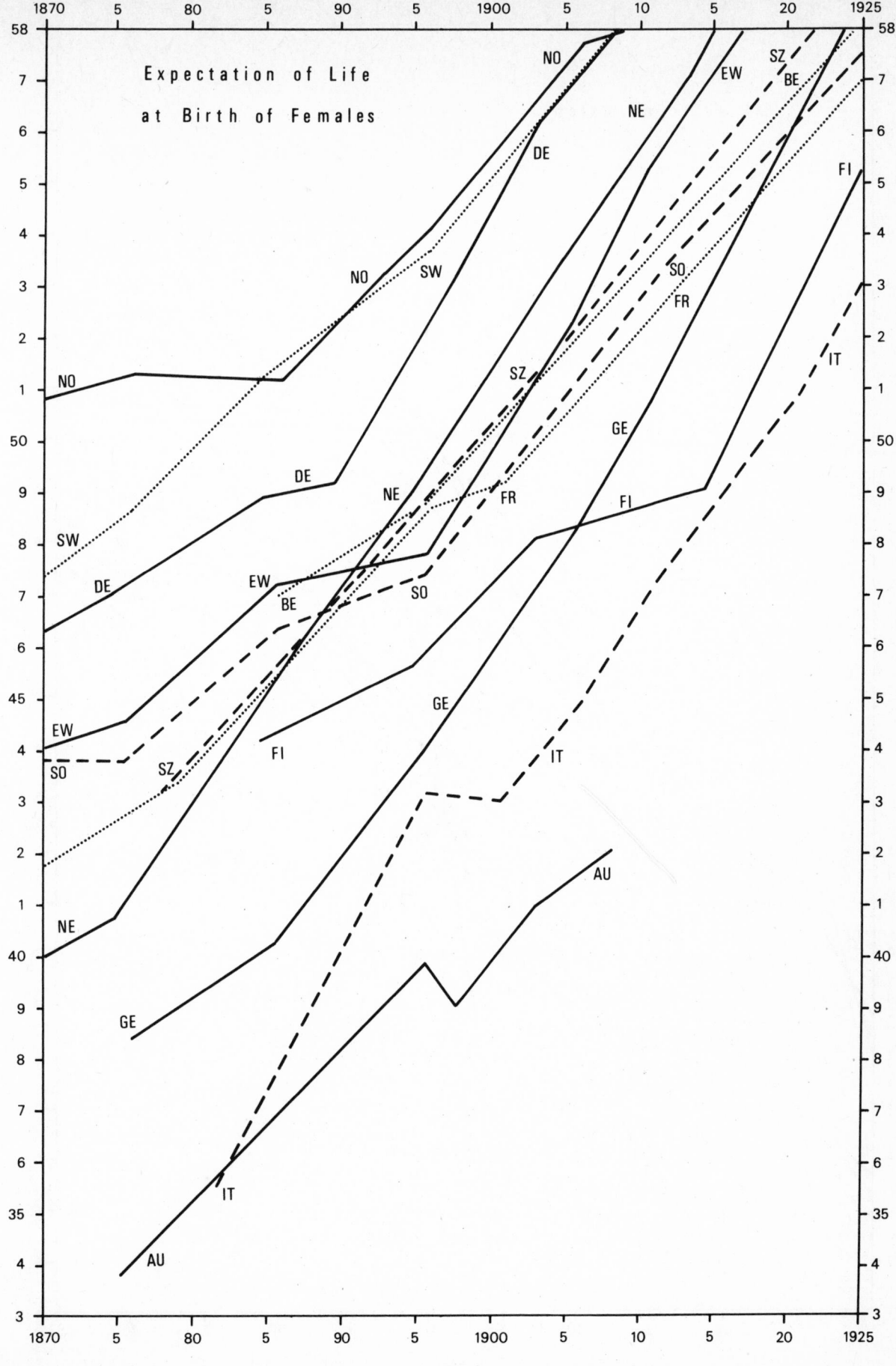

Expectation of Life
at Birth of Females

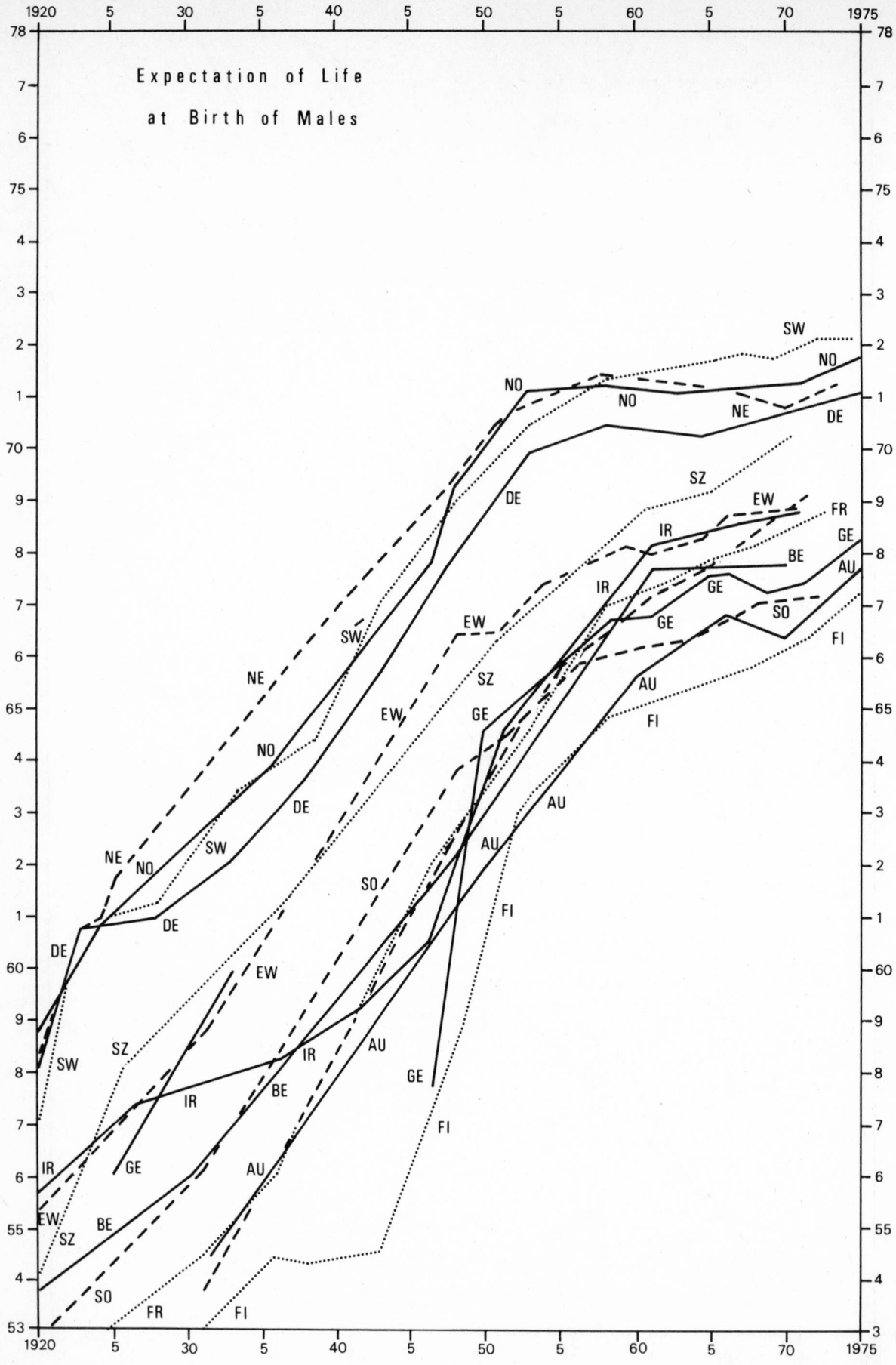

Expectation of Life
at Birth of Males

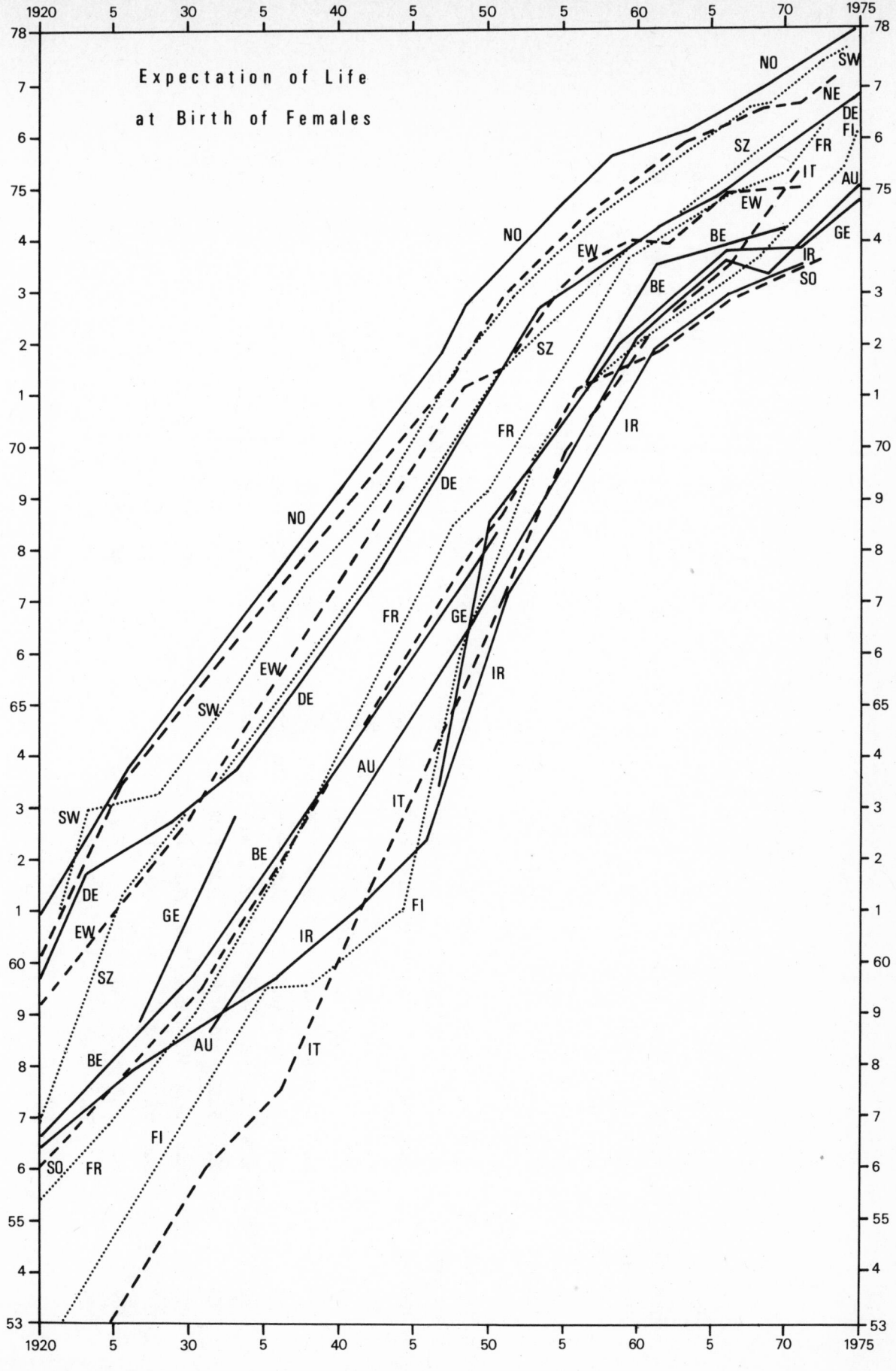

Expectation of Life at Birth of Females

Austria

Expectation of Life at Specific Ages

Age	Males 0	10	20	30	40	50	60	70	80	Females 0	10	20	30	40	50	60	70	80
1870–1880	30.98	44.21	36.80	30.53					4.42	33.77	45.52	38.28	31.52			12.37		4.44
1891–1900	37.77	48.22	40.08	32.86	25.51	18.64	12.58	7.61	4.39	39.87	48.54	40.78	33.70	26.64	19.40	12.77	7.65	4.47
1895–1900	36.78	48.20	40.17	33.03			12.69		4.45	38.97	48.55	40.86	33.84			12.96		4.65
1901–1905	39.14	48.59	40.50	33.27			12.78		4.39	41.05	48.81	41.22	34.22			13.07		4.49
1906–1910	40.69	49.08	40.90	33.49	26.01	19.04	12.86	7.85	4.41	42.08	49.71	41.93	34.80			13.32		4.47
1930–1933	54.47	54.08	45.18	36.86	28.65	20.96	14.15	8.56	4.60	58.53	56.96	48.03	39.59	31.13	22.94	15.42	9.21	4.97
1949–1951	61.91	58.02	48.68	39.71	30.74	22.31	15.12	9.27	5.05	66.97	62.15	52.62	43.37	34.20	25.42	17.27	10.37	5.57
1959–1961	65.60	59.11	49.60	40.54	31.42	22.70	15.25	9.46	5.24	72.03	65.00	55.26	45.64	36.19	27.11	18.67	11.30	5.98
1966	66.82	59.54	50.03	40.81	31.72	23.03	15.41	9.67	5.45	73.54	65.71	55.95	46.26	36.76	27.62	19.12	11.71	6.31
1967	66.57	59.14	49.67	40.46	31.36	22.68	15.01	9.27	5.21	73.41	65.40	55.75	46.04	36.52	27.43	18.93	11.46	6.12
1968	66.73	59.13	49.61	40.39	31.27	22.64	14.98	9.23	5.22	73.50	65.56	55.86	46.17	36.62	27.48	18.94	11.53	6.14
1969	66.46	58.96	49.44	40.19	31.08	22.48	14.76	9.08	5.31	73.34	65.33	55.59	45.87	36.35	27.24	18.77	11.43	6.20
1970	66.34	58.80	49.36	40.17	31.08	22.50	14.84	9.10	5.23	73.52	65.57	55.81	46.07	36.51	27.40	18.86	11.47	6.19
1971	66.57	59.02	49.60	40.49	31.41	22.84	15.18	9.26	5.24	73.72	65.67	56.00	46.30	36.76	27.67	19.05	11.58	6.09
1972	66.8	64.0	54.3	45.3	36.0	27.2	19.0	12.2		74.1	71.0	61.2	51.6	41.9	32.5	23.6	15.4	
1973	67.4	59.7	50.3	41.1	32.0	23.4	15.7	9.6		74.7	66.5	56.8	47.1	37.5	28.3	19.8	12.2	
1974	67.4	59.7	50.2	41.0	31.8	23.3	15.7	9.5		74.7	66.5	56.7	47.1	37.5	28.3	19.8	12.1	
1975	67.7	59.7	50.2	41.0	31.8	23.3	15.6	9.4		74.9	66.5	56.7	47.1	37.4	28.2	19.6	12.0	

Belgium

Expectation of Life at Specific Ages

Males

Age	0	10	20	30	40	50	60	70	80
1881–1890	43.84	49.26	40.96	33.96			13.73		4.39
1891–1900	45.39	50.32	41.83	34.22	26.71	19.69	13.43	8.13	4.56
1928–1932	56.02	54.88	46.04	37.78	29.48	21.61	14.53	6.69	4.65
1946–1949	62.04	57.36	48.02	39.30	30.61	22.52	15.45	9.50	5.18
1959–1963	67.74	59.87	50.26	40.94	31.66	22.93	15.52	9.70	5.29
1968–1972	67.79	59.86	50.29	40.93	31.58	22.79	15.22	9.47	5.41

Females

Age	0	10	20	30	40	50	60	70	80
1881–1890	46.98	51.51	43.56	36.36			14.70		4.86
1891–1900	48.84	52.78	44.44	36.96	29.46	21.87	14.78	8.87	4.91
1928–1932	59.79	57.25	48.43	40.17	31.77	23.55	15.93	9.60	5.20
1946–1949	67.26	61.71	52.27	43.22	34.20	25.47	17.45	10.66	5.79
1959–1963	73.51	65.32	55.53	45.86	36.34	27.20	18.69	11.36	6.07
1968–1972	74.21	65.88	56.11	46.43	36.86	27.69	19.19	11.77	6.33

Denmark

Expectation of Life at Specific Ages

Females

Age	0	10	20	30	40	50	60	70	80
1835–1844	44.7	48.9	41.6	34.2			14.3		
1840–1849	43.5	49.1	41.8	34.5	27.8	20.8	14.2	8.8	
1860–1869	45.5	50.2	43.2	36.1	29.1	21.9	14.8	9.0	5.0
1870–1879	47.4	50.6		36.3		22.0		9.2	
1880–1889	48.9	52.1	44.9	37.6			15.8		5.3
1885–1894	49.2	52.6	45.4	37.9			15.8		5.5
1895–1900	53.2	54.7	46.7	38.9	31.2	23.4	16.0	9.8	5.3
1901–1905	56.2	55.8	47.5	39.6	31.7	23.8	16.3	10.0	5.5
1906–1910	57.9	56.7	48.2	40.1	32.0	24.1	16.5	10.0	5.5
1911–1915	59.2	57.2	48.4	40.2	32.0	24.0	16.4	9.9	5.3
1916–1920	58.1	55.6	47.2	39.6	32.0	24.0	16.4	10.0	5.4
1921–1925	61.9	58.4	49.3	40.8	32.3	24.1	16.5	10.0	5.4
1926–1930	62.6	58.8	49.6	42.0	32.4	24.1	16.3	9.8	5.2
1931–1935	63.8	59.4	50.0	41.2	32.5	24.1	16.4	9.9	5.4
1936–1940	65.8	60.6	51.1	42.0	33.1	24.5	16.6	10.0	5.3
1941–1945	67.70	61.52	52.03	42.91	33.88	25.16	17.14	10.38	5.56
1946–1950	70.14	63.29	53.62	44.22	35.00	26.13	17.88	10.90	5.88
1951–1955	72.60	64.79	54.99	45.34	35.89	26.85	18.44	11.17	6.01
1956–1960	73.76	65.60	55.79	46.08	36.59	27.47	18.97	11.53	6.14
1962–1963	74.4	66.1	56.3	46.5	37.0	27.9	19.3	11.8	6.3
1964–1965	74.7	66.3	56.4	46.7	37.2	28.0	19.4	11.9	6.3
1970–1971	75.9	67.2	57.4	47.7	38.1	29.1	20.6	13.1	7.2
1972–1973	76.3	67.4	57.6	47.8	38.3	29.2	20.8	13.2	7.3
1975–1976	76.8	67.7	57.9	48.1	38.5	29.5	21.1	13.5	7.4

Males

Age	0	10	20	30	40	50	60	70	80
1835–1844	42.6	47.7	39.8	32.6			13.2		
1840–1849	40.9	47.8	40.1	33.0	25.8	19.1	13.2	8.0	
1860–1869	43.6	49.1	41.6	34.5	27.0	19.9	13.5	8.5	4.6
1870–1879	45.6	49.8		34.7		20.1		8.5	
1880–1889	46.8	51.0	43.2	35.9			14.4		4.8
1885–1894	46.9	51.3	43.6	36.2			14.6		5.0
1895–1900	50.2	52.8	44.5	36.8	28.9	21.5	14.7	9.0	4.9
1901–1905	52.9	54.0	45.4	37.4	29.4	21.8	15.0	9.2	5.0
1906–1910	54.9	55.1	46.3	38.0	29.7	22.1	15.2	9.3	5.1
1911–1915	56.2	55.6	46.7	38.4	30.2	22.4	15.3	9.4	5.1
1916–1920	55.8	54.6	46.1	38.9	31.1	23.1	15.8	9.7	5.1
1921–1925	60.6	58.4	49.4	40.8	32.1	23.7	16.0	9.8	5.2
1926–1930	60.9	58.7	49.6	40.8	32.0	23.6	15.9	9.6	5.1
1931–1935	62.0	59.0	49.8	41.0	32.1	23.6	16.0	9.7	5.2
1936–1940	63.5	59.6	50.3	41.2	32.2	23.7	16.0	9.6	5.2
1941–1945	65.62	60.46	51.12	42.20	33.16	24.51	16.69	10.13	5.40
1946–1950	67.75	61.37	52.20	43.00	33.81	25.05	17.11	10.44	5.55
1951–1955	69.79	62.65	53.01	43.65	34.30	25.37	17.40	10.70	5.80
1956–1960	70.38	62.77	53.12	43.66	34.25	25.25	17.51	10.71	5.81
1962–1963	70.3	62.4	52.8	43.3	33.8	24.9	17.0	10.5	5.7
1964–1965	70.2	62.2	52.6	43.1	33.6	24.7	16.8	10.5	5.7
1970–1971	70.7	62.4	52.8	43.3	33.8	25.0	17.1	10.8	6.1
1972–1973	70.8	62.2	52.6	43.1	33.7	24.8	17.0	10.8	6.3
1975–1976	71.1	62.3	52.6	43.2	33.7	24.9	17.1	10.7	6.2

Finland

Expectation of Life at Specific Ages

Age	Males									Females								
	0	10	20	30	40	50	60	70	80	0	10	20	30	40	50	60	70	80
1881–1890	41.4	49.3	41.5	34.3	26.9	19.7	13.2	8.0	4.5	44.2	50.9	43.3	36.0	28.8	21.3	14.3	8.6	5.0
1891–1900	42.9	49.9	42.0	34.8	27.3	20.1	13.5	8.0	4.3	45.6	51.6	44.2	36.8	29.5	21.9	14.6	8.7	4.9
1901–1910	45.33	49.94	42.16	34.94	27.38	20.03	13.56	8.27	4.51	48.10	51.74	44.54	37.30	29.92	22.31	15.08	9.00	4.94
1911–1920	43.41	45.24	37.91	32.49	25.87	19.36	13.37	8.25	4.76	49.12	51.11	43.82	36.96	29.73	22.29	15.05	8.92	4.87
1921–1930	50.68	49.98	41.89	35.13	27.55	20.32	13.99	8.98	5.49	55.14	53.78	46.00	38.71	31.01	23.27	15.82	9.61	5.35
1931–1940	54.45	51.73	43.34	35.89	28.12	20.86	14.57	9.51	5.91	59.55	56.24	47.89	40.15	32.07	23.97	16.41	10.06	5.72
1936–1940	54.32	51.54	42.99	35.33	27.38	19.95	13.60	8.59	5.16	59.48	56.03	47.56	39.69	31.57	23.40	15.79	9.50	5.29
1941–1945	54.62	51.27	42.90	35.36	27.52	20.16	13.78	8.80	5.48	61.14	57.42	48.91	40.96	32.68	24.41	16.58	10.03	5.59
1946–1950	58.59	53.44	44.40	36.30	28.02	20.28	13.75	8.65	4.98	65.87	60.18	51.02	42.36	33.59	24.88	16.79	10.04	5.42
1951–1953	62.89	56.15	46.67	37.74	28.94	20.79	13.94	8.59	4.80	69.12	62.08	52.46	43.13	33.93	24.97	16.75	9.90	5.23
1951–1955	63.4	56.5	47.0	38.0	29.2	21.0	14.1	8.7	4.8	69.8	62.5	52.8	43.4	34.2	25.2	16.9	10.0	5.6
1956–1960	64.90	57.37	47.81	38.63	29.72	21.41	14.38	8.91	5.04	71.57	63.68	53.94	44.35	34.96	25.92	17.51	10.36	5.46
1961–1965	65.4	57.3	47.8	38.5	29.5	21.2	14.3	8.9	4.9	72.6	64.2	54.4	44.7	35.2	26.0	17.5	10.3	5.3
1966–1970	65.88	57.39	47.78	38.46	29.44	21.23	14.25	8.77	4.86	73.57	64.86	55.07	45.35	35.79	26.60	18.01	10.62	5.42
1972	66.57	57.90	48.37	39.12	30.11	21.91	14.85	9.29	5.10	74.87	65.87	56.11	46.39	36.81	27.52	18.81	11.21	5.63
1974	66.90	58.07	48.51	39.23	30.14	21.91	14.87	9.22	5.07	75.41	66.46	56.69	46.95	37.33	28.08	19.36	11.69	5.89
1975	67.38	58.49	48.93	39.74	30.62	22.27	15.04	9.46	5.26	75.93	66.83	57.02	47.28	37.66	28.38	19.70	11.97	6.11

France

Expectation of Life at Specific Ages

Males

Age	0	10	20	30	40	50	60	70	80
1817–1831	38.33	47.00	40.00	34.00	27.00	19.91	13.25	8.08	4.75
1861–1865	39.10	48.70	41.20	34.65			13.55		4.40
1877–1881	40.83	48.25	40.42	33.83		20.00	13.58	8.33	4.83
1891–1900	45.35	49.25	41.03	33.86	26.65	19.76	13.31	7.92	4.37
1898–1903	45.74	49.75	41.53	34.35	27.15	20.26	13.81	8.42	4.87
1908–1913	48.49	49.90	41.39	34.03	26.67	19.69	13.74	8.00	4.39
1920–1923	52.19	51.51	42.93	35.50	27.84	20.45	13.84	8.25	4.33
1928–1933	54.30	52.06	43.30	35.42	27.62	20.33	13.76	8.29	4.44
1933–1938	55.94	52.57	43.62	35.52	27.71	20.43	13.92	8.50	4.61
1946–1949	61.87	57.61	48.28	39.44	30.69	22.53	15.31	9.28	5.00
1950–1951	63.6	57.9	48.4	39.3	30.4	22.2	15.1	9.1	4.8
1952–1956	65.04	58.48	48.90	39.69	30.68	22.36	15.24	9.26	4.90
1957	65.7	58.5	49.0	39.8	30.8	22.4	15.3	9.4	
1958	67.0	59.6	50.0	40.8	31.8	23.2	15.9	9.8	
1959	67.0	59.5	49.9	40.7	31.6	23.1	15.8	9.6	
1960	67.2	59.5	49.9	40.5	31.4	22.9	15.6	9.6	
1961	67.6	59.8	50.2	40.9	31.8	23.3	16.0	10.0	
1962	67.29	59.45	49.86	40.54	31.47	22.97	15.68	9.75	5.28
1963	67.2	59.3	49.7	40.4	31.3	22.8	15.5	9.6	5.3
1964	68.0	59.9	50.3	41.1	31.9	23.4	16.0	10.1	5.6
1965	67.8	59.6	50.0	40.7	31.6	23.1	15.8	9.9	5.5
1966	68.2	60.0	50.4	41.1	32.0	23.5	16.1	10.2	5.8
1968	68.0	59.7	50.2	40.9	31.7	23.3	15.9	10.0	5.6
1969	67.6	59.3	49.8	40.5	31.4	22.9	15.5	9.8	5.6
1970	68.6	60.2	50.6	41.4	32.2	23.7	16.2	10.2	5.8
1971	68.5	60.0	50.5	41.2	32.1	23.6	16.2	10.2	5.7
1972	68.6	60.0	50.5	41.3	32.2	23.7	16.3	10.3	5.9
1974	69.0	60.3	50.8	41.5	32.3	23.9	16.4	10.3	5.9

Females

Age	0	10	20	30	40	50	60	70	80
1817–1831	40.83	47.42	40.08	33.41	26.58	19.58	13.16	8.08	4.75
1861–1865	40.55	48.75	41.60	35.10			13.90		4.66
1877–1881	43.42	49.75	42.25	35.50		21.42	14.58	8.83	5.00
1891–1900	48.72	51.53	43.59	36.44	29.10	21.64	14.58	8.72	4.89
1898–1903	49.13	52.03	44.02	36.93	29.60	22.14	15.08	9.21	5.38
1908–1913	52.41	53.08	44.83	37.37	29.75	22.13	14.95	8.95	4.96
1920–1923	55.87	54.49	46.16	38.61	30.82	22.99	15.63	9.33	5.04
1928–1933	59.02	55.95	47.40	39.54	31.37	23.39	15.94	9.58	5.09
1933–1938	61.64	57.50	48.64	40.46	32.10	24.01	16.50	10.06	5.46
1946–1949	67.43	62.36	52.92	43.92	34.97	26.24	18.13	11.08	5.95
1950–1951	69.3	63.0	53.4	44.1	35.0	26.2	18.1	11.1	5.9
1952–1956	71.15	64.09	54.36	44.84	35.58	26.73	18.54	11.31	5.95
1957	72.4	64.9	55.1	45.5	36.2	27.3	19.0	11.7	
1958	73.4	65.7	56.0	46.3	36.9	27.9	19.5	12.0	
1959	73.6	65.7	55.9	46.4	37.0	28.0	19.5	12.0	
1960	73.8	65.7	55.9	46.4	36.9	27.9	19.5	12.0	
1961	74.5	66.4	56.6	47.0	37.5	28.5	20.0	12.5	
1962	74.14	65.95	56.19	46.56	37.13	28.08	19.61	12.10	6.41
1963	74.1	65.9	56.1	46.5	37.1	28.0	19.6	12.0	6.4
1964	75.1	66.7	56.9	47.3	37.8	28.8	20.3	12.7	6.9
1965	75.0	66.5	56.7	47.1	37.6	28.6	20.1	12.5	6.7
1966	75.4	66.9	57.1	47.5	38.0	29.0	20.5	12.8	7.0
1968	75.5	67.0	57.2	47.6	38.1	29.0	20.4	12.8	6.9
1969	75.3	66.7	57.0	47.3	37.8	28.8	20.3	12.7	7.0
1970	76.1	67.4	57.6	48.0	38.5	29.4	20.8	13.1	7.2
1971	76.1	67.4	57.7	48.0	38.5	29.4	20.9	13.1	7.1
1972	76.4	67.6	57.9	48.2	38.7	29.6	21.1	13.3	7.3
1974	76.9	68.0	58.3	48.6	39.1	29.9	21.3	13.5	7.3

Germany

Expectation of Life at Specific Ages

Age	Males									Females								
Age	0	10	20	30	40	50	60	70	80	0	10	20	30	40	50	60	70	80
1871–1881	35.58	46.51	38.45	31.41	24.46	17.98	12.11	7.34	4.10	38.45	48.18	40.19	33.07	26.32	19.29	12.71	7.60	4.22
1881–1890	37.17	47.75	39.52	32.11	25.03	18.41	12.43	7.51	4.11	40.25	49.69	41.62	34.21	27.16	19.89	13.14	7.84	4.37
1891–1900	40.56	49.66	41.23	33.46	25.89	19.00	12.82	7.76	4.23	43.97	51.71	43.37	35.62	28.14	20.58	13.60	8.10	4.48
1901–1910	44.82	51.16	42.56	34.55	26.64	19.43	13.14	7.99	4.38	48.33	53.35	44.84	36.94	29.16	21.35	14.17	8.45	4.65
1910–1911	47.41	52.08	43.43	35.29	27.18	19.71	13.18	7.90	4.25	50.68	53.99	45.35	37.30	29.38	21.45	14.17	8.35	4.52
1924–1926	55.97	55.63	46.70	38.56	30.05	21.89	14.60	8.74	4.77	58.82	57.11	48.09	39.76	31.37	23.12	15.51	9.27	5.06
1932–1934	59.86	57.28	48.16	39.47	30.83	22.54	15.11	9.05	4.84	62.81	59.09	49.84	41.05	32.33	23.85	16.07	9.58	5.15
1946–1947	57.72	56.20	47.22	39.20	30.86	22.69	15.18	8.85	4.74	63.44	60.76	51.51	42.72	33.81	25.11	16.99	10.02	5.11
1949–1951	64.56	59.76	50.34	41.32	32.32	23.75	16.20	9.84	5.24	68.48	62.84	53.24	43.89	34.67	25.75	17.46	10.42	5.57
1958–1959	66.75	60.08	50.56	41.39	32.18	23.35	15.74	9.66	5.19	71.88	64.67	54.91	45.30	35.86	26.77	18.27	10.91	5.71
1959–1960	66.69	59.92	50.38	41.21	31.98	23.16	15.53	9.54	5.11	71.94	64.65	54.89	45.27	35.83	26.74	18.22	10.86	5.63
1960–1962	66.84	59.86	50.31	41.11	31.87	23.06	15.45	9.55	5.19	72.34	64.87	55.11	45.48	36.03	26.94	18.42	11.05	5.77
1964–1965	67.59	60.00	50.47	41.21	31.96	23.17	15.51	9.71	5.43	73.45	65.48	55.70	46.03	36.54	27.44	18.93	11.55	6.17
1965–1967	67.62	59.94	50.41	41.13	31.89	23.10	15.41	9.57	5.36	73.57	65.50	55.73	46.06	36.55	27.45	18.92	11.52	6.13
1968–1970	67.24	59.52	50.03	40.75	31.51	22.76	15.02	9.20	5.24	73.44	65.32	55.58	45.90	36.38	27.29	18.77	11.36	6.01
1970–1972	67.41	59.68	50.21	41.00	31.77	23.05	15.31	9.35	5.36	73.83	65.70	55.97	46.30	36.77	27.65	19.12	11.63	6.16
1971–1973	67.61	59.84	50.36	41.12	31.88	23.16	15.42	9.39	5.36	74.09	65.93	56.19	46.32	36.98	27.85	19.30	11.77	6.23
1973–1975	68.04	60.10	50.59	41.27	32.01	23.30	15.54	9.42	5.37	74.54	66.25	56.49	46.80	37.24	28.10	19.53	11.92	6.31
1974–1976	68.30	60.21	50.69	41.36	32.09	23.40	15.64	9.47	5.40	74.81	66.40	56.65	46.95	37.39	28.23	19.66	12.02	6.37

Ireland

Expectation of Life at Specific Ages

Males

Age	0	10	20	30	40	50	60	70	80
1900–1902	49.3	50.5	42.1	31.0	23.8	16.9	10.8	5.8	
1910–1912	53.6	53.7	45.0	33.5	25.9	18.9	13.0	8.0	
1925–1927	57.37	55.20	46.40	38.39	30.43	22.67	15.75	10.02	5.81
1935–1937	58.20	55.75	46.83	38.53	30.26	22.41	15.46	9.99	6.00
1940–1942	59.01	56.25	47.24	38.92	30.58	22.53	15.37	9.60	5.68
1945–1947	60.47	56.89	47.77	39.22	30.60	22.43	15.12	9.21	5.27
1950–1952	64.53	58.81	49.31	40.25	31.31	22.84	15.40	9.23	4.98
1960–1962	68.13	60.83	51.14	41.66	32.35	23.50	15.83	9.70	5.06
1965–1967	68.58	60.84	51.15	41.65	32.24	23.35	15.63	9.65	5.23
1970–1972	68.77	60.62	50.97	41.52	32.06	23.28	15.60	9.66	5.35

Females

Age	0	10	20	30	40	50	60	70	80
1900–1902	49.6	50.4	42.2	30.9	23.7	16.7	10.6	5.9	
1910–1912	54.1	53.7	45.4	33.8	26.4	19.2	13.4	8.2	
1925–1927	57.93	54.92	46.36	38.60	30.83	23.19	16.36	10.72	6.47
1935–1937	59.62	56.10	47.26	39.22	31.18	23.28	16.17	10.59	6.46
1940–1942	61.02	56.94	48.04	39.89	31.63	23.54	16.31	10.42	6.39
1945–1947	62.43	57.90	48.84	40.53	32.10	23.88	16.41	10.19	5.99
1950–1952	67.08	60.61	51.15	42.16	33.28	24.68	16.83	10.17	5.64
1960–1962	71.86	64.11	54.31	44.65	35.28	26.28	18.10	11.00	5.87
1965–1967	72.85	64.75	54.93	45.21	35.68	26.64	18.37	11.18	6.06
1970–1972	73.52	65.11	55.32	45.62	36.04	26.96	18.68	11.54	6.19

Italy

Expectation of Life at Specific Ages

Males

Age	0	10	20	30	40	50	60	70	80
1876–1887	35.1	47.1	40.4	33.6	26.3	19.5	13.1	8.0	
1881–1882	35.16	48.16	40.58	33.81	26.44	19.47	13.18	8.16	4.99
1891–1900	42.83	51.25	43.08	35.67	28.00	20.50	13.58	7.92	4.33
1899–1902	42.59	51.21	43.02	35.68	27.94	20.42	13.47	7.74	3.98
1901–1910	44.24	51.44	43.27	35.94	28.23	20.73	13.78	8.02	4.06
1910–1912	46.57	52.48	44.15	36.70	28.88	21.23	14.10	8.15	4.15
1921–1922	49.27	53.53	45.15	37.63	29.63	21.76	14.49	8.38	4.26
1930–1932	53.76	55.46	46.75	38.58	30.39	22.45	15.16	9.05	4.85
1935–1937									
1950–1953	63.75	59.80	50.37	41.18	32.07	23.52	16.01	9.58	5.04
1954–1957	65.75	60.53	51.04	41.74	32.52	23.80	16.23	9.87	5.17
1960–1962	67.24	61.19	51.67	42.32	33.06	24.29	16.65	10.44	5.70
1964–1967	67.87	61.15	51.57	42.14	32.84	24.07	16.35	10.29	5.69
1970–1972	68.97	61.56	52.00	42.55	33.18	24.41	16.66	10.34	5.82

Females

Age	0	10	20	30	40	50	60	70	80
1876–1887	35.5	47.3	40.0	33.5	26.8	19.7	12.1	7.8	
1881–1882	35.65	47.61	40.38	33.70	26.86	19.64	12.91	7.79	4.89
1891–1900	43.17	51.00	43.17	36.00	28.67	21.08	13.67	7.83	4.17
1899–1902	43.00	51.00	43.13	36.01	28.68	21.01	13.60	7.65	3.99
1901–1910	44.83	51.53	43.69	36.58	29.18	21.47	14.02	8.02	4.11
1910–1912	47.33	52.69	44.64	37.30	29.76	21.91	14.36	8.18	4.20
1921–1922	50.75	54.18	45.96	38.37	30.51	22.48	14.84	8.48	4.45
1930–1932	56.00	57.15	48.49	40.41	32.14	23.89	16.13	9.61	5.18
1935–1937	57.49	57.86	49.05	40.72	32.30	23.96	16.15	9.63	5.2
1950–1953	67.25	62.88	53.32	43.97	34.73	25.80	17.48	10.36	5.55
1954–1957	70.02	64.37	54.68	45.14	35.76	26.67	18.20	10.90	5.75
1960–1962	72.27	65.80	56.07	46.43	36.97	27.82	19.27	11.79	6.35
1964–1967	73.36	66.22	56.45	46.77	37.23	28.06	19.46	11.92	6.38
1970–1972	74.88	67.13	57.34	47.63	38.05	28.81	20.16	12.44	6.71

Netherlands

Expectation of Life at Specific Ages

Males

Age	0	10	20	30	40	50	60	70	80
1816–1825	29.32	40.67	32.87	27.60	21.86	16.41	11.60	7.47	4.77
1840–1851	34.94	44.39	36.86	30.71	24.06	17.98	12.14	7.22	4.02
1850–1859	36.44	45.59	37.95	31.44	24.71	18.25	12.57	7.75	4.23
1860–1869	37.2	46.7	39.2	32.7	25.8	19.2	13.2	8.1	4.6
1870–1879	38.4	48.0	40.3	33.7	26.5	19.6	13.3	8.2	4.6
1880–1889	42.5	50.4	42.3	35.1	27.6	20.5	13.9	8.5	4.7
1890–1899	46.2	51.7	43.4	35.9	28.1	20.7	14.0	8.6	4.7
1900–1909	51.0	54.3	45.7	37.8	29.5	21.8	14.7	8.9	4.9
1910–1920	55.1	55.4	46.7	38.8	30.5	22.4	15.1	9.1	5.0
1921–1930	61.9	58.7	49.7	41.0	32.1	23.5	15.9	9.6	5.2
1931–1940	65.5	60.1	50.8	41.8	32.8	24.1	16.2	9.8	5.2
1931–1940	65.7	60.3	51.0	41.9	32.9	24.1	16.3	9.8	5.2
1947–1949	69.4	62.7	53.2	43.8	34.5	25.6	17.5	10.7	5.8
1950–1952	70.6	63.4	53.7	44.3	34.9	25.9	17.8	10.9	5.8
1951–1955	70.9	63.4	53.8	44.3	34.8	25.8	17.7	10.9	5.8
1953–1955	71.0	63.4	53.7	44.2	34.8	25.7	17.8	10.8	5.8
1956–1960	71.4	63.4	53.7	44.2	34.7	25.7	17.7	10.9	5.9
1961–1965	71.1	63.0	53.3	43.8	34.3	25.3	17.4	11.0	6.0
1966	71.1	62.7	53.1	43.6	34.1	25.1	17.2	10.9	6.1
1967	71.0	62.7	53.1	43.6	34.2	25.2	17.3	11.0	6.4
1968	71.0	62.5	52.9	43.4	33.9	24.9	17.0	11.0	6.0
1970	70.7	62.3	52.7	43.2	33.7	24.7	16.8	10.7	6.2
1971	71.0	62.4	52.8	43.3	33.8	24.8	16.9	10.7	6.2
1972	70.8	62.2	52.6	43.1	33.6	24.6	16.7	10.5	6.1
1971–1975	71.2	62.6	52.9	43.4	33.9	24.9	17.0	10.7	6.2

Females

Age	0	10	20	30	40	50	60	70	80
1816–1825	35.12	45.03	36.99	30.68	24.84	18.70	12.84	8.01	4.76
1840–1851	37.76	46.07	38.71	31.98	25.77	19.34	12.94	7.57	4.14
1850–1859	38.21	46.26	38.92	32.16	26.13	19.51	13.12	7.95	4.41
1860–1869	39.1	47.4	40.1	33.3	27.1	20.4	13.8	8.4	4.8
1870–1879	40.7	48.7	41.2	34.3	27.9	21.0	14.1	8.4	4.7
1880–1889	45.0	51.5	43.5	36.1	29.2	21.9	14.8	9.0	4.9
1890–1899	49.0	53.0	44.8	37.1	29.7	22.2	15.0	9.0	5.0
1900–1909	53.4	55.4	46.9	38.8	30.8	22.9	15.5	9.4	5.2
1910–1920	57.1	56.0	47.5	39.5	31.4	23.4	15.9	9.6	5.3
1921–1930	63.5	58.9	49.8	41.1	32.5	24.1	16.4	10.5	5.5
1931–1940	67.2	60.8	51.5	42.3	33.3	24.7	16.8	10.2	5.5
1947–1949	71.5	64.1	54.5	45.0	35.6	26.5	18.2	11.1	6.1
1950–1952	72.9	65.1	55.4	45.7	36.3	27.1	18.6	11.3	6.1
1951–1955	73.5	65.6	55.8	46.1	36.6	27.4	18.8	11.5	6.1
1953–1955	73.9	65.7	56.0	46.2	36.7	27.5	18.9	11.5	6.2
1956–1960	74.8	66.5	56.7	46.9	37.3	28.1	19.5	11.8	6.2
1961–1965	75.9	67.3	57.5	47.7	38.1	28.8	20.1	12.3	6.6
1966	76.1	67.4	57.6	47.9	38.3	29.0	20.3	12.5	6.7
1967	76.5	67.8	58.0	48.3	38.6	29.4	20.6	12.9	7.0
1968	76.4	67.7	57.9	48.1	38.5	29.2	20.5	12.7	6.8
1970	76.5	67.7	57.9	48.1	38.5	29.2	20.5	12.8	6.9
1971	76.7	67.9	58.1	48.3	38.7	29.4	20.6	12.8	6.9
1972	76.8	67.9	58.1	48.3	38.7	29.4	20.7	10.7	6.8
1971–1975	77.2	68.3	58.5	48.7	39.0	29.8	21.0	13.1	7.1

Norway

Expectation of Life at Specific Ages

Age	Males 0	10	20	30	40	50	60	70	80	Females 0	10	20	30	40	50	60	70	80
1821–1830	45.0	50.3	42.5	35.6	28.3	21.4	15.2	9.7		48.0	52.4	44.5	37.0	29.8	22.4	15.8	10.0	
1831–1840	41.8	47.4	39.5	32.9	26.2	19.6	13.8	8.8		45.6	50.4	42.4	35.1	28.2	21.4	14.8	9.3	
1841–1850	44.5	49.4	41.5	34.6	27.5	20.7	14.4	9.1		47.9	51.8	43.9	36.2	29.4	22.2	15.2	9.5	
1846–1855	44.9	49.4	42.0	34.8	28.0	21.0	14.6	9.0		47.9	52.0	44.5	36.9	29.7	22.5	15.5	9.4	
1856–1865	47.40	50.81	43.16	36.28	29.1	22.0	15.19	9.4	5.43	49.95	52.83	45.27	37.31	30.7	23.4	16.24	10.1	6.05
1871–1881	48.33	50.76	43.14	36.82	29.69	22.49	15.63	9.89	5.67	51.30	53.10	45.39	38.19	31.14	23.84	16.67	10.55	6.05
1881–1891	48.73	51.25	43.89	37.68	30.43	23.08	16.13	10.11	5.63	51.21	53.32	45.90	38.81	31.81	24.45	17.18	10.88	6.01
1891–1901	50.41	51.05	43.58	37.69	30.62	23.34	16.39	10.29	5.64	54.14	54.11	46.54	39.43	31.31	24.86	17.46	10.97	6.14
1901–1911	54.82	52.92	45.16	38.85	31.49	23.95	16.80	10.59	5.85	57.70	55.08	47.34	40.24	32.92	25.30	17.85	11.24	6.28
1911–1921	55.62	52.65	44.85	38.83	31.64	24.10	16.98	10.40	5.73	58.71	54.98	47.19	40.35	32.96	25.28	17.78	11.15	6.19
1921–1931	60.98	56.27	47.73	40.39	32.40	24.41	16.97	10.63	5.87	63.84	58.35	49.85	42.14	34.00	25.87	18.16	11.40	6.31
1931–1941	64.08	58.56	49.59	41.48	33.15	24.90	17.22	10.71	5.84	67.55	61.25	52.12	43.55	34.89	26.35	18.38	11.38	6.22
1945–1948	67.76	61.52	52.32	43.72	34.99	26.44	18.46	11.54	6.41	71.68	64.66	55.20	46.10	36.98	28.12	19.70	12.35	6.76
1946–1950	69.25	62.63	53.25	44.22	35.16	26.43	18.39	11.43	6.30	72.65	65.24	55.64	46.29	36.96	27.95	19.45	12.03	6.51
1951–1955	71.11	63.65	54.11	44.81	35.54	26.60	18.52	11.60	6.39	74.70	66.72	56.96	47.31	37.79	28.57	19.93	12.30	6.60
1956–1960	71.32	63.50	53.93	44.57	35.19	26.21	18.12	11.38	6.28	75.57	67.30	57.49	47.74	38.14	28.84	20.06	12.36	6.64
1961–1965	71.03	62.94	53.34	43.93	34.58	25.62	17.60	11.04		75.97	67.49	57.66	47.87	38.22	28.88	20.06	12.29	
1966–1970	71.09	62.69	53.08	43.61	34.22	25.32	17.33	10.87	6.14	76.83	68.10	58.28	48.49	38.81	29.47	20.64	12.83	6.97
1971–1972	71.24	62.72	53.12	43.67	34.32	25.38	17.39	10.86	6.16	77.43	68.52	58.69	48.90	39.24	29.87	21.00	13.04	7.03
1972–1973	71.32	62.72	53.13	43.68	34.31	25.34	17.37	10.82	6.14	77.60	68.66	58.82	49.02	39.33	29.96	21.09	13.11	7.06
1973–1974	71.50	62.85	53.27	43.81	34.40	25.44	17.49	10.89	6.19	77.83	68.83	59.00	49.19	39.51	30.14	21.26	13.25	7.17
1975–1976	71.85	63.05	53.44	43.98	34.54	25.55	17.55	11.00	6.26	78.12	69.12	59.32	49.53	39.81	30.39	21.57	13.57	7.32

Sweden

Expectation of Life at Specific Ages

Males

Age	0	10	20	30	40	50	60	70	80
1755–1776	33.20	43.94	36.95	30.34	23.75	17.72	12.24	7.60	4.27
1816–1840	39.50	45.21	37.32	30.25	23.66	17.55	12.07	7.35	4.03
1841–1845	41.94	46.98	38.95	31.60			12.49		3.84
1846–1850	41.38	46.57	38.58	31.18			12.17		3.73
1851–1855	40.51	45.90	38.11	30.89			12.23		4.09
1856–1860	40.48	47.32	39.99	32.91			13.12		3.12
1861–1870	42.80	48.90	41.00	33.60	26.30	19.40	13.10	8.00	4.30
1871–1880	45.3	50.3	42.3	35.1	27.8	20.8	14.2	8.5	4.6
1881–1890	48.55	52.16	44.18	36.87	29.27	21.94	15.07	9.14	4.81
1891–1900	50.94	52.79	44.75	37.50	29.90	22.44	15.44	9.36	4.88
1901–1910	54.53	54.03	45.88	38.57	30.77	23.17	16.06	9.85	5.22
1911–1915	56.49	54.36	46.11	38.78	30.97	23.22	16.04	9.81	5.23
1916–1920	54.81	52.14	44.52	38.37	31.16	23.47	16.20	9.93	5.28
1921–1925	60.72	57.09	48.49	40.66	32.39	24.22	16.70	10.28	5.51
1926–1930	61.19	57.32	48.56	40.50	32.16	24.04	16.50	10.11	5.37
1931–1935	63.22	58.37	49.44	41.07	32.50	24.21	16.59	10.12	5.37
1936–1940	64.30	58.77	49.70	41.13	32.37	23.97	16.35	9.92	5.25
1941–1945	67.06	60.45	51.23	42.57	33.64	25.02	17.19	10.52	5.61
1946–1950	69.04	61.62	52.14	43.02	33.84	24.99	17.05	10.40	5.50
1951–1955	70.49	62.67	53.10	43.74	34.42	25.45	17.38	10.63	5.65
1956–1960	71.23	63.07	53.47	44.04	34.66	25.62	17.46	10.70	5.74
1961–1965	71.60	63.20	53.57	44.12	34.72	25.65	17.45	10.71	5.82
1967	71.85	63.18	53.48	44.04	34.70	25.74	17.56	10.86	6.05
1969	71.69	63.04	53.40	43.90	34.57	25.60	17.40	10.70	5.95
1970–1974	72.11	63.25	53.61	44.16	34.79	25.86	17.71	10.97	6.17
1971–1975	72.07	63.16	53.51	44.06	34.70	25.79	17.65	10.90	6.08
1972–1976	72.10	63.13	53.47	44.03	34.66	25.74	17.62	10.86	6.05

Females

Age	0	10	20	30	40	50	60	70	80
1755–1776	35.70	46.25	39.15	32.17	25.21	19.26	13.08	7.91	4.47
1816–1840	43.56	48.59	40.75	33.40	26.41	19.60	13.22	8.03	4.46
1841–1845	46.60	50.52	42.60	34.95			13.77		4.35
1846–1850	45.59	50.10	42.21	34.48			13.41		4.16
1851–1855	44.64	49.39	41.57	33.95			13.28		4.48
1856–1860	44.15	49.99	42.60	35.06			14.04		4.91
1861–1870	46.40	51.80	43.90	36.20	28.70	21.30	14.40	8.80	4.70
1871–1880	48.60	52.90	45.00	37.50	30.10	22.60	15.40	9.40	5.20
1881–1890	51.47	54.22	46.40	38.82	31.28	23.64	16.25	9.96	5.40
1891–1900	53.63	54.61	46.76	39.31	31.75	24.04	16.56	10.08	5.40
1901–1910	56.98	55.58	47.66	40.20	32.53	24.74	17.19	10.53	5.64
1911–1915	59.24	56.27	48.13	40.49	32.66	24.79	17.13	10.47	5.59
1916–1920	57.62	54.45	46.70	39.89	32.55	24.78	17.24	10.59	5.75
1921–1925	62.95	58.29	49.73	41.68	33.43	25.26	17.51	10.75	5.78
1926–1930	63.33	58.43	49.73	41.60	33.25	25.01	17.29	10.56	5.67
1931–1935	65.33	59.49	50.55	42.15	33.54	25.14	17.29	10.51	5.62
1936–1940	66.92	60.46	51.27	42.48	33.67	25.12	17.19	10.37	5.49
1941–1945	69.71	62.40	53.02	44.01	34.97	26.20	18.04	11.00	5.91
1946–1950	71.58	63.58	53.95	44.57	35.29	26.32	18.02	10.89	5.76
1951–1955	73.43	65.12	55.36	45.72	36.22	27.07	18.61	11.28	5.98
1956–1960	74.72	66.14	56.36	46.63	37.06	27.83	19.19	11.66	6.20
1961–1965	75.70	66.98	57.18	47.45	37.84	28.56	19.84	12.13	6.44
1967	76.54	67.64	57.81	48.10	38.50	29.22	20.42	12.57	6.77
1969	76.50	67.46	57.66	47.91	38.31	29.07	20.30	12.45	6.55
1970–1974	77.51	68.43	58.64	48.89	39.28	29.98	21.20	13.28	7.23
1971–1975	77.65	68.54	58.74	48.99	39.38	30.08	21.29	13.36	7.28
1972–1976	77.75	68.61	58.81	49.07	39.46	30.15	21.35	13.40	7.28

Switzerland

Expectation of Life at Specific Ages

Males

Age	0	10	20	30	40	50	60	70	80
1876–1880	40.6	46.9	38.8	31.7	24.8	18.1	12.2	7.4	4.1
1881–1888	43.3	47.9	39.6	32.2	25.1	18.4	12.4	7.4	4.2
1889–1900	45.7	49.0	40.5	32.9	25.5	18.6	12.5	7.6	4.1
1901–1910	49.25	50.34	41.70	33.80	26.03	18.90	12.73	7.78	4.27
1910–1911	50.65	51.07	42.37	34.32	26.48	19.18	12.81	7.83	4.32
1920–1921	54.48	52.53	43.85	35.56	27.47	19.89	13.26	8.01	4.34
1921–1930	58.15	54.13	45.16	36.76	28.74	20.52	13.76	8.30	4.57
1931–1941	60.93	55.75	46.66	38.10	29.47	21.34	14.29	8.63	4.64
1939–1944	62.68	57.08	47.92	39.26	30.42	22.08	14.75	8.85	4.75
1948–1953	66.36	59.64	50.16	41.01	31.88	23.22	15.69	9.53	5.24
1958–1963	68.72	61.00	51.45	42.17	32.84	23.99	16.24	10.02	5.47
1960–1970	69.21	61.23	51.65	42.33	32.99	24.11	16.30	10.06	5.55
1968–1973	70.29	61.97	52.39	43.06	33.64	24.69	16.74	10.35	5.78

Females

Age	0	10	20	30	40	50	60	70	80
1876–1880	43.2	48.2	40.3	33.2	26.3	19.1	12.5	7.5	4.2
1881–1888	45.7	49.0	41.0	33.8	26.7	19.4	12.7	7.5	4.2
1889–1900	48.5	50.3	42.2	34.7	27.3	19.8	13.0	7.7	4.2
1901–1910	52.15	51.98	43.69	36.10	28.43	20.71	13.67	8.15	4.51
1910–1911	53.89	53.17	44.74	36.88	28.91	21.13	14.61	8.18	4.12
1920–1921	57.50	54.48	45.85	37.79	29.66	21.71	14.40	8.39	4.20
1921–1930	61.41	56.54	47.63	39.31	30.86	22.60	15.12	9.01	4.89
1931–1941	64.84	58.94	49.73	41.03	32.26	23.73	15.95	9.52	5.09
1939–1944	66.96	60.62	51.28	42.32	33.35	24.65	16.65	9.97	5.32
1948–1953	70.85	63.55	53.86	44.36	35.02	26.04	17.77	10.72	5.74
1958–1963	74.13	65.98	56.21	46.52	36.96	27.75	19.16	11.67	6.10
1960–1970	75.03	66.67	56.87	47.15	37.54	28.28	19.62	12.01	6.34
1968–1973	76.22	67.56	57.79	48.05	38.41	29.11	20.39	12.60	6.68

England and Wales

Expectation of Life at Specific Ages

Age	Males									Females								
	0	10	20	30	40	50	60	70	80	0	10	20	30	40	50	60	70	80
1841	40.19	47.08	39.88	33.13	26.56	20.02	13.50	8.51	4.92	42.18	47.81	40.81	34.25	27.72	21.07	14.40	9.03	5.20
1838–1844	40.36	47.47	39.99	33.21	26.46	19.87	13.60	8.55	4.97	42.04	47.86	40.65	34.06	27.50	20.84	14.49	9.12	5.34
1838–1854	39.91	47.05	39.48	32.76	26.06	19.54	13.53	8.45	4.93	41.85	47.67	40.29	33.81	27.34	20.75	14.34	9.02	5.26
1871–1880	41.35	47.60	39.40	32.10	25.30	18.93	13.14	8.27	4.79	44.62	49.76	41.66	34.41	27.46	20.68	14.24	8.95	5.20
1876–1880	41.92	48.16	39.86	32.47	25.59	19.14	13.31	8.44	4.96	45.25	50.32	42.10	34.75	27.68	20.80	14.32	9.08	5.38
1881–1890	43.66	49.00	40.27	32.52	25.42	18.82	12.88	8.04	4.52	47.18	51.10	42.42	34.76	27.60	20.56	14.10	8.77	5.00
1891–1900	44.13	49.63	41.02	33.07	25.64	18.90	12.93	8.05	4.62	47.77	51.97	43.44	35.39	27.82	20.64	14.10	8.78	5.05
1901–1910	48.53	51.81	43.01	34.76	26.96	19.76	13.49	8.39	4.86	52.38	54.53	45.77	37.36	29.37	21.81	15.01	9.25	5.36
1910–1912	51.50	53.08	44.21	35.81	27.74	20.29	13.78	8.53	4.90	55.35	55.91	47.10	38.54	30.30	22.51	15.48	9.58	5.49
1920–1922	55.62	54.64	45.78	37.40	29.19	21.36	14.36	8.75	4.93	59.58	57.53	48.73	40.26	31.86	23.69	16.22	9.95	5.56
1930–1932	58.74	55.79	46.81	38.21	29.62	21.60	14.43	8.62	4.74	62.88	58.87	49.88	41.22	32.55	24.13	16.50	10.02	5.46
1948	66.39	59.76	50.29	41.04	31.86	23.25	15.82	10.03	5.92	71.15	63.94	54.43	45.26	36.04	27.15	18.96	11.91	6.95
1950–1952	66.42	59.24	49.64	40.27	30.98	22.23	14.79	9.00	4.86	71.54	63.87	54.17	44.68	35.32	26.34	18.07	10.97	5.83
1953–1955	67.46	59.92	50.27	40.81	31.42	22.56	15.04	9.24	5.17	72.86	64.93	55.15	45.52	36.08	27.04	18.67	11.48	6.25
1954–1956	67.62	59.98	50.32	40.84	31.43	22.55	15.02	9.20	5.15	73.11	65.07	55.28	45.62	36.15	27.10	18.70	11.49	6.23
1956–1958	67.85	60.08	50.42	40.92	31.49	22.60	15.06	9.29	5.28	73.53	65.39	55.59	45.90	36.39	27.23	18.90	11.66	6.38
1958–1960	68.1	60.2	50.6	41.1	31.6	22.7	15.2	9.4	5.3	73.9	65.7	55.9	46.1	36.6	27.5	19.1	11.8	6.4
1960–1962	68.0	60.2	50.6	41.1	31.6	22.7	15.1	9.3	5.2	74.0	65.7	55.9	46.2	36.6	27.5	19.0	11.7	6.3
1961–1963	68.0	60.0	50.4	40.9	31.4	22.5	14.9	9.1	5.1	73.9	65.0	55.8	46.1	36.5	27.4	18.9	11.6	6.2
1963–1965	68.3	60.3	50.6	41.1	31.6	22.8	15.1	9.4	5.3	74.4	66.1	56.3	46.5	37.0	27.9	19.4	12.1	6.7
1965–1967	68.7	60.5	50.9	41.4	31.9	23.0	15.3	9.5	5.5	74.9	66.4	56.6	46.9	37.3	28.2	19.8	12.4	6.9
1967–1969	68.7	60.5	50.9	41.3	31.8	22.9	15.2	9.4	5.4	74.9	66.4	56.6	46.9	37.3	28.2	19.7	12.4	6.8
1968–1970	68.6	60.4	50.8	41.2	31.7	22.8	15.1	9.3	5.3	74.9	66.4	56.6	46.8	37.2	28.1	19.7	12.3	6.8
1969–1971	68.8	60.5	50.9	41.3	31.8	22.9	15.2	9.4	5.5	75.1	66.5	56.7	47.0	37.4	28.3	19.8	12.5	6.9
1970–1972	68.9	60.6	52.0	41.4	31.9	23.0	15.3	9.4	5.5	75.1	66.6	56.8	47.0	37.4	28.3	19.9	12.5	7.0

Scotland

Expectation of Life at Specific Ages

Age	Males									Females								
	0	10	20	30	40	50	60	70	80	0	10	20	30	40	50	60	70	80
1861–1870	40.33	46.10	38.75	32.20			13.30		4.59	43.85	48.26	41.05	34.26			14.38		4.89
1871–1880	40.95	46.07	38.68	32.05			13.18		4.68	43.80	48.19	40.94	34.25			14.48		5.16
1881–1890	43.92	47.10	40.19	33.06			13.52		5.00	46.33	49.54	41.93	34.95			14.82		5.46
1891–1900	44.41	48.60	40.43	33.02	25.71	18.91	13.12	8.28	4.91	47.47	50.39	42.41	34.92	27.83	20.74	14.33	9.19	5.26
1910–1912	50.10	51.86	43.27	35.17	27.25	19.91	13.54	8.38	4.94	53.18	53.83	45.35	37.22	29.48	21.91	15.17	9.38	5.51
1920–1922	53.08	53.55	44.82	36.52	28.43	20.68	13.82	8.40	4.78	56.35	55.53	46.82	38.63	30.68	22.79	15.64	9.65	5.36
1930–1932	56.0	54.9	46.0	37.4	29.1	21.3	14.1	8.4	4.6	59.5	57.2	48.3	39.8	31.4	23.3	15.9	9.6	5.2
1948	63.76	58.12	48.75	39.70	30.79	22.54	15.53	9.73	5.64	67.63	60.97	51.77	43.10	34.29	25.59	17.63	11.08	6.46
1950–1952	64.4	57.9	48.3	39.1	29.9	21.4	14.3	8.8	4.6	68.7	61.5	51.9	42.7	33.6	24.8	16.8	10.1	5.4
1955–1957	65.90	58.66	49.03	39.57	30.29	21.65	14.50	9.04	5.10	71.07	63.33	53.56	43.95	34.57	25.63	17.46	10.64	5.72
1957–1959	66.05	58.71	49.06	39.56	30.25	21.60	14.40	9.03	5.15	71.40	63.57	53.79	44.14	34.72	25.81	17.62	10.75	5.75
1958–1960	66.21	58.78	49.11	39.62	30.30	21.62	14.39	9.01	5.18	71.57	63.72	53.92	44.25	34.81	25.86	17.65	10.76	5.74
1960–1962	66.20	58.73	49.05	39.57	30.26	21.56	14.34	8.95	5.15	71.87	63.94	54.13	44.42	34.95	25.99	17.79	10.87	5.85
1961–1963	66.01	58.52	48.85	39.36	30.06	21.39	14.15	8.80	4.93	71.93	63.95	54.13	44.43	34.97	26.03	17.83	10.92	5.9
1963–1965	66.34	58.63	48.97	39.48	30.13	21.51	14.24	8.93	5.14	72.45	64.36	54.57	44.88	35.39	26.45	18.25	11.34	6.30
1964–1966	66.60	58.81	49.16	39.68	30.33	21.70	14.38	9.02	5.21	72.64	64.15	54.36	44.57	35.04	26.36	18.39	11.42	6.35
1967–1969	67.06	59.08	49.46	39.96	30.62	21.97	14.63	9.13	5.37	73.21	64.90	55.08	45.04	35.54	26.58	18.70	11.64	6.42
1968–1970	66.90	58.92	49.29	39.79	30.45	21.81	14.47	8.98	5.27	73.08	64.72	54.91	45.32	35.80	26.84	18.62	11.57	6.35
1969–1971	67.10	59.04	49.40	39.91	30.56	21.92	14.57	9.04	5.33	73.36	64.97	55.16	45.15	35.66	26.72	18.85	11.81	6.55
1970–1972	67.17	58.98	49.30	39.79	30.46	21.78	14.43	8.86	5.17	73.54	65.06	55.22	45.40	35.87	26.94	18.87	11.83	6.60
1971–1973	67.23	59.24	49.79	40.57	31.27	22.49	14.99	9.27	5.15	73.61	65.40	55.62	45.89	36.33	27.28	18.94	11.71	6.45

Northern Ireland

Expectation of Life at Specific Ages

Males

Age	0	10	20	30	40	50	60	70	80
1911	50.7	51.5	43.2	31.9	24.4	17.6	12.1	8.0	
1925–1927	55.42	54.42	45.63	37.46	29.28	21.55	14.79	9.36	5.43
1936–1938	57.8	55.4	46.4	33.6	25.4	18.0	11.6	7.0	
1950–1952	65.5	59.2	49.6	40.4	31.3	22.7	15.3	9.4	5.3
1954–1956	67.36	60.21	50.52	40.99	31.69	22.93	15.33	9.50	5.28
1956–1958	67.55	60.16	50.47	40.93	31.56	22.79	15.33	9.50	5.29
1957–1959	67.44	59.97	50.31	40.80	31.42	22.65	15.16	9.41	5.26
1958–1960	67.51	60.04	50.40	40.88	31.47	22.69	15.17	9.33	5.25
1960–1962	67.64	60.21	50.53	41.01	31.63	22.80	15.28	9.51	5.40
1961–1963	67.64	60.15	50.45	40.9	31.54	22.70	15.29	9.58	5.39
1963–1965	67.84	60.23	50.53	40.97	31.56	22.79	15.34	9.60	5.37
1964–1966	67.79	60.15	50.46	40.90	31.50	22.73	15.19	9.47	5.25
1965–1967	68.09	60.35	50.66	41.11	31.71	22.91	15.36	9.58	5.33
1966–1968	68.19	60.44	50.77	41.24	31.81	22.99	15.38	9.58	5.38
1967–1969	68.30	60.52	50.85	41.32	31.88	23.11	15.50	9.69	5.68
1968–1970	67.92	60.13	50.44	40.92	31.48	22.74	15.14	9.47	5.57
1969–1971	67.75	59.96	50.29	40.81	31.40	22.68	15.10	9.45	5.46
1970–1972	67.63	59.71	50.14	40.74	31.33	22.58	15.03	9.38	5.26
1972–1974	64.97	58.73	49.32	40.20	30.95	22.25	14.87	9.12	5.00
1973–1975	67.24	59.16	49.73	40.64	31.11	22.37	14.93	9.15	4.92
1974–1976	66.76	59.01	49.54	40.57	31.10	22.44	14.93	9.15	4.82

Females

Age	0	10	20	30	40	50	60	70	80
1911	51.0	50.7	42.8	31.9	24.7	18.1	12.8	8.5	
1925–1927	56.11	53.73	45.22	37.42	29.65	22.18	15.55	10.20	6.25
1936–1938	59.2	56.1	47.1	34.6	26.4	18.8	12.4	7.6	
1950–1952	68.8	62.0	52.3	42.9	33.8	25.0	17.0	10.4	5.8
1954–1956	71.05	63.52	53.75	44.09	34.74	25.77	17.56	10.72	3.68
1956–1958	71.79	64.07	54.26	44.54	35.13	26.10	17.79	10.91	5.87
1957–1959	71.82	64.15	54.35	44.59	35.15	26.13	17.83	10.91	5.84
1958–1960	71.94	64.21	54.39	44.64	35.14	26.13	17.86	10.86	5.89
1960–1962	72.40	64.59	54.76	45.05	35.54	26.49	18.10	10.99	6.00
1961–1963	72.54	64.71	54.88	45.16	35.66	26.59	18.22	11.10	6.02
1963–1965	72.89	64.96	55.11	45.35	35.84	26.81	18.53	11.34	6.21
1964–1966	72.98	65.02	55.20	45.45	35.91	26.87	18.52	11.28	6.13
1965–1967	73.34	65.39	55.57	45.82	36.30	27.22	18.83	11.58	6.45
1966–1968	73.45	65.43	55.62	45.87	36.33	27.28	18.86	11.69	6.54
1967–1969	73.70	65.62	55.77	46.03	36.49	27.43	19.03	11.94	6.77
1968–1970	73.45	65.29	55.45	45.68	36.15	27.11	18.80	11.74	6.63
1969–1971	73.66	65.51	55.67	45.91	36.34	27.27	18.95	11.79	6.56
1970–1972	73.67	65.45	55.64	45.90	36.31	27.27	18.94	11.74	6.48
1972–1974	73.64	65.79	56.01	46.29	36.76	27.71	19.44	12.37	6.27
1973–1975	73.55	65.36	55.58	45.83	36.29	27.21	18.87	11.64	6.18
1974–1976	73.72	65.49	55.71	45.97	36.41	27.30	19.00	11.76	6.14

A g e   D i s t r i b u t i o n   a t   S u c c e s s i v e   C e n s u s e s

Census	1869	1880	1890	1900	1910	1910[a]	1920	1934	1951	1961	1971	Census
Age group	A g e	o f	t o t a l	p o p u l a t i o n		(proportions per 10.000 population)						Age group
0–4	1 304	1 316	1 285	1 305	1 242	1 051	627	693	764	825	796	0–4
5–9	1 085	1 094	1 102	1 113	1 155	999	935	797	740	689	863	5–9
10–14	995	990	1 028	1 023	1 087	953	976	875	784	726	785	10–14
15–19	930	942	950	954	964	916	1009	581	635	731	686	15–19
20–24	854	878	858	874	831	890	905	872	701	730	709	20–24
25–29	819	742	765	756	734	805	790	879	746	579	652	25–29
30–34	723	692	710	681	674	756	764	867	537	651	675	30–34
35–39	660	649	602	612	617	674	723	761	668	697	546	35–39
40–44	576	603	567	576	555	589	695	665	774	490	610	40–44
45–49	557	504	518	475	497	529	603	642	781	634	645	45–49
50–54	462	451	465	444	453	477	525	588	712	713	455	50–54
55–59	376	379	361	375	362	406	454	540	591	697	555	55–59
60–64	267	322	302	314	301	343	369	433	504	603	599	60–64
65–69	205	210	220	216	231	271	284	335	421	467	539	65–69
70–74	103	129	153	148	158	182	183	237	318	352	410	70–74
75+	84	99	114	133	139	157	156	219	319	416	475	75+
Unknown							1	18	6	1		Unknown
Age group			A g e	o f	m a l e s	(proportions per 10.000 males)						Age group
0–4	1 324	1 339	1 307	1 329	1 267	1 066	661	731	842	904	868	0–4
5–9	1 097	1 117	1 130	1 139	1 186	1 014	979	839	812	754	940	5–9
10–14	1 021	1 007	1 045	1 033	1 104	964	1 026	920	858	796	856	10–14
15–19	923	944	950	949	961	929	1 058	605	696	798	742	15–19
20–24	855	879	859	881	834	917	892	903	757	803	767	20–24
25–29	801	740	763	758	726	808	741	905	695	629	702	25–29
30–34	714	686	706	677	665	755	722	885	494	694	726	30–34
35–39	647	646	603	615	618	679	707	728	631	639	584	35–39
40–44	560	593	561	576	554	589	684	623	751	445	642	40–44
45–49	547	497	515	473	498	530	609	603	791	590	584	45–49
50–54	465	430	451	432	446	466	532	566	705	679	405	50–54
55–59	376	369	353	369	356	393	455	518	549	684	500	55–59
60–64	270	316	284	301	289	327	360	420	463	564	539	60–64
65–69	208	211	212	207	222	256	269	321	384	399	482	65–69
70–74	108	127	149	138	148	167	168	223	286	291	335	70–74
75+	84	99	111	123	127	140	135	194	280	329	329	75+
Unknown							1	16	6	1		Unknown
Age group			A g e	o f	f e m a l e s	(proportions per 10.000 females)						Age group
0–4	1 285	1 294	1 265	1 283	1 217	1 036	596	659	697	756	732	0–4
5–9	1 073	1 071	1 075	1 087	1 126	985	895	758	679	632	795	5–9
10–14	970	973	1 011	1 013	1 071	942	929	833	719	664	722	10–14
15–19	936	940	950	958	967	903	964	559	582	672	637	15–19
20–24	852	878	857	867	829	862	918	842	653	666	659	20–24
25–29	836	744	767	754	742	803	834	854	790	535	608	25–29
30–34	732	699	714	686	682	757	802	850	574	615	629	30–34
35–39	671	651	600	609	616	669	737	792	700	747	511	35–39
40–44	592	612	572	577	556	589	706	704	794	529	582	40–44
45–49	567	510	522	476	497	529	598	677	772	672	699	45–49
50–54	459	471	479	455	461	487	519	608	717	743	500	50–54
55–59	376	389	370	381	367	419	453	560	627	707	603	55–59
60–64	266	328	319	328	313	359	377	445	540	638	653	60–64
65–69	203	209	228	226	239	287	298	348	453	526	590	65–69
70–74	98	130	156	158	168	198	197	249	345	405	476	70–74
75+	84	100	116	143	150	173	176	243	352	491	604	75+
Unknown							1	19	6	1		Unknown

a) approximate territory of later Republic

Austria

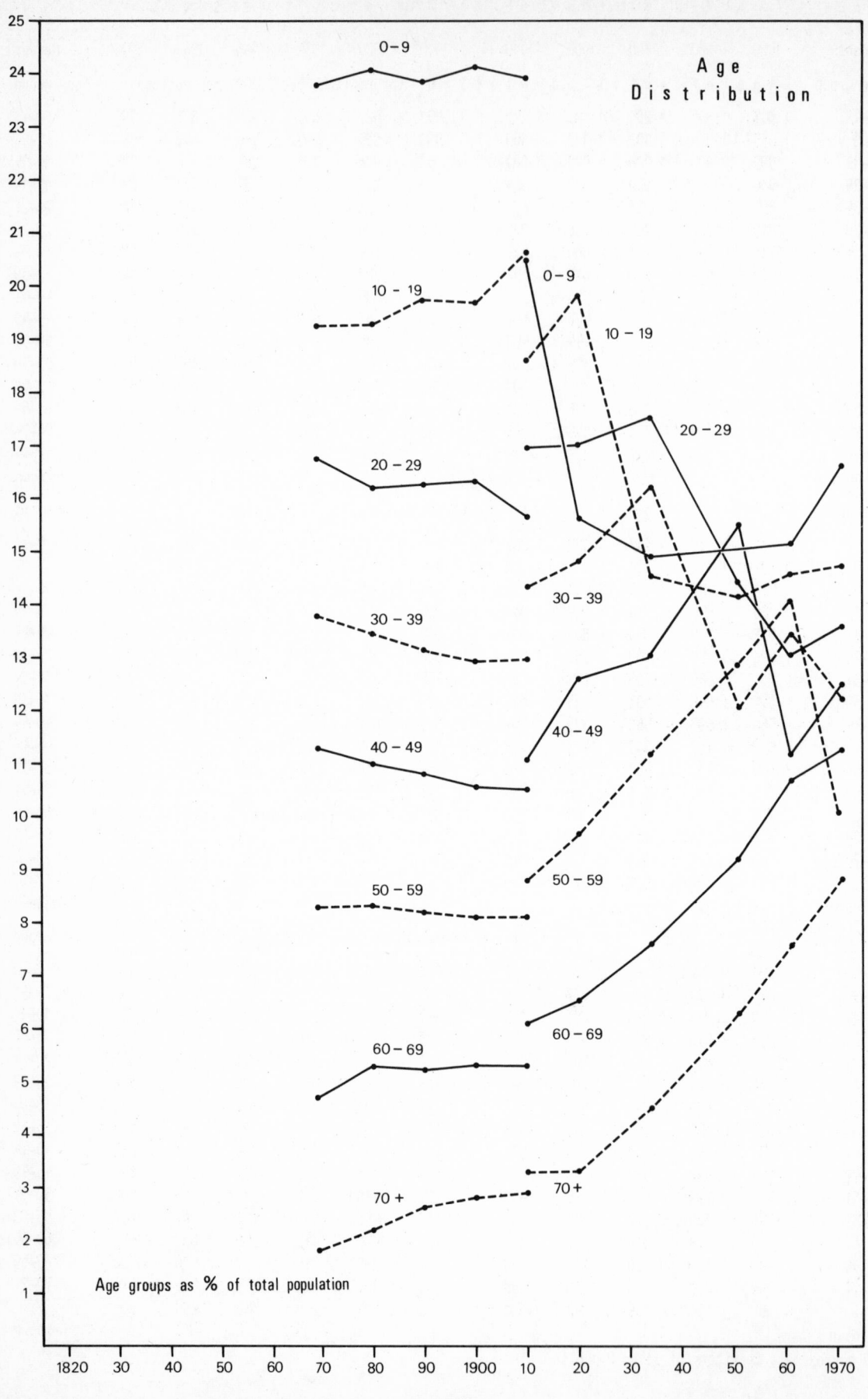

Age Distribution

0 - 9

10 - 19

0 - 9

10 - 19

20 - 29

20 - 29

30 - 39

30 - 39

40 - 49

40 - 49

50 - 59

50 - 59

60 - 69

60 - 69

70 +

70 +

Age groups as % of total population

1820 30 40 50 60 70 80 90 1900 10 20 30 40 50 60 1970

Age Distribution at Successive Censuses

Census	1846	1856	1866	1880	1890	1900	1910	1920	1930	1947	1961	1970	Census
Age group	Age	of	total	population			(proportions per 10.000 population)						Age group
0–4	1 164	1 078	1 202	1 237	1 159	1 171	1 023	694	825	753	832	737	0–4
5–9	1 091	984	1 046	1 111	1 083	1 033	1 031	863	854	622	790	817	5–9
10–14	978	968	920	1 002	1 036	967	1 000	941	618	683	762	801	10–14
15–19	899	943	877	920	984	963	925	982	803	764	659	754	15–19
20–24	908	867	844	839	896	905	852	927	870	798	600	748	20–24
25–29	754	778	781	706	759	823	816	811	890	710	656	597	25–29
30–34	694	741	694	637	678	721	759	747	830	619	711	612	30–34
35–39	657	659	628	630	577	630	693	727	726	760	726	652	35–39
40–44	602	605	599	576	518	560	607	682	663	776	569	672	40–44
45–49	577	553	519	498	511	471	524	621	639	746	602	679	45–49
50–54	441	501	479	458	453	414	457	535	586	653	657	468	50–54
55–59	340	441	416	408	378	394	369	446	516	552	643	563	55–59
60–64	307	317	361	333	327	328	306	366	421	494	572	555	60–64
65–70	242	231	296	262	270	250	266	267	322	419	453	500	65–70
70–74	164	164	172	191	185	182	187	187	226	324	338	384	70–74
75+	181	169	164	192	187	187	184	195	211	326	431	461	75+
Unknown													Unknown

Age group			Age	of	males		(proportions per 10.000 males)						Age group
0–4	1 175	1 078	1 203	1 246	1 165	1 185	1 037	713	838	778	871	770	0–4
5–9	1 107	987	1 048	1 119	1 092	1 043	1 043	879	870	637	824	854	5–9
10–14	1 002	979	923	1 010	1 044	976	1 012	958	630	700	793	836	10–14
15–19	912	954	883	929	994	974	936	999	815	780	685	786	15–19
20–24	914	886	844	840	922	916	861	938	891	828	615	781	20–24
25–29	762	790	787	711	763	831	827	801	914	734	670	621	25–29
30–34	700	748	699	636	677	728	766	745	838	634	728	632	30–34
35–39	667	665	640	634	578	634	700	734	715	773	742	669	35–39
40–44	619	607	608	576	516	560	612	687	656	785	578	686	40–44
45–49	590	555	523	500	509	469	524	624	637	746	609	687	45–49
50–54	420	511	479	460	449	406	451	534	583	631	656	469	50–54
55–59	299	444	413	405	374	386	357	440	510	527	632	553	55–59
60–64	283	301	362	325	319	317	291	352	411	471	541	528	60–64
65–69	226	201	292	252	259	239	250	248	307	395	404	453	65–69
70–74	155	146	159	180	174	170	173	169	208	300	294	323	70–74
75+	167	150	137	178	166	165	159	167	176	280	358	351	75+
Unknown													Unknown

Age group			Age	of	females		(proportions per 10.000 females)						Age group
0–4	1 154	1 079	1 202	1 227	1 153	1 156	1 009	675	812	729	795	705	0–4
5–9	1 074	981	1 044	1 103	1 074	1 024	1 019	847	839	607	756	782	5–9
10–14	954	957	916	993	1 029	957	989	924	607	668	732	767	10–14
15–19	886	932	870	911	974	953	915	966	792	749	634	724	15–19
20–24	902	849	845	838	869	894	843	917	848	769	585	717	20–24
25–29	746	766	774	702	755	815	806	820	867	686	641	573	25–29
30–34	689	734	690	638	679	714	752	750	822	603	695	594	30–34
35–39	647	653	617	627	576	626	687	721	737	747	711	636	35–39
40–44	586	602	589	576	520	561	603	676	669	767	561	660	40–44
45–49	565	551	516	495	513	474	524	617	640	747	595	670	45–49
50–54	461	492	480	457	457	422	464	535	589	674	658	467	50–54
55–59	381	438	420	412	382	403	381	452	522	577	654	572	55–59
60–64	330	333	360	341	335	339	320	380	431	517	602	581	60–64
65–69	258	262	300	272	281	262	282	285	337	442	499	545	65–69
70–74	173	182	186	201	196	193	202	204	244	347	380	441	70–74
75+	195	189	192	206	208	208	208	222	245	372	501	566	75+
Unknown													Unknown

Belgium

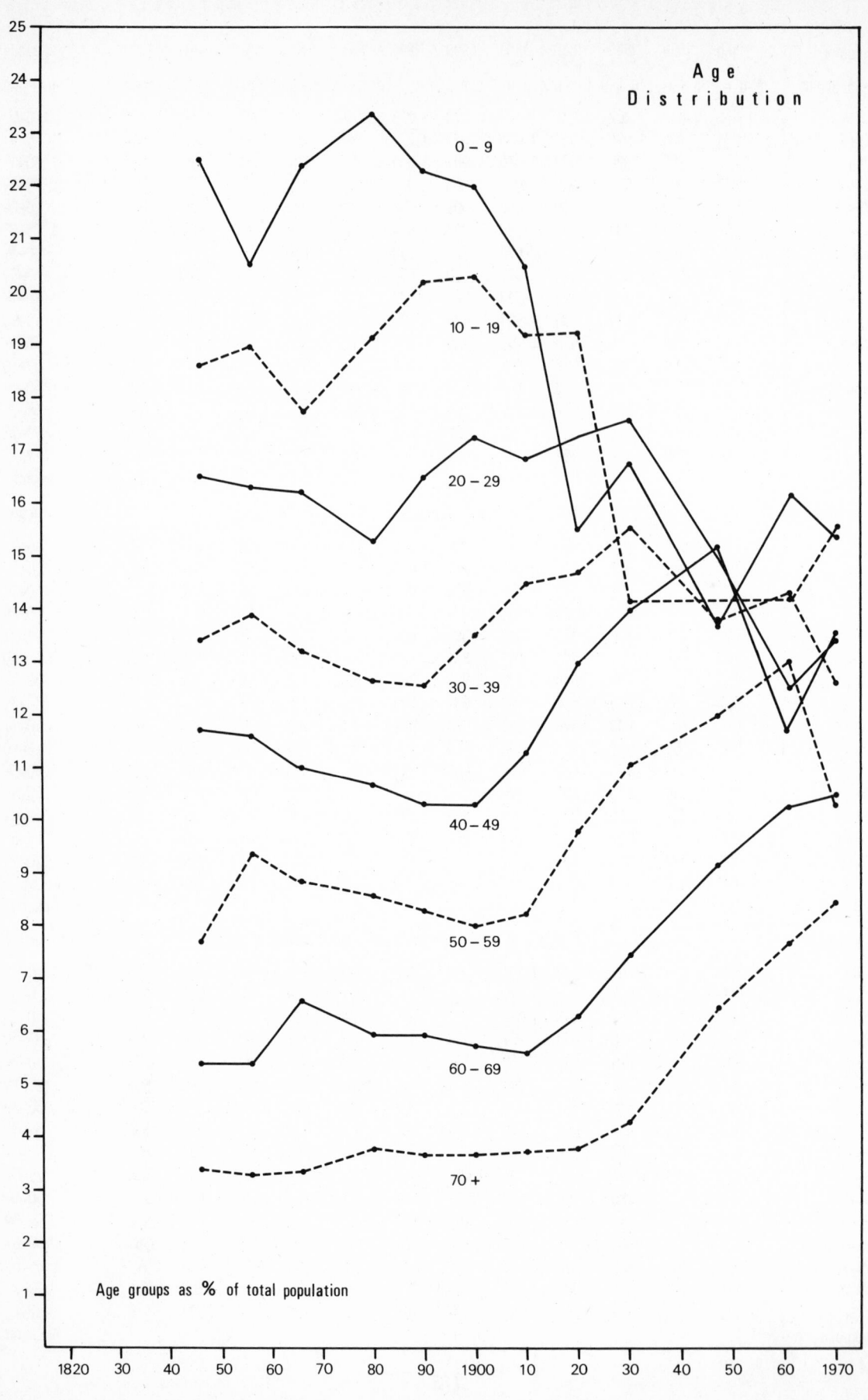

Age
Distribution

0 – 9

10 – 19

20 – 29

30 – 39

40 – 49

50 – 59

60 – 69

70 +

Age groups as % of total population

1820 30 40 50 60 70 80 90 1900 10 20 30 40 50 60 1970

Age Distribution at Successive Censuses

Census	1801	1834	1840	1845	1855	1860	1870	1880	1890	Census
Age group	Age of total population					(proportions per 10.000 population)				Age group
0-4	2 310	2 322	1 241	1 249	1 289	1 315	1 244	1 285	1 278	0-4
5-9			1 033	1 075	1 062	1 101	1 068	1 089	1 158	5-9
10-14	1 745	2 105	1 008	952	976	953	1 025	1 004	1 043	10-14
15-19			1 034	947	925	907	927	897	898	15-19
20-24	1 614	1 627	935	955	827	846	810	855	785	20-24
25-29			769	851	789	754	746	749	703	25-29
30-34	1 330	1 339	667	663	763	695	675	645	682	30-34
35-39			677	636	691	705	629	600	606	35-39
40-44	1 160	982	543	579	545	601	574	546	520	40-44
45-49			500	509	502	497	564	491	488	45-49
50-54	901	797	386	415	458	424	479	451	437	50-54
55-59			360	331	360	391	374	427	374	55-59
60-64	615	521	302	290	288	290	303	350	324	60-64
65-69			227	239	212	226	255	252	294	65-69
70-74	324	307	158	148	151	141	162	171	206	70-74
75+			160	161	160	153	164	185	196	75+
Unknown							2	6	7	Unknown

Age group	1801	1834	1840	1845	1855	1860	1870	1880	1890	Age group
	Age of males			(proportions per 10.000 males)						
0-4	2 332	2 367	1 265	1 274	1 316	1 338	1 273	1 320	1 322	0-4
5-9			1 054	1 097	1 077	1 124	1 097	1 119	1 201	5-9
10-14	1 754	2 151	1 034	974	1 002	969	1 045	1 034	1 085	10-14
15-19			1 054	964	940	923	945	919	922	15-19
20-24	1 583	1 630	939	960	820	837	797	842	760	20-24
25-29			769	853	783	756	738	739	674	25-29
30-34	1 352	1 355	670	668	765	697	663	630	663	30-34
35-39			690	641	702	712	633	594	603	35-39
40-44	1 184	960	544	586	548	607	578	540	512	40-44
45-49			487	501	502	495	566	491	487	45-49
50-54	910	775	372	404	457	418	478	449	430	50-54
55-59			347	316	351	385	369	423	371	55-59
60-64	596	487	286	272	271	278	289	340	318	60-64
65-69			209	220	194	207	240	236	282	65-69
70-74	289	276	143	134	136	126	148	156	192	70-74
75+			138	136	136	129	139	160	169	75+
Unknown							2	6	8	Unknown

Age group	1801	1834	1840	1845	1855	1860	1870	1880	1890	Age group
	Age of females			(proportions per 10.000 females)						
0-4	2 289	2 278	1 218	1 225	1 263	1 292	1 216	1 250	1 236	0-4
5-9			1 013	1 053	1 048	1 079	1 040	1 060	1 117	5-9
10-14	1 737	2 061	982	930	951	937	1 005	975	1 008	10-14
15-19			1 015	930	911	891	909	875	875	15-19
20-24	1 645	1 625	932	950	835	856	823	867	809	20-24
25-29			768	849	795	751	754	759	731	25-29
30-34	1 308	1 324	665	659	761	694	687	659	699	30-34
35-39			663	631	680	699	625	606	609	35-39
40-44	1 137	1 003	541	572	541	594	570	551	526	40-44
45-49			513	516	503	498	561	490	489	45-49
50-54	892	818	399	427	459	430	480	452	445	50-54
55-59			374	345	369	397	379	430	377	55-59
60-64	634	554	318	308	305	303	316	359	331	60-64
65-69			244	257	230	245	270	266	306	65-69
70-74	359	337	173	162	165	155	175	186	218	70-74
75+			182	186	183	178	189	209	223	75+
Unknown							1	5	7	Unknown

Age Distribution at Successive Censuses

Census	1901	1911	1921	1930	1935	1945	1950	1960	1965	1970	Census
Age group	Age of total population (proportions per 10.000 population)										Age group
0-4	1 246	1 209	1 045	876	807	958	976	801	828	774	0-4
5-9	1 102	1 097	1 030	941	831	778	921	806	773	800	5-9
10-14	1 038	1 045	1 034	923	900	728	737	902	777	747	10-14
15-19	967	923	955	922	873	748	683	843	865	754	15-19
20-24	842	820	872	895	881	806	691	663	799	834	20-24
25-29	725	757	762	818	868	782	739	607	635	777	25-29
30-34	644	696	698	761	790	799	728	622	585	617	30-34
35-39	576	602	646	673	726	770	734	673	598	567	35-39
40-44	566	525	590	613	640	701	719	661	644	575	40-44
45-49	487	470	503	559	574	635	648	665	626	613	45-49
50-54	428	454	440	504	522	549	587	639	625	591	50-54
55-59	372	379	372	416	456	482	500	565	591	579	55-59
60-64	319	318	343	348	369	416	426	490	510	537	60-64
65-69	258	256	266	273	292	339	353	394	425	445	65-69
70-74	186	191	196	219	210	237	266	301	319	347	70-74
75+	219	215	220	236	248	259	292	369	399	444	75+
Unknown	25	36	29	23	12	11					Unknown

Age group	Age of males (proportions per 10.000 males)										Age group
0-4	1 287	1 254	1 084	905	831	986	1 006	827	853	800	0-4
5-9	1 142	1 141	1 065	973	854	799	948	833	798	825	5-9
10-14	1 076	1 083	1 068	954	923	747	755	930	803	770	10-14
15-19	995	949	980	944	893	762	697	868	894	781	15-19
20-24	840	804	861	898	892	810	699	677	822	864	20-24
25-29	713	738	745	808	869	786	738	609	648	804	25-29
30-34	626	689	684	744	786	804	730	621	589	632	30-34
35-39	558	559	639	660	712	771	736	670	598	572	35-39
40-44	552	523	587	602	631	695	717	661	641	576	40-44
45-49	482	456	503	553	562	621	640	663	625	609	45-49
50-54	420	441	430	501	514	536	571	634	621	587	50-54
55-59	364	370	359	416	452	469	485	550	581	570	55-59
60-64	308	306	327	337	365	403	411	467	488	517	60-64
65-69	245	244	254	259	279	332	340	371	395	412	65-69
70-74	176	177	184	206	196	229	257	280	290	306	70-74
75+	192	190	200	217	227	236	271	339	353	374	75+
Unknown	26	36	33	24	13	11					Unknown

Age group	Age of females (proportions per 10.000 females)										Age group
0-4	1 207	1 166	1 008	848	784	930	945	776	803	748	0-4
5-9	1 065	1 057	998	911	809	758	894	779	747	776	5-9
10-14	1 002	1 009	1 002	894	878	709	720	873	751	723	10-14
15-19	940	898	931	901	853	734	669	818	837	727	15-19
20-24	845	835	882	893	871	802	684	650	777	804	20-24
25-29	736	774	778	827	866	777	740	604	622	749	25-29
30-34	662	702	711	776	794	793	726	623	582	602	30-34
35-39	593	605	654	685	740	770	733	677	598	561	35-39
40-44	579	545	592	623	650	708	720	662	647	574	40-44
45-49	492	483	503	566	585	649	656	666	627	617	45-49
50-54	435	466	449	506	529	562	602	644	629	595	50-54
55-59	379	387	384	417	460	495	516	579	601	588	55-59
60-64	330	329	359	359	373	428	441	513	532	557	60-64
65-69	271	266	278	286	305	346	367	417	455	477	65-69
70-74	196	204	208	232	224	246	275	321	348	387	70-74
75+	246	238	239	254	269	282	312	399	444	514	75+
Unknown	23	35	26	21	11	11					Unknown

Denmark

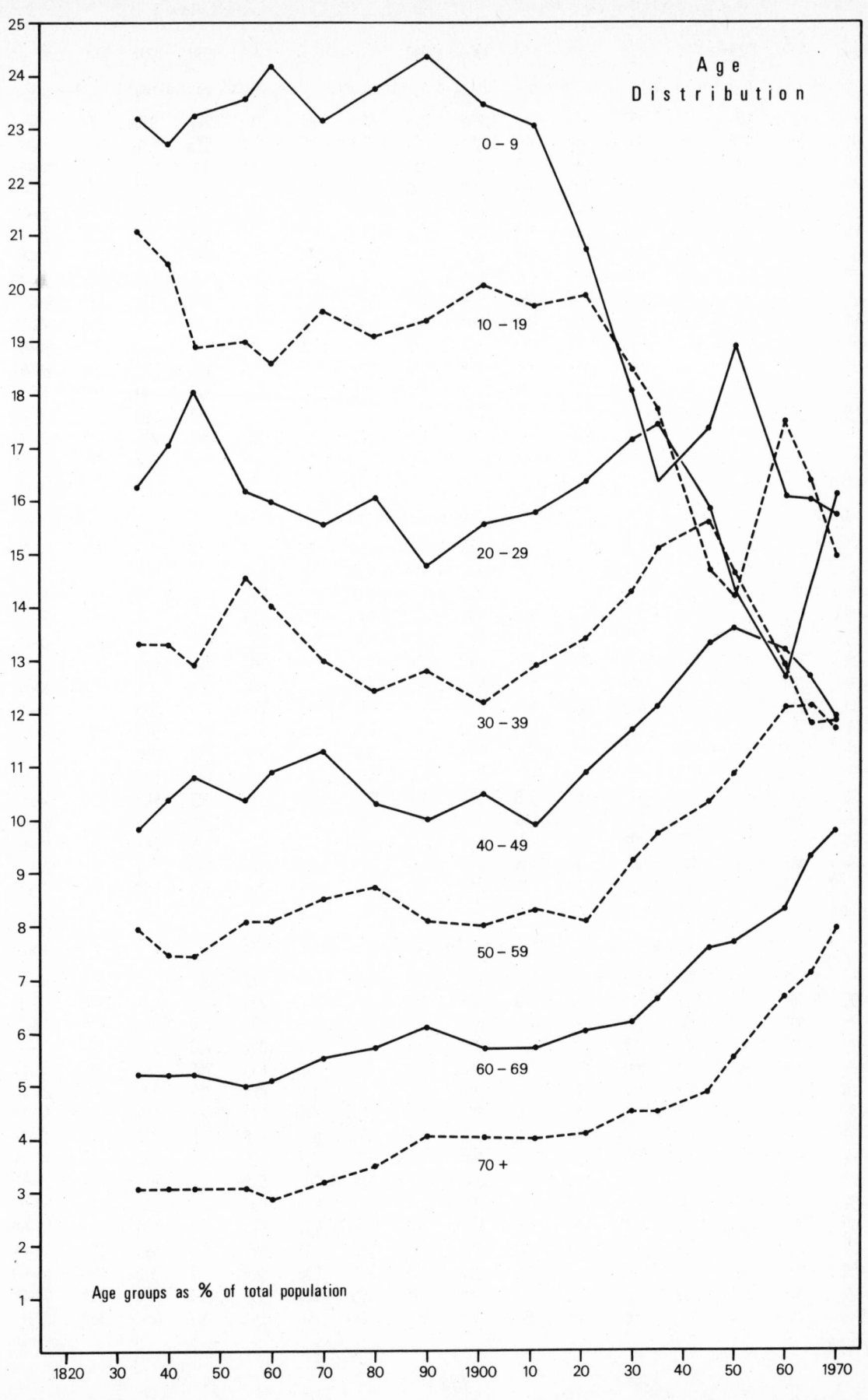

A g e
D i s t r i b u t i o n

Age groups as **%** of total population

Finland

Age Distribution at Successive Censuses

Census / Age group	1800	1825	1850	1870	1880	1890	1900	1910	1920	1930	1940	1950	1960	1970
Age of total population (proportions per 10.000 population)														
0-4	1 530	1 464	1 395	1 263	1 402	1 364	1 299	1 279	999	948	914	1 247	918	734
5-9	1 109	1 077	1 106	1 113	1 164	1 163	1 101	1 118	1 070	969	858	935	987	825
10-14	984	980	952	1 012	894	1 051	1 054	1 022	1 101	884	921	816	1 106	861
15-19	923	841	878	974	935	959	970	910	983	957	937	773	837	921
20-24	888	907	893	900	847	740	875	871	867	966	832	812	703	974
25-29	795	842	838	839	799	761	791	795	763	844	867	765	650	721
30-34	736	760	747	718	715	672	604	715	731	744	866	664	693	625
35-39	646	629	621	625	671	634	616	641	671	653	742	714	662	595
40-44	579	588	506	607	560	564	539	487	596	622	643	718	575	638
45-49	485	512	514	529	469	520	503	489	530	562	542	611	614	605
50-54	395	418	466	445	451	425	438	417	394	490	481	516	608	518
55-59	299	346	379	334	384	344	389	376	381	419	413	414	501	537
60-64	243	264	266	237	298	308	297	308	308	294	345	349	400	507
65-69	182	186	201	193	198	236	219	251	253	259	273	271	295	386
70-74	117	109	136	124	109	149	162	165	175	182	167	195	216	271
75+	89	77	102	87	104	111	142	157	177	207	198	196	226	279
Unknown												5	9	1
Age of males (proportions per 10.000 males)														
0-4	1 576	1 505	1 434	1 303	1 445	1 395	1 326	1 304	1 030	977	959	1 332	973	775
5-9	1 132	1 108	1 136	1 145	1 193	1 187	1 119	1 137	1 103	999	900	1 001	1 044	870
10-14	1 000	1 008	970	1 042	917	1 073	1 072	1 039	1 130	911	964	867	1 171	909
15-19	933	857	895	993	954	980	990	928	1 006	988	979	820	884	974
20-24	888	913	905	909	865	754	891	883	868	989	853	859	742	1 035
25-29	798	853	852	844	809	770	802	806	762	856	883	766	690	763
30-34	731	768	757	719	714	678	611	723	733	740	880	644	724	654
35-39	639	625	622	619	669	636	618	647	674	648	747	703	653	624
40-44	575	576	501	600	556	558	539	490	596	617	631	711	547	658
45-49	473	497	505	519	459	510	497	487	528	558	527	599	590	586
50-54	382	403	452	429	434	411	425	407	387	481	455	488	582	478
55-59	287	326	360	314	363	328	371	362	365	400	382	383	468	493
60-64	230	241	243	217	273	286	279	286	287	276	310	306	352	453
65-69	168	163	176	172	175	214	200	227	230	232	237	224	247	325
70-74	108	94	113	107	92	131	143	145	153	155	140	153	166	208
75+	80	63	79	68	81	89	116	130	148	172	153	140	157	190
Unknown												4	9	
Age of females (proportions per 10.000 females)														
0-4	1 487	1 425	1 357	1 225	1 361	1 333	1 272	1 253	968	919	873	1 169	867	696
5-9	1 087	1 048	1 077	1 083	1 136	1 139	1 083	1 099	1 038	940	819	875	934	782
10-14	969	955	936	984	872	1 030	1 037	1 006	1 073	858	881	770	1 046	816
15-19	914	826	863	955	916	938	951	893	961	927	897	730	793	872
20-24	888	901	881	891	829	725	860	859	866	943	811	768	666	918
25-29	793	831	825	832	790	751	780	784	763	832	853	764	613	681
30-34	740	753	738	717	716	665	598	707	730	748	853	683	664	598
35-39	652	634	620	630	674	632	613	634	668	658	738	724	670	569
40-44	583	599	510	614	564	570	540	484	597	627	655	725	602	620
45-49	497	526	522	540	479	530	508	492	532	566	555	622	636	623
50-54	406	432	480	461	467	439	451	427	401	499	506	542	632	554
55-59	311	364	397	354	404	360	406	390	398	437	441	442	531	578
60-64	255	287	288	257	321	330	315	331	329	311	377	389	445	557
65-69	195	207	225	213	219	258	237	275	276	286	306	313	340	442
70-74	126	122	157	139	125	167	181	183	196	208	193	233	262	331
75+	97	90	124	105	126	132	168	183	206	240	241	247	290	362
Unknown												5	9	

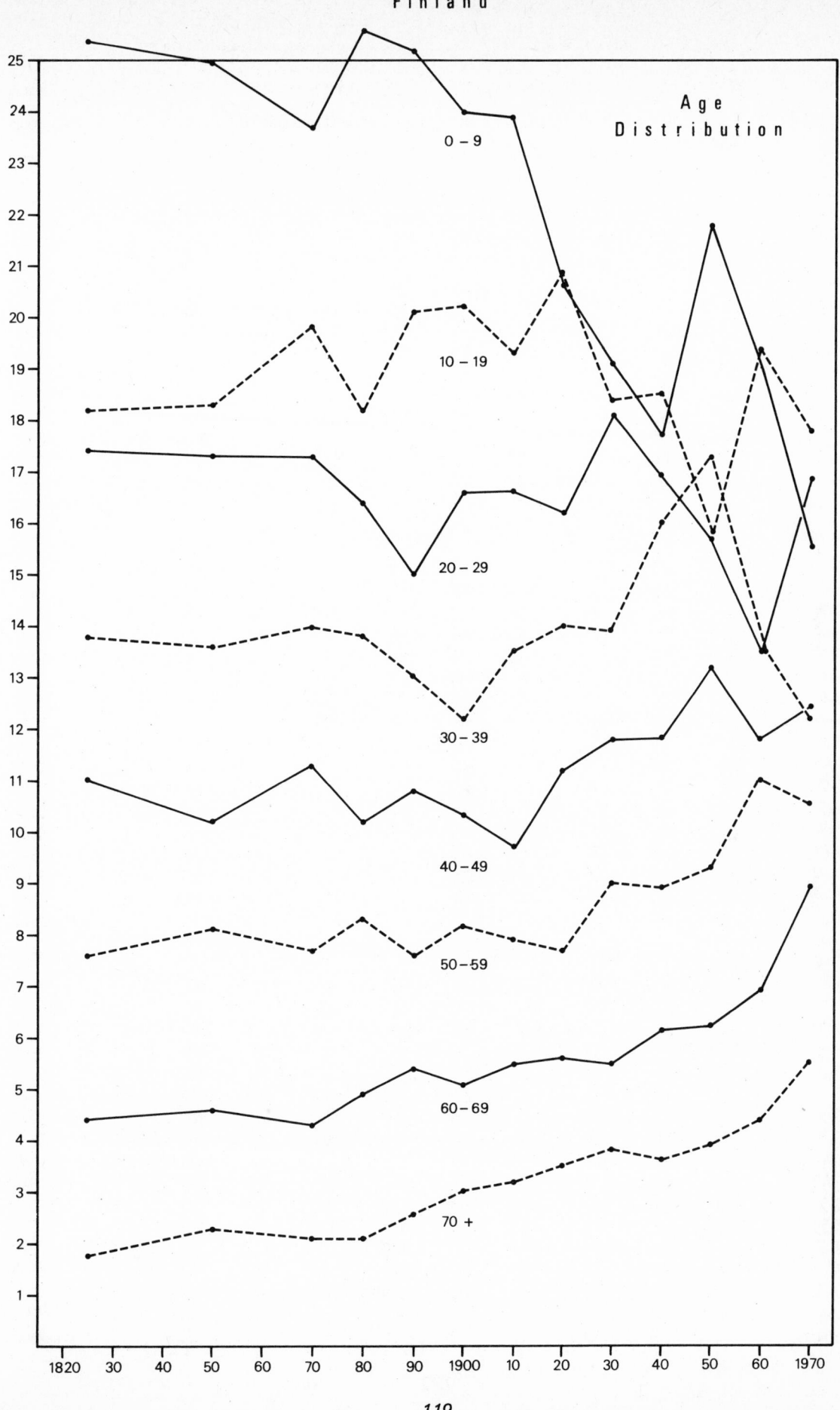

Finland

Age
Distribution

0 – 9

10 – 19

20 – 29

30 – 39

40 – 49

50 – 59

60 – 69

70 +

A g e   D i s t r i b u t i o n   a t   S u c c e s s i v e   C e n s u s e s

Census	1851	1856	1861	1866	1872	1876	1881	1886	1891	1896	Census
Age group	A g e	o f	t o t a l	p o p u l a t i o n		(proportions per 10.000 population)					Age group
0–4	928	955	966	976	928	975	923	920	871	862	0–4
5–9	921	910	875	881	905	867	910	896	880	863	5–9
10–14	879	880	865	835	870	869	840	881	872	872	10–14
15–19	880	851	869	849	844	858	867	847	876	876	15–19
20–24	832	806	822	825	879	875	904	945	860	874	20–24
25–29	801	806	784	785	721	709	682	714	766	750	25–29
30–34	756	756	741	731	704	707	697	682	712	729	30–34
35–39	718	724	709	705	688	682	678	670	667	690	35–39
40–44	659	664	661	652	645	641	640	625	630	623	40–44
45–49	586	603	615	616	608	603	596	589	602	594	45–49
50–54	578	531	537	546	547	546	546	536	537	541	50–54
55–59	439	483	455	464	495	483	483	475	471	474	55–59
60–64	367	373	415	395	416	415	421	414	422	414	60–64
65–69	278	275	294	327	305	318	332	327	333	336	65–69
70–74	195	190	194	210	232	222	235	235	245	244	70–74
75+	174	173	181	183	204	226	244	241	250	256	75+
Unknown	8	20	16	21	7	2	3	3	5	3	Unknown

Age group	A g e	o f	m a l e s	(proportions per 10.000 males)							Age group
0–4	946	975	978	990	944	990	934	930	881	873	0–4
5–9	942	929	884	893	922	880	919	900	886	873	5–9
10–14	900	903	879	848	889	886	852	890	882	884	10–14
15–19	896	860	875	855	851	866	874	848	882	885	15–19
20–24	817	757	804	813	839	847	875	922	838	858	20–24
25–29	806	792	783	786	718	710	694	731	781	758	25–29
30–34	760	765	750	735	710	713	705	690	725	739	30–34
35–39	727	738	718	712	634	691	687	675	676	700	35–39
40–44	666	679	670	659	650	649	646	631	629	630	40–44
45–49	592	610	619	618	610	602	593	591	606	592	45–49
50–54	584	536	541	547	547	543	540	531	538	538	50–54
55–59	415	481	452	463	495	474	478	474	466	470	55–59
60–64	332	352	413	396	416	411	419	406	416	405	60–64
65–69	264	253	273	322	297	314	324	320	324	325	65–69
70–74	188	181	175	195	226	215	229	230	238	234	70–74
75+	155	159	165	160	184	207	227	229	230	235	75+
Unknown	10	32	21	9	8	2	3	3	5	2	Unknown

Age group	A g e	o f	f e m a l e s	(proportions per 10.000 females)							Age group
0–4	911	935	954	962	913	961	913	910	862	852	0–4
5–9	900	892	867	870	888	855	900	891	873	853	5–9
10–14	858	858	852	821	852	852	828	871	862	861	10–14
15–19	864	843	863	843	837	850	860	846	870	868	15–19
20–24	847	854	841	837	918	902	932	968	882	889	20–24
25–29	796	819	786	784	725	708	670	696	751	743	25–29
30–34	752	747	732	726	698	701	689	674	699	719	30–34
35–39	709	711	700	697	683	674	669	665	659	680	35–39
40–44	652	650	653	646	640	633	634	618	631	616	40–44
45–49	581	596	610	615	606	605	598	588	599	596	45–49
50–54	571	526	534	545	547	549	552	542	537	544	50–54
55–59	462	485	458	464	495	492	489	477	477	477	55–59
60–64	401	393	418	394	416	419	423	422	428	422	60–64
65–69	292	297	314	333	314	323	339	335	342	347	65–69
70–74	202	199	213	226	238	229	240	240	253	253	70–74
75+	194	187	197	206	224	245	260	254	271	276	75+
Unknown	6	9	10	32	7	2	3	3	6	3	Unknown

France

Age Distribution at Successive Censuses

Census	1901	1911	1921	1926	1931	1936	1946	1954	1962	1968	Census
Age group	Age of total population (proportions per 10.000 population)										Age group
0–4	932	886	618	908	872	801	721	874	727	700	0–4
5–9	838	848	774	567	857	818	687	893	865	843	5–9
10–14	841	842	878	768	566	849	774	862	891	827	10–14
15–19	852	813	888	851	741	550	802	673	739	851	15–19
20–24	828	791	785	835	821	717	785	713	592	762	20–24
25–29	783	784	717	815	847	804	525	738	652	579	25–29
30–34	725	760	712	698	793	817	696	762	711	625	30–34
35–39	698	715	714	691	677	766	779	419	701	676	35–39
40–44	642	655	710	669	651	641	782	694	606	670	40–44
45–49	582	616	670	659	626	615	711	705	476	622	45–49
50–54	544	553	602	606	604	584	590	685	630	397	50–54
55–59	492	481	545	534	547	555	548	586	605	567	55–59
60–64	425	421	465	465	464	485	499	485	550	538	60–64
65–69	332	346	363	374	382	389	432	427	432	476	65–69
70–74	252	250	} 540	} 539	277	} 595	327	343	336	360	70–74
75+	236	240			276		334	443	488	507	75+
Unknown			19	21		14	8				Unknown

Age group	Age of males (proportions per 10.000 males)										Age group
0–4	947	907	657	954	913	838	774	933	760	734	0–4
5–9	850	867	815	597	898	856	730	954	909	881	5–9
10–14	857	862	927	806	595	892	824	921	931	865	10–14
15–19	864	826	938	893	773	578	839	706	776	888	15–19
20–24	827	796	762	858	863	748	790	729	631	803	20–24
25–29	793	790	667	842	902	844	546	779	690	614	25–29
30–34	729	769	679	657	815	864	723	793	744	658	30–34
35–39	706	726	690	659	631	784	817	432	727	706	35–39
40–44	649	658	713	645	615	595	823	715	620	693	40–44
45–49	587	618	689	653	593	575	718	726	482	632	45–49
50–54	529	548	613	612	588	548	533	703	636	395	50–54
55–59	486	473	550	530	538	531	496	557	601	560	55–59
60–64	413	396	458	455	446	467	444	412	527	517	60–64
65–69	318	327	349	353	358	363	387	362	360	435	65–69
70–74	236	229	} 474	} 466	249	} 504	288	277	263	285	70–74
75+	209	205			223		259	338	344	335	75+
Unknown			19	20		12	8				Unknown

Age group	Age of females (proportions per 10.000 females)										Age group
0–4	918	865	583	866	833	767	674	819	696	669	0–4
5–9	825	830	736	538	819	784	648	837	823	807	5–9
10–14	826	822	833	734	538	810	730	808	853	792	10–14
15–19	840	800	843	812	711	524	770	642	704	815	15–19
20–24	828	786	805	814	781	688	780	698	555	722	20–24
25–29	774	778	762	790	796	767	505	700	615	545	25–29
30–34	720	751	743	735	772	774	672	734	681	594	30–34
35–39	690	704	735	721	719	749	744	406	676	647	35–39
40–44	635	652	707	692	684	684	744	675	592	649	40–44
45–49	578	614	654	665	657	651	705	685	470	612	45–49
50–54	557	556	591	600	619	617	643	668	625	398	50–54
55–59	497	489	541	538	555	577	595	613	609	574	55–59
60–64	436	444	471	474	481	502	548	551	572	559	60–64
65–69	346	364	377	393	405	413	472	488	500	514	65–69
70–74	267	271	} 600	} 605	304	} 678	363	404	405	431	70–74
75+	263	274			325		401	539	625	672	75+
Unknown			19	23		15	7				Unknown

France

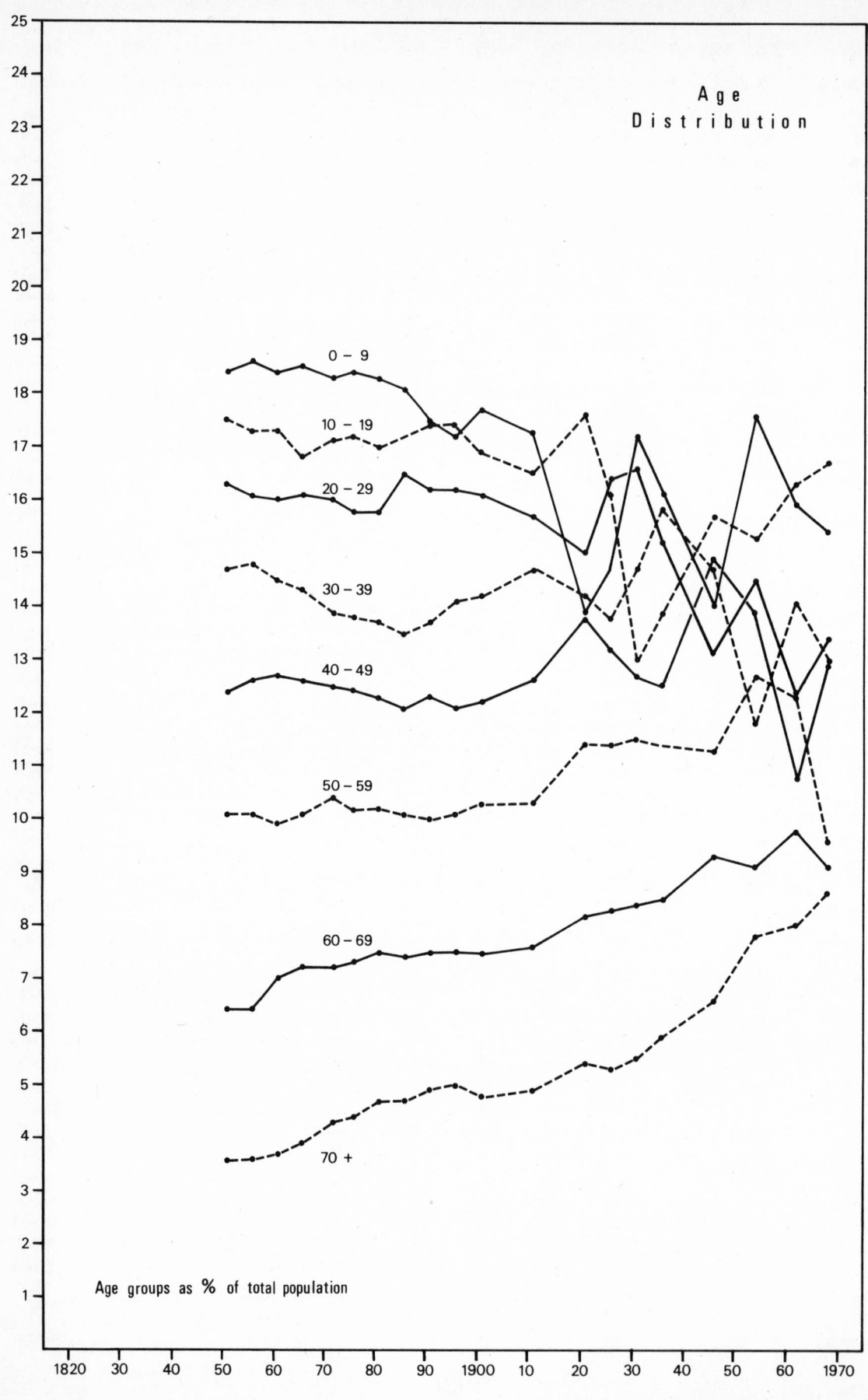

Age
Distribution

0 – 9

10 – 19

20 – 29

30 – 39

40 – 49

50 – 59

60 – 69

70 +

Age groups as % of total population

1820 30 40 50 60 70 80 90 1900 10 20 30 40 50 60 1970

Germany

Age Distribution at Successive Censuses [a]

Census	1871	1880	1885	1890	1900	1910	1925	1933	1939	1950	1961	1970	Census
Age group	Age of total population						(proportions per 10.000 population)						Age group
0–4	1 265	1 364	1 287	1 301	1 308	1 200	941	658	742	702	797	777	0–4
5–9	1 127	1 143	1 184	1 119	1 137	1 139	639	818	698	749	697	823	5–9
10–14	1 040	1 034	1 066	1 095	1 036	1 066	996	876	771	904	676	718	10–14
15–19	912	934	947	972	944	968	1 048	627	864	728	656	659	15–19
20–24	864	856	847	861	905	864	985	943	554	750	847	614	20–24
25–29	783	733	759	758	793	774	850	947	882	744	693	708	25–29
30–34	704	682	660	685	701	743	734	886	907	519	691	817	30–34
35–39	629	619	608	591	612	647	686	749	854	756	677	648	35–39
40–44	547	565	561	544	548	565	626	660	729	808	519	647	40–44
45–49	519	472	497	494	462	434	616	612	621	774	653	629	45–49
50–54	472	422	418	433	416	423	518	554	570	657	728	416	50–54
55–59	364	376	354	350	360	340	437	523	502	530	685	619	55–59
60–64	307	315	312	288	292	284	347	410	463	451	568	608	60–64
65–69	214	218	235	232	213	221	259	316	351	370	428	521	65–69
70–74	142	138	147	156	148	151	169	219	248	289	318	374	70–74
75+	104	116	119	122	123	131	147	202	243	269	361	422	75+
Unknown	7	13								6			Unknown
Age group	Age of males						(proportions per 10.000 males)						Age group
0–4	1 292	1 394	1 318	1 331	1 333	1 224	988	689	776	768	868	837	0–4
5–9	1 148	1 164	1 210	1 143	1 156	1 159	670	855	728	816	759	886	5–9
10–14	1 064	1 056	1 088	1 119	1 055	1 083	1 038	917	801	983	737	774	10–14
15–19	919	947	961	987	961	983	1 088	653	899	792	713	708	15–19
20–24	854	857	850	869	916	876	1 015	973	578	794	923	660	20–24
25–29	767	730	757	760	802	783	817	973	910	680	758	771	25–29
30–34	701	677	659	686	707	751	671	903	934	471	741	896	30–34
35–39	625	616	603	590	616	654	651	695	875	698	623	709	35–39
40–44	544	559	555	535	544	566	614	606	688	779	464	675	40–44
45–49	513	468	488	485	454	480	616	582	562	789	592	562	45–49
50–54	467	408	408	418	398	409	526	541	531	636	680	366	50–54
55–59	358	363	338	336	342	322	439	519	479	483	671	545	55–59
60–64	297	302	296	270	272	262	341	408	448	421	526	541	60–64
65–69	208	208	223	216	196	200	245	307	340	354	359	468	65–69
70–74	137	131	138	145	129	134	155	206	235	282	269	297	70–74
75+	98	107	109	110	117	113	126	176	215	256	312	305	75+
Unknown	8	13								6			Unknown
Age group	Age of females						(proportions per 10.000 females)						Age group
0–4	1 239	1 335	1 257	1 271	1 283	1 176	896	628	710	644	733	723	0–4
5–9	1 106	1 123	1 159	1 096	1 117	1 120	609	784	670	690	641	766	5–9
10–14	1 017	1 012	1 044	1 071	1 017	1 049	956	838	742	835	622	666	10–14
15–19	906	922	934	957	927	954	1 011	603	831	672	605	614	15–19
20–24	873	856	844	854	894	852	958	915	531	712	780	573	20–24
25–29	799	736	760	755	784	765	881	922	855	799	636	650	25–29
30–34	707	687	661	685	695	735	792	871	882	562	647	745	30–34
35–39	632	621	613	592	608	640	720	801	835	807	724	592	35–39
40–44	550	571	567	553	551	563	638	711	768	834	568	622	40–44
45–49	524	477	504	503	470	488	617	641	677	761	707	689	45–49
50–54	477	435	429	447	433	436	511	567	607	675	771	462	50–54
55–59	370	388	369	363	378	357	435	526	524	571	698	686	55–59
60–64	316	327	328	305	311	307	353	412	478	477	606	668	60–64
65–69	221	227	247	247	229	241	272	324	361	383	489	571	65–69
70–74	147	145	156	167	156	167	183	231	260	296	362	444	70–74
75+	109	124	129	134	148	149	167	226	270	280	405	529	75+
Unknown	6	14								6			Unknown

a) age groups 1871–1910: 0–4 = 0 – 4 years and 11 months, etc.

Germany

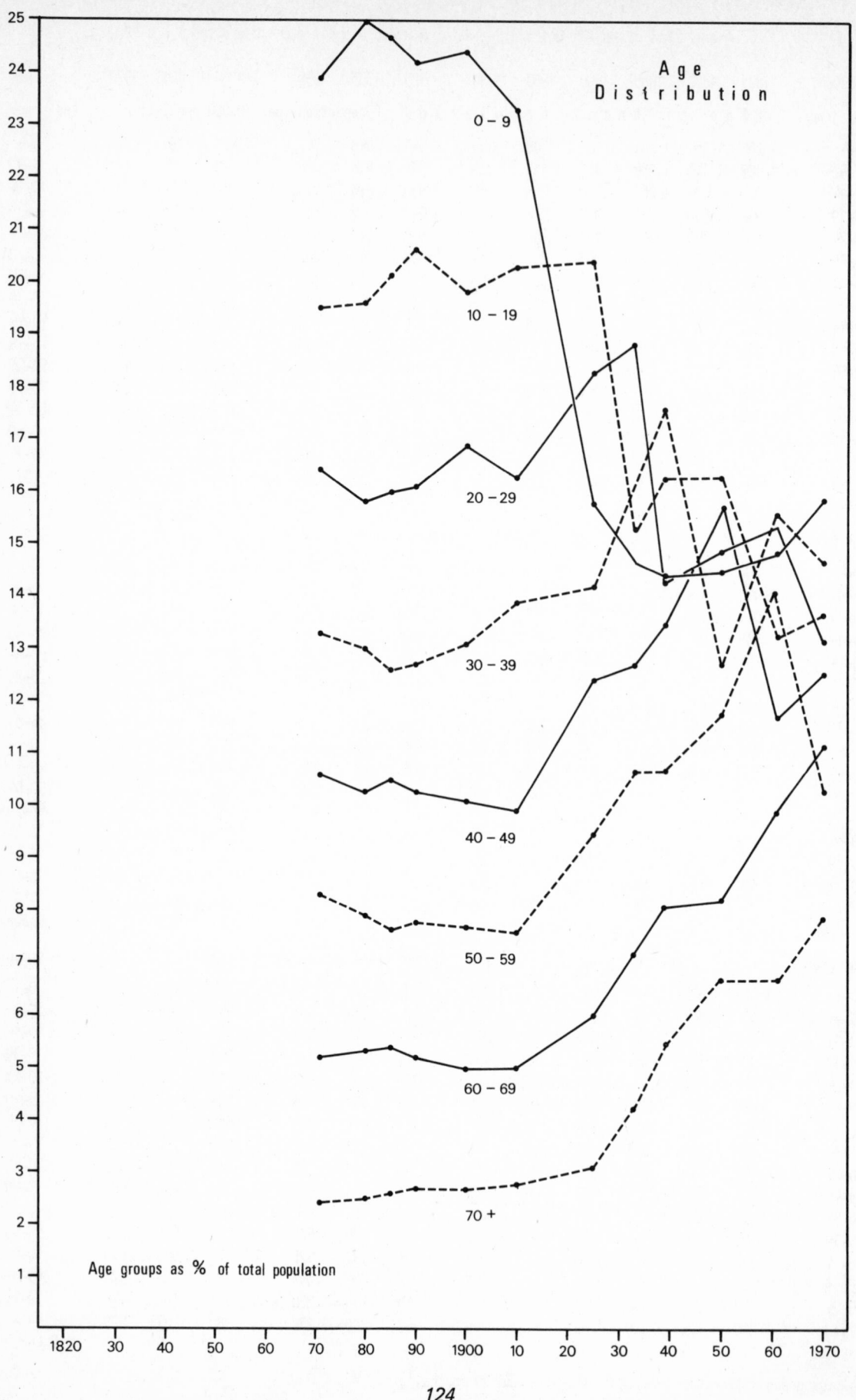

Age Distribution

Age groups as % of total population

Ireland [a)]

Age Distribution at Successive Censuses

Census	1861	1871	1881	1881	1901	1911	1926	1936	1946	1951	1961	1966	1971	Census
Age group	Age of total population						(proportions per 10.000 population)							Age group
0–4	1 188	1 205	1 116	988	968	978	968	904	997	1 057	1 067	1 095	1 060	0–4
5–9	1 036	1 176	1 219	1 095	1 009	988	958	907	900	949	1 021	1 037	1 064	5–9
10–14	1 028	1 171	1 202	1 196	1 044	966	994	953	888	881	1 025	990	1 002	10–14
15–19	1 173	967	1 084	1 192	1 083	966	963	904	851	815	830	899	899	15–19
20–24	1 071	839	919	937	1 005	857	808	857	783	683	561	642	723	20–24
25–29	702	687	624	661	802	753	725	730	705	670	516	518	581	25–29
30–34	590	654	577	580	644	694	617	617	693	647	542	508	508	30–34
35–39	1 041 }	994 }	1 068 }	1 018 }	1 062 }	1 212 }	591	648	849	679	592	535	501	35–39
40–44							569	549	560	609	604	566	513	40–44
45–49	959 }	893 }	843 }	969 }	926 }	889 }	568	1 042 }	586	544	620	577	538	45–49
50–54							548 }		465	551	557	572	534	50–54
55–59	750 }	813 }	721 }	714 }	807 }	646 }	423	922 }	456	435	483	510	520	55–59
60–64							354 }		403	412	465	429	450	60–64
65–69	308 }	413 }	416 }	410 }	434 }	750 }	341	670 }	388	363	367	396	375	65–69
70–74							277 }		338	338	329	312	332	70–74
75+	147	180	206	236	216	301	297	296	338	367	421	412	400	75+
Unknwon	7	8	5	4										Unknown

Age group	1861	1871	1881	1881	1901	1911	1926	1936	1946	1951	1961	1966	1971	Age group
	Age of males						(proportions per 10.000 males)							
0–4	1 223	1 241	1 144	1 007	982	981	970	897	1 007	1 064	1 083	1 113	1 082	0–4
5–9	1 066	1 210	1 248	1 116	1 023	991	961	897	904	952	1 038	1 052	1 082	5–9
10–14	1 070	1 219	1 244	1 223	1 066	970	1 001	945	892	881	1 047	1 005	1 017	10–14
15–19	1 176	965	1 083	1 211	1 087	978	969	908	855	835	850	920	914	15–19
20–24	1 080	819	930	981	1 016	889	826	886	790	699	568	654	735	20–24
25–29	717	668	614	647	797	738	708	745	697	661	510	518	587	25–29
30–34	583	642	553	573	657	701	614	619	694	640	531	509	514	30–34
35–39	984 }	981 }	1 031 }	964 }	1 047 }	1 248 }	580	637	652	679	576	528	505	35–39
40–44							571	551	564	624	599	559	511	40–44
45–49	933 }	855 }	831 }	935 }	881 }	899 }	577 }	1 047 }	582	547	629	577	532	45–49
50–54							568 }		468	550	577	582	535	50–54
55–59	726 }	799 }	689 }	706 }	787 }	630 }	445 }	942 }	453	432	484	523	524	55–59
60–64							356 }		401	407	455	425	455	60–64
65–69	296 }	420 }	420 }	399 }	444 }	687 }	342 }	663 }	391	359	361	380	364	65–69
70–74							249 }		334	326	311	292	298	70–74
75+	137	172	207	233	213	288	263	263	316	344	382	363	345	75+
Unknown	9	9	6	4										Unknown

Age group	1861	1871	1881	1881	1901	1911	1926	1936	1946	1951	1961	1966	1971	Age group
	Age of females						(proportions per 10.000 females)							
0–4	1 153	1 169	1 088	969	954	976	966	911	988	1 050	1 051	1 078	1 038	0–4
5–9	1 007	1 143	1 191	1 075	995	984	955	919	996	946	1 004	1 021	1 046	5–9
10–14	987	1 124	1 160	1 170	1 022	961	988	960	883	882	1 002	974	988	10–14
15–19	1 170	970	1 086	1 173	1 080	954	957	899	847	794	810	878	883	15–19
20–24	1 062	859	908	893	995	824	790	828	775	666	553	631	710	20–24
25–29	688	705	633	674	806	768	742	715	713	680	521	518	575	25–29
30–34	597	667	601	587	631	687	620	616	691	654	553	508	503	30–34
35–39	1 096 }	1 006 }	1 103 }	1 071 }	1 078 }	1 174 }	603	660	646	678	608	542	497	35–39
40–44							567	547	557	594	610	574	515	40–44
45–49	985 }	928 }	855 }	1 002 }	970 }	880 }	559 }	1 037 }	589	540	611	578	544	45–49
50–54							526 }		463	551	538	562	533	50–54
55–59	774 }	827 }	754 }	723 }	827 }	663 }	400 }	902 }	459	439	482	497	515	55–59
60–64							351 }		406	418	475	434	445	60–64
65–69	319 }	407 }	412 }	421 }	423 }	815 }	339 }	677 }	384	367	373	412	386	65–69
70–74							306 }		342	351	347	333	367	70–74
75+	157	189	205	238	219	314	332	329	361	392	462	460	456	75+
Unknown	5	6	4	4										Unknown

a) 1861–1911: territory of later Republic

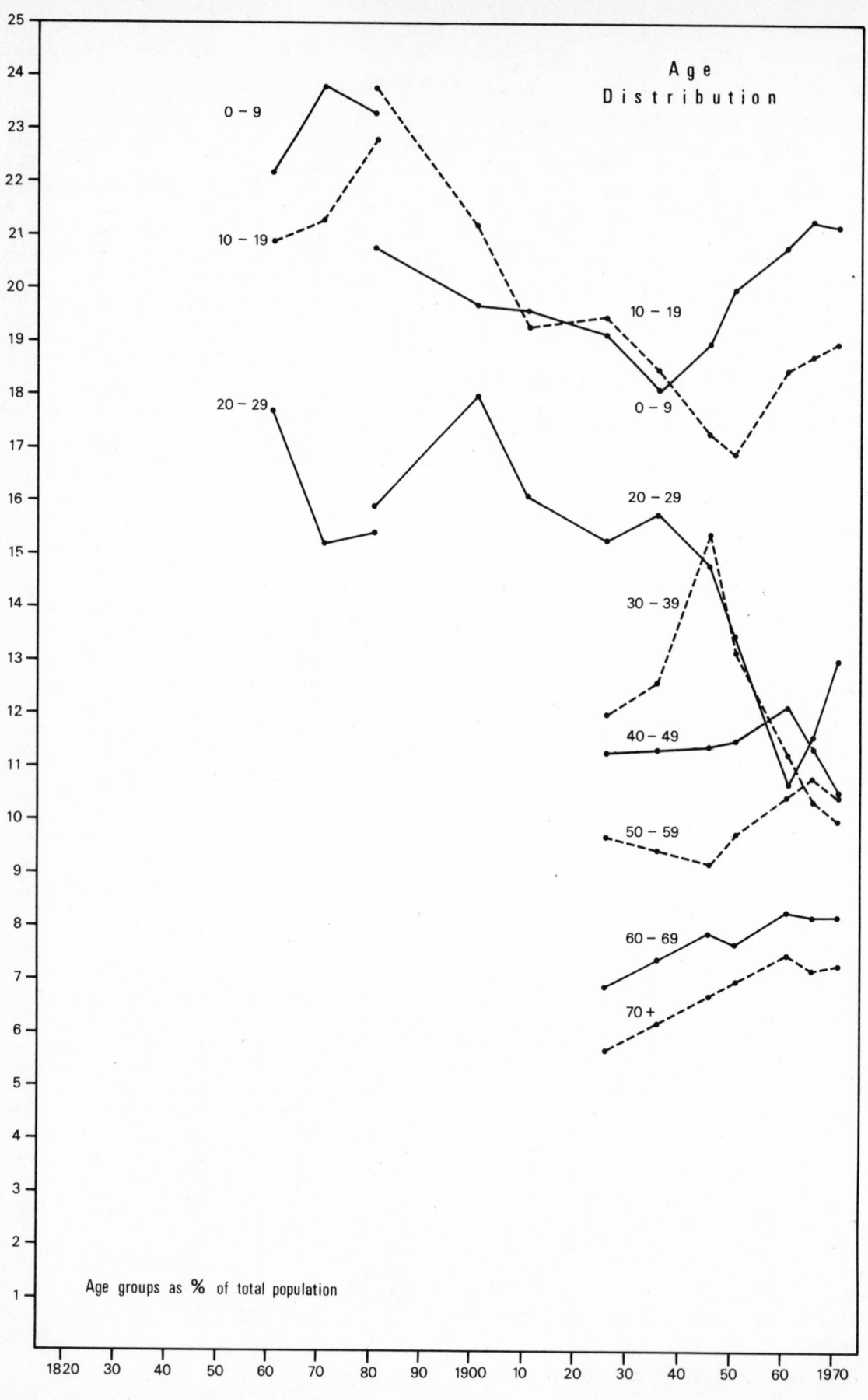

Age
Distribution

Age groups as % of total population

Italy

Age Distribution at Successive Censuses

Census	1861	1871	1881	1901	1911	1921	1931	1936	1951	1961	1971	Census
Age group	Age	of	total	population			(proportions per 10.000 population)					Age group
0–4	1 359	1 155	1 209	1 296	1 244	935	1 111	1 014	919	841	821	0–4
5–9	1 077	1 088	1 057	1 097	1 082	1 067	1 088	1 016	821	800	860	5–9
10–14	983	1 003	952	1 043	1 058	1 103	774	1 032	893	850	781	10–14
15–19	936	902	926	1 102	932	985	983	724	849	736	702	15–19
20–24	849	875	860	641	840	877	929	919	855	773	740	20–24
25–29	853	773	748	679	703	739	781	856	827	720	635	25–29
30–34	654	718	723	631	626	679	697	725	597	749	705	30–34
35–39	777	621	624	596	562	608	609	649	719	743	672	35–39
40–44	511	632	631	560	520	554	569	566	709	540	687	40–44
45–49	557	516	485	504	498	504	515	523	608	654	671	45–49
50–54	386	516	514	479	474	448	458	471	530	637	480	50–54
55–59	403	328	376	412	402	410	404	409	450	532	559	55–59
60–64	237	363	383	353	368	369	349	352	398	447	543	60–64
65–69	204	208	206	258	276	275	299	286	325	356	432	65–69
70–74	103	165	173	184	196	207	218	225	238	282	319	70–74
75+	111	138	134	165	175	189	213	232	263	336	394	75+
Unknown					35	53	3	1				Unknown

Age group			Age	of	males	(proportions per 10.000 males)						Age group
0–4	1 372	1 166	1 228	1 329	1 291	968	1 156	1 051	966	890	866	0–4
5–9	1 091	1 101	1 073	1 122	1 123	1 101	1 131	1 048	862	843	906	5–9
10–14	994	1 016	970	1 061	1 094	1 138	804	1 063	931	899	824	10–14
15–19	880	873	912	1 096	916	1 003	1 009	746	876	764	730	15–19
20–24	839	868	851	637	818	869	949	943	877	786	765	20–24
25–29	837	763	736	663	664	698	777	871	822	717	643	25–29
30–34	660	711	711	616	601	644	671	727	585	750	712	30–34
35–39	780	620	621	589	547	584	566	627	713	741	677	35–39
40–44	524	629	626	553	519	546	532	527	711	530	693	40–44
45–49	552	519	485	501	497	506	493	488	605	649	664	45–49
50–54	402	520	507	471	473	449	449	449	511	638	465	50–54
55–59	398	333	378	411	405	414	402	399	411	523	544	55–59
60–64	248	362	380	346	367	367	345	346	364	420	525	60–64
65–69	202	214	211	256	280	276	296	279	300	313	402	65–69
70–74	108	167	174	184	196	206	214	219	224	246	277	70–74
75+	113	140	137	165	175	186	203	217	241	291	307	75+
Unknown					34	45	3	1				Unknown

Age group			Age	of	females	(proportions per 10.000 females)						Age group
0–4	1 347	1 145	1 190	1 263	1 199	902	1 067	979	873	795	778	0–4
5–9	1 063	1 076	1 042	1 072	1 042	1 033	1 048	985	781	759	816	5–9
10–14	971	990	935	1 026	1 024	1 069	744	1 002	856	804	741	10–14
15–19	992	931	940	1 108	948	967	957	703	823	710	675	15–19
20–24	858	882	869	645	862	885	910	895	834	760	716	20–24
25–29	869	784	760	695	741	779	784	841	831	722	627	25–29
30–34	648	725	734	646	650	714	722	723	609	748	699	30–34
35–39	774	622	627	602	577	631	651	671	725	754	667	35–39
40–44	497	634	636	568	536	561	605	604	708	550	681	40–44
45–49	562	513	486	507	499	502	538	556	610	658	678	45–49
50–54	370	512	520	488	475	447	466	493	548	637	494	50–54
55–59	408	322	374	413	398	406	407	418	487	540	573	55–59
60–64	227	364	386	360	369	370	353	358	430	472	560	60–64
65–69	207	201	200	259	271	274	301	293	349	396	460	65–69
70–74	98	163	172	185	197	208	222	231	250	316	360	70–74
75+	109	136	131	164	175	192	222	247	284	377	476	75+
Unknown				1	36	60	3	1				Unknown

Italy

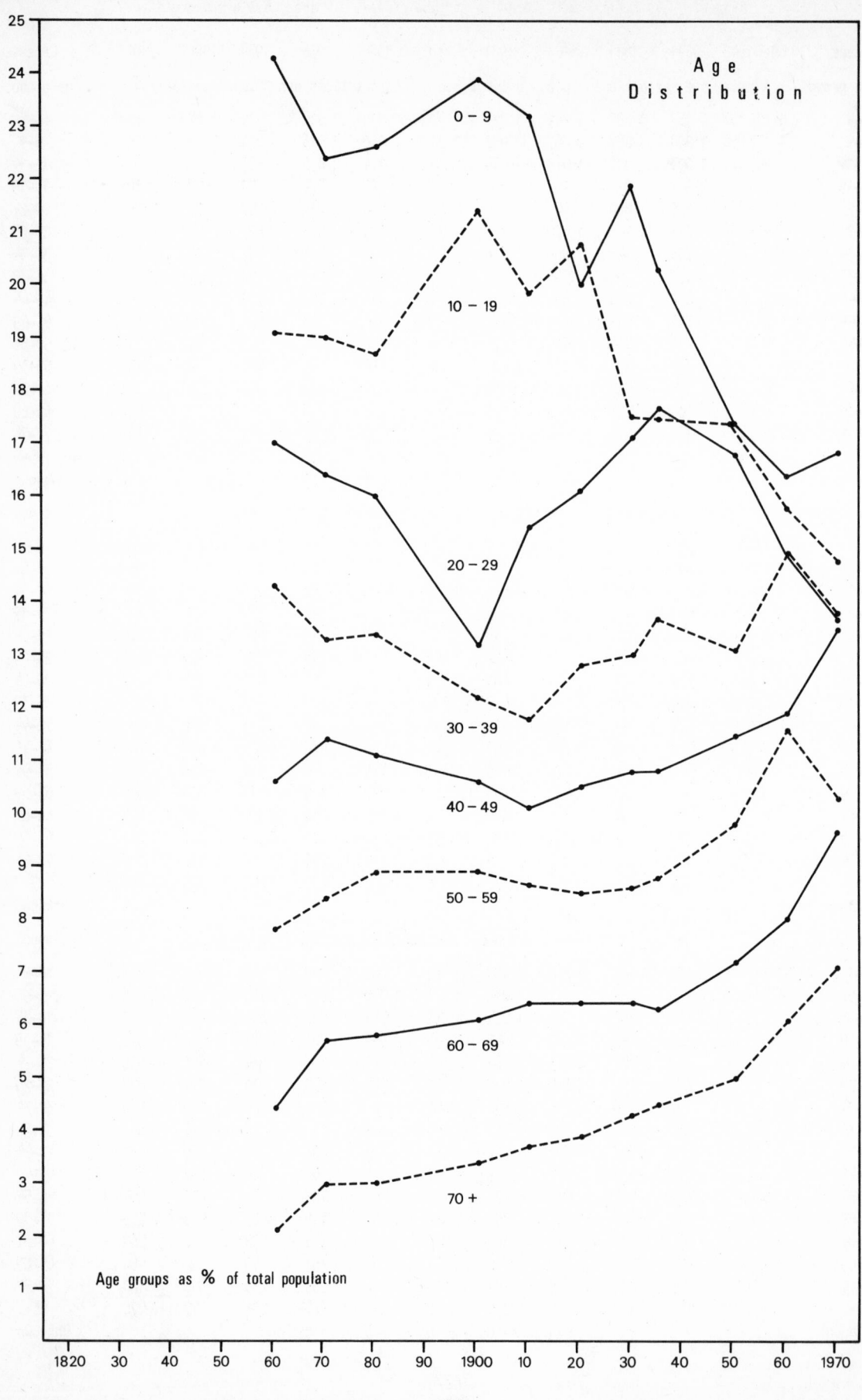

Age
Distribution

0 - 9

10 - 19

20 - 29

30 - 39

40 - 49

50 - 59

60 - 69

70 +

Age groups as % of total population

Netherlands

Age Distribution at Successive Censuses

Census	1830	1840	1849	1859	1869	1879	1889	1899	1909	1920	1930	1947	1960	1970	Census
Age group	Age	of	total	population			(proportions per 10.000 population)								Age group
0-4	1 293	1 322	1 127	1 213	1 303	1 369	1 314	1 299	1 259	1 132	1 054	1 212	1 087	902	0-4
5-9	1 197	1 090	1 133	1 032	1 091	1 123	1 131	1 129	1 141	1 083	1 058	878	963	930	5-9
10-14	1 936	2 039	1 077	951	944	1 020	1 077	1 054	1 053	1 045	953	837	1 018	886	10-14
15-19			928	969	916	915	943	953	949	982	938	847	791	848	15-19
20-24	829	887	900	911	790	780	833	875	848	872	894	833	694	918	20-24
25-29	797	756	843	773	735	731	732	750	756	778	821	762	673	707	25-29
30-34	714	664	714	722	723	629	623	670	704	692	728	727	655	629	30-34
35-39	632	654	630	690	632	631	590	595	613	630	650	690	670	590	35-39
40-44	550	572	540	583	585	582	506	503	545	583	574	645	573	579	40-44
45-49	430	483	522	504	548	495	501	471	478	508	519	568	576	572	45-49
50-54			456	416	458	451	455	398	396	436	471	503	543	504	50-54
55-59	1 061	1 014	359	385	379	410	373	379	359	378	398	426	482	478	55-59
60-64			295	309	290	319	321	324	286	291	324	362	408	435	60-64
65-69			199	225	244	238	265	242	249	235	260	292	329	370	65-69
70-74	533	518	136	144	164	152	175	176	183	166	172	212	249	282	70-74
75+			139	119	143	155	161	182	180	187	188	206	289	370	75+
Unknown	26	2	1	4	4	1	1								Unknown

Age group			Age	of	males		(proportions per 10.000 males)								Age group
0-4	1 337	1 359	1 158	1 240	1 329	1 393	1 342	1 327	1 285	1 161	1 082	1 250	1 118	921	0-4
5-9	1 238	1 125	1 168	1 109	1 118	1 137	1 148	1 149	1 165	1 105	1 083	901	992	955	5-9
10-14	1 983	2 094	1 109	975	965	1 035	1 093	1 075	1 073	1 064	975	860	1 047	910	10-14
15-19			948	991	933	932	954	967	964	998	949	866	811	869	15-19
20-24	819	887	900	914	786	784	830	871	848	873	889	836	708	944	20-24
25-29	796	747	848	768	776	728	728	737	747	771	812	758	682	738	25-29
30-34	708	657	716	720	717	624	622	661	695	684	717	720	654	658	30-34
35-39	607	655	627	692	631	631	591	594	605	624	640	679	662	607	35-39
40-44	526	569	535	585	587	583	506	505	539	576	568	633	566	581	40-44
45-49	420	463	515	497	552	495	502	472	477	501	514	554	565	561	45-49
50-54			446	407	456	448	452	394	395	430	466	492	528	492	50-54
55-59	1 025	965	335	371	367	403	366	375	355	373	392	418	465	460	55-59
60-64			269	293	278	308	311	315	278	285	318	354	389	408	60-64
65-70			181	202	227	221	252	231	240	227	253	284	311	335	65-70
70-74	495	474	122	127	152	141	163	164	173	157	167	205	235	246	70-74
75+			123	104	123	137	141	163	162	170	175	191	267	315	75+
Unknown	45	1	1	4	4	1									Unknown

Age group			Age	of	females		(proportions per 10.000 males)								Age group
0-4	1 251	1 286	1 098	1 187	1 278	1 345	1 287	1 271	1 232	1 104	1 025	1 174	1 056	884	0-4
5-9	1 057	1 056	1 099	1 056	1 065	1 109	1 115	1 110	1 118	1 062	1 033	856	934	905	5-9
10-14	1 894	1 986	1 047	927	923	1 005	1 060	1 034	1 033	1 026	932	815	990	862	10-14
15-19			909	947	899	899	933	939	935	966	927	829	771	827	15-19
20-24	840	887	900	909	795	775	835	878	848	871	899	830	679	891	20-24
24-29	798	765	839	777	794	734	736	763	764	786	830	765	664	676	24-29
30-34	720	670	713	725	729	635	625	678	714	700	738	734	657	600	30-34
35-39	656	652	633	687	632	630	589	595	622	637	659	702	679	573	35-39
40-44	573	574	544	581	583	582	506	501	550	589	580	658	579	577	40-44
45-49	440	503	529	511	545	496	500	469	480	515	524	582	588	583	45-49
50-54			465	424	461	454	458	402	398	441	476	513	557	516	50-54
55-59	1 094	1 062	382	399	391	416	380	383	363	384	404	434	499	497	55-59
60-64			321	325	303	330	331	333	293	297	330	369	428	463	60-64
65-69			217	247	261	254	278	254	258	244	266	299	347	404	65-69
70-74	570	560	149	161	175	163	186	187	193	175	177	220	262	317	70-74
75+			155	134	163	172	180	202	198	203	202	220	310	425	75+
Unknown	7		1	4	5	1	1								Unknown

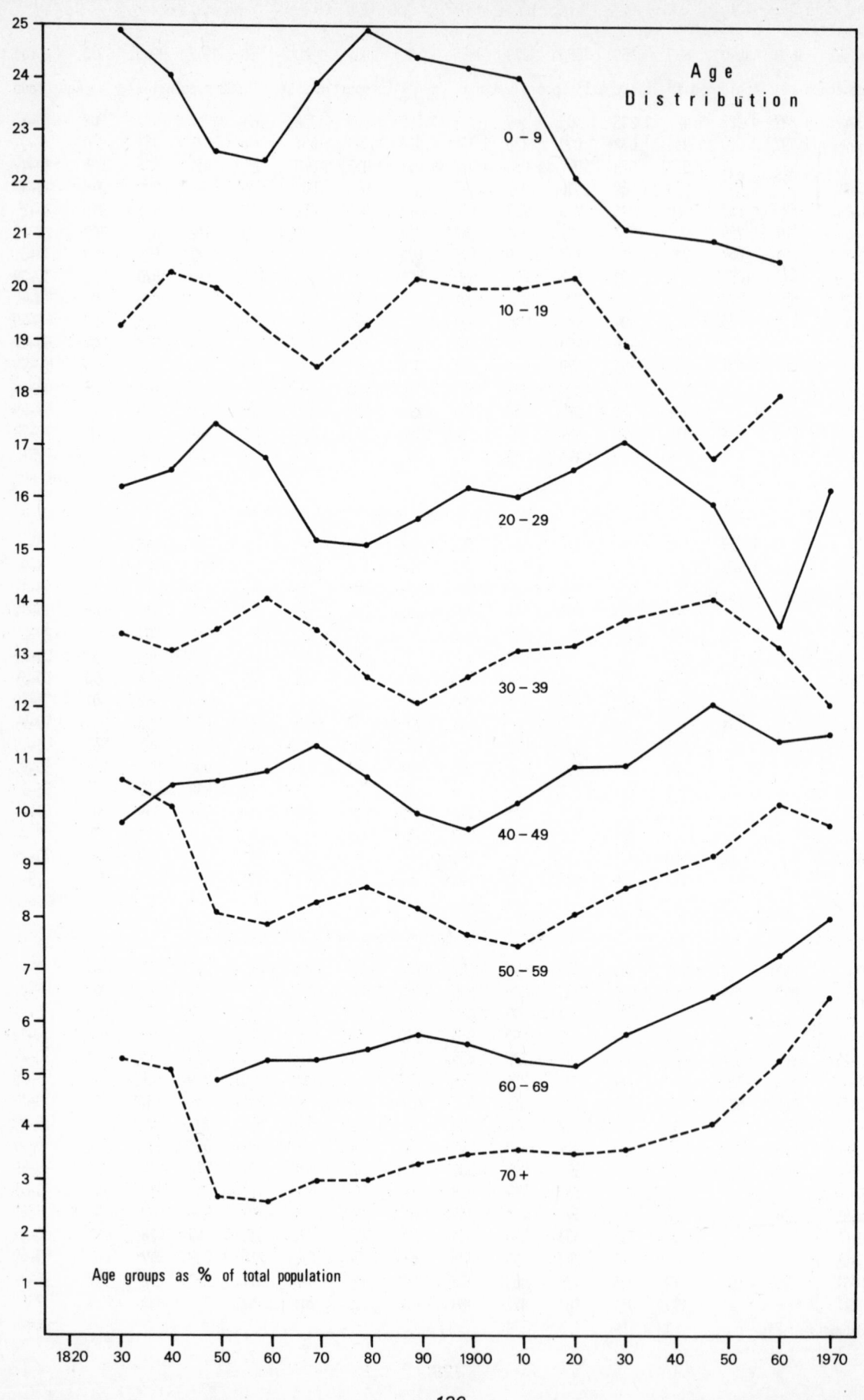

Age
Distribution

0 - 9

10 - 19

20 - 29

30 - 39

40 - 49

50 - 59

60 - 69

70 +

Age groups as % of total population

1820 30 40 50 60 70 80 90 1900 10 20 30 40 50 60 1970

Age Distribution at Successive Censuses

Age of total population (proportions per 10.000 population)

Census / Age group	1801	1865	1875	1890	1900	1910	1920	1930	1946	1950	1960	1970
0-4	2 473	1 354	2 353	1 315	1 294	1 200	1 107	844	934	974	858	847
5-9		1 193		1 179	1 176	1 188	1 061	992	689	815	843	806
10-14	1 822	1 057	2 091	1 089	1 085	1 140	1 039	1 013	642	651	883	791
15-19		944		922	958	980	1 010	960	752	623	736	778
20-24	1 550	812	1 595	749	821	764	910	874	835	700	584	806
25-29		697		681	636	653	772	810	863	798	553	670
30-34	1 288	650	1 150	622	589	622	647	760	809	803	622	532
35-39		657		577	554	548	564	664	762	763	714	504
40-44	1 148	555	1 048	503	509	490	536	567	705	712	717	565
45-49		516		457	472	465	464	491	658	659	678	643
50-54	830	361	867	396	415	434	408	465	572	608	627	641
55-59		306		379	356	389	378	392	470	512	568	594
60-64	535	272	495	362	294	326	333	333	394	416	506	530
65-69		251		308	274	270	284	290	328	334	406	454
70-74	354	176	401	222	229	200	211	231	263	274	302	366
75+		196		232	288	307	272	307	341	356	404	474
Unknown				9		24	3	7	11	1		

Age of males (proportions per 10.000 males)

Census / Age group	1801	1865	1875	1890	1900	1910	1920	1930	1946	1950	1960	1970
0-4	2 590	1 400	2 442	1 403	1 370	1 286	1 161	884	972	1 009	882	875
5-9		1 237		1 256	1 250	1 270	1 112	1 035	712	843	868	833
10-14	1 907	1 094	2 166	1 157	1 153	1 215	1 088	1 058	664	668	910	813
15-19		964		945	990	1 013	1 047	1 000	747	640	756	801
20-24	1 512	799	1 547	700	793	725	917	889	859	722	598	837
25-29		673		621	652	602	773	803	879	818	564	695
30-34	1 271	644	1 119	583	556	590	633	755	825	814	636	543
35-39		655		548	517	525	542	664	770	775	724	513
40-44	1 115	561	1 037	484	487	466	521	552	697	714	720	575
45-49		509		445	451	438	452	469	646	647	683	649
50-54	815	352	857	385	398	415	388	449	562	593	621	639
55-59		294		379	346	373	353	377	451	498	549	587
60-64	490	259	475	357	284	316	312	312	368	393	481	509
65-70		232		304	267	259	264	266	305	307	383	417
70-74	300	162	357	215	220	190	195	210	241	251	274	322
75+		165		210	266	284	241	269	290	308	350	391
Unknown				10		35	3	7	11	1		

Age of females (proportions per 10.000 females)

Census / Age group	1801	1865	1875	1890	1900	1910	1920	1930	1946	1950	1960	1970
0-4	2 366	1 310	2 267	1 233	1 225	1 121	1 056	806	898	940	835	819
5-9		1 151		1 107	1 108	1 114	1 014	950	666	787	818	780
10-14	1 743	1 021	2 020	1 026	1 022	1 072	993	969	620	633	856	769
15-19		926		900	929	950	975	922	705	607	715	755
20-24	1 586	825	1 641	794	847	799	903	860	811	678	569	776
25-29		721		737	717	700	771	816	847	779	542	647
30-34	1 303	656	1 179	658	619	651	661	766	794	793	609	520
35-39		659		604	588	569	586	665	755	752	704	495
40-44	1 179	550	1 059	521	529	512	550	580	712	711	713	554
45-49		524		468	491	490	476	512	669	671	674	636
50-54	843	369	876	405	430	452	428	480	582	623	632	643
55-59		317		380	365	403	401	406	488	526	586	600
60-64	576	285	514	366	304	335	352	353	419	439	530	550
65-69		270		312	281	281	304	314	350	360	429	491
70-74	404	189	443	229	237	209	227	251	284	297	330	410
75+		226		252	308	327	302	343	390	403	459	556
Unknown				8		14	3	7	11	1		

Norway

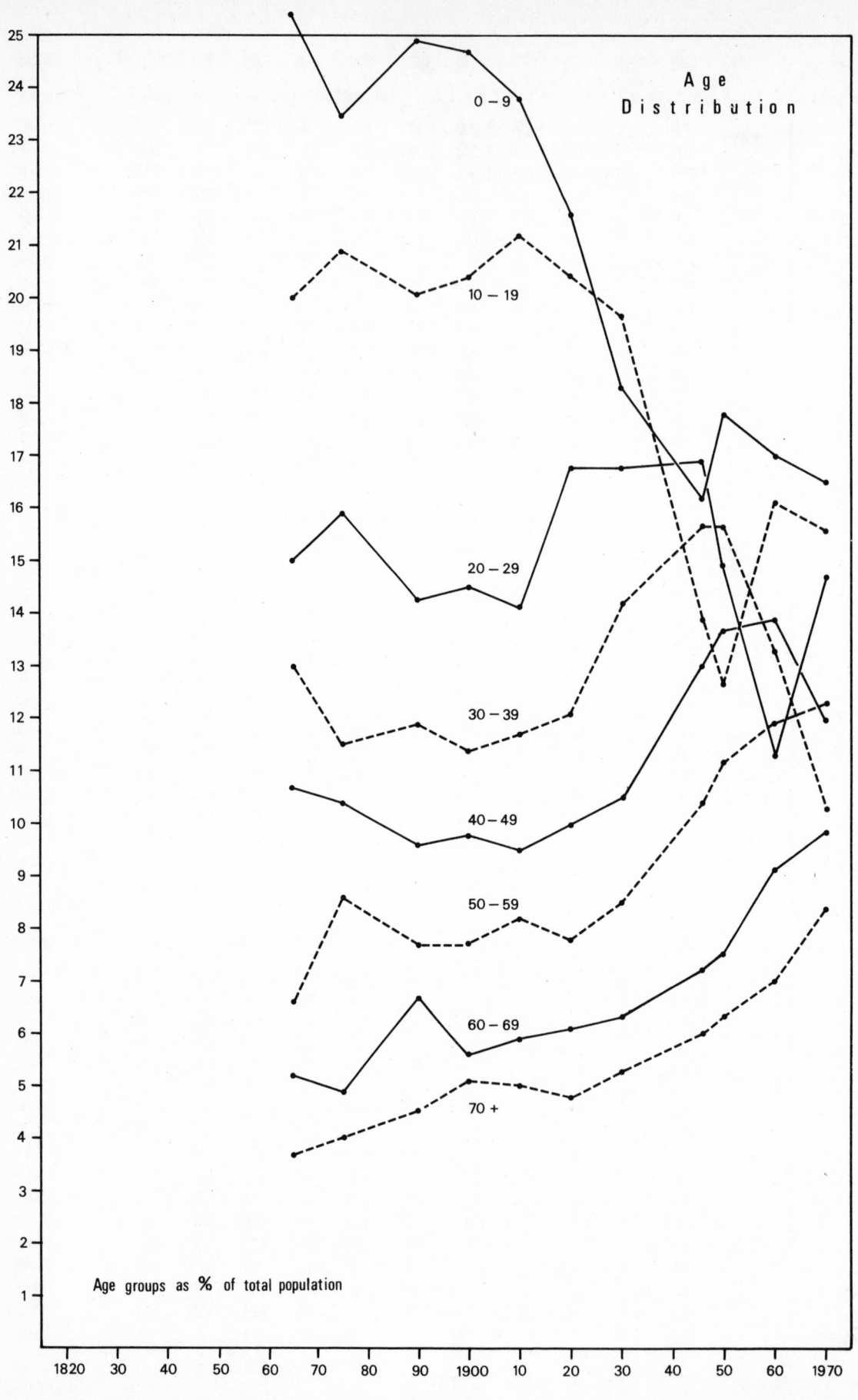

Age Distribution

0 – 9

10 – 19

20 – 29

30 – 39

40 – 49

50 – 59

60 – 69

70 +

Age groups as **%** of total population

1820 30 40 50 60 70 80 90 1900 10 20 30 40 50 60 1970

132

Sweden

Age Distribution at Successive Censuses

Census	1800	1820	1830	1840	1850	1860	1870	1880	1890	Census
Age group	Age of total population (proportions per 10.000 population)									Age group
0–4	1 191	1 285	1 285	1 188	1 243	1 331	1 178	1 233	1 218	0–4
5–9	1 086	1 053	1 239	1 122	1 086	1 057	1 163	1 065	1 093	5–9
10–14	958	893	1 023	1 049	964	963	1 065	962	1 019	10–14
15–19	886	904	892	1 077	958	917	906	990	904	15–19
20–24	862	868	752	883	892	812	786	861	729	20–24
25–29	708	838	752	760	899	794	729	709	725	25–29
30–34	702	713	712	631	737	738	658	631	663	30–34
35–39	669	641	676	620	625	734	651	598	579	35–39
40–44	618	603	563	574	508	596	601	541	529	40–44
45–49	577	482	492	533	484	495	592	530	505	45–49
50–54	482	447	449	429	440	388	471	482	453	50–54
55–59	383	403	342	354	390	353	378	461	435	55–59
60–64	311	327	293	301	291	300	279	348	378	60–64
65–69	255	259	232	200	211	241	229	255	336	65–69
70–74	171	161	159	145	147	148	161	160	221	70–74
75+	141	121	139	133	124	132	153	174	212	75+
Unknown							1			Unknown
Age group	Age of males (proportions per 10.000 males)									Age group
0–4	1 305	1 371	1 410	1 276	1 308	1 401	1 232	1 286	1 273	0–4
5–9	1 068	1 053	1 228	1 138	1 099	1 109	1 207	1 109	1 144	5–9
10–14	999	947	1 052	1 072	1 003	958	1 103	1 002	1 064	10–14
15–19	916	940	920	1 113	990	943	938	1 025	946	15–19
20–24	882	896	770	904	913	823	793	872	734	20–24
25–29	706	851	773	770	917	803	719	707	716	25–29
30–34	700	704	721	636	744	738	648	620	643	30–34
35–39	659	629	675	626	622	737	645	583	567	35–39
40–44	606	590	545	568	501	593	592	526	515	40–44
45–49	559	462	468	516	471	482	584	517	487	45–49
50–54	468	431	415	399	424	368	457	466	435	50–54
55–59	362	367	315	320	354	331	358	443	419	55–59
60–64	291	304	265	275	265	277	258	329	359	60–64
65–69	221	224	201	170	177	213	205	233	316	65–69
70–74	141	136	136	118	118	123	141	142	204	70–74
75+	115	96	107	98	94	101	120	140	178	75+
Unknown							1			Unknown
Age group	Age of females (proportions per 10.000 females)									Age group
0–4	1 212	1 255	1 300	1 185	1 210	1 283	1 127	1 183	1 165	0–4
5–9	985	877	1 138	1 049	1 031	1 021	1 120	1 023	1 045	5–9
10–14	911	872	975	1 006	941	936	1 028	926	977	10–14
15–19	859	871	866	1 042	929	894	876	957	865	15–19
20–24	843	842	735	863	873	801	780	850	724	20–24
25–29	710	826	732	751	882	786	738	711	734	25–29
30–34	705	721	703	627	731	737	669	641	682	30–34
35–39	678	653	677	615	628	732	657	612	590	35–39
40–44	630	616	580	580	514	599	609	554	543	40–44
45–49	592	501	515	549	497	507	600	542	522	45–49
50–54	503	476	469	456	462	404	484	498	470	50–54
55–59	402	431	369	382	406	374	397	478	451	55–59
60–64	344	357	329	345	334	324	298	366	396	60–64
65–69	276	283	261	222	239	268	251	276	355	65–69
70–74	193	178	181	167	172	172	181	178	237	70–74
75+	159	141	168	160	150	162	184	205	244	75+
Unknown							2			Unknown

Sweden

Age Distribution at Successive Censuses

Census Age group	1900	1910	1920	1930	1935	1940	1945	1950	1960	1965	1970	1975	Census Age group
0–4	1 147	1 122	956	737	660	699	880	865	674	707	694	652	0–4
5–9	1 067	1 053	971	855	717	642	665	839	712	674	712	700	5–9
10–14	1 031	996	1 002	892	836	701	614	641	814	690	656	699	10–14
15–19	945	928	944	909	870	816	670	591	793	797	682	650	15–19
20–24	829	829	861	904	881	845	778	652	622	792	814	684	20–24
25–29	692	731	767	825	880	855	804	757	581	620	785	798	25–29
30–34	587	667	700	755	806	855	813	771	627	568	607	761	30–34
35–39	605	581	630	686	735	782	810	774	712	607	551	588	35–39
40–44	562	502	579	632	664	710	739	767	715	684	584	535	40–44
45–49	490	517	504	568	607	637	667	694	712	684	653	566	45–49
50–54	443	475	431	516	540	576	592	618	696	675	646	628	50–54
55–59	413	404	433	440	482	504	527	540	616	651	630	615	55–59
60–64	355	351	382	361	401	438	450	468	529	563	595	588	60–64
65–69	317	305	304	339	314	348	375	383	435	466	496	537	65–69
70–74	242	234	235	266	273	251	277	297	338	360	386	423	70–74
75+	278	305	301	316	334	341	337	344	424	464	508	578	75+
Unknown													Unknown

Age group	Age of males (proportions per 10.000 males)												Age group
0–4	1 196	1 173	994	762	632	719	907	891	695	726	714	672	0–4
5–9	1 111	1 094	1 008	885	737	661	682	862	733	694	731	722	5–9
10–14	1 069	1 036	1 041	925	861	718	630	655	836	710	676	721	10–14
15–19	988	965	977	942	897	837	683	602	811	815	699	670	15–19
20–24	860	842	886	927	906	865	793	657	631	815	834	701	20–24
25–29	699	735	770	829	898	875	819	768	588	638	816	822	25–29
30–34	575	667	691	753	810	870	828	782	632	577	627	792	30–34
35–39	584	577	623	677	732	784	821	786	719	611	561	607	35–39
40–44	539	487	574	619	653	706	737	775	724	689	588	543	40–44
45–49	472	496	497	560	592	624	659	690	719	689	656	568	45–49
50–54	424	451	415	509	529	559	577	609	699	678	648	629	50–54
55–59	390	385	410	431	472	489	508	522	605	647	627	613	55–59
60–64	332	330	356	343	389	425	433	446	511	544	582	578	60–64
65–69	296	282	283	315	295	334	360	364	408	439	467	513	65–69
70–74	222	213	214	244	250	233	262	280	310	325	350	382	70–74
75+	243	267	261	280	296	302	300	311	380	401	425	467	75+
Unknown													Unknown

Age group	Age of females (proportions per 10.000 females)												Age group
0–4	1 101	1 073	918	712	639	679	854	839	653	687	674	632	0–4
5–9	1 024	1 014	936	825	698	624	649	816	690	654	692	678	5–9
10–14	994	958	964	861	813	684	599	627	792	671	637	677	10–14
15–19	903	892	912	878	843	796	656	581	775	778	666	630	15–19
20–24	799	815	837	882	856	825	764	648	613	768	794	667	20–24
25–29	684	727	764	820	861	836	789	747	574	602	753	775	25–29
30–34	599	666	708	756	803	840	798	759	623	558	586	730	30–34
35–39	624	586	636	694	737	780	800	761	705	603	541	569	35–39
40–44	584	517	584	645	675	715	741	759	707	679	581	526	40–44
45–49	506	537	511	577	622	649	674	697	705	678	650	564	45–49
50–54	462	498	447	523	551	592	607	627	694	672	644	627	50–54
55–59	434	423	456	448	492	517	546	557	626	655	632	616	55–59
60–64	377	372	407	378	412	451	467	490	547	582	607	598	60–64
65–69	337	327	325	362	333	361	390	402	461	493	526	560	65–69
70–74	261	254	254	288	296	270	292	313	367	394	423	464	70–74
75+	311	341	341	351	371	380	374	376	468	527	592	687	75+
Unknown													Unknown

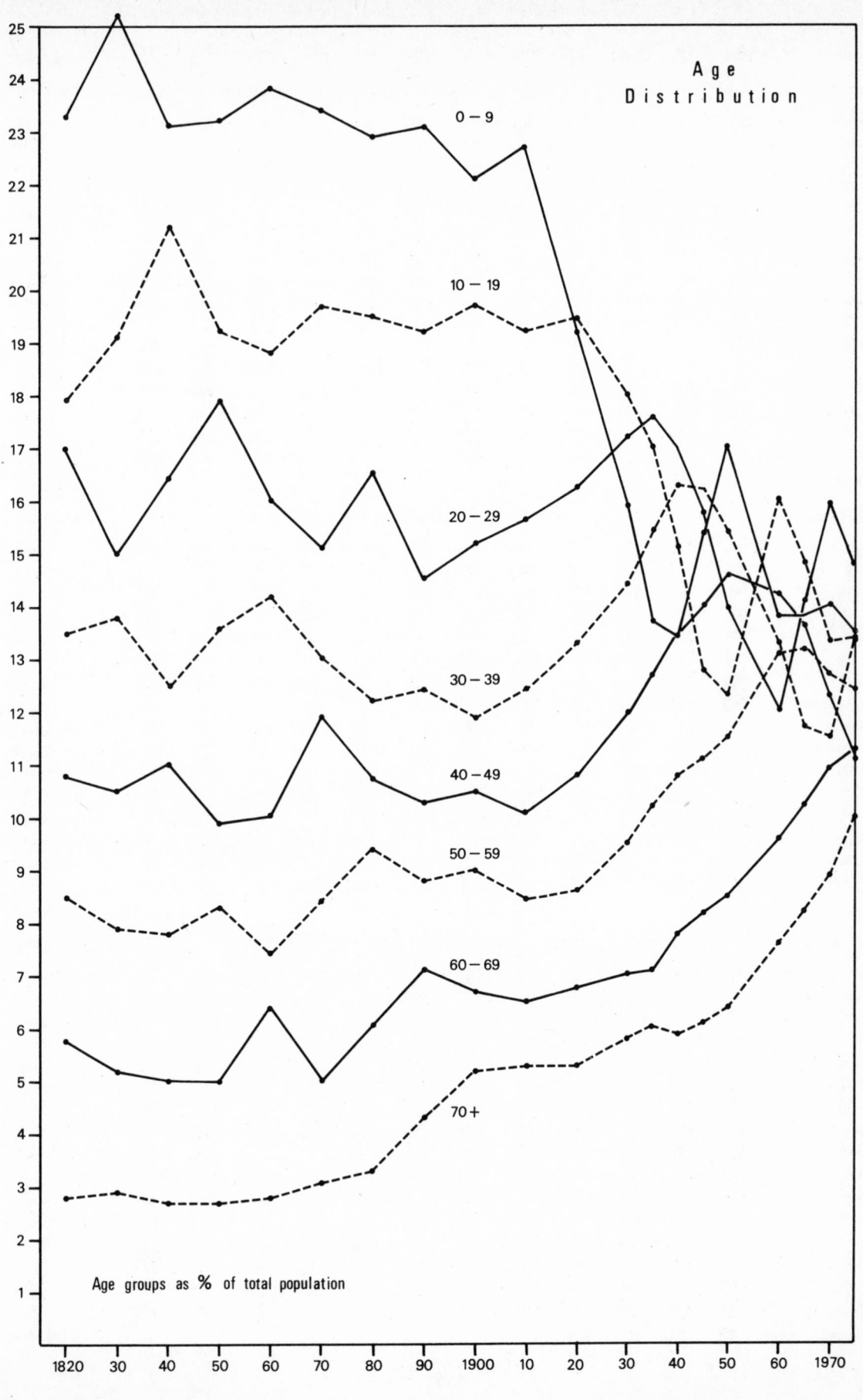

A g e
D i s t r i b u t i o n

Age groups as % of total population

Age Distribution at Successive Censuses

Census	1860	1870	1880	1888	1900	1910	1920	1930	1941	1950	1960	1970	Census
Age group	Age	of	total	population			(proportions per 10.000 population)						Age group
0–4	1 096	1 110	1 175	1 109	1 141	1 076	848	800	716	874	809	782	0–4
5–9	923	1 056	1 051	1 061	1 016	1 051	938	855	736	831	757	816	5–9
10–14	933	964	964	1 052	945	999	1 006	801	760	650	783	741	10–14
15–19	971	834	948	928	952	950	997	893	798	695	787	719	15–19
20–24	909	803	830	834	907	841	899	924	764	742	747	816	20–24
25–29	797	801	699	773	826	809	786	872	785	759	749	830	25–29
30–34	767	741	681	646	718	773	713	792	842	676	711	719	30–34
35–39	685	663	675	603	659	685	688	699	809	733	692	673	35–39
40–44	599	629	621	578	576	592	668	633	746	761	597	630	40–44
45–49	541	561	542	565	473	533	591	603	648	713	635	603	45–49
50–54	496	476	500	493	444	452	501	570	566	631	643	507	50–54
55–59	428	411	428	417	417	353	436	484	516	530	580	522	55–59
60–64	333	346	331	360	345	306	345	385	458	443	489	503	60–64
65–69	221	266	249	278	255	255	242	304	367	375	384	426	65–69
70–74	162	161	167	161	177	173	172	204	243	290	285	323	70–74
75+	127	124	138	142	151	152	171	180	246	297	352	391	75+
Unknown	15	55											Unknown

Age group	Age	of	males	(proportions per 10.000 males)									Age group
0–4	1 109	1 132	1 200	1 143	1 164	1 101	889	841	753	928	844	813	0–4
5–9	932	1 079	1 075	1 092	1 036	1 070	980	897	775	879	788	845	5–9
10–14	945	983	982	1 082	964	1 017	1 046	839	798	685	814	768	10–14
15–19	982	846	963	950	978	973	1 019	922	833	723	817	746	15–19
20–24	898	775	818	822	907	839	882	930	792	738	781	837	20–24
25–29	787	783	701	763	844	827	762	867	804	761	788	871	25–29
30–34	759	727	678	641	727	786	700	776	848	692	728	756	30–34
35–39	683	660	674	600	660	697	692	683	805	743	698	700	35–39
40–44	594	625	614	568	569	593	672	623	727	765	605	638	40–44
45–49	539	557	537	554	464	526	597	602	626	705	638	601	45–49
50–55	489	468	487	478	425	435	497	564	545	609	633	506	50–55
55–59	425	408	415	404	397	334	422	476	499	503	554	509	55–59
60–64	330	340	317	344	322	280	323	368	434	415	447	470	60–64
65–69	221	264	242	266	239	231	221	280	341	348	339	378	65–69
70–74	161	164	162	155	165	156	152	180	218	259	244	267	70–74
75+	131	129	136	137	140	135	146	151	202	247	282	293	75+
Unknown	15	60											Unknown

Age group	Age	of	females	(proportions per 10.000 females)									Age group
0–4	1 083	1 088	1 152	1 076	1 118	1 052	809	761	682	824	776	751	0–4
5–9	914	1 035	1 029	1 031	996	1 033	900	816	700	787	727	787	5–9
10–14	921	946	948	1 025	927	982	969	765	726	618	752	716	10–14
15–19	960	822	933	908	926	928	977	866	765	670	757	692	15–19
20–24	920	829	842	847	908	842	914	919	738	745	715	796	20–24
25–29	806	818	698	782	808	792	807	877	768	756	712	790	25–29
30–34	774	754	685	651	710	759	726	807	837	662	695	683	30–34
35–39	687	667	677	606	658	673	685	714	812	723	686	646	35–39
40–44	604	632	628	587	582	591	664	643	763	759	588	623	40–44
45–49	542	564	547	575	481	541	586	603	669	720	633	604	45–49
50–54	503	483	512	506	462	469	505	576	585	651	653	508	50–54
55–59	431	414	440	428	436	371	448	491	532	555	606	534	55–59
60–64	336	352	344	374	367	332	364	402	480	469	530	535	60–64
65–69	221	267	255	289	271	278	260	326	391	400	427	473	65–69
70–74	162	159	171	167	188	190	192	226	267	318	325	377	70–74
75+	122	120	139	147	161	169	194	208	286	343	419	485	75+
Unknown	15	51											Unknown

Switzerland

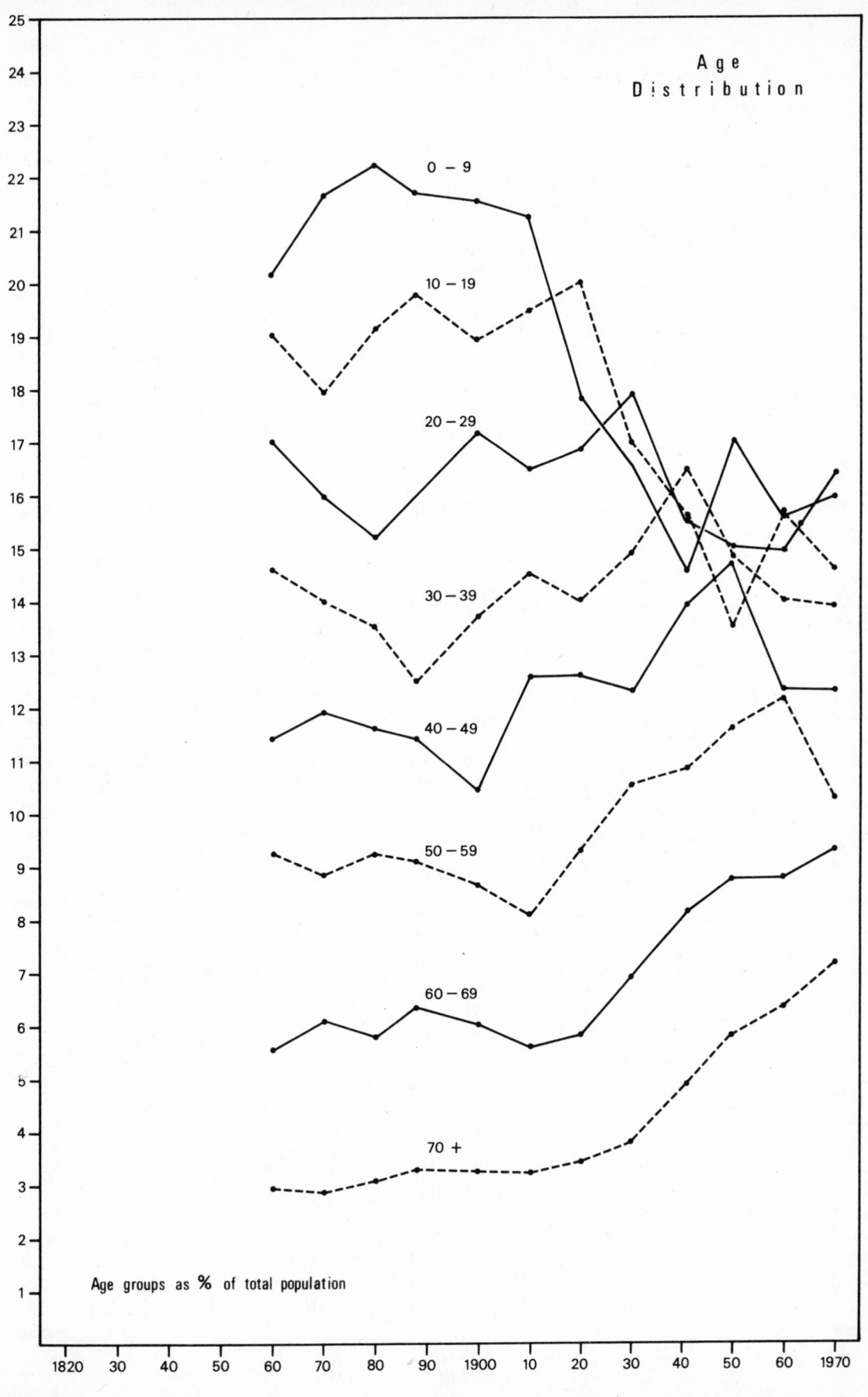

Age
Distribution

0 – 9

10 – 19

20 – 29

30 – 39

40 – 49

50 – 59

60 – 69

70 +

Age groups as % of total population

1820 30 40 50 60 70 80 90 1900 10 20 30 40 50 60 1970

England and Wales

Age Distribution at Successive Censuses

Age of total population (proportions per 10.000 population)

Age group	1841	1851	1861	1871	1881	1891	1901	1911	1921	1931	1951	1961	1966	1971	Age group
0-4	1 324	1 310	1 346	1 349	1 356	1 225	1 143	1 069	877	748	850	780	852	801	0-4
5-9	1 197	1 167	1 168	1 189	1 212	1 171	1 072	1 025	929	832	723	708	758	830	5-9
10-14	1 089	1 067	1 049	1 065	1 078	1 111	1 027	970	966	803	643	808	690	744	10-14
15-19	997	980	963	958	981	1 017	998	925	925	860	618	694	781	680	15-19
20-24	974	930	912	903	896	912	959	880	832	875	669	624	667	765	20-24
25-29	}1 534	820	782	782	788	810	868	854	781	840	750	617	603	655	25-29
30-34		712	691	685	672	699	747	798	747	765	704	647	593	589	30-34
35-39	}1 114	607	610	589	593	614	660	724	717	702	759	703	625	572	35-39
40-44		540	565	540	539	533	569	619	687	667	769	659	675	602	40-44
45-49	}800	446	464	463	443	461	484	534	635	639	725	700	631	643	45-49
50-54		395	402	415	393	400	409	444	532	596	646	699	661	594	50-54
55-59	}522	294	306	315	310	305	324	354	430	518	554	635	647	610	55-59
60-64		268	277	274	280	266	274	283	338	415	490	533	574	583	60-64
65-69	}304	183	188	194	193	197	194	224	260	318	418	429	457	492	65-69
70-74		140	140	142	135	144	137	153	173	218	326	335	340	365	70-74
75+	140	141	137	136	129	132	136	144	171	206	358	429	445	475	75+
Unknown															Unknown

Age of males (proportions per 10.000 males)

Age group	1841	1851	1861	1871	1881	1891	1901	1911	1921	1931	1951	1961	1966	1971	Age group
0-4	1 348	1 340	1 386	1 383	1 391	1 258	1 180	1 110	930	789	906	828	902	846	0-4
5-9	1 225	1 196	1 200	1 216	1 241	1 205	1 106	1 059	977	877	769	749	804	876	5-9
10-14	1 132	1 098	1 084	1 099	1 109	1 146	1 062	1 002	1 016	847	680	855	728	788	10-14
15-19	1 005	995	980	976	1 003	1 043	1 022	949	956	893	635	727	819	716	15-19
20-24	930	906	880	902	880	888	936	861	801	888	679	643	689	792	20-24
25-29	}1 512	796	751	759	776	791	845	834	741	851	774	648	632	681	25-29
30-34		704	677	672	665	696	736	789	709	749	720	673	617	617	30-34
35-39	}1 120	607	604	577	589	616	658	723	704	671	777	725	647	595	35-39
40-44		540	564	531	532	531	571	616	677	643	789	670	689	619	40-44
45-49	}798	447	464	456	433	457	483	531	643	620	741	710	637	655	45-49
50-54		394	401	410	384	391	405	440	537	583	627	706	666	596	50-54
55-59	}513	290	306	311	302	294	316	349	432	516	518	631	643	605	55-59
60-64		259	271	265	269	254	261	274	333	407	447	492	552	562	60-64
65-69	}289	173	179	185	183	185	180	210	249	302	371	367	399	449	65-69
70-74		131	131	135	125	132	124	136	155	197	281	269	271	292	70-74
75+	128	125	122	122	115	115	116	118	139	166	286	307	306	311	75+
Unknown															Unknown

Age of females (proportions per 10.000 females)

Age group	1841	1851	1861	1871	1881	1891	1901	1911	1921	1931	1951	1961	1966	1971	Age group
0-4	1 300	1 281	1 308	1 317	1 322	1 195	1 108	1 030	828	711	798	736	805	759	0-4
5-9	1 170	1 139	1 138	1 163	1 184	1 138	1 041	993	885	790	680	669	715	786	5-9
10-14	1 047	1 038	1 016	1 033	1 048	1 079	995	941	920	762	608	764	655	703	10-14
15-19	990	966	947	940	959	994	975	903	896	829	602	663	746	645	15-19
20-24	1 016	952	942	903	912	936	981	898	860	862	660	607	646	740	20-24
25-29	}1 566	843	811	804	800	829	891	872	818	880	727	588	577	630	25-29
30-34		720	705	698	679	702	758	806	782	779	688	623	570	563	30-34
35-39	}1 108	608	616	601	597	613	661	726	728	730	743	683	605	549	35-39
40-44		540	567	549	545	536	567	621	696	689	751	648	661	586	40-44
45-49	}802	444	464	469	453	465	484	537	628	657	710	691	625	632	45-49
50-54		397	403	420	402	408	412	448	527	608	663	691	657	592	50-54
55-59	}532	297	306	319	318	315	330	360	429	519	586	639	651	615	55-59
60-64		278	283	281	290	278	286	291	344	422	529	572	595	603	60-64
65-69	}318	192	195	202	203	209	207	237	271	333	461	487	512	533	65-69
70-74		148	149	149	144	156	149	170	190	237	368	396	404	433	70-74
75+	151	157	150	150	143	148	154	167	201	242	425	543	577	631	75+
Unknown															Unknown

England and Wales

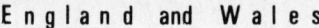

Age
Distribution
0 – 9
10 – 19
20 – 29
30 – 39
40 – 49
50 – 59
60 – 69
70 +
Age groups as % of total population
25
24
23
22
21
20
19
18
17
16
15
14
13
12
11
10
9
8
7
6
5
4
3
2
1
1820
30
40
50
60
70
80
90
1900
10
20
30
40
50
60
1970

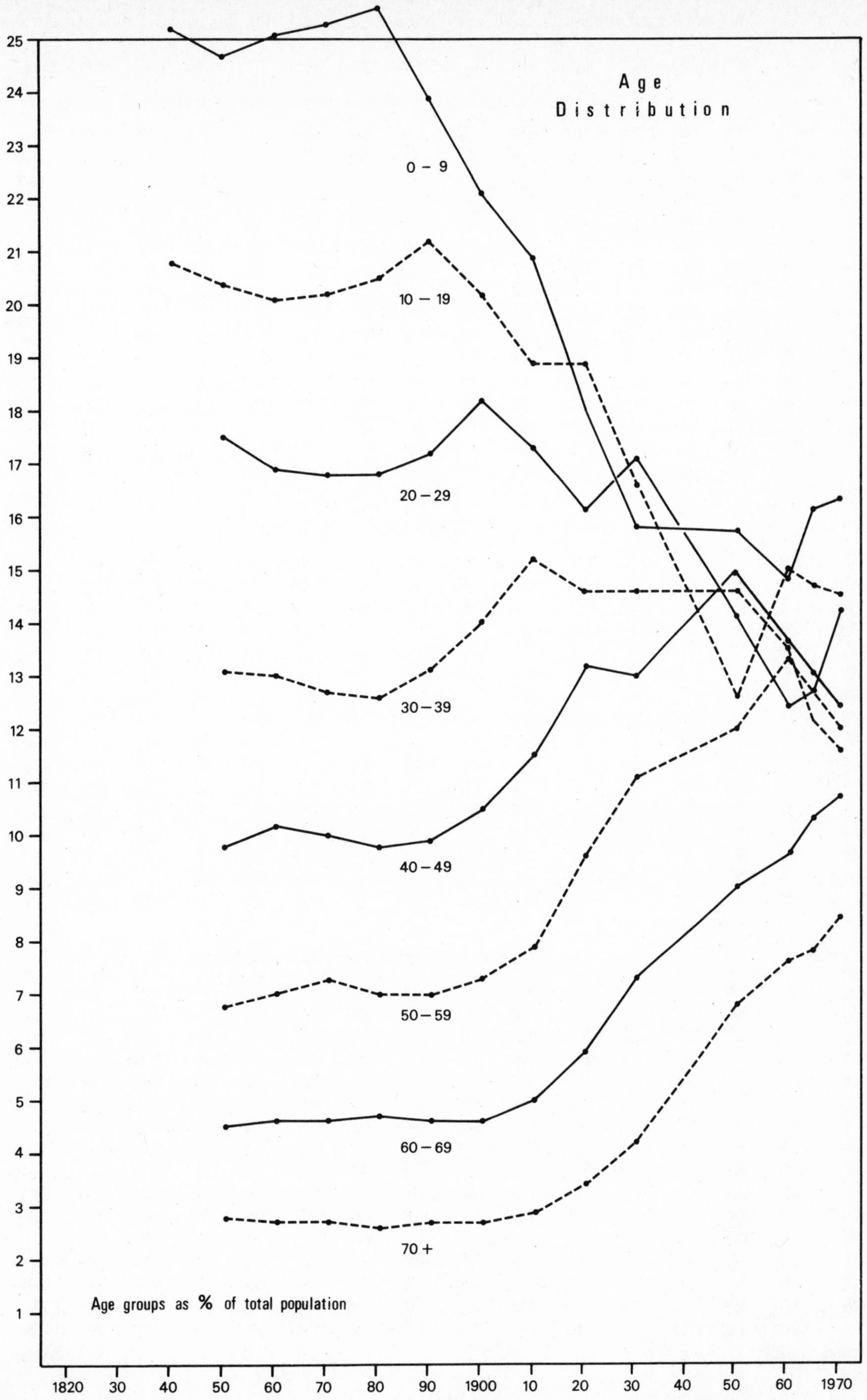

Scotland

Age Distribution at Successive Censuses

Census	1841	1851	1861	1871	1881	1891	1901	1911	1921	1931	1951	1961	1966	1971	Census
Age group	Age	of	total	population				(proportions	per	10.000	population)				Age group
0-4	1 308	1 286	1 363	1 356	1 367	1 248	1 192	1 119	967	874	924	906	923	850	0-4
5-9	1 197	1 176	1 186	1 205	1 205	1 186	1 102	1 079	978	941	781	812	863	896	5-9
10-14	1 133	1 099	1 054	1 107	1 084	1 123	1 049	1 029	1 004	879	758	867	794	845	10-14
15-19	1 031	1 038	1 004	999	1 013	1 039	1 020	972	979	907	710	722	811	750	15-19
20-24	971	971	915	870	920	903	969	881	878	870	714	643	630	747	20-24
25-29	786	797	760	758	772	777	847	810	771	803	748	631	598	605	25-29
30-34	717	670	660	655	635	672	705	747	692	722	677	642	595	575	30-34
35-39	541	571	568	563	567	590	621	682	664	653	723	671	622	575	35-39
40-44	557	532	531	523	526	510	549	579	632	603	726	619	644	595	40-44
45-49	376	422	442	440	434	454	467	506	594	579	686	662	595	617	45-49
50-54	387	411	406	401	395	404	395	432	501	550	604	661	636	566	50-54
55-59	240	280	308	312	303	308	319	349	411	491	511	603	617	586	55-59
60-64	292	270	307	293	282	282	281	272	331	396	441	501	545	560	60-64
65-69	149	177	187	201	195	197	194	220	253	307	377	395	434	473	65-69
70-74	143	144	142	162	148	151	143	169	171	219	297	297	314	343	70-74
75+	153	156	158	155	155	157	147	152	174	203	321	368	380	417	75+
Unknown	19		9						1	2	2				Unknown
Age group	Age	of	males	(proportions	per	10.000	males)								Age group
0-4	1 399	1 374	1 462	1 440	1 436	1 311	1 235	1 161	1 016	918	990	967	986	909	0-4
5-9	1 278	1 251	1 271	1 277	1 266	1 244	1 147	1 117	1 023	986	832	866	918	955	5-9
10-14	1 215	1 182	1 139	1 185	1 143	1 180	1 096	1 069	1 051	923	804	927	853	901	10-14
15-19	1 032	1 060	1 038	1 044	1 054	1 086	1 060	1 011	1 017	942	711	755	861	793	15-19
20-24	913	936	879	864	926	896	968	874	864	885	708	642	648	782	20-24
25-29	747	759	698	724	762	747	834	788	735	802	769	649	607	630	25-29
30-34	691	645	625	624	623	664	694	737	660	698	682	655	610	589	30-34
35-39	522	552	541	528	544	585	610	683	640	619	730	687	631	586	35-39
40-44	537	515	509	499	504	501	546	577	621	578	739	617	652	602	40-44
45-49	370	411	430	420	409	436	462	499	605	559	693	660	587	624	45-49
50-54	362	389	389	380	370	381	385	425	508	545	581	662	628	555	50-54
55-59	232	265	296	296	283	286	302	343	411	497	476	593	606	569	55-59
60-64	269	242	281	268	253	255	256	260	323	394	402	456	519	532	60-64
65-69	140	160	170	182	173	174	170	200	242	293	342	336	371	424	65-69
70-74	130	127	123	142	127	128	121	139	148	198	270	242	250	270	70-74
75+	137	132	132	128	128	126	114	116	134	163	270	286	275	279	75+
Unknown	26		17						1	2	2				Unknown
Age group	Age	of	females	(proportions	per	10.000	females)								Age group
0-4	1 226	1 206	1 273	1 280	1 302	1 189	1 152	1 079	922	833	863	850	864	795	0-4
5-9	1 123	1 108	1 109	1 139	1 148	1 132	1 059	1 043	936	899	734	763	812	841	5-9
10-14	1 060	1 024	977	1 037	1 029	1 071	1 005	993	960	839	717	812	740	794	10-14
15-19	1 030	1 018	974	958	974	996	982	935	944	874	709	693	765	711	15-19
20-24	1 024	1 003	948	876	915	910	970	888	891	857	720	644	614	714	20-24
25-29	821	832	816	790	782	804	860	831	804	804	729	615	589	583	25-29
30-34	740	694	692	684	646	679	715	756	722	744	672	629	582	562	30-34
35-39	558	589	593	596	588	594	632	681	687	684	717	656	614	565	35-39
40-44	575	547	550	545	546	518	551	582	641	627	714	620	637	589	40-44
45-49	381	433	453	456	458	470	471	513	584	599	679	663	603	611	45-49
50-54	409	430	421	420	418	425	404	438	494	555	626	660	644	575	50-54
55-59	248	293	318	327	322	328	336	355	411	486	544	613	628	601	55-59
60-64	313	295	331	315	309	307	305	284	337	398	476	543	569	587	60-64
65-69	158	193	204	218	215	218	217	238	262	321	409	449	492	518	65-69
70-74	154	159	159	180	168	172	165	197	192	239	322	347	372	410	70-74
75+	168	177	181	179	180	186	177	186	212	240	367	443	477	544	75+
Unknown	12		1						1	2	2				Unknown

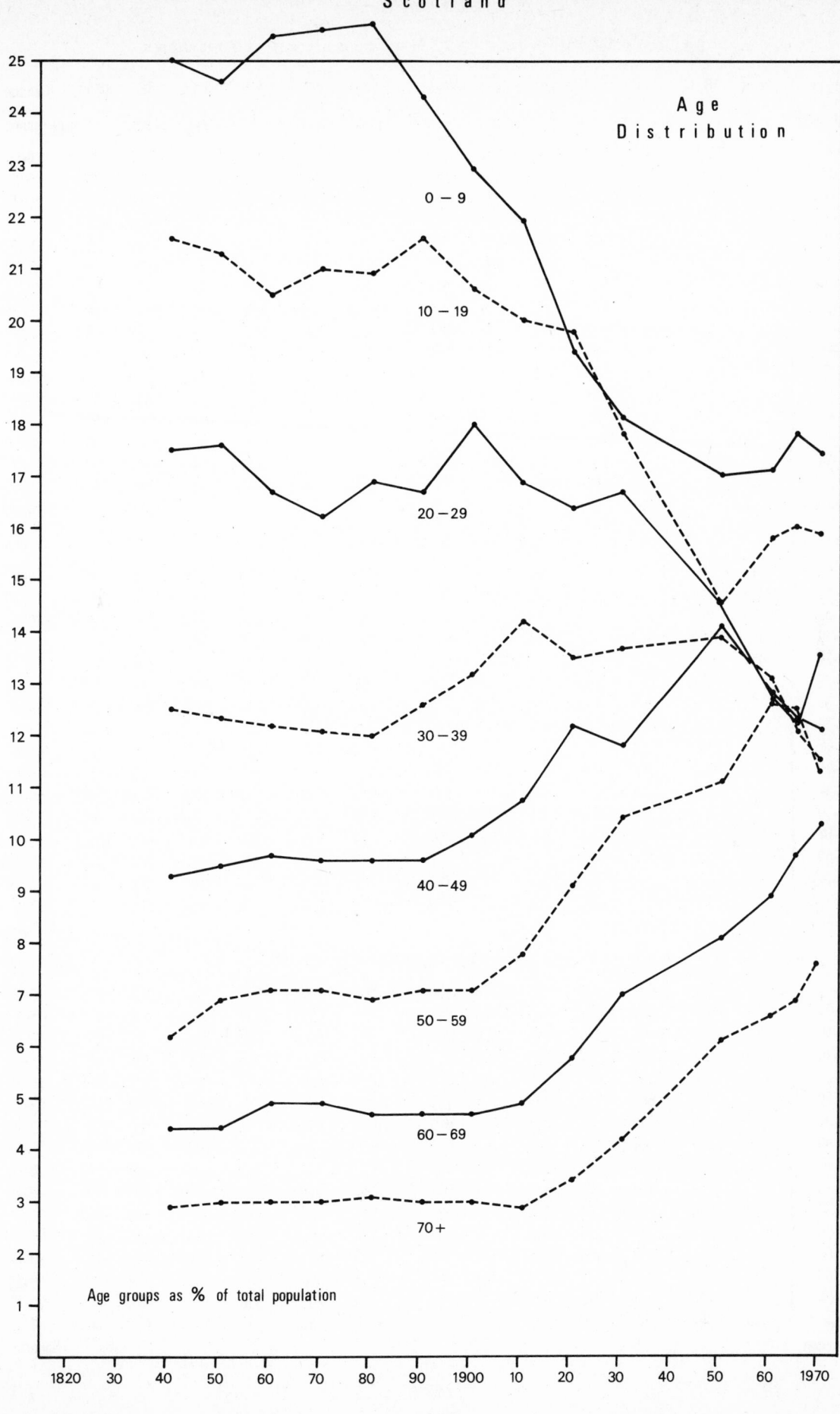

Scotland

Age Distribution

0 — 9

10 — 19

20 — 29

30 — 39

40 — 49

50 — 59

60 — 69

70 +

Age groups as % of total population

Age Distribution at Successive Censuses

Census	1861	1871	1881	1891	1901	1911	1926	1926	1937	1951	1961	1966	1971	Census
Age group	Age of total population							(proportions per 10.000 population)						Age group
0–4	1 197	1 207	1 113	1 000	993	932	983	1 017	875	1 006	1 028	1 081	1 017	0–4
5–9	1 055	1 168	1 201	1 081	1 011	997	950	931	893	942	929	986	1 023	5–9
10–14	1 029	1 163	1 191	1 169	1 031	973	982	953	944	815	935	889	935	10–14
15–19	1 160	982	1 080	1 169	1 060	964	960	954	889	791	844	847	823	15–19
20–24	1 060	846	922	945	996	857	826	869	822	736	658	717	748	20–24
25–29	1 307	697	640	678	813	754	744	788	792	726	598	591	663	25–29
30–34		657	585	593	659	694	628	655	709	665	607	564	564	30–34
35–39	1 028	470	486	485	537	656	596	608	689	686	638	571	537	35–39
40–44		535	594	552	546	567	566	557	593	650	597	594	549	40–44
45–49	945	362	381	431	422	460	566	557	528	590	611	563	560	45–49
50–54		519	476	544	505	437	540	552	485	557	576	561	521	50–54
55–59	740	313	269	303	331	334	426	433	454	454	509	522	511	55–59
60–64		472	435	407	457	310	352	346	424	398	461	462	469	60–64
65–69	317	189	194	188	218	332	332	311	368	346	366	392	392	65–69
70–74		227	219	218	210	383	267	252	276	296	281	291	312	70–74
75+	155	186	209	232	210	289	282	248	260	343	362	370	376	75+
Unknown	7	7	6	4										Unknown

Age group	Age of males							(proportions per 10.000 males)						Age group
0–4	1 241	1 254	1 154	1 030	1 022	1 007	998	1 069	917	1 058	1 085	1 147	1 064	0–4
5–9	1 093	1 211	1 241	1 114	1 038	1 013	965	976	932	989	981	1 038	1 075	5–9
10–14	1 079	1 221	1 243	1 209	1 065	991	998	992	987	852	981	936	976	10–14
15–19	1 160	980	1 082	1 192	1 068	980	971	977	909	830	868	877	863	15–19
20–24	1 050	811	915	965	988	873	837	864	819	729	675	724	785	20–24
25–29	1 294	663	616	654	794	729	726	754	779	717	599	600	683	25–29
30–34		635	553	581	664	694	617	625	700	669	599	568	576	30–34
35–39	976	468	466	465	530	665	580	581	668	681	633	564	539	35–39
40–44		519	571	514	532	582	561	539	575	645	600	590	539	40–44
45–49	923	354	380	414	409	469	569	551	512	582	606	565	552	45–49
50–54		497	464	526	475	435	557	531	472	540	570	555	517	50–54
55–59	723	318	267	307	322	332	444	441	448	433	495	511	496	55–59
60–64		458	411	396	447	297	354	350	427	366	424	432	438	60–64
65–69	307	197	200	189	227	320	332	309	366	324	331	349	350	65–69
70–74		227	219	209	210	337	242	226	258	274	245	250	258	70–74
75+	144	179	212	231	207	276	249	217	230	312	306	295	284	75+
Unknown	11	8	7	4										Unknown

Age group	Age of females							(proportions per 10.000 females)						Age group
0–4	1 154	1 162	1 074	970	965	978	968	968	835	956	974	1 018	972	0–4
5–9	1 019	1 127	1 163	1 049	985	981	935	888	855	898	880	936	973	5–9
10–14	982	1 109	1 141	1 130	998	954	967	915	902	779	890	845	895	10–14
15–19	1 161	985	1 079	1 147	1 053	947	950	932	869	755	820	818	784	15–19
20–24	1 070	878	930	925	1 005	841	817	875	826	743	641	710	712	20–24
25–29	1 320	729	662	702	831	779	767	819	805	734	597	583	644	25–29
30–34		678	616	605	655	695	640	683	718	662	614	561	553	30–34
35–39	1 077	473	504	505	543	647	613	633	710	691	643	577	534	35–39
40–44		550	617	590	559	552	555	575	610	654	594	597	558	40–44
45–49	965	369	381	448	435	452	561	564	544	597	615	561	568	45–49
50–54		540	487	561	535	440	523	514	496	573	581	568	524	50–54
55–59	756	309	271	299	340	336	408	426	460	474	522	533	526	55–59
60–64		485	457	418	466	322	349	342	421	428	497	491	499	60–64
65–69	328	181	188	187	209	345	332	313	370	366	400	432	433	65–69
70–74		226	219	226	210	430	297	275	293	316	316	329	364	70–74
75+	165	193	207	234	212	301	316	277	288	373	415	441	466	75+
Unknown	3	6	5	4										Unknown

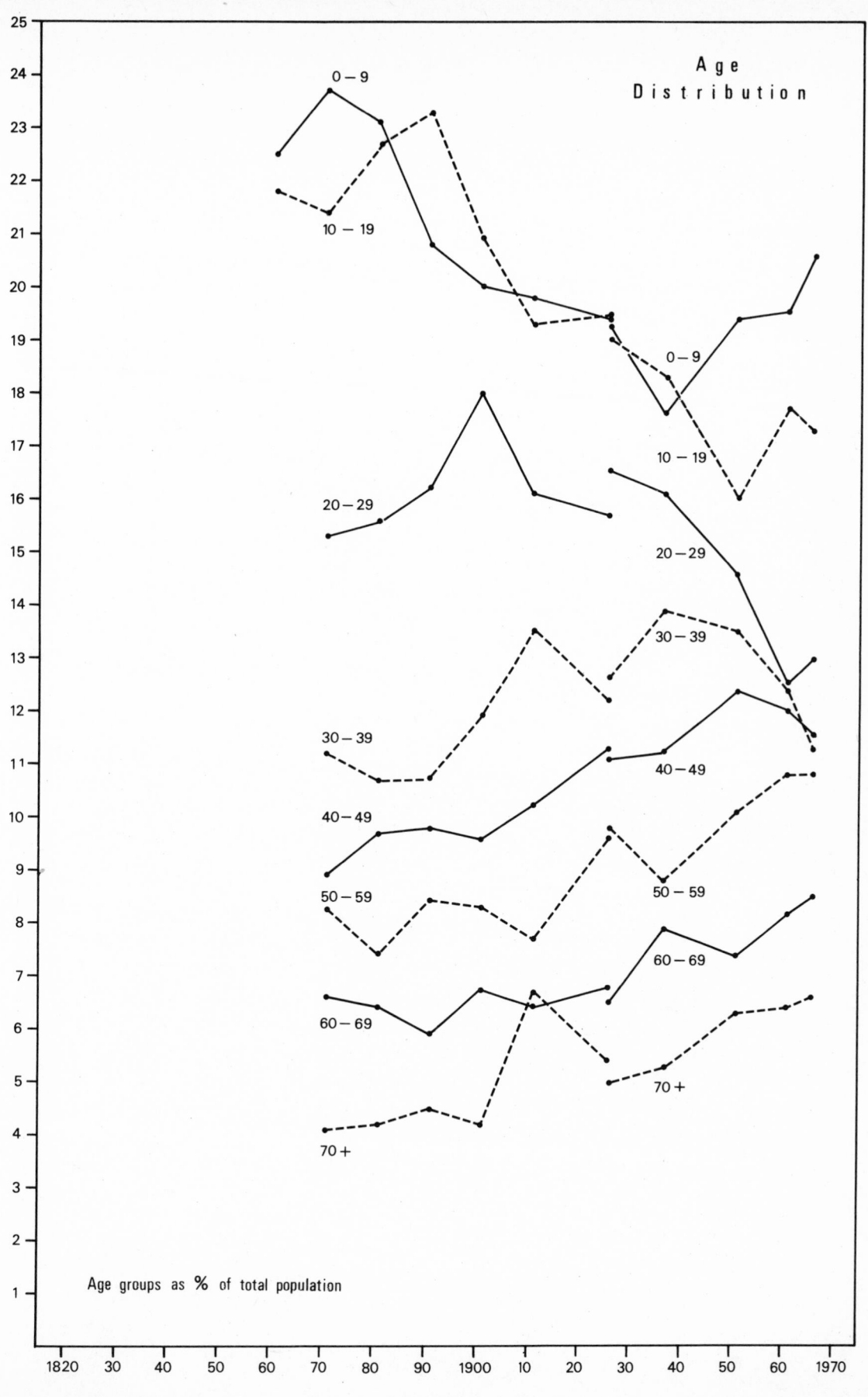

Age
Distribution

0 − 9

10 − 19

0 − 9

20 − 29

10 − 19

20 − 29

30 − 39

30 − 39

40 − 49

40 − 49

50 − 59

50 − 59

60 − 69

60 − 69

70 +

70 +

Age groups as % of total population

1820   30   40   50   60   70   80   90   1900   10   20   30   40   50   60   1970

Chapter 2

MARRIAGES AND FAMILIES

Birth and death rates may be unreliable, but they do not create problems as to their 'meaning'. Obviously, the same does not hold true for a distinction between legitimate births, for marriage and divorce rates. Not only would an explanation of levels and changes in these rates require, as a first step, an understanding of institutional regulations, but the statistics themselves are already dependent upon these definitions.

Family and marriage are pre-legal institutions. For the Romans and the Germanic peoples, marriage and divorce were de facto rather than de jure matters, regulated by religious and group norms. After the breakdown of the Roman Empire in the West and the spread of Christianity, however, a long-term process of juridification began, from the extension of ecclesiastical jurisdiction over matrimonial matters to direct marriage regulation through State laws. This development of a marriage law common to all groups of a society was a unique European phenomenon. Only recently, this long-term development seems to have been reversed by a process of – at least partial – dejuridification.

The spread of Christianity eventually resulted in marriage being treated not only as a civil contract but also as a sacrament, a holy bond which was indissoluble. From the time that Christianity became the established religion until the eighteenth century, divorce a vincolo matrimonii (i.e. from the bonds of marriage), permitting remarriage, was generally not obtainable. Only divorce a mensa et thoro (i.e. separation from board and bed) was obtainable, but it did not permit remarriage. To some extent, however, the principle of indissolubility was mitigated by the possibility of an annulment, on the basis of grounds which pre-dated the marriage. The establishment of the doctrine of indissolubility and of ecclesiastical jurisdiction over matrimonial causes took centuries. For a long time marriage continued to be considered as basically a private and secular matter. Until the Council of Trent, there were two equally valid sorts of marriage, one public and formal, the other private and informal. Then the Tridentine Decree Tametsi provided that henceforth no marriage was valid unless it had been celebrated in the presence of a priest, and it prescribed the keeping of official records of marriages. What the Church established at the Council of Trent has never been repealed.

The Council was the outcome of the crisis which faced the Church in the sixteenth century. Among the churches which developed out of the Reformation, the attitude towards divorce varied, but in general it was accepted. Neither Luther nor Calvin considered marriage a sacrament. Only the Church of England inherited Roman canon law unchanged and divorce a vincolo did not exist until 1858. Protestantism, however, did not 'privatize' divorce. Instead it defined it as a sanction for marital misconduct to be granted by an ecclesiastical or civil official. Divorce by mutual consent was not recognized and the rules governing annulment were tightened up.

With the exception of England (where ecclesiastical jurisdiction over marriage survived until 1858), Protestantism accepted the notion of civil jurisdiction over marriage. Yet when the State first assumed this jurisdiction, it simply applied ecclesiastical norms. During the absolutist period, special exemption procedures were introduced, either by royal jurisdiction, as in most countries, or by private acts of parliament, as in England. These procedures, however, were of limited importance, and it was only during the Enlightenment that a new strand of thought, reviving Roman legal ideas, came to influence divorce legislation (especially in Prussia and Austria).

The influence of these ideas on divorce was only fully realized in the French Revolution. A law of 1792 defined marriage as a civil contract and permitted divorce by mutual consent. Although divorce by mutual consent was severely restricted by the Code Napoleon of 1804 and divorce abolished altogether in 1816, the revolutionary legislation was an indication of the future development of divorce law in Europe. These developments varied greatly across Europe, but in general they conformed to the following steps: introduction of divorce on the grounds of guilt and successive extensions of these grounds; introduction of divorce on the grounds of marital breakdown and successive efforts to make it more easily obtainable; finally, divorce by mutual consent, and corresponding efforts to make it available more quickly. The following table gives a synopsis of the major steps in divorce legislation in our European countries.

Austria

1811   Divorce introduced for non-Catholics (General Civil Code)
1855   Concordat abolished divorce
1868   Divorce reintroduced for non-Catholics
1934   Divorce abolished
1938   German law adopted extending divorce to Catholics; on the combined grounds of guilt and marital breakdown; still basically in force today

Belgium

1804   Divorce on the grounds of guilt and (very restricted) mutual consent (Code Napoleon)
1969
1972   Divorce on the grounds of mutual consent more accessible
1974   Divorce on the grounds of marital breakdown introduced (retained some element of the guilt principle)

Denmark

Divorce on the grounds of guilt allowed since the Reformation, and exemptions made by the King.

1922   Divorce on the grounds of guilt, marital breakdown or by mutual consent (but only indirectly, after a period of legal separation)
1969   Divorce legislation similar to that of Sweden prior to 1973

Finland

Divorce on the grounds of one-sided guilt allowed since the Reformation; exemptions made by the King, by the parliament in the nineteenth century, and by the High Court since independence.

1929   Divorce on the combined grounds of guilt and marital breakdown
1948   Legal separation added, indirectly introducing divorce by mutual consent

France

1804   Divorce on the grounds of guilt and (very restricted) mutual consent (Code Napoleon)
1816   Divorce abolished
1884   Divorce reintroduced on the grounds of guilt
1975   Divorce on the grounds of marital breakdown and by mutual consent, in addition to guilt

Germany

Prior to the founding of the Empire in 1871, divorce legislation varied by province and denomination.

1875   Divorce introduced for Catholics; guilt the only grounds for divorce for Catholics and non-Catholics
1938   Divorce on the grounds of marital breakdown and guilt; law in force, with minor changes, until the 1976 reform

Ireland

Divorce not allowed, as the indissolubility of marriage is guaranteed by the Constitution.

Italy

1970   Divorce on the grounds of guilt or marital breakdown introduced

Netherlands

1838   Divorce on the grounds of guilt and (very limited) by mutual consent (but only indirectly, after a period of legal separation)

1883   Supreme Court decision making (indirect) divorce by mutual consent easier
1971   Marital breakdown introduced as sole grounds for divorce

Norway

Since the Reformation divorce available on the grounds of guilt or by royal decree.

1909   Divorce on the grounds of guilt, marital breakdown and by mutual consent after a certain period of legal separation; still in force with minor amendments

Sweden

Since the Reformation divorce available on the grounds of guilt or by royal decree.

1915   Divorce on the grounds of guilt and marital breakdown, after a certain period of legal separation
1973   Divorce on the grounds of marital breakdown or by mutual consent, with no or only short period of separation

Switzerland

Since the Reformation divorce available on the grounds of guilt.

1912   Divorce on the grounds of guilt or marital breakdown

England and Wales

Since the break with Rome divorce was only possible by private acts of parliament.

1857   Divorce on the grounds of guilt
1923   Grounds for divorce equalized for men and women
1937   Extension of the grounds for divorce
1971   Marital breakdown the sole grounds for divorce

Northern Ireland

1939   Divorce on the grounds of guilt introduced (according the English law of 1937), still in force

Chapter 2 consists of two data sets. One is based on the statistics of civil registration, the other on population census results. First, the figures for marriages, divorces, legitimate and illegitimate births are presented, in absolute as well as in relative terms. In addition to three simple ratios (marriages per 1,000 population, divorces per 100 marriages, and illegitimate births per 100 legitimate births), five more complicated indicators have been calculated:

(a)   persons marrying per 10,000 non-married persons aged 15 years and over as a more refined marriage rate; in order to have some control for the ageing of the population (as old people marry much less frequently), a second indicator using the age group 15—49 has been calculated;

(b)   persons divorcing per 10,000 married persons as a more refined divorce rate;

(c)   legitimate births per 10,000 married women in the child-bearing age of 15—44, and illegitimate births per 10,000 non-married women of the same age, as more adequate indicators of fertility inside and outside marriage. We have calculated the respective population categories for these indicators on the basis of population census results. Their relative shares of total population have been interpolated for the intercensus years (except, in some countries, for the two World Wars) and extrapolated for the years after the latest census around 1970.

The tables present these data in the form of time series for each country in alphabetical order. They are preceded by a series of comparative graphs on the development of marriage, divorce, legitimate and illegitimate births. They are followed by the second set of data which consists of detailed breakdowns of the population by sex, civil status and ten age groups. These data are calculated from census results and are, for comparative reasons, given as relative figures, i.e. the respective distribution for each male or female by civil status.

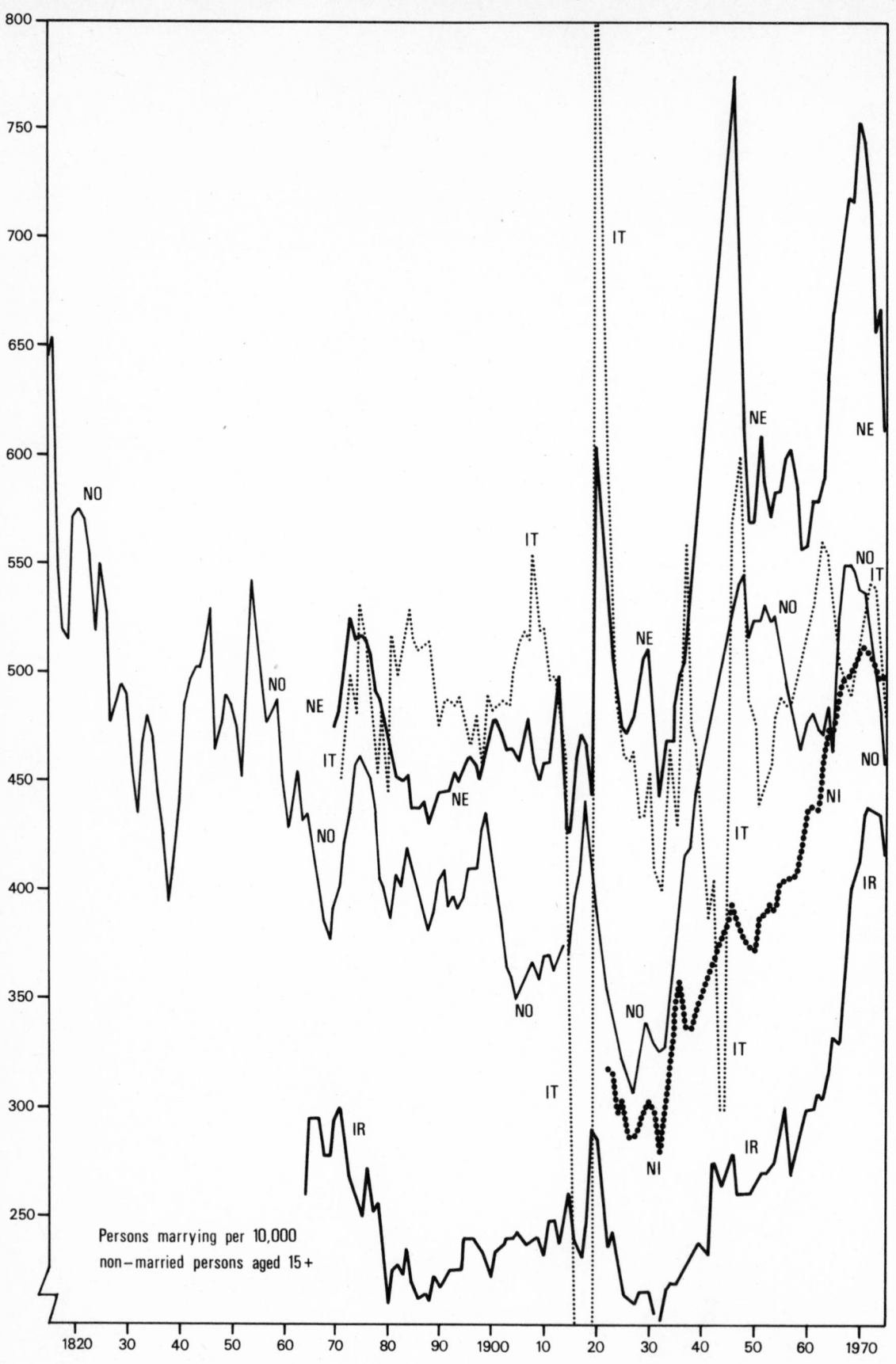

Persons marrying per 10,000
non-married persons aged 15+

M a r r i a g e s

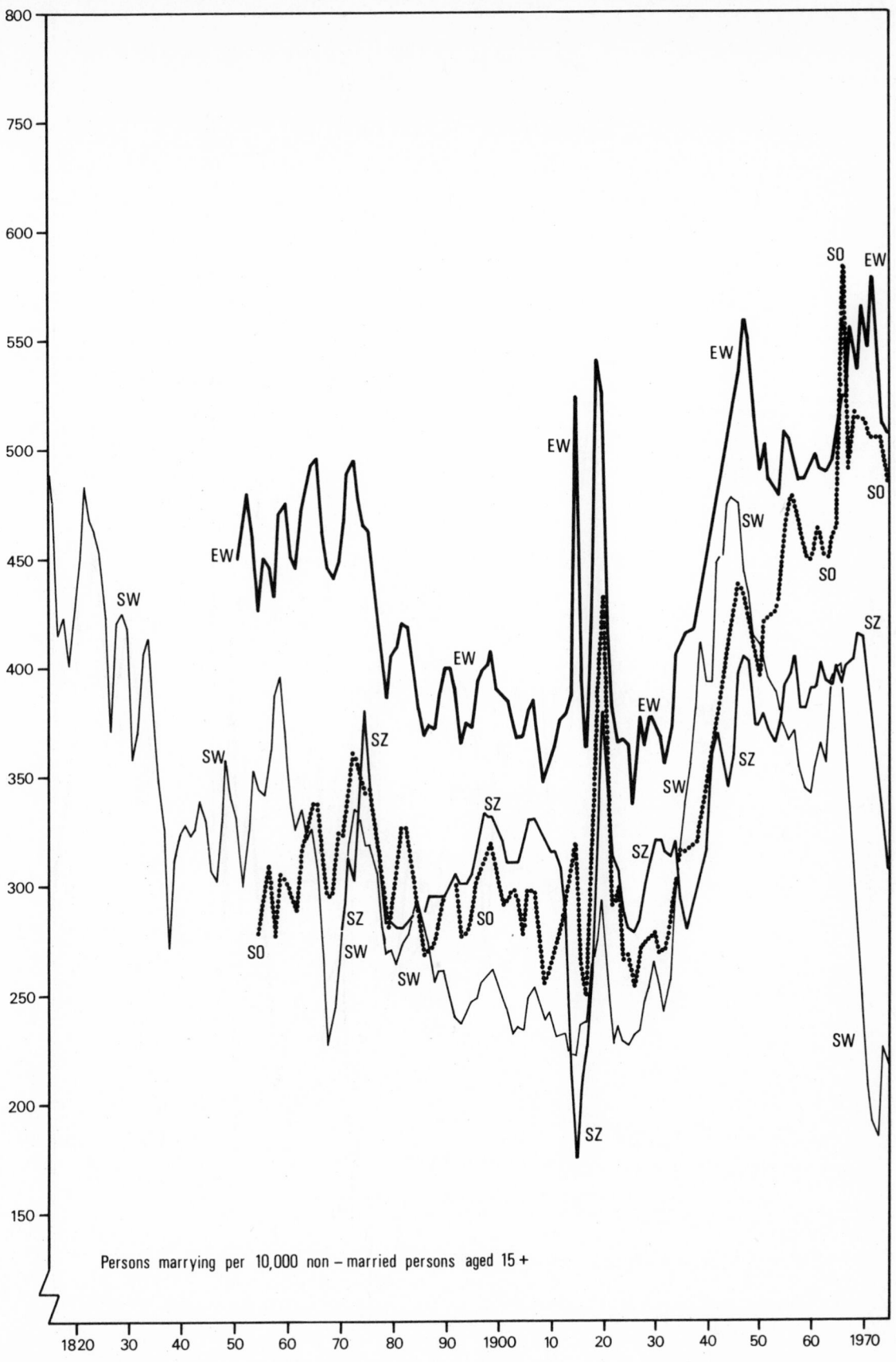

Persons marrying per 10,000 non – married persons aged 15 +

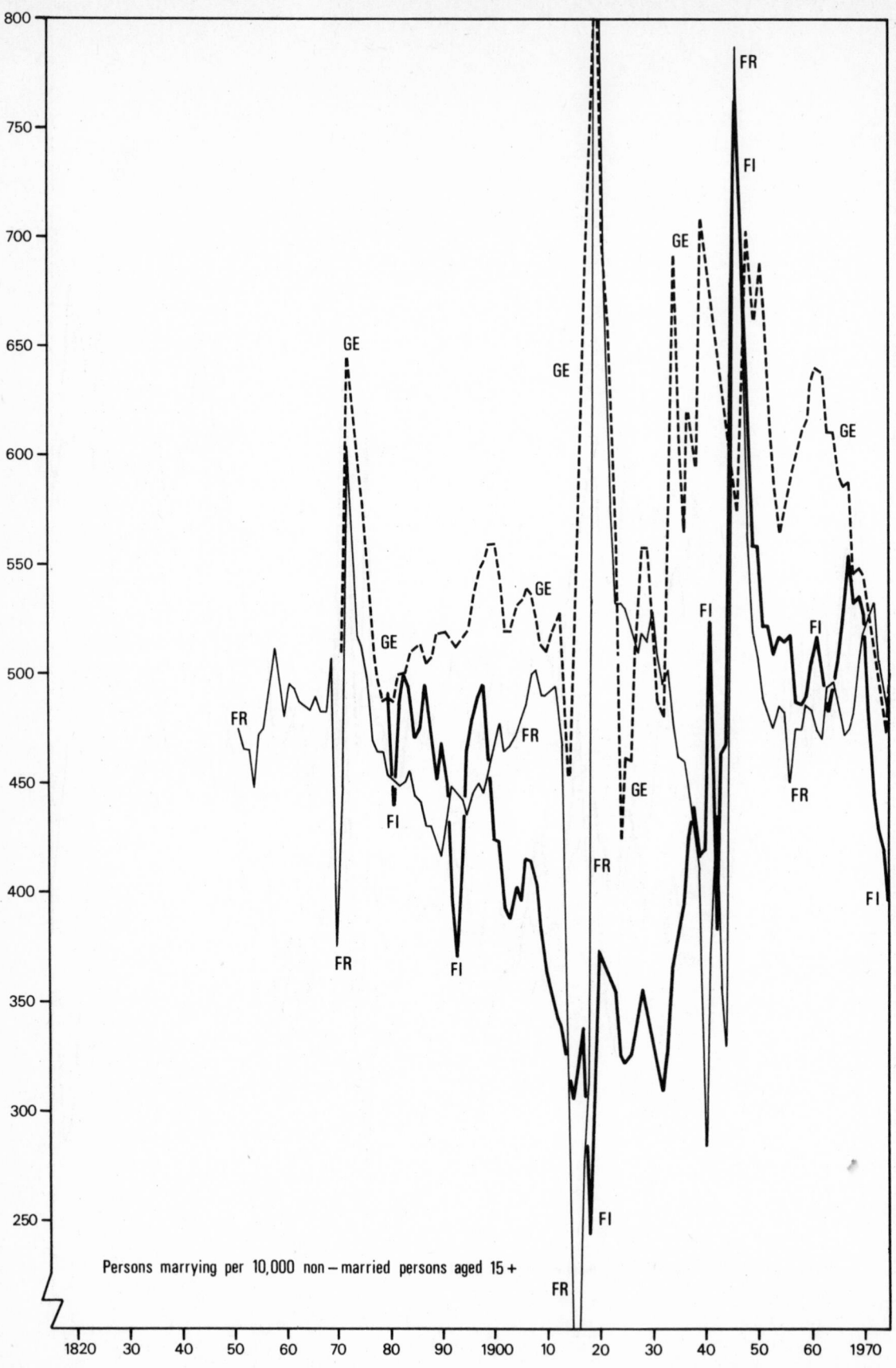

Persons marrying per 10,000 non–married persons aged 15 +

Marriages

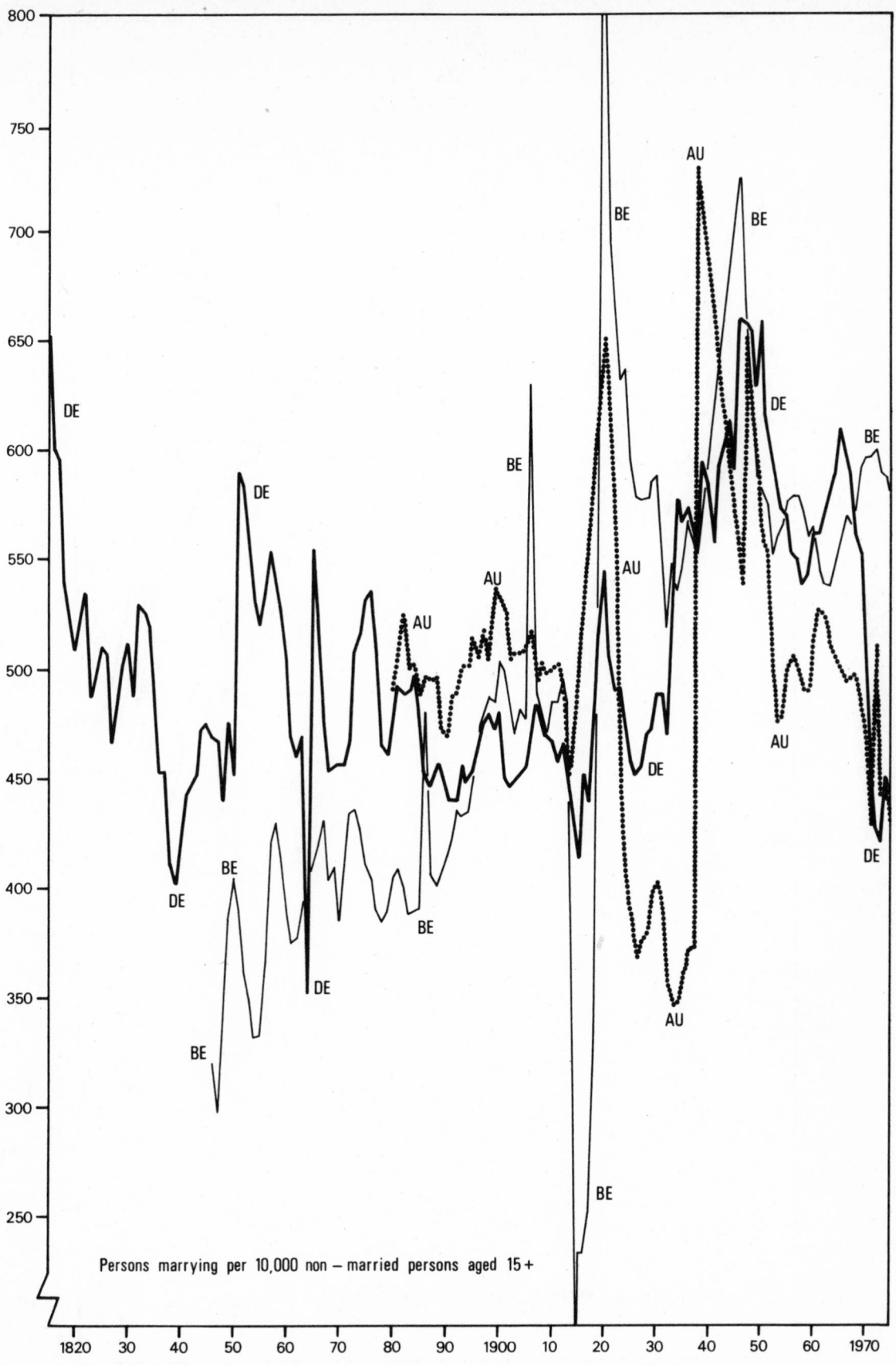

Persons marrying per 10,000 non – married persons aged 15 +

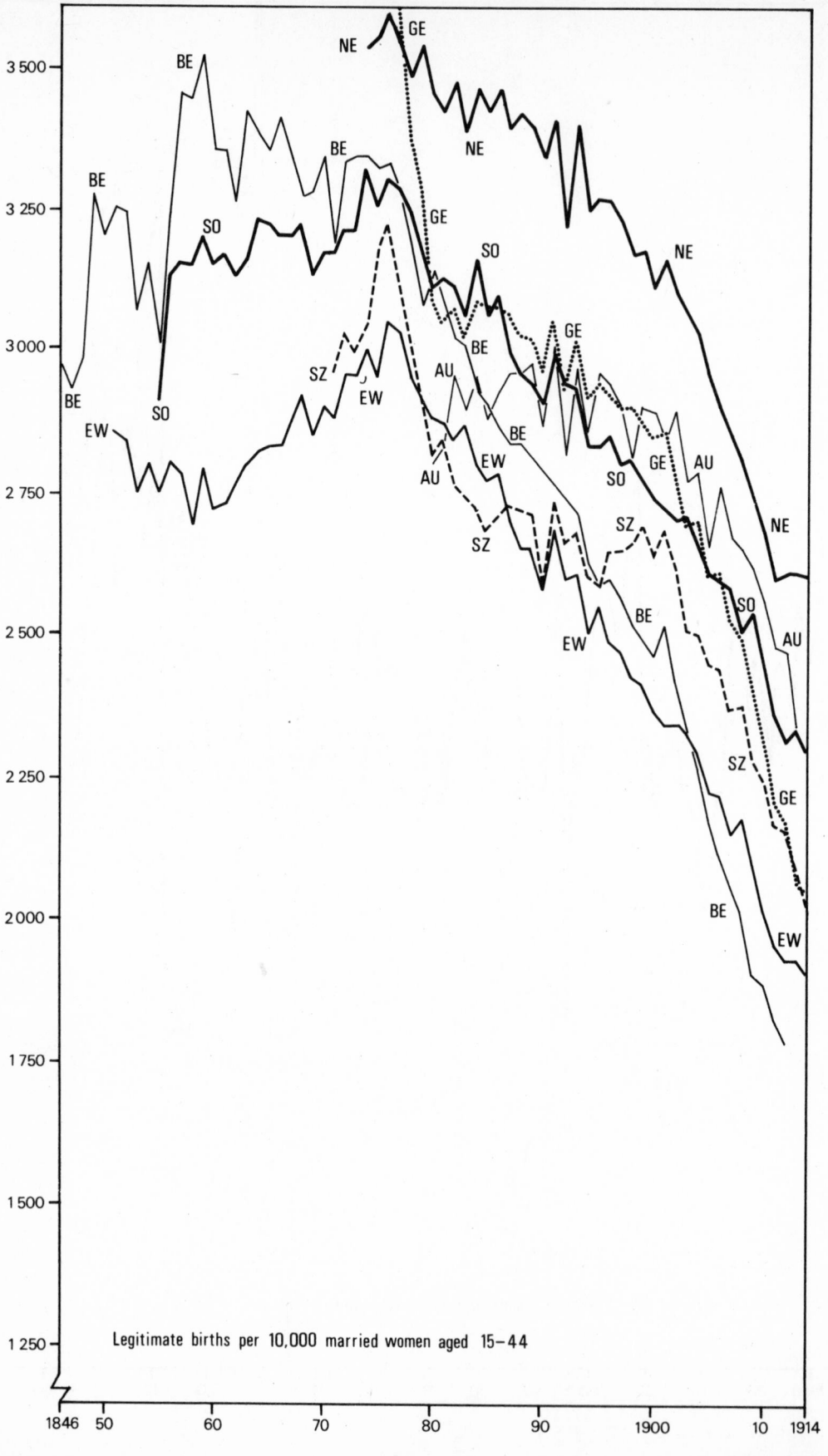

Legitimate births per 10,000 married women aged 15–44

1846 50   60   70   80   90   1900   10 1914

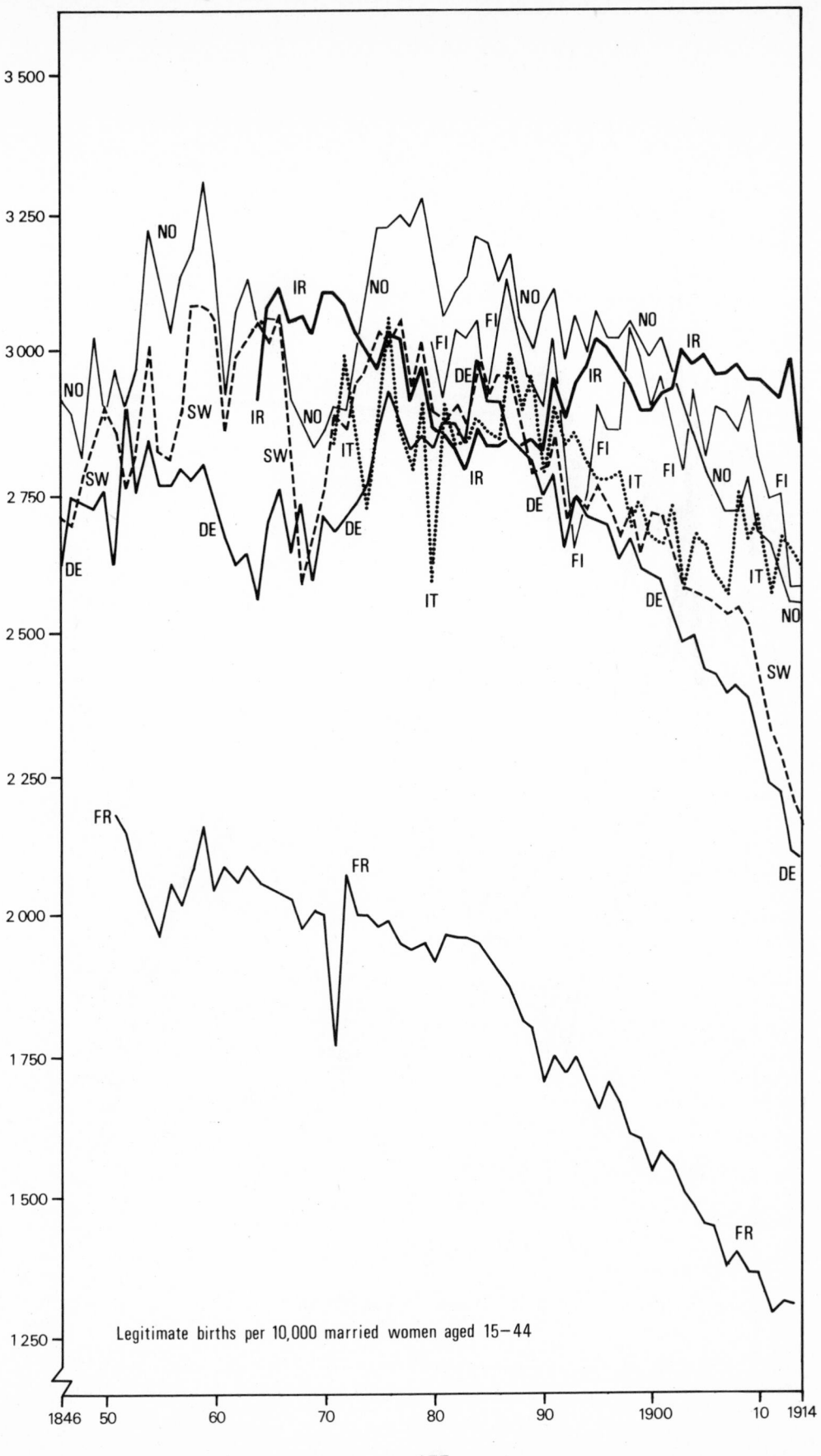

Legitimate births per 10,000 married women aged 15—44

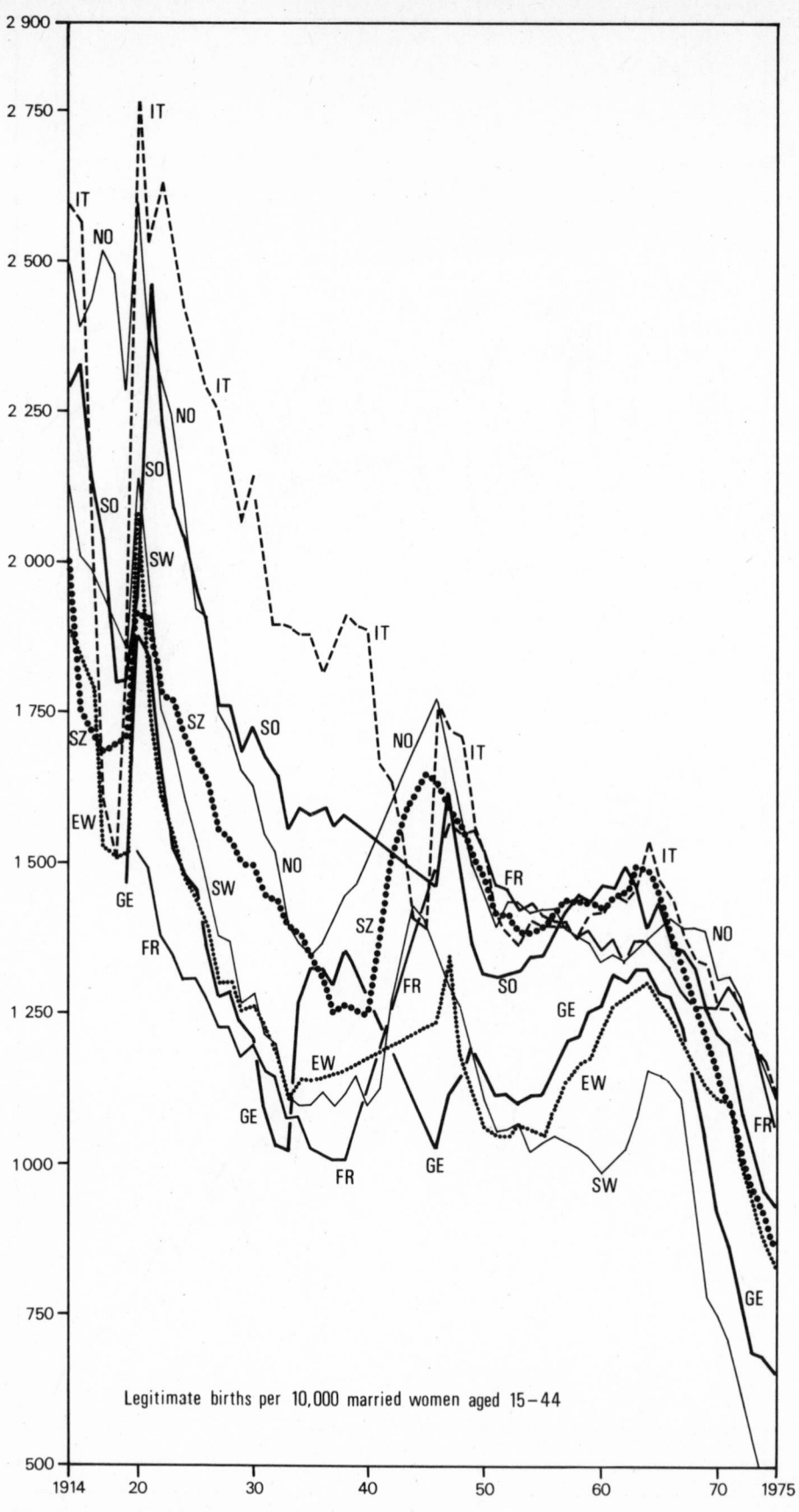

Legitimate births per 10,000 married women aged 15−44

Legitimate Births

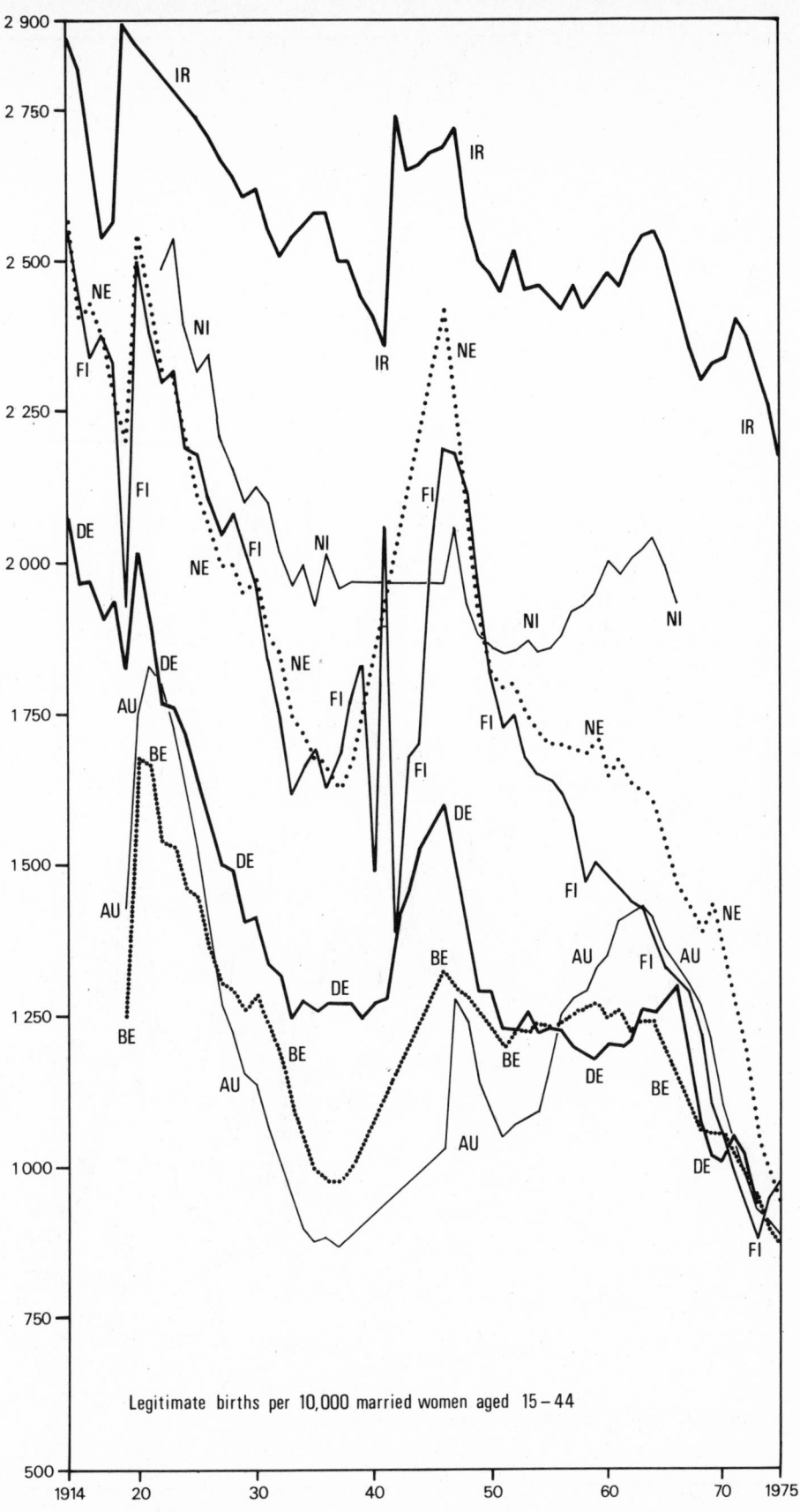

Legitimate births per 10,000 married women aged 15-44

Illegitimate Births

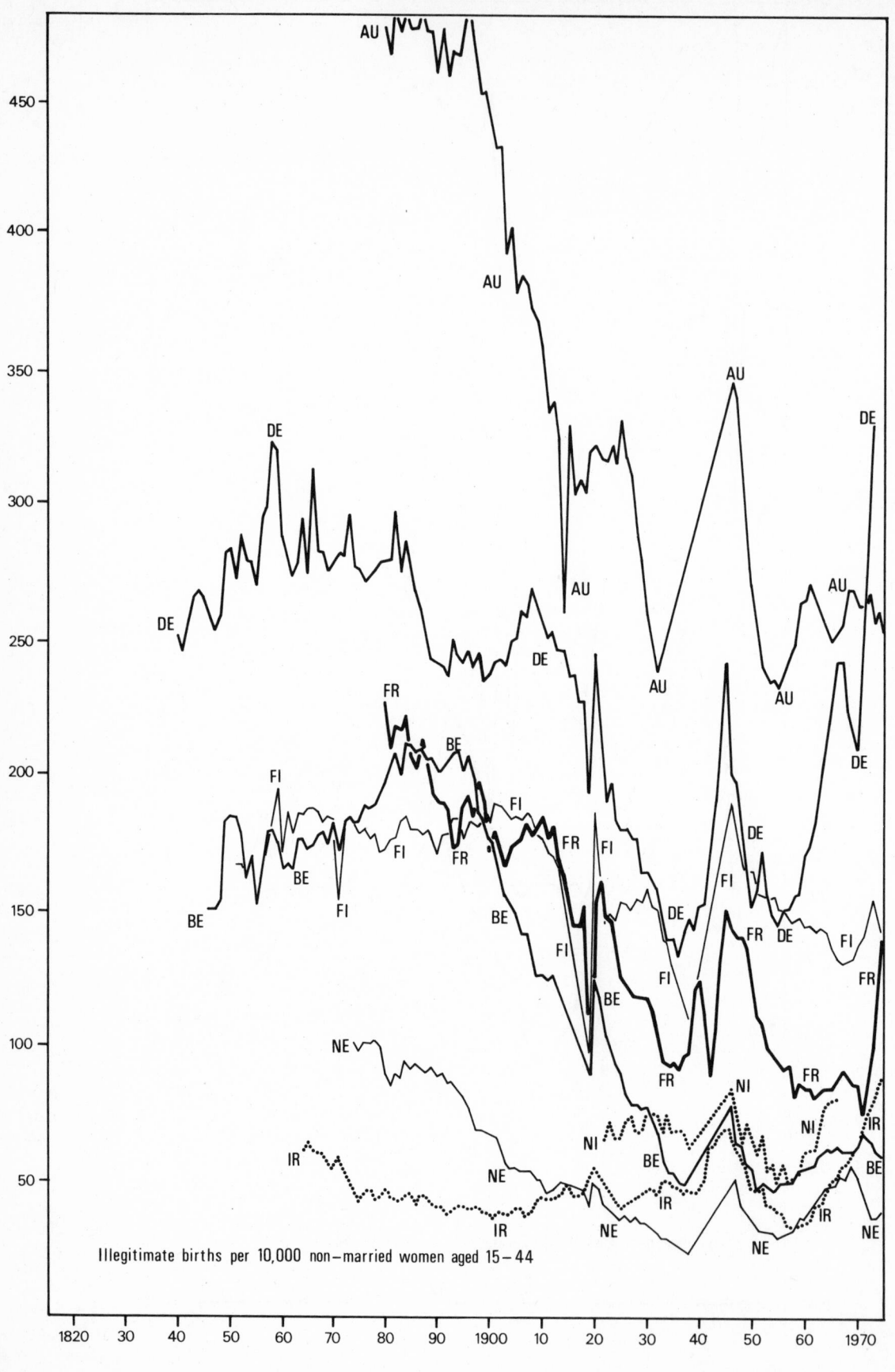

Illegitimate births per 10,000 non-married women aged 15–44

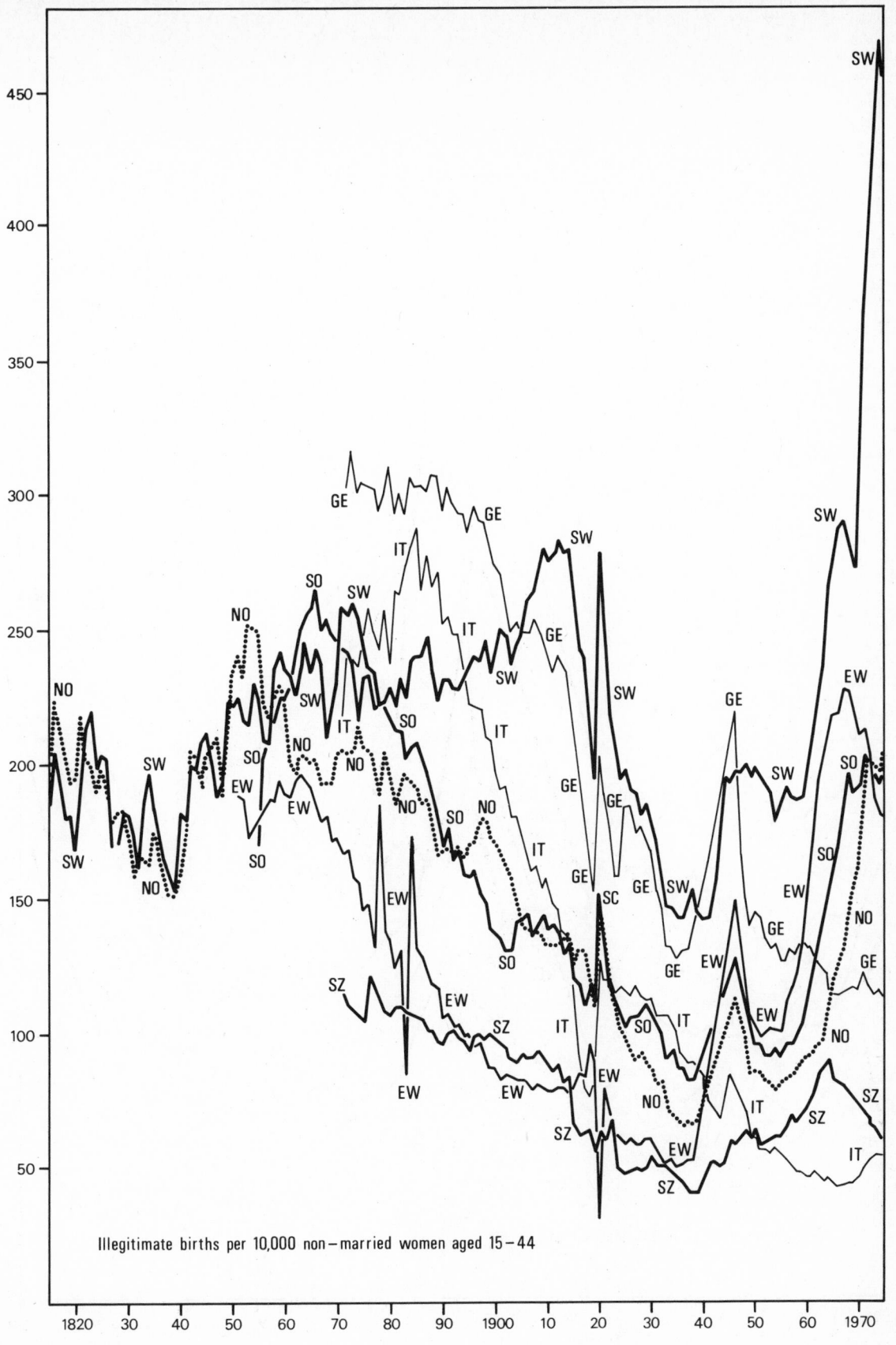

Illegitimate births per 10,000 non-married women aged 15-44

Divorces

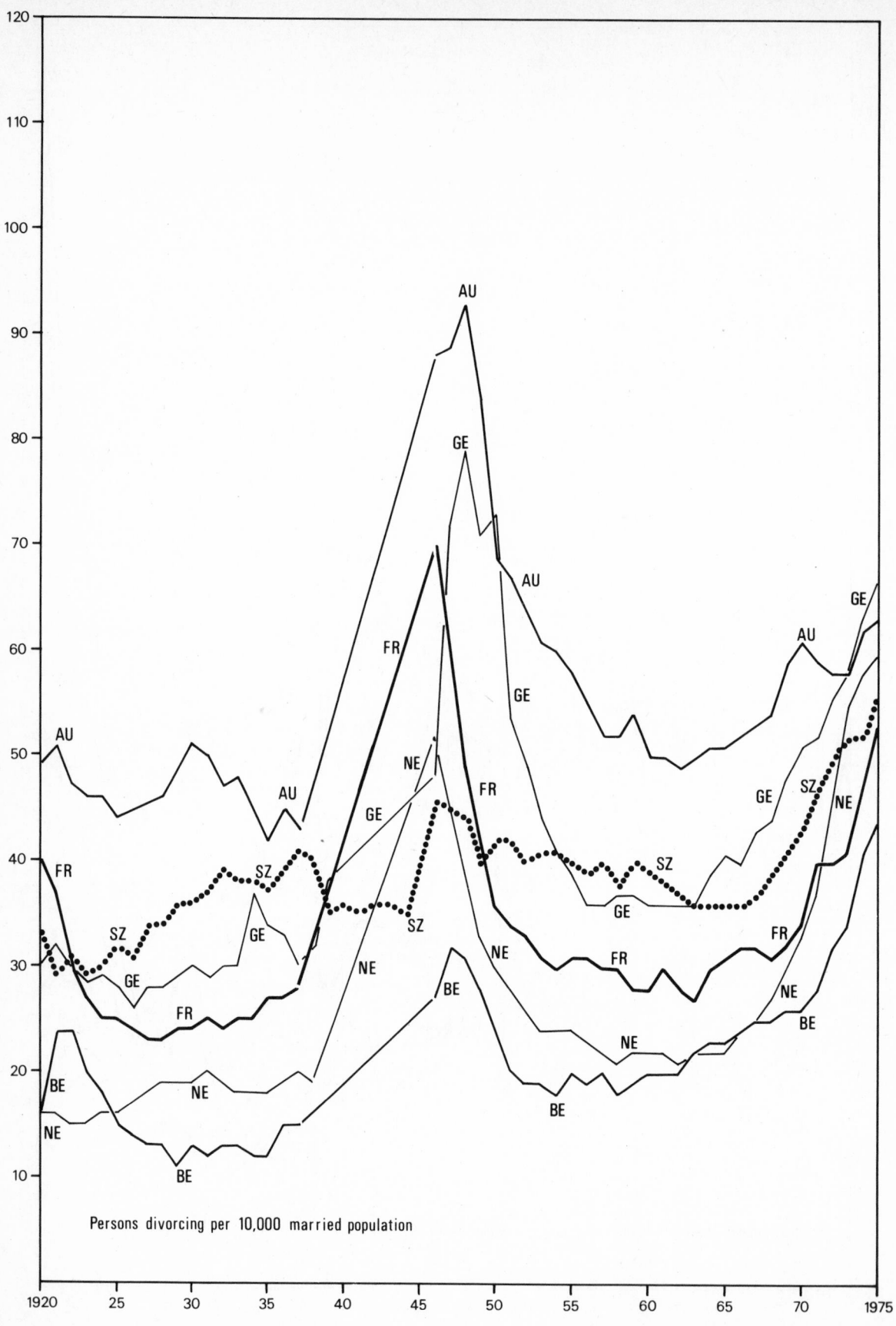

Persons divorcing per 10,000 married population

Divorces

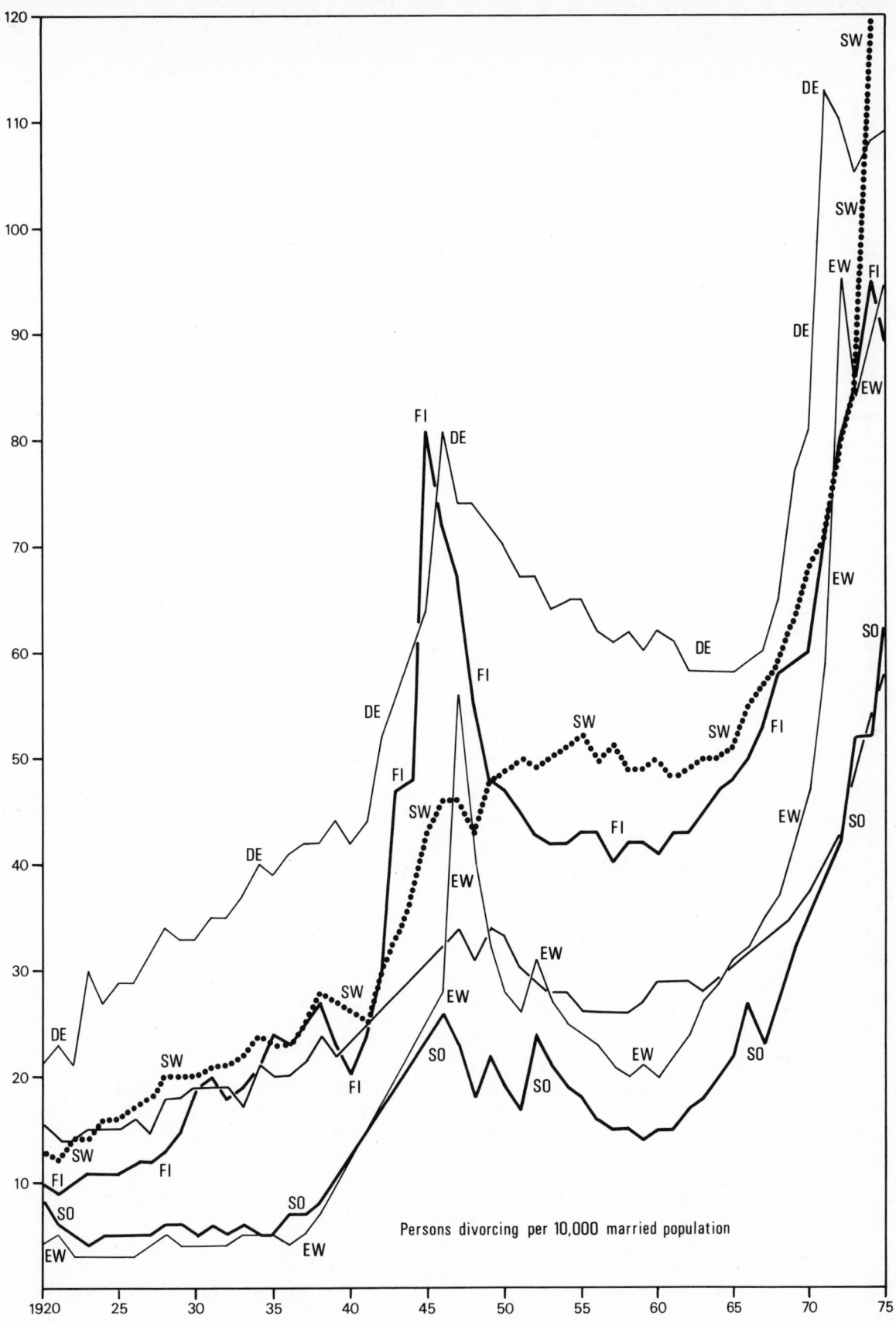

Persons divorcing per 10,000 married population

Austria

Marriages, Divorces, Illegitimacy

Year	Marriages		persons marrying per 10.000 non-married persons		Divorces a)			Births			births per 10.000 women age 15-44		Year
		marr. per 1.000 pop.				divorces per 100 marr.	persons divorcing per 10.000 married pop.	Legitimate	Illegit.	illeg. births per 100 legit. births	leg. births/ married women	ill. births/ non-marr. w.	
			age 15+	age 15-49									
	Total				Total			Total	Total				
1975	46 542	6.2	425	750	10 763	23.1	63	81 092	12 665	15.6	880	253	1975
1974	49 296	6.5	446	783	10 630	21.6	62	84 018	13 412	16.0	914	262	1974
1973	49 430	6.6	444	776	9 972	20.2	58	84 636	13 405	15.8	926	257	1973
1972	57 372	7.7	514	894	9 939	17.3	58	89 818	14 215	15.8	991	269	1972
1971	48 166	6.5	430	745	10 005	20.8	59	94 411	14 099	14.9	1052	263	1971
1970	52 773	7.1	470	810	10 356	19.6	61	97 958	14 343	14.6	1100	263	1970
1969	54 559	7.4	485	831	9 969	18.3	59	106 514	14 863	14.0	1207	269	1969
1968	56 001	7.6	496	847	9 705	17.3	58	110 978	15 137	13.6	1269	270	1968
1967	56 091	7.7	496	843	8 880	15.8	53	112 799	14 605	12.9	1302	257	1967
1966	55 816	7.7	492	833	8 643	15.5	52	113 937	14 640	12.8	1327	255	1966
1965	56 738	7.8	499	841	8 423	14.8	51	115 350	14 574	12.6	1355	250	1965
1964	57 533	8.0	505	848	8 390	14.6	51	118 688	15 153	12.8	1408	257	1964
1963	58 415	8.1	513	857	8 150	14.0	50	119 140	15 669	13.2	1430	263	1963
1962	59 705	8.4	523	872	7 969	13.3	49	117 203	16 050	13.7	1421	267	1962
1961	60 001	8.5	526	872	8 045	13.4	50	115 020	16 543	14.4	1409	272	1961
1960	58 508	8.3	514	845	8 011	13.7	50	109 541	16 404	15.0	1348	266	1960
1959	55 514	7.9	489	796	8 474	15.3	54	107 780	16 597	15.4	1333	265	1959
1958	55 407	7.9	489	789	8 238	14.9	52	103 894	15 861	15.3	1289	249	1958
1957	56 510	8.1	499	798	8 177	14.5	52	102 927	15 785	15.3	1279	244	1957
1956	57 383	8.3	506	803	8 488	14.8	55	100 140	15 687	15.7	1247	238	1956
1955	56 689	8.2	499	785	8 994	15.9	58	92 980	15 595	16.8	1158	233	1955
1954	54 289	7.8	477	744	9 227	17.0	60	87 761	16 134	18.4	1093	236	1954
1953	54 202	7.8	476	735	9 417	17.4	61	86 554	16 313	18.8	1078	235	1953
1952	57 571	8.3	505	773	9 833	17.1	64	86 036	16 976	19.7	1072	241	1952
1951	63 167	9.1	552	839	10 295	16.3	67	84 476	18 288	21.6	1051	255	1951
1950	64 621	9.3	563	849	10 534	16.3	69	88 070	19 784	22.5	1095	271	1950
1949	68 974	9.9	599	896	12 776	18.5	84	91 955	21 420	23.3	1142	288	1949
1948	71 904	10.3	622	923	14 162	19.7	93	99 658	23 563	23.6	1235	311	1948
1947	75 484	10.9	654	964	13 465	17.8	89	102 858	26 095	25.4	1279	341	1947
1946	62 791	9.0	537	784	13 351	21.3	88	84 031	27 271	32.5	1033	346	1946
1945	62 791				4 554	7.3		75 554	25 815	34.2			1945
1944	31 363												1944
1943	41 107												1943
1942	48 588				6 552	13.5							1942
1941	56 504				6 917	12.2							1941
1940	78 204				6 574	8.4							1940
1939	117 076				8 226	7.0							1939
1938	89 994	13.3	729	1006									1938
1937	46 289	6.9	373	511	5 843	12.6	43	66 663	19 688	29.5	873	239	1937
1936	46 293	6.8	370	505	5 980	12.9	45	67 190	21 074	31.4	885	252	1936
1935	45 673	6.8	363	492	5 571	12.2	42	66 455	22 234	33.5	881	261	1935
1934	43 979	6.5	347	469	5 918	13.5	45	67 412	24 155	35.8	901	279	1934
1933	43 902	6.5	345	463	6 228	14.2	48	70 989	25 380	35.8	957	289	1933
1932	45 356	6.7	355	474	6 048	13.3	47	74 601	27 676	31.1	1015	311	1932
1931	49 717	7.4	388	516	6 357	12.8	50	77 735	28 589	36.8	1069	317	1931
1930	51 583	7.7	402	531	6 424	12.5	51	81 830	30 400	37.2	1136	332	1930
1929	51 293	7.7	398	523	5 906	11.5	48	82 782	29 265	35.4	1161	316	1929
1928	49 305	7.4	381	499	5 561	11.3	46	86 451	30 278	35.0	1224	323	1928

162

Austria

Marriages, Divorces, Illegitimacy

Year	Marriages Total	marr. per 1.000 pop.	persons marrying per 10.000 non-married persons age 15+	age 15-49	Divorces [a] Total	divorces per 100 marr.	persons divorcing per 10.000 married pop.	Births Legitimate Total	Illegit. Total	illeg. births per 100 legit. births	leg. births/married women	ill. births/non-marr. w.	Year
1927	48 493	7.3	374	487				88 682	29 986	33.8	1269	316	1927
1926	47 886	7.3	368	477				96 773	30 477	31.5	1400	317	1926
1925	50 842	7.7	390	503	5 193	10.2	44	104 484	31 357	30.0	1526	323	1925
1924	52 845	8.1	404	519	5 356	10.1	46	110 736	31 405	28.4	1635	320	1924
1923	56 594	8.6	431	552	5 297	9.4	46	116 613	30 272	26.0	1729	305	1923
1922	74 274	11.4	564	719	5 350	7.2	47	119 770	31 188 [b]	26.0	1804	310	1922
1921	81 223	12.5	615	781	5 654	7.0	51	120 171	30 967	25.7	1829	305	1921
1920	85 866	13.3	652	823	5 358	6.2	49	112 900	33 744	29.9	1746	330	1920
1919	80 363	12.5	610	767	4 159	5.2	39	91 456	27 062	29.6	1433	262	1919

a) First steps towards a secularization of marriage law were taken as early as 1783 and 1811. The General Civil Code of 1811 introduced divorce for the non-Catholic population. Catholics were only allowed separation a mensa et thoro, apart from the limited practice of marriage invalidation by the Church. This legal situation did not basically change until 1938. After World War I, however, legal separation (then referred to as 'divorce' in Austria) became almost identical with divorce (then referred to as 'separation'), as remarriage after separation was allowed by edict in some provinces. In 1938, after annexation, civil marriage was made obligatory and divorce was also introduced for Catholics. The new Austrian state took over the 1938 law with only a few changes regarding divorce. Divorce law is based on the principles of guilt and marital breakdown.
In the tables, divorce figures for the period 1882 to 1937 include divorces (D) for non-Catholics together with separations (S) for Catholics and other groups, but do not include invalidations (I). Figures for the latter are given below. From 1938 figures refer to divorces in the stricter sense.

Year	D	S		Year	D	S	I		Year	D	S	I
1882	97	651		1898	149	1 117			1919	272	3 887	12
1883	81	616		1899	156	1 190			1920	365	4 993	14
1884	65	656		1900	163	1 310			1921	436	5 218	21
1885	91	654		1901	187	1 508			1922	436	4 914	44
1886	90	670		1902	222	1 725			1923	459	4 836	39
1887	111	671		1903	206	1 827			1924	520	4 836	152
1888	86	671		1904	285	1 876			1925	475	4 718	157
1889	103	702		1905	262	1 885			1926	-	-	-
1890	106	702		1906	290	2 019			1927	455	4 634	59
1891	116	767		1907	330	2 040			1928	535	5 026	142
1892	129	777		1908	346	2 110			1929	547	5 359	97
1893	130	801		1909	380	2 433	36		1930	650	5 774	149
1894	133	856		1910	364	2 437	30		1931	654	5 703	373
1895	136	858		1911	437	2 599	32		1932	578	5 470	255
1896	139	838		1912	489	2 709	39		1933	618	5 610	327
1897	150	837		1913	339	2 903	36		1934	784	5 134	397
									1935	728	4 843	397

b) Excluding Burgenland

Austria

Marriages, Divorces, Illegitimacy

Year	Marriages Total	marr. per 1.000 pop.	persons marrying per 10.000 non-married persons age 15+	age 15–49	Divorces Total	divorces per 100 marr.	persons divorcing per 10.000 married pop.	Births Legitimate Total	Illegit. Total	illeg. births per 100 legit. births	births per 10.000 women age 15–44 leg. births/ married women	ill. births/ non-marr. w.	Year
1913	195 846	6.8	448	563	3 242	1.7	7	761 918	102 845	13.5	2339	325	1913
1912	212 187	7.4	487	613	3 188	1.5	7	796 606	106 801	13.4	2466	339	1912
1911	217 373	7.6	502	631	3 036	1.4	6	793 563	105 139	13.2	2475	335	1911
1910	214 970	7.6	499	628	2 781	1.3	6	811 815	111 730	13.8	2555	358	1910
1909	213 083	7.6	498	626	2 813	1.3	6	826 859	114 380	13.8	2624	368	1909
1908	213 670	7.7	502	631	2 456	1.1	5	826 029	115 346	14.0	2646	373	1908
1907	209 514	7.6	495	623	2 370	1.1	5	825 250	116 919	14.2	2667	381	1907
1906	217 317	8.0	517	650	2 219	1.0	5	843 853	117 405	13.9	2756	385	1906
1905	212 927	7.9	510	641	2 147	1.0	5	806 809	114 955	14.2	2656	379	1905
1904	210 146	7.8	506	636	2 161	1.0	5	839 643	121 787	14.5	2788	403	1904
1903	209 135	7.9	507	637	2 033	1.0	4	825 842	118 111	14.3	2767	393	1903
1902	206 577	7.9	504	633	1 947	0.9	4	854 960	129 280	15.1	2894	433	1902
1901	213 757	8.2	525	660	1 695	0.8	4	833 345	128 156	15.4	2849	432	1901
1900	214 214	8.3	531	666	1 473	0.7	3	837 170	130 769	15.6	2893	444	1900
1899	213 751	8.4	534	669	1 446	0.7	3	827 981	132 224	16.0	2899	452	1899
1898	199 661	7.9	502	629	1 266	0.6	3	791 885	131 356	16.6	2807	452	1898
1897	203 943	8.1	516	647	987	0.5	2	809 224	135 540	16.7	2905	469	1897
1896	198 461	8.0	506	634	977	0.5	2	808 869	139 750	17.3	2941	487	1896
1895	199 505	8.1	512	642	987	0.5	2	805 101	136 083	16.9	2963	477	1895
1894	194 233	8.0	501	628	986	0.5	2	768 594	132 804	17.3	2857	467	1894
1893	193 235	8.0	501	628	931	0.5	2	790 967	132 503	16.8	2972	468	1893
1892	187 707	7.8	489	612	906	0.5	2	741 825	129 453	17.5	2815	459	1892
1891	186 418	7.8	488	611	883	0.5	2	785 754	133 749	17.0	3011	476	1891
1890	178 906	7.6	470	588	808	0.5	2	740 233	128 702	17.4	2866	460	1890
1889	177 771	7.6	472	591	810	0.5	2	766 491	131 859	17.2	2975	475	1889
1888	185 991	8.0	500	626	757	0.4	2	759 656	130 245	17.1	2958	475	1888
1887	182 088	7.9	495	619	782	0.4	2	758 763	130 715	17.2	2963	481	1887
1886	180 191	7.9	496	619	760	0.4	2	747 687	128 376	17.2	2928	477	1886
1885	175 233	7.7	487	608	745	0.4	2	733 871	126 792	17.3	2881	476	1885
1884	179 171	8.0	503	628	721	0.4	2	750 018	128 303	17.1	2951	486	1884
1883	176 018	7.9	500	624	697	0.4	2	734 691	124 141	16.9	2897	475	1883
1882	183 378	8.3	526	656	748	0.4	2	747 737	125 785	16.8	2955	486	1882
1881	176 983	8.0	513	640				713 888	119 588	16.8	2826	466	1881
1880	167 200	7.6	490	610				706 823	121 157	17.1	2802	476	1880
1879	169 088	7.8						732 849	122 744	16.7			1879
1878	164 233	7.6						716 156	117 095	16.4			1878
1877	161 337	7.5						715 704	115 072	16.1			1877
1876	176 148	8.3						747 925	105 511	14.1			1876
1875	180 349	8.6						742 065	100 238	13.5			1875
1874	189 017	9.1						730 696	99 013	13.6			1874
1873	194 815	9.4						727 772	100 258	13.8			1873
1872	192 406	9.3						711 421	98 726	13.9			1872
1871	194 591	9.5						697 544	103 971	14.9			1871
1870	199 083	9.8						782 488	105 793	13.5			1870
1869	208 787	10.4						685 862	109 498	16.0			1869
1868	182 940	9.2											1868
1867	191 661	9.7						671 355	106 702	15.9			1867
1866	128 051	6.5											1866

Austria

Marriages, Divorces, Illegitimacy

Year	Marriages Total	marr. per 1.000 pop.	persons marrying per 10.000 non-married persons age 15+	persons marrying per 10.000 non-married persons age 15–49	Divorces Total	divorces per 100 marr.	persons divorcing per 10.000 married pop.	Births[b] Legitimate Total	Illegit. Total	illeg. births per 100 legit. births	births per 10.000 women age 15–44 leg. births/married women	births per 10.000 women age 15–44 ill. births/non-marr. w.	Year
1865	153 492	7.9											1865
1864	160 740	8.3						645 827	112 325	17.4			1864
1863	162 958	8.5											1863
1862	168 684	8.9											1862
1861	151 440	8.0											1861
1860	158 340	8.5											1860
1859	130 656	7.1						614 184	112 355	18.3			1859
1858	155 073	8.5											1858
1857	147 657	8.1											1857
1856	147 474	8.2											1856
1855	115 223	6.4											1855
1854	124 258	6.9						573 681	88 500	15.4			1854
1853	137 621	7.7											1853
1852	140 379	7.9											1852
1851	154 481	8.8											1851
1850	168 818	9.6											1850
1849	161 273	9.2						571 030	86 027	15.1			1849
1848	152 240	8.7											1848
1847	128 389	7.3											1847
1846	141 738	8.1											1846
1845	133 446	7.6											1845
1844	141 874	8.2						587 631	93 758	16.0			1844
1843	145 960	8.5											1843
1842	138 020	8.1											1842
1841	142 000	8.4											1841
1840	132 253	7.9											1840
1839	130 025	7.9						552 750	81 484	14.7			1839
1838	127 888	7.8											1838
1837	141 572	8.8											1837
1836	139 538	8.7											1836
1835	127 760	8.0											1835
1834	132 080	8.4						535 655	72 869	13.6			1834
1833	135 745	8.6											1833
1832	151 188	9.7											1832
1831	113 331	7.2											1831
1830	126 373	8.1											1830
1829	134 947	8.7											1829
1828	130 553	8.5											1828
1827	131 255	8.6											1827
1826	120 026	8.0											1826
1825	115 898	7.8											1825
1824	114 670	7.8											1824
1823	104 395	7.2											1823
1822	107 822	7.6											1822
1821	111 414	7.9											1821
1820	121 982	8.8											1820
1819	121 713	8.9											1819

a) See footnote for the years 1919–1975.
b) From 1832 to 1868 figures have only been available as five-year-averages.

M a r r i a g e s ,   D i v o r c e s ,   I l l e g i t i m a c y

Year	Marriages				Divorces [a]			Births		illeg. births per 100 legit. births	birth per 10,000 women age 15-44		Year
	Total	marr. per 1,000 pop.	persons marrying per 10,000 non-married persons age 15+	age 15-49	Total	divorces per 100 marr.	persons divorcing per 10,000 married pop.	Legitimate Total	Illegit. Total		leg. births/ married women	ill. births/ on-marr. women	
1975	73 363	7.5	582	944	10 977	15.0	44	115 576	3 697	3.2	862	58	1975
1974	73 567	7.5	587	954	10 133	13.8	41	119 378	3 777	3.2	895	60	1974
1973	73 664	7.6	591	963	8 336	11.3	34	125 546	3 879	3.1	946	62	1973
1972	74 352	7.7	600	980	7 832	10.5	32	130 326	4 111	3.2	986	66	1972
1971	73 644	7.6	598	979	7 024	9.5	28	134 906	4 198	3.1	1026	68	1971
1970	73 261	7.6	597	981	6 403	8.7	26	137 178	3 941	2.9	1047	64	1970
1969	72 330	7.5	592	974	6 458	8.9	26	137 055	3 779	2.8	1049	62	1969
1968	69 713	7.2	573	947	6 057	8.7	25	137 472	3 770	2.7	1056	62	1968
1967	68 309	7.1	565	936	6 023	8.8	25	142 177	3 722	2.6	1098	62	1967
1966	68 330	7.2	570	947	5 826	8.5	24	146 886	3 750	2.6	1143	63	1966
1965	66 535	7.0	560	932	5 520	8.3	23	151 179	3 677	2.4	1187	62	1965
1964	65 008	6.9	553	924	5 470	8.4	23	156 691	3 680	2.3	1243	63	1964
1963	62 449	6.7	538	901	5 171	8.3	22	154 705	3 491	2.3	1241	61	1963
1962	62 086	6.7	539	906	4 697	7.6	20	151 076	3 262	2.2	1220	57	1962
1961	62 371	6.8	545	918	4 607	7.4	20	155 246	3 185	2.1	1260	56	1961
1960	65 220	7.1	565	941	4 589	7.0	20	152 320	3 200	2.1	1245	55	1960
1959	65 135	7.2	560	921	4 406	6.8	19	154 955	3 282	2.1	1273	55	1959
1958	67 193	7.4	573	932	4 261	6.3	18	151 933	3 115	2.1	1256	51	1958
1957	68 338	7.6	580	932	4 527	6.6	20	149 787	3 084	2.1	1247	50	1957
1956	68 700	7.7	579	922	4 313	6.3	19	147 091	3 119	2.1	1235	50	1956
1955	68 881	7.8	577	909	4 416	6.4	20	146 026	3 169	2.2	1233	50	1955
1954	67 931	7.7	566	881	3 999	5.9	18	145 453	3 085	2.1	1236	47	1954
1953	67 742	7.7	560	864	4 163	6.1	19	142 864	3 261	2.3	1221	49	1953
1952	67 340	7.7	553	845	4 211	6.3	19	142 668	3 396	2.4	1226	50	1952
1951	70 541	8.1	575	872	4 366	6.2	20	138 999	3 315	2.4	1202	48	1951
1950	72 023	8.3	583	876	5 100	7.1	24	141 895	3 777	2.7	1233	54	1950
1949	73 453	8.5	589	878	5 988	8.2	28	143 914	3 940	2.7	1255	56	1949
1948	79 737	9.3	636	941	6 518	8.2	31	145 889	4 527	3.1	1281	63	1948
1947	83 665	9.9	669	980	6 825	8.2	32	145 497	4 730	3.3	1295	65	1947
1946	90 909	10.9	725	1055	5 653	6.2	27	147 171	5 791	3.9	1324	79	1946
1945	83 077	10.0			3 178	3.8		124 966	5 560	4.4			1945
1944	45 352	5.5			3 398	7.5		122 759	4 363	3.6			1944
1943	52 056	6.3			3 430	6.6		120 163	3 186	2.7			1943
1942	61 834	7.5			2 971	4.8		106 011	2 592	2.4			1942
1941	52 697	6.4			2 623	5.0		97 608	3 008	3.1			1941
1940	35 685	4.3			1 803	5.1		109 010	3 487	3.2			1940
1939	54 871	6.5			3 423	6.2		126 819	3 200	2.5			1939
1938	61 549	7.4	553	805	3 501	5.7	16	130 251	3 359	2.6	996	52	1938
1937	63 435	7.6	563	811	3 208	5.1	15	125 443	3 253	2.6	975	49	1937
1936	64 749	7.8	567	811	3 093	4.8	15	124 310	3 441	2.8	982	50	1936
1935	63 160	7.6	546	774	2 575	4.1	12	124 665	3 767	3.0	1000	54	1935
1934	62 692	7.6	535	753	2 441	3.9	12	129 578	3 936	3.0	1055	54	1934
1933	65 098	7.9	549	766	2 616	4.0	13	132 434	4 323	3.3	1097	58	1933
1932	62 186	7.6	519	720	2 522	4.1	13	140 647	5 188	3.7	1187	68	1932
1931	66 168	8.1	548	754	2 351	3.6	12	144 068	5 589	3.9	1241	72	1931
1930	71 624	8.9	588	804	2 491	3.5	13	146 366	6 164	4.2	1285	78	1930
1929	71 811	8.9	584	793	2 134	3.0	11	141 076	6 235	4.4	1263	77	1929
1928	71 485	9.0	578	780	2 351	3.3	13	141 565	6 506	4.6	1295	79	1928

Marriages, Divorces, Illegitimacy

Year	Marriages				Divorces [a]			Births			births per 10.000 women		Year
	Total	marr. per 1.000 pop.	persons marrying per 10.000 non-married persons age 15+	age 15-49	Total	divorces per 100 marr.	persons divorcing per 10.000 married pop.	Legitimate Total	Illegit. Total	illeg. births per 100 legit. births	leg. births/ married women	ill. births/ non-marr. women	
1927	71 921	9.1	578	775	2 351	3.3	13	139 682	6 614	4.7	1306	79	1927
1926	72 517	9.2	579	772	2 349	3.2	14	143 908	7 101	4.9	1375	83	1926
1925	74 761	9.6	596	790	2 503	3.3	15	147 578	7 752	5.3	1448	90	1925
1924	80 088	10.5	638	841	2 956	3.7	18	145 917	8 166	5.6	1471	94	1924
1923	79 786	10.5	633	830	3 253	4.1	20	147 791	8 809	6.0	1527	100	1923
1922	82 806	11.0	654	853	3 718	4.5	24	145 443	9 338	6.4	1538	104	1922
1921	88 456	11.9	695	902	3 665	4.1	24	153 963	10 640	6.9	1668	118	1921
1920	106 514	14.2	821	1061	2 195	2.1	15	153 302	11 648	7.6	1676	125	1920
1919	97 084	12.8	746	963	623	0.6	4	114 973	8 341	7.3	1249	89	1919
1918	43 558	5.7	335	433									1918
1917	32 974	4.3	253	327									1917
1916	30 458	4.0	234	302									1916
1915	24 654	3.2	191	246									1915
1914	41 095	5.4	321	415									1914
1913	61 096	8.0	485	626	1 207	2.0	8	160 124	10 975	6.9	1766	123	1913
1912	61 278	8.1	494	638	1 159	1.9	8	160 080	11 107	6.9	1791	127	1912
1911	59 370	8.0	486	628	1 081	1.8	8	161 035	10 767	6.7	1825	125	1911
1910	58 776	7.9	486	628	1 089	1.9	8	165 576	10 837	6.5	1888	127	1910
1909	57 126	7.7	471	608	1 039	1.8	8	165 599	10 832	6.5	1909	127	1909
1908	57 564	7.8	477	615	892	1.5	7	172 509	11 325	6.6	2023	133	1908
1907	58 660	8.1	489	630	841	1.4	6	173 134	12 004	6.9	2069	142	1907
1906	58 388	8.1	630	618	618	1.1	5	174 338	11 933	6.8	2124	142	1906
1905	56 679	8.0	478	616	901	1.6	7	175 028	12 409	7.1	2176	148	1905
1904	56 740	8.1	483	621	932	1.6	8	179 093	12 628	7.1	2273	151	1904
1903	54 946	7.9	471	605	734	1.3	6	179 414	12 887	7.2	2327	156	1903
1902	56 157	8.2	486	624	703	1.3	6	182 514	13 357	7.3	2421	163	1902
1901	57 131	8.5	499	641	821	1.4	7	185 940	14 137	7.6	2524	174	1901
1900	57 711	8.6	504	647	690	1.2	6	179 352	14 437	8.0	2467	177	1900
1899	55 765	8.3	486	623	563	1.0	5	179 349	14 919	8.3	2504	183	1899
1898	55 444	8.4	487	624	747	1.3	7	175 869	15 052	8.6	2517	186	1898
1897	54 198	8.3	481	616	625	1.2	6	175 102	15 885	9.1	2574	198	1897
1896	52 585	8.1	471	604	548	1.0	5	172 023	16 510	9.6	2598	208	1896
1895	49 712	7.8	449	575	492	1.0	5	167 204	15 811	9.5	2591	201	1895
1894	47 735	7.6	435	557	477	1.0	5	165 150	16 316	9.9	2626	209	1894
1893	47 065	7.6	432	553	497	1.1	5	166 976	16 086	9.6	2724	208	1893
1892	47 209	7.7	436	558	441	0.9	4						1892
1891	45 449	7.4	423	541	402	0.9	4						1891
1890	44 596	7.3	415	530	373	0.8	4	161 349	15 246	9.4	2816	201	1890
1889	43 759	7.2	409	524	379	0.9	4	161 939	15 603	9.6	2839	206	1889
1888	42 427	7.1	401	514	356	0.8	4	160 250	15 336	9.6	2840	206	1888
1887	42 491	7.2	406	522	292	0.7	3	160 017	15 449	9.7	2871	210	1887
1886	49 642	8.4	481	618	286	0.6	3	159 918	15 173	9.5	2902	209	1886
1885	39 910	6.9	391	503	230	0.6	2	159 903	15 140	9.5	2936	211	1885
1884	39 205	6.8	390	501	221	0.6	2	161 734	14 987	9.3	3007	212	1884
1883	38 666	6.8	389	502	209	0.5	2	160 518	13 966	8.7	3021	200	1883
1882	39 214	7.0	400	516	216	0.6	2	162 066	14 279	8.8	3094	208	1882
1881	39 487	7.1	409	528	202	0.5	2	161 644	13 767	8.5	3127	203	1881
1880	38 926	7.0	405	524	214	0.5	2	158 580	13 284	8.4	3084	197	1880
1879	37 421	6.8	390	503	151	0.4	2						1879

Belgium

Marriages, Divorces, Illegitimacy

Year	Marriages		persons marrying per 10.000 non-married persons		Divorces a)			Births		illeg. births per 100 legit. births	births per 10.000 women age 15-44		Year
		marr. per 1.000 pop.	age 15+	age 15-49		divorces per 100 marr.	persons divorcing per 10.000 married pop.	Legitimate	Illegit.		leg. births/ married women	ill. births/ non-marr. women	
	Total				Total			Total	Total				
1878	36 669	6.7	385	496	143	0.4	2	160 070	12 660	7.9	3178	189	1878
1877	36 964	6.9	391	504	118	0.3	1	162 602	12 475	7.7	3281	188	1877
1876	38 228	7.1	404	519	135	0.4	2	164 348	12 567	7.6	3327	189	1876
1875	39 050	7.3	411	528	126	0.3	1	163 348	12 204	7.5	3317	183	1875
1874	40 328	7.6	428	550	120	0.3	1	161 882	12 096	7.5	3341	183	1874
1873	40 598	7.8	436	560	114	0.3	1	158 585	12 123	7.6	3335	185	1873
1872	40 084	7.8	435	558	109	0.3	1	155 528	11 849	7.6	3326	183	1872
1871	37 538	7.4	409	524	75	0.2	1	147 599	11 161	7.6	3190	173	1871
1870	35 263	7.0	386	494	81	0.2	1	152 792	11 780	7.7	3344	183	1870
1869	37 134	7.4	410	525	82	0.2	1	147 583	11 104	7.5	3278	174	1869
1868	36 271	7.4	404	516	60	0.2	1	144 831	11 303	7.8	3268	179	1868
1867	38 244	7.9	431	549	64	0.2	1	146 053	11 096	7.6	3348	177	1867
1866	37 783	7.7	420	535	70	0.2	1	147 134	10 876	7.4	3409	174	1866
1865	37 671	7.6	411	522	51	0.1	1	145 313	11 010	7.6	3345	173	1865
1864	36 959	7.5	405	512	66	0.2	1	144 635	11 237	7.8	3377	176	1864
1863	35 813	7.4	393	497	65	0.2	1	144 284	11 280	7.8	3422	177	1863
1862	34 146	7.1	377	475	57	0.2	1	135 032	10 536	7.8	3256	165	1862
1861	33 802	7.1	375	471	56	0.2	1	136 606	10 647	7.8	3348	167	1861
1860	35 112	7.5	391	490	55	0.2	1	134 196	10 472	7.8	3345	165	1860
1859	36 941	7.9	414	517	47	0.1	1	138 701	11 111	8.0	3515	175	1859
1858	38 237	8.3	430	535	55	0.1	1	133 673	11 401	8.5	3440	180	1858
1857	37 292	8.2	421	523	50	0.1	1	131 934	11 357	8.6	3449	179	1857
1856	32 926	7.2	368	456	42	0.1	1	123 652	10 535	8.5	3238	164	1856
1855	29 815	6.5	333	412	37	0.1	1	116 096	9 859	8.5	3013	153	1855
1854	29 485	6.5	333	412	44	0.1	1	120 932	10 905	9.0	3149	170	1854
1853	30 636	6.8	350	433	20	0.1		117 451	10 277	8.8	3073	162	1853
1852	31 251	7.0	362	447	35	0.1	1	123 254	11 143	9.0	3242	178	1852
1851	33 169	7.5	390	481	27	0.1		122 854	11 394	9.3	3254	184	1851
1850	33 766	7.7	404	497	29	0.1		120 107	11 309	9.4	3206	185	1850
1849	31 788	7.3	385	474	23	0.1		121 994	11 111	9.1	3271	183	1849
1848	28 656	6.6	351	431	22	0.1		111 091	9 292	8.4	2985	154	1848
1847	24 145	5.6	298	366	21	0.1		109 108	8 998	8.2	2930	150	1847
1846	25 670	5.9	320	392	29	0.1		110 661	8 949	8.1	2977	150	1846
1845	29 210	6.8			22	0.1		127 288	9 724	7.6			1845
1844	29 326	6.9			16	0.1		124 552	9 424	7.6			1844
1843	28 220	6.7			20	0.1		123 603	9 308	7.5			1843
1842	29 023	7.0			21	0.1		125 541	9 486	7.6			1842
1841	29 876	7.3			21	0.1		128 781	9 354	7.3			1841
1840	30 551	7.5			26	0.1							1840
1839	29 758	7.4			9								1839
1838	31 604	7.4			20	0.1							1838
1837	32 213	7.6			18	0.1							1837
1836	29 439	7.0			15	0.1							1836
1835	33 778	8.0			11								1835
1834	30 455	7.3			12								1834
1833	26 770	6.5			10								1833
1832	27 511	6.7			3								1832
1831	30 951	7.6			7								1831

a) Until 1974 divorce law was based on the Code Napoleon which allowed divorce on the grounds of guilt and by mutual consent. The latter was initially very limited, but became increasingly feasible, particularly as a result of the 1969 and 1972 amendments. A 1974 law (effective from 1975) introduced marital breakdown (as evidenced by a certain period of separation) as grounds for divorce. However, it retained some element of the guilt principle. Legal separation is obtainable on grounds similar to those for divorce, and may be turned into divorce after three years.

Divorce is granted by the courts but must be registered with the local Registrar's Office to become effective, thus giving us two sets of statistics, judicial and administrative, the latter being slightly lower. In the tables, divorce figures refer to registered divorces only. Figures on legal separations are not included. They are not available for the whole period and are of relatively minor importance.

Marriages, Divorces, Illegitimacy

Year	Marriages Total	marr. per 1.000 pop.	persons marrying per 10.000 non-married persons age 15+	age 15-49	Divorces [a] Total	divorces per 100 marr.	persons divorcing per 10.000 married pop.	Births Legitimate Total	Illegit. Total	illeg. births per 100 legit. births	births per 10.000 women age 15-44 leg. births/married women	ill. births/non-marr. w.	Year
1975	31 782	6.3	430	680	13 264	41.7	109						1975
1974	33 182	6.6	451	711	13 132	39.6	108						1974
1973	30 813	6.1	422	662	12 637	41.0	105	59 569	12 326	20.7	938	330	1973
1972	31 073	6.2	429	670	13 134	42.3	110	64 628	10 877	16.8	1023	292	1972
1971	32 801	6.6	456	710	13 401	40.9	113	66 074	9 285	14.1	1051	249	1971
1970	36 376	7.4	510	792	9 524	26.2	81	62 991	7 811	12.4	1008	210	1970
1969	39 158	8.0	554	858	8 955	22.9	77	63 244	8 054	12.7	1019	217	1969
1968	39 457	8.1	562	867	7 572	19.2	65	66 233	8 310	12.5	1071	224	1968
1967	41 158	8.5	591	908	6 939	16.9	60	72 388	9 022	12.5	1176	243	1967
1966	41 424	8.6	601	920	6 726	16.2	59	79 349	8 983	11.3	1298	243	1966
1965	41 693	8.8	611	932	6 527	15.7	58	77 684	8 112	10.4	1281	220	1965
1964	39 565	8.4	588	896	6 483	16.4	58	75 572	7 784	10.3	1256	214	1964
1963	38 580	8.2	581	883	6 460	16.7	58	75 096	7 317	9.7	1257	203	1963
1962	37 513	8.1	573	869	6 409	17.1	58	71 318	6 490	9.1	1205	182	1962
1961	36 364	7.9	563	853	6 606	18.2	61	70 286	6 153	8.8	1197	175	1961
1960	35 897	7.8	563	851	6 682	18.6	62	70 124	5 953	8.5	1202	171	1960
1959	34 414	7.6	544	819	6 457	18.8	60	68 500	5 428	7.9	1175	156	1959
1958	33 795	7.5	539	807	6 571	19.4	62	69 288	5 393	7.8	1190	156	1958
1957	34 310	7.6	551	820	6 439	18.8	61	70 035	5 229	7.5	1202	151	1957
1956	34 215	7.7	553	819	6 499	19.0	62	71 489	5 236	7.3	1226	151	1956
1955	35 027	7.9	570	840	6 771	19.3	65	71 791	5 054	7.0	1232	146	1955
1954	34 973	7.9	574	842	6 686	19.1	65	71 235	5 130	7.2	1224	149	1954
1953	35 293	8.1	584	854	6 515	18.5	64	72 893	5 368	7.4	1255	156	1953
1952	35 724	8.2	597	868	6 735	18.9	67	71 020	5 923	8.3	1226	173	1952
1951	36 575	8.5	616	891	6 681	18.3	67	71 175	5 384	7.6	1230	157	1951
1950	38 838	9.1	659	950	6 868	17.7	70	74 350	5 208	7.0	1287	152	1950
1949	37 496	8.9	630	897	6 991	18.6	72	73 995	5 924	8.0	1294	168	1949
1948	39 279	9.4	654	920	7 120	18.1	74	78 388	6 550	8.4	1384	181	1948
1947	39 910	9.6	659	917	6 943	17.4	74	84 334	7 380	8.8	1506	198	1947
1946	40 257	9.8	660	909	7 500	18.6	81	88 474	7 637	8.6	1597	200	1946
1945	36 341	9.0	593	809	5 849	16.1	64	85 624	9 438	11.0	1568	242	1945
1944	37 524	9.4	614	834	5 365	14.3	60	82 293	8 348	10.1	1534	212	1944
1943	36 738	9.3	604	816	4 913	13.4	56	76 790	7 529	9.8	1457	190	1943
1942	35 825	9.2	592	794	4 450	12.4	52	72 821	6 724	9.2	1406	169	1942
1941	33 719	8.7	558	746	3 761	11.2	44	65 154	6 152	9.4	1278	153	1941
1940	35 262	9.2	584	777	3 472	9.8	42	63 958	6 163	9.6	1272	152	1940
1939	35 856	9.4	594	785	3 647	10.2	44	62 035	5 879	9.5	1250	144	1939
1938	33 625	8.9	557	733	3 394	10.1	42	62 328	6 135	9.8	1272	148	1938
1937	34 130	9.1	565	740	3 344	9.8	42	61 488	5 952	9.7	1272	143	1937
1936	34 680	9.3	574	749	3 210	9.3	41	60 774	5 644	9.3	1274	134	1936
1935	34 327	9.3	568	738	2 992	8.7	39	59 281	5 942	10.0	1259	140	1935
1934	34 759	9.5	577	748	3 032	8.7	40	59 121	5 995	10.1	1284	140	1934
1933	31 958	8.8	533	690	2 762	8.6	37	56 363	6 417	11.4	1254	150	1933
1932	28 133	7.8	471	609	2 514	8.9	35	57 826	6 824	11.8	1317	159	1932
1931	29 027	8.1	489	630	2 472	8.5	35	57 379	6 887	12.0	1340	160	1931
1930	28 973	8.2	489	630	2 300	7.9	33	59 207	7 096	12.0	1414	164	1930
1929	27 725	7.9	473	609	2 265	8.2	33	58 264	7 033	12.1	1410	164	1929
1928	27 300	7.8	471	605	2 307	8.5	34	60 955	7 561	12.4	1492	177	1928

Denmark

Marriages, Divorces, Illegitimacy

Year	Marriages Total	marr. per 1.000 pop.	persons marrying per 10.000 non-married persons age 15+	age 15-49	Divorces[a] Total	divorces per 100 marr.	persons divorcing per 10.000 married pop.	Births Legitimate Total	Illegit. Total	illeg. births per 100 legit. births	births per 10.000 women age 15-44 leg. births/married women	ill. births/non-marr. w.	Year
1927	26 199	7.5	456	586	2 135	8.1	32	60 508	7 516	12.4	1500	177	1927
1926	25 733	7.5	453	581	1 904	7.4	29	63 146	7 588	12.0	1585	180	1926
1925	25 786	7.5	459	589	1 889	7.3	29	64 394	7 503	11.7	1641	180	1925
1924	26 482	7.8	479	613	1 707	6.4	27	66 263	7 573	11.4	1717	184	1924
1923	26 842	8.0	493	630	1 872	7.0	30	66 772	8 055	12.1	1760	198	1923
1922	26 354	7.9	491	627	1 308	5.0	21	66 202	7 684	11.6	1774	191	1922
1921	26 768	8.2	506	645	1 390	5.2	23	70 178	8 637	12.3	1912	217	1921
1920	26 991	8.8	546	697	1 197	4.4	21	69 091	9 139	13.2	2016	245	1920
1919	25 073	8.2	515	658	1 294	5.2	23	61 550	7 172	11.7	1828	195	1919
1918	22 976	7.6	479	612	1 098	4.8	20	64 262	8 243	12.8	1940	228	1918
1917	20 810	7.0	440	563	1 012	4.9	19	62 201	8 105	13.0	1908	227	1917
1916	21 071	7.2	452	579	917	4.4	17	63 218	8 341	13.2	1974	237	1916
1915	18 985	6.5	414	530	878	4.6	17	61 991	8 201	13.2	1968	237	1915
1914	19 757	6.9	437	561	887	4.5	17	64 900	8 394	12.9	2095	246	1914
1913	20 463	7.2	459	590	801	3.9	16	64 162	8 313	13.0	2105	247	1913
1912	20 537	7.3	467	601	724	3.5	15	66 282	8 377	12.6	2211	253	1912
1911	19 879	7.2	459	591	736	3.7	15	65 740	8 193	12.5	2228	251	1911
1910	19 986	7.3	466	600	749	3.7	16	66 973	8 324	12.4	2304	257	1910
1909	19 944	7.4	471	606	734	3.7	15	67 952	8 349	12.3	2375	261	1909
1908	20 011	7.5	478	614	651	3.3	14	67 697	8 536	12.6	2403	270	1908
1907	20 103	7.6	485	623	662	3.3	14	66 208	8 116	12.3	2386	259	1907
1906	19 358	7.4	472	606	590	3.0	13	66 129	8 088	12.2	2422	261	1906
1905	18 479	7.2	455	584	549	3.0	12	65 386	7 696	11.8	2429	251	1905
1904	18 225	7.2	453	581	473	2.6	11	66 102	7 589	11.5	2489	250	1904
1903	17 926	7.1	449	575	449	2.5	10	65 070	7 278	11.2	2478	241	1903
1902	17 649	7.1	447	572	481	2.7	11	65 542	7 253	11.1	2534	243	1902
1901	17 599	7.1	451	576	375	2.1	9	66 069	7 142	10.8	2594	242	1901
1900	18 498	7.6	481	615	381	2.1	9	65 219	6 910	10.6	2599	238	1900
1899	17 937	7.5	473	605	368	2.1	9	64 611	6 744	10.4	2610	235	1899
1898	17 897	7.5	480	614	349	2.0	9	64 730	6 940	10.7	2658	246	1898
1897	17 464	7.5	476	609	344	2.0	9	62 897	6 679	10.6	2625	240	1897
1896	16 823	7.3	466	597	316	1.9	8	63 518	6 753	10.6	2693	247	1896
1895	16 147	7.1	455	582				62 385	6 486	10.4	2685	241	1895
1894	15 687	7.0	449	574				61 813	6 487	10.5	2698	245	1894
1893	15 739	7.1	456	583				61 956	6 574	10.6	2737	251	1893
1892	15 039	6.8	440	563				59 310	6 158	10.4	2647	237	1892
1891	14 941	6.8	441	565				61 764	6 173	10.0	2780	240	1891
1890	14 975	6.9	447	572				60 218	6 158	10.2	2736	242	1890
1889	15 233	7.0	457	584				61 232	6 153	10.0	2808	243	1889
1888	15 091	7.0	455	581				61 158	6 269	10.3	2828	249	1888
1887	14 725	6.9	447	569				60 909	6 508	10.7	2845	261	1887
1886	14 834	7.1	454	577				61 454	6 608	10.8	2900	267	1886
1885	15 645	7.5	483	613				60 727	6 737	11.1	2905	275	1885
1884	15 970	7.8	498	631				61 375	6 965	11.3	2975	287	1884
1883	15 642	7.7	491	622				57 853	6 621	11.4	2834	275	1883
1882	15 496	7.7	489	618				57 979	7 091	12.2	2866	297	1882
1881	15 529	7.8	493	622				57 510	6 635	11.5	2868	279	1881
1880	14 959	7.6	479	602				56 044	6 568	11.7	2825	279	1880

Denmark

Marriages, Divorces, Illegitimacy

Year	Marriages				Divorces[a]			Births			births per 10.000 women age 15-44		Year
			persons marrying per 10.000 non-married persons										
	Total	marr. per 1.000 pop.	age 15+	age 15-49	Total	divorces per 100 marr.	persons divorcing per 10.000 married pop.	Legitimate Total	Illegit. Total	illeg. births per 100 legit. births	leg. births/married women	ill. births/non-marr. w.	
1879	14 287	7.3	460	578				55 940	6 515	11.6	2846	278	1879
1878	14 295	7.4	465	582				55 910	6 380	11.6	2825	275	1878
1877	15 428	8.0	507	634									1877
1876	16 180	8.5	537	671				55 612	6 176	11.1	2933	271	1876
1875	15 915	8.5	533	665				53 530	6 219	11.6	2856	275	1875
1874	15 260	8.2	516	642				51 076	6 202	12.1	2755	277	1874
1873	14 903	8.1	508	631				49 990	6 581	13.2	2725	296	1873
1872	13 627	7.5	468	580				49 035	6 186	12.6	2698	280	1872
1871	13 207	7.3	457	565				48 203	6 193	12.8	2676	282	1871
1870	13 134	7.3	457	564				48 349	6 071	12.6	2707	278	1870
1869	12 971	7.3	456	562				46 162	5 947	12.9	2590	275	1869
1868	12 769	7.3	454	560				48 488	6 002	12.4	2729	282	1868
1867	13 225	7.6	476	586				46 762	5 938	12.7	2638	282	1867
1866	14 354	8.3	523	643				48 628	6 513	13.4	2756	313	1866
1865	15 056	8.8	554	681				47 588	5 630	11.8	2702	274	1865
1864	9 466	5.6	353	433				44 832	5 965	13.3	2559	294	1864
1863	12 456	7.4	470	576				46 150	5 551	12.0	2641	277	1863
1862	12 044	7.3	461	564				45 539	5 403	11.9	2622	273	1862
1861	12 097	7.4	469	574				46 169	5 447	11.8	2673	279	1861
1860	12 849	8.0	505	618				46 995	5 541	11.8	2731	288	1860
1859	13 334	8.4	528	644				47 238	6 123	13.0	2798	319	1859
1858	13 626	8.7	543	662				45 935	6 180	13.5	2773	323	1858
1857	13 847	8.9	555	675				45 365	5 689	12.5	2789	298	1857
1856	13 175	8.6	532	646				43 972	5 581	12.7	2759	294	1856
1855	12 821	8.5	521	633				43 059	5 109	11.9	2758	270	1855
1854	12 994	8.7	532	646				43 509	5 216	12.0	2841	278	1854
1853	13 521	9.2	557	674				41 434	5 180	12.5	2748	278	1853
1852	14 153	9.7	585	708				43 000	5 390	12.5	2895	289	1852
1851	14 205	9.9	591	715				38 298	5 040	13.2	2624	272	1851
1850	10 824	7.6	453	547				39 549	5 219	13.2	2754	283	1850
1849	11 329	8.0	477	575				38 447	5 198	13.5	2721	282	1849
1848	10 447	7.5	441	532				38 002	4 745	12.5	2728	258	1848
1847	11 022	8.0	467	562				37 663	4 628	12.3	2742	253	1847
1846	11 039	8.1	469	564				36 489	4 736	13.0	2576	259	1846
1845	11 131	8.2	475	571				36 776	4 825	13.1	2755	265	1845
1844	10 942	8.1	472	568				35 934	4 812	13.4	2722	268	1844
1843	10 344	7.8	452	543				34 849	4 702	13.5	2669	265	1843
1842	10 157	7.7	448	539				35 010	4 524	12.9	2706	257	1842
1841	9 921	7.6	442	532				34 461	4 257	12.4	2687	245	1841
1840	9 426	7.3	424	511				34 876	4 334	12.4	2744	252	1840
1839	8 824	6.9	403	486				33 207	3 844	11.6			1839
1838	8 868	7.0	411	496				33 954	3 809	11.2			1838
1837	9 620	7.6	453	547				33 990	3 765	11.1			1837
1836	9 480	7.6	452	547				34 206	3 844	11.2			1836
1835	10 088	8.1	488	591				35 031	4 270	12.2			1835
1834	10 558	8.6	519	629				36 601	4 043	11.1			1834
1833	10 594	8.7	526	638				35 741	3 586	10.0			1833
1832	10 591	8.7	530	643				29 467	3 298	11.2			1832

Marriages, Divorces, Illegitimacy

Year	Marriages		persons marrying per 10.000 non-married persons		Divorces a)			Births			births per 10.000 women age 15-44		Year
	Total	marr. per 1.000 pop.	age 15+	age 15-49	Total	divorces per 100 marr.	persons divorcing per 10.000 married pop.	Legitimate Total	Illegit. Total	illeg. births per 100 legit. births	leg. births/ married women	ill. births/ non marr. w.	
1831	9 747	8.0	489	593				32 459	3 538	10.9			1831
1830	10 170	8.4	512	621				31 705	3 264	10.3			1830
1829	9 935	8.2	503	610				32 613	3 129	9.6			1829
1828	9 520	7.9	485	588				32 962	3 382	10.3			1828
1827	9 085	7.6	467	566				31 545	3 268	10.4			1827
1826	9 769	8.3	508	616				33 767	3 295	9.8			1826
1825	9 676	8.3	510	619				33 295	3 156	9.5			1825
1824	9 316	8.1	498	605				32 826	3 246	9.9			1824
1823	8 984	7.9	488	592				33 711	3 310	9.8			1823
1822	9 695	8.7	535	650				34 579	3 207	9.0			1822
1821	9 325	8.4	522	633				32 447	3 089	9.5			1821
1820	9 014	8.2	510	619				31 500	3 051	9.7			1820
1819	9 206	8.5	529	642				32 174	3 022	9.4			1819
1818	9 262	8.7	540	656				31 409	2 902	9.2			1818
1817	8 363	7.9	495	601				31 753	2 857	9.0			1817
1816	10 003	9.6	601	730				31 276	3 010	9.6			1816
1815	10 872	10.6	663	806				31 964	3 064	9.6			1815

a) Since the Reformation divorce was obtainable on the grounds of guilt. In addition, there was an exemption procedure by royal jurisdiction. A 1922 law introduced divorce on the grounds of marital breakdown, after a longer period of separation. Divorce by mutual consent was not permitted, but was indirectly obtainable after a period of legal separation. A 1969 law made divorce legislation similar to that of Sweden prior to 1973. In the tables, figures refer to divorces only, i.e. they do not include legal separations.

Finland

Marriages, Divorces, Illegitimacy

Year	Marriages	marr. per 1.000 pop.	persons marrying per 10.000 non-married persons		Divorces[a]	divorces per 100 marr.	persons divorcing per 10.000 married pop.	Births		illeg. births per 100 legit. births	births per 10.000 women age 15-44		Year
			age 15+	age 15-49				Legitimate	Illegit.		leg. births/ married women	ill. births/ non-marr. w.	
	Total				Total			Total	Total				
1975	31 547	6.7	376	577	9 358	29.7	88	59 049	6 670	11.3	981	144	1975
1974	34 533	7.4	419	640	10 019	29.0	95	56 824	5 648	9.9	952	123	1974
1973	34 883	7.5	430	656	8 831	25.3	85	52 286	4 501	8.6	884	100	1973
1972	35 467	7.6	445	677	8 254	23.3	80	54 930	3 934	7.2	938	88	1972
1971	37 925	8.2	485	735	7 175	18.9	71	57 699	3 368	5.8	995	76	1971
1970	40 730	8.8	528	798	6 044	14.8	60	60 793	3 766	6.2	1054	86	1970
1969	40 910	8.8	535	806	5 895	14.4	59	63 643	3 807	6.0	1104	87	1969
1968	40 251	8.7	533	800	5 416	13.5	54	69 753	3 901	5.6	1214	90	1968
1967	41 273	9.0	556	832	5 209	12.6	53	73 381	3 908	5.3	1289	92	1967
1966	38 252	8.4	525	783	4 854	12.7	50	73 989	3 708	5.0	1312	88	1966
1965	36 214	7.9	506	751	4 594	12.7	48	74 331	3 554	4.8	1329	85	1965
1964	34 520	7.6	490	725	4 458	12.9	47	76 915	3 513	4.6	1385	85	1964
1963	33 361	7.4	483	712	4 188	12.6	45	78 824	3 427	4.3	1433	84	1963
1962	34 251	7.6	506	744	4 004	11.7	43	78 175	3 279	4.2	1438	82	1962
1961	34 222	7.7	517	755	3 931	11.5	43	78 645	3 351	4.3	1463	85	1961
1960	32 834	7.4	506	738	3 655	11.1	41	78 810	3 319	4.2	1483	85	1960
1959	31 712	7.2	491	711	3 697	11.7	42	79 827	3 426	4.3	1505	87	1959
1958	31 360	7.2	487	702	3 662	11.7	42	77 911	3 237	4.2	1472	82	1958
1957	31 333	7.2	488	700	3 522	11.2	40	83 236	3 749	4.5	1577	94	1957
1956	33 004	7.7	517	737	3 674	11.1	43	85 178	3 718	4.4	1620	93	1956
1955	32 640	7.7	515	730	3 611	11.1	43	85 929	3 811	4.4	1643	95	1955
1954	32 599	7.8	518	730	3 492	10.7	42	85 936	3 909	4.5	1651	97	1954
1953	31 807	7.7	509	714	3 442	10.8	42	86 781	4 085	4.7	1677	101	1953
1952	32 414	7.9	523	729	3 481	10.7	43	89 928	4 386	4.9	1749	108	1952
1951	32 206	8.0	523	725	3 602	11.2	45	88 512	4 551	5.1	1730	112	1951
1950	34 205	8.5	558	771	3 687	10.8	47	92 922	5 143	5.5	1824	125	1950
1949	34 806	8.8	558	768	3 693	10.6	48	97 791	5 724	5.9	1971	137	1949
1948	38 977	10.0	615	844	4 170	10.7	55	101 828	5 931	5.8	2111	140	1948
1947	43 518	11.3	677	926	4 944	11.4	67	102 132	6 036	5.9	2178	140	1947
1946	49 743	13.1	763	1042	5 164	10.4	72	99 732	6 343	6.4	2191	145	1946
1945	44 380	11.8	672	915	5 605	12.6	81	89 081	6 677	7.5	2014	151	1945
1944	31 535	8.4	468	636	3 246	10.3	48	73 578	5 868	8.0	1701	130	1944
1943	31 954	8.6	464	629	3 166	9.9	47	71 203	4 909	6.9	1680	106	1943
1942	26 891	7.3	383	517	1 954	7.3	30	57 427	4 245	7.4	1381	90	1942
1941	37 662	10.2	524	707	1 580	4.2	24	84 155	5 410	6.4	2063	112	1941
1940	30 778	8.3	419	564	1 325	4.3	20	59 690	6 159	10.3	1491	125	1940
1939	30 614	8.3	417	558	1 433	4.6	23	72 156	6 008	8.3	1828	121	1939
1938	33 609	8.8	441	587	1 784	5.3	27	71 632	5 063	7.1	1773	98	1938
1937	32 464	8.5	426	562	1 627	5.0	25	67 269	5 050	7.5	1683	97	1937
1936	29 841	7.9	393	516	1 435	4.8	23	64 092	4 803	7.5	1634	92	1936
1935	28 758	7.6	380	496	1 517	5.3	24	64 978	4 964	7.6	1686	95	1935
1934	27 505	7.3	366	474	1 298	4.7	21	62 829	4 884	7.8	1662	93	1934
1933	24 472	6.6	327	421	1 177	4.8	19	60 070	4 977	8.3	1617	95	1933
1932	23 029	6.2	309	395	1 107	4.8	18	63 778	5 574	8.7	1749	106	1932
1931	23 836	6.5	321	409	1 203	5.0	20	65 863	6 003	9.1	1842	114	1931
1930	24 841	6.8	337	426	1 106	4.5	19	69 008	6 228	9.0	1971	118	1930
1929	25 060	6.9	344	435	855	3.4	15	69 879	6 132	8.8	2018	118	1929
1928	25 520	7.1	356	448	734	2.9	13	71 399	6 124	8.6	2085	119	1928

Marriages, Divorces, Illegitimacy

Year	Marriages Total	marr. per 1.000 pop.	persons marrying per 10.000 non-married persons age 15+	age 15-49	Divorces[a] Total	divorces per 100 marr.	persons divorcing per 10.000 married pop.	Births Legitimate Total	Illegit. Total	illeg. births per 100 legit. births	births per 10.000 women age 15-44 leg. births/married women	ill. births/non-marr. w.	Year
1927	24 105	6.7	341	429	672	2.8	12	69 521	6 090	8.8	2053	119	1927
1926	22 695	6.4	326	409	670	3.0	12	70 631	6 244	8.8	2112	124	1926
1925	22 103	6.3	322	404	626	2.8	11	71 906	6 354	8.8	2179	127	1925
1924	22 048	6.3	326	408	578	2.6	11	71 281	6 776	9.5	2187	137	1924
1923	23 634	6.8	355	443	608	2.6	11	74 764	7 197	9.6	2324	147	1923
1922	23 524	6.9	360	447	510	2.2	10	73 025	7 115	9.7	2302	148	1922
1921	23 719	7.0	369	458	466	2.0	9	74 362	7 803	10.5	2379	162	1921
1920	23 604	7.0	374	463	517	2.2	10	77 439	7 275	9.4	2502	154	1920
1919	18 831	5.7	303	376	441	2.4	4	59 584	4 312	7.2	1930	94	1919
1918	15 008	4.5	244	303	219	1.5	4	72 513	6 981	9.6	2326	153	1918
1917	20 604	6.2	339	421	308	1.5	6	74 556	6 490	8.7	2376	145	1917
1916	19 297	5.8	324	402	363	1.9	7	73 316	6 337	8.6	2336	145	1916
1915	17 785	5.4	305	379	333	1.9	6	76 547	6 659	8.7	2441	156	1915
1914	18 381	5.7	322	401	294	1.6	6	80 731	6 846	8.5	2582	164	1914
1913	18 923	5.9	339	423	273	1.4	5	80 408	6 842	8.5	2582	168	1913
1912	18 653	5.9	343	427	265	1.4	5	85 077	7 198	8.5	2745	182	1912
1911	18 735	6.0	353	441	258	1.4	5	84 449	6 789	8.0	2740	177	1911
1910	18 781	6.1	364	454	184	1.0	4	86 100	6 884	8.0	2812	185	1910
1909	19 418	6.4	383	478	204	1.1	4	88 359	6 646	7.5	2917	181	1909
1908	20 091	6.7	404	504	173	0.9	4	85 763	6 383	7.4	2858	178	1908
1907	20 266	6.8	415	518	126	0.6	3	85 983	6 474	7.5	2893	183	1907
1906	19 937	6.8	416	519	141	0.7	3	85 218	6 183	7.3	2898	178	1906
1905	18 632	6.5	396	494	153	0.8	3	81 878	5 963	7.3	2812	175	1905
1904	18 646	6.6	403	503	128	0.7	3	84 425	5 828	6.9	2925	174	1904
1903	17 651	6.3	388	485	119	0.7	3	79 615	5 505	6.9	2786	167	1903
1902	17 508	6.3	392	490	114	0.7	2	81 488	5 594	6.9	2878	173	1902
1901	18 535	6.8	422	528	105	0.6	2	82 902	5 735	6.9	2952	180	1901
1900	18 295	6.8	424	529	121	0.7	3	80 908	5 431	6.7	2904	173	1900
1899	19 539	7.3	460	575	124	0.6	3	82 511	5 847	7.1	2990	190	1899
1898	20 611	7.9	496	620	142	0.7	3	83 117	5 989	7.2	3050	198	1898
1897	19 913	7.7	489	611	108	0.5	2	76 848	5 482	7.1	2858	185	1897
1896	19 189	7.5	481	601	112	0.6	3	76 018	5 638	7.4	2860	194	1896
1895	18 256	7.3	466	583	92	0.5	2	76 415	5 368	7.0	2912	189	1895
1894	16 113	6.5	419	524	81	0.5	2	71 338	4 868	6.8	2748	174	1894
1893	14 095	5.8	372	466	72	0.5	2	68 257	4 773	7.0	2650	173	1893
1892	14 825	6.1	397	497	96	0.6	2	71 352	5 081	7.1	2788	187	1892
1891	16 572	6.9	451	565	77	0.5	2	77 045	5 075	6.6	3035	190	1891
1890	16 885	7.1	469	587	91	0.5	2	72 873	4 987	6.8	2903	190	1890
1889	16 099	6.9	452	565	82	0.5	2	72 832	5 049	6.9	2926	194	1889
1888	16 748	7.3	476	595	65	0.4	2	74 840	5 332	7.1	3035	207	1888
1887	17 179	7.6	495	619	64	0.4	2	76 283	5 441	7.1	3128	213	1887
1886	16 248	7.3	474	593	62	0.4	2	73 453	5 123	7.0	3042	203	1886
1885	15 978	7.3	471	589	63	0.4	2	69 903	5 226	7.5	2920	209	1885
1884	16 585	7.7	495	618	30	0.2	1	72 612	5 535	7.6	3060	223	1884
1883	16 546	7.8	500	624	34	0.2	1	71 041	5 337	7.5	3024	217	1883
1882	15 928	7.6	487	608	30	0.2	1	70 727	5 326	7.5	3040	219	1882
1881	14 283	6.9	441	550	28	0.2	1	67 370	5 066	7.5	2917	210	1881
1880	15 816	7.7	493	615				69 336	5 448	7.9	3022	227	1880

Finland

Marriages, Divorces, Illegitimacy

Year	Marriages		Divorces			Births			births per 10.000 women age 15-44		Year
		marr. per 1.000 pop.	persons marrying per 10.000 non-married persons			Legitimate	Illegit.	illeg. births per 100 legit. births	leg. births/ married women		
			age 15+	age 15-44					ill. births/ non-marr. w.		
	Total				Total	divorces per 100 marr.	persons divorcing per 10.000 married pop.	Total	Total		
1879	14 987	7.4						70 673	5 477	7.7		1879
1878	15 261	7.7						65 052	5 223	8.0		1878
1877	16 116	8.2						69 541	5 290	7.6		1877
1876	15 807	8.2						65 419	5 340	8.2		1876
1875	15 940	8.4						64 000	5 521	8.6		1875
1874	16 852	9.0						65 065	5 743	8.8		1874
1873	15 634	8.5						62 713	5 709	9.1		1873
1872	15 796	8.7						60 327	5 862	9.7		1872
1871	17 318	9.7						60 385	6 182	10.2		1871
1870	17 917	10.2						57 860	5 888	10.2		1870
1869	17 238	9.9						54 207	4 188	7.7		1869
1868	10 121	5.7						40 541	3 216	7.9		1868
1867	11 729	6.4						55 091	4 073	7.4		1867
1866	11 140	6.1						54 826	4 027	7.3		1866
1865	12 824	7.0						58 152	4 628	8.0		1865
1864	14 065	7.8						66 353	4 954	7.5		1864
1863	13 205	7.4						60 459	4 529	7.5		1863
1862	14 103	7.9						61 777	4 551	7.4		1862
1861	15 067	8.6						61 722	4 812	7.8		1861
1860	15 516	8.9						58 718	4 465	7.6		1860
1859	13 759	8.0						57 148	4 306	7.5		1859
1858	13 104	7.7						58 733	3 937	6.7		1858
1857	11 995	7.1						51 779	3 831	7.4		1857
1856	13 433	7.9						56 923	4 396	7.7		1856
1855	13 301	7.9						56 015	4 355	7.8		1855
1854	13 008	7.8						58 542	4 407	7.5		1854
1853	12 265	7.4						54 187	4 211	7.8		1853
1852	11 990	7.2						53 620	4 449	8.3		1852
1851	13 723	8.3						58 612	4 343	7.4		1851
1850	13 147	8.1						54 175	4 094	7.6		1850
1849	13 892	8.6						56 016	4 304	7.7		1849
1848	14 718	9.3						53 789	4 232	7.9		1848
1847	12 650	8.1						49 462	3 749	7.6		1847
1846	11 438	7.4						47 827	3 777	7.9		1846
1845	11 668	7.6						50 945	3 939	7.7		1845
1844	12 338	8.1						49 202	3 922	8.0		1844
1843	12 040	8.0						49 699	3 898	7.8		1843
1842	12 193	8.3						50 798	4 008	7.9		1842
1841	11 610	8.0						45 953	3 487	7.6		1841
1840	11 131	7.7						46 293	3 501	7.6		1840
1839	10 873	7.7						44 365	3 439	7.8		1839
1838	9 985	7.1						41 872	2 780	6.6		1838
1837	10 145	7.3						41 614	2 466	5.9		1837
1836	9 001	6.5						40 646	2 644	6.5		1836
1835	9 656	7.0						44 652	2 873	6.4		1835
1834	10 428	7.6						47 534	2 704	5.7		1834
1833	9 318	6.8						39 514	1 978	5.0		1833
1832	8 926	6.5						45 087	2 609	5.8		1832

Finland

Marriages, Divorces, Illegitimacy

Year	Marriages Total	marr. per 1.000 pop.	persons marrying per 10.000 non-married persons age 15+	age 15-49	Divorces Total	divorces per 100 marr.	persons divorcing per 10.000 married pop.	Births Legitimate Total	Illegit. Total	illeg. births per 100 legit. births	leg. births/ married women	ill. births/ non-marr. w.	Year
1831	11 852	8.5						45 884	2 647	5.8			1831
1830	10 172	7.5						46 027	2 937	6.4			1830
1829	10 937	8.3						48 214	2 988	6.2			1829
1828	11 776	9.0						48 122	3 140	6.5			1828
1827	11 653	9.1						44 309	2 833	6.4			1827
1826	10 460	8.3						44 605	3 070	6.9			1826
1825	10 221	8.2						45 028	3 092	6.9			1825
1824	10 684	8.6						43 708	3 054	7.0			1824
1823	10 764	8.8						46 145	3 023	6.6			1823
1822	9 809	8.1						40 004	2 894	7.2			1822
1821	11 240	9.5						46 003	3 162	6.9			1821
1820	10 894	9.3						40 276	2 513	6.2			1820
1819	8 817	7.6						39 070	2 677	6.9			1819
1818	9 808	8.6						41 066	2 852	6.9			1818
1817	9 660	8.6						41 172	2 691	6.5			1817
1816	9 817	8.9						40 254	2 609	6.5			1816
1815	9 516	8.7						38 602	2 296	5.9			1815

a) Divorce has been possible since the Reformation. A law of 1734 transferred jurisdiction over marriage from the Lutheran Church to the state. This law remained in force for almost two hundred years. It based divorce on a strict notion of one-sided guilt, but this restriction was eased by an additional exemption procedure which was a matter of free deliberation, first of royal jurisdiction, then of the Senate, in the nineteenth century, and finally of the Supreme Court after independence. This procedure introduced in practice the principle of marital breakdown. A law of 1929 (effective from 1930), codified this practice and based divorce legislation on a combination of the principles of guilt and marital breakdown. In 1948 provisions for legal separation were added, separation also being granted by mutual consent after a conciliation procedure, divorce being made possible after one year's legal separation.

In the tables divorce figures do not include these separations, the figures for which are given below.

Year	Number of separations	Year	Number of separations	Year	Number of separations
1949	462	1958	1 737	1967	2 501
1950	635	1959	1 731	1968	2 932
1951	727	1960	1 757	1969	3 263
1952	861	1961	1 832	1970	3 840
1953	1 391	1962	2 163	1971	4 313
1954	1 565	1963	2 153	1972	4 775
1955	1 488	1964	1 926	1973	5 084
1956	1 541	1965	2 048	1974	5 461
1957	1 591	1966	2 281	1975	5 002

Year	Marriages Total	marr. per 1.000 pop.	persons marrying per 10.000 non-married persons age 15+	persons marrying per 10.000 non-married persons age 15-49	Divorces a) Total	divorces per 100 marr.	persons divorcing per 10.000 married pop.	Births Legitimate Total	Births Illegit. Total	illeg. births per 100 legit. births	leg. births/ married women	ill. births/ non-marr. w.	Year
1975	387 400	7.3	477	698	67 000	17.3	54	580 100	63 100	9.3	1052	134	1975
1974	394 800	7.5	493	726	50 000	12.7	41	731 700	67 900	9.3	1139	147	1974
1973	400 700	7.7	505	749	50 000	12.5	41	784 900	70 000	8.9	1226	155	1973
1972	416 500	8.1	532	796	48 400	11.6	40	809 300	65 800	8.1	1274	149	1972
1971	406 400	7.9	527	793	47 700	11.7	40	816 900	61 100	7.5	1297	142	1971
1970	393 700	7.8	518	786	40 000	10.2	34	789 900	57 900	7.3	1265	138	1970
1969	380 800	7.6	508	778	37 500	9.8	32	784 900	54 600	7.0	1267	133	1969
1968	356 600	7.1	482	745	36 100	10.1	31	779 800	53 000	6.8	1268	132	1968
1967	345 600	7.0	474	737	37 200	10.8	32	786 100	51 400	6.5	1287	131	1967
1966	339 700	6.9	472	741	36 500	10.7	32	809 100	51 100	6.3	1334	133	1966
1965	346 300	7.1	488	772	34 900	10.1	31	811 400	50 900	6.3	1349	136	1965
1964	347 500	7.2	496	792	33 300	9.6	30	822 600	51 600	6.3	1376	142	1964
1963	339 500	7.1	493	794	30 300	8.9	27	814 300	51 000	6.3	1377	144	1963
1962	316 900	6.7	471	766	30 600	9.7	28	779 900	49 000	6.3	1341	143	1962
1961	314 800	6.8	474	769	32 700	10.7	30	785 900	49 300	6.3	1380	145	1961
1960	319 900	7.0	483	784	30 200	9.4	28	766 900	49 400	6.4	1364	145	1960
1959	320 800	7.1	486	787	29 900	9.3	28	775 200	50 400	6.5	1395	148	1959
1958	312 100	7.0	475	768	31 300	10.0	30	759 000	49 600	6.5	1382	146	1958
1957	310 500	7.0	475	767	30 700	9.9	30	762 500	50 100	6.6	1407	147	1957
1956	293 500	6.7	451	727	31 300	10.7	31	752 200	50 900	6.8	1406	150	1956
1955	312 700	7.2	482	776	31 300	10.0	31	751 000	51 300	6.8	1421	151	1955
1954	314 500	7.3	486	782	30 200	9.6	30	754 100	53 100	7.0	1443	156	1954
1953	308 400	7.2	475	759	31 000	10.1	31	747 700	53 400	7.1	1432	154	1953
1952	313 900	7.4	482	764	33 000	10.5	33	763 400	55 100	7.2	1463	156	1952
1951	319 700	7.6	489	770	33 400	10.4	34	766 600	56 200	7.3	1471	157	1951
1950	331 100	7.9	506	790	34 700	10.5	36	798 100	60 000	7.5	1534	165	1950
1949	341 100	8.2	520	807	40 300	11.8	42	808 000	60 600	7.5	1557	165	1949
1948	370 800	9.0	565	871	45 900	12.4	49	804 300	62 800	7.8	1555	168	1948
1947	427 000	10.6	657	1006	56 300	13.2	61	801 000	66 000	8.2	1569	177	1947
1946	516 900	12.8	788	1199	64 100	12.4	70	767 400	72 800	9.5	1496	191	1946
1945	393 000	9.9	615	938									1945
1944	205 000	5.3	331	506									1944
1943	219 000	5.6	357	547									1943
1942	267 000	6.8	435	670									1942
1941	226 000	5.7	371	572									1941
1940	177 000	4.3	284	439									1940
1939	258 400	6.2	410	637									1939
1938	273 900	6.5	439	685				573 800	38 400	6.7	1008	111	1938
1937	274 500	6.5	446	698	27 100	9.9	28	578 000	40 100	6.9	1008	118	1937
1936	279 900	6.7	461	723	25 900	9.3	27	589 800	41 000	7.0	1022	123	1936
1935	284 900	6.8	463	717	26 100	9.2	27	595 700	44 800	7.5	1029	130	1935
1934	298 500	7.1	479	733	24 000	8.0	25	629 100	48 800	7.8	1084	138	1934
1933	315 700	7.5	502	758	24 000	7.6	25	627 900	50 800	8.1	1082	140	1933
1932	315 000	7.5	495	740	23 700	7.5	24	666 300	56 100	8.4	1147	150	1932
1931	326 700	7.8	508	750	24 600	7.5	25	675 700	58 200	8.6	1160	152	1931
1930	342 100	8.2	529	779	23 400	6.8	24	687 800	62 200	9.0	1197	159	1930
1929	334 300	8.1	516	757	22 200	6.6	24	669 000	61 100	9.1	1184	154	1929
1928	338 800	8.3	519	760	21 900	6.5	23	686 400	62 900	9.2	1229	155	1928

Marriages, Divorces, Illegitimacy

Year	Marriages Total	marr. per 1.000 pop.	persons marrying per 10.000 non-married persons age 15+	age 15-49	Divorces Total	divorces per 100 marr.	persons divorcing per 10.000 married pop.	Births Legitimate Total	Births Illegit. Total	illeg. births per 100 legit. births	leg. births/ married women	ill. births/ non-marr. w.	Year
1927	336 400	8.2	511	746	21 600	6.4	23	681 500	62 300	9.1	1233	151	1927
1926	345 400	8.5	520	756	22 400	6.5	24	702 700	64 800	9.2	1283	153	1926
1925	352 800	8.7	530	768	22 600	6.4	25	704 000	66 100	9.4	1309	154	1925
1924	355 400	8.8	532	769	22 600	6.4	25	689 300	64 200	9.3	1307	147	1924
1923	355 100	8.9	532	768	23 500	6.6	27	695 300	66 000	9.5	1350	149	1923
1922	384 600	9.8	578	831	25 700	6.7	30	694 300	65 400	9.4	1381	147	1922
1921	455 500	11.6	681	977	31 100	6.8	37	738 800	73 000	9.9	1495	161	1921
1920	622 700	16.0	943	1352	34 800	5.6	41	750 800	82 700	11.0	1522	187	1920
1919 b)	552 700	14.3	850	1216	19 600	3.5	24						1919
1918 b)	178 300	5.4	312	447	9 800	5.5							1918
1917 b)	158 400	4.9	275	393	8 900	5.6							1917
1916 b)	108 100	3.3	190	271	4 900	4.5							1916
1915 b)	75 200	2.3	130	185	2 000	2.7							1915
1914	168 900	5.1	304	432	10.200	6.0							1914
1913	298 900	7.5	468	667	16 300	5.5	19	680 400	65 600	9.6	1306	166	1913
1912	312 100	7.9	494	701	16 700	5.4	20	685 000	65 400	9.5	1311	170	1912
1911	308 000	7.8	492	697	15 300	5.0	18	677 600	64 800	9.6	1293	172	1911
1910	307 700	7.8	491	695	14 300	4.6	17	707 400	67 000	9.5	1357	177	1910
1909	307 700	7.8	490	693	13 900	4.5	17	702 100	67 500	9.6	1357	178	1909
1908	315 600	8.0	502	709	13 300	4.2	16	721 800	70 400	9.8	1403	185	1908
1907	314 100	8.0	500	704	12 600	4.0	15	701 600	71 100	10.1	1372	186	1907
1906	306 500	7.8	486	684	11 600	3.8	14	735 900	70 900	9.6	1446	184	1906
1905	302 600	7.7	479	673	10 900	3.6	13	735 800	71 500	9.7	1453	185	1905
1904	298 700	7.6	472	662	10 900	3.6	13	746 500	71 700	9.6	1481	184	1904
1903	296 000	7.6	467	654	10 200	3.4	13	754 000	72 700	9.6	1505	186	1903
1902	294 800	7.5	465	650	9 400	3.2	12	771 300	74 100	9.6	1549	189	1902
1901	303 500	7.8	478	667	8 800	2.9	11	782 600	74 700	9.5	1581	190	1901
1900	299 100	7.7	468	650	7 800	2.6	10	754 200	73 100	9.7	1542	183	1900
1899	295 800	7.6	460	636	8 000	2.7	10	772 600	75 000	9.7	1600	186	1899
1898	287 200	7.4	445	611	8 100	2.8	10	769 300	74 600	9.7	1614	182	1898
1897	291 500	7.5	450	614	8 000	2.7	10	783 100	76 000	9.7	1667	184	1897
1896	290 200	7.5	446	607	7 900	2.7	10	789 300	76 300	9.7	1706	183	1896
1895	282 900	7.4	436	592	7 700	2.7	10	760 900	73 300	9.6	1654	176	1895
1894	286 700	7.5	443	601	7 900	2.8	10	778 900	76 500	9.8	1701	184	1894
1893	287 300	7.5	444	603	6 900	2.4	9	798 100	76 600	9.6	1750	184	1893
1892	290 300	7.6	449	609	7 000	2.4	9	782 000	73 800	9.4	1722	178	1892
1891	285 500	7.4	442	599	6 400	2.2	8	792 500	73 900	9.3	1751	178	1891
1890	269 300	7.0	417	564	6 600	2.5	9	767 000	71 100	9.3	1701	171	1890
1889	272 900	7.1	423	571	6 200	2.3	8	806 900	73 600	9.1	1797	177	1889
1888	276 800	7.2	430	579	5 500	2.0	7	807 700	74 900	9.3	1812	180	1888
1887	277 100	7.2	431	579	5 800	2.1	8	825 400	73 900	9.0	1861	178	1887
1886	283 200	7.4	441	592	4 000	1.4	5	838 000	74 800	8.9	1899	180	1886
1885	283 200	7.4	444	597	4 100	1.4	5	850 400	74 200	8.7	1927	180	1885
1884	289 600	7.6	456	615				862 000	75 800	8.8	1952	185	1884
1883	284 500	7.5	451	609				863 700	74 200	8.6	1958	183	1883
1882	281 100	7.5	449	607				864 300	71 300	8.2	1960	177	1882
1881	282 100	7.5	453	615				867 000	70 100	8.1	1966	176	1881
1880	279 000	7.4	454	616				852 000	68 200	8.0	1921	173	1880

Year	Marriages Total	marr. per 1.000 pop.	persons marrying per 10.000 non-married persons age 15+	age 15-49	Divorces Total	divorces per 100 marr.	persons divorcing per 10.000 married pop.	Births Legitimate Total	Illegit. Total	illeg. births per 100 legit. births	leg. births/married women (births per 10.000 women age 15-44)	ill. births/non-marr. w.	Year
1879	282 800	7.6	465	632				869 500	67 000	7.7	1950	172	1879
1878	279 600	7.5	465	632				868 800	68 500	7.9	1939	178	1878
1877	278 100	7.5	469	638				877 700	66 900	7.6	1951	176	1877
1876	291 400	7.9	497	677				899 400	67 300	7.5	1990	180	1876
1875	300 400	8.2	513	697				884 100	66 900	7.6	1977	178	1875
1874	303 100	8.3	518	702				885 400	69 300	7.8	1999	183	1874
1873	321 200	8.8	549	742				875 800	70 600	8.1	1997	185	1873
1872	352 800	9.8	604	814				896 300	69 700	7.8	2067	182	1872
1871	262 500	7.3	448	602				767 000	59 100	7.7	1768	154	1871
1870	233 800	6.1	375	502				920 800	75 100	8.2	2000	184	1870
1869	316 700	8.2	508	678				924 200	75 600	8.2	2011	185	1869
1868	301 200	7.9	483	643				909 100	75 000	8.2	1983	183	1868
1867	300 300	7.9	482	640				927 000	76 800	8.3	2029	187	1867
1866	303 600	8.0	489	647				929 600	76 700	8.3	2045	188	1866
1865	299 200	7.9	482	636				928 800	77 000	8.3	2048	188	1865
1864	299 600	7.9	484	638				930 000	75 900	8.2	2061	185	1864
1863	301 400	8.0	488	642				936 300	76 500	8.2	2085	186	1863
1862	303 500	8.1	493	647				921 300	73 900	8.0	2063	179	1862
1861	305 200	8.2	496	651				928 400	76 700	8.3	2088	186	1861
1860	288 900	7.9	481	630				887 600	69 300	7.8	2046	171	1860
1859	298 400	8.2	496	650				937 500	80 400	8.6	2164	196	1859
1858	307 100	8.5	512	670				894 700	74 600	8.3	2078	182	1858
1857	295 500	8.1	493	644				869 800	70 900	8.2	2024	171	1857
1856	284 400	7.9	475	621				883 800	68 300	7.7	2064	164	1856
1855	283 300	7.9	473	616				838 100	64 200	7.7	1972	154	1855
1854	270 900	7.5	449	583				853 400	70 100	8.2	2010	167	1854
1853	280 600	7.8	465	603				868 700	68 300	7.9	2064	163	1853
1852	281 500	7.8	466	603				895 200	69 800	7.8	2145	167	1852
1851	286 900	8.0	475	613				901 500	69 800	7.7	2178	167	1851
1850	297 700	8.4						884 500	69 700	7.9			1850
1849	278 900	7.8						915 500	70 300	7.7			1849
1848	293 600	8.3						873 300	66 900	7.7			1848
1847	249 600	7.0						837 700	64 200	7.7			1847
1846	268 300	7.6						897 000	68 900	7.7			1846
1845	283 200	8.1						913 900	68 600	7.5			1845
1844	279 800	8.0						890 100	69 400	7.8			1844
1843	285 500	8.2						908 900	69 500	7.6			1843
1842	280 600	8.1						912 800	70 200	7.7			1842
1841	282 400	8.3						905 600	71 200	7.9			1841
1840	283 300	8.3						881 400	71 000	8.1			1840
1839	267 200	7.9						888 100	70 100	7.9			1839
1838	273 300	8.1						892 200	70 900	7.9			1838
1837	266 800	7.9						873 700	70 000	8.0			1837
1836	274 100	8.2						906 100	73 600	8.1			1836
1835	275 500	8.3						919 100	74 700	8.1			1835
1834	271 200	8.2						912 900	73 600	8.1			1834
1833	263 600	8.0						898 700	71 500	8.0			1833
1832	242 500	7.4						869 900	67 500	7.8			1832

France

Marriages, Divorces, Illegitimacy

Year	Marriages Total	marr. per 1.000 pop.	persons marrying per 10.000 non-married persons age 15+	persons marrying per 10.000 non-married persons age 15–49	Divorces Total	divorces per 100 marr.	persons divorcing per 10.000 married pop.	Births Legitimate Total	Births Illegit. Total	illeg. births per 100 legit. births	leg. births/ married women	ill. births/ non-marr. w.	Year
1831	245 700	7.5						915 500	71 300	7.8			1831
1830	270 400	8.4						899 000	69 000	7.7			1830
1829	250 600	7.8						896 200	69 300	7.7			1829
1828	246 400	7.7						906 100	70 800	7.8			1828
1827	255 900	8.0						909 400	70 700	7.8			1827
1826	247 400	7.8						920 200	72 100	7.8			1826
1825	243 400	7.7						904 200	69 300	7.7			1825
1824	237 800	7.6						913 200	71 000	7.8			1824
1823	261 800	8.5						893 700	69 600	7.8			1823
1822	235 800	7.7						902 900	69 700	7.7			1822
1821	222 700	7.3						897 200	68 200	7.6			1821
1820	209 000	6.9						893 700	66 300	7.4			1820
1819	215 300	7.2						922 100	65 500	7.1			1819
1818	213 300	7.1						856 000	58 600	6.8			1818
1817	205 900	6.9						881 600	62 900	7.1			1817
1816	249 200	8.5						906 300	62 600	6.9			1816
1815	246 000	8.4						893 000	60 100	6.7			1815

a) Under the Old Regime only legal separation and annulment were allowed. The 1804 Civil Code introduced divorce on the grounds of guilt, and by mutual consent (very restricted). During the Restoration the ecclesiastical marriage law was reintroduced and divorce abolished. In 1884, a new law reintroduced divorce, but only on the grounds of guilt. This remained in force until 1975 when a new law (effective from 1976) allowed divorce by mutual consent and on the grounds of marital breakdown (in addition to guilt).
Divorce is granted by the courts but must be registered within a certain period in order to be effective. Thus, there are judicial and administrative divorce statistics, the latter being slightly lower. In the tables divorce figures refer to divorces granted by the courts. Legal separations have not been taken into account.

b) Present territory. Figures are official estimates on the basis of statistics for 77 departments.

Marriages, Divorces, Illegitimacy

Year	Marriages Total	marr. per 1.000 pop.	persons marrying per 10.000 non-married persons age 15+	age 15-49	Divorces[a] Total	divorces per 100 marr.	persons divorcing per 10.000 married pop.	Births Legitimate Total	Illegit. Total	illeg. births per 100 legit. births	births per 10.000 women age 15-44 leg. births/ married women	ill. births non-marr. w.	Year
1975	386 681	6.3	492	890	106 829	27.6	68	563 738	36 774	6.5	649	114	1975
1974	377 265	6.1	473	846	98 584	26.1	63	587 096	39 277	6.7	678	116	1974
1973	394 603	6.4	490	866	90 164	22.8	58	595 790	39 843	6.7	693	114	1973
1972	415 132	6.7	512	896	86 614	20.9	56	658 804	42 410	6.4	775	117	1972
1971	432 030	7.0	530	918	80 444	18.6	52	733 263	45 263	6.2	872	122	1971
1970	444 510	7.3	545	935	76 500	17.2	51	766 528	44 280	5.8	928	116	1970
1969	446 586	7.4	547	930	72 300	16.2	48	857 958	45 498	5.3	1056	117	1969
1968	444 150	7.5	544	915	65 264	14.7	44	923 616	46 209	5.0	1154	116	1968
1967	483 101	8.1	587	979	62 835	13.0	43	972 495	46 964	4.8	1228	115	1967
1966	484 562	8.2	584	966	58 730	12.1	40	1 002 491	47 854	4.8	1276	114	1966
1965	492 128	8.4	592	971	58 718	11.9	41	995 351	48 977	4.9	1287	114	1965
1964	506 182	8.7	610	991	55 710	11.0	39	1 012 306	53 131	5.2	1332	122	1964
1963	507 644	8.8	609	982	50 833	10.0	36	999 003	55 120	5.5	1332	124	1963
1962	530 640	9.3	638	1020	49 508	9.3	36	961 904	56 648	5.9	1305	126	1962
1961	529 901	9.4	640	1015	49 271	9.3	36	952 418	60 269	6.3	1319	132	1961
1960	521 445	9.4	634	993	48 874	9.4	36	907 299	61 330	6.8	1273	132	1960
1959	503 981	9.2	616	953	48 848	9.7	37	888 226	63 716	7.2	1262	135	1959
1958	494 110	9.1	609	931	48 050	9.7	37	842 551	61 914	7.3	1214	129	1958
1957	482 590	9.0	600	906	46 352	9.6	36	828 056	64 172	7.7	1211	131	1957
1956	478 352	8.9	591	882	46 101	9.6	36	791 933	63 954	8.1	1159	127	1956
1955	461 818	8.7	575	849	48 277	10.5	39	755 701	64 427	8.5	1122	126	1955
1954	453 168	8.6	567	827	50 670	11.2	41	747 295	68 733	9.2	1122	133	1954
1953	462 101	8.9	582	839	53 876	11.7	44	727 091	69 005	9.5	1105	131	1953
1952	483 358	9.4	613	875	57 933	12.0	49	726 940	72 140	9.9	1120	136	1952
1951	522 946	10.2	666	940	64 009	12.2	54	718 905	76 703	10.7	1119	142	1951
1950	535 708	10.6	688	961	84 740	15.8	73	733 760	79 075	10.8	1158	145	1950
1949	506 199	10.2	661	919	80 139	15.8	71	755 300	77 503	10.3	1196	140	1949
1948	525 160	10.7	699	969	87 593	16.7	79	723 626	82 448	11.4	1152	148	1948
1947	482 193	10.1	660	912	76 597	15.9	72	688 819	92 602	13.4	1115	166	1947
1946	400 399	8.8	576	792	48 601	12.1	48	612 914	120 084	19.6	1028	220	1946
1945													1945
1944													1944
1943	514 095	7.3											1943
1942	525 459	7.4											1942
1941	504 200	7.2			52 872	10.5							1941
1940	613 103	8.8			49 278	8.0							1940
1939	774 163	11.2	708	948	61 789	8.0	38						1939
1938	645 062	9.4	594	790	49 497	7.7	32	1 246 041	102 493	8.2	1356	139	1938
1937	670 265	9.9	619	818	46 786	7.0	30	1 179 278	97 768	8.3	1304	131	1937
1936	609 770	9.1	565	740	50 357	8.3	33	1 180 198	98 385	8.3	1326	130	1936
1935	651 435	9.7	604	787	50 259	7.7	34	1 165 782	98 194	8.4	1330	128	1935
1934	732 147	11.2	689	891	54 402	7.4	37	1 081 895	100 894	9.3	1268	132	1934
1933	631 152	9.7	594	763	42 485	6.7	30	854 854	102 117	11.9	1016	132	1933
1932	509 597	7.9	480	614	42 202	8.3	30	864 379	113 831	13.2	1036	145	1932
1931	515 403	8.0	486	618	39 971	7.8	29	910 545	121 225	13.3	1101	153	1931
1930	562 648	8.8	532	672	40 722	7.2	30	992 158	135 292	13.6	1211	169	1930
1929	589 611	9.2	558	702	39 424	6.7	29	1 008 927	138 531	13.7	1243	172	1929

Germany

Marriages, Divorces, Illegitimacy a)

Year	Marriages Total	marr. per 1.000 pop.	persons marrying per 10.000 non-married persons age 15+	age 15-49	Divorces Total	divorces per 100 marr.	persons divorcing per 10.000 married pop.	Births Legitimate Total	Illegit. Total	illeg. births per 100 legit. births	leg. births/married women	ill. births non-marr. w.	Year
1928	587 175	9.2	557	697	36 928	6.3	28	1 038 434	144 381	13.9	1291	177	1928
1927	538 463	8.5	512	637	36 449	6.8	28	1 018 974	142 745	14.0	1280	174	1927
1926	483 198	7.7	461	570	34 105	7.1	26	1 075 972	151 928	14.1	1366	184	1926
1925	482 792	7.7	462	569	35 451	7.3	28	1 139 832	152 667	13.4	1463	184	1925
1924	440 039	7.1	423	518	35 936	8.2	29	1 138 488	132 332	11.6	1478	158	1924
1923	581 277	9.4	560	683	33 939	5.8	28	1 163 779	133 670	11.5	1527	159	1923
1922	681 891	11.1	659	800	36 587	5.4	30	1 254 977	149 238	11.9	1665	176	1922
1921	740 330	11.9	698	844	38 726	5.2	32	1 416 326	164 804	11.6	1848	188	1921
1920	894 978	14.5	850	1023	36 542	4.1	30	1 419 865	179 422	12.6	1880	204	1920
1919	844 339	13.4	786	940	22 022	2.6	18	1 121 510	138 990	12.4	1465	153	1919
1918	352 543	5.3			13 344	3.8		806 691	120 122	14.9			1918
1917	308 446	4.6			11 603	3.8		808 043	104 066	12.9			1917
1916	279 076	4.1			10 494	3.8		916 781	112 703	12.3			1916
1915	278 208	4.1			10 791	3.9		1 229 403	153 143	12.5			1915
1914	460 608	6.8	452	558	17 740	3.9	14	1 642 326	176 270	10.7	2041	235	1914
1913	513 283	7.7	509	629	17 835	3.5	15	1 662 171	176 579	10.6	2096	238	1913
1912	523 491	7.9	526	650	16 911	3.2	14	1 693 121	176 515	10.4	2169	241	1912
1911	512 819	7.8	521	644	15 780	3.1	13	1 700 815	169 914	10.0	2211	234	1911
1910	496 396	7.7	510	631	15 016	3.0	13	1 752 394	172 384	9.8	2312	241	1910
1909	494 127	7.8	514	636	14 730	3.0	13	1 801 895	176 383	9.8	2415	249	1909
1908	500 620	8.0	527	653	13 327	2.7	12	1 838 367	176 685	9.6	2504	253	1908
1907	503 964	8.1	537	666	12 489	2.5	11	1 828 027	171 906	9.4	2532	249	1907
1906	498 990	8.2	539	669	12 180	2.4	11	1 852 457	170 020	9.2	2609	249	1906
1905	485 906	8.1	532	660	11 215	2.3	11	1 819 652	167 501	9.2	2605	249	1905
1904	477 822	8.0	530	659	11 868	2.5	11	1 857 408	168 439	9.1	2704	253	1904
1903	463 150	7.9	520	647	9 933	2.1	10	1 819 716	163 362	9.0	2694	249	1903
1902	457 208	7.9	521	648	9 069	2.0	9	1 854 949	169 786	9.2	2797	262	1902
1901	468 329	8.2	542	674	7 964	1.7	8	1 859 993	172 320	9.3	2856	270	1901
1900	476 491	8.5	559	696	7 928	1.7	8	1 823 932	172 207	9.4	2850	274	1900
1899	471 519	8.5	560	698	9 433	2.0	10	1 804 461	175 843	9.7	2873	283	1899
1898	458 877	8.4	552	689	9 008	2.0	10	1 787 336	177 395	9.9	2900	289	1898
1897	447 770	8.4	547	682	8 878	2.0	10	1 750 647	176 043	10.1	2897	291	1897
1896	432 107	8.2	535	668	8 460	2.0	9	1 737 327	177 422	10.2	2933	297	1896
1895	414 218	8.0	519	649	8 326	2.0	9	1 708 703	168 575	9.9	2939	286	1895
1894	408 066	7.9	517	646	7 502	1.8	9	1 670 650	170 555	10.2	2921	292	1894
1893	401 234	7.9	513	642	6 694	1.7	8	1 696 796	168 919	10.0	3013	292	1893
1892	398 775	7.9	515	644	6 513	1.6	8	1 626 303	169 668	10.4	2930	296	1892
1891	399 398	8.0	520	651	6 677	1.7	8	1 667 716	172 456	10.3	3046	303	1891
1890	395 356	8.0	519	650	6 220	1.6	7	1 593 581	165 672	10.4	2956	294	1890
1889	389 339	8.0	519	651	6 457	1.7	8	1 601 998	170 572	10.6	3019	307	1889
1888	376 654	7.8	508	637	6 618	1.8	8	1 591 762	169 645	10.7	3033	308	1888
1887	370 650	7.8	505	633				1 592 917	164 162	10.3	3066	302	1887
1886	372 326	7.9	513	643				1 582 296	163 837	10.4	3076	304	1886
1885	368 619	7.9	513	643				1 567 903	162 024	10.3	3077	303	1885
1884	362 596	7.8	509	639				1 562 943	162 640	10.4	3083	307	1884
1883	352 999	7.7	499	628				1 530 015	153 684	10.0	3031	293	1883
1882	350 457	7.7	500	629				1 545 822	156 526	10.1	3071	301	1882
1881	338 909	7.5	487	613				1 531 266	150 883	9.9	3053	293	1881

M a r r i a g e s ,   D i v o r c e s ,   I l l e g i t i m a c y

Year	Marriages				Divorces a)			Births			births per 10.000 women age 15-44		Year
	Total		persons marrying per 10.000 non-married persons		Total	divorces per 100 marr.	persons divorcing per 10.000 married pop.	Legitimate Total	Illegit. Total	illeg. births per 100 legit. births	leg. births/ married women	ill. births non-marr. w.	
			age 15+	age 15-49									
1880	337 342	7.5	489	616				1 537 466	158 709	10.3	3080	311	1880
1879	335 113	7.5	488	614				1 583 914	151 957	9.6	3292	300	1879
1878	340 016	7.7	498	626				1 567 406	147 027	9.4	3383	294	1878
1877	347 792	8.0	513	643				1 594 969	149 690	9.4	3582	302	1877
1876	366 930	8.5	545	683									1876
1875	386 746	9.1	578	724				1 576 805	147 607	9.4	3848	305	1875
1874	400 282	9.5	603	753				1 539 286	144 154	9.4	3921	301	1874
1873	416 049	10.0	630	786				1 497 677	150 440	10.0	3980	317	1873
1872	423 900	10.3	644	803				1 483 362	142 675	9.6	4102	303	1872
1871	336 745	8.2	511	636									1871
1870	313 961	7.7											1870
1869	384 267	9.5											1869
1868	357 916	8.9											1868
1867	363 491	9.1											1867
1866	314 202	7.9											1866
1865	353 807	8.9											1865
1864	334 613	8.5											1864
1863	330 335	8.5											1863
1862	312 247	8.1											1862
1861	295 434	7.8											1861
1860	302 397	8.0											1860
1859	298 639	8.0											1859
1858	313 652	8.5											1858
1857	304 558	8.3											1857
1856	272 853	7.5											1856
1855	252 503	7.0											1855
1854	255 278	7.1											1854
1853	274 580	7.6											1853
1852	274 404	7.7											1852
1851	296 753	8.3											1851
1850	299 916	8.5											1850
1849	287 389	8.2											1849
1848	265 151	7.6											1848
1847	250 689	7.2											1847
1846	273 129	7.9											1846
1845	278 899	8.1											1845
1844	278 355	8.2											1844
1843	275 363	8.2											1843
1842	278 023	8.3											1842
1841	270 713	8.2											1841

a) Prior to the founding of the German Empire in 1871, divorce law differed by province and denomination. In principle, the Protestant states allowed divorce on the grounds of guilt (in Prussia, to a limited extent, also by mutual consent), whereas the Catholic states prohibited divorce for the Catholic population. In 1875, a uniform law made divorce obtainable for Catholics, but only on the grounds of guilt. In 1938, compulsory civil marriage was introduced and marital breakdown became an additional grounds for divorce. The 1938 law remained in force, with minor changes, until the 1976 reform.
In the tables, figures refer to divorces only.

Marriages, Divorces, Illegitimacy

Year	Marriages				Divorces a)			Births			births per 10.000 women age 15-44		Year
	Total	marr. per 1.000 pop.	persons marrying per 10.000 non-married persons age 15+	age 15-49	Total	divorces per 100 marr.	persons divorcing per 10.000 married pop.	Legitimate Total	Illegit. Total	illeg. births per 100 legit. births	leg. births/ married women	ill. births/ non-marr.w.	
1975	21 280	6.8	415	643				64 663	2 515	3.9	2145	91	1975
1974	22 833	7.4	447	691				66 598	2 309	3.5	2262	84	1974
1973	22 816	7.5	449	692				66 546	2 167	3.3	2315	79	1973
1972	22 302	7.4	440	678				66 522	2 005	3.0	2371	74	1972
1971	22 014	7.4	436	670				65 709	1 842	2.8	2398	68	1971
1970	20 778	7.0	412	633				62 673	1 709	2.7	2337	63	1970
1969	20 304	6.9	403	617				61 270	1 642	2.7	2332	60	1969
1968	18 993	6.5	376	574				59 446	1 558	2.6	2301	57	1968
1967	17 788	6.1	351	535				59 767	1 540	2.6	2353	56	1967
1966	16 849	5.8	331	505				60 779	1 436	2.4	2436	52	1966
1965	16 946	5.9	332	507				62 122	1 403	2.3	2506	51	1965
1964	16 128	5.6	316	482				62 780	1 292	2.1	2552	47	1964
1963	15 556	5.5	305	465				62 089	1 157	1.9	2542	42	1963
1962	15 627	5.5	307	468				60 671	1 111	1.8	2510	41	1962
1961	15 329	5.4	301	459				58 850	975	1.7	2454	36	1961
1960	15 465	5.5	299	452				59 767	968	1.6	2483	35	1960
1959	15 420	5.4	293	441				59 229	959	1.6	2448	34	1959
1958	15 061	5.3	282	421				58 534	976	1.7	2417	33	1958
1957	14 657	5.1	269	398				60 210	1 032	1.7	2458	34	1957
1956	16 761	5.8	303	446				59 567	1 173	2.0	2424	38	1956
1955	16 443	5.6	291	426				60 388	1 234	2.0	2441	39	1955
1954	15 831	5.4	276	401				61 224	1 310	2.1	2458	41	1954
1953	15 888	5.4	273	394				61 218	1 340	2.2	2454	41	1953
1952	15 876	5.4	270	387				63 012	1 619	2.6	2522	48	1952
1951	16 017	5.4	269	383				61 290	1 588	2.6	2450	47	1951
1950	16 018	5.4	265	376				61 938	1 627	2.6	2484	47	1950
1949	16 009	5.4	261	368				62 147	2 006	3.2	2497	56	1949
1948	16 115	5.4	259	364				63 765	2 165	3.4	2574	59	1948
1947	16 290	5.5	260	363				66 630	2 348	3.5	2716	63	1947
1946	17 525	5.9	279	387				65 280	2 642	4.0	2692	70	1946
1945	17 301	5.9	275	381				64 235	2 626	4.1	2683	70	1945
1944	16 772	5.7	266	368				62 858	2 567	4.1	2659	68	1944
1943	17 328	5.9	274	378				61 927	2 448	4.0	2647	64	1943
1942	17 470	5.9	274	376				63 698	2 419	3.8	2739	63	1942
1941	15 021	5.0	232	319				54 805	1 975	3.6	2360	50	1941
1940	15 212	5.1	237	325				54 770	1 824	3.3	2411	47	1940
1939	15 204	5.2	238	325				54 289	1 781	3.3	2438	46	1939
1938	14 893	5.1	232	316				55 047	1 878	3.4	2499	48	1938
1937	14 780	5.0	229	311				54 675	1 813	3.3	2500	46	1937
1936	14 763	5.0	226	307				56 207	1 908	3.4	2584	48	1936
1935	14 336	4.8	220	298				56 320	1 946	3.5	2583	49	1935
1934	14 251	4.8	219	296				55 867	2 030	3.6	2562	51	1934
1933	13 992	4.7	216	292				55 360	2 004	3.6	2543	50	1933
1932	13 029	4.4	203	273				54 421	1 819	3.3	2511	45	1932
1931	13 133	4.5	206	277				55 161	1 925	3.5	2555	48	1931
1930	13 631	4.7	214	288				56 490	1 863	3.3	2622	47	1930
1929	13 593	4.6	214	286				56 427	1 853	3.3	2607	46	1929
1928	13 716	4.7	215	288				57 388	1 788	3.1	2645	44	1928

Ireland

Marriages, Divorces, Illegitimacy

Year	Marriages		persons marrying per 10.000 non-married persons		Divorces a)			Births			births per 10.000 women age 15-44		Year
	Total	marr. per 1.000 pop.	age 15+	age 15-49	Total	divorces per 100 marr.	persons divorcing per 10.000 married pop.	Legitimate Total	Illegit. Total	illeg. births per 100 legit. births	leg. births/ married women	ill. births/ non-marr. w.	
1927	13 418	4.5	210	281				58 296	1 758	3.0	2671	43	1927
1926	13 570	4.6	212	283				59 460	1 716	2.9	2712	42	1926
1925	13 820	4.6	215	287				60 407	1 662	2.8	2738	41	1925
1924	14 822	4.9	230	306									1924
1923	15 632	5.2	242	322									1923
1922	15 141	5.0	235	311									1922
1921	15 102	4.9											1921
1920	17 276	5.6											1920
1919	17 201	5.5											1919
1918	14 773	4.8											1918
1917	14 201	4.6											1917

a) Legal marriage is indissoluble in Ireland, and the Constitution expressly provides that no law shall be enacted providing for the dissolution of marriage. The only forms of marriage dissolution available are the very limited ones afforded under ecclesiastical law.

Marriages, Divorces, Illegitimacy

Year	Marriages Total	marr. per 1.000 pop.	persons marrying per 10.000 non-married persons age 15+	age 15-49	Divorces[a] Total	divorces per 100 marr.	persons divorcing per 10.000 married pop.	Births Legitimate Total	Births Illegit. Total	illeg. births per 100 legit. births	births per 10.000 women age 15-44 leg. births/ married women	ill. births/ non-marr. w.	Year
1975	374 364	6.8	481	755				806 391	21 461	2.7	1109	54	1975
1974	403 215	7.4	519	808				846 558	22 324	2.6	1175	55	1974
1973	418 334	7.7	540	833				852 427	22 119	2.6	1195	54	1973
1972	418 944	7.8	542	829				866 255	21 948	2.5	1226	53	1972
1971	404 464	7.5	524	796				885 192	20 990	2.4	1266	50	1971
1970	395 321	7.4	514	774				880 430	19 640	2.2	1272	46	1970
1969	385 044	7.3	502	751				915 203	19 075	2.1	1336	44	1969
1968	374 097	7.1	489	726				911 158	19 014	2.1	1344	44	1968
1967	380 178	7.3	499	734				929 724	19 048	2.0	1386	43	1967
1966	384 802	7.4	507	740				960 825	19 115	2.0	1449	43	1966
1965	399 009	7.8	527	764				970 850	19 608	2.0	1480	44	1965
1964	417 486	8.2	554	798				995 422	20 698	2.1	1536	46	1964
1963	420 300	8.3	561	801				939 761	20 575	2.2	1468	45	1963
1962	406 370	8.1	544	771				915 399	21 858	2.4	1444	48	1962
1961	397 461	8.0	533	751				907 619	22 038	2.4	1446	47	1961
1960	387 683	7.8	519	726				888 154	22 038	2.5	1424	47	1960
1959	381 105	7.7	510	708				878 338	22 679	2.6	1418	48	1959
1958	373 752	7.6	500	690				847 391	23 077	2.7	1379	48	1958
1957	365 243	7.5	488	670				854 195	24 711	2.9	1401	51	1957
1956	363 734	7.5	486	662				847 764	25 844	3.0	1400	53	1956
1955	366 718	7.6	489	663				842 419	26 914	3.2	1400	55	1955
1954	359 911	7.5	480	646				842 788	27 901	3.3	1412	56	1954
1953	342 814	7.2	457	612				811 538	27 940	3.4	1370	56	1953
1952	337 047	7.1	449	597				815 664	28 783	3.5	1386	57	1952
1951	330 650	7.0	440	582				831 819	29 179	3.5	1423	57	1951
1950	356 079	7.6	478	632				877 736	30 886	3.5	1517	61	1950
1949	359 722	7.8	488	644				904 932	32 214	3.6	1583	64	1949
1948	385 034	8.4	527	694				971 099	34 752	3.6	1717	70	1948
1947	437 915	9.5	600	790				974 087	37 403	3.8	1728	75	1947
1946	415 641	9.0	571	751				996 210	39 888	4.0	1773	80	1946
1945	308 831	6.7	428	561				773 811	41 867	5.4	1392	85	1945
1944	215 384	4.7	300	393				777 232	37 514	4.8	1407	76	1944
1943	215 122	4.7	301	394				849 016	33 089	3.9	1546	67	1943
1942	287 375	6.3	404	529				891 375	34 688	3.9	1635	71	1942
1941	273 695	6.1	388	507				901 164	36 382	4.0	1671	75	1941
1940	314 167	7.0	450	587				1 006 530	39 949	4.0	1889	83	1940
1939	322 515	7.3	467	610				998 132	42 081	4.2	1900	88	1939
1938	324 844	7.4	476	621				995 046	42 134	4.2	1920	89	1938
1937	377 219	8.7	559	728				950 676	41 191	4.3	1857	88	1937
1936	316 514	7.4	473	615				919 260	43 426	4.7	1816	93	1936
1935	287 653	6.7	429	557				949 337	47 371	5.0	1886	101	1935
1934	312 702	7.4	466	603				942 770	50 196	5.3	1885	106	1934
1933	289 915	6.9	432	557				944 922	51 057	5.4	1903	107	1933
1932	267 771	6.4	399	512				939 098	51 897	5.5	1903	107	1932
1931	276 035	6.7	411	526				973 893	52 304	5.4	1986	107	1931
1930	303 214	7.4	455	584				1 037 983	54 695	5.3	2151	113	1930
1929	287 800	7.1	436	559				983 363	54 337	5.5	2070	113	1929
1928	285 248	7.1	436	558				1 018 072	54 244	5.3	2175	114	1928

Italy

Marriages, Divorces, Illegitimacy

Year	Marriages				Divorces a)			Births			births per 10.000 women age 15-44		Year
	Total	marr. per 1.000 pop.	persons marrying per 10.000 non-married persons age 15+	age 15-49	Total	divorces per 100 marr.	persons divorcing per 10.000 married pop.	Legitimate Total	Illegit. Total	illeg. births per 100 legit. births	leg. births/ married women	ill. births/ non-marr. w.	
1927	302 564	7.6	466	597				1 037 878	55 894	5.4	2253	118	1927
1926	295 566	7.5	459	588				1 041 371	53 295	5.1	2295	114	1926
1925	295 769	7.5	463	593				1 054 025	54 540	5.2	2357	117	1925
1924	306 830	7.9	485	621				1 070 651	53 999	5.0	2432	117	1924
1923	334 306	8.7	533	682				1 102 263	52 894	4.8	2545	115	1923
1922	365 460	9.6	589	753				1 121 308	54 526	4.9	2633	120	1922
1921	438 535	11.6	714	913				1 064 414	53 930	5.1	2544	120	1921
1920	508 834	14.2	879	1128				1 103 946	54 095	4.9	2765	128	1920
1919	332 576	9.3	583	750				735 388	35 232	4.8	1843	85	1919
1918	107 131	3.0	188	243				608 520	31 743	5.2	1510	77	1918
1917	98 920	2.7	173	224				658 274	32 933	5.0	1607	80	1917
1916	105 882	2.9	186	242				844 742	36 884	4.4	2046	91	1916
1915	185 675	5.1	331	432				1 060 937	48 246	4.5	2573	121	1915
1914	252 187	7.1	461	603				1 061 278	52 813	5.0	2603	136	1914
1913	264 235	7.5	492	646				1 070 263	52 219	4.9	2640	138	1913
1912	264 657	7.5	499	657				1 079 669	54 316	5.0	2659	146	1912
1911	260 198	7.4	498	658				1 039 559	53 986	5.2	2565	148	1911
1910	269 024	7.7	519	686				1 087 795	56 615	5.2	2706	158	1910
1909	266 334	7.7	519	685				1 061 362	54 469	5.1	2662	154	1909
1908	283 160	8.3	556	734				1 082 087	56 726	5.2	2737	162	1908
1907	260 104	7.7	515	679				1 006 762	55 571	5.5	2565	161	1907
1906	260 780	7.7	520	686				1 013 816	57 162	5.6	2601	167	1906
1905	255 873	7.6	514	677				1 025 663	58 855	5.7	2649	174	1905
1904	247 808	7.5	502	661				1 025 278	60 153	5.9	2668	180	1904
1903	237 211	7.2	484	637				982 922	59 168	6.0	2579	180	1903
1902	237 513	7.2	488	642				1 030 543	62 531	6.1	2721	192	1902
1901	234 819	7.2	486	640				996 475	61 288	6.2	2651	191	1901
1900	232 631	7.2	483	635				1 003 970	63 406	6.3	2678	197	1900
1899	235 665	7.3	490	644				1 021 706	66 852	6.5	2732	209	1899
1898	219 597	6.9	458	601				1 002 812	67 262	6.7	2690	210	1898
1897	229 041	7.2	480	628				1 031 649	70 199	6.8	2778	220	1897
1896	222 603	7.0	468	612				1 025 227	70 278	6.9	2772	221	1896
1895	228 152	7.3	481	629				1 021 563	70 539	6.9	2768	222	1895
1894	231 581	7.4	490	639				1 028 242	74 693	7.3	2796	236	1894
1893	228 103	7.4	484	632				1 048 190	78 106	7.5	2863	248	1893
1892	228 572	7.4	487	635				1 032 617	77 956	7.5	2832	248	1892
1891	227 656	7.4	487	634				1 052 098	80 041	7.6	2897	255	1891
1890	221 972	7.3	477	620				1 004 255	78 848	7.9	2776	252	1890
1889	230 451	7.6	497	646				1 064 798	84 399	7.9	2959	271	1889
1888	236 883	7.9	514	667				1 037 150	82 413	7.9	2898	266	1888
1887	235 629	7.9	513	666				1 067 002	85 904	8.1	2995	278	1887
1886	233 310	7.9	510	661				1 005 402	81 558	8.1	2835	265	1886
1885	233 931	8.0	514	665				1 040 868	85 102	8.2	2947	278	1885
1884	239 513	8.2	530	685				1 045 080	85 661	8.2	2979	281	1884
1883	231 945	8.1	516	667				988 375	83 077	8.4	2835	274	1883
1882	224 041	7.8	501	646				981 451	79 643	8.1	2830	264	1882
1881	230 143	8.1	517	667				1 001 617	79 508	7.9	2904	265	1881
1880	196 738	7.0	444	572				886 821	71 079	8.0	2591	237	1880

Italy

Marriages, Divorces, Illegitimacy

Year	Marriages				Divorces [a]			Births			births per 10.000 women age 15-44		Year
	Total	marr. per 1.000 pop.	persons marrying per 10.000 non-married persons age 15+	age 15-49	Total	divorces per 100 marr.	persons divorcing per 10.000 married pop.	Legitimate Total	Illegit. Total	illeg. births per 100 legit. births	leg. births/ married women	ill. births/ non-marr. w.	
1879	213 096	7.6	482	619				986 889	77 264	7.8	2904	258	1879
1878	199 885	7.2	454	583				940 022	72 453	7.7	2791	243	1878
1877	214 972	7.8	491	630				954 913	74 124	7.8	2861	249	1877
1876	225 453	8.2	518	664				1 007 487	76 234	7.6	3055	258	1876
1875	230 486	8.4	533	682				963 324	72 053	7.5	2950	245	1875
1874	207 997	7.7	482	616				882 403	69 255	7.8	2722	236	1874
1873	214 906	8.0	500	638				915 112	70 076	7.7	2842	239	1873
1872	202 361	7.5	472	602				949 775	70 907	7.5	2977	242	1872
1871	192 839	7.2	452	576				896 440	63 580	7.1	2835	218	1871
1870	188 986	7.4						890 459	61 036	6.9			1870
1869	295 287	8.1						895 141	56 993	6.4			1869
1868	182 743	7.2						845 991	54 425	6.4			1868
1867	170 456	6.8						875 584	51 812	5.9			1867
1866	142 024	6.0						831 020	45 897	5.5			1866
1865	226 458	10.2						821 521	43 866	5.3			1865
1864	198 759	9.0						802 376	43 078	5.4			1864
1863	201 225	9.2						819 856	42 504	5.2			1863
1862	198 666	9.1											1862

a) Divorce was not obtainable prior to a 1970 law, effective from 1971, which introduced civil marriage and permitted divorce on the grounds of guilt and marital breakdown, as evidenced by a legal separation of five years. Prior to 1971, only separation a mensa et thoro was obtainable.

Number of legal separations

Year	No.	Year	No.	Year	No.	Year	No.	Year	No.	Year	No.
1880	615	1896	717	1911	971	1926	1 321	1941	1 694	1960	4 997
1881	717	1897	775	1912	1 003	1927	1 421			1961	4 695
1882	630	1898	783	1913	1 012	1928	1 600	1947	7 296	1962	4 955
1883	597	1899	798	1914	979	1929	1 514	1948	6 302	1963	5 288
1884	479	1900	826	1915	867	1930	1 391	1949	5 506	1964	5 177
1885	556	1901	814	1916	767	1931	1 329	1950	5 050	1965	5 644
1886	596	1902	839	1917	703	1932	1 354	1951	5 212	1966	6 269
1887	570	1903	819	1918	725	1933	1 389	1952	5 187	1967	6 838
1888	620	1904	879	1919	1 390	1934	1 351	1953	4 742	1968	7 459
1889	591	1905	847	1920	1 641	1935	1 276	1954	5 225	1969	8 636
1890	591	1906	913	1921	1 334	1936	1 433	1955	5 373	1970	10 269
1891	628	1907	878	1922	1 337	1937	1 901	1956	4 420	1971	11 693
1892	652	1908	810	1923	1 286	1938	2 016	1957	4 387	1972	12 662
1893	686	1909	1 009	1924	1 291	1939	2 002	1958	4 594	1973	13 150
1894	683	1910	906	1925	1 399	1940	1 767	1959	4 803	1974	15 012
1895	728									1975	19 132

Marriages, Divorces, Illegitimacy

Year	Marriages Total	marr. per 1.000 pop.	persons marrying per 10.000 non-married persons age 15+	age 15-49	Divorces Total	divorces per 100 marr.	persons divorcing per 10.000 married pop.	Births Legitimate Total	Illegit. Total	illeg. births per 100 legit. births	leg. births/married women (per 10.000 women age 15-44)	ill. births/non-marr. w.	Year
1975	100 081	7.3	614	814	20 093	20.1	60	174 007	3 869	2.2	932	39	1975
1974	109 607	8.1	671	899	19 167	17.5	58	182 252	3 730	2.0	991	37	1974
1973	107 642	8.0	657	890	17 913	16.6	55	191 268	3 725	1.9	1054	37	1973
1972	117 532	8.8	715	980	14 938	12.7	46	209 999	4 134	2.0	1174	42	1972
1971	122 395	9.3	745	1031	11 572	9.5	37	222 642	4 538	2.0	1266	46	1971
1970	123 631	9.5	754	1054	10 317	8.3	33	233 872	5 040	2.2	1354	52	1970
1969	117 397	9.1	717	1013	9 080	7.7	30	242 122	5 466	2.3	1428	56	1969
1968	117 534	9.2	719	1026	8 148	6.9	27	232 213	4 899	2.1	1395	51	1968
1967	115 115	9.1	705	1016	7 464	6.5	25	233 725	4 953	2.1	1428	52	1967
1966	111 912	9.0	686	998	6 797	6.1	24	234 915	4 696	2.0	1460	49	1966
1965	108 517	8.8	668	981	6 206	5.7	22	240 705	4 511	1.9	1526	48	1965
1964	102 913	8.5	636	943	6 203	6.0	22	246 553	4 361	1.8	1595	47	1964
1963	95 360	8.0	591	885	5 851	6.1	22	245 888	3 991	1.6	1622	43	1963
1962	93 144	7.9	580	877	5 711	6.1	21	242 440	3 710	1.5	1631	41	1962
1961	92 583	8.0	579	884	5 704	6.2	22	243 491	3 518	1.4	1674	39	1961
1960	89 100	7.8	559	862	5 672	6.4	22	235 575	3 214	1.4	1651	36	1960
1959	88 007	7.8	557	844	5 530	6.3	22	238 872	3 326	1.4	1698	37	1959
1958	91 508	8.2	585	873	5 280	5.8	21	233 625	2 918	1.2	1686	32	1958
1957	93 592	8.5	604	887	5 342	5.7	22	230 697	2 911	1.3	1691	31	1957
1956	92 272	8.5	601	869	5 548	6.0	23	228 341	2 863	1.3	1697	30	1956
1955	89 037	8.3	585	833	5 498	6.2	24	226 116	2 762	1.2	1704	29	1955
1954	88 103	8.3	584	819	5 525	6.3	24	224 912	2 933	1.3	1718	31	1954
1953	85 739	8.2	572	792	5 471	6.4	24	225 632	2 977	1.3	1747	31	1953
1952	87 402	8.4	587	801	5 831	6.7	26	229 424	3 172	1.4	1797	32	1952
1951	90 225	8.8	610	822	6 075	6.7	28	225 401	3 230	1.4	1788	33	1951
1950	83 110	8.2	569	755	6 462	7.8	30	225 960	3 409	1.5	1821	34	1950
1949	82 261	8.3	569	746	7 004	8.5	33	232 404	3 773	1.6	1906	38	1949
1948	87 719	9.0	614	795	8 038	9.2	39	243 712	4 211	1.7	2032	42	1948
1947	98 683	10.2	700	895	8 847	9.0	45	262 193	5 155	2.0	2228	51	1947
1946	107 221	11.4	774	977	10 116	9.4	52	277 415	7 041	2.5	2413	70	1946
1945	72 191	7.8			4 598	6.4		202 285	7 322	3.6			1945
1944	50 446	5.5			4 654	9.2		215 445	4 501	2.1			1944
1943	65 436	7.2			4 543	6.9		205 663	3 716	1.8			1943
1942	87 559	9.7			3 795	4.3		186 742	3 233	1.7			1942
1941	65 717	7.3			3 308	5.0		178 828	3 131	1.8			1941
1940	67 220	7.6			2 947	4.4		182 313	2 533	1.4			1940
1939	80 597	9.2			3 256	4.0		178 552	2 365	1.3			1939
1938	67 040	7.7	504	627	3 262	4.9	19	175 865	2 557	1.5	1682	25	1938
1937	66 040	7.7	500	623	3 420	5.2	20	167 865	2 355	1.4	1631	24	1937
1936	63 486	7.5	485	603	3 203	5.0	19	169 063	2 612	1.5	1667	26	1936
1935	61 057	7.2	470	585	2 971	4.9	18	167 798	2 627	1.6	1679	27	1935
1934	60 631	7.3	471	586	2 959	4.8	18	169 417	2 797	1.7	1723	29	1934
1933	59 245	7.2	465	578	2 916	4.9	18	168 450	2 839	1.7	1743	29	1933
1932	55 846	6.9	444	552	2 917	5.2	19	175 434	3 091	1.8	1852	32	1932
1931	59 422	7.4	479	595	3 007	5.1	20	174 316	3 071	1.8	1879	33	1931
1930	62 911	8.0	513	638	2 815	4.5	19	179 065	3 245	1.8	1968	35	1930
1929	61 482	7.9	508	630	2 741	4.5	19	174 035	3 181	1.8	1948	35	1929
1928	59 128	7.7	494	613	2 708	4.6	19	175 702	3 326	1.9	2004	37	1928

a) Divorces

Netherlands

Marriages, Divorces, Illegitimacy

Year	Marriages Total	marr. per 1.000 pop.	persons marrying per 10.000 non-married persons age 15+	age 15-49	Divorces [a] Total	divorces per 100 marr.	persons divorcing per 10.000 married pop.	Births Legitimate Total	Illegit. Total	illeg. births per 100 legit. births	births per 10.000 women age 15-44 leg. births/ married women	illeg. births/ non-marr. w.	Year
1927	56 642	7.5	479	594	2 571	4.5	18	171 940	3 158	1.8	2000	35	1927
1926	55 299	7.4	473	586	2 368	4.3	17	174 154	3 344	1.9	2065	38	1926
1925	54 768	7.4	475	588	2 198	4.0	16	175 363	3 182	1.8	2120	36	1925
1924	56 433	7.8	495	613	2 102	3.7	16	179 153	3 277	1.8	2208	38	1924
1923	57 167	8.0	508	630	2 024	3.5	15	184 065	3 447	1.9	2317	40	1923
1922	61 151	8.7	552	683	1 954	3.2	15	178 324	3 562	2.0	2297	42	1922
1921	63 572	9.2	582	720	1 988	3.1	16	185 560	3 986	2.1	2442	48	1921
1920	65 325	9.6	606	749	1 962	3.0	16	188 875	4 112	2.2	2536	50	1920
1919	58 270	8.6	546	676	1 527	2.6	13	161 112	3 335	2.1	2195	41	1919
1918	49 527	7.4	468	579	1 404	2.8	12	163 848	3 788	2.3	2257	47	1918
1917	49 344	7.5	472	585	1 354	2.7	12	169 309	3 803	2.2	2375	48	1917
1916	46 990	7.3	459	569	1 301	2.8	11	168 777	3 795	2.2	2427	49	1916
1915	42 651	6.7	424	526	1 166	2.7	10	163 666	3 760	2.3	2406	49	1915
1914	42 539	6.8	431	535	1 122	2.6	11	173 103	3 728	2.2	2603	50	1914
1913	48 387	7.9	499	619	1 108	2.3	11	169 950	3 591	2.1	2609	49	1913
1912	46 163	7.6	483	600	1 046	2.3	10	166 869	3 400	2.0	2612	47	1912
1911	43 248	7.2	459	570	965	2.2	10	163 200	3 327	2.0	2601	46	1911
1910	42 740	7.2	459	571	859	2.0	8	165 380	3 514	2.1	2680	50	1910
1909	41 687	7.1	451	561	860	2.1	9	167 172	3 594	2.1	2740	51	1909
1908	41 932	7.2	458	570	818	2.0	8	168 098	3 763	2.2	2807	54	1908
1907	43 379	7.6	479	597	829	1.9	9	167 808	3 698	2.2	2853	54	1907
1906	42 223	7.5	472	588	770	1.8	8	167 284	3 668	2.2	2901	54	1906
1905	40 732	7.3	461	574	724	1.8	8	167 082	3 685	2.2	2957	55	1905
1904	40 574	7.4	465	580	656	1.6	7	167 836	3 659	2.2	3032	55	1904
1903	40 049	7.4	465	580	618	1.5	7	166 342	3 766	2.3	3065	58	1903
1902	40 255	7.6	473	591	581	1.4	7	164 742	3 986	2.4	3102	62	1902
1901	40 261	7.7	480	600	561	1.4	7	164 099	4 281	2.6	3159	67	1901
1900	39 419	7.7	476	595	549	1.4	6	158 364	4 247	2.7	3111	68	1900
1899	37 990	7.5	462	578	484	1.3	6	158 999	4 290	2.7	3175	69	1899
1898	36 813	7.3	453	567	509	1.4	6	156 560	4 205	2.7	3167	69	1898
1897	36 796	7.4	460	576	453	1.2	6	157 034	4 407	2.8	3233	73	1897
1896	36 490	7.5	463	581	463	1.3	6	155 636	4 611	3.0	3265	78	1896
1895	35 598	7.4	458	575	473	1.3	6	153 351	4 779	3.1	3271	82	1895
1894	34 470	7.2	450	565	391	1.1	5	149 889	4 833	3.2	3250	84	1894
1893	34 311	7.3	455	571	405	1.2	5	154 073	4 932	3.2	3396	87	1893
1892	33 330	7.2	447	563	354	1.1	5	143 952	4 762	3.3	3221	86	1892
1891	32 707	7.1	444	559	414	1.3	5	149 774	4 913	3.3	3404	90	1891
1890	32 304	7.1	445	560	383	1.2	5	144 574	4 755	3.3	3336	88	1890
1889	31 494	7.0	437	551	360	1.1	5	145 626	4 903	3.4	3393	92	1889
1888	30 862	6.9	432	545	409	1.3	6	146 347	4 747	3.2	3415	90	1888
1887	30 924	7.0	439	554	333	1.1	5	144 346	4 811	3.3	3391	92	1887
1886	30 298	6.9	437	552	315	1.0	4	146 023	4 828	3.3	3457	94	1886
1885	29 894	6.9	437	553	261	0.9	4	143 379	4 649	3.2	3421	92	1885
1884	30 528	7.2	453	573	196	0.6	3	143 749	4 731	3.3	3457	95	1884
1883	29 815	7.1	449	568	189	0.6	3	139 814	4 288	3.1	3384	88	1883
1882	29 571	7.1	453	573	168	0.6	2	142 149	4 305	3.0	3469	90	1882
1881	29 849	7.3	464	588	187	0.6	3	138 954	4 015	2.9	3420	85	1881
1880	30 349	7.5	477	605	151	0.5	2	139 702	4 153	3.0	3450	89	1880

Marriages, Divorces, Illegitimacy

Year	Marriages Total	marr. per 1.000 pop.	persons marrying per 10.000 non-married persons age 15+	age 15-49	Divorces [a] Total	divorces per 100 marr.	persons divorcing per 10.000 married pop.	Births Legitimate Total	Illegit. Total	illeg. births per 100 legit. births	births per 10.000 women age 15-44 leg. births/married women	ill. births/non-marr. w.	Year
1879	30 655	7.6	488	618	155	0.5	2	142 456	4 558	3.2	3535	99	1879
1878	30 711	7.8	492	623	163	0.5	2	138 050	4 696	3.4	3482	102	1878
1877	31 470	8.1	508	642	155	0.5	2	138 030	4 588	3.3	3537	101	1877
1876	31 699	8.3	516	651	153	0.5	2	137 616	4 594	3.3	3586	101	1876
1875	31 553	8.3	517	651	151	0.5	2	134 063	4 406	3.3	3546	98	1875
1874	31 353	8.4	516	650	154	0.5	2	131 524	4 548	3.5	3529	101	1874
1873	31 671	8.6	524	659									1873
1872	30 189	8.3	501	630									1872
1871	28 991	8.0	482	605									1871
1870	28 632	8.0	476	597									1870
1869													1869
1868													1868
1867													1867
1866													1866
1865													1865
1864													1864
1863	28 419	8.3	473	634	103	0.4	2	119 874	4 884	4.1	3586	106	1863
1862	26 541	7.8	444	581	78	0.3	1	108 427	4 341	4.0	3292	94	1862
1861	27 172	8.1	456	585	87	0.3	2	114 045	4 642	4.1	3508	101	1861
1860	27 108	8.2	457	573	92	0.3	2	104 662	4 188	4.0	3261	92	1860
1859	27 007	8.2	454	556	82	0.3	2	110 837	4 732	4.3	3472	103	1859
1858	26 342	8.0	445	545	73	0.3	1	102 454	4 392	4.3	3244	96	1858
1857	25 950	7.9	442	541	73	0.3	1	108 768	4 658	4.3	3490	103	1857
1856	24 509	7.6	421	516	70	0.3	1	101 487	4 521	4.5	3306	101	1856
1855	23 367	7.3	405	490	81	0.3	2	98 066	3 749	3.8	3240	84	1855
1854	23 855	7.5	417	510	79	0.3	2	100 113	4 131	4.1	3353	93	1854
1853	24 487	7.8	451	529	80	0.3	2	99 997	4 300	4.3	3404	98	1853
1852	25 530	8.2	457	559	71	0.3	1	105 170	4 897	4.7	3647	112	1852
1851	26 786	8.8	487	595	76	0.3	2	102 129	5 240	5.1	3618	123	1851
1850	27 386	9.0	499	611	67	0.2	1	100 115	5 223	5.2	3579	123	1850
1849	25 081	8.2	455	557	54	0.2	1	104 601	5 331	5.1	3740	125	1849
1848	21 906	7.2	388	471	52	0.2	1	92 191	4 426	4.8	3283	104	1848
1847	19 280	6.3	332	401	66	0.3	1	87 242	4 428	5.1	3080	105	1847
1846	20 633	6.7	347	416	67	0.3	1	95 434	5 268	5.5	3346	125	1846
1845	22 854	7.5	377	451	62	0.3	1	103 640	5 684	5.5	3231	136	1845
1844	22 381	7.4	365	433	38	0.2	1	103 131	5 467	5.3	3629	133	1844
1843	21 212	7.1	341	403	36	0.2	1	99 874	5 476	5.5	3525	135	1843
1842	21 064	7.2	334	394	33	0.2	1	100 113	5 516	5.5	3546	138	1842
1841	21 727	7.5	341	400	19	0.1	0	102 806	5 520	5.4	3654	141	1841
1840	22 337	7.8	349	408	48	0.2	1	100 830	4 868	4.8	3622	127	1840

a) The 1838 Civil Code basically reaffirmed the 1810 Code Napoleon in that it allowed divorce on the grounds of guilt. Divorce by mutual consent was not completely excluded, because divorce could be obtained after a legal separation of five years. In 1883, a Supreme Court decision made divorce (indirectly by mutual consent) easier. This situation lasted until 1971 when a new law made marital breakdown the sole grounds for divorce. In the tables figures refer to divorces only, i.e. they do not include legal separations, the figures of which are given below.

Number of legal separations

1874	29	1894	137	1914	212	1934	647	1954	913
1875	35	1895	125	1915	263	1935	688	1955	891
1876	25	1896	134	1916	260	1936	618	1956	918
1877	51	1897	147	1917	240	1937	718	1957	877
1878	71	1898	145	1918	234	1938	663	1958	896
1879	59	1899	159	1919	245	1939	666	1959	918
1880	75	1900	144	1920	288	1940	567	1960	1 038
1881	94	1901	165	1921	239	1941	661	1961	1 030
1882	84	1902	188	1922	241	1942	645	1962	973
1883	82	1903	161	1923	230	1943	684	1963	1 015
1884	95	1904	150	1924	314	1944	583		
1885	78	1905	172	1925	370	1945	325	1965	1 039
1886	103	1906	172	1926	418	1946	538		
1887	105	1907	179	1927	426	1947	685	1968	1 043
1888	133	1908	174	1928	452	1948	765	1969	1 046
1889	121	1909	174	1929	491	1949	732	1970	880
1890	100	1910	220	1930	490	1950	785	1971	886
1891	117	1911	218	1931	504	1951	899	1972	884
1892	120	1912	248	1932	503	1952	1 008	1973	488
1893	131	1913	215	1933	582	1953	928	1974	391
								1975	445

Marriages, Divorces, Illegitimacy

Year	Marriages				Divorces a)			Births			births per 10.000 women age 15-44		Year
	Total	marr. per 1.000 pop.	persons marrying per 10.000 non-married persons age 15+	age 15-49	Total	divorces per 100 marr.	persons divorcing per 10.000 married pop.	Legitimate Total	Illegit. Total	illeg. births per 100 legit. births	leg. births/married women	ill. births/non-marr. w.	
1975	25 898	6.5	456	731	5 577	21.5	58	50 555	5 790	11.5	1096	204	1975
1974	27 344	6.9	485	776	5 156	18.9	54	54 060	5 543	10.3	1172	197	1974
1973	28 141	7.1	503	804	4 664	16.6	49	55 656	5 552	10.0	1208	199	1973
1972	28 596	7.3	516	823	4 022	14.1	43	58 692	5 568	9.5	1277	201	1972
1971	29 510	7.6	537	856	3 731	12.6	40	60 353	5 197	8.6	1316	189	1971
1970	29 370	7.6	539	858	3 429	11.7	37	60 120	4 431	7.4	1313	163	1970
1969	29 630	7.7	548	872	3 146	10.6	35	63 583	4 163	6.5	1391	154	1969
1968	29 441	7.7	550	875	3 058	10.4	34	63 580	3 770	5.9	1396	141	1968
1967	29 154	7.7	550	874	2 876	9.9	32	63 351	3 428	5.4	1396	130	1967
1966	27 680	7.4	528	838	2 672	9.7	30	63 776	3 285	5.2	1410	125	1966
1965	24 185	6.5	465	738	2 581	10.6	29	63 220	3 057	4.8	1402	118	1965
1964	25 005	6.8	486	769	2 556	10.2	29	62 812	2 758	4.4	1397	107	1964
1963	24 096	6.6	472	747	2 439	10.1	28	60 853	2 437	4.0	1357	96	1963
1962	24 070	6.6	476	753	2 439	10.1	29	59 864	2 390	4.0	1339	95	1962
1961	24 142	6.7	482	761	2 465	10.2	29	60 248	2 307	3.8	1351	92	1961
1960	23 651	6.6	477	752	2 379	10.1	29	59 603	2 277	3.8	1341	92	1960
1959	23 237	6.5	465	726	2 219	9.5	27	60 738	2 267	3.7	1375	89	1959
1958	23 931	6.8	476	735	2 093	8.7	26	60 745	2 240	3.7	1385	86	1958
1957	24 472	7.0	484	740	2 036	8.3	26	60 838	2 225	3.7	1397	84	1957
1956	25 163	7.3	495	750	2 071	8.2	26	61 935	2 236	3.6	1433	83	1956
1955	26 156	7.6	513	769	1 982	7.6	26	61 308	2 244	3.7	1431	81	1955
1954	26 977	7.9	527	783	2 102	7.8	28	60 510	2 229	3.7	1424	79	1954
1953	27 032	8.0	526	774	2 076	7.7	28	60 667	2 318	3.8	1439	81	1953
1952	27 499	8.3	533	779	2 119	7.7	29	60 153	2 390	4.0	1439	82	1952
1951	27 180	8.2	525	761	2 151	7.9	30	58 069	2 502	4.3	1401	85	1951
1950	27 222	8.3	524	753	2 324	8.5	33	59 833	2 577	4.3	1454	86	1950
1949	27 469	8.5	517	732	2 350	8.6	34	60 363	2 689	4.5	1499	85	1949
1948	29 558	9.2	545	762	2 128	7.2	31	62 396	3 222	5.2	1585	98	1948
1947	29 923	9.5	542	747	2 236	7.5	34	64 027	3 598	5.6	1666	105	1947
1946	29 688	9.5	530	720	2 064	7.0	32	66 647	4 080	6.1	1778	114	1946
1945	23 504	7.6			1 917	8.2		57 266	4 548	7.9			1945
1944	21 996	7.2			1 540	7.0		57 695	4 546	7.9			1944
1943	24 021	7.9			1 303	5.4		52 978	4 303	8.1			1943
1942					1 200			49 312	3 913	7.9			1942
1941	26 459	8.8			1 106	4.2		42 595	3 178	7.5			1941
1940	27 983	9.4			965	3.4		44 863	3 080	6.9			1940
1939	26 095	8.8	445	573	1 149	4.4	22	43 728	2 875	6.6	1473	68	1939
1938	24 335	8.3	420	541	1 241	5.1	24	42 603	2 716	6.4	1448	65	1938
1937	23 959	8.2	418	538	1 046	4.4	21	41 039	2 769	6.7	1409	67	1937
1936	22 375	7.7	395	507	1 006	4.5	20	39 567	2 673	6.8	1371	65	1936
1935	20 511	7.1	366	470	983	4.8	20	38 548	2 773	7.2	1348	68	1935
1934	19 235	6.7	347	445	1 043	5.4	21	38 989	2 844	7.3	1374	70	1934
1933	17 995	6.3	328	421	837	4.7	17	39 144	2 970	7.6	1393	74	1933
1932	17 612	6.2	325	416	935	5.3	19	42 191	3 260	7.7	1517	82	1932
1931	17 666	6.3	330	422	908	5.1	19	42 781	3 208	7.5	1552	81	1931
1930	18 064	6.4	341	436	879	4.9	19	44 447	3 397	7.6	1629	87	1930
1929	17 795	6.4	339	434	829	4.7	18	44 913	3 459	7.7	1660	89	1929
1928	16 683	6.0	321	410	841	5.0	18	46 308	3 573	7.7	1723	93	1928

Norway

Marriages, Divorces, Illegitimacy

Year	Marriages Total	marr. per 1.000 pop.	persons marrying per 10.000 non-married persons age 15+	age 15-49	Divorces [a] Total	divorces per 100 marr.	persons divorcing per 10.000 married pop.	Births Legitimate Total	Illegit. Total	illeg. births per 100 legit. births	births per 10.000 women age 15-44 leg. births/married women	ill. births non-marr. w.	Year
1927	15 803	5.7	307	392	626	4.0	14	46 724	3 451	7.4	1752	90	1927
1926	15 948	5.8	313	399	738	4.6	16	50 618	3 545	7.0	1914	94	1926
1925	16 214	5.9	322	410	687	4.2	15	50 505	3 561	7.1	1929	95	1925
1924	16 586	6.1	333	425	680	4.1	15	54 242	3 779	7.0	2092	102	1924
1923	16 963	6.3	345	439	662	3.9	15	57 658	4 073	7.1	2246	110	1923
1922	17 185	6.4	354	450	630	3.7	14	58 575	4 333	7.4	2307	119	1922
1921	18 063	6.8	378	480	612	3.4	14	59 725	4 885	8.2	2384	136	1921
1920	18 460	7.0	393	500	660	3.6	16	64 065	5 261	8.2	2601	148	1920
1919	15 379	5.9	334	425	593	3.9	14	55 600	3 886	7.0	2292	111	1919
1918	20 019	7.8	442	565	618	3.1	15	59 274	4 212	7.1	2478	122	1918
1917	18 086	7.1	407	520	563	3.1	14	59 516	4 453	7.5	2523	131	1917
1916	17 312	6.9	397	509	513	3.0	13	56 753	4 367	7.7	2443	131	1916
1915	15 940	6.4	372	478	561	3.5	14	54 881	4 094	7.5	2393	125	1915
1914	15 773	6.4	374	482	424	2.7	11	57 608	4 503	7.8	2546	139	1914
1913	15 262	6.2	369	476	501	3.3	13	56 881	4 413	7.8	2552	138	1913
1912	14 797	6.1	364	471	490	3.3	13	57 207	4 202	7.3	2600	133	1912
1911	14 826	6.2	371	481	411	2.8	11	57 602	4 125	7.2	2654	133	1911
1910	14 566	6.1	370	481	412	2.8	11	57 445	4 041	7.0	2675	132	1910
1909	14 080	5.9	361	468	358	2.5	10	59 180	4 144	7.0	2768	136	1909
1908	14 153	6.0	367	475	292	2.1	8	57 513	4 173	7.3	2709	138	1908
1907	13 953	6.0	365	372	314	2.3	8	57 176	4 126	7.2	2707	138	1907
1906	13 590	5.9	357	462	216	1.6	6	57 946	4 145	7.2	2749	139	1906
1905	13 269	5.7	351	453	234	1.8	6	58 394	4 207	7.2	2780	142	1905
1904	13 481	5.9	359	462	180	1.3	5	59 773	4 370	7.3	2853	148	1904
1903	13 566	5.9	364	467	185	1.4	5	60 802	4 668	7.7	2908	159	1903
1902	14 385	6.3	388	498	139	1.0	4	61 741	4 753	7.7	2962	163	1902
1901	14 760	6.5	403	516	138	0.9	4	62 509	4 794	7.7	3020	166	1901
1900	15 222	6.8	421	538				61 427	4 872	7.9	2993	171	1900
1899	15 530	7.0	435	557				61 137	4 831	7.9	3015	172	1899
1898	15 039	6.9	428	548				60 902	5 024	8.2	3045	181	1898
1897	14 220	6.6	411	527				59 453	4 880	8.2	3017	178	1897
1896	13 962	6.6	410	526				58 615	4 639	7.9	3017	172	1896
1895	13 339	6.4	398	510				58 803	4 515	7.7	3068	170	1895
1894	12 966	6.3	392	504				56 555	4 334	7.7	2989	165	1894
1893	12 974	6.4	397	510				57 387	4 436	7.7	3061	170	1893
1892	12 742	6.3	393	505				55 640	4 293	7.7	2985	166	1892
1891	13 179	6.5	410	526				57 557	4 344	7.5	3109	169	1891
1890	12 922	6.5	405	521				56 461	4 286	7.6	3073	168	1890
1889	12 416	6.3	390	501				54 594	4 217	7.7	2997	166	1889
1888	12 154	6.1	382	488				55 473	4 579	8.3	3064	180	1888
1887	12 491	6.3	392	500				57 048	4 779	8.4	3169	188	1887
1886	12 819	6.5	403	512				55 740	4 726	8.5	3118	186	1886
1885	13 024	6.7	411	521				56 422	4 809	8.5	3186	191	1885
1884	13 247	6.9	420	530				56 167	4 852	8.6	3203	193	1884
1883	12 710	6.6	403	507				54 555	4 885	9.0	3134	195	1883
1882	12 874	6.7	407	510				53 933	4 829	9.0	3104	192	1882
1881	12 316	6.4	387	484				53 068	4 710	8.9	3056	186	1881
1880	12 751	6.6	400	498				54 373	4 942	9.1	3145	195	1880

Marriages, Divorces, Illegitimacy

Year	Marriages Total	marr. per 1.000 pop.	persons marrying per 10.000 non-married persons age 15+	persons marrying per 10.000 non-married persons age 15-49	Divorces[a) Total	divorces per 100 marr.	persons divorcing per 10.000 married pop.	Births Legitimate Total	Births Illegit. Total	illeg. births per 100 legit. births	births per 10.000 women age 15-44 leg. births/ married women	births per 10.000 women age 15-44 ill. births/ non-marr. w.	Year
1879	12 850	6.8	405	503				55 955	5 151	9.2	3272	205	1879
1878	13 681	7.3	435	539				54 340	4 726	8.7	3224	190	1878
1877	14 022	7.6	450	557				53 736	4 981	9.3	3239	202	1877
1876	14 049	7.7	455	561				52 699	5 000	9.5	3223	205	1876
1875	14 177	7.9	463	570				51 858	4 998	9.6	3224	207	1875
1874	13 713	7.7	457	561				50 195	5 064	10.1	3131	214	1874
1873	12 822	7.3	434	533				47 975	4 774	10.0	2997	205	1873
1872	12 302	7.0	422	518				47 894	4 698	9.8	2989	204	1872
1871	11 610	6.7	403	495				46 511	4 652	10.0	2897	205	1871
1870	11 176	6.4	393	482				46 049	4 569	9.9	2862	204	1870
1869	10 635	6.2	378	463				45 677	4 308	9.4	2825	194	1869
1868	10 709	6.2	385	471				46 628	4 244	9.1	2871	194	1868
1867	11 105	6.5	404	494				47 399	4 208	8.9	2910	194	1867
1866	11 434	6.7	421	515				49 856	4 310	8.6	3055	202	1866
1865	11 593	6.9	435	531				49 734	4 205	8.5	3056	200	1865
1864	11 371	6.8	432	528				48 937	4 221	8.6	3043	204	1864
1863	11 808	7.2	455	555				49 740	4 165	8.4	3134	203	1863
1862	11 221	6.9	437	534				48 197	3 993	8.3	3070	197	1862
1861	10 909	6.8	429	524				45 473	4 073	9.0	2917	203	1861
1860	11 413	7.2	453	554				48 641	4 433	9.1	3155	223	1860
1859	12 083	7.7	488	597				50 067	4 489	9.0	3298	230	1859
1858	11 722	7.6	482	589				47 392	4 279	9.0	3176	223	1858
1857	11 447	7.5	477	584				46 095	4 103	8.9	3131	217	1857
1856	11 599	7.7	490	600				44 125	4 186	9.5	3035	224	1856
1855	12 009	8.1	515	630				44 855	4 583	10.2	3130	249	1855
1854	12 479	8.6	543	665				45 363	4 533	10.0	3210	250	1854
1853	11 257	7.8	496	607				41 506	4 533	10.9	2969	252	1853
1852	10 179	7.1	453	555				40 075	4 144	10.3	2895	233	1852
1851	10 575	7.5	476	583				40 679	4 220	10.4	2970	240	1851
1850	10 648	7.6	486	595				38 992	4 090	10.5	2879	235	1850
1849	10 629	7.7	490	600				40 398	3 715	9.2	3016	216	1849
1848	10 187	7.5	475	581				37 334	3 220	8.6	2811	189	1848
1847	9 890	7.3	465	569				38 049	3 561	9.4	2888	211	1847
1846	11 152	8.3	530	649				38 072	3 456	9.1	2921	207	1846
1845	10 570	8.0	509	624				37 843	3 357	8.9	2939	204	1845
1844	10 290	7.9	502	615				35 816	3 157	8.8	2819	194	1844
1843	10 173	7.9	503	616				35 543	3 257	9.2	2828	203	1843
1842	9 962	7.8	498	611				35 779	3 277	9.2	2879	206	1842
1841	9 595	7.6	486	596				34 689	2 683	7.7	2828	171	1841
1840	8 601	6.9	441	540				32 074	2 474	7.7	2640	159	1840
1839	7 949	6.4	410	503				30 549	2 332	7.6	2529	151	1839
1838	7 584	6.2	394	483				31 661	2 324	7.3	2639	152	1838
1837	8 123	6.7	426	522				32 459	2 383	7.3	2726	157	1837
1836	8 424	7.0	446	547				32 868	2 499	7.6	2784	166	1836
1835	8 784	7.4	470	577				36 165	2 615	7.2	3100	176	1835
1834	8 872	7.6	480	590				34 845	2 395	6.9	3017	163	1834
1833	8 548	7.3	467	574				33 319	2 399	7.2	2911	165	1833
1832	7 839	6.8	434	532				32 001	2 399	7.5	2827	166	1832

Norway

Marriages, Divorces, Illegitimacy

Year	Marriages Total	marr. per 1.000 pop.	persons marrying per 10.000 non-married persons age 15+	persons marrying per 10.000 non-married persons age 15–49	Divorces a) Total	divorces per 100 marr.	persons divorcing per 10.000 married pop.	Births Legitimate Total	Births Illegit. Total	illeg. births per 100 legit. births	births per 10.000 women age 15–44 leg. births/married women	births per 10.000 women age 15–44 ill. births/non-marr. w.	Year
1831	8 190	7.2	458	563				32 978	2 247	6.8	2944	158	1831
1830	8 669	7.7	491	603				33 852	2 455	7.3	3058	174	1830
1829	8 639	7.8	496	609				34 741	2 539	7.3	3179	183	1829
1828	8 358	7.6	487	598				32 264	2 503	7.8	2990	182	1828
1827	8 087	7.5	477	587				32 119	2 419	7.5	3017	179	1827
1826	8 806	8.3	528	649				34 473	2 533	7.3	3286	190	1826
1825	9 020	8.6	550	676				33 236	2 620	7.9	3218	200	1825
1824	8 376	8.1	519	638				30 939	2 449	7.9	3043	190	1824
1823	8 841	8.7	556	684				31 836	2 539	8.0	3175	200	1823
1822	8 949	9.0	571	703				30 338	2 531	8.3	3068	202	1822
1821	8 895	9.0	576	708				31 457	2 709	8.6	3226	219	1821
1820	8 712	9.0	572	704				29 929	2 380	8.0	3110	195	1820
1819	7 721	8.1	514	633				28 205	2 332	8.3	2970	194	1819
1818	7 713	8.2	520	640				26 718	2 384	8.9	2845	200	1818
1817	8 010	8.6	547	673				27 845	2 455	8.8	3001	209	1817
1816	9 427	10.3	654	805				29 674	2 585	8.7	3248	224	1816
1815	9 171	10.1	645	794				25 287	1 866	7.4	2801	163	1815

a) Since the Reformation divorce was allowed on the grounds of guilt. In addition, marriage could be dissolved by royal exemption. In the same period, legal separation was introduced. It was first intended as a final solution, but gradually became a step towards divorce. In 1909, a new law gave the right to divorce after a certain period of legal separation. This law basically is still in force and combines the three main grounds for divorce, guilt, marital breakdown and mutual consent.

In the tables figures refer to divorces only, i.e. they do not include legal separations, the figures for which are given below.

Number of legal separations

Year	No.	Year	No.	Year	No.	Year	No.	Year	No.
1895	109	1911	419	1927	905	1944	1 791	1960	2 411
1896	94	1912	417	1928	906	1945	1 843	1961	2 338
1897	94	1913	532	1929	953	1946	1 975	1962	2 436
1898	142	1914	570	1930	1 018	1947	2 081	1963	2 462
1899	125	1915	533	1931	1 012	1948	1 922	1964	2 672
1900	107	1916	495	1932	950	1949	1 783	1965	2 824
1901	135	1917	500	1933	951	1950	1 941	1966	2 969
1902	139	1918	528	1934	1 030	1951	1 818	1967	3 110
1903	185	1919	597	1935	1 020	1952	2 023	1968	3 439
1904	176	1920	701	1936	1 070	1953	1 998	1969	3 496
1905	173			1937	1 094	1954	2 065	1970	4 157
1906	158	1922	699	1938	1 240	1955	2 101	1971	4 741
1907	162	1923	858	1939	1 252	1956	2 180	1972	5 691
1908	182	1924	936			1957	2 189	1973	6 185
1909	255	1925	824	1942	1 125	1958	2 218	1974	6 460
1910	384	1926	965	1943	1 473	1959	2 249	1975	6 943

Marriages, Divorces, Illegitimacy

Year	Marriages		persons marrying per 10.000 non-married persons		Divorces[a]			Births		illeg. births per 100 legit. births	births per 10.000 women age 15-44		Year
		marr. per 1.000 pop.				divorces per 100 marr.	persons divorcing per 10.000 married pop.	Legitimate	Illegit.		leg. births/ married women	ill. births/ non-marr. w.	
	Total		age 15+	age 15-49	Total			Total	Total				
1975	44 103	5.4	314	487	25 383	57.6	137	36 546	33 543	91.8	431	443	1975
1974	44 864	5.5	326	506	26 802	59.7	144	40 972	34 451	84.1	475	468	1974
1973	38 251	4.7	283	441	16 021	41.9	85	47 435	31 114	65.6	540	435	1973
1972	38 636	4.8	291	455	15 179	39.3	80	55 989	28 142	50.3	624	404	1972
1971	39 918	4.9	307	481	13 540	33.9	71	64 922	24 781	38.2	711	366	1971
1970	43 278	5.4	341	536	12 943	29.9	68	69 640	20 255	29.1	753	310	1970
1969	48 357	6.1	385	606	12 140	25.1	63	72 588	17 517	24.1	786	271	1969
1968	52 291	6.6	421	662	11 228	21.5	59	77 305	17 891	23.1	837	280	1968
1967	56 561	7.2	459	722	10 722	19.0	57	103 037	18 323	17.8	1114	289	1967
1966	61 101	7.8	501	788	10 228	16.8	55	105 392	17 962	17.0	1139	286	1966
1965	59 963	7.8	497	783	9 563	15.9	51	104 856	16 950	16.0	1146	274	1965
1964	58 439	7.6	492	774	9 169	15.7	50	106 547	16 117	15.1	1159	264	1964
1963	53 480	7.0	455	717	8 996	16.8	50	98 731	14 172	14.4	1077	235	1963
1962	53 913	7.1	464	731	8 849	16.4	49	93 987	13 297	14.1	1026	223	1962
1961	52 449	7.0	456	718	8 696	16.6	48	92 285	12 216	13.2	1008	207	1961
1960	50 149	6.7	440	694	8 958	17.9	50	90 684	11 535	12.7	991	198	1960
1959	50 168	6.7	443	695	8 761	17.5	49	93 833	10 910	11.6	1021	187	1959
1958	50 785	6.9	450	705	8 657	17.0	49	94 701	10 801	11.4	1027	186	1958
1957	52 529	7.1	469	730	8 858	16.9	51	96 318	10 850	11.3	1042	187	1957
1956	51 719	7.1	465	721	8 608	16.6	50	96 910	11 050	11.4	1047	191	1956
1955	52 250	7.2	473	731	8 785	16.8	52	96 631	10 674	11.0	1042	186	1955
1954	53 008	7.3	483	744	8 588	16.2	51	94 811	10 285	10.8	1020	179	1954
1953	53 152	7.4	487	748	8 393	15.8	50	99 383	10 761	10.8	1067	188	1953
1952	53 314	7.5	492	752	8 159	15.3	49	99 258	10 934	11.0	1064	192	1952
1951	54 247	7.7	504	768	8 114	15.0	50	99 073	11 095	11.2	1061	196	1951
1950	54 222	7.7	509	772	8 008	14.8	49	104 155	11 259	10.8	1116	199	1950
1949	55 288	7.9	512	768	7 609	13.8	48	109 889	11 383	10.4	1190	196	1949
1948	58 009	8.4	532	789	6 782	11.7	43	114 763	11 920	10.4	1257	199	1948
1947	59 670	8.8	543	797	7 058	11.8	46	116 697	12 082	10.4	1297	197	1947
1946	63 800	9.5	576	837	6 988	11.0	46	120 214	12 383	10.3	1354	197	1946
1945	64 280	9.7	577	830	6 463	10.1	43	122 990	12 383	10.1	1406	193	1945
1944	64 627	9.9	572	814	5 428	8.4	37	122 009	12 982	10.6	1434	195	1944
1943	62 803	9.7	549	771	4 747	7.6	33	113 173	12 219	10.8	1365	178	1943
1942	63 659	9.9	548	762	4 180	6.6	30	102 915	11 046	10.7	1274	155	1942
1941	58 102	9.1	492	678	3 430	5.9	25	89 214	10 513	11.8	1130	143	1941
1940	59 166	9.3	493	672	3 489	5.9	26	84 938	10 840	12.8	1100	142	1940
1939	61 373	9.7	509	689	3 541	5.8	27	86 115	11 265	13.1	1146	145	1939
1938	58 130	9.2	479	645	3 484	6.0	28	81 891	12 055	14.7	1121	153	1938
1937	55 606	8.9	456	609	3 128	5.6	25	78 413	11 960	15.3	1103	149	1937
1936	53 276	8.5	434	576	2 874	5.4	23	77 248	11 690	15.1	1117	143	1936
1935	51 306	8.2	415	548	2 718	5.3	23	74 019	11 887	16.1	1100	143	1935
1934	48 095	7.7	391	515	2 737	5.7	24	72 876	12 216	16.8	1101	146	1934
1933	43 437	7.0	355	467	2 558	5.9	22	72 726	12 294	16.9	1117	147	1933
1932	41 673	6.7	343	450	2 384	5.7	21	76 610	13 169	17.2	1198	157	1932
1931	42 908	7.0	356	465	2 344	5.5	21	76 748	14 326	18.7	1222	171	1931
1930	43 858	7.2	366	477	2 218	5.1	20	79 363	14 857	18.7	1285	177	1930
1929	41 719	6.8	351	457	2 188	5.2	20	77 456	15 405	19.9	1268	185	1929
1928	40 507	6.6	343	447	2 141	5.3	20	82 816	15 052	18.2	1369	181	1928

Sweden

Marriages, Divorces, Illegitimacy

Year	Marriages Total	marr. per 1.000 pop.	persons marrying per 10.000 non-married persons age 15+	age 15-49	Divorces[a] Total	divorces per 100 marr.	persons divorcing per 10.000 married pop.	Births Legitimate Total	Illegit. Total	illeg. births per 100 legit. births	births per 10.000 women age 15-44 leg. births/married women	ill. births/non-marr.w.	Year
1927	38 999	6.4	333	433	1 973	5.1	18	82 398	15 596	18.9	1377	189	1927
1926	38 268	6.3	329	428	1 780	4.7	17	86 316	15 691	18.2	1457	191	1926
1925	37 419	6.2	324	422	1 748	4.7	16	90 188	16 104	17.9	1540	197	1925
1924	37 385	6.2	327	425	1 634	4.4	16	93 252	15 803	16.9	1612	195	1924
1923	37 829	6.3	334	434	1 444	3.8	14	97 037	16 398	16.9	1696	204	1923
1922	36 806	6.2	328	426	1 455	4.0	14	99 610	17 336	17.4	1763	217	1922
1921	39 550	6.7	357	463	1 265	3.2	12	107 999	19 724	18.3	1940	249	1921
1920	42 918	7.3	393	509	1 325	3.1	13	116 946	21 807	18.6	2138	279	1920
1919	40 289	6.9	373	484	1 204	3.0	12	100 130	15 063	15.0	1857	195	1919
1918	38 645	6.7	361	468	1 098	2.8	11	101 607	16 348	16.1	1904	213	1918
1917	35 524	6.1	335	434	1 043	2.9	11	102 795	18 060	17.6	1946	238	1917
1916	35 024	6.1	335	434	772	2.2	8	103 553	18 126	17.5	1989	242	1916
1915	33 182	5.8	321	416	847	2.6	9	103 503	19 494	18.8	2014	263	1915
1914	32 932	5.8	322	417	785	2.4	8	108 977	20 481	18.8	2149	279	1914
1913	33 329	5.9	329	427	770	2.3	8	110 040	20 160	18.3	2199	278	1913
1912	33 149	5.9	331	430	659	2.0	7	112 509	20 359	18.1	2277	283	1912
1911	32 614	5.9	330	428	603	1.8	7	113 267	19 710	17.4	2325	278	1911
1910	33 162	6.0	340	441	609	1.8	7	116 303	19 322	16.6	2422	275	1910
1909	32 546	6.0	337	437	530	1.6	6	120 009	19 496	16.2	2518	280	1909
1908	33 084	6.1	346	450	506	1.5	6	120 279	18 595	15.5	2544	270	1908
1907	33 251	6.2	352	457	498	1.5	6	118 851	17 942	15.1	2532	263	1907
1906	32 583	6.1	348	452	534	1.6	6	119 063	17 557	14.7	2554	260	1906
1905	30 888	5.9	333	432	448	1.5	5	118 761	16 648	14.0	2563	248	1905
1904	30 683	5.9	334	433	442	1.4	5	118 725	16 227	13.7	2574	244	1904
1903	30 088	5.8	330	428	418	1.4	5	118 247	15 649	13.2	2576	237	1903
1902	30 896	6.0	342	443	391	1.3	5	121 146	16 218	13.4	2648	247	1902
1901	31 278	6.1	349	452	359	1.1	4	122 985	16 385	13.3	2701	251	1901
1900	31 478	6.2	354	459	405	1.3	5	122 380	15 759	12.9	2706	244	1900
1899	31 710	6.2	361	467	387	1.2	5	118 888	14 994	12.6	2644	234	1899
1898	30 900	6.1	356	461	409	1.3	5	120 882	15 641	12.9	2706	247	1898
1897	30 221	6.1	354	458	349	1.2	4	118 066	14 933	12.6	2667	238	1897
1896	29 376	5.9	348	451	349	1.2	4	119 453	14 855	12.4	2719	240	1896
1895	28 728	5.9	345	447	305	1.1	4	120 161	14 438	12.0	2757	236	1895
1894	27 851	5.7	339	439	292	1.0	4	117 451	13 958	11.9	2716	231	1894
1893	27 219	5.7	335	434	293	1.1	4	118 113	13 616	11.5	2747	227	1893
1892	27 338	5.7	339	439	316	1.2	4	116 027	13 595	11.7	2701	228	1892
1891	27 940	5.8	349	452	276	1.0	3	121 798	13 718	11.3	2836	231	1891
1890	28 611	6.0	360	466	296	1.0	4	119 949	13 648	11.4	2798	231	1890
1889	28 478	6.0	359	463	240	0.8	3	118 781	13 288	11.2	2778	224	1889
1888	28 075	5.9	354	455	252	0.9	3	122 579	13 872	11.3	2872	233	1888
1887	29 517	6.2	372	477	233	0.8	3	125 384	14 785	11.8	2945	248	1887
1886	30 133	6.4	381	467	226	0.3	3	125 545	14 337	11.4	2958	240	1886
1885	30 911	6.6	393	500	229	0.7	3	123 014	14 294	11.6	2918	240	1885
1884	30 200	6.5	386	490	241	0.8	3	124 562	14 183	11.4	2977	239	1884
1883	29 449	6.4	378	478	218	0.7	3	119 514	13 361	11.2	2870	225	1883
1882	28 967	6.3	372	469	195	0.7	3	120 522	13 778	11.4	2901	232	1882

Marriages, Divorces, Illegitimacy

Year	Marriages Total	marr. per 1,000 pop.	persons marrying per 10,000 non-married persons age 15+	age 15-49	Divorces[a] Total	divorces per 100 marr.	persons divorcing per 10,000 married pop.	Births Legitimate Total	Illegit. Total	illeg. births per 100 legit. births	births per 10,000 women age 15-44 leg. births/married women	ill. births/non-marr. w.	Year
1881	28 301	6.2	363	456	214	0.8	3	119 527	13 277	11.1	2875	222	1881
1880	28 919	6.3	370	463	217	0.8	3	120 530	13 732	11.4	2894	228	1880
1879	28 635	6.3	368	461	206	0.7	3	125 236	13 807	11.0	3008	231	1879
1878	29 151	6.5	380	475	205	0.7	3	121 358	13 106	10.8	2936	222	1878
1877	30 674	6.9	406	507	211	0.7	3	124 805	13 671	11.0	3047	234	1877
1876	31 184	7.1	418	522	212	0.7	3	122 275	13 615	11.1	3010	236	1876
1875	30 762	7.1	418	521	181	0.6	3	122 077	13 881	11.4	3025	244	1875
1874	31 422	7.3	432	539	216	0.7	3	119 000	14 249	12.0	2969	253	1874
1873	31 257	7.3	436	543	190	0.6	3	117 159	14 484	12.4	2944	260	1873
1872	29 470	7.0	417	518	154	0.5	2	112 989	13 994	12.4	2865	255	1872
1871	27 187	6.5	389	484	135	0.5	2	113 291	14 042	12.4	2891	258	1871
1870	25 072	6.0	362	449	126	0.5	2	107 420	12 418	11.6	2748	230	1870
1869	23 503	5.6	339	421	115	0.5	2	105 712	11 965	11.3	2674	221	1869
1868	22 833	5.5	328	406	115	0.5	2	103 551	11 404	11.0	2581	210	1868
1867	25 440	6.1	366	453	128	0.5	2	116 005	12 827	11.1	2865	237	1867
1866	27 797	6.7	404	500	137	0.5	2	123 919	13 070	10.5	3059	243	1866
1865	28 944	7.1	425	525	127	0.4	2	121 841	12 440	10.2	3014	234	1865
1864	28 248	7.0	419	518	135	0.5	2	123 085	12 919	10.5	3048	246	1864
1863	29 013	7.3	436	538	148	0.5	2	122 076	12 203	10.0	3032	235	1863
1862	27 825	7.1	424	523	120	0.4	2	119 984	11 600	9.7	2990	226	1862
1861	28 272	7.3	437	538	150	0.5	2	114 819	11 815	10.3	2872	233	1861
1860	29 839	7.8	469	577	119	0.4	2	121 380	11 782	9.7	3058	236	1860
1859	31 125	8.3	495	610	132	0.4	2	119 702	11 903	9.9	3078	242	1859
1858	30 092	8.1	484	595	124	0.4	2	117 604	11 435	9.7	3077	235	1858
1857	28 531	7.8	461	567	119	0.4	2	109 328	10 021	9.2	2893	207	1857
1856	27 221	7.4	441	543	130	0.5	2	104 990	10 092	9.6	2806	209	1856
1855	27 253	7.5	444	546	115	0.4	2	104 269	10 803	10.4	2823	225	1855
1854	27 585	7.7	453	557	124	0.4	2	109 121	10 986	10.1	2998	230	1854
1853	25 596	7.2	423	520	106	0.4	2	101 263	10 144	10.0	2820	214	1853
1852	24 150	6.8	400	492	112	0.5	2	98 066	10 239	10.4	2757	217	1852
1851	25 750	7.4	429	527	122	0.5	2	100 459	10 606	10.6	2859	225	1851
1850	26 267	7.6	441	542				100 079	10 320	10.3	2891	221	1850
1849	26 891	7.9	458	563				102 062	10 242	10.0	2979	223	1849
1848	24 729	7.3	428	526				93 792	8 732	9.3	2767	193	1848
1847	22 858	6.8	400	492				90 774	8 405	9.3	2694	188	1847
1846	22 981	6.9	406	500				90 832	8 871	9.8	2712	200	1846
1845	24 009	7.3	429	529				94 392	9 268	9.8	2841	212	1845
1844	24 208	7.4	439	542				95 755	8 938	9.3	2912	208	1844
1843	23 167	7.2	426	526				90 753	8 401	9.3	2786	198	1843
1842	22 691	7.1	423	522				92 619	8 357	9.0	2866	200	1842
1841	22 619	7.2	427	528				88 395	7 339	8.3	2762	178	1841
1840	22 071	7.1	422	523				90 781	7 379	8.1	2861	182	1840
1839	20 963	6.8	409	507				85 249	6 114	7.2	2687	154	1839
1838	18 774	6.1	372	463				84 398	6 167	7.3	2650	158	1838
1837	21 153	6.9	426	532				88 353	6 263	7.1	2767	164	1837
1836	21 816	7.2	448	561				90 351	6 506	7.2	2828	174	1836

Sweden

Marriages, Divorces, Illegitimacy

Year	Marriages		persons marrying per 10.000 non-married persons		Divorces[a]			Births		illeg. births per 100 legit. births	births per 10.000 women age 15–44		Year
	Total	marr. per 1.000 pop.	age 15+	age 15–49	Total	divorces per 100 marr.	persons divorcing per 10.000 married pop.	Legitimate Total	Illegit. Total		leg. births/ married women	ill. births/ non-marr. w.	
1835	22 533	7.5	474	595				91 470	6 674	7.3	2878	183	1835
1834	23 803	8.0	512	645				93 235	6 996	7.5	2944	197	1834
1833	23 029	7.8	506	640				93 921	6 388	6.8	2971	185	1833
1832	20 935	7.2	470	597				84 402	5 460	6.5	2676	162	1832
1831	19 983	6.9	457	582				82 482	5 771	7.0	2609	175	1831
1830	22 222	7.7	517	662				88 779	5 847	6.6	2807	181	1830
1829	22 581	7.9	525	670				93 525	5 963	6.4	2981	183	1829
1828	22 440	7.9	520	663				89 775	5 579	6.2	2879	171	1828
1827	20 339	7.2	471	599				82 550	5 588	6.8	2670	170	1827
1826	22 525	8.1	523	664				90 481	6 644	7.3	2956	202	1826
1825	23 640	8.6	552	699				93 614	6 701	7.2	3104	204	1825
1824	23 907	8.8	562	711				87 083	6 494	7.5	2934	199	1824
1823	23 993	9.0	568	717				91 079	7 180	7.9	3115	220	1823
1822	24 431	9.3	582	734				87 384	6 925	7.9	3036	213	1822
1821	22 890	8.8	547	689				85 806	6 266	7.3	3016	193	1821
1820	21 722	8.4	520	654				79 345	5 496	6.9	2819	169	1820
1819	20 795	8.1	502	632				78 390	5 860	7.5	2808	182	1819
1818	21 427	8.5	522	657				79 960	5 754	7.2	2892	180	1818
1817	20 938	8.3	516	649				77 842	5 979	7.7	2846	189	1817
1816	23 069	9.3	576	724				81 255	6 389	7.9	3010	205	1816
1815	23 553	9.6	596	749				79 579	5 660	7.1	2986	184	1815

a) Since the Reformation divorce was allowed on the grounds of guilt. In addition, divorce was possible by royal exemption. In 1915, a new law based divorce on the two principles of guilt and marital breakdown. Divorce was possible after one year's legal separation. In 1974, marital breakdown became the only grounds for divorce, making it much easier to obtain.

In the tables figures refer to divorces only, i.e. they do not include legal separations, the figures for which are given below.

Number of legal separations

1916	744	1926	1 924	1936	3 380	1946	7 830	1956	9 248	1966	11 537
1917	799	1927	2 201	1937	3 630	1947	7 753	1957	9 048	1967	12 201
1918	1 019	1928	2 319	1938	3 963	1948	7 761	1958	9 233	1968	13 622
1919	1 191	1929	2 319	1939	4 019	1949	8 608	1959	9 657	1969	14 347
1920	1 326	1930	2 510	1940	3 775	1950	8 512	1960	9 221	1970	15 374
1921	1 234	1931	2 622	1941	4 377	1951	8 566	1961	9 113	1971	16 699
1922	1 364	1932	2 653	1942	5 091	1952	8 576	1962	9 425	1972	18 059
1923	1 483	1933	2 726	1943	6 069	1953	9 149	1963	9 640	1973	16 997
1924	1 545	1934	2 929	1944	7 046	1954	9 163	1964	10 537	1974	903
1925	1 854	1935	3 226	1945	7 652	1955	9 333	1965	10 942	1975	20

Marriages, Divorces, Illegitimacy

Year	Marriages Total	marr. per 1.000 pop.	persons marrying per 10.000 non-married persons age 15+	age 15-49	Divorces a) Total	divorces per 100 marr.	persons divorcing per 10.000 married pop.	Births Legitimate Total	Illegit. Total	illeg. births per 100 legit. births	births per 10.000 women age 15-44 leg. births/married women	ill. births/non-marr. w.	Year
1975	35 189	5.5	395	593	8 917	25.3	57	75 537	2 927	3.9	847	60	1975
1974	38 499	6.0	426	638	8 193	21.3	52	81 419	3 088	3.8	917	61	1974
1973	40 768	6.3	448	669	8 030	19.7	52	84 187	3 331	4.0	960	65	1973
1972	43 081	6.7	472	705	7 650	17.8	50	87 942	3 400	3.9	1020	66	1972
1971	44 881	7.1	492	733	7 035	15.7	47	92 677	3 584	3.9	1097	70	1971
1970	46 693	7.5	512	761	6 405	13.7	43	95 470	3 746	3.9	1152	73	1970
1969	46 886	7.5	514	763	5 980	12.8	41	98 649	3 871	3.9	1214	75	1969
1968	45 711	7.5	503	746	5 599	12.2	39	101 096	4 034	4.0	1274	78	1968
1967	45 269	7.5	500	740	5 198	11.5	37	103 276	4 141	4.0	1331	80	1967
1966	44 266	7.4	490	724	4 944	11.2	36	105 527	4 211	4.0	1390	81	1966
1965	45 082	7.6	499	736	4 977	11.0	36	107 477	4 358	4.1	1446	83	1965
1964	44 172	7.5	490	722	4 865	11.0	36	108 157	4 733	4.4	1489	90	1964
1963	43 946	7.6	492	724	4 711	10.7	36	105 448	4 545	4.3	1494	87	1963
1962	44 323	7.8	502	738	4 724	10.7	37	99 914	4 408	4.4	1460	85	1962
1961	42 257	7.7	489	717	4 737	11.2	38	95 311	3 927	4.1	1451	77	1961
1960	41 574	7.8	489	716	4 656	11.2	39	90 762	3 610	4.0	1433	72	1960
1959	40 164	7.6	479	700	4 683	11.7	40	89 477	3 496	3.9	1441	70	1959
1958	39 975	7.7	480	700	4 400	11.0	38	88 086	3 335	3.8	1436	67	1958
1957	41 669	8.1	505	734	4 545	10.9	40	87 348	3 475	4.0	1444	70	1957
1956	40 488	8.0	496	719	4 293	10.6	39	84 636	3 276	3.9	1423	66	1956
1955	39 713	8.0	490	709	4 416	11.1	40	82 228	3 103	3.8	1400	62	1955
1954	38 247	7.8	474	685	4 437	11.6	41	80 657	3 084	3.8	1388	62	1954
1953	37 392	7.7	466	672	4 406	11.8	41	80 048	2 981	3.7	1393	60	1953
1952	37 471	7.8	471	677	4 188	11.2	40	80 593	2 956	3.7	1421	59	1952
1951	37 719	7.9	478	686	4 295	11.4	42	79 008	2 895	3.7	1413	58	1951
1950	37 108	7.9	473	678	4 241	11.4	42	81 560	3 216	3.9	1476	65	1950
1949	36 993	8.0	472	672	4 111	11.1	41	82 249	3 059	3.7	1506	61	1949
1948	39 274	8.6	502	710	4 292	10.9	44	84 546	3 217	3.8	1568	64	1948
1947	39 401	8.7	504	709	4 280	10.9	45	84 644	3 080	3.6	1590	61	1947
1946	38 768	8.7	497	695	4 298	11.1	46	86 118	3 008	3.5	1638	59	1946
1945	35 640	8.1	457	636	3 726	10.5	40	85 457	3 065	3.6	1647	60	1945
1944	34 765	8.0	446	617	3 138	9.0	35	82 918	2 709	3.3	1616	52	1944
1943	35 694	8.3	457	629	3 211	9.0	36	80 380	2 669	3.3	1581	51	1943
1942	36 820	8.6	471	644	3 199	8.7	36	76 169	2 706	3.6	1511	52	1942
1941	36 130	8.5	460	627	3 066	8.5	35	69 215	2 711	3.9	1384	51	1941
1940	32 472	7.7	416	563	3 093	9.5	36	61 656	2 459	4.0	1248	46	1940
1939	31 513	7.5	404	546	2 996	9.5	35	61 616	2 221	3.6	1261	41	1939
1938	31 031	7.4	399	535	3 390	10.9	40	61 558	2 232	3.6	1271	41	1938
1937	30 394	7.3	391	522	3 379	11.1	41	60 185	2 295	3.8	1254	42	1937
1936	29 633	7.1	381	507	3 219	10.9	39	62 480	2 486	4.0	1314	45	1936
1935	30 495	7.3	392	520	3 015	9.9	37	63 763	2 615	4.1	1352	47	1935
1934	32 492	7.8	419	553	3 034	9.3	38	64 614	2 663	4.1	1384	48	1934
1933	31 969	7.8	413	543	2 992	9.4	38	64 695	2 814	4.3	1400	50	1933
1932	31 959	7.8	414	542	3 041	9.5	39	65 794	2 856	4.3	1440	51	1932
1931	32 269	7.9	419	546	2 875	8.9	37	65 359	2 890	4.4	1447	51	1931
1930	32 132	7.9	419	545	2 723	8.5	36	66 797	3 058	4.6	1499	54	1930
1929	31 238	7.8	411	533	2 733	8.7	36	66 157	2 849	4.3	1504	50	1929
1928	30 050	7.5	399	516	2 545	8.5	34	66 831	2 763	4.1	1540	49	1928

Switzerland

Marriages, Divorces, Illegitimacy

Year	Marriages Total	marr. per 1.000 pop.	persons marrying per 10.000 non-married persons age 15+	age 15-49	Divorces[a] Total	divorces per 100 marr.	persons divorcing per 10.000 married pop.	Births Legitimate Total	Births Illegit. Total	illeg. births per 100 legit. births	births per 10.000 women age 15-44 leg. births/ married women	ill. births non-marr. w.	Year
1927	28 585	7.2	383	494	2 500	8.7	34	66 740	2 793	4.2	1558	50	1927
1926	28 079	7.1	378	488	2 213	7.9	31	69 390	2 728	3.9	1639	49	1926
1925	28 110	7.2	381	490	2 223	7.9	32	69 927	2 643	3.8	1670	48	1925
1924	28 510	7.3	388	498	2 119	7.4	30	70 820	2 688	3.8	1707	49	1924
1923	29 561	7.6	404	518	2 005	6.8	29	72 791	2 760	3.8	1770	50	1923
1922	30 063	7.8	412	527	2 108	7.0	31	72 456	3 834	5.3	1775	70	1922
1921	32 624	8.4	447	571	1 979	6.1	29	77 491	3 317	4.3	1908	60	1921
1920	34 975	9.0	480	611	2 241	6.4	34	77 599	3 591	4.6	1921	65	1920
1919	30 751	7.9	425	542	1 977	6.4	30	69 001	3 124	4.5	1707	57	1919
1918	26 117	6.7	362	462	1 699	6.5	26	69 165	3 493	5.1	1703	64	1918
1917	23 254	6.0	324	413	1 640	7.1	25	68 705	3 360	4.9	1683	63	1917
1916	22 251	5.7	312	398	1 562	7.0	24	70 404	3 256	4.6	1724	62	1916
1915	19 527	5.0	276	352	1 472	7.5	22	72 102	3 443	4.8	1760	66	1915
1914	22 245	5.7	315	402	1 455	6.5	22	82 989	4 341	5.2	2013	84	1914
1913	26 841	6.9	385	492	1 616	6.0	25	85 579	4 178	4.9	2089	82	1913
1912	27 843	7.3	407	519	1 514	5.4	24	87 801	4 395	5.0	2163	89	1912
1911	27 809	7.4	414	528	1 623	5.8	26	87 165	4 155	4.8	2168	86	1911
1910	27 346	7.3	414	529	1 527	5.6	24	89 310	4 204	4.7	2239	89	1910
1909	27 470	7.4	420	536	1 534	5.6	25	89 865	4 247	4.7	2286	91	1909
1908	27 634	7.6	426	545	1 551	5.6	26	91 904	4 341	4.7	2375	94	1908
1907	27 660	7.7	430	551	1 494	5.4	25	90 341	4 167	4.6	2369	91	1907
1906	27 298	7.7	429	549	1 343	4.9	23	91 427	4 168	4.6	2437	91	1906
1905	26 272	7.5	417	535	1 206	4.6	21	90 437	4 216	4.7	2447	93	1905
1904	25 502	7.3	409	524	1 243	4.9	22	90 905	3 962	4.4	2501	89	1904
1903	25 283	7.4	409	526	1 182	4.7	21	89 843	3 981	4.4	2510	90	1903
1902	25 078	7.4	410	527	1 105	4.4	20	92 296	4 185	4.5	2622	95	1902
1901	25 378	7.6	419	539	1 027	4.0	19	92 811	4 217	4.5	2679	97	1901
1900	25 537	7.7	426	548	1 028	4.0	19	90 102	4 214	4.7	2643	98	1900
1899	25 412	7.8	429	553	1 095	4.3	21	90 212	4 260	4.7	2690	100	1899
1898	25 114	7.8	430	554	1 018	4.1	19	87 678	4 115	4.7	2660	98	1898
1897	24 954	7.8	433	559	1 011	4.1	20	85 914	4 164	4.8	2650	100	1897
1896	23 784	7.5	418	540	1 057	4.4	21	84 375	4 053	4.8	2646	99	1896
1895	22 682	7.3	404	523	897	4.0	18	81 212	3 761	4.6	2592	93	1895
1894	22 188	7.2	400	519	932	4.2	19	80 270	3 872	4.8	2606	97	1894
1893	21 884	7.2	400	519	903	4.1	18	81 033	3 864	4.8	2677	98	1893
1892	21 884	7.3	406	527	881	4.0	18	79 199	3 926	5.0	2665	101	1892
1891	21 264	7.2	400	520	877	4.1	18	79 762	3 834	4.8	2731	100	1891
1890	20 836	7.1	394	513	880	4.2	19	74 907	3 641	4.9	2591	96	1890
1889	20 691	7.0	394	513	865	4.2	18	77 514	3 662	4.7	2707	97	1889
1888	20 706	7.1	396	516	841	4.1	18	77 284	3 814	4.9	2723	101	1888
1887	20 646	7.1	396	516	925	4.5	20	77 489	3 798	4.9	2727	101	1887
1886	20 080	6.9	387	503	899	4.5	19	76 857	3 906	5.1	2703	105	1886
1885	20 105	6.9	388	505	920	4.6	20	76 423	3 926	5.1	2684	106	1885
1884	19 898	6.9	386	502	907	4.6	20	77 611	3 960	5.1	2725	107	1884
1883	19 696	6.9	383	498	898	4.6	19	78 001	3 973	5.1	2736	108	1883
1882	19 414	6.8	379	492	964	5.0	21	78 666	4 023	5.1	2758	110	1882
1881	19 425	6.8	381	494	945	4.9	21	81 133	4 009	4.9	2841	110	1881
1880	19 413	6.8	382	496	856	4.4	19	80 306	3 859	4.8	2815	107	1880

Marriages, Divorces, Illegitimacy

Year	Marriages	marr. per 1.000 pop.	persons marrying per 10.000 non-married persons		Divorces a)	divorces per 100 marr.	persons divorcing per 10.000 married pop.	Births		illeg. births per 100 legit. births	births per 10.000 women age 15-44		Year
	Total		age 15+	age 15-49	Total			Legitimate Total	Illegit. Total		leg. births/ married women	ill. births/ non-marr. w.	
1879	19 450	6.9	382	496	938	4.8	21	82 282	3 898	4.7	2928	108	1879
1878	20 590	7.3	404	524	1 036	5.0	23	83 728	4 105	4.9	3026	113	1878
1877	21 871	7.9	428	556	1 036	4.7	24	84 968	4 276	5.0	3119	117	1877
1876	22 376	8.1	437	568				86 321	4 465	5.2	3218	122	1876
1875	24 629	9.0	481	624				83 780	3 799	4.5	3173	104	1875
1874	22 655	8.3	441	574				79 132	3 919	5.0	3045	107	1874
1873	20 649	7.6	402	523				76 597	3 975	5.2	2995	108	1873
1872	21 212	7.9	412	536				76 247	4 082	5.4	3030	110	1872
1871	19 514	7.3	379	493				73 373	4 260	5.8	2964	115	1871

a) Since the Reformation divorce was obtainable on the grounds of guilt. In 1912, divorce on the grounds of marital breakdown was introduced. In addition, a legal separation is allowable on the same grounds as divorce.

In the tables, figures refer to divorces only, i.e. they do not include legal separations, the number of which always amounted to less than 10 percent of divorces.

Marriages, Divorces, Illegitimacy

Year	Marriages Total	marr. per 1.000 pop.	persons marrying per 10.000 non-married persons age 15+	age 15-49	Divorces Total a)	divorces per 100 marr.	persons divorcing per 10.000 married pop.	Births Legitimate Total	Births Illegit. Total	illeg. births per 100 legit. births	births per 10.000 women age 15-44 leg. births/married women	ill. births/non-marr. w.	Year
1975	380 620	7.7	605	1013	120 522	31.7	95	548 000	55 000	10.0	826	179	1975
1974	384 389	7.8	610	1021	113 500	29.5	90	584 000	56 000	9.6	883	181	1974
1973	400 435	8.1	635	1061	106 003	26.5	84	618 000	58 000	9.4	937	187	1973
1972	426 241	8.7	678	1130	119 025	27.9	95	662 000	63 000	9.5	1010	203	1972
1971	404 737	8.3	645	1075	74 437	18.4	59	717 000	66 000	9.2	1100	213	1971
1970	415 487	8.5	664	1106	58 239	14.0	47	719 000	65 000	9.0	1110	210	1970
1969	396 746	8.2	635	1057	51 310	12.9	41	731 000	67 000	9.2	1135	216	1969
1968	407 822	8.4	655	1088	45 794	11.2	37	749 000	70 000	9.3	1170	226	1968
1967	386 052	8.0	622	1033	43 093	11.2	35	762 000	70 000	9.2	1200	227	1967
1966	384 497	8.0	623	1033	39 067	10.2	32	783 000	67 000	8.6	1243	218	1966
1965	371 000	7.8	605	1007	37 785	10.2	31	797 000	66 000	8.3	1269	217	1965
1964	359 000	7.6	593	991	34 868	9.7	29	813 000	63 000	7.7	1306	212	1964
1963	351 000	7.5	588	986	32 052	9.1	27	795 000	59 000	7.4	1290	203	1963
1962	348 000	7.5	590	993	28 935	8.3	24	784 000	55 000	7.0	1283	193	1962
1961	347 000	7.5	598	1011	25 394	7.3	22	763 000	48 000	6.3	1264	172	1961
1960	344 000	7.5	593	994	23 868	6.9	20	742 000	43 000	5.8	1232	152	1960
1959	340 000	7.5	586	974	24 286	7.1	21	711 000	38 000	5.3	1182	132	1959
1958	340 000	7.5	584	963	22 654	6.7	20	705 000	36 000	5.1	1171	122	1958
1957	347 000	7.7	594	971	23 785	6.9	21	688 000	35 000	5.1	1140	117	1957
1956	353 000	7.9	602	977	26 265	7.4	23	666 000	34 000	5.1	1101	111	1956
1955	358 000	8.1	608	981	26 816	7.5	24	637 000	31 000	4.9	1051	100	1955
1954	342 000	7.7	578	926	28 027	8.2	25	642 000	32 000	5.0	1056	101	1954
1953	345 000	7.8	581	922	30 326	8.8	27	651 000	33 000	5.1	1067	102	1953
1952	349 000	7.9	585	922	33 922	9.7	31	641 000	33 000	5.1	1048	100	1952
1951	361 000	8.2	602	943	28 767	8.0	26	645 000	33 000	5.1	1050	98	1951
1950	358 000	8.1	589	917	30 870	8.6	28	662 000	35 000	5.3	1065	102	1950
1949	375 000	8.6	615	952	34 856	9.3	32	694 000	37 000	5.3	1115	106	1949
1948	397 000	9.1	650	999	43 698	11.0	40	733 000	42 000	5.7	1177	118	1948
1947	401 000	9.3	659	1005	60 254	15.0	56	834 000	47 000	5.6	1345	131	1947
1946	386 000	9.0	634	962	29 829	7.7	28	767 000	54 000	7.0	1239	149	1946
1945	398 000	9.3			15 634	3.9		617 000	63 000	10.2			1945
1944	303 000	7.1			12 312	4.1		696 000	55 000	7.9			1944
1943	296 000	7.0			10 012	3.4		640 000	44 000	6.9			1943
1942	370 000	8.8			7 618	2.1		616 000	36 000	5.8			1942
1941	389 000	9.3			6 368	1.6		548 000	31 000	5.7			1941
1940	471 000	11.3			7 755	1.6		564 000	26 000	4.6			1940
1939	440 000	10.6			7 955	1.8		588 000	26 000	4.4			1939
1938	362 000	8.8	517	701	6 250	1.7	7	595 000	26 000	4.4	1160	53	1938
1937	359 000	8.7	516	697	4 886	1.4	5	585 000	26 000	4.4	1148	53	1937
1936	355 000	8.7	514	692	4 057	1.1	4	580 000	25 000	4.3	1145	51	1936
1935	350 000	8.6	510	685	4 069	1.2	5	574 000	25 000	4.4	1141	51	1935
1934	342 000	8.5	502	672	4 287	1.3	5	572 000	26 000	4.5	1144	53	1934
1933	318 000	7.9	470	626	4 042	1.3	5	555 000	25 000	4.5	1114	51	1933
1932	307 000	7.6	456	606	3 894	1.3	4	587 000	27 000	4.6	1184	55	1932
1931	312 000	7.8	467	618	3 764	1.2	4	604 000	28 000	4.6	1227	57	1931
1930	315 000	7.9	475	627	3 563	1.1	4	619 000	30 000	4.8	1265	61	1930
1929	313 000	7.9	476	625	3 396	1.1	4	614 000	30 000	4.9	1264	61	1929
1928	303 000	7.7	463	607	4 018	1.3	5	631 000	29 000	4.6	1304	59	1928

Marriages, Divorces, Illegitimacy

Year	Marriages Total	marr. per 1.000 pop.	persons marrying per 10.000 non-married persons age 15+	age 15-49	Divorces a) Total	divorces per 100 marr.	persons divorcing per 10.000 married pop.	Births Legitimate Total	Illegit. Total	illeg. births per 100 legit. births	births per 10.000 women age 15-44 leg. births/married women	ill. births/non-marr. w.	Year
1927	308 000	7.8	475	619	3 190	1.0	4	625 000	29 000	4.6	1300	59	1927
1926	280 000	7.2	435	565	2 622	0.9	3	665 000	30 000	4.5	1391	61	1926
1925	296 000	7.6	463	599	2 605	0.9	3	682 000	29 000	4.3	1436	59	1925
1924	296 000	7.6	466	601	2 286	0.8	3	700 000	30 000	4.3	1481	61	1924
1923	292 000	7.6	465	598	2 667	0.9	3	727 000	31 000	4.3	1554	63	1923
1922	300 000	7.9	482	617	2 588	0.9	3	746 000	34 000	4.6	1607	70	1922
1921	321 000	8.5	520	665	3 522	1.1	5	810 000	39 000	4.8	1760	80	1921
1920	380 000	10.2	626	797	3 090	0.8	4	943 000	15 000	1.6	2091	31	1920
1919	369 000	10.4	639	810	1 657	0.4	2	651 000	41 000	6.3	1521	90	1919
1918	287 000	8.4	517	653	1 111	0.4	2	621 000	42 000	6.8	1513	96	1918
1917	259 000	7.6	463	583	703	0.3	1	631 000	37 000	5.9	1534	84	1917
1916	280 000	8.1	494	619	990	0.4	2	748 000	38 000	5.1	1798	85	1916
1915	361 000	10.2	624	780	680	0.2	1	778 000	37 000	4.8	1839	81	1915
1914	294 000	8.0	484	603	856	0.3	1	842 000	37 000	4.4	1904	77	1914
1913	287 000	7.8	477	592	577	0.2	1	844 000	38 000	4.5	1933	80	1913
1912	284 000	7.8	475	588	587	0.2	1	835 000	38 000	4.6	1930	80	1912
1911	275 000	7.6	462	569	580	0.2	1	844 000	37 000	4.4	1964	79	1911
1910	268 000	7.5	454	560	581	0.2	1	860 000	37 000	4.3	2024	79	1910
1909	261 000	7.4	447	550	694	0.3	1	877 000	37 000	4.2	2089	80	1909
1908	265 000	7.6	459	564	672	0.3	1	903 000	37 000	4.1	2177	81	1908
1907	276 000	8.0	484	593	644	0.2	1	882 000	36 000	4.1	2152	79	1907
1906	271 000	7.9	480	588	650	0.2	1	898 000	37 000	4.1	2218	82	1906
1905	261 000	7.7	468	571	623	0.2	1	892 000	37 000	4.1	2230	83	1905
1904	258 000	7.7	467	570	634	0.2	1	908 000	37 000	4.1	2297	83	1904
1903	261 000	7.8	478	582	614	0.2	1	911 000	37 000	4.1	2333	84	1903
1902	262 000	8.0	486	591	608	0.2	1	904 000	37 000	4.1	2345	85	1902
1901	259 000	7.9	485	589	601	0.2	1	894 000	36 000	4.0	2345	83	1901
1900	257 000	8.0	489	594	494	0.2	1	890 000	37 000	4.2	2371	87	1900
1899	262 000	8.2	507	615	526	0.2	1	892 000	37 000	4.1	2414	88	1899
1898	255 000	8.1	501	608	436	0.2	1	885 000	38 000	4.3	2433	92	1898
1897	249 000	8.0	497	604	583	0.2	1	883 000	39 000	4.4	2466	96	1897
1896	243 000	7.9	493	599	486	0.2	1	877 000	38 000	4.3	2491	95	1896
1895	228 000	7.5	470	571	478	0.2	1	883 000	39 000	4.4	2548	100	1895
1894	226 000	7.5	474	575	381	0.2	1	852 000	38 000	4.5	2498	99	1894
1893	219 000	7.4	466	566	362	0.2	1	876 000	39 000	4.5	2609	103	1893
1892	227 000	7.7	491	597	354	0.2	1	860 000	38 000	4.4	2603	102	1892
1891	227 000	7.8	499	607	342	0.2	1	875 000	39 000	4.5	2691	107	1891
1890	223 000	7.8	499	606	400	0.2	1	832 000	38 000	4.6	2583	106	1890
1889	214 000	7.5	487	592	370	0.2	1	845 000	41 000	4.9	2650	116	1889
1888	204 000	7.3	471	574	392	0.2	1	839 000	41 000	4.9	2655	118	1888
1887	201 000	7.2	472	575	390	0.2	1	844 000	42 000	5.0	2698	123	1887
1886	196 000	7.1	468	570	387	0.2	1	861 000	43 000	5.0	2778	128	1886
1885	198 000	7.3	481	586	316	0.2	1	851 000	43 000	5.1	2774	131	1885
1884	204 000	7.6	503	614	337	0.2	1	851 000	56 000	6.6	2800	173	1884
1883	206 000	7.7	517	631	361	0.2	1	864 000	27 000	3.1	2872	85	1883
1882	204 000	7.7	520	635	345	0.2	1	848 000	41 000	4.8	2845	132	1882
1881	197 000	7.6	511	624	302	0.2	1	846 000	38 000	4.5	2867	124	1881
1880	192 000	7.5	504	617	340	0.2	1	841 000	41 000	4.9	2884	136	1880

England and Wales

Marriages, Divorces, Illegitimacy

Year	Marriages Total	marr. per 1.000 pop.	persons marrying per 10.000 non-married persons age 15+	age 15–49	Divorces [a] Total	divorces per 100 marr.	persons divorcing per 10.000 married pop.	Births Legitimate Total	Illegit. Total	illeg. births per 100 legit. births	leg. births/ married women	ill. births/ non-marr. w.	Year
1879	182 000	7.2	485	593	300	0.2	1	839 000	41 000	4.9	2914	138	1879
1878	190 000	7.6	513	628	380	0.2	1	838 000	54 000	6.4	2947	185	1878
1877	194 000	7.9	531	651	322	0.2	1	850 000	38 000	4.5	3027	132	1877
1876	202 000	8.3	560	687	283	0.1	1	846 000	42 000	5.0	3051	148	1876
1875	201 000	8.4	565	693	304	0.2	1	810 000	41 000	5.1	2956	146	1875
1874	202 000	8.5	576	707	281	0.1	1	812 000	43 000	5.3	3002	156	1874
1873	206 000	8.8	595	732	238	0.1	1	787 000	43 000	5.5	2947	158	1873
1872	201 000	8.7	589	724	203	0.1	1	781 000	45 000	5.8	2961	168	1872
1871	190 000	8.3	564	694	190	0.1		753 000	44 000	5.8	2891	167	1871
1870	182 000	8.1	547	673	194	0.1	1	748 000	45 000	6.0	2896	172	1870
1869	177 000	8.0	539	663	186	0.1		729 000	44 000	6.0	2848	171	1869
1868	177 000	8.1	546	671	181	0.1		741 000	46 000	6.2	2918	181	1868
1867	179 000	8.3	559	686	144	0.1		723 000	45 000	6.2	2873	179	1867
1866	188 000	8.8	594	730	146	0.1		708 000	46 000	6.5	2836	185	1866
1865	185 000	8.7	592	726	147	0.1		701 000	47 000	6.7	2834	191	1865
1864	180 000	8.6	583	715	166	0.1		693 000	47 000	6.8	2824	194	1864
1863	174 000	8.4	571	700	160	0.1		680 000	47 000	6.9	2796	196	1863
1862	164 000	8.1	545	667	153	0.1		667 000	46 000	6.9	2765	194	1862
1861	164 000	8.2	551	675	118	0.1		652 000	44 000	6.7	2728	188	1861
1860	170 000	8.5	574	703	127	0.1		640 000	44 000	6.9	2723	189	1860
1859	168 000	8.5	571	697	141	0.1		645 000	45 000	7.0	2791	194	1859
1858	156 000	8.0	533	650	179	0.1		612 000	43 000	7.0	2693	186	1858
1857	159 000	8.3	546	665				620 000	43 000	6.9	2776	187	1857
1856	159 000	8.3	549	669				615 000	42 000	6.8	2801	183	1856
1855	152 000	8.1	528	642				594 000	41 000	6.9	2753	180	1855
1854	160 000	8.6	559.	679				594 000	40 000	6.7	2801	176	1854
1853	165 000	9.0	580	703				573 000	39 000	6.8	2750	173	1853
1852	159 000	8.7	563	681				582 000	42 000	7.2	2844	187	1852
1851	154 000	8.6	548	663				574 000	42 000	7.3	2855	188	1851
1850	153 000	8.6						553 000	40 000	7.2			1850
1849	142 000	8.1						539 000	39 000	7.2			1849
1848	138 000	8.0						526 000	37 000	7.0			1848
1847	136 000	7.9						504 000	36 000	7.1			1847
1846	146 000	8.6						534 000	39 000	7.3			1846
1845	144 000	8.6						505 000	39 000	7.7			1845
1844	132 000	8.0											1844
1843	124 000	7.6											1843
1842	119 000	7.4											1842
1841	122 000	7.7											1841
1840	123 000	7.8											1840
1839	123 000	7.9											1839
1838	118 000	7.7											1838

a) In general, divorce was not obtainable prior to 1859, but only separation a mensa et thoro. To a limited extent, however, divorce was obtainable by private acts of parliament. In 1859, civil marriage was introduced and divorce was permitted on the grounds of guilt. In 1923, the existing grounds for divorce were equalized for men and women, and in 1937, they were considerably extended. Finally, a 1971 law made marital breakdown the sole grounds for divorce.
In the tables, divorce figures include until 1938 the small number of annulments, but they do not include legal separations, the number of which was always less than 1 percent of divorces.

Marriages, Divorces, Illegitimacy

Year	Marriages Total	marr. per 1.000 pop.	persons marrying per 10.000 non-married persons age 15+	age 15-49	Divorces[a] Total	divorces per 100 marr.	persons divorcing per 10.000 married pop.	Births Legitimate Total	Illegit. Total	illeg. births per 100 legit. births	leg. births/ married women age 15-44	illeg.births/ non-marr. w.	Year
1975	39 191	7.5	570	996	7 795	19.9	63	61 600	6 300	10.2	929	195	1975
1974	41 174	7.9	595	1035	6 745	16.4	54	63 800	6 300	9.9	961	191	1974
1973	42 018	8.1	605	1047	6 670	15.9	54	67 900	6 500	9.6	1023	195	1973
1972	42 139	8.1	604	1041	5 155	12.2	42	71 900	6 700	9.3	1085	198	1972
1971	42 500	8.1	606	1039	4 485	10.6	36	79 700	7 000	8.8	1202	203	1971
1970	43 203	8.3	613	1048	4 270	9.9	35	80 600	6 700	8.3	1217	192	1970
1969	43 294	8.3	612	1042	3 911	9.0	32	83 600	6 700	8.0	1265	189	1969
1968	43 696	8.4	616	1043	4 446	10.2	36	87 800	7 000	8.0	1331	195	1968
1967	42 116	8.1	592	997	2 765	6.6	23	89 500	6 700	7.5	1358	184	1967
1966	48 851	9.4	683	1146	3 276	6.7	27	90 300	6 200	6.9	1370	168	1966
1965	40 500	7.8	564	944	2 688	6.6	22	94 800	5 900	6.2	1436	159	1965
1964	40 200	7.7	559	932	2 446	6.1	20	98 800	5 600	5.7	1493	150	1964
1963	39 700	7.6	550	916	2 235	5.6	18	97 400	5 300	5.4	1470	141	1963
1962	40 200	7.7	556	924	2 035	5.1	17	99 300	5 000	5.0	1499	132	1962
1961	40 600	7.8	562	931	1 825	4.5	15	96 600	4 600	4.8	1459	121	1961
1960	40 100	7.7	549	900	1 823	4.5	15	96 900	4 400	4.5	1465	113	1960
1959	40 400	7.8	548	889	1 699	4.2	14	95 200	4 100	4.3	1443	103	1959
1958	41 200	8.0	555	891	1 781	4.3	15	95 400	4 100	4.3	1451	100	1958
1957	42 700	8.3	570	907	1 739	4.1	15	94 000	4 000	4.3	1434	96	1957
1956	44 000	8.6	581	916	1 883	4.3	16	91 200	4 100	4.5	1392	96	1956
1955	43 200	8.5	565	883	2 073	4.8	18	88 500	4 000	4.5	1351	91	1955
1954	42 000	8.2	544	842	2 216	5.3	19	88 100	4 200	4.8	1347	94	1954
1953	40 900	8.0	524	805	2 365	5.8	21	86 700	4 200	4.8	1326	92	1953
1952	41 200	8.1	522	795	2 714	6.6	24	86 100	4 300	5.0	1317	92	1952
1951	41 400	8.1	519	784	1 944	4.7	17	86 000	4 600	5.3	1314	96	1951
1950	40 500	7.8	496	743	2 196	5.4	19	87 700	4 800	5.5	1322	96	1950
1949	41 700	8.1	506	753	2 438	5.8	22	90 500	5 200	5.7	1367	102	1949
1948	43 700	8.5	526	776	2 047	4.7	18	94 500	5 800	6.1	1428	112	1948
1947	44 400	8.7	532	779	2 513	5.7	23	106 800	6 300	5.9	1623	120	1947
1946	45 800	8.9	538	783	2 924	6.4	26	97 500	6 900	7.1	1467	128	1946
1945	48 600	9.4			2 223	4.6		89 400					1945
1944	37 000	7.1			1 731	4.7		88 300	7 600	8.6			1944
1943	38 200	7.4			1 312	3.4		87 500	7 200	8.2			1943
1942	47 400	9.2			1 017	2.1		84 200	6 500	7.7			1942
1941	47 600	9.2			762	1.6		83 800	5 900	7.0			1941
1940	53 500	10.6			780	1.5		81 300	5 100	6.3			1940
1939	46 200	9.2			884	1.9		81 700	5 200	6.4			1939
1938	38 700	7.8	419	570	788	2.0	8	83 200	5 400	6.5	1585	83	1938
1937	38 400	7.7	417	566	649	1.7	7	82 400	5 400	6.6	1575	83	1937
1936	37 900	7.6	414	558	642	1.7	7	83 200	5 700	6.9	1594	87	1936
1935	38 000	7.7	416	560	498	1.3	5	82 200	5 700	6.9	1579	87	1935
1934	36 900	7.5	406	545	468	1.3	5	82 700	6 100	7.4	1595	94	1934
1933	34 200	7.0	379	506	510	1.5	6	80 600	5 900	7.3	1563	91	1933
1932	33 200	6.8	370	493	488	1.5	5	84 500	6 500	7.7	1648	100	1932
1931	32 700	6.8	368	488	569	1.7	6	85 600	6 600	7.7	1683	102	1931
1930	33 300	6.9	377	497	469	1.4	5	87 600	6 900	7.9	1728	106	1930
1929	33 000	6.8	374	492	519	1.6	6	85 700	7 200	8.4	1689	111	1929
1928	32 900	6.8	372	487	504	1.5	6	89 700	7 100	7.9	1764	108	1928

M a r r i a g e s , D i v o r c e s , I l l e g i t i m a c y

Year	Marriages Total	marr. per 1.000 pop.	persons marrying per 10.000 non-married persons age 15+	age 15-49	Divorces a) Total	divorces per 100 marr.	persons divorcing per 10.000 married pop.	Births Legitimate Total	Illegit. Total	illeg. births per 100 legit. births	leg. births/ married women	ill. births/ non-marr. w.	Year
1927	32 600	6.7	368	481	474	1.5	5	89 700	7 000	7.8	1762	106	1927
1926	31 200	6.4	352	458	425	1.4	5	97 300	7 000	7.2	1907	106	1926
1925	32 500	6.7	367	476	451	1.4	5	99 800	6 800	6.8	1955	102	1925
1924	32 300	6.6	366	473	438	1.4	5	104 400	7 100	6.8	2047	107	1924
1923	35 200	7.2	397	511	363	1.0	4	107 200	7 500	7.0	2093	112	1923
1922	34 400	7.0	388	497	382	1.1	5	114 200	7 900	6.9	2225	117	1922
1921	39 200	8.0	444	567	500	1.3	6	126 300	8 800	7.0	2469	130	1921
1920	46 800	9.6	532	678	776	1.7	9	98 800	10 200	10.3	1942	151	1920
1919	44 100	9.1	506	643	829	1.9	10	90 700	7 500	8.3	1804	112	1919
1918	34 500	7.2	397	502	485	1.4	6	90 100	7 900	8.8	1799	119	1918
1917	30 400	6.3	350	442	297	1.0	4	102 100	7 300	7.1	2043	110	1917
1916	31 400	6.5	363	456	267	0.9	3	106 300	7 800	7.3	2140	118	1916
1915	36 200	7.6	420	528	242	0.7	3	115 100	7 900	6.9	2333	120	1915
1914	35 000	7.4	408	511	347	1.0	5	112 000	8 800	7.9	2286	134	1914
1913	33 800	7.1	396	495	250	0.7	3	113 800	8 500	7.5	2337	130	1913
1912	32 500	6.9	380	473	249	0.8	3	112 700	9 000	8.0	2315	137	1912
1911	31 800	6.7	371	461	234	0.7	3	115 000	9 200	8.0	2362	140	1911
1910	30 900	6.5	362	448	223	0.7	3	119 300	9 100	7.6	2458	139	1910
1909	30 100	6.4	355	439	192	0.6	3	122 300	9 400	7.7	2539	144	1909
1908	31 600	6.8	375	463	189	0.6	3	120 000	9 100	7.6	2509	140	1908
1907	33 300	7.2	397	491	200	0.6	3	122 700	8 800	7.2	2584	136	1907
1906	33 100	7.2	398	490	173	0.5	2	122 300	9 300	7.6	2595	145	1906
1905	31 300	6.8	378	466	167	0.5	2	122 300	9 100	7.4	2611	142	1905
1904	32 300	7.1	393	483	182	0.6	3	123 600	9 000	7.3	2658	141	1904
1903	32 400	7.1	397	487	194	0.6	3	125 200	8 300	6.6	2711	131	1903
1902	31 900	7.1	393	482	204	0.6	3	124 000	8 300	6.7	2705	131	1902
1901	31 400	7.0	390	477	158	0.5	2	123 700	8 500	6.9	2718	135	1901
1900	32 400	7.3	407	499	144	0.4	2	122 900	8 500	6.9	2740	137	1900
1899	33 000	7.5	421	516	176	0.5	3	122 200	8 500	7.0	2769	139	1899
1898	32 100	7.4	415	509	135	0.4	2	122 000	8 900	7.3	2808	147	1898
1897	31 100	7.2	408	501	142	0.5	2	119 800	9 100	7.6	2804	152	1897
1896	30 300	7.1	403	495	133	0.4	2	119 800	9 400	7.8	2847	160	1896
1895	28 400	6.7	383	471	117	0.4	2	117 300	9 200	7.8	2832	158	1895
1894	27 600	6.6	377	465	120	0.4	2	115 300	9 100	7.9	2830	159	1894
1893	27 100	6.6	375	463	112	0.4	2	117 600	9 500	8.1	2932	168	1893
1892	28 700	7.0	403	498	118	0.4	2	115 800	9 200	7.9	2936	165	1892
1891	28 000	6.9	399	493	107	0.4	2	116 300	9 700	8.3	2995	176	1891
1890	27 500	6.9	396	490	87	0.3	1	112 300	9 200	8.2	2907	169	1890
1889	26 300	6.6	383	474	100	0.4	2	113 000	9 800	8.7	2941	182	1889
1888	25 300	6.4	372	461	107	0.4	2	113 300	10 000	8.8	2962	188	1888
1887	24 900	6.4	370	459	80	0.3	1	114 000	10 400	9.1	2993	197	1887
1886	24 500	6.3	368	457	97	0.4	2	117 400	10 500	8.9	3099	201	1886
1885	25 300	6.6	384	477	76	0.3	1	115 400	10 700	9.3	3060	208	1885
1884	26 100	6.8	400	497	87	0.3	2	118 700	10 500	8.8	3162	206	1884
1883	26 900	7.1	417	519	65	0.2	1	114 300	10 200	8.9	3058	202	1883
1882	26 600	7.1	417	518	69	0.3	1	115 600	10 600	9.2	3109	212	1882
1881	26 000	6.9	411	512	71	0.3	1	115 700	10 500	9.1	3125	213	1881
1880	24 500	6.6	392	488	80	0.3	1	114 000	10 600	9.3	3110	217	1880

Marriages, Divorces, Illegitimacy

Year	Marriages Total	marr. per 1,000 pop.	persons marrying per 10.000 non-married persons age 15+	age 15–49	Divorces[a] Total	divorces per 100 marr.	persons divorcing per 10.000 married pop.	Births Legitimate Total	Illegit. Total	illeg. births per 100 legit. births	births per 10.000 women age 15–44 leg. births/ married women	ill. births/ non-marr. w.	Year
1879	23 500	6.4	380	474	55	0.2	1	115 000	10 700	9.3	3174	221	1879
1878	24 400	6.7	399	498	66	0.3	1	116 100	10 700	9.2	3239	223	1878
1877	25 800	7.2	426	533	29	0.1	1	116 300	10 500	9.0	3282	220	1877
1876	26 600	7.5	444	556	40	0.2	1	115 500	11 000	9.5	3295	233	1876
1875	26 000	7.4	439	550	33	0.1	1	112 800	10 800	9.6	3251	231	1875
1874	26 400	7.6	450	565	38	0.1	1	113 700	10 000	8.8	3316	216	1874
1873	26 700	7.8	460	578	25	0.1		108 800	10 900	10.0	3207	237	1873
1872	25 600	7.5	446	561	12			107 800	11 000	10.2	3214	241	1872
1871	24 000	7.1	423	532	11			105 100	11 000	10.5	3167	243	1871
1870	23 900	7.2	424	534	17	0.1		104 400	11 000	10.5	3173	245	1870
1869	22 100	6.7	395	497	7			102 300	11 100	10.9	3135	248	1869
1868	21 900	6.7	395	497	13	0.1		104 200	11 300	10.8	3217	254	1868
1867	22 600	7.0	410	516	5			102 900	11 100	10.8	3203	250	1867
1866	23 700	7.4	434	545	4			102 000	11 700	11.5	3201	265	1866
1865	23 600	7.4	435	547	.4			101 800	11 300	11.1	3222	257	1865
1864	22 700	7.2	422	530	2			101 100	11 200	11.1	3226	255	1864
1863	22 200	7.1	415	522	9			98 400	10 900	11.1	3163	250	1863
1862	20 600	6.6	388	488	26	0.1	1	96 700	10 400	10.8	3134	239	1862
1861	20 900	6.8	397	499	27	0.1	1	97 100	9 900	10.2	3173	229	1861
1860	21 200	6.9	403	505	23	0.1	1	95 900	9 700	10.1	3152	224	1860
1859	21 200	7.0	403	504	24	0.1	1	96 800	9 700	10.0	3198	225	1859
1858	19 700	6.5	375	468	12	0.1		94 700	9 300	9.8	3146	215	1858
1857	21 400	7.1	408	508	18	0.1		94 200	9 200	9.8	3150	213	1857
1856	20 700	6.9	396	492	16	0.1		93 100	8 700	9.3	3133	202	1856
1855	19 700	6.6	377	468	11	0.1		86 000	7 300	8.5	2911	170	1855

a) Figures refer to divorces only, i.e. they do not include legal separations, the number of which is negligible.

Marriages, Divorces, Illegitimacy

Year	Marriages Total	marr. per 1.000 pop.	persons marrying per 10.000 non-married persons age 15+	persons marrying per 10.000 non-married persons age 15-49	Divorces Total	divorces per 100 marr.	persons divorcing per 10.000 married pop.	Births Legitimate Total	Illegit. Total	illeg. births per 100 leg. births	births per 10.000 women age 15-44 leg. births/married women	leg. births/married women	ill. births/non-marr. w.	Year
1927	7 200	5.8	288	386				25 400	1 300	5.1	2211		74	1927
1926	7 200	5.7	287	384				26 900	1 300	4.8	2347		73	1926
1925	7 700	6.1	306	409				26 500	1 200	4.5	2319		67	1925
1924	7 500	6.0	298	397				27 300	1 200	4.4	2398		67	1924
1923	8 000	6.4	317	422				28 800	1 300	4.5	2542		72	1923
1922	8 100	6.4	318	423				28 300	1 200	4.2	2492		66	1922

Ireland

Year	Marriages Total	marr. per 1.000 pop.	age 15+	age 15-49	Divorces Total	divorces per 100 marr.	persons divorcing per 10.000 married pop.	Legitimate Total	Illegit. Total	illeg. births per 100 leg. births	leg. births/married women	leg. births/married women	ill. births/non-marr. w.	Year
1920	26 800	6.1	285	384				96 200	3 300	3.4	2861		56	1920
1919	27 200	6.3	290	389				97 300			2904			1919
1918	22 600	5.3	245	327				84 600	2 700	3.2	2567		46	1918
1917	21 100	4.9	229	305				83 700	2 700	3.2	2544		45	1917
1916	22 200	5.2	241	320				88 700	2 700	3.0	2699		45	1916
1915	24 200	5.7	262	347				92 600	3 000	3.2	2815		50	1915
1914	23 700	5.5	253	334				95 900	2 900	3.0	2877		47	1914
1913	22 300	5.1	238	312				97 300	2 800	2.9	2911		45	1913
1912	23 300	5.3	247	323				98 200	2 800	2.9	2927		44	1912
1911	23 500	5.4	248	324				99 000	2 800	2.8	2942		44	1911
1910	22 100	5.0	233	303				99 100	2 900	2.9	2943		45	1910
1909	22 700	5.2	239	310				100 000	2 800	2.8	2972		43	11909
1908	22 700	5.2	239	309				99 400	2 600	2.6	2955		39	1908
1907	22 500	5.1	237	305				99 200	2 500	2.5	2947		38	1907
1906	22 700	5.2	238	306				100 800	2 700	2.7	2992		40	1906
1905	23 100	5.3	242	310				100 100	2 700	2.7	2971		40	1905
1904	23 000	5.2	241	307				101 200	2 600	2.6	2997		38	1904
1903	23 000	5.2	240	305				99 200	2 600	2.6	2931		38	1903
1902	22 900	5.2	238	302				99 200	2 700	2.7	2924		39	1902
1901	22 600	5.1	234	296				98 400	2 600	2.6	2892		37	1901
1900	21 300	4.8	221	279				98 800	2 700	2.7	2890		38	1900
1899	22 300	5.0	231	292				101 200	2 700	2.7	2942		38	1899
1898	22 600	5.0	234	296				102 600	2 900	2.8	2972		41	1898
1897	22 900	5.1	238	301				103 900	2 800	2.7	3002		40	1897
1896	23 100	5.1	241	304				104 800	2 800	2.7	3024		40	1896
1895	23 100	5.1	241	305				103 200	2 900	2.8	2966		41	1895
1894	21 600	4.7	225	285				102 500	2 900	2.8	2927		41	1894
1893	21 700	4.7	226	287				103 300	2 800	2.7	2939		40	1893
1892	21 500	4.6	224	284				101 600	2 600	2.6	2877		37	1892
1891	21 500	4.6	223	283				105 200	2 900	2.8	2950		41	1891
1890	21 000	4.5	218	276				102 400	2 900	2.8	2822		41	1890
1889	21 500	4.5	223	283				104 800	3 000	2.9	2835		42	1889
1888	20 100	4.2	209	264				106 400	3 200	3.0	2827		45	1888
1887	20 900	4.3	216	274				109 200	3 200	2.9	2842		45	1887
1886	20 600	4.2	213	270				110 900	3 000	2.7	2833		42	1886
1885	21 200	4.3	220	279				112 700	3 300	2.9	2831		46	1885
1884	22 600	4.5	234	297				115 700	3 200	2.8	2861		45	1884
1883	21 400	4.3	222	281				115 100	3 100	2.7	2794		43	1883
1882	22 000	4.3	227	288				119 400	3 200	2.7	2827		44	1882
1881	21 800	4.2	225	285				122 600	3 200	2.6	2853		44	1881

Marriages, Divorces, Illegitimacy

Year	Marriages Total	marr. per 1.000 pop.	persons marrying per 10.000 non-married persons age 15+	age 15-49	Divorces[a] Total	divorces per 100 marr.	persons divorcing per 10.000 married pop.	Births Legitimate Total	Illegit. Total	illeg. births per 100 legit. births	births per 10.000 women age 15-44 leg. births/ married women	ill. births/ non-marr. w.	Year
1975	10 867	7.1	506	906	572	5.3	18	24 800	1 300	5.2	1380	117	1975
1974	10 783	7.0	496	871	464	4.3	14	25 900	1 300	5.0	1437	114	1974
1973	11 212	7.2	512	884	460	4.1	14	28 000	1 200	4.3	1559	104	1973
1972	11 905	7.7	541	917	494	4.2	15	28 700	1 300	4.5	1606	111	1972
1971	12 152	7.9	551	919	535	4.4	17	30 600	1 200	3.9	1727	101	1971
1970	12 297	8.1	557	914	384	3.1	12	30 900	1 200	3.9	1763	100	1970
1969	11 587	7.7	525	849	397	3.4	13	31 200	1 200	3.8	1801	99	1969
1968	11 240	7.5	509	811	298	2.7	10	32 000	1 200	3.7	1868	98	1968
1967	10 924	7.3	496	778	272	2.5	9	32 200	1 200	3.7	1905	98	1967
1966	10 735	7.3	488	756	262	2.4	9	32 200	1 000	3.1	1929	81	1966
1965	10 500	7.1	474	731	130	1.2	4	32 900	1 000	3.0	1991	80	1965
1964	10 600	7.3	476	732	162	1.5	6	33 300	1 000	3.0	2043	79	1964
1963	10 200	7.1	457	699	118	1.2	4	32 500	900	2.8	2021	71	1963
1962	9 800	6.8	437	667	128	1.3	5	31 800	800	2.5	2005	62	1962
1961	9 900	6.9	439	667	123	1.2	4	31 100	800	2.6	1983	62	1961
1960	9 900	7.0	437	659	152	1.5	5	31 200	800	2.6	2001	61	1960
1959	9 600	6.8	422	634	118	1.2	4	30 100	700	2.3	1949	53	1959
1958	9 300	6.6	407	606	146	1.6	5	29 600	700	2.4	1926	52	1958
1957	9 400	6.7	408	604	124	1.3	5	29 400	700	2.4	1919	51	1957
1956	9 400	6.7	404	595	115	1.2	4	28 700	800	2.8	1878	57	1956
1955	9 500	6.8	405	594	116	1.2	4	28 300	700	2.5	1857	50	1955
1954	9 200	6.6	390	569	136	1.5	5	28 000	800	2.9	1849	56	1954
1953	9 400	6.8	395	573	169	1.8	6	28 200	800	2.8	1868	55	1953
1952	9 300	6.8	390	562	159	1.7	6	27 800	1 000	3.6	1855	68	1952
1951	9 400	6.8	391	561	173	1.8	7	27 600	900	3.3	1846	60	1951
1950	9 100	6.6	373	534	154	1.7	6	27 800	1 000	3.6	1856	66	1950
1949	9 200	6.7	375	534	187	2.0	7	28 000	1 100	3.9	1879	72	1949
1948	9 400	6.9	382	541	180	1.9	7	28 500	1 000	3.5	1927	65	1948
1947	9 500	7.0	386	544	196	2.1	8	30 100	1 200	4.0	2055	77	1947
1946	9 800	7.3	395	554	217	2.2	9	28 800	1 300	4.5	1968	82	1946
1945	10 500	7.7			174	1.7		27 400	1 600	5.8			1945
1944	9 500	7.0			131	1.4		29 200	1 700	5.8			1944
1943	10 200	7.6			119	1.2		29 800	1 700	5.7			1943
1942	11 700	8.8			117	1.0		28 200	1 400	5.0			1942
1941	12 000	9.2			67	0.6		25 600	1 300	5.1			1941
1940	9 800	7.5			107	1.1		24 200	1 200	5.0			1940
1939	9 200	7.1			31	0.4		24 100	1 100	4.6			1939
1938	8 600	6.7	337	459				24 600	1 100	4.5	1972	63	1938
1937	8 600	6.7	338	460				24 200	1 200	5.0	1958	69	1937
1936	9 100	7.1	359	487				24 700	1 200	4.9	2016	69	1936
1935	8 800	6.9	348	472				23 500	1 200	5.1	1934	69	1935
1934	8 200	6.5	326	441				24 100	1 300	5.4	2003	75	1934
1933	7 600	6.0	303	410				23 400	1 200	5.1	1966	69	1933
1932	7 000	5.6	281	379				23 800	1 300	5.5	2020	75	1932
1931	7 400	6.0	298	402				24 400	1 300	5.3	2095	75	1931
1930	7 500	6.1	304	409				24 600	1 300	5.3	2131	75	1930
1929	7 400	6.0	299	402				24 200	1 200	5.0	2103	69	1929
1928	7 300	5.9	293	393				24 800	1 200	4.8	2155	68	1928

Ireland

Marriages, Divorces, Illegitimacy

Year	Marriages Total	marr. per 1.000 pop.	persons marrying per 10.000 non-married persons age 15+	persons marrying per 10.000 non-married persons age 15-49	Divorces Total	divorces per 100 marr.	persons divorcing per 10.000 married pop.	Births Legitimate Total	Births Illegit. Total	illeg. births per 100 legit. births	births per 10.000 women age 15-44 leg. births/married women	births per 10.000 women age 15-44 illeg. births/non-marr. w.	Year
1880	20 400	3.9	209	266				124 900	3 200	2.6	2858	47	1880
1879	23 300	4.4	237	302				132 000	3 300	2.5	2970	45	1879
1878	25 300	4.8	258	330				131 000	3 100	2.4	2921	42	1878
1877	24 700	4.7	253	324				136 300	3 400	2.5	3023	47	1877
1876	26 400	5.0	273	350				137 200	3 300	2.4	3030	46	1876
1875	24 000	4.5	249	320				135 200	3 100	2.3	2971	43	1875
1874	24 500	4.6	255	328				138 000	3 300	2.4	3004	46	1874
1873	25 700	4.8	267	345				140 900	3 500	2.5	3033	49	1873
1872	26 900	5.0	279	361				145 500	3 800	2.6	3081	54	1872
1871	29 000	5.4	301	390				147 200	4 200	2.9	3095	59	1871
1870	28 700	5.3	295	378				145 800	4 000	2.7	3096	55	1870
1869	27 300	5.0	277	352				141 500	4 200	3.0	3030	56	1869
1868	27 700	5.1	278	350				141 500	4 600	3.3	3060	60	1868
1867	29 700	5.4	295	368				139 700	4 700	3.4	3053	60	1867
1866	30 100	5.4	295	365				141 200	4 900	3.5	3110	61	1866
1865	30 800	5.5	296	363				139 600	5 400	3.9	3080	65	1865
1864	27 400	4.9	259	315				131 200	5 200	4.0	2915	61	1864

a) Divorce was introduced as late as 1937. In the tables figures refer to divorces only, i.e. they do not include legal separations, the number of which is insignificant.

Austria

Civil Status of Males by Age

Census	1869	1880	1890	1900	1910	1910 b)	1920 a)	1934	1951	1961	1971
Age group					(Civil status per 10.000 of respective age group)						
15 +											
single	4 091	4 112	4 294	4 194	4 104	4 770	4 647	9 345	3 035	2 912	2 738
married	5 451	5 436	5 256	5 359	5 422	4 719	4 773	5 374	6 296	6 444	6 611
widowed	454	446	450	447	474	511	580	445	442	399	381
divorced	4	6						227	227	244	270
Unknown								9			
15-19											
single		9 989	9 996	9 982	9 981	10 000	9 983	9 988	9 967	9 934	9 941
married		11	4	17	18		15	8	33	66	59
widowed				1	1		2				
divorced										1	
20-24											
single		9 059	9 334	9 335	9 328	9 668		9 449	8 392	8 176	7 417
married		934	657	654	661	324		529	1 577	1 789	2 510
widowed		6	9	11	11	8	8 295	4	4	3	3
divorced							1 654	10	27	32	70
25-34							50				
single		3 930	4 122	3 923	3 901	5 379		5 306	3 848	2 808	2 549
married		5 993	5 798	6 002	6 010	4 527		4 480	5 921	6 977	7 119
widowed		74	80	75	88	95		43	30	16	13
divorced		4					3 430	162	201	198	318
35-44							6 280				
single		1 497	1 710	1 501	1 410	2 307	291	1 749	1 315	988	1 007
married		8 302	8 074	8 298	8 361	7 407		7 699	8 214	8 623	8 606
widowed		192	217	201	229	286		130	101	46	47
divorced		8					1 836	415	370	342	339
45-54							7 674				
single		1 054	1 242	1 114	1 007	1 685	490	1 136	928	792	668
married		8 486	8 284	8 417	8 502	7 762		8 171	8 511	8 613	8 826
widowed		449	474	469	490	553		296	237	169	131
divorced		11					1 469	392	325	426	374
55-64							7 669				
single		942	1 125	1 000	924	1 600	862	1 041	808	753	679
married		7 871	7 764	7 905	7 960	7 242		7 876	8 334	8 420	8 506
widowed		1 176	1 111	1 095	1 116	1 159		786	588	485	437
divorced		12						291	270	342	378
65-69							1 389				
single		939	1 086	974	902	1 555	6 830	1 049	830	712	713
married		6 815	6 833	6 973	7 045	6 365	1 781	7 044	7 698	7 975	8 025
widowed		2 236	2 080	2 053	2 053	2 079		1 708	1 255	1 055	955
divorced		10						190	217	258	308
70-74											
single		978	1 082	1 011	912	1 544		1 091	862	736	664
married		5 852	5 894	6 007	6 118	5 484		6 091	6 848	7 261	7 399
widowed		3 161	3 023	2 982	2 970	2 972	1 222	2 659	2 111	1 782	1 682
divorced		9					5 005	148	179	221	255
75 +							3 773				
single		846	1 094	1 000	880	1 450		996	854	741	665
married		4 371	4 403	4 507	4 599	4 083		4 477	5 116	5 529	5 774
widowed		4 773	4 503	4 493	4 521	4 467		4 415	3 904	3 575	3 380
divorced		11						93	126	155	181

a) age groups: 15 + , 15 - 19 , 20 - 29 , 30 - 39 , 40 - 49 , 50 - 59 , 60 - 69 , 70 +

b) approximate territory of later Republic

Austria

Civil Status of Females by Age

Census	1869	1880	1990	1900	1910	1910 b)	1920 a)	1934	1951	1961	1971
Age group	(Civil status per 10.000 of respective age group)										
15 +											
single	3 811	3 653	3 808	3 665	3 537	4 222	4 257	3 561	2 754	2 489	2 189
married	5 047	5 126	4 970	5 103	5 203	4 564	4 312	4 835	5 244	5 353	5 537
widowed	1 136	1 213	1 222	1 232	1 260	1 214	1 431	1 346	1 697	1 807	1 874
divorced	6	8						249	305	351	400
Unknown								9			
15–19											
single		9 536	9 593	9 557	9 587	9 856	9 866	9 832	9 647	9 398	9 298
married		460	403	434	402	138	127	160	348	591	691
widowed		4	4	10	10	6	7	2	1	1	1
divorced								2	3	10	9
20–24											
single		6 773	6 928	6 609	6 664	8 044		8 105	6 616	5 798	4 498
married		3 184	3 028	3 339	3 286	1 923		1 830	3 280	4 082	5 278
widowed		41	45	52	50	33	7 013	13	21	14	20
divorced		3					2 803	43	83	105	205
25–34							183				
single		3 034	3 277	3 100	2 828	4 120		4 110	2 934	1 973	1 539
married		6 728	6 505	6 691	6 945	5 676		5 496	6 337	7 632	7 948
widowed		230	218	210	228	204		120	384	82	77
divorced		8					3 046	267	344	313	437
35–44							6 223				
single		1 638	1 746	1 610	1 493	2 231	730	2 159	1 494	1 356	1 052
married		7 591	7 500	7 687	7 805	7 125		6 904	7 112	7 582	8 176
widowed		759	754	703	702	644		503	963	541	291
divorced		12					1 903	428	431	521	480
45–54							6 781				
single		1 408	1 508	1 328	1 227	1 879	1 316	1 699	1 429	1 218	1 128
married		6 756	6 724	6 929	7 084	6 611		6 506	6 818	6 672	7 207
widowed		1 825	1 768	1 742	1 689	1 509		1 429	1 324	1 590	1 066
divorced		12					1 663	359	429	521	598
55–64							5 890				
single		1 360	1 545	1 362	1 198	1 830	2 447	1 516	1 506	1 339	1 147
married		5 203	5 095	5 332	5 483	5 153		5 324	5 479	5 589	5 492
widowed		3 427	3 360	3 306	3 318	3 018		2 911	2 669	2 628	2 853
divorced		11						242	346	444	508
65–69							1 614				
single		1 411	1 580	1 446	1 273	1 900	4 089	1 490	1 508	1 455	1 275
married		3 688	3 634	3 786	3 877	3 616	4 297	3 860	3 924	4 067	4 122
widowed		4 891	4 786	4 768	4 850	4 484		4 499	4 331	4 142	4 195
divorced		10						141	237	336	408
70–74											
single		1 456	1 618	1 559	1 359	2 012		1 498	1 458	1 495	1 319
married		2 648	2 600	2 622	2 741	2 567		2 782	2 830	2 924	2 957
widowed		5 889	5 782	5 818	5 900	5 421	1 588	5 610	5 547	5 330	5 382
divorced		7					1 988	94	165	251	342
75 +							6 424				
single		1 339	1 608	1 521	1 382	2 060		1 425	1 422	1 432	1 422
married		1 523	1 484	1 482	1 472	1 375		1 423	1 472	1 411	1 401
widowed		7 132	6 908	6 997	7 146	6 565		7 074	7 021	7 011	6 951
divorced		6						53	85	146	227

a) age groups: 15 + , 15 – 19 , 20 – 29 , 30 – 39 , 40 – 49 , 50 – 59 , 60 – 69 , 70 +

b) approximate territory of later Republic

Civil Status of Males by Age

Census	1846	1856	1866	1880	1890	1900	1910	1920	1930	1947	1961	1970
Age group	(Civil status per 10.000 respective age group)											
15 +												
single	4 860	5 049	4 711	4 543	4 619	4 347	4 056	3 940	3 254	2 953	2 417	2 503
married	4 555	4 380	4 637	4 808	4 770	5 076	5 391	5 513	6 186	6 414	6 980	6 919
widowed	585	571	652	643	603	562	528	517	511	542	497	458
divorced				6	8	15	25	31	50	91	105	121
15-19												
single	9 991	9 991	9 983	9 967	9 984	9 977	9 973	9 962	9 950	9 929	9 936	9 898
married	8	9	16	33	16	23	27	38	49	71	63	102
widowed			1	1					1			1
divorced												
20-24												
single	9 475	9 505	9 246	8 947	8 999	8 509	8 385	8 330	8 006	7 807	7 074	6 459
married	519	490	737	1 035	990	1 477	1 603	1 652	1 980	2 183	2 920	3 529
widowed	6	5	17	17	11	13	11	16	12	6	2	4
divorced				1		1	1	2	2	4	4	8
25-34												
single	5 945	6 113	5 553	4 763	4 562	4 047	3 712	3 791	2 855	3 012	2 038	1 714
married	3 967	3 814	4 322	5 106	5 325	5 848	6 178	6 095	7 030	6 868	7 876	8 168
widowed	88	74	125	126	109	96	92	95	79	44	16	18
divorced				4	5	9	17	19	36	76	70	101
35-44												
single	2 588	3 034	2 630	2 438	2 210	1 961	1 779	1 643	1 159	1 340	1 011	967
married	7 107	6 687	7 041	7 221	7 463	7 744	7 939	8 061	8 581	8 370	8 786	8 791
widowed	306	279	329	331	312	269	239	246	178	134	58	57
divorced				9	16	27	43	50	82	156	145	185
45-54												
single	1 554	1 950	1 941	1 815	1 732	1 591	1 449	1 297	1 054	849	912	802
married	7 757	7 348	7 380	7 495	7 586	7 761	7 958	8 125	8 436	8 683	8 710	8 844
widowed	690	702	679	679	667	611	541	523	418	328	198	167
divorced				11	15	37	52	56	92	140	180	187
55-64												
single	1 194	1 561	1 652	1 701	1 603	1 559	1 438	1 287	1 092	803	785	817
married	7 337	6 986	6 885	6 916	7 020	7 103	7 295	7 509	7 814	8 270	8 466	8 478
widowed	1 469	1 453	1 463	1 375	1 365	1 316	1 225	1 153	1 026	821	596	532
divorced				8	12	23	42	51	67	105	153	172
65-69												
single	1 035	1 400	1 422	1 683	1 593	1 526	1 502	1 330	1 132	901	654	754
married	6 580	6 134	5 995	6 029	6 080	6 166	6 243	6 503	6 826	7 335	7 954	7 937
widowed	2 385	2 466	2 584	2 281	2 321	2 293	2 229	2 125	1 990	1 679	1 287	1 169
divorced				6	6	16	26	42	52	85	103	140
70-74												
single	1 052	1 344	1 281	1 636	1 685	1 555	1 500	1 402	1 192	925	690	662
married	5 623	5 390	5 155	5 173	5 139	5 211	5 344	5 503	5 768	6 361	7 083	7 228
widowed	3 325	3 266	3 565	3 185	3 168	3 222	3 136	3 061	2 996	2 646	2 143	1 998
divorced				6	9	12	19	33	44	69	84	113
75 +												
single	1 082	1 307	1 156	1 453	1 587	1 557	1 479	1 412	1 178	923	761	649
married	4 166	4 037	3 719	3 659	3 604	3 690	3 759	3 974	4 076	4 477	4 891	5 285
widowed	4 752	4 655	5 125	4 881	4 804	4 743	4 747	4 591	4 717	4 553	4 287	3 998
divorced				7	5	9	14	22	29	47	60	68

C i v i l   S t a t u s   o f   F e m a l e s   b y   A g e

Census	1846	1856	1866	1880	1890	1900	1910	1920	1930	1947	1961	1970
Age group	(Civil status per 10.000 of respective age group)											
15 +												
single	4 478	4 581	4 275	4 138	4 165	3 943	3 686	3 649	2 919	2 501	1 969	1 937
married	4 459	4 376	4 631	4 749	4 703	4 946	5 245	5 261	5 988	6 132	6 504	6 451
widowed	1 063	1 043	1 094	1 106	1 122	1 091	1 036	1 049	1 026	1 251	1 392	1 461
divorced				7	10	20	32	41	67	116	135	151
15-19												
single	9 945	9 924	9 876	9 824	9 848	9 745	9 735	9 777	9 588	9 539	9 417	9 315
married	54	76	122	171	150	253	264	221	410	459	581	680
widowed	1	1	2	5	1	2	1	1	2	1	1	3
divorced										1	1	1
20-24												
single	8 705	8 711	8 204	7 630	7 679	7 138	6 880	6 949	5 946	5 631	4 353	4 015
married	1 280	1 277	1 769	2 330	2 295	2 836	3 095	3 010	4 023	4 326	5 615	5 936
widowed	15	12	27	38	25	24	22	36	22	22	12	16
divorced				2	1	2	4	5	9	21	20	32
25-34												
single	4 943	5 138	4 590	3 997	3 811	3 427	3 080	3 249	2 217	1 982	1 212	937
married	4 929	4 739	5 239	5 793	6 010	6 420	6 780	6 502	7 614	7 736	8 619	8 842
widowed	128	123	171	202	170	134	112	212	112	144	57	64
divorced				7	9	19	29	37	57	138	111	158
35-44												
single	2 391	2 629	2 325	2 192	2 079	1 974	1 825	1 710	1 458	1 112	924	684
married	7 158	6 890	7 175	7 247	7 334	7 504	7 737	7 770	8 068	8 324	8 667	8 883
widowed	451	481	500	550	566	486	385	453	360	378	218	212
divorced				11	21	37	54	67	113	186	191	221
45-54												
single	1 777	1 921	1 824	1 886	1 753	1 678	1 641	1 538	1 331	1 062	915	777
married	7 041	6 816	6 942	6 865	6 928	6 976	7 197	7 368	7 652	7 850	8 088	8 309
widowed	1 182	1 263	1 235	1 236	1 300	1 305	1 105	1 027	902	939	779	689
divorced				13	19	41	57	67	114	149	218	225
55-64												
single	1 585	1 728	1 679	1 782	1 728	1 629	1 634	1 557	1 371	1 186	931	837
married	5 732	5 776	5 798	5 677	5 617	5 638	5 721	5 978	6 461	6 598	6 880	6 995
widowed	2 683	2 497	2 523	2 531	2 641	2 709	2 596	2 407	2 091	2 091	2 026	1 975
divorced				10	14	25	49	58	77	126	164	193
65-69												
single	1 426	1 654	1 609	1 728	1 684	1 659	1 604	1 626	1 477	1 229	1 047	891
married	4 275	4 297	4 393	4 373	4 249	4 146	4 205	4 254	4 758	5 178	5 302	5 376
widowed	4 299	4 049	3 998	3 893	4 060	4 179	4 164	4 071	3 703	3 484	3 529	3 580
divorced				6	8	16	27	49	62	109	122	153
70-74												
single	1 408	1 606	1 621	1 745	1 712	1 694	1 656	1 594	1 487	1 260	1 163	949
married	3 181	3 272	3 403	3 451	3 158	3 034	3 066	3 111	3 464	3 947	4 009	4 030
widowed	5 411	5 121	4 976	4 799	5 124	5 259	5 255	5 258	4 996	4 703	4 714	4 895
divorced				5	6	14	23	37	53	90	114	126
75 +												
single	1 388	1 485	1 467	1 606	1 622	1 602	1 636	1 577	1 485	1 339	1 213	1 145
married	1 789	1 912	1 883	2 050	1 744	1 692	1 575	1 671	1 682	2 045	2 097	2 069
widowed	6 823	6 603	6 650	6 336	6 631	6 698	6 775	6 727	6 793	6 550	6 589	6 684
divorced				7	4	7	14	26	40	66	101	102

Civil Status of Males by Age

Census	1840	1860	1870	1880	1890	1901	1911	1921	1930	1935	1945	1950	1960	1965	1970
Age group					(Civil status per 10.000 of respective age group)										
15 +															
single	4 493	4 139	4 126	4 013	3 860	3 952	3 873	3 918	3 784	3 676	3 241	2 784	2 872	2 909	2 846
married	5 002	5 345	5 329	5 392	5 522	5 439	5 555	5 504	5 573	5 748	6 092	6 368	6 405	6 360	6 352
widowed	505	471	500	555	583	567	521	505	484	475	456	449	424	406	397
divorced		45	45	40	35	42	52	58	115	74	194	241	300	326	405
15-19															
single	9 998	9 998	9 999	9 999	9 999	9 995	9 982	9 993	9 990	9 993	9 983	9 605	9 964	9 939	9 969
married	2	2	1	1	1	5	17	7	5	7	15	20	35	60	31
widowed							1						2		
divorced												1	1	1	1
20-24															
single	9 533	9 293	9 400	9 236	9 127	8 809	8 762	8 779	8 965	8 884	8 468	7 644	7 721	7 350	7 284
married	462	701	594	758	867	1 181	1 220	1 198	988	1 107	1 480	1 732	2 220	2 587	2 611
widowed	5	5	4	6	5	7	10	11	3	3	4	8	2	2	3
divorced		1	2	1	1	3	8	7	14	4	38	51	58	62	103
25-34															
single	5 105	4 721	4 886	4 374	4 000	3 793	3 660	3 762	3 764	3 852	3 337	2 790	2 463	2 218	2 296
married	4 804	5 184	5 015	5 522	5 892	6 102	6 233	6 088	6 032	6 036	6 395	6 780	7 245	7 459	7 239
widowed	91	70	77	84	91	82	69	89	49	38	31	23	14	12	13
divorced		26	22	19	17	23	37	51	120	55	219	255	278	311	451
35-44															
single	1 487	1 462	1 460	1 388	1 297	1 285	1 311	1 362	1 242	1 289	1 362	1 187	1 127	1 107	1 115
married	8 243	8 295	8 272	8 313	8 400	8 419	8 405	8 316	8 369	8 442	8 268	8 327	8 402	8 405	8 270
widowed	270	178	206	245	259	231	204	215	160	134	87	72	51	47	50
divorced		65	63	54	43	65	79	94	189	111	268	351	420	441	565
45-54															
single	752	835	835	824	845	833	905	949	911	921	923	926	949	928	943
married	8 588	8 614	8 612	8 557	8 559	8 558	8 528	8 498	8 470	8 569	8 531	8 488	8 419	8 400	8 297
widowed	560	462	463	540	530	525	464	440	388	356	262	207	164	154	163
divorced		90	90	79	66	84	103	99	185	130	270	329	469	518	597
55-64															
single	561	640	684	685	704	720	769	841	796	789	831	777	875	891	899
married	8 151	8 055	8 076	8 054	8 057	8 010	8 079	8 024	8 048	8 160	8 137	8 250	8 238	8 171	8 100
widowed	1 288	1 209	1 154	1 173	1 166	1 195	1 069	1 027	948	898	767	640	490	457	445
divorced		96	86	88	73	75	83	97	158	125	249	288	397	481	556
65-69															
single	454	526	616	629	632	679	760	800	787	755	758	775	771	821	878
married	7 165	7 082	7 126	7 116	7 130	7 133	7 208	7 241	7 147	7 245	7 375	7 456	7 777	7 761	7 717
widowed	2 381	2 315	2 183	2 185	2 169	2 112	1 963	1 871	1 843	1 858	1 631	1 454	1 125	1 052	964
divorced		77	75	69	69	76	68	72	143	98	217	252	327	367	441
70-74															
single	402	442	554	592	653	626	725	759	760	740	719	716	778	747	812
married	6 402	6 181	6 081	6 141	6 240	6 126	6 267	6 362	6 259	6 306	6 458	6 609	6 974	7 161	7 191
widowed	3 196	3 311	3 293	3 211	3 044	3 190	2 951	2 787	2 786	2 800	2 621	2 387	1 969	1 783	1 655
divorced		65	73	56	63	58	57	72	106	83	177	213	279	309	341
75 +															
single	362	352	408	490	607	617	763	831	754	683	678	687	750	717	718
married	5 044	4 682	4 654	4 440	4 479	4 411	4 426	4 535	4 406	4 375	4 478	4 621	4 994	5 165	5 410
widowed	4 594	4 931	4 887	5 018	4 865	4 923	4 767	4 575	4 644	4 752	4 687	4 419	4 954	3 889	3 630
divorced		34	51	52	49	50	44	36	66	57	119	145	202	228	242

Denmark

Civil Status of Females by Age

Census	1840	1860	1870	1880	1890	1901	1911	1921	1930	1935	1945	1950	1960	1965	1970
Age group						(Civil status per 10.000 of respective age group)									
15 +															
single	3 963	3 671	3 742	3 700	3 661	3 753	3 730	3 753	3 603	3 419	2 891	2 427	2 359	2 313	2 153
married	4 742	5 138	5 059	5 062	5 063	4 996	5 064	5 092	5 226	5 497	5 867	6 147	6 169	6 125	6 115
widowed	1 295	1 135	1 143	1 186	1 229	1 190	1 128	1 050	955	938	947	963	1 039	1 096	1 177
divorced		56	56	51	47	62	79	89	168	123	278	352	432	466	555
15-19															
single	9 910	9 869	9 901	9 897	9 902	9 856	9 810	9 825	9 815	9 781	9 643	9 270	9 505	9 413	9 586
married	89	130	98	102	98	143	181	173	176	218	348	453	485	575	403
widowed						1	7	1	1		1	2	1	1	
divorced							2		2		6	7	9	11	12
20-24															
single	8 454	7 950	8 219	7 982	7 830	7 463	7 265	7 226	7 117	6 840	5 902	4 868	4 585	4 538	4 472
married	1 524	2 029	1 760	1 997	2 149	2 509	2 688	2 714	2 791	3 133	3 948	4 680	5 221	5 256	5 215
widowed	22	14	14	15	16	19	26	31	12	9	20	13	11	9	11
divorced		7	6	6	5	9	20	2	50	13	124	165	183	197	302
25-34															
single	3 971	3 640	3 834	3 615	3 499	3 391	3 305	3 219	3 074	2 922	2 100	1 557	1 192	1 062	1 095
married	5 843	6 186	5 974	6 209	6 311	6 424	6 490	6 516	6 616	6 898	7 486	7 909	8 335	8 438	8 221
widowed	186	132	152	143	156	138	124	169	93	70	86	69	50	47	46
divorced		42	40	33	33	47	81	90	186	98	319	390	424	454	638
35-44															
single	1 348	1 431	1 434	1 523	1 581	1 736	1 843	1 855	1 788	1 777	1 554	1 156	816	724	647
married	7 953	8 031	7 959	7 874	7 805	7 618	7 556	7 534	7 556	7 708	7 819	8 086	8 400	8 469	8 446
widowed	698	457	524	527	543	548	465	448	356	305	247	223	182	179	181
divorced		81	84	76	71	97	136	154	259	190	367	481	601	628	726
45-54															
single	843	984	1 013	1 039	1 164	1 314	1 466	1 564	1 563	1 549	1 536	1 409	1 031	827	712
married	7 417	7 582	7 639	7 487	7 396	7 261	7 147	7 192	7 208	7 361	7 290	7 380	7 727	7 843	7 908
widowed	1 740	1 331	1 247	1 375	1 354	1 314	1 249	1 076	903	851	765	671	601	605	586
divorced		102	101	99	86	111	137	156	271	213	393	476	641	726	794
55-64															
single	726	802	927	945	951	1 144	1 287	1 421	1 458	1 489	1 490	1 450	1 377	1 197	977
married	5 756	6 070	6 145	6 241	6 140	6 030	6 046	6 056	6 155	6 295	6 277	6 309	6 458	6 557	6 645
widowed	3 518	3 025	2 833	2 729	2 826	2 731	2 574	2 394	2 094	1 980	1 863	1 748	1 626	1 640	1 674
divorced		103	94	86	83	95	94	115	222	201	346	415	539	606	704
65-69															
single	674	709	888	983	900	1 011	1 231	1 315	1 437	1 444	1 496	1 457	1 473	1 417	1 295
married	4 289	4 353	4 573	4 558	4 717	4 583	4 644	4 803	4 725	4 833	4 916	5 040	5 111	5 087	5 113
widowed	5 037	4 860	4 465	4 374	4 313	4 314	4 056	3 788	3 580	3 533	3 285	3 085	2 980	2 994	3 063
divorced		79	74	85	70	92	69	76	159	139	272	327	436	502	529
70-74															
single	605	660	813	938	1 022	984	1 170	1 337	1 379	1 414	1 486	1 477	1 483	1 466	1 410
married	3 211	3 290	3 464	3 478	3 572	3 398	3 497	3 570	3 640	3 675	3 882	3 881	3 992	3 955	3 964
widowed	6 184	5 984	5 655	5 529	5 352	5 542	5 284	5 015	4 757	4 741	4 402	4 249	4 157	4 178	4 173
divorced		66	68	54	53	76	48	56	99	99	197	269	368	402	453
75 +															
single	606	598	662	877	1 021	1 013	1 116	1 307	1 352	1 298	1 439	1 464	1 536	1 511	1 494
married	2 024	1 896	1 960	1 949	1 957	1 926	1 870	2 000	1 945	1 975	1 997	2 109	2 168	2 072	2 052
widowed	7 371	7 449	7 328	7 138	6 978	7 000	6 969	6 628	6 503	6 572	6 412	6 124	6 057	6 127	6 126
divorced		57	50	37	44	60	45	37	59	57	105	144	239	291	328

Finland

Civil Status of Males by Age

Census	1800	1825	1850	1870	1880	1890	1900	1910	1920	1930	1940	1950	1960	1970
Age group					(Civil status per 10.000 of respective age group)									
15 +														
single	3 823	3 760	4 030	4 174	4 112	4 115	4 320	4 519	4 915	5 014	4 719	3 474	3 336	3 444
married	5 760	5 727	5 437	5 174	5 393	5 399	5 211	5 001	4 596	4 503	4 799	6 052	6 179	6 055
widowed	417 }	513 }	533 }	652 }	495	486	462	470	470	446	416	361	308	280
divorced							7	10	19	37	66	112	177	220
15–19														
single					9 951	9 947	9 954	9 957	9 965	9 974	9 965	9 899	9 886	9 887
married					48	53	45	42	35	26	35	100	112	110
widowed					1		1		1			1		
divorced												1	2	1
20–24														
single					8 381	8 425	8 355	8 592	8 939	8 974	8 917	7 863	7 505	7 160
married					1 601	1 554	1 626	1 394	1 041	1 014	1 071	2 110	2 454	2 782
widowed					19	21	19	14	19	11	8	8	2	2
divorced									1	1	4	19	39	55
25–34														
single					3 913	4 006	4 249	4 711	5 289	5 024	4 657	3 049	2 949	2 639
married					5 970	5 887	5 641	5 168	4 577	4 850	5 232	6 797	6 889	7 140
widowed					117	107	106	115	122	101	74	44	17	11
divorced							3	6	12	25	38	110	145	209
35–44														
single					1 613	1 767	1 944	2 256	2 990	3 128	2 729	1 359	1 349	1 559
married					8 114	7 966	7 795	7 448	6 686	6 552	6 963	8 350	8 346	8 085
widowed					273	267	250	278	292	258	203	112	64	49
divorced							11	17	32	63	105	178	241	307
45–54														
single					1 044	1 180	1 363	1 579	1 912	2 550	2 686	1 176	1 006	1 107
married					8 321	8 277	8 121	7 841	7 513	6 858	6 768	8 367	8 499	8 372
widowed					635	543	502	558	539	520	423	283	193	159
divorced							15	22	36	72	123	174	302	360
55–64														
single					898	960	1 118	1 296	1 565	1 837	2 545	1 077	1 022	943
married					7 711	7 796	7 783	7 633	7 342	7 104	6 439	7 981	8 155	8 228
widowed					1 390	1 244	1 088	1 054	1 058	1 000	904	798	558	476
divorced							11	17	34	59	113	144	265	352
65–69														
single					887	923	1 022	1 215	1 454	1 722	2 042	983	1 021	977
married					6 558	6 858	6 941	6 892	6 685	6 419	6 184	7 277	7 496	7 674
widowed					2 555	2 220	2 031	1 880	1 838	1 805	1 689	1 621	1 258	1 057
divorced							6	13	23	55	85	119	225	290
70–74														
single					922	964	975	1 179	1 564	1 726	2 134	915	973	985
married					5 536	5 805	5 987	6 060	5 742	5 607	5 482	6 428	6 669	7 007
widowed					3 541	3 231	3 028	2 745	2 676	2 622	2 312	2 561	2 177	1 776
divorced							10	16	18	45	71	96	181	230
75 +														
single					945	1 094	1 069	1 376	1 888	2 330	2 922	857	902	1 167
married					3 737	4 058	4 383	4 382	4 151	3 964	3 738	4 677	4 890	5 130
widowed					5 317	4 849	4 543	4 230	3 940	3 664	3 267	4 395	4 073	3 521
divorced							4	12	21	42	73	71	135	180

Finland

Civil Status of Females by Age

Census	1800	1825	1850	1870	1880	1890	1900	1910	1920	1930	1940	1950	1960	1970
Age group	(Civil status per 10.000 of respective age group)													
15 +														
single	3 557	3 549	3 727	3 843	3 697	3 659	3 796	3 963	4 354	4 452	4 159	3 156	2 905	3 105
married	5 315	5 192	5 024	4 764	5 034	5 115	5 012	4 851	4 372	4 290	4 513	5 271	5 484	5 949
widowed	1 241	1 259	1 249	1 393	1 269	1 226	1 183	1 173	1 251	1 212	1 241	1 384	1 326	1 396
divorced							9	13	23	46	87	189	285	385
15–19														
single					9 606	9 609	9 651	9 707	9 811	9 787	9 772	9 565	9 489	9 457
married					391	389	347	292	187	212	224	432	505	533
widowed					4	2	1	2	2	1	4	2	1	1
divorced												1	5	7
20–24														
single					6 761	6 795	6 815	7 154	7 679	7 628	7 128	5 899	5 399	5 233
married					3 198	3 166	3 148	2 815	2 260	2 340	2 758	4 032	4 503	4 625
widowed					41	40	36	30	59	27	106	25	10	13
divorced							1	1	2	5	8	44	87	128
25–34														
single					3 320	3 241	3 417	3 809	4 434	4 361	3 801	2 462	2 017	1 825
married					6 457	6 538	6 389	5 986	5 234	5 422	5 845	7 162	7 659	7 773
widowed					223	220	188	195	314	179	294	185	80	63
divorced							7	9	18	38	60	191	245	338
35–44														
single					1 828	1 868	1 903	2 183	2 721	3 111	2 876	1 772	1 401	1 195
married					7 440	7 479	7 459	7 202	6 492	6 176	6 428	7 294	7 841	8 052
widowed					732	653	622	592	750	632	558	644	358	275
divorced							16	23	37	81	138	290	401	477
45–54														
single					1 405	1 441	1 491	1 616	1 965	2 455	2 799	1 897	1 501	1 229
married					6 799	7 012	7 056	6 941	6 477	5 984	5 725	6 454	6 858	7 283
widowed					1 796	1 546	1 438	1 417	1 514	1 480	1 320	1 363	1 177	944
divorced							15	26	44	82	156	286	464	543
55–64														
single					1 303	1 305	1 340	1 432	1 486	1 887	2 390	1 872	1 801	1 467
married					5 171	5 548	5 665	5 669	5 443	5 133	4 702	4 900	5 248	5 622
widowed					3 526	3 146	2 981	2 880	2 934	2 912	2 780	2 994	2 567	2 395
divorced							14	19	37	68	129	234	384	514
65–69														
single					1 266	1 247	1 288	1 365	1 460	1 654	1 972	1 662	1 879	1 762
married					3 447	3 953	4 152	4 248	4 073	3 868	3 619	3 411	3 596	3 973
widowed					5 287	4 800	4 549	4 372	4 442	4 426	4 311	4 765	4 234	3 831
divorced							11	15	25	52	97	162	291	430
70–74														
single					1 234	1 250	1 259	1 333	1 487	1 607	1 921	1 567	1 805	1 909
married					2 534	2 877	3 042	3 207	3 051	2 889	2 738	2 441	2 492	2 744
widowed					6 231	5 873	5 690	5 444	5 444	5 460	5 260	5 872	5 495	5 006
divorced							8	17	19	44	82	120	209	339
75 +														
single					1 106	1 262	1 282	1 369	1 576	1 793	2 147	1 434	1 636	2 010
married					1 424	1 534	1 742	1 869	1 856	1 741	1 807	1 246	1 213	1 292
widowed					7 470	7 204	6 968	6 750	6 550	6 440	5 996	7 233	7 023	6 443
divorced							9	12	18	25	50	87	128	251

France

Civil Status of Males by Age

(Civil status per 10.000 of respective age group)

Census	1851	1861	1872	1881	1891	1901 a)	1911	1921	1931	1936	1946	1954	1962	1968
15 +														
single	3 904	3 764	3 590	3 721	3 757	3 563	3 413	3 206	3 047	2 748	3 048	2 539	2 962	3 075
married	5 444	5 548	5 637	5 525	5 489	5 709	5 877	5 959	6 304	6 495	6 232	6 763	6 479	6 416
widowed	652	688	773	754	742	728	664	670	576	587	550	497	421	367
divorced					12		46	64	73	88	118	141	139	142
Unknown (b)								101		82	52	60		
15–19														
single	9 981	9 973	9 979	9 982	9 984	9 964	9 971	9 945	9 943	9 949	9 857	9 894	9 964	9 961
married	18	26	21	18	16	35	28	55	57	50	83	34	36	39
widowed	1		1			1	1				1			
divorced											1			
20–24														
single	8 940	8 730	8 262	8 706	9 038	9 032	8 895		7 798	8 613	7 654	8 115	8 443	7 921
married	1 040	1 251	1 702	1 260	934	950	1 092	5 441	2 179	1 378	2 219	1 802	1 546	2 066
widowed	20	19	36	34	27	19	10	4 267	14	6	12	4	3	3
divorced					1		3	41	9	3	14	8	8	10
25–34														
single	4 565	4 329	3 870	3 863	3 937	3 632	3 362	23	2 776	3 178	3 339	2 813	2 913	2 531
married	5 308	5 532	5 946	5 978	5 888	6 231	6 498		7 069	6 678	6 404	7 003	6 989	7 363
widowed	127	139	184	159	164	137	103	1 553	92	77	71	30	16	17
divorced							11	8 122	62	67	124	95	82	89
35–44														
single	1 737	1 671	1 686	1 797	1 721	1 463	1 429	83	1 146	1 272	1 445	1 299	1 339	1 351
married	7 927	7 961	7 887	7 810	7 855	8 175	8 205	141	8 542	8 401	8 139	8 332	8 416	8 405
widowed	336	368	426	393	400	362	285		203	191	195	100	61	57
divorced						25		81	1 017	109	135	183	211	185	187
45–54														
single	1 063	1 100	1 135	1 235	1 252	1 062	1 070	332	912	870	887	1 029	1 065	1 020
married	8 207	8 174	8 082	8 013	7 943	8 207	8 224	123	8 489	8 589	8 500	8 386	8 459	8 567
widowed	729	726	783	752	784	731	621	8 455	467	406	406	299	228	165
divorced						21		85	910	132	137	175	239	248	248
55–64														
single	837	862	952	995	1 023	910	894	755	849	827	732	737	911	937
married	7 672	7 657	7 547	7 558	7 545	7 686	7 742	106	7 997	8 115	8 193	8 351	8 261	8 327
widowed	1 491	1 481	1 500	1 447	1 420	1 404	1 306	8 170	1 053	936	903	691	603	488
divorced						11		59	837	100	120	141	174	226	248
65–69														
single	695	729	880	921	925	810	799	1 637	811	812	713	665	726	806
married	6 832	6 784	6 562	6 750	6 812	6 871	6 909	72	7 215	7 386	7 458	7 821	7 947	7 977
widowed	2 473	2 487	2 557	2 329	2 255	2 319	2 258	7 398	1 902	1 707	1 683	1 328	1 157	1 022
divorced						7		34		72	89	114	137	171	195
70–74														
single	648	674	750	878	867	758	733		746	789	685	644	671	697
married	5 929	5 820	5 740	5 925	6 044	5 961	6 061		6 482	6 656	6 707	7 139	7 423	7 534
widowed	3 423	3 506	3 510	3 197	3 084	3 281	3 182	885	2 715	2 490	2 480	2 040	1 779	1 615
divorced						5		23	5 496	57	68	94	122	127	153
75 +														
single	720	641	708	853	871	708	631	37	630	662	607	616	639	626
married	4 481	4 342	4 367	4 395	4 579	4 314	4 492	3 717	4 812	5 101	5 143	5 499	5 820	6 122
widowed	4 800	5 017	4 925	4 751	4 547	4 978	4 863		4 526	4 184	4 154	3 742	3 454	3 152
divorced						3		13		32	45	56	76	88	100

a) 'widowed' including 'divorced'

b) 1851 – 1911, 1931, 1962, 1968: persons with unknown civil status distributed among the other categories

France

Civil Status of Females by Age

Census	1851	1861	1872	1881	1891	1901a)	1911	1921	1931	1936	1946	1954	1962	1968
Age group					(Civil status per 10.000 of respective age group)									
15 +														
single	3 450	3 262	3 033	3 138	3 150	2 875	2 700	2 790	2 465	2 215	2 495	2 044	2 239	2 381
married	5 270	5 434	5 496	5 438	5 386	5 473	5 613	5 256	5 740	5 840	5 491	5 951	5 931	5 841
widowed	1 280	1 304	1 471	1 424	1 450	1 653	1 630	1 774	1 692	1 747	1 790	1 762	1 626	1 564
divorced					14		58	76	103	121	151	204	204	214
Unknown (b)								104		77	73	39		
15-19														
single	9 661	9 459	9 416	9 389	9 527	9 348	9 356	9 442	9 274	9 378	9 135	9 611	9 673	9 672
married	336	536	574	605	467	638	637	555	724	619	532	322	325	325
widowed	4	5	10	5	6	14	5	2	1	2	6	2	1	1
divorced							2	1	1	2	2	2	1	2
20-24														
single	6 954	6 511	5 878	6 017	6 198	5 818	5 500		5 056	5 644	5 694	5 712	5 574	5 607
married	2 992	3 430	3 961	3 865	3 703	4 102	4 427	3 868	4 871	4 307	4 110	4 218	4 385	4 350
widowed	54	59	162	119	93	80	52	5 785	40	27	59	10	13	13
divorced					6	-	22	93	34	21	40	27	28	31
25-34														
single	3 348	3 096	2 675	2 707	2 691	2 433	2 211	50	2 075	2 142	2 035	1 801	1 584	1 422
married	6 400	6 631	6 893	6 936	6 933	7 243	7 472		7 615	7 573	7 461	7 909	8 212	8 358
widowed	252	273	433	357	353	324	243	1 615	200	162	279	95	66	66
divorced					23		73	7 464	110	123	183	168	138	154
35-44														
single	1 752	1 633	1 503	1 649	1 605	1 374	1 340	687	1 354	1 398	1 236	1 015	980	915
married	7 537	7 623	7 552	7 562	7 528	7 737	7 811	138	7 591	7 840	7 918	8 180	8 482	8 573
widowed	711	745	944	789	841	889	745	1 136	890	587	593	437	259	235
divorced					26		104	7 353	165	176	220	336	279	277
45-54														
single	1 416	1 300	1 194	1 295	1 314	1 148	1 122	1 286	1 091	1 145	1 215	1 039	914	873
married	7 082	7 156	7 078	7 106	7 036	7 001	7 045	146	7 009	6 986	7 093	7 569	7 820	7 998
widowed	1 502	1 544	1 728	1 599	1 633	1 851	1 746	1 087	1 745	1 688	1 449	1 069	903	770
divorced					17		87	6 493	154	181	208	294	363	360
55-64														
single	1 247	1 182	1 085	1 195	1 185	1 089	1 044	2 236	1 070	1 067	1 075	1 146	1 014	925
married	5 900	5 997	5 943	5 925	5 893	5 565	5 534	110	5 750	5 873	5 496	6 070	6 575	6 736
widowed	2 853	2 821	2 972	2 880	2 914	3 345	3 372		3 071	2 924	3 212	2 522	2 133	1 999
divorced					9		50	1 045	109	135	180	227	278	341
65-69														
single	1 139	1 121	1 072	1 170	1 155	1 056	1 012	4 652	1 044	1 076	1 029	1 093	1 146	1 021
married	4 462	4 615	4 631	4 571	4 596	4 023	3 970	4 154	4 106	4 348	4 070	4 263	4 863	5 181
widowed	4 399	4 264	4 296	4 259	4 245	4 920	4 992	74	4 772	4 478	4 721	4 390	3 771	3 534
divorced					5		26		78	98	141	211	219	263
70-74														
single	1 136	1 095	1 024	1 152	1 146	1 052	1 024		1 024	1 048	1 018	1 009	1 124	1 136
married	3 299	3 508	3 687	3 581	3 556	2 811	2 751		2 919	3 229	2 953	3 187	3 477	3 766
widowed	5 565	5 397	5 289	5 267	5 295	6 138	6 210	985	5 994	5 642	5 872	5 572	5 207	4 880
divorced					3		15	2 106	63	80	113	186	192	218
75 +														
single	1 027	1 023	1 025	1 184	1 169	1 035	967	6 791	969	992	962	1 033	1 043	1 075
married	1 976	2 196	2 389	2 391	2 327	1 452	1 445	35	1 439	1 533	1 497	1 550	1 628	1 690
widowed	6 997	6 780	6 586	6 425	6 501	7 512	7 579		7 556	7 427	7 415	7 216	7 183	7 063
divorced					2		8		36	54	79	135	146	172

a) 'widowed' including 'divorced'
b) 1851 - 1911, 1931, 1962, 1968: persons with unknown civil status distributed among the other categories

Civil Status of Males by Age

Census	1871	1880	1890	1900	1910	1925	1933	1939	1950	1961	1970
Age group				(Civil status per 10.000 of respective age group)							
15 +											
single	4 210	4 058	4 092	4 059	4 017	3 786	3 523	3 307	2 965	2 680	2 430
married	5 247	5 414	5 393	5 472	5 546	5 771	5 991	6 179	6 454	6 782	7 039
widowed	525	513	499	452	414	397	410	408	452	388	204
divorced	18	15	16	17	23	46	77	105	129	146	177
15-19											
single	9 987	9 990	9 995	9 992	9 995	9 995	9 996	9 997	9 979	9 961	9 921
married	13	9	5	7	5	7	4	3	21	38	73
widowed											5
divorced											1
20-24											
single		9 228	9 205	9 073	9 167	8 918	9 313	9 516	8 339	7 933	7 468
married		765	789	921	828	1 071	681	480	1 642	2 041	2 492
widowed	7 766	7	5	6	4	7	3	2	4	3	7
divorced	2 206	1	1	1	1	4	3	3	15	18	33
25-34	25										
single	3	3 838	3 769	3 599	3 599	3 353	4 320	4 070	3 699	2 497	2 333
married		6 078	6 155	6 334	6 331	6 546	5 586	5 833	6 136	7 367	7 462
widowed	2 226	75	67	57	54	54	35	29	31	16	15
divorced	7 624	10	9	10	16	46	59	68	135	177	190
35-44	132										
single	18	1 209	1 212	1 176	1 165	917	971	1 159	1 017	661	756
married		8 574	8 564	8 632	8 647	8 881	8 795	8 597	8 632	9 112	8 977
widowed	1 112	195	198	164	148	122	98	83	105	41	43
divorced	8 546	22	26	27	40	80	136	160	245	184	225
45- 54	312										
single	30	860	833	851	824	653	597	606	614	491	445
married		8 630	8 633	8 665	8 738	8 966	9 028	8 994	8 997	9 091	9 206
widowed	930	482	501	447	390	304	243	209	216	151	114
divorced	8 207	29	33	37	48	77	132	191	173	265	235
55-64	825										
single	38	806	737	742	731	645	577	562	470	468	433
married		7 854	7 959	8 030	8 141	8 380	8 574	8 600	8 819	8 850	8 912
widowed	904	1 310	1 272	1 193	1 086	911	744	677	590	457	395
divorced	6 872	29	33	35	42	65	105	161	121	223	260
65-69	2 188										
single	36	799	725	702	675	625	594	580	495	397	458
married		6 561	6 759	6 919	7 093	7 314	7 613	7 753	8 018	8 363	8 398
widowed		2 617	2 487	2 349	2 199	2 013	1 716	1 545	1 389	1 075	936
divorced		23	29	30	33	48	76	121	99	163	208
70-74											
single		788	715	714	644	630	594	584	520	400	401
married		5 375	5 660	5 773	6 037	6 217	6 591	6 766	6 945	7 596	7 763
widowed	788	3 815	3 599	3 486	3 293	3 115	2 758	2 561	2 454	1 875	1 673
divorced	4 609	22	26	27	26	38	58	89	81	127	163
75 +	4 572										
single	31	707	699	709	629	637	577	578	565	414	411
married		3 748	3 919	4 046	4 263	4 365	4 630	4 854	4 917	5 448	5 888
widowed		5 528	5 365	5 227	5 087	4 972	4 757	4 517	4 466	4 042	3 593
divorced		18	17	19	21	26	35	52	53	91	108

Civil Status of Females by Age

Census	1871	1880	1890	1900	1910	1925	1933	1939	1950	1961	1970
Age group	(Civil status per 10.000 of respective age group)										
15 +											
single	3 791	3 579	3 585	3 522	3 469	3 536	3 207	2 911	2 708	2 270	1 892
married	4 974	5 120	5 080	5 197	5 310	5 234	5 509	5 730	5 568	5 769	6 033
widowed	1 202	1 273	1 305	1 249	1 181	1 155	1 165	1 204	1 528	1 699	1 777
divorced	33	27	30	32	41	75	120	155	195	260	297
15-19											
single	9 850	9 848	9 866	9 840	9 861	9 883	9 878	9 859	9 751	9 488	9 187
married	146	149	132	158	137	115	120	140	245	504	799
widowed	3	3	2	2	1	1	1	1	2	3	7
divorced	1						1	1	2	4	7
20-24											
single		7 427	7 381	7 126	7 137	7 529	7 936	7 186	6 755	5 481	4 159
married		2 538	2 591	2 845	2 836	2 436	2 037	2 774	3 166	4 440	5 694
widowed	6 089	30	24	24	20	19	10	13	22	15	22
divorced	3 807	5	4	4	7	16	17	27	56	62	125
25-34											
single	19	2 772	2 827	2 709	2 573	3 001	3 384	2 671	2 783	1 713	1 135
married	13	6 992	6 959	7 105	7 252	6 725	6 413	7 131	6 511	8 015	8 516
widowed	1 979	211	188	158	136	184	89	75	444	71	66
divorced	7 591	26	26	28	40	90	113	124	263	199	283
35-44											
single	390	1 298	1 239	1 302	1 297	1 381	1 646	1 625	1 193	1 192	876
married	40	7 941	7 965	8 011	8 107	7 721	7 700	7 794	7 485	7 889	8 538
widowed	1 338	718	743	633	526	767	450	338	1 026	547	246
divorced	7 535	43	53	54	70	132	204	243	297	370	340
45-54											
single	1 071	1 132	1 049	1 026	1 074	1 044	1 147	1 322	1 261	956	986
married	56	7 076	7 091	7 186	7 345	7 526	7 358	7 250	7 276	6 864	7 463
widowed	1 193	1 745	1 806	1 728	1 511	1 315	1 308	1 168	1 218	1 766	1 105
divorced	6 354	47	53	60	70	115	186	259	245	412	446
55-64											
single	2 395	1 101	1 051	999	957	992	994	1 074	1 217	1 169	910
married	58	5 396	5 380	5 489	5 660	6 131	6 423	6 202	6 028	5 927	5 812
widowed	1 204	3 460	3 525	3 464	3 327	2 795	2 448	2 535	2 565	2 570	2 881
divorced	4 321	42	44	48	56	82	134	190	190	332	397
65-69											
single	4 428	1 112	1 073	1 028	954	959	985	1 018	1 073	1 238	1 130
married	47	3 626	3 698	3 744	3 936	4 296	4 746	4 858	4 573	4 458	4 462
widowed		5 230	5 193	5 192	5 070	4 691	4 183	3 999	4 227	4 040	4 096
divorced		31	35	36	41	54	87	124	128	260	313
70-74											
single		1 124	1 068	1 082	987	944	995	1 014	1 035	1 168	1 192
married		2 521	2 597	2 585	2 732	2 932	3 417	3 556	3 439	3 259	3 285
widowed	1 146	6 329	6 306	6 305	6 251	6 085	5 529	5 344	5 439	5 364	5 255
divorced	2 073	26	29	28	31	38	60	86	87	205	269
75 +											
single	6 748	1 063	1 072	1 088	1 004	948	948	1 011	1 043	1 069	1 194
married	33	1 310	1 313	1 357	1 400	1 484	1 652	1 782	1 784	1 650	1 637
widowed		7 605	7 594	7 533	7 575	7 542	7 363	7 158	7 123	7 145	6 977
divorced		22	21	21	21	26	36	49	50	132	192

Ireland

Civil Status of Males by Age

Census	1911[a]	1926	1936	1946	1951	1961	1966	1971
Age group	(Civil status per 10.000 of respective age group)							
15 +								
single	5 719	5 619	5 682	5 507	5 288	4 840	4 765	4 568
married	3 693	3 826	3 787	3 950	4 194	4 687	4 824	5 048
widowed	588	555	531	544	518	473	411	384
divorced								
15-19								
single	9 994	9 994	9 992	9 978	9 986	9 983	9 968	9 953
married	6	5	8	20	13	17	32	47
widowed				1				
divorced								
20-24								
single	9 661	9 600	9 618	9 500	9 486	9 251	8 960	8 458
married	335	395	379	495	510	747	1 038	1 542
widowed	4	5	4	5	4	2	1	1
divorced								
25-34								
single	7 453	7 173	7 379	7 035	6 741	5 802	4 978	4 125
married	2 491	2 768	2 573	2 925	3 225	4 185	5 012	5 863
widowed	56	58	48	40	34	12	10	11
divorced								
35-44								
single	4 447	4 497	4 417	4 298	4 045	3 621	3 336	2 895
married	5 329	5 289	5 390	5 563	5 836	6 309	6 610	7 058
widowed	223	214	194	138	119	71	54	47
divorced								
45-54								
single	2 861	3 139	3 346	3 213	3 100	2 967	2 914	2 810
married	6 594	6 359	6 204	6 390	6 563	6 813	6 888	7 009
widowed	545	502	450	397	337	219	198	182
divorced								
55-64								
single	2 269	2 617	2 823	2 998	2 880	2 815	2 769	2 715
married	6 647	6 411	6 253	6 108	6 299	6 554	6 714	6 777
widowed	1 084	972	925	894	821	632	517	508
divorced								
65-69								
single		2 337	2 607	2 804	2 932	2 744	2 771	2 738
married		6 000	5 838	5 632	5 629	6 026	6 135	6 242
widowed	1 875	1 662	1 555	1 565	1 439	1 230	1 094	1 020
divorced	5 937							
70-74	2 188							
single		2 121	2 478	2 610	2 785	2 826	2 716	2 789
married		5 463	5 231	5 117	5 077	5 283	5 562	5 604
widowed		2 417	2 291	2 273	2 137	1 891	1 722	1 607
divorced								
75 +								
single	1 511	1 625	1 871	2 152	2 243	2 484	2 557	2 513
married	4 635	4 305	4 375	4 256	4 246	4 258	4 422	4 552
widowed	3 854	4 070	3 754	3 591	3 512	3 258	3 021	2 935
divorced								

a) territory of later Republic

Civil Status of Females by Age

Census	1911 [a]	1926	1936	1946	1951	1961	1966	1971
Age group		(Civil status per 10.000 of respective age group)						
15 +								
single	4 811	4 694	4 719	4 488	4 278	3 899	3 817	3 644
married	3 829	4 009	4 067	4 273	4 481	4 811	4 916	5 093
widowed	1 360	1 297	1 214	1 239	1 241	1 290	1 267	1 264
divorced								
15-19								
single	9 950	9 930	9 906	9 840	9 886	9 889	9 840	9 788
married	49	70	94	158	113	111	159	212
widowed		1	1	2	1		1	
divorced								
20-24								
single	8 844	8 702	8 642	8 252	8 226	7 821	7 478	6 890
married	1 144	1 285	1 351	1 733	1 762	2 175	2 515	3 104
widowed	12	14	8	15	12	4	6	6
divorced								
25-34								
single	5 545	5 260	5 484	4 827	4 559	3 713	3 101	2 568
married	4 324	4 606	4 430	5 081	5 367	6 242	6 855	7 390
widowed	130	134	86	91	74	45	43	41
divorced								
35-44								
single	3 098	2 951	3 016	3 000	2 764	2 274	2 036	1 745
married	6 342	6 506	6 570	6 639	6 913	7 478	7 733	8 035
widowed	560	543	415	361	323	248	231	220
divorced								
45-54								
single	2 396	2 394	2 510	2 565	2 565	2 306	2 076	1 884
married	6 159	6 334	6 346	6 339	6 415	6 858	7 104	7 312
widowed	1 445	1 272	1 144	1 096	1 020	837	820	804
divorced								
55-64								
single	2 075	2 357	2 367	2 442	2 474	2 570	2 439	2 204
married	5 233	5 131	5 300	5 153	5 205	5 354	5 545	5 766
widowed	2 692	2 512	2 333	2 405	2 321	2 077	2 016	2 031
divorced								
55-69								
single		2 185	2 354	2 391	2 457	2 501	2 506	2 536
married		4 011	4 097	3 992	4 002	3 997	4 007	4 094
widowed		3 804	3 549	3 617	3 540	3 501	3 487	3 370
divorced	1 829							
70-74	3 627							
single	4 544	2 067	2 399	2 378	2 408	2 497	2 573	2 514
married		2 904	2 891	3 010	3 028	2 954	2 995	2 924
widowed		5 030	4 710	4 612	4 564	4 549	4 432	4 562
divorced								
75 +								
single	1 900	1 681	2 063	2 225	2 261	2 324	2 394	2 472
married	1 703	1 474	1 638	1 723	1 825	1 686	1 652	1 617
widowed	6 397	6 845	6 299	6 052	5 914	5 990	5 955	5 911
divorced								

a) territory of later Republic

Italy

Civil Status of Males by Age

Census	1861	1871	1881	1901	1911	1921	1931	1936	1951	1961	1971
Age group				(Civil status per 10.000 of respective age group)							
15 +											
single	4 039	4 135	4 040	3 903	3 803	4 004	3 950	3 835	3 711	3 335	3 195
married	5 353	5 255	5 364	5 484	5 550	5 392	5 501	5 651	5 857	6 266	6 392
widowed	607	609	595	613	588	571	526	513	409	368	350
divorced					14	16	18	1	24	31	64
unknown					45						
15-19											
single	9 807	9 966	9 971	9 875	9 953	9 935	9 953	9 960	9 957	9 948	9 935
married	189	33	29	123	47	63	46	39	42	50	61
widowed	3	1	1	2		1	1		1	1	2
divorced											1
20-24											
single	8 172	8 956	8 916	8 401	8 637	8 579	8 844	9 077	9 072	9 076	8 654
married	1 795	1 028	1 072	1 578	1 344	1 394	1 146	916	923	920	1 333
widowed	31	15	13	20	11	16	7	6	4	3	7
divorced					1	1	1		1	1	6
25-34											
single	4 013	4 373	4 049	3 824	3 582	4 140	3 676	4 199	4 393	3 907	3 288
married	5 833	5 497	5 833	6 065	6 306	5 738	6 240	5 742	5 570	6 068	6 662
widowed	153	131	118	110	96	100	69	58	23	14	14
divorced					8	12	10		13	10	35
35-44											
single	1 805	1 735	1 666	1 573	1 506	1 538	1 289	1 290	1 350	1 323	1 379
married	7 937	7 927	8 010	8 126	8 200	8 137	8 478	8 535	8 529	8 592	8 505
widowed	357	339	324	301	263	292	195	172	85	45	43
divorced					21	25	32	1	36	40	73
45-54											
single	1 399	1 297	1 197	1 127	1 065	1 059	952	920	872	887	1 094
married	7 803	8 015	8 109	8 239	8 315	8 319	8 514	8 639	8 822	8 886	8 667
widowed	796	688	693	634	583	587	490	439	263	169	127
divorced					27	28	39	2	44	58	112
55-64											
single	1 200	1 181	1 087	1 034	917	903	873	837	726	747	1 069
married	7 297	7 358	7 549	7 700	7 878	7 905	8 019	8 149	8 505	8 650	8 382
widowed	1 502	1 461	1 363	1 266	1 171	1 157	1 072	1 012	725	547	438
divorced					25	28	32	1	44	57	111
65-69											
single	1 049	1 097	1 127	972	899	832	820	826	732	661	1 196
married	6 173	6 486	6 556	6 819	7 058	7 196	7 255	7 341	7 761	8 116	7 755
widowed	2 775	2 417	2 317	2 209	2 013	1 939	1 899	1 831	1 473	1 173	960
divorced					22	23	24	1	34	50	89
70-74											
single	1 201	992	1 069	965	888	814	762	771	711	675	1 008
married	5 318	5 686	5 686	5 912	6 153	6 353	6 473	6 565	6 958	7 391	7 259
widowed	3 481	3 322	3 244	3 123	2 932	2 803	2 742	2 663	2 306	1 893	1 657
divorced					17	18	19		25	41	75
75 +											
single	1 231	921	980	953	840	842	691	673	684	710	972
married	4 326	4 341	4 328	4 441	4 605	4 819	4 854	4 944	5 211	5 605	5 551
widowed	4 442	4 737	4 692	4 606	4 535	4 302	4 441	4 381	4 091	3 659	3 427
divorced					11	15	11		14	26	50

Italy

Civil Status of Females by Age

Census	1861	1871	1881	1901	1911	1921	1931	1936	1951	1961	1971
Age group				(Civil status per 10.000 of respective age group)							
15 +											
single	3 262	3 366	3 265	3 178	3 242	3 514	3 435	3 304	3 205	2 870	2 600
married	5 349	5 284	5 372	5 480	5 436	5 184	5 252	5 392	5 501	5 796	5 988
widowed	1 387	1 350	1 363	1 343	1 263	1 273	1 291	1 303	1 271	1 296	1 341
divorced					16	18	19	1	24	38	70
unknown					43						
15–19											
single	8 966	9 556	9 516	9 123	9 540	9 623	9 590	9 624	9 617	9 558	9 366
married	1 015	437	478	864	453	370	406	374	377	438	627
widowed	18	7	7	13	4	5	2	1	6	3	4
divorced										1	3
20–24											
single	5 388	6 250	6 089	5 365	6 049	6 775	6 677	6 938	6 751	6 514	5 637
married	4 493	3 675	3 855	4 566	3 893	3 157	3 291	3 039	3 225	3 469	4 319
widowed	117	75	56	69	45	59	28	23	19	13	26
divorced					4	4	4		4	5	18
25–34											
single	2 478	2 608	2 445	2 440	2 502	3 123	2 920	3 193	2 886	2 462	1 853
married	7 107	7 060	7 270	7 312	7 263	6 432	6 879	6 654	6 932	7 435	8 016
widowed	414	332	285	248	211	421	181	151	157	77	68
divorced					16	18	19	1	25	26	63
35–44											
single	1 517	1 499	1 389	1 350	1 373	1 529	1 646	1 752	1 624	1 510	1 285
married	7 407	7 562	7 713	7 929	7 943	7 631	7 528	7 649	7 827	8 070	8 352
widowed	1 075	938	898	721	649	805	787	597	511	352	263
divorced					27	30	46	2	38	67	100
45–54											
single	1 217	1 266	1 215	1 115	1 091	1 167	1 236	1 309	1 478	1 381	1 394
married	6 449	6 749	6 795	7 225	7 378	7 359	7 204	7 152	7 330	7 538	7 645
widowed	227	1 985	1 990	1 660	1 496	1 438	1 523	1 536	1 154	1 015	834
divorced					27	30	35	2	38	66	126
55–64											
single	1 126	1 163	1 143	1 116	1 002	1 015	1 086	1 131	1 352	1 401	1 499
married	4 893	5 227	5 279	5 637	5 964	6 181	6 054	6 101	6 044	6 310	6 315
widowed	3 980	3 610	3 577	3 247	3 005	2 773	2 833	2 766	2 574	2 239	2 098
divorced					21	23	25	1	29	50	89
65–69											
single	1 109	1 085	1 184	1 132	1 034	968	1 003	1 054	1 198	1 368	1 652
married	3 430	4 133	3 915	4 057	4 347	4 707	4 557	4 569	4 625	4 823	4 825
widowed	5 461	4 783	4 901	4 812	4 597	4 300	4 423	4 375	4 159	3 774	3 464
divorced					13	15	15	1	18	35	60
70–74											
single	1 232	1 032	1 161	1 173	1 093	978	984	1 004	1 160	1 271	1 576
married	3 047	2 914	2 697	2 881	3 005	3 467	3 276	3 401	3 445	3 569	3 663
widowed	5 720	6 054	6 142	5 947	5 882	5 527	5 730	5 594	5 382	5 135	4 716
divorced					11	12	9		12	25	45
75 +											
single	1 274	1 031	1 098	1 191	1 116	1 031	951	968	1 085	1 192	1 524
married	2 046	1 966	1 674	1 666	1 683	2 049	1 652	1 705	1 722	1 850	1 785
widowed	6 677	7 002	7 227	7 143	7 185	6 889	7 390	7 325	7 187	6 946	6 662
divorced					6	9	5		6	13	28

Civil Status of Males by Age

Census	1830	1840	1849	1859	1869	1879	1889	1899	1909	1920	1930	1947	1960	1970
Age groups	(Civil status per 10.000 of respective age groups)													
15 +														
single	5 142	5 271	4 625	4 577	4 321	4 151	4 253	4 276	4 181	4 098	3 909	3 538	3 015	2 944
married	4 312	4 228	4 744	4 805	5 080	5 272	5 169	5 161	5 286	5 395	5 607	5 948	6 529	6 649
widowed	546	501	630	615	597	573	569	550	513	479	439	415	361	308
divorced				2	3	4	8	13	20	28	45	99	93	98
15-19														
single	9 983	9 984	9 987	9 987	9 988	9 983	9 982	9 981	9 986	9 978	9 979	9 940	9 945	9 934
married	16	16	13	13	12	17	17	19	14	22	21	59	54	65
widowed							1	1						
divorced													1	1
20-24														
single	8 936	9 025	9 364	9 358	9 256	9 005	8 960	8 902	8 874	8 768	8 962	8 628	8 330	7 163
married	1 043	962	623	630	736	988	1 032	1 090	1 119	1 223	1 031	1 354	1 657	2 818
widowed	21	12	13	11	8	7	8	7	5	7	3	3	1	1
divorced								1	2	3	4	15	11	18
25-34														
single	4 457	4 609	5 244	4 990	4 756	4 252	4 334	4 140	3 952	3 770	3 614	3 461	2 634	1 998
married	5 395	5 273	4 613	4 880	5 141	5 648	5 567	5 777	5 971	6 130	6 308	6 405	7 300	7 902
widowed	148	118	143	127	101	98	92	74	62	76	40	29	9	8
divorced				1	1	2	6	8	15	24	38	105	56	93
35-44														
single	1 726	1 776	1 885	1 965	1 852	1 786	1 782	1 777	1 633	1 523	1 220	1 237	880	955
married	7 893	7 892	7 697	7 668	7 856	7 948	7 934	7 982	8 150	8 246	8 579	8 547	8 980	8 881
widowed	381	332	418	363	288	261	269	220	184	189	129	79	32	28
divorced				3	4	5	14	21	32	42	72	137	107	135
45-54														
single	1 140	1 190	1 170	1 221	1 276	1 226	1 293	1 284	1 268	1 195	1 084	856	764	668
married	8 226	8 224	7 986	7 989	8 072	8 203	8 115	8 150	8 242	8 344	8 486	8 761	8 962	9 078
widowed	634	586	844	785	646	564	576	538	450	412	353	237	115	101
divorced				4	6	7	16	28	39	49	77	147	158	154
55-64														
single	1 008	1 038	960	997	1 101	1 101	1 089	1 121	1 110	1 120	1 034	861	734	691
married	7 643	7 680	7 344	7 312	7 437	7 610	7 669	7 634	7 723	7 836	7 988	8 252	8 683	8 808
widowed	1 349	1 282	1 695	1 687	1 456	1 282	1 229	1 223	1 129	994	903	739	415	339
divorced				5	6	7	13	23	37	50	74	149	167	162
65-69														
single			886	904	1 023	1 024	1 013	1 017	1 033	1 069	1 029	919	691	724
married			6 427	6 266	6 293	6 509	6 692	6 737	6 768	6 867	7 091	7 270	8 103	8 359
widowed			2 687	2 825	2 678	2 463	2 284	2 224	2 165	2 023	1 814	1 678	1 048	784
divorced				5	6	5	10	22	32	41	66	133	157	133
70-74														
single	996	992	872	885	947	1 029	1 035	971	984	993	1 001	919	764	673
married	5 521	5 488	5 327	5 257	5 256	5 424	5 670	5 714	5 781	5 891	6 079	6 254	7 093	7 761
widowed	3 483	3 520	3 801	3 853	3 793	3 543	3 284	3 298	3 213	3 076	2 865	2 712	2 002	1 446
divorced				4	5	4	11	16	21	39	55	115	140	119
75 +														
single			906	836	920	903	914	903	846	893	896	860	782	666
married			3 979	3 883	3 812	3 662	3 855	3 998	3 989	3 985	4 106	4 345	4 839	5 579
widowed			5 115	5 281	5 262	5 433	5 227	5 087	5 147	5 100	4 961	4 721	4 280	3 681
divorced					6	2	4	12	18	23	37	75	97	74

Netherlands

Civil Status of Females by Age

Census	1830	1840	1849	1859	1869	1879	1889	1899	1909	1920	1930	1947	1960	1970
Age group				(Civil status per 10.000 of respective ag group)										
15 +														
single	4 813	4 938	4 305	4 241	4 003	3 794	3 917	3 992	3 931	3 857	3 727	3 242	2 637	2 396
married	4 041	3 980	4 445	4 553	4 833	5 071	4 960	4 937	5 084	5 227	5 433	5 776	6 321	6 444
widowed	1 147	1 082	1 250	1 202	1 159	1 128	1 109	1 049	954	870	773	841	891	1 005
divorced				4	6	7	15	22	31	46	67	141	150	155
15-19														
single	9 935	9 945	9 938	9 937	9 922	9 899	9 900	9 893	9 894	9 843	9 835	9 681	9 629	9 506
married	64	54	61	62	77	100	98	106	106	157	164	315	367	492
widowed	1	1	1	1	1	1	2	1			1	1		
divorced											1	3	3	2
20-24														
single	8 092	8 178	8 662	8 539	8 317	7 834	7 846	7 858	7 750	7 477	7 545	6 918	5 944	4 635
married	1 874	1 793	1 309	1 434	1 661	2 144	2 131	2 124	2 234	2 497	2 436	3 009	4 016	5 311
widowed	34	29	29	26	22	21	20	16	11	15	7	20	7	7
divorced				1	1	1	2	2	4	11	12	54	33	47
25-34														
single	3 989	4 015	4 560	4 281	3 997	3 484	3 618	3 583	3 438	3 268	3 031	2 571	1 632	1 121
married	5 773	5 789	5 211	5 520	5 835	6 363	6 226	6 279	6 445	6 585	6 844	7 149	8 240	8 697
widowed	238	196	229	196	164	149	143	120	91	106	64	124	37	38
divorced				3	4	5	14	17	25	41	61	156	91	144
35-44														
single	1 848	1 875	1 890	1 939	1 843	1 735	1 736	1 851	1 844	1 803	1 684	1 526	1 028	762
married	7 326	7 397	7 338	7 374	7 579	7 755	7 736	7 678	7 762	7 820	7 963	7 990	8 620	8 894
widowed	826	727	772	682	570	498	506	436	346	313	253	304	169	160
divorced				5	8	11	23	35	47	63	101	180	182	184
45-54														
single	1 365	1 435	1 408	1 378	1 404	1 359	1 366	1 398	1 495	1 517	1 493	1 331	1 139	838
married	7 081	7 159	6 837	6 942	7 162	7 343	7 394	7 400	7 467	7 578	7 712	7 742	8 021	8 372
widowed	1 554	1 406	1 756	1 671	1 422	1 285	1 217	1 159	978	829	685	727	591	558
divorced				8	12	13	24	42	59	76	110	201	248	232
55-64														
single	1 194	1 309	1 304	1 268	1 274	1 265	1 266	1 257	1 295	1 398	1 413	1 342	1 190	1 038
married	5 782	5 792	5 348	5 463	5 720	5 977	6 074	6 192	6 313	6 460	6 727	6 790	7 021	7 142
widowed	3 024	2 899	3 348	3 261	2 996	2 746	2 638	2 514	2 337	2 062	1 760	1 670	1 550	1 582
divorced				7	10	13	22	37	55	81	101	198	238	239
65-69														
single			1 259	1 265	1 303	1 238	1 225	1 217	1 228	1 278	1 395	1 335	1 238	1 165
married			3 853	3 948	4 108	4 234	4 565	4 631	4 805	4 928	5 240	5 462	5 719	5 739
widowed			4 889	4 781	4 581	4 519	4 188	4 120	3 925	3 724	3 271	3 036	2 819	2 885
divorced				7	8	9	22	31	42	71	94	167	223	211
70-74														
single	1 133	1 146	1 208	1 256	1 269	1 253	1 245	1 223	1 201	1 266	1 367	1 322	1 306	1 168
married	3 066	2 966	2 849	2 809	3 081	3 140	3 357	3 426	3 632	3 697	3 953	4 226	4 546	4 563
widowed	5 801	5 889	5 944	5 928	5 643	5 597	5 383	5 329	5 134	4 985	4 597	4 310	3 955	4 063
divorced				6	7	10	16	22	34	51	84	143	194	205
75 +														
single			1 186	1 157	1 313	1 241	1 186	1 204	1 165	1 154	1 254	1 283	1 355	1 290
married			1 683	1 641	1 660	1 648	1 740	1 885	1 903	1 945	2 039	2 239	2 476	2 519
widowed			7 131	7 200	7 024	7 105	7 063	6 893	6 909	6 861	6 644	6 383	6 021	6 039
divorced				2	3	6	11	18	23	40	64	95	147	152

Norway

Civil Status of Males by Age

Census	1801a)	1865	1875a)	1890	1900	1910	1920	1930	1946	1950	1960	1970
Age group	(Civil status per 10.000 of respective age group)											
15 +												
single	4 690	4 178	5 176	3 971	4 123	4 142	4 387	4 491	3 947	3 542	3 101	3 066
married	4 907	5 263	4 338	5 362	5 270	5 212	4 991	4 916	5 494	5 896	6 347	6 374
widowed	403	559	486	640	603	597	577	527	439	436	400	530
divorced				5	5	11	41	61	102	124	153	30
Unknown				9	38	4	5	18	2			
15-19												
single	9 980	9 985	9 981	9 976	9 958	9 954	9 982	9 988	9 975	9 966	9 937	9 919
married	20	15	19	24	41	45	18	12	24	34	63	81
widowed			1		1	1						1
divorced												
20-24												
single		9 122		8 852	8 614	8 729	8 848	9 346	9 047	8 803	7 894	7 175
married		870		1 121	1 372	1 236	1 130	645	929	1 179	2 068	2 768
widowed	7 333	9	7 620	16	14	12	13	4	4	2	2	58
divorced	2 621		2 344			1	8	4	13	15	36	
	46		36									
25-34												
single		4 535		4 304	4 272	4 332	4 487	5 110	4 698	4 248	3 156	2 525
married		5 352		5 551	5 621	5 527	5 346	4 782	5 168	5 634	6 709	7 234
widowed		113		121	104	106	131	61	31	21	12	240
divorced	2 257		2 580	2	3	7	33	45	88	96	123	
	7 558		7 116									
35-44												
single	185	1 504	204	1 592	1 667	1 790	1 867	2 047	2 076	1 854	1 609	1 373
married		8 195		8 063	8 039	7 886	7 750	7 629	7 685	7 910	8 162	8 313
widowed		300		319	287	278	313	223	92	72	43	313
divorced	872		1 281	7	7	19	68	99	132	163	186	
	8 832		8 297									
45-54												
single	296	898	422	1 096	1 090	1 185	1 222	1 385	1 531	1 509	1 333	1 251
married		8 501		8 288	8 356	8 223	8 124	7 997	8 025	8 082	8 302	8 329
widowed		602		589	545	544	565	494	268	217	138	420
divorced	577		921	10	9	24	84	120	162	191	227	
	8 783		8 238									
55-64												
single	640	726	841	883	971	982	996	1 104	1 350	1 347	1 356	1 207
married		8 011		7 949	7 971	7 957	7 817	7 741	7 728	7 816	7 984	8 156
widowed		1 262		1 139	1 050	1 023	1 107	1 039	748	652	439	637
divorced				11	8	18	76	112	155	183	221	
65-69	430		570									
single	7 971	570	7 489	760	869	890	903	1 013	1 211	1 294	1 301	1 278
married	1 599	7 253	1 727	7 252	7 324	7 352	7 180	7 101	7 116	7 170	7 471	7 710
widowed		2 177		1 958	1 801	1 725	1 855	1 789	1 500	1 371	1 031	774
divorced				8	6	12	55	89	154	164	197	237
70-74												
single		551		730	829	951	802	965	1 107	1 153	1 309	1 296
married		6 346		6 474	6 551	6 518	6 438	6 389	6 430	6 457	6 723	7 106
widowed	372	3 103	631	2 755	2 615	2 486	2 710	2 572	2 315	2 244	1 810	1 397
	6 142											
divorced	3 485		5 425	12	6	7	39	66	121	146	159	202
			3 944									
75 +												
single		477		607	728	787	722	924	1 006	1 006	1 194	1 206
married		4 924		4 792	4 937	4 889	4 805	4 764	4 712	4 723	4 879	5 405
widowed		4 599		4 549	4 329	4 265	4 442	4 249	4 163	4 177	3 814	3 230
divorced				10	6	8	19	43	78	90	113	159

a) age groups: 15+, 15-19, 20-29, 30-39, 40-49, 50-59, 60-69, 70+

Norway

Civil Status of Females by Age

Census	1801[a]	1865	1875[a]	1890	1900	1910	1920	1930	1946	1950	1960	1970
Age group	(Civil status per 10.000 of respective age group)											
15 +												
single	4 555	3 989	4 956	4 071	4 141	4 198	4 283	4 323	3 601	3 151	2 600	2 425
married	4 383	4 882	4 063	4 739	4 699	4 631	4 540	4 539	5 240	5 683	6 181	6 186
widowed	1 062	1 130	981	1 171	1 154	1 139	1 120	1 048	994	992	1 012	1 334
divorced				6	6	17	55	86	147	173	207	55
Unknown				13		15	2	5	19	1		
15-19												
single	9 876	9 892	9 916	9 873	9 822	9 822	9 844	9 886	9 779	9 693	9 523	9 439
married	123	107	82	126	175	175	154	111	216	304	473	554
widowed	1	1	2	1	3	2	1	1	2			7
divorced								1	2	2	4	
20-24												
single		8 016		7 986	7 683	7 761	7 647	8 127	7 326	6 565	4 974	4 618
married	6 442	1 961	6 676	1 985	2 287	2 199	2 303	1 848	2 607	3 384	4 927	5 241
widowed	3 832	24	3 258	27	29	31	32	12	17	7	11	142
divorced	75		66	1	1	2	18	12	44	44	88	
25-34												
single		3 990		4 195	4 067	4 088	4 048	4 279	3 250	2 668	1 453	1 282
married		5 832		5 606	5 744	5 720	5 703	5 529	6 501	7 114	8 333	8 376
widowed		178		187	185	166	194	106	96	64	47	343
divorced	2 663		2 808	6	5	16	55	85	143	154	167	
35-44	6 956		6 814									
single	381	1 855	378	2 178	2 341	2 433	2 483	2 562	2 184	1 783	1 104	689
married		7 592		7 217	7 093	6 991	6 904	6 855	7 317	7 742	8 478	8 812
widowed		553		588	555	534	516	438	302	252	167	499
divorced	1 532		1 712	8	12	32	96	144	185	222	251	
45-54	7 578		7 372									
single	890	1 288	917	1 702	1 780	1 988	2 075	2 184	2 184	2 071	1 425	898
married		7 419		6 993	6 957	6 805	6 653	6 625	6 769	6 960	7 722	8 191
widowed		1 293		1 278	1 250	1 161	1 166	1 027	797	704	552	912
divorced	1 291		1 333	12	13	32	103	161	237	265	301	
55-64	6 668		6 850									
single	2 041	1 096	1 818	1 417	1 608	1 676	1 887	2 004	2 164	2 150	1 938	1 324
married		6 177		6 154	6 021	5 998	5 769	5 728	5 824	5 935	6 301	6 838
widowed		2 727		2 396	2 362	2 285	2 266	2 135	1 789	1 674	1 469	1 839
divorced				12	10	21	74	127	206	240	291	
65-69	1 059		1 160									
single	5 030	1 047	5 385	1 229	1 450	1 596	1 642	1 941	2 075	2 133	2 093	1 832
married	3 911	4 738	3 455	5 030	4 934	4 840	4 690	4 646	4 718	4 796	5 001	5 181
widowed		4 215		3 707	3 613	3 525	3 614	3 327	3 014	2 876	2 653	2 665
divorced				9	3	12	49	78	170	194	254	322
70-74												
single		980		1 195	1 392	1 584	1 594	1 900	2 014	2 076	2 162	1 986
married		3 913		4 033	4 055	3 830	3 724	3 651	3 762	3 804	3 972	3 969
widowed	906	5 107	1 022	4 734	4 548	4 540	4 644	4 385	4 068	3 965	3 671	3 737
divorced	2 981		2 911	5	5	12	30	52	122	154	195	307
75 +	6 113		6 067									
single		949		999	1 241	1 368	1 428	1 688	1 916	1 961	2 104	2 153
married		2 295		2 315	2 425	2 281	2 052	2 133	2 035	2 085	2 148	2 159
widowed		6 756		6 636	6 331	6 304	6 493	6 128	5 936	5 874	5 620	5 443
divorced				5	3	5	15	22	65	78	128	245

a) age groups: 15+, 15-19, 20-29, 30-39, 40-49, 50-59, 60-69, 70+

C i v i l   S t a t u s   o f   M a l e s   b y   A g e

Census	1800	1850	1870	1880	1890	1900	1910	1920	1930	1940	1950	1960	1965	1970	1975
Age group	(Civil status per 10.000 of respective age group)														
15 +															
single	3 782	4 379	4 219	4 295	4 138	4 342	4 421	4 504	4 471	4 074	3 281	3 189	3 230	3 226	3 369
married	5 697	5 106	5 213	5 166	5 267	5 053	4 981	4 892	4 916	5 325	6 099	6 160	6 121	6 071	5 763
widowed	521	515	561	532	586	594	582	577	558	517	473	424	359	377	372
divorced			7	7	9	12	16	27	54	84	148	227	255	326	496
15-19															
single	9 981	9 997	9 999	9 999	9 998	9 998	9 998	9 998	9 999	9 994	9 968	9 979	9 968	9 986	9 989
married	19	3	1	1	2	2	2	2	1	6	32	21	32	14	11
widowed															
divorced															
20-24															
single	8 677	9 211	9 361	9 230	9 163	9 189	9 319	9 353	9 430	9 151	8 448	8 245	8 072	8 425	9 146
married	1 314	783	633	764	832	805	676	642	567	844	1 538	1 739	1 913	1 555	826
widowed	9	7	5	6	5	6	5	4	3	3	2	1	1		
divorced										2	12	15	14	19	28
25-34															
single	3 861	4 552	4 881	4 695	4 800	4 917	4 978	5 112	5 378	4 723	3 770	3 227	2 979	3 274	4 229
married	6 041	5 356	5 029	5 220	5 113	5 002	4 937	4 781	4 540	5 203	6 093	6 594	6 836	6 455	5 320
widowed	98	93	87	83	83	76	77	93	53	32	19	10	9	9	9
divorced			3	2	4	6	8	14	29	42	118	169	177	262	442
35-44															
single	1 211	1 375	1 638	1 705	1 865	2 017	2 149	2 218	2 221	2 272	1 848	1 660	1 591	1 499	1 538
married	8 516	8 323	8 079	8 046	7 885	7 733	7 595	7 484	7 505	7 505	7 980	7 987	8 018	7 987	7 587
widowed	273	302	275	239	237	233	230	258	193	118	70	44	39	39	38
divorced			8	11	12	17	25	41	80	105	193	308	352	476	838
45-54															
single	689	896	942	1 001	1 144	1 265	1 433	1 531	1 575	1 607	1 569	1 437	1 357	1 336	1 344
married	8 810	8 536	8 440	8 467	8 335	8 216	8 042	7 916	7 867	7 897	8 027	8 058	8 089	8 011	7 731
widowed	501	568	605	519	503	494	492	498	452	346	203	146	133	125	125
divorced			13	13	18	25	33	55	106	151	200	359	421	528	800
55-64															
single			776	782	881	991	1 129	1 294	1 348	1 430	1 512	1 425	1 384	1 321	1 254
married			7 824	8 020	7 991	7 914	7 821	7 622	7 539	7 503	7 735	7 820	7 839	7 833	7 761
widowed			1 385	1 183	1 112	1 071	1 019	1 031	1 010	903	649	450	395	373	359
divorced			15	15	16	24	32	53	103	163	204	305	382	473	626
65-69															
single	575	715	688	732	749	880	968	1 117	1 244	1 339	1 384	1 347	1 371	1 376	1 301
married	7 747	7 451	6 700	6 991	7 166	7 156	7 151	6 971	6 819	6 752	6 969	7 349	7 411	7 449	7 457
widowed	1 678	1 834	2 599	2 264	2 072	1 947	1 855	1 868	1 850	1 763	1 445	1 067	922	814	755
divorced			12	13	13	16	27	44	86	145	203	246	296	360	487
70-74															
single			599	702	726	770	920	1 039	1 141	1 256	1 317	1 320	1 317	1 335	1 344
married			5 712	6 003	6 238	6 293	6 326	6 226	6 077	5 910	6 121	6 580	6 810	6 943	7 013
widowed			3 679	3 286	3 025	2 924	2 729	2 700	2 707	2 708	2 376	1 869	1 624	1 425	1 269
divorced			11	10	11	14	25	35	75	126	187	231	249	297	374
75 +															
single			458	583	668	693	789	900	958	1 117	1 156	1 205	1 220	1 231	1 243
married			4 329	4 287	4 539	4 650	4 560	4 427	4 342	4 180	4 310	4 707	4 941	5 205	5 444
widowed			5 206	5 122	4 783	4 645	4 638	4 639	4 654	4 621	4 388	3 900	3 633	3 342	3 054
divorced			7	9	10	11	14	24	47	82	146	189	206	222	259

Civil Status of Females by Age

Census	1800	1850	1870	1880	1890	1900	1910	1920	1930	1940	1950	1960	1965	1970	1975
Age group						(Civil status per 10.000 of respective age group)									
15 +															
single	3 621	4 039	4 031	4 115	4 010	4 124	4 208	4 264	4 227	3 713	2 842	2 654	2 597	2 512	2 596
married	5 011	4 652	4 717	4 706	4 786	4 682	4 636	4 599	4 680	5 179	5 962	6 034	6 017	5 967	5 615
widowed	1 368	1 309	1 240	1 166	1 189	1 174	1 130	1 092	1 011	978	981	1 010	1 047	1 106	1 194
divorced			11	13	15	20	27	45	82	130	215	302	339	416	596
15–19															
single	9 727	9 915	9 901	9 892	9 891	9 887	9 889	9 893	9 896	9 814	9 631	9 728	9 625	9 806	9 886
married	271	84	99	108	109	113	111	107	104	186	368	272	374	193	112
widowed	3	1	1												
divorced													1	1	2
20–24															
single	7 762	8 350	8 429	8 228	8 158	8 041	8 024	7 971	8 037	7 159	5 969	5 747	5 741	6 157	7 599
married	2 215	1 633	1 555	1 757	1 827	1 944	1 961	2 006	1 949	2 821	3 977	4 195	4 197	3 757	2 297
widowed	22	16				14	13		9	10	10	6	7	7	4
divorced			1	1	1	1	2	4	6	10	44	51	54	78	100
25–34															
single	3 899	4 073	4 409	4 256	4 365	4 737	4 339	4 309	4 329	3 330	2 109	1 610	1 567	1 840	2 553
married	5 909	5 731	5 420	5 606	5 503	5 494	5 530	5 513	5 529	6 518	7 650	8 099	8 125	7 744	6 748
widowed	192	196	164	132	124	122	114	148	88	72	60	44	42	43	40
divorced			7	6	8	11	16	30	55	80	181	246	266	373	659
35–44															
single	1 733	1 717	2 072	2 169	2 281	2 452	2 585	2 627	2 588	2 390	1 510	974	857	794	851
married	7 610	7 574	7 316	7 305	7 220	7 077	6 961	6 885	6 932	7 161	8 025	8 456	8 526	8 465	8 045
widowed	657	709	599	508	478	442	413	422	358	281	203	162	157	162	158
divorced			13	18	22	30	41	66	122	168	263	407	460	579	947
45–54															
single	1 170	1 232	1 476	1 587	1 763	1 877	2 071	2 219	2 247	2 220	1 912	1 233	952	800	730
married	7 388	7 393	7 055	7 093	7 024	6 972	6 858	6 722	6 716	6 737	7 164	7 809	8 022	8 063	7 887
widowed	1 442	1 375	1 448	1 297	1 185	1 112	1 018	973	885	811	633	511	494	491	497
divorced			22	22	28	39	53	86	152	232	291	447	532	646	886
55–64															
single			1 201	1 358	1 508	1 663	1 779	1 978	2 117	2 150	2 085	1 787	1 478	1 146	889
married			5 721	5 980	6 057	6 012	6 008	5 886	5 842	5 787	5 959	6 388	5 582	6 925	7 032
widowed			3 053	2 638	2 407	2 292	2 165	2 056	1 902	1 838	1 662	1 445	1 386	1 372	1 373
divorced			25	24	27	33	48	80	139	225	303	381	454	556	706
65–69															
single	847	1 074	1 034	1 221	1 371	1 518	1 660	1 772	1 981	2 095	2 109	1 999	1 871	1 632	1 270
married	5 196	4 889	4 124	4 487	4 838	4 829	4 826	4 776	4 758	4 658	4 685	4 941	5 073	5 323	5 580
widowed	3 957	4 027	4 825	4 268	3 769	3 626	3 477	3 390	3 151	3 066	2 928	2 718	2 675	2 611	2 597
divorced			18	24	22	27	38	62	111	181	278	342	381	434	553
70–74															
single			972	1 088	1 275	1 429	1 605	1 704	1 905	2 085	2 104	2 108	1 987	1 851	1 610
married			3 075	3 361	3 752	3 837	3 821	3 782	3 772	3 586	3 676	3 768	3 898	4 013	4 205
widowed			5 938	5 533	4 955	4 707	4 543	4 466	4 229	4 177	3 974	3 799	3 766	3 749	3 736
divorced			15	18	19	26	31	48	94	153	247	326	349	388	449
75 +															
single			854	942	1 129	1 294	1 445	1 592	1 690	1 899	2 070	2 112	2 107	2 042	1 929
married			1 752	1 811	2 083	2 283	2 182	2 064	2 116	2 035	1 993	2 062	2 026	2 047	2 057
widowed			7 385	7 230	6 767	6 404	6 350	6 314	6 133	5 964	5 761	5 561	5 562	5 581	5 657
divorced			9	16	21	19	24	31	61	103	177	264	305	330	358

Civil Status of Males by Age

Census	1860 a)	1870	1880	1888	1900	1910	1920	1930	1941	1950	1960	1970
Age group	(Civil status per 10.000 respective age group)											
15 +												
single	4 910	4 602	4 482	4 444	4 530	4 441	4 391	4 196	3 917	3 494	3 387	3 076
married	4 247	4 700	4 871	4 914	4 875	4 999	5 045	5 272	5 525	5 959	6 127	6 462
widowed	634	660	610	600	549	501	489	438	423	391	325	280
divorced	210	38	37	42	46	58	75	94	136	157	161	183
15-19												
single	9 985	9 976	9 979	9 989	9 990	9 990	9 991	9 994	9 996	9 993	9 985	9 973
married	11	22	20	11	10	10	8	6	4	7	14	27
widowed	1	1	1									
divorced	3											
20-24												
single	9 319	9 208	8 995	9 033	9 087	9 154	9 202	9 310	9 360	9 029	8 608	8 125
married	605	776	988	951	901	835	784	679	633	961	1 380	1 857
widowed	10	12	15	13	10	7	8	4	2	2	2	2
divorced	66	3	3	3	3	4	6	6	5	8	10	16
25-34												
single	5 709	5 371	4 777	4 768	4 628	4 516	4 728	4 589	4 709	4 145	3 498	2 780
married	3 966	4 506	5 089	5 104	5 265	5 368	5 140	5 295	5 175	5 731	6 382	7 068
widowed	90	101	110	102	82	81	81	46	28	17	12	9
divorced	235	22	24	26	25	35	51	70	87	106	108	143
35-44												
single	2 871	2 612	2 342	2 142	2 030	1 973	1 955	1 769	1 884	1 682	1 398	1 103
married	6 562	7 043	7 316	7 509	7 658	7 718	7 718	7 960	7 832	8 055	8 353	8 622
widowed	281	297	289	290	244	223	223	136	88	57	38	33
divorced	286	48	52	59	68	86	105	135	196	206	212	242
36-54												
single	1 895	1 921	1 760	1 688	1 586	1 522	1 456	1 377	1 343	1 301	1 181	979
married	7 060	7 365	7 565	7 623	7 743	7 852	7 940	8 110	8 179	8 282	8 434	8 630
widowed	717	645	611	608	580	511	468	356	252	171	126	103
divorced	328	68	63	80	91	115	136	158	227	246	259	288
55-64												
single	1 486	1 560	1 575	1 483	1 476	1 420	1 348	1 282	1 281	1 196	1 149	1 034
married	6 619	6 815	7 012	7 121	7 116	7 214	7 386	7 617	7 736	8 008	8 180	8 342
widowed	1 592	1 548	1 341	1 319	1 314	1 250	1 122	939	769	558	411	333
divorced	303	77	73	78	94	115	143	162	214	238	259	291
65-69												
single	1 188	1 374	1 380	1 402	1 363	1 364	1 237	1 251	1 206	1 222	1 091	1 052
married	5 689	5 783	5 955	6 126	6 116	6 261	6 465	6 646	6 932	7 231	7 665	7 912
widowed	2 870	2 785	2 605	2 402	2 431	2 278	2 173	1 963	1 671	1 329	1 014	782
divorced	254	57	60	70	90	96	124	140	190	218	229	253
70-74												
single	1 164	1 217	1 284	1 320	1 357	1 357	1 278	1 222	1 178	1 113	1 119	1 046
married	4 638	4 793	4 904	5 130	5 148	5 215	5 395	5 760	6 034	6 391	6 929	7 304
widowed	3 983	3 945	3 763	3 486	3 413	3 348	3 217	2 886	2 616	2 299	1 732	1 414
divorced	215	45	49	64	83	80	110	132	172	197	220	236
70 +												
single	1 111	1 033	1 192	1 134	1 212	1 198	1 152	1 117	1 085	1 053	1 016	950
married	3 273	3 338	3 436	3 522	3 652	3 678	3 850	4 047	4 306	4 632	5 104	5 645
widowed	5 471	5 591	5 335	5 295	5 081	5 056	4 929	4 727	4 483	4 157	3 708	3 219
divorced	145	39	38	49	55	69	69	110	126	157	173	186

a) 'divorced' including married couples not living together

Switzerland

Civil Status of Females by Age

Census	1860 a)	1870	1880	1888	1900	1910	1920	1930	1941	1950	1960	1970
Age group	(Civil status per 10.000 of respective age group)											
15 +												
single	4 529	4 274	4 073	4 094	4 098	3 994	4 185	4 026	3 640	3 306	3 038	2 642
married	4 102	4 471	4 622	4 563	4 593	4 720	4 546	4 730	5 026	5 335	5 597	5 955
widowed	1 112	1 202	1 244	1 270	1 230	1 191	1 152	1 098	1 133	1 121	1 098	1 100
divorced	256	55	61	74	79	95	117	146	200	238	267	304
15-19												
single	9 886	9 871	9 855	9 894	9 889	9 889	9 927	9 930	9 916	9 877	9 813	9 628
married	101	125	144	105	111	110	72	69	83	122	186	371
widowed	3	3	1	1		1	1					1
divorced	10	1									1	1
20-24												
single	8 265	8 059	7 661	7 877	7 777	7 761	8 185	8 240	7 986	7 387	6 531	5 482
married	1 572	1 903	2 296	2 095	2 199	2 211	1 782	1 734	1 988	2 575	3 424	4 451
widowed	24	31	32	20	17	18	20	10	7	8	7	8
divorced	139	6	11	8	7	10	14	17	19	30	37	58
25-34												
single	4 676	4 348	3 659	3 863	3 710	3 484	4 049	3 941	3 634	3 066	2 323	1 776
married	4 879	5 422	6 078	5 899	6 090	6 313	5 683	5 862	6 160	6 706	7 443	7 949
widowed	156	189	212	183	147	135	182	90	65	62	47	43
divorced	288	41	51	56	53	68	86	108	140	166	187	232
35-44												
single	2 615	2 540	2 167	2 056	2 087	2 021	2 096	2 257	2 262	1 916	1 526	1 135
married	6 433	6 743	7 069	7 133	7 206	7 326	7 204	7 142	7 191	7 561	7 940	8 312
widowed	591	639	679	702	591	518	533	402	293	231	199	178
divorced	362	78	85	109	116	136	168	199	255	293	335	375
45-54												
single	1 918	2 036	1 941	1 828	1 738	1 780	1 772	1 793	1 965	1 920	1 594	1 260
married	6 121	6 293	6 351	6 446	6 475	6 592	6 731	6 807	6 781	6 986	7 373	7 688
widowed	1 567	1 570	1 602	1 603	1 642	1 453	1 292	1 151	943	743	629	592
divorced	394	101	106	123	145	175	204	249	311	351	403	461
55-64												
single	1 727	1 754	1 848	1 797	1 684	1 666	1 748	1 704	1 751	1 874	1 808	1 488
married	4 860	4 990	4 927	4 945	4 979	4 927	5 197	5 462	5 579	5 752	6 086	6 452
widowed	3 095	3 166	3 126	3 134	3 195	3 238	2 851	2 592	2 357	2 020	1 717	1 611
divorced	318	89	99	124	142	169	204	241	314	354	390	449
65-69												
single	1 589	1 648	1 693	1 815	1 708	1 609	1 664	1 749	1 679	1 781	1 851	1 737
married	3 495	3 507	3 432	3 415	3 415	3 399	3 484	3 828	4 091	4 290	4 597	4 931
widowed	4 683	4 773	4 796	4 655	4 754	4 854	4 681	4 210	3 941	3 598	3 186	2 921
divorced	233	72	79	114	123	138	171	213	290	331	367	411
70-74												
single	1 640	1 616	1 702	1 721	1 824	1 694	1 685	1 750	1 716	1 667	1 826	1 804
married	2 475	2 529	2 403	2 377	2 375	2 344	2 365	2 653	2 884	3 193	3 362	3 690
widowed	5 721	5 806	5 829	5 827	5 694	5 846	5 805	5 410	5 164	4 839	4 466	4 132
divorced	163	49	66	76	107	116	146	186	236	301	347	374
75 +												
single	1 551	1 515	1 585	1 660	1 761	1 722	1 686	1 706	1 763	1 727	1 749	1 827
married	1 342	1 347	1 362	1 234	1 243	1 202	1 189	1 247	1 429	1 588	1 731	1 856
widowed	7 000	7 089	6 999	7 029	6 910	6 976	7 002	6 906	6 607	6 441	6 230	5 982
divorced	107	48	55	77	86	100	123	141	201	244	290	335

a) 'divorced' including married couples not living together

England and Wales

Civil Status of Males by Age

Census	1851	1861	1871	1881	1891	1901	1911	1921	1931	1951	1961	1966	1971
Age group	(Civil status per 10.000 of respective age group)												
15 +													
single	4 112	3 838	3 884	3 918	4 058	4 111	4 031	3 647	3 562	2 647	2 556	2 576	2 454
married	5 290	5 539	5 547	5 532	5 402	5 363	5 452	5 844	5 927	6 843	6 998	6 962	7 064
widowed	598	624	569	550	540	526	517	502	502	460	390	392	482
divorced								7	9	49	56	70	
15–19													
single	9 960	9 950	9 944	9 953	9 962	9 972	9 980	9 959	9 972	9 949	9 895	9 829	9 716
married	40	50	55	46	38	28	19	40	28	50	105	171	283
widowed			1	1									1
divorced													
20–24													
single	7 970	7 750	7 787	7 771	8 056	3 262	8 572	8 221	8 612	7 621	6 900	6 693	6 006
married	2 000	2 230	2 188	2 207	1 927	1 726	1 418	1 767	1 381	2 372	3 095	3 299	3 973
widowed	30	20	25	22	17	13	10	11	7	4	2	1	21
divorced								1		3	4	6	
25–34													
single	3 560	3 190	3 159	3 170	3 426	3 589	3 855	3 411	3 523	2 721	2 335	2 046	1 907
married	6 270	6 660	6 683	6 685	6 455	6 312	6 063	6 494	6 403	7 197	7 609	7 873	7 958
widowed	170	150	157	145	120	99	82	86	65	29	13	13	136
divorced								9	9	53	43	68	
35–44													
single	1 620	1 420	1 370	1 378	1 466	1 584	1 687	1 501	1 254	1 205	1 202	1 149	1 074
married	7 950	8 210	8 258	8 257	8 189	8 114	8 058	8 273	8 546	8 617	8 657	8 694	8 719
widowed	430	370	372	365	345	302	254	214	182	86	54	52	207
divorced								11	18	92	87	105	
44–54													
single	1 150	740	973	963	999	1 104	1 211	1 199	1 084	925	922	882	921
married	8 020	8 210	8 320	8 322	8 273	8 187	8 174	8 309	8 473	8 679	8 810	8 832	8 764
widowed	830	1 050	707	715	728	709	615	483	427	237	171	171	315
divorced								8	16	69	97	115	
55–64													
single	980	900	894	829	844	887	987	1 037	1 024	781	828	788	795
married	7 480	7 610	7 715	7 788	7 710	7 639	7 626	7 827	7 952	8 503	8 609	8 641	8 620
widowed	1 540	1 490	1 391	1 384	1 446	1 475	1 388	1 128	1 014	676	493	481	586
divorced								7	10	41	69	90	
65–69													
single	850	840	833			799	877	939	961	839	733	703	758
married	6 260	6 270	6 792			6 688	6 650	6 885	7 077	7 705	8 116	8 115	8 147
widowed	2 890	2 890	2 375			2 513	2 473	2 170	1 954	1 429	1 111	1 124	1 095
divorced								6	9	27	39	58	
70–74													
single			800	764	731	742	802	861	852	848	761	629	675
married			5 816	5 873	5 904	5 760	5 768	5 992	6 208	6 821	7 340	7 513	7 511
widowed			3 384	3 363	3 365	3 498	3 430	3 141	2 932	2 312	1 872	1 817	1 814
divorced								6	7	18	27	42	
75 +													
single	742	740	705			653	678	724	705	779	778	642	617
married	4 378	4 199	4 253			4 259	4 228	4 486	4 542	5 079	5 453	5 593	5 784
widowed	4 880	5 061	5 043			5 088	5 094	4 786	4 747	4 128	3 754	3 743	3 599
divorced								4	6	14	15	22	

England and Wales

Civil Status of Females by Age

Census	1851	1861	1871	1881	1891	1901	1911	1921	1931	1951	1961	1966	1971
Age group	(Civil status per 10.000 of respective age group)												
15 +													
single	3 854	3 737	3 614	3 674	3 867	3 954	3 899	3 683	3 540	2 477	2 190	2 152	1 950
married	5 041	5 134	5 223	5 164	4 992	4 964	5 059	5 200	5 341	6 162	6 363	6 363	6 466
widowed	1 104	1 129	1 163	1 162	1 142	1 082	1 041	1 111	1 107	1 288	1 356	1 380	1 584
divorced								6	12	72	91	105	
15–19													
single	9 750	9 700	9 682	9 745	9 805	9 844	9 880	9 823	9 819	9 558	9 344	9 205	8 918
married	250	300	316	253	194	155	120	175	180	441	656	794	1 079
widowed			3	2	1	1	1	1		1		1	3
divorced													
20–24													
single	6 870	6 640	6 517	6 654	7 011	7 259	7 570	7 264	7 419	5 179	4 204	4 127	3 689
married	3 080	3 310	3 432	3 306	2 962	2 717	2 415	2 700	2 568	4 798	5 774	5 839	6 241
widowed		50	51	40	27	23	15	34	12	11	9	9	70
divorced								2	1	12	13	25	
25–34													
single	3 290	3 246	2 946	2 922	3 260	3 398	3 553	3 340	3 300	1 824	1 325	1 117	1 022
married	6 430	6 457	6 757	6 815	6 526	6 430	6 316	6 342	6 577	7 975	8 555	8 728	8 725
widowed	280	298	297	264	214	172	131	310	110	96	44	43	253
divorced								8	13	105	76	112	
35–44													
single	1 630	1 590	1 556	1 535	1 644	1 853	1 963	1 942	1 940	1 375	974	836	716
married	7 570	7 620	7 624	7 650	7 607	7 508	7 531	7 427	7 522	8 203	8 673	8 823	8 874
widowed	800	790	820	815	749	639	506	622	515	291	200	184	409
divorced								9	23	131	154	157	
45–54													
single	1 220	1 190	1 205	1 193	1 241	1 362	1 578	1 639	1 636	1 510	1 138	927	804
married	7 160	7 200	7 162	7 108	7 059	7 051	7 088	7 211	7 204	7 592	8 029	8 233	8 340
widowed	1 620	1 610	1 633	1 699	1 700	1 586	1 334	1 143	1 142	800	673	662	856
divorced								7	18	98	160	179	
55–64													
single	1 152	1 090	1 090	1 089	1 102	1 169	1 320	1 531	1 563	1 554	1 408	1 258	1 055
married	5 888	5 890	5 896	5 808	5 726	5 693	5 839	5 997	6 190	6 238	6 607	6 811	6 944
widowed	2 960	3 020	3 014	3 103	3 172	3 138	2 841	2 466	2 236	2 153	1 874	1 792	2 001
divorced								5	10	55	111	139	
65–69													
single			1 043			1 105	1 201	1 392	1 584	1 542	1 523	1 407	1 324
married			4 414			4 169	4 243	4 412	4 607	4 769	4 927	5 067	5 191
widowed	1 110	1 051	4 543			4 726	4 556	4 192	3 803	3 660	3 487	3 446	3 485
divorced	4 000	4 000						4	6	30	63	80	
70–74													
single	4 890	4 950	1 037	1 036	1 075	1 122	1 226	1 394	1 563	1 573	1 547	1 500	1 385
married			3 266	3 262	3 186	3 010	3 070	3 252	3 418	3 683	3 667	3 758	3 779
widowed			5 697	5 702	5 739	5 868	5 705	5 351	5 014	4 725	4 747	4 685	4 836
divorced									3	5	19	39	57
75 +													
single	1 087	1 005	958			1 115	1 211	1 322	1 468	1 649	1 597	1 541	1 536
married	1 929	1 854	1 868			1 624	1 612	1 714	1 752	2 015	1 905	1 892	1 866
widowed	6 984	7 141	7 174			7 261	7 177	6 963	6 778	6 326	6 481	6 542	6 599
divorced								2	3	10	17	25	

Scotland

Civil Status of Males by Age

Census	1851	1861	1871	1881	1891	1901	1911	1921	1931	1951	1961	1966	1971
Age group	(Civil status per 10.000 of respective age group)												
15 +													
single	4 634	4 425	4 441	4 521	4 627	4 709	4 613	4 306	4 185	3 212	2 897	2 850	2 699
married	4 818	5 041	5 019	4 946	4 847	4 778	4 842	5 137	5 241	6 194	6 608	6 663	6 797
widowed	549	534	540	533	526	513	538	547	562	537	458	448	504
divorced								7	9	31		39	
Unknown							7	3	4	26			
15-19													
single	9 958	9 965	9 966	9 972	9 979	9 975	9 978	9 953	9 961	9 961	9 884	9 808	9 683
married	41	34	34	28	21	25	21	46	38	39	116	191	316
widowed		1											1
divorced													
20-24													
single	8 343	8 326	8 416	8 480	8 664	8 736	8 836	8 533	8 815	7 967	7 041	6 781	5 845
married	1 635	1 650	1 564	1 501	1 320	1 253	1 146	1 452	1 172	1 981	2 954	3 213	4 130
widowed	22	23	20	19	15	11	10	11	9	4	2	2	25
divorced								1	1	2	3	3	
25-34													
single	4 250	3 854	3 937	4 005	4 333	4 520	4 741	4 328	4 443	3 337	2 483	2 112	1 894
married	5 590	6 002	5 905	5 838	5 532	5 364	5 146	5 564	5 469	6 558	7 476	7 843	8 001
widowed	160	144	158	157	135	116	104	98	77	41	15	14	105
divorced								8	7	33	26	32	
35-44													
single	2 054	1 817	1 795	1 785	1 946	2 112	2 291	2 139	1 858	1 582	1 434	1 287	1 156
married	7 520	7 820	7 824	7 834	7 682	7 551	7 387	7 576	7 885	8 218	8 440	8 594	8 676
widowed	427	362	381	381	372	338	316	271	237	125	71	60	167
divorced								11	17	57	55	59	
45-54													
single	1 466	1 353	1 319	1 275	1 336	1 462	1 603	1 685	1 618	1 300	1 224	1 137	1 128
married	7 713	7 918	7 956	7 996	7 928	7 795	7 686	7 714	7 830	8 315	8 481	8 581	8 558
widowed	821	729	724	729	736	743	704	588	531	320	229	218	314
divorced								9	15	46	66	63	
55-64													
single	1 197	1 262	1 212	1 117	1 147	1 210	1 280	1 424	1 500	1 176	1 204	1 125	1 093
married	7 357	7 390	7 444	7 503	7 461	7 331	7 281	7 263	7 313	7 906	8 100	8 207	8 227
widowed	1 446	1 348	1 344	1 380	1 391	1 459	1 433	1 302	1 172	867	647	609	680
divorced								8	11	30	49	59	
65-69													
single	1 015	1 125	1 190	1 095	1 058	1 072	1 167	1 224	1 363	1 302	1 122	1 096	1 130
married	6 749	6 684	6 729	6 700	6 712	6 551	6 387	6 504	6 493	6 880	7 419	7 498	7 565
widowed	2 237	2 191	2 081	2 205	2 230	2 377	2 436	2 261	2 128	1 767	1 430	1 369	1 305
divorced								7	8	18	29	37	
70-74													
single	1 004	1 104	1 205	1 079	1 059	1 069	1 110	1 141	1 226	1 298	1 167	973	1 069
married	6 030	6 004	5 942	5 881	5 878	5 732	5 595	5 605	5 731	5 912	6 541	6 795	6 808
widowed	2 966	2 892	2 853	3 040	3 063	3 199	3 285	3 244	3 026	2 727	2 270	2 211	2 123
divorced								5	9	15	22	21	
75 +													
single	837	917	1 069	1 051	1 012	1 004	1 000	944	1 055	1 132	1 219	1 052	1 022
married	4 844	4 707	4 661	4 510	4 582	4 330	4 228	4 163	4 209	4 343	4 597	4 789	4 993
widowed	4 318	4 376	4 271	4 440	4 405	4 667	4 759	4 886	4 719	4 456	4 171	4 145	3 984
divorced								2	7	9	9	15	

Scotland

Civil Status of Females by Age

Census	1851	1861	1871	1881	1891	1901	1911	1921	1931	1951	1961	1966	1971
Age group	(Civil status per 10.000 of respective age group)												
15 +													
single	4 554	4 428	4 323	4 303	4 422	4 447	4 401	4 239	4 147	3 157	2 555	2 589	2 356
married	4 189	4 305	4 388	4 441	4 385	4 428	4 518	4 639	4 751	5 551	5 919	5 968	6 089
widowed	1 258	1 267	1 289	1 256	1 193	1 125	1 075	1 113	1 088	1 220	1 312	1 370	1 555
divorced								7	12	48	66	73	
Unknown							6	3	3	24			
15-19													
single	9 787	9 787	9 782	9 817	9 876	9 835	9 854	9 788	9 772	9 647	9 419	9 318	9 008
married	209	211	216	182	124	165	143	210	227	352	580	679	987
widowed	3	2	2	1	1		1	1	1			1	5
divorced												1	
20-24													
single	7 484	7 409	7 379	7 351	7 642	7 643	7 813	7 541	7 704	6 010	4 816	4 599	3 908
married	2 468	2 548	2 577	2 615	2 333	2 337	2 162	2 420	2 278	3 945	5 162	5 372	6 020
widowed	48	42	44	34	25	21	18	35	13	12	10	10	72
divorced								2	2	8	12	19	
25-34													
single	3 978	3 915	3 773	3 663	4 019	4 038	4 213	4 049	4 127	2 417	1 669	1 370	1 150
married	5 674	5 771	5 911	6 069	5 776	5 791	5 650	5 649	5 743	7 383	8 224	8 499	8 623
widowed	348	313	316	268	205	171	132	289	115	111	53	57	228
divorced								10	13	72	54	74	
35-44													
single	2 366	2 372	2 351	2 198	2 240	2 388	2 427	2 431	2 471	1 785	1 338	1 188	948
married	6 618	6 675	6 721	6 915	7 003	6 956	7 036	6 936	6 978	7 780	8 278	8 466	8 646
widowed	1 016	953	928	888	757	656	533	617	526	343	259	230	406
divorced								13	22	79	124	116	
45-54													
single	2 078	2 014	2 004	1 935	1 867	1 917	2 081	2 069	2 151	2 028	1 545	1 312	1 158
married	5 919	6 095	6 115	6 211	6 380	6 454	6 527	6 719	6 698	6 955	7 515	7 749	7 874
widowed	2 002	1 891	1 881	1 854	1 753	1 629	1 388	1 201	1 130	933	832	819	968
divorced								9	18	65	108	120	
55-64													
single	2 078	2 049	1 977	1 943	1 862	1 807	1 887	2 046	2 066	2 082	1 973	1 769	1 502
married	4 514	4 615	4 763	4 780	4 971	5 002	5 263	5 414	5 656	5 563	5 839	6 075	6 254
widowed	3 409	3 336	3 260	3 277	3 167	3 191	2 846	2 531	2 263	2 282	2 114	2 071	2 244
divorced								7	13	42	74	86	
65-69													
single	2 045	2 074	2 006	1 955	1 897	1 844	1 866	1 978	2 157	2 143	2 128	2 014	1 925
married	3 363	3 353	3 489	3 492	3 611	3 563	3 691	3 883	4 099	4 181	4 184	4 248	4 360
widowed	4 591	4 572	4 505	4 553	4 491	4 593	4 438	4 130	3 733	3 612	3 643	3 672	3 715
divorced								6	8	22	45	67	
70-74													
single	2 106	2 141	2 094	2 051	2 002	1 966	1 959	1 998	2 182	2 174	2 197	2 098	2 054
married	2 503	2 441	2 509	2 520	2 595	2 499	2 592	2 780	2 970	3 188	3 046	3 107	3 071
widowed	5 391	5 418	5 397	5 429	5 403	5 535	5 439	5 214	4 835	4 569	4 723	4 755	4 876
divorced								4	8	15	34	40	
75 +													
single	2 083	2 058	2 080	2 016	1 993	2 026	2 045	1 931	2 101	2 202	2 301	2 246	2 264
married	1 330	1 338	1 357	1 380	1 463	1 260	1 306	1 335	1 449	1 643	1 551	1 544	1 481
widowed	6 587	6 604	6 563	6 603	6 544	6 714	6 638	6 730	6 440	6 070	6 131	6 196	6 255
divorced								2	4	10	16	13	

Ireland and Northern Ireland

Civil Status of Males by Age

Census	1871	1881	1891	1901	1911	1926	1937	1951	1961	1966	1971
Age group					(Civil status per 10.000 of respective age group)						
15 +											
single	4 785	5 080	5 425	5 593	5 552	4 889	4 755	4 205	3 821	3 631	3 509
married	4 633	4 322	3 981	3 825	3 851	4 527	4 684	5 298	5 760	5 977	6 113
widowed	582	595	594	582	597	583	561	487	408	380	357
divorced								10	11	12	20
15–19											
single	9 977	9 986	9 988	9 989	9 991	9 979	9 981	9 967	9 935	9 903	9 869
married	23	14	12	11	9	21	19	33	65	97	131
widowed											
divorced											
20–24											
single	9 128	9 275	9 430	9 484	9 513	9 032	8 978	8 702	7 900	7 456	7 134
married	861	713	563	508	481	956	1 017	1 294	2 099	2 542	2 862
widowed	11	12	8	8	6	11	5	3	1	1	2
divorced						1				1	2
25–34											
single	5 577	6 000	6 435	6 796	7 008	5 277	5 526	4 625	3 681	2 936	2 631
married	4 339	3 899	3 469	3 127	2 922	4 626	4 406	5 336	6 301	7 045	7 336
widowed	83	102	96	76	69	97	68	29	11	9	11
divorced								10	7	10	22
35–44											
single	2 573	2 716	3 256	3 681	4 149	3 068	2 905	2 477	2 190	1 923	1 656
married	7 167	6 972	6 413	6 018	5 603	6 644	6 865	7 387	7 728	8 004	8 259
widowed	259	313	332	301	248	287	231	116	61	54	49
divorced								20	21	18	36
45–54											
single	1 701	1 708	1 998	2 378	2 726	2 391	2 264	1 998	1 840	1 759	1 680
married	7 685	7 622	7 284	6 901	6 703	7 016	7 221	7 671	7 928	8 026	8 106
widowed	613	670	718	721	571	594	515	313	212	192	179
divorced								17	19	23	35
55–64											
single	1 330	1 421	1 610	1 864	2 232	2 118	2 145	1 902	1 806	1 753	1 675
married	7 419	7 253	7 061	6 736	6 650	6 760	6 805	7 309	7 578	7 705	7 794
widowed	1 251	1 326	1 329	1 400	1 118	1 123	1 050	781	601	526	509
divorced								8	16	16	21
65–69											
single	1 214	1 275	1 558			2 122	2 108	2 055	1 894	1 823	1 788
married	6 805	6 642	6 436			5 999	6 141	6 440	6 904	7 005	7 169
widowed	1 980	2 083	2 007	1 704	1 901	1 879	1 751	1 498	1 193	1 153	1 019
divorced				5 938	5 863	1		5	10	18	24
70–74				2 357	2 233						
single	1 158	1 215	1 416			2 132	2 118	2 071	1 940	1 849	1 756
married	5 940	6 007	5 839			5 261	5 341	5 670	6 138	6 384	6 534
widowed	2 902	2 778	2 744			2 607	2 541	2 252	1 915	1 756	1 693
divorced								7	7	11	17
75 +											
single	1 115	1 104	1 284	1 504	1 571	1 767	1 866	1 791	1 843	1 793	1 736
married	4 646	4 926	4 693	4 556	4 528	4 094	4 201	4 413	4 613	4 863	5 000
widowed	4 240	3 970	4 024	3 940	3 901	4 139	3 933	3 792	3 540	3 338	3 257
divorced								3	4	6	7

(Note: for 1901 and 1911, the 65–69 and 70–74 age groups are combined by a brace, with single = 1 704 / 1 901, married = 5 938 / 5 863, widowed = 2 357 / 2 233.)

Ireland and Northern Ireland

Civil Status of Females by Age

Census	1871	1881	1891	1901	1911	1926	1937	1951	1961	1966	1971
Age group	(Civil status per 10.000 of respective age group)										
15+											
single	4 238	4 479	4 750	4 966	4 826	4 623	4 464	3 814	3 405	3 184	2 961
married	4 329	4 073	3 830	3 709	3 860	4 221	4 420	5 024	5 373	5 574	5 726
widowed	1 433	1 447	1 420	1 325	1 314	1 155	1 115	1 145	1 200	1 218	1 259
divorced								16	22	24	35
15–19											
single	9 808	9 881	9 910	9 924	9 937	9 829	9 808	9 767	9 667	9 557	9 508
married	190	117	89	74	63	169	192	232	333	442	491
widowed		2	1	2		1				1	1
divorced											
20–24											
single	7 813	8 210	8 462	8 644	8 654	7 976	7 720	7 081	6 132	5 657	5 333
married	2 154	1 759	1 514	1 333	1 333	2 009	2 266	2 909	3 860	4 336	4 653
widowed	34	31	25	23	13	15	14	8	5	6	8
divorced								2	3	1	6
25–34											
single	4 036	4 309	4 889	5 234	5 374	4 539	4 659	3 401	2 583	2 032	1 736
married	5 706	5 404	4 874	4 564	4 486	5 302	5 241	6 476	7 355	7 907	8 183
widowed	258	286	237	202	139	159	100	95	46	42	42
divorced								27	16	19	39
35–44											
single	2 166	2 141	2 551	2 945	3 118	2 927	2 879	2 333	1 826	1 579	1 324
married	6 933	6 868	6 535	6 265	6 302	6 477	6 669	7 323	7 889	8 167	8 420
widowed	901	991	914	789	581	596	452	317	238	216	203
divorced								27	47	38	53
45–54											
single	1 646	1 714	1 852	2 195	2 488	2 509	2 507	2 361	1 966	1 687	1 544
married	6 356	6 214	6 134	5 892	6 070	6 209	6 332	6 691	7 197	7 486	7 658
widowed	1 998	2 072	2 014	1 913	1 442	1 282	1 161	923	798	779	732
divorced								25	39	47	66
55–64											
single	1 437	1 492	1 729	1 904	2 222	2 584	2 447	2 427	2 320	2 121	1 895
married	4 997	4 780	4 689	4 648	5 120	4 981	5 227	5 386	5 612	5 874	6 069
widowed	3 566	3 728	3 582	3 448	2 658	2 435	2 326	2 175	2 044	1 969	1 991
divorced								11	25	35	44
65–69											
single	1 458	1 381	1 665			2 708	2 599	2 479	2 374	2 352	2 289
married	4 087	3 978	3 682			3 698	3 945	4 049	4 126	4 189	4 322
widowed	4 455	4 642	4 654	1 925	2 005	3 594	3 457	3 465	3 487	3 441	3 357
divorced				3 075	3 509			7	13	18	31
70–74				5 002	4 485						
single	1 497	1 408	1 620			2 657	2 741	2 516	2 483	2 324	2 357
married	2 655	2 853	2 614			2 662	2 812	3 041	3 017	3 186	3 108
widowed	5 847	5 739	5 766			4 681	4 447	4 438	4 493	4 480	4 518
divorced								4	7	10	17
75 +											
single	1 486	1 444	1 537	1 869	2 053	2 373	2 625	2 474	2 424	2 405	2 361
married	1 469	1 677	1 597	1 443	1 672	1 451	1 591	1 745	1 535	1 676	1 610
widowed	7 045	6 879	6 866	6 688	6 274	6 176	5 784	5 778	6 037	5 913	6 023
divorced								2	3	6	7

VII

Urbanization and Housing

Chapter 3

CITIES AND URBANIZATION

This chapter contains data on the growth of cities and the process of urbanization. Urban growth is not the same as urbanization. Cities have a history of almost ten thousand years, whereas urbanization is a more recent phenomenon. Urbanization implies the relative growth of the urban population, i.e. the increase in the proportion of the total population of an area living in cities. In this simple ecological sense, urban growth can occur without urbanization, if the rest of the population increases at the same or a faster rate; and urbanization may occur without urban growth, if there is a faster decline of the rural population (as happened in Ireland in the last century).

Urban growth may be the result of one or more of four factors: (1) the natural increase of the urban population, (2) the net migration into cities, (3) the annexation of inhabited areas or communities adjacent to existing cities, (4) the transformation of non-urban communities into cities. How can one distinguish cities from non-urban communities? The easiest way, in principle, is to define the difference in terms of size and density. Urban growth then may simply mean that during a given interval some communities pass a statistical threshold.

Even if one applies only a numerical standard, however, one has to solve the problem of how to define the boundaries of a community or city. There are in principle two alternative solutions. One is to define the boundaries in terms of the economic interdependence and social interrelations of a population in a territory, using indicators of processes of exchange, communication and mobility. This is obviously difficult; and it is not feasible for a data set covering more than a dozen countries and one and a half centuries. The second alternative is to simply accept the boundaries of incorporated communities which underlie the official statistics. This has been done here.

One must be aware, however, that these official boundaries frequently do not correspond with the 'real boundaries' of communities. Three typical cases can be distinguished. The first refers to local communities which as administrative units embrace a number of separate settlements. The average number of such settlements varies greatly between and even within countries, but sometimes we know at least the size of the central settlement. This problem arises mainly with the smaller communities, and one may reasonably assume that from 20,000 and more inhabitants, communities are largely identical with the central settlement. We have therefore used this criterion (in addition to 100,000 and more inhabitants) in our comparative tables at the beginning of the chapter, which show the relative increase of the urban population across Europe.

The second case where official and 'real' boundaries do not correspond is the case of suburbanization. Many suburbs which have outgrown the boundaries of the city to which they belong, have been incorporated with a considerable time lag only, and then this incorporation produces an artificial jump in the rate of urbanization. To some extent, this can be seen from the tables which give population figures for individual cities.

The third case, the development of metropolitan areas, poses more fundamental problems. One approach to the study of cities lies in the analysis of the distribution of activities within a territory. From this perspective, cities consist of nodes with a higher density and specialization of activities, and tributary areas. Increasing urbanization produces a growing interrelatedness of urban communities and leads to the development of new urban systems at a higher level: the development of metropolitan areas. With our simple data this complex process cannot be measured. Any attempt to do so would require detailed studies which are available for a few countries and periods only.

The boundary problems in a quantitative study of urbanization are not merely problems of relatively arbitrary statistical classifications, but reflect historical changes. The medieval town was an organism in itself, clearly separated from the rural areas. Until the nineteenth century, the European cities remained separate entities, even when the walls had been torn down. However, this changed with the process of industrialization. Industrial urbanization differs from other forms of urbanization not only in quantity but also in quality. The city increasingly lost its specific social form; networks of interaction and communication became more diffused; and the urban-rural differences in the way of life tended to become less profound. For all these reasons urbanization rates have lost much of their former significance, at least since World War II.

Even if cities as single units have changed their character, the networks of cities still exhibit characteristics which they acquired centuries ago. We therefore present two comparative tables at the beginning with measures of the monocephality or polycephality of the city networks: the population of the capital as a percentage of the total population and as a percentage of the five biggest cities including the capital. Together with the other two comparative tables with measures of the degree of urbanization, they depict the basic outline of the urban structure of a country.

The comparative tables are followed by national tables, two for each country. First, population shares by size of locality are given in tabular and graphical form. Localities or communities are usually classified according to the following categories (number of inhabitants): 0—2,000, 2,000—5,000, 5,000—20,000, 20,000—100,000, 100,000—1,000,000, 1,000,000 and over. The second table contains population figures for the major cities of each country. For the majority of countries, the criterion of 20,000 inhabitants in 1910 has been chosen for selecting the cities. For the Austrian Empire, France, Germany, Great Britain and Italy a different criterion has been utilized in order to reduce the number of cities.

U r b a n i z a t i o n

Distribution of total population by size of locality (number of inhabitants)
in 1,000s and as % of total population

Year	0–2,000	2–5,000		5–10,000		10–20,000		20–100,000		100–1,000,000		1,000,000+		Year
	%	1,000	%	1,000	%	1,000	%	1,000	%	1,000	%	1,000	%	
1837						162	1.0	216	1.3	439	2.7			1837
1843	80.7	1 815	10.6	532	3.1	264	1.5	236	1.3	485	2.8			1843
1851	77.2	2 343	13.3	498	2.8	317	1.8	332	1.8	550	3.1			1851
1857								375	2.0	619	3.3			1857
1869						918	4.5	577	2.8	765	3.7			1869
1880	70.6	2 805	12.6	912	4.1	1 065	4.8	794	3.5	978	4.4			1880
1890	68.0	3 014	12.6	967	4.0	908	3.8	900	3.7	543	2.2	1 365	5.7	1890
1900	62.0	3 876	14.8	1 340	5.1	1 003	3.8	1 356	5.1	743	2.8	1 675	6.4	1900
1910	57.2	4 523	15.8	1 688	5.9	1 217	4.2	1 815	6.3	1 020	3.5	2 032	7.1	1910

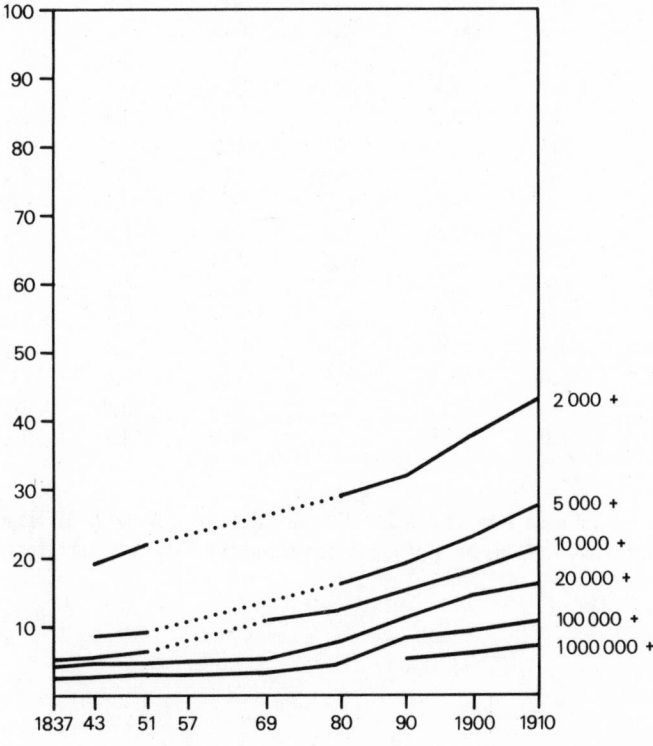

Cumulative percent distribution of population
by size of locality

249

Growth of Cities (a)

	1837	1843	1851	1857	1869	1880	1890	1900	1910
Vienna	333.6	373.2	431.1	476.2	607.5	705.7	1.364.5	1.675.0	2.031.5
					(880.1)	(1.136.7)	(1.399.9)	(1.728.7)	(2.031.5)
Prague	105.5	111.7	118.4	142.6	157.7	162.3	182.5	201.6	223.7
Lemberg	58.7	66.0	68.3	70.8	87.1	109.7	127.9	159.9	206.1
Trieste	52.6	54.7	63.9		70.3	74.5	120.3	134.1	161.0
Cracow			50.3	41.1	49.8	60.7	74.6	91.3	151.9
Graz	43.8	47.5	55.4	63.2	81.1	97.8	112.1	138.1	151.8
Brno	37.2	41.4	47.4	58.8	73.8	82.7	94.5	109.3	125.7
Cernowitz	10.7	12.6	20.5	26.3	33.9	45.6	54.2	67.6	87.1
Pilsen	8.9	9.8	11.5	14.3	23.7	38.9	50.2	68.1	80.3
Kgl. Weinberge					5.6	14.6	34.5	52.5	77.1
Zizkow					4.3	21.2	41.2	59.3	72.2
Linz	23.4	26.1	26.6	27.6	30.5	36.1	43.3	58.8	67.8
Pola				3.2	10.5	25.2	31.6	36.2	58.6
Przemysl	8.7	10.3	8.6	9.8	15.2	22.0	35.2	46.3	54.1
Innsbruck	10.8	11.8	13.1	14.2	16.3	19.1	23.3	26.9	53.2
Smichov		4.3	5.3	9.1	15.4	24.9	32.6	47.1	51.8
Budweis	7.6	10.0	12.3	14.8	17.4	23.8	28.5	39.3	44.5
Kolomea	8.7	10.5	13.1	14.8	17.7	23.1	30.2	34.2	42.7
Laibach	14.9	15.8	17.3	20.7	22.6	26.3	30.5	36.5	41.7
Außig	2.0	2.4	3.1	7.0	10.9	16.5	23.6	29.1	39.3
Mährisch-Ostrau				4.1	6.9	13.4	19.2	30.1	36.8
Tarnow	4.7	6.6	7.4	8.5	21.8	24.6	27.6	31.7	36.7
Reichenberg	12.4	12.1	13.1	18.9	22.4	28.1	30.9	34.1	36.4
Salzburg	12.1	14.5	17.0	17.3	20.3	25.0	27.2	33.1	36.2
Drohobyez	7.9	11.9	12.0	11.3	16.9	18.2	17.9	19.4	34.7
Tarnopol	13.3	16.2	16.5	16.5	20.1	25.8	27.4	30.4	33.9
Stanislav	10.5	11.7	10.9	13.0	14.5	18.6	22.4	30.4	33.3
Wiener Neustadt	10.3	10.3	12.8	14.5	19.2	23.8	25.0	28.7	32.9
Proßnitz	10.8	8.5	11.4	12.5	15.8	18.4	21.2	25.5	31.0
Görz	9.4	8.1	10.9	13.3	16.7	20.9	21.8	25.4	31.0
Stryj	6.5	7.8	7.8	9.2	9.9	12.6	16.5	23.2	30.9
Troppau	9.9	12.6	10.1	13.9	16.6	20.6	22.9	26.7	30.8
Trent	12.6	9.0	8.9	14.3	17.1	19.6	21.5	24.9	30.0
Gablonz		3.8	3.9	4.6	6.8	9.0	14.7	21.1	29.5
Klagenfurt	11.9	12.0	12.1	13.5	15.3	18.7	19.8	24.3	28.9
Marburg	5.3	6.1	6.9	6.3	12.8	17.6	19.9	24.6	28.0
Treplitz-Schönau	2.7	2.3	3.6	6.9	10.2	14.8	17.5	23.5	26.8
Eger	9.9	10.3	11.2	11.0	13.5	17.1	18.7	23.5	26.6
Iglau	15.3	16.9	18.1	17.4	20.0	22.4	23.7	24.4	25.9
Brüx	3.0		3.6	5.0	6.3	10.1	14.1	21.4	25.6
Neusandez	5.5	7.0	6.2	7.1	9.4	11.2	12.7	15.7	25.0

(a) All cities with 25,000 and more inhabitants in 1910 (in 1,000s); 1837-1869: civilian population only; bracketed figures for Vienna are numbers of inhabitants for the 1910 city territory of Vienna.

Austria

Urbanization

Distribution of total population by size of locality (number of inhabitants)
in 1,000s and as % of total population

Year	0-2,000		2-5,000		5-10,000		10-100,000		100-1,000,000		1,000,000+		Year
	1,000	%	1,000	%	1,000	%	1,000	%	1,000	%	1,000	%	
1920	2 415	39.8	854	14.1	293	4.8	503	8.3	158	2.6	1 842	30.4	1920
1934	2 652	39.3	1 058	15.6	374	5.6	535	7.9	262	3.9	1 874	27.7	1934
1951	2 383	34.4	1 140	16.5	428	6.2	703	10.1	514	7.4	1 766	25.4	1951
1961	2 349	33.2	1 186	16.8	505	7.1	760	10.7	640	9.0	1 628	23.0	1961
1971	1 936	26.0	1 653	22.2	598	8.0	958	12.9	695	9.3	1 615	21.6	1971

Cumulative percent distribution
of population by size of locality

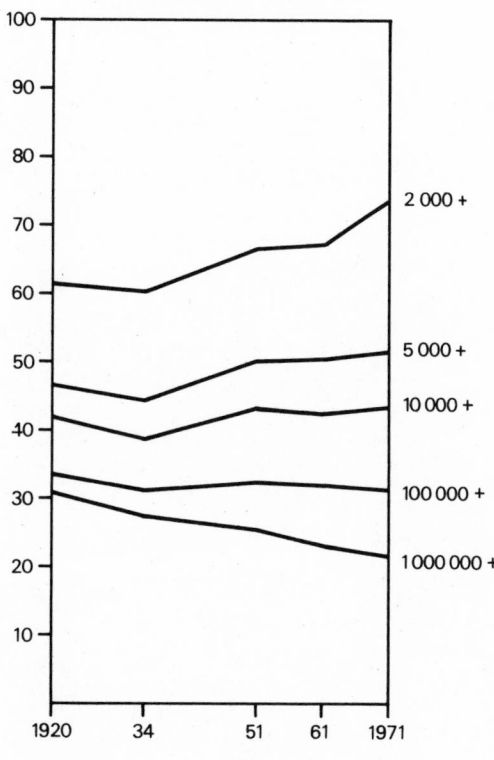

Austria

Growth of Cities (a)

	1920	1923	1934	1951	1961	1971
Wien	1 841.3	1 863.8	1 874.1	1 616.1	1 627.6	1 614.8
Graz	157.6	152.7	152.8	226.5	237.1	248.5
Linz	100.1	101.3	109.0	184.7	196.0	202.9
Innsbruck	55.1	56.4	61.0	95.1	100.7	115.2
Salzburg	36.7	37.8	40.2	102.7	108.1	128.8
Wiener Neustadt	35.3	36.9	36.8	30.6	33.8	34.8
St. Pölten	28.4	31.6	36.2	37.7	40.1	50.1
Klagenfurt	26.1	27.4	29.7	62.8	69.2	74.3

(a) Cities with 20,000 and more inhabitants in 1920.

Belgium

Urbanization

Distribution of total population by size of locality (number of inhabitants)
in 1,000s and as % of total population

Year	0-2,000		2-5,000		5-10,000		10-25,000		25-100,000		100,000+		Year
	1,000	%	1,000	%	1,000	%	1,000	%	1,000	%	1,000	%	
1831			3 172	83.8			202	5.3	412	10.9			1831
1846			3 460	79.8			346	8.0	304	7.0	227	5.2	1846
1856			3 501	77.3			380	8.4	284	6.3	365	8.0	1856
1866			3 639	75.4			525	10.9	274	5.7	391	8.1	1866
1880	1 745	31.6	1 403	25.4	691	12.5	612	11.1	482	8.7	565	10.6	1880
1890	1 736	28.6	1 527	25.2	710	11.7	704	11.6	696	11.5	697	11.5	1890
1900	1 670	25.0	1 524	22.8	942	14.1	914	13.7	869	13.0	774	11.6	1900
1910	1 654	22.3	1 578	21.3	1 143	15.4	1 079	14.5	1 157	15.6	813	11.0	1910
1920	1 649	22.1	1 539	20.6	1 132	15.2	1 159	15.5	1 098	14.7	889	11.9	1920
1930	1 579	19.5	1 619	20.0	1 182	14.6	1 373	17.0	1 400	17.3	940	11.6	1930
1947	1 504	17.7	1 668	19.6	1 369	16.1	1 448	17.0	1 629	19.1	894	10.5	1947
1961	1 386	15.1	1 701	18.5	1 583	17.2	1 774	19.3	1 894	20.6	852	9.3	1961
1970	1 103	11.6	1 692	17.5	1 659	17.2	2 112	22.0	2 047	21.2	1 020	10.6	1970

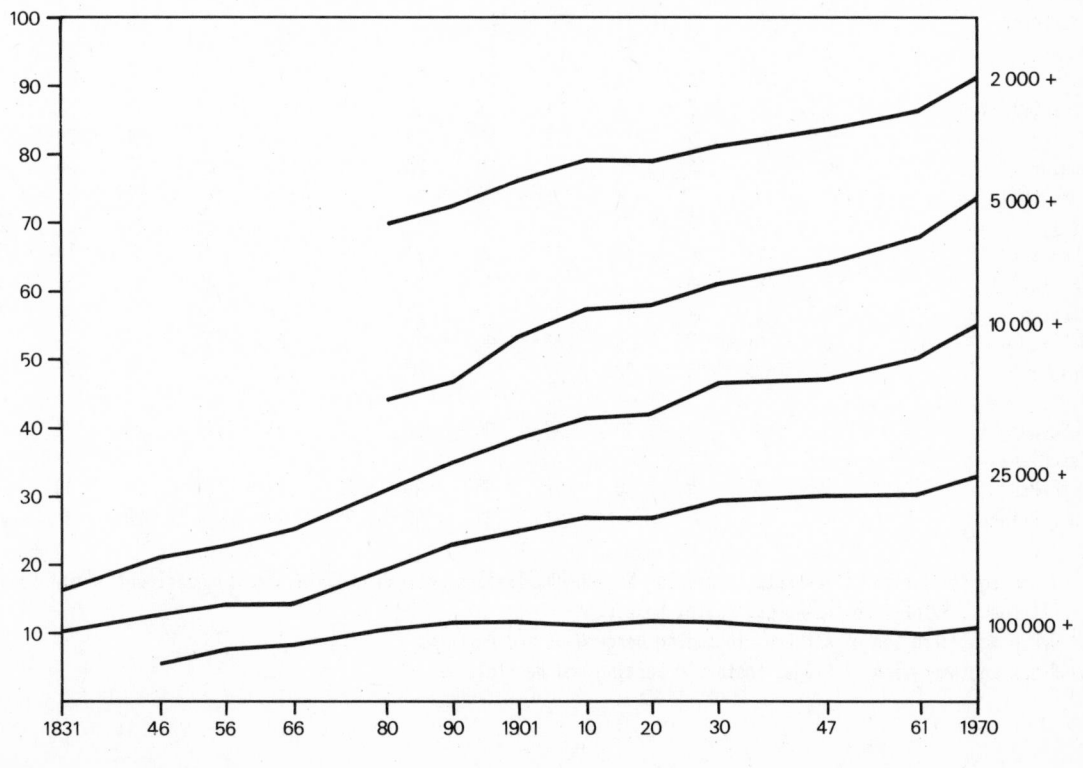

Cumulative percent distribution of population by size of locality

Belgium

Growth of Cities

	1831	1846	1856	1866	1880	1890	1900	1910	1920	1930	1947	1961	1970
Brussels	100	124	153	158	163	176	219	219	203	200	185	171	161
(a)	(140)	(212)	(261)	(309)	(437)	(520)	(626)	(762)	(807)	(892)	(967)	(1 023)	(1 075)
Antwerp	74	89	103	117	169	224	284	313	313	291	270	253	225
(b)	(105)	(127)	(145)	(162)	(241)	(323)	(406)	(487)	(512)	(582)	(597)	(652)	(671)
Ghent	86	103	109	115	131	149	160	166	167	170	166	158	149
	(91)	(110)	(117)	(126)	(157)	(184)	(203)	(217)	(217)	(225)	(228)	(229)	(225)
Liège	59	76	89	99	123	148	158	168	163	166	156	153	146
(c)	(104)	(143)	(138)	(196)	(258)	(299)	(355)	(399)	(395)	(427)	(425)	(445)	(441)
Scharbeck(a)	2	6	11	19	41	51	64	82	102	119	124	117	–
Ixelles(a)	5	14	18	23	36	45	59	73	81	84	91	94	–
Molenbeck-Saint-Jean(a)	4	12	16	24	42	49	58	73	71	69	64	64	–
Anderlecht	4	6	8	12	23	32	48	64	67	80	86	95	–
Saint-Gilles(a)	2	4	6	10	33	40	52	63	69	64	61	55	–
Malines	23	30	31	34	42	51	56	60	58	60	60	65	66
Bruges	42	49	49	47	45	48	52	53	52	51	53	52	117
Borgerhout(b)	–	5	7	11	20	29	38	49	53	56	51	51	49
Verviers	20	23	27	32	41	49	49	47	42	44	41	36	34
Ostende	12	14	16	16	19	25	40	42	45	47	50	57	71
Louvain	26	30	31	31	36	41	42	42	38	39	37	36	31
Seraing(c)	3	11	17	20	27	34	38	41	38	45	42	41	41
Tournai	27	30	31	30	33	34	35	37	35	35	32	33	33
Courtrai	19	22	22	23	27	30	33	36	36	39	40	44	45
Alost	15	17	18	19	21	26	29	33	35	38	42	45	47
Saint Nicholas	17	20	22	23	26	28	31	35	34	39	44	48	49
Etterbeck(a)	2	3	3	5	12	18	21	33	40	45	50	53	–
Namur	19	22	25	23	25	30	31	32	31	31	31	33	32
Saint-Jose-Ten-Noode(a)	3	15	17	22	28	30	32	32	32	31	28	25	–
Berchem(b)	3	4	5	5	9	16	20	30	35	42	45	49	50
Charleroi	6	8	11	12	16	21	25	28	28	29	26	26	24
Jumet	7	9	13	15	21	24	26	28	28	30	29	29	28
Mons	23	24	26	22	24	25	27	28	27	28	26	27	28
Veele(a)	5	6	7	8	11	13	18	27	32	43	56	72	–
Lierre	13	14	15	15	17	20	23	26	25	28	28	29	28
Roulers	10	11	11	14	17	20	23	25	22	27	32	36	40
Forest(a)	1	1	2	2	4	6	10	24	31	40	47	52	–
Gilly	6	8	12	15	18	20	23	24	25	26	24	24	23
Turnhout	13	14	15	14	17	19	21	24	24	27	32	36	38
Herstal(c)	6	8	8	9	11	14	18	23	23	26	27	30	30
Lokeren	16	17	17	17	18	20	21	23	23	24	26	26	27
Molskaoen	6	6	7	8	11	14	19	23	24	33	36	37	–
Renaix	12	12	11	12	14	17	20	22	22	24	26	25	29
Montignies-Sur-Sambre	3	5	8	10	13	16	18	22	23	25	23	24	24
Marchienne-Au-Pont	1	3	4	8	12	15	19	22	22	24	21	19	18
La Louvière	–	–	–	–	12	14	18	21	22	24	22	23	24

a) Urban agglomeration of Brussels, including Scharbeck, Ixelles, Molenbeck-Saint-Jean, Anderlecht, Saint-Gilles, Etterbeck, Saint-Jose-Ten-Noode, Veele, Forest.

b) Urban agglomeration of Antwerp, including Borgerhout and Berchem.

c) Urban agglomeration of Liège, including Seraing and Herstal.

Distribution of total population by size of locality (number of inhabitants)
in 1,000s and as % of total population

Year	0–2,000		2–5,000		5–10,000		10–20,000		20–100,000		100,000+		Year
	1,000	%	1,000	%	1,000	%	1,000	%	1,000	%	1,000	%	
1801	789	85.2	19	2.1	17	1.8					101	10.9	1801
1834	1 020	83.4	49	4.0	36	2.9					119	9.7	1834
1845	1 115	82.5	63	4.7	36	2.6	10	0.8			127	9.4	1845
1860	1 276	79.7	81	5.1	53	3.3	35	2.2			155	9.7	1860
1870	1 385	77.6	79	4.4	57	3.2	82	4.6			181	10.2	1870
1880	1 459	74.2	87	4.4	76	3.8	40	2.0	72	3.7	235	11.9	1880
1890	1 481	68.2	99	4.6	94	4.3	75	3.4	111	5.1	313	14.4	1890
1901	1 511	61.6	118	4.8	100	4.1	79	3.2	242	9.9	401	16.4	1901
1911	1 666	60.3	102	3.7	123	4.5	123	4.5	281	10.2	462	16.8	1911
1921	1 870	57.3	78	2.4	159	4.9	197	6.0	263	8.0	701	21.4	1921
1930	2 025	57.0	80	2.3	136	3.8	227	6.4	311	8.8	771	21.7	1930
1940	2 041	53.0	82	2.1	138	3.6	260	6.8	434	11.3	890	23.2	1940
1950	2 207	51.6	76	1.8	147	3.4	280	6.5	406	9.5	1 165	27.2	1950
1960	2 436	53.2	66	1.4	144	3.1	248	5.4	536	11.7	1 155	25.2	1960
1965	2 588	54.3	68	1.4	115	2.4	271	5.7	626	13.1	1 100	23.1	1965

a) After 1965 available figures not comparable.

Cumulative percent distribution of population by size of locality

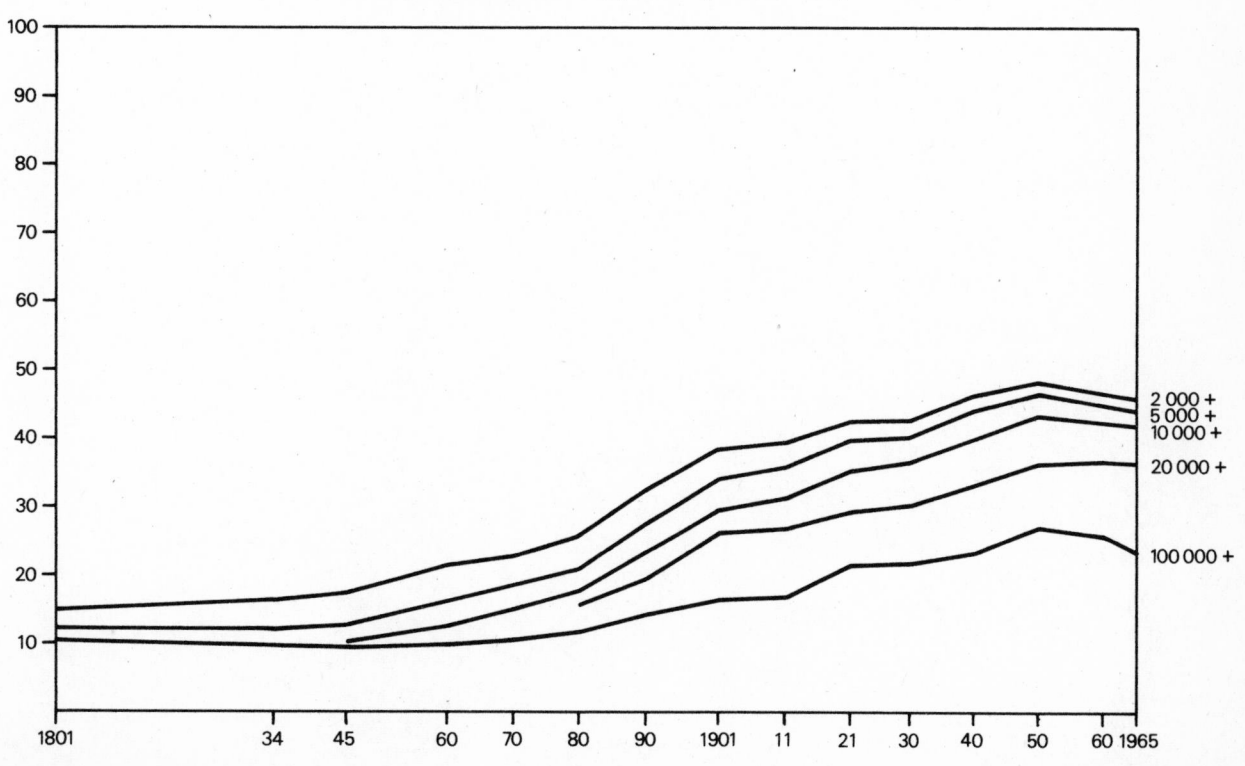

Denmark
Growth of Cities ^{a)}

	1801	1834	1845	1860	1870	1880	1890	1901	1910
Copenhagen	101.0	119.3	126.8	155.1	181.3	234.9	312.9	400.6	462.2
Frederiksberg	1.2	1.9	2.5	8.2	16.9	26.5	47.0	76.2	97.2
Aarhus	4.1	6.8	7.9	11.0	15.0	24.8	33.3	51.8	61.8
Odense	5.8	8.7	10.2	14.3	17.0	20.8	30.3	40.1	42.2
Aalborg	5.6	7.0	7.5	10.1	11.7	14.2	19.5	31.5	33.4
Horsens	2.4	4.8	5.1	9.0	10.5	12.7	17.3	22.2	23.8
Randers	4.6	6.4	7.1	9.7	11.4	13.5	16.6	20.1	23.0

	1916	1921	1930	1940	1950	1960	1965	1970	1975
Copenhagen	506.4 }	700.6	771.2	890.1	974.9	924.0	874.4	662.8	562.4
Frederiksberg	99.4 ⌡								
Aarhus	65.9	74.3	81.3	99.9	116.2	119.6	117.7	237.5	246.3
Odense	45.3	49.5	56.8	87.5	100.9	111.1	107.5	164.9	168.5
Aalborg	38.1	41.6	44.4	55.7	79.8	85.8	85.6	154.3	154.7
Horsens	25.1	27.6	28.4	30.4	35.9	37.3	37.1	52.2	54.1
Randers	24.4	26.5	27.7	32.9	40.1	42.2	42.9	64.2	64.5
Esbjerg	18.9	21.3	27.4	33.2	48.2	55.2	55.9	76.4	78.8

a) Local communities with 20,000 and mor inhabitants in 1911.

Finland

Urbanization

Distribution of total population by size of locality (number of inhabitants)
in 1,000s and as % of total population

Year	0-2,000		2-5,000		5-10,000		10-20,000		20-100,000		100,000+		Year
	1,000	%	1,000	%	1,000	%	1,000	%	1,000	%	1,000	%	
1810	839	97.2	14	1.6			10	1.2					1810
1840	1 377	95.3	28	1.9	10	0.7	30	2.1					1840
1850	1 544	94.2	34	2.1	21	1.3	17	1.1	21	1.3			1850
1860	1 650	94.3	32	1.9	25	1.5	17	1.0	22	1.3			1860
1870	1 653	93.4	30	1.7	28	1.6	30	1.7	29	1.6			1870
1880	1 906	92.6	30	1.4	32	1.5	28	1.3	66	3.2			1880
1890	2 162	90.8	44	1.8	9	0.4	33	1.4	133	5.6			1890
1900	2 405	88.6	42	1.6	22	0.8	43	1.6	200	7.4			1900
1910	2 669	85.7	56	1.8	36	1.2	63	2.0	144	4.6	147	4.7	1910
1920	2 829	84.1	62	1.8	47	1.4	48	1.4	182	5.4	198	5.9	1920
1930	3 003	81.9	49	1.3	72	2.0	47	1.3	252	6.9	244	6.6	1930
1940	2 789	75.4	71	1.9	129	3.5	76	2.1	158	4.3	473	12.8	1940
1950	2 735	67.8	55	1.4	119	3.0	225	5.6	323	8.0	572	14.2	1950
1960	2 742	61.6	38	0.9	111	2.5	225	5.1	625	14.1	704	15.8	1960
1970	2 261	49.2	10	0.2	156	3.4	330	7.2	1 023	22.2	818	17.8	1970

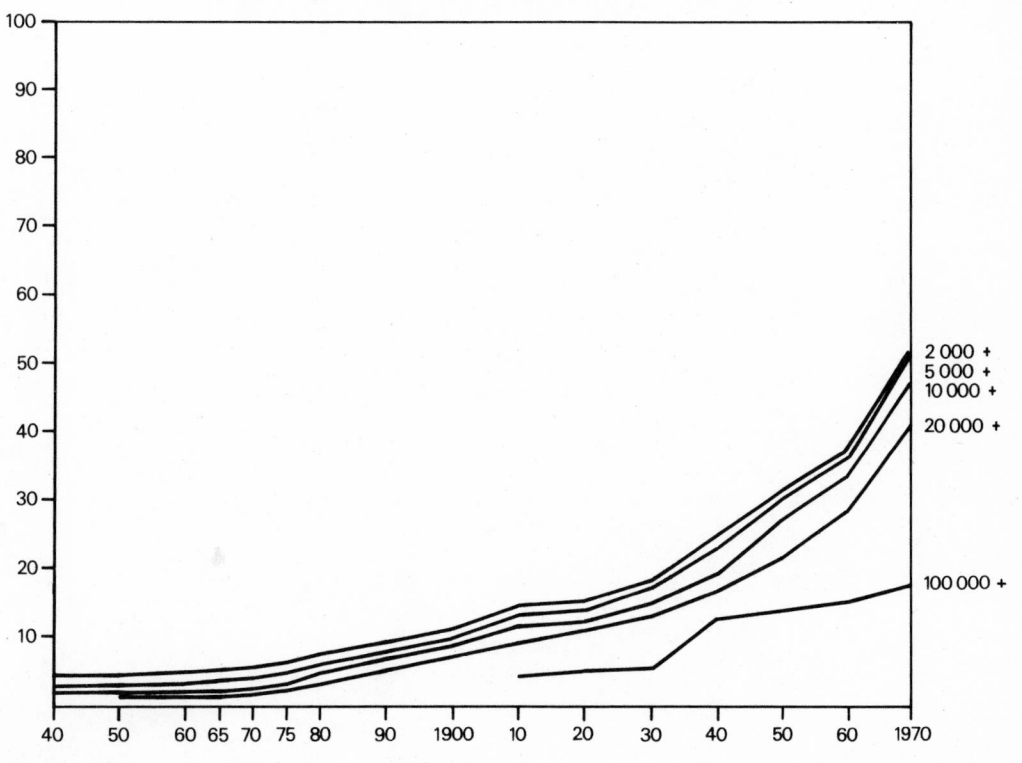

Cumulative percent distribution of population by size of locality

Finland

Growth of Cities [a)]

	1810	1840	1850	1860	1870	1880	1890	1900
Helsinki	4.1	16.6	20.7	22.2	28.5	43.3	61.5	93.6
Turku	10.2	13.1	17.2	16.9	19.6	22.7	30.1	38.2
Tampere	0.7	1.8	3.2	5.2	7.0	13.6	20.1	36.3
Viipuri	–	4.7	8.6	5.4	10.6	14.1	20.8	32.3
Vaasa	2.4	3.0	3.7	4.0	4.6	6.3	10.3	15.3
Oulu	3.0	5.1	5.8	7.0	8.0	9.7	12.7	16.3
Pori	2.5	5.4	6.2	7.1	7.0	8.7	10.0	15.0
Kuopio	–	2.1	2.8	4.0	5.6	6.9	8.9	11.8

	1910	1920	1930	1940	1950	1960	1970
Helsinki	147.2	197.8	243.6	317.3	369.4	452.8	510.4
Viipuri	27.5	30.1	55.8				
Turku	49.7	58.4	66.7	74.8	101.8	124.4	152.2
Tampere	45.4	47.8	56.0	80.8	101.1	127.3	155.4
Vaasa	21.8	24.0	26.1	33.3	35.0	42.7	48.2
Oulu	19.8	21.3	24.2	28.0	37.9	58.2	85.0
Pori	16.9	17.1	18.4	21.6	43.2	54.1	73.4
Kuopio	15.8	18.7	24.1	25.2	33.4	44.9	63.8

a) Local communities with 15,000 and more inhabitants in 1910.

France

Urbanization

Distribution of total population by size of locality (number of inhabitants)
in 1,ooos and as % of total population

Year	0–5,000		5–10,000		10–50,000		50–100,000		100–1,000,000		1,000,000+		Year
	1,000	%	1,000	%	1,000	%	1,000	%	1,000	%	1,000	%	
1851	30 285	81.7	1 650	4.6	2 610	7.3	634	1.8	604	1.7	1 053	2.9	1851
1861	28 676	76.7	1 182	5.3	2 992	8.0	836	2.2	1 203	3.2	1 696	4.5	1861
1866	31 011	81.5			2 985	7.8	836	2.2	1 410	3.7	1 825	4.8	1866
1872	28 828	79.8			3 092	8.6	887	2.5	1 444	4.0	1 852	5.1	1872
1876	29 007	78.6			3 356	9.1	1 029	2.8	1 525	4.1	1 989	5.4	1876
1881	29 405	78.6			3 425	9.2	676	1.8	1 630	4.4	2 269	6.1	1881
1886	29 217	77.0			3 456	9.1	1 094	2.9	1 819	4.8	2 345	6.2	1886
1891	28 897	75.8			3 697	9.7	1 046	2.7	2 045	5.4	2 448	6.4	1891
1901	24 680	64.1	2 405	6.3	4 531	11.8	1 485	3.9	2 636	6.9	2 714	7.1	1901
1906	24 458	63.0	2 525	6.5	4 808	12.4	1 584	4.1	2 707	7.0	2 763	7.1	1906
1911	23 942	61.1	2 559	6.5	5 194	13.3	1 720	4.4	2 889	7.4	2 888	7.4	1911
1921	22 684	58.5	2 659	6.9	5 157	13.3	2 306	5.9	3 086	8.0	2 906	7.5	1921
1926	21 776	54.1	3 611	9.0	6 184	15.4	2 347	5.8	3 439	8.5	2 871	7.1	1926
1931	22 233	53.9	2 948	7.2	6 708	16.3	2 754	6.7	3 694	9.0	2 891	7.0	1931
1936	21 546	52.4	3 142	7.6	6 915	16.8	2 889	7.0	3 861	9.4	2 830	6.9	1936
1946	21 504	53.1	3 246	8.0	6 965	17.2	2 195	5.4	3 868	9.5	2 725	6.7	1946
1962	20 264	43.6	3 977	8.6	10 091	21.7	3 409	7.3	5 940	12.8	2 811	6.1	1962
1968	20 909	41.2	4 376	8.6	11 973	23.5	3 941	7.8	7 033	13.8	2 608	5.1	1968
1975	20 853	38.8	4 969	9.3	13 618	25.4	4 590	8.5	7 350	13.7	2 317	4.3	1975

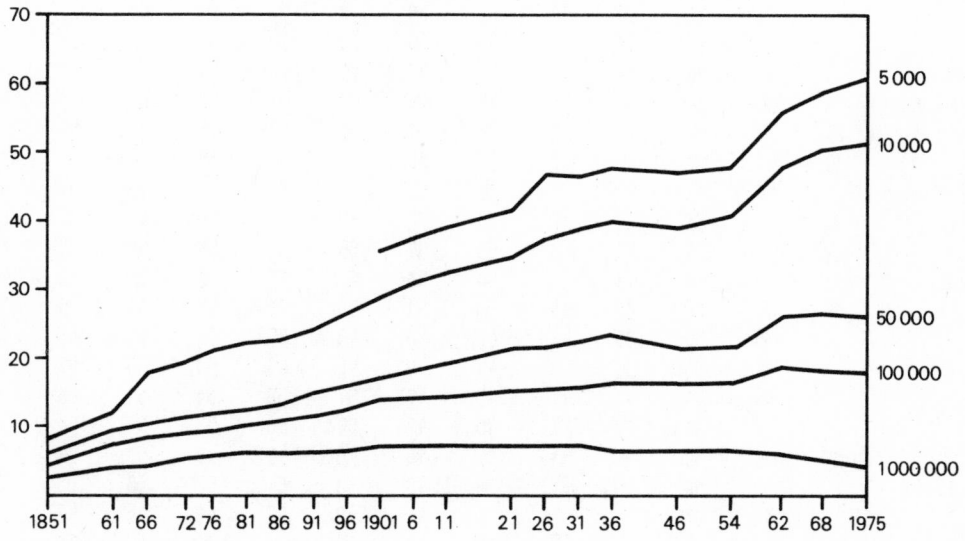

Cumulative percent distribution of population by size of locality

Growth of Cities (a)

	1801	1851	1866	1876	1886	1901	1911	1921	1931	1936	1946	1954	1962	1968
Paris	547	1 053	1 825	1 989	2 345	2 714	2 888	2 907	2 891	2 830	2 725	2 850	2 790	2 591
Marseille	111	195	300	319	376	491	551	586			636	662	778	889
Lyon	110	177	324	343	402	459	524	562	480	460	461	471	536	528
Bordeaux	91	131	194	215	241	257	262	267	263	258	254	258	278	267
Lille	55	76	155	163	188	211	218	201	202	201	189	195	193	191
Strasbourg	49	76		94		151	179	169	182	193	176	201	229	249
Nantes	74	96	112	122	127	133	171	184	187	195	200	223	240	259
Toulouse	50	93	127	132	148	150	150	175	195	213	264	269	324	371
St. Etienne	16	56	97	126	118	147	149	168	141	190	178	182	201	214
Nice			50	53	77	105	143	156	220	242	211	244	293	322
Le Havre	16	29	75	92	112	131	136	163	165	164	107	140	185	200
Rouen	87	100	101	105	107	116	125	124	123	123	108	117	121	121
Roubaix	8	35	65	84	100	124	123	113	117	107	101	110	113	115
Nancy	30	45	50	66	79	103	120	113	121	121	114	125	129	123
Reims	20	46	61	81	98	108	115	77	113	117	111	121	134	153
Toulon	21	70	77	71	70	102	105	106	133	150	126	141	162	175
Mulhouse	7	30		57		89	95	99	100	101	92	99	109	116
Amiens	40	52	61	67	80	91	93	93	90	94	85	93	105	118
Limoges	21	42	53	59	68	84	92	90	93	95	108	106	119	133
Brest	27	61	80	67	71	84	91	74	70	79	75	111	136	154
Angers	33	47	55	57	73	82	84	86	86	88	94	102	115	129
Tourcoing		28	38	49	58	79	83	79	82	78	76	83	89	99
Nimes	39	54	60	63	70	81	80	83	89	94	92	89	100	123
Montpellier	34	46	56	55	57	76	80	82	87	91	93	98	119	162
Rennes	26	40	49	57	66	75	79	82	89	99	114	124	152	181
Grenoble	24	31	51	45	52	67	77	77	91	96	102	116	157	162
Dijon	21	32	39	48	61	71	77	79	91	96	101	113	136	145
Tours	22	34	43	48	60	65	73	75	79	84	80	84	108	128
Calais		11	13	13	59	60	72	73	70	68	50	60	70	75
Orléans	36	47	49	52	61	67	72	69	72	73	70	76	84	96
St. Denis	4	16	26	35	48	61	72	76	82	78	70	81	94	99
Le Mans	17	27	45	50	58	63	69	72	77	85	101	112	132	143
Metz	32	58		50		59	69	62	79	83	70	86	62	108
Levallois-Perret			16	23	36	58	79	74	71	65	62	63	128	59
Clermont-Ferrand	25	34	38	42	47	53	65	83	103	101	108	113	87	149
Versailles	25	35	44	50	50	55	61	65	67	74	70	84	96	91
Besancon	30	41	47	54	57	55	58	56	60	65	64	73	107	113
Boulogne-Billancourt		8	17	22		44	57	68	86	97	79	94	61	109
St. Quentin	11	25	33	39	47	50	56	37	49	49	49	54	61	64
Troyes	24	27	36	41	47	53	56	55	59	58	59	59	68	75
Boulogne s.M.		31	40	41		50	53	55	52	52	35	42	49	49
Béziers	14	19	28	31	43	53	51	56	72	73	65	65	74	81
Avignon		36	36	38	41	47	49	48	57	60	60	63	73	86
Lorient		26	38	35	40	45	49	46	43	51	19	47	61	66
Caen	31	45	41	41	44	45	47	54	58	61	51	68	92	110
Clichy		6	18	17	27	40	47	50	56	57	53	56	56	53
Bourges	15	25	30	15	43	47	46	46	45	49	51	54	61	71
Neuilly s.S.		16	18	21	27	38	45	52	54	57	60	66	73	71
Colmar		21	23				44	42	47	49	46	47	52	60
Cherbourg		28	37		37	43	44	38	38	39	40	38	38	38

(a) Cities with 25,000 and more inhabitants in 1911.

France

Growth of Cities

	1801	1851	1866	1876	1886	1901	1911	1921	1931	1936	1946	1954	1962	1968
Montreuil s.B.		4	9	14	22	32	43	51	70	72	70	76	92	96
Asnières		1	6	8	15	31	43	50	64	72	72	78	82	80
Villeurbanne		5	7	9	15	29	43	56	82	81	82	82	105	120
St. Ouen			6	11	21	35	42	51	53	51	46	48	52	49
Poitiers	18	29	31	33	37	40	41	38	42	44	49	53	62	71
Perpignan	11	22	25	28	34	36	40	54	74	72	75	70	83	102
Belfort		8	8	15	22	33	39	39	43	46	37	43	48	53
Dunkerque		29	33	15	38	39	39	35	32	31	11	21	28	28
Vincennes		9	15	18	22	31	39	42	47	49	46	50	50	
Ivry s.S.		9	10	15	21	29	38	44	49	45	42	48	55	61
St. Nazaire		5	19		26	36	38	42	41	43	12	39	58	63
Angoulême		21	25	31	35	38	38	35	37	39	44	43	48	48
Courbevoie		6	10	12	16	25	38	46	54	59	55	60	60	58
Aubervilliers		3	9	14	22	31	38	41	56	56	53	59	71	74
Pau		16	25	29	31	34	37	36	39	41	46	48	60	74
Roanne		13	19	23	30	35	37	38	41	42	45	47	52	53
La Rochelle	18	17	19	20	24	32	36	40	45	48	49	59	67	73
Pantin		3	9	14	19	30	36	39	37	38	36	37	46	48
Douai		21	24	27	30	34	36	34	42	42	37	43	48	49
Le Creusot		8	29	26	27	31	36	38	32	29	24	29	34	34
Rochefort		24	30	27	31	37	35	30	27	30	30	31	29	29
Valenciennes		33	24	26	28	31	35	34	42	43	39	43	45	47
St.-Maur-des Fossés		2	6	8	16	23	34	40	57	57	56	64	70	77
Montlucon		9	19	23	28	35	34	36	41	43	47	49	55	58
Périgueux		14	20	24	30	32	33	33	34	38	41	41	39	38
Cette (Sètte)		19	24	29	37	33	33	37	37	37	32	34	36	41
Puteaux		4	9	12	16	24	32	34	38	44	37	41	40	38
Lens		10	6	9	12	24	32	14	34	33	34	41	43	42
Chalon s.S.		17	20	21	23	29	32	32	33	33	36	37	44	51
Châlon s.M.		16	18	20	24	27	31	31	32	36	31	37	42	51
Arles		23	26	25	23	29	31	31	33	29	35	37	42	46
Carcassonne		20	22	26	29	31	31	29	35	33	38	37	41	44
Laval		19	27	27	31	30	30	28	28	28	33	35	39	46
Epinal		11	12	15	21	28	30	28	27	28	23	29	33	37
Aix en Provence		27	28	29	29	29	30	30	38	43	46	54	68	90
Alais (Alès)		19	20	21	23	25	30	37	43	41	35	37	41	43
Montauban		25	26	27	30	31	30	26	30	32	36	38	41	46
Cannes		6	10	14	20	30	30	31	47	49	46	50	58	47
Bastia		16	22	18	21	25	29	33	45	52	49	43	50	49
Wattrelos		9	13	15		26	29	28	31	31	29	32	41	42
Valence		16	20	23	25	27	29	29	34	37	40	42	53	62
Armentières		9	16	22	28	29	29	15	23	24	23	25	25	27
Tarbes		14	16	21	25	26	29	27	33	35	45	40	47	55
Narbonne		13	17	20	30	29	28	29	32	30	30	32	34	38
Cambrai		21	22	22	24	27	28	26	29	30	26	30	33	38
Bayonne		18	26	27	27	28	28	28	32	31	33	33	37	43
Castres		21	21	26	27	27	28	26	28	29	31	34	37	41
Nevers		17	21	23	25	28	28	30	32	34	34	35	39	42
Manceau-les-Mines			5	11		29	27	25	28	27	27	28	29	27
Denain		9	11	11	18	23	27	24	28	27	25	27	30	28
Châteauroux		16	17	19	23	25	25	27	27	29	35	36	45	49
Arras		25	26	27	27	26	25	25	30	32	34	36	42	49
Vienne		13	25	27	25	25	25	24	26	25	24	26	27	29

Germany

Urbanization

Distribution of total population by size of locality (number of inhabitants)
in 1,000s and as % of total population

Year	0-2,000		2-5,000		5-20,000		20-100,000		100-1,000,000		1,000,000+		Year
	1,000	%	1,000	%	1,000	%	1,000	%	1,000	%	1,000	%	
1871	26 219	63.9	5 087	12.4	4 588	11.2	3 147	7.7	1 969	4.8			1871
1875	26 070	61.0	5 379	12.6	5 124	12.0	3 488	8.2	2 666	6.2			1875
1880	26 514	58.6	5 749	12.7	5 671	12.6	4 027	8.9	2 151	4.7	1 122	2.5	1880
1885	26 377	56.3	5 806	12.4	6 055	12.9	4 172	8.9	3 131	6.7	1 315	2.8	1885
1890	26 185	53.0	5 935	12.0	6 481	13.1	4 829	8.9	4 419	8.9	1 579	3.2	1890
1895	26 023	49.8	6 277	12.0	7 119	13.6	5 584	10.7	5 600	10.7	1 677	3.2	1895
1900	25 734	45.6	6 816	12.1	7 585	13.5	7 111	12.6	7 232	12.8	1 888	3.4	1900
1905	25 822	42.6	7 159	11.8	8 334	13.7	7 817	12.9	9 469	15.6	2 040	3.4	1905
1910	25 955	40.0	7 298	11.2	9 172	14.1	8 678	13.4	11 752	18.1	2 071	3.2	1910
1925	22 219	35.6	6 753	10.8	8 196	13.1	8 196	13.1	11 619	18.6	5 093	8.2	1925
1933	21 481	32.9	6 907	10.6	8 581	13.1	8 447	13.0	14 430	22.1	5 372	8.3	1933
1939	25 025	31.6	9 144	11.5	10 604	13.3	10 388	13.1	18 136	22.8	6 051	7.6	1939
1950	13 757	27.6	6 494	13.0	7 649	15.3	6 754	13.5	11 428	23.0	3 753	7.5	1950
1961	12 487	22.2	6 745	12.0	9 041	16.1	9 100	16.2	13 685	24.4	5 115	9.1	1961
1970	11 353	18.7	6 772	11.1	11 466	19.0	11 417	18.8	14 423	23.8	5 221	8.6	1970

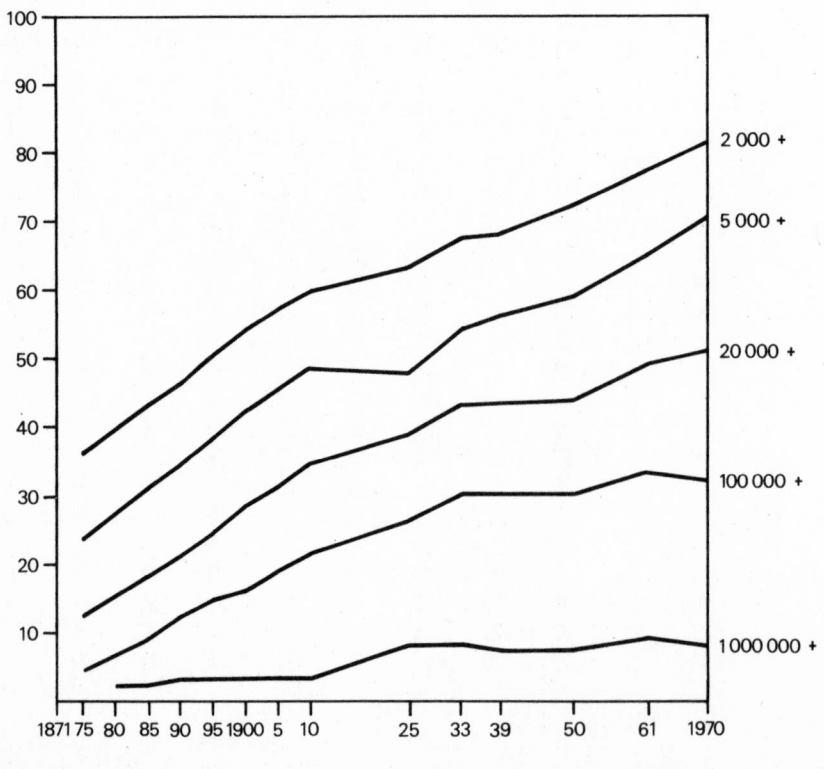

Cumulative percent distribution of population by size of locality

Growth of Cities (a)

	1880	1890	1900	1910	1925	1933	1939	1950	1961	1970
Berlin	1 122	1 579	1 888	2 071	4 013	4 242	4 338	2 146	2 198	2 115
suburbs (b)	100	220	504	942						
Hamburg	290	324	706	931	1 079	1 129	1 712	1 606	1 832	1 794
München	230	349	500	590	681	735	829	832	1 085	1 312
Leipzig	149	295	455	590	679	713	707			
Dresden	221	277	395	548	619	642	630			
Köln	144	282	372	517	698	757	772	595	809	850
Breslau	273	335	423	512	555	625	630			
Frankfurt/M.	137	180	288	415	462	556	553	532		666
Düsseldorf	95	145	214	359	431	499	541	501	703	661
Nürnberg	100	143	261	333	392	410	423	362	455	478
Hannover	123	164	236	302	422	444	471	444	573	521
Essen	57	78	119	295	469	654	667	605	727	696
Chemnitz	95	139	207	288	332	351	338			
Stuttgart	117	140	176	286	341	415	458	498	638	634
Magdeburg	98	202	230	280	292	307	337			
Bremen	112	126	163	247	295	323	424	445	565	593
Königsberg	141	162	188	246	280	316	372			
Stettin	92	116	211	236	254	271	383			
Duisburg	41	59	93	229	272	440	435	411	503	453
Dortmund	67	90	142	214	320	541	542	507	642	641
Kiel	44	69	108	212	214	218	274	254	273	272
Halle	71	101	157	181	194	209	220			
Straßburg	104	124	150	179						
Altona	91	143	162	173	185	242				
Elberfeld	94	126	157	170	167					
Barmen	96	116	142	169	187					
Danzig	109	120	141	170			250			
Gelsenkirchen	15	28	37	170	207	333	318	315	383	347
Posen	66	70	117	157			280			
Aachen	86	103	135	156	155	163	162	130	170	176
Kassel	58	72	106	153	171	175	216	162	208	215
Braunschweig	75	101	128	143	146	157	196	224	246	223
Mannheim	53	79	140	140	247	275	285	246	314	332
Bochum	33	48	66	137	157	315	305	290	361	344
Karlsruhe	49	74	97	134	146	155	190	197	242	259
Krefeld	74	105	107	130	130	165	171	172	213	223
Plauen	35	47	74	121	111	114	112			
Mülheim (Ruhr)	22	28	38	113	127	133	138	150	186	192
Erfurt	53	72	81	111	135	145	166			
Mainz	61	71	84	111	109	143	159	88	134	175
Wiesbaden	50	65	86	109	103	160	170	221	253	251
Saarbrücken		14	23	105			133		131	128
Augsburg	61	76	89	102	166	177	185	185	209	213
Hamborn			33	102	126					
Lübeck	51	64	82	97	121	129	155	238	235	240
Münster	40	49	64	90	106	122	141	118	183	199
Oberhausen	17	25	42	90	105	192	192	203	257	246
Hagen	26	35	51	89	99	148	152	146	196	201
Bonn	32	40	51	88	90	99	101	115	144	276
Darmstadt	41	56	72	87	89	93	115	95	136	142

Growth of Cities (a)

	1880	1890	1900	1910	1925	1933	1939	1950	1961	1970
Görlitz	50	62	81	86	86	94	94			
Würzburg	51	61	75	84	90	101	108	78	117	116
Freiburg	36	49	62	83	90	99	110	110	145	164
Ludwigshafen	15	29	62	83	102	107	144	124	165	176
Bielefeld	31	40	63	78	86	121	129	154	175	169
Offenbach	28	35	51	76	79	81	85	89	116	118
Zwickau	35	44	56	74	81	85	85			
Linden in Hannover	22	28	51	73						
Königshütte	28	37	58	73			115			
Remscheid	30	40	58	72	76	101	104	103	127	137
Borbeck	21	29	47	71						
Pforzheim	24	30	43	69	79	80	79	54	83	68
Metz	53	60	58	69						
Frankfurt/O.	51	56	62	68	71	76	84			
Beuthen(i.o.S.)	23	37	51	68	63	101	101			
Hamburg	19	35	50	67	73	113				
Gleiwitz	15	20	52	67	82	111	117			
Liegnitz	37	47	55	67	73	77	84			
Fürth	31	43	54	67	74	77	82	100	98	94
Mönchen-Gladbach	37	50	58	66	115	127	125	125	152	151
Osnabrück	33	40	52	66	89	94	107	110	135	145
Rostock	37	44	55	65	78	90	121			
Zabrze Hindenburg				63	73	130	126			
Potsdam	48	54	60	62	64	74	136			
Buer		11	29	62	99					
Flensburg	31	37	49	61	63	67	71	103	99	95
Elbing	36	42	53	59	68	73	86			
Bromberg	34	41	52	58						
Herne		14	28	57	67	99	95	112		
Dessau	23	35	51	57	71	79	119			
Koblenz	31	32	45	56	58	65	91	66	99	120
Ulm	33	36	43	56	57	62	74	71	93	93
Heidelberg	24	32	40	56	73	84	86	116	125	121
Kaiserslautern	26	37	48	55	60	63	71	63	86	107
Recklinghausen		14	34	54	60	87	86	105	131	125
Brandenburg	29	38	50	54	60	64	84			
Mühlheim a. Rhein	20	31	45	53						
Regensburg	35	38	46	53	77	81	96	117	125	131
Solingen	17	37	45	51	52	140	140	148	170	177
Hildesheim	26	33	43	50	58	63	72	72	93	93

a) Local communities with 50,000 and more inhabitants in 1910.

Ireland

Urbanization

Distribution of total population by size of locality (number of inhabitants)
in 1,000s and as % of total population

Year	0-2,000		2-5,000		5-10,000		10-20,000		20-100,000		100,000+		Year
	1,000	%	1,000	%	1,000	%	1,000	%	1,000	%	1,000	%	
1821	5 884	86.5	218	3.2	184	2.7	54	0.8	176	2.6	287	4.2	1821
1831	6 658	85.7	259	3.3	222	2.9	113	1.4	206	2.6	311	4.0	1831
1841	7 046	86.2	291	3.6	206	2.5	172	2.1	228	2.8	233	2.8	1841
1851	5 417	82.7	263	4.0	181	2.8	122	1.9	272	4.2	298	4.5	1851
1861	4 693	80.9	249	4.3	167	2.9	107	1.8	167	2.9	416	7.2	1861
1871	4 221	78.0	232	4.3	194	3.6	137	2.5	208	3.8	421	7.8	1871
1881	3 934	76.0	240	4.6	185	3.6	139	2.7	218	4.2	458	8.8	1881
1891	3 464	73.6	218	4.6	178	3.8	125	2.7	219	4.6	501	10.6	1891
1901	3 060	68.6	206	4.6	158	3.5	156	3.5	239	5.4	640	14.3	1901
1911	2 923	66.6	203	4.6	152	3.5	170	3.9	251	5.7	692	15.8	1911

Republic of Ireland

Year	0-2,000		2-5,000		5-10,000		10-20,000		20-100,000		100,000+		Year
1926	1 802	60.6	146	4.9	80	2.7	85	2.9	180	6.0	680	22.9	1926
1936	1 952	65.8	142	4.8	96	3.2	103	3.5	202	6.8	473	15.9	1936
1946	1 881	63.6	156	5.3	104	3.5	81	2.7	227	7.7	506	17.1	1946
1951	1 758	59.4	152	5.1	97	3.3	106	3.6	159	5.4	688	23.2	1951
1961	1 581	56.1	124	4.4	108	3.8	100	3.6	193	6.7	711	25.2	1961
1971	1 457	48.9	176	5.9	152	5.1	105	3.5	268	9.0	814	27.3	1971

Northern Ireland

Year	0-2,000		2-5,000		5-10,000		10-20,000		20-100,000		100,000+		Year
1926	620	49.3	56	4.5	36	2.8	85	6.7	45	3.6	415	33.0	1926
1937	599	46.8	54	4.3	38	3.0	102	8.0	48	3.8	438	34.2	1937
1951	622	45.4	48	3.5	56	4.1	111	8.1	91	6.6	444	32.4	1951
1961	643	45.1	64	4.5	44	3.1	143	10.0	115	8.1	416	29.2	1961
1971	542	37.4	54	3.5	113	7.4	95	6.2	283	18.4	417	27.1	1971

Cumulative percent distribution of population by size of locality

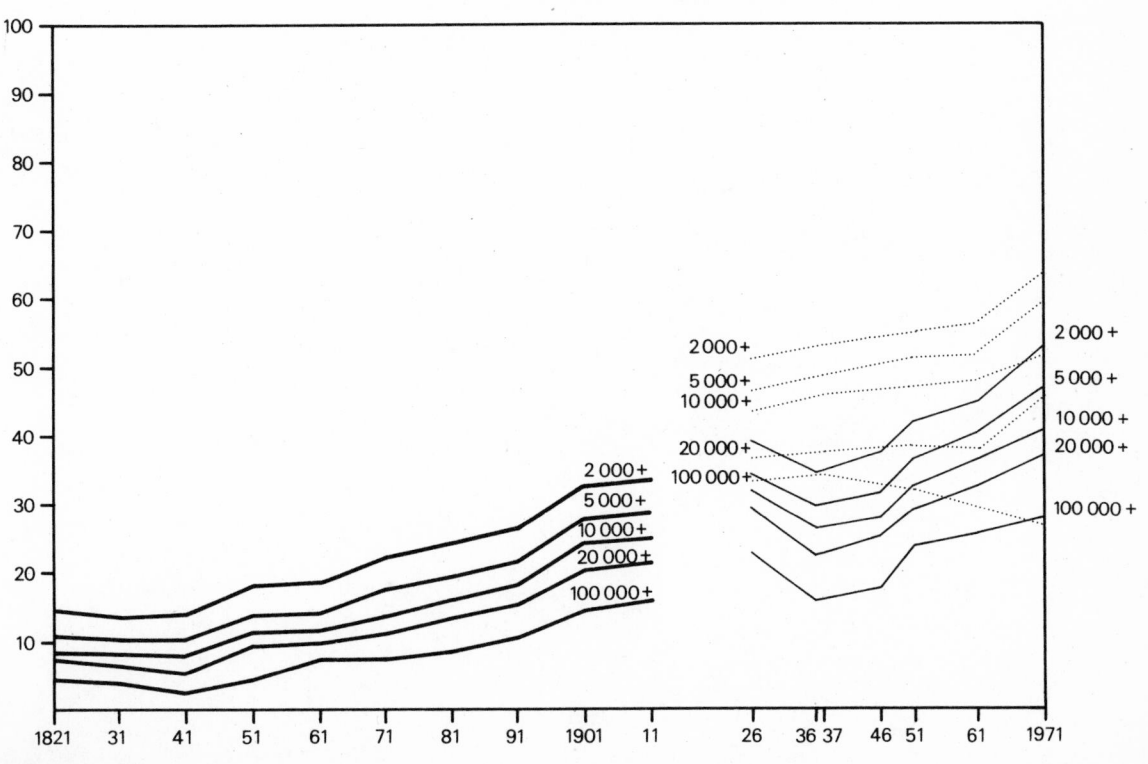

265

Ireland

Growth of Cities [a]

	1821	1831	1841	1851	1861	1871	1881	1891	1901	1911
Dublin	185.9	204.2	232.7	246.7	246.5	246.3	249.6	245.0	290.6	304.8
Belfast	37.3	52.3	75.3	97.8	119.4	174.4	208.1	256.0	349.2	386.9
Cork	100.7	107.0	80.7	82.6	79.6	78.6	80.1	73.3	76.1	76.7
Londonderry	9.3	19.6	15.2	19.7	20.5	25.2	29.1	33.2	39.9	40.8
Limerik	59.0	66.6	48.4	48.8	43.9	39.4	38.6	37.1	38.2	38.5
Rathmines/Rathgar b)						20.6	24.4	27.8	32.6	37.8
Pembroke b)						21.0	23.2	24.3	25.8	29.3
Waterford	28.7	28.8	23.2	23.0	22.9	23.3	22.5	20.9	26.8	27.5
Kingstown	1.5	5.7	7.2	10.5	12.5	16.3	18.6	17.4	17.4	16.9

Republik of Ireland

	1926	1936	1946	1951	1961	1971
Dublin c)	394.1	472.9	506.1	576.0	595.3	679.7
Cork c)	78.5	99.3	89.9	112.0	115.7	134.4
Limerik	39.4	41.1	43.0	50.8	51.7	63.0
Dun Laoghaire d)	35.1	39.8	44.7	58.5	68.1	98.4
Waterford	26.6	28.0	29.3	28.7	28.2	33.7

Northern Ireland

	1926	1937		1951	1961	1971
Belfast	415.2	438.1		443.7	415.9	416.7
Derry	45.2	47.8		50.1	53.8	66.5

a) Towns with 15,000 and more inhabitants in 1911.
b) From 1926 included in Dublin.
c) From 1951 including suburbs.
d) Former Kingstown, but including other urban districts.

Italy

Urbanization

Distribution of total population by size of locality (number of inhabitants)
in 1,000s and as % of total population

Year	2-2,000		2-5,000		5-10,000		10-20,000		20-50,000		50-100,000		100 000+		1,000,000+		Year
	1,000	%	1,000	%	1,000	%	1,000	%	1,000	%	1,000	%	1,000	%	1,000	%	
1861	16 236	73.2			1 883	8.5	1 613	7.3	943	4.3	301	1.4	1 206	5.4			1861
1881	4 518	15.1	8 873	29.6	5 713	19.1	3 792	12.7	2 775	9.3	892	3.0	2 390	8.0			1881
1901	4 146	12.4	9 437	28.3	6 375	19.1	4 502	13.5	4 274	12.8	1 564	4.7	3 106	9.3			1901
1911	3 957	11.1	9 517	26.6	7 139	19.9	5 086	14.2	4 316	12.1	1 866	5.2	3 906	10.9			1911
1921	4 407	11.0	9 573	23.9	7 792	19.5	5 667	14.2	4 559	11.4	2 683	6.7	5 308	13.3			1921
1931	3 137	7.6	9 248	22.4	7 959	19.3	5 763	14.0	5 135	12.5	2 816	6.8	7 172	17.4	1 000	2.4	1931
1936	3 012	7.0	9 297	21.6	8 439	19.6	6 319	14.7	5 433	12.6	2 831	6.6	7 662	17.8	2 287	5.3	1936
1951							6 737	14.3	6 221	13.2	3 610	7.7	9 390	19.9	4 003	0.4	1951
1961	3 658	7.2	8 634	17.1	7 979	15.8	6 573	13.0	6 864	13.6	4 385	8.7	12 530	24.8	6 094	12.0	1961
1971	3 815	7.1	7 768	14.4	7 430	13.8	6 695	12.4	8 191	15.2	4 327	8.0	15 798	29.2	7 014	13.0	1971

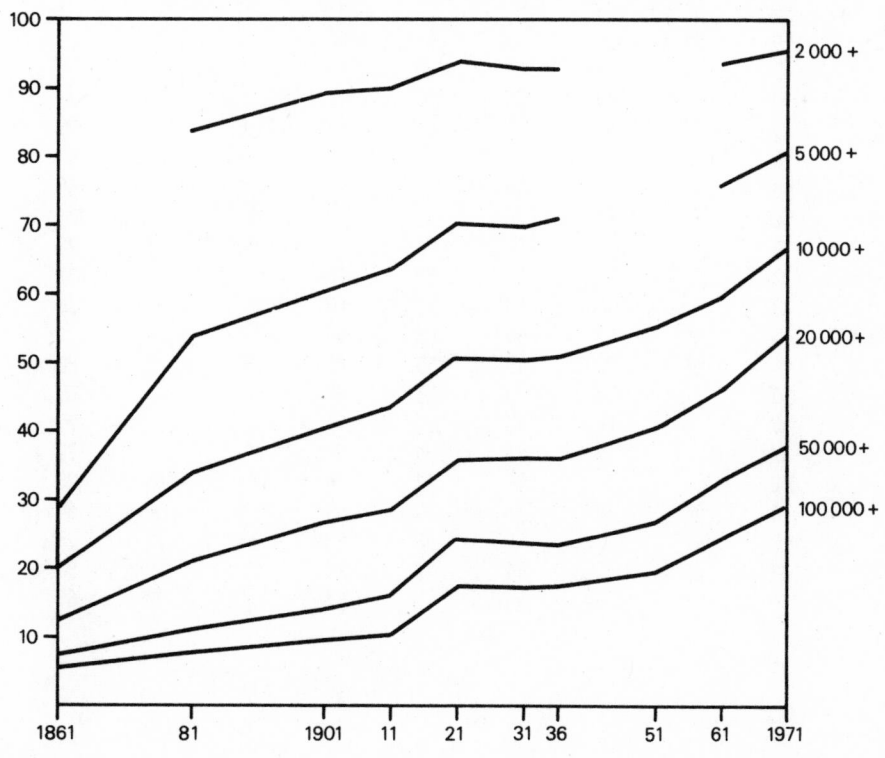

Cumulative percent distribution of population by size of locality

Growth of Cities [a]

	1861	1871	1881	1901	1911	1921	1931	1936	1951	1961	1971
Napoli	491	494	548	637	761	861	839	876	1 025	1 197	1 259
Milano	269	291	356	540	700	835	991	1 114	1 277	1 599	1 725
Roma		243	298	460	538	687	1 000	1 173	1 702	2 247	2 843
Genova	235	260	291	395	473	554	608	631	688	796	822
Torino	205	213	254	336	427	502	597	637	722	1 051	1 188
Palermo	197	222	248	314	345	398	390	417	503	593	657
Firenze	170	197	200	244	266	286	316	330	391	459	482
Trieste		123	145	179	229	239	250	252	270	273	274
Catania	70	85	101	151	212	254	228	244	302	364	402
Venezia		165	169	192	211	229	260	270	323	359	378
Bologna	114	121	128	157	179	219	256	289	351	456	502
Messina	104	113	127	150	127	177	183	195	223	258	262
Bari	44	62	73	93	121	135	174	198	274	316	365
Verona		87	91	100	114	129	148	162	186	230	264
Livorno	97	97	98	99	106	115	125	129	146	166	178
Padova		66	72	82	96	112	131	143	173	206	238
Ferrara	64	68	71	82	95	108	116	120	135	154	155
Brescia	59	58	64	75	88	106	119	128	147	180	215
Spezia	15	28	35	73	82	99	108	112	112	125	128
Parma	67	65	65	73	80	91	101	107	117	143	178
Cagliari	38	40	47	66	74	77	99	109	143	188	232
Reggio di Calabria	58	62	68	76	74	95	109	118	140	152	163
Foggia	34	38	40	53	77	67	57	64	98	118	139
Lucca	65	68	68	75	76	79	82	82	90	89	91
Alessandria	55	56	61	70	74	77	83	84	84	95	105
Ravenna	57	59	61	64	72	72	78	81	92	116	133
Modena	56	57	58	65	71	84	93	100	115	144	174
Regio nell'Emilia	50	51	51	59	70	83	91	94	107	118	130
Pistoia	49	51	51	62	67	70	70	71	79	85	94
Perugia	15		51	61	66	73			97	114	132
Marsala	18		40	58	66	73			74		
Taranto	25	25	32	57	65	104	106	138	175	201	236
Pisa	46	50	54	61	65	69	73	76	81	97	112
Ancona	48	48	50	59	65	69	75	81	86	102	113
Bergamo	42	41	44	53	63	71	82	89	105	119	131
Trapani	31	34	38	60	60	71	60	63	73	76	70
Prato	12		42	52	57	61			77		
Modica	27		41	49	56	60			38		
Cremona (ed Uniti)	43	41	42	50	55	59	64	65	71	76	85
Vicenza		38	39	45	55	60	65	71	82	104	121
Andria	30		37	50	53	59			65		
Monza	16		28	43	53	57			74		
Rimini	17		37	43	51	58			77		
Como	32	33	35	44	51	55	63	66	76	86	99
Savona	20	26	30	38	50	59	61	64	69	73	81
Piacenza	48	44	44	46	50	58	66	71	76	92	103
Ragusa	22	29	31	41	47	49	50	49	50	57	59
Trento		33	35	40	47	53	57	59	65	82	95

Growth of Cities [a]

	1861	1871	1881	1901	1911	1921	1931	1936	1951	1961	1971
Terni	22	23	34	42	46	50	58	64	84	94	106
Forli	39	39	41	44	46	52	61	65	79	93	106
Salerno	29	28	31	43	46	52	63	69	92	124	158
Cesena	8		38	42	46	51			70		
Corato			25	42	45	49			45		
Asti	35	36	38	43	45	45	49	50	53	62	77
Pavia	38	37	38	39	44	46	55	51	66	78	90
Barletta	27		33	42	44	51			66		
Molfetta	25		30	40	43	46			55		
Sassari	25	33	36	38	43	43	54	56	72	91	109
Caltagirone	22		32	45	43	38			44		
San Pier d´Arena	13		22	35	42	52					
Siena	31	33	34	39	42	44	48	50	58	64	69
Treviso		29	32	35	42	50	54	57	66	80	95
Caltanissetta	24	26	31	43	41	60	44	50	51	63	61
Siracusa	21	22	24	32	41	50	50	54	72	90	109
Faenza	18		36	40	40	43			48		
Cerignola			24	34	40	39			51		
Mantova		32	34	36	40	45	49	49	55	64	67
Piazza Armerina	20	20	24	32	38						
Torre el Greco			28	40	37	46			62		
Lecce	21	23	26	33	36	39	47	51	67	78	85
Acireale	24		39	35	36	35			39		
Chioggia			28	31	35	36			48		
Imola											
Catanzaro	23	25	29	32	34	36	42	46	61	75	86
Casale Monferrato	17		29	32	34	34			42		
Castellamare di Stabia	14		33	33	34	39			56		
Bisceglie	16		24	31	34	38			39		
Caserta	11		31	33	33	35			52	54	67
San Severo	17		20	30	32	35			50		
Vercelli	25	27	29	31	32	33	40	41	44	55	59
Noto	13		18	23	32	32					
Torre Annunziata	15		22	28	31	35			51		
Trani	22		26	32	31	35			35		
Massa	15	18	20	26	31	34	40	41	50	57	63
Ascoli Piceno	23	23	23	29	31	32	37	39	44	50	56
Canicatti	20		20	25	30	31					
Aderno	13		20	26	30	40					

a) Cities with 3o,ooo and more inhabitants in 1911.

Urbanization

Distribution of total population by size of locality (number of inhabitants)

in 1,000s and as % of total population

Year	0-5,000		5-10,000		10-20,000		20-50,000		50-100,000		100,000+		Year
	1,000	%	1,000	%	1,000	%	1,000	%	1,000	%	1,000	%	
1899	1 751	34.3	873	17.1	623	12.2	480	9.4	240	4.7	1 138	22.3	1899
1909	1 740	29.7	1 037	17.7	715	12.2	627	10.7	369	6.3	1 371	23.4	1909
1920	1 737	25.3	1 098	16.0	892	13.0	934	13.6	542	7.9	1 661	24.2	1920
1930	1 682	21.2	1 206	15.2	1 182	14.9	913	11.5	794	10.0	2 158	27.2	1930
1940	1 597	17.9	1 303	14.6	1 428	16.0	1 115	12.5	1 026	11.5	2 454	27.5	1940
1947	1 477	15.2	1 331	13.7	1 516	15.6	1 380	14.2	1 020	10.5	2 954	30.4	1947
1960	1 340	11.6	1 514	13.1	1 768	15.3	1 791	15.5	1 364	11.8	3 779	32.7	1960
1966	1 204	9.6	1 543	12.3	2 070	16.5	2 153	17.2	1 591	12.7	3 969	31.7	1966
1971	953	7.3	1 515	11.6	2 338	17.9	2 612	20.0	1 841	14.1	3 800	29.1	1971

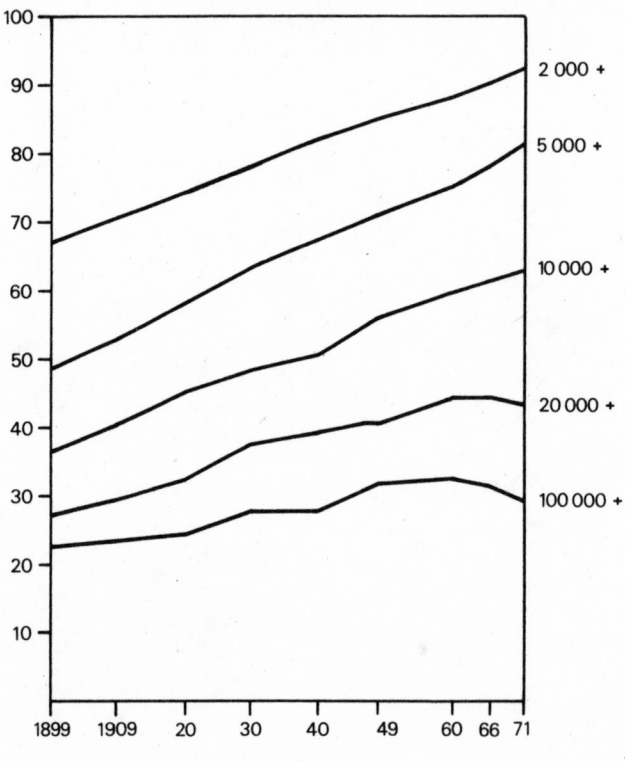

Cumulative percent distribution of population
by size of locality

G r o w t h   o f   C i t i e s   (a)

	1830	1840	1849	1859	1869	1879	1889	1899	1909	1920	1930	1947	1960	1971
Amsterdam	202	211	224	243	265	317	408	511	566	647	757	814	866	820
Rotterdam	72	78	90	106	116	148	202	319	418	516	587	653	730	679
S'Gravenhage	56	64	72	78	90	114	157	206	271	355	438	542	606	538
Utrecht	43	49	48	53	59	68	84	102	119	140	155	187	256	278
Groningen	30	34	34	36	39	46	56	67	75	91	105	133	146	171
Haarlem	22	24	26	28	31	37	51	64	69	77	120	159	170	173
Arnhem	15	17	19	25	32	41	50	57	64	72	78	99	125	132
Leiden	35	38	36	37	39	41	43	54	58	66	71	88	97	100
Nijmegen	18	21	21	22	23	24	32	43	55	67	82	107	132	150
Tilburg	12	14	15	16	21	28	34	41	50	63	79	116	139	154
Dordrecht	20	21	21	23	25	27	33	38	46	54	56	69	84	101
Maastricht	24	26	25	27	28	29	32	34	38	54	61	75	91	113
Leuwarden	21	23	25	26	25	29	30	32	37	43	49	77	83	87
Appeldoorn	7	8	10	11	13	15	19	26	36	48	61	85	105	126
S'Hertogenbosch	21	22	22	23	24	25	27	31	35	38	42	55	73	81
Enschede	3	4	4	4	5	5	15	24	34	42	52	102	126	141
Delft	15	17	18	20	22	25	29	32	34	39	51	63	75	86
Zwolle	16	17	18	19	20	23	26	31	34	36	41	48	56	77
Schiedam	12	12	13	15	19	23	26	27	32	41	53	70	90	83
Hilversum	4	5	6	6	7	9	13	19	32	39	57	86	102	99
Deventer	14	14	15	16	18	19	23	26	28	32	36	44	57	66
Emmen	2	2	3	4	6	10	14	19	28	41	41	55	67	81
Breda	13	15	15	15	15	17	22	26	27	30	45	86	109	122
Helder	6	9	12	15	18	20	22	25	27	29	29	33	49	61
Gouda	13	15	14	15	16	18	20	22	25	27	29	38	43	47
Zaandam	11	11	11	12	12	13	15	21	25	29	33	42	50	66
Amersfoort	12	13	12	13	13	14	15	19	24	31	39	57	71	79
Vlardingen	7	7	8	8	9	10	13	17	22	26	28	44	69	81
Vlissingen	8	9	10	11	10	10	13	19	21	23	22		29	41
Alkmaar	9	10	10	10	11	13	16	18	21	24	28	38	44	52
Hengelo	3	4	4	4	6	7	10	15	20	26	34	46	62	70
Eindhoven	3	3	3	3	3	4	5	5	6	48	95	136	169	190

a) Local communities with 2o,ooo and more inhabitants in 1909.

Urbanization [a]

Distribution of total population by size of locality (number of inhabitants)
in 1,000s and as % of total population

Year	0–2,000		2–5,000		5–10,000		10–20,000		20–100,000		100,000+		Year
	1,000	%	1,000	%	1,000	%	1,000	%	1,000	%	1,000	%	
1801	842	95.3	7	0.8	5	0.6	29	3.3					1801
1815	829	93.7	5	0.5	22	2.5	29	3.3					1815
1825	974	92.6	11	1.0	14	1.4	31	3.0	21	2.0			1825
1835	1 108	92.8	13	1.1	15	1.2	13	1.1	46	3.8			1835
1845	1 232	92.7	10	0.7	17	1.3	15	1.1	56	4.2			1845
1855	1 368	91.8	12	0.8	28	1.9	16	1.1	66	4.4			1855
1865	1 540	90.5	16	1.0	6	0.3	54	3.2	85	5.0			1865
1875	1 601	87.9	4	0.3	28	1.6	31	1.7	154	8.5			1875
1890	1 542	77.6	48	2.4	62	3.2	58	2.9	125	6.3	150	7.6	1890
1900	1 613	72.5	62	2.8	65	3.0	89	4.0	164	7.4	229	10.3	1900
1910	1 687	71.6	69	2.9	67	2.8	108	4.6	184	7.8	243	10.3	1910
1920	1 886	71.1	55	2.1	55	2.1	175	6.6	219	8.3	260	9.8	1920
1930	2 038	72.5	55	1.9	68	2.4	175	6.2	225	8.0	253	9.0	1930
1946	2 289	72.5	70	2.2	57	1.8	185	5.9	159	5.0	397	12.6	1946
1950	2 242	68.4	77	2.3	61	1.9	192	5.9	161	4.9	546	16.6	1950
1960	2 460	68.5	58	1.6	80	2.2	188	5.2	218	6.1	587	16.4	1960

a) After 1960 available data not comparable.

Cumulative percent distribution of population by size of locality

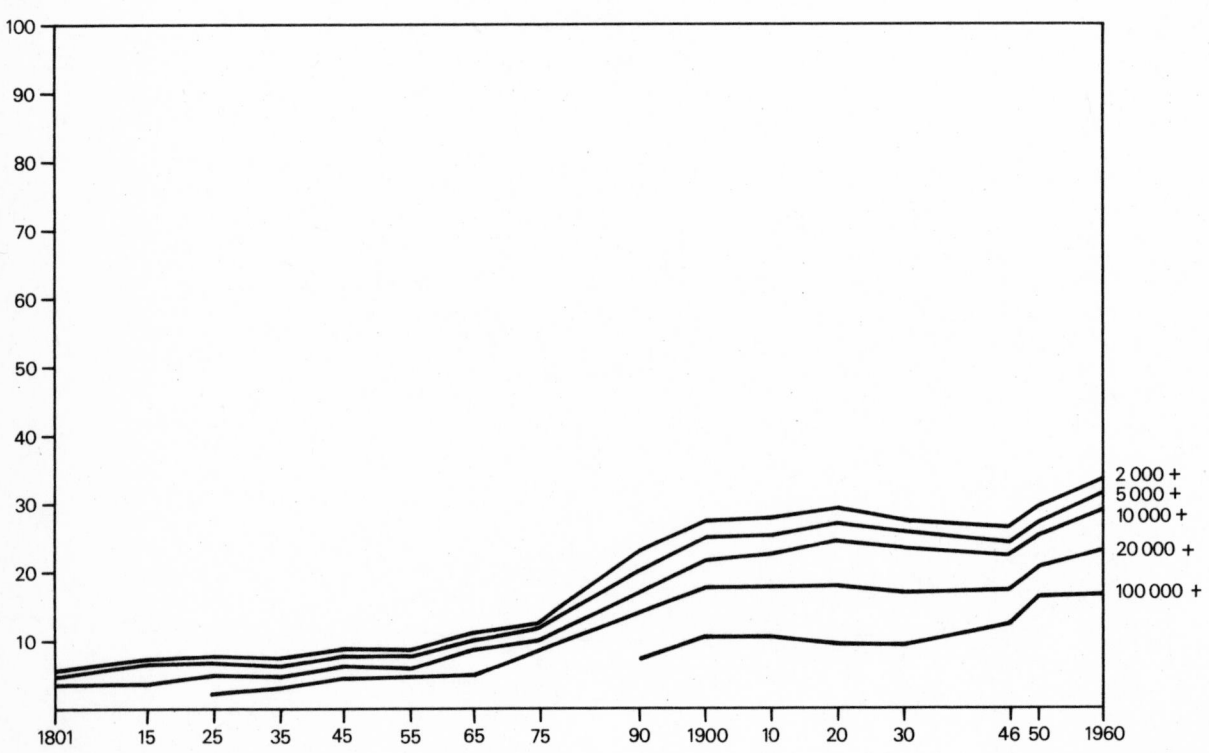

Norway

Growth of Cities [a]

	1801	1815	1825	1835	1845	1855	1865	1875
Oslo	11.9	13.6	20.8	24.4	33.2	41.3	57.4	76.9
Bergen	16.9	15.9	19.6	21.5	22.3	24.5	27.7	34.4
Trondheim	8.8	9.8	11.9	12.9	14.8	16.0	19.3	22.5
Stavanger	2.5	2.5	3.8	4.9	6.6	8.6	11.7	20.3
Drammen	5.4	5.4	6.9	7.3	8.4	9.9	13.0	18.9
Kristiansand	4.8	7.2	7.5	7.7	8.3	9.5	10.9	12.2
Frederikstad	2.2	1.9	2.4	2.4	2.7	3.5	4.8	9.7

	1890	1900	1910	1920	1930	1946	1950	1960
Oslo	151.2	227.6	241.8	258.5	253.1	286.2	433.3	471.5
Bergen	53.7	72.3	76.9	91.4	98.3	110.4	112.7	115.8
Trondheim	25.1	38.2	45.3	55.0	54.5	57.1	56.7	59.3
Stavanger	23.9	30.6	37.3	43.8	46.8	50.3	50.6	52.8
Drammen	20.7	23.1	24.9	26.2	25.5	27.0	27.4	30.9
Kristiansand	12.8	14.7	15.3	16.6	14.6	13.2	25.9	27.8
Frederikstad	12.5	14.6	15.6	15.6	14.1	14.4	14.3	13.7

a) Cities with 15,000 and more inhabitants in 1910; after 1960 available figures not comparable.

Sweden

Urbanization [a]

Distribution of total population by size of locality (number of inhabitants)
in 1,000s and as % of total population

Year	0–2,000		2–5,000		5–10,000		10–20,000		20–100,000		100,000+		Year
	1,000	%	1,000	%	1,000	%	1,000	%	1,000	%	1,000	%	
1800	2 173	93.0	56	2.4	20	0.9	23	1.0	76	2.7			1800
1840	2 889	92.0	84	2.7	25	0.8	35	1.1	106	3.4			1840
1860	3 490	90.4	77	2.0	79	2.0	65	1.7	37	1.0	112	2.9	1860
1870	3 675	88.1	69	1.7	119	2.9	63	1.5	106	2.5	136	3.3	1870
1880	3 912	85.6	88	1.9	138	3.0	117	2.6	141	3.1	169	3.8	1880
1890	3 926	82.0	76	1.6	122	2.6	143	3.0	167	3.5	351	7.3	1890
1900	4 067	79.2	84	1.6	143	2.8	163	3.2	248	4.8	431	8.4	1900
1910	4 183	75.7	80	1.5	179	3.2	191	3.5	379	6.9	510	9.2	1910
1920	4 178	70.7	120	2.0	225	3.8	222	3.8	424	7.2	735	12.5	1920
1930	4 159	67.7	96	1.6	241	3.9	282	4.6	498	8.1	866	14.1	1930
1940	4 004	62.9	85	1.3	234	3.7	403	6.3	547	8.6	1 098	17.2	1940
1950	3 773	53.5	76	1.1	249	3.5	545	7.8	1 110	15.8	1 290	18.3	1950
1960	3 632	48.5	54	0.7	259	3.5	579	7.7	1 529	20.4	1 442	19.2	1960

a) After 1960 available figures not comparable.

Cumulative percent distribution of population by size of locality

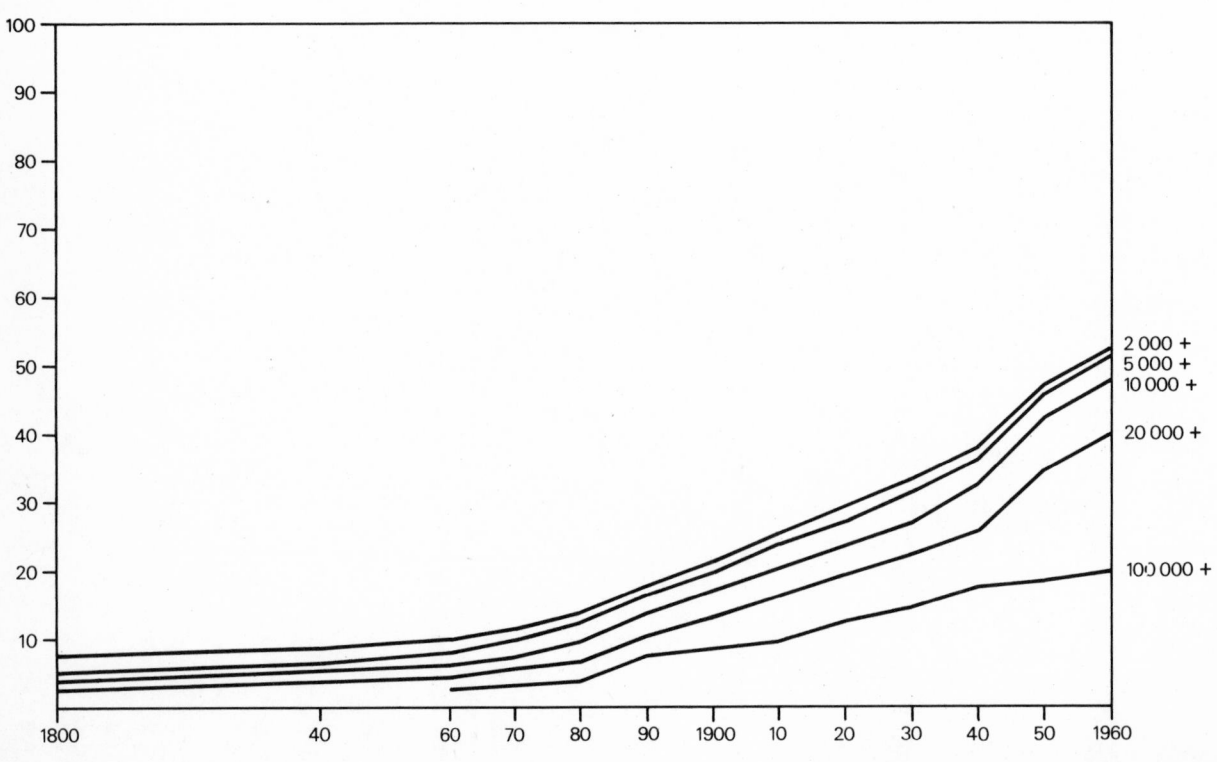

Sweden

Growth of Cities [a]

	1800	1810	1820	1830	1840	1850	1860	1870	1880
Stockholm	75.5	65.5	75.6	80.6	84.2	93.1	112.4	136.0	168.8
Gothenburg	12.8	14.3	16.5	21.0	21.6	26.1	37.0	56.3	76.4
Malmö	4.0	5.8	6.7	8.7	10.2	13.1	18.9	25.6	38.1
Norköpping	9.1	9.0	9.7	10.0	12.8	16.9	20.0	23.9	26.7
Gävle	5.4	5.6	7.0	7.8	8.1	9.3	11.0	13.8	18.8
Helsingborg	1.7	2.1	2.4	3.0	3.2	4.1	5.3	7.9	11.6
Örebro	3.3	3.0	3.4	4.1	4.2	5.2	7.4	9.1	11.8
Eskilstuna	1.3	1.9	2.0	2.7	3.3	4.0	4.6	5.7	8.2
Karlskrona	10.2	10.6	11.6	11.7	12.5	14.1	15.3	16.6	18.3
Jonköpping	2.7	3.0	3.5	4.2	4.7	6.0	7.4	11.9	16.1
Uppsala	5.1	4.1	4.5	4.5	5.2	7.0	8.5	11.4	15.7
Linköpping	2.7	3.3	3.4	4.0	4.8	5.2	6.1	7.3	8.8
Boras	1.8	1.8	2.1	2.2	2.4	2.7	3.0	3.3	4.7
Lund	3.1	3.1	3.6	4.2	5.3	6.7	8.4	10.7	14.3

	1890	1900	1910	1920	1930	1940	1950	1960	1970
Stockholm	246.5	300.6	342.3	419.4	502.2	590.5	744.1	808.3	740.5
Gothenburg	104.7	130.6	167.8	202.3	243.4	281.3	353.6	404.7	451.8
Malmö	48.5	60.9	83.4	111.6	120.3	155.5	191.8	229.4	265.5
Norköpping	32.8	41.0	46.4	58.7	61.5	70.8	84.6	91.0	115.8
Gävle	23.5	29.5	35.2	37.8	38.9	39.7	46.9	54.8	84.6
Helsingborg	20.4	24.7	33.3	47.1	47.1	55.9	71.6	76.6	100.6
Örebro	14.5	22.0	30.1	36.0	37.5	49.2	66.8	75.4	115.7
Eskilstuna	10.9	13.7	28.4	30.3	32.7	40.7	53.4	59.1	94.1
Karlskrona	20.6	24.0	27.4	27.1	25.5	29.6	31.2	33.0	36.4
Jonköpping	19.7	23.1	27.0	29.3	30.9	36.3	43.8	50.7	107.8
Uppsala	21.5	22.9	26.0	28.9	30.3	38.4	63.0	77.5	127.4
Linköpping	12.6	14.6	22.2	26.9	29.8	38.7	54.5	65.2	104.6
Boras	8.1	15.8	21.5	28.2	38.2	48.3	58.0	67.1	74.5
Lund	15.0	16.6	20.1	23.1	24.5	28.0	33.8	40.4	56.0

a) Local communities with 20,000 and more inhabitants in 1910.

Distribution of total population by size of locality (number of inhabitants)

in 1,000s and as % of total population

Year	0-2,000		2-5,000		5-10,000		10-20,000		20-100,000		100,000+		Year
	1,000	%	1,000	%	1,000	%	1,000	%	1,000	%	1,000	%	
1850	1 612	67.4	495	20.7	131	5.5	68	2.8	86	3.9			1850
1860	1 610	64.2	531	21.1	158	6.3	83	3.3	129	5.1			1860
1870	1 599	60.0	591	22.6	200	7.5	94	3.5	170	6.4			1870
1880	1 567	55.4	683	24.1	205	7.2	128	4.5	250	8.8			1880
1888	1 563	53.5	671	23.0	243	8.3	138	4.7	305	10.5			1888
1900	1 570	47.4	731	22.0	287	8.6	135	4.1	334	10.1	260	7.8	1900
1910	1 530	40.8	832	22.2	422	11.2	177	4.7	468	12.5	323	8.6	1910
1920	1 522	39.2	854	22.0	433	11.2	186	4.8	437	11.3	448	11.5	1920
1930	1 486	36.6	907	22.3	435	10.7	225	5.5	379	9.3	634	15.6	1930
1941	1 508	29.5	855	20.0	500	11.7	424	9.9	389	9.1	846	19.8	1941
1950	1 502	28.1	942	20.0	551	11.7	485	10.3	441	9.3	972	20.6	1950
1960	1 465	27.0	1 023	18.8	662	12.2	647	11.9	520	9.6	1 113	20.5	1960
1970	1 398	22.3	1 192	19.0	838	13.4	842	13.4	892	14.2	1 109	17.7	1970

Cumulative percent distribution of population by size of locality

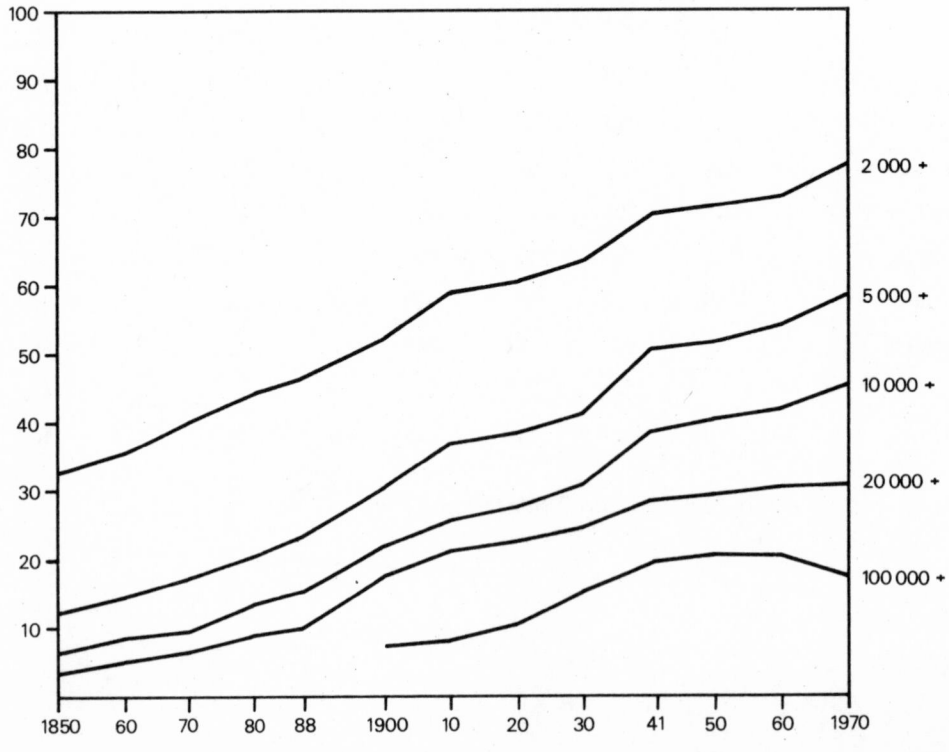

Growth of Cities (a)

	1850	1860	1870	1880	1888	1900	1910	1920	1930	1941	1950	1960	1970
Zürich	17.0	19.8	20.8	24.5	27.6	150.1	190.7	207.2	249.8	336.4	390.0	440.2	442.6
	41.6	51.6	65.7	86.9	103.9	168.0	215.5	234.8	290.9	336.4	390.0	440.2	442.6
Basel	27.3	37.9	44.1	60.6	69.9	109.2	132.3	136.0	148.1	162.1	183.5	206.7	212.9
	27.8	38.7	44.9	61.7	71.1	109.2	132.3	136.0	148.1	162.1	183.5	206.7	212.9
Genève	31.2	41.4	44.2	48.8	52.0	59.4	58.3	56.3	124.1	124.4	145.5	176.2	173.6
	37.7	54.0	60.0	70.4	75.7	97.4	115.2	126.6	124.1	124.4	145.5	176.2	173.6
Bern	27.6	29.0	35.5	43.2	46.0	64.2	85.7	104.6	111.8	130.3	146.5	163.2	162.4
	29.7	31.1	37.5	45.7	48.6	67.6	90.9	104.6	111.8	130.3	146.5	163.2	162.4
Lausanne	17.1	20.5	25.8	29.4	33.3	46.7	64.4	68.5	75.9	92.4	106.8	126.3	137.4
	17.1	20.5	25.8	29.4	33.3	46.7	64.4	68.5	75.9	92.4	106.8	126.3	137.4
Winterthur	5.3	6.5	9.3	13.5	15.8	22.3	25.3	26.6	53.9	58.9	66.9	80.4	92.7
	13.7	15.6	19.5	25.9	29.5	41.0	46.6	50.0	53.9	58.9	66.9	80.4	92.7
St. Gallen	11.2	14.5	16.5	21.0	27.4	33.1	37.9	70.4	63.9	62.5	68.0	76.3	80.6
	17.9	23.1	26.4	34.3	43.3	53.8	75.5	70.4	63.9	62.5	68.0	76.3	80.6
Luzern	10.1	11.5	14.4	17.8	20.3	29.3	39.3	44.0	47.1	54.7	60.5	67.4	69.9
	10.1	11.5	14.4	17.8	20.3	29.3	39.3	44.0	47.1	54.7	60.5	67.4	69.9
Biel	3.5	6.0	7.9	11.6	15.3	22.0	23.7	34.6	37.7	41.2	48.3	59.2	64.3
	5.6	8.8	11.7	16.6	21.2	29.6	32.1	34.6	37.7	41.2	48.3	59.2	64.3
La Chaux-de-Fonds	12.6	16.8	19.6	22.3	25.6	36.0	37.8	37.7	35.3	30.9	33.3	38.9	42.3
	12.6	17.9	20.8	23.6	26.9	36.0	37.8	37.7	35.3	30.9	33.3	38.9	42.3
Fribourg	9.1	10.4	10.6	11.4	12.2	15.8	20.3	20.6	21.6	26.0	29.0	32.6	39.7
	9.1	10.4	10.6	11.4	12.2	15.8	20.3	20.6	21.6	26.0	29.0	32.6	39.7
Neuchâtel	7.2	10.4	12.7	15.4	16.3	20.8	23.7	23.2	22.7	23.8	28.0	33.3	38.8
	7.9	10.6	12.9	15.7	16.6	21.2	24.2	23.6	22.7	23.8	28.0	33.3	38.8

(a) All cities with 20,000 and more inhabitants in 1910 (in 1,000s); upper figures of inhabitants refer to the city territory of the respective year, lower figures to the city territory of 1970.

Distribution of total population by size of locality (number of inhabitants)

in 1,000s and as % of total population

Year	0-2,000		2-20,000		20-100,000		100-1,000,000		1,000,000+		Year
	1,000	%	1,000	%	1,000	%	1,000	%	1,000	%	
1801		8 144	77.0		1 476	14.0	959	9.1			1801
1811		9 112	75.6			1 799	14.9		1 139	9.5	1811
1821		10 505	74.1			2 297	16.2		1 379	9.7	1821
1831		11 699	71.5			3 011	18.4		1 655	10.1	1831
1841		12 926	69.3			3 784	20.3		1 948	10.4	1841
1851		13 915	66.4			4 682	22.3		2 362	11.3	1851
1861		12 399	61.8		2 653	13.2	2 211	11.0	2 804	14.0	1861
1871		13 168	58.0		3 672	16.2	2 618	11.5	3 254	14.3	1871
1881		13 521	52.1		4 754	18.3	3 883	15.0	3 816	14.7	1881
1891		13 439	46.3		6 310	21.8	5 022	17.3	4 232	14.6	1891
1901		13 586	41.8		7 452	22.9	6 954	21.4	4 537	14.0	1901
1911	8 044	22.3	6 152	17.1	8 179	22.7	9 173	25.4	4 522	12.5	1911
1921	7 988	21.1	6 238	16.5	8 824	23.3	10 355	27.3	4 483	11.8	1921
1931	7 061	17.7	4 437	11.1	11 229	28.1	11 825	29.6	5 400	13.5	1931
1951	8 480	19.4	4 974	11.4	13 491	30.8	12 352	28.2	4 461	10.2	1951

Cumulative percent distribution of population by size of locality

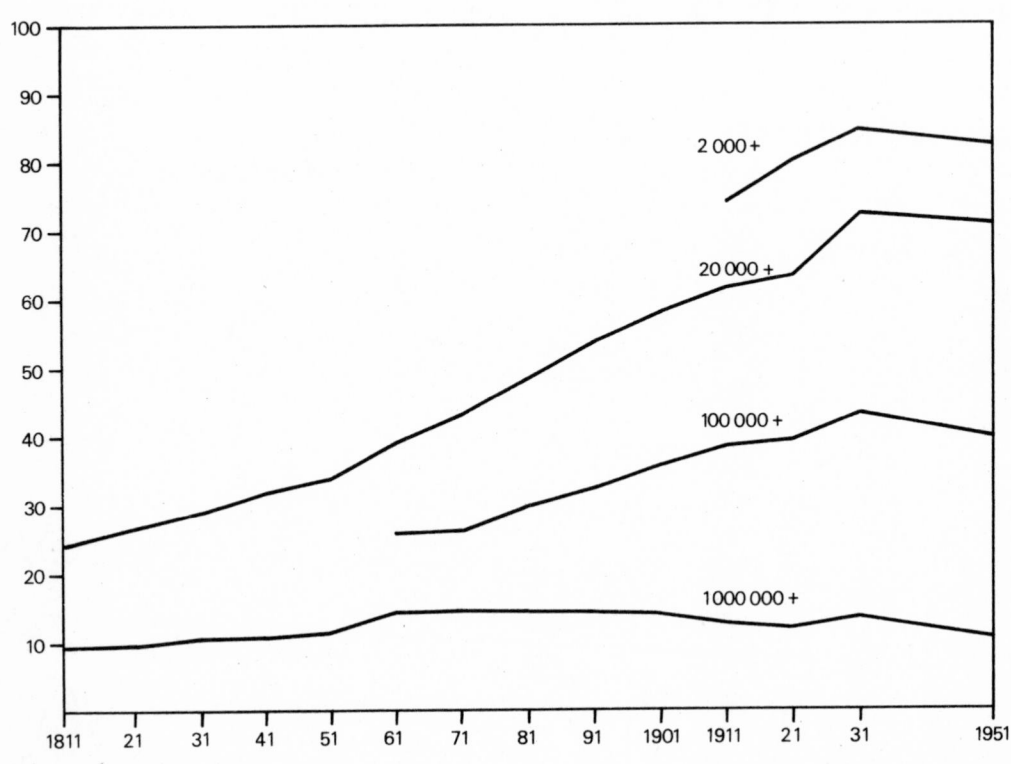

England and Wales
Growth of Cities[a]

	1801	1811	1821	1831	1841	1851	1861	1871	1881	1891	1901	1911	1921	1931	1951	1961	1971
Greater London	1 117	1 327	1 600	1 907	2 239	2 685	3 227	3 890	4 770	5 638	6 586	7 256	7 488	8 216	8 348	8 183	7 452
Liverpool	82	104	138	202	286	376	444	439	553	518	685	746	803	856	789	746	610
Manchester	75	89	126	182	235	303	339	351	341	505	544	714	730	766	703	662	544
Birmingham	71	83	102	144	183	233	296	344	401	478	522	526	919	1 003	1 113	1 107	1 015
Sheffield	46	53	65	92	111	135	185	240	285	324	381	455	491	512	513	494	520
Leeds	53	63	84	123	152	172	207	259	309	368	429	446	458	483	505	511	496
Bristol	61	71	85	104	124	137	154	183	207	222	289	357	377	397	443	437	427
Bradford	13	16	26	44	67	104	106	146	183	216	280	288	286	298	292	296	294
Kingston-upon-Hull	30	37	45	52	67	85	98	122	154	200	240	278	287	314	299	303	286
Newcastle-upon-Tyne	33	33	42	54	70	88	109	128	145	186	215	267	275	283	292	267	284
Nottingham	29	34	40	50	52	57	75	87	187	214	240	260	263	269	306	312	301
Stoke-upon-Trent		28	35	35	54	66	78	101	113	145	215	235	240	277	275	265	265
Portsmouth	33	42	47	50	53	72	95	114	128	159	188	231	247	249	234	215	197
Salford	14	19	26	41	53	64	102	125	176	198	221	231	234	223	178	155	131
Leicester	17	19	26	41	53	61	68	95	122	175	212	227	234	239	285	273	284
Plymouth	40	51	55	66	70	90	113	118	123	139	178	194	210	208	208	204	213
Cardiff	2	2	4	6	10	18	33	40	83	129	164	182	200	224	244	257	279
Bolton	18	25	32	42	51	61	70	83	105	115	168	181	179	177	167	161	154
Sunderland	24	25	31	39	43	65	78	98	117	131	146	151	159	186	182	190	188
Oldham	12	17	22	32	43	53	72	83	111	131	137	147	145	140	121	115	105
Blackburn	12	15	22	27	37	47	63	76	101	120	128	133	127	123	111	106	101
Brighton	7	12	24	41	47	66	78	90	108	116	123	131	142	147	156	163	160
Birkenhead				3	8	24	38	45	84	100	111	131	146	148	143	142	138
Derby	11	13	17	24	33	41	43	50	81	94	106	123	130	142	141	132	139
Norwich	36	37	50	61	62	68	75	80	88	101	112	121	121	126	121	120	121
Southampton	8	10	13	19	28	35	47	54	60	65	105	119	161	176	178	205	215
Gates Head	9	9	12	15	20	26	34	49	66	86	110	117	125	125	115	103	
Preston	12	17	25	34	51	70	83	85	97	108	113	117	117	119	119	113	
Swansea	10	12	15	20	25	31	42	52	66	91	95	115	158	165	161	167	172
South Shields	11	15	17	19	23	29	35	45	57	78	97	109	117	113	107	110	
Stockport	17	21	27	36	50	54	55	53	60	70	79	109	123	125	142	143	140
Huddersfield	7	10	13	19	25	31	35	70	82	95	95	108	110	113	129	130	130
Coventry	16	18	21	17	31	36	41	38	42	53	70	106	128	167	258	306	324
Middlesbrough					6	8	19	40	55	76	91	105	131	138	147	157	
Halifax	12	13	17	22	28	34	57	66	74	90	105	102	99	98	98	96	

a) Cities of 100,000 and more inhabitants in 1911.

Scotland

Urbanization

Distribution of total population by size of locality (number of inhabitants in 1,000s and as % of total population

Year	0–20,000		20–100,000		100–1,000,000		1,000,000+		Year
	1,000	%	1,000	%	1,000	%	1,000	%	
1851	2 149	74.4	250	8.7	489	16.9			1851
1861	2 231	72.9	313	10.2	518	16.9			1861
1871	2 292	68.2	305	9.1	763	22.7			1871
1881	2 396	64.1	378	10.1	962	25.7			1881
1891	2 417	60.0	507	12.6	1 101	27.4			1891
1901	2 332	52.1	747	16.7	1 393	31.2			1901
1911	2 406	50.5	921	19.4	1 434	30.1			1911
1921	2 404	49.2	697	14.3	748	15.3	1 034	21.2	1921
1931	2 249	46.4	724	14.9	782	16.1	1 089	22.5	1931
1951	2 352	46.1	828	16.3	827	16.2	1 090	21.4	1951
1961	2 414	46.6	874	16.9	836	16.1	1 055	20.4	1961
1971	2 538	48.5	975	18.7	1 715	32.8			1971

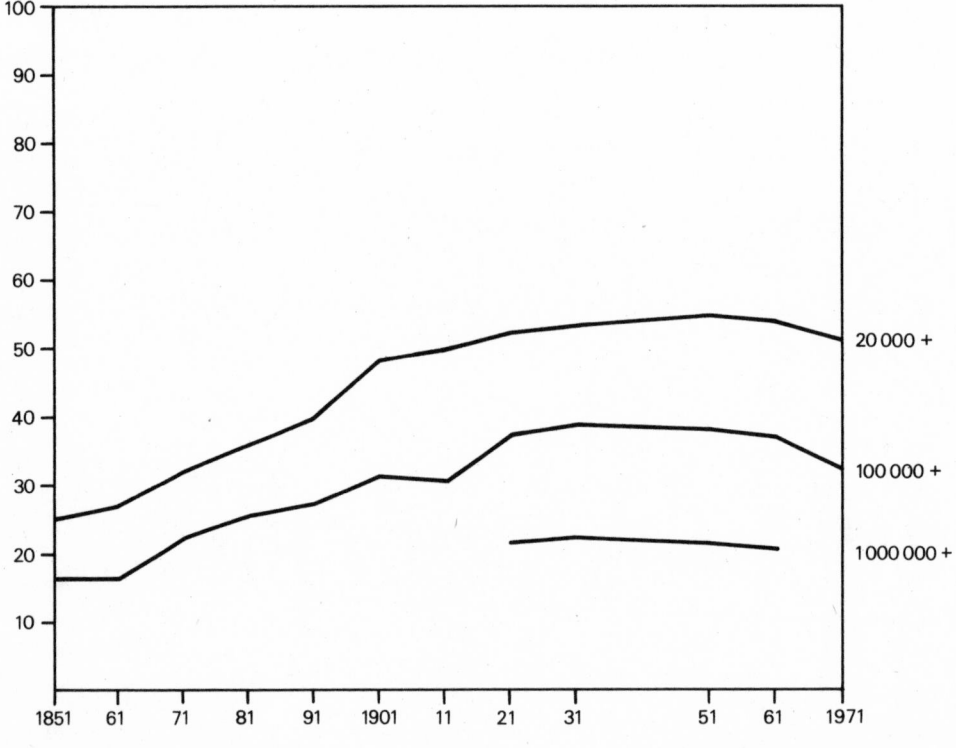

Cumulative percent distribution of population by size of locality

Growth of Cities [a)]

	1851	1861	1871	1881	1891	1901	1911	1921	1931	1951	1961	1971
Glasgow	330	350	477	488	565	762	785	1 034	1 089	1 090	1 055	898
Govan			19	50	62	77	90					
Partik			18	27	37	54	67					
Edinburgh	160	168	197	228	261	317	320	420	439	467	468	454
Leith	31	35	45	60	69	78	81					
Dundee	79	92	119	140	154	161	165	168	176	177	183	182
Aberdeen	72	74	88	105	122	154	164	159	167	183	185	182
Paisley	32	47	48	56	66	79	85	85	86	94	96	95
Greenock	37	43	58	67	63	68	75	81	79	76	75	70
Coatbridge	9	11	16	18	30	37	43	44	43	48	54	52
Motherwell	1	3	7	13	19	30	40	69	65	68	73	74
Wishaw	3	6	11	13	15	21	25					
Kirkcaldy	5	5	6	23	27	34	40	32	44	49	52	50
Hamilton	10	11	12	19	25	33	39	39	38	40	42	46
Core/ Kilcreggan					10	19	38	47	47	45	50	48
Perth	15	14	22	27	30	33	36	33	35	41	41	43
Kilmarnock	19	23	24	26	28	34	35	36	38	42	48	49
Falkirk	9	9	12	16	20	29	34	33	37	38	38	38
Ayr	9	8	8	21	25	29	33	36	37	42	45	48
Dunfermline	9	8	17	20	22	25	28	40	35	45	47	50
Airdrie	14	13	14	13	19	22	24	25	26	30	34	38
Rutherglen	7	8	9	12	12	16	24	25	25	24	25	25
Inverness	10	10	15	17	19	21	22	21	23	18	30	35
Dumbarton	5	6	11	14	17	20	22	23	22	24	26	26
Sterling	9	10	11	16	17	18	21	21	23	27	28	30
Arbroath	8	8	20	22	23	22	21	20	18	20	20	23

a) Cities with 20,000 and more inhabitants in 1911; 1851-1891: parliamentary burgh; 1901-1971: municipal burgh.

Chapter 4

HOUSING CONDITIONS

This chapter provides basic data on the long-term development of housing conditions of the total population or the urban population or both. Mass housing has improved since the nineteenth century in size, fittings, and standards of layout, but it is only for the size that quantitative data are available during the period under consideration. Thus, the main measure of housing conditions used here is the number of persons per habitable room which gives a rather good indication of the amount of space and degree of privacy these persons have. One must be aware, however, that the person/room ratio takes no account of other qualitative improvements in housing which may have occurred at the same time.

Buildings have been enumerated in population censuses from the very beginning, normally as a by-product of the enumeration of the population. In counting people one used to ask how many buildings were inhabited and by how many families/households they were occupied. More detailed data, however, especially on the size of dwellings, did not become available at the national level prior to the end of the nineteenth century, at a time when rapid population growth and urbanization reached a peak volume, intensifying housing problems.

Governments took little direct responsibility for housing before the turn of the century, with the exception of protective legislation against the worst and unacceptable housing and health conditions. Later, some countries also encouraged self-help schemes through cooperatives and unions in working-class housing construction. It is therefore not surprising that more detailed housing statistics did not become available before the turn of the century and frequently only after World War I, when the disruption of housing production during the war and an increased household formation after the war created severe housing shortages.

However, even if we limit ourselves to questions of size and density of housing, difficulties of data comparability are not negligible. A major problem lies in the fact that there are two units of analysis in housing inquiries which do not coincide: the dwelling, and the family or the group of individuals who occupy in common a dwelling or part of it. In general, a dwelling is any room or suite of rooms intended or used for habitation which has a separate access to the street or to a common landing or staircase. Usually, a dwelling lodges only one household, but it may also contain two or more households or families. The definition of a separate dwelling may vary, but the definition of a household is usually more problematic. In general it includes, in addition to the nuclear family, other relatives and indoor domestic servants. Other categories of people, such as lodgers, however, may be treated rather differently from census to census. In more recent times, the increasing share of households formed by persons without kinship or marriage ties creates new problems of comparability.

Housing statistics are normally confined to private households and thus exclude individuals in hotels or boarding houses, in hospitals or institutions for the old, infirm or poor, in schools and prisons, etc. However, on average private households comprise more than 95 percent of the total population. In the enumeration of dwellings a first distinction has to be made between vacant and occupied dwellings. Vacant dwellings may be tenantless or simply not occupied at the time of the census. For these dwellings the information on the number of rooms and persons is of course less reliable and less complete. Data on the distribution of dwellings by size, therefore, frequently refer to occupied dwellings only.

For each (occupied) dwelling usually the following information is collected: the number of households/families living in the dwelling, the number of persons and rooms per household/family. The enumeration of rooms is not without problems: living and bedrooms are always counted, sculleries, landings, lobbies, closets and bathrooms are never counted, but the kitchen may be treated rather differently. In dwellings with more than one household, the treatment of rooms used in common may also vary. Normally, however, more than 90 percent of all dwellings are occupied by one household only.

In the main table on the housing conditions in each country, four data sets are presented:

(1)   the distribution of households or dwellings by the number of rooms;

(2)   the distribution of households by size, i.e. by the number of persons;

(3)   the density of occupation, i.e. the number of persons per room, by household size;

(4)   the distribution of all households by density of occupation.

The improvement of housing conditions in terms of the density of occupation is not only the result of an expanding living space of households. It is also the product of a shrinking household size. The same spatial separation of functions implies much lower ratios of persons to rooms for smaller than for larger households. On the basis of the four data sets, it becomes possible to distinguish and weight the two factors in the development of occupancy rates. No attempt has been made to develop a consistent measure of 'over-crowding' which usually is defined as a person/room ratio in excess of a certain arbitrary limit. Frequently the share of households with ratios of more than two persons per room is taken as an index of overcrowding. Sometimes, however, children are counted differently, and the requirement of a sex separation of unmarried people above a certain age is used in addition to a simple person/room ratio.

In addition to the main tables with the basic housing statistics, more complex cross-tabulations are given for most countries which show the distribution of dwellings by the number of persons *and* the number of rooms. These tables represent the most important general source for an analysis of the inequality of housing conditions among households. Of course, one would have to know more about the households than only their size in order to derive from these housing statistics a more concrete idea of the social structure of the population. However, the complexity of housing statistics has discouraged such an attempt from the very beginning.

Whenever possible, housing statistics are presented for the total population, but sometimes they are only available for the urban population or perhaps only for single cities (which have been included in cases where they represent a larger proportion of the total population, such as Vienna or Copenhagen).

Austria

Housing Conditions

	1890 [a]	1910 [a]	1951	1961	1971 [b]	1975 [b]
Total number of						
– occupied dwellings	552	847	2 138	2 153	2 436	2 589
– persons		3 509	6 923	6 805		
– rooms		2 591		5 458		
Average number of						
– persons per dwelling		4.14		3.16		
– rooms per dwelling		3.06		2.54		
– persons per room		1.35		1.25		
Dwellings by number of room (percent distribution)						
1 room	14.9	14.5	8.4	26.3	7.5	7.3
2 rooms	34.1	38.4	35.9	33.6	25.0	23.1
3		20.3	19.7	20.3	29.9	28.8
4	} 40.6	9.1	14.8	9.7	17.8	19.1
5		6.3	7.6	5.1		
6		4.1	5.5	2.6		
7			2.7	1.2	} 18.8	} 21.5
8	} 10.5	} 7.4	2.1	0.6		
9			1.1	0.3		
10+			2.2	0.3		
Dwellings by number of persons (percent distribution)						
1 person	5.4	6.3		16.7	21.6	25.0
2 persons	15.9	17.9		26.9	27.3	26.5
3		20.0		21.3	17.7	17.0
4	} 48.0	18.4		15.7	14.6	15.2
5		14.4		9.0		
6		9.8		5.0		
7		6.0		2.6	} 18.0	} 16.4
8	} 30.7	3.4		1.4		
9		1.8		0.7		
10+		2.0		0.8		
Persons per room in dwellings with						
1 person		0.50		0.56	0.43	0.37
2 persons		0.82		0.93	0.69	0.63
3		1.04		1.21	0.89	0.85
4		1.29		1.42	1.03	1.02
5		1.50		1.57		
6		1.70		1.69		
7		1.97		1.81	} 1.33	} 1.35
8		2.09		1.91		
9		2.22		2.01		
10+		2.32		2.17		

a) Major cities of the Austrian monarchy; see the following table

b) Microcensus; density for category 5+ estimated according to the percentage distribution in the 1961 housing census

Housing Conditions in Cities [a]

Distribution of dwellings by number of units and occupants, per 1,000 dwellings (o/oo)

1890

Number of occupants	1	2	3	4	5	3-5	6	7-10	6-10	11+	Total o/oo	Total 1,000
1	21.6	18.1				13.2			1.3	0.1	54.3	30.0
2	42.2	65.8				46.1			4.5	0.3	158.9	87.7
3-5	65.4	180.2				193.4			38.4	2.6	479.9	264.9
6-10	18.4	74.1				141.1			39.6	6.2	279.6	154.3
11+	0.8	2.6				11.5			7.7	4.6	27.3	15.1
Total												
o/oo	148.5	340.8				405.5			91.4	13.8	1,000.0	
1,000	81.9	188.1				223.8			50.5	7.6		551.9

1910

Number of occupants	1	2	3	4	5	3-5	6	7-10	6-10	11+	Total o/oo	Total 1,000
1	27.3	21.0	7.2	3.7	1.8	12.7	0.9	0.7	1.6	.0	62.6	53.1
2	39.4	82.1	27.8	14.3	7.9	50.0	4.0	3.7	7.7	0.1	179.2	151.8
3	29.0	85.9	37.3	17.6	11.9	66.9	7.7	10.5	18.2	0.4	200.3	169.7
4	21.0	74.1	38.1	16.7	12.4	85.4	8.2	12.5	20.5	0.8	183.9	155.8
5	13.1	53.3	32.1	13.7	10.5	56.4	7.3	12.6	19.9	1.1	143.7	121.8
3-5	63.0	213.3	107.6	48.0	14.9	190.5	23.1	35.6	58.8	2.3	528.0	447.2
6	7.6	33.0	23.9	9.8	7.1	40.8	5.2	10.0	15.1	1.3	97.8	82.8
7	4.1	14.5	15.7	6.3	4.6	26.5	3.3	6.4	9.6	1.2	59.9	50.7
8	1.9	9.3	9.8	3.9	2.8	16.5	1.9	3.7	5.6	1.0	34.3	29.1
9	0.8	4.3	5.5	2.3	1.6	9.4	1.1	2.0	3.1	0.8	18.4	15.6
10	0.3	1.8	2.8	1.3	0.9	5.0	0.7	1.2	1.9	0.4	9.4	8.0
6-10	14.7	66.9	57.7	23.6	16.9	98.2	12.1	23.3	35.4	4.6	219.8	186.2
11+	0.1	1.1	2.4	1.4	1.3	5.1	1.0	2.0	3.0	1.0	10.4	8.8
Total												
o/oo	144.5	384.4	202.6	91.1	62.8	356.5	41.1	65.4	106.5	8.1	1,000.0	
1,000	122.4	325.6	171.6	77.2	53.2	302.0	34.8	55.4	90.2	6.9		847.1

a) Vienna incl. suburbs, Prague incl. suburbs, Lemberg, Trieste incl. suburbs, Cracow, Graz, Brno, Pilsen, Linz, Innsbruck, Laibach, Reichenberg incl. suburbs, Salzburg, Wiener Neustadt, Troppau, Trent, Klagenfurt, Marburg, Olmütz.

Austria

Housing Conditions in Cities [a]

Distribution of dwellings by number of units and occupants, per 1,000 dwellings (o/oo)

1900

Number of occupants	1	2	3	4	5	6	7	8	9	10	11+	Total o/oo	Total 1,000
1	18.8	22.1	8.9	3.7	1.2				0.3			55.0	17.5
2	28.4	88.3	31.5	13.7	9.2				1.8			173.1	55.2
3													
4	31.9	229.3	133.7	46.1	58.2				19.9			519.2	165.7
5													
6													
7													
8	3.5	82.3	88.1	23.7	31.9				23.2			252.8	80.7
9													
10+													
Total o/oo	82.7	422.0	262.2	87.3	100.6				45.2			1,000.0	
Total 1,000	26.4	134.7	83.7	27.9	32.1				14.4				319.1

1910

Number of occupants	1	2	3	4	5	6	7	8	9	10	11+	Total o/oo	Total 1,000
1	22.6	23.8	7.7	4.1	1.8	0.9			0.8			61.8	27.1
2	25.5	99.0	32.1	15.1	6.9	3.5			4.0			186.1	81.5
3	13.6	101.3	45.1	18.2	10.9	6.6			10.9			206.7	90.6
4	6.5	83.7	46.6	16.8	11.4	6.7			13.7			185.4	81.2
5	3.1	57.6	39.2	12.8	9.5	5.8			13.5			141.2	61.9
6	1.4	34.7	29.2	8.8	6.2	3.9			10.7			94.9	41.6
7	0.8	18.6	19.4	5.3	3.8	2.5			7.0			57.3	25.1
8	0.3	8.8	12.3	3.3	2.2	1.3			4.0			32.2	14.1
9	0.1	3.7	6.9	1.9	1.3	0.7			2.4			17.0	7.4
10+	0.1	2.3	6.4	2.0	1.5	1.1			4.0			17.4	7.6
Total o/oo	74.1	433.4	244.9	88.2	55.6	32.9			70.9			1,000.0	
Total 1,000	32.5	189.9	107.3	38.6	24.3	14.4			31.1				438.1

1934

Number of occupants	1	2	3	4	5	6	7	8	9	10	11+	Total 1,000
1	1.9	26.3	49.2	20.0	39.1	22.8	21.5	10.5	9.2	4.8	10.3	
2	2.5	32.2	131.5	67.7								
3	0.6	18.0	109.0	75.6	47.9	36.0	16.8	10.8	4.7	3.3		
4			51.6	50.6							5.4	
5	0.5	10.6	19.0	23.6	15.9	11.6						
6												
7+			11.7	17.7	4.0	2.9	1.7	1.2				
Total o/oo	5.5	87.1	372.0	255.2	106.9	73.3	40.0	22.5	13.9	8.1	15.7	
Total 1,000	3.3	52.7	224.8	154.2	64.6	44.3	24.2	13.6	8.4	4.9	9.5	604.4

a) Vienna only

H o u s i n g   C o n d i t i o n s

Distribution of dwellings by number of units and occupants, per 1,000 dwellings (o/oo)

1961

Number of occupants	Number of units										Total	
	1	2	3	4	5	6	7	8	9	10+	o/oo	1,000
1	84.0	53.6	18.5	6.6	2.5	1.0	0.4	0.2	0.1	0.1	167.1	359.8
2	90.2	101.7	46.4	17.8	7.2	3.0	1.2	0.6	0.2	0.3	268.6	578.2
3	47.9	81.4	47.3	19.9	9.1	4.0	1.6	0.7	0.3	0.3	212.5	457.5
4	24.3	52.8	41.8	19.6	10.0	4.8	2.0	0.9	0.4	0.4	157.1	338.1
5	9.8	25.7	24.2	14.1	8.3	4.4	2.0	0.9	0.4	0.4	90.1	194.1
6	3.9	11.9	12.6	9.1	5.7	3.3	1.7	0.9	0.4	0.4	50.0	107.5
7	1.6	5.3	6.2	5.0	3.6	2.2	1.2	0.6	0.3	0.3	26.4	56.7
8	0.7	2.3	2.9	2.6	2.1	1.5	0.7	0.4	0.2	0.3	13.7	29.5
9	0.3	1.0	1.4	1.3	1.1	0.9	0.5	0.3	0.1	0.2	7.1	15.3
10+	0.2	0.8	1.2	1.2	1.2	1.0	0.7	0.5	0.3	0.4	7.5	16.2
Total												
o/oo	262.9	336.4	202.5	97.4	50.7	26.2	12.0	6.0	2.7	3.2	1,000.0	
1,000	565.9	724.2	436.0	209.6	109.2	56.4	25.8	13.0	5.9	6.8		2,152.8

1971

Number of occupants	Number of units				5 6 7 8 9 10+	Un- known	Total	
	1	2	3	4			o/oo	1,000
1	45	91	54	15	9	1	216	592.2
2	21	93	93	40	25	1	273	670.3
3	6	39	66	38	28		177	433.9
4	2	18	48	39	39		146	359.6
5 6 7 8 9 10+	1	9	38	46	87		188	443.0
Total								
o/oo	75	250	299	178	188	2	1,000	
1,000	185.3	612.5	734.2	435.6	462.5	73		2,436.9

1975

Number of occupants	Number of units				5 6 7 8 9 10+	Total	
	1	2	3	4		o/o	1,000
1	39	86	69	31	23	250	646.3
2	19	74	86	45	40	265	685.7
3	8	36	53	37	35	170	439.0
4	4	21	45	37	45	152	394.2
5 6 7 8 9 10+	3	14	34	40	72	164	423.9
Total							
o/oo	73	231	288	191	215	1,000.0	
1,000	187.8	599.1	745.4	494.5	557.9		2 589.0

Housing Conditions[a]

	1910	1920	1930	1947	1947	1961	1970
Total number (in 1,000) of							
- dwellings[b]	832	953	1 113	1 435	2 816	3 016	3 135
- persons	2 979	3 080	3 507	3 833	8 338	8 998	9 493
- rooms	3 310	3 492	4 669	5 322	10 890	14 444	15 865
Average number of							
- persons per dwelling	3.58	3.23	3.15	2.67	2.96	2.98	2.95
- rooms per dwelling	3.98	3.67	4.20	3.71	3.87	4.79	4.92
- persons per room	0.90	0.88	0.75	0.72	0.77	0.62	0.60
Dwellings by number of rooms (percent distribution)							
1 room	13.4	13.2	7.2	7.9	5.8	2.3	0.7
2 rooms	19.7	22.3	18.6	21.1	19.7	8.1	5.4
3	16.6	18.2	18.3	22.2	20.1	14.5	12.6
4	19.7	20.6	19.8	21.9	24.6	23.5	23.9
5	9.8	9.2	13.2	12.5	13.6	19.8	24.3
6	6.9	6.4	8.9	7.0	8.4	16.3	18.0
7	3.7	3.0	4.7	3.1	3.4	7.2	7.8
8	3.0	2.5	3.1	1.9	2.2	4.0	4.1
9	1.8	1.2	1.9	0.9	0.9	1.8	1.6
10+	5.5	3.3	4.2	1.6	1.4	2.4	1.7
Dwellings by number of persons (percent distribution)							
1 person	14.2	15.0	11.3	20.7	16.7	16.8	18.0
2 persons	20.5	25.2	28.9	33.4	30.7	31.0	30.4
3	21.7	24.3	26.6	23.9	23.9	21.6	20.3
4	16.8	16.3	16.6	12.1	14.1	14.6	15.0
5	10.9	9.0	8.5	5.1	7.0	7.9	8.2
6	6.7	4.8	4.1	2.3	3.6	4.1	4.3
7	4.0	2.5	2.0	1.1	1.8	2.0	2.0
8	2.4	1.5	1.0	0.6	1.0	1.0	0.9
9	1.4	0.7	0.5	0.3	0.5	0.5	0.5
10+	1.5	0.8	0.6	0.4	0.7	0.5	0.4
Persons per room in dwellings with							
1 person	0.52	0.49	0.41	0.40	0.38	0.29	0.26
2 persons	0.57	0.61	0.54	0.56	0.55	0.45	0.43
3	0.74	0.71	0.71	0.76	0.75	0.61	0.59
4	0.89	0.94	0.83	0.90	0.91	0.74	0.73
5	1.04	1.09	0.95	1.03	1.06	0.87	0.85
6	1.20	1.25	1.07	1.14	1.21	0.98	0.97
7	1.38	1.42	1.18	1.26	1.35	1.10	1.08
8	1.55	1.60	1.32	1.41	1.51	1.22	1.20
9	1.68	1.76	1.41	1.50	1.64	1.32	1.31
10+	1.74	1.82	1.56	1.53	1.73	1.53	1.51

a) 1910-1947: cities of 10,000 and more inhabitants; 1947-1970: total population
b) 1910-1961: occupied dwellings; 1970: private households

Housing Conditions in Cities 1910

Distribution of dwellings by number of units and occupants, per 1,000 dwellings (o/oo)

Number of occupants	Number of units 1	2	3	4	5	6	7	8	9	10+	Total o/oo	1,000
Cities of 10,000 – 25,000 inhabitants												
1	28.1	21.1	8.5	9.6	3.9	3.0	1.3	1.1	0.4	0.7	77.7	21.0
2	8.1	40.9	30.4	47.5	21.3	16.1	7.3	5.6	2.8	4.2	184.1	49.8
3	4.0	35.3	36.6	65.6	29.2	21.7	10.4	7.4	3.9	7.0	221.0	59.8
4	1.3	22.5	28.5	60.0	27.0	19.4	9.4	6.6	3.9	7.1	158.8	50.2
5	0.5	12.7	19.8	41.4	19.1	13.2	6.4	4.7	2.7	6.0	126.6	34.2
6	0.2	6.9	13.0	27.1	12.6	8.4	4.2	3.2	1.8	4.3	81.8	22.1
7	0.1	4.2	7.8	16.8	8.5	5.7	2.6	2.0	1.0	2.7	51.3	13.9
8	0.1	2.1	5.0	10.8	5.3	3.3	1.7	1.1	0.7	1.9	32.1	8.7
9	0.0	1.2	3.0	6.0	3.3	2.2	1.1	0.7	0.4	1.2	19.0	5.1
10+	0.0	0.9	2.4	5.9	3.4	2.4	1.2	1.0	0.5	3.0	20.6	5.6
Total o/oo	42.3	147.7	154.9	290.7	133.6	95.5	45.6	33.5	18.0	38.2	1,000.0	
1,000	11.4	39.9	41.9	78.6	36.1	25.8	12.3	9.0	4.9	10.3		270.4
Cities of 25,000 – 100,000 inhabitants												
1	90.3	29.8	13.1	8.0	3.4	2.4	1.3	1.0	0.4	1.3	151.0	48.4
2	26.6	66.3	40.0	32.6	15.6	10.7	6.6	5.6	3.0	6.8	213.9	68.5
3	12.3	57.3	44.2	40.1	19.4	14.3	8.1	7.0	4.1	11.6	218.5	70.0
4	5.0	32.9	31.8	53.3	17.2	12.4	7.2	6.2	3.9	12.1	164.1	52.6
5	1.8	16.0	19.6	23.1	12.8	8.7	5.1	4.4	2.8	10.1	104.4	33.5
6	0.6	8.1	11.0	15.0	8.2	5.8	3.2	2.6	1.7	7.3	63.5	20.3
7	0.2	4.2	6.4	9.4	4.9	3.3	1.9	1.5	1.0	4.5	37.2	11.9
8	0.1	2.1	3.5	6.1	3.1	1.9	1.0	0.8	0.5	2.8	22.0	7.0
9	0.1	1.0	1.7	3.2	1.8	1.2	0.6	0.4	0.3	1.7	12.1	3.9
10+	0.0	0.7	1.3	3.0	2.0	1.3	0.6	0.5	0.3	3.7	13.4	4.3
Total o/oo	137.0	218.4	172.6	176.0	88.3	62.0	35.6	30.1	18.1	61.8	1,000.0	
1,000	43.9	70.0	55.3	56.4	28.3	19.9	11.4	9.7	5.8	19.8		320.4
Cities of 100,000 and more inhabitants												
1	142.9	31.2	13.2	6.6	3.0	1.9	1.0	0.8	0.5	1.1	202.3	48.8
2	47.2	66.9	39.7	23.3	12.8	7.9	4.7	4.1	2.4	5.9	214.9	51.8
3	23.6	56.0	45.5	30.2	16.3	11.2	6.3	6.1	3.8	11.1	210.1	50.7
4	10.8	33.1	31.6	25.3	14.7	10.0	5.9	5.4	3.6	11.9	152.4	36.8
5	4.8	17.1	18.1	15.5	10.3	6.9	4.3	4.1	2.9	11.0	95.0	22.9
6	2.1	9.1	10.2	8.9	6.0	4.2	2.6	2.3	1.8	8.3	55.5	13.4
7	0.9	4.9	5.8	4.9	3.4	2.5	1.4	1.3	1.1	5.7	31.7	7.7
8	0.3	2.7	3.2	2.7	2.1	1.4	0.8	0.8	0.5	3.6	18.0	4.4
9	0.1	1.2	1.6	1.3	1.0	0.6	0.3	0.3	0.3	2.3	9.2	2.2
10+	0.1	0.7	1.3	1.1	1.0	0.7	0.5	0.4	0.4	4.6	10.8	2.6
Total o/oo	233.0	233.0	170.2	119.7	70.8	47.2	27.6	25.8	17.3	65.5	1,000.0	
1,000	56.2	53.8	41.1	28.9	17.1	11.4	6.7	6.2	4.2	15.8		241.2

Belgium

Housing Conditions in Cities 1920

Distribution of dwellings by number of units and occupants, per 1,000 dwellings (o/oo)

Number of occupants	Number of units										Un-known	Total	
	1	2	3	4	5	6	7	8	9	10+		o/oo	1,000
Cities of 10,000 - 25,000 inhabitants													
1	33.1	25.3	10.9	14.8	5.3	3.8	1.7	1.5	0.5	1.7		98.5	31.3
2	14.2	58.6	37.3	60.0	23.5	17.4	6.9	4.9	1.9	3.7		228.5	72.5
3	7.4	45.7	44.2	76.5	30.7	21.9	8.3	6.1	2.3	4.7		247.9	78.7
4	2.0	24.3	30.2	61.3	24.9	17.2	6.9	4.7	2.2	4.4		178.1	56.5
5	0.7	11.8	17.8	37.4	15.7	10.3	5.0	3.2	1.5	3.0		106.4	33.8
6	0.3	5.9	11.0	20.5	8.6	5.9	2.4	2.1	0.9	2.4		59.9	19.0
7	0.1	3.4	6.5	12.0	5.1	3.4	1.7	1.2	0.5	1.4		35.3	11.2
8	0.1	1.9	3.9	7.0	3.0	1.9	0.9	0.7	0.3	0.9		20.4	6.5
9	0.0	0.9	2.1	3.9	1.8	1.1	0.5	0.3	0.2	0.5		11.4	3.6
10+	0.0	0.9	1.8	4.0	2.1	1.3	0.6	0.4	0.2	2.1		13.4	4.3
Total o/oo	58.0	178.7	165.8	297.3	120.7	84.2	34.8	25.1	10.6	24.7		1,000.0	
1,000	18.4	56.7	52.6	94.4	38.3	26.7	11.1	8.0	3.4	7.8			317.4
Cities of 25,000 - 100,000 inhabitants													
1	81.7	37.2	15.8	9.4	3.6	2.5	1.7	0.9	0.4	1.0	0.8	155.1	53.0
2	32.3	85.0	55.1	40.2	17.7	12.6	5.8	5.1	2.2	4.4	1.0	261.3	89.3
3	13.5	62.3	54.3	48.3	22.7	15.9	8.1	6.1	3.1	7.3	1.0	242.6	82.9
4	3.6	33.2	32.5	36.9	18.0	13.3	6.7	5.5	2.8	7.4	0.6	160.5	54.9
5	1.3	12.6	15.8	20.4	10.6	7.6	4.3	3.8	2.0	5.9	0.4	84.5	28.9
6	0.5	5.2	8.1	11.3	5.7	4.3	2.1	2.1	1.3	3.9	0.2	44.8	15.3
7	0.3	2.4	3.7	5.9	2.8	2.2	1.2	1.1	0.6	2.4	0.1	22.8	7.8
8	0.1	1.4	2.0	3.4	1.7	1.1	0.6	0.6	0.4	1.6	0.1	12.9	4.4
9	0.1	0.6	1.1	1.8	1.0	0.6	0.3	0.3	0.2	1.0	0.1	7.2	2.5
10+	0.1	0.4	0.9	1.6	0.9	0.5	0.3	0.3	0.2	2.4	0.5	8.2	2.8
Total o/oo	133.5	240.4	189.4	179.2	84.7	60.6	31.1	25.7	13.3	37.3	4.8	1,000.0	
1,000	45.6	82.1	64.7	61.2	28.9	20.7	10.6	8.8	4.5	12.7	1.6		341.6
Cities of 100,000 and more inhabitants													
1	126.1	39.1	16.7	8.0	2.9	1.8	1.0	0.8	0.4	0.8	0.6	198.0	58.2
2	49.0	90.6	54.2	32.4	14.0	9.0	4.1	3.5	1.9	3.7	1.3	263.7	77.5
3	23.1	66.0	54.9	39.0	19.0	12.1	5.9	5.5	3.0	6.5	1.3	236.1	69.4
4	7.7	30.7	32.9	28.1	15.0	10.5	5.6	5.1	2.9	7.3	0.9	146.7	43.1
5	2.7	12.9	15.7	14.6	9.3	6.0	3.4	3.7	2.0	6.5	0.7	77.4	22.7
6	1.0	5.7	7.0	6.7	4.2	3.0	1.8	2.1	1.3	4.6	0.4	37.8	11.1
7	0.4	2.8	3.4	3.2	1.9	1.6	1.0	0.9	0.7	3.1	0.3	19.2	5.6
8	0.1	1.2	1.7	1.6	1.0	0.8	0.5	0.6	0.4	1.9	0.2	9.9	2.9
9	0.0	0.6	0.8	0.8	0.5	0.3	0.2	0.3	0.3	1.2	0.1	5.1	1.5
10+	0.0	0.3	0.6	0.7	0.4	0.4	0.2	0.3	0.2	2.6	0.5	6.2	1.8
Total o/oo	210.0	249.9	187.8	135.0	68.0	45.5	23.8	22.6	13.0	38.1	6.1	1,000.0	
1,000	61.7	73.4	55.2	39.7	20.0	13.4	7.0	6.6	3.8	11.2	1.8		293.8

Housing Conditions in Cities 1930

Distribution of dwellings by number of units and occupants, per 1,000 dwellings (o/oo)

Number of occupants	Number of units										Total	
	1	2	3	4	5	6	7	8	9	10+	o/oo	1,000
Cities of 10,000 − 25,000 inhabitants												
1	14.3	18.6	10.2	10.8	4.8	3.1	1.7	1.0	0.5	0.7	65.7	24.9
2	8.3	54.1	44.7	61.0	35.9	22.5	10.8	6.4	3.1	4.2	251.0	94.9
3	4.3	40.1	45.2	73.7	48.2	29.3	13.4	8.4	4.3	5.9	272.9	103.2
4	1.5	17.2	26.9	55.5	36.7	24.2	12.0	7.4	3.8	6.0	191.1	72.3
5	0.4	6.4	13.3	29.8	22.5	14.2	7.5	4.8	2.7	4.9	106.6	40.3
6	0.2	2.7	6.4	15.0	11.1	7.8	3.9	2.8	1.6	3.1	54.7	20.7
7	0.1	1.0	3.0	7.0	5.8	4.0	2.2	1.5	0.9	2.0	27.5	10.4
8	0.0	0.4	1.4	3.6	3.1	2.3	1.3	0.9	0.4	1.2	14.6	5.5
9	0.0	0.2	0.7	1.6	1.6	1.2	0.7	0.5	0.2	0.8	7.7	2.9
10+	0.0	0.2	0.6	1.5	1.6	1.4	0.9	0.6	0.3	1.0	8.2	3.1
Total												
o/oo	29.1	140.9	152.4	259.6	171.4	110.0	54.5	34.4	17.9	29.7	1,000.0	
1,000	11.0	53.3	57.6	98.2	64.8	41.6	20.6	13.0	6.8	11.2		378.2
Cities of 25,000 − 100,000 inhabitants												
1	46.4	32.7	16.7	10.4	5.4	3.3	1.8	1.3	0.7	1.4	120.1	51.6
2	16.7	82.2	67.3	51.1	31.3	20.2	10.2	6.5	3.7	7.0	296.2	127.2
3	5.9	51.1	59.2	54.2	36.8	25.2	12.7	7.8	5.0	9.9	267.7	114.9
4	1.9	19.4	29.4	34.2	26.8	19.7	10.2	6.8	4.4	9.7	162.3	69.7
5	0.7	5.7	12.1	16.0	14.7	10.9	6.0	4.1	3.0	7.6	80.8	34.7
6	0.2	2.1	4.5	7.2	6.8	5.1	3.0	2.2	1.7	4.9	37.6	16.1
7	0.1	0.8	1.7	3.0	3.4	2.5	1.5	1.1	0.9	3.0	18.1	7.8
8	0.0	0.3	0.8	1.3	1.7	1.1	0.7	0.6	0.4	1.3	8.3	3.5
9	0.0	0.2	0.4	0.6	0.7	0.5	0.3	0.3	0.2	1.0	4.4	1.9
10+	0.0	0.1	0.2	0.5	0.7	0.5	0.4	0.3	0.2	1.6	4.5	1.9
Total												
o/oo	71.9	194.7	192.4	178.6	128.2	89.1	46.7	30.9	20.1	47.3	1,000.0	
1,000	30.9	83.6	82.6	76.7	55.0	38.3	20.1	13.3	8.6	20.3		429.3
Cities of 100,000 and more inhabitants												
1	74.1	40.8	21.7	10.6	4.9	2.9	1.5	1.0	0.7	1.2	160.0	48.8
2	32.5	101.2	78.3	46.2	25.5	15.9	9.0	5.8	3.7	6.4	324.6	99.1
3	11.6	57.1	62.8	44.6	26.9	18.5	10.9	7.3	4.8	9.8	254.2	77.6
4	4.0	21.0	28.7	27.2	17.5	13.0	8.4	6.0	4.4	10.2	140.4	42.9
5	1.1	6.7	10.6	11.7	8.5	6.8	4.6	3.9	2.8	8.1	64.8	19.8
6	0.5	2.4	3.8	4.8	3.5	3.0	2.3	1.9	1.6	5.5	29.4	9.0
7	0.1	0.8	1.4	1.9	1.5	1.2	1.0	0.9	0.8	3.6	13.3	4.1
8	0.0	0.4	0.5	0.8	0.6	0.6	0.5	0.4	0.3	2.2	6.2	1.9
9	0.0	0.2	0.3	0.4	0.3	0.3	0.2	0.2	0.2	1.4	3.5	1.1
10+	0.0	0.0	0.1	0.3	0.2	0.2	0.2	0.2	0.2	2.1	3.6	1.1
Total												
o/oo	124.5	230.6	208.3	184.4	89.6	62.5	38.4	27.6	19.6	50.5	1,000.0	
1,000	38.0	70.4	63.6	45.3	27.4	19.1	11.7	8.4	6.0	15.4		305.3

Housing Conditions in Cities 1947

Distribution of dwellings by number of units and occupants, per 1,000 dwellings (o/oo)

Number of occupants	Number of units										Total	
	1	2	3	4	5	6	7	8	9	10+	o/oo	1,000
Cities of 5,000 - 20,000 inhabitants												
1	31.0	53.3	21.5	21.1	9.1	5.0	1.8	1.1	0.5	0.6	145.0	122.4
2	9.8	77.1	63.5	77.4	41.1	21.5	7.7	4.6	1.7	2.0	306.3	258.6
3	5.4	44.7	49.9	70.8	39.6	22.0	8.2	4.6	1.8	2.2	249.1	210.3
4	1.9	17.6	26.6	44.7	26.7	16.3	6.6	3.7	1.5	2.1	147.9	124.8
5	0.7	6.0	11.8	21.0	14.6	9.0	3.9	2.5	1.1	1.5	72.2	60.9
6	0.4	2.4	5.3	10.4	7.3	5.1	2.2	1.5	0.6	1.1	36.5	30.8
7	0.2	1.0	2.5	5.2	4.2	2.8	1.3	0.9	0.5	0.7	19.3	16.3
8	0.2	0.6	1.2	2.7	2.3	1.6	0.7	0.6	0.2	0.5	10.7	9.1
9	0.0	0.2	0.5	1.3	1.2	0.9	0.4	0.3	0.1	0.3	5.4	4.5
10+	0.3	0.3	0.5	1.4	1.4	1.1	0.6	0.4	0.2	1.4	7.6	6.4
Total												
o/oo	50.0	203.3	183.4	256.0	147.4	85.4	33.6	20.3	8.3	12.4	1,000.0	
1,000	42.2	171.6	154.8	216.0	124.4	72.0	28.4	17.1	7.0	10.5		844.0
Cities of 20,000 - 100,000 inhabitants												
1	52.2	69.3	38.4	22.7	9.4	4.9	2.0	1.1	0.6	0.8	201.5	134.8
2	11.9	80.3	91.9	75.9	40.3	20.4	8.1	4.5	2.0	2.9	338.3	226.3
3	4.7	38.6	60.3	62.4	36.8	20.2	8.2	4.6	2.1	3.0	241.0	161.3
4	1.4	12.6	23.8	32.7	22.1	14.0	6.5	3.8	1.8	2.7	121.4	81.2
5	0.4	3.6	7.8	12.0	10.3	6.9	3.7	2.3	1.4	2.1	50.5	33.8
6	0.2	1.2	2.8	5.0	4.7	3.5	2.0	1.5	0.9	1.7	23.3	15.6
7	0.1	0.5	1.1	2.1	2.1	1.7	1.1	0.8	0.5	1.1	11.1	7.4
8	0.2	0.2	0.5	1.0	1.0	0.9	0.5	0.5	0.3	0.7	5.8	3.9
9	0.0	0.1	0.2	0.5	0.5	0.4	0.3	0.2	0.1	0.4	2.8	1.9
10+	0.1	0.1	0.2	0.5	0.6	0.5	0.3	0.3	0.2	1.6	4.4	2.9
Total												
o/oo	71.2	206.5	227.0	214.7	127.9	73.5	32.7	19.5	9.9	17.0	1,000.0	
1,000	47.7	138.2	151.9	143.6	85.6	49.2	21.9	13.0	6.6	11.4		669.1
Cities of 100,000 and more inhabitants												
1	89.8	87.8	51.0	23.9	9.3	4.3	2.0	1.2	0.7	1.2	270.9	97.2
2	19.3	86.3	106.4	70.2	32.4	16.1	7.2	4.3	2.0	2.8	346.9	124.5
3	6.5	34.7	63.8	53.6	27.5	14.6	6.7	4.2	2.1	2.8	216.6	77.7
4	1.8	11.2	23.1	53.3	14.9	9.4	4.9	3.3	1.7	2.8	98.4	35.3
5	0.5	3.1	6.9	8.7	6.1	4.2	2.6	1.9	1.1	2.2	37.4	13.4
6	0.2	1.0	2.4	3.1	2.4	2.0	1.2	0.9	0.7	1.5	15.4	5.5
7	0.1	0.4	0.9	1.3	1.0	0.8	0.6	0.6	0.3	1.0	6.9	2.5
8	0.1	0.2	0.4	0.6	0.5	0.4	0.3	0.3	0.2	0.6	3.4	1.2
9	0.0	0.1	0.1	0.3	0.2	0.2	0.1	0.1	0.1	0.4	1.7	0.6
10+	0.0	0.0	0.1	0.2	0.3	0.2	0.1	0.1	0.1	1.2	2.4	0.9
Total												
o/oo	118.3	224.9	255.2	187.2	94.5	52.1	25.7	16.8	9.0	16.3	1,000.0	
1,000	42.5	80.7	91.5	67.1	33.9	18.7	9.2	6.0	3.2	5.9		338.8

Housing Conditions

Distribution of dwellings by number of units and occupants, per 1,000 dwellings (o/oo)

1947

Number of occupants	Number of units										Total	
	1	2	3	4	5	6	7	8	9	10+	o/oo	1,000
1	39.3	57.8	28.7	22.6	9.0	5.1	2.0	1.4	.5	.7	167.1	470.6
2	10.5	74.8	72.1	75.0	37.3	20.7	7.7	4.9	1.8	2.4	306.6	863.5
3	5.0	40.3	53.0	66.5	35.9	21.0	7.9	4.9	1.9	2.4	238.8	672.4
4	1.7	15.7	26.4	42.3	24.7	16.1	6.6	4.1	1.6	2.2	141.4	398.2
5	0.6	5.4	11.3	19.8	13.8	9.3	4.2	2.8	1.2	1.7	70.1	197.3
6	0.3	2.1	5.1	9.7	7.0	5.3	2.4	1.7	0.7	1.2	35.5	100.0
7	0.1	0.9	2.3	4.8	3.8	2.8	1.4	1.0	0.5	0.9	18.5	52.0
8	0.1	0.5	1.1	2.5	2.0	1.5	.8	.6	0.3	0.6	10.0	28.2
9		0.2	0.5	1.2	1.0	0.8	0.4	0.4	0.2	0.4	5.1	14.3
10+		0.1	0.5	1.2	1.3	1.1	0.6	0.4	0.2	1.5	6.9	19.6
Total												
o/oo	57.6	197.2	201.0	245.6	135.8	83.7	34.0	22.2	8.9	14.0	1,000.0	
1,000	162.3	555.3	565.9	691.4	382.5	235.7	95.7	62.5	25.0	39.3		2,816.0

1961

Number of occupants	Number of units										Total	
	1	2	3	4	5	6	7	8	9	10+	o/oo	1,000
1	20.3	40.3	36.9	32.6	17.5	10.7	4.4	2.7	1.2	1.7	168.4	507.8
2	2.3	27.6	62.2	86.0	59.9	39.3	15.3	8.4	3.6	4.8	309.6	933.6
3	0.7	8.7	28.0	59.4	50.2	37.9	15.1	7.9	3.3	4.2	215.5	650.1
4	0.1	3.0	11.5	33.4	35.6	33.1	14.3	7.6	3.2	4.2	146.1	440.7
5	0.0	0.9	4.0	14.0	18.7	20.5	9.7	5.5	2.4	3.2	78.9	238.1
6	0.0	0.1	1.5	5.8	8.9	11.2	6.0	3.6	1.6	2.3	41.1	124.0
7	0.0	0.0	0.6	2.3	4.1	5.4	3.4	2.0	1.0	1.4	20.2	60.9
8	0.0	0.0	0.2	1.0	1.9	2.8	1.8	1.2	0.6	0.9	10.4	31.3
9	0.0	0.0	0.0	0.4	0.8	1.3	0.9	0.6	0.3	0.5	4.8	14.5
10+	0.0	0.0	0.0	0.2	0.6	1.2	1.0	0.9	0.4	0.7	5.0	15.4
Total												
o/oo	23.4	80.6	144.9	235.1	198.2	163.4	71.9	40.4	17.6	23.9	1,000.0	
1,000	70.6	243.3	437.1	709.2	598.1	492.5	216.8	121.8	53.1	72.0		3,016.4

1970

Number of occupants	Number of units										Total	
	1	2	3	4	5	6	7	8	9	10+	o/oo	1,000
1	5.9	32.9	45.1	44.9	25.4	14.4	5.4	3.1	1.3	1.4	179.8	563.6
2	0.6	14.3	51.7	93.1	72.4	43.2	15.5	7.9	2.7	2.7	304.1	953.2
3	0.2	3.9	17.9	54.9	59.6	39.6	15.0	7.1	2.6	2.4	203.3	637.1
4	0.0	1.6	6.9	29.0	45.6	37.2	15.8	7.8	2.7	2.8	149.5	468.6
5	0.0	0.7	2.4	10.5	23.2	23.0	11.7	6.2	2.4	2.5	82.5	258.6
6	0.0	0.3	0.9	3.9	9.9	12.5	7.2	4.1	1.7	1.9	42.5	133.3
7	0.0	0.1	0.4	1.5	3.9	5.7	3.9	2.4	1.0	1.2	20.2	63.2
8	0.0	0.1	0.1	0.6	1.5	2.5	1.9	1.3	0.6	0.7	9.4	29.3
9	0.0	0.0	0.1	0.2	0.7	1.2	1.0	0.7	0.3	0.4	4.6	14.3
10+	0.0	0.0	0.0	0.2	0.5	0.9	0.9	0.8	0.4	0.6	4.3	13.3
Total												
o/oo	6.7	53.9	125.5	238.8	242.5	180.3	78.5	41.3	15.8	16.7	1,000.0	
1,000	21.1	168.9	393.3	748.4	760.3	565.1	246.0	129.5	49.5	52.3		3,134.6

Housing Conditions [a]

	1901	1916	1930	1960	1965	1970
Total number (in 1,000) of						
- occupied dwellings	119	165	238	1 463	1 578	1 743
- persons	456	569	767	4 466	4 629	4 780
- rooms	361	494	735	4 941	5 510	6 251
Average number of						
- persons	3.84	3.45	3.22	3.05	2.93	2.74
- rooms	3.04	2.99	3.08	3.38	3.49	3.59
- persons per room	1.26	1.15	1.04	0.90	0.84	0.76
Dwellings by number of rooms (percent distribution)						
1 room	11.5	8.6	7.2	3.5	3.5	3.7
2 rooms	39.4	39.2	38.2	25.0	22.9	20.9
3	18.4	22.1	23.1	30.6	30.8	28.1
4	15.5	17.1	17.2	21.0	23.5	24.7
5	6.5	6.4	6.9	9.3	10.2	11.2
6	3.8	3.4	3.7	} 8.9	} 8.9	} 10.5
7	2.2	1.6	1.9			
8	1.2	0.7	0.9			
9	0.6	0.3	0.4			
10+	1.0	0.6	0.6			
Dwellings by number of persons (percent distribution)						
1 person	10.7	13.6	14.0	16.0	18.2	21.4
2 persons	19.2	22.0	25.6	27.4	27.8	30.4
3	20.6	22.0	24.4	20.9	20.6	19.1
4	17.1	17.3	17.2	18.9	18.5	17.2
5	12.7	11.4	9.4	9.7	9.2	7.9
6	8.6	6.6	4.6	4.2	3.6	2.8
7	5.3	3.6	2.2	1.7	1.3	0.9
8	3.0	1.8	1.0	} 1.2	} 1.2	} 4.3
9	1.5	0.9	0.4			
10+	1.4	0.8	1.2			
Persons per room in dwellings with						
1 person	.59	.55	.49	0.41	0.40	0.39
2 persons	.79	.75	.71	0.63	0.61	0.59
3	1.01	.98	.95	0.88	0.83	0.79
4	1.25	1.22	1.18	1.09	1.03	0.95
5	1.47	1.42	1.36	1.23	1.16	1.08
6	1.67	1.63	1.53	1.35	1.29	1.21
7	1.86	1.85	1.68	1.51	1.39	1.34
8+	1.96	2.12	2.20	1.77	1.72	1.66

a) 1901–1930: Copenhagen; 1960–1970: whole country.

Denmark

Housing Conditions in Cities [a]

Distribution of dwellings by number of units and occupants, per 1,000 dwellings (o/oo)

1901

Number of occupants	Number of units										Total	
	1	2	3	4	5	6	7	8	9	10+	o/oo	1,000
1	55.8	37.3	7.2	4.8	1.3	0.5	0.1	0.0	0.0	0.0	107.1	12.7
2	27.3	95.5	29.0	25.8	9.3	3.2	0.9	0.4	0.2	0.1	191.6	22.7
3	14.3	88.9	40.6	32.8	15.6	7.8	3.3	1.3	0.6	0.3	205.5	24.4
4	8.5	67.5	34.6	30.5	13.5	8.2	4.3	2.0	0.8	0.8	170.7	20.3
5	4.9	46.2	27.7	23.1	10.0	6.9	4.3	2.3	1.0	1.0	127.3	15.1
6	2.4	28.3	19.4	16.4	6.7	4.7	3.3	2.0	1.1	1.3	85.5	10.1
7	1.2	16.3	12.8	10.1	4.0	3.1	2.3	1.4	0.9	1.3	53.3	6.3
8	0.4	8.3	6.7	6.0	2.3	1.7	1.4	1.0	0.7	1.3	29.9	3.5
9	0.2	3.5	3.4	3.3	1.2	0.8	0.9	0.5	0.6	0.9	15.3	1.8
10+	1.0	2.1	2.4	2.2	1.2	0.9	0.8	0.8	1.2	2.3	13.8	1.6
Total o/oo	115.1	394.0	183.7	155.0	65.2	37.7	21.8	11.7	6.1	9.7	1,000.0	
1,000	13.7	46.7	21.8	18.4	7.7	4.5	2.6	1.4	0.7	1.2		118.7

1916

Number of occupants	Number of units										Total	
	1	2	3	4	5	6	7	8	9	10+	o/oo	1,000
1	58.3	57.6	10.9	7.2	1.6	0.5	0.1	0.1	0.0	0.0	136.3	22.4
2	16.2	112.2	42.9	32.8	10.7	3.6	1.1	0.3	0.1	0.2	219.9	36.2
3	6.4	91.4	53.4	39.7	16.2	7.9	3.1	0.9	0.3	0.2	219.5	36.1
4	2.8	61.6	44.4	36.5	14.0	7.9	3.4	1.4	0.5	0.6	173.1	28.5
5	1.3	34.9	30.4	24.7	10.2	6.5	3.4	1.4	0.6	0.8	114.1	18.8
6	0.7	17.9	18.3	14.5	5.7	4.1	2.4	1.3	0.7	0.7	66.1	10.9
7	0.2	9.1	10.3	7.9	3.0	2.0	1.5	0.9	0.4	0.7	36.2	6.0
8	0.1	4.3	5.3	4.0	1.3	0.9	0.7	0.5	0.3	0.7	18.2	3.0
9	0.0	1.8	2.7	1.9	0.6	0.4	0.4	0.3	0.2	0.8	8.7	1.4
10+	0.0	1.1	1.9	1.5	0.5	0.4	0.3	0.1	0.2	1.0	7.9	1.3
Total o/oo	86.1	391.9	220.5	170.7	63.8	34.3	16.4	7.2	3.4	5.8	1,000.0	
1,000	14.2	64.5	36.3	28.1	10.5	5.6	2.7	1.2	0.6	1.0		164.6

1930

Number of occupants	Number of units										Total	
	1	2	3	4	5	6	7	8	9	10+	o/oo	1,000
1	46.0	64.7	15.7	9.9	2.6	1.1	0.2	0.1	0.0	0.1	140.3	33.4
2	13.2	116.5	61.8	43.7	13.5	5.0	1.7	0.4	0.1	0.2	256.2	61.0
3	6.2	91.3	64.2	49.3	18.4	8.8	3.7	1.2	0.4	0.5	244.0	58.1
4	3.6	56.6	43.4	36.1	15.6	8.7	4.3	1.7	0.7	0.8	171.5	40.9
5	1.4	27.5	23.4	18.5	9.8	6.5	3.9	1.8	0.8	0.9	94.4	22.5
6	0.7	12.5	11.4	7.9	4.6	3.5	2.6	1.5	0.7	0.9	46.3	11.0
7	0.3	5.7	5.3	3.3	1.8	1.5	1.3	0.9	0.6	0.8	21.7	5.2
8	0.1	2.7	2.3	1.2	0.8	0.7	0.5	0.5	0.2	0.5	9.5	2.3
9	0.0	1.1	1.0	0.6	0.3	0.3	0.2	0.2	0.1	0.3	4.3	1.0
10+	0.8	3.1	2.5	1.6	0.9	0.7	0.5	0.4	0.3	1.3	11.9	2.8
Total o/oo	72.3	381.6	231.0	172.1	68.5	36.6	19.0	8.6	4.0	6.2	1,000.0	
1,000	17.2	90.9	55.0	41.0	16.3	8.7	4.5	2.1	0.9	1.5		238.3

a) Copenhagen only

H o u s i n g   C o n d i t i o n s

Distribution of dwellings by number of units and occupants, per 1,000 dwellings (o/oo)

1960

Number of occupants	Number of units 1	2	3	4	5	6	7	8	9	10+	Total o/oo	Total 1,000
1	27.9	66.2	39.7	16.8	5.1			2.9			160.4	234.5
2	4.7	83.8	94.7	53.2	20.0			13.6			274.1	401.0
3	1.4	51.5	69.9	47.0	19.6			15.5			208.6	305.2
4	0.5	34.0	60.5	48.6	23.2			18.5			188.6	275.9
5	0.2	10.1	26.6	27.1	14.1			16.6			97.2	142.2
6	0.1	3.3	9.3	11.0	6.6			11.0			42.4	62.1
7	0.0	1.0	3.3	4.1	2.6			5.4			17.0	24.8
8+	0.0	0.5	1.8	2.2	1.3			5.3			11.6	17.0
Total o/oo	34.6	250.4	305.9	210.1	92.8			88.7			1,000.0	
1,000	50.7	366.2	447.4	307.3	135.7			129.7				1,462.6

1965

Number of occupants	Number of units 1	2	3	4	5	6	7	8	9	10+	Total o/oo	Total 1,000
1	30.4	75.4	46.4	20.1	6.2			3.2			181.9	287.2
2	3.5	80.8	98.4	58.4	21.7			14.8			278.0	438.9
3	0.9	40.5	71.6	52.6	22.7			17.0			205.7	324.7
4	0.2	23.4	57.6	58.0	25.5			20.3			185.3	292.5
5	0.0	6.3	23.4	29.4	16.1			16.6			92.3	145.6
6	0.0	1.7	7.5	11.0	6.4			9.7			36.4	57.5
7	0.0	0.3	2.0	3.7	2.4			4.6			13.1	20.6
8+	0.0	0.3	1.0	1.8	0.9			3.2			7.2	11.4
Total o/oo	35.0	228.7	307.8	235.0	101.9			89.4			1,000.0	
1,000	55.3	361.0	485.8	371.0	160.8			141.1				1,578.4

1970

Number of occupants	Number of units 1	2	3	4	5	6	7	8	9	10+	Total o/oo	Total 1,000
1	33.1	86.7	53.2	24.9	8.2			5.6			213.6	372.2
2	3.3	80.8	100.9	68.3	27.1			20.8			303.6	529.1
3	0.5	26.9	62.2	56.0	24.0			20.1			191.0	332.9
4	0.1	11.6	44.7	60.5	28.7			25.7			172.4	300.5
5	0.0	2.6	14.5	26.0	16.3			18.7			78.7	137.1
6	0.0	0.6	3.8	8.3	5.7			9.1			27.8	48.4
7	0.0	0.2	0.9	2.3	1.7			3.5			8.7	15.2
8+	0.0	0.1	0.4	1.0	0.8			2.0			4.3	7.4
Total o/oo	37.1	209.4	280.5	247.4	112.4			105.4			1,000.0	
1,000	64.6	364.9	488.9	431.2	195.9			183.7				1,742.8

Finland

Housing Conditions [a]

	1900	1910	1930	1950	1960	1960	1970
Total number (in 1,000) of							
– occupied dwellings	43	62	58	998	1 204		
– private households						1 276	1 495
– persons	197	273	209	3 954	4 352	4 352	4 516
– rooms	97	141	139	2 607	3 297	3 299	4 340
Average number of							
– persons	4.57	4.42	3.58	3.96	3.61	3.41	3.02
– rooms	2.25	2.29	2.38	2.61	2.74	2.58	2.90
– persons per room	2.03	1.94	1.51	1.52	1.32	1.32	1.04
Dwellings by number of rooms [b] (percent distribution)							
1 room	45.8	36.7	35.9	19.7	14.9	20.7	15.2
2 rooms	28.6	36.8	32.7	37.5	33.6	32.1	24.6
3	8.9	10.6	13.0	23.2	29.4	27.2	27.4
4	6.1	6.6	7.0	10.1	12.4	11.5	16.8
5	3.6	3.5	4.8	4.9	6.0	5.4	9.7
6	2.8	2.5	3.3	2.2	2.1		2.9
7	1.7	1.6	2.0	1.1	0.8	} 3.1	0.9
8	1.0	.8	0.8	0.6	} 0.6		0.3
9	} 1.5	1.0	0.6	0.7			0.2
10+							
Dwellings by number of persons [b] (percent distribution)							
1 person	6.7	7.5	8.7	10.3	14.1	19.3	22.9
2 persons	15.0	15.7	23.0	18.2	20.5	19.9	22.4
3	17.2	17.5	23.3	19.7	19.2	18.3	19.4
4	16.3	16.5	18.7	18.2	17.8	16.7	17.1
5	13.6	13.7	12.2	13.0	12.1	11.1	9.4
6	10.8	10.7	6.8	8.3	7.3	6.6	4.7
7	7.6	7.4	3.7	5.1	4.2		2.2
8	5.2	4.7	1.9	3.2	2.3	} 8.0	1.1
9	} 7.7	6.2	0.9	1.9	1.3		0.9
10+			0.8	2.3	1.3		
Persons per room in dwellings [b] with							
1 person	0.74	0.70	0.73	0.61	0.57	0.64	0.57
2 persons	1.26	1.15	1.17	0.96	0.86	0.88	0.77
3	1.62	1.52	1.46	1.26	1.12	1.15	0.99
4	1.99	1.86	1.60	1.50	1.34	1.36	1.13
5	2.23	2.10	1.66	1.68	1.53	1.56	1.29
6	2.44	2.35	1.68	1.85	1.74	1.79	1.48
7	2.52	2.46	1.78	2.05	1.97		1.71
8	2.66	2.68	1.81	2.23	2.21	} 2.29	1.95
9	} 2.26	2.46	2.00	2.44	2.46		2.40
10+			2.07	2.70	2.89		

a) 1900 and 1910: Helsinki, Turku, Tampere, Uleaborg; 1930: Helsinki; 1950–1970: whole country.
b) 1900–1960: dwellings; 1960–1970: households.

Finland

Housing Conditions in Cities [a]

Distribution of dwellings by number of units and occupants, per 1,000 dwellings (o/oo)

1900

Number of occupants	Number of units									Total	
	1	2	3	4	5	6	7	8	9+	o/oo	1,000
1	51.0	12.1	2.5	0.8	0.4	0.3	0.0	0.0	0.1	67.2	2.9
2	95.6	37.6	9.6	4.0	2.2	0.9	0.5	0.1	0.2	150.2	6.5
3	94.1	44.8	14.4	9.2	4.9	2.5	1.2	0.3	0.3	171.6	7.4
4	80.2	47.7	13.0	9.8	5.4	3.5	1.8	0.8	0.6	163.0	7.0
5	57.3	42.8	11.7	9.9	5.8	4.0	1.9	1.0	1.2	135.6	5.8
6	39.1	35.7	11.3	7.8	4.8	3.9	2.3	1.4	1.5	108.0	4.7
7	21.2	27.3	8.2	6.1	3.7	3.8	2.6	1.6	1.3	75.6	3.3
8	12.1	17.9	6.6	4.6	3.0	2.7	2.0	1.2	1.4	51.5	2.2
9+	7.5	20.5	11.2	8.5	7.7	6.1	4.7	3.6	8.8	77.2	3.3
Total o/oo	458.1	286.0	88.6	60.7	36.3	27.8	17.1	10.1	15.4	1,000.0	
1,000	19.7	12.3	3.8	2.6	1.6	1.2	0.7	0.4	0.7		43.1

1910

Number of occupants	Number of units									Total	
	1	2	3	4	5	6	7	8	9+	o/oo	1,000
1	50.7	19.9	3.1	1.2	0.3	0.2	0.0	0.0	0.0	75.4	4.7
2	79.4	56.8	11.6	5.5	2.1	1.0	0.4	0.1	0.3	157.2	9.7
3	75.2	64.8	16.3	9.8	4.5	2.5	1.5	0.4	0.2	175.2	10.8
4	61.8	63.6	17.3	10.8	5.2	3.4	1.9	0.7	0.5	165.2	10.2
5	43.7	53.2	16.0	10.9	5.6	3.7	2.4	1.1	0.9	137.4	8.5
6	28.2	43.6	12.9	8.5	5.1	3.8	2.5	1.3	0.8	106.8	6.6
7	15.2	29.1	10.6	6.5	4.1	3.5	2.2	1.4	1.1	73.7	4.6
8	7.6	19.4	7.4	4.4	2.9	2.1	1.6	0.8	0.9	47.0	2.9
9+	5.0	18.0	10.6	8.0	4.9	4.5	3.4	2.4	5.3	62.0	3.8
Total o/oo	366.8	368.3	105.7	65.5	34.7	24.6	16.0	8.3	10.0	1,000.0	
1,000	22.6	22.7	6.5	4.0	2.1	1.5	0.1	0.5	0.6		61.7

1930

Number of occupants	Number of units									Total	
	1	2	3	4	5	6	7	8	9+	o/oo	1,000
1	63.7	17.5	3.6	1.3	0.5	0.2	0.1	0.0	0.0	86.8	5.1
2	124.9	71.2	20.7	7.4	3.3	1.5	0.7	0.1	0.2	230.0	13.4
3	93.2	84.5	28.2	13.0	7.6	3.9	1.9	0.4	0.2	232.8	13.6
4	46.3	74.8	29.8	15.5	9.7	6.6	3.2	0.8	0.5	187.3	10.9
5	19.6	42.9	22.9	13.1	10.2	7.1	4.0	1.5	0.8	122.0	7.1
6	6.7	20.1	12.5	8.7	7.5	6.1	4.2	1.7	0.8	68.3	4.0
7	3.0	9.2	6.8	5.3	4.2	3.4	2.9	1.3	1.2	37.3	2.2
8	0.8	3.9	3.3	3.0	2.4	1.8	1.6	1.0	1.2	19.0	1.1
9	0.3	1.8	1.6	1.2	1.0	0.9	0.9	0.4	0.5	8.5	0.5
10+	0.1	1.0	1.1	1.2	1.1	1.0	0.7	0.5	1.0	7.8	0.5
Total o/oo	358.6	326.9	130.4	69.6	47.5	32.6	20.3	7.8	6.3	1,000.0	
1,000	20.9	19.0	7.6	4.1	2.8	1.9	1.2	0.5	0.4		58.3

a) 1900 and 1910: Helsinki, Turku, Tampere, Uleaborg; 1930: Helsinki only

Finland

Housing Conditions

Distribution of dwellings by number of units and occupants, per 1,000 dwellings (o/oo)

1950

Number of occupants	Number of units 1	2	3	4	5	6	7	8	9+	Unknown	Total o/oo	Total 1,000
1	55.8	32.6	9.6	2.7	0.9	0.4	0.2	0.1	0.1	0.4	102.6	102.5
2	55.1	80.1	31.3	9.3	3.3	1.3	0.6	0.3	0.3	0.2	181.7	181.4
3	39.3	85.8	45.5	15.7	6.0	2.3	1.0	0.5	0.5	0.1	196.8	196.5
4	23.7	74.7	48.2	20.1	8.6	3.6	1.4	0.7	0.8	0.1	181.9	181.6
5	11.5	45.6	37.7	17.8	9.0	4.1	1.9	0.9	0.9	0.1	129.5	129.3
6	5.7	25.6	24.4	13.1	7.1	3.6	1.8	0.9	1.1	0.0	83.2	83.1
7	2.9	14.2	15.0	8.5	5.0	2.6	1.4	0.7	0.9	0.0	51.2	51.1
8	1.7	8.0	9.0	5.5	3.4	1.8	1.0	0.6	0.8	0.0	31.8	31.7
9	0.9	4.3	5.2	3.4	2.2	1.1	0.6	0.4	0.5	0.0	18.5	18.5
10+	0.8	4.2	5.9	4.4	3.2	1.7	1.0	0.6	1.1	0.0	22.8	22.7
Total												
o/oo	197.4	375.1	231.7	100.5	48.7	22.4	10.7	5.6	6.9	1.0	1,000.0	
1,000	197.1	374.5	231.3	100.3	48.7	22.4	10.7	5.6	6.9	1.0		998.4

1960

Number of occupants	Number of units 1	2	3	4	5	6	7	8 – 9+	Unknown	Total o/oo	Total 1,000
1	66.9	49.5	17.6	4.1	1.3	0.4	0.1	0.1	0.4	140.5	169.2
2	42.8	88.1	51.7	14.6	5.2	1.6	0.5	0.4	0.2	205.3	247.2
3	21.4	74.8	61.2	22.1	8.5	2.6	0.9	0.7	0.2	192.3	231.6
4	10.1	57.7	63.1	28.1	12.6	3.9	1.3	0.9	0.1	177.7	214.1
5	4.2	32.0	43.7	22.0	12.0	4.1	1.6	1.2	0.1	120.9	145.6
6	1.9	16.4	26.0	14.5	8.4	3.2	1.4	1.1	0.0	73.0	87.9
7	1.0	8.8	14.5	8.6	5.2	2.1	0.9	0.8	0.0	41.9	50.4
8	0.5	4.5	7.9	4.8	3.0	1.2	0.5	0.5	0.0	22.9	27.6
9	0.2	2.4	4.3	2.7	1.7	0.7	0.3	0.3	0.0	12.5	15.1
10+	0.2	2.1	4.3	2.9	1.9	0.9	0.4	0.4	0.0	13.0	15.6
Total											
o/oo	149.2	336.3	294.2	124.4	59.9	20.7	8.0	6.3	1.1	1,000.0	
1,000	179.7	405.0	354.3	149.8	72.1	24.9	9.6	7.6	1.3		1 204.4

Housing Conditions

Distribution of households by number of units and occupants, per 1,000 dwellings (o/oo)

1960

Number of occupants	\\	\\	\\	Number of units	\\	6	7	8	9+	Un-known	Total o/oo	Total 1,000
	1	2	3	4	5							
1	118.9	50.4	17.5	4.2	1.3		0.7			0.3	193.4	246.8
2	45.6	83.4	48.4	14.0	4.9		2.4			0.1	198.9	253.9
3	23.4	70.9	56.7	20.7	7.7		3.7			0.1	183.2	233.8
4	10.8	54.5	58.2	26.2	11.6		5.5			0.1	166.8	213.0
5	4.4	30.0	39.6	20.2	10.8		6.2			0.0	111.3	142.1
6	1.9	15.3	23.4	13.0	7.4		5.0			0.0	66.1	84.3
7+	1.8	16.5	27.9	16.6	9.9		7.6			0.0	80.4	102.6
Total o/oo	206.9	321.0	271.7	115.0	53.6		31.1			0.7	1,000.0	
1,000	264.1	409.8	346.9	146.7	68.5		39.7			0.9		1,276.6

1970

Number of occupants	1	2	3	4	Number of units 5	6	7	8	9+	Un-known	Total o/oo	Total 1,000
1	97.7	67.6	34.6	9.4	3.2	0.9	0.3	0.1	0.1	14.5	228.5	341.8
2	33.4	74.9	71.5	26.9	10.5	2.7	0.8	0.3	0.2	2.7	224.0	334.9
3	14.4	52.3	65.9	37.4	16.6	4.2	1.2	0.4	0.3	1.7	194.4	290.7
4	4.5	30.2	54.2	44.1	26.4	7.1	2.1	0.7	0.5	1.1	170.9	255.6
5	1.2	11.7	25.5	26.7	19.3	6.1	2.0	0.7	0.5	0.5	94.3	141.0
6	0.4	4.9	11.6	12.9	10.6	3.7	1.2	0.5	0.3	0.2	46.6	69.6
7	0.2	2.3	5.4	5.8	5.1	2.0	0.6	0.3	0.2	0.1	22.0	32.9
8	0.1	1.1	2.7	2.7	2.6	1.0	0.3	0.1	0.1	0.1	10.8	16.1
9+	0.1	0.8	2.1	2.1	2.1	0.9	0.3	0.1	0.1	0.1	8.6	12.8
Total o/oo	152.0	245.8	273.5	168.1	96.5	28.5	8.8	3.3	2.4	21.1	1,000.0	
1,000	227.3	367.5	409.0	251.4	144.3	42.7	13.1	4.9	3.6	31.6		1,495.4

Housing Conditons[a]

	1901	1911	1901	1946	1954	1962	1968	1975
Total number (in 1,000) of								
- occupied dwellings	1 915	2 299	9 690	12 672	13 402	14 565	15 778	17 744
- persons	5 689	6 706	33 480	38 742	41 109	45 169	48 255	51 214
- rooms	5 564	6 873	29 133	33 951	45 785	45 111	52 206	61 828
Average number of								
- person	2.97	2.91	3.46	3.06	3.07	3.10	3.06	2.89
- rooms	2.90	2.99	3.01	2.68	3.42	3.10	3.31	3.48
- persons per room	1.02	0.98	1.15	1.14	0.90	1.00	0.92	0.83
Dwellings by number of rooms (percent distribution)								
1 room	22.2	19.6	17.8	21.1	13.0	14.7	11.6	9.3
2 rooms	29.6	29.5	31.6	29.7	25.7	24.1	20.6	17.4
3	21.3	22.4	21.0	25.1	25.2	26.8	27.2	27.0
4	12.3	13.5	14.3	13.7	17.3	19.0	22.3	25.1
5	5.6	5.7	5.9	5.4	7.8	8.7	10.7	13.0
6	3.7	3.8	4.1	2.4	3.5	}		
7	1.6	1.7	1.6	0.9	1.5 }			
8	1.4	1.5	1.6	0.5	0.7	} 6.7	7.7	8.3
9	} 2.4	2.5	2.2	0.2	0.8			
10+				0.3		}		
Dwellings by number of persons (percent distribution)								
1 person	21.1	20.0	15.1	18.6	19.2	19.6	20.3	22.2
2 persons	26.8	27.9	22.7	26.6	27.3	26.9	26.9	27.8
3	21.0	22.4	20.5	21.7	19.8	18.7	18.7	19.2
4	14.2	14.4	16.3	14.9	14.7	14.7	15.1	15.4
5	8.2	7.7	10.9	8.5	9.2	9.4	9.2	8.2
6	4.4	3.9	6.6	4.5	5.0	}		
7	2.2	1.9	3.7	2.4	2.5			
8	1.1	.9	2.0	1.3	1.2	} 10.7	9.9	7.3
9	} 1.1	.9	2.2	0.6	1.2			
10+				0.7		}		
Persons per room in dwellings with								
1 person	0.57	0.59	0.49	0.51	0.33	0.45	0.42	0.41
2 persons	0.79	0.77	0.73	0.80	0.63	0.71	0.67	0.62
3	0.98	0.95	0.98	1.09	0.89	0.96	0.90	0.83
4	1.17	1.11	1.23	1.34	1.12	1.16	1.07	0.98
5	1.30	1.22	1.46	1.55	1.31	1.32	1.21	1.11
6	1.42	1.31	1.68	1.75	1.47	}		
7	1.50	1.39	1.89	1.94	1.63			
8	1.57	1.47	2.09	2.14	1.80	} 1.65	1.53	1.42
9	} 1.60	1.53	2.33	2.34	2.11			
10+				2.61		}		

a) 1901-1911: cities of 50,000 and more inhabitants; 1901-1975: whole country.

Housing Conditions in Cities [a)

Distribution of dwellings by number of units and occupants, per 1,000 dwellings (o/oo)

1901

Number of occupants	Number of units									Total	
	1	2	3	4	5	6	7	8	9+	o/oo	1,000
1	123.0	49.0	21.7	10.0	3.5	1.8	0.6	0.5	0.5	210.5	403.1
2	60.8	98.8	56.7	28.0	11.0	6.4	2.3	1.7	1.7	267.5	512.3
3	22.4	72.4	55.2	29.7	12.7	7.9	3.3	2.6	3.3	209.5	401.2
4	9.3	41.3	39.1	24.1	10.8	7.4	3.1	2.7	3.9	141.7	271.3
5	3.9	19.2	21.5	15.5	8.0	5.7	2.6	2.3	3.7	82.3	157.6
6	1.6	8.7	10.3	8.4	4.6	3.7	1.7	1.7	3.2	44.0	84.3
7	0.7	3.8	4.5	4.0	2.5	1.9	1.1	1.1	2.5	22.1	42.3
8	0.3	1.7	2.0	1.9	1.2	1.1	0.5	0.7	1.8	11.2	21.4
9+	0.2	1.1	1.5	1.5	1.1	1.0	0.6	0.7	3.5	11.1	21.2
Total o/oo	222.1	296.1	212.5	123.0	55.5	36.9	15.8	13.9	24.1	1,000.0	
1,000	425.3	567.0	406.9	235.6	106.2	70.7	30.2	26.7	46.2		1,914.6

1911

Number of occupants	Number of units									Total	
	1	2	3	4	5	6	7	8	9+	o/oo	1,000
1	119.8	47.2	18.6	9.1	2.9	1.5	0.5	0.3	0.3	200.3	460.4
2	50.5	112.0	61.5	31.3	11.5	6.8	2.5	1.8	1.5	279.4	642.2
3	16.2	74.4	65.1	35.0	14.0	8.8	3.9	3.0	3.2	223.5	513.9
4	5.8	36.3	42.7	27.9	12.2	8.3	3.5	3.1	4.0	143.9	330.9
5	2.1	14.5	20.6	16.5	8.0	6.0	3.0	2.6	4.1	77.4	178.0
6	0.8	6.0	8.7	8.4	4.3	3.3	1.8	2.0	3.5	38.8	89.2
7	0.3	2.5	3.7	3.8	2.1	1.6	0.9	1.1	2.8	18.7	43.1
8	0.1	1.1	1.7	1.7	1.0	0.8	0.4	0.5	1.9	9.3	21.3
9+	0.1	0.6	1.1	1.2	0.9	0.7	0.4	0.5	3.1	8.6	19.9
Total o/oo	195.7	294.6	223.5	134.9	56.7	37.9	17.1	15.0	24.5	1,000.0	
1,000	449.9	677.3	513.8	310.1	130.4	87.1	39.4	34.5	56.3		2,298.8

a) 1901 and 1911: cities of 50,000 and more inhabitants.

H o u s i n g   C o n d i t i o n s

Distribution of dwellings by number of units and occupants, per 1,000 dwellings (o/oo)

1901

Number of occupants	Number of units 1	2	3	4	5	6	7	8	9	10+	Total o/oo	1,000
1	65.6	47.6	19.3	10.4	3.4	2.1	0.7	0.6	0.6		150.5	1,458.4
2	42.2	83.8	46.7	28.9	10.9	7.4	2.7	2.6	2.3		227.4	2,203.9
3	26.1	68.6	48.9	30.7	12.3	8.2	3.3	3.0	3.5		204.7	1,983.7
4	18.0	49.5	38.7	27.8	11.3	7.6	3.0	2.9	3.7		162.5	1,574.1
5	11.4	30.3	25.4	19.5	8.8	5.9	2.4	2.3	3.3		109.3	1,059.1
6	6.8	17.3	14.5	12.0	5.4	4.1	1.7	1.6	2.6		66.1	640.1
7	3.8	9.4	7.8	6.6	3.3	2.3	1.1	1.0	1.9		37.2	360.6
8	1.9	5.0	4.1	3.6	1.8	1.3	0.6	0.6	1.3		20.2	196.2
9+	1.7	4.9	4.1	3.7	2.1	1.6	0.8	0.8	2.5		22.0	213.6
Total o/oo	177.6	316.4	209.5	143.2	59.3	40.5	16.3	15.5	21.7		1,000.0	
1,000	1,721.2	3,065.3	2,029.8	1,387.4	574.7	392.5	158.3	149.9	210.7			9,689.7

1946

Number of occupants	Number of units 1	2	3	4	5	6	7	8	9	10+	Total o/oo	1,000
1	81.3	58.0	27.6	11.0	3.5	1.6	0.6	0.3	0.1	0.2	186.1	2,357.7
2	57.8	92.9	67.4	30.7	9.6	3.9	1.4	0.8	0.2	0.4	266.2	3,373.5
3	34.3	67.3	64.2	32.0	11.3	4.3	1.5	0.8	0.3	0.4	217.1	2,751.2
4	19.0	40.0	43.6	27.6	10.8	4.6	1.6	0.8	0.3	0.4	149.0	1,888.7
5	9.3	19.7	24.1	16.9	8.2	3.8	1.5	0.8	0.3	0.4	85.1	1,078.4
6	4.5	9.5	12.2	9.3	4.7	2.7	1.1	0.7	0.2	0.3	45.4	575.8
7	2.2	4.6	6.0	4.8	2.6	1.5	0.8	0.5	0.2	0.3	23.6	298.5
8	1.1	2.3	3.1	2.5	1.4	0.8	0.4	0.3	0.1	0.2	12.5	157.8
9	0.6	1.1	1.5	1.3	0.7	0.4	0.2	0.2	0.1	0.2	6.2	79.1
10+	0.5	1.1	1.5	1.3	0.7	0.5	0.3	0.2	0.1	0.4	6.6	83.5
Total o/oo	210.7	296.5	251.2	137.4	53.6	24.0	9.3	5.3	1.9	3.2	1,000.0	
1,000	2,669.5	3,757.5	3,183.3	1,741.6	679.1	304.5	118.1	67.1	24.6	40.7		12,671.7

1954

Number of occupants	Number of units 1	2	3	4	5	6	7	8	9+	Un-known	Total o/oo	1,000
1	55.5	58.2	34.5	16.8	5.9	2.4	1.0	0.5	0.5	16.1	191.5	2,565.9
2	36.7	80.8	73.4	43.2	16.2	6.4	2.5	1.1	1.1	11.5	272.8	3,656.2
3	19.2	52.5	55.7	36.7	15.7	6.5	2.5	1.1	1.1	6.7	197.8	2,650.7
4	10.6	33.8	41.3	31.1	14.6	6.3	2.5	1.1	1.1	4.7	147.3	1,974.1
5	4.8	17.4	24.3	21.7	11.3	5.5	2.4	1.0	1.0	2.7	92.1	1,234.6
6	2.0	7.8	12.0	12.1	7.0	3.6	1.8	0.9	0.9	1.5	49.5	663.4
7	0.8	3.5	5.6	6.3	3.7	2.2	1.1	0.6	0.7	0.7	25.2	337.1
8	0.3	1.6	2.6	3.0	1.7	1.1	0.6	0.4	0.5	0.3	12.1	162.7
9+	0.2	1.3	2.3	2.7	1.9	1.1	0.7	0.4	0.8	0.3	11.7	156.7
Total o/oo	130.2	257.0	251.7	173.4	78.0	35.1	15.1	7.1	7.8	44.6	1,000.0	
1,000	1,744.3	3,444.8	3,373.6	2,324.5	1,045.5	469.9	202.0	95.8	104.1	597.1		13,401.5

France

Housing Conditions

Distribution of dwellings by number of units and occupants, per 1,000 dwellings (o/oo)

1962

Number of occupants	Number of units 1	2	3	4	5	6+	Total o/oo	1,000
1	70.7	60.2	37.1	17.3	6.3	4.8	196.4	2,860.7
2	41.2	81.0	77.9	42.0	15.9	10.8	268.7	3,913.6
3	19.0	47.6	58.8	36.3	14.7	10.3	186.7	2,719.6
4	9.2	27.7	46.6	36.7	16.1	11.1	147.3	2,145.2
5	3.9	13.0	25.8	27.4	13.7	10.3	94.1	1,370.3
6+	3.1	11.0	21.9	30.7	20.7	19.5	106.8	1,555.8
Total o/oo	147.1	240.5	268.1	190.3	87.4	66.7	1,000.0	
1,000	2,142.1	3,502.5	3,905.3	2,771.1	1,272.8	971.3		14,565.2

1968

Number of occupants	Number of units 1	2	3	4	5	6+	Total o/oo	1,000
1	64.1	61.7	42.6	20.7	8.0	5.7	202.7	3,198.3
2	31.5	73.5	82.8	49.1	18.9	12.8	268.6	4,237.8
3	12.1	38.0	63.3	43.3	17.8	11.9	186.5	2,942.2
4	5.0	18.8	46.5	46.9	20.4	13.1	150.7	2,377.4
5	1.9	7.4	21.3	32.1	17.3	12.3	92.3	1,456.0
6+	1.4	6.1	15.2	30.3	24.7	21.6	99.3	1,566.3
Total o/oo	115.9	205.5	271.6	222.5	107.1	77.4	1,000.0	
1,000	1 828.7	3,242.9	4,286.1	3,509.9	1,689.9	1,220.6		15,778.1

1975

Number of occupants	Number of units 1	2	3	4	5	6+	Total o/oo	1,000
1	62.1	68.3	50.5	25.2	9.4	6.4	221.8	3,935.1
2	21.4	64.9	93.2	60.2	24.1	14.4	278.2	4,936.8
3	6.0	25.3	66.9	56.6	23.9	13.0	191.7	3,400.9
4	2.1	9.8	39.0	57.6	29.2	16.1	153.8	2,729.6
5	0.7	3.1	12.7	30.8	21.0	13.6	81.9	1,452.6
6+	0.4	2.1	7.2	20.9	22.5	19.5	72.6	1,288.7
Total o/oo	92.6	173.5	269.6	251.2	130.1	83.0	1,000.0	
1,000	1,643.8	3,078.5	4,783.5	4,457.6	2,308.5	1,471.9		17,743.8

Housing Conditions

	1927[a]	1950[b]	1956[c]	1968[d]
Total number (in 1,000) of				
– dwellings		10 082	13 483	19 640
– occupied dwellings	8 709			19 154
– private households [e]		15 534		20 664
– persons	33 192	47 060		58 613
– rooms		41 057	50 965	81 013
Dwellings by number of rooms (percent distribution)				
1 room	3.1	0.9	2.0	1.4
2 rooms	16.1	13.5	15.7	8.9
3	29.6	28.6	31.9	26.6
4	23.9	25.9	26.2	31.8
5	12.7	14.6	} 24.3	16.0
6	7.0	8.2		
7	} 6.4			} 15.4
8		8.3		
9				
10+	1.2			
Households by number of persons (percent distribution)				
1 person			19.1	21.6
2 persons			26.1	27.8
3			22.8	20.8
4			16.4	15.9
5			} 15.5	} 13.9
6				
7				
8				
9				
10+				
Persons per room in households with				
1 person			0.60	
2 persons			0.74	
3			0.94	
4			1.09	
5			} 1.35	
6				
7				
8				
9				
10+				

a) Municipalities of 5,000 and more inhabitants
b) Including West-Berlin
c) 10% sample, incl. West-Berlin but excl. the Saare
d) Housing census
e) Private households = Wohnparteien

Housing Conditions

Distribution of households by number of units and occupants, per 1,000 households (o/oo)

1956

Number of occupants	\multicolumn{10}{c}{Number of units}	\multicolumn{2}{c}{Total}
	1	2	3	4	5	6	7	8	9	10+	o/oo	1,000
1	97.5	49.6	25.4	5.9			2.0				180.4	288.1
2	32.3	81.1	95.7	36.0			11.8				256.9	410.1
3	17.0	52.5	80.7	56.6			24.2				231.0	368.8
4	6.7	26.1	52.0	49.8			34.7				169.3	270.2
5												
6												
7	3.0	13.1	32.8	42.7			70.9				162.4	259.3
8												
9												
10+												
Total												
o/oo	156.3	222.3	286.6	191.0			143.6				1,000.0	
1,000	149.6	354.9	457.6	305.0			229.3					1,596.4

Housing Conditions

	1926	1936	1946	1961	1971
Total number (in 1,000) of					
- private households	622	647	622	676	705
- persons	2 791	2 791	2 756	2 686	2 859
- rooms	2 354	2 564	2 734	2 945	3 311
Average number of					
- persons	4.49	4.31	4.16	3.97	4.05
- rooms	3.78	3.96	4.13	4.35	4.69
- persons per room	1.19	1.09	1.01	0.91	0.86
Dwellings by number of rooms (percent distribution)					
1 room	7.5	6.7	5.2	2.3	0.8
2 rooms	18.0	14.0	10.6	6.5	4.6
3	28.1	26.2	23.3	17.8	15.1
4	21.1	24.2	29.7	33.0	30.9
5	9.4	11.3	12.8	17.3	21.7
6	6.3	7.4	8.4	12.2	15.7
7	3.5	4.0	4.4	4.9	6.1
8	2.5	2.7	2.6	2.4	2.6
9	1.4	1.3	1.3	1.0	1.0
10+	2.2	2.2	1.8	1.2	1.2
Households by number of persons (percent distribution)					
1 person	8.3	9.4	10.4	12.6	12.9
2 persons	15.8	17.2	17.9	20.3	20.0
3	16.5	17.2	17.6	17.3	15.9
4	15.5	15.5	15.6	14.5	14.3
5	13.2	12.8	12.8	11.6	11.9
6	10.5	9.7	9.5	8.8	9.3
7	7.8	7.1	6.7	6.1	6.3
8	5.4	4.8	4.3	3.9	3.9
9	3.4	3.1	2.7	2.3	2.4
10+	3.7	3.3	2.6	2.7	3.2
Persons per room in households with					
1 person	0.38	0.35	0.33	0.30	0.27
2 persons	0.59	0.56	0.52	0.49	0.46
3	0.81	0.76	0.73	0.68	0.64
4	1.02	0.97	0.93	0.87	0.82
5	1.25	1.18	1.13	1.07	1.00
6	1.48	1.40	1.34	1.26	1.17
7	1.70	1.62	1.55	1.47	1.35
8	1.92	1.84	1.77	1.68	1.53
9	2.12	2.04	1.97	1.89	1.71
10+	2.39	2.38	2.37	2.31	2.04

Ireland

Housing Conditions

Distribution of households by number of units and occupants, per 1,000 households (o/oo)

1926

Number of occupants	Number of units										Total	
	1	2	3	4	5	6	7	8	9	10+	o/oo	1,000
1	21.4	24.2	17.7	11.6	3.4	2.0	1.0	0.7	0.3	0.5	82.8	51.5
2	17.2	36.7	45.1	29.7	11.6	7.9	4.3	2.7	1.3	1.8	158.2	98.4
3	12.2	30.0	49.0	34.1	14.6	10.0	5.7	4.1	2.1	3.1	165.0	102.7
4	8.9	25.1	44.8	33.5	15.8	10.5	6.0	4.1	2.4	3.5	154.7	96.2
5	6.3	20.5	38.0	29.6	14.0	9.4	5.3	3.8	2.1	3.3	132.3	82.3
6	4.4	15.8	30.0	23.8	11.3	7.6	4.3	3.1	1.8	2.9	105.0	65.3
7	2.6	11.4	21.9	18.3	8.6	5.8	3.2	2.4	1.3	2.4	77.8	48.4
8	1.3	7.6	15.3	12.9	6.0	4.0	2.1	1.6	0.9	1.7	53.5	33.3
9	0.7	4.4	9.8	8.3	3.9	2.6	1.4	1.0	0.6	1.2	33.9	21.1
10+	0.4	3.7	9.7	8.9	4.5	3.2	1.9	1.4	0.8	2.0	36.6	22.8
Total												
o/oo	75.4	179.6	281.3	210.6	93.8	63.0	35.2	25.0	13.7	22.4	1,000.0	
1,000	46.9	111.7	175.0	131.0	58.4	39.2	21.9	15.5	8.5	13.9		622.1

1936

Number of occupants	Number of units										Total	
	1	2	3	4	5	6	7	8	9	10+	o/oo	1,000
1	21.3	23.4	22.5	15.6	4.9	2.9	1.4	0.8	0.4	0.5	93.6	60.8
2	15.0	32.1	48.3	37.2	15.7	10.7	5.5	3.5	1.5	2.0	171.6	111.0
3	10.1	24.0	48.4	40.7	19.3	12.6	7.0	4.7	2.4	3.2	172.4	111.5
4	7.4	18.6	40.8	39.0	19.0	12.8	6.9	4.6	2.2	3.5	154.8	100.1
5	5.2	14.3	32.3	32.9	17.0	11.0	6.1	4.2	2.1	3.3	128.2	82.9
6	3.4	10.5	24.0	25.6	13.0	8.5	4.6	3.1	1.6	2.8	97.0	62.8
7	2.2	7.1	17.9	19.5	9.2	5.9	3.3	2.3	1.2	2.2	70.8	45.8
8	1.3	4.6	12.3	13.3	6.1	4.0	2.2	1.6	0.8	1.5	47.9	31.0
9	0.6	2.8	7.6	8.8	4.0	2.6	1.4	1.0	0.5	1.0	30.4	19.7
10+	0.4	2.6	8.0	9.6	4.5	3.1	1.6	1.2	0.7	1.6	33.3	21.6
Total												
o/oo	66.9	140.0	262.3	242.2	112.7	74.0	40.1	27.0	13.4	21.6	1,000.0	
1,000	43.2	90.5	169.6	156.7	72.9	47.9	26.0	17.4	8.6	14.0		646.8

1946

Number of occupants	Number of units										Total	
	1	2	3	4	5	6	7	8	9	10+	o/oo	1,000
1	19.3	22.7	26.6	21.4	6.7	3.8	1.6	0.9	0.4	0.6	104.0	68.9
2	11.4	25.9	48.6	46.6	19.2	13.3	6.7	3.7	1.7	2.0	179.2	118.7
3	8.1	18.2	44.1	49.4	22.6	15.2	8.1	4.8	2.4	3.0	175.7	116.4
4	5.7	13.9	34.9	47.3	21.9	14.9	7.7	4.4	2.2	3.1	156.1	103.4
5	3.5	9.6	26.7	40.2	19.1	12.8	6.6	4.0	2.1	2.9	127.5	84.4
6	1.9	6.4	19.4	31.8	14.5	9.5	4.9	2.9	1.6	2.2	95.0	63.0
7	1.0	4.1	13.4	23.5	9.9	6.2	3.5	2.1	1.1	1.7	66.5	44.0
8	0.6	2.4	8.6	15.8	6.2	4.0	2.1	1.4	0.8	1.2	43.0	28.5
9	0.3	1.3	5.5	10.3	3.8	2.4	1.3	0.9	0.5	0.9	27.1	18.0
10+	0.1	1.1	5.0	10.4	3.5	2.2	1.3	0.9	0.5	1.0	25.9	17.1
Total												
o/oo	51.9	105.6	232.6	296.7	127.5	84.2	43.9	26.1	13.1	18.4	1,000.0	
1,000	34,4	70,0	154,1	196,5	84,4	55,8	29,1	17,3	8,7	12,2		662,5

Housing Conditions

Distribution of households by number of units and occupants, per 1,000 households (o/oo)

1961

Number of occupants	Number of units										Un-known	Total	
	1	2	3	4	5	6	7	8	9	10+		o/oo	1,000
1	14.0	22.0	31.2	32.5	12.0	6.9	2.7	1.4	0.5	0.6	2.5	126.2	85.4
2	4.4	18.8	46.7	62.6	30.2	21.7	8.3	4.0	1.5	1.7	3.3	203.0	137.3
3	2.2	9.6	33.3	56.5	30.9	21.8	8.5	3.9	1.8	1.8	2.5	172.8	116.9
4	1.2	6.1	22.3	48.5	28.0	21.5	8.2	3.9	1.5	1.8	2.2	145.2	98.2
5	0.6	3.6	15.8	39.8	23.4	17.7	6.9	3.5	1.4	1.6	1.7	116.0	78.4
6	0.2	2.1	10.9	31.5	18.0	13.0	5.4	2.7	1.2	1.3	1.3	87.5	59.2
7	0.1	1.2	7.2	22.6	12.6	8.2	3.7	1.9	1.0	1.1	0.9	60.5	40.9
8	0.1	0.7	4.5	15.1	7.7	5.0	2.3	1.3	0.6	0.8	0.6	38.7	26.2
9	0.0	0.4	2.7	9.2	4.8	2.8	1.3	0.7	0.4	0.5	0.4	23.1	15.6
10+	0.0	0.4	2.9	11.5	5.4	3.0	1.4	0.8	0.4	0.7	0.6	27.0	18.2
Total o/oo	22.8	64.9	177.5	329.7	172.8	121.6	48.6	24.2	10.2	11.8	15.9	1 000.0	
1,000	15.4	43.9	120.1	223.0	116.9	82.2	32.9	16.4	6.9	8.0	10.8		676.4

1971

Number of occupants	Number of units										Un-known	Total	
	1	2	3	4	5	6	7	8	9	10+		o/oo	1,000
1	5.9	19.1	33.2	38.4	16.5	9.3	3.3	1.4	0.5	0.6	0.5	128.6	90.7
2	1.4	13.5	42.4	64.3	37.3	25.2	9.1	3.5	1.2	1.3	0.5	199.8	140.9
3	0.4	5.8	26.1	50.7	34.4	25.5	9.1	3.5	1.3	1.4	0.3	158.5	111.7
4	0.3	3.8	17.5	43.3	34.3	27.3	9.9	3.8	1.3	1.5	0.2	143.0	100.8
5	0.1	1.9	12.0	35.3	30.4	23.8	9.4	3.5	1.3	1.4	0.2	119.3	84.2
6	0.1	1.0	8.0	27.9	23.8	18.4	7.7	3.3	1.3	1.4	0.1	93.2	65.7
7	0.0	0.6	5.0	18.7	16.5	12.0	5.4	2.5	1.1	1.1	0.1	63.1	44.5
8	0.0	0.3	2.9	12.2	10.2	6.8	3.3	1.6	0.8	1.0	0.1	39.3	27.7
9	0.0	0.2	1.8	7.6	6.1	3.9	1.7	1.1	0.5	0.8	0.0	23.6	16.7
10+	0.0	0.2	2.2	10.5	7.6	4.5	2.2	1.5	0.8	1.9	0.1	31.5	22.2
Total o/oo	8.3	46.4	151.1	308.8	217.1	156.7	61.2	25.6	10.1	12.4	2.2	1 000.0	
1,000	5.8	32.7	106.6	217.8	153.1	110.5	43.2	18.1	7.1	8.8	1.6		705.2

Italy

Housing Conditions

	1911[a]	1931[b]	1931	1961	1971
Total number (in 1,000) of					
- dwellings			9 644	14 214	17 434
- occupied dwellings	430	1 263	9 070	13 032	15 301
- persons		5 220		49 314	53 157
- rooms		4 161	30 078	43 424	56 242
Average number of					
- persons		4.13		3.78	3.47
- rooms		3.29	3.32	3.33	3.67
- persons per room		1.25		1.14	0.95
Dwellings by number of rooms (percent distribution)					
1 room	19.9	17.9		8.6	3.9
2 rooms	25.2	25.6		24.8	18.0
3	14.7	18.5		26.5	26.9
4	13.1	15.0		21.9	28.2
5	9.6	10.0		9.6	13.3
6	6.5	5.7		4.6	5.6
7	3.8	3.0		1.9	2.0
8	2.5	1.8		1.1	1.2
9	1.4	0.9		0.5	0.5
10+	3.1	1.5		0.4	0.6
Dwellings by number of persons (percent distribution)					
1 person	9.2	6.7			11.3
2 persons	17.8	17.7			21.1
3	19.7	21.4			22.2
4	16.9	18.8			21.5
5	12.6	13.4			12.6
6	8.6	8.7			5.9
7	5.5	5.4			2.7
8	3.6	3.3			1.3
9	2.1	2.0			} 1.3
10+	4.1	2.8			
Persons per room in dwellings with					
1 person	0.52	0.47			0.36
2 persons	0.85	0.75			0.60
3	1.04	0.98			0.82
4	1.22	1.18			1.03
5	1.35	1.35			1.21
6	1.49	1.57			1.40
7	1.63	1.77			1.61
8	1.76	1.97			1.81
9	1.85	2.17			} 2.16
10+	2.14	2.31			

a) Florence, Milan, Rome, Turin, and Venice.
b) Bologna, Catania, Florence, Genova, Milan, Naples, Palermo, Rome, Trieste, Turin, and Venice.

Italy

Housing Conditions a)

Distribution of dwellings by number of units and occupants, per 1,000 dwellings (o/oo)

1911

Number of occupants				Number of units							Total	
	1	2	3	4	5	6	7	8	9	10+	o/oo	1,000
1	56.1	15.9	7.7	5.4	3.1	1.8	0.9	0.5	0.0	0.6	92.4	39.7
2	54.6	54.2	24.5	18.5	11.8	6.7	3.5	1.9	0.9	1.7	178.3	76.6
3	39.9	59.4	30.8	24.1	16.6	10.8	6.2	3.8	1.7	3.2	196.5	84.4
4	24.3	49.5	26.7	23.5	16.3	11.4	6.5	4.3	2.2	4.3	168.9	72.6
5	12.5	33.0	20.4	18.4	14.3	9.8	6.4	4.2	2.4	4.7	126.0	54.1
6	5.9	19.7	14.2	13.3	10.2	7.6	4.6	3.4	2.0	4.6	85.6	36.8
7	2.8	10.3	9.4	9.3	7.1	5.0	3.4	2.3	1.5	3.6	54.7	23.5
8	1.5	5.4	5.9	6.6	5.1	3.4	2.2	1.7	1.0	2.8	35.5	15.2
9	0.6	2.4	3.3	4.0	3.6	2.4	1.4	0.9	0.7	2.0	21.4	9.2
10+	1.0	2.0	4.3	7.7	7.7	5.9	3.2	2.6	1.1	4.4	40.6	17.5
Total												
o/oo	199.2	251.9	147.1	130.8	95.9	64.8	38.3	25.1	13.7	31.0	1,000.0	
1,000	85.6	108.2	63.2	56.2	41.2	27.8	16.5	10.8	5.9	13.3		429.5

1931

Number of occupants				Number of units							Total	
	1	2	3	4	5	6	7	8	9	10+	o/oo	1,000
1	32.9	15.0	7.5	4.8	2.7	1.3	0.7	0.4	0.2	0.3	65.7	83.0
2	44.1	57.3	31.7	20.8	11.7	5.5	2.7	1.4	0.6	0.9	176.8	223.3
3	36.2	66.6	41.9	30.5	18.6	9.8	4.9	2.7	1.2	1.6	214.1	270.4
4	24.9	49.0	37.9	31.1	20.3	11.4	5.9	3.4	1.6	2.2	187.6	237.0
5	16.3	29.0	26.2	23.3	16.7	9.7	5.3	3.4	1.7	2.5	134.2	169.5
6	10.9	17.1	16.4	14.8	11.1	6.9	3.8	2.5	1.3	2.2	87.0	109.9
7	6.6	10.0	9.7	9.3	7.1	4.3	2.6	1.6	0.9	1.8	53.8	68.0
8	3.7	5.8	5.8	5.9	4.4	2.8	1.6	1.1	0.6	1.2	32.8	41.5
9	2.0	3.3	3.5	3.7	2.8	1.7	0.9	0.6	0.4	0.8	19.6	24.7
10+	1.5	3.1	4.3	5.6	5.0	3.5	2.0	1.2	0.7	1.5	28.3	35.8
Total												
o/oo	179.0	256.2	185.0	149.8	100.3	56.9	30.4	18.3	9.2	15.0	1,000.0	
1,000	226.0	323.6	233.7	189.2	126.7	71.9	38.3	23.1	11.6	19.0		1,263.0

1971

Number of occupants				Number of units							Total	
	1	2	3	4	5	6	7	8	9	10+	o/oo	1,000
1	17.1	39.8	27.8	17.4	6.3	2.7	1.0	0.6	0.3	0.4	113.4	1 734.8
2	9.2	51.9	65.3	52.9	19.4	7.3	2.4	1.4	0.6	0.8	211.1	3 230.8
3	4.6	36.5	67.2	69.0	27.7	10.1	3.3	1.7	0.7	0.8	221.6	3 391.0
4	3.4	26.6	56.7	71.6	34.9	13.3	4.5	2.3	0.9	1.1	215.4	3 295.7
5	2.1	13.3	29.0	39.6	23.5	10.5	3.8	2.2	0.9	1.0	126.1	1 929.8
6	1.0	6.0	12.2	17.6	11.5	5.9	2.4	1.4	0.6	0.7	59.4	909.1
7	0.6	2.9	5.4	7.4	5.0	2.8	1.2	0.8	0.3	0.4	26.8	410.2
8	0.3	1.4	2.5	3.3	2.3	1.4	0.6	0.5	0.2	0.3	12.7	194.5
9+	0.3	1.4	2.5	3.3	2.4	1.5	0.8	0.6	0.3	0.5	13.4	205.4
Total												
o/oo	38.6	179.8	268.5	282.1	133.1	55.6	20.0	11.5	4.8	6.0	1,000.0	
1,000	590.6	2 751.5	4,108.9	4,316.2	2,036.8	850.2	306.3	175.6	74.1	91.1		15,301.4

a) 1911: Florence, Milan, Rome, Turin, Venice; 1931: Bologna, Catania, Florence, Genova, Milan, Naples, Palermo, Rome, Trieste, Turin, Venice; 1971: whole country.

Housing Conditions a)

	1899	1909	1930	1947	1971
Total number (in 1,000) of					
- occupied dwellings	1 089	1 267	1 886	2 050	3 894
- persons				9 138	12 589
- rooms			8 079	10 120	18 847
Average number of					
- persons				4.46	3.23
- rooms			4.28	4.94	4.84
- persons per room				0.90	0.67
Dwellings by number of rooms (percent distribution)					
1 room	28.3	18.7	8.0	2.2	1.3
2 rooms	30.7	29.2	14.5	8.2	6.0
3	17.6	20.0	16.3	11.4	9.9
4	15.3	21.3	18.3	17.8	18.2
5			18.1	24.0	35.8
6	4.2	6.1	12.2	20.1	19.1
7			6.0	8.9	6.6
8				3.7	
9	3.9	4.7	7.1	1.7	3.2
10+				2.0	
Dwellings by number of persons (percent distribution)					
1 person				3.8	15.9
2 persons				15.8	25.6
3				18.9	18.3
4				20.3	19.4
5				15.0	10.7
6				10.0	5.2
7				6.3	2.5
8				4.0	1.2
9				2.5	0.6
10+				3.6	0.6
Persons per room in dwellings with					
1 person				0.31	0.29
2 persons				0.47	0.44
3				0.64	0.61
4				0.81	0.76
5				0.97	0.90
6				1.12	1.03
7				1.27	1.16
8				1.42	1.30
9				1.56	1.41
10+				1.80	1.67

a) 1899–1947: dwellings; 1971 private households.

Netherlands

Housing Conditions

Distribution of dwellings by number of units and densitiy of occupation, per 1,000 dwellings (o/oo)

1899

Number of occupants per unit	1	2	3	4 – 5	6 – 7	8+	Total o/oo	Total 1,000
< 1–1 person	43.1	72.3	60.9	77.8	31.7	36.7	320.3	348.7
> 1–2 persons	54.0	98.7	75.1	63.8	10.1	2.3	303.9	330.8
> 2–3	47.9	74.8	34.4	11.2	0.3	.0	168.6	183.6
> 3–4	41.9	41.8	7.0	0.5	.0		91.1	99.2
> 4–6	57.4	18.9	0.6	.0			76.9	83.8
> 6	38.4	0.6	.0				39.1	42.6
Total o/oo	282.8	307.1	175.8	153.2	42.0	39.0	1,000.0	
Total 1,000	307.9	334.4	191.4	166.9	45.7	42.5		1,088.7

1909

Number of occupants per unit	1	2	3	4 – 5	6 – 7	8+	Total o/oo	Total 1,000
< 1–1 person	37.9	77.7	72.6	117.2	47.6	44.3	397.3	503.5
> 1–2 persons	34.8	95.3	84.2	82.2	12.7	2.3	311.6	394.8
> 2–3	29.9	66.5	35.2	13.1	0.3	0.3	145.1	183.9
> 3–4	25.7	35.0	7.6	0.6	.0		68.9	87.3
> 4–6	35.5	16.9	0.6	.0			53.1	67.2
> 6	23.4	0.6	.0				24.0	30.5
Total o/oo	187.3	292.0	200.2	213.2	60.7	46.7	1,000.0	
Total 1,000	237.3	370.0	253.7	270.1	76.9	59.2		1,267.3

1930

Number of occupants per unit	1	2	3	4	5	6	7	8+	Total o/oo	Total 1,000
< 1–1 person	34.9	59.3	84.2	120.3	135.8	99.1	52.0	66.8	652.6	1 230.8
> 1–2 persons	12.8	48.2	58.8	54.3	42.7	22.4	7.9	4.0	251.1	473.6
> 2–3	9.1	23.6	16.5	8.1	2.8	0.6	0.1	.0	61.0	115.0
> 3–4	6.7	9.4	3.4	0.5	.0	.0			20.0	37.8
> 4–5	4.3	3.2	0.4	.0					7.9	14.9
> 5–6	2.6	0.9	.0						3.6	6.7
> 6	3.4	0.1	.0						3.6	6.8
Total o/oo	79.9	144.9	163.4	183.3	181.4	122.2	59.9	70.8	1 000.0	
Total 1,000	139.4	273.2	308.2	345.6	342.2	230.4	113.0	133.5		1 885.6

Netherlands

Housing Conditions [a]

Distribution of dwellings by number of units and occupants, per 1,000 dwellings (o/oo)

1947

Number of occupants	Number of units										Total	
	1	2	3	4	5	6	7	8	9	10+	o/oo	1,000
1	4.7	9.2	9.7	6.8	4.3	1.8	0.6	0.2	0.1	0.1	37.6	77.0
2	4.4	17.3	27.5	37.1	38.0	22.7	7.2	2.1	0.8	0.7	157.6	323.0
3	3.8	15.1	22.7	39.4	50.7	37.0	13.2	4.1	1.5	1.4	188.9	387.2
4	3.4	14.0	19.8	37.0	53.5	45.7	18.5	6.4	2.5	2.1	202.9	415.8
5	2.3	10.0	13.3	23.2	37.2	35.0	16.4	6.8	2.9	2.6	149.7	306.8
6	1.5	6.5	8.5	14.0	22.9	23.1	11.9	5.7	2.7	2.8	99.5	203.9
7	0.8	4.0	5.2	8.3	13.7	14.3	8.1	4.1	2.2	2.5	63.2	129.5
8	0.5	2.4	3.2	5.1	8.2	8.7	5.2	2.9	1.6	2.0	39.7	81.4
9	0.3	1.4	1.9	3.0	4.8	5.3	3.3	1.9	1.1	1.6	24.5	50.3
10+	0.3	1.8	2.6	4.2	6.6	7.4	4.9	3.0	1.8	3.9	36.4	74.7
Total												
o/oo	22.0	81.6	114.3	178.2	239.8	201.1	89.3	37.1	17.1	19.5	1,000.0	
1,000	45.1	167.3	234.2	365.3	491.5	412.2	183.0	76.0	35.1	40.1		2 049.7

1971

Number of occupants	Number of units							8	9	10+	Total	
	1	2	3	4	5	6	7				o/oo	1,000
1	10.7	39.5	36.4	30.7	25.6	11.2	3.5		1.8		159.3	620.5
2	1.1	12.2	38.4	67.9	85.5	36.1	10.4		4.7		256.4	998.4
3	0.4	5.0	12.2	40.8	77.2	33.1	9.6		4.3		182.7	711.4
4	0.2	1.9	7.4	27.3	92.8	45.2	13.2		5.5		193.6	753.8
5	0.1	0.8	2.8	9.1	46.0	31.9	11.1		5.3		107.2	417.5
6	0.0	0.3	1.1	3.5	18.5	16.8	7.6		4.1		52.0	202.5
7	0.0	0.2	0.5	1.4	6.8	8.4	4.5		2.6		24.5	95.3
8	0.0	0.1	0.2	0.6	3.0	4.0	2.4		1.6		11.9	46.4
9	0.0	0.0	0.1	0.3	1.2	2.0	1.6		1.0		6.2	24.3
10+	0.0	0.0	0.1	0.2	1.0	1.9	1.5		1.4		6.1	23.9
Total												
o/oo	12.5	60.2	99.2	181.9	357.7	190.5	65.6		32.3		1,000.0	
1,000	48.6	234.3	386.5	708.4	1 392.8	741.9	255.6		125.8			3 894.0

a) 1947: dwellings; 1971: private households.

Norway

Housing Conditions [a]

	1910	1920	1933	1930	1946	1960	1970
Total number (in 1,000) of							
– occupied dwellings	53	57	64	201	244	1 075	1 297
– persons			245	772	815	3 521	3 819
– rooms			165	713	825	4 551	5 674
Average number of							
– persons			3.83	3.84	3.34	3.28	2.94
– rooms			2.58	3.55	3.38	4.23	4.37
– persons per room			1.48	1.08	0.99	0.77	0.67
Dwellings by number of rooms (percent distribution)							
1 room	31.6	31.5	29.2	6.2	4.9	3.7	6.0
2 rooms	30.5	30.5	32.4	19.4	18.1	9.3	7.7
3	13.8	14.1	14.4	31.8	37.2	22.5	15.9
4	10.7	11.0	10.7	21.0	24.3	26.8	23.6
5	6.6	6.8	7.0	10.6	9.4	18.1	24.9
6	3.6	3.4	3.5	5.5	4.0	10.1	11.9
7	1.7	1.6	1.6	2.9	1.5	5.0	5.7
8	0.7	0.6	0.6	1.5	0.6	2.3	2.4
9	0.3	0.3	0.6	0.7	0.2	1.1	1.1
10+	0.5	0.3		0.5	0.1	1.0	0.8
Dwellings by number of persons (percent distribution)							
1 person			8.0	11.3	11.1	13.9	21.1
2 persons			19.2	18.4	22.3	23.5	25.4
3			22.2	20.0	26.1	21.2	18.8
4			19.9	17.8	20.2	20.3	17.9
5			13.6	13.2	10.7	11.6	10.2
6			8.2	8.6	5.3	5.5	4.3
7			4.3	4.9	2.4	2.4	1.5
8			2.2	2.8	1.0	1.0	0.6
9			1.2	1.5	0.5	0.4	0.2
10+			1.1	1.4	0.4	0.3	0.1
Persons per room in dwellings with							
1 person			0.69	0.47	0.47	0.36	0.34
2 persons			0.97	0.65	0.68	0.52	0.47
3			1.25	0.87	0.91	0.71	0.65
4			1.49	1.07	1.09	0.88	0.81
5			1.67	1.24	1.22	1.00	0.93
6			1.83	1.42	1.35	1.11	1.05
7			2.02	1.59	1.47	1.22	1.17
8			2.31	1.79	1.61	1.34	1.28
9			2.42	2.01	1.74	1.47	1.40
10+			2.49	2.32	1.89	1.76	1.65

a) 1910–1933: Oslo; 1930–1946: all cities; 1960–1970: whole country.

H o u s i n g   C o n d i t i o n s [a)]

Distribution of dwellings by number of units and occupants, per 1,000 dwellings (o/oo)

1933

Number of occupants	Number of units 1	2	3	4	5	6	7	8	9 10+	Total o/oo	1,000
1	55.8	17.0	4.4	1.8	0.7	0.2	0.0	0.0	0.0	80.1	5.1
2	72.9	69.2	27.1	15.3	5.5	1.6	0.5	0.2	0.1	192.4	12.4
3	64.7	78.4	34.9	24.5	13.4	4.2	1.6	0.4	0.2	222.3	14.3
4	45.3	68.4	31.4	27.1	15.6	7.2	2.4	0.7	0.5	198.6	12.8
5	25.7	43.0	21.4	18.6	14.6	7.9	3.3	0.9	0.7	136.1	8.7
6	13.8	23.8	12.2	10.3	10.2	6.4	3.1	1.1	0.8	81.8	5.3
7	7.1	12.1	6.1	4.7	5.1	3.8	2.2	1.1	0.8	43.0	2.8
8	3.6	6.4	3.2	2.5	2.6	1.8	1.4	0.5	0.4	22.3	1.4
9	1.9	3.2	2.0	1.3	1.3	0.9	0.9	0.3	0.6	12.4	0.8
10+	1.4	2.6	1.4	0.8	1.1	0.9	0.9	0.5	1.3	11.0	0.7
Total o/oo	292.3	324.1	144.3	107.0	70.0	34.9	16.3	5.6	5.5	1,000.0	
1,000	18.8	20.8	9.3	6.9	4.5	2.2	1.0	0.4	0.4		64.3

1930

Number of occupants	Number of units 1	2	3	4	5	6	7	8	9	10+	Total o/oo	1,000
1	35.2	42.1	24.8	7.6	2.3	0.7	0.2	0.1	0.0	0.0	113.1	22.8
2	12.8	47.0	68.3	34.9	13.5	4.8	1.9	0.7	0.2	0.2	184.2	37.1
3	7.1	40.1	71.7	45.3	20.2	8.9	3.8	1.6	0.6	0.5	199.7	40.2
4	3.6	27.9	60.4	42.0	23.6	11.1	5.3	2.3	1.0	0.7	178.0	35.8
5	1.7	16.7	40.3	33.1	18.2	11.5	5.7	2.8	1.2	0.8	132.0	26.6
6	0.9	9.7	24.3	20.8	12.8	8.1	5.3	2.6	1.2	0.7	86.4	17.4
7	0.3	5.2	13.1	11.5	7.0	4.7	3.3	2.1	1.0	0.7	48.9	9.9
8	0.1	2.8	7.5	7.0	4.1	2.7	1.8	1.2	0.7	0.6	28.3	5.8
9	0.1	1.4	4.1	3.7	2.1	1.4	0.9	0.6	0.4	0.3	15.1	3.0
10+	0.1	1.1	3.5	3.5	2.2	1.3	1.0	0.7	0.4	0.5	14.3	2.9
Total o/oo	61.9	193.9	317.9	209.5	106.0	55.2	29.2	14.7	6.7	5.0	1,000.0	
1,000	12.5	39.0	64.0	42.2	21.3	11.1	5.9	3.0	1.3	1.0		201.4

1946

Number of occupants	Number of units 1	2	3	4	5	6	7	8	9	10+	Total o/oo	1,000
1	29.2	48.1	27.7	5.3	0.9	0.2	0.1	0.0	0.0	0.0	111.4	27.2
2	11.2	56.2	103.1	42.9	7.4	1.8	0.5	0.1	0.0	0.0	223.4	54.6
3	5.7	45.4	110.5	72.6	20.1	4.8	1.3	0.4	0.1	0.1	261.1	63.8
4	1.9	21.7	77.8	60.6	27.1	9.6	2.3	0.7	0.2	0.1	202.0	49.4
5	0.4	6.2	32.0	34.1	19.2	10.2	3.3	1.0	0.3	0.1	106.9	26.1
6	0.1	2.0	12.7	15.8	10.3	6.5	3.5	1.2	0.3	0.2	52.5	12.8
7	0.0	0.6	4.6	6.7	4.8	3.4	2.1	0.9	0.3	0.1	23.6	5.8
8	0.0	0.2	1.8	2.8	2.1	1.5	1.1	0.6	0.3	0.1	10.4	2.5
9	0.0	0.1	0.7	1.1	0.9	0.8	0.5	0.3	0.1	0.1	4.6	1.1
10+	0.0	0.0	0.5	0.8	0.7	0.7	0.6	0.4	0.2	0.2	4.1	1.0
Total o/oo	48.6	180.5	371.5	242.7	93.6	39.6	15.2	5.5	1.9	1.1	1,000.0	
1,000	11.9	44.1	90.7	59.3	22.9	9.7	3.7	1.3	0.5	0.3		244.3

a) 1933: Oslo; 1930-1946: all cities.

Housing Conditions

Distribution of dwellings by number of units and occupants, per 1,000 dwellings (o/oo)

1960

Number of occupants	Number of units										Total	
	1	2	3	4	5	6	7	8	9	10+	o/oo	1,000
1	26.7	38.2	37.9	20.1	8.7	4.3	1.8	0.8	0.4	0.3	139.2	149.7
2	5.8	25.8	73.0	67.8	33.5	16.5	7.2	3.1	1.2	1.1	235.0	252.7
3	2.6	15.6	52.5	66.5	39.3	19.9	8.8	3.9	1.7	1.6	212.4	228.4
4	1.1	8.7	38.3	64.7	46.8	23.5	10.8	4.7	2.1	1.8	202.6	217.9
5	0.4	3.1	14.6	30.9	30.0	18.3	9.7	4.5	2.1	1.9	115.5	124.1
6	0.1	1.2	5.2	11.5	13.7	10.4	6.2	3.2	1.6	1.5	54.7	58.8
7	0.1	0.5	1.8	4.0	5.5	4.8	3.3	1.8	1.0	1.0	23.8	25.5
8	0.0	0.2	0.7	1.5	2.2	2.2	1.6	0.9	0.5	0.6	10.3	11.1
9	0.0	0.1	0.2	0.5	0.8	0.8	0.5	0.4	0.2	0.3	3.8	4.1
10+	0.0	0.1	0.2	0.3	0.5	0.6	0.4	0.3	0.2	0.3	2.7	2.9
Total												
o/oo	36.9	93.4	224.5	267.8	181.0	101.4	50.3	23.4	10.9	10.3	1,000.0	
1,000	39.7	100.4	241.4	288.0	194.6	109.0	54.1	25.2	11.7	11.0		1,075.1

1970

Number of occupants	Number of units										Total	
	1	2	3	4	5	6	7	8	9	10+	o/oo	1,000
1	49.9	43.4	49.9	35.0	18.1	8.5	3.8	1.5	0.7	0.5	211.4	274.1
2	6.8	18.9	55.7	76.4	53.4	24.3	10.6	4.3	1.8	1.4	253.6	328.9
3	2.0	9.0	28.5	53.6	53.7	23.1	10.4	4.1	1.9	1.4	187.8	243.5
4	0.6	4.0	17.0	44.0	65.1	27.1	12.2	5.0	2.1	1.6	178.5	231.5
5	0.2	1.3	5.5	18.8	38.0	20.1	10.2	4.5	1.9	1.5	102.0	132.3
6	0.1	0.4	1.6	6.0	14.3	9.5	5.7	2.8	1.3	1.0	42.6	55.2
7	0.0	0.1	0.5	1.7	4.3	3.8	2.4	1.3	0.7	0.6	15.4	19.9
8	0.0	0.0	0.1	0.5	1.4	1.4	1.0	0.5	0.3	0.3	5.5	7.2
9	0.0	0.0	-0.0	0.2	0.4	0.5	0.4	0.2	0.1	0.1	2.0	2.6
10+	0.0	0.0	0.0	0.1	0.2	0.3	0.2	0.2	0.1	0.1	1.3	1.7
Total												
o/oo	59.5	77.1	158.9	236.3	248.9	118.5	57.0	24.4	10.8	8.4	1,000.0	
1,000	77.2	100.0	206.1	306.4	322.8	153.7	73.9	31.7	14.1	10.9		1,296.8

Sweden

Housing Conditions [a]

	1930	1945	1960	1965	1970	1975
Total number (in 1,000) of						
– private households b)	143	2 082	2 582	2 778	3 050	3 325
– persons	473			7 624	7 915	8 016
– rooms	412			10 015	11 731	13 263
Average number of						
– persons	3.30			2.74	2.60	2.41
– rooms	2.88			3.61	3.85	4.00
– persons per room	1.15			0.76	0.68	0.60
Households by number of rooms (percent distribution)						
1 room	16.3	} 37.1	25.5	6.4	4.7	4.9
2 room	35.5			15.2	13.2	10.0
3	24.3	31.1	31.7	29.1	26.7	24.9
4	9.9	16.3	23.4	25.1	26.5	26.5
5	5.6	8.2	11.7	14.3	16.3	18.4
6	4.1			6.1		10.1
7	2.4			2.1		
8	1.0	} 7.4	7.5	0.7	} 12.2	
9	0.5					} 5.2
10+	0.5			0.6		
Households by number of persons (percent distribution)						
1 person	12.2	14.3	20.2	22.4	25.3	30.0
2 persons	25.8	24.9	27.2	27.7	29.6	30.8
3	23.4	25.6	21.9	21.1	19.4	16.9
4	17.6	17.7	17.5	17.3	16.3	15.2
5	10.4			7.5	6.5	5.4
6	5.5			2.7	2.1	1.3
7	1.2			0.9		0.3
8	0.6	} 17.5	13.1	0.3	} 0.9	
9	0.7			0.1		} 0.1
10+				0.1		
Persons per room in households with						
1 person	0.64			0.40	0.38	0.35
2 persons	0.87			0.58	0.54	0.51
3	1.07			0.77	0.71	0.66
4	1.24			0.93	0.84	0.79
5	1.35			1.06	0.97	0.91
6	1.43			1.21	1.12	1.05
7	1.52			1.36		1.20
8	1.61			1.52	} 1.43	
9	1.70			1.69		} 1.40
10+	2.18			1.93		

a) 1930: Stockholm only, dwellings; 1945: whole country, private households; 1960–1975: whole country, 'dwelling households', i.e. all persons living in a dwelling

Sweden

Housing Conditions [a]

Distribution of households by number of units and occupants, per 1,000 households (o/oo)

1930

Number of occupants	Number of units										Unknown	Total	
	1	2	3	4	5	6	7	8	9	10+		o/oo	1,000
1	76.1	32.6	9.2	2.7	1.4	0.5	0.2	0.0	0.0	0.0		122.9	17.7
2	59.2	116.3	52.4	16.3	7.8	3.9	1.5	0.4	0.2	0.1		258.0	37.0
3	18.8	104.0	64.1	22.8	11.6	7.6	3.6	1.2	0.3	0.3		234.3	33.6
4	5.9	60.1	56.3	23.7	13.4	8.8	4.6	1.5	0.7	0.6		175.7	25.2
5	1.5	25.2	33.6	16.3	10.1	8.6	4.8	1.8	0.9	0.7		103.5	14.9
6	0.5	9.7	15.7	9.1	6.0	5.5	4.2	1.9	1.0	0.8		54.5	7.8
7	0.1	4.0	6.7	4.3	3.1	2.8	2.6	1.4	0.7	0.8		26.5	3.8
8	0.0	1.5	2.6	2.0	1.5	1.6	1.0	0.8	0.5	0.6		12.0	1.7
9	0.0	0.7	1.2	0.8	0.7	0.6	0.5	0.4	0.3	0.5		5.7	0.8
10+	0.6	1.0	1.1	0.7	0.7	0.7	0.7	0.4	0.2	0.7		6.8	1.0
Total o/oo	162.9	355.1	242.8	98.8	56.3	40.6	23.7	9.9	4.8	5.2		1,000.0	
1,000	23.4	51.0	34.9	14.2	8.1	5.8	3.4	1.4	0.7	0.7			143.3

1945

Number of occupants	Number of units					6 7 8 9 10+					Unknown	Total	
	1	2	3	4	5	6	7	8	9	10+		o/oo	1,000
1		98.9	27.4	10.1	4.3			2.9				143.1	298
2		109.5	79.7	35.1	14.9			10.1				248.8	518
3		92.2	89.8	40.8	17.8			15.4				256.0	533
4		44.2	62.0	37.0	17.8			15.9				177.2	369
5 } 6 } 7 } 8 } 9 } 10+		26.4	52.4	40.3	26.4			29.8				174.8	364
Total o/oo		370.8	310.8	163.3	81.2			74.0				1,000.0	
1,000		772	647	340	169			154					2,082

1960

Number of occupants	Number of units					6 7 8 9 10+					Unknown	Total	
	1	2	3	4	5	6	7	8	9	10+		o/oo	1,000
1		124.7	47.6	19.0	6.6			3.5			0.8	202.2	552
2		74.4	102.6	59.6	22.9			12.4			0.4	271.9	702
3		35.2	82.1	61.2	26.7			13.9			0.4	219.2	566
4		14.7	56.5	55.0	30.6			19.0			0.4	175.4	453
5 } 6 } 7 } 8 } 9 } 10+		5.4	27.5	40.3	30.2			27.5			0.0	131.3	339
Total o/oo		254.5	316.8	234.3	116.6			75.9			1.5	1,000.0	
1,000		657	818	605	301			196					2,582

a) 1930: Stockholm only, dwellings; 1945: whole country, private households; 1960: whole country, 'dwelling households'

Sweden

Housing Conditions

Distribution of households by number of units and occupants, per 1,000 households (o/oo)

1965

Number of occupants	Number of units										Unknown	Total	
	1	2	3	4	5	6	7	8	9	10+		o/oo	1,000
1	53.5	75.9	56.0	23.3	8.6	3.0	1.1	0.4		0.4	1.2	223.5	620.9
2	8.2	49.8	103.7	69.2	29.7	10.3	3.3	1.2		1.0	0.9	277.3	770.2
3	1.8	18.0	70.7	56.4	34.1	12.7	3.9	1.3		1.0	0.6	210.6	585.0
4	0.4	6.4	43.3	56.7	39.1	17.4	5.5	1.9		1.3	0.4	172.5	479.0
5	0.1	1.6	12.4	23.5	19.4	10.6	4.0	1.6		1.3	0.2	74.5	207.0
6	0.0	0.4	3.3	8.1	7.5	4.4	1.8	0.8		0.8	0.1	27.1	75.3
7	0.0	0.1	0.9	2.4	2.7	1.7	0.7	0.3		0.3	0.0	9.2	25.6
8	0.0	0.0	0.3	0.8	1.0	0.6	0.3	0.1		0.1	0.0	3.3	9.2
9	0.0	0.0	0.1	0.3	0.4	0.3	0.1	0.0		0.0	0.0	1.2	3.3
10+	0.0	0.0	0.1	0.1	0.2	0.2	0.1	0.0		0.1	0.0	0.8	2.1
Total													
o/oo	64.1	152.3	290.7	250.8	142.8	61.2	20.8	7.7		6.2	3.4	1,000.0	
1,000	178.0	423.0	807.4	696.5	696.7	170.1	57.8	21.4		17.3	9.4		1,777.7

1970

Number of occupants	Number of units					6 7 8 9 10+	Unknown	Total	
	1	2	3	4	5			o/oo	1,000
1	42.6	87.4	73.7	30.5	11.3	6.3	1.1	252.9	771.3
2	4.0	34.7	111.2	84.7	38.7	21.7	0.9	295.9	902.6
3	0.5	7.0	52.0	69.0	39.4	25.1	0.5	193.5	590.4
4	0.1	1.9	23.8	55.5	44.8	36.4	0.4	163.0	497.1
5	0.0	0.4	4.8	18.8	19.5	21.2	0.2	64.9	198.1
6	0.0	0.1	1.0	5.1	6.5	7.8	0.1	20.6	62.8
7 8 9 10+	0.0	0.0	0.3	1.6	3.2	4.0	0.0	9.2	28.1
Total									
o/oo	47.2	131.6	266.8	265.2	163.4	122.4	3.3	1,000.0	
1,000	144.1	401.5	813.8	808.9	498.5	373.5			3,050.4

1975

Number of occupants	Number of units						7 8 9 10+	Unknown	Total	
	1	2	3	4	5	6			o/oo	1,000
1	42.0	81.9	107.9	43.2	15.6	5.9	2.8	0.4	299.7	996.5
2	5.3	15.5	104.4	102.3	49.9	21.7	9.1	0.2	308.4	1,025.5
3	1.1	1.8	26.6	63.9	43.3	22.4	10.0	0.1	169.1	562.1
4	0.5	0.5	8.0	42.5	51.5	32.1	16.2	0.1	151.5	503.6
5	0.2	0.1	1.3	10.3	17.7	14.3	9.6	0.1	53.5	177.8
6	0.0	0.0	0.2	2.0	4.3	3.6	3.0	0.0	13.3	44.2
7	0.0	0.0	0.1	0.4	1.1	0.9	0.8	0.0	3.3	10.8
8 9 10+	0.0	0.0	0.0	0.1	0.4	0.4	0.4	0.0	1.4	4.5
Total										
o/oo	49.1	99.8	248.5	264.6	183.8	101.3	51.9	0.9	1,000.0	
1,000	163.3	331.9	826.3	879.8	611.1	336.9	172.6	3.0		3,325.0

	1930	1920	1930	1960	1970
Total numer (in 1,000) of					
- private households	136	883	995	1 581	2 052
- persons	497	3 743	3 904	5 162	6 009
- rooms	519			5 987	7 603
Average number of					
- persons	3.65			3.27	2.93
- rooms	3.81			3.79	3.71
- persons per room	0.96			0.86	0.79
Households by number of rooms (percent distribution)					
1 room	2.8			5.9	7.9
2 rooms	18.2			15.2	14.6
3	33.7			29.9	29.5
4	20.9			22.5	23.1
5	10.3			12.5	11.9
6	5.5			6.5	6.2
7	3.0			3.3	3.2
8	2.1			1.9	1.7
9	1.1				
10+	2.3			2.3	2.0
Households by number of persons (percent distribution)					
1 person	5.4	8.5	8.5	14.2	19.6
2 persons	21.7	16.7	19.8	26.8	28.5
3	25.8	18.7	20.9	20.6	19.3
4	21.5	17.6	18.4	17.2	16.9
5	13.0	13.8	12.9	10.2	8.8
6	6.5	9.5		5.5	3.9
7	3.0	6.1		2.7	1.6
8	1.5	3.8	19.6	1.4	0.8
9	0.7	2.3		0.7	0.3
10+	1.0	3.1		0.7	0.3
Persons per room in households with					
1 person	0.43			0.41	0.42
2 persons	0.67			0.60	0.58
3	0.85			0.80	0.78
4	1.01			0.98	0.95
5	1.11			1.09	1.05
6	1.19			1.16	1.12
7	1.27			1.25	1.18
8	1.35			1.32	1.25
9	1.39			1.39	1.33
10+	1.51			1.53	1.50

a) 1930: Bâle, Berne, Zurich; dwellings; 1920-1970: whole country; households.

Switzerland

Housing Conditions [a]

Distribution of dwellings/households by number of units and occupants, per 1,000 dwellings (o/oo)

1930

Number of occupants	\ Number of units 1	2	3	4	5	6	7	8	9	10+	Total o/oo	Total 1,000
1	15.0	20.6	10.7	4.5	1.8	0.6	0.3	0.2	0.1	0.1	53.8	7.3
2	8.8	77.0	78.5	30.4	13.0	4.9	2.1	1.2	0.6	0.7	217.3	29.5
3	3.0	49.7	110.2	50.7	21.8	10.4	5.0	3.5	1.5	2.5	258.2	35.1
4	0.8	23.4	79.7	56.7	25.9	12.3	6.2	3.9	2.1	3.7	214.8	29.2
5	0.2	7.9	36.3	36.9	20.4	12.3	6.1	4.1	2.1	3.7	130.0	17.7
6	0.0	2.4	13.6	17.4	10.9	7.1	4.6	3.2	1.6	3.6	64.6	8.8
7	0.0	0.6	4.9	7.2	5.1	3.7	2.7	1.8	1.0	2.6	29.6	4.0
8	0.0	0.2	1.9	2.9	2.7	1.8	1.5	1.0	0.7	1.7	14.5	2.0
9	0.0	0.1	0.7	1.2	0.9	0.9	0.8	0.8	0.5	1.0	6.9	0.9
10+	0.1	0.3	1.0	1.1	1.0	0.9	1.0	1.1	0.9	3.0	10.3	1.4
Total o/oo	27.9	182.3	337.4	209.1	103.4	54.9	30.4	20.9	11.0	22.7	1,000.0	
Total 1,000	3.8	24.8	45.9	28.4	14.1	7.5	4.1	2.8	1.5	3.1		136.0

1960

Number of occupants	\ Number of units 1	2	3	4	5	6	7	8	9 10+	Total o/oo	Total 1,000
1	41.2	43.6	32.5	14.1	5.9	2.4	1.1	0.6	0.6	141.9	224.3
2	13.5	63.4	97.7	51.0	23.5	9.9	4.5	2.2	2.3	268.0	423.5
3	3.3	27.4	79.1	50.4	24.4	10.8	5.1	2.6	3.0	206.1	325.7
4	0.9	12.1	55.9	52.4	26.7	12.3	5.6	2.8	3.1	171.8	271.6
5	0.2	3.7	22.2	32.2	21.1	11.2	5.6	2.9	3.3	102.3	161.7
6	0.1	1.2	7.5	14.8	12.3	8.2	4.6	2.8	3.3	54.9	86.7
7	0.0	0.4	2.4	5.8	6.3	4.8	3.1	1.9	2.4	27.1	42.8
8	0.0	0.2	0.9	2.3	2.8	2.6	1.8	1.2	1.8	13.6	21.6
9	0.0	0.1	0.3	0.9	1.3	1.3	1.0	0.8	1.3	7.0	11.0
10+	0.0	0.1	0.2	0.6	1.0	1.2	1.0	0.9	2.3	7.4	11.6
Total o/oo	59.4	152.1	298.8	224.5	125.2	64.7	33.3	18.7	23.3	1,000.0	
Total 1,000	93.8	240.3	472.1	354.8	197.9	102.2	52.7	29.6	36.8		1,580.4

1970

Number of occupants	\ Number of units 1	2	3	4	5	6	7	8	9 10+	Total o/oo	Total 1,000
1	62.3	57.0	43.2	18.9	8.4	3.5	1.5	0.7	0.8	196.3	402.6
2	12.9	58.0	105.4	57.5	27.7	12.1	5.4	2.7	2.9	284.6	583.5
3	2.8	20.1	74.4	49.8	23.7	11.2	5.2	2.6	3.0	192.7	395.1
4	0.3	8.2	51.8	57.5	26.3	12.9	6.1	3.0	3.1	169.1	346.8
5	0.1	1.8	14.7	31.3	18.2	10.6	5.6	2.9	3.1	88.3	181.0
6	0.0	0.4	3.7	11.0	8.8	6.3	3.9	2.2	2.7	39.1	80.1
7	0.0	0.1	0.9	3.2	3.6	3.0	2.2	1.3	1.8	16.3	33.4
8	0.0	0.0	0.3	1.1	1.5	1.4	1.2	0.8	1.2	7.5	15.4
9	0.0	0.0	0.1	0.3	0.6	0.6	0.5	0.4	0.7	3.2	6.7
10+	0.0	0.0	0.1	0.2	0.4	0.5	0.4	0.4	0.9	2.8	5.8
Total o/oo	78.5	145.6	294.6	230.7	119.1	62.1	32.0	17.1	20.3	1,000.0	
Total 1,000	161.0	298.7	604.0	473.1	244.2	127.3	65.6	35.1	41.5		2,050.5

a) 1930: Bâle, Berne, Zurich; dwellings; 1960 and 1970: whole country; households.

Housing Conditions

	1911	1921	1931	1961	1971
Total number (in 1,000) of					
- private households	7 943	8 739	10 233	14 641	16 434
- persons	34 606	36 180	38 042	44 543	47 119
- rooms	37 800	39 786	46 036	67 009	80 692
Average number of					
- persons	4.36	4.14	3.72	3.04	2.87
- rooms	4.76	4.55	4.50	4.58	4.91
- persons per room	0.91	0.90	0.82	0.66	0.58
Households by number of rooms (percent distribution)					
1 room	3.2	3.6	3.4	2.2	2.1
2 rooms	8.3	10.5	9.9	4.9	3.7
3	14.0	15.6	15.1	11.4	8.2
4	24.9	24.5	24.6	26.8	22.4
5	20.6	20.8	23.7	36.0	30.5
6	13.7	12.9	13.2	12.6	24.2
7	5.9	5.0	4.6	3.3	5.1
8	3.5	3.0	2.4	1.5	2.1
9	2.0	1.5	1.2	0.6	0.8
10+	3.8	2.6	1.9	0.7	0.8
Households by number of persons (percent distribution)					
1 person	5.3	6.0	6.7	13.4	18.1
2 persons	16.2	17.7	21.9	29.9	31.9
3	19.3	20.9	24.0	22.9	19.1
4	18.1	18.6	19.4	18.3	16.9
5	14.4	13.9	13.4	8.8	8.1
6	10.4	9.4	7.3	3.8	3.5
7	6.9	6.0	4.1	1.7	1.3
8	4.3	3.6	2.1	0.7	0.6
9	2.5	2.0	1.1	0.3	0.2
10+	2.5	2.0	0.1	0.3	0.2
Persons per room in households with					
1 person	0.35	0.34	0.33	0.27	0.25
2 persons	0.48	0.50	0.48	0.46	0.42
3	0.65	0.68	0.67	0.65	0.59
4	0.82	0.85	0.85	0.82	0.74
5	0.98	1.02	1.03	0.97	0.89
6	1.15	1.20	1.20	1.13	1.04
7	1.31	1.37	1.38	1.28	1.20
8	1.47	1.53	1.53	1.43	1.35
9	1.61	1.67	1.67	1.59	1.50
10+	1.76	1.81	1.67	1.81	1.73

England and Wales

Housing Conditions

Distribution of households by number of rooms and occupants, per 1,000 households (o/oo)

1911

Number of occupants	Number of rooms										Total	
	1	2	3	4	5	6	7	8	9	10+	o/oo	1,000
1	15.5	12.9	7.6	8.7	4.0	2.5	1.0	0.5	0.2	0.3	53.3	423.2
2	9.3	22.4	27.6	41.9	27.0	18.9	7.2	3.6	1.6	2.1	161.6	1,283.6
3	4.2	18.0	30.4	51.3	37.7	25.9	11.2	6.5	3.3	4.3	192.8	1,531.4
4	2.0	12.8	25.6	47.4	39.0	26.2	11.5	7.0	3.9	6.1	181.2	1,439.5
5	0.8	8.0	19.0	36.5	32.9	21.3	9.8	6.1	3.6	6.3	144.2	1,145.6
6	0.3	4.7	12.9	25.8	24.5	15.6	7.0	4.5	2.8	5.7	103.6	823.0
7	0.1	2.5	8.1	17.1	17.1	10.6	4.7	3.0	1.8	4.5	69.4	551.2
8	0.0	1.2	4.6	10.5	11.1	7.0	2.9	1.9	1.1	3.2	43.4	344.8
9	0.0	0.5	2.3	5.8	6.7	4.4	1.8	1.1	0.7	2.1	25.3	200.7
10+	0.0	0.2	1.4	4.5	6.4	4.8	2.1	1.4	0.8	3.5	25.2	200.0
Total												
o/oo	32.1	83.2	139.5	249.5	206.4	137.1	59.2	35.4	19.7	38.1	1,000.0	
1,000	254.7	660.5	1,107.9	1,981.4	1,639.1	1,089.3	469.9	281.3	156.7	302.3		7,943.1

1921

Number of occupants	Number of rooms										Total	
	1	2	3	4	5	6	7	8	9	10+	o/oo	1,000
1	16.5	14.0	9.4	9.9	4.9	3.1	1.2	0.7	0.3	0.4	60.3	526.9
2	10.3	31.6	31.4	41.5	28.5	18.9	7.3	3.9	1.7	2.1	177.0	1,546.9
3	5.9	26.0	34.9	52.3	40.8	26.3	10.3	5.8	2.8	3.6	208.7	1,823.6
4	2.3	15.4	28.8	48.2	41.6	26.0	10.2	6.0	3.0	4.4	186.0	1,625.3
5	0.8	8.7	20.4	35.7	33.3	20.1	8.0	4.9	2.6	4.2	138.9	1,213.5
6	0.3	4.7	13.3	24.0	23.2	13.8	5.5	3.5	1.9	3.5	93.7	818.4
7	0.1	2.5	8.3	15.2	15.1	8.8	3.5	2.2	1.2	2.6	59.5	520.1
8	0.0	1.3	4.8	9.2	9.4	5.4	2.1	1.4	0.7	1.8	36.0	314.8
9	0.0	0.5	2.4	5.2	5.5	3.2	1.2	0.8	0.4	1.2	20.5	179.3
10+	0.0	0.3	1.7	4.2	5.3	3.3	1.3	0.9	0.5	1.9	19.5	170.4
Total												
o/oo	36.3	105.0	155.5	245.4	207.7	128.9	50.5	30.0	15.0	25.6	1,000.0	
1,000	317.4	918.0	1,358.7	2,144.2	1,815.1	1,126.2	441.7	262.6	131.4	224.1		8,739.2

1931

Number of occupants	Number of rooms										Total	
	1	2	3	4	5	6	7	8	9	10+	o/oo	1,000
1	17.3	14.6	10.9	11.5	6.9	3.9	1.3	0.6	0.2	0.3	67.3	688.7
2	8.3	32.3	38.2	52.7	45.3	27.0	8.1	3.8	1.5	1.6	218.9	2,239.8
3	4.5	24.9	38.2	60.7	57.5	32.9	11.0	5.5	2.4	2.8	240.4	2,459.9
4	2.2	13.7	27.5	49.8	50.9	28.2	10.1	5.2	2.5	3.4	193.5	1,980.5
5	1.0	6.9	16.6	31.5	34.0	18.0	7.1	3.9	2.1	3.2	134.3	1,271.5
6	0.4	3.6	9.5	18.7	19.8	10.4	4.1	2.5	1.4	2.5	73.0	746.6
7	0.2	1.9	5.3	10.7	11.2	5.6	2.2	1.4	0.8	1.8	41.2	421.8
8	0.0	0.8	2.6	5.5	5.7	2.8	1.0	0.7	0.4	1.2	20.9	214.4
9	0.0	0.4	1.3	2.9	3.0	1.5	0.5	0.4	0.2	0.7	10.9	112.0
10+	0.0	0.2	0.9	2.3	2.6	1.4	0.5	0.4	0.2	1.1	9.6	87.2
Total												
o/oo	34.0	99.3	150.9	246.3	236.7	131.8	46.1	24.4	11.8	18.6	1,000.0	
1,000	347.8	1,016.5	1,544.7	2,520.3	2,422.6	1,349.2	471.5	249.8	120.3	190.4		10,233.1

England

Housing Conditions

Distribution of households by number of units and occupants, per 1,000 households (o/oo)

1961

Number of occupants	Number of units										Total o/oo	Total 1,000
	1	2	3	4	5	6	7	8	9	10+	o/oo	1,000
1	14.3	20.2	23.5	34.6	27.4	10.0	2.2	0.9	0.3	0.3	133.9	1,959.8
2	4.7	19.3	44.4	90.5	94.6	32.8	7.6	3.1	1.1	1.2	299.4	4,383.3
3	1.7	5.9	26.1	68.4	85.4	29.1	7.1	3.0	1.2	1.3	229.1	3,353.6
4	0.7	2.6	13.3	45.4	81.2	26.9	7.2	3.1	1.2	1.4	183.1	2,680.9
5	0.2	0.9	4.2	17.9	41.7	14.4	4.7	2.2	1.0	1.1	88.4	1,294.3
6	0.1	0.3	1.4	6.8	17.5	6.9	2.4	1.3	0.6	0.8	38.0	555.7
7	0.0	0.1	0.5	2.6	7.1	3.0	1.1	0.6	0.3	0.4	15.7	229.3
8	0.0	0.0	0.2	1.1	3.1	1.5	0.5	0.3	0.1	0.2	7.2	104.8
9	0.0	0.0	0.1	0.4	1.2	0.7	0.2	0.1	0.1	0.1	2.9	42.1
10+	0.0	0.0	0.0	0.3	0.9	0.7	0.3	0.1	0.1	0.1	2.5	37.3
Total o/oo	21.9	49.4	113.7	268.0	359.9	126.0	33.4	14.8	5.9	7.0	1,000.0	
Total 1,000	320.3	722.8	1,665.3	3,923.3	5,269.7	1,844.1	489.3	216.8	86.9	102.5		14,640.9

1971

Number of occupants	Number of units										Total o/oo	Total 1,000
	1	2	3	4	5	6	7	8	9	10+	o/oo	1,000
1	17.5	20.9	31.3	45.8	32.9	25.7	4.3	1.8	0.6	0.6	181.4	2,980.4
2	2.8	12.1	32.9	92.0	90.4	68.4	11.9	4.9	1.7	1.8	318.7	5,238.2
3	0.6	2.4	10.6	45.9	64.5	50.4	9.7	4.0	1.5	1.5	190.9	3,137.5
4	0.2	1.0	4.8	26.3	64.8	53.0	11.4	4.6	1.7	1.7	169.3	2,782.7
5	0.1	0.4	1.6	8.7	31.7	25.9	7.1	3.2	1.3	1.4	81.3	1,335.3
6	0.0	0.2	0.6	3.3	13.1	11.1	3.6	1.7	0.8	0.9	35.3	580.4
7	0.0	0.0	0.2	1.1	4.7	4.1	1.5	0.6	0.3	0.4	12.9	211.2
8	0.0	0.0	0.1	0.4	1.9	1.9	0.8	0.3	0.1	0.2	5.7	94.0
9	0.0	0.0	0.0	0.2	0.8	0.8	0.4	0.1	0.1	0.1	2.5	40.9
10+	0.0	0.0	0.0	0.1	0.5	0.7	0.4	0.2	0.1	0.1	2.0	33.4
Total o/oo	21.1	37.0	82.2	223.8	305.3	241.8	51.0	21.4	8.0	8.5	1,000.0	
Total 1,000	347.2	607.9	1,350.1	3,678.1	5,018.0	3,973.8	837.3	351.1	131.4	139.0		16,434.1

Scotland

Housing Conditions

	1881	1891	1901	1911	1921	1931	1951	1961	1971
Total number of									
- private households	811	874	965	1 011	1 055	1 147	1 440	1 570	1 681
- persons	3 679	3 960	4 377	4 606	4 700	4 683	4 883	5 003	5 037
- rooms	3 044	2 533	2 893	3 139	3 281	3 652	4 630	5 394	6 537
Average number of									
- persons per dwelling	4.54	4.53	4.54	4.56	4.45	4.08	3.39	3.19	3.00
- rooms per dwelling	3.75	2.90	3.00	3.10	3.11	3.18	3.22	3.44	3.89
- persons per room	1.65	1.56	1.51	1.47	1.43	1.28	1.05	0.93	0.77
Households by number of rooms (percent distribution)									
1 room	26.0	22.1	17.6	12.8	11.8	9.6	8.7	4.0	2.2
2 rooms	38.9	39.1	39.9	40.5	40.2	36.9	26.9	19.5	12.7
3	14.7	16.4	18.5	20.3	21.1	24.9	29.9	35.2	28.0
4	6.8	7.5	8.5	9.4	10.2	11.9	20.0	25.8	29.9
5	3.7	4.1	4.5	5.4	5.6	6.2	7.0	8.7	16.6
6	2.7	2.9	3.1	3.6	3.7	3.7	3.0	3.1	5.9
7	1.7	1.9	2.1	2.4	2.4	2.3	1.9	1.6	2.3
8	1.3	1.5	1.6	1.9	1.8	1.7	1.1	1.0	1.3
9	1.0	1.1	1.2	1.3	1.2	1.1	0.6	0.5	0.6
10+	3.2	3.4	3.1	2.4	2.1	1.8	0.7	0.6	0.7
Households by number of persons (percent distribution)									
1 person	9.2	9.5	8.4	6.2	6.5	6.9	11.1	14.1	18.5
2 persons	15.4	15.7	15.3	14.8	15.1	17.9	24.2	26.5	28.5
3	15.3	15.3	16.1	17.0	17.9	20.7	23.6	22.0	18.8
4	14.6	14.4	15.2	16.6	17.3	18.7	19.0	18.5	17.0
5	13.1	12.7	13.3	14.3	14.3	13.8	10.7	10.0	9.3
6	11.0	10.7	10.8	11.2	10.7	9.2	5.6	4.8	4.5
7	8.4	8.2	8.1	8.0	7.4	5.7	2.9	2.2	1.9
8	5.8	5.9	5.6	5.4	4.8	3.4	1.4	1.1	0.8
9	3.5	3.6	3.5	3.2	2.9	1.9	0.7	0.5	0.4
10+	3.8	4.0	3.8	3.3	3.1	1.9	0.7	0.4	0.3
Persons per room in households with									
1 person	0.62	0.59	0.56	0.48	0.44	0.42	0.39	0.36	0.33
2 persons	0.90	0.85	0.79	0.73	0.69	0.66	0.65	0.62	0.54
3	1.17	1.10	1.06	1.00	0.98	0.95	0.96	0.88	0.75
4	1.49	1.37	1.33	1.28	1.27	1.24	1.21	1.10	0.93
5	1.78	1.66	1.59	1.54	1.55	1.51	1.41	1.28	1.11
6	2.04	1.91	1.83	1.80	1.84	1.79	1.60	1.48	1.30
7	2.23	2.13	2.07	2.06	2.13	2.08	1.80	1.68	1.51
8	2.36	2.30	2.26	2.33	2.41	2.34	1.99	1.88	1.72
9	2.39	2.37	2.43	2.56	2.62	2.57	2.17	2.09	1.92
10+	2.10	2.20	2.40	2.75	2.78	2.68	2.54	2.46	2.20

Scotland

Housing Conditions

Distribution of households by number of rooms and occupants, per 1,000 households (o/oo)

1881

Number of occupants	Number of rooms										Total	
	1	2	3	4	5	6	7	8	9	10+	o/oo	1,000
1	58.5	23.1	5.4	2.3	1.0	0.6	0.3	0.2	0.1	0.5	92.2	74.7
2	60.8	54.0	17.8	8.7	4.2	2.9	1.5	1.2	0.7	1.9	153.9	124.7
3	44.4	59.4	21.8	9.8	5.2	3.6	2.2	1.8	1.3	3.0	152.6	123.7
4	35.1	60.7	22.5	10.2	5.2	3.6	2.2	1.7	1.3	3.4	146.1	118.5
5	25.4	57.4	21.4	9.5	5.1	3.6	2.2	1.7	1.3	3.5	131.1	106.3
6	17.4	49.1	18.6	8.4	4.5	3.3	2.0	1.6	1.1	3.4	109.6	88.9
7	10.0	37.2	15.3	6.9	3.8	2.8	1.8	1.4	1.0	3.2	83.5	67.7
8	5.2	24.7	11.2	5.1	2.8	2.3	1.5	1.2	0.8	2.8	57.7	46.8
9	2.1	13.8	6.9	3.5	2.1	1.6	1.1	0.9	0.7	2.4	35.1	28.5
10+	1.1	9.9	6.4	3.6	2.6	2.4	1.8	1.6	1.4	7.3	38.2	30.9
Total o/oo	260.0	389.4	147.4	68.1	36.5	26.7	16.7	13.4	9.8	31.5	1,000.0	
1,000	210.8	315.7	119.5	55.2	29.6	21.7	13.5	10.8	7.9	25.5		810.7

1891

Number of occupants	Number of rooms										Total	
	1	2	3	4	5	6	7	8	9	10+	o/oo	1,000
1	57.9	24.9	6.5	2.8	1.3	0.7	0.3	0.3	0.2	0.5	95.3	83.3
2	54.6	57.0	20.7	9.7	5.0	3.3	1.9	1.3	0.9	2.1	156.5	136.8
3	36.9	60.8	24.2	11.2	6.2	4.2	2.7	2.1	1.4	3.4	153.2	133.9
4	27.4	59.6	24.5	11.2	6.0	4.3	2.6	2.1	1.6	4.5	143.9	125.8
5	19.2	55.1	23.0	10.3	5.6	4.1	2.6	2.0	1.5	4.0	127.4	111.4
6	12.3	47.2	20.1	9.2	5.1	3.6	2.3	1.8	1.4	3.7	106.7	93.3
7	7.1	36.0	16.6	7.5	4.0	2.9	1.9	1.6	1.1	3.5	82.2	71.9
8	3.5	25.1	12.6	5.4	3.0	2.4	1.6	1.2	0.9	3.0	58.8	51.4
9	1.4	14.4	7.9	3.7	2.0	1.6	1.1	0.9	0.7	2.5	36.3	31.8
10+	0.7	10.9	7.8	4.2	2.6	2.3	1.7	1.6	1.2	6.7	39.7	34.7
Total o/oo	221.2	391.0	164.0	75.2	40.8	29.4	18.9	15.0	10.9	33.8	1,000.0	
1,000	193.3	341.8	143.4	65.7	35.6	25.7	16.5	13.1	9.5	29.6		874.2

1901

Number of occupants	Number of rooms										Total	
	1	2	3	4	5	6	7	8	9	10+	o/oo	1,000
1	46.9	23.4	6.9	3.1	1.5	0.9	0.4	0.3	0.2	0.4	83.9	81.0
2	42.8	58.8	23.3	11.4	5.8	3.8	2.2	1.5	1.0	2.0	152.6	147.3
3	31.0	66.2	28.5	12.9	7.0	4.8	3.1	2.5	1.7	3.2	161.0	155.4
4	22.5	64.0	28.6	13.2	7.3	4.9	3.2	2.6	1.8	4.0	152.1	146.8
5	15.3	56.6	26.3	11.9	6.6	4.5	3.2	2.4	1.7	4.0	132.6	128.0
6	9.0	46.5	22.6	10.2	5.5	3.9	2.6	2.2	1.6	3.9	107.9	104.1
7	4.8	35.0	17.8	7.7	4.2	3.0	2.1	1.7	1.2	3.4	81.0	78.1
8	2.3	23.6	13.1	5.8	2.9	2.1	1.5	1.3	1.0	2.8	56.4	54.4
9	0.9	13.8	8.4	3.9	2.0	1.4	1.0	0.8	0.6	2.0	34.8	33.6
10+	0.5	11.0	9.0	4.5	2.4	1.9	1.4	1.2	0.9	4.9	37.6	36.3
Total o/oo	176.0	398.9	184.6	84.5	45.2	31.2	20.8	16.5	11.6	30.6	1,000.0	
1,000	169.8	384.9	178.1	81.6	43.7	30.1	20.0	15.9	11.2	29.6		964.9

Scotland

Housing Conditions

Distribution of households by number of rooms and occupants, per 1,000 households (o/oo)

1911

Number of occupants	Number of rooms										Total	
	1	2	3	4	5	6	7	8	9	10+	o/oo	1,000
1	26.3	20.7	7.4	3.4	1.8	1.0	0.5	0.3	0.2	0.3	62.0	62.6
2	31.0	58.4	26.1	13.0	7.6	4.8	2.8	1.9	1.0	1.7	148.2	149.8
3	25.7	68.5	32.9	15.6	9.3	6.2	4.2	3.2	2.0	2.8	170.4	172.2
4	19.6	68.2	33.4	16.0	9.5	6.3	4.2	3.3	2.2	3.6	166.2	168.0
5	12.7	59.8	29.7	13.8	8.4	5.6	3.9	3.0	2.1	3.7	142.7	144.2
6	7.3	47.7	24.3	11.0	6.3	4.4	3.0	2.5	1.8	3.4	111.7	112.9
7	3.5	34.6	18.7	8.1	4.4	3.0	2.1	1.7	1.2	2.9	80.3	81.1
8	1.6	23.4	13.0	5.4	2.9	2.0	1.4	1.2	0.8	2.1	53.7	54.2
9	0.6	13.2	8.4	3.5	1.8	1.2	0.9	0.6	0.5	1.4	32.1	32.4
10+	0.3	10.7	9.1	4.2	2.0	1.6	1.1	0.9	0.7	2.3	32.7	33.1
Total												
o/oo	128.4	405.1	203.2	93.9	54.0	36.0	24.2	18.6	12.6	24.1	1,000.0	
1,000	129.7	409.4	205.3	94.9	54.6	36.4	24.4	18.8	12.7	24.4		1,010.5

1921

Number of occupants	Number of rooms										Total	
	1	2	3	4	5	6	7	8	9	10+	o/oo	1,000
1	23.8	22.6	8.6	4.3	2.3	1.3	0.7	0.5	0.3	0.4	64.8	68.3
2	26.0	59.5	28.8	14.5	8.4	5.4	3.3	2.4	1.3	1.8	151.4	159.7
3	24.0	69.4	38.2	18.1	10.1	6.6	4.4	3.3	2.0	2.9	179.0	188.8
4	18.0	69.8	36.9	19.1	10.0	6.5	4.2	3.3	2.1	3.4	173.2	182.7
5	12.0	58.9	31.6	14.8	9.0	5.5	3.6	2.7	1.8	3.3	143.1	151.0
6	7.3	45.2	24.3	11.0	6.0	4.5	2.7	2.0	1.4	2.6	107.1	113.0
7	3.8	32.1	16.9	7.6	4.1	2.8	2.0	1.4	1.0	2.0	73.8	77.8
8	1.9	20.9	11.2	5.0	2.5	1.8	1.2	1.0	0.6	1.4	47.5	50.1
9	0.8	12.4	6.9	3.2	1.6	1.1	0.7	0.6	0.5	1.0	28.6	30.2
10+	0.4	11.4	7.4	3.9	2.1	1.6	1.0	0.9	0.7	2.1	31.4	33.2
Total												
o/oo	117.9	402.2	210.8	101.5	56.0	37.2	23.7	18.1	11.7	21.0	1,000.0	
1,000	124.4	424.2	222.3	107.0	59.1	39.3	25.0	19.1	12.4	22.1		1,054.9

1931

Number of occupants	Number of rooms										Total	
	1	2	3	4	5	6	7	8	9	10+	o/oo	1,000
1	21.7	24.0	10.9	5.9	3.0	1.7	0.8	0.5	0.2	0.3	69.1	79.3
2	21.6	65.3	40.9	22.3	12.1	6.7	4.1	2.5	1.3	1.7	178.6	204.8
3	19.6	76.1	51.6	24.8	13.6	7.8	4.9	3.6	2.1	2.8	206.9	237.3
4	14.1	69.4	47.8	23.3	12.2	6.9	4.6	3.4	2.1	3.1	187.0	214.5
5	8.7	51.8	36.2	16.2	8.8	5.1	3.6	2.7	1.8	3.0	138.0	158.3
6	5.0	34.8	24.4	10.7	5.3	3.7	2.3	1.8	1.3	2.4	91.6	105.1
7	2.6	22.0	15.9	6.7	3.1	1.9	1.5	1.0	0.8	1.7	57.3	65.7
8	1.2	12.7	9.7	4.1	1.8	1.2	0.8	0.7	0.4	1.1	33.7	38.7
9	0.5	7.0	5.5	2.3	1.0	0.7	0.4	0.4	0.3	0.8	18.8	21.6
10+	0.3	5.5	5.5	2.5	1.2	0.9	0.6	0.5	0.3	1.6	18.9	21.7
Total												
o/oo	95.5	368.7	248.5	118.9	62.2	36.6	23.5	17.1	10.6	18.5	1,000.0	
1,000	109.5	422.8	284.9	136.3	71.4	42.0	27.0	19.6	12.2	21.2		1,146.9

Scotland

Housing Conditions

Distribution of households by number of rooms and occupants, per 1,000 households (o/oo)

1951

Number of occupants	1	2	3	4	5	6	7	8	9	10+	Total o/oo	1,000
1	25.6	40.0	22.7	12.3	5.4	2.5	1.2	0.7	0.3	0.4	111.1	160.0
2	25.3	78.1	67.7	36.5	16.3	7.6	5.6	2.6	1.2	1.3	242.1	348.6
3	20.3	68.2	77.2	39.1	15.1	7.2	4.0	2.5	1.3	1.5	236.4	340.4
4	10.5	46.8	66.0	40.4	12.4	5.9	3.5	2.2	1.2	1.4	190.3	274.1
5	3.5	21.3	35.3	30.3	7.6	3.5	2.2	1.5	0.8	1.1	107.3	154.4
6	1.2	8.6	16.6	19.6	4.7	1.9	1.3	0.9	0.5	0.7	56.1	80.8
7	0.5	3.6	7.8	11.2	3.2	0.9	0.6	0.5	0.3	0.4	29.0	41.8
8	0.2	1.4	3.4	5.5	2.1	0.4	0.2	0.2	0.1	0.2	13.8	19.9
9	0.1	0.6	1.5	2.8	1.4	0.2	0.1	0.1	0.1	0.1	7.0	10.1
10+	0.0	0.4	1.3	2.5	1.9	0.2	0.1	0.1	0.0	0.2	6.9	9.9
Total o/oo	87.2	269.1	299.4	200.2	70.1	30.3	19.0	11.4	5.8	7.4	1,000.0	
1,000	125.6	387.4	431.2	288.2	101.0	43.7	27.3	16.4	8.4	10.7		1,439.9

1961

Number of occupants	1	2	3	4	5	6	7	8	9	10+	Total o/oo	1,000
1	19.3	50.7	39.0	18.5	7.4	3.0	1.3	0.7	0.3	0.4	140.6	220.7
2	10.5	68.8	99.5	50.1	19.8	7.7	3.8	2.2	0.9	1.1	264.5	415.2
3	6.0	38.3	92.6	51.3	17.9	6.6	3.4	2.0	0.9	1.1	220.1	345.5
4	2.9	22.9	71.4	56.3	17.3	6.3	3.4	2.0	0.9	1.1	184.6	289.8
5	1.1	8.9	30.9	39.3	10.9	3.8	2.4	1.5	0.8	0.8	100.3	157.4
6	0.4	3.4	11.4	22.2	5.9	1.9	1.2	0.8	0.4	0.6	48.2	75.6
7	0.2	1.3	4.3	10.8	3.6	0.8	0.5	0.4	0.2	0.3	22.4	35.1
8	0.1	0.6	1.7	5.3	2.1	0.4	0.2	0.2	0.1	0.2	10.8	17.0
9	0.0	0.2	0.6	2.2	1.2	0.2	0.1	0.0	0.0	0.1	4.7	7.4
10+	0.0	0.1	0.5	1.6	1.3	0.2	0.1	0.0	0.0	0.1	3.9	6.2
Total o/oo	40.5	195.3	351.9	257.7	87.5	30.8	16.3	9.9	4.6	5.6	1,000.0	
1,000	63.5	306.5	552.5	404.6	137.3	48.3	25.6	15.6	7.2	8.8		1,569.8

1971

Number of occupants	1	2	3	4	5	6	7	8	9	10+	Total o/oo	1,000
1	15.4	55.2	56.4	35.2	13.6	5.4	2.0	1.1	0.5	0.6	185.4	311.4
2	3.8	44.3	96.2	80.4	35.1	13.7	5.4	3.0	1.4	1.6	284.9	478.6
3	1.4	14.2	58.1	63.0	31.1	11.2	4.3	2.3	1.1	1.3	188.1	316.1
4	0.6	7.5	41.5	58.4	37.8	13.6	5.3	2.8	1.3	1.3	170.1	285.8
5	0.3	3.2	17.0	32.5	24.8	9.4	3.4	2.1	1.0	1.1	93.0	156.3
6	0.1	1.4	6.8	16.7	12.5	3.8	1.5	1.0	0.6	0.7	45.2	75.9
7	0.0	0.5	2.3	6.9	5.6	1.7	0.5	0.4	0.2	0.3	18.5	31.1
8	0.0	0.3	0.9	3.0	2.7	0.9	0.2	0.1	0.1	0.1	8.5	14.2
9	0.0	0.1	0.4	1.3	1.3	0.5	0.1	0.1	0.0	0.0	3.8	6.3
10+	0.0	0.1	0.2	0.8	1.1	0.4	0.1	0.0	0.0	0.0	2.9	4.8
Total o/oo	21.7	126.8	279.8	298.5	165.7	58.9	22.8	13.0	6.2	7.0	1,000.0	
1,000	36.4	213.1	470.0	501.4	278.3	98.9	38.3	21.8	10.5	11.7		1,680.5

Housing Conditions

	1926	1937	1951	1961
Total number (in 1,000) of				
- private households	274	303	338	373
- persons	1 193	1 229	1 321	1 378
- rooms	1 179	1 343	1 453	1 670
Average number of				
- persons	4.35	4.06	3.91	3.69
- rooms	4.30	4.43	4.30	4.48
- persons per room	1.01	0.92	0.91	0.83
Households by number of rooms (percent distribution)				
1 room	2.6	1.6	1.8	0.7
2 rooms	15.3	10.4	8.1	4.9
3	18.5	16.0	15.8	14.1
4	29.4	34.2	34.3	33.7
5	12.2	16.7	20.0	26.2
6	} 14.5	} 14.8	15.0	15.8
7			3.7	3.5
8	} 5.0	} 4.4	} 1.3	1.2
9				
10+	2.5	1.9		
Households by number of persons (percent distribution)				
1 person	7.8	8.5	9.3	11.5
2 persons	16.4	18.9	19.7	22.6
3	17.5	19.5	20.0	19.8
4	16.3	17.2	18.1	17.3
5	13.6	12.9	12.8	11.7
6	10.3	9.1	8.3	7.0
7	7.3	5.9	5.1	4.2
8	4.8	3.7	3.1	2.6
9	2.9	2.2	1.7	1.4
10+	2.9	2.2	2.0	1.9
Persons per room in households with				
1 person	0.33	0.30	0.28	0.26
2 persons	0.51	0.47	0.47	0.46
3	0.70	0.67	0.69	0.66
4	0.90	0.87	0.90	0.86
5	1.10	1.06	1.12	1.07
6	1.30	1.28	1.35	1.28
7	1.52	1.52	1.58	1.50
8	1.72	1.72	1.82	1.73
9	1.89	1.92	2.04	1.94
10+	2.10	2.21	2.47	2.37

Northern Ireland

Housing Conditions

Distribution of households by number of units and occupants, per 1,000 households (o/oo)

1926

Number of occupants	Number of units 1	2	3	4	5	6 — 7	8 — 9	10+	Total o/oo	1,000
1	9.5	26.7	16.0	14.2	5.0	4.6	1.4	0.4	77.9	21.3
2	6.4	34.5	33.4	42.4	18.7	20.4	6.4	2.2	164.4	45.0
3	4.5	27.5	32.8	48.9	22.4	26.1	9.1	3.9	175.3	48.0
4	2.8	21.8	29.0	49.3	21.0	25.8	9.3	4.2	163.2	44.7
5	1.6	15.7	24.2	43.1	17.7	22.0	7.7	4.0	136.1	37.2
6	0.8	11.3	18.4	33.6	13.3	16.7	5.9	3.6	103.7	28.4
7	0.5	7.1	13.1	25.1	9.2	11.8	3.9	2.4	73.1	20.0
8	0.2	4.0	8.8	17.0	6.5	7.5	2.5	1.8	48.4	13.2
9	0.1	2.2	5.0	10.2	4.1	4.6	1.6	1.0	28.7	7.9
10+	0.1	1.7	4.5	10.1	4.1	5.1	2.0	1.5	29.1	8.0
Total o/oo	26.4	152.6	185.4	294.0	122.2	144.7	49.8	25.0	1,000.0	
Total 1,000	7.2	41.8	50.7	80.4	33.4	39.6	13.6	6.8		273.7

1937

Number of occupants	Number of units 1	2	3	4	5	6 — 7	8 — 9	10+	Total o/oo	1,000
1	7.7	22.9	17.3	21.3	8.0	5.9	1.5	0.4	85.2	25.8
2	3.7	24.4	32.4	61.7	32.6	25.6	6.7	2.1	189.2	57.3
3	2.1	17.8	30.0	67.7	35.1	29.7	8.8	3.5	194.8	58.9
4	1.1	13.8	24.9	60.6	31.9	27.2	8.3	3.7	171.6	51.9
5	0.6	9.5	19.0	45.4	22.9	21.4	7.1	3.0	128.9	39.0
6	0.4	6.5	14.1	32.7	15.1	15.1	4.9	2.4	91.2	27.6
7	0.2	3.9	9.6	21.7	9.3	9.8	3.0	1.5	59.2	17.9
8	0.1	2.4	5.9	14.0	5.8	5.9	1.7	1.0	36.8	11.1
9	0.0	1.4	3.4	8.5	3.3	3.5	1.0	0.5	21.7	6.6
10+	0.0	1.1	3.3	8.1	3.3	3.8	1.2	0.7	21.6	6.5
Total o/oo	16.0	103.8	159.9	341.7	167.3	148.1	44.3	18.9	1,000.0	
Total 1,000	4.8	31.4	48.4	103.4	50.6	44.8	13.4	5.7		302.6

Housing Conditions

Distribution of households by number of units and occupants, per 1,000 households (o/oo)

1951

Number of occupants	Number of units								Total	
	1	2	3	4	5	6	7	8 +	o/oo	1,000
1	7.3	18.6	18.6	26.6	11.5	8.7	1.8	0.4	93.4	31.5
2	4.1	19.9	31.9	62.2	40.1	30.1	6.7	2.1	197.2	66.6
3	2.7	14.0	31.1	67.5	43.0	31.6	7.7	2.5	200.0	67.5
4	1.7	10.6	25.4	65.1	40.3	28.1	7.3	2.4	180.9	61.1
5	0.9	6.9	18.5	46.8	27.2	20.4	5.5	2.1	128.3	43.3
6	0.4	4.7	12.8	30.6	16.0	12.9	3.7	1.4	82.5	27.9
7	0.3	2.9	8.3	18.7	9.8	7.7	2.2	1.0	50.8	17.2
8	0.1	1.7	5.2	11.7	5.6	4.6	1.2	0.5	30.7	10.4
9	0.0	0.9	2.7	6.4	3.1	2.5	0.7	0.3	16.6	5.6
10+	0.0	1.0	3.1	7.7	3.4	3.0	0.8	0.4	19.5	6.6
Total										
o/oo	17.6	81.1	157.7	343.2	200.1	149.8	37.4	13.2	1,000.0	
1,000	5.9	27.4	53.3	115.9	67.5	50.6	12.6	4.4		337.6

1961

Number of occupants	Number of units								Total	
	1	2	3	4	5	6	7	8 +	o/oo	1,000
1	3.8	16.4	23.9	37.0	18.8	12.4	1.9	0.6	114.9	42.8
2	1.6	14.2	35.4	75.2	56.7	34.2	6.8	2.1	226.2	84.3
3	0.6	6.5	28.4	67.5	54.7	31.2	7.1	1.6	197.7	73.7
4	0.4	4.3	19.7	57.9	53.1	29.3	6.1	2.1	172.9	64.5
5	0.3	2.8	13.3	39.0	33.9	20.1	5.0	2.2	116.6	43.4
6	0.1	1.8	8.3	23.6	19.2	12.7	3.4	1.3	70.4	26.2
7	0.1	1.1	5.1	14.9	10.7	7.7	2.1	0.7	42.2	15.7
8	0.1	0.8	3.3	9.2	6.6	4.6	1.2	0.4	26.1	9.7
9	0.0	0.3	1.7	5.3	3.5	2.6	0.6	0.2	14.2	5.3
10+	0.0	0.5	2.1	7.1	4.7	3.4	0.7	0.3	18.8	7.0
Total										
o/oo	7.0	48.7	141.2	336.5	262.0	158.1	34.9	11.5	1,000.0	
1,000	2.6	18.2	52.6	125.5	97.7	58.9	13.0	4.3		372.8

VIII

Economic Growth

Chapter 5

GROWTH OF NATIONAL PRODUCT

This chapter presents data on the growth of national product in the form of aggregates and per capita values. Figures are usually given for the following concepts: the GDP (m) or gross domestic product at market prices which is the broadest concept, the NDP (m) or net domestic product at market prices, and NDP (f) or net domestic product at factor cost which is the most narrow concept. In addition, per capita figures are given for the GDP (m) and the NDP (f) in order to standardize for differences in population size. Two tables are included for each country with figures at current and at constant prices.

Attempts to estimate a country's economic performance can be traced back as far as the seventeenth century, the most famous examples being the estimates developed for England by William Petty and Gregory King. These early estimators were modern in following a comprehensive production concept which later, mainly under the influence of Adam Smith, narrowed in scope to the production of material commodities. This restricted concept was only overcome in the late nineteenth century, above all by Alfred Marshall who identified production with the creation of utility, thus encompassing services as well as commodities. Since then the comprehensive production concept has become the accepted approach in Western countries.

Until World War I, estimates of national product were largely undertaken by individual investigators. Following the earlier attempts in England and France, first estimates were prepared in Austria in 1861, in Norway in 1893, in Germany in 1899 (there were earlier estimates for single German countries), in Switzerland in 1902, in the Netherlands in 1910 and in Italy in 1911 (cf. Paul Studenski, The Income of Nations, 2 vols, New York 1961). In the interwar period, central governments increasingly took over national product estimation and put it on a regular basis. The conceptual as well as empirical foundations were considerably improved. The real breakthrough, however, only occurred after World War II. In 1953 the UN Statistical Office published 'A System of National Accounts and Supporting Tables' which provided a standardized framework (SNA) also for the collection of data on the origin, distribution and use of national product, a decisive step in promoting consistency in national accounting estimates.

National product estimates are pieced together from a variety of sources by different methods. Major sources are, among others, tax statistics and government budget reports, occupational, industrial and other economic censuses, production, price and wage statistics, household and other sample surveys, foreign trade and payments statistics. Prior to World War II, only single estimates were usually made which combined partial and complementary information on the origin, distribution and use of national product. With the improvement of the data basis, however, it became possible to estimate the national product in three largely independent ways using the sector value-added (origin), the income (distribution), and the expenditure (use) approach. This procedure normally leads to different estimates of national product and the statistical discrepancies may be used for a judgement of the reliability and a further refinement of the estimates. Unfortunately, however, they are separately shown only recently. In the former SNA, the value-added approach and the expenditure approach have been adjusted to each other (the statistical discrepancy increasingly being allocated to changes in stocks, i.e. to the expenditure side), whereas deviations of the income approach estimates have frequently been included under the statistically less reliable category of entrepreneurial income.

The elaboration of the basic sector accounts and the improvements in the quality of data since the early 1950s have made the current national product figures in general sufficiently reliable and comparable. For the period prior to World War II, however, one has to rely on a variety of historical studies. Many of them were carried out in the 1960s under the auspices of Simon Kuznets. These studies, in contrast to earlier estimates, all depart from a common framework of national accounts concepts. However, given the scarcity of adequate data, they too have to rely to large extent on indirect and partial evidence and simple estimation procedures (sometimes considerable shares of the national product have been linearly interpolated over decades!). These national product figures obviously do not allow for analyses of annual changes, but only of broad trends and patterns.

Relying on a variety of historical studies, we have tried to link series for different periods whenever figures for overlapping years have been available. Data from SNA have not been linked, however, to those from historical studies. Respective figures for overlapping years instead are given in the notes. Chaining has also been applied to the time series at constant prices when different price bases overlapped. Only in a few cases (e.g. Italy) small modifications have been made to improve comparability. Such changes or combinations of various series are documented in the notes to the tables. For a fuller explanation of the problems involved in statistical definitions, the empirical basis and the estimation procedures, we must refer to the sources which we have used and which are documented in the appendix.

It is difficult to adequately solve the various measurement problems, but it may be even more problematic to find an acceptable definition of the national product which can be used over long stretches of space and time. According to Simon Kuznets (Economic Growth of Nations. Harvard University Press 1971), these problems may be grouped under three headings:

(1)   the distinction between economic activity and social life (questions of scope or of inclusion and exclusion);
(2)   the distinction between costs and net returns of economic activity (questions of grossness and netness);
(3)   the definition of a common denominator of economic activities and their products (questions of valuation or weighting).

National product estimators have in general tended to delimit economic activities in terms of transactions which are channeled through markets or through other social institutions (e.g. governments) which also are extraneous to the family or household. In addition, value imputations may be made for various non-market activities that have market counterparts (e.g. food produced and consumed on farms, the rental value of owner-occupied houses, etc.). Usually, however, such imputations fall considerably short of measuring all activities that contribute to economic welfare (e.g. the services of housewives). As economic growth is often accompanied by a shift in economic activities from the household to the marketplace, it follows that long-term product estimates closely tied to market criteria tend to exaggerate the rate of growth.

National product is defined as the total production of final goods (commodities and services, net of imports) within a period. Intermediate goods, i.e. products which are used up in the production of other goods, should be excluded, but the distinction between costs and net returns of economic activity is far from being unambiguous. Final goods must be related to basic goals of economic activity. Even if one sees the basic purpose as lying in the satisfaction of human wants, present and future, through the production of consumer goods (and by additions to capital stock), important conceptual problems remain. These refer above all to government activities which may be considered instrumental for the production of goods. In practice, final products are simply defined as those which have not been purchased and charged to current cost by other producers in the same accounting period, and intermediate products as those which are consumed in the production process. For this reason, products which could not be sold are counted as investment (i.e. changes in stocks), and the cost of governmental activity is counted either as public consumption or as public investment.

Conceptually, net measures are preferable to gross measures. Frequently, however, product estimates are presented gross of the fixed capital outlays which are required to offset the consumption of fixed capital goods. This is done because of the difficulties in measuring depreciation in current market values. For this reason, we present in the tables figures for the gross as well as the net domestic product and we also include the depreciation estimates. Both product figures are given at market prices. These are not equal to relative factor costs because of the influence of indirect taxes and subsidies. We have therefore included a third time series with estimates for the net domestic product at factor cost, and we have also given the net figures of indirect taxes and subsidies.

All three product figures refer to the domestic and not to the national product. We thus focus on the productive activity carried out within the boundaries of a country, regardless of the residence of the owners of the factors of production. If we had been interested in studying income and expenditure, it would have been more meaningful to use the concept of national product, i.e. to add the income of a country's residents from their property or labour used abroad and to subtract the income paid to foreign residents. With few exceptions, however, the differences between the national and the domestic product are insignificant for most purposes.

The goods and services subsumed under the national product are weighted by a price system which reflects socially set priorities. Real product is generally obtained by dividing the current value of goods and services by appropriate price indexes. In using such price deflators for long-term records of national product, two main problems are encountered. First, these indexes may not adequately reflect changes in the quality of goods and services, leading to an underestimation of the rate of economic growth. Secondly, the real growth rate may also depend on the time point which is chosen for the common system of price weights, since price relations change during economic growth. The domestic product figures at constant prices must therefore be interpreted with great caution. The use of price deflators for different time points and the simple chaining of price indexes for different periods set limits to their intertemporal and international comparability.

Time series of product estimates at internationally comparable constant prices, the so-called constant purchasing power units, have not been included here. They only cover the period after World War II, and comparative collections are already easily available (I. B. Kravis, A. Heston and R. Summers: World Product and Income, Baltimore 1982; R. Summers and A. Heston: Improved International Comparisons of Real Product and its Composition 1950–1980, The Review of Income and Wealth, 30,2,1984). The following data collection on domestic product was finished in 1977 and no attempt has been made to update it although additional material has become available in the meantime.

National Product at Current Prices

Year	GDP (m)	– Depreci- ation	NDP (m)	– Ind.Taxes + Subsidies	NDP (f)	GDP(m) per cap.	NDP(f) per cap.	Year
	(in million schillings)					(in schillings)		
1975	654 420	73 460	580 960	97 600	483 360	87 023	64 276	1975
1974	613 460	65 590	547 870	87 720	460 150	81 436	61 084	1974
1973	533 270	56 540	476 730	80 150	396 580	70 866	52 701	1973
1972	469 410	49 210	420 200	70 930	349 270	62 629	46 600	1972
1971	412 700	43 250	369 450	60 740	308 710	55 351	41 404	1971
1970	371 240	38 830	332 410	53 770	278 640	49 991	37 522	1970
1969	331 730	35 230	296 500	47 640	248 860	44 870	33 661	1969
1968	302 760	32 590	270 170	43 270	226 900	41 135	30 828	1968
1967	283 160	31 120	252 040	38 300	213 740	38 667	29 187	1967
1966	267 570	29 200	238 370	36 620	201 750	36 703	27 674	1966
1965	247 430	27 080	220 350	32 640	187 710	34 104	25 873	1965
1964	227 140	24 350	202 790	29 700	173 090	31 481	23 990	1964
1963	207 320	22 560	184 760	26 190	158 570	28 906	22 109	1963
1962	192 350	20 380	171 970	24 420	147 550	26 977	20 694	1962
1961	180 760	18 740	162 020	23 260	138 760	25 505	19 579	1961
1960	163 250	17 070	146 180	20 570	125 610	23 162	17 822	1960
1959	146 330	15 660	130 670	18 350	112 320	20 758	15 934	1959
1958	137 420	14 610	122 810	16 630	106 180	19 572	15 123	1958
1957	131 950	13 590	118 360	15 990	102 370	18 855	14 628	1957
1956	119 190	12 430	106 760	14 190	92 570	17 068	13 256	1956
1955	107 160	11 130	96 030	13 150	82 880	15 365	11 884	1955
1954	93 590	10 420	83 170	10 810	72 360	13 431	10 384	1954
1953	82 520	9 930	72 590	9 480	63 110	11 859	9 070	1953
1952	80 010	8 730	71 280	8 360	62 920	11 515	9 055	1952
1951 a)	69 080	7 040	62 040	6 310	55 730	9 963	8 038	1951 a)
1950	52 313	5 117	47 196	4 738	42 458	7 543	6 122	1950
1949	41 990	3 990	38 000	3 000	35 000	6 048	5 041	1949
1948	32 537	2 930	29 607	7 050	22 557	4 680	3 244	1948
1937	9 822	773	9 049	1 214	7 835	1 454	1 159	1937
1936	9 319	771	8 548	1 200	7 348	1 378	1 087	1936
1935	9 140	772	8 368	1 125	7 243	1 352	1 071	1935
1934	8 980	780	8 200	1 080	7 120	1 329	1 054	1934
1933	9 020	783	8 237	1 115	7 122	1 337	1 055	1933
1932	9 550	809	8 741	1 191	7 550	1 420	1 122	1932
1931	10 360	802	9 558	1 104	8 454	1 545	1 261	1931
1930	11 560	798	10 762	1 300	9 462	1 729	1 415	1930
1929	12 087	818	11 269	1 320	9 949	1 814	1 493	1929
1928	11 678	796	10 882	1 240	9 642	1 757	1 451	1928
1927	11 110	763	10 347	1 150	9 197	1 677	1 388	1927
1926	10 283	768	9 515	1 040	8 475	1 557	1 283	1926
1925	10 296	762	9 534	980	8 554	1 564	1 299	1925
1924	9 257	701	8 556	850	7 706	1 410	1 174	1924
1913	10 116	598	9 518	825	8 693			1913

a) Figures for 1913-1950 refer not to Domestic Product but to National Product; the corresponding figures are
   69 608; 6 482; 63 126; 6 239; 56 887; 10 040; 8 205.

Ireland

National Product at Current Prices

Year	GDP (m)	– Depreciation	NDP (m)	– Ind. Taxes + Subsidies	NDP [b] (f)	GDP(m) per cap.	NDP(f) [b] per cap.	Year
			(in million pounds)			(in pounds)		
1975	3 621	290	3 331	398	2 933	1 158	938	1975
1974	2 920	250	2 670	363	2 307	945	747	1974
1973	2 689	213	2 477	374	2 103	881	689	1973
1972	2 223	182	2 042	319	1 722	738	571	1972
1971	1 860	153	1 706	272	1 435	625	482	1971
1970	1 626	133	1 493	235	1 257	551	426	1970
1969	1 446	121	1 324	205	1 120	494	383	1969
1968	1 251	101	1 150	169	982	430	337	1968
1967	1 109	87	1 022	149	874	383	301	1967
1966	1 016	78	938	141	797	352	276	1966
1965	962	73	890	123	766	335	266	1965
1964	904	65	839	115	724	316	253	1964
1963	795	59	736	96	639	279	224	1963
1962	739	52	687	85	602	261	213	1962
1961	683	45	638	81	558	242	198	1961
1960	635	40	595	80	515	224	182	1960
1959	608	37	570	87	483	213	170	1959
1958	568	34	535	82	452	199	158	1958
1957	549	32	517	79	438	190	152	1957
1956	530	30	500	73	428	183	148	1956
1955	522	25	497	65	432	179	148	1955
1954	498	24	474	63	412	169	140	1954
1953	496	22	474	63	411	168	139	1953
1952	450	19	431	55	377	153	128	1952
_ _ [a]					_ _ [c]		_ _ [d]	[a] _ _
1951					372		126	1951
1950					357		120	1950
1949					347		116	1949
1948					334		112	1948
1947					310		104	1947
1946					297		100	1946
1945					284		96	1945
1944					260		88	1944
1943					246		84	1943
1942					222		75	1942
1941					200		67	1941
1940					184		62	1940
1939					169		58	1939
1938					161		55	1938
1937					158		54	1937
1936					156		53	1936
1935					152		51	1935
1934					147		49	1934
1933					142		48	1933
1932					146		50	1932
1931					150		51	1931
1930					156		53	1930

Ireland

National Product at Current Prices

Year	G D P (m)	– Depreci- ation	N D P (m)	– Ind.Taxes + Subsidies	N D P b) (f)	GDP(m) per cap.	NDP(f) b) per cap.	Year
			(in million pounds)				(in pounds)	
1929					161		55	1929
1928					159		54	1928
1927					157		53	1927
1926					154		52	1926

a) Figures are from different sources which are not strictly comparable.
b) Figures for 1926 to 1951 are for GNP at factor cost.
c) For 1952 the corresponding figure for GNP at factor cost is 413.
d) For 1952 the corresponding figure for GNP (f) per capita is 140.

Belgium

National Product at Current Prices

Year	G D P (m)	− Depreci- ation	N D P (m)	− Ind.Taxes + Subsidies	N D P (f)	GDP(m) per cap.	NDP(f) per cap.	Year
			(in million francs)			(in francs)		
1975	2 289 400	211 100	2 078 300	233 900	1 844 400	233 303	187 914	1975
1974	2 080 300	191 200	1 889 100	215 500	1 673 600	212 535	170 984	1974
1973	1 774 000	161 900	1 612 100	181 000	1 431 100	181 836	146 689	1973
1972	1 560 700	149 400	1 411 300	165 000	1 246 300	160 466	128 141	1972
1971	1 402 300	137 800	1 264 500	159 700	1 104 800	144 641	113 955	1971
1970	1 280 900	124 600	1 156 300	148 200	1 008 100	132 735	104 466	1970
1969	1 151 300	108 900	1 042 400	134 300	908 100	119 182	94 006	1969
1968	1 037 500	99 000	938 500	122 900	815 600	107 725	84 684	1968
1967	969 700	92 400	877 300	117 900	759 400	100 957	79 062	1967
1966	905 000	86 100	818 900	107 100	711 800	94 704	74 487	1966
1965	842 100	80 000	762 100	92 200	669 900	88 651	70 523	1965
1964	773 400	74 300	699 100	86 300	612 800	82 032	64 997	1964
1963	691 100	67 200	623 900	77 800	546 100	74 088	58 544	1963
1962	642 700	62 000	580 700	71 600	509 100	69 473	55 031	1962
1961	600 200	58 600	541 600	66 500	475 100	65 041	51 484	1961
1960	564 000	56 300	507 700	57 700	450 000	61 451	49 030	1960
1959	531 100	53 300	477 800	53 200	424 600	58 183	46 516	1959
1958	512 800	50 600	462 200	48 300	413 900	56 488	45 593	1958
1957	508 700	50 300	458 400	47 700	410 700	56 359	45 501	1957
1956	479 600	47 200	432 400	44 300	388 100	53 580	43 358	1956
1955	451 100	42 900	408 200	42 100	366 100	50 708	41 153	1955
1954	424 300	40 600	383 700	36 700	347 000	47 997	39 253	1954
1953	407 500	38 300	369 200	37 300	331 900	46 317	37 724	1953
a)								a)
1952	429 000					48 989		1952
1951	408 000					46 800		1951
1950	354 000					40 910		1950
1949	347 000					40 231		1949
1948	339 000		248 000			39 409	28 830	1948
1947			218 000				25 610	1947
1946			194 000				23 128	1946
1943			55 000				6 699	1943
1941			46 000				5 571	1941
1939			65 000				7 741	1939
1938			65 200				7 774	1938
1937			65 300				7 810	1937
1936			59 800				7 178	1936
1935			50 700				6 109	1935
1934			49 400				5 969	1934
1930			66 500				8 217	1930
1927			48 200				6 076	1927
1924			31 300					1924
1913			6 500				851	1913

a) Figures are not strictly comparable because of differences in accounting systems. According to the earlier
system the corresponding figures for 1953 are 433 000 and 49 215.

National Product at Current Prices

Year	G D P (m)	- Depreci- ation	N D P (m)	- Ind.Taxes + Subsidies	N D P (f)	GDP(m) per cap.	NDP(f) per cap.	Year
			(in million kroner)			(in kroner)		
1975	203 781	20 165	183 616	28 111	155 505	40 272	30 732	1975
1974	183 854	17 489	166 365	24 890	141 475	36 442	28 042	1974
1973	164 931	13 868	151 063	24 830	126 233	32 841	25 136	1973
1972	145 432	11 881	133 551	22 701	110 850	29 133	22 205	1972
1971	128 400	10 406	117 994	19 975	98 019	25 871	19 749	1971
1970	116 801	9 323	107 478	18 184	89 294	23 696	18 116	1970
1969	105 599	8 271	97 328	16 110	81 218	21 590	16 605	1969
1968	92 399	7 510	84 889	13 799	71 090	18 984	14 606	1968
1967	83 817	6 779	77 038	11 765	65 273	17 321	13 488	1967
1966	76 503	6 207	70 296	10 550	59 746	15 948	12 454	1966
1965	69 700	5 565	64 135	9 083	55 052	14 649	11 570	1965
1964	62 049	4 905	57 144	7 894	49 250	13 145	10 434	1964
1963	54 282	4 446	49 836	6 907	42 929	11 588	9 165	1963
1962	50 995	3 962	47 033	6 025	41 008	10 973	8 824	1962
1961	45 257	3 554	41 703	5 033	36 670	9 817	7 954	1961
1960	40 786	3 145	37 641	4 833	32 808	8 903	7 161	1960
1959	37 812	2 879	34 933	4 472	30 461	8 315	6 699	1959
1958	34 097	2 691	31 406	3 899	27 507	7 551	6 092	1958
1957	32 647	2 548	30 099	3 596	26 503	7 274	5 905	1957
1956	30 721	2 343	28 378	3 406	24 972	6 878	5 591	1956
1955	28 732	2 124	26 608	3 147	23 461	6 472	5 285	1955
1954	27 524	1 923	25 601	2 808	22 793	6 246	5 173	1954
1953	26 272	1 794	24 478	2 533	21 945	6 013	5 022	1953
1952	24 529	1 706	22 823	2 189	20 634	5 659	4 760	1952
1951	22 995	1 499	21 496	2 093	19 403	5 342	4 508	1951
_ _a)								a)_ _
1950	23 132	1 184	21 948	1 514	20 434	5 416	4 784	1950
1949	20 201	1 054	19 147	1 306	17 841	4 775	4 217	1949
1948	18 843	881	17 962	1 181	16 781	4 497	4 005	1948
1947	17 292	708	16 584	1 018	15 566	4 170	3 754	1947
1946	15 626			856		3 810		1946
1945	14 390			430		3 552		1945
1944	14 437			587		3 611		1944
1943	12 938			458		3 276		1943
1942	11 466			446		2 937		1942
1941	10 207			417		2 642		1941
1940	9 048			428		2 361		1940
1939	8 577	461	8 116	450	7 666	2 254	2 014	1939
1938	7 936	425	7 511	422	7 089	2 101	1 876	1938
1937	7 559	421	7 138	418	6 720	2 016	1 792	1937
1936	7 080	376	6 704	390	6 314	1 902	1 696	1936
1935	6 734	353	6 381	354	6 027	1 822	1 631	1935
1934	6 328	331	5 997	361	5 636	1 726	1 537	1934
1933	5 829	307	5 522	323	5 199	1 604	1 431	1933
1932	5 384	287	5 097	272	4 825	1 494	1 339	1932
1931	5 665	297	5 368	296	5 072	1 587	1 421	1931
1930	6 000	314	5 686	295	5 391	1 693	1 522	1930
1929	6 087	318	5 769	285	5 484	1 730	1 558	1929
1928	5 695	302	5 393	258	5 135	1 628	1 468	1928

National Product at Current Prices

Year	G D P (m)	– Depreci- ation	N D P (m)	– Ind.Taxes + Subsidies	N D P (f)	GDP(m) per cap.	NDP(f) per cap.	Year
			(in million kroner)			(in kroner)		
1927	5 568	292	5 276	250	5 026	1 602	1 446	1927
1926	5 765	304	5 461	236	5 225	1 670	1 513	1926
1925	6 392	346	6 046	239	5 807	1 866	1 695	1925
1924	6 814	365	6 449	248	6 201	2 010	1 829	1924
1923	6 275	328	5 947	245	5 702	1 872	1 701	1923
1922	5 614	301	5 313	208	5 105	1 691	1 538	1922
1921b)	6 204	364	5 840	147	5 693	1 889	1 734	b)1921
1914	2 593	135	2 458	64	2 394	904	835	1914
1913	2 368	125	2 243	67	2 176	835	768	1913
1912	2 323	120	2 203	64	2 139	829	763	1912
1911	2 108	110	1 998	57	1 941	761	700	1911
1910	1 976	105	1 871	54	1 817	721	663	1910
1909	1 879	105	1 774	51	1 723	695	636	1909
1908	1 837	100	1 737	64	1 673	688	627	1908
1907	1 801	100	1 701	62	1 639	683	622	1907
1906	1 687	95	1 592	60	1 532	648	588	1906
1905	1 611	90	1 521	53	1 468	625	570	1905
1904	1 531	85	1 446	52	1 394	601	547	1904
1903	1 513	80	1 433	51	1 382	599	547	1903
1902	1 445	75	1 370	49	1 321	579	529	1902
1901	1 419	75	1 344	47	1 297	576	526	1901
1900	1 368	70	1 298	46	1 252	562	514	1900
1899	1 264	65	1 199	47	1 152	526	479	1899
1898	1 202	60	1 142	45	1 097	506	462	1898
1897	1 139	55	1 084	42	1 042	487	445	1897
1896	1 097	50	1 047	38	1 009	475	437	1896
1895	1 076	50	1 026	37	989	472	434	1895
1894	1 024	45	979	34	945	455	420	1894
1893	1 034	45	989	34	955	464	429	1893
1892	1 037	45	992	32	960	469	434	1892
1891	1 041	45	996	33	963	474	438	1891
1890	997	45	952	32	920	457	422	1890
1889	924	40	884	32	852	427	394	1889
1888	873	40	833	32	801	407	373	1888
1887	857	40	817	30	787	403	370	1887
1886	848	35	813	29	784	403	372	1886
1885	850	40	810	30	780	409	375	1885
1884	869	40	829	30	799	423	389	1884
1883	898	40	858	30	828	442	408	1883
1882	879	40	839	29	810	436	402	1882
1881	867	40	827	28	799	434	400	1881
1880	866	40	826	26	800	438	404	1880
1879	785	40	745	26	719	400	366	1879
1878	782	40	742	24	718	403	370	1878
1877	798	35	763	25	738	416	384	1877
1876	858	40	818	26	792	453	418	1876
1875	835	35	800	27	773	445	412	1875
1874	834	35	799	25	774	449	417	1874

National Product at Current Prices

Year	G D P (m)	– Depreci- ation	N D P (m)	– Ind.Taxes + Subsidies	N D P (f)	GDP(m) per cap.	NDP(f) per cap.	Year
			(in million kroner)			(in kroner)		
1873	803	35	768	22	746	436	405	1873
1872	744	35	709	22	687	408	377	1872
1871	704	30	674	19	655	389	362	1871
1870	687	30	657	18	639	383	356	1870
1869	659	29	630	18	612	370	344	1869
1868	670	29	641	18	623	380	354	1868
1867	651	28	623	17	606	373	348	1867
1866	608	26	582	17	565	352	327	1866
1865	592	26	566	17	549	346	321	1865
1864	518	23	495	13	482	306	285	1864
1863	508	22	486	13	473	303	282	1863
1862	504	22	482	12	470	305	284	1862
1861	511	22	489	11	478	313	293	1861
1860	475	21	454	11	443	294	274	1860
1859	478	22	456	11	445	300	279	1859
1858	465	20	445	10	435	296	277	1858
1857	504	22	482	12	470	324	302	1857
1856	491	21	470	13	457	320	298	1856
1855	482	21	461	13	448	319	296	1855
1854	437	19	418	11	407	293	273	1854
1853	418	18	400	11	389	283	263	1853
1852	356	16	340	10	330	244	226	1852
1851	329	14	315	10	305	228	211	1851
1850	326	14	312	11	301	228	211	1850
1849	315	14	301	12	289	223	205	1849
1848	322	14	308	11	297	230	212	1848
1847	331	14	317	10	307	239	221	1847
1846	324	14	310	10	300	236	218	1846
1845	279	12	267	10	257	205	189	1845
1844	260	11	249	9	240	193	178	1844
	__c)					__c)		
1843	239	11			228	180	171	1843
1842	236	11			225	179	171	1842
1841	234	11			223	179	171	1841
1840	236	11			225	184	174	1840
1839	229	10			219	179	171	1839
1838	220	10			210	174	165	1838
1837	216	10			206	172	163	1837
1836	216	10			206	173	164	1836
1835	198	9			189	160	152	1835
1834	184					149		1834
1833	188					146		1833
1832	199					164		1832
1831	200					165		1831
1830	194					160		1830
1829	185					153		1829
1828	183					152		1828
1827	185					155		1827
1826	173					147		1826

National Product at Current Prices

Year	G D P (m)	– Depreci- ation	N D P (m)	– Ind.Taxes + Subsidies	N D P (f)	GDP(m) per cap.	NDP(f) per cap.	Year
		(in million kroner)				(in kroner)		
1825	175					150		1825
1824	156					135		1824
1823	157					138		1823
1822	153					137		1822
1821	169					153		1821
1820	188					171		1820
1819	221					204		1819
1818	230					215		1818

a) Figures are not strictly comparable because of differences in accounting systems. According to the earlier system the corresponding figures for 1951 are 25 050; 1 499; 23 551; 1 647; 21 904; 5 820; 5 089.

b) Small changes in territory.

c) Figures for 1818–1843 no longer refer to Domestic Product at market prices but to Domestic Product at factor cost.

National Product at Current Prices

Year	G D P (m)	– Depreci- ation	N D P (m)	– Ind.Taxes + Subsidies	N D P (f)	GDP(m) per cap.	NDP(f) per cap.	Year
			(in million markaas)			(in markaas)		
1975	97 961	9 130	88 831	8 317	80 514	20 794	17 090	1975
1974	84 174	8 461	75 713	7 801	67 912	19 947	14 480	1974
1973	66 746	6 311	60 435	7 588	52 847	14 304	11 325	1973
1972	54 909	5 113	49 796	6 207	43 589	11 836	9 396	1972
1971	47 661	4 569	43 092	5 440	37 652	10 334	8 163	1971
1970	43 592	4 524	39 068	4 685	34 383	9 464	7 464	1970
1969	39 013	3 923	35 090	4 414	30 676	8 438	6 635	1969
1968	34 148	3 119	31 029	4 084	26 945	7 381	5 824	1968
1967	30 109	2 748	27 361	3 429	23 932	6 538	5 196	1967
1966	27 777	2 567	25 210	3 031	22 179	6 064	4 842	1966
1965	25 828	2 454	23 374	2 682	20 692	5 660	4 534	1965
1964	23 553	2 268	21 285	2 413	18 872	5 178	4 149	1964
1963	20 541	2 056	18 485	2 009	16 476	4 541	3 642	1963
1962	18 856	1 902	16 954	2 086	14 868	4 198	3 310	1962
1961	17 625	1 834	15 791	1 917	13 874	3 950	3 110	1961
1960	15 824	1 618	14 206	1 742	12 464	3 572	2 814	1960
1959	14 079	1 350	12 729	1 575	11 154	3 204	2 538	1959
1958	12 954	1 196	11 758	1 577	10 181	2 971	2 335	1958
1957	12 025	1 035	10 990	1 474	9 516	2 780	2 200	1957
1956	11 031	845	10 186	1 120	9 066	2 576	2 117	1956
1955	9 922	697	9 225	929	8 296	2 343	1 959	1955
1954	8 969	603	8 366	1 018	7 348	2 142	1 755	1954
1953	8 074	570	7 504	972	6 532	1 950	1 578	1953
1952	8 181	468	7 713	1 021	6 692	2 000	1 636	1952
1951	7 901	406	7 495	926	6 569	1 952	1 623	1951
1950	5 424	296	5 128	652	4 476	1 279	1 116	1950
1949	4 391	272	4 169	627	3 543	1 052	894	1949
1948	4 089	194	3 895	544	3 351	995	856	1948
a)								a)
1947			2 541	298	2 243		581	1947
1946			1 815	251	1 564		410	1946
1945			1 083	91	992		263	1945
1944			796	92	704		188	1944
1943			739	98	641		172	1943
1942			580	80	500		134	1942
1941			461	51	410		110	1941
1940			364	26	338		91	1940
1939			328	28	300		81	1939
1938			325	28	297		77	1938
1937			313	27	286		74	1937
1936			262	24	238		62	1936
1935			236	22	214		56	1935
1934			224	20	204		54	1934
1933			196	16	180		48	1933
1932			185	13	172		46	1932
1931			186	15	171		46	1931
1930			211	18	193		52	1930
1929			227	18	209		57	1929
1928			235	18	217		60	1928
1927			221	17	204		57	1927
1926			198	14	184		51	1926

a) Figures are not strictly comparable because of differences in accounting systems.

National Product at Current Prices

Year	G D P (m)	- Depreci- ation	N D P (m)	- Ind.Taxes + Subsidies	N D P (f)	GDP(m) per cap.	NDP(f) per cap.	Year
			(in million new francs)			(in new francs)		
1975	1 437 150	161 000	1 276 150	199 921	1 076 229	27 245	20 403	1975
1974	1 271 810	138 180	1 133 630	181 556	952 047	24 299	18 190	1974
1973	1 114 200	112 430	1 001 770	163 241	838 529	21 373	16 085	1973
1972	981 120	99 160	881 960	131 380	750 580	18 976	14 517	1972
1971	872 430	89 370	783 060	116 270	666 790	17 023	13 010	1971
1970	782 560	80 570	701 990	103 640	598 350	15 414	11 785	1970
1969	700 690	70 100	630 590	97 180	533 410	13 926	10 601	1969
1968	614 520	61 720	552 800	82 050	470 750	12 311	9 431	1968
1967	565 390	56 880	508 510	80 520	427 990	11 410	8 637	1967
1966	523 420	51 890	471 530	76 950	394 580	10 646	8 025	1966
1965	483 490	47 620	435 870	71 080	364 790	9 916	7 481	1965
1964	449 160	43 430	405 730	67 360	338 370	9 278	6 989	1964
1963	404 880	39 320	365 560	59 230	306 330	8 461	6 401	1963
1962	361 160	34 970	326 190	51 980	274 210	7 684	5 834	1962
1961	323 460	31 740	291 720	46 830	244 890	7 007	5 305	1961
1960	296 510	29 010	267 500	43 490	224 010	6 491	4 903	1960
1959	272 560	28 250	244 310	40 650	203 660	6 024	4 501	1959
1958	248 500	24 600	223 900	35 400	188 500	5 548	4 208	1958
1957	215 900	22 000	193 900	30 500	163 400	4 872	3 687	1957
1956	192 100	19 900	172 200	26 100	146 100	4 381	3 332	1956
1955	172 800	18 200	154 600	23 900	130 700	3 978	3 009	1955
1954	161 700	17 900	143 800	23 500	120 300	3 844	2 860	1954
1953	152 600	17 600	135 000	22 500	112 500	3 569	2 631	1953
1952	146 400	17 500	128 900	21 400	107 500	3 447	2 531	1952
a)								a)
1949			74 840	9 450	65 390	1 804	1 576	1949
1948			59 190	4 890	54 300	1 439	1 320	1948
1947			36 010	2 980	33 030			1947
1938			3 580	310	3 270	85	77	1938
1937			2 940	280	2 660	70	63	1937
1936			2 490	280	2 210	59	52	1936
1935			2 210	280	1 930	52	46	1935
1934			2 250	290	1 960	53	46	1934
1933			2 440	250	2 190	58	52	1933
1932			2 520	250	2 270	60	54	1932
1931			2 900	380	2 520	69	60	1931
1930			3 000	330	2 670	72	64	1930
1929			3 000	300	2 700	72	65	1929
1928			2 800	300	2 500	68	60	1928
1927			2 590	280	2 310	63	56	1927
1926			2 550	260	2 290	62	56	1926
1925			2 080	190	1 890	51	46	1925
1924			1 880	180	1 700	46	42	1924
1923			1 630	160	1 470	40	36	1923
1922			1 460	150	1 310	37	33	1922
1921			1 400	140	1 260	35	32	1921
1920			1 330	120	1 210	34	31	1920
1913			386	25	361	9	8	1913

a) Figures are not strictly comparable because of differences in accounting systems.

National Product at Current Prices

Year	G D P (m)	– Depreci-ation	N D P (m)	– Ind.Taxes + Subsidies	N D P (f)	GDP(m)[d] per cap.	NDP(f) per cap.	Year
	(in million marks)					(in marks)		
1975	1 030 020	117 030	912 990	111 590	801 400	16 659	12 961	1975
1974	987 130	107 260	879 870	107 360	772 510	15 907	12 448	1974
1973	918 600	95 740	822 860	103 440	719 420	14 821	11 608	1973
1972	825 990	86 330	739 660	95 380	644 280	13 393	10 446	1972
1971	754 880	78 450	676 430	86 480	589 950	12 314	9 623	1971
1970	678 750	68 350	610 400	77 540	532 860	11 191	8 785	1970
1969	596 950	58 120	538 830	76 750	462 080	9 938	7 692	1969
1968	534 900	53 380	481 520	61 920	419 600	8 989	7 052	1968
1967	494 460	50 520	443 940	62 330	381 610	8 340	6 436	1967
1966	488 340	47 770	440 570	59 680	380 890	8 256	6 439	1966
1965	459 270	43 310	415 960	56 330	359 630	7 834	6 135	1965
1964	420 280	38 960	381 320	53 340	327 980	7 249	5 657	1964
1963	382 470	34 990	347 480	49 180	298 300	6 639	5 178	1963
1962	360 880	31 230	329 650	47 190	282 460	6 337	4 960	1962
1961	331 800	27 120	304 680	43 540	261 140	5 906	4 648	1961
1960	302 800	23 630	279 170	39 280	239 890	5 448	4 316	1960
1959	255 140	21 470	233 670	34 940	198 730	4 637	3 612	1959
1958	234 370	19 590	214 780	31 430	183 350	4 310	3 372	1958
1957	218 890	17 740	201 150	29 470	171 680	4 076	3 197	1957
1956	200 950	15 790	185 160	28 170	156 990	3 735	2 918	1956
1955	182 000	14 050	167 950	26 370	141 580	3 422	2 662	1955
1954	159 060	12 650	146 410	23 420	122 990	3 019	2 334	1954
1953	147 720	11 990	135 730	21 800	113 930	2 830	2 182	1953
1952 a)	136 970	11 550	125 420	19 740	105 680	2 654	2 047	1952 a)
1951	120 000	10 100	109 900	16 700	93 200	2 344	1 820	1951
1950 b)	98 100	8 300	89 800	12 900	76 900	1 938	1 519	b) 1950
1939	109 300	8 100	101 200	14 000	87 200	1 576	1 258	1939
1938	100 200	7 800	92 400	12 600	79 800	1 464	1 166	1938
1937	90 900	7 400	83 500	12 000	71 500	1 340	1 054	1937
1936	81 200	7 000	74 200	10 600	63 600	1 205	944	1936
1935	73 100	6 400	66 700	9 800	56 900	1 093	850	1935
1934	65 500	5 800	59 700	9 200	50 500	998	769	1934
1933	58 400	5 800	52 600	8 500	44 100	895	676	1933
1932	56 700	5 800	50 900	8 300	42 600	873	656	1932
1931	69 000	6 400	62 600	8 800	53 800	1 067	832	1931
1930	82 400	6 900	75 500	9 300	66 200	1 281	1 029	1930
1929	88 400	7 000	81 400	9 100	72 300	1 382	1 130	1929
1928	88 100	6 700	81 400	9 000	72 400	1 384	1 138	1928
1927	82 300	6 400	75 900	8 600	67 300	1 301	1 063	1927
1926	73 700	5 900	67 800	7 700	60 100	1 172	956	1926
1925	70 400	5 600	64 800	7 400	57 400	1 128	919	1925
b)	c)	c)				c)	b)	
1913	57 764	5 894	51 870	3 634	48 236	862	720	1913
1912	56 713	5 702	51 011	4 265	46 746	857	706	1912

National Product at Current Prices

Year	G D P (m)	- Depreci- ation	N D P (m)	- Ind.Taxes + Subsidies	N D P (f)	GDP(m) per cap.	NDP(f) per cap.	Year
			(in million marks)			(in marks)		
1911	53 668	6 106	47 562	3 912	43 650	821	667	1911
1910	51 371	6 115	45 256	3 900	41 356	795	640	1910
1909	49 339	5 492	43 847	4 850	38 997	774	612	1909
1908	46 699	4 758	41 941	3 899	38 042	742	605	1908
1907	47 119	4 636	42 483	4 312	38 171	759	615	1907
1906	46 585	6 430	40 155	4 473	35 682	761	583	1906
1905	42 187	3 790	38 397	4 568	33 829	699	560	1905
1904	40 118	4 277	35 841	4 261	31 580	674	530	1904
1903	38 162	4 195	33 967	3 897	30 070	650	512	1903
1902	35 373	3 872	31 501	2 800	28 701	612	496	1902
1901	35 465	4 259	31 206	3 376	27 830	623	489	1901
1900	36 089	4 045	32 044	3 593	28 451	643	507	1900
1899	35 293	3 925	31 368	4 286	27 082	638	490	1899
1898	33 635	2 997	30 638	4 525	26 113	618	479	1898
1897	31 422	3 068	28 354	3 982	24 372	586	454	1897
1896	30 165	3 522	26 643	4 001	22 642	571	429	1896
1895	28 357	3 416	24 941	3 470	21 471	545	412	1895
1894	27 165	3 103	24 062	3 064	20 998	529	409	1894
1893	26 830	2 756	24 074	3 213	20 861	528	410	1893
1892	26 250	2 457	23 793	3 018	20 775	522	413	1892
1891	25 193	2 830	22 363	2 154	20 209	506	406	1891
1890	25 935	2 510	23 425	3 086	20 339	526	413	1890
1889	25 254	3 242	22 012	3 091	18 921	520	390	1889
1888	23 850	3 349	20 501	2 665	17 836	496	371	1888
1887	22 649	3 560	19 089	2 140	16 949	476	356	1887
1886	22 582	3 821	18 761	2 656	16 105	479	341	1886
1885	22 250	3 672	18 578	2 803	15 775	476	337	1885
1884	21 831	3 422	18 409	2 762	15 647	471	337	1884
1883	21 332	3 428	17 904	2 542	15 362	463	333	1883
1882	21 097	3 705	17 392	2 694	14 698	461	321	1882
1881	20 802	3 550	17 252	2 680	14 572	457	320	1881
1880	20 305	3 465	16 840	2 467	14 373	450	318	1880
1879	20 483	3 854	16 629	2 932	13 697	458	306	1879
1878	21 232	3 396	17 836	3 870	13 966	481	316	1878
1877	20 466	3 081	17 385	3 195	14 190	469	325	1877
1876	20 606	2 665	17 941	3 431	14 510	478	336	1876
1875	20 993	2 766	18 227	4 008	14 219	493	334	1875
1874	21 617	2 082	19 535	4 826	14 709	514	350	1874
1873	20 267	2 321	17 946	3 971	13 975	487	336	1873
1872	19 879	3 252	16 627	3 879	12 748	482	309	1872
							_ _d)	
1871			14 013	2 684	11 329	341	276	1871
1870			12 876	2 443	10 433	315	255	1870
1869			11 750	1 573	10 177	290	251	1869
1868			12 967	2 511	10 456	322	259	1968
1867			11 558	2 171	9 387	288	234	1967
1866			10 714	1 836	8 878	269	223	1866
1865			10 279	1 820	8 459	259	213	1865
1864			10 207	1 625	8 582	260	219	1864

National Product at Current Prices

Year	G D P (m)	– Depreci- ation	N D P (m)	– Ind.Taxes + Subsidies	N D P (f)	GDP(m)d) per cap.	NDP(f) per cap.	Year
			(in million marks)			(in marks)		
1863			10 372	1 837	8 535	267	220	1863
1862			10 050	1 784	8 266	261	215	1862
1861			9 379	1 386	7 993	246	210	1861
1860			9 630	1 693	7 937	256	211	1860
1859			8 134	973	7 161	218	192	1859
1858			8 334	1 303	7 031	226	190	1858
1857			8 581	1 199	7 382	234	202	1857
1856			9 139	1 625	7 514	252	207	1856
1855			7 882	1 061	6 821	218	188	1855
1854			8 203	1 206	6 997	222	189	1854
1853			7 189	1 011	6 178	199	171	1853
1852			7 296	1 453	5 843	203	162	1852
1851			6 431	1 074	5 357	180	150	1851
1850			6 070	1 140	4 930	171	139	1850

a) Figures are not strictly comparable because of differences in accounting systems. Corresponding figures for
   1952 are 137 000, 11 500, 125 500, 19 800, 1o5 700, 2 654, 2 048.
b) Considerable changes in territory.
c) Figures for GDP and NDP at market prices are from different sources which are not strictly comparable;
   depreciation figures therefore are only crude estimates.
d) Figures for 1850–1871 refer to NDP.

National Product at Current Prices

Year	G D P (m)	– Depreci- ation	N D P (m)	– Ind.Taxes + Subsidies	N D P (f)	GDP(m) per cap.	NDP(f) per cap.	Year
			(in thousand million lire)				(in thousand lire)	
1975	114 215	11 602	102 613	7 982	94 631	2 039	1 689	1975
1974	100 911	9 818	91 093	9 137	81 956	1 813	1 472	1974
1973	82 503	7 336	75 167	7 207	67 960	1 495	1 231	1973
1972	69 080	5 953	63 127	6 141	56 986	1 264	1 042	1972
1971	63 056	5 415	57 641	6 323	51 318	1 163	947	1971
1970	57 937	5 003	52 934	6 092	46 842	1 085	877	1970
1969	51 691	4 281	47 410	5 425	41 985	974	791	1969
1968	46 953	3 857	43 096	5 095	38 001	889	720	1968
1967	43 517	3 622	39 895	4 944	34 951	829	666	1967
1966	39 521	3 375	36 146	4 287	31 859	758	611	1966
1965	36 530	3 141	33 389	4 009	29 380	705	567	1965
1964	33 941	2 908	31 033	3 763	27 270	660	530	1964
1963	31 053	2 588	28 465	3 486	24 979	608	489	1963
1962	27 117	2 289	24 828	3 098	21 730	535	428	1962
1961	24 118	2 065	22 053	2 843	19 210	475	378	1961
1960	21 632	1 858	19 774	2 496	17 278	434	347	1960
1959	20 029	1 709	18 320	2 212	16 108	404	325	1959
1958	18 862	1 609	17 253	2 081	15 172	383	308	1958
1957	17 565	1 528	16 037	1 986	14 051	359	287	1957
1956	16 360	1 384	14 976	1 866	13 110	336	269	1956
1955	15 032	1 284	13 748	1 651	12 097	310	250	1955
1954	13 634	1 201	12 433	1 516	10 917	283	227	1954
1953	12 795	1 153	11 642	1 314	10 328	267	216	1953
1952	11 570	1 116	10 454	1 157	9 297	243	195	1952
– – a)			(in million lire)				(in lire)	a) – –
1951	10 013 000	925 000	9 088 000	1 222 000	7 866 000	212 032	166 568	1951
1950	8 629 999	748 000	7 881 000	1 028 000	6 853 000	183 756	145 936	1950
1949	7 758 000	664 000	7 094 000	891 000	6 203 000	166 556	133 172	1949
1948	7 345 000	621 000	6 724 000	715 000	5 009 000	158 917	130 011	1948
1947	6 206 000	513 000	5 693 000	442 000	5 251 000	135 263	114 448	1947
1946	3 179 000	215 000	2 964 000	197 000	2 767 000	68 760	60 308	1946
1945	1 346 235	70 084	1 276 151	75 654	1 200 497	29 354	26 176	1945
1944	743 700	29 690	714 010	28 801	685 209	16 287	15 006	1944
1943	419 028	23 837	395 191	26 442	368 749	9 199	8 095	1943
1942	311 370	21 347	290 023	26 130	263 893	6 853	5 808	1942
1941	249 258	20 630	228 628	22 651	205 977	5 515	4 557	1941
1940	214 458	19 576	194 882	18 714	176 168	4 780	3 927	1940
1939	185 362	16 761	168 601	19 085	149 516	4 174	3 366	1939
1938	167 378	15 110	152 268	16 990	135 278	3 813	3 082	1938
1937	155 779	13 757	142 022	15 102	126 920	3 580	2 917	1937
1936	132 143	12 150	119 993	13 409	106 584	3 060	2 468	1936
1935	121 785	11 148	110 637	12 729	97 908	2 841	2 284	1935
1934	108 070	9 980	98 090	12 378	85 712	2 541	2 015	1934
1933	107 536	9 952	97 584	12 272	85 312	2 549	2 022	1933
1932	114 989	10 129	104 860	13 003	91 857	2 748	2 195	1932
1931	118 343	10 660	107 674	13 616	94 058	2 850	2 265	1931
1930	130 813	11 761	119 052	13 205	105 847	3 178	2 571	1930
1929	145 742	12 452	133 290	12 911	120 379	3 575	2 953	1929
1928	145 810	12 208	133 602	13 114	120 488	3 604	2 978	1928

Italy

National Product at Current Prices

Year	G D P (m)	- Depreci- ation	N D P (m)	- Ind.Taxes + Subsidies	N D P (f)	GDP(m) per cap.	NDP(f) per cap.	Year
			(in million lire)			(in lire)		
1927	145 818	12 555	133 263	13 594	119 669	3 635	2 983	1927
1926	165 835	14 551	151 284	11 710	139 574	4 172	3 511	1926
1925	156 677	13 645	143 032	10 852	132 180	3 973	3 352	1925
1924	126 557	10 930	115 627	10 760	104 867	3 237	2 682	1924
1923	122 176	9 892	112 284	10 006	102 278	3 152	2 638	1923
1922	115 015	9 132	105 883	9 156	96 727	2 996	2 519	1922
1921	107 801	8 575	99 226	8 278	90 948	2 836	2 392	1921
1920	103 775	8 066	95 709	8 226	87 483	2 883	2 430	1920
1919	76 449	6 125	70 324	5 788	64 536	2 134	1 802	1919
1918	69 577	6 012	63 565	4 615	58 950	1 953	1 654	1918
1917	51 770	4 425	47 345	3 748	43 597	1 429	1 203	1917
1916	37 974	3 062	34 912	2 764	32 148	1 041	881	1916
1915	26 470	2 108	24 362	1 659	22 703	725	622	1915
1914	21 439	1 527	19 912	1 488	18 424	594	511	1914
1913	21 498	1 566	19 932	1 621	18 311	608	517	1913
1912	20 709	1 490	19 219	1 569	17 650	585	499	1912
1911	19 788	1 396	18 392	2 108	16 284	563	463	1911
1910	17 835	1 306	16 529	1 397	15 132	510	433	1910
1909	17 974	1 370	16 604	1 289	15 315	519	442	1909
1908	16 478	1 271	15 207	1 221	13 986	480	407	1908
1907	17 122	1 246	15 876	1 148	14 728	502	432	1907
1906	15 136	1 039	14 097	1 213	12 884	447	380	1906
1905	14 273	960	13 313	1 084	12 229	424	363	1905
1904	13 777	898	12 879	992	11 887	412	356	1904
1903	13 921	893	13 028	1 002	12 026	420	363	1903
1902	12 770	869	11 901	995	10 906	388	331	1902
1901	13 318	876	12 442	954	11 488	407	351	1901
1900	13 052	818	12 234	944	11 290	402	348	1900
1899	12 248	747	11 501	878	10 623	378	328	1899
1898	12 234	723	11 511	858	10 653	380	331	1898
1897	10 947	659	10 288	866	9 422	342	294	1897
1896	11 272	679	10 593	887	9 706	355	306	1896
1895	11 272	657	10 615	855	9 760	357	309	1895
1894	10 942	644	10 298	843	9 455	349	301	1894
1893	11 301	665	10 636	809	9 827	362	315	1893
1892	11 123	650	10 473	800	9 673	359	312	1892
1891	12 329	688	11 641	848	10 793	401	351	1891
1890	11 837	690	11 147	871	10 276	387	336	1890
1889	10 896	624	10 272	917	9 355	359	308	1889
1888	10 783	620	10 163	925	9 238	358	307	1888
1887	10 831	621	10 210	878	9 332	362	312	1887
1886	11 598	638	10 960	839	10 121	391	341	1886
1885	11 178	615	10 563	850	9 713	379	329	1885
1884	10 464	594	9 870	820	9 050	358	310	1884
1883	10 561	590	9 971	755	9 216	365	318	1883
1882	11 190	614	10 576	752	9 824	390	342	1882
1881	10 380	575	9 805	747	9 058	364	318	1881
1880	11 485	625	10 860	700	10 160	407	360	1880
1879	10 774	596	10 178	704	9 474	382	336	1879
1878	10 969	611	10 358	692	9 666	391	345	1878

National Product at Current Prices

Year	G D P (m)	– Depreciation	N D P (m)	– Ind.Taxes + Subsidies	N D P (f)	GDP(m) per cap.	NDP(f) per cap.	Year
	(in million lire)					(in lire)		
1877	11 547	626	10 921	716	10 205	415	366	1877
1876	10 307	578	9 729	663	9 066	373	328	1876
1875	10 238	608	9 630	639	8 991	374	328	1875
1874	11 597	632	10 965	589	10 376	426	381	1874
1873	12 146	613	11 533	591	10 942	448	403	1873
1872	10 717	547	10 170	584	9 586	397	355	1872
1871	9 619	504	9 115	565	8 550	358	319	1871
1870	8 996	473	8 523	519	8 004	348	310	1870
1869	9 058	444	8 614	560	8 054	353	314	1869
1868	9 310	444	8 866	592	8 274	366	325	1868
1867	8 282	415	7 867	459	7 408	327	293	1867
1866	8 026	404	7 622	662	6 960	318	276	1866
1865	7 165	368	6 797	593	6 204	319	277	1865
1864	6 935	358	6 577	479	6 098	312	274	1864
1863	6 720	342	6 378	387	5 991	304	271	1863
1862	7 259	348	6 911	387	6 524	331	297	1862
1861	6 903	334	6 569	359	6 210	316	285	1861

a) Figures are not strictly comparable because of differences in accounting systems. According to the earlier system the corresponding figures (in million Lire) for 1952 are 10 610; 973; 9 637; 1 332; 8 305; 225; 175.

National Product at Current Prices

Year	G D P (m)	– Depreci- ation	N D P (m)	– Ind.Taxes + Subsidies	N D P (f)	GDP(m) per cap.	NDP(f) per cap.	Year
			(in million guilders)			(in guilders)		
1975	208 930	19 930	189 000	20 210	168 790	15 214	12 291	1975
1974	190 290	17 090	173 200	17 960	155 240	13 993	11 416	1974
1973	168 110	14 560	153 550	17 020	136 530	12 461	10 120	1973
1972	146 730	12 910	133 820	15 770	118 050	10 961	8 818	1972
1971	129 650	11 340	118 310	13 790	104 520	9 770	7 877	1971
1970	114 573	9 727	104 846	11 553	93 293	8 733	7 112	1970
1969	101 715	8 568	93 147	9 684	83 463	7 850	6 442	1969
1968	89 811	7 749	82 062	9 335	72 727	7 017	5 683	1968
1967	80 997	7 166	73 831	7 988	65 843	6 397	5 200	1967
1966	73 829	6 595	67 234	7 179	60 055	5 927	4 821	1966
1965	67 802	6 010	61 792	6 370	55 422	5 515	4 508	1965
1964	60 708	5 455	55 253	5 596	49 657	5 006	4 094	1964
1963	51 592	4 940	46 652	4 773	41 879	4 311	3 500	1963
1962	47 554	4 545	43 009	4 377	38 632	4 028	3 272	1962
1961	44 173	4 206	39 967	4 032	35 935	3 795	3 087	1961
1960	41 840	3 909	37 931	3 675	34 256	3 642	2 982	1960
1959	37 829	3 708	34 121	3 291	30 830	3 333	2 717	1959
1958	35 437	3 523	31 914	2 847	29 067	3 167	2 598	1958
1957	35 145	3 324	31 821	2 996	28 825	3 187	2 614	1957
1956	32 278	2 981	29 297	3 094	26 203	2 964	2 406	1956
1955	29 747	2 748	26 999	3 003	23 996	2 767	2 232	1955
1954	26 602	2 484	24 118	2 951	21 167	2 506	1 994	1954
1953	23 805	2 400	21 405	2 690	18 715	2 268	1 783	1953
1952	22 375	2 403	19 972	2 596	17 376	2 155	1 673	1952
1951	21 433	2 189	19 244	2 544	16 680	1 874	1 625	1951
1950	18 770	1 851	16 919	2 131	14 788	1 672	1 462	1950
1949	16 783	1 706	15 077	1 808	13 269	1 514	1 332	1949
1948	14 966	1 612	13 354	1 369	11 985	1 362	1 222	1948
						– – a)		
1939			5 360	536	4 824	610	549	1939
1938			4 993	491	4 502	574	518	1938
1937			4 942	508	4 434	574	515	1937
1936			4 517	448	4 069	530	477	1936
1935			4 463	431	4 032	529	478	1935
1934			4 570	414	4 156	547	498	1934
1933			4 552	388	4 164	552	505	1933
1932			4 659	370	4 289	573	528	1932
1931			5 119	271	4 848	640	606	1931
1930			5 658	377	5 281	717	669	1930
1929			5 922	388	5 534	761	711	1929
1928			5 691	379	5 312	741	691	1928
1927			5 359	362	4 997	707	659	1927
1926			5 240	347	4 893	701	654	1926
1925			5 181	330	4 851	703	658	1925
1924			5 053	303	4 750	695	653	1924
1923			4 862	296	4 566	680	638	1923
1922			4 957	300	4 657	704	662	1922
1921			5 228	300	4 928	755	712	1921

National Product at Current Prices

Year	G D P (m)	- Depreci- ation	N D P (m)	- Ind.Taxes + Subsidies	N D P (f)	GDP(m) per cap.	NDP(f) per cap.	Year
		(in million guilders)				(in guilders)		
b)								b)
1917			3 405	73	3 332	514	503	1917
1916			3 428	142	3 286	529	507	1916
1915			3 015	134	2 881	473	452	1915
1914			2 505	135	2 370	400	379	1914
1913			2 535	137	2 398	412	390	1913
1912			2 464	132	2 332	407	385	1912
1911			2 309	127	2 182	386	365	1911
1910			2 220	125	2 095	376	355	1910
1909			2 149	120	2 029	366	346	1909
1908			2 082	115	1 967	359	339	1908
1907			2 031	115	1 916	355	335	1907
1906			1 974	115	1 859	350	330	1906
1905			1 909	110	1 799	343	324	1905
1904			1 844	109	1 735	337	317	1904
1903			1 793	107	1 686	332	312	1903
1902			1 765	104	1 661	332	313	1902
1901			1 725	102	1 623	330	310	1901
1900			1 658	97	1 561	322	303	1900

a) Figures for 1900 to 1939 are not for GDP(m) but for NDP(m).

b) Prior to the First World War data for National Product do not include Public Consumption and Public Investment. Hence, comparability over time and between countries is severely impaired.

National Product at Current Prices

Year	G D P (m)	- Depreci- ation	N D P (m)	- Ind.Taxes + Subsidies	N D P (f)	GDP(m) per cap.	NDP(f) per cap.	Year
			(in million kroner)			(in kroner)		
1975	148 237	21 056	127 181	17 132	110 049	36 994	27 464	1975
1974	130 159	18 827	111 332	15 231	96 101	32 662	24 115	1974
1973	111 773	15 307	96 466	14 356	82 110	28 225	20 734	1973
1972	98 397	13 576	84 821	12 960	71 861	25 018	18 271	1972
1971	89 156	12 460	76 696	11 882	64 814	22 842	16 606	1971
1970	79 872	11 086	68 786	10 450	58 336	20 601	15 046	1970
1969	69 447	9 572	59 875	7 490	52 385	18 038	13 606	1969
1968	63 798	8 858	54 940	6 317	48 623	16 709	12 735	1968
1967	59 913	7 970	51 943	6 078	45 865	15 829	12 117	1967
1966	55 459	6 924	48 535	5 951	42 584	14 781	11 349	1966
1965	50 909	6 318	44 591	5 244	39 347	13 674	10 568	1965
1964	45 929	5 591	40 338	4 904	35 434	12 433	9 592	1964
1963	41 531	5 232	36 299	4 167	32 132	11 328	8 764	1963
1962	38 442	4 942	33 500	4 042	29 458	10 566	8 097	1962
1961	35 632	4 670	30 962	3 672	27 290	9 873	7 561	1961
1960	32 676	4 386	28 290	3 274	25 016	9 124	6 985	1960
1959	30 701	4 178	26 523	3 152	23 371	8 643	6 579	1959
1958	28 924	3 847	25 077	2 885	22 192	8 212	6 300	1958
1957	29 018	3 587	25 431	2 634	22 797	8 312	6 530	1957
1956	27 306	3 181	24 125	2 514	21 611	7 894	6 247	1956
1955	24 150	2 856	21 294	2 225	19 069	7 046	5 564	1955
1954	22 682	2 634	20 048	2 084	17 964	6 682	5 292	1954
1953	20 937	2 466	18 471	1 884	16 587	6 231	4 936	1953
1952	20 688	2 390	18 298	1 974	16 324	6 218	4 906	1952
1951	18 747	2 098	16 649	1 636	15 013	5 689	4 556	1951
a)	b)	c)				b)		a)
1950	16 425	2 965	13 460	833	12 627	5 030	3 867	1950
1949	14 917	2 765	12 152	541	11 611	4 612	3 590	1949
1948	13 904	2 441	11 463	458	11 005	4 343	3 437	1948
1947	12 687	2 098	10 589	763	9 826	4 008	3 104	1947
1946	10 778	1 798	8 980	703	8 277	3 447	2 647	1946
1939	6 253	839	5 414	346	5 068	2 116	1 715	1939
1938	5 827	765	5 062	342	4 720	1 985	1 608	1938
1937	5 581	697	4 884	332	4 552	1 912	1 559	1937
1936	4 850	590	4 260	295	3 965	1 670	1 365	1936
1935	4 362	544	3 818	259	3 559	1 509	1 231	1935
1934	4 068	524	3 544	238	3 306	1 415	1 150	1934
1933	3 866	503	3 363	227	3 136	1 352	1 097	1933
1932	3 862	513	3 349	216	3 133	1 359	1 102	1932
1931	3 842	504	3 338	213	3 125	1 360	1 106	1931
1930	4 377	500	3 877	218	3 659	1 559	1 303	1930
1929	4 345	491	3 854			1 554		1929
1928	4 221	483	3 738			1 516		1928
1927	4 218	493	3 725			1 520		1927
1926	4 646	575	4 071			1 681		1926
1925	5 633	673	4 960			2 051		1925
1924	5 576	669	4 907			2 043		1924
1923	4 997	639	4 358			1 841		1923

National Product at Current Prices

Year	G D P (m)	- Depreci- ation	N D P (m)	- Ind.Taxes + Subsidies	N D P (f)	GDP(m) per cap.	NDP(f) per cap.	Year
			(in million kroner)			(in kroner)		
1922	4 980	704	4 276			1 848		1922
1921	5 448	954	4 494			2 042		1921
1920	7 500	1 027	6 473			2 847		1920
1919	6 195	821	5 374			2 380		1919
1918	5 048	755	4 293			1 958		1918
1917	4 489	692	3 797			1 760		1917
1916	3 871	428	3 443			1 534		1916
1915	2 594	279	2 315			1 038		1915
1914	1 919	218	1 701			776		1914
1913	1 857	202	1 655			759		1913
1912	1 680	185	1 495			693		1912
1911	1 530	170	1 360			637		1911
1910	1 435	156	1 279			602		1910
1909	1 316	149	1 167			555		1909
1908	1 299	152	1 147			553		1908
1907	1 265	148	1 117			543		1907
1906	1 187	140	1 047			511		1906
1905	1 105	128	977			478		1905
1904	1 081	122	959			470		1904
1903	1 081	121	960			472		1903
1902	1 088	119	969			478		1902
1901	1 101	118	983			488		1901
1900	1 115	125	990			500		1900
1899	1 065	117	948			483		1899
1898	998	103	895			459		1898
1897	919	95	824			429		1897
1896	875	91	784			414		1896
1895	832	85	747			399		1895
1894	816	85	731			396		1894
1893	809	86	723			397		1893
1892	799	87	712			394		1892
1891	802	88	714			398		1891
1890	780	86	694			390		1890
1889	770	79	691			388		1889
1888	710	71	639			359		1888
1887	659	68	591			334		1887
1886	667	69	598			340		1886
1885	679	71	608			349		1885
1884	721	73	648			373		1884
1883	750	75	675			390		1883
1882	760	74	686			396		1882
1881	739	72	667			384		1881
1880	720	71	649			375		1880
1879	662	69	593			348		1879
1878	706	73	633			376		1878
1877	797	78	719			430		1877
1876	799	78	721			437		1876
1875	771	77	694			427		1875
1874	790	79	711			443		1874
1873	729	69	660			412		1873

National Product at Current Prices

Year	G D P (m)	– Depreci- ation	N D P (m)	– Ind.Taxes + Subsidies	N D P (f)	GDP(m) per cap.	NDP(f) per cap.	Year
			(in million kroner)			(in kroner)		
1872	640	60	580			364		1872
1871	562	49	513			322		1871
1870	542	46	496			312		1870
1869	537	44	493			310		1869
1868	524	45	479			304		1868
1867	518	44	474			301		1867
1866	492	42	450			288		1866
1865	480	42	438			284		1865

a) Figures are not strictly comparable because of differences in accounting systems.

b) Figures for 1865 to 1950 are not for GDP(m) but for Gross-GDP(m), i. e. are inclusive of repair and maintenance. For 1951 Gross-GDP(m) amounts to 20 456 and Gross-GDP(m) p.c. to 6 208.

c) Figures for 1865 to 1950 in addition include repair and maintenance.
For 1951 the corresponding figure is 3 705.

National Product at Current Prices

Year	G D P (m)	– Depreci- ation	N D P (m)	– Ind.Taxes + Subsidies	N D P (f)	GDP(m) per cap.	NDP(f) per cap.	Year
			(in million kroner)			(in kroner)		
1975	286 477	30 023	256 454	34 943	221 511	34 970	27 039	1975
1974	249 346	26 072	223 274	30 397	192 877	30 557	23 636	1974
1973	220 176	21 852	198 324	29 765	168 559	27 061	20 717	1973
1972	199 426	19 342	180 084	26 579	153 505	24 553	18 899	1972
1971	183 791	17 620	166 171	24 368	141 803	22 695	17 510	1971
1970	170 883	16 113	154 770	19 384	135 386	21 248	16 834	1970
1969	153 369	14 617	138 752	16 992	121 760	19 248	15 281	1969
1968	141 676	14 291	127 385	16 448	110 937	17 906	14 021	1968
1967	133 368	13 549	119 819	14 941	104 878	16 952	13 331	1967
1966	123 289	12 645	110 644	13 647	96 997	15 792	12 424	1966
1965	113 316	11 479	101 837	12 049	89 788	14 653	11 611	1965
1964	102 685	10 371	92 314	10 408	81 906	13 403	10 691	1964
1963	92 109	9 512	82 597	9 445	73 152	12 113	9 620	1963
1962	85 196	8 793	76 403	8 641	67 762	11 267	8 962	1962
1961	78 522	7 996	70 526	7 194	63 332	10 443	8 422	1961
1960	72 160	7 350	64 810	6 506	58 304	9 647	7 794	1960
1959	66 245	6 632	59 613	5 121	54 492	8 896	7 318	1959
1958	62 269	6 362	55 907	4 629	51 278	8 404	6 921	1958
1957	58 963	6 070	52 893	4 314	48 579	8 008	6 597	1957
1956	55 241	5 564	49 677	4 069	45 608	7 552	6 235	1956
1955	50 827	5 084	45 743	3 656	42 087	6 999	5 795	1955
1954	47 279	4 630	42 649	3 090	39 559	6 554	5 484	1954
1953	44 437	4 553	39 884	2 725	37 159	6 196	5 181	1953
1952	43 159	4 462	38 697	2 519	36 178	6 058	5 078	1952
1951	41 023			1 938	39 085	5 800	5 526	1951
a)	b)				c)	b)	c)	a)
1950	33 605			1 677	31 928	4 791	4 552	1950
1949	30 871			1 577	29 294	4 438	4 211	1949
1948	29 142			1 544	27 598	4 233	4 009	1948
1947	26 463			1 440	25 023	3 890	3 678	1947
1946	24 310			1 595	22 715	3 618	3 381	1946
1945	21 930			1 273	20 657	3 305	3 113	1945
1944	20 282			1 236	19 046	3 091	2 903	1944
1943	19 270			1 123	18 147	2 969	2 796	1943
1942	17 789			975	16 814	2 765	2 614	1942
1941	16 452			848	15 604	2 575	2 442	1941
1940	14 685			644	14 041	2 310	2 209	1940
1939	13 301			516	12 785	2 102	2 021	1939
1938	12 205			446	11 759	1 938	1 867	1938
1937	11 547			418	11 129	1 840	1 773	1937
1936	10 548			372	10 176	1 685	1 626	1936
1935	9 719			350	9 369	1 557	1 501	1935
1934	9 037			322	8 715	1 452	1 400	1934
1933	8 244			278	7 966	1 329	1 284	1933
1932	8 271			262	8 009	1 339	1 296	1932
1931	8 817			278	8 539	1 433	1 388	1931
1930	10 063			293	9 770	1 641	1 593	1930
1929	9 937			297	9 640	1 625	1 577	1929
1928	9 343			281	9 062	1 532	1 486	1928

National Product at Current Prices

Year	G D P (m)	– Depreci- ation	N D P (m)	– Ind.Taxes + Subsidies	N D P (f)	GDP(m) per cap.	NDP(f) per cap.	Year
			(in million kroner)			(in kroner)		
1927	9 194			273	8 921	1 511	1 467	1927
1926	8 938			252	8 686	1 474	1 432	1926
1925	8 756			241	8 515	1 448	1 408	1925
1924	8 140			254	7 886	1 352	1 309	1924
1923	7 889			252	7 637	1 315	1 273	1923
1922	7 852			228	7 624	1 315	1 277	1922
1921	9 639			221	9 418	1 625	1 588	1921
1920	12 568			250	12 318	2 139	2 096	1920
1919	10 892			196	10 696	1 868	1 834	1919
1918	9 179			80	9 099	1 580	1 566	1918
1917	7 104			73	7 031	1 229	1 216	1917
1916	6 051			91	5 960	1 055	1 039	1916
1915	4 812			78	4 734	844	831	1915
1914	4 062			78	3 984	717	704	1914
1913	4 020			90	3 930	715	699	1913
1912	3 694			75	3 619	661	648	1912
1911	3 455			80	3 375	623	608	1911
1910	3 378			80	3 298	614	599	1910
1909	3 136			75	3 061	575	561	1909
1908	3 108			69	3 039	575	562	1908
1907	3 056			75	2 981	570	556	1907
1906	2 863			73	2 790	538	524	1906
1905	2 558			73	2 485	484	470	1905
1904	2 468			72	2 396	470	457	1904
1903	2 440			68	2 372	468	455	1903
1902	2 256			65	2 191	435	422	1902
1901	2 240			54	2 186	434	424	1901
1900	2 316			68	2 248	452	439	1900
1899	2 202			71	2 131	433	419	1899
1898	2 035			63	1 972	404	391	1898
1897	1 891			54	1 837	379	368	1897
1896	1 758			52	1 706	355	345	1896
1895	1 681			48	1 633	343	333	1895
1894	1 579			46	1 533	325	316	1894
1893	1 570			43	1 527	326	317	1893
1892	1 573			44	1 529	327	318	1892
1891	1 562			46	1 516	325	316	1891
1890	1 489			47	1 442	311	301	1890
1889	1 432			47	1 385	300	290	1889
1888	1 344			42	1 302	283	274	1888
1887	1 266			35	1 231	267	260	1887
1886	1 323			37	1 286	281	273	1886
1885	1 381			38	1 343	296	288	1885
1884	1 397			39	1 358	302	293	1884
1883	1 422			38	1 384	309	301	1883
1882	1 369			34	1 335	299	291	1882
1881	1 384			35	1 349	302	295	1881
1880	1 320			33	1 287	288	281	1880
1879	1 258			29	1 229	276	269	1879

National Product at Current Prices

Year	G D P (m)	– Depreci- ation	N D P (m)	– Ind.Taxes + Subsidies	N D P (f)	GDP(m) per cap.	NDP(f) per cap.	Year
			(in million kroner)			(in kroner)		
1878	1 289			28	1 261	285	279	1878
1877	1 401			30	1 371	314	307	1877
1876	1 429			30	1 399	324	317	1876
1875	1 332			27	1 305	305	299	1875
1874	1 389			32	1 357	321	314	1874
1873	1 305			24	1 281	305	299	1873
1872	1 112			21	1 091	263	258	1872
1871	987			20	967	235	231	1871
1870	933			19	914	224	219	1870
1869	859			17	842	206	202	1869
1868	866			15	851	206	203	1868
1867	869			14	855	207	204	1867
1866	840			13	827	203	199	1866
1865	808			12	796	197	194	1865
1864	808			11	797	199	196	1864
1863	823			12	811	206	203	1863
1862	826			11	815	209	206	1862
1861	787			11	776	202	199	1861

a) Figures are not strictly comparable because of differences in accounting system.

b) Figures for 1910-1950 are not for Domestic Product but for National Product. For 1951 the corresponding figures are 39 593 and 5 998.

c) Figures for 1861-1950 are not for NDP(f) but for Gross-GDP(f), i.e. inclusive of depreciation, repair and maintenance. For 1951 the corresponding figures are 2 307 and 4 740.

National Product at Current Prices

Year	G D P (m)	– Depreci- ation	N D P (m)	– Ind.Taxes + Subsidies	N D P (f)	GDP(m) per cap.	NDP(f) per cap.	Year
			(in million francs)			(in francs)		
1975	139 920	15 245	124 675	7 200	117 475	21 845	18 341	1975
1974	141 100	16 225	124 875	7 400	117 475	21 903	18 235	1974
1973	130 060	15 250	114 810	7 545	107 265	20 223	16 679	1973
1972	116 710	14 090	102 620	7 015	95 605	18 278	14 973	1972
1971	102 995	12 250	90 745	6 005	84 740	16 286	13 399	1971
1970	90 665	10 770	79 895	5 615	74 280	14 467	11 852	1970
1969	81 395	9 290	72 105	5 045	67 060	13 102	10 795	1969
1968	75 120	8 525	66 595	4 395	62 200	12 250	10 143	1968
1967	70 350	7 810	62 540	4 200	58 340	11 603	9 622	1967
1966	65 355	7 235	58 120	4 015	54 105	10 899	9 023	1966
1965	60 860	6 590	54 270	3 780	50 490	10 240	8 495	1965
1964	56 825	6 070	50 755	3 675	47 080	9 673	8 014	1964
1963	51 265	5 330	45 935	3 350	42 585	8 884	7 380	1963
1962	46 620	4 890	41 730	3 030	38 700	8 236	6 837	1962
1961	42 040	4 505	37 535	2 730	34 805	7 649	6 332	1961
1960	37 370	3 975	33 395	2 345	31 050	6 969	5 790	1960
1959	33 975	3 310	30 665	1 945	28 720	6 460	5 461	1959
1958	31 990	2 870	29 120	1 850	27 270	6 153	5 245	1958
1957	31 115	2 960	28 155	1 860	26 295	6 070	5 129	1957
1956	29 250	2 785	26 465	1 865	24 600	5 797	4 876	1956
1955	27 205	2 535	24 670	1 625	23 045	5 462	4 627	1955
1954	25 220	2 280	22 940	1 540	21 400	5 116	4 341	1954
1953	23 800	2 225	21 575	1 440	20 135	4 879	4 127	1953
1952	22 675	2 070	20 605	1 335	19 270	4 709	4 002	1952
1951	21 460	1 855	19 605	1 305	18 300	4 518	3 853	1951
a)			b)		b)	b)	b)	a)
1950					17 250		3 674	1950
1949			17 530	1 115	16 415	3 778	3 537	1949
1948			18 100	1 215	16 885	3 950	3 685	1948
1947			17 390			3 843		1947
1946			15 450			3 458		1946
1945			13 860			3 141		1945
1944			12 960			2 969		1944
1943			12 440			2 877		1943
1942			11 490			2 680		1942
1941			10 640			2 501		1941
1940			9 690			2 292		1940
1939			9 040			2 149		1939
1938	9 580	710	8 870	340	8 530	2 285	2 035	1938
c)								c)
1937			8 780	620	8 160	2 100	1 952	1937
1936			8 020	563	7 457	1 924	1 789	1936
1935			8 040	611	7 429	1 935	1 787	1935
1934			8 110	511	7 599	1 958	1 835	1934
1933			8 190	492	7 698	1 987	1 867	1933
1932			8 140	455	7 685	1 984	1 873	1932
1931			9 170	561	8 609	2 248	2 110	1931

National Product at Current Prices

Year	G D P (m)	- Depreci- ation	N D P (m)	- Ind.Taxes + Subsidies	N D P (f)	GDP(m) per cap.	NDP(f) per cap.	Year
		(in million francs)					(in francs)	
1930			9 950	606	9 344	2 456	2 306	1930
1929			10 000	531	9 469	2 486	2 354	1929
1924			8 150	412	7 738	2 092	1 986	1924
1913			3 960			1 024		1913
			- - - d)		- - - d)			
1910			4 324		4 222			1910

a) Figures are not strictly comparable because of differences in accounting systems.

b) Figures for 1910-1950 are not for Domestic Product but for National Product. For 1951 the corresponding figures are 21 935; 19 190; 4 618; 4 040.

c) Figures are not strictly comparable.

d) Figures are not strictly comparable.

National Product at Current Prices

Year	G D P (m)	− Depreci- ation	N D P (m)	− Ind.Taxes + Subsidies	N D P (f)	GDP(m) per cap.	NDP(f) per cap.	Year
			(in million pounds)			(in pounds)		
1975	103 139	10 918	92 221	9 888	82 333	1 844	1 472	1975
1974	81 932	8 384	73 548	8 132	65 416	1 464	1 169	1974
1973	71 963	6 900	65 063	8 354	56 709	1 287	1 014	1973
1972	62 881	5 813	57 068	7 830	49 238	1 127	883	1972
1971	56 826	5 082	51 744	7 681	44 063	1 022	792	1971
1970	50 724	4 437	46 287	7 273	39 014	915	704	1970
1969	46 109	3 899	42 210	6 695	35 515	834	643	1969
1968	43 146	3 577	39 569	5 686	33 883	784	616	1968
1967	39 960	3 272	36 688	5 024	31 664	729	578	1967
1966	37 850	3 090	34 760	4 707	30 053	694	551	1966
1965	35 521	2 852	32 669	4 255	28 414	655	524	1965
1964	33 047	2 653	30 394	3 811	26 583	613	493	1964
1963	30 276	2 478	27 798	3 357	24 441	565	456	1963
1962	28 486	2 324	26 162	3 180	22 982	535	431	1962
1961	27 209	2 192	25 017	2 959	22 058	515	418	1961
1960	25 489	2 042	23 447	2 824	20 623	487	394	1960
__ a)								a) __
1959	23 860	1 844	22 016	2 831	19 185	459	369	1959
1958	22 601	1 791	20 810	2 655	18 155	438	351	1958
1957	21 692	1 691	20 001	2 559	17 442	422	339	1957
1956	20 569	1 584	18 985	2 468	16 517	402	323	1956
1955	19 112	1 461	17 651	2 305	15 346	375	301	1955
1954	17 700	1 340	16 360	2 082	14 278	349	281	1954
1953	16 728	1 289	15 439	2 003	13 436	331	266	1953
1952	15 625	1 240	14 385	1 875	12 510	310	248	1952
1951	14 411	1 101	13 310	1 803	11 507	287	229	1951
1950	12 945	953	11 992	1 591	10 401	256	206	1950
1949	12 420	893	11 527	1 470	10 057	247	200	1949
1948	11 700	848	10 852	1 442	9 410	234	188	1948
1947	10 655	770	9 885	1 347	8 538	215	172	1947
1946	9 959	690	9 269	1 189	8 080	202	164	1946
1945	9 888	640	9 248	1 157	8 091	201	165	1945
1944	10 084	650	9 434	1 212	8 222	206	168	1944
1943	9 937	620	9 317	1 218	8 099	204	166	1943
1942	9 311	530	8 781	1 151	7 630	192	158	1942
1941	8 481	500	7 981	1 050	6 931	176	144	1941
1940	7 065	440	6 625	803	5 822	146	121	1940
1939	5 865	390	5 475	640	4 835	123	101	1939
1938	5 546	370	5 176	587	4 589	117	97	1938
1937	5 290	357	4 933	582	4 351	112	92	1937
1936	4 946	317	4 629	557	4 072	105	86	1936
1935	4 719	298	4 421	522	3 899	101	83	1935
1934	4 523	282	4 241	207	3 734	97	80	1934
1933	4 262	283	3 979	486	3 493	92	75	1933
1932	4 236	283	3 953	490	3 463	91	75	1932
1931	4 302	290	4 012	459	3 553	93	77	1931
1930	4 642	291	4 351	457	3 894	101	85	1930

National Product at Current Prices

Year	G D P (m)	- Depreci- ation	N D P (m)	- Ind.Taxes + Subsidies	N D P (f)	GDP(m) per cap.	NDP(f) per cap.	Year
			(in million pounds)			(in pounds)		
1929	4 690	293	4 397	476	3 921	103	86	1929
1928	4 596	284	4 312	493	3 819	101	84	1928
1927	4 553	279	4 279	479	3 800	100	84	1927
1926	4 319	283	4 036	449	3 587	95	79	1926
1925	4 542	283	4 259	429	3 830	101	85	1925
1924	4 307	283	4 024	430	3 594	96	80	1924
1923	4 247	288	3 959	454	3 505	95	79	1923
1922	4 434	314	4 120	439	3 681	100	83	1922
b)								b)
1921	4 980	352	4 628	402	4 226	106	90	1921
1920	5 809	435	5 374	370	5 004	125	108	1920
1919	5 348	321	5 027	283	4 744	120	106	1919
1918	5 010	264	4 746	181	4 565	116	106	1918
1917	4 246	229	4 017	199	3 818	98	88	1917
1916	3 393	191	3 202	222	2 980	78	68	1916
1915	2 929	159	2 770	208	2 562	66	58	1915
1914	2 441	116	2 325	171	2 154	53	47	1914
1913	2 407	116	2 291	175	2 116	53	46	1913
1912	2 303	110	2 193	172	2 021	51	44	1912
1911	2 217	103	2 114	167	1 947	49	43	1911
1910	2 135	100	2 035	164	1 871	48	42	1910
1909	2 047	97	1 950	151	1 799	46	40	1909
1908	2 003	97	1 906	150	1 756	45	40	1908
1907	2 093	98	1 995	155	1 840	48	42	1907
1906	2 027	93	1 934	153	1 781	47	41	1906
1905	1 951	89	1 862	152	1 710	45	40	1905
1904	1 894	87	1 807	151	1 656	44	39	1904
1903	1 889	86	1 803	146	1 657	45	39	1903
1902	1 905	85	1 820	146	1 674	46	40	1902
1901	1 902	87	1 815	136	1 679	46	40	1901
1900	1 879	88	1 791	128	1 663	46	40	1900
1899	1 804	80	1 724	121	1 603	44	39	1899
1898	1 692	73	1 619	115	1 504	42	37	1898
1897	1 600	69	1 531	113	1 418	40	35	1897
1896	1 562	66	1 496	111	1 385	39	35	1896
1895	1 508	64	1 444	107	1 337	38	34	1895
1894	1 474	64	1 410	102	1 308	38	34	1894
1893	1 398	64	1 334	98	1 236	36	32	1893
1892	1 404	65	1 339	97	1 242	37	33	1892
1891	1 438	66	1 372	96	1 276	38	34	1891
1890	1 425	67	1 358	95	1 263	38	34	1890
1889	1 388	63	1 325	93	1 232	37	33	1889
1888	1 319	60	1 259	90	1 169	36	32	1888
1887	1 273	60	1 213	88	1 125	35	31	1887
1886	1 220	60	1 160	87	1 073	34	30	1886
1885	1 216	62	1 154	87	1 067	34	30	1885
1884	1 247	63	1 184	88	1 096	35	31	1884

National Product at Current Prices

Year	GDP (m)	− Depreciation	NDP (m)	− Ind.Taxes + Subsidies	NDP (f)	GDP(m) per cap.	NDP(f) per cap.	Year
			(in million pounds)			(in pounds)		
1883	1 288	65	1 223	87	1 136	36	32	1883
1882	1 274	65	1 209	87	1 122	36	32	1882
1881	1 235	64	1 171	85	1 086	35	31	1881
1880	1 228	64	1 164	82	1 082	35	31	1880
1879	1 134	61	1 073	82	991	33	29	1879
1878	1 188	63	1 125	85	1 040	35	31	1878
1877	1 210	64	1 146	84	1 062	36	32	1877
1876	1 223	64	1 159	83	1 076	37	32	1876
1875	1 236	64	1 172	81	1 091	38	33	1875
1874	1 261	67	1 194	80	1 114	39	34	1874
1873	1 259	66	1 193	80	1 113	39	35	1873
1872	1 205	61	1 144	78	1 066	38	33	1872
1871	1 142	56	1 086	75	1 011	36	32	1871
1870	1 056	54	1 002	74	928	34	30	1870
1869	983	52	931	73	858	32	28	1869
1868	952	51	901	70	831	31	27	1868
1867	953	51	902	69	833	31	27	1867
1866	965	52	913	66	847	32	28	1866
1865	944	51	893	65	827	32	28	1865
1864	914	50	864	66	797	31	27	1864
1863	885	48	837	67	770	30	26	1863
1862	851	46	805	65	739	29	25	1862
1861	829	45	784	65	720	29	25	1861
1860	796	45	751	67	685	28	24	1860
1859	770	45	725	65	660	27	23	1859
1858	742	46	696	64	632	26	22	1858
1857	752	46	706	64	642	27	23	1857
1856	764	47	717	63	655	27	23	1856
1855	731	47	684	59	625	27	23	1855
c)								c)
1854	715			59		26		1854
1853	672			57		24		1853
1852	602			57		22		1852
1851	599			58		22		1851
1850	576			59		21		1850
1849	618			60		22		1849
1848	599			57		22		1848
1847	635			58		23		1847
1846	593			57		21		1846
1845	563			59		20		1845
1844	533			57		19		1844
1843	493			57		18		1843
1842	503			59		19		1842
1841	528			58		20		1841
1840	540			56		20		1840

National Product at Current Prices

Year	G D P (m)	– Depreci- ation	N D P (m)	– Ind.Taxes + Subsidies	N D P (f)	GDP(m) per cap.	NDP(f) per cap.	Year
			(in million pounds)			(in pounds)		
1839	571			55		22		1839
1838	542			54		21		1838
1837	517			56		20		1837
1836	539			54		21		1836
1835	501			56		20		1835
1834	479			59		19		1834
1833	455			58		18		1833
1832	462			57		19		1832
1831	477			56		20		1831
1830	483			61		20		1830

a) Figures are not strictly comparable because of differences in sources. According to the historical source the corresponding figures for 1960 are: 25 412; 1 933; 23 479; 2 904; 20 575; 485; 393.

b) For 1830 to 1921 Southern Ireland is included.

c) Figures for 1830 to 1854 are not for Domestic Product but for National Product, which, in addition, does not include changes in stocks.
   For 1855 the corresponding figures for National Product are: 744; 47; 697; 59; 638; 27; 23.

Austria

National Product at Constant Prices

Year	G D P a) (m)	– Depreci- ation	N D P (m)	– Ind.Taxes + Subsidies	N D P (f)	GDP(m) a) per cap.	NDP(f) per cap.	Year
			(in million schillings)			(in schillings)		
			1 9 7 0 p r i c e s					
1975	448 780					59 678		1975
1974	457 890					60 784		1974
1973	439 740					58 437		1973
1972	415 670					55 459		1972
1971	390 850					52 420		1971
1970	371 240					49 991		1970
1969	344 500					46 598		1969
1968	325 450					44 218		1968
1967	311 610					42 552		1967
1966	304 360					41 750		1966
1965	289 870					39 954		1965
1964	280 250					38 842		1964
1963	263 920					36 798		1963
1962	253 400					35 539		1962
1961	246 930					34 842		1961
1960	233 940					33 192		1960
1959	216 130					30 661		1959
1958	210 170					29 934		1958
1957	202 740					28 971		1957
1956	191 040					27 357		1956
1955	178 770					25 633		1955
1954	160 950					23 098		1954
1953	146 070					20 993		1953
1952	139 900					20 135		1952
1951 b)	139 830					20 168		b) 1951
			1 9 5 4 p r i c e s					
1950	77 062					11 112		1950
1949	68 582					9 877		1949
1948	57 660					8 292		1948
			1 9 3 7 p r i c e s					
1937 c)	9 822					1 454		c) 1937
1936	9 321					1 379		1936
1935	9 056					1 339		1935
1934	8 875					1 314		1934
1933	8 803					1 305		1933
1932	9 107					1 354		1932
1931	10 154					1 514		1931
1930	11 042					1 652		1930
1929	11 358					1 704		1929
1928	11 194					1 685		1928
1927	10 697					1 615		1927
1926	10 378					1 571		1926
1925	10 211					1 551		1925

Austria

National Product at Constant Prices

Year	G D P[a] (m)	− Depreci- ation	N N P (m)	− Ind.Taxes + Subsidies	N N P (f)	GDP(m)[a] per cap.	NNP(f) per cap.	Year
			(in million schillings)			(in schillings)		
1924	9 565					1 457		1924
1923	8 562					1 308		1923
1922	8 657					1 326		1922
1921	7 942					1 221		1921
1920	7 175					1 111		1920
1913	10 802							1913

a) Figures for 1913–1950 refer not to Domestic Product but to National Product. According to the Austrian Statistical Bureau, the difference is of negligible magnitude.
b) For 1951 the corresponding figures at 1954-prices are 82 404 and 11 886.
c) For 1937 the respective figures at 1954-prices are 63 910 and 9 462.

National Product at Constant Prices

Year	G D P (m)	– Depreci- ation	N N P (m)	– Ind.Taxes + Subsidies	N N P (f)	GDP(m) per cap.	NNP(m) per cap.	Year
			(in million francs)			(in francs)		
			1 9 7 0 p r i c e s					
1975	1 522 800					155 181		1975
1974	1 554 200					158 786		1974
1973	1 494 400					153 177		1973
1972	1 405 200					144 478		1972
1971	1 332 300					137 421		1971
1970	1 280 900					132 735		1970
1969	1 204 500					124 689		1969
1968	1 130 200					117 350		1968
1967	1 084 100					112 868		1967
1966	1 042 800					109 125		1966
1965	1 011 900					106 527		1965
1964	975 800					103 500		1964
1963	912 100					97 780		1963
1962	873 900					94 465		1962
1961	829 700					90 292		1961
1960	789 800					86 053		1960
1959	749 500					82 109		1959
1958	726 500					80 028		1958
1957	727 600					80 611		1957
1956	714 300					79 801		1956
1955	694 200					78 035		1955
1954 a)	662 600					74 954		a) 1954
1953 a)	636 400					72 334		a) 1953
			1 9 4 8 p r i c e s					
1952	405 000					46 248		1952
1951	388 000					44 582		1951
1950	369 000					42 644		1950
1949	358 000					41 507		1949
1948	339 000		248 000			39 409	28 830	1948
1947			250 000				29 370	1947
1938			241 000				28 738	1938
1937			250 000				29 900	1937
1936			246 000				29 531	1936
1935			219 000				26 388	1935
1934			209 000				25 256	1934
1930			215 000				26 569	1930
1927			173 000				21 810	1927
1924			176 000					1924

a) For 1953 the corresponding figures at 1948-prices are 410 000 and 46 601.

Denmark

National Product at Constant Prices

Year	G D P (m)	– Depreci- ation	N D P (m)	– Ind.Taxes + Subsidies	N D P (f)	GDP(m) per cap.	NDP(m) per cap.	Year
			(in million kroner)			(in kroner)		
				1970 prices				
1975	128 549					25 404		1975
1974	129 981					25 764		1974
1973	129 764					25 839		1973
1972	126 212					25 282		1972
1971	120 966					24 373		1971
1970	116 801					23 696		1970
1969	113 717					23 250		1969
1968	104 735					21 519		1968
1967	100 884					20 848		1967
1966	96 780					20 175		1966
1965	94 198					19 797		1965
1964	90 094					19 087		1964
1963	82 451					17 602		1963
1962	81 929					17 630		1962
1961	77 535					16 818		1961
1960	72 886					15 910		1960
1959	68 804					15 131		1959
1958	64 389					14 261		1958
1957	62 645					13 958		1957
1956	60 035					13 442		1956
1955	58 853					13 258		1955
1954	59 067					13 406		1954
1953	57 082					13 065		1953
1952 a)	53 966					12 451		a) 1952
				1929 prices				
1951	9 941	384	9 557			2 309	2 220	1951
1950	9 877	395	9 482			2 312	2 220	1950
1949	9 211	345	8 866			2 177	2 095	1949
1948	8 811	283	8 528			2 102	2 035	1948
1947	8 542	268	8 274			2 060	1 995	1947
1946	8 099	274	7 825			1 974	1 908	1946
1945	6 973	336	6 637			1 723	1 640	1945
1944	7 482	341	7 141			1 871	1 786	1944
1943	6 787	333	6 454			1 718	1 634	1943
1942	6 136	315	5 821			1 572	1 491	1942
1941	5 996	307	5 689			1 552	1 472	1941
1940	6 658	291	6 367			1 737	1 661	1940
1939	7 764	381	7 383			2 040	1 940	1939
1938	7 409	354	7 055			1 961	1 867	1938
1937	7 241	363	6 878			1 931	1 834	1937
1936	7 070	351	6 719			1 899	1 805	1936
1935	6 892	336	6 556			1 865	1 774	1935
1934	6 746	325	6 421			1 840	1 751	1934
1933	6 549	295	6 254			1 802	1 721	1933
1932	6 351	302	6 049			1 762	1 678	1932
1931	6 520	303	6 217			1 826	1 741	1931
1930	6 444	311	6 133			1 819	1 731	1930
1929	6 087	318	5 769			1 730	1 639	1929

National Product at Constant Prices

Year	G D P (m)	– Depreci- ation	N D P (m)	– Ind.Taxes + Subsidies	N D P (f)	GDP(m) per cap.	NDP(m) per cap.	Year
			(in million kroner)			(in kroner)		
			1929 prices					
1928	5 719	305	5 414			1 635	1 548	1928
1927	5 531	292	5 239			1 591	1 507	1927
1926	5 421	289	5 132			1 570	1 486	1926
1925	5 127	264	4 863			1 496	1 419	1925
1924	5 249	267	4 982			1 548	1 470	1924
1923	5 236	256	4 980			1 562	1 485	1923
1922 b)	4 729	239	4 490			1 425	1 353	b) 1922
1921 b)	4 298	208	4 090			1 309	1 245	1921
1914	4 057	210	3 847			1 415	1 342	1914
1913	3 836	200	3 636			1 354	1 283	1913
1912	3 697	190	3 507			1 319	1 251	1912
1911	3 680	185	3 495			1 328	1 261	1911
1910	3 491	185	3 306			1 275	1 207	1910
1909	3 388	180	3 208			1 253	1 187	1909
1908	3 265	175	3 090			1 223	1 158	1908
1907	3 173	170	3 003			1 204	1 139	1907
1906	3 057	165	2 892			1 174	1 111	1906
1905	2 971	155	2 816			1 154	1 094	1905
1904	2 920	145	2 775			1 146	1 089	1904
1903	2 853	140	2 713			1 129	1 074	1903
1902	2 694	140	2 554			1 080	1 024	1902
1901	2 634	135	2 499			1 069	1 014	1901
1900	2 531	125	2 406			1 040	989	1900
1899	2 449	120	2 329			1 019	969	1899
1898	2 349	115	2 234			990	942	1898
1897	2 305	110	2 195			985	938	1897
1896	2 254	105	2 149			977	931	1896
1895	2 175	100	2 075			955	911	1895
1894	2 059	100	1 959			915	871	1894
1893	2 017	95	1 922			906	863	1893
1892	1 980	90	1 890			895	855	1892
1891	1 934	90	1 844			881	840	1891
1890	1 897	90	1 807			870	829	1890
1889	1 792	90	1 702			829	787	1889
1888	1 766	90	1 676			824	782	1888
1887	1 747	85	1 662			822	782	1887
1886	1 689	85	1 604			803	763	1886
1885	1 627	85	1 542			783	742	1885
1884	1 616	85	1 531			787	746	1884
1883	1 606	80	1 526			791	752	1883
1882	1 552	80	1 472			770	731	1882
1881	1 496	75	1 421			749	712	1881
1880	1 480	75	1 405			748	711	1880
1879	1 445	75	1 370			737	698	1879
1878	1 399	75	1 324			721	682	1878
1877	1 346	70	1 276			702	665	1877
1876	1 384	70	1 314			730	693	1876
1875	1 355	65	1 290			723	688	1875

National Product at Constant Prices

Year	G D P (m)	– Depreci- ation	N D P (m)	– Ind.Taxes + Subsidies	N D P (f)	GDP(m) per cap.	NDP(m) per cap.	Year
			(in million kroner)			(in kroner)		
				1 9 2 9 p r i c e s				
1874	1 333	65	1 268			718	683	1874
1873	1 299	60	1 239			706	674	1873
1872	1 302	60	1 242			714	682	1872
1871	1 238	60	1 178			685	651	1871
1870	1 227	60	1 167			684	650	1870
1869	1 178					662		1869
1868	1 116					634		1868
1867	1 097					630		1867
1866	1 095					635		1866
1865	1 094					640		1865
1864	1 055					625		1864
1863	1 066					637		1863
1862	1 004					608		1862
1861	973					596		1861
1860	955					592		1860
1859	962					605		1859
1858	903					575		1858
1857	911					586		1857
1856	896					585		1856
1855	947					627		1855
1854	852					571		1854
1853	849					575		1853
1852	846					579		1852
1851	820					569		1851
1850	858					602		1850
1849	815					578		1849
1848	771					552		1848
1847	733					530		1847
1846	735					536		1846
1845	721					530		1845
1844	699					520		1844
	– – c)					– – c)		
1843	637					480		1843
1842	607					462		1842
1841	603					467		1841
1840	602					467		1840
1839	585					457		1839
1838	576					454		1838
1837	573					455		1837
1836	558					447		1836
1835	560					452		1835
1834	562					457		1834
1833	534					438		1833
1832	536					442		1832
1831	523					432		1831
1830	526					435		1830
1829	522					433		1829

National Product at Constant Prices

Year	G D P[c] (m)	- Depreci- ation	N D P (m)	- Ind.Taxes + Subsidies	N D P (f)	GDP(m)[c] per cap.	NDP(m) per cap.	Year
		(in million kroner)				(in kroner)		
			1 9 2 9 p r i c e s					
1828	535					445		1828
1827	526					441		1827
1826	511					433		1826
1825	503					431		1825
1824	502					436		1824
1823	486					428		1823
1822	487					435		1822
1821	480					433		1821
1820	456					416		1820
1819	454					419		1819
1818	441					413		1818

a) For 1952 the corresponding figures at 1929 prices are 10 096 and 2 329.

b) Small change in territory.

c) Figures for 1818 to 1843 refer not to GDP(m) but to GDP(f). The figure for GDP(f) in 1844 is 670 million and for GDP(f) per cap. 499 Kroner.

N a t i o n a l   P r o d u c t   a t   C o n s t a n t   P r i c e s

Year	G D P (m)	– Depreci- ation	N D P (m)	– Ind.Taxes + Subsidies	N D P (f)	GDP(m) per cap.	NDP(f) per cap.	Year
			(in million markaas)			(in markaas)		
			1 9 7 0 p r i c e s					
1975	53 515					11 359		1975
1974	53 038					11 308		1974
1973	50 871					10 902		1973
1972	47 773					10 298		1972
1971	44 641					9 679		1971
1970	43 592					9 464		1970
1969	40 263					8 709		1969
1968	36 458					7 881		1968
1967	35 605					7 731		1967
1966	34 687					7 573		1966
1965	33 884					7 425		1965
1964	32 226					7 085		1964
1963	30 239					6 685		1963
1962	29 504					6 569		1962
1961	28 292					6 342		1961
1960	26 184					5 911		1960
1959	23 819					5 420		1959
1958	22 209					5 094		1958
1957	22 226					5 140		1957
1956	21 893					5 113		1956
1955	21 467					5 070		1955
1954	19 960					4 768		1954
1953	18 303					4 422		1953
1952	18 280					4 469		1952
1951[a]	17 672					4 366		[a]1951
			1 9 5 4 p r i c e s					
1950	7 264					1 812		1950
1949	6 769					1 708		1949
1948	6 529					1 669		1948
			1 9 3 8 p r i c e s					
1947					3 100		800	1947
1946					2 910		760	1946
1945					2 580		680	1945
1944					3 030		810	1944
1943					3 080		820	1943
1942					2 830		760	1942
1941					2 700		720	1941
1940					2 550		680	1940
1939					2 890		780	1939
1938					2 970		770	1938
1937					2 950		770	1937
1936					2 690		700	1936
1935					2 510		660	1935
1934					2 450		650	1934
1933					2 180		580	1933
1932					2 040		550	1932
1931					2 000		540	1931
1930					2 080		560	1930
1929					2 130		580	1929
1928					2 140		590	1928
1927					2 070		570	1927
1926					1 910		530	1926

a) The corresponding figures at 1954-prices are 7 941 and 1 962.

National Product at Constant Prices

Year	GDP (m)	- Depreci- ation	NNP (m)	- Ind.Taxes + Subsidies	NNP (f)	GDP(m) per cap.	NNP(f) per cap.	Year
			(in million new francs)				(in new Francs)	

1970 prices

Year	GDP (m)					GDP(m) per cap.		Year
1975	953 880					18 083		1975
1974	947 520					18 103		1974
1973	922 070					17 687		1973
1972	874 580					16 915		1972
1971	824 140					16 081		1971
1970	782 560					15 414		1970
1969	740 140					14 710		1969
1968	691 780					13 859		1968
1967	663 470					13 390		1967
1966	633 820					12 891		1966
1965	602 360					12 354		1965
1964	574 930					11 876		1964
1963	541 050					11 307		1963
1962	513 680					10 929		1962
1961	481 460					10 430		1961
1960	456 350					9 990		1960
1959	428 310					9 467		1959
1958	415 190					9 269		1958
1957	403 400					9 104		1957
1956	380 610					8 681		1956
1955	359 280					8 272		1955
1954	343 250					8 160		1954
1953	329 480					7 707		1953
1952 a)	321 400					7 569		a) 1952

1938 prices

Year					NNP (f)		NNP(f) per cap.	Year
1949 b)					4 140		99	b) 1949
1948					3 660		89	1948
1947					3 410		88	1947
1946					3 150		78	1946
1945					2 070		52	1945
1944					1 910		49	1944
1943					2 260		57	1943
1942					2 380		60	1942
1941					2 660		67	1941
1940					3 360		81	1940
1939					4 070		97	1939
1938					3 800		90	1938
1937					3 840		91	1937
1936					3 710		88	1936
1935					3 750		89	1935
1934					3 920		93	1934
1933					4 000		95	1933
1932					3 980		95	1932
1931					4 280		102	1931
1930					4 470		107	1930
1929					4 530		109	1929
1928					4 100		99	1928
1927					3 870		94	1927

National Product at Constant Prices

Year	G D P (m)	− Depreciation	N N P (m)	− Ind.Taxes + Subisides	N N P (f)	GDP(m) per cap.	NDP(f) per cap.	Year
			(in million new francs)				(in new francs)	
				1 9 3 8 p r i c e s				
1926					4 010		98	1926
1925					3 840		94	1925
1924					3 810		94	1924
1923					3 290		82	1923
1922					3 040		77	1922
1921					2 500		63	1921
1920					2 700		69	1920
1913					3 280		82	1913
1912					3 280		82	1912
1911					3 000		75	1911
1910					2 880		72	1910
1909					2 880		73	1909
1908					2 790		70	1908
1907					2 770		70	1907
1906					2 700		68	1906
1905					2 640		67	1905
1904					2 670		68	1904
1903					2 470		63	1903
1902					2 400		61	1902
1901					2 400		61	1901

a) Figures are not comparable to previous years.
b) The figures for 1952 are 4 920 resp. 116.

National Product at Constant Prices

Year	GDP (m)	– Depreci- ation	NDP (m)	– Ind.Taxes + Subsidies	NDP (f)	GDP(m) per cap.	NDP(f) per cap.	Year
			(in million marks)			(in marks)		

1970 prices

Year	GDP (m)	NDP (m)	NDP (f)	GDP(m) per cap.	NDP(f) per cap.	Year
1975	746 150			12 067		1975
1974	765 950			12 343		1974
1973	761 840			12 292		1973
1972	726 280			11 776		1972
1971	700 680			11 429		1971
1970	678 750			11 191		1970
1969	640 460			10 662		1969
1968	593 970			9 982		1968
1967	558 840			9 426		1967
1966	559 750			9 463		1966
1965	546 120			9 316		1965
1964	517 010			8 918		1964
1963	484 500			8 410		1963
1962	470 460			8 261		1962
1961	450 580			8 021		1961
1960	428 740			7 714		1960
1959	367 890			6 687		1959
1958	342 510			6 299		1958
1957	330 820			6 161		1957
1956	313 200			5 821		1956
1955	292 220			5 495		1955
1954	260 820			4 950		1954
1953	242 270			4 641		1953
1952	223 720			4 335		1952

1900 prices b)   1913 prices   c)

Year	GDP (m) 1900 prices	GDP (m) 1913 prices	NDP (f)	GDP(m) per cap.	NDP(f) per cap.	Year
1951 a)	40 600	48 312	44 151	943	862	1951 a)
1950	37 200	44 904	40 052	887	791	1950
1938	61 100		67 967		993	1938
1937	55 000		63 098		930	1937
1936	49 700		59 511		883	1936
1935	45 600	58 658	53 856	877	805	1935
1934	41 300	52 102	49 395	794	753	1934
1933	37 800	47 375	45 068	726	691	1933
1932	35 500	41 760	41 011	643	631	1932
1931	39 200	43 913	45 223	679	699	1931
1930	43 200	49 289	50 326	766	782	1930
1929	44 400	51 694	53 596	808	838	1929
1928	44 600	53 950	52 969	848	832	1928
1927	42 600	53 108	51 806	839	819	1927
1926	38 800	46 587	43 688	741	694	1926
1925	37 300	46 897	45 515	751	729	1925
1913	45 100	52 440	48 480	782	723	1913
1912	42 400	51 914	46 388	784	701	1912
1911	43 400	49 648	44 476	759	680	1911

National Product at Constant Prices

Year	G D P (m)	– Depreci- ation	N D P (m)	– Ind.Taxes + Subsidies	N D P (f)	GDP(m) per cap.	NDP(f) per cap.	Year
			(in million marks)			(in marks)		
	1900 prices			1913 prices				
1910	42 700		47 457		42 981	734	665	1910
1909	40 600		47 512		41 482	745	651	1909
1908	39 900		46 410		40 665	738	646	1908
1907	38 800		46 181		39 993	744	644	1907
1906	39 200		44 299		38 283	724	626	1906
1905	36 700		43 346		37 189	718	616	1905
1904	37 000		42 263		36 405	710	612	1904
1903	35 700		40 132		34 979	684	596	1903
1902	34 000		36 918		33 142	639	573	1902
1901	33 200		36 197		32 406	636	569	1901
1900	32 900		36 466		33 169	650	591	1900
1899	32 600		36 860		31 818	667	575	1899
1898	30 900		36 813		30 703	676	564	1898
1897	30 600		34 739		29 437	648	549	1897
1896	29 900		33 377		28 615	632	542	1896
1895	28 200		32 079		27 621	616	531	1895
1894	27 000		30 196		26 383	588	513	1894
1893	25 800		30 606		25 760	602	507	1893
1892	24 100		28 390		24 537	564	488	1892
1891	23 700		26 822		23 579	538	473	1891
1890	23 500		27 754		23 589	563	479	1890
1889	23 400		26 478		22 859	545	471	1889
1888	23 600		25 840		22 266	538	463	1888
1887	22 900		24 558		21 362	516	449	1887
1886	22 800		24 142		20 548	512	436	1886
1885	21 800		23 452		20 417	502	437	1885
1884	21 200		22 712		19 923	490	429	1884
1883	20 200		21 909		19 427	476	422	1883
1882	19 800		20 444		18 441	447	403	1882
1881	19 000		20 616		18 122	453	398	1881
1880	17 000		19 874		17 679	440	392	1880
1879	18 400				17 839		399	1879
1878	17 700				18 257		413	1878
1877	15 900				17 438		399	1877
1876	15 200				17 548		407	1876
1875	14 300				17 651		415	1875
1874	12 700				17 545		417	1874
1873	11 400				16 347		393	1873
1872	11 900				15 683		380	1872
1871					14 653		357	1871
1870					14 169		347	1870
1869					14 188		350	1869
1868					14 099		350	1868
1867					13 318		332	1867
1866					13 293		334	1866
1865					13 167		332	1865
1864					13 127		334	1864
1863					12 729		328	1863

National Product at Constant Prices

Year	G D P (m)	– Depreci- ation	N D P (m)	– Ind.Taxes + Subsidies	N D P (f)	GDP(m) per cap.	NDP(f) per cap.	Year
			(in million marks)			(in marks)		
	1 9 0 0 p r i c e s			1 9 1 3 p r i c e s				
1862					11 872		309	1862
1861					11 364		299	1861
1860					11 577		307	1860
1859					10 938		294	1859
1858					10 888		295	1858
1857					10 948		299	1857
1856					10 442		287	1856
1855					9 657		267	1855
1854					9 793		265	1854
1853					9 565		265	1853
1852					9 578		267	1852
1851					9 390		263	1851
1850					9 449		267	1850

a) For 1952 the corresponding figures are 43 700; 51 660; 46 278; 1 001; 896.
b) Figures for 1850 to 1951 are not for GDP(m) but for GDP(f).
c) Figures for 1850 to 1951 are not for GDP(m) p.c. but for NDP(m) p.c.

National Product at Constant Prices

Year	G D P (m)	– Depreci-ation	N D P (m)	– Ind.Taxes + Subsidies	N D P [a] (f)	GDP(m) per cap.	NDP(f) [a] per cap.	Year
			(in million pounds)			(in pounds)		
			1 9 7 0 p r i c e s					
1975	1 892	152	1 740			605		1975
1974	1 887	161	1 725			611		1974
1973	1 861	147	1 714			610		1973
1972	1 783	146	1 637			592		1972
1971	1 691	139	1 552			568		1971
1970	1 626	133	1 493			551		1970
1969	1 575	132	1 442			538		1969
1968	1 484	119	1 365			510		1968
1967	1 374	108	1 266			474		1967
1966	1 305	100	1 205			453		1966
1965	1 288	97	1 191			448		1965
1964	1 263	91	1 172			441		1964
1963	1 212	90	1 122			425		1963
1962	1 156	81	1 075			409		1962
1961	1 116	74	1 042			396		1961
1960	1 065	67	998			376		1960
1959	1 022	63	959			359		1959
1958	982	58	923			344		1958
1957	1 003	58	944			348		1957
1956	1 004	56	948			346		1956
1955	1 017	49	968			348		1955
1954	992	47	945			337		1954
1953	983	43	939			333		1953
1952	957	41	916			324		1952
			1 9 2 6 p r i c e s					
1950					203		68	1950
1949					197		66	1949
1948					193		65	1948
1947					117		60	1947
1946					179		61	1946
1945					183		62	1945
1944					160		54	1944
1943					159		54	1943
1942					160		54	1942
1941					160		53	1941
1940					163		55	1940
1939					179		61	1939
1938					170		58	1938
1937					170		58	1937
1936					179		60	1936
1935					177		60	1935
1934					177		60	1934
1933					173		58	1933
1932					174		59	1932
1931					174		59	1931
1930					170		58	1930

National Product at Constant Prices

Year	G D P (m)	– Depreci- ation	N D P (m)	– Ind.Taxes + Subsidies	N D P [a] (f)	GDP(m) per cap.	NDP(f) [a] per cap.	Year
			(in million pounds)				(in pounds)	
			1 9 2 6 p r i c e s					
1929					168		57	1929
1928					168		57	1928
1927					166		56	1927
1926					154		52	1926

a) Figures for 1926 to 1950 are not for NDP(f) but for GNP(f).

Italy

National Product at Constant Prices

Year	GDP (m)	– Depreci- ation	NDP (m)	– Ind.Taxes + Subsidies	NDP (f)	GDP(m) per cap.	NDP(f) per cap.	Year
	(in thousand million lire)					(in thousand lire)		
			1970 prices					
1975	65 086					1 161		1975
1974	67 459					1 212		1974
1973	64 905					1 176		1973
1972	60 689					1 110		1972
1971	58 836					1 085		1971
1970	57 937					1 085		1970
1969	55 182					1 039		1969
1968	52 221					989		1968
1967	49 117					936		1967
1966	45 896					880		1966
1965	43 392					838		1965
1964	42 062					818		1964
1963	40 983					803		1963
1962	38 827					766		1962
1961	36 574					721		1961
1960	33 807					679		1960
1959	31 658					639		1959
1958	29 719					604		1958
1957	28 345					579		1957
1956	26 918					553		1956
1955	25 716					531		1955
1954	24 106					501		1954
1953	23 258					487		1953
1952 a)	21 635					455		a) 1952
	(in million lire)					(in lire)		
			1938 prices					
1951	207 540	17 476	190 064		165 258	4 394	3 499	1951
1950	191 499	16 018	175 481		153 186	4 078	3 262	1950
1949	176 754	14 678	162 076		142 324	3 794	3 055	1949
1948	162 579	13 832	148 747		133 409	3 517	2 886	1948
1947	149 356	13 668	135 688		125 358	3 255	2 732	1947
1946	126 157	10 365	115 792		108 168	2 728	2 339	1946
1945	96 297	5 057	91 240		85 866	2 099	1 872	1945
1944	120 579	6 589	113 990		109 353	2 640	2 394	1944
1943	150 766	11 486	139 280		129 770	3 309	2 848	1943
1942	169 757	14 596	155 161		140 926	3 736	3 102	1942
1941	173 617	15 376	158 241		142 471	3 841	3 152	1941
1940	175 040	15 646	159 394		143 774	3 901	3 204	1940
1939	176 790	16 185	160 605		142 291	3 981	3 204	1939
1938	165 053	14 900	150 153		133 173	3 760	3 034	1938
1937	163 117	14 547	148 570		132 705	3 749	3 050	1937
1936	152 673	14 104	138 569		123 186	3 535	2 852	1936
1935	152 387	13 900	138 487		122 589	3 555	2 860	1935
1934	141 681	12 472	129 209		113 112	3 331	2 659	1934
1933	141 305	12 113	129 192		113 111	3 350	2 681	1933
1932	141 668	11 771	129 897		114 291	3 386	2 732	1932
1931	138 113	11 159	126 954		111 826	3 326	2 693	1931

Italy

National Product at Constant Prices

Year	G D P (m)	– Depreci- ation	N D P (m)	– Ind.Taxes + Subsidies	N D P (f)	GDP(m) per cap.	NDP(f) per cap.	Year
			(in million lire)			(in lire)		
			1938 prices					
1930	137 749	11 704	126 045		113 911	3 346	2 767	1930
1929	143 355	11 764	131 591		120 488	3 517	2 956	1929
1928	139 044	11 264	127 780		116 787	3 436	2 886	1928
1927	130 475	10 132	120 343		109 583	3 253	2 732	1927
1926	130 066	9 832	120 234		113 143	3 272	2 846	1926
1925	128 561	9 273	119 288		112 062	3 260	2 841	1925
1924	122 502	8 687	113 815		105 322	3 133	2 693	1924
1923	120 343	8 345	111 998		103 927	3 105	2 681	1923
1922	113 159	7 615	105 544		98 287	2 948	2 560	1922
1921	106 787	7 161	99 626		93 315	2 809	2 455	1921
1920	109 262	7 080	102 182		96 245	3 035	2 674	1920
1919	117 744	6 920	110 824		103 898	3 288	2 901	1919
1918	138 184	6 672	131 512		121 853	3 878	3 420	1918
1917	137 358	7 081	130 277		120 306	3 792	3 321	1917
1916	133 450	7 833	125 617		115 961	3 659	3 179	1916
1915	119 342	7 792	111 550		104 369	3 270	2 859	1915
1914	106 812	7 205	99 607		93 987	2 963	2 607	1914
1913	108 516	7 280	101 236		95 885	3 069	2 712	1913
1912	103 779	7 037	96 742		91 410	2 936	2 586	1912
1911	101 768	6 716	95 052		89 656	2 895	2 550	1911
1910	95 694	6 380	89 314		84 446	2 740	2 418	1910
1909	100 114	6 406	93 708		88 626	2 894	2 562	1909
1908	94 563	6 085	88 478		83 895	2 754	2 443	1908
1907	93 995	6 057	87 938		84 384	2 759	2 476	1907
1906	86 639	5 438	81 201		77 653	2 560	2 294	1906
1905	84 490	5 142	79 348		76 104	2 514	2 265	1905
1904	81 352	5 022	76 330		72 161	2 437	2 161	1904
1903	81 345	4 897	76 448		72 425	2 457	2 188	1903
1902	79 136	4 737	74 399		70 253	2 404	2 134	1902
1901	79 805	4 582	75 223		71 574	2 443	2 191	1901
1900	75 946	4 207	71 739		67 392	2 341	2 077	1900
1899	70 957	3 969	66 988		62 786	2 195	1 942	1899
1898	69 906	3 915	65 991		61 792	2 176	1 924	1898
1897	66 301	3 676	62 625		57 785	2 075	1 808	1897
1896	69 079	3 893	65 186		59 961	2 178	1 891	1896
1895	67 637	3 811	63 826		58 721	2 146	1 863	1895
1894	66 312	3 722	62 590		57 242	2 115	1 825	1894
1893	66 640	3 765	62 875		57 846	2 139	1 857	1893
1892	64 656	3 667	60 989		56 012	2 091	1 811	1892
1891	66 938	3 763	63 175		58 454	2 178	1 902	1891
1890	66 699	3 698	63 001		57 753	2 185	1 892	1890
1889	62 953	3 542	59 411		53 828	2 075	1 774	1889
1888	65 191	3 624	61 567		55 216	2 169	1 837	1888
1887	65 518	3 659	61 859		55 785	2 194	1 868	1887
1886	64 556	3 620	60 936		55 739	2 179	1 882	1886
1885	63 714	3 360	60 354		54 982	2 163	1 867	1885
1884	63 239	3 295	59 944		54 559	2 167	1 869	1884
1883	62 005	3 226	58 779		54 020	2 145	1 869	1883
1882	62 113	3 200	58 913		54 372	2 165	1 895	1882

National Product at Constant Prices

Year	G D P (m)	– Depreciation	N D P (m)	– Ind.Taxes + Subsidies	N D P (f)	GDP(m) per cap.	NDP(f) per cap.	Year
		(in million lire)				(in lire)		
		1 9 3 8 p r i c e s						
1881	59 440	2 985	56 455		51 845	2 088	1 821	1881
1880	61 670	3 043	58 627		54 607	2 185	1 935	1880
1879	61 107	2 923	58 184		53 891	2 168	1 912	1879
1878	60 342	2 862	57 480		53 436	2 155	1 909	1878
1877	60 083	2 891	57 192		53 270	2 159	1 914	1877
1876	60 286	2 730	57 556		53 572	2 183	1 940	1876
1875	60 879	2 754	58 125		54 237	2 225	1 982	1875
1874	58 547	2 787	55 760		52 602	2 152	1 934	1874
1873	58 425	2 832	55 593		52 456	2 155	1 935	1873
1872	56 541	2 652	53 889		50 290	2 096	1 865	1872
1871	57 397	2 681	54 716		50 588	2 141	1 887	1871
1870	57 712	2 533	55 179		51 282	2 237	1 988	1870
1869	57 274	2 538	54 736		50 531	2 235	1 972	1869
1868	56 173	2 388	53 785		49 551	2 213	1 952	1868
1867	54 000	2 323	51 677		47 851	2 137	1 894	1867
1866	60 667	2 530	58 137		52 411	2 406	2 079	1866
1865	58 101	2 346	55 755		50 368	2 594	2 249	1865
1864	54 886	2 273	52 613		48 248	2 470	2 171	1864
1863	52 783	2 193	50 590		47 058	2 393	2 134	1863
1862	53 490	2 249	51 241		47 984	2 442	2 191	1862
1861	52 307	2 155	50 152		47 142	2 401	2 164	1861

a) For 1952 the corresponding figures at 1938-prices are 214 725; 17 870; 196 855; 170 572; 4 523; 3 593.

National Product at Constant Prices

Year	G D P a) (m)	− Depreci- ation	N D P (m)	− Ind.Taxes − Subsidies	N D P (f)	GDP(m) a) per cap.	NDP(f) per cap.	Year
		(in million guilders)				(in guilders)		
1 9 7 0 p r i c e s								
1975	135 530					9 869		1975
1974	137 140					10 104		1974
1973	131 610					9 755		1973
1972	124 280					9 284		1972
1971	119 590					9 013		1971
1970	114 580					8 734		1970
1969	107 210					8 274		1969
1968	100 400					7 845		1968
1967	94 080					7 431		1967
1966	89 310					7 170		1966
1965	86 850					7 064		1965
1964	82 490					6 802		1964
1963	75 980					6 350		1963
1962	73 540					6 229		1962
1961	70 510					6 058		1961
1960	68 500					5 963		1960
1959	62 911					5 544		1959
1958	60 085					5 371		1958
1957	60 682					5 503		1957
1956	58 920					5 410		1956
1955	56 414					5 247		1955
1954	52 715					4 966		1954
1953	49 408					4 708		1953
1952 c)	45 650					4 397		c)1952
1 9 6 3 p r i c e s								
1951	34 021					3 314		1951
1950	29 709					2 937		1950
1949	27 313					2 743		1949
1948	25 396					2 591		1948
1939	13 417					1 527		1939
1938	12 937					1 489		1938
1937	12 937					1 504		1937
1936	12 458					1 463		1936
1935	12 458					1 477		1935
1934	12 937					1 551		1934
1933	12 937					1 570		1933
1932	12 937					1 592		1932
1931	13 896					1 737		1931
1930	14 854					1 884		1930
1929	15 812					2 032		1929
1928	15 812					2 059		1928
1927	15 333					2 023		1927
1926	15 812					2 116		1926
1925	16 292					2 212		1925
1924	16 292					2 243		1924
1923	16 292					2 278		1923
1921	18 688					2 700		1921

National Product at Constant Prices

Year	G D P[a] (m)	– Depreciation	N D P (m)	– Ind.Taxes + Subsidies	N D P (f)	GDP(m)[a] per cap.	NDP(f) per cap.	Year
		(in million guilders)				(in guilders)		
			1 9 6 3 p r i c e s					
1920	22 042					3 232		1920
1919	19 646					2 909		1919
1918 b)	18 208					2 716		b) 1918
1917	15 333					2 319		1917
1916	14 375					2 218		1916
1915	12 937					2 033		1915
1914	11 500					1 839		1914
1913	11 500					1 871		1913
1912	11 250					1 849		1912
1911	11 500					1 924		1911
1910	11 021					1 868		1910
1909	10 541					1 798		1909
1908	10 541					1 821		1908
1907	10 541					1 846		1907
1906	10 541					1 872		1906
1905	10 541					1 899		1905
1904	10 541					1 927		1904
1903	10 062					1 867		1903
1902	10 062					1 896		1902
1901	10 541					2 019		1901
1900	9 583					1 864		1900

a) Figures for 1900 to 1939 are not for GDP(m) but for NDP(m).

b) Prior to the First World War data for National Product do not include Public Consumption and Public Investment. Hence, comparability over time and between countries is severely impaired.

c) For 1952 the corresponding figures at 1963-prices are 34 500 and 3 323.

National Product at Constant Prices

Year	G D P [a)] (m)	- Depreci- [b)] ation	N D P (m)	- Ind.Taxes + Subsidies	N D P (f)	GDP(m) [a)] per cap.	NDP(m) per cap.	Year
			(in million kroner)			(in kroner)		
			1 9 7 0 p r i c e s					
1975	99 677					24 875		1975
1974	96 305					24 166		1974
1973	91 461					23 096		1973
1972	87 847					22 335		1972
1971	83 580					21 414		1971
1970	79 872					20 601		1970
1969	76 625					19 902		1969
1968	72 934					19 102		1968
1967	70 493					18 624		1967
1966	66 650					17 763		1966
1965	63 764					17 127		1965
1964	60 614					16 408		1964
1963	57 534					15 693		1963
1962	54 589					15 005		1962
1961	52 143					14 448		1961
1960	49 626					13 858		1960
1959	47 392					13 342		1959
1958	46 057					13 076		1958
1957	45 459					13 021		1957
1956	44 437					12 846		1956
1955	42 275					12 335		1955
1954	41 391					12 195		1954
1953	39 858					11 862		1953
1952	37 963					11 410		1952
1951	36 646					11 121		1951
			1 9 5 5 p r i c e s					
1950	21 646	4 030	17 616			6 629	5 395	1950
1949	20 625	3 878	16 747			6 377	5 178	1949
1948	20 115	3 609	16 506			6 283	5 156	1948
1947	18 797	3 375	15 422			5 939	4 872	1947
1946 [c)]	16 533	3 089	13 444			5 288	4 300	[c)]1946
			1 9 3 8 p r i c e s					
1939	6 110	800	5 310			2 068	1 797	1939
1938	5 827	765	5 062			1 985	1 724	1938
1937	5 697	728	4 969			1 952	1 702	1937
1936	5 459	697	4 762			1 880	1 640	1936
1935	5 114	674	4 440			1 770	1 536	1935
1934	4 870	660	4 210			1 694	1 464	1934
1933	4 699	651	4 048			1 644	1 416	1933
1932	4 595	641	3 954			1 617	1 391	1932
1931	4 368	627	3 741			1 547	1 325	1931
1930	4 746	598	4 148			1 690	1 477	[d)] 1930
			1 9 1 0 p r i c e s					
1929	2 607	304	2 303			932	823	1929
1928	2 382	290	2 092			855	751	1928

National Product at Constant Prices

Year	G D P [a) (m)	- Depreci- [b) ation	N D P (m)	- Ind.Taxes + Subsidies	N D P (f)	GDP(m) [a) per cap.	NDP(m) per cap.	Year
			(in million kroner)			(in kroner)		
			1910 prices					
1927	2 281	282	1 999			822	720	1927
1926	2 198	274	1 924			795	696	1926
1925	2 166	266	1 900			788	691	1925
1924	2 040	257	1 783			747	653	1924
1923	2 041	251	1 790			752	659	1923
1922	1 987	243	1 744			737	647	1922
1921	1 795	239	1 556			673	583	1921
1920	1 987	226	1 761			754	668	1920
1919	1 865	211	1 654			716	635	1919
1918	1 592	205	1 387			617	538	1918
1917	1 659	208	1 451			650	569	1917
1916	1 825	207	1 618			723	641	1916
1915	1 757	199	1 558			703	623	1915
1914	1 683	192	1 491			680	603	1914
1913	1 649	183	1 466			674	599	1913
1912	1 564	172	1 392			645	574	1912
1911	1 491	163	1 328			621	553	1911
1910	1 435	156	1 279			602	536	1910
1909	1 378	151	1 227			582	518	1909
1908	1 349	148	1 201			575	512	1908
1907	1 307	143	1 164			561	500	1907
1906	1 253	139	1 114			540	480	1906
1905	1 203	134	1 069			521	463	1905
1904	1 194	130	1 064			519	463	1904
1903	1 192	128	1 064			521	465	1903
1902	1 199	125	1 074			527	472	1902
1901	1 181	123	1 058			523	469	1901
1900	1 152	121	1 031			516	462	1900
1899	1 138	116	1 022			516	463	1899
1898	1 104	112	992			508	456	1898
1897	1 095	109	986			511	460	1897
1896	1 040	106	934			492	442	1896
1895	1 011	104	907			485	435	1895
1894	999	101	898			485	436	1894
1893	993	100	893			487	438	1893
1892	967	99	868			477	428	1892
1891	949	97	852			471	423	1891
1890	940	94	846			470	423	1890
1889	915	91	824			461	415	1889
1888	881	88	793			445	401	1888
1887	842	85	757			427	384	1887
1886	831	84	747			424	381	1886
1885	827	83	744			425	382	1885
1884	819	81	738			424	382	1884
1883	805	81	724			419	377	1883
1882	808	78	730			421	380	1882
1881	809	76	733			420	381	1881
1880	802	75	727			417	378	1880
1879	777	73	704			408	370	1879

National Product at Constant Prices

Year	GDP[a] (m)	- Depreci-[b] ation	NDP (m)	- Ind.Taxes + Subsidies	NDP (f)	GDP(m)[a] per cap.	NDP(m) per cap.	Year
			(in million kroner)			(in kroner)		
			1910 prices					
1878	770	71	699			410	372	1878
1877	798	70	728			431	393	1877
1876	792	67	725			433	396	1876
1875	769	64	705			426	391	1875
1874	748	63	685			419	384	1874
1873	721	60	661			408	374	1873
1872	704	59	645			401	367	1872
1871	661	57	605			379	346	1871
1870	650	55	595			374	342	1870
1869	651	53	598			376	345	1869
1868	627	52	575			363	333	1868
1867	628	51	577			365	336	1867
1866	613	49	564			359	330	1866
1865	601	48	553			355	327	1865

a) For 1865 to 1950 figures are not for GDP(m) but for Gross-GDP(m), i.e. inclusive of repair and maintenance.

b) For 1865 to 1950 figures in addition include repair and maintenance.

c) For 1951 the corresponding figures at 1955-prices are 22 813; 4 247; 18 566; 6 923; 5 634.

National Product at Constant Prices

Year	G D P (m)	- Depreci- ation	G D P [a] (f)	- Ind.Taxes + Subsidies	N D P (f)	GDP(m) per cap.	GDP(f) [a] per cap.	Year
			(in million kroner)				(in kroner)	

1 9 7 0   p r i c e s

Year	G D P (m)					GDP(m) per cap.		Year
1975	191 712					23 402		1975
1974	190 016					23 286		1974
1973	182 738					22 460		1973
1972	176 521					21 733		1972
1971	172 114					21 253		1971
1970	170 883					21 248		1970
1969	162 785					20 429		1969
1968	154 929					19 581		1968
1967	148 934					18 931		1967
1966	144 056					18 452		1966
1965	140 709					18 195		1965
1964	135 034					17 626		1964
1963	126 422					16 625		1963
1962	120 160					15 892		1962
1961	115 218					15 323		1961
1960	108 992					14 571		1960
1959	104 989					14 100		1959
1958	99 786					13 468		1958
1957	97 486					13 239		1957
1956	95 235					13 020		1956
1955	92 171					12 692		1955
1954	89 482					12 405		1954
1953	84 435					11 774		1953
1952	81 792					11 481		1952
1951 [b]	80 408					11 369		[b] 1951

1 9 0 8 / 0 9   p r i c e s [c]

Year	G D P (m)		G D P (f)			GDP(m) per cap.	GDP(f) per cap.	Year
1950	10 472		10 191			1 493	1 452	1950
1949	9 860		9 665			1 417	1 389	1949
1948	9 480		9 178			1 377	1 333	1948
1947	9 177		8 817			1 349	1 296	1947
1946	8 715		8 469			1 297	1 260	1946
1945	8 044		8 050			1 212	1 213	1945
1944	7 363		7 561			1 122	1 152	1944
1943	7 030		7 294			1 083	1 123	1943
1942	6 717		7 173			1 044	1 115	1942
1941	6 745		6 954			1 055	1 088	1941
1940	6 861		6 958			1 079	1 094	1940
1939	7 119		7 277			1 125	1 150	1939
1938	6 820		7 033			1 083	1 116	1938
1937	6 630		6 810			1 056	1 085	1937
1936	6 307		6 704			1 007	1 071	1936
1935	5 837		6 301			935	1 009	1935
1934	5 521		5 957			887	957	1934
1933	5 089		5 609			820	904	1933
1932	4 945		5 482			800	887	1932
1931	5 220		5 614			848	912	1931
1930	5 790		6 038			944	984	1930

National Product at Constant Prices

Year	G D P (m)	– Depreci- ation	G D P [a] (f)	– Ind.Taxes + Subsidies	N D P (f)	GDP(m) per cap.	GDP(f) [a] per cap.	Year
			(in million kroner)			(in kroner)		
			1908/09 prices [c]					
1929	5 574		5 711			911	934	1929
1928	5 177		5 303			849	869	1928
1927	5 136		5 288			844	869	1927
1926	4 871		5 061			803	834	1926
1925	4 601		4 757			761	787	1925
1924	4 326		4 352			718	722	1924
1923	4 179		4 264			696	711	1923
1922	3 868		4 079			647	683	1922
1921	3 763		3 866			634	652	1921
1920	4 008		3 751			682	638	1920
1919	3 562		3 520			610	603	1919
1918	3 447		3 358			593	578	1918
1917	3 790		3 375			655	584	1917
1916	4 244		3 794			740	661	1916
1915	3 881		3 595			681	631	1915
1914	3 762		3 658			664	646	1914
1913	3 833		3 649			681	649	1913
1912	3 547		3 507			635	628	1912
1911	3 450		3 378			622	609	1911
1910	3 363		3 240			611	589	1910
1909	3 096		3 052			567	559	1909
1908	3 145		3 045			582	563	1908
1907	3 141		3 033			586	566	1907
1906	3 086		2 912			580	547	1906
1905	2 823		2 675			534	506	1905
1904	2 788		2 624			531	500	1904
1903	2 736		2 542			525	487	1903
1902	2 584		2 418			498	466	1902
1901	2 575		2 330			499	451	1901
1900	2 578		2 356			503	460	1900
1899	2 486		2 299			489	452	1899
1898	2 416		2 254			479	447	1898
1897	2 336		2 195			468	440	1897
1896	2 239		2 110			453	427	1896
1895	2 142		2 039			437	416	1895
1894	2 060		1 926			424	397	1894
1893	1 965		1 876			408	389	1893
1892	1 912		1 825			398	379	1892
1891	1 863		1 800			388	375	1891
1890	1 808		1 729			378	361	1890
1889	1 776		1 679			373	352	1889
1888	1 728		1 659			364	349	1888
1887	1 689		1 595			357	337	1887
1886	1 700		1 618			361	344	1886
1885	1 711		1 597			366	342	1885
1884	1 663		1 577			359	341	1884
1883	1 640		1 576			357	343	1883

National Product at Constant Prices

Year	G D P (m)	– Depreci- ation	G D P [a] (f)	– Ind.Taxes + Subsidies	N D P (f)	GDP(m) per cap.	GDP(f)[a] per cap.	Year
			(in million kroner)			(in kroner)		
			1 9 0 8 / 0 9 p r i c e s [c]					
1882	1 571		1 495			343	326	1882
1881	1 561		1 491			341	326	1881
1880	1 522		1 471			332	321	1880
1879	1 506		1 461			330	320	1879
1878	1 454		1 374			322	304	1878
1877	1 494		1 379			335	309	1877
1876	1 494		1 380			339	313	1876
1875	1 410		1 300			323	298	1875
1874	1 465		1 326			339	307	1874
1873	1 424		1 311			333	306	1873
1872	1 343		1 240			317	293	1872
1871	1 243		1 169			296	279	1871
1870	1 225		1 128			294	270	1870
1869	1 090		1 012			261	242	1869
1868	1 033		964			246	230	1868
1867	1 066		1 019			255	243	1867
1866	1 085		1 011			262	244	1866
1865	1 082		975			264	238	1865
1864	1 076		954			265	235	1864
1863	1 054		935			263	234	1863
1862	1 009		910			256	230	1862
1861	982		879			252	226	1861

a) For 1861 to 1950 figures are not for NDP(m) but for GDP(f).

b) For 1951 the corresponding figures at 1908/09-prices are 10 770; 10 019; 1 522; 1 416.

c) Linked deflators, based on 1908/09 = 100.

National Product at Constant Prices

Year	G D P[a] (m)	– Depreci- ation	N D P (m)	– Ind.Taxes + Subsidies	N D P (f)	GDP(m)[a] per cap.	NDP(f) per cap.	Year
			(in million francs)			(in francs)		
			1 9 7 0 p r i c e s					
1975	94 245					14 714		1975
1974	101 810					15 804		1974
1973	100 350					15 604		1973
1972	97 380					15 251		1972
1971	94 360					14 920		1971
1970	90 665					14 467		1970
1969	85 230					13 720		1969
1968	80 685					13 158		1968
1967	77 890					12 846		1967
1966	75 580					12 605		1966
1965	73 765					12 412		1965
1964	71 490					12 170		1964
1963	67 920					11 771		1963
1962	64 760					11 441		1962
1961	61 800					11 244		1961
1960	57 165					10 661		1960
1959	53 430					10 159		1959
1558	50 255					9 666		1958
1957	51 355					10 018		1957
1956	49 390					9 789		1956
1955	46 320					9 301		1955
1954	43 390					8 803		1954
1953	41 090					8 423		1953
1952	39 685					8 241		1952
1951[b]	39 360					8 288		[b] 1951
			1 9 5 8 p r i c e s					
1950	22 920					4 882		1950
1949	21 465					4 626		1949
1948	22 235					4 852		1948
1938	17 370					4 144		1938

a) Figures for 1938 to 1950 are not for Domestic Product but for National Product.
b) For 1951 the corresponding figures at 1958-prices are 24 845 and 5 232.

National Product at Constant Prices

Year	GDP[a] (m)	– Depreci- ation	N D P (m)	– Ind.Taxes + Subsidies	N D P (f)	GDP(m)[a] per cap.	NDP(f) per cap.	Year
			(in million pounds)			(in pounds)		

1 9 7 0   p r i c e s

Year	GDP[a] (m)	– Depreci- ation	N D P (m)	– Ind.Taxes + Subsidies	N D P (f)	GDP(m)[a] per cap.	NDP(f) per cap.	Year
1975	55 652	5 891	49 761			995		1975
1974	56 551	5 787	50 764			1 010		1974
1973	56 916	5 457	51 459			1 018		1973
1972	53 404	4 937	48 467			957		1972
1971	52 127	4 662	47 465			937		1971
1970	50 724	4 437	46 287			915		1970
1969	49 489	4 185	45 304			896		1969
1968	48 821	4 047	44 774			887		1968
1967	47 209	3 866	43 343			861		1967
1966	46 000	3 755	42 245			844		1966
1965	45 163	3 626	41 537			833		1965
1964	44 164	3 545	40 619			820		1964
1963	41 814	3 422	38 392			781		1963
1962	40 222	3 281	36 941			755		1962
1961	39 883	3 213	36 670			755		1961
1960[b]	38 601	3 092	35 509			737		[b] 1960

1 9 0 0   p r i c e s [d]

Year	GDP[a] (m)	– Depreci- ation	N D P (m)	– Ind.Taxes + Subsidies	N D P (f)	GDP(m)[a] per cap.	NDP(f) per cap.	Year
1959	4 362	307	4 057	246	3 811	84	73	1959
1958	4 175	296	3 881	208	3 673	81	71	1958
1957	4 165	285	3 882	184	3 698	81	72	1957
1956	4 096	274	3 824	178	3 646	80	71	1956
1955	4 049	266	3 785	183	3 602	79	71	1955
1954	3 900	255	3 647	175	3 472	77	68	1954
1953	3 747	244	3 504	165	3 339	74	66	1953
1952	3 604	236	3 370	157	3 212	71	64	1952
1951	3 612	229	3 384	164	3 220	72	64	1951
1950	3 492	221	3 271	157	3 114	69	62	1950
1949	3 392	214	3 179	155	3 025	67	60	1949
1948	3 277	206	3 072	155	2 917	66	58	1948
1947	3 201	204	2 998	161	2 837	65	57	1947
1946	3 280	202	3 079	159	2 920	67	59	1946
1945	3 319	202	3 118	150	2 968	67	60	1945
1944	3 453	208	3 245	136	3 109	70	63	1944
1943	3 586	214	3 373	130	3 243	74	66	1943
1942	3 512	213	3 299	131	3 168	73	65	1942
1941	3 439	218	3 222	139	3 083	71	64	1941
1940	3 173	217	2 958	142	2 815	66	58	1940
1939	2 906	211	2 697	160	2 538	61	53	1939
1938	2 828	205	2 624	157	2 467	60	52	1938
1937	2 759	200	2 561	155	2 406	58	51	1937
1936	2 669	192	2 479	149	2 329	57	49	1936
1935	2 565	187	2 380	145	2 235	55	48	1935
1934	2 479	183	2 298	139	2 159	53	46	1934
1933	2 319	182	2 138	138	2 000	50	43	1933
1932	2 270	180	2 092	134	1 957	49	42	1932
1931	2 254	177	2 079	143	1 936	49	42	1931

National Product at Constant Prices

Year	GDP a) (m)	− Depreci- ation	N D P (m)	− Ind.Taxes + Subsidies	N D P (f)	GDP(m) a) per cap.	NDP(f) per cap.	Year
			(in million pounds)			(in pounds)		
			1 9 0 0 p r i c e s					
1930	2 384	174	2 212	140	2 072	52	45	1930
1929	2 391	168	2 224	139	2 085	52	46	1929
1928	2 322	162	2 161	138	2 024	51	44	1928
1927	2 284	160	2 128	137	1 991	50	44	1927
1926	2 126	157	1 970	135	1 835	47	41	1926
1925	2 219	155	2 065	134	1 931	49	43	1925
1924	2 106	151	1 956	135	1 821	47	41	1924
1923	2 032	147	1 887	131	1 755	46	39	1923
1922	1 971	144	1 828	130	1 698	44	38	1922
_ _ c)								c) _ _
1921	1 908	142	1 767	135	1 632	40	35	1921
1920	2 028	140	1 889	144	1 744	44	38	1920
1919	2 236	127	2 109	121	1 988	50	45	1919
1918	2 445	126	2 318	71	2 247	57	52	1918
1917	2 438	127	2 311	76	2 235	56	52	1917
1916	2 451	128	2 323	112	2 211	56	51	1916
1915	2 422	128	2 294	132	2 162	55	49	1915
1914	2 255	113	2 142	138	2 004	49	44	1914
1913	2 239	114	2 125	141	1 984	49	43	1913
1912	2 154	111	2 044	137	1 907	47	42	1912
1911	2 137	109	2 028	136	1 892	47	42	1911
1910	2 085	108	1 978	132	1 845	46	41	1910
1909	2 014	106	1 907	130	1 777	45	40	1909
1908	1 966	106	1 861	133	1 728	45	39	1908
1907	2 053	99	1 954	135	1 820	47	42	1907
1906	2 024	102	1 922	133	1 789	47	41	1906
1905	1 957	99	1 857	132	1 725	46	40	1905
1904	1 909	96	1 812	131	1 682	45	39	1904
1903	1 909	96	1 813	130	1 683	45	40	1903
1902	1 921	94	1 828	131	1 697	46	41	1902
1901	1 894	89	1 805	130	1 674	46	40	1901
1900	1 863	88	1 775	128	1 647	45	40	1900
1899	1 905	85	1 820	127	1 693	47	42	1899
1898	1 817	83	1 734	122	1 612	45	40	1898
1897	1 725	81	1 644	119	1 525	43	38	1897
1896	1 703	79	1 624	117	1 507	43	38	1896
1895	1 639	77	1 563	114	1 449	42	37	1895
1894	1 588	77	1 511	111	1 400	41	36	1894
1893	1 486	76	1 411	108	1 303	39	34	1893
1892	1 485	74	1 411	109	1 302	39	34	1892
1891	1 521	74	1 447	108	1 339	40	35	1891
1890	1 498	72	1 426	105	1 322	40	35	1890
1889	1 488	71	1 417	103	1 314	40	35	1889
1888	1 433	71	1 362	100	1 263	39	34	1888
1887	1 380	69	1 311	100	1 212	38	33	1887
1886	1 328	68	1 260	98	1 163	37	32	1886
1885	1 306	69	1 237	98	1 139	36	32	1885

National Product at Constant Prices

Year	GDP [a) (m)	− Depreci- ation	NDP (m)	− Ind.Taxes + Subsidies	NDP (f)	GDP(m) [a) per cap.	NDP(f) per cap.	Year
	(in million pounds)					(in pounds)		
			1 9 0 0 p r i c e s					
1884	1 305	67	1 238	98	1 141	37	32	1884
1883	1 313	66	1 247	97	1 150	37	32	1883
1882	1 285	65	1 220	96	1 124	36	32	1882
1881	1 264	65	1 199	95	1 103	36	32	1881
1880	1 234	64	1 170	95	1 075	36	31	1880
1879	1 184	62	1 122	94	1 028	35	30	1879
1878	1 185	61	1 124	95	1 029	35	30	1878
1877	1 190	60	1 130	95	1 035	35	31	1877
1876	1 172	59	1 113	95	1 018	35	31	1876
1875	1 160	58	1 102	94	1 008	35	31	1875
1874	1 138	57	1 081	92	990	35	30	1874
1873	1 103	57	1 046	89	957	34	30	1873
1872	1 089	55	1 034	86	948	34	30	1872
1871	1 090	54	1 036	83	953	35	30	1871
1870	1 033	54	979	80	900	33	29	1870
1869	1 014					33		1869
1868	994					32		1868
1867	959					32		1867
1866	947					31		1866
1865	936					31		1865
1864	886					30		1864
1863	868					29		1863
1862	838					29		1862
1861	838					29		1861
1860	818					28		1860
1859	810					28		1859
1858	766					27		1858
1857	781					28		1857
1856	768					27		1856
1855	735					26		1855
1854	717					26		1854
1853	701					25		1853
1852	682					25		1852
1851	672					25		1851
1850	649					24		1850
1849	562					24		1849
1848	640					23		1848
1847	630					23		1847
1846	629					22		1846
1845	596					21		1845
1844	566					21		1844
1843	539					20		1843
1842	531					20		1842
1841	537					20		1841
1840	546					21		1840
1839	558					21		1839
1838	535					21		1838

National Product at Constant Prices

Year	G D P a) (m)	– Depreci- ation	N D P (m)	– Ind.Taxes + Subsidies	N D P (f)	GDP(m) a) per cap.	NDP(f) per cap.	Year
			(in million pounds)				(in pounds)	
				1 9 0 0 p r i c e s				
1837	511					20		1837
1836	515					20		1836
1835	502					20		1835
1834	481					19		1834
1833	465					19		1833
1832	460					19		1832
1831	460					19		1831
1830	444					19		1830

a) Figures for 1830 to 1869 are not for Domestic Product but for National Product.
b) For 1960 the corresponding figures at 1900-prices are 4 584; 320; 4 264; 88.
c) For 1830 to 1921 Southern Ireland is included.
d) Figures are based on linked deflators.

Chapter 6

ORIGIN AND USE OF NATIONAL PRODUCT

Modern economic growth is more than growth of aggregate or per capita national product. It is usually accompanied by far-reaching structural changes which may be grasped in terms of changes in the origin, distribution, and use of national product. Modern economic growth implies a shift from agricultural to industrial production and to services, changes in the distribution of national income among social classes as well as changes in the use of national product for private household or government consumption or for capital formation. This chapter presents basic data on the origin and use of national product. Data on the distribution of national income are given in Chapter 8, Income Distribution.

The changes in the sectoral origin of national product reflect changes in the structure of final demand. To some extent, these changes are influenced by political decisions (consider the growing importance of government consumption), but on the whole they are mainly a product of the overall rise in per capita income as well as of the different impact of technological progress on the production of the various categories of finished goods. As income elasticities of demand for these goods differ, productivity increases lead to a changing structure of domestic final demand and hence to changes in the production structure.

A wide variety of industrial sectors could be distinguished on the basis of the characteristics of their products and of the technology and organization utilized in the production of these goods. Typically, industrial sectors differ markedly in the institutional setting of production and the character of work, in the level of productivity and the prospects of growth, and hence the positions and opportunities of the people working in them. A major problem in the identification of production sectors lies in the rather loose correspondence between types of economic activity (such as extracting, manufacturing, distributing, and financing) and statistically classifiable industrial groupings (such as mining, manufacture, commerce, etc.). Thus, activities subsumed under a certain industrial sector may greatly vary, especially with regard to applied technology. In this sense, measures of the change in sectoral shares of national product may rather underestimate the long-term changes in the production structure.

The estimation of the value added of the industrial sectors raises problems of its own. In principle, there are two basic methods of measurement. A sector's contribution may be measured in terms of the value of its total product net of purchases or in terms of the total income from work or property within the respective sector. The first method requires a full statistical account of input-output flows among the various industrial sectors. It involves a high risk of double counting, and adequate statistics are usually not available for the period prior to World War II. Therefore, this method has only recently become a major tool for independent estimation. The second method, the income approach, relies on a piecing together of various income and employment statistics (and supplementary information from production and price statistics). Historical estimates are mainly based on this approach which suffers from the fragmentary nature of the statistical materials.

Because of the above mentioned conceptual and empirical problems, only three major economic sectors are distinguished (cf. also Chapter 7, Labour Force): a primary (agriculture, forestry, and fishing), a secondary (mining, manufacture, construction, and utilities), and a tertiary sector (commerce, transport and communication, banking, private services and public administration.). Figures are provided in the form of percentage distributions. They usually refer to the time series of domestic product at current market prices (see Chapter 5), but sometimes to the gross or even the net domestic product at factor cost (cf. notes to the tables). A more comprehensive analysis of sectoral changes would certainly have to consider not only nominal but also real changes in sectoral value added. Because of the great index problems involved in such historical estimates, however, we have not included these figures.

The national product may be used in two principle ways: it may be consumed or added to capital stocks. Usually a further distinction is made between private and public consumption Private consumption, by far the largest component, covers the expenditure on all consumer goods by private households and non-profit institutions, but excludes the purchase of land and dwellings. Public consumption comprises the cost of services provided free of charge by general government (excluding government enterprises and public corporations) and all military expenditure. Finally, gross capital formation is the gross value of goods added to the capital stock, including residential construction, but excluding defense equipment.

Defining consumption as the use of goods to satisfy demands of ultimate consumers, and capital formation as additions to the stock of tools used to produce other goods, the line of distinction seems to be easily drawn. In reality, however, this distinction involves several conceptual problems. Investment in human capital (education, medical services etc.) is considered in national accounts as consumption, whereas investment in physical capital, including housing, is always classified as investment. Similarly the consumption of capital (depreciation) is included under gross investment, while the reproduction costs of human labour are defined as consumption. Changes in stocks are in principle classified as investment, even if they consist of consumer goods which have not been sold in the period of observation.

Perhaps the greatest conceptual problem refers to that varying part of private and public consumption expenditure which may be interpreted as individual or social costs of production. Public services, such as general administration, legislation, education or defense, cannot easily be understood as goods which satisfy the demands of final consumers. They rather represent intermediate goods (cf. the introduction to Chapter 5) or social production costs. And the same holds true for many expenditure items of private households (e.g. transportation) which represent individual production costs in a modern economy.

Consumption and investment are the basic categories of the use of national product. In order to arrive at the national product, one has to add the net balance between exports and imports to the domestic products. From the expenditure side, national product is defined as the sum of domestic consumption (private and public), domestic investment (private and public), and exports (net of imports). The following tables give the percentage distribution of national product according to these main categories of use. Figures usually refer to domestic product at current market prices, and in some cases to national product. In the latter case, exports (net of imports) include not only goods and services, but also the balance of factor remuneration to and from abroad (cf. notes to the tables). It should be noted that the share of total consumption, being the largest single category, can exceed the 100 % mark, when a country has become a net importer of goods and services.

An evaluation of changes in the allocation of production resources would have to take into account not only nominal changes, but in addition changes in the relative price relations between consumer and investment goods. Deflation raises a number of severe conceptual problems. Historical estimates also suffer from the insufficiency of the date basis. For these reasons, we have not included distributions at constant prices.

Austria

Origin and Use of National Product

| Year | GDP at market prices [a] | | | Gross National Product at market prices [b] | | | | | | | | | Year |
| | Agriculture | Industry | Services | Consumption | | | Investment | | | | Ex-ports | Im-ports | |
				Private	Public	Total	Net cap. formation	Gross cap. form.	Changes in stocks [c]	Total			
1975	5.2	44.3	50.5	56.3	16.6	72.9	15.4	26.7	0.3	27.0	33.4	33.3	1975
1974	8.7	46.0	45.3	54.2	15.7	69.9	17.5	28.2	2.9	31.0	36.4	37.3	1974
1973	5.8	45.5	48.6	55.0	15.3	70.3	17.3	27.9	2.2	30.1	34.0	34.4	1973
1972	5.9	48.8	45.3	56.2	14.6	70.8	19.7	30.2	-0.8	29.4	33.0	33.2	1972
1971	6.1	48.0	46.0	55.9	14.7	70.6	17.6	28.1	1.1	29.2	32.6	32.5	1971
1970	7.0	47.4	45.6	56.4	14.8	71.2	15.8	26.3	2.2	28.5	31.5	31.3	1970
1969	7.1	47.3	45.6	57.5	15.0	72.4	14.3	25.0	1.7	26.7	28.3	27.5	1969
1968	8.1	50.3	41.6	59.0	14.8	73.8	15.1	25.9	1.0	27.0	25.8	26.5	1968
1967	8.9	50.6	40.5	59.5	14.6	74.1	16.0	27.1	0.3	27.4	24.8	26.2	1967
1966	8.7	52.3	39.0	58.9	13.8	72.7	17.2	28.3	1.4	29.7	25.0	27.4	1966
1965	9.0	52.3	38.7	59.4	13.3	72.7	16.4	27.4	1.1	28.5	25.1	26.3	1965
1964	10.6	51.4	38.0	58.9	13.1	72.0	15.5	26.2	2.5	28.6	24.5	25.1	1964
1963	10.4	50.9	38.7	60.6	13.1	73.6	15.1	25.9	0.2	26.1	24.6	24.4	1963
1962	10.7	51.4	37.9	60.4	12.7	73.1	15.2	25.8	0.2	26.0	24.7	23.8	1962
1961	12.0	51.4	36.6	58.8	12.5	71.2	15.9	26.3	1.7	28.1	24.4	23.6	1961
1960	11.5	52.5	35.9	59.9	12.8	72.7	14.6	25.1	2.7	27.8	24.7	25.2	1960
1959	11.8	51.6	36.6	61.4	13.4	74.8	12.9	23.6	0.6	24.3	23.7	22.8	1959
1958	13.9	50.6	35.5	61.4	13.7	75.0	12.0	22.7	0.8	23.5	23.9	22.4	1958
1957	13.7	51.7	34.6	60.3	13.5	73.8	12.3	22.7	1.9	24.6	25.5	23.9	1957
1956	14.2	51.9	33.9	62.0	12.6	74.6	11.3	21.8	2.3	24.1	24.3	23.0	1956
1955	15.4	51.8	32.8	62.3	12.4	74.7	12.0	22.3	6.4	28.7	19.6	23.0	1955
1954	16.7	49.9	33.4	63.5	13.2	76.7	9.2	20.3	2.7	23.0	19.8	19.5	1954
1953	15.8	50.3	33.9	65.0	13.8	78.8	6.0	18.1	0.8	18.9	18.4	16.0	1953
1952	15.9	50.8	33.3	65.0	13.4	78.4	8.7	19.6	2.5	22.1	15.1	15.5	1952
1951	16.3	51.2	32.5	64.9	13.1	78.0	9.6	19.8	9.0	28.8	15.4	22.2	1951
1950	16.4	50.3	33.3	67.4	12.0	79.4	7.1	16.9	8.7	25.6	14.5	19.5	1950
1949	15.4	50.0	34.6	70.7	12.1	82.9	5.3	14.8	9.7	24.5	9.1	16.5	1949
1948	14.5	49.0	36.5	73.2	12.2	85.4	3.3	12.3	7.3	19.7	7.2	12.2	1948
1937	14.3	42.0	43.6	78.4	13.8	92.2	-0.5	7.3	0.1	7.5	17.6	17.2	1937
1936	14.1	40.9	45.0	81.2	13.4	94.6	-1.3	7.0	-0.4	6.6	14.8	16.0	1936
1935	13.6	41.1	45.3	82.4	13.0	95.4	-2.2	6.2	0.1	6.3	14.1	15.9	1935
1934	15.0	40.4	44.6	83.0	13.1	96.1	-3.0	5.7	0.2	5.9	13.5	15.5	1934
1933	14.9	38.9	46.1	86.1	13.0	99.1	-3.4	5.2	-2.1	3.1	13.1	15.4	1933
1932	13.8	40.5	45.8	87.2	12.9	100.0	-2.4	6.1	-2.3	3.8	13.2	17.0	1932
1931	10.9	42.8	46.3	89.0	12.9	101.8	0.7	8.5	-4.6	3.9	17.8	23.5	1931
1930	11.4	44.9	43.8	84.8	11.7	96.5	2.5	9.4	-0.8	8.6	20.9	26.1	1930
1929	12.8	46.5	40.7	82.1	10.9	93.0	3.7	10.5	3.1	13.6	23.1	29.7	1929
1928	13.0	46.0	40.9	81.0	10.7	91.8	2.9	9.7	4.4	14.1	24.5	30.4	1928
1927	14.9	44.4	40.7	79.9	10.1	90.0	1.2	8.0	8.5	16.5	23.7	30.2	1927
1926	12.4	46.6	40.9	82.0	9.9	91.9	1.8	9.3	6.1	15.4	21.9	29.3	1926
1925	14.6	45.6	39.6	80.2	9.4	89.5	0.8	8.2	9.3	17.5	23.4	30.4	1925
1924	14.6	45.0	40.4	82.3	8.9	91.2	-0.8	6.8	15.5	22.3	26.3	39.8	1924
1913	11.2	45.0	43.8	76.9	10.9	87.7	7.0	12.9	-0.7	12.3	22.8	22.8	1913

a) Figures for 1913–1950 refer to GNP at market prices. Figures for 1951–1968 refer to GDP at factor cost.
b) Figures for 1913–1950 refer to GNP.
c) Figures for 1913–1953 and for 1973–1975 include statistical discrepancies.

Austria

Origin of National Product

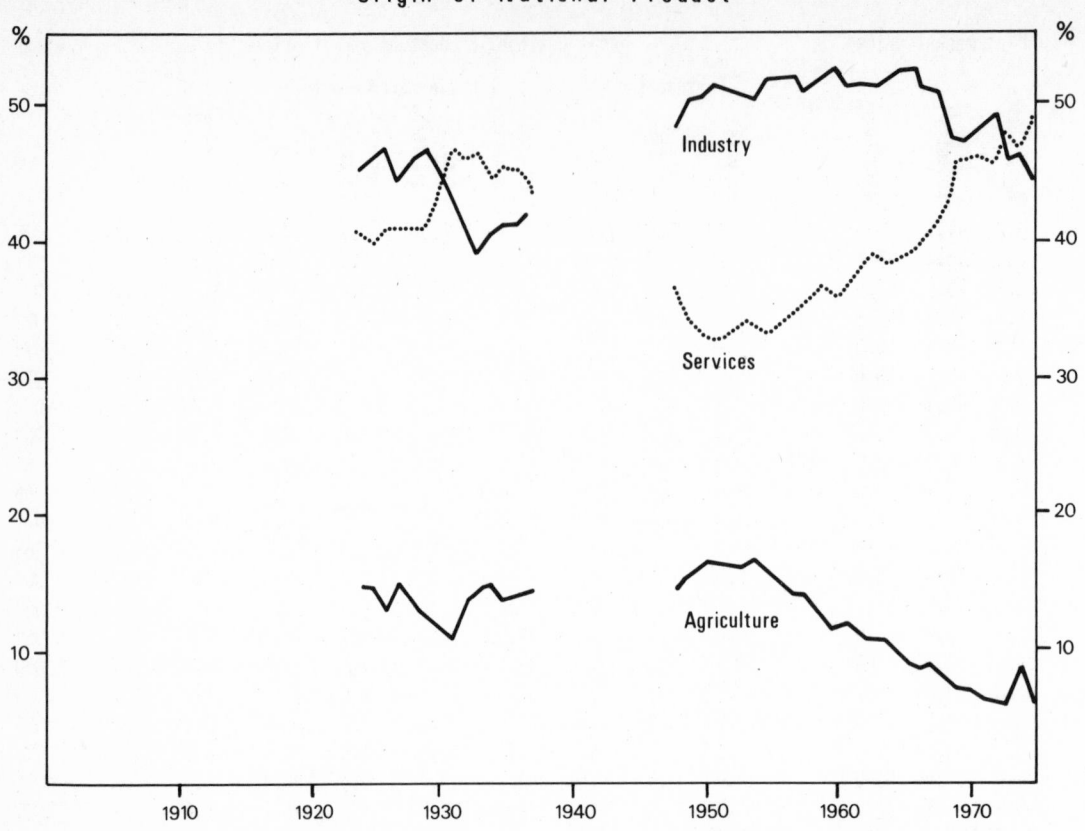

Industry

Services

Agriculture

Use of National Product

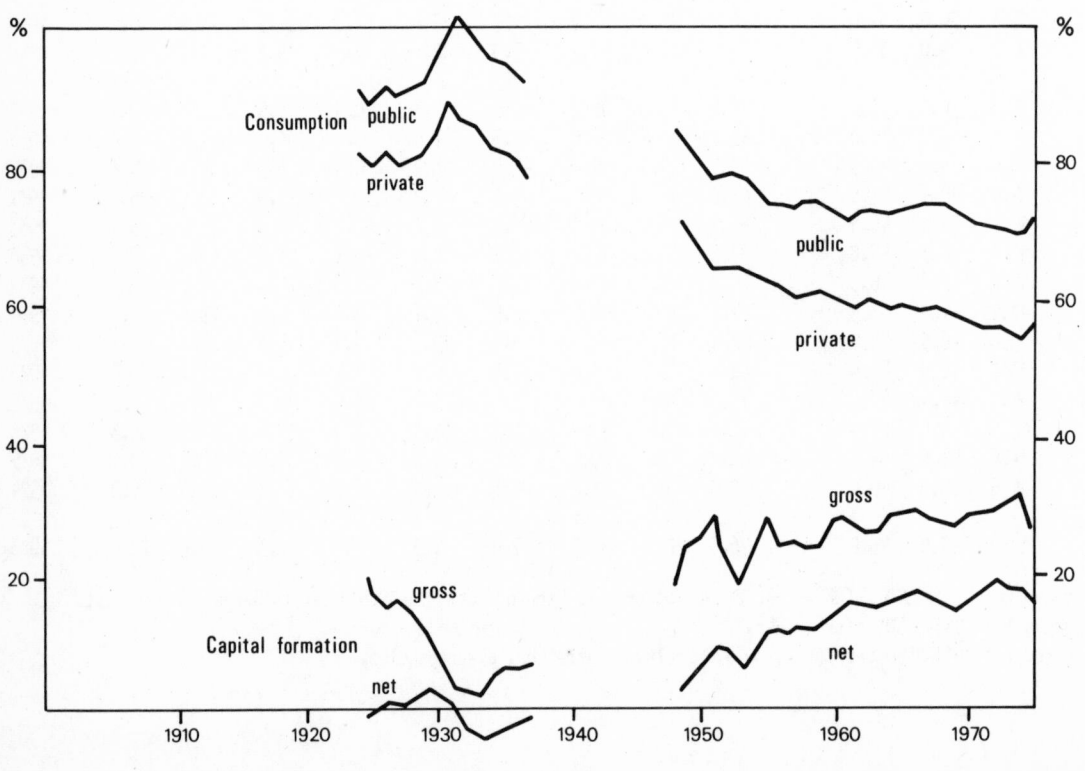

Consumption

public

private

public

private

gross

Capital formation

net

gross

net

Origin and Use of National Product

Year	GDP at market prices [a]			Gross Domestic Product at market prices									Year
				Consumption			Investment				Ex-ports	Im-ports	
	Agriculture	Industry	Services	Private	Public	Total	Net cap. formation	Gross cap. form.	Changes in stocks	Total			
1975	3.3	40.5	56.2	61.4	17.1	78.5	12.7	22.0	-0.5	21.4	46.4	46.3	1975
1974	3.2	43.4	53.4	59.8	15.0	74.9	13.3	22.5	2.3	24.8	53.7	53.3	1974
1973	4.1	42.2	53.8	60.6	14.8	75.4	12.0	21.1	1.5	22.6	47.7	45.7	1973
1972	4.2	42.0	53.9	60.2	14.9	75.1	11.5	21.1	0.6	21.6	43.8	40.5	1972
1971	3.7	42.5	53.8	60.4	14.4	74.8	12.0	21.8	1.4	23.2	43.4	41.4	1971
1970	3.8	44.4	51.8	60.0	13.7	73.7	12.7	22.4	1.6	24.0	43.9	41.6	1970
1969	4.6	43.3	52.0	62.4	13.9	76.3	11.5	20.9	2.0	22.9	41.9	41.1	1969
1968	5.4	41.1	53.5	63.9	13.9	77.8	11.5	21.1	1.0	22.1	38.7	38.6	1968
1967	5.3	41.3	53.4	63.1	13.8	76.8	13.0	22.5	0.5	23.1	36.3	36.2	1967
1966	5.5	41.9	52.7	64.1	13.4	77.4	13.1	22.6	1.0	23.6	36.2	37.2	1966
1965	6.1	41.8	52.1	64.2	13.1	77.3	12.5	22.0	0.5	22.5	36.3	36.2	1965
1964	6.4	42.8	50.7	64.2	12.8	77.0	12.4	22.0	1.6	23.6	35.9	36.6	1964
1963	6.8	41.5	51.6	67.2	13.3	80.5	10.8	20.5	0.2	20.8	34.6	35.8	1963
1962	6.9	41.0	52.2	66.7	12.6	79.3	11.3	20.9	0.1	21.0	34.0	34.3	1962
1961	7.6	40.5	51.9	68.4	12.3	80.6	10.6	20.4	0.1	20.5	33.9	35.0	1961
1960	7.3	40.5	52.2	69.3	12.8	82.0	9.1	19.1	-0.1	19.1	32.9	33.9	1960
1959	7.5	39.4	53.2	70.0	12.7	82.7	7.6	17.6	0.7	18.3	30.8	31.8	1959
1958	7.4	40.2	52.5	69.1	12.2	81.3	7.0	16.8	0.0	16.8	31.9	30.1	1958
1957	7.7	42.4	49.9	69.8	11.4	81.2	7.9	17.8	1.4	19.2	33.7	34.0	1957
1956	7.3	41.6	51.1	68.9	11.5	80.4	8.6	18.5	0.7	19.2	34.8	34.4	1956
1955	7.9	41.0	51.1	70.3	11.6	81.9	7.7	17.2	0.0	17.2	32.1	31.3	1955
1954	8.0	41.1	51.0	71.1	12.5	83.7	7.7	17.2	0.7	17.9	28.3	29.9	1954
1953	8.4	41.6	49.9	71.0	12.9	83.8	6.9	16.3	0.5	16.8	28.0	28.7	1953

a) Figures for 1953–1968 refer to GDP at factor cost.

Belgium

Origin of National Product

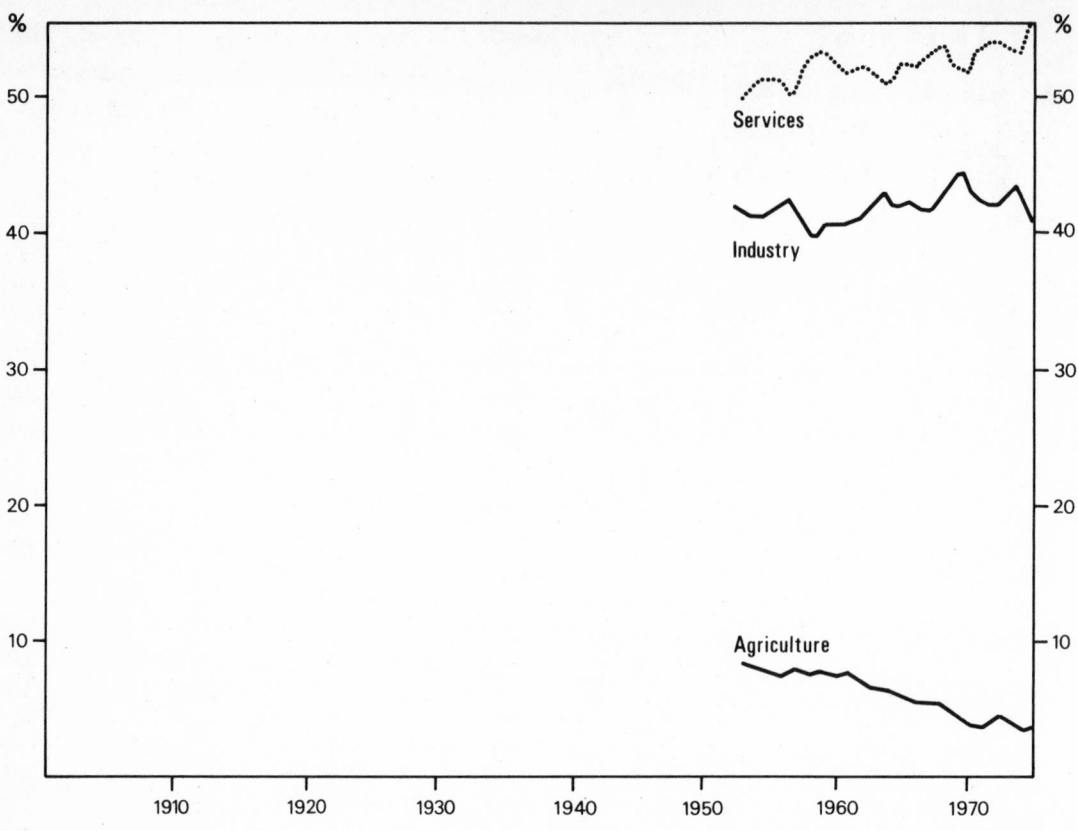

Use of National Product

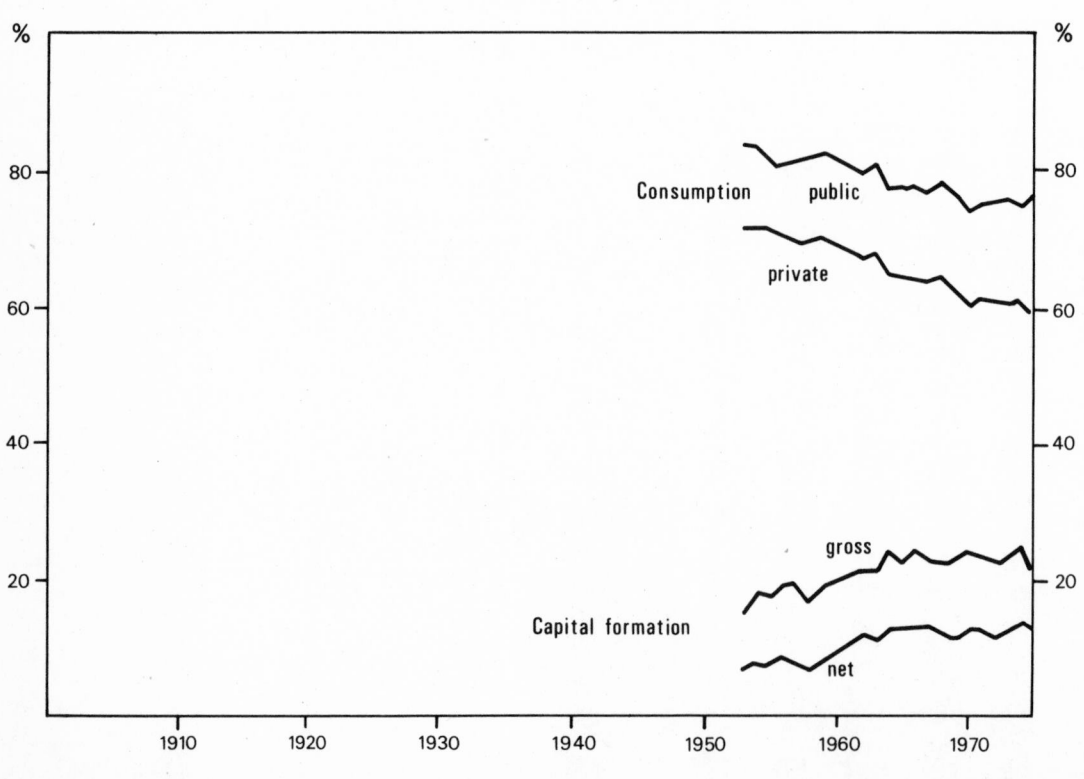

Origin and Use of National Product

| Year | GDP at market prices a) | | | Gross Domestic Product at market prices b) | | | | | | | | | Year |
| | Agriculture c) | Industry | Services | Consumption | | | Investment | | | | Ex-ports | Im-ports | |
				Private	Public	Total	Net cap. formation	Gross cap. form.	Changes in stocks	Total			
1975	7.4	37.1	55.5	57.8	24.6	82.5	9.9	19.8	-1.7	18.1	34.3	34.9	1975
1974	8.3	38.0	53.6	56.4	22.9	79.4	12.7	22.2	1.1	23.3	35.9	38.6	1974
1973	8.3	39.6	52.1	56.4	21.0	77.4	14.6	23.0	1.4	24.4	32.1	33.9	1973
1972	8.0	40.0	52.1	55.9	21.2	77.1	13.7	21.8	0.1	22.0	30.3	29.4	1972
1971	7.7	40.0	52.3	58.3	21.3	79.6	13.4	21.5	0.4	21.9	30.5	32.0	1971
1970	8.0	40.8	51.2	60.1	19.8	79.9	13.7	21.7	1.1	22.8	29.6	32.3	1970
1969	9.1	41.1	49.8	62.2	17.3	79.5	14.0	21.8	0.8	22.6	29.1	31.2	1969
1968	9.1	40.7	50.1	62.6	17.5	80.1	12.8	20.9	0.1	21.1	29.4	30.6	1968
1967	9.3	40.0	50.7	63.3	16.8	80.1	14.1	22.1	-0.4	21.7	28.8	30.6	1967
1966	10.2	40.0	49.8	63.2	15.9	79.0	13.5	21.7	0.6	22.3	30.0	31.3	1966
1965	11.0	40.1	48.9	62.4	15.1	77.5	13.7	21.7	2.1	23.8	30.8	32.1	1965
1964	12.3	39.8	47.9	63.9	14.4	78.3	14.1	22.0	1.5	23.5	31.3	33.2	1964
1963	12.4	39.2	48.4	65.1	14.3	79.5	11.6	19.8	0.2	19.9	31.9	31.3	1963
1962	12.6	39.8	47.6	65.6	14.1	79.7	13.0	20.8	2.5	23.3	30.0	33.1	1962
1961	13.5	39.2	47.3	65.8	13.4	79.2	13.0	20.9	1.4	22.2	31.5	32.9	1961
1960	14.4	39.1	46.5	65.7	12.3	78.0	11.7	19.4	3.6	23.0	33.9	34.9	1960
1959	15.3	38.2	46.5	65.9	12.5	78.3	11.3	18.9	2.3	21.2	34.1	33.6	1959
1958	16.0	36.9	47.1	67.6	12.8	80.4	9.5	17.4	-0.5	16.9	34.8	32.1	1958
1957	17.0	36.4	46.6	67.1	12.5	79.7	9.2	17.0	2.2	19.2	35.2	34.0	1957
1956	18.5	35.6	45.9	69.6	12.6	82.2	8.8	16.4	1.5	17.9	34.3	34.4	1956
1955	18.4	36.1	45.5	70.3	12.6	82.9	8.7	16.1	0.0	16.1	34.0	33.0	1955
1954	18.6	36.8	44.6	70.2	12.5	82.7	10.5	17.5	1.4	18.9	32.0	33.6	1954
1953	20.8	35.8	43.4	68.5	12.0	80.4	10.3	17.1	1.8	18.9	31.3	30.6	1953
1952	21.3	35.0	43.7	70.3	11.7	82.0	10.2	17.1	-0.1	17.1	32.5	31.6	1952
1951	19.9	35.9	44.1	72.8	11.1	83.9	9.9	16.4	0.6	17.0	34.0	34.9	1951
1950	21.2	35.8	43.0	73.2	10.2	83.4	10.2	15.7	4.3	20.0	-3.4		1950
1949	21.3	35.3	43.4	72.9	11.0	83.9	9.3	15.0	2.2	17.2	-1.1		1949
1948	20.9	34.9	44.2	72.8	11.3	84.1	8.1	13.2	4.3	17.5	-1.6		1948
1947	20.7	33.6	45.7	75.7	11.9	87.7	7.4	11.8	2.7	14.6	-2.2		1947
1939	18.6	32.1	49.3	75.2	9.9	85.1	7.1	12.0			2.1		1939
1938	18.5	31.9	49.6	76.1	9.3	85.4	6.4	12.1			2.5		1938
1937	17.4	31.4	51.1	76.5	9.0	85.6	5.9	11.8			2.7		1937
1936	18.0	31.6	50.4	77.8	9.0	86.8	6.1	11.8			1.4		1936
1935	18.0	32.1	49.9	76.1	9.1	85.2	6.6	12.2			2.6		1935
1934	18.2	31.1	50.7	78.1	8.8	86.9	6.8	12.3			0.8		1934
1933	18.5	29.9	51.7	78.0	8.9	87.0	5.6	11.1			1.9		1933
1932	18.2	29.8	52.0	78.2	9.4	87.6	4.4	10.0			2.3		1932
1931	17.7	29.7	52.6	77.6	9.1	86.7	7.8	13.4			-0.1		1931
1930	21.1	27.7	51.3	77.4	8.6	86.0	7.8	13.5			0.5		1930
1929	23.2	25.9	50.9	78.8	8.8	87.7	5.0	10.7			1.7		1929
1928	22.4	25.4	52.2	79.7	9.3	89.0	3.8	9.5			1.5		1928
1927	20.9	25.1	54.0	79.2	10.2	89.5	3.6	9.3			1.2		1927
1926	21.6	25.2	53.2	78.0	11.2	89.2	3.9	9.6			1.2		1926
1925	24.5	23.7	51.9	79.2	9.3	88.5	4.5	10.3			1.1		1925
1924	26.6	23.0	50.4	81.1	7.9	89.0	4.9	10.6			0.4		1924
1923	24.9	22.3	52.8	83.0	9.1	92.1	4.7	10.3			-2.4		1923
1922	23.7	22.6	53.7	80.3	11.2	91.5	4.6	10.5			-1.9		1922
1921	26.1	23.2	50.6	79.6	8.8	88.4	4.7	11.0			0.6		1921
1920	23.6	27.3	49.2										1920
1919	24.7	25.3	50.0										1919

Denmark

Origin and Use of National Product

| Year | GDP at market prices a) | | | Gross Domestic Product at market prices b) | | | | | | | | | Year |
| | | | | Consumption | | | Investment | | | | Ex-ports | Im-ports | |
	Agriculture	Industry	Services	Private	Public	Total	Net cap. formation	Gross cap. form.	Changes in stocks	Total			
1918	31.9	20.5	47.6										1918
1917	32.0	21.4	46.7										1917
1916	31.8	22.6	45.7										1916
1915	30.5	22.3	47.2										1915
1914	31.8	22.7	45.6	74.6	7.4	82.0	5.7	11.2			6.8		1914
1913	29.9	24.0	46.1	82.1	6.3	89.1	6.9	12.5			-1.6		1913
1912	29.1	24.3	46.6	83.2	6.5	89.7	6.4	12.2			-1.9		1912
1911	30.6	23.8	45.6	81.8	6.9	88.7	5.7	11.3			0.0		1911
1910	30.3	24.3	45.4	81.6	7.0	88.6	5.9	11.7			-0.3		1910
1909	29.6	24.2	46.2	82.3	7.7	90.0	6.2	12.3			-2.3		1909
1908	29.8	24.8	45.3	81.6	7.1	88.6	7.2	13.1			-1.8		1908
1907	29.6	25.3	45.1	83.3	6.5	89.7	9.1	15.1			-4.8		1907
1906	30.2	25.0	44.8	82.6	6.6	89.6	9.2	15.3			-4.5		1906
1905	31.5	24.7	43.8	81.5	6.4	87.9	6.4	12.5			-0.3		1905
1904	30.9	25.5	43.6	80.8	6.9	87.8	7.6	13.6			-1.4		1904
1903	32.2	25.4	42.4	79.6	6.6	86.2	8.1	13.8			0.0		1903
1902	30.7	26.2	43.1	80.9	6.8	87.7	8.6	14.2			-1.9		1902
1901	31.5	26.0	42.5	81.9	6.7	88.6	7.2	12.9			-1.5		1901
1900	30.2	26.2	43.6	82.4	6.9	89.3	9.2	14.7			-3.9		1900
1899	28.0	27.0	45.1	80.8	6.8	87.6	10.6	16.2			-3.8		1899
1898	29.9	26.5	43.6	82.0	6.7	88.7	10.9	16.2			-4.9		1898
1897	31.0	25.7	43.3	80.8	6.9	87.7	8.1	13.2			-0.9		1897
1896	33.1	24.5	42.4	83.6	7.1	90.8	6.8	11.7			-2.4		1896
1895	34.7	23.2	42.1	86.1	6.8	92.9	4.2	9.1			-2.0		1895
1894	33.6	23.2	43.3	86.2	7.5	93.7	3.2	7.8			-1.5		1894
1893	35.7	22.9	41.4	86.5	7.7	94.2	3.3	7.9			-2.0		1893
1892	37.8	22.4	39.8	86.1	7.6	93.7	3.3	7.8			-1.5		1892
1891	39.0	22.2	38.8	86.6	7.3	93.9	3.5	8.1			-2.0		1891
1890	37.9	22.2	39.9	85.2	7.8	93.0	3.8	8.5			-1.6		1890
1889	36.0	22.6	41.4	87.6	8.1	95.7	3.8	8.3			-4.0		1889
1888	34.7	22.5	42.8	87.8	8.2	96.0	2.8	7.6			-3.6		1888
1887	37.0	21.8	41.2	85.1	8.2	93.4	2.3	7.2			-0.6		1887
1886	38.2	21.5	40.3	84.6	7.8	92.4	2.0	6.3			1.2		1886
1885	37.4	22.1	40.5	88.4	7.2	95.5	3.2	8.2			-3.7		1885
1884	38.9	21.5	39.7	38.5	6.8	95.3	4.4	9.2			-4.5		1884
1883	41.2	20.7	38.0	88.2	6.3	94.5	4.7	9.3			-3.8		1883
1882	42.2	20.4	37.4	86.3	6.4	92.8	4.0	8.8			-1.5		1882
1881	43.0	20.4	36.6	87.7	6.0	93.8	3.6	8.4			-2.2		1881
1880	44.9	19.4	35.7	85.9	6.1	92.1	2.3	7.1			0.8		1880
1879	42.6	20.3	37.2	86.9	6.8	93.7	1.2	6.5			-0.3		1879
1878	43.0	20.2	36.8	86.8	6.6	93.4	0.8	6.2			0.4		1878
1877	42.0	20.8	37.1	88.4	6.6	95.0	2.6	7.3			-2.2		1877
1876	45.3	19.6	35.1	86.3	6.3	92.5	3.8	8.7			-1.2		1876
1875	44.9	20.3	34.9	85.9	5.9	91.8	5.7	10.1			-1.9		1875
1874	46.8	20.5	32.6	87.0	5.5	92.5	5.8	10.2			-2.6		1874
1873	47.8	20.6	31.6	87.4	5.7	93.1	5.2	9.7			-2.9		1873
1872	48.6	20.4	31.0	85.1	5.6	90.7	3.8	8.7			0.6		1872
1871	49.3	20.4	30.3	85.9	6.1	92.0	3.9	8.3			-0.3		1871
1870	50.1	20.0	29.9	83.6	6.2	89.8	3.5	8.0			2.1		1870
1869	48.5	20.6	30.9	87.5	6.8	94.3	3.5	8.1			-2.4		1869
1868	50.2	19.9	29.9	88.5	6.8	95.3	2.6	7.2			-2.5		1868

Denmark

Origin and Use of National Product

Year	GDP at market prices [a]			Gross Domestic Product at market prices [b]									Year
				Consumption			Investment				Ex-ports	Im-ports	
	Agriculture	Industry	Services	Private	Public	Total	Nat. cap. formation	Gross cap. form.	Changes in stocks	Total			
1867	50.3	20.5	29.2	88.8	6.7	95.5	3.2	7.7			-3.2		1867
1866	48.6	22.1	29.2	85.2	6.2	91.4	4.8	9.3			-0.7		1866
1865	48.7	21.4	29.9	83.2	8.0	91.2	4.8	9.4			-0.5		1865
1864	42.4	24.0	33.7	78.7	12.6	91.3	4.3	8.9			-0.2		1864
1863	44.8	23.4	31.7	82.4	9.3	91.7	5.2	9.7			-1.4		1863
1862	47.4	23.4	29.3	83.2	7.1	90.2	5.6	10.2			-0.4		1862
1861	49.6	22.4	28.0	81.4	7.2	88.5	4.5	9.0			2.5		1861
1860	48.1	23.5	28.4	81.2	6.4	87.6	4.0	8.6			3.8		1860
1859	49.7	22.5	27.8	81.8	6.2	87.9	3.1	7.9			4.2		1859
1858	49.7	23.1	27.3	80.7	6.3	87.1	4.5	9.1			3.9		1858
1857	50.0	22.6	27.4	85.6	5.8	91.5	6.5	11.0			-2.5		1857
1856	50.8	22.2	27.0	82.9	6.0	88.9	6.4	10.9			0.2		1856
1855	55.7	19.8	24.5	82.5	5.6	88.1	5.6	10.2			1.7		1855
1854	54.2	20.7	25.1	79.4	6.2	85.6	6.7	11.2			3.1		1854
1853	56.2	19.5	24.4	82.8	6.0	88.8	5.0	9.5			1.7		1853
1852	52.0	21.1	26.9	81.8	7.3	89.1	5.0	9.7			1.2		1852
1851	49.7	21.9	28.4	84.8	7.6	92.4	6.0	10.5			-2.9		1851
1850	44.8	21.3	34.0	77.2	15.4	92.6	5.1	9.6			-2.2		1850
1849	46.5	21.1	32.3	82.1	13.6	95.7	3.3	7.9			3.6		1849
1848	50.3	20.8	28.8	82.8	9.7	92.6	3.6	8.1			-0.6		1848
1847	51.7	21.5	26.8	85.0	6.9	91.8	4.7	9.1			-0.9		1847
1846	54.5	20.4	25.2	85.3	6.4	91.7	4.2	8.7			-0.3		1846
1845	51.7	20.8	27.5	85.5	7.4	92.9	4.1	8.6			-1.5		1845
1844	51.8	20.3	27.9	81.3	7.6	88.8	3.6	8.0			3.2		1844
1843	51.0	20.5	28.5										1843
1842	50.4	21.6	28.0										1842
1841	51.9	20.9	27.2										1841
1840	53.0	19.9	27.1										1840
1839	53.7	19.2	27.1										1839
1838	52.0	20.4	27.6										1838
1837	51.9	19.9	27.3										1837
1836	52.8	19.9	27.3										1836
1835	52.3	19.3	28.4										1835
1834	52.2	18.5	29.3										1834
1833	52.7	19.1	28.2										1833
1832	55.8	17.6	26.6										1832
1831	56.5	17.5	26.0										1831
1830	55.7	18.0	26.3										1830
1829	53.5	18.9	27.6										1829
1828	54.1	18.6	27.3										1828
1827	55.2	18.0	26.8										1827
1826	52.9	19.8	27.3										1826
1825	51.4	20.6	28.0										1825
1824	50.0	21.2	28.8										1824
1823	49.7	21.0	29.3										1823
1822	48.4	22.2	29.4										1822
1821	51.5	20.7	27.8										1821
1820	54.8	18.6	26.6										1820
1819	58.8	16.7	24.4										1819
1818	62.2	14.3	23.5										1818

a) Figures refer to Gross-GDP (i.e., are inclusive of repair and maintenance) at factor cost.

b) Prior to 1947, GDP at market prices is without changes in stocks.

c) Prior to 1947, agriculture is without fisheries.

Denmark

Origin of National Product

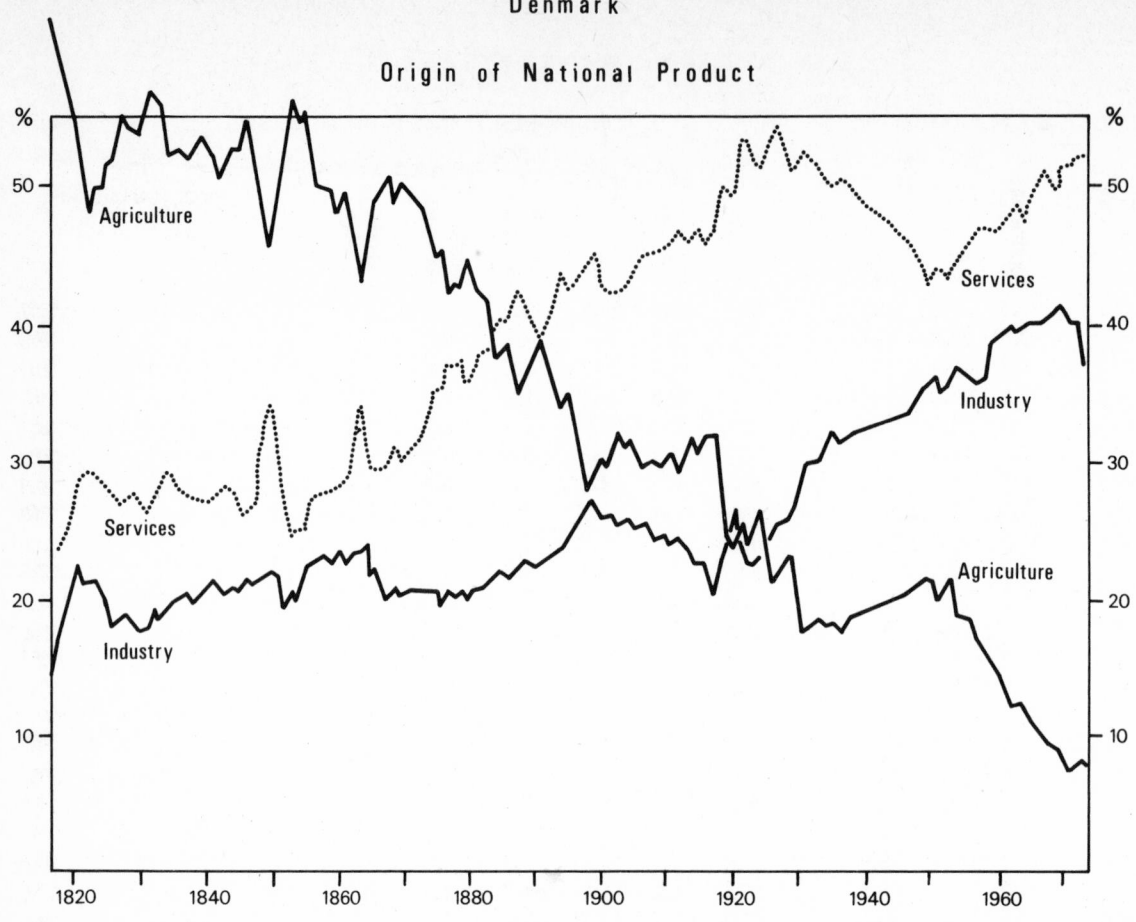

Use of National Product

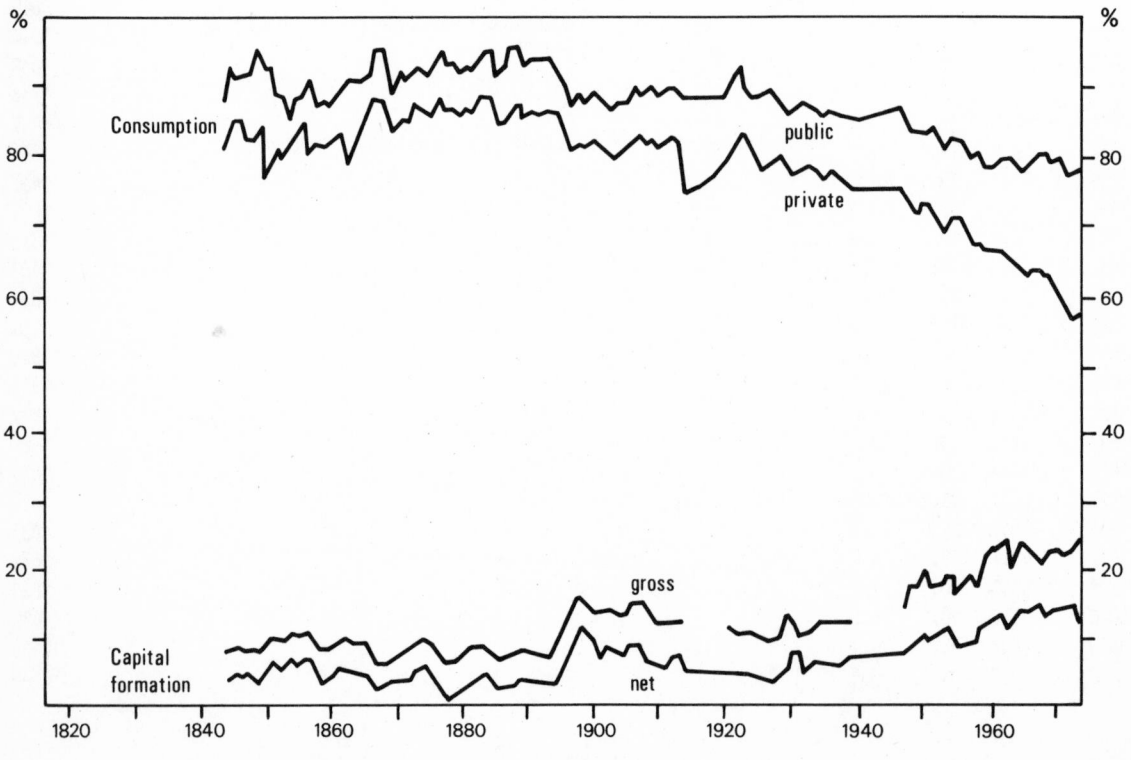

Finland

Origin and Use of National Product

Year	GDP at market prices [a]			Gross Domestic Product at market prices									Year
				Consumption			Investment				Ex-ports	Im-ports	
	Agriculture	Industry	Services	Private	Public	Total	Net cap. formation	Gross cap. form.	Changes in stocks	Total			
1975	12.3	44.2	43.5	50.8	18.7	69.5	21.5	30.8	6.3	31.7	25.4	32.0	1975
1974	12.0	46.2	41.9	48.8	16.9	65.7	18.4	28.4	10.1	38.6	29.6	33.8	1974
1973	12.0	44.3	43.7	51.0	16.7	67.7	18.3	27.8	5.6	33.4	27.3	28.4	1973
1972	12.6	43.3	44.2	52.8	16.9	69.7	18.2	27.5	2.7	30.2	27.6	27.5	1972
1971	13.9	42.0	44.2	52.3	16.7	69.0	17.6	27.2	5.8	33.1	26.1	28.1	1971
1970	13.9	43.2	42.9	52.5	15.9	68.4	15.5	25.8	7.1	33.0	27.4	28.8	1970
1969	14.5	41.8	43.7	53.8	15.9	69.7	13.5	23.5	5.9	29.4	25.9	25.0	1969
1968	15.4	39.2	45.5	54.7	16.7	71.4	13.7	22.8	4.2	27.0	24.3	22.7	1968
1967	15.3	39.1	45.6	57.1	16.1	73.2	15.1	24.2	3.5	27.7	21.1	22.0	1967
1966	16.2	39.0	44.8	57.1	15.2	72.3	16.5	25.7	3.7	29.4	21.0	22.7	1966
1965	17.8	38.6	43.5	58.0	14.6	72.6	16.5	26.0	3.4	29.3	21.3	23.2	1965
1964	18.5	38.5	42.9	58.2	14.2	72.4	14.8	24.4	5.1	29.6	21.2	23.1	1964
1963	18.3	38.9	42.8	58.7	14.2	72.9	15.6	25.7	1.4	27.1	21.7	21.7	1963
1962	18.6	39.6	41.9	58.6	13.4	72.0	17.3	27.4	1.9	29.3	22.6	23.9	1962
1961	20.1	39.7	40.2	57.3	12.5	69.8	17.6	28.0	3.3	31.3	22.7	23.8	1961
1960	19.8	39.7	40.4	58.1	12.6	70.7	17.1	27.3	2.7	30.0	23.5	24.2	1960
1959	19.6	39.2	41.2	59.4	13.2	72.6	15.9	25.5	1.2	26.6	22.4	21.6	1959
1958	20.9	38.0	41.1	59.5	12.8	72.3	15.6	24.8	0.6	25.5	22.6	20.4	1958
1957	20.6	38.7	40.7	61.3	12.5	73.9	15.7	24.3	1.8	26.1	21.5	21.5	1957
1956	21.7	38.8	39.6	61.4	12.3	73.7	18.3	26.0	1.3	27.2	19.7	20.7	1956
1955	23.8	39.3	36.9	59.8	11.5	71.3	18.5	25.5	1.5	27.1	21.7	20.1	1955
1954	23.9	40.1	35.9	61.1	11.1	72.2	19.5	26.3	-0.2	26.1	20.6	18.8	1954
1953	24.8	38.6	36.6	63.8	12.2	76.0	20.2	27.3	-5.0	22.3	19.4	17.7	1953
1952	29.4	35.9	34.7	63.5	11.1	74.5	20.9	26.6	-0.1	26.5	24.1	25.1	1952
1951	26.7	41.1	32.2	59.8	10.2	70.0	17.9	23.0	0.6	23.6	28.9	22.5	1951
1950	26.3	40.2	33.5	63.9	11.6	75.5	17.0	22.	0.8	23.3	20.0	18.8	1950
1949	28.4	40.1	31.5	63.5	10.7	74.2	17.4	22.5	-0.5	22.0	21.7	17.9	1949
1948	33.9	38.3	27.8	64.6	10.0	74.5	16.9	21.7	1.4	23.1	20.2	17.8	1948
1947	37.1	34.9	28.0										
1946	36.8	34.9	28.3										
1945	35.5	34.0	30.5										
1944	29.7	26.3	44.0										
1943	31.6	27.9	40.5										
1942	29.7	26.6	43.7										
1941	29.2	26.8	44.0										
1940	30.0	26.2	43.8										
1939	34.4	28.6	37.0										
1938	35.4	29.8	34.8										
1937	35.0	31.3	33.7										
1936	33.5	30.2	36.3										
1935	33.9	28.5	37.6										
1934	33.8	28.6	37.6										
1933	31.7	27.4	40.9										
1932	31.5	25.8	42.7										
1931	31.1	24.9	44.1										
1930	32.8	25.9	41.3										
1929	33.0	28.4	38.5										
1928	34.2	29.8	36.0										
1927	36.3	28.3	35.4										
1926	36.6	27.7	35.6										

a) Figures for 1926-1947 refer to NDP at factor cost. Figures for
1948-1975 refer to GDP at factor cost.

Finland

Origin of National Product

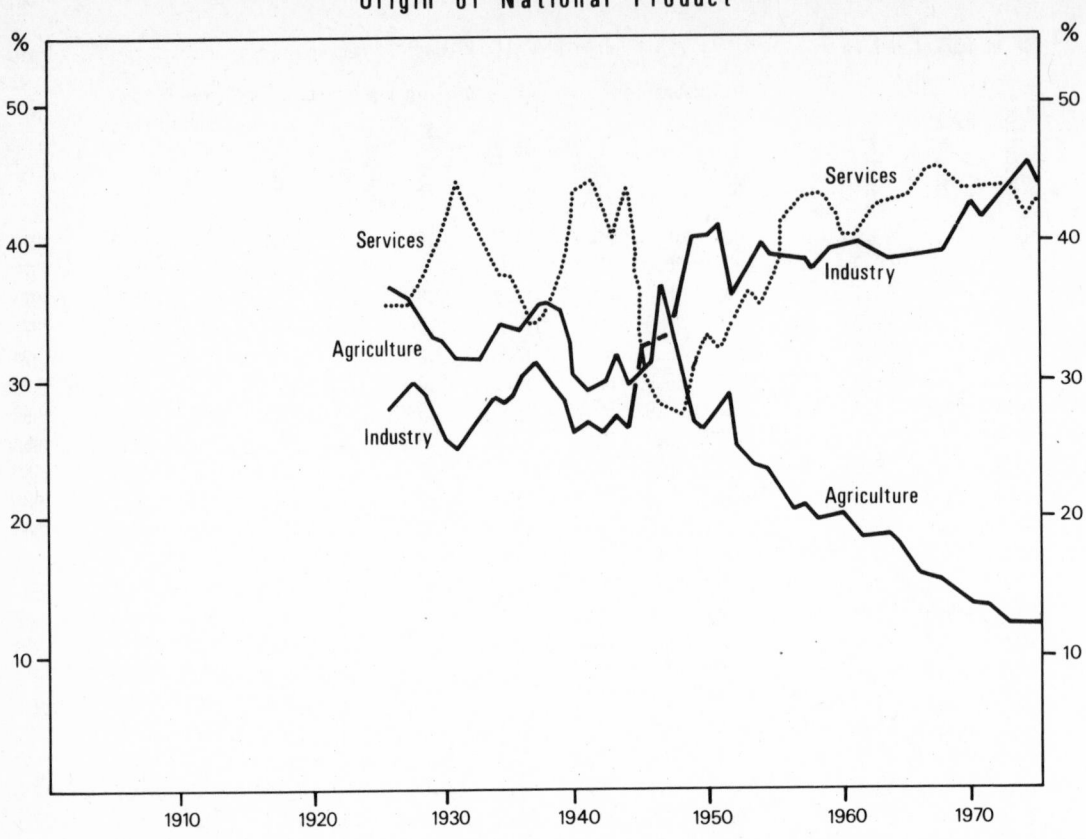

Use of National Product

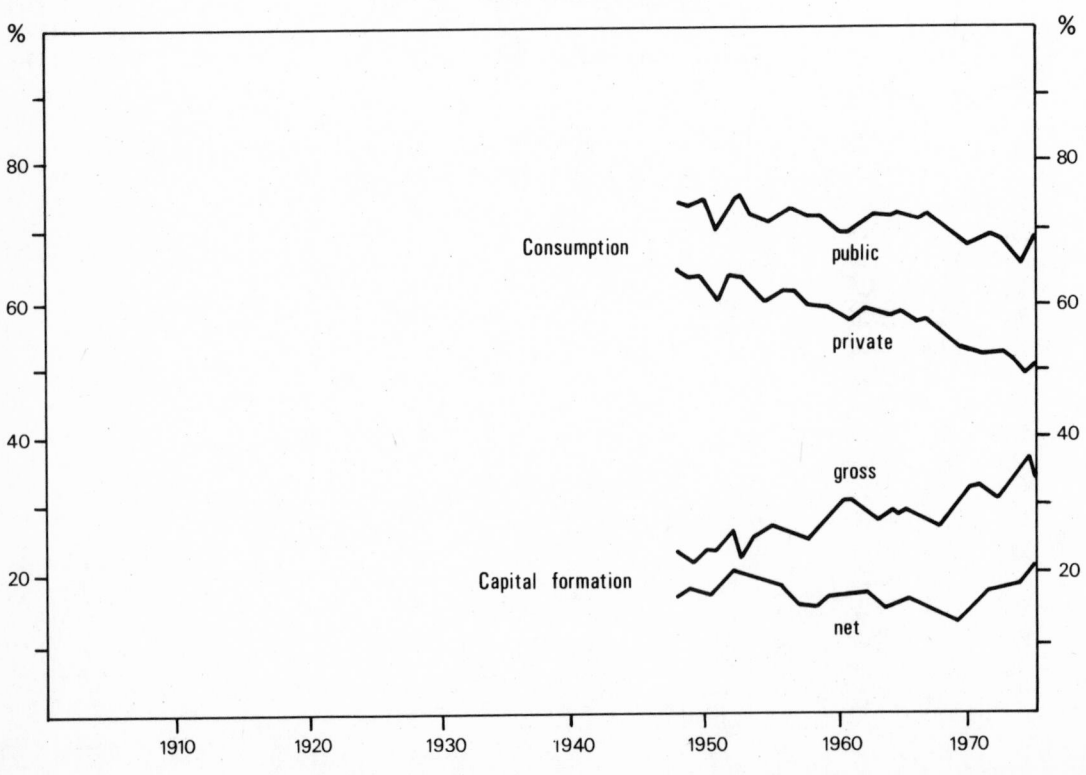

France

Origin and Use of National Product

Year	GDP at market prices [a)			Gross Domestic Product at market prices									Year
				Consumption			Investment				Ex-ports	Im-ports	
	Agriculture	Industry	Services	Private	Public	Total	Net cap. formation	Gross cap. form.	Changes in stocks	Total			
1975	5.6	41.2	53.2	62.1	14.6	76.7	12.1	23.3	-0.9	22.4	19.8	19.0	1975
1974	6.3	41.7	52.0	61.1	13.7	74.8	13.7	24.5	2.2	26.7	21.6	23.1	1974
1973	7.4	41.7	50.9	60.0	13.2	73.2	13.7	23.8	2.4	26.2	18.2	17.6	1973
1972	7.1	42.2	50.7	60.4	13.2	73.5	13.5	23.7	1.9	25.5	17.2	16.3	1972
1971	6.7	42.4	50.8	60.5	13.4	74.0	13.4	23.6	1.5	25.1	17.1	16.1	1971
1970	7.1	42.8	50.1	60.0	13.4	73.4	13.1	23.4	2.7	26.1	16.3	15.8	1970
1969				61.2	13.3	74.5	13.4	23.4	2.6	26.1	14.6	15.2	1969
1968	6.6	47.8	45.6	61.4	13.5	74.9	13.3	23.2	1.8	25.1	13.7	13.8	1968
1967	7.0	48.1	44.9	61.2	13.0	74.1	13.8	23.8	1.8	25.6	13.7	13.4	1967
1966	7.1	48.5	44.5	61.0	13.0	74.0	13.8	23.7	2.0	25.7	13.8	13.6	1966
1965	7.4	48.2	44.4	61.1	13.1	74.2	13.5	23.3	1.6	24.9	13.8	12.9	1965
1964	7.5	48.3	44.2	61.6	13.3	74.9	13.2	22.9	2.4	25.3	13.2	13.4	1964
1963	8.4	47.6	44.0	62.6	13.4	76.0	12.4	22.1	1.5	23.6	13.1	12.8	1963
1962	8.9	47.4	43.3	62.1	13.3	75.4	11.7	21.4	2.3	23.6	13.4	12.4	1962
1961	8.5	48.2	43.3	62.1	13.1	75.2	11.4	21.2	1.7	22.9	14.5	12.6	1961
1960	9.5	48.0	42.5	61.9	13.0	74.9	10.3	20.1	3.0	23.0	15.0	12.9	1960
1959	9.2	48.1	42.7	62.4	13.5	75.9	10.0	20.3	2.3	22.6	13.8	12.3	1959
1958	10.7	47.5	41.8	63.1	13.0	76.1	10.6	20.5	3.9	24.4	12.3	12.8	1958
1957	10.1	47.9	42.0	64.0	13.8	77.9	10.3	20.5	3.2	23.8	12.3	13.9	1957
1956	10.2	47.6	42.2	63.8	13.9	77.7	9.1	19.5	4.5	23.9	12.3	14.0	1956
1955	11.4	46.5	42.1	63.9	12.8	76.7	8.6	19.1	3.0	22.1	13.7	12.6	1955
1954	11.9	46.6	41.5	63.6	13.7	77.2	6.8	17.9	3.7	21.6	13.9	12.7	1954
1953	12.0	47.0	40.9	64.0	14.9	78.8	6.0	17.6	3.3	20.8	13.4	13.1	1953
1952	12.6	48.0	39.4	63.7	14.6	78.3	6.4	18.3	4.2	22.5	13.9	14.7	1952

a) Figures for 1952–1968 refer to GDP at factor cost.
   For 1969–1975 market prices are net of value added tax.

France

Origin of National Product

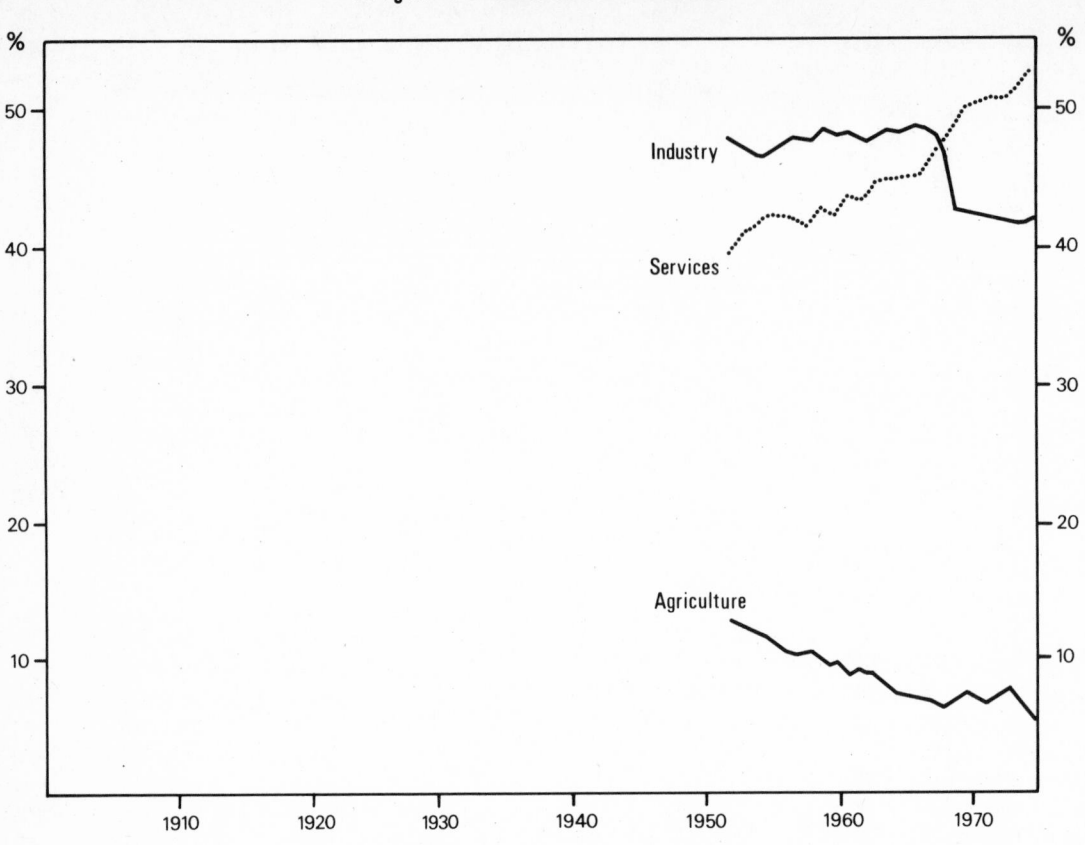

Use of National Product

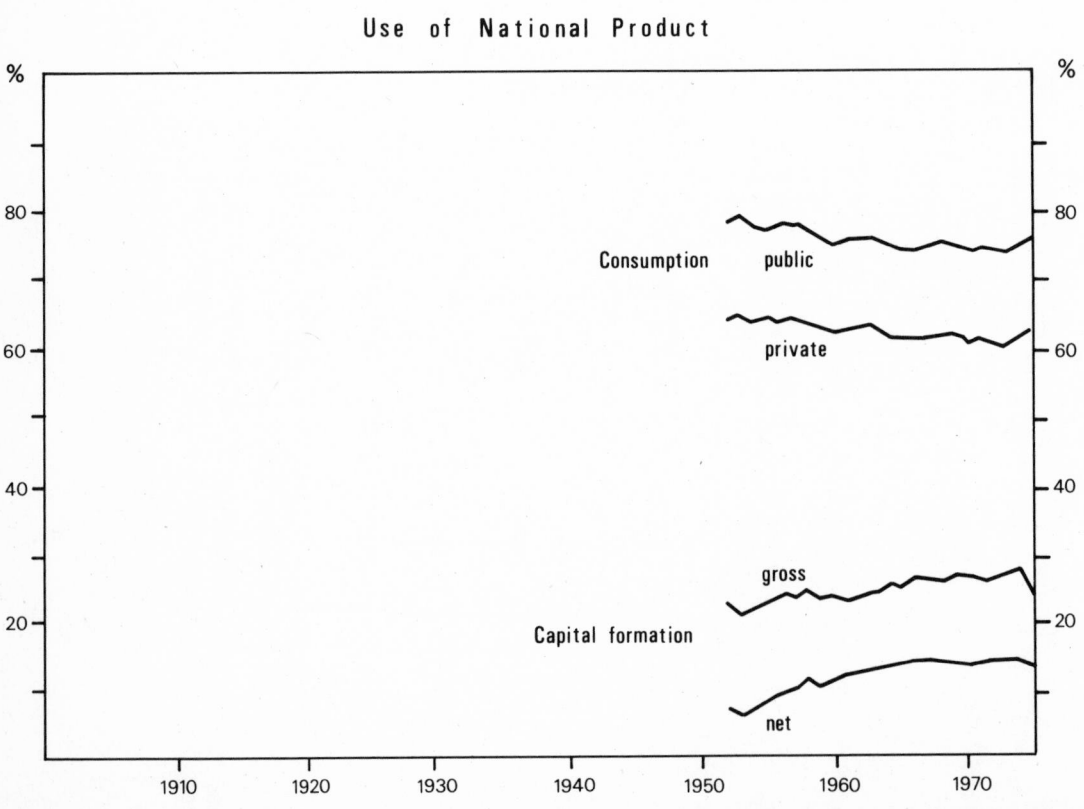

414

Origin and Use of National Product

Year	GNP at market prices			Gross National Product at market prices [a]									Year
				Consumption			Investment				Ex-ports	Im-ports	
	Agriculture	Industry	Services	Private	Public	Total	Net cap. formation	Gross cap. form.	Changes in stocks	Total			
1975	3.0	48.8	48.2	55.8	21.0	76.8	9.5	20.8	−0.3	20.5	24.8	22.1	1975
1974	2.8	51.0	46.2	53.4	19.7	73.1	11.1	21.9	0.6	22.5	26.3	21.9	1974
1973	3.2	51.5	45.3	53.5	18.1	71.7	14.1	24.5	0.8	25.3	21.9	18.9	1973
1972	3.3	51.9	44.8	54.2	17.4	71.6	15.5	25.9	0.3	26.3	20.7	18.6	1972
1971	3.3	52.9	43.8	54.0	17.1	71.1	16.0	26.4	0.5	26.9	20.8	18.8	1971
1970	3.5	54.0	42.5	54.2	15.9	70.1	15.5	25.6	2.3	27.9	21.1	19.0	1970
1969	4.0	53.4	42.6	55.4	15.8	71.2	13.6	23.4	2.6	26.0	21.7	18.8	1969
1968	4.3	52.9	42.8	56.2	15.6	71.9	12.5	22.5	2.0	24.5	21.3	17.7	1968
1967	4.3	49.8	45.9	57.2	16.3	73.5	12.9	23.1	−0.2	22.9	20.5	16.8	1967
1966	4.2	51.6	44.2	56.3	15.6	71.9	15.6	25.4	1.0	26.4	19.2	17.5	1966
1965	4.4	52.6	42.9	56.1	15.3	71.4	16.7	26.1	2.2	28.3	18.1	17.8	1965
1964	4.9	52.8	42.3	55.6	14.9	70.4	17.3	26.6	1.4	28.0	18.1	16.5	1964
1963	5.1	52.7	42.2	56.7	15.6	72.3	16.4	25.5	0.6	26.1	17.9	16.3	1963
1962	5.1	53.5	41.4	56.7	14.7	71.5	17.1	25.7	1.5	27.2	17.4	16.1	1962
1961	5.5	53.5	41.0	56.8	13.9	70.6	17.0	25.2	1.9	27.1	18.1	15.8	1961
1960	6.0	53.3	40.7	56.8	13.5	70.2	16.5	24.3	2.9	27.2	19.0	16.5	1960
1959	6.7	52.5	40.7	57.9	13.4	71.3	15.1	23.5	1.5	25.0	22.8	19.1	1959
1958	7.1	52.1	40.8	59.1	13.3	72.4	14.0	22.3	1.5	23.9	22.1	18.4	1958
1957	7.2	52.3	40.5	58.7	12.7	71.4	14.2	22.3	2.2	24.5	23.3	19.2	1957
1956	7.5	52.9	39.6	58.7	12.8	71.5	15.7	23.6	1.5	25.1	21.3	17.9	1956
1955	8.0	53.0	39.0	58.3	13.3	71.6	15.7	23.4	2.5	26.0	19.6	17.1	1955
1954	8.7	52.2	39.1	59.5	14.0	73.5	13.5	21.4	1.6	23.1	18.9	15.5	1954
1953	9.1	51.8	39.1	60.1	14.5	74.6	12.5	20.6	1.3	21.9	16.8	13.2	1953
1952 [b]	9.8	50.8	39.5	59.3	15.2	74.4	11.2	19.6	3.7	23.3	15.8	13.6	1952 [b]
1951				57.4	14.1	71.5	18.5			26.7	1.8		1951
1950				63.1	14.0	77.1	15.8			24.0	−1.2		1950
1938				55.2	24.4	79.6	13.3			20.7	−0.3		1938
1937				58.0	19.7	77.7	14.3			22.0	0.3		1937
1936				60.3	20.6	80.9	10.5			18.6	0.5		1936
1935				64.6	17.8	82.4	9.6			17.7	−0.1		1935
1934				70.3	15.5	85.8	6.7			15.0	−0.8		1934
1933				73.0	14.1	87.2	3.1			12.4	0.4		1933
1932				79.4	13.3	92.7	−3.6			6.6	0.7		1932
1931				78.8	13.1	91.9	−4.9			5.0	3.1		1931
1930				74.2	12.3	86.5	3.3			12.1	1.4		1930
1929				73.9	11.5	85.4	6.7			14.8	−0.2		1929
1928				70.9	10.9	81.8	12.1			19.5	−1.3		1928
1927				71.4	10.2	81.6	14.1			21.5	−3.1		1927
1926				72.6	11.5	84.1	6.0			14.3	1.6		1926
1925				72.4	10.9	83.2	11.8			19.5	−2.7		1925
1913				66.3	8.9	75.2	14.2			23.2	1.6		1913
1912				66.5	8.0	74.5	15.0			24.7	0.8		1912
1911				67.5	8.0	75.5	13.7			23.3	1.2		1911
1910				69.0	8.1	77.1	12.1			21.4	1.5		1910
1909				70.5	8.3	78.8	12.6			20.3	0.9		1909
1908				70.5	8.1	78.7	12.2			20.1	1.2		1908

Germany

Origin and Use of National Product

Year	GNP at market prices			Gross National Product at market prices[a]									Year
	Agriculture	Industry	Services	Consumption			Investment				Exports	Imports	
				Private	Public	Total	Net cap. formation	Gross cap. form.	Changes in stocks	Total			
1907				65.9	7.8	73.8	15.9			25.9	0.3		1907
1906				64.6	7.5	72.1	14.4			26.8	1.1		1906
1905				66.2	7.5	73.7	14.1			23.3	3.1		1905
1904				67.6	7.4	74.9	14.1			23.5	1.6		1904
1903				69.2	7.3	76.6	13.1			22.3	1.2		1903
1902				72.5	7.8	80.2	10.1			18.3	1.4		1902
1901				71.3	7.9	79.2	11.3			19.6	1.2		1901
1900				67.8	7.3	75.0	14.2			23.8	1.1		1900
1899				67.9	6.8	74.8	15.5			24.2	1.1		1899
1898				67.4	6.7	74.1	15.9			23.5	2.4		1898
1897				70.5	7.1	77.6	13.5			20.2	2.2		1897
1896				71.9	7.1	79.1	12.5			18.9	2.0		1896
1895				75.2	7.3	82.5	10.6			16.3	1.3		1895
1894				74.6	7.5	82.0	9.8			15.5	2.5		1894
1893				74.3	7.5	81.8	11.4			16.8	1.4		1893
1892				74.4	7.2	81.6	12.4			17.7	0.7		1892
1891				76.9	7.4	83.2	8.7			14.4	1.4		1891
1890				71.2	7.7	78.9	13.3			19.4	1.7		1890
1889				71.6	7.3	78.9	12.4			18.6	2.5		1889
1888				72.0	7.8	79.8	10.9			17.1	3.1		1888
1887				73.7	6.7	80.4	10.8			17.5	2.1		1887
1886				74.7	6.4	81.0	9.7			16.6	2.4		1886
1885				74.6	6.3	80.8	9.7			16.6	2.5		1885
1884				74.7	6.3	81.0	9.9			16.5	2.5		1884
1883				76.0	6.3	82.3	9.3			16.3	1.4		1883
1882				76.1	6.5	82.6	8.2			15.0	2.4		1882
1881				76.1	6.6	82.7	8.5			15.4	1.9		1881
1880				77.7	6.7	84.4	7.3			14.0	1.6		1880
1879				77.8	6.8	84.5	6.8			13.5	1.9		1879
1878				75.7	6.2	82.0	9.5			15.8	2.2		1878
1877				75.9	6.5	82.5	9.8			16.8	1.3		1877
1876				73.9	6.1	80.0	12.5			18.7	1.3		1876
1875				73.8	6.6	80.4	12.8			18.7	0.8		1875
1874				71.3	6.2	77.5	16.3			21.9	0.6		1874
1873				73.6	5.7	79.3	12.4			18.2	2.5		1873
1872				72.2	6.1	78.2	14.7			20.8	0.9		1872

a) Net National Product prior to 1952.
b) Figures are from different sources which are not strictly comparable.

Germany

Origin of National Product

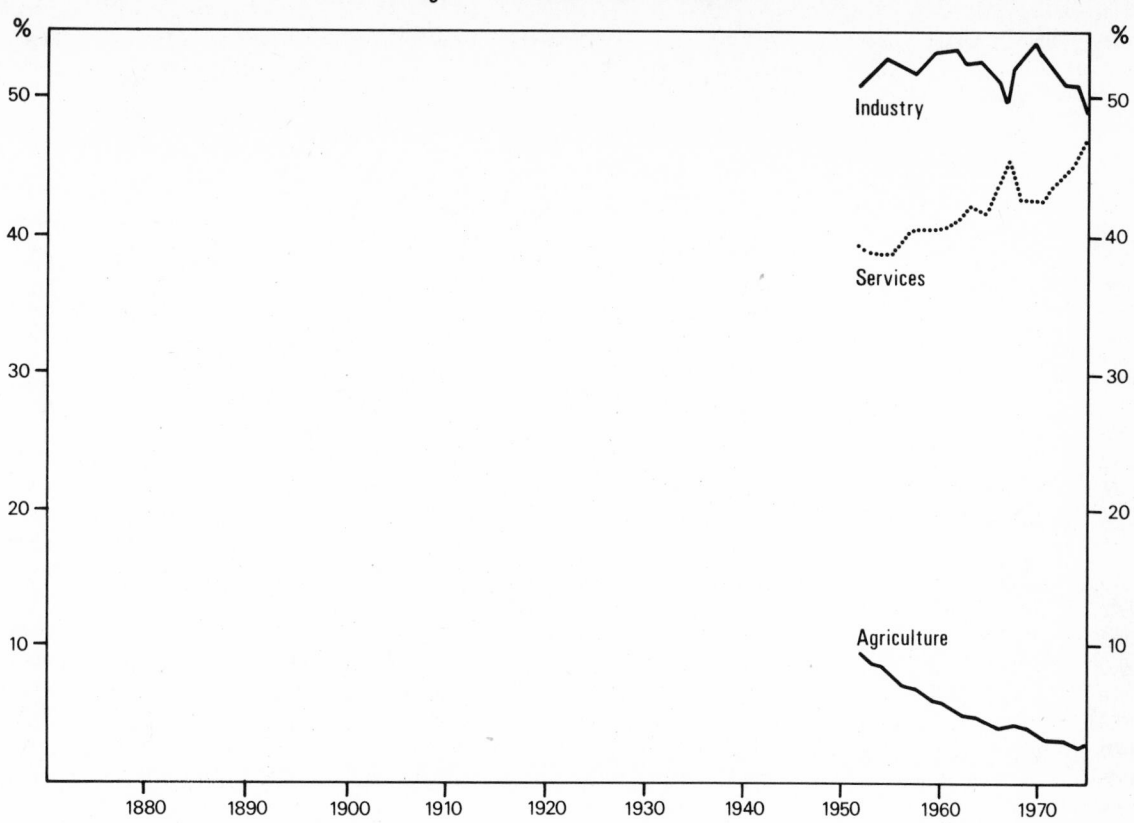

Use of National Product

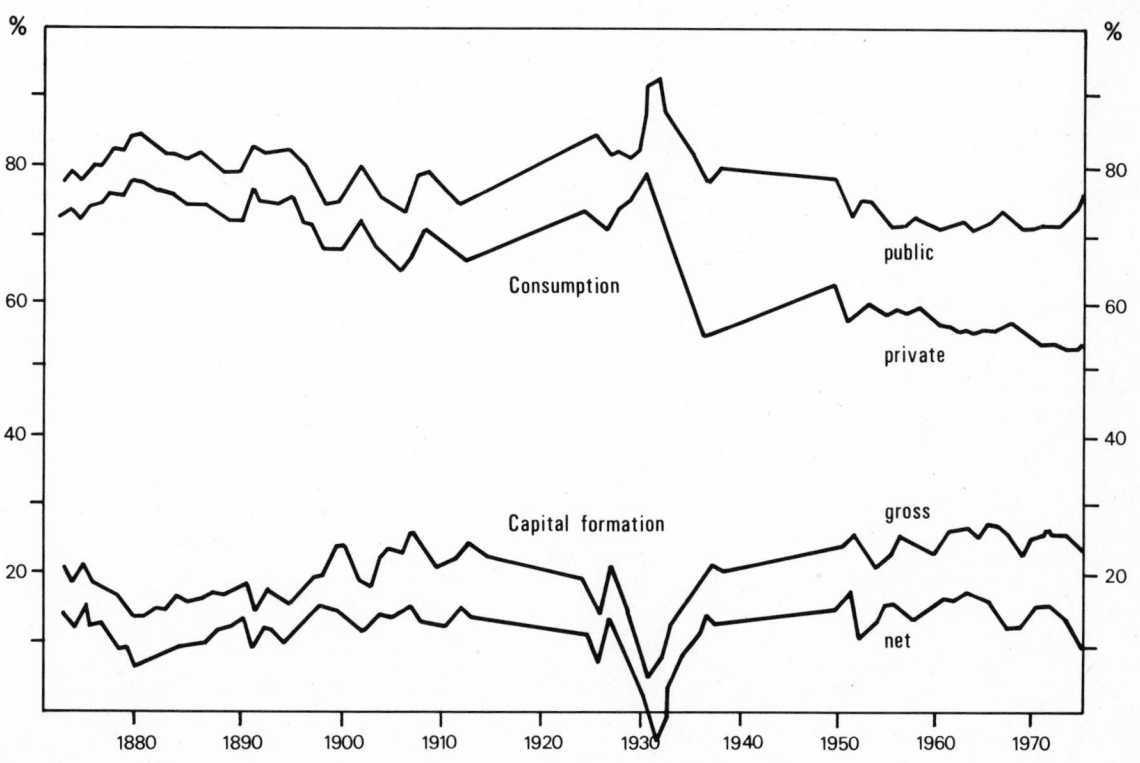

Ireland

Origin and Use of National Product

Year	GDP at market prices [a]			Gross Domestic Product at market prices								
				Consumption			Investment				Exports	Imports
	Agriculture	Industry	Services	Private	Public	Total	Net cap. formation	Gross ca. form.	Changes in stocks	Total		
1975				63.9	19.5	83.4	15.4	23.4	-1.2	22.2	45.0	50.7
1974				67.3	18.1	85.4	17.5	26.1	3.7	29.8	43.6	58.8
1973				63.7	16.1	79.8	17.4	25.3	1.8	27.1	38.2	45.0
1972				65.2	15.6	80.8	15.3	23.4	1.1	24.5	34.8	40.2
1971				67.7	15.4	83.1	15.5	23.8	0.4	24.1	36.0	43.2
1970				68.8	14.8	83.6	14.5	22.6	1.7	24.4	36.8	44.8
1969				69.8	13.5	83.4	14.8	23.2	2.4	25.6	37.1	46.1
1968				71.1	13.3	84.4	12.8	20.8	1.1	21.9	38.7	45.0
1967	19.5	33.5	47.0	70.2	13.3	83.5	12.1	19.9	-0.4	19.5	37.7	40.7
1966	19.6	33.1	47.3	71.9	13.6	85.5	12.0	19.7	0.8	20.5	37.0	42.9
1965	21.1	32.5	46.3	71.7	13.6	85.4	13.8	21.3	2.3	23.6	34.7	43.7
1964	22.1	31.6	46.3	72.6	13.3	86.0	13.2	20.4	1.2	21.6	33.3	40.8
1963	21.5	32.6	45.9	74.1	12.7	86.8	12.0	19.4	0.9	20.4	33.4	40.5
1962	23.2	31.8	45.0	74.7	12.5	87.2	10.8	17.8	1.6	19.4	32.1	38.1
1961	24.3	30.7	44.9	75.1	12.5	87.5	9.6	16.2	1.4	17.6	34.4	39.6
1960	25.1	29.7	45.1	76.6	12.4	89.1	8.1	14.3	2.0	16.3	31.7	37.1
1959	26.3	28.9	44.8	76.7	12.1	88.8	7.6	13.8	4.0	17.8	29.7	36.2
1958	26.0	29.0	45.0	80.8	12.4	93.2	8.1	14.1	-1.4	12.7	30.4	36.2
1957	29.1	27.8	43.2	78.4	12.3	90.7	8.8	14.6	-1.2	13.4	31.0	35.1
1956				79.4	12.9	92.3	11.7	17.3	-1.5	15.8	28.0	36.1
1955				80.4	12.4	92.8	12.8	17.6	1.9	19.5	29.2	41.4
1954				78.2	12.6	90.8	12.6	17.3	-1.1	16.2	31.0	38.0
1953				76.0	12.4	89.4	12.0	16.4	1.4	17.8	31.4	38.6
1952				78.3	12.5	90.8	13.8	18.1	-0.9	17.2	32.6	40.5

a) Figures refer to GDP at factor cost.

Ireland

Origin of National Product

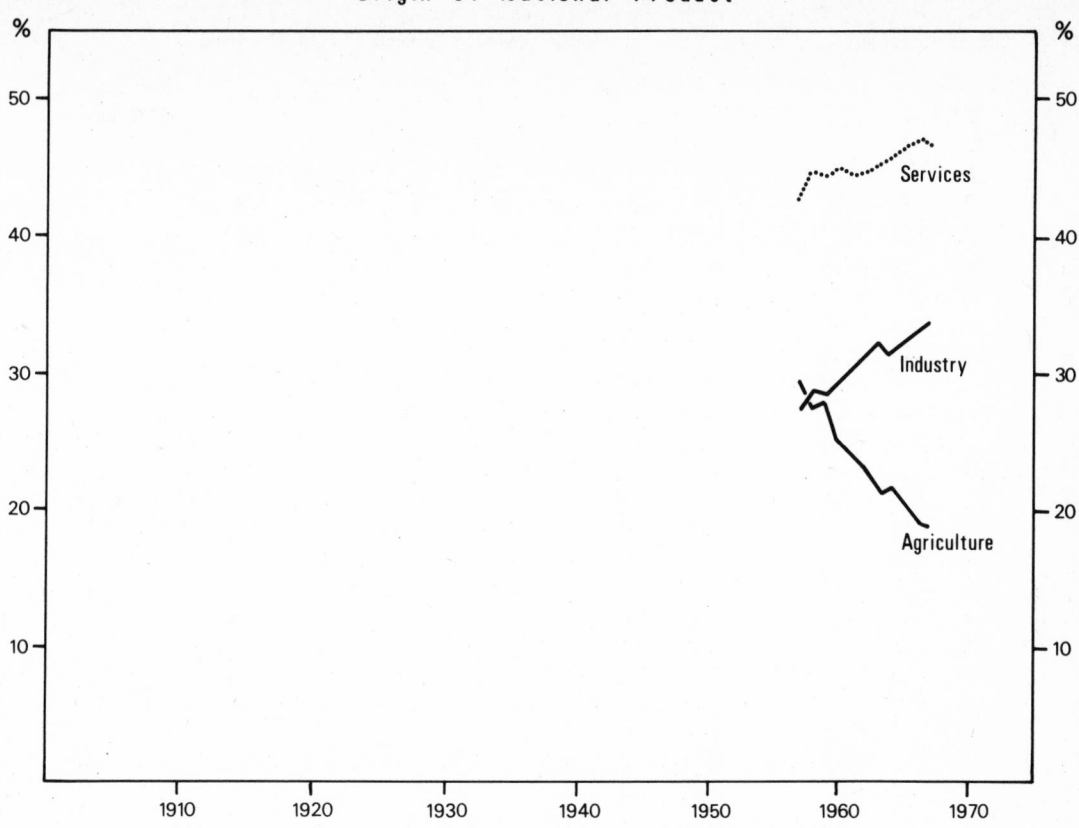

Use of National Product

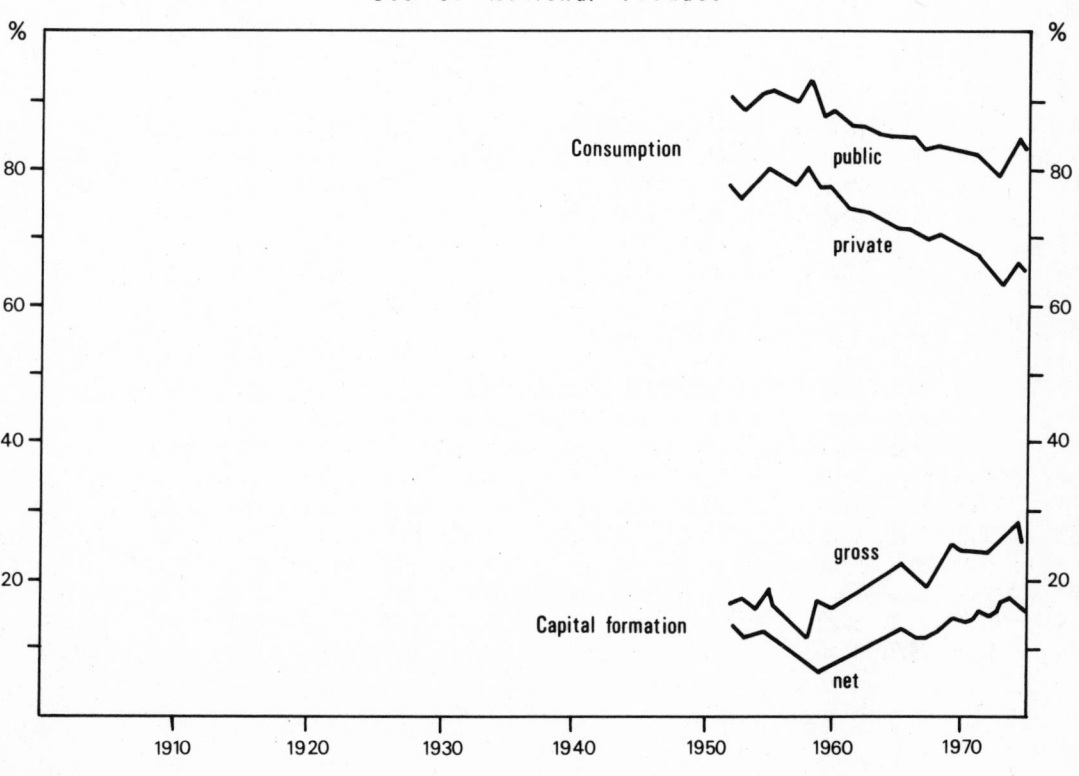

Origin and Use of National Product

Year	GDP at market prices a)			Gross Domestic Product at market prices b)									Year
	Agriculture	Industry	Services	Private	Public	Total	Net cap. formation	Gross cap. form.	Changes in stocks	Total	Exports	Imports	
1975	8.7	43.0	48.3	66.1	13.9	80.0	10.6	20.8	-0.8	20.0	25.0	25.0	1975
1974	8.3	44.4	47.3	64.7	13.7	78.3	12.9	22.6	4.0	26.6	24.5	29.4	1974
1973	8.7	42.8	48.5	63.9	14.0	77.9	11.9	20.8	3.6	24.4	20.4	22.7	1973
1972	8.0	41.6	50.4	64.1	14.6	78.6	11.1	19.7	0.6	20.4	20.5	19.5	1972
1971	8.6	42.1	49.3	63.7	14.1	77.8	11.7	20.3	0.7	21.0	19.8	18.6	1971
1970	9.0	43.1	47.9	63.7	12.7	76.3	12.7	21.3	1.8	23.1	19.3	18.7	1970
1969	11.1	39.2	49.6	63.0	13.3	76.4	12.6	20.9	0.9	21.8	19.3	17.4	1969
1968	11.1	38.6	50.3	63.6	13.6	77.2	12.0	20.2	0.0	20.2	18.5	15.9	1968
1967	12.6	38.0	49.4	64.4	13.6	77.9	10.9	19.2	1.5	20.7	17.5	16.1	1967
1966	12.7	37.5	49.8	64.2	14.2	78.3	10.0	18.5	0.9	19.4	17.7	15.5	1966
1965	13.3	37.5	49.2	63.1	14.5	77.6	10.4	19.0	0.7	19.6	17.2	14.4	1965
1964	13.4	38.4	48.1	63.6	13.7	77.3	13.3	21.9	0.5	22.4	15.4	15.1	1964
1963	13.9	38.9	47.3	64.2	13.3	77.5	15.3	23.6	1.3	24.9	14.6	17.0	1963
1962	15.0	38.5	46.6	63.0	12.4	75.4	14.8	23.2	1.7	25.0	15.2	15.7	1962
1961	15.4	38.3	46.4	62.9	12.0	75.0	14.3	22.9	2.0	24.9	15.4	15.3	1961
1960	14.8	37.9	47.3	64.2	12.2	76.3	13.7	22.3	1.6	23.9	15.1	15.3	1960
1959	16.8	36.6	46.6	64.9	12.1	76.9	12.4	20.9	1.0	21.9	12.9	11.8	1959
1958	18.5	35.9	45.6	66.1	12.0	78.0	12.1	20.6	0.8	21.5	12.5	12.0	1958
1957	17.9	36.3	45.8	66.8	11.7	78.5	13.0	21.7	0.9	22.5	13.1	14.1	1957
1956	19.2	35.8	45.1	67.7	11.9	79.6	12.1	20.6	1.1	21.7	11.6	13.0	1956
1955	20.2	36.1	43.8	67.2	11.8	79.0	12.0	20.6	1.5	22.1	10.9	12.1	1955
1954	20.7	36.2	43.2	69.0	12.1	81.1	11.3	20.1	0.0	20.1	10.7	11.9	1954
1953	22.4	35.3	42.2	70.8	11.6	82.4	10.4	19.4	0.6	20.0	10.4	12.8	1953
1952	21.5	36.0	42.5	72.0	12.2	84.3	9.5	19.1	0.0	19.1	9.9	13.3	1952
1951	26.5	42.6	30.8	70.7	10.1	80.8	9.3	18.6	2.2	20.8	12.8	14.3	1951
1950	29.4	38.8	31.9	72.1	9.6	81.7	9.0	17.7	1.4	19.1	11.1	12.0	1950
1949	30.0	37.9	32.2	73.8	10.0	83.8	8.9	17.5	0.9	18.4	10.4	12.5	1949
1948	33.9	36.6	29.5	72.7	11.9	84.6	10.3	18.7	-0.5	18.2	10.0	12.9	1948
1947	37.2	36.2	26.7	72.8	11.0	83.8	10.6	18.9	7.1	26.0	6.3	16.1	1947
1946	43.6	31.5	25.0	69.2	15.3	84.6	11.1	17.9	2.1	20.0	4.0	8.5	1946
1945	52.9	20.5	26.7	89.7	17.4	107.0	3.5	8.7	-5.6	3.1	0.9	11.0	1945
1944	55.6	17.8	26.7	84.4	19.4	103.7	2.0	6.0	-4.9	1.1	2.4	7.3	1944
1943	42.8	20.4	36.8	72.2	24.0	96.3	3.2	8.9	-4.6	4.3	5.0	5.6	1943
1942	38.2	22.2	39.7	71.0	20.4	91.4	4.1	11.0	-2.4	8.5	4.7	4.6	1942
1941	31.6	27.9	40.5	68.5	18.3	86.8	6.3	14.6	-2.0	12.7	5.4	4.9	1941
1940	26.8	31.1	42.1	68.5	17.6	86.1	7.7	16.8	-1.6	15.2	5.4	6.8	1940
1939	26.7	30.8	42.5	64.4	16.7	81.1	7.4	16.5	2.6	19.1	6.4	6.6	1939
1938	27.1	30.8	42.1	67.2	15.9	83.1	6.9	16.0	1.5	17.4	7.4	7.9	1938
1937	27.2	30.7	42.2	64.6	17.3	81.8	8.2	17.1	2.7	19.7	8.4	9.9	1937
1936	24.4	29.7	46.0	64.7	18.8	83.4	9.4	18.6	-1.9	16.7	5.5	5.6	1936
1935	27.6	28.9	43.5	67.4	14.8	82.2	8.1	17.2	2.1	19.3	6.0	7.5	1935
1934	25.9	29.4	44.7	72.4	14.2	86.5	6.4	15.7	-1.3	14.4	7.6	8.5	1934
1933	26.3	29.3	44.4	73.0	14.5	87.5	5.2	14.4	-0.9	13.6	8.7	9.8	1933
1932	30.7	26.7	42.6	72.4	13.2	85.6	4.6	13.4	1.0	14.4	8.9	8.8	1932
1931	28.9	28.5	42.6	73.0	12.5	85.5	6.9	15.9	-1.9	14.0	12.2	11.7	1931
1930	29.4	30.5	40.1	76.2	10.4	86.6	8.8	17.7	-2.7	14.9	13.2	14.8	1930
1929	34.7	29.8	35.5	74.0	9.0	83.1	8.7	17.2	1.9	19.1	14.3	16.5	1929
1928	35.6	29.9	34.5	73.6	8.9	82.5	8.4	16.7	3.6	20.3	14.2	16.9	1928

Italy[c]

Origin and Use of National Product

Year	GDP at market prices [a]			Gross Domestic Product at market prices [b]									Year
				Consumption			Investment				Ex-ports	Im-ports	
	Agriculture	Industry	Services	Private	Public	Total	Net cap. formation	Gross cap. form.	Changes in stocks	Total			
1927	34.4	30.3	35.6	76.8	9.3	86.1	9.0	17.5	-2.5	15.0	14.7	15.8	1927
1926	38.0	31.5	30.5	74.7	8.4	83.1	10.6	19.2	-1.0	18.2	16.1	17.4	1926
1925	36.8	33.1	30.0	72.7	7.9	80.5	10.4	19.0	1.8	20.8	17.2	18.6	1925
1924	34.9	33.0	32.1	71.7	9.9	81.6	9.5	18.0	1.3	19.3	17.3	18.1	1924
1923	39.5	29.2	31.3	74.2	10.7	84.9	6.7	14.7	2.5	17.2	14.5	16.5	1923
1922	40.6	27.6	31.8	74.4	15.3	89.7	5.6	13.4	0.0	13.4	12.9	16.0	1922
1921	43.8	23.9	32.3	75.6	20.5	96.1	3.8	11.7	-1.9	9.8	12.6	18.4	1921
1920	46.4	27.5	26.0	79.6	17.5	97.1	5.4	13.0	1.2	14.3	16.4	27.8	1920
1919	41.3	25.7	33.1	70.8	32.0	102.8	3.1	11.0	-3.9	7.1	12.4	22.3	1919
1918	39.5	25.2	35.2	70.1	42.6	112.7	-2.1	6.5	-3.6	2.9	6.8	22.4	1918
1917	36.6	26.0	37.4	70.1	44.3	114.3	-0.9	7.6	-4.6	3.0	8.8	26.1	1917
1916	35.9	25.2	38.9	68.0	41.3	109.3	-1.5	6.5	-5.0	1.4	11.1	21.9	1916
1915	35.2	24.3	40.5	66.7	32.7	99.4	1.4	9.3	-4.2	5.0	13.2	17.7	1915
1914	39.3	22.9	37.9	73.1	14.3	87.5	6.7	13.6	-2.1	11.5	16.3	15.3	1914
1913	43.0	23.4	33.6	72.9	9.4	82.3	7.2	14.2	3.5	17.7	18.8	18.8	1913
1912	42.0	24.3	33.6	74.4	9.6	84.0	8.0	15.0	2.2	17.2	18.6	19.8	1912
1911	43.4	23.4	33.2	73.5	9.3	82.8	8.1	14.9	2.6	17.6	18.4	18.8	1911
1910	40.3	24.4	35.3	76.8	9.1	85.9	9.6	16.7	-2.3	14.4	19.7	20.0	1910
1909	43.2	23.5	33.4	73.8	7.7	81.5	9.6	17.0	3.1	20.1	17.4	18.9	1909
1908	41.2	24.9	33.9	76.2	7.8	84.0	10.2	17.7	-0.6	17.1	18.1	19.2	1908
1907	45.3	24.0	30.7	72.4	7.0	79.4	8.6	15.7	4.7	20.4	18.5	18.3	1907
1906	44.2	22.8	33.0	76.4	7.7	83.9	7.6	14.2	-0.9	13.3	21.1	18.3	1906
1905	44.9	21.2	33.9	75.1	8.1	83.2	6.0	12.5	0.0	12.5	20.3	16.1	1905
1904	46.6	19.8	33.6	76.3	8.3	84.5	4.3	10.7	2.1	12.8	18.2	15.5	1904
1903	47.7	19.8	32.5	76.8	8.0	84.8	3.8	10.0	2.7	12.8	17.4	15.0	1903
1902	44.0	21.2	34.8	76.5	8.6	85.1	3.7	10.3	1.7	11.9	18.6	15.7	1902
1901	48.8	19.3	32.0	73.4	8.1	81.4	3.8	10.1	6.1	16.2	17.1	14.7	1901
1900	48.8	19.2	32.0	77.3	8.2	85.5	4.0	10.1	3.3	13.4	15.8	14.7	1900
1899	48.2	19.3	32.5	78.9	8.5	87.4	3.6	9.6	-0.1	9.5	17.3	14.2	1899
1898	50.5	17.2	23.3	79.3	8.4	87.7	2.4	8.3	2.2	10.5	15.0	13.3	1898
1897	44.9	19.0	36.1	83.3	9.5	92.8	2.9	8.8	-4.0	4.9	15.4	13.1	1897
1896	46.9	18.5	34.6	81.1	9.5	90.5	2.8	8.8	-0.9	7.9	14.5	12.9	1896
1895	47.0	18.6	34.4	83.2	9.4	92.6	3.2	9.0	-2.8	6.1	14.1	12.8	1895
1894	46.6	18.4	34.9	81.8	10.1	91.9	3.3	9.2	-2.7	6.5	14.2	12.5	1894
1893	48.3	18.2	33.6	79.9	9.7	89.5	3.1	8.9	1.4	10.4	13.4	13.3	1893
1892	47.5	18.4	34.1	82.2	9.7	91.9	3.1	9.0	-1.1	7.8	13.7	13.5	1892
1891	52.4	16.9	30.7	78.9	8.8	87.7	2.7	8.2	4.1	12.4	11.7	11.7	1891
1890	49.1	18.9	32.1	82.3	9.5	91.8	3.6	9.4	0.6	10.0	11.9	13.7	1890
1889	45.5	20.7	33.8	86.3	10.5	96.8	5.5	11.2	-6.2	5.0	13.3	15.2	1889
1888	46.4	19.9	33.7	78.1	10.4	88.5	6.3	12.1	0.7	12.8	13.0	14.3	1888
1887	47.1	20.7	32.1	80.8	9.5	90.3	6.7	12.5	1.4	13.9	13.8	18.0	1887
1886	51.1	19.9	29.0	77.8	8.5	86.3	6.1	11.7	4.7	16.3	12.4	14.9	1886
1885	49.8	20.6	29.6	80.4	8.8	89.2	6.0	11.6	2.4	14.0	12.1	15.3	1885
1884	48.4	19.8	31.8	79.9	9.2	89.1	5.9	11.6	0.1	11.7	14.1	14.9	1884
1883	49.7	19.5	30.8	78.9	8.8	87.7	5.5	11.1	0.7	11.7	14.9	14.3	1883
1882	52.3	18.9	28.8	77.7	8.1	85.8	5.1	10.6	3.1	13.7	13.6	13.0	1882
1881	48.9	20.1	31.0	85.1	8.3	93.4	5.6	11.1	-5.3	5.8	14.7	13.9	1881
1880	55.3	16.7	28.0	79.0	7.4	86.4	4.6	10.1	2.8	12.9	12.7	12.0	1880

Italy [c]

Origin and Use of National Product

Year	GDP at market prices [a]			Gross Domestic Product at market prices [b]									Year
				Consumption			Investment				Exports	Imports	
	Agriculture	Industry	Services	Private	Public	Total	Net cap. formation	Gross cap. form.	Changes in stocks	Total			
1879	53.2	17.7	29.1	82.3	8.3	90.7	4.5	10.0	-0.3	9.7	12.9	13.3	1879
1878	53.1	18.8	28.2	82.8	8.2	91.0	3.9	9.4	-1.3	8.2	12.1	11.2	1878
1877	53.6	19.4	27.1	85.2	8.0	93.2	3.2	8.6	-1.2	7.4	10.6	11.3	1877
1876	51.8	19.4	28.9	85.4	8.1	93.5	3.1	8.7	-2.7	6.9	14.6	14.1	1876
1875	52.4	19.7	28.0	82.4	8.0	90.4	3.0	8.9	0.9	9.8	12.6	12.9	1875
1874	56.3	17.8	25.9	85.6	7.2	92.7	1.7	7.2	1.7	8.8	10.7	12.3	1874
1873	57.6	18.0	24.4	82.0	7.1	89.1	2.1	7.1	4.1	11.2	11.5	11.8	1873
1872	55.7	17.9	26.4	83.8	7.8	91.6	2.2	7.4	0.6	8.0	13.1	12.7	1872
1871	55.0	17.8	27.2	81.8	8.3	90.0	2.1	7.4	1.1	8.5	13.4	11.9	1871
1870	54.6	18.8	26.5	83.2	9.1	92.3	1.9	7.2	1.6	8.8	10.5	11.5	1870
1869	56.2	19.0	24.7	81.6	8.5	90.1	2.7	7.6	3.5	11.2	10.8	12.0	1869
1868	56.6	17.5	25.8	82.1	8.3	90.3	2.8	7.6	3.3	10.9	10.0	11.2	1868
1867	52.6	19.3	28.1	84.3	8.9	93.1	3.2	8.2	0.5	8.7	10.4	12.3	1867
1866	52.2	19.0	28.8	79.8	12.7	92.5	3.0	8.0	2.3	10.3	8.4	11.3	1866
1865	53.8	19.3	26.9	83.2	9.7	92.9	3.3	8.4	3.4	11.8	8.6	13.3	1865
1864	53.9	18.8	27.4	84.0	10.2	94.2	3.3	8.4	2.4	10.9	8.8	13.8	1864
1863	54.3	18.8	27.0	84.7	10.2	94.9	3.4	8.4	-0.1	8.3	9.7	12.9	1863
1862	56.5	17.9	25.6	83.4	9.6	93.0	3.0	7.8	2.0	9.8	8.0	10.9	1862
1861	54.9	19.3	25.8	87.9	9.1	97.0	3.2	8.0	-1.0	7.0	7.1	11.1	1861

a) Figures for 1861–1969 refer to GDP at factor cost.
b) Figures for 1861–1951 refer to GNP.
c) Refers to present-day boundaries.

Italy

Origin of National Product

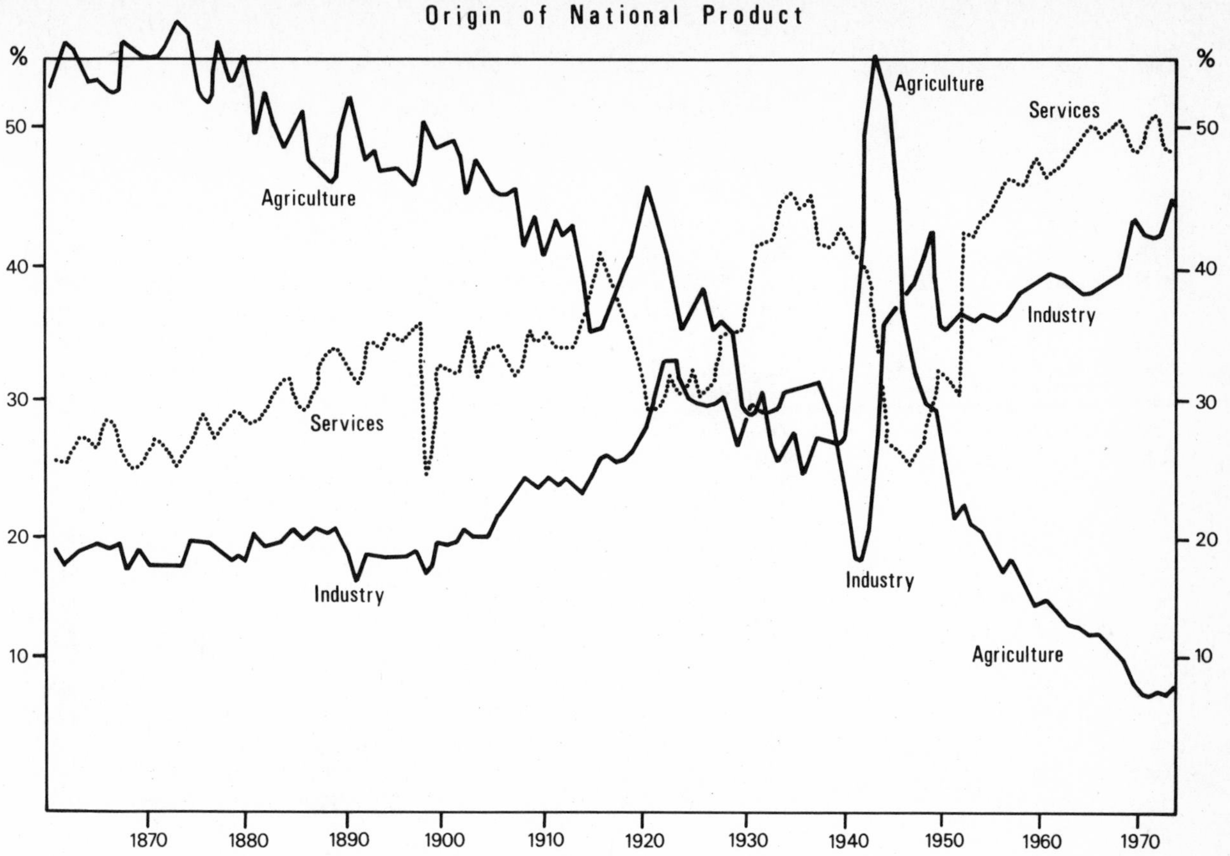

Use of National Product

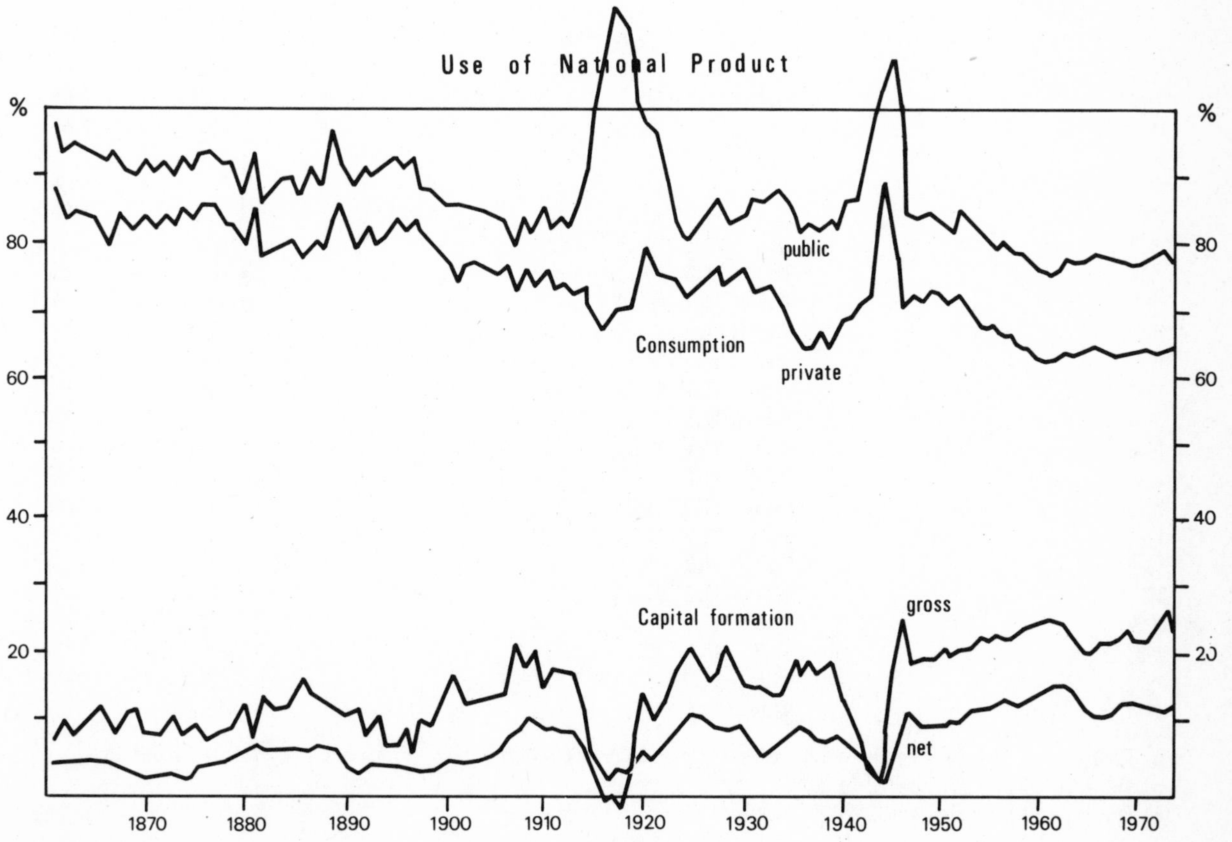

423

Origin and Use of National Product

Year	GDP at market prices [a]			Gross Domestic Product at market prices [b]									Year
				Consumption			Investment				Ex-ports	Im-ports	
	Agriculture	Industry	Services	Private	Public	Total	Net cap. formation [c]	Gross cap. form.	Changes in stocks	Total			
1975				57.8	18.4	72.6	11.5	21.0	-0.7	20.3	52.4	48.9	1975
1974	4.7	41.2	52.9	55.4	17.0	72.5	12.8	21.8	2.9	24.7	56.5	53.6	1974
1973	5.9	41.2	52.9	55.5	16.3	71.8	14.4	23.0	1.8	24.8	49.6	46.3	1973
1972	5.9	41.6	52.5	56.0	16.7	72.7	14.9	23.7	0.7	24.4	47.3	44.4	1972
1971	5.9	41.6	52.3	56.6	16.7	73.2	17.0	25.8	1.4	27.2	47.7	48.0	1971
1970	6.3	42.1	51.6	57.2	16.3	73.6	17.2	25.7	2.5	28.2	47.2	49.0	1970
1969	7.0	42.6	50.4	57.4	16.0	73.3	16.0	24.5	2.4	26.9	45.1	45.3	1969
1968	7.0	42.2	50.8	56.8	15.9	72.6	18.1	26.8	0.6	27.4	43.4	43.5	1968
1967	7.2	41.9	50.9	57.6	16.2	73.8	17.4	26.2	0.9	27.1	42.9	43.9	1967
1966	7.4	42.3	50.3	58.2	15.9	74.0	17.2	26.1	1.3	27.4	44.2	45.7	1966
1965	8.3	41.8	49.9	58.2	15.5	73.7	16.2	25.0	1.9	27.0	45.4	46.1	1965
1964	8.8	41.5	49.7	58.2	15.5	73.7	16.4	25.4	3.0	28.4	46.1	48.3	1964
1963	8.8	41.2	49.9	60.6	15.4	75.9	14.1	23.7	1.1	24.8	47.6	48.3	1963
1962	9.1	41.7	49.2	59.2	14.5	73.7	14.8	24.4	1.5	25.9	47.5	47.1	1962
1961	9.8	42.5	47.7	58.5	14.0	72.5	15.2	24.7	2.7	27.4	48.2	48.1	1961
1960	10.5	42.6	46.9	57.3	13.4	70.8	14.7	24.0	3.3	27.3	50.5	48.6	1960
1959	9.9	42.4	47.7	59.0	13.6	72.6	13.6	23.4	0.7	24.1	49.6	46.3	1959
1958	11.2	41.3	47.5	59.6	14.5	74.1	12.7	22.6	0.3	22.8	48.3	45.3	1958
1957	11.0	41.5	47.5	59.0	15.0	74.0	16.1	25.6	2.6	28.2	48.5	50.6	1957
1956	10.7	41.4	47.9	60.8	15.1	75.9	15.8	25.0	2.2	27.2	47.8	50.9	1956
1955	11.4	41.2	47.4	59.8	14.5	74.3	13.5	22.7	2.2	24.9	47.9	47.0	1955
1954	12.2	41.7	46.1	61.4	14.2	75.6	12.0	21.3	3.8	25.1	47.3	47.9	1954
1953	12.4	41.6	46.0	61.8	13.9	75.7	11.1	21.2	-0.8	20.4	48.3	44.4	1953
1952	14.7	38.7	46.6	62.7	13.6	76.3	8.1	18.9	-1.4	17.5	50.4	44.1	1952
1951	13.7	39.5	46.7	65.0	12.9	77.8	14.4			24.6	-2.4		1951
1950	14.2	39.7	46.1	68.4	12.2	80.6	16.8			26.7	-7.3		1950
1949				69.3	12.2	81.4	12.3			22.5	-3.9		1949
1948				71.0	13.6	84.5	15.5			26.3	-10.8		1948
1939							0.1						1939
1938				88.1	14.0	102.1	1.2				-3.3		1938
1937				87.0	12.3	99.3	4.5				-3.8		1937
1936				91.1	13.2	104.3	-1.2				-3.1		1936
1935				92.4	13.7	106.1	-2.6				-3.5		1935
1934				93.3	14.1	107.5	-2.3				-5.1		1934
1933				96.8	14.3	111.1	-2.6				-8.6		1933
1932				97.6	15.4	113.0	-5.7				-7.3		1932
1931				96.3	15.5	111.9	-3.8				-8.0		1931
1930				91.6	13.4	105.0	3.4				-8.4		1930
1929				86.8	12.2	99.0	9.2				-8.2		1929
1928				88.3	11.3	99.6	7.6				-7.2		1928
1927				89.5	11.8	101.3	5.5				-6.8		1927
1926				89.3	11.4	100.6	7.4				-8.1		1926
1925				90.4	11.2	101.6	6.1				-7.7		1925
1924				91.8	11.5	103.3	6.0				-9.2		1924
1923				94.2	12.4	106.6	2.9				-9.5		1923
1922				96.6	13.1	109.6	2.1				-11.8		1922
1921				92.4	13.6	106.0	6.3				-12.3		1921

a) Figures for 1950–1968 refer to GDP at factor cost. For 1969–1975 market prices are net of value added tax.
b) Prior to 1948 figures refer to NDP.
c) Prior to 1948 public investment not included here or in NDP.

Netherlands

Origin of National Product

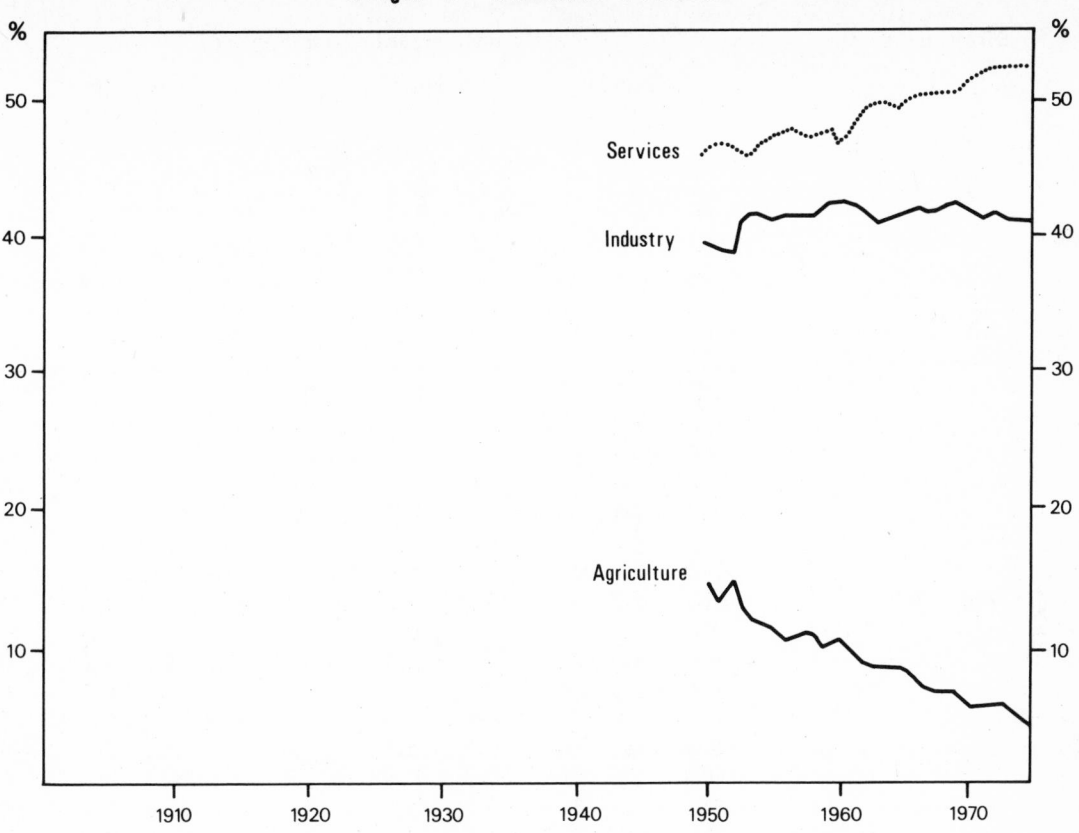

Use of National Product

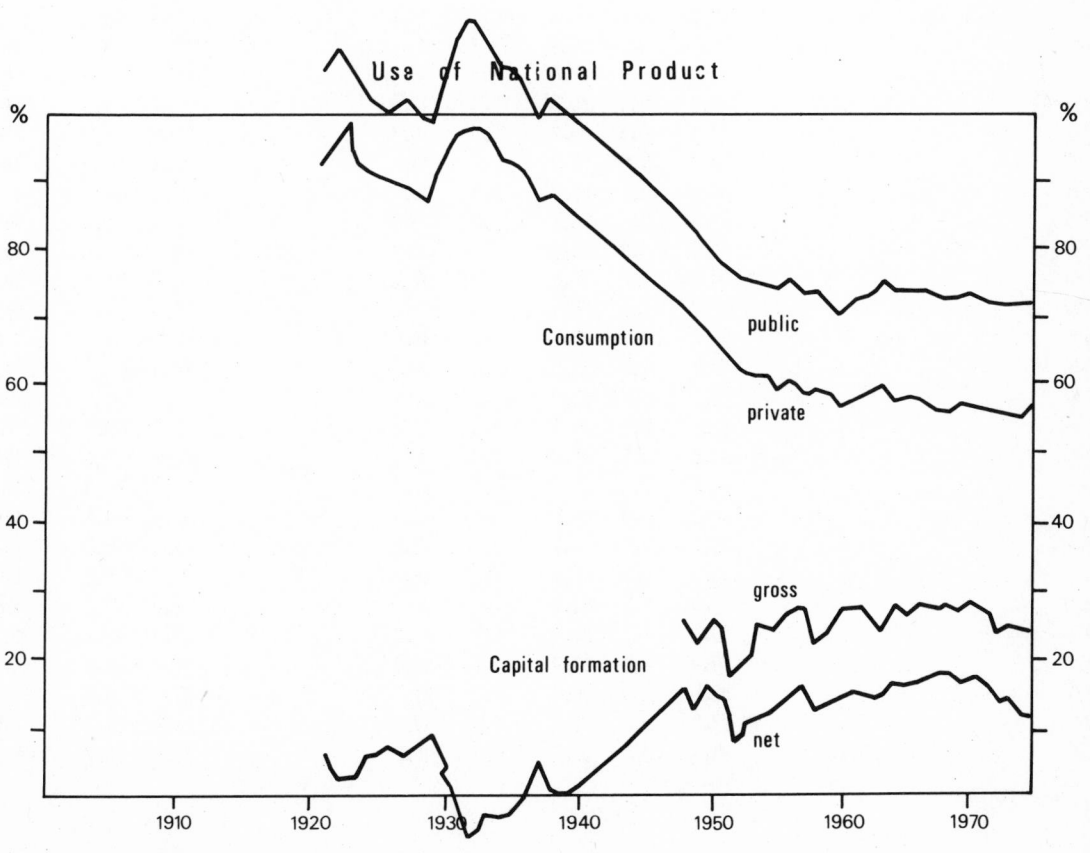

Origin and Use of National Product

Year	GDP at market prices [a]			Gross Domestic Product at market prices [b],[c]									Year
				Consumption			Investment				Exports	Imports	
	Agriculture	Industry	Services	Private	Public	Total	Net cap. formation	Gross cap. form.	Changes in stocks	Total			
1922				75.4	10.4	85.8	4.6	18.7	0.6	19.3	27.1	32.2	1922
1921				75.5	10.2	85.7	7.3	24.8	-1.1	23.7	23.7	33.0	1921
1920				73.7	7.0	80.7	14.8	28.5	2.1	30.6	35.3	46.6	1920
1919				73.8	7.5	81.3	13.0	26.2	9.6	35.8	30.7	47.8	1919
1918				73.5	7.8	81.3	9.8	24.8	-9.1	15.7	34.3	31.3	1918
1917				71.2	6.5	77.6	11.8	27.2	-3.1	24.2	44.0	45.8	1917
1916				63.7	5.2	68.8	11.2	22.3	-1.3	21.0	54.9	44.7	1916
1915				68.8	6.1	74.9	9.2	19.9	-0.2	19.8	45.8	40.5	1915
1914				73.8	6.6	80.4	9.4	20.7	-0.1	20.6	35.2	36.2	1914
1913				73.0	5.8	78.8	10.1	20.9	-0.3	20.7	37.0	36.5	1913
1912				75.0	6.0	81.0	10.6	21.6	-0.2	21.4	35.6	38.0	1912
1911				76.6	5.8	82.4	9.8	20.9	-0.2	20.7	33.9	37.0	1911
1910	23.3	26.0	50.7	77.2	5.9	83.1	7.6	18.5	-0.1	18.3	32.8	34.1	1910
1909				79.3	6.1	85.4	6.1	17.4	-0.1	17.3	31.2	34.0	1909
1908				79.0	5.9	84.8	7.4	19.1			29.8	33.7	1908
1907				78.4	5.8	84.3	7.5	19.2			31.6	35.1	1907
1906				78.4	6.0	84.4	5.6	17.4			33.5	35.3	1906
1905				80.4	6.3	86.7	4.2	15.7			32.2	34.7	1905
1904				79.6	6.4	85.9	5.6	16.8			30.8	33.6	1904
1903				81.5	6.6	88.1	4.7	15.9			29.0	33.0	1903
1902				80.9	6.7	87.6	5.9	16.8			28.4	32.8	1902
1901				80.7	6.6	87.4	6.9	17.6			27.5	32.5	1901
1900	25.0	28.0	47.0	80.3	6.4	86.6	7.4	18.7			29.6	34.9	1900
1899				80.5	6.5	86.9	9.7	20.7			28.3	35.9	1899
1898				81.0	6.0	87.0	8.6	18.9			28.8	34.7	1898
1897				80.2	6.3	86.5	7.3	17.6			31.4	35.6	1897
1896				81.9	6.3	88.2	5.9	16.3			29.8	34.4	1896
1895				82.1	5.8	87.9	6.6	16.8			28.8	33.5	1895
1894				81.6	5.4	87.0	6.0	16.4			28.7	32.1	1894
1893				81.1	5.3	86.4	5.7	16.3			29.4	32.1	1893
1892				81.6	5.1	86.7	5.4	16.3			29.3	32.3	1892
1891				83.2	4.6	87.8	6.2	17.2			30.3	35.3	1891
1890	31.6	24.3	44.1	79.7	4.6	84.4	6.8	17.8			32.6	34.7	1890
1889				78.1	4.7	82.7	6.1	16.4			34.2	33.2	1889
1888				78.7	4.8	83.5	4.6	14.6			31.5	29.7	1888
1887				78.8	5.2	83.9	3.9	14.3			29.1	27.3	1887
1886				80.4	4.9	85.3	3.4	13.8			28.0	27.1	1886
1885				81.1	4.7	85.9	3.8	14.3			28.4	28.6	1885
1884				80.6	4.3	84.9	4.6	14.7			29.7	29.3	1884
1883				80.0	4.3	84.3	5.1	15.1			30.3	29.6	1883
1882				78.2	4.2	82.4	5.3	15.0			31.2	28.6	1882
1881				80.6	4.2	84.8	4.9	14.6			29.8	29.2	1881
1880				79.6	4.2	83.8	4.9	14.7			29.9	28.3	1880
1879				80.1	4.5	84.6	4.4	14.8			27.9	27.3	1879
1878				79.9	4.0	83.9	5.4	15.7			27.6	27.2	1878
1877				82.4	4.0	86.4	7.3	17.1			27.1	30.6	1877
1876				78.5	3.8	82.2	7.3	17.0			28.8	28.0	1876
1875	35.4	21.8	42.8	81.5	3.8	85.2	8.2	18.2			26.3	29.7	1875

Origin and Use of National Product

| Year | GDP at market prices a) | | | Gross Domestic Product at market prices b),c) | | | | | | | | | Year |
| | Agriculture | Industry | Services | Consumption | | | Investment | | | | Ex-ports | Im-ports | |
				Private	Public	Total	Net cap. formation	Gross cap. form.	Changes in stocks	Total			
1975	5.8	38.0	56.1	54.7	17.0	71.7	20.0	34.2	0.7	34.9	41.9	48.6	1975
1974	6.1	35.8	56.0	52.7	16.0	68.8	16.1	30.6	3.4	34.0	46.0	48.9	1974
1973	6.0	35.2	58.8	54.0	16.1	70.2	15.8	29.5	0.8	30.3	43.6	44.1	1973
1972	6.1	35.8	58.1	55.1	16.2	71.3	14.2	28.0	-0.1	27.9	40.7	39.9	1972
1971	6.8	35.4	57.8	55.3	16.1	71.4	15.9	29.9	2.0	31.9	40.2	43.5	1971
1970	6.8	35.7	57.5	55.3	15.3	70.6	12.9	26.7	3.9	30.7	41.8	43.1	1970
1969	5.9	34.4	59.7	56.6	15.8	72.4	10.8	24.6	0.9	25.4	42.3	40.1	1969
1968	6.8	37.2	56.0	55.6	15.6	71.2	13.2	27.1	-0.3	26.8	43.1	41.1	1968
1967	7.4	38.3	54.3	55.6	15.1	70.7	16.5	29.8	1.3	31.1	41.8	43.6	1967
1966	8.3	38.6	53.1	56.0	14.5	70.5	16.0	28.6	2.3	30.9	40.7	42.1	1966
1965	8.9	37.9	53.2	56.6	14.3	70.9	15.6	28.2	1.9	30.1	40.9	41.9	1965
1964	8.3	37.8	53.6	58.6	13.8	72.4	15.4	27.8	0.6	28.4	41.5	42.3	1964
1963	8.5	38.1	53.4	59.5	13.7	73.2	16.8	29.6	0.1	29.7	40.1	42.9	1963
1962	9.2	38.2	52.6	60.3	13.4	73.7	16.1	29.2	0.4	29.5	39.3	42.6	1962
1961	10.4	37.7	51.9	60.0	12.5	72.5	16.1	29.4	2.0	31.4	40.5	44.4	1961
1960	10.7	37.6	51.6	60.4	12.4	72.8	14.7	28.3	1.6	29.9	41.9	44.6	1960
1959	11.8	37.1	51.1	60.6	12.7	73.3	15.6	29.4	-0.9	28.5	41.9	43.7	1959
1958	11.9	37.0	51.1	60.7	12.3	73.0	18.6	32.2	-1.2	30.9	41.5	45.5	1958
1957	12.6	36.3	51.1	58.1	11.5	69.6	16.2	28.7	1.3	30.0	45.5	45.2	1957
1956	13.7	36.9	49.4	58.3	11.1	69.3	15.8	27.6	2.9	30.5	44.5	44.3	1956
1955	13.5	38.8	47.7	61.9	11.2	73.1	18.4	30.3	0.4	30.8	41.6	45.5	1955
1954	13.9	39.5	46.5	62.7	11.9	74.7	18.4	30.2	1.0	31.2	38.6	44.5	1954
1953	13.9	38.6	47.4	63.7	12.2	75.8	18.0	30.0	-0.7	29.3	39.1	44.2	1953
1952	15.1	36.9	48.0	60.5	10.8	71.3	14.7	26.3	3.1	29.4	42.9	43.6	1952
1951	14.4	37.7	47.9	59.5	9.6	69.1	12.7	23.9	6.2	30.0	47.0	46.1	1951
1950				64.3	11.2	75.5	16.8	27.9	2.0	29.9	38.5	43.8	1950
1949				64.9	11.4	76.3	17.9	29.4	3.1	32.5	32.5	41.3	1949
1948				62.8	11.6	74.4	17.1	27.9	3.4	31.3	33.0	38.7	1948
1947				66.1	12.3	78.4	19.7	28.2	4.1	32.4	30.3	41.1	1947
1946				66.3	14.8	81.1	11.6	21.8	3.8	25.6	24.2	30.9	1946
1939	11.5	33.6	54.9	70.1	10.8	80.8	12.7	18.7	0.4	19.1	30.6	30.5	1939
1938	13.7	32.7	53.6	69.5	9.5	79.0	12.4	18.1	0.9	19.0	31.1	29.0	1938
1937	13.3	31.9	54.8	69.6	9.2	78.8	13.1	18.2	1.0	19.1	34.0	31.9	1937
1936	13.1	33.4	53.6	70.6	9.8	80.7	10.2	15.6	0.7	16.3	29.7	26.7	1936
1935	13.6	32.3	54.0	73.0	10.1	83.1	8.0	13.8	1.3	15.1	28.6	26.8	1935
1934	12.7	32.7	54.6	74.0	10.2	84.2	5.6	11.9	0.9	12.8	29.1	26.0	1934
1933	12.4	32.6	55.0	75.0	10.5	85.4	3.9	10.2	0.1	10.4	29.3	25.0	1933
1932	12.0	32.1	55.9	76.1	10.6	86.7	3.5	10.1	-0.1	10.0	28.7	25.4	1932
1931	13.8	29.2	57.1	78.6	11.2	89.8	7.6	13.8	-1.3	12.5	28.5	30.8	1931
1930	16.7	30.3	53.0	73.3	9.9	83.2	10.4	15.4	2.2	17.6	31.6	32.4	1930
1929				72.4	7.8	80.2	8.4	19.7	-0.2	19.0	31.1	30.8	1929
1928				74.5	8.3	82.8	7.4	18.8	0.0	18.8	28.8	30.4	1928
1927				74.9	8.8	83.8	4.5	16.2	0.1	16.2	29.6	29.6	1927
1926				73.5	8.5	82.1	4.5	16.9	0.3	17.2	30.2	29.4	1926
1925				74.0	7.7	81.7	6.7	18.7	0.0	18.7	30.1	30.4	1925
1924				76.2	8.0	84.3	6.5	18.5	-0.2	18.3	31.2	33.8	1924
1923				75.9	9.3	85.2	6.1	18.9	0.3	19.2	28.7	33.1	1923

O r i g i n   a n d   U s e   o f   N a t i o n a l   P r o d u c t

Year	GDP at market prices [a]			Gross Domestic Product at market prices [b],[c]									Year
	Agriculture	Industry	Services	Consumption			Investment				Exports	Imports	
				Private	Public	Total	Net cap. formation	Gross cap. form.	Changes in stocks	Total			
1874				79.2	3.3	82.5	8.4	18.4			30.0	30.9	1974
1873				78.2	3.3	81.5	7.4	16.9			32.2	30.6	1873
1872				78.8	3.4	82.2	5.6	15.0			31.3	28.4	1872
1871				79.5	3.9	83.5	3.7	12.5			29.0	24.9	1871
1870				80.4	3.9	84.3	3.7	12.2			29.2	25.6	1870
1869				79.9	3.7	83.6	3.6	12.1			27.7	23.5	1869
1868				83.6	4.0	87.6	4.4	13.0			25.0	25.6	1868
1867				81.9	4.1	85.9	4.4	12.9			25.3	24.1	1867
1866				83.5	4.1	87.6	4.9	13.4			25.6	26.6	1866
1865	45.3	17.8	36.9	83.8	4.0	87.7	4.2	12.9			26.5	27.1	1865

a) Figures for 1930–1939 refer to Gross–GDP (i.e. are inclusive of repair and maintenance).
   For 1951–1968 they refer to GDP at factor cost. For 1969–1975 market prices are net of value added tax.
b) Figures for 1865–1950 refer to Gross–GDP. Prior to 1908 without changes in stocks.
c) Prior to 1951 repair and maintenance are included.

Norway

Origin of National Product

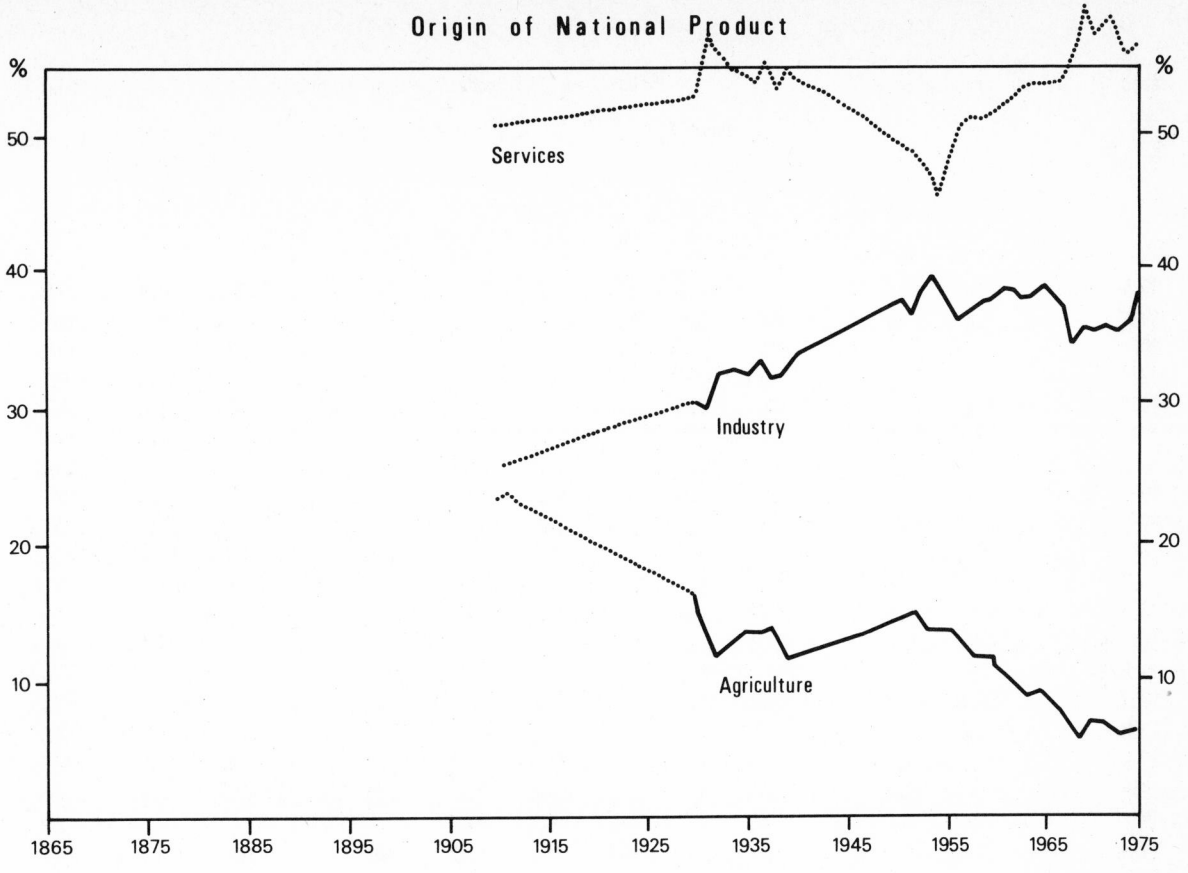

Services

Industry

Agriculture

Use of National Product

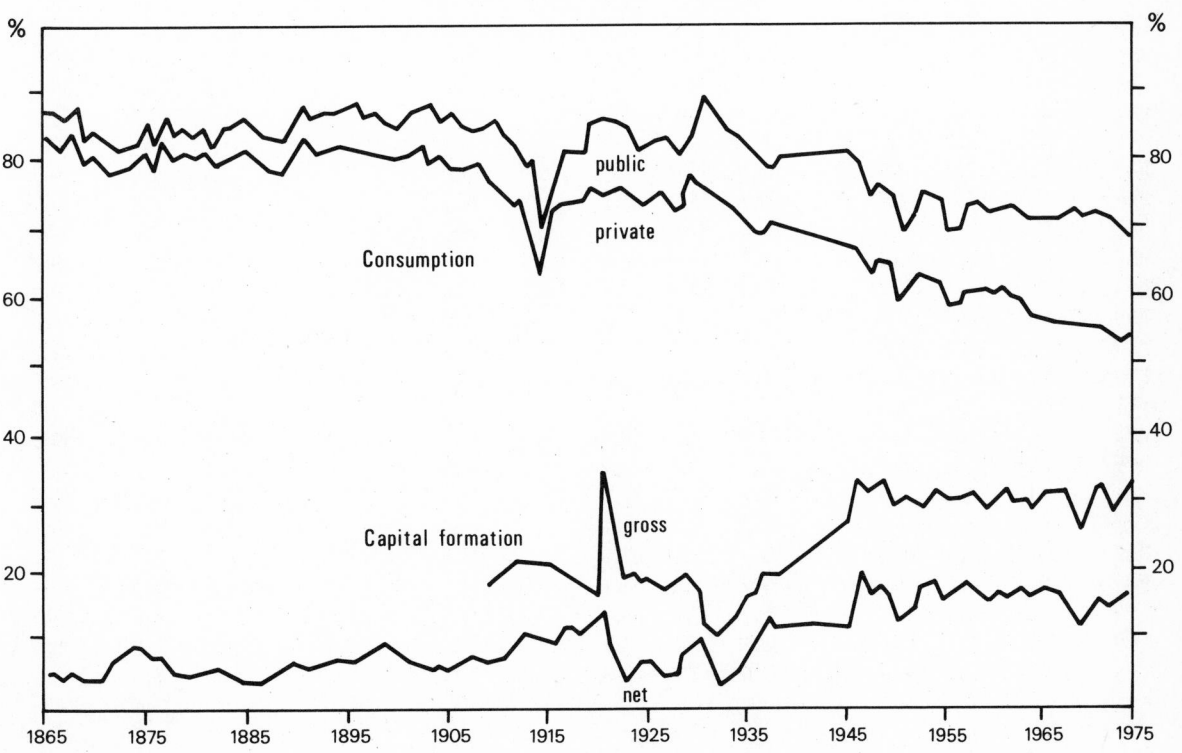

public

private

Consumption

Capital formation

gross

net

Origin and Use of National Product

Year	GDP at market prices [a]			Gross Domestic Product at market prices [b]									Year
				Consumption			Investment				Ex-ports	Im-ports	
	Agriculture	Industry	Services	Private	Public	Total	Net cap. formation	Gross cap. form.	Changes in stocks	Total			
1975	5.2	41.5	55.3	52.5	22.8	77.3	10.6	21.1	2.9	24.0	28.8	30.1	1975
1974	5.3	43.4	51.3	53.0	23.7	76.7	11.5	22.0	2.2	24.2	23.6	33.4	1974
1973	4.3	41.8	53.9	52.7	23.0	75.7	11.9	21.8	-0.6	21.3	27.8	24.8	1973
1972	4.3	40.9	54.8	53.5	23.0	76.5	12.6	23.3	-0.1	22.2	24.4	23.1	1972
1971	4.8	40.7	54.5	53.6	22.7	76.3	12.0	21.6	1.0	24.5	24.5	23.5	1971
1970	4.5	42.7	52.8	54.0	21.4	75.4	12.9	22.3	2.8	25.1	24.3	24.8	1970
1969	4.4	42.6	53.0	55.7	20.7	76.4	13.2	22.8	1.2	24.0	22.8	23.2	1969
1968	4.9	42.7	52.4	56.0	20.5	76.4	13.3	23.4	0.3	23.7	21.5	21.6	1968
1967	5.0	40.4	54.7	56.0	19.5	75.6	14.2	24.4	0.1	24.5	21.1	21.1	1967
1966	5.1	41.6	53.2	56.5	18.8	75.3	13.9	24.2	1.2	25.3	21.3	21.9	1966
1965	5.7	42.7	51.6	56.4	17.7	74.1	14.0	24.2	2.5	26.7	21.8	22.6	1965
1964	6.2	43.1	50.8	56.7	17.2	73.8	13.9	24.0	1.9	25.8	22.3	22.0	1964
1963	5.9	43.0	51.1	58.5	17.3	75.8	13.3	23.6	0.3	23.9	21.9	21.6	1963
1962	6.7	43.1	50.1	58.8	16.7	75.6	12.8	23.1	1.0	24.1	21.8	21.5	1962
1961	7.3	42.9	49.8	59.4	15.9	75.3	12.5	22.6	1.6	24.2	22.3	21.8	1961
1960	7.4	42.9	49.7	60.0	15.8	75.9	11.9	22.1	2.6	24.7	22.9	23.5	1960
1959	7.1	43.5	49.3	61.9	16.2	78.1	11.8	21.8	0.0	21.8	21.7	21.7	1959
1958	8.2	43.1	48.8	62.7	16.2	78.9	10.9	21.1	0.6	21.7	22.2	22.8	1958
1957	8.8	43.1	48.1	61.9	16.1	78.0	9.9	20.2	2.0	22.2	24.4	24.6	1957
1956	10.0	42.5	47.5	62.7	15.4	78.1	10.2	20.2	2.0	22.2	23.5	23.9	1956
1955	9.9	42.9	47.3	63.1	15.1	78.3	10.3	20.3	2.3	22.6	22.4	23.3	1955
1954	10.9	43.4	45.8	63.8	15.0	78.8	11.4	21.2	0.4	21.5	22.1	22.4	1954
1953	10.6	42.8	46.5	64.2	15.2	79.4	10.7	20.9	-1.2	19.7	21.5	20.7	1953
1952	13.6	41.7	44.6	63.4	14.3	77.6	9.3	19.6	2.3	21.9	23.6	23.2	1952
1951	11.2	45.6	43.2	62.4	12.8	75.8	8.9	18.4	4.1	22.4	28.3	25.9	1951
1950	11.6	48.7	39.8	69.1	10.5	79.5		19.9			18.7	18.2	1950
1949	10.3	49.2	40.5	68.6	10.6	79.3		19.1			15.6	14.0	1949
1948	10.0	48.2	41.8	71.1	10.5	81.6		19.6			15.8	17.0	1948
1947	10.9	46.8	42.2	73.6	10.0	83.5		21.8			14.4	19.7	1947
1946	11.3	47.0	41.7	71.2	9.8	81.0		19.9			13.0	13.9	1946
1945	11.1	47.9	41.0	67.1	11.8	78.9		16.7			9.4	4.9	1945
1944	11.4	45.6	43.0	69.7	13.1	82.8		19.5			5.9	8.3	1944
1943	11.3	45.3	43.4	68.3	13.6	81.9		19.5			8.0	9.4	1943
1942	11.0	44.9	44.0	68.3	13.9	82.2		18.4			9.4	10.0	1942
1941	11.5	43.7	44.7	70.1	13.9	84.0		15.8			10.4	10.2	1941
1940	12.1	42.3	45.6	72.0	12.9	85.0		17.0			11.6	13.6	1940
1939	12.1	44.4	43.5	72.4	10.3	82.7		19.9			16.2	18.8	1939
1938	12.9	44.2	42.9	72.7	8.6	81.3		19.0			16.7	17.1	1938
1937	14.3	42.4	43.3	73.8	8.2	82.0		17.5			18.9	18.4	1937
1936	14.4	41.4	44.2	74.6	8.3	82.9		16.9			15.7	15.6	1936
1935	14.3	40.0	45.7	75.4	8.5	83.9		16.5			14.7	15.2	1935
1934	14.6	38.9	46.6	75.7	8.8	84.5		14.1			15.9	14.5	1934
1933	14.9	37.3	47.8	77.1	9.3	86.4		12.3			14.6	13.3	1933
1932	13.9	37.9	48.2	78.3	9.6	87.9		13.0			13.0	14.0	1932
1931	13.3	39.1	47.6	77.7	9.1	86.7		15.0			14.5	16.2	1931
1930	13.1	43.3	43.7	75.7	7.6	83.4		15.9			17.4	16.6	1930
1929	14.4	42.1	43.5	76.2	7.6	83.7		14.1			20.1	18.0	1929
1928	15.1	40.6	44.4	78.0	7.8	85.8		13.9			18.7	18.3	1928

Origin and Use of National Product

Year	GDP at market prices [a]			Gross Domestic Product at market prices [b]									Year
				Consumption			Investment				Ex-ports	Im-ports	
	Agriculture	Industry	Services	Private	Public	Total	Net cap. formation	Gross cap. form.	Changes in stocks	Total			
1927	15.4	40.4	44.2	77.3	7.6	84.8		12.7			19.7	17.2	1927
1926	16.1	39.9	44.0	78.2	7.9	86.1		12.8			17.8	16.7	1926
1925	17.5	38.8	43.7	77.9	8.2	86.1		13.2			17.3	16.5	1925
1924	17.9	36.1	46.0	78.6	8.5	87.1		13.1			17.3	17.5	1924
1923	18.5	35.2	46.2	78.1	8.9	87.0		13.1			16.3	16.4	1923
1922	17.5	35.6	46.8	76.9	9.6	86.5		11.4			16.3	14.2	1922
1921	19.4	37.5	43.1	79.4	8.7	88.1		12.2			12.8	13.1	1921
1920	22.4	34.5	43.0	85.1	7.2	92.3		13.3			20.8	26.4	1920
1919	24.4	33.1	42.6	85.5	6.7	92.3		13.2			17.8	23.3	1919
1918	28.5	32.6	38.8	77.5	6.3	83.8		12.3			18.7	14.8	1918
1917	25.8	37.3	36.9	73.1	5.0	78.1		12.4			21.9	12.4	1917
1916	26.2	34.1	39.7	73.4	5.2	78.6		11.0			30.6	20.2	1916
1915	25.5	31.4	43.1	76.7	5.8	82.6		10.8			31.0	24.4	1915
1914	24.2	34.4	41.5	77.7	6.1	83.6		12.9			21.2	17.8	1914
1913	23.7	34.7	41.6	80.2	5.9	86.1		12.7			22.3	21.0	1913
1912	21.4	36.1	42.5	81.3	6.2	87.5		11.3			22.4	21.2	1912
1911	23.6	34.2	42.2	80.8	6.3	87.1		11.6			21.3	20.0	1911
1910	25.5	32.2	42.3	83.2	6.2	89.4		10.8			19.5	19.7	1910
1909	26.2	31.1	42.6	85.8	6.5	92.3		10.3			16.9	19.6	1909
1908	26.5	31.9	41.6	84.4	6.0	90.4		11.5			17.3	19.3	1908
1907	24.8	34.3	41.0	83.7	5.7	89.4		13.4			19.1	22.0	1907
1906	23.7	33.9	42.4	83.5	5.8	89.3		13.5			19.6	22.4	1906
1905	23.3	33.3	43.4	83.8	6.1	90.0		12.9			19.6	22.4	1905
1904	25.0	32.0	43.0	84.8	6.1	90.9		13.5			18.8	23.2	1904
1903	27.0	30.4	42.6	83.0	5.8	88.8		13.0			19.9	21.7	1903
1902	26.2	31.2	42.6	85.6	6.0	91.6		11.4			19.3	22.3	1902
1901	27.6	30.9	41.4	84.7	5.8	90.5		11.7			18.3	20.6	1901
1900	28.0	31.2	40.8	84.4	5.5	89.9		13.0			19.8	22.7	1900
1899	27.4	30.2	42.4	85.2	5.4	90.7		13.1			19.0	22.8	1899
1898	28.4	28.9	42.7	84.4	5.6	90.0		12.2			19.7	21.9	1898
1897	29.3	28.4	42.3	81.3	5.9	87.3		12.0			21.9	21.2	1897
1896	30.2	26.7	43.1	81.7	6.0	87.8		10.2			22.3	20.3	1896
1895	30.5	26.8	42.7	82.5	6.2	88.7		10.3			21.2	20.2	1895
1894	31.4	25.4	43.1	84.9	6.5	91.4		8.4			21.8	21.5	1894
1893	32.8	24.4	42.8	84.9	6.4	91.3		7.2			22.0	20.4	1893
1892	34.4	22.9	42.7	87.0	6.2	93.1		8.0			20.9	22.0	1892
1891	36.1	20.0	43.9	87.5	6.2	93.7		7.8			21.6	23.2	1891
1890	33.2	21.5	45.3	87.0	6.4	93.4		10.0			21.6	24.9	1890
1889	32.1	23.3	44.5	86.4	6.5	92.9		10.2			22.6	25.7	1889
1888	33.5	21.2	45.3	85.0	6.8	91.8		9.3			22.6	23.7	1888
1887	31.2	23.6	45.2	86.4	7.0	93.4		8.1			21.1	22.7	1887
1886	31.7	24.4	43.9	85.3	6.8	92.1		10.9			18.9	21.9	1886
1885	34.0	22.2	43.9	88.3	6.4	94.7		9.8			19.6	24.1	1885
1884	35.6	21.5	42.9	86.8	6.2	93.0		10.5			19.2	22.7	1884
1883	35.6	21.9	42.5	87.1	6.0	93.0		9.4			20.5	22.9	1883
1882	37.5	20.8	41.7	85.4	6.1	91.5		8.9			21.0	21.4	1882
1881	35.1	23.6	41.3	85.8	5.9	91.7		9.9			18.6	20.2	1881
1880	38.1	20.6	41.3	84.7	5.8	90.5		9.5			20.5	20.5	1880

Sweden

Origin and Use of National Product

Year	GDP at market prices [a)			Gross Domestic Product at market prices [b)									Year
				Consumption			Investment				Exports	Imports	
	Agriculture	Industry	Services	Private	Public	Total	Net cap. formation	Gross cap. form.	Changes in stocks	Total			
1879	36.9	22.5	40.6	83.9	6.1	90.1		9.8			17.0	16.9	1879
1878	37.0	22.8	40.3	84.2	5.8	90.0		11.2			16.8	18.0	1878
1877	36.7	23.0	40.3	86.2	5.0	91.2		12.0			18.1	21.3	1877
1876	36.2	23.8	40.0	84.8	4.8	89.6		11.9			18.2	19.7	1876
1875	36.2	24.6	39.2	83.8	4.7	88.4		13.4			17.7	19.5	1875
1874	37.2	24.3	38.5	84.9	4.1	89.0		13.5			18.5	21.4	1874
1873	39.6	22.2	38.2	84.5	4.4	88.9		11.9			19.3	20.1	1873
1872	39.6	20.6	39.8	84.4	4.8	89.2		8.8			20.6	18.6	1872
1871	40.5	18.8	40.6	84.9	5.5	90.4		7.3			18.9	16.6	1871
1870	40.9	18.3	40.8	83.5	5.3	88.7		7.2			19.3	15.2	1870
1869	39.8	19.1	41.1	85.7	5.7	91.4		7.7			16.5	15.6	1869
1868	40.1	17.9	42.1	91.0	5.5	96.5		4.5			14.5	15.6	1868
1867	38.7	18.9	42.3	87.8	5.2	93.0		7.2			15.1	15.3	1867
1866	37.7	20.4	41.8	85.6	5.5	91.1		9.0			13.3	13.5	1866
1865	35.9	20.4	43.7	86.9	5.4	92.3		6.7			14.4	13.4	1865
1864	36.1	20.8	43.0	85.5	5.6	91.1		8.8			12.7	12.6	1864
1863	37.5	20.0	42.5	86.5	5.3	91.9		7.8			12.5	12.2	1863
1862	37.3	20.7	42.0	86.6	5.0	91.5		9.2			11.5	12.2	1862
1861	38.5	18.3	43.2	89.7	5.2	94.9		6.4			13.1	14.4	1861

a) Figures for 1961-1951 refer to GDP at factor cost.
   For 1968-1975 market prices are net of value added tax.
b) Prior to 1950 GDP is without changes in stocks.

Sweden

Origin of National Product

Use of National Product

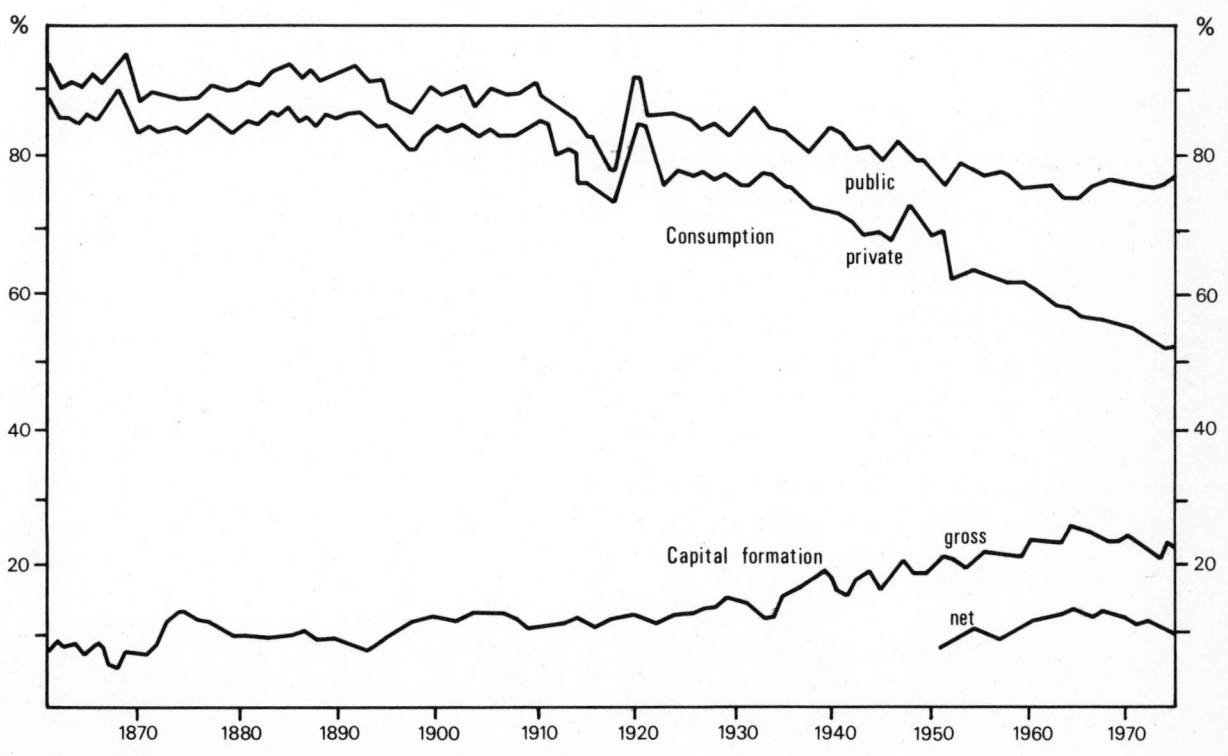

Switzerland

Origin and Use of National Product

Year	GNP at market prices			Gross National Product at market prices[a]									Year
				Consumption			Investment				Ex-ports	Im-ports	
	Agriculture	Industry	Services	Private	Public	Total	Net cap. formation	Gross cap. form.	Changes in stocks	Total			
1975				61.7	12.6	74.3	13.2	24.1	-1.2	22.8	31.5	28.6	1975
1974				59.1	11.6	70.7	16.1	27.6	3.7	31.2	32.5	34.5	1974
1973				58.5	11.2	69.8	17.7	29.4	1.9	31.3	30.9	32.0	1973
1972				58.2	10.9	69.1	17.6	29.7	2.1	31.8	30.6	31.5	1972
1971				58.1	10.9	69.1	17.4	29.2	3.2	32.5	31.1	32.7	1971
1970				59.0	10.5	69.4	15.6	27.5	4.7	32.3	32.8	34.5	1970
1969				59.9	10.5	70.5	14.4	25.8	2.5	28.3	32.7	31.5	1969
1968				59.9	10.4	70.3	14.2	25.6	2.5	28.1	30.8	29.3	1968
1967				60.1	10.3	70.3	14.9	26.0	3.1	29.1	29.1	28.6	1967
1966				60.2	10.4	70.6	16.3	27.4	1.9	29.3	29.4	29.3	1966
1965				59.9	10.5	70.4	17.9	28.7	1.7	30.4	28.7	29.6	1965
1964				59.7	10.4	70.1	20.0	30.7	2.5	33.2	28.1	31.3	1964
1963				60.6	10.5	71.1	19.6	30.0	2.1	32.1	28.1	31.3	1963
1962				61.3	10.1	71.5	18.3	28.8	3.3	32.1	28.4	31.9	1962
1961				60.9	9.7	70.6	16.7	27.4	5.0	32.4	28.7	31.7	1961
1960				62.4	8.8	71.3	14.2	24.8	4.2	29.0	29.3	29.6	1960
1959				64.6	9.6	74.2	13.2	22.9	2.1	25.0	28.8	28.1	1959
1958				65.6	10.4	76.1	12.0	21.0	1.5	22.5	27.9	26.5	1958
1957				64.9	9.8	74.7	13.3	22.8	4.6	27.4	28.5	30.6	1957
1956				65.7	9.1	74.9	12.5	22.1	4.3	26.4	28.2	29.4	1956
1955				66.0	9.2	75.2	11.4	20.7	3.4	24.1	27.6	26.9	1955
1954				67.4	9.6	77.0	10.9	19.9	1.0	20.9	27.5	25.5	1954
1953				67.8	10.2	78.0	10.0	19.3	-1.2	18.2	28.0	24.2	1953
1952				69.3	11.0	80.3	9.6	18.8	0.2	18.9	27.0	26.2	1952
1951				70.6	10.3	81.0	9.8	18.5	3.6	22.1	27.7	30.8	1951
1950				71.2			7.2	14.7	1.3	16.0			1950
1949				72.6			8.3	15.2	-1.6	13.6			1949
1948				72.2			10.4	16.2	2.6	18.8			1948
1938				74.9			-0.2	9.1	-0.3	8.8			1938

a) Figures for 1951 to 1975 refer to GDP.

Switzerland

Use of National Product

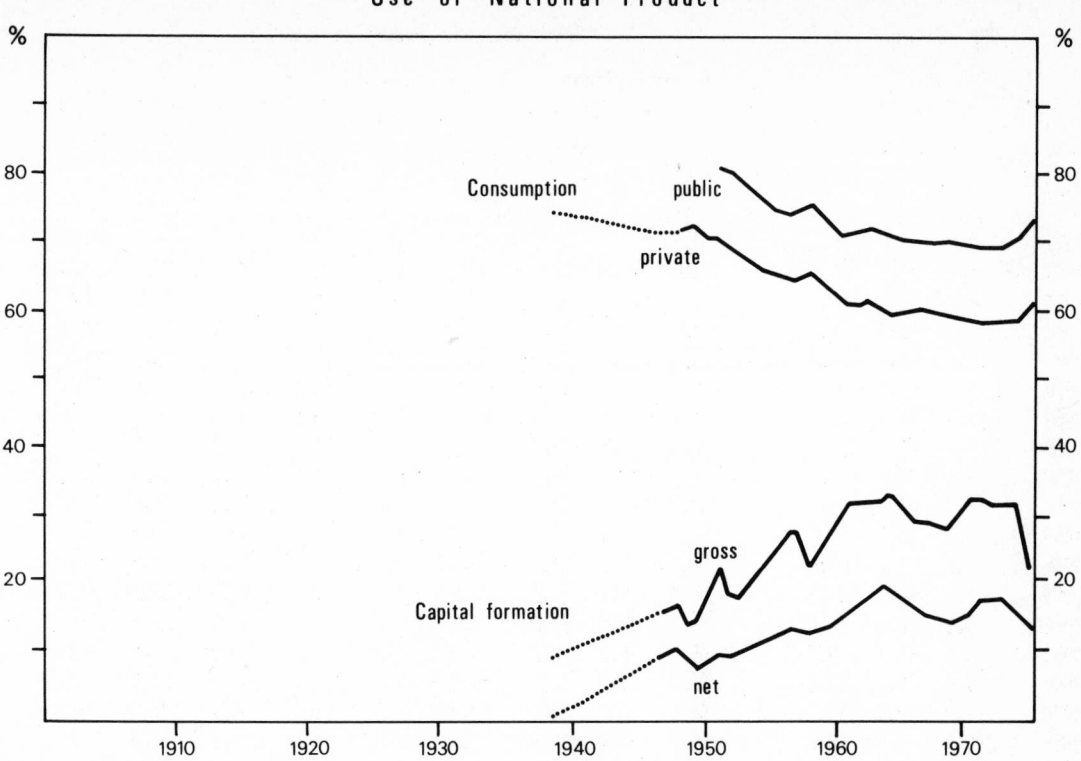

Origin and Use of National Product

Year	GNP at market prices [a]			Gross National Product at market prices [b]							Ex-ports	Im-ports	Year
				Consumption			Investment						
	Agriculture	Industry	Services	Private	Public	Total	Net cap. formation	Gross cap. form.	Changes in stocks	Total			
1975	2.8	41.0	56.3	61.2	22.1	83.3	9.4	20.0	-1.3	18.6	26.5	28.4	1975
1974	2.9	42.5	54.6	63.0	20.2	83.2	10.4	20.7	1.4	22.1	28.6	33.9	1974
1973	3.0	42.5	54.6	62.4	18.4	80.7	10.1	19.7	1.9	21.6	24.5	26.8	1973
1972	2.7	42.1	55.1	63.0	18.5	81.6	9.3	18.6	0.0	18.6	22.2	22.3	1972
1971	2.8	42.9	54.3	61.8	18.0	79.8	9.6	18.6	0.1	18.7	23.5	21.9	1971
1970	2.8	43.9	53.2	61.9	17.7	79.6	9.9	18.7	0.8	19.5	23.4	22.5	1970
1969	2.9	44.5	52.5	62.6	17.3	79.9	10.2	18.7	0.9	19.6	22.6	22.1	1969
1968	3.0	45.8	51.2	62.9	17.7	80.7	10.7	19.0	1.1	20.1	21.6	22.4	1968
1967	3.3	45.5	51.2	63.3	18.0	81.3	10.6	18.8	0.8	19.7	19.3	20.2	1967
1966	3.3	46.0	50.8	63.7	17.2	80.9	10.1	18.3	0.9	19.2	19.6	19.6	1966
1965	3.3	46.8	49.9	64.1	16.8	80.9	10.3	18.3	1.4	19.7	19.5	20.1	1965
1964	3.5	46.6	49.9	64.6	16.5	81.1	10.3	18.3	2.2	20.5	19.5	21.1	1964
1963	3.6	45.8	50.5	66.1	16.9	83.0	8.5	16.7	0.5	17.3	20.1	20.3	1963
1962	3.9	46.1	50.0	66.1	17.1	33.2	8.8	17.0	0.0	16.9	20.3	20.4	1962
1961	3.9	46.7	49.3	65.3	16.7	82.0	9.3	17.3	1.0	18.3	20.7	21.0	1961
1960	4.0	47.5	48.5	66.2	16.5	82.7	8.4	16.4	2.2	18.6	21.3	22.6	1960
1959	4.2	47.5	48.3	66.8	16.2	82.9	7.8	15.4	0.7	16.1	24.8	23.9	1959
1958	4.4	47.6	48.0	66.6	15.9	82.6	7.4	15.1	0.5	15.6	25.3	23.5	1958
1957	4.5	48.0	47.5	66.0	16.2	82.2	7.6	15.3	1.1	16.4	26.5	25.1	1957
1956	4.5	47.9	47.6	66.2	16.4	82.6	7.3	14.9	1.2	16.1	26.6	25.3	1956
1955	4.7	47.8	47.5	68.0	16.4	84.4	7.1	14.7	1.6	16.2	26.2	26.8	1955
1954	5.0	47.8	47.2	67.6	17.3	84.8	6.7	14.2	0.3	14.5	25.9	25.2	1954
1953	5.4	47.2	47.4	67.2	17.7	85.0	6.3	13.8	0.7	14.6	26.3	25.9	1953
1952	5.6	46.2	48.1	67.8	18.2	85.9	5.5	13.3	0.3	13.6	28.9	28.4	1952
1951	5.5	46.3	48.2	69.2	16.4	85.6	5.3	12.8	3.9	16.7	30.5	32.8	1951
1950	5.7	45.8	48.5	71.0	15.5	86.5	5.6	12.8	-1.6	11.2	28.6	26.2	1950
1949				71.2	15.7	86.8	5.4	12.5	0.5	13.0	24.3	24.2	1949
1948				72.0	14.7	86.7	4.8	11.9	1.5	13.4	23.1	23.1	1948
1947				74.3	16.1	90.4	4.0	11.1	2.5	13.6	19.1	23.1	1947
1946				72.4	22.7	95.1	2.3	9.2	-1.3	8.0	17.7	20.8	1946
1945				64.5	42.3	106.3	-2.9	3.5	-2.0	1.5	11.2	19.5	1945
1944				56.5	48.8	105.3	-3.4	2.9	-1.9	1.0	12.2	18.5	1944
1943				53.7	48.4	102.0	-2.5	3.5	1.0	4.5	9.9	16.4	1943
1942				55.8	47.3	103.1	-0.8	4.6	-1.0	3.6	9.0	15.7	1942
1941				56.9	45.7	102.6	-0.6	5.4	1.1	6.5	9.7	18.7	1941
1940				62.5	38.4	100.9	1.0	6.8	2.6	9.4	11.2	21.5	1940
1939				74.2	19.3	93.5	2.5	8.8	1.6	10.5	15.5	19.5	1939
1938				76.2	13.0	89.2	3.9	10.3	1.4	11.7	17.5	18.4	1938
1937				78.1	11.2	89.3	3.9	10.4	1.1	11.5	20.3	21.1	1937
1936				80.0	10.5	90.5	3.9	10.1	-0.1	10.0	18.6	19.1	1936
1935				80.3	9.9	90.1	3.2	9.3	0.1	9.4	18.8	18.3	1935
1934				81.2	9.5	90.8	3.1	9.1	0.6	9.7	17.5	18.1	1934
1933				83.8	9.7	93.5	1.7	8.1	-1.3	6.8	17.5	17.5	1933
1932				83.6	9.8	93.4	1.5	7.9	0.0	7.9	17.4	18.7	1932
1931				84.1	9.8	93.9	2.6	9.0	-0.1	9.0	19.0	21.9	1931
1930				80.2	9.0	89.3	2.9	8.9	1.9	10.7	24.2	24.2	1930
1929				80.1	8.8	88.9	3.0	8.9	0.8	9.7	28.8	27.3	1929
1928				80.4	8.7	89.1	2.8	8.6	0.4	8.9	29.0	27.0	1928

Origin and Use of National Product

Year	GNP at market prices a)			Gross National Product at market prices b)									Year
				Consumption			Investment				Ex-ports	Im-ports	
	Agriculture	Industry	Services	Private	Public	Total	Net cap. formation	Gross cap. form.	Changes in stocks	Total			
1927				80.1	8.7	88.8	3.0	8.8	0.9	9.7	29.2	27.7	1927
1926				82.7	9.1	91.8	2.5	8.7	0.4	9.0	29.0	29.8	1926
1925				79.5	8.4	88.0	2.8	8.6	2.7	11.3	30.4	29.7	1925
1924				81.8	8.6	90.5	2.0	8.1	-0.1	8.0	32.2	30.6	1924
1923				81.5	8.7	90.2	1.0	7.3	-1.4	5.9	31.2	27.3	1923
1922				80.8	9.1	89.9	1.4	8.0	-1.9	6.1	28.8	24.8	1922
1921				81.2	9.2	90.4	2.0	8.6	-1.9	6.7	26.4	23.6	1921
1920				80.6	7.6	88.4	0.8	7.7	-1.6	6.1	39.3	33.8	1920
1919				78.9	16.3	95.1	-1.7	3.9	1.7	5.7	29.6	30.3	1919
1918				66.4	34.0	100.4	-1.9	3.0	1.8	4.8	21.8	27.0	1918
1917				63.0	35.6	98.6	-1.7	3.1	-2.1	1.0	27.9	27.5	1917
1916				68.1	35.2	103.3	-2.0	3.0	-7.9	-4.9	32.5	30.9	1916
1915				72.2	31.6	103.8	-0.9	3.9	-6.1	-2.1	28.5	30.1	1915
1914				75.6	11.8	87.4	1.6	5.8	1.8	7.7	32.8	27.9	1914
1913				76.2	7.5	83.7	1.6	5.9	1.7	7.5	38.3	29.5	1913
1912				78.2	7.6	85.8	1.0	5.3	0.8	6.1	38.1	30.0	1912
1911				77.7	7.5	85.2	1.2	5.3	1.2	6.5	36.6	28.3	1911
1910				78.1	7.6	85.7	1.5	5.7	1.2	6.9	36.6	29.2	1910
1909				79.6	7.5	87.1	1.5	5.7	0.9	6.6	34.3	28.0	1909
1908				81.3	7.5	88.8	1.4	5.7	-1.3	4.4	34.3	27.5	1908
1907				78.7	7.1	85.8	2.3	6.5	0.4	7.0	36.1	28.9	1907
1906				78.6	7.3	85.8	3.6	7.8	0.9	8.7	33.3	27.8	1906
1905				79.6	7.5	87.0	4.0	8.1	0.7	8.8	30.7	26.5	1905
1904				80.8	7.7	88.4	4.7	8.8	0.2	9.0	28.9	26.4	1904
1903				80.6	8.0	88.6	5.3	9.4	-0.2	9.2	28.5	26.2	1903
1902				79.9	9.0	88.9	5.3	9.3	0.2	9.6	27.4	25.9	1902
1901				78.9	9.5	88.4	5.2	9.3	1.2	10.4	27.0	25.8	1901
1900				79.7	8.9	88.6	5.4	9.7	0.0	9.7	28.2	26.4	1900
1899				79.5	6.9	86.4	5.2	9.3	1.8	11.1	27.6	25.2	1899
1898				81.7	6.1	87.8	4.6	8.6	1.9	10.5	27.5	25.8	1898
1897				82.9	6.1	89.1	3.6	7.6	0.9	8.5	28.7	26.3	1897
1896				82.4	6.0	88.3	2.8	6.6	2.1	8.7	29.1	26.1	1896
1895				82.8	5.9	88.7	2.1	6.0	1.8	7.9	29.1	25.7	1895
1894				83.2	5.7	88.9	2.2	6.2	1.9	8.0	28.8	25.7	1894
1893				84.5	5.7	90.3	1.9	6.0	0.0	6.0	30.1	26.4	1893
1892				83.9	5.6	89.4	2.0	6.2	0.3	6.5	31.4	27.3	1892
1891				82.5	5.5	88.0	1.8	5.9	1.6	7.5	32.1	27.5	1891
1890				80.8	5.5	86.3	1.4	5.7	1.0	6.7	34.5	27.5	1890
1889				81.7	5.3	87.1	1.4	5.6	1.7	7.3	34.5	28.8	1889
1888				81.7	5.4	87.1	1.0	5.1	1.4	6.5	33.5	27.1	1888
1887				81.4	5.5	86.8	0.6	4.8	2.1	6.9	32.1	25.8	1887
1886				82.9	5.9	88.7	0.7	5.1	0.4	5.4	32.0	26.2	1886
1885				83.4	6.1	89.5	1.3	5.9	0.0	5.9	32.1	27.5	1885
1884				82.8	5.4	88.2	2.1	6.6	0.0	6.6	33.3	28.2	1884
1883				82.1	5.2	87.3	2.6	7.0	2.1	9.1	33.3	29.7	1883
1882				82.3	5.3	87.6	2.2	6.8	1.1	7.9	34.2	29.7	1882
1881				82.6	5.2	87.8	2.2	6.9	0.7	7.6	33.9	29.4	1881
1880				82.6	5.0	87.6	2.4	7.0	2.9	9.9	32.3	29.8	1880

United Kingdom

Origin and Use of National Product

Year	GNP at market prices a)			Gross National Product at market prices b)									Year
				Consumption			Investment				Ex-ports	Im-ports	
	Agriculture	Industry	Services	Private	Public	Total	Net cap. formation	Gross cap. form.	Changes in stocks	Total			
1879				85.0	5.6	90.6	2.3	7.2	-0.4	6.8	31.9	29.4	1879
1878				84.7	4.8	89.5	3.6	8.3	0.4	8.7	29.8	28.0	1878
1877				84.9	4.6	89.5	4.2	9.0	0.7	9.7	30.4	29.7	1877
1876				83.0	4.5	87.5	4.4	9.1	1.1	10.2	30.0	27.7	1876
1875				81.5	4.4	85.9	3.7	8.4	1.5	9.8	31.7	27.4	1875
1874				79.9	4.1	84.1	3.0	7.8	2.5	10.2	32.3	26.6	1874
1873				82.3	4.0	86.3	2.1	6.9	0.4	7.3	34.0	27.5	1873
1872				80.6	4.3	84.9	2.3	6.9	0.8	7.6	34.6	27.2	1872
1871				79.7	4.4	84.2	2.0	6.4	3.2	9.6	32.7	26.5	1871
1870				82.6	4.8	87.4	0.9	5.5	2.2	7.7	31.4	26.5	1870
1869				84.6	5.6	90.2		5.7			4.2		1869
1868				84.9	6.0	90.9		5.7			3.3		1868
1867				84.8	5.7	90.5		5.6			3.9		1867
1866				85.3	5.4	90.7		6.3			3.0		1866
1865				83.7	5.5	89.2		7.4			3.4		1865
1864				85.5	5.9	91.4		6.3			2.3		1864
1863				84.9	6.3	91.2		5.9			2.8		1863
1862				87.0	6.6	93.6		5.1			1.3		1862
1861				86.6	6.8	93.4		5.0			1.6		1861
1860				85.3	7.0	92.3		4.9			2.8		1860
1959				84.0	6.9	91.0		4.7			4.4		1859
1858				85.2	7.0	92.2		4.9			2.9		1858
1857				85.1	6.9	92.0		4.7			3.3		1857
1856				84.4	7.6	92.0		5.3			2.7		1856
1855				83.1	9.3	92.4		5.7			1.8		1855
1854				85.9	7.4	93.3		5.9			0.8		1854
1853				87.0	6.5	93.6		6.0			0.5		1853
1852				85.4	7.3	92.7		6.1			1.2		1852
1851				85.9	7.2	93.2		5.3			1.5		1851
1850				85.4	7.4	92.8		5.5			1.8		1850
1849				85.6	7.4	93.0		6.4			0.6		1849
1848				84.3	7.6	91.8		7.8			0.3		1848
1847				84.6	6.4	91.0		9.2			-0.2		1847
1846				84.3	6.7	90.9		7.8			1.3		1846
1845				86.2	6.8	93.0		5.4			1.6		1845
1844				86.9	7.5	94.4		3.7			1.9		1844
1843				86.5	8.0	94.5		3.6			1.8		1843
1842				88.5	7.6	96.1		4.1			-0.1		1842
1841				88.5	7.0	95.4		4.4			0.2		1841
1840				87.8	6.8	94.6		5.8			-0.4		1840
1839				87.8	6.0	93.8		5.6			0.5		1839
1838				87.5	6.1	93.6		5.6			0.8		1838
1837				88.2	6.3	94.4		5.1			0.4		1837
1836				88.7	5.9	94.6		4.4			1.0		1836
1835				86.6	6.4	93.1		4.5			2.5		1835
1834				88.8	6.7	95.6		3.0			1.4		1834
1833				89.1	7.4	96.6		2.7			0.8		1833
1832				88.6	7.5	96.1		2.6			1.3		1832
1831				89.1	7.0	96.2		3.3			0.5		1831
1830				89.7	7.2	96.9		3.0			0.1		1830

a) Figures refer to GDP at factor cost.
b) Figures for 1830-1960 refer to GNP. Prior to 1870 GNP is without changes in stocks.

United Kingdom

Origin of National Product

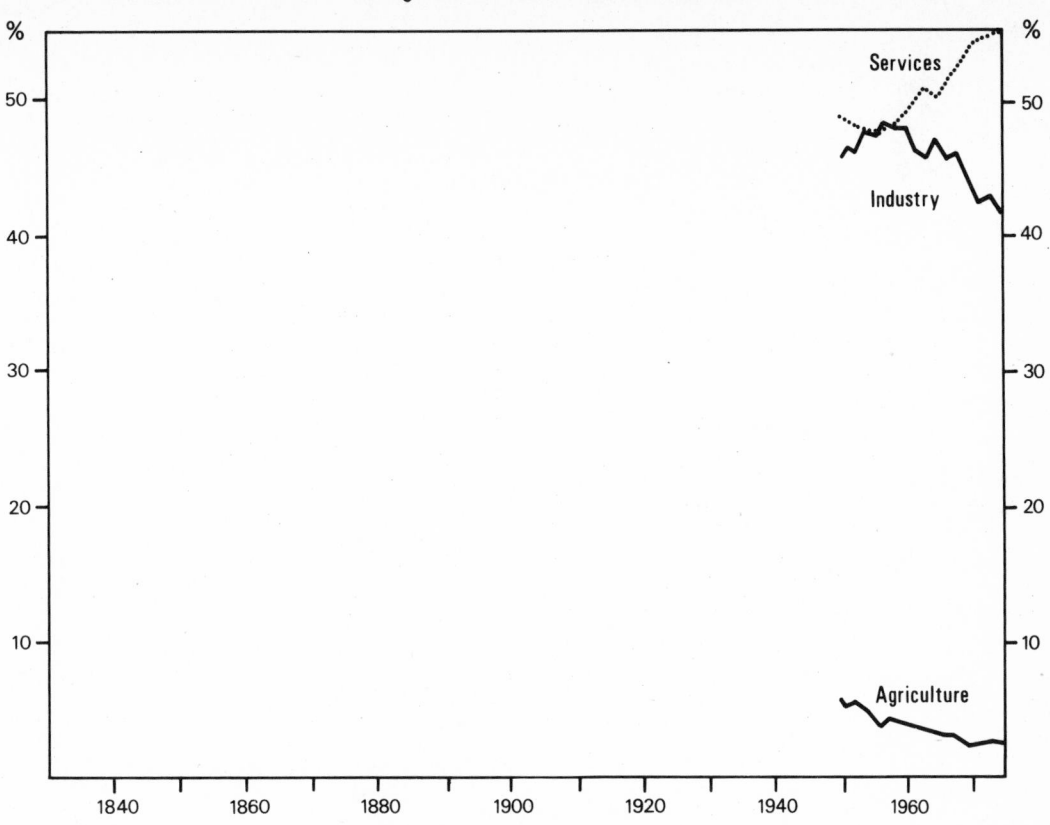

Use of National Product

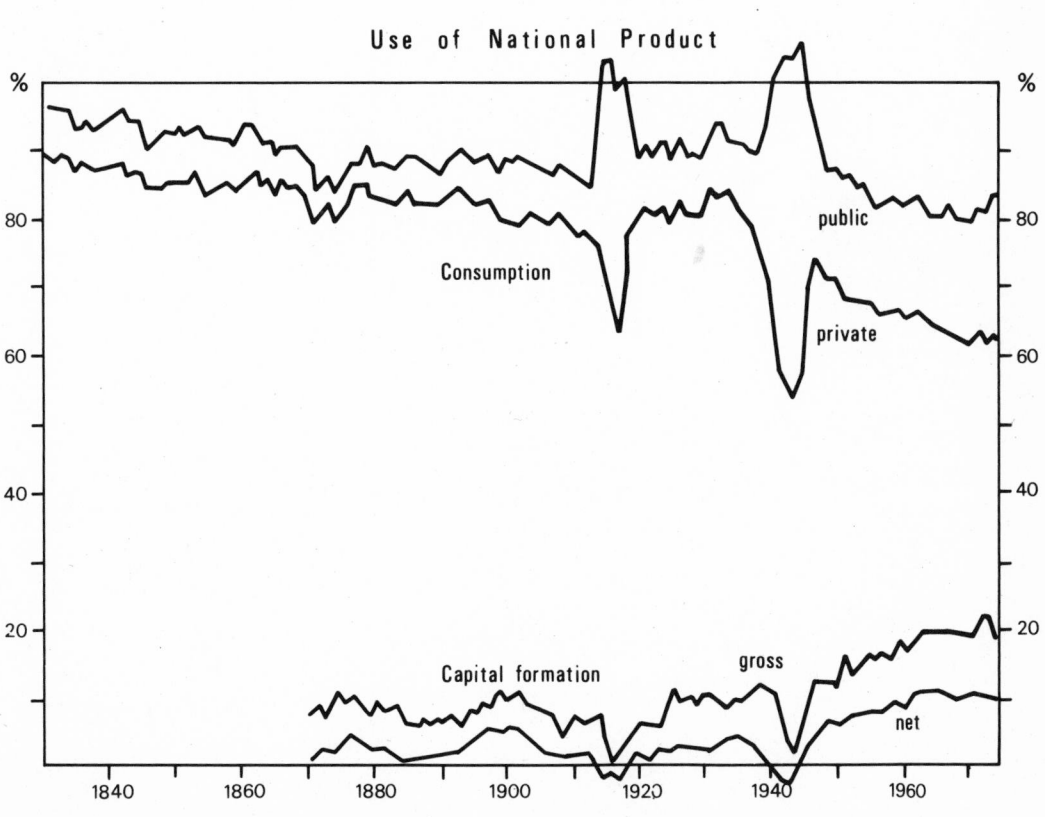

IX

Division of Labour and Inequality

Chapter 7

LABOUR FORCE

This chapter presents basic data on the differentiation of the working population by economic sector and occupational status. This comes perhaps closest to the idea of a 'social structure' of the population as defined by the extent and form of the social division of labour.

One of the earliest attempts to describe the social structure of a country is Gregory King's famous study of the English population in 1688. He classified all English families/households (around 1,35 million with ca. 5,5 million people) by the position of the head of household, distinguishing between 26 social categories. Basically, they represented a mixture of social status (e.g. the distinctions within the gentry), occupation (e.g. merchant), branch of activity (e.g. 'persons in offices'), and industrial status (independents or dependents). He then estimated the average household size and the average annual income per household in each category. Of course, King could not rely on an occupational census, but had to utilize a variety of sources, above all tax statistics.

The first occupational censuses were carried out in the eighteenth century and became a regular practice in the nineteenth century. Up to the last third of the nineteenth century it was common to ask only for the occupation of the head of the family/household as the main provider and to classify the other family/household members (including domestic personnel) accordingly. Only gradually a clearer distinction was drawn between the main breadwinner and the others, until it was finally required to state the occupation of all persons who worked for pay or profit. This transition from counting families to the enumeration of individuals, and the increasing differentiation between occupation, branch and status is a watershed in the history of the occupational census. In principle, the enumeration of individuals instead of families now makes it possible to identify the working population out of the total population of a country. For this reason we have not tried to include censuses prior to around 1880.

In modern censuses, the economically active population is classified according to:

a)	occupation, i.e. the kind of work from which a person earns his main income and/or in which he spends most of his work time,

b)	the branch or industry in which a person pursues his occupation,

c)	industrial status, i.e. the role a person assumes within his place of work such as employer, employee, apprentice etc.

This threefold classification must be seen as a product of a long-term process of increasing differentiation between the three dimensions. Originally, a mixed classification in which occupational aspects predominated was common. Frequently as a first step, the classification by status became more clearly separated, whereas an unambiguous distinction between the occupational and the industrial principle of classification was not normally made prior to World War I.

This differentiation between an occupational and an industrial principle was enhanced by the introduction of industrial censuses in which data are collected on the basis of productive units such as firms, and not on the basis of housholds as in the case of general population and/or occupational censuses. These special censuses frequently produce figures on the size and structure of the economically active population which differ markedly from those of the general censuses. On the one hand, industrial censuses may understimate the working population, not only because they are usually partial enumerations, but also because they focus on clearly defined productive units. On the other hand, they may also overestimate the economically active population, because they enumerate positions and not persons, and persons may have more than one occupation.

We therefore have relied exclusively on general censuses. These are mainly general population censuses and only in a few cases separate occupational censuses which also cover the total population (see the following table for all censuses which have been utilized). The main data presented in this chapter refer to the classification of the economically active population by branch or sector of activity and by industrial status (cross-tabulations). The classification by occupation has been excluded because it poses insurmountable problems of comparability, even for the period after World War II.

Census Dates (a)

	AU	BE	DE	FI	FR	GE	IR	IT	NE	NO	SW	SZ	EW	SO
1975	1975				1975						1975		⌒	
1970	1970	1971	1970	1970	1968	1970	1971	1971	1971	1970	1970	1970	1971	
1965	1965		1965				1966				1965			
1960	1960	1961	1961	1960	1962	1961	1961	1961	1961	1960	1960	1960	1961	1961
1955	1955		1955		1954									
1950	1950	1951		1950		1950	1951	1951		1950	1950	1950	1951	1951
1945		1947			1946		1946		1947	1946	1945			
1940	1939		1940	1940		1939					1940	1941		
1935	1934				1936	1933	1936	1936						
1930		1930	1930	1930	1931			1931	1931	1930	1930	1930	1931	1931
1925					1926	1925	1926							
1920		1920	1921	1920	1921			1921	1920	1920	1920	1920	1921	1921
1915			1916											
1910	1910	1910	1910	1911	1910			1911	1909	1910	1910	1910	1911	1911
1905					1906	1907								
1900	1900	1900	1900	(1900)	1901			1901	1899	1900	1900	1900	1901	1901
1895						1895								
1890	1890	1890	1890	1890	1891				(1889)	1890	1890	1888	1891	1891
1885					1886									
1880	1880	1880	1880	1880	1881	1882		1881			1880	(1880)		

(a) For censuses in brackets, only classifications by sector are available.

Unless due care is exercised, comparisons of labour force statistics over time and across countries may be rendered wholly invalid. It starts with the relatively simple difficulties of an 'operational-statistical' nature. Thus, a first problem stems from differences in the definition of the total population: the choice between utilization of the present or the resident population, and the choice between including or excluding foreigners, has consequences not only for the size of the economically active population, but also for its structure. The size of the labour force may be influenced by the definition of a minimum age (usually varying from nine to fifteen years), because young people under this age limit are automatically excluded even if they are 'economically active'. The census date may also have an impact, since no distinction is normally made between 'permanent' and 'occasional/seasonal' work at the time of the census.

More serious, however, are the conceptual problems in comparing labour force statistics. They refer first of all to the term 'economically active', which must be regarded in terms of the specific organization of work in a particular society. To some extent, therefore, the economically active population will always remain a statistical artifact which should be defined differently for different purposes. However, the conceptual problems refer more to the concept's boundaries and less to its core, because there is a structural equivalent to the statistical artifact: the process of capitalist industrialization has made the labour force more visible as a distinctive population category. Labour and its products are increasingly exchanged in markets, and 'economically active' has largely become synonymous with 'active in markets'. This process of commercialization was related to an increasing separation of household and work place, and to a corresponding spatial and temporal concentration of the working population.

The following figure shows the major classification problems of the labour force concept (here used interchangeably with the concepts of 'economically active population' or 'working population'). The core of the economically active population consists of all those who are gainfully occupied full-time as employees, self-employed or employers in the private or public sector.

PRIVATE HOUSEHOLDS

	Not: housewives	
	— Family Workers —	
	Domestic personnel	
Part- time work	Private sector FULL-TIME GAINFULLY OCCUPIED Public sector	Temporar- ily out of work
	— Apprentices — — Recruits —	
	Not: pupils/ Not: persons in	
	students other institutions	

(INSTITUTIONAL HOUSEHOLDS)

A first category of boundary problems refers to the required duration and regularity of this gainful occupation, i.e. the treatment of those who work part-time, who are temporarily out of work, or who are looking for a job for the first time. In this respect the comparability is very limited. Definitions vary greatly and are often vague, and their operationalization and the actual coding are frequently unknown. Usually, all persons whose work only contributes to a minor degree to their living are excluded. Definitions of minimum weekly working hours are found only in recent censuses and vary a great deal. Any such criteria is, of course, relatively arbitrary and must be regarded in terms of the existing social division of labour. With the spread of gainful part-time work, this boundary problem will become even more problematic. In historical perspective, however, the differences in the treatment of persons temporarily out of work are probably more relevant. In early censuses it was frequently the case that all persons who had worked at any point in time were included among the working population (i.e. also retired people). Later, pensioners, invalids, persons in hospitals or other institutional households were excluded. This has also been done in our tables. The two most important categories of people 'temporarily out of work' which have usually been included are the sick and the unemployed. In early censuses the treatment of unemployed persons is frequently unknown, but after the turn of the century they are normally included, even though they were only coded separately later on. Today, there is still the problem of how to distinguish between temporary and long-term sickness and unemployment, and how to classify the — usually young — persons who are unemployed without previous occupation.

A second category of boundary problems refers to the element of 'gainful' work, i.e. the exchange of labour or its product for income. This produces difficulties in all situations in which economic exchange is incomplete or mixed. The most problematic cases are found in private households which have remained productive units, above all in agriculture, among artisans, and in the retail trade. The most frequent census categories, which of course simplify a great variety of work forms in these households, are 'housewives', 'family workers', and 'domestic personnel'. Whenever available as separate categories, housewives have been excluded from the economically active population, and domestic personnel have been classified as workers in the service sector.

The classification of family workers, who may be paid or unpaid family members or other relatives, is much more problematic. The actual treatment has varied greatly and these differences pose enormous problems for comparability. Sometimes it is not even known whether family workers are included or not; sometimes they are included but their classification is unknown; and sometimes they are coded as workers or as self-employed or are distributed among the various status categories.

With respect to the 'gainful' aspect of work, boundary problems are not only created by the differentiation of private households and units of production. They are also produced by the differentiation of the educational system and the labour market, and by the development of public institutional households. As to the educational system, pupils and students are consistently excluded, but apprentices in part-time vocational schools are classified as economically active, and as a separate category where the relevant information was available. Among the persons working in public institutional households without corresponding pay, only conscripts have usually been included, all others (e.g. prisoners) being classified as economically inactive.

This introduction is only intended as a brief explanation of our general guidelines in delineating the economically active population, and its indicates only the most serious problems encountered in comparing labour force statistics. Some additional information can be found in the notes to the tables, but more complete information will only be given in the computer documentation.

For altogether 131 censuses, the data are presented in a standard table in which the total labour force is classified according to ten sectors of economic activity, six status categories, and sex (separate data are given for the male labour force only).

The classification of economic activities relies on the UN International Standard Industrial Classification (ISIC), with a few modifications:

(1)   The ISIC category 'services' has been split into a general service sector and into public administration.
(2)   Some activities have been reclassified in order to create more homogeneous sectors. The most important cases are given in the following table.

Classification of economic activities by sector

I	Agriculture:	agriculture forestry fishing
II	Mining:	mining quarrying
III	Manufacturing:	basic mineral products basic metal products fabricated metal products, machinery and equipment fabricated non-metallic mineral products chemicals, rubber and plastic products paper, printing and publishing furniture and wood products textiles, wearing apparel and leather products food, beverage, and tobacco other manufacturing industries
IV	Construction:	building construction of communication networks
V	Utilities:	electricity, gas and steam water works and supply
VI	Commerce:	wholesale trade retail trade
VII	Transport:	transport and storage communication
VIII	Banking:	banking insurance (except social security institutions)
IX	Services:	restaurants and hotels (ISIC: VI) laundry, cleaning, repair, sanitary services domestic services real estate and business services (ISIC: VIII)

		private non-profit organizations
		recreational and cultural services
		education
		health
		social security institutions
		religion
		international organizations and extraterritorial bodies
X	Public ad-ministration:	civil administration
		police
		military
XI	Unknown	industry unknown
		not adequately described (not: unknown whether active or not

This standard classification has been applied to all 131 censuses. Differences in the definition of sectors could be minimized by regrouping the economic activities on the basis of the most detailed census table. With few exceptions, therefore, the actual classification comes very close to the above standard classification. Where problems arise, they are mainly found in delimiting mining and manufacturing, in creating a utility sector (often included in other sectors), and a more homogeneous banking sector (which often includes very heterogeneous activities).

The transition from occupational to industrial classification entails a break in the series. Whenever possible, occupational classifications have been transformed into pseudo-industrial classifications, which assume that certain types of occupations are typically performed in a specific industry. This presupposes a low level of vertical integration of production. While the resulting figures are fairly reliable for a distinction between the primary (I), secondary (II to V), and tertiary sectors (VI to X), they are far less reliable for more detailed analyses. This holds especially true for the tertiary sector.

The classification of day-labourers varies considerably between censuses. Sometimes they are considered a separate category, and sometimes they are assigned to the temporary occupation at census time or their dominant occupation during the previous year. They account for a large proportion of 'industry unknown' in our tables.

With respect to status, no standard classification could be applied because the definition of status categories differs markedly between censuses. Whenever possible, data have been re-arranged to meet the following distinctions:

Definitions of status categories

Employers	those employing other than family workers
Self-employed	those working on their own account without help except for family workers
Employees	higher-status dependent labourer or white collar personnel, including civil servants
Workers	lower-status dependent labourers or blue collar personnel, including home-workers
Apprentices	persons in vocational training in firms
Family Workers	assisting spouses, children or relatives

With respect to the comparability of these status categories, three general observations can be made:

(1) The major distinction between an independent labour force (employers and self-employed) and a dependent labour force (employees and workers) is fairly consistent and comparable. Sometimes managers and directors are included among the employers, but this bias is not very significant.

(2) Within these two major groups, however, the categories are not strictly comparable. This is especially true for the distinction between workers and employees which, to a varying degree, combines differences in the type of work (manual versus non-manual), the work place (factory versus office), and the legal status (in labour and social security law). Here, comparisons must be limited to relatively stable contexts.

(3) In general, data on family workers are much less reliable and comparable than for any other category because their definition and coverage varies greatly (which sometimes causes breaks in comparability even for the figures on 'total labour force').

For some of the earlier censuses, it is not possible to cross-tabulate the labour force by sector and status, but only to give separate totals for the different categories. These data are included in the summary table for each country which precedes the census tables.

The summary table gives an overview with respect to the development of:

(a)   the total labour force and the activity ratios;
(b)   the distribution of the labour force among the three major sectors: the primary (sector I), secondary (II—IV), and tertiary (VI—X) sectors;
(c)   the distribution of the labour force among dependent, independent, and family workers;
(d)   the domestic personnel and military personnel.

Data on the two specific groups in (d) have been included in order to improve the comparability of the two sectors Services (IX) and Administration (X). With regard to the latter, the classification of conscripts differs from one census to another. Sometimes they have been included in the sector, sometimes they have been excluded from the labour force. In many censuses, however, they have been coded according to their previous status and sector of activity. Thus, on the basis of the figures given in the summary table, it is possible to construct a more comparable public administration sector by excluding the military personnel.

The sector Services poses still greater problems. It comprises much more heterogeneous activities than any other sector and one may doubt whether it is meaningful to group all these activities together. In order to reduce the heterogeneity somewhat, we give separate figures for the domestic personnel as they form a distinctive and, in earlier times, quantitatively important group within the service sector. However, we have not done what would have been necessary: to reclassify the various activities according to a more detailed and theoretically meaningful classification scheme (as suggested for example by Siegelman in his book From Agriculture to Services. The Transformation of Industrial Employment. London: Sage 1978). Such a re-classification would have required a separate project which we are glad to leave to all people who are crazy enough to follow us.

Austria

The Development of the Labour Force

Year	by Status				by Sector				Total labour force	Domestic services	Military personnel	Year
	Inde-pendent (IN)	Depend-ent (DE)	Family worker	Un-known	Agricul-ture (A)	Indus-try (I)	Serv-ices (S)	Un-known				
	percent distribution				percent distribution				in thousands			
1971	13.8	78.8	7.4		13.8	41.6	42.7	2.0	3 098.0	21.8		1971
1961	15.8	70.8	13.3		22.8	40.6	35.4	1.1	3 369.8	47.0		1961
1951	17.6	64.7	17.7		32.3	37.1	29.4	1.2	3 347.1	76.3		1951
1939	16.9	60.9	22.2		39.0	31.7	28.6	0.7	3 648.9	126.0	69.7[a]	1939
1934	20.6	67.3	12.0		31.9	33.3	31.8	3.0	3 149.5	157.8	30.9	1934
1910	25.9	46.3	27.8		56.9	23.5	16.4	3.1	14 951.1	636.5	246.9	1910
1900	23.7	45.9	30.3		60.9	21.3	16.3	1.5	13 476.8	595.7	229.0	1900
1890	23.1	76.9			64.1	20.4	13.7	1.8	13 216.0	549.6	187.5	1890
1880	28.9	71.1			55.6	20.5	15.9	8.0	11 079.0	890.2	162.4	1880

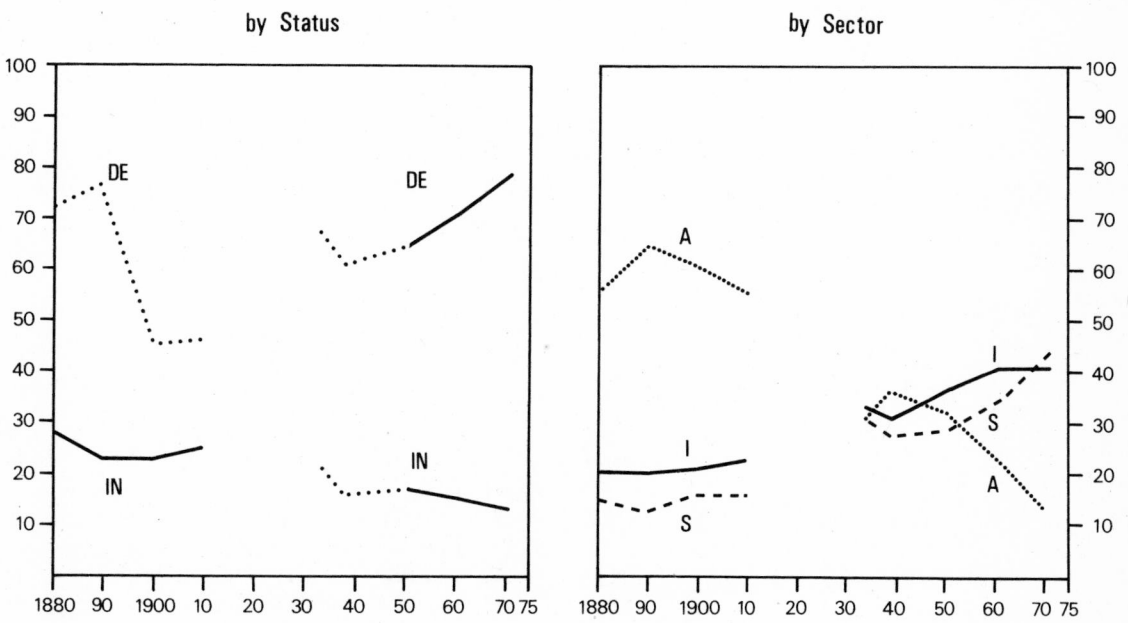

by Status   by Sector

449

Austria

Labour Force by Sector and Status 1880

Absolute figures in thousands

Sector			Employ-ers	Self-employed	Employ-ees	Workers	Apprent-ices	Family-workers	Un-known	Total	%
			EM	SE	EE	WO	AP	FW[a]	U	T	
I	Agriculture	Total	2 366.7		56.2	3 738.3				6 161.2	55.6
		males	1 736.6		46.5	1 649.2				3 432.3	51.9
II	Mining	Total	1.3		4.9	111.6				117.9	1.1
		males	1.2		4.9	102.2				108.2	1.6
III	Manufacturing	Total									
		males									
IV	Construction	Total	575.8		49.9	1 531.4				2 157.1	19.5
		males	498.4		42.9	1 091.1				1 632.4	24.7
V	Utilities	Total									
		males									
VI	Commerce	Total	185.4	33.1		91.5				310.1	2.8
		males	139.2	28.9		63.2				231.2	3.5
VII	Transport	Total	18.2	28.0		69.3				115.5	1.0
		males	17.1	26.9		66.7				110.7	1.7
VIII	Banking	Total	1.5	7.1		1.2				9.8	.1
		males	1.4	6.9		1.2				9.5	.1
IX	Services	Total	57.5	93.4		912.5				1 063.4	9.6
		males	38.2	71.5		262.0				371.7	5.6
X	Public admin.[b]	Total	.0	60.6		200.9				261.4	2.4
		males	.0	60.1		200.5				260.5	3.9
U	Unknown[c]	Total				882.6				882.6	8.0
		males				454.2				454.2	6.9
T	All sectors	Total	3 206.4	333.2		7 539.3				11 079.0	100.0
		males	2 432.0	288.5		3 890.2				6 610.8	100.0

Percent distributions

Total labour force

	EM	SE	EE	WO	AP	FW	U	T
I	38.4		.9	60.7				100.0
II	1.1		4.2	94.7				100.0
III								
IV	26.7		2.3	71.0				100.0
V								
VI	59.8		10.7	29.5				100.0
VII	15.7		24.2	60.0				100.0
VIII	15.2		72.3	12.5				100.0
IX	5.4		8.8	85.8				100.0
X	.0		23.2	76.8				100.0
U				100.0				100.0
T	28.9		3.0	68.1				100.0

Male labour force

	EM	SE	EE	WO	AP	FW	U	T
I	50.6		1.4	48.0				100.0
II	1.1		4.5	94.4				100.0
III								
IV	30.5		2.6	66.8				100.0
V								
VI	60.2		12.5	27.3				100.0
VII	15.4		24.3	60.3				100.0
VIII	14.7		73.1	12.2				100.0
IX	10.3		19.2	70.5				100.0
X	.0		23.0	77.0				100.0
U				100.0				100.0
T	36.8		4.4	58.8				100.0

450

Austria

Labour Force by Sector and Status 1890

Absolute figures in thousands

Sector			Employers	Self-employed	Employees	Workers	Apprentices	Family-workers [a]	Unknown	Total	%
			EM	SE	EE	WO	AP	FW	U	T	
I	Agriculture	Total	2 006.7	22.4		5 615.0	824.8			8 468.9	64.1
		males	1 766.8	21.5		1 962.5	413.6			4 164.4	56.2
II	Mining	Total	1.9	2.4		114.0	11.6			129.9	1.0
		males	1.7	2.4		103.4	9.2			116.7	1.6
III	Manufacturing	Total	488.6	28.4		1 684.2	68.2			2 269.4	17.2
		males	392.9	26.8		1 181.0	46.9			1 647.6	22.2
IV	Construction	Total	35.9	4.8		235.1	17.8			293.6	2.2
		males	34.3	4.7		221.4	12.9			273.3	3.7
V	Utilities	Total	.1	.3		2.2	.6			3.2	.0
		males	.1	.3		2.1	.5			3.0	.0
VI	Commerce	Total	206.1	55.3		89.1	5.2			355.8	2.7
		males	158.5	51.1		55.0	4.1			268.7	3.6
VII	Transport	Total	20.3	42.5		123.2	11.2			197.1	1.5
		males	18.1	38.9		116.4	10.0			183.5	2.5
VIII	Banking	Total	2.0	10.3		2.5	.0			14.8	.1
		males	1.8	9.9		2.2	.0			13.9	.2
IX	Services	Total	219.0	120.9		611.4	3.6			955.0	7.2
		males	124.2	90.9		113.4	2.3			330.8	4.5
X	Public admin. [b]	Total	.0		250.4	37.7	1.5			289.6	2.2
		males	.0		249.2	34.6	1.3			285.1	3.8
U	Unknown	Total	69.8			12.1	156.9			238.7	1.8
		males	19.9			6.1	93.0			119.0	1.6
T	All sectors	Total	3 050.4	537.7		8 526.4	1 101.4			13 216.0	100.0
		males	2 518.4	495.6		3 798.2	593.9			7 406.0	100.0

Percent distributions

Total labour force

	EM	SE	EE	WO	AP	FW	U	T
I	23.7	.3		66.3	9.7			100.0
II	1.5	1.8		87.7	8.9			100.0
III	21.5	1.3		74.2	3.0			100.0
IV	12.2	1.6		80.1	6.1			100.0
V	2.8	10.6		68.3	18.3			100.0
VI	57.9	15.5		25.0	1.5			100.0
VII	10.3	21.6		62.5	5.7			100.0
VIII	13.7	69.3		16.9	.1			100.0
IX	22.9	12.7		64.0	.4			100.0
X	.0		86.5	13.0	.5			100.0
U	29.2			5.1	65.7			100.0
T	23.1	4.1		64.5	8.3			100.0

Male labour force

	EM	SE	EE	WO	AP	FW	U	T
I	42.4	.5		47.1	9.9			100.0
II	1.5	2.0		88.6	7.9			100.0
III	23.8	1.6		71.7	2.8			100.0
IV	12.6	1.7		81.0	4.7			100.0
V	2.7	10.9		68.7	17.7			100.0
VI	59.0	19.0		20.5	1.5			100.0
VII	9.9	21.2		63.4	5.5			100.0
VIII	12.7	71.3		15.9	.1			100.0
IX	37.5	27.5		34.3	.7			100.0
X	.0		87.4	12.1	.5			100.0
U	16.8			5.1	78.2			100.0
T	34.0	6.7		51.3	8.0			100.0

L a b o u r   F o r c e   b y   S e c t o r   a n d   S t a t u s   1 9 0 0

Absolute figures in thousands

Sector			Employ-ers EM	Self-employed SE	Employ-ees EE	Workers WO	Apprent-ices AP	Family-workers FW[a]	Un-known U	Total T	%
I	Agriculture	Total	2 164.6	20.7	2 085.5		3 934.7		8 205.6	60.9
		males	1 906.3	20.3	1 133.0		1 023.2		4 082.7	52.4
II	Mining	Total	1.3	3.6	165.0		.6		170.4	1.3
		males	1.2	3.5	156.0		.1		160.8	2.1
III	Manufacturing	Total	448.7	57.8	1 759.7		62.1		2 328.3	17.3
		males	375.4	54.0	1 306.9		20.8		1 757.0	22.5
IV	Construction	Total	37.4	8.6	322.0		3.5		371.5	2.8
		males	35.9	8.5	310.2		1.3		356.0	4.6
V	Utilities	Total	.1	.5	4.6		.0		5.3	.0
		males	.1	.5	4.4		.0		5.1	.1
VI	Commerce	Total	213.2	31.1	119.4		41.5		405.2	3.0
		males	151.1	27.7	95.0		10.5		284.3	3.6
VII	Transport	Total	21.1	58.1	182.9		2.4		264.5	2.0
		males	19.1	49.8	178.9		1.0		248.9	3.2
VIII	Banking	Total	1.9	20.7	4.2		.1		26.9	.2
		males	1.6	19.3	3.8		.0		24.8	.3
IX	Services	Total	311.9	158.6	632.8		39.1		1 142.4	8.5
		males	159.5	109.6	111.8		7.2		388.1	5.0
X	Public admin.[b]	Total	.0	84.9	275.2		.5		360.6	2.7
		males	.0	83.6	273.5		.1		357.2	4.6
U	Unknown	Total				196.1			196.1	1.5
		males				127.0			127.0	1.6
T	All sectors	Total	3 200.1	444.8	5 747.4		4 084.5		13 476.8	100.0
		males	2 650.1	376.8	3 700.6		1 064.2		7 791.8	100.0

Percent distributions

Total labour force

	EM	SE	EE	WO	AP	FW	U	T
I	26.4	.3	25.4			48.0		100.0
II	.7	2.1	96.8			.3		100.0
III	19.3	2.5	75.6			2.7		100.0
IV	10.1	2.3	86.7			.9		100.0
V	2.0	10.3	86.9			.8		100.0
VI	52.6	7.7	29.5			10.2		100.0
VII	8.0	22.0	69.2			.9		100.0
VIII	7.0	77.0	15.6			.4		100.0
IX	27.3	13.9	55.4			3.4		100.0
X	.0	23.5	76.3			.1		100.0
U				100.0				100.0
T	23.7	3.3	42.6			30.3		100.0

Male labour force

	EM	SE	EE	WO	AP	FW	U	T
I	46.7	.5	27.8			25.1		100.0
II	.7	2.2	97.0			.1		100.0
III	21.4	3.1	74.4			1.2		100.0
IV	10.1	2.4	87.1			.4		100.0
V	1.9	10.5	87.4			.3		100.0
VI	53.1	9.8	33.4			3.7		100.0
VII	7.7	20.0	71.9			.4		100.0
VIII	6.5	77.9	15.5			.1		100.0
IX	41.1	28.2	28.8			1.9		100.0
X	.0	23.4	76.6			.0		100.0
U				100.0				100.0
T	34.0	4.8	47.5			13.7		100.0

L a b o u r   F o r c e   b y   S e c t o r   a n d   S t a t u s   1 9 1 0

Absolute figures in thousands

Sector			Employ-ers	Self-employed	Employ-ees	Workers	Apprent-ices	Family-workers	Un-known	Total	%
			EM	SE	EE	WO	AP	FW	U	T	
I	Agriculture	Total	2 598.8	22.3	1 951.4	2.9	3 930.9		8 506.5	56.9
		males	1 996.8	21.8	1 020.9	2.8	1 170.1		4 212.5	48.8
II	Mining	Total	1.4	4.7	176.5	.4	.4		183.4	1.2
		males	1.3	4.5	168.3	.4	.2		174.7	2.0
III	Manufacturing	Total	536.2	84.4	1 909.1	255.9	69.1		2 854.6	19.1
		males	410.6	71.9	1 331.1	206.8	17.9		2 038.2	23.6
IV	Construction	Total	46.3	12.5	371.5	32.4	1.7		464.4	3.1
		males	45.2	11.7	357.5	32.2	1.1		447.7	5.2
V	Utilities	Total	.2	2.7	12.3	.2	.0		15.4	.1
		males	.1	2.4	11.8	.2	.0		14.5	.2
VI	Commerce	Total	258.8	58.2	146.5	27.8	89.5		580.9	3.9
		males	179.7	42.5	108.2	23.7	17.9		372.0	4.3
VII	Transport	Total	22.6	67.1	306.4	.4	2.0		398.6	2.7
		males	20.9	52.6	301.0	.4	1.4		376.3	4.4
VIII	Banking	Total	1.8	39.9	6.9	.1	.1		48.8	.3
		males	1.5	34.6	6.4	.1	.0		42.6	.5
IX	Services	Total	404.6	199.3	747.0	15.0	61.7		1 427.7	9.5
		males	175.8	123.0	172.6	13.6	8.3		493.2	5.7
X	Public admin. [a)]	Total	.0	129.4	341.2	.0	.4		470.9	3.1
		males	.0	124.2	337.1	.0	.1		461.3	5.3
U	Unknown	Total								
		males								
T	All sectors	Total	3 870.9	620.5	5 968.7	335.3	4 155.8		14 951.1	100.0
		males	2 832.0	489.3	3 814.8	280.1	1 216.9		8 633.1	100.0

Percent distributions

	Total labour force									Male labour force							
	EM	SE	EE	WO	AP	FW	U	T		EM	SE	EE	WO	AP	FW	U	T
I	30.6	.3	22.9	.0	46.2		100.0	I	47.4	.5	24.2	.1	27.8		100.0
II	.8	2.6	96.2	.2	.2		100.0	II	.8	2.6	96.3	.2	.1		100.0
III	18.8	3.0	66.9	9.0	2.4		100.0	III	20.1	3.5	65.3	10.1	.9		100.0
IV	10.0	2.7	80.0	7.0	.4		100.0	IV	10.1	2.6	79.8	7.2	.2		100.0
V	1.2	17.8	79.7	1.2	.0		100.0	V	.9	16.8	81.3	1.1	.0		100.0
VI	44.6	10.0	25.2	4.8	15.4		100.0	VI	48.3	11.4	29.1	6.4	4.8		100.0
VII	5.7	16.8	76.9	.1	.5		100.0	VII	5.5	14.0	80.0	.1	.4		100.0
VIII	3.7	81.7	14.1	.2	.2		100.0	VIII	3.5	81.2	15.0	.2	.1		100.0
IX	28.3	14.0	52.3	1.1	4.3		100.0	IX	35.6	24.9	35.0	2.8	1.7		100.0
X	.0	27.5	72.5	.0	.1		100.0	X	.0	26.9	73.1	.0	.0		100.0
U								U							
T	25.9	4.2	39.9	2.2	27.8		100.0	T	32.8	5.7	44.2	3.2	14.1		100.0

Labour Force by Sector and Status 1934 [a]

Absolute figures in thousands

Sector			Employ-ers EM	Self-employed SE	Employ-ees [b] EE	Workers WO	Apprent-ices AP	Family-workers [c] FW	Un-known U	Total T	%
I	Agriculture	Total	290.7	11.5	347.0	1.0	353.8		1 004.0	31.9
		males	250.2	10.7	214.3	.9	178.1		654.2	31.1
II	Mining	Total	.7	2.3	28.4	.2	.0		31.7	1.0
		males	.7	2.1	27.4	.2	.0		30.5	1.5
III	Manufacturing	Total	149.0	87.4	566.4	38.5	7.3		848.6	26.9
		males	118.6	62.1	396.9	30.5	4.3		612.3	29.2
IV	Construction	Total	12.6	9.5	132.1	4.3	.5		158.9	5.0
		males	12.1	8.7	128.0	4.2	.4		153.5	7.3
V	Utilities	Total	.1	3.3	7.1	.1	.0		10.6	.3
		males	.1	3.0	6.9	.1	.0		10.1	.5
VI	Commerce	Total	91.1	95.3	29.8	9.9	9.1		235.1	7.5
		males	58.7	57.7	23.0	6.3	3.7		149.3	7.1
VII	Transport	Total	9.3	43.0	90.5	.1	.3		143.3	4.5
		males	8.6	34.8	88.6	.1	.3		132.3	6.3
VIII	Banking	Total	.7	27.7	2.6	.1	.0		31.1	1.0
		males	.6	21.5	1.6	.1	.0		23.8	1.1
IX	Services	Total	94.5	124.1	259.4	6.5	8.2		492.9	15.6
		males	55.5	60.3	63.0	4.3	2.4		185.5	8.8
X	Public admin. [d]	Total	.0	39.8	58.9	.0	.0		98.7	3.1
		males	.0	32.7	56.5	.0	.0		89.2	4.2
U	Unknown	Total	.9	11.5	81.0	1.3			94.7	3.0
		males	.1	5.4	53.5	.7			59.6	2.8
T	All sectors	Total	649.7	455.4	1 603.1	62.1	379.3		3 149.5	100.0
		males	505.1	298.9	1 059.6	47.4	189.3		2 100.3	100.0

Percent distributions

Total labour force

	EM	SE	EE	WO	AP	FW	U	T
I	29.0	1.1	34.6	.1	35.2		100.0
II	2.3	7.2	89.6	.7	.2		100.0
III	17.6	10.3	66.7	4.5	.9		100.0
IV	7.9	6.0	83.1	2.7	.3		100.0
V	.9	31.5	66.5	1.1	.1		100.0
VI	38.7	40.5	12.7	4.2	3.9		100.0
VII	6.5	30.0	63.2	.1	.2		100.0
VIII	2.4	88.9	8.3	.3	.1		100.0
IX	19.2	25.2	52.6	1.3	1.7		100.0
X	.0	40.3	59.7	.0	.0		100.0
U	1.0	12.1	85.5	1.4			100.0
T	20.6	14.5	50.9	2.0	12.0		100.0

Male labour force

	EM	SE	EE	WO	AP	FW	U	T
I	38.2	1.6	32.8	.1	27.2		100.0
II	2.3	6.8	90.0	.8	.1		100.0
III	19.4	10.1	64.8	5.0	.7		100.0
IV	7.9	5.7	83.4	2.8	.2		100.0
V	.9	29.3	68.7	1.1	.0		100.0
VI	39.3	38.7	15.4	4.2	2.5		100.0
VII	6.5	26.3	66.9	.1	.2		100.0
VIII	2.4	90.5	6.9	.3	.0		100.0
IX	29.9	32.5	33.9	2.3	1.3		100.0
X	.0	36.7	63.3	.0	.0		100.0
U	.2	9.0	89.6	1.2			100.0
T	24.0	14.2	50.4	2.3	9.0		100.0

L a b o u r   F o r c e   b y   S e c t o r   a n d   S t a t u s   1 9 3 9 [a]

Absolute figures in thousands

Sector			Employ- ers	Civil servants	Employ- ees	Workers	Apprent- ices	Family- workers	Un- known	Total	%
			EM	CS	EE	WO	AP	FW	U	T	
I	Agriculture	Total	340.1	1.3	9.2	322.5		749.7		1 422.8	39.0
		males	281.8	1.3	8.5	185.0		178.9		655.3	30.5
II	Mining	Total	2.3	.1	5.6	68.4		.3		76.8	2.1
		males	2.1	.1	4.6	60.8		.1		67.7	3.1
III	Manufacturing	Total	123.5	.3	85.3	577.9		15.8		802.9	22.0
		males	97.9	.3	54.1	394.5		2.1		548.8	25.5
IV	Construction	Total	14.9	1.8	15.5	227.4		.9		260.4	7.1
		males	14.2	1.8	13.2	221.3		.2		250.6	11.7
V	Utilities	Total	.1	1.7	5.0	10.0		.0		16.8	.5
		males	.1	1.6	4.4	9.7		.0		15.7	.7
VI	Commerce	Total	71.1	.0	79.9	31.7		23.7		206.3	5.7
		males	42.4	.0	41.3	23.9		3.1		110.7	5.1
VII	Transport	Total	8.3	64.9	32.2	84.7		.6		190.7	5.2
		males	7.7	59.7	22.2	81.8		.3		171.7	8.0
VIII	Banking	Total	.5	1.5	24.8	1.9		.1		28.7	.8
		males	.3	1.3	18.3	.8		.0		20.7	1.0
IX	Services	Total	54.2	25.8	102.2	237.3		20.2		439.7	12.0
		males	37.1	22.2	38.8	41.1		1.7		141.0	6.6
X	Public admin.[b]	Total	.0	102.9	37.0	39.2[c]		.0		179.1	4.9
		males	.0	92.5	29.7	29.7[c]		.0		151.9	7.1
U	Unknown	Total	.1		5.1	19.5				24.8	.7
		males	.1		2.0	14.2				16.4	.8
T	All sectors	Total	615.0	200.3	401.8	1 620.6		811.2		3 648.9	100.0
		males	483.5	180.7	237.2	1 062.9		186.2		2 150.6	100.0

Percent distributions

Total labour force

	EM	CS	EE	WO	AP	FW	U	T
I	23.9	.1	.6	22.7		52.7		100.0
II	3.0	.1	7.3	89.2		.4		100.0
III	15.4	.0	10.6	72.0		2.0		100.0
IV	5.7	.7	5.9	87.3		.3		100.0
V	.5	10.0	29.9	59.5		.1		100.0
VI	34.4	.0	38.7	15.3		11.5		100.0
VII	4.4	34.1	16.9	44.4		.3		100.0
VIII	1.6	5.2	86.3	6.7		.2		100.0
IX	12.3	5.9	23.2	54.0		4.6		100.0
X	.0	57.5	20.6	21.9		.0		100.0
U	.4		20.6	79.0				100.0
T	16.9	5.5	11.0	44.4		22.2		100.0

Male labour force

	EM	CS	EE	WO	AP	FW	U	T
I	43.0	.2	1.3	28.2		27.3		100.0
II	3.2	.1	6.8	89.8		.1		100.0
III	17.8	.0	9.9	71.9		.4		100.0
IV	5.7	.7	5.3	88.3		.1		100.0
V	.5	9.9	27.9	61.7		.0		100.0
VI	38.3	.0	37.3	21.6		2.8		100.0
VII	4.5	34.8	12.9	47.7		.2		100.0
VIII	1.2	6.3	88.5	3.9		.0		100.0
IX	26.3	15.8	27.5	29.2		1.2		100.0
X	.0	60.9	19.6	19.5		.0		100.0
U	.5		12.5	87.0				100.0
T	22.5	8.4	11.0	49.4		8.7		100.0

L a b o u r   F o r c e   b y   S e c t o r   a n d   S t a t u s   1 9 5 1

Absolute figures in thousands

Sector			Employ-ers	Self-employed	Employ-ees	Workers	Appren-ices	Family-workers	Un-known	Total	%
			EM	SE	EE a)	WO	AP	FW b)	U	T	
I	Agriculture	Total	311.5	9.5	217.1	2.3	539.3		1 079.6	32.3
		males	232.7	8.4	122.1	1.9	147.5		512.5	25.0
II	Mining	Total	.4	4.2	42.6	.5	.1		47.9	1.4
		males	.4	3.4	40.6	.5	.0		45.0	2.2
III	Manufacturing	Total	116.0	106.8	625.0	61.8	17.5		927.1	27.7
		males	95.7	69.1	434.4	51.0	8.6		658.7	32.2
IV	Construction	Total	13.7	21.5	193.3	11.5	1.3		241.3	7.2
		males	13.4	17.9	188.9	11.3	.7		232.2	11.3
V	Utilities	Total	.1	11.5	13.8	.4	.0		25.8	.8
		males	.1	9.9	13.3	.4	.0		23.7	1.2
VI	Commerce	Total	68.9	90.2	38.8	11.9	18.4		228.1	6.8
		males	42.1	46.5	29.2	5.3	5.5		128.6	6.3
VII	Transport	Total	9.5	116.3	47.4	.4	.9		174.4	5.2
		males	8.7	102.8	43.8	.3	.6		156.3	7.6
VIII	Banking	Total	.4	22.5	1.6	.0	.0		24.6	.7
		males	.2	14.8	.6	.0	.0		15.6	.8
IX	Services	Total	66.7	165.5	191.0	5.2	15.5		443.9	13.3
		males	44.5	74.8	35.9	2.0	2.6		159.8	7.8
X	Public admin.	Total	.0	101.8	12.9	.0	.0		114.7	3.4
		males	.0	81.9	8.1	.0	.0		90.0	4.4
U	Unknown	Total	.7	12.5	25.7	.4	.2		39.5	1.2
		males	.3	6.4	18.3	.2	.0		25.4	1.2
T	All sectors	Total	587.9	662.4	1 409.3	94.4	593.1		3 347.1	100.0
		males	438.0	436.0	935.3	73.0	165.6		2 047.9	100.0

Percent distributions

	Total labour force								Male labour force						
	EM	SE	EE	WO	AP	FW	U	T		EM	SE	EE	WO	AP	FW	U	T
I	28.9	.9	20.1	.2	50.0		100.0	I	45.4	1.6	23.8	.4	28.8		100.0
II	.9	8.8	89.0	1.1	.1		100.0	II	.9	7.6	90.3	1.2	.1		100.0
III	12.5	11.5	67.4	6.7	1.9		100.0	III	14.5	10.5	65.9	7.7	1.3		100.0
IV	5.7	8.9	80.1	4.8	.5		100.0	IV	5.8	7.7	81.4	4.9	.3		100.0
V	.3	44.5	53.5	1.7	.1		100.0	V	.3	41.9	56.0	1.8	.0		100.0
VI	30.2	39.6	17.0	5.2	8.0		100.0	VI	32.7	36.2	22.7	4.1	4.2		100.0
VII	5.4	66.7	27.2	.2	.5		100.0	VII	5.6	65.8	28.0	.2	.4		100.0
VIII	1.8	91.4	6.6	.1	.1		100.0	VIII	1.1	94.8	4.0	.1	.1		100.0
IX	15.0	37.3	43.0	1.2	3.5		100.0	IX	27.8	46.8	22.5	1.2	1.7		100.0
X	.0	88.8	11.2	.0	.0		100.0	X	.0	91.0	9.0	.0	.0		100.0
U	1.8	31.6	65.1	1.0	.5		100.0	U	1.4	25.4	72.2	.9	.1		100.0
T	17.6	19.8	42.1	2.8	17.7		100.0	T	21.4	21.3	45.7	3.6	8.1		100.0

Austria

Labour Force by Sector and Status 1961

Absolute figures in thousands

Sector			Employers EM	Self-employed SE	Employees EE [a]	Workers WO	Apprentices AP	Family-workers FW [b]	Unknown U	Total T	%
I	Agriculture	Total	278.5		9.8	107.6	3.8	368.0		767.6	22.8
		males	198.5		8.5	62.8	2.6	88.2		360.6	17.9
II	Mining	Total	.6		6.2	41.6	.9	.2		49.5	1.5
		males	.5		4.8	39.8	.9	.1		46.1	2.3
III	Manufacturing	Total	90.3		154.8	690.8	76.9	26.5		1 039.4	30.8
		males	74.2		93.5	456.1	62.5	8.7		694.9	34.6
IV	Construction	Total	10.3		27.1	195.3	13.7	2.3		248.8	7.4
		males	9.6		22.0	190.6	13.3	.9		236.4	11.8
V	Utilities	Total	.0		16.5	14.4	1.1	.0		32.1	1.0
		males	.0		13.9	13.7	1.0	.0		28.6	1.4
VI	Commerce	Total	71.9		137.6	50.6	28.7	27.3		316.2	9.4
		males	43.9		57.8	33.0	9.4	5.2		149.3	7.4
VII	Transport	Total	9.5		138.2	45.5	2.2	1.9		197.3	5.9
		males	8.7		121.2	40.0	1.9	.9		172.6	8.6
VIII	Banking	Total	.2		36.3	1.9	.3	.0		38.7	1.1
		males	.2		21.6	.5	.2	.0		22.4	1.1
IX	Services	Total	71.8		214.4	181.1	13.2	23.4		504.0	15.0
		males	46.7		84.1	32.3	4.8	3.5		171.3	8.5
X	Public admin.	Total	.0		123.5	14.5	.0	.0		138.1	4.1
		males	.0		98.2	8.5	.0	.0		106.7	5.3
U	Unknown	Total	.1		7.5	27.9	2.6			38.2	1.1
		males	.1		3.4	16.1	1.3			21.0	1.0
T	All sectors	Total	533.3		872.2	1 371.4	143.3	449.6		3 369.8	100.0
		males	382.4		528.9	893.3	97.8	107.4		2 009.9	100.0

Percent distributions

Total labour force

	EM	SE	EE	WO	AP	FW	U	T
I	36.3		1.3	14.0	.5	47.9		100.0
II	1.2		12.6	83.9	1.9	.4		100.0
III	8.7		14.9	66.5	7.4	2.5		100.0
IV	4.1		10.9	78.5	5.5	.9		100.0
V	.1		51.6	45.0	3.3	.0		100.0
VI	22.7		43.5	16.0	9.1	8.6		100.0
VII	4.8		70.1	23.1	1.1	.9		100.0
VIII	.6		93.8	4.9	.7	.1		100.0
IX	14.2		42.5	35.9	2.6	4.6		100.0
X	.0		89.5	10.5	.0	.0		100.0
U	.3		19.7	73.0	6.9			100.0
T	15.8		25.9	40.7	4.3	13.3		100.0

Male labour force

	EM	SE	EE	WO	AP	FW	U	T
I	55.0		2.3	17.4	.7	24.5		100.0
II	1.2		10.5	86.3	1.9	.2		100.0
III	10.7		13.5	65.6	9.0	1.2		100.0
IV	4.1		9.3	80.6	5.6	.4		100.0
V	.1		48.4	48.0	3.4	.0		100.0
VI	29.4		38.7	22.1	6.3	3.5		100.0
VII	5.1		70.2	23.1	1.1	.5		100.0
VIII	.8		96.3	2.1	.8	.0		100.0
IX	27.2		49.1	18.9	2.8	2.0		100.0
X	.0		92.1	7.9	.0	.0		100.0
U	.4		16.2	77.1	6.3			100.0
T	19.0		26.3	44.4	4.9	5.3		100.0

Austria

Labour Force by Sector and Status 1971[a]

Absolute figures in thousands

Sector			Employers EM	Self-employed SE	Employees EE[b]	Workers WO	Apprentices AP[d]	Family-workers FW[c]	Unknown U	Total T	%
I	Agriculture	Total	204.7	8.6		52.0		161.2		426.5	13.8
		males	148.0	7.0		33.8		38.7		227.5	12.0
II	Mining	Total	.3	5.4		21.3		.1		27.1	.9
		males	.3	4.0		20.4		.1		24.8	1.3
III	Manufacturing	Total	57.7	207.3		682.4		15.7		963.0	31.1
		males	48.8	129.9		461.4		4.6		644.7	34.0
IV	Construction	Total	13.5	38.6		207.2		2.8		262.1	8.5
		males	13.0	29.2		203.2		.8		246.2	13.0
V	Utilities	Total	.0	17.6		17.9		.0		35.5	1.1
		males	.0	14.4		16.8		.0		31.2	1.6
VI	Commerce	Total	63.9	202.9		69.8		20.1		356.7	11.5
		males	39.4	82.7		44.7		4.1		170.9	9.0
VII	Transport	Total	9.2	133.5		50.4		1.7		194.9	6.3
		males	8.3	112.6		44.7		.9		166.6	8.8
VIII	Banking	Total	.2	59.9		3.2		.1		63.5	2.1
		males	.1	34.3		.7		.0		35.1	1.8
IX	Services	Total	67.8	275.9		185.3		20.4		549.5	17.7
		males	40.7	116.0		48.0		4.0		208.6	11.0
X	Public admin.	Total	.0	136.7		21.7		.0		158.4	5.1
		males	.0	101.2		13.3		.0		114.5	6.0
U	Unknown	Total	10.5	13.3		30.9		6.0		60.8	2.0
		males	6.1	7.0		17.2		2.4		32.8	1.7
T	All sectors	Total	427.9	1 099.7		1 342.2		228.1		3 098.0	100.0
		males	304.7	638.2		904.2		55.7		1 898.3	100.0

Percent distributions

	Total labour force								Male labour force						
	EM	SE	EE	WO	AP	FW	U	T		EM	SE	EE	WO	AP	FW	U	T
I	48.0	2.0		12.2		37.8		100.0	I	65.1	3.1		14.8		17.0		100.0
II	1.1	20.0		78.4		.4		100.0	II	1.2	16.2		82.4		.2		100.0
III	6.0	21.5		70.9		1.6		100.0	III	7.6	20.2		71.6		.7		100.0
IV	5.2	14.7		79.1		1.1		100.0	IV	5.3	11.9		82.5		.3		100.0
V	.0	49.5		50.5		.0		100.0	V	.0	46.2		53.8		.0		100.0
VI	17.9	56.9		19.6		5.6		100.0	VI	23.0	48.4		26.2		2.4		100.0
VII	4.7	68.5		25.9		.9		100.0	VII	5.0	67.6		26.9		.5		100.0
VIII	.3	94.4		5.1		.2		100.0	VIII	.4	97.6		1.9		.1		100.0
IX	12.3	50.2		33.7		3.7		100.0	IX	19.5	55.6		23.0		1.9		100.0
X	.0	86.3		13.7		.0		100.0	X	.0	88.4		11.6		.0		100.0
U	17.3	21.9		50.9		9.9		100.0	U	18.8	21.4		52.5		7.3		100.0
T	13.8	35.5	43.3			7.4		100.0	T	16.1	33.6	47.6			2.9		100.0

458

Notes:

1880–1910   Present population aged 10 years and over

1880   a) Included mainly among Workers
            b) Including conscripts
            c) Including a large proportion of day-labourers

1890   a) Included mainly among Workers
            b) Including conscripts

1900   a) Restricted enumeration as compared to 1880 and 1890
            b) Including conscripts

1910   a) Including conscripts

1934–1971   Resident population
1934–1939   Unemployed classified according to their previous occupation; conscripts included in the public
            sector
1951–1971   Conscripts and unemployed classified according to their previous occupation; persons seeking work
            for the first time excluded from the labour force

1934   a) Excluding persons under the age of 14 (except those living outside the parental household) and
               domestic servants of economically non-active persons
            b) Including civil servants
            c) In agriculture all persons aged 14 to 60 classified as family workers, except housewives, sick
               persons and those in vocational training
            d) Including conscripts

1939   a) German census for the territory of the former Austrian Republic
            b) Including enterprises under military control
            c) Including conscripts

1951   a) Including civil servants
            b) Farmers' wives are classified as family workers, except for large land-holdings

1961   a) Including civil servants
            b) Farmers' wives classified as family workers

1971   a) Persons aged 15 years and over working at least 14 hours a week
            b) Including civil servants
            c) Farmers' wives included only if explicitly stated that they assist their husbands
            d) Included among Employees or Workers

Belgium

The Development of the Labour Force

Year	by Status				by Sector				Total labour force	Domestic services	Military personnel	Year
	Inde-pendent (IN)	Depend-ent (DE)	Family worker	Un-known	Agricul-ture (A)	Indus-try (I)	Serv-ices (S)	Un-known				
	percent distribution				percent distribution				in thousands			
1970	15.1	81.5	3.3	0.1	4.6	43.7	49.6	2.0	3 637.8	30.9	89.4	1970
1961	18.9	73.6	4.6	2.9	7.2	45.7	44.1	3.0	3 512.5		100.8	1961
1947	22.0	71.6	6.4		12.1	48.3	36.8	2.8	3 506.0	75.1	57.2	1947
1930	20.1	68.5	10.0	1.4	17.0	47.8	34.5	0.8	3 750.3	175.7	54.4	1930
1920	20.5	70.8	5.6	3.1	19.1	45.9	33.0	2.0	3 205.5	168.6	67.6	1920
1910	20.6	66.3	10.7	2.5	22.4	45.1	30.9	1.6	3 491.8	197.9	39.7	1910
1900	29.3	68.7		2.0	21.9	41.3	27.4	9.5	3 190.7	169.9	33.4	1900
1890	30.1	68.2		1.7	23.1	37.2	26.9	12.8	2 830.2	176.5	48.3	1890
1880	31.6	67.0		1.4	30.3	34.9	22.1	12.8	2 681.3	156.3	30.3	1880

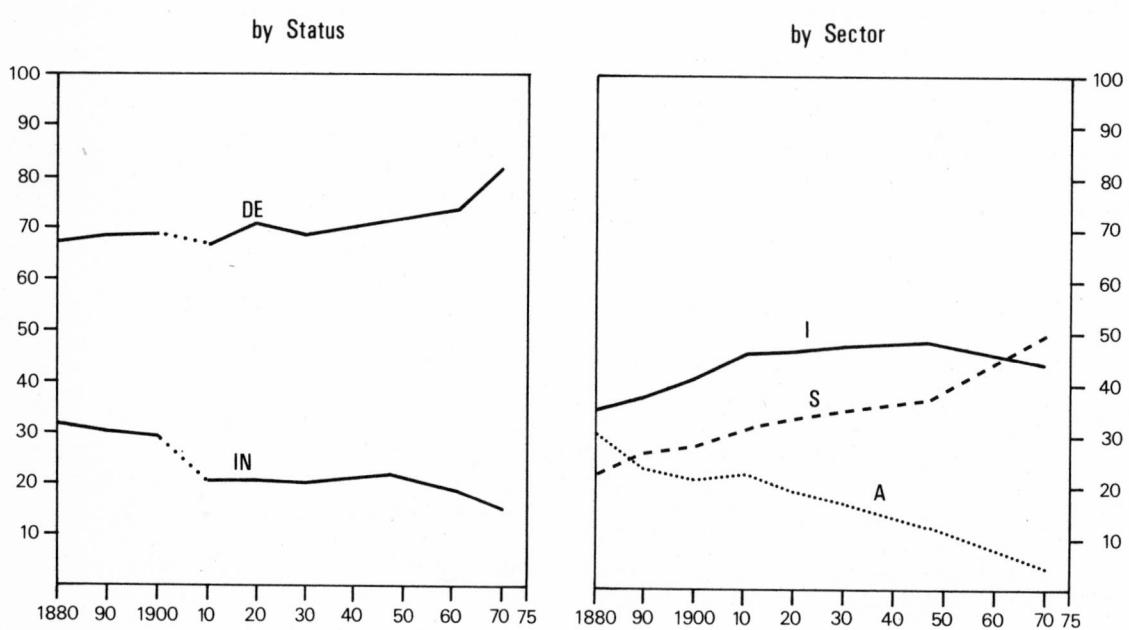

by Status   by Sector

460

Belgium

Labour Force by Sector and Status 1880 [a)]

Absolute figures in thousands

Sector			Employers	Self-employed	Employees	Workers	Apprentices	Family-workers	Unknown	Total	%
			EM	SE	EE	WO	AP	FW [b)]	U	T	
I	Agriculture	Total	480.2		331.3					811.5	30.3
		males	326.3		219.7					546.0	31.0
II	Mining	Total	2.0		112.7					114.7	4.3
		males	1.9		102.5					104.4	5.9
III	Manufacturing	Total	168.8		565.3					734.1	27.4
		males	122.3		364.6					486.9	27.7
IV	Construction	Total	17.4		67.4					84.7	3.2
		males	17.2		67.0					84.2	4.8
V	Utilities	Total	.1		.9					1.1	.0
		males	.1		.9					1.1	.1
VI	Commerce	Total	118.5		88.2					206.7	7.7
		males	71.0		48.7					119.7	6.8
VII	Transport	Total	6.8		11.6					18.4	.7
		males	6.2		11.3					17.5	1.0
VIII	Banking	Total	1.7		[d)]					1.7	.1
		males	1.7							1.7	.1
IX	Services	Total	48.8		229.8				35.3	313.8	11.7
		males	31.1		90.0				19.7	140.9	8.0
X	Public admin. [c)]	Total	.0		52.5					52.5	2.0
		males	.0		52.3					52.3	3.0
U	Unknown	Total	2.4		336.5				3.3	342.2	12.8
		males	2.3		198.9				3.3	204.5	11.6
T	All sectors	Total	846.6		1 796.1				38.6	2 681.3	100.0
		males	580.2		1 155.9				23.0	1 759.1	100.0

Percent distributions

	Total labour force								Male labour force							
	EM	SE	EE	WO	AP	FW	U	T		EM	SE	EE	WO	AP	FW	U	T
I	59.2		40.8					100.0	I	59.8		40.2					100.0
II	1.7		98.3					100.0	II	1.9		98.1					100.0
III	23.0		77.0					100.0	III	25.1		74.9					100.0
IV	20.5		79.5					100.0	IV	20.4		79.6					100.0
V	11.5		88.5					100.0	V	11.3		88.7					100.0
VI	57.3		42.7					100.0	VI	59.3		40.7					100.0
VII	37.0		63.0					100.0	VII	35.3		64.7					100.0
VIII	100.0		.0					100.0	VIII	100.0		.0					100.0
IX	15.5		73.2				11.2	100.0	IX	22.1		63.9				14.0	100.0
X	.0		100.0					100.0	X	.0		100.0					100.0
U	.7		98.3				1.0	100.0	U	1.1		97.2				1.6	100.0
T	31.6		67.0				1.4	100.0	T	33.0		65.7				1.3	100.0

Belgium

Labour Force by Sector and Status 1890 [a]

Absolute figures in thousands

Sector			Employ-ers	Self-employed	Employ-ees	Workers	Apprent-ices	Family-workers	Un-known	Total	%
			EM	SE	EE	WO	AP	FW [b]	U	T	
I	Agriculture	Total	425.9		4.0	223.4				653.2	23.1
		males	321.8		4.0	167.7				493.5	24.8
II	Mining	Total	1.1		4.2	133.9				139.3	4.9
		males	1.1		4.2	125.1				130.4	6.5
III	Manufacturing	Total	168.4		9.9	641.1				819.4	29.0
		males	126.5		9.1	439.1				574.8	28.8
IV	Construction	Total	20.0		.7	73.2				94.0	3.3
		males	19.9		.7	72.8				93.4	4.7
V	Utilities	Total	.1		.1	1.0				1.2	.0
		males	.1		.1	1.0				1.2	.1
VI	Commerce	Total	157.3		34.0	81.7				273.0	9.6
		males	106.3		22.0	51.2				179.5	9.0
VII	Transport	Total	7.9		1.4	18.5				27.7	1.0
		males	7.3		1.4	18.1				26.8	1.3
VIII	Banking	Total	1.7		d)	d)				1.7	.1
		males	1.6							1.6	.1
IX	Services	Total	65.7		74.1	178.6			44.1	362.6	12.8
		males	43.6		31.2	57.5			26.5	158.7	8.0
X	Public admin. [c]	Total	.0		49.4	46.3				95.7	3.4
		males	.0		48.8	46.3				95.1	4.8
U	Unknown	Total	3.0		33.9	321.4			4.0	362.5	12.8
		males	3.0		31.5	200.0			4.0	238.6	12.0
T	All sectors	Total	851.1		211.8	1 719.2			48.2	2 830.2	100.0
		males	631.2		153.0	1 178.8			30.5	1 993.6	100.0

Percent distributions

Total labour force

	EM	SE	EE	WO	AP	FW	U	T
I	65.2	.6	34.2					100.0
II	.8	3.1	96.2					100.0
III	20.6	1.2	78.2					100.0
IV	21.3	.7	77.9					100.0
V	5.7	7.5	86.8					100.0
VI	57.6	12.5	29.9					100.0
VII	28.4	5.0	66.6					100.0
VIII	100.0	.0	.0					100.0
IX	18.1	20.4	49.3				12.2	100.0
X	.0	51.6	48.4					100.0
U	.8	9.4	88.7				1.1	100.0
T	30.1	7.5	60.7				1.7	100.0

Male labour force

	EM	SE	EE	WO	AP	FW	U	T
I	65.2	.8	34.0					100.0
II	.8	3.3	95.9					100.0
III	22.0	1.6	76.4					100.0
IV	21.3	.7	77.9					100.0
V	5.5	7.6	86.9					100.0
VI	59.2	12.3	28.5					100.0
VII	27.3	5.1	67.6					100.0
VIII	100.0	.0	.0					100.0
IX	27.5	19.6	36.2				16.7	100.0
X	.0	51.3	48.7					100.0
U	1.3	13.2	83.8				1.7	100.0
T	31.7	7.7	59.1				1.5	100.0

Belgium

Labour Force by Sector and Status 1900 [a]

Absolute figures in thousands

Sector			Employers EM	Self-employed SE	Employees EE	Workers WO	Apprentices AP	Family-workers FW [b]	Unknown U	Total T	%
I	Agriculture	Total	449.9		.0	247.5				697.4	21.9
		males	341.7		.0	192.0				533.7	23.6
II	Mining	Total	1.4		4.9	167.0				173.3	5.4
		males	1.4		4.9	160.1				166.3	7.4
III	Manufacturing	Total	183.8		12.5	814.8				1 011.0	31.7
		males	130.8		12.0	555.1				697.9	30.9
IV	Construction	Total	23.2		.9	107.7				131.9	4.1
		males	23.1		.9	107.2				131.2	5.8
V	Utilities	Total	.1		.1	1.7				1.9	.1
		males	.1		.1	1.7				1.9	.1
VI	Commerce	Total	189.0		40.0	98.2				327.2	10.3
		males	125.0		25.0	60.2				210.2	9.3
VII	Transport	Total	9.6		2.2	42.3				54.1	1.7
		males	8.7		2.2	41.3				52.2	2.3
VIII	Banking	Total	2.5		d)	d)				2.5	.1
		males	2.5							2.5	.1
IX	Services	Total	71.4		86.3	179.1			58.0	394.8	12.4
		males	47.1		35.1	57.1			32.9	172.2	7.6
X	Public admin. [c]	Total	.0		63.3	31.0				94.2	3.0
		males	.0		62.3	31.0				93.2	4.1
U	Unknown	Total	4.5		50.1	242.7			5.2	302.4	9.5
		males	4.4		45.9	141.9			5.2	197.4	8.7
T	All sectors	Total	935.3		260.3	1 931.9			63.2	3 190.7	100.0
		males	684.7		188.4	1 347.6			38.2	2 258.7	100.0

Percent distributions

	Total labour force								Male labour force							
	EM	SE	EE	WO	AP	FW	U	T		EM	SE	EE	WO	AP	FW	U	T
I	64.5		.0	35.5				100.0	I	64.0		.0	36.0				100.0
II	.8		2.8	96.4				100.0	II	.8		3.0	96.2				100.0
III	18.2		1.2	80.6				100.0	III	18.7		1.7	79.5				100.0
IV	17.6		.7	81.7				100.0	IV	17.6		.7	81.7				100.0
V	3.7		5.9	90.4				100.0	V	3.7		5.9	90.4				100.0
VI	57.8		12.2	30.0				100.0	VI	59.5		11.9	28.6				100.0
VII	17.7		4.1	78.2				100.0	VII	16.7		4.2	79.1				100.0
VIII	100.0		.0	.0				100.0	VIII	100.0		.0	.0				100.0
IX	18.1		21.9	45.4			14.7	100.0	IX	27.3		20.4	33.2			19.1	100.0
X	.0		67.1	32.9				100.0	X	.0		66.8	33.2				100.0
U	1.5		16.6	80.2			1.7	100.0	U	2.2		23.2	71.9			2.6	100.0
T	29.3		8.2	60.5			2.0	100.0	T	30.3		8.3	59.7			1.7	100.0

Absolute figures in thousands

Sector			Employers	Self-employed	Employees	Workers	Apprentices	Family-workers	Unknown	Total	%
			EM	SE	EE	WO	AP	FW	U	T	
I	Agriculture	Total	245.1		1.0	272.0		263.8		782.0	22.4
		males	215.0		1.0	225.5		125.5		566.9	23.6
II	Mining	Total	1.8		5.3	192.3		.7		200.1	5.7
		males	1.8		5.3	184.7		.4		192.3	8.0
III	Manufacturing	Total	174.0		30.6	947.5		36.1		1 188.2	34.0
		males	120.9		27.2	632.8		24.0		805.0	33.6
IV	Construction	Total	26.3		2.1	144.4		5.2		178.0	5.1
		males	26.2		2.0	144.1		4.6		176.8	7.4
V	Utilities	Total	.2		1.1	7.3		.0		8.7	.2
		males	.2		1.1	7.3		.0		8.6	.4
VI	Commerce	Total	146.5		32.3	41.2		36.2		256.2	7.3
		males	86.4		17.9	32.7		8.9		145.9	6.1
VII	Transport	Total	12.8		43.8	133.0		4.2		193.8	5.6
		males	12.0		42.4	130.3		2.3		187.0	7.8
VIII	Banking	Total	2.9		13.8	.2		.1		17.1	.5
		males	2.8		13.6	.2		.1		16.7	.7
IX	Services	Total	108.0		122.8	246.9		25.7	31.2	534.7	15.3
		males	45.7		58.8	53.0		1.5	29.0	188.0	7.8
X	Public admin.	Total	.0		42.3	35.7		.0		78.0	2.2
		males	.0		41.9	35.7		.0		77.6	3.2
U	Unknown	Total							55.1	55.1	1.6
		males							32.7	32.7	1.4
T	All sectors	Total	717.6		295.2	2 020.7		372.0	86.3	3 491.8	100.0
		males	511.0		211.2	1 446.3		167.3	61.7	2 397.5	100.0

Percent distributions

	Total labour force								Male labour force							
	EM	SE	EE	WO	AP	FW	U	T		EM	SE	EE	WO	AP	FW	U	T
I	31.3		.1	34.8		33.7		100.0	I	37.9		.2	39.8		22.1		100.0
II	.9		2.7	96.1		.3		100.0	II	.9		2.8	96.1		.2		100.0
III	14.6		2.6	79.7		3.0		100.0	III	15.0		3.4	78.6		3.0		100.0
IV	14.8		1.2	81.1		2.9		100.0	IV	14.8		1.1	81.5		2.6		100.0
V	1.7		12.9	84.8		.5		100.0	V	1.8		12.8	85.0		.4		100.0
VI	57.2		12.6	16.1		14.1		100.0	VI	59.2		12.3	22.4		6.1		100.0
VII	6.6		22.6	68.7		2.1		100.0	VII	6.4		22.7	69.7		1.2		100.0
VIII	17.0		81.0	1.4		.7		100.0	VIII	17.0		81.3	1.2		.5		100.0
IX	20.2		23.0	46.2		4.8	5.8	100.0	IX	24.3		31.3	28.2		.8	15.4	100.0
X	.0		54.2	45.8		.0		100.0	X	.0		54.0	46.0		.0		100.0
U							100.0	100.0	U							100.0	100.0
T	20.6		8.5	57.9		10.7	2.5	100.0	T	21.3		8.8	60.3		7.0	2.6	100.0

Belgium

Labour Force by Sector and Status 1920 [a]

Absolute figures in thousands

Sector			Employ-ers EM	Self-employed SE	Employ-ees EE	Workers WO	Apprent-ices AP	Family-workers FW	Un-known U	Total T	%
I	Agriculture	Total	252.7	.6		226.1		132.9		612.3	19.1
		males	214.3	.6		191.6		76.5		483.0	20.1
II	Mining	Total	1.7		5.6	204.7		.7		212.8	6.6
		males	1.7		5.3	195.6		.6		203.1	8.5
III	Manufacturing	Total	140.6		37.7	860.4		19.3		1 058.0	33.0
		males	108.1		30.7	616.2		14.4		769.4	32.0
IV	Construction	Total	20.5		2.4	162.9		4.3		190.0	5.9
		males	20.1		2.1	161.0		4.1		187.4	7.8
V	Utilities	Total	.3		1.4	10.1		.1		11.9	.4
		males	.2		1.3	9.9		.0		11.5	.5
VI	Commerce	Total	149.4		31.4	30.6		13.9		225.2	7.0
		males	94.1		18.1	24.1		5.1		141.4	5.9
VII	Transport	Total	12.0		61.4	166.1		2.3		241.8	7.5
		males	10.9		57.2	159.9		1.5		229.4	9.5
VIII	Banking	Total	2.4		27.9	.7		.2		31.2	1.0
		males	2.2		23.4	.6		.1		26.4	1.1
IX	Services	Total	77.9		125.1	186.2		5.9	36.5	431.7	13.5
		males	39.6		63.0	51.2		.8	32.1	186.7	7.8
X	Public admin.	Total	.0		65.5	62.2		.0		127.6	4.0
		males	.0		61.0	62.2		.0		123.2	5.1
U	Unknown	Total							63.0	63.0	2.0
		males							41.4	41.4	1.7
T	All sectors	Total	657.4		359.1	1 910.0		179.5	99.5	3 205.5	100.0
		males	491.3		262.7	1 472.2		103.1	73.4	2 402.7	100.0

Percent distributions

Total labour force

	EM	SE	EE	WO	AP	FW	U	T
I	41.3	.1		36.9		21.7		100.0
II	.8		2.7	96.2		.3		100.0
III	13.3		3.6	81.3		1.8		100.0
IV	10.8		1.3	85.7		2.2		100.0
V	2.1		12.2	85.2		.5		100.0
VI	66.3		13.9	13.6		6.2		100.0
VII	5.0		25.4	68.7		1.0		100.0
VIII	7.8		89.4	2.3		.6		100.0
IX	18.1		29.0	43.1		1.4		100.0
X	.0		51.3	48.7		.0		100.0
U							100.0	100.0
T	20.5		11.2	59.6		5.6	3.1	100.0

Male labour force

	EM	SE	EE	WO	AP	FW	U	T
I	44.4	.1		39.7		15.8		100.0
II	.8		2.6	96.3		.3		100.0
III	14.1		4.0	80.1		1.9		100.0
IV	10.8		1.1	85.9		2.2		100.0
V	2.1		11.4	86.1		.4		100.0
VI	66.5		12.8	17.0		3.6		100.0
VII	4.8		24.9	69.7		.6		100.0
VIII	8.5		88.6	2.4		.5		100.0
IX	21.2		33.8	27.4		.4	17.2	100.0
X	.0		49.5	50.5		.0		100.0
U							100.0	100.0
T	20.4		10.9	61.3		4.3	3.1	100.0

Labour Force by Sector and Status 1930 [a]

Absolute figures in thousands

Sector			Employ-ers	Self-employed	Employ-ees	Workers	Apprent-ices	Family-workers	Un-known	Total	%
			EM[b]	SE[b]	EE	WO	AP	FW	U	T	
I	Agriculture	Total	267.4	.7	130.5			239.1		637.6	17.0
		males	242.8	.6	117.9			135.7		497.1	18.0
II	Mining	Total	1.3		8.6	211.6		.1		221.7	5.9
		males	1.3		8.1	205.8		.1		215.3	7.8
III	Manufacturing	Total	162.6		76.9	1 045.7		37.2		1 322.4	35.3
		males	128.8		58.0	754.0		24.8		965.6	35.0
IV	Construction	Total	33.0		4.5	186.6		6.0		230.1	6.1
		males	32.8		3.7	185.8		5.7		228.0	8.3
V	Utilities	Total	.2		3.7	13.6		.0		17.5	.5
		males	.2		3.3	13.5		.0		17.0	.6
VI	Commerce	Total	200.7		54.1	37.2		60.6		352.6	9.4
		males	125.2		24.3	31.2		16.5		197.2	7.1
VII	Transport	Total	19.6		61.6	168.1		6.7		256.1	6.8
		males	18.7		56.2	165.6		3.7		244.3	8.9
VIII	Banking	Total	3.9		44.8	1.2		.2		50.2	1.3
		males	3.9		37.2	1.0		.1		42.1	1.5
IX	Services[c]	Total	64.6		235.6	173.5		23.6	25.8	523.0	13.9
		males	30.8		141.8	29.3		2.1	18.7	222.7	8.1
X	Public admin.[d]	Total	.0		60.6	50.1		.0		110.8	3.0
		males	.0		57.9	50.1		.0		108.1	3.9
U	Unknown	Total							28.2	28.2	.8
		males							20.6	20.6	.7
T	All sectors	Total	753.2		551.2	2 018.2		373.6	54.0	3 750.3	100.0
		males	584.5		391.2	1 554.2		188.8	39.3	2 758.0	100.0

Percent distributions

	Total labour force									Male labour force							
	EM	SE	EE	WO	AP	FW	U	T		EM	SE	EE	WO	AP	FW	U	T
I	41.9		.1	20.5		37.5		100.0	I	48.9		.1	23.7		27.3		100.0
II	.6		3.9	95.5		.1		100.0	II	.6		3.8	95.6		.1		100.0
III	12.3		5.8	79.1		2.8		100.0	III	13.3		6.0	78.1		2.6		100.0
IV	14.3		2.0	81.1		2.6		100.0	IV	14.4		1.6	81.5		2.5		100.0
V	1.3		20.9	77.7		.1		100.0	V	1.3		19.4	79.2		.1		100.0
VI	56.9		15.4	10.5		17.2		100.0	VI	63.5		12.3	15.8		8.4		100.0
VII	7.6		24.1	65.7		2.6		100.0	VII	7.6		23.0	67.8		1.5		100.0
VIII	7.8		89.4	2.3		.5		100.0	VIII	9.1		88.2	2.3		.3		100.0
IX	12.3		45.0	33.2		4.5	4.9	100.0	IX	13.8		63.7	13.2		.9	8.4	100.0
X	.0		54.7	45.3		.0		100.0	X	.0		53.6	46.4		.0		100.0
U							100.0	100.0	U							100.0	100.0
T	20.1		14.7	53.8		10.0	1.4	100.0	T	21.2		14.2	56.4		6.8	1.4	100.0

L a b o u r   F o r c e   b y   S e c t o r   a n d   S t a t u s   1 9 4 7

Absolute figures in thousands

Sector		Status	Employers EM[a]	Self-employed SE[a]	Employees EE	Workers WO[b]	Apprentices AP	Family-workers FW	Unknown U	Total T	%
I	Agriculture	Total	230.9		1.8	58.4		131.7		422.8	12.1
		males	212.3		1.6	55.7		92.0		361.6	13.5
II	Mining	Total	.9		9.3	180.2		.2		190.6	5.4
		males	.9		8.6	177.9		.1		187.6	7.0
III	Manufacturing	Total	168.4		127.9	962.6		23.8		1 282.7	36.6
		males	146.5		96.1	711.0		17.5		971.1	36.2
IV	Construction	Total	44.6		6.6	136.9		4.2		192.3	5.5
		males	44.2		5.4	136.5		4.2		190.3	7.1
V	Utilities	Total	.3		8.5	19.0		.0		27.9	.8
		males	.3		7.7	18.7		.0		26.7	1.0
VI	Commerce	Total	204.3		85.3	58.0		43.3		390.8	11.1
		males	135.1		44.4	45.7		14.4		239.7	8.9
VII	Transport	Total	19.2		80.7	137.1		6.3		243.2	6.9
		males	18.3		73.0	134.2		3.1		228.6	8.5
VIII	Banking	Total	3.1		45.9	2.5		.1		51.7	1.5
		males	3.0		34.3	1.3		.0		38.7	1.4
IX	Services	Total	98.1		161.2	136.5		13.6		409.4	11.7
		males	60.2		81.6	37.9		2.7		182.3	6.8
X	Public admin.[c]	Total	.0		136.1	59.7		.0		195.8	5.6
		males	.0		121.2	56.0		.0		177.2	6.6
U	Unknown[d]	Total	1.8		15.0	81.7		.2		98.7	2.8
		males	1.6		9.9	69.7		.1		81.3	3.0
T	All sectors	Total	771.5		678.3	1 832.7		223.4		3 506.0	100.0
		males	622.4		483.8	1 444.7		134.2		2 685.1	100.0

Percent distributions

	Total labour force								Male labour force							
	EM	SE	EE	WO	AP	FW	U	T	EM	SE	EE	WO	AP	FW	U	T
I	54.6		.4	13.8		31.1		100.0	58.7		.4	15.4		25.4		100.0
II	.5		4.9	94.5		.1		100.0	.5		4.6	94.8		.1		100.0
III	13.1		10.0	75.0		1.9		100.0	15.1		9.9	73.2		1.8		100.0
IV	23.2		3.4	71.2		2.2		100.0	23.2		2.8	71.7		2.2		100.0
V	1.0		30.6	68.2		.2		100.0	1.0		28.7	70.1		.2		100.0
VI	52.3		21.8	14.8		11.1		100.0	56.4		18.5	19.1		6.0		100.0
VII	7.9		33.2	56.4		2.6		100.0	8.0		31.9	58.7		1.3		100.0
VIII	6.1		88.9	4.9		.1		100.0	7.8		88.7	3.3		.1		100.0
IX	24.0		39.4	33.3		3.3		100.0	33.0		44.8	20.8		1.5		100.0
X	.0		69.5	30.5		.0		100.0	.0		68.4	31.6		.0		100.0
U	1.9		15.2	82.7		.2		100.0	1.9		12.1	85.8		.2		100.0
T	22.0		19.3	52.3		6.4		100.0	23.2		18.0	53.8		5.0		100.0

Labour Force by Sector and Status 1961

Absolute figures in thousands

Sector			Employers	Directors	Employees	Workers	Apprentices	Family-workers	Unknown	Total	%
			EM	DR	EE	WO[a)	AP	FW	U	T	
I	Agriculture	Total	170.5	.4	1.4	24.3		57.3		253.9	7.2
		males	150.1	.4	1.2	23.2		37.6		212.6	8.2
II	Mining	Total	.5	.1	8.1	101.3		.1		110.1	3.1
		males	.5	.1	7.4	100.6		.0		108.7	4.2
III	Manufacturing	Total	98.7	5.0	177.9	919.8		15.3		1 216.7	34.6
		males	89.1	4.7	134.3	694.1		10.8		932.9	36.2
IV	Construction	Total	45.3	.9	11.2	187.1		5.5		250.0	7.1
		males	44.6	.8	9.1	186.7		5.2		246.4	9.6
V	Utilities	Total	.2	.1	13.2	15.5		.0		29.0	.8
		males	.2	.1	12.2	15.2		.0		27.7	1.1
VI	Commerce	Total	202.9	9.4	117.9	74.6		41.7		446.5	12.7
		males	125.5	4.6	56.2	56.7		13.2		256.2	9.9
VII	Transport	Total	16.1	1.0	111.6	105.2		4.7	.2	238.7	6.8
		males	15.1	.9	100.0	101.7		2.0	.1	219.8	8.5
VIII	Banking	Total	5.9	1.0	58.7	3.6		.3		69.6	2.0
		males	4.4	1.0	41.6	1.5		.1		48.5	1.9
IX	Services	Total	123.2	3.8	243.2	136.6		38.3	.1	545.1	15.5
		males	61.3	1.5	111.1	39.8		7.6	.1	221.4	8.6
X	Public admin.[b)	Total	.0	.0	181.5	67.5		.0		249.0	7.1
		males	.0	.0	163.4	62.3		.0		225.7	8.8
U	Unknown[c)	Total	.1	.0	1.5	.7			101.5	104.0	3.0
		males	.1	.0	1.0	.6			78.1	79.7	3.1
T	All sectors	Total	663.4	21.7	926.1	1 636.2		163.2	101.9	3 512.5	100.0
		males	490.8	14.1	637.6	1 282.3		76.5	78.3	2 579.6	100.0

Percent distributions

Total labour force

	EM	DR	EE	WO	AP	FW	U	T
I	67.1	.2	.6	9.6		22.6		100.0
II	.5	.1	7.3	92.0		.1		100.0
III	8.1	.4	14.6	75.6		1.3		100.0
IV	18.1	.4	4.5	74.9		2.2		100.0
V	.5	.3	45.6	53.5		.1		100.0
VI	45.4	2.1	26.4	16.7		9.3		100.0
VII	6.7	.4	46.8	44.1		2.0	.1	100.0
VIII	8.5	1.5	84.4	5.2		.4		100.0
IX	22.6	.7	44.6	25.1		7.0		100.0
X	.0	.0	72.9	27.1		.0		100.0
U	.1		1.5	.7		.0	97.7	100.0
T	18.9	.6	26.4	46.6		4.6	2.9	100.0

Male labour force

	EM	DR	EE	WO	AP	FW	U	T
I	70.6	.2	.6	10.9		17.7		100.0
II	.5	.1	6.8	92.5		.0		100.0
III	9.5	.5	14.4	74.4		1.2		100.0
IV	18.1	.3	3.7	75.8		2.1		100.0
V	.5	.3	44.2	54.8		.1		100.0
VI	49.0	1.8	21.9	22.1		5.1		100.0
VII	6.9	.4	45.5	46.2		.9	.1	100.0
VIII	9.0	2.0	85.8	3.1		.2		100.0
IX	27.7	.7	50.2	18.0		3.4		100.0
X	.0	.0	72.4	27.6		.0		100.0
U	.2	.0	1.2	.7		.0	97.9	100.0
T	19.0	.5	24.7	49.7		3.0	3.0	100.0

Belgium

Labour Force by Sector and Status 1970

Absolute figures in thousands

Sector			Employ-ers	Self-employed	Direc-tors	Employ-ees	Workers	Family-workers	Un-known	Total	%
			EM	SE	DR	EE	WO	FW	U	T	
I	Agriculture	Total	5.9	110.1	.1	1.4	13.5	31.1	.1	162.1	4.5
		males	5.5	97.2	.1	1.2	12.6	16.5	.1	133.1	5.2
II	Mining	Total	.2	.1	.2	4.6	45.0	.0	.0	50.1	1.4
		males	.2	.1	.2	4.1	44.6	.0	.0	49.2	1.9
III	Manufacturing	Total	25.0	30.6	7.6	234.5	856.6	10.1	.4	1 164.8	32.0
		males	23.2	27.3	7.0	171.7	635.3	4.3	.2	868.9	33.9
IV	Construction	Total	19.9	23.6	1.8	25.6	216.3	4.4	.1	291.6	8.0
		males	19.4	23.3	1.7	20.5	214.6	3.2	.1	282.7	11.0
V	Utilities	Total	.0	.1	.2	17.5	16.4	.0	.0	34.2	0.9
		males	.0	.1	.2	15.8	15.9	.0	.0	32.0	1.2
VI	Commerce	Total	33.6	129.5	13.4	155.0	84.3	45.7	.2	461.7	12.7
		males	27.8	81.2	7.4	72.6	60.5	8.8	.1	258.3	10.1
VII	Transport	Total	3.6	9.1	1.1	107.5	95.7	3.8	.1	220.8	6.1
		males	3.3	8.7	1.0	95.4	91.8	1.4	.1	201.7	7.9
VIII	Banking	Total	1.4	5.9	2.2	88.5	5.2	1.0	.0	104.1	2.9
		males	1.3	3.5	2.1	57.1	2.5	.2	.0	66.6	2.6
IX	Services	Total	27.8	100.1	7.5	394.1	178.3	20.8	.6	729.2	20.0
		males	22.7	54.3	4.5	177.8	85.9	4.8	.3	350.3	13.7
X	Public admin. a)	Total	.2	.4	.2	197.9	67.6	.1	.2	266.6	7.3
		males	.2	.3	.2	164.1	57.2	.0	.1	222.2	8.7
U	Unknown b)	Total	.6	3.7	1.4	34.9	28.5	.8	82.6	152.5	4.2
		males	.5	2.6	1.1	19.7	21.2	.2	49.3	94.7	3.7
T	All sectors	Total	118.2	413.2	35.6	1 261.5	1 607.2	117.9	84.3	3 637.8	100.0
		males	104.0	298.6	25.4	799.9	1 242.0	39.4	50.4	2 559.7	100.0

Percent distributions

Total labour force

	EM	SE	DR	EE	WO	FW	U	T
I	3.6	67.9	.1	.9	8.3	19.2	.0	100.0
II	.4	.3	.3	9.2	89.7	.1	.0	100.0
III	2.1	2.6	.7	20.1	73.5	.9	.0	100.0
IV	6.8	8.1	.6	8.8	74.2	1.5	.0	100.0
V	.1	.2	.5	51.2	47.8	.0	.1	100.0
VI	7.3	28.0	2.9	33.6	18.3	9.9	.0	100.0
VII	1.6	4.1	.5	48.7	43.3	1.7	.1	100.0
VIII	1.3	5.7	2.1	85.0	5.0	.9	.0	100.0
IX	3.8	13.7	1.0	54.0	24.4	2.9	.1	100.0
X	.1	.2	.1	74.2	25.4	.1	.1	100.0
U	.4	2.4	.9	22.9	18.7	.6	54.2	100.0
T	3.2	11.4	1.0	34.7	44.2	3.2	2.3	100.0

Male labour force

	EM	SE	DR	EE	WO	FW	U	T
I	4.1	73.0	.1	.9	9.5	12.4	.0	100.0
II	.4	.3	.3	8.4	90.6	.0	.0	100.0
III	2.7	3.1	.8	19.8	73.1	.5	.0	100.0
IV	6.8	8.2	.6	7.2	75.9	1.1	.0	100.0
V	.1	.2	.5	49.4	49.7	.0	.1	100.0
VI	10.8	31.4	2.9	28.1	23.4	3.4	.0	100.0
VII	1.6	4.3	.5	47.3	45.5	.7	.1	100.0
VIII	1.9	5.2	3.1	85.7	3.8	.2	.0	100.0
IX	6.5	15.5	1.3	50.8	24.5	1.4	.1	100.0
X	.1	.2	.1	73.9	25.7	.0	.1	100.0
U	.6	2.8	1.1	20.8	22.4	.3	52.1	100.0
T	4.1	11.7	1.0	31.2	48.5	1.5	2.0	100.0

Notes:

1880–1970	Resident population of age 15 and over (1880–1961) and of age 14 and over (1970)
1880–1900	Labour force refers to jobs and not to persons; the status distribution must be regarded as a crude estimate
1930–1970	Conscripts included under Public Administration
1947–1970	Unemployed as separate census category included under Unknown

1880–1900   a) Status distribution partially estimated; in Commerce, the percentage distribution of the 1910 census has been used; in Services and Public Administration, the distribution has been inferred from the nature of occupation
b) Not included in the labour force
c) Including conscripts
d) No separate figures available

1910–1920   a) Status distribution for Services and Public Administration partially estimated on the basis of the nature of occupation; conscripts allocated according to their previous occupation

1930   a) Unemployed classified according to their previous occupation
b) Including directors and managers
c) For liberal professions, status partially inferred from the nature of occupation
d) Including military personnel

1947   a) Including directors and managers
b) Including home-workers
c) Including military personnel
d) Mainly unemployed

1961   a) Including home-workers
b) Including military personnel
c) Mainly unemployed

1970   a) Including conscripts
b) Mainly unemployed

The Development of the Labour Force

Year	by Status				by Sector				Total labour force	Domestic services	Military personnel	Year
	Inde-pendent (IN)	Depend-ent (DE)	Family worker	Un-known	Agricul-ture (A)	Indus-try (I)	Serv-ices (S)	Un-known				
	percent distribution				percent distribution				in thousands			
1970	14.8	81.1	4.1		10.6	37.7	48.8	2.9	2 310.0	24.6	28.3	1970
1965	18.1	78.3	3.6		14.6	37.9	44.8	2.7	2 233.1	41.2	25.4	1965
1960	20.8	77.0	2.2		17.8	37.0	42.5	2.7	2 063.6	58.6	19.3	1960
1950	21.6	72.0	6.3		25.6	34.1	38.3	2.0	2 023.7	104.2	10.2	1950
1940	22.3	71.7	6.0		29.9	32.2	37.1	.7	1 880.1	125.4	4.9	1940
1930	26.6	65.4	6.6	1.3	35.2	26.8	36.6	1.3	1 588.4	192.3	10.6	1930
1921	27.4	63.4	7.9	1.2	35.2	26.9	36.6	1.2	1 347.6	180.6	8.7	1921
1916	28.1	65.9	6.0		38.2	27.8	32.4	1.6	1 155.5	127.9	4.0	1916
1911	27.9	66.9	5.2		42.7	24.0	31.4	1.9	1 200.0	126.0	8.8	1911
1901	28.8	64.5	5.7		47.5	25.0	25.7	1.8	1 100.6	93.8	7.9	1901
1890	39.4	57.2		3.4	44.8	25.5	20.8	8.8	842.1	84.2	9.4	1890
1880	37.3	60.7		2.0	50.3	23.7	17.1	8.9	738.9	92.2	8.0	1880

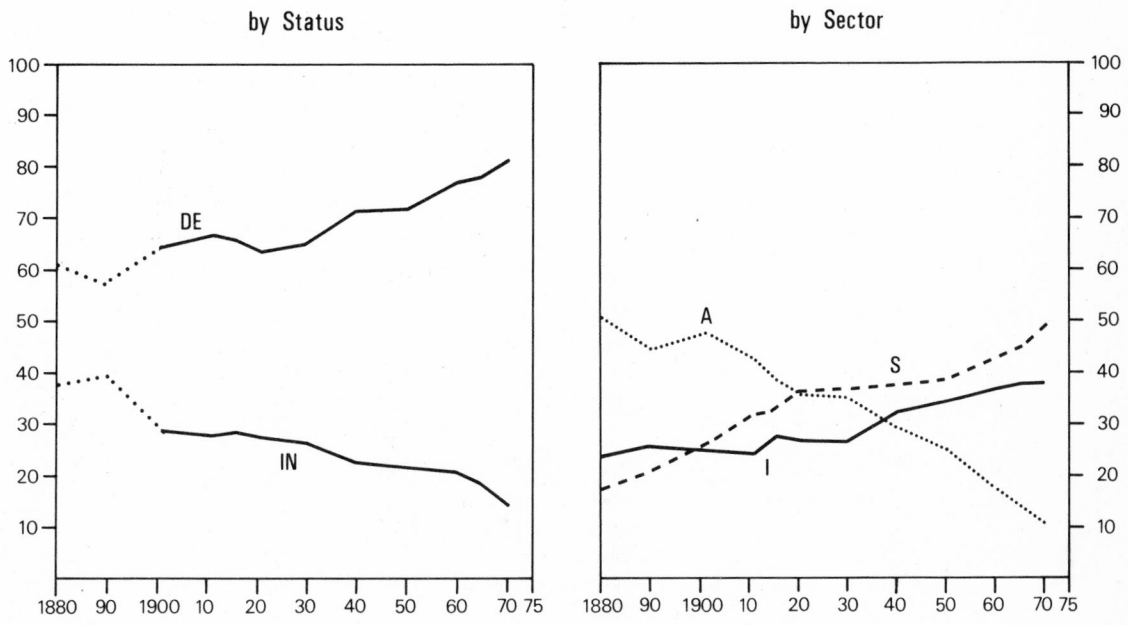

by Status   by Sector

Denmark

Labour Force by Sector and Status 1880 [a]

Absolute figures in thousands

Sector			Employ-ers EM	Self-employed SE	Employ-ees EE	Workers WO	Servants SV [b]	Family-workers FW [c]	Un-known U	Total T	%
I	Agriculture	Total	156.4		49.9		156.5			371.8	50.3
		males	139.6		45.8		89.4			274.8	50.8
II	Mining	Total	1.7		.6		.0			2.3	.3
		males	1.7		.6		.0			2.3	.4
III	Manufacturing	Total	74.2		59.3		14.6			148.0	20.0
		males	57.5		48.4		4.6			110.6	20.4
IV	Construction	Total	14.2		9.4		1.1			24.7	3.3
		males	14.2		9.4		.1			23.7	4.4
V	Utilities [d]	Total									
		males									
VI	Commerce	Total	20.1		9.9		13.5			43.5	5.9
		males	16.4		9.1		3.4			28.9	5.4
VII	Transport	Total	1.8		.9		.7			3.4	.5
		males	1.8		.9		.4			3.0	.6
VIII	Banking	Total	.3		.2		.3			.8	.1
		males	.3		.2		.0			.5	.1
IX	Services	Total	6.8		11.4		22.0		7.6	47.8	6.5
		males	5.3		7.9		3.9		6.6	23.7	4.4
X	Public admin.	Total	.0		24.7		6.3			31.0	4.2
		males	.0		23.3		1.0			24.3	4.5
U	Unknown [e]	Total			54.5		4.1		6.9	65.5	8.9
		males			46.1		1.3		1.6	49.1	9.1
T	All sectors	Total	275.5		220.7		228.2		14.5	738.9	100.0
		males	236.8		191.7		104.2		8.2	540.8	100.0

Percent distributions

		Total labour force								Male labour force					
	EM	SE	EE	WO	SV	FW	U	T		EM	SE	EE	WO	SV	FW	U	T
I	42.1		13.4		44.5			100.0	I	50.8		16.7		32.5			100.0
II	72.9		25.0		2.1			100.0	II	74.3		25.4		.3			100.0
III	50.1		40.1		9.8			100.0	III	52.0		43.8		4.2			100.0
IV	57.4		38.0		4.6			100.0	IV	59.9		39.6		.5			100.0
V									V								
VI	46.3		22.7		31.1			100.0	VI	56.8		31.6		11.7			100.0
VII	53.3		25.6		21.1			100.0	VII	58.1		29.0		13.0			100.0
VIII	32.4		25.2		42.4			100.0	VIII	54.1		41.0		5.0			100.0
IX	14.2		23.8		46.0		16.0	100.0	IX	22.5		33.2		16.5		27.8	100.0
X	.0		79.7		20.3			100.0	X	.0		95.9		4.1			100.0
U			83.2		6.2		10.6	100.0	U			94.0		2.7		3.3	100.0
T	37.3		29.9		30.9		2.0	100.0	T	43.8		35.4		19.3		1.5	100.0

L a b o u r   F o r c e   b y   S e c t o r   a n d   S t a t u s   1 8 9 0

Absolute figures in thousands

Sector			Employ-ers EM	Self-employed SE	Employ-ees EE	Workers WO	Servants SV[a]	Family-workers FW[b]	Un-known U	Total T	%
I	Agriculture	Total	189.9		35.9		151.6			377.4	44.8
		males	172.0		23.5		82.7			278.2	45.7
II	Mining	Total	1.7		.3		.0			2.1	.2
		males	1.7		.3		.0			2.1	.3
III	Manufacturing	Total	81.3		84.3		15.9			181.6	21.6
		males	59.3		69.6		4.6			133.4	21.9
IV	Construction	Total	15.6		14.3		1.4			31.3	3.7
		males	15.6		14.3		.1			30.0	4.9
V	Utilities[c]	Total									
		males									
VI	Commerce	Total	26.7		19.4		15.0			61.1	7.3
		males	22.3		17.1		3.1			42.5	7.0
VII	Transport	Total	6.6		14.5		2.4			23.5	2.8
		males	6.5		14.3		.5			21.3	3.5
VIII	Banking	Total	.3		.6		.6			1.4	.2
		males	.3		.6		.0			.9	.1
IX	Services	Total	10.1		15.7		24.2		11.4	61.3	7.3
		males	4.9		9.9		3.3		9.2	27.3	4.5
X	Public admin.	Total	.0		22.8		5.1			27.9	3.3
		males	.0		21.2		.7			21.9	3.6
U	Unknown[d]	Total			51.7		5.6		17.2	74.5	8.8
		males			44.8		2.0		4.2	51.1	8.4
T	All sectors	Total	332.1		259.7		221.7		28.5	842.1	100.0
		males	282.5		215.6		97.1		13.4	608.6	100.0

Percent distributions

	Total labour force								Male labour force						
	EM	SE	EE	WO	SV	FW	U	T		EM	SE	EE	WO	SV	FW	U	T
I	50.3		9.5		40.2			100.0	I	61.8		8.4		29.7			100.0
II	83.0		15.0		2.0			100.0	II	84.4		15.1		.4			100.0
III	44.8		46.5		8.7			100.0	III	44.4		52.1		3.4			100.0
IV	49.8		45.8		4.3			100.0	IV	51.9		47.7		.4			100.0
V									V								
VI	43.7		31.8		24.6			100.0	VI	52.5		40.3		7.2			100.0
VII	28.0		61.8		10.2			100.0	VII	30.6		67.1		2.3			100.0
VIII	18.5		42.6		38.8			100.0	VIII	29.9		68.0		2.2			100.0
IX	16.4		25.5		39.5		18.5	100.0	IX	17.9		36.2		12.2		33.7	100.0
X	.0		81.8		18.2			100.0	X	.0		96.9		3.1			100.0
U			69.5		7.5		23.0	100.0	U			87.8		4.0		8.3	100.0
T	39.4		30.8		26.3		3.4	100.0	T	46.4		35.4		16.0		2.2	100.0

Labour Force by Sector and Status 1901

Absolute figures in thousands

Sector		EM	SE	EE	WO[a]	AP	FW[b]	U	T	%
I Agriculture	Total	163.5		10.3	349.4		(65.7)		523.2	47.5
	males	150.1		10.1	215.9		(36.3)		367.1	50.3
II Mining	Total	.8		.0	1.7				2.6	.2
	males	.8		.0	1.7				2.6	.3
III Manufacturing	Total	86.1		11.5	136.2				233.8	21.2
	males	56.3		8.2	106.5		(6.2)		171.0	22.9
IV Construction	Total	11.2		.2	24.9		(5.5)		36.2	3.3
	males	11.1		.1	24.8				36.0	4.8
V Utilities	Total	.0		.2	1.9				2.1	.2
	males	.0		.2	1.9				2.1	.3
VI Commerce	Total	29.8		17.5	10.7				58.0	5.3
	males	23.4		13.6	9.4		(1.5)		46.5	6.2
VII Transport	Total	4.1		15.5	34.8		(1.0)		54.4	4.9
	males	3.9		11.4	33.8				49.2	6.6
VIII Banking	Total	.4		1.9	.2				2.5	.2
	males	.4		1.7	.2				2.3	.3
IX Services	Total	21.5		24.4	104.7				150.6	13.7
	males	11.8		11.6	12.2		(.0)		35.6	4.8
X Public admin.	Total	.0		7.0	10.1		(.0)		17.1	1.6
	males	.0		6.8	9.8				16.7	2.2
U Unknown	Total				19.9				19.9	1.8
	males				9.6				9.6	1.3
T All sectors	Total	317.4		88.4	694.6		(73.4)		1 100.6	100.0
	males	257.9		63.9	425.9		(42.8)		747.6	100.0

Percent distributions

Total labour force

	EM	SE	EE	WO	AP	FW	U	T
I	31.2		2.0	66.8		(12.6)		100.0
II	31.9		1.5	66.6				100.0
III	36.8		4.9	58.3				100.0
IV	30.9		.5	68.7				100.0
V	1.0		8.9	90.1				100.0
VI	51.4		30.2	18.4				100.0
VII	7.5		28.5	64.0				100.0
VIII	15.0		76.0	9.0				100.0
IX	14.3		16.2	69.5				100.0
X	.0		40.9	59.1				100.0
U			.0	100.0				100.0
T	28.8		8.0	63.1		(6.7)		100.0

Male labour force

	EM	SE	EE	WO	AP	FW	U	T
I	39.9		2.7	57.4		(9.9)		100.0
II	31.9		1.3	66.8				100.0
III	32.9		4.8	62.3				100.0
IV	30.8		.4	68.8				100.0
V	.9		8.6	90.5				100.0
VI	50.4		29.3	20.3				100.0
VII	8.0		23.2	68.8				100.0
VIII	16.0		74.7	9.3				100.0
IX	33.2		23.6	34.2				100.0
X	.0		40.9	59.1				100.0
U			.0	100.0				100.0
T	34.5		8.5	57.0		(5.7)		100.0

Denmark

Labour Force by Sector and Status 1911

Absolute figures in thousands

Sector		Employers / Self-employed EM SE	Employees EE	Workers WO a)	Apprentices AP b)	Family-workers FW c)	Unknown U	Total T	%
I Agriculture	Total	184.2	10.3	263.7		54.5		512.8	42.7
	males	172.1	10.1	190.8		29.7		402.7	48.6
II Mining	Total	.7	.0	1.6		.0		2.3	.2
	males	.7	.0	1.5		.0		2.2	.3
III Manufacturing	Total	71.0	13.8	152.5		5.6		243.0	20.2
	males	55.4	9.3	114.1		4.8		183.6	22.1
IV Construction	Total	14.6	.3	24.5		.0		39.4	3.3
	males	14.5	.2	24.3		.0		39.1	4.7
V Utilities	Total	.0	.3	2.4		.0		2.8	.2
	males	.0	.3	2.4		.0		2.7	.3
VI Commerce	Total	35.0	37.4	23.5		1.5		97.5	8.1
	males	28.1	23.6	21.4		.9		74.0	8.9
VII Transport	Total	4.3	10.7	36.8		.2		52.1	4.3
	males	4.2	8.1	35.9		.2		48.4	5.8
VIII Banking	Total	.5	4.2	.4		.0		5.2	.4
	males	.5	3.5	.4		.0		4.4	.5
IX Services	Total	24.3	31.3	145.6		.1		201.2	16.8
	males	14.8	14.3	11.7		.0		40.9	4.9
X Public admin.	Total	.0	8.1	12.8		.0		21.0	1.7
	males	.0	7.7	11.9		.0		19.5	2.4
U Unknown	Total			22.8				22.8	1.9
	males			11.3				11.3	1.4
T All sectors	Total	334.7	116.6	686.8		61.9		1 200.0	100.0
	males	290.4	77.1	425.8		35.6		828.9	100.0

Percent distributions

Total labour force

	EM SE	EE	WO	AP	FW	U	T
I	35.9	2.0	51.4		10.6		100.0
II	29.9	1.6	68.5		.0		100.0
III	29.2	5.7	62.8		2.3		100.0
IV	37.1	.8	62.1		.0		100.0
V	1.0	11.3	87.6		.0		100.0
VI	35.9	38.4	24.2		1.6		100.0
VII	8.3	20.6	70.7		.4		100.0
VIII	10.4	81.3	8.3		.0		100.0
IX	12.1	15.6	72.3		.0		100.0
X	.0	38.8	61.2		.0		100.0
U			100.0				100.0
T	27.9	9.7	57.2		5.2		100.0

Male labour force

	EM SE	EE	WO	AP	FW	U	T
I	42.7	2.5	47.4		7.4		100.0
II	30.0	1.3	68.7		.0		100.0
III	30.2	5.1	62.1		2.6		100.0
IV	37.1	.6	62.3		.0		100.0
V	1.1	10.6	88.4		.0		100.0
VI	38.0	31.9	28.9		1.2		100.0
VII	8.6	16.8	74.1		.4		100.0
VIII	11.8	78.9	9.3		.0		100.0
IX	36.3	35.0	28.6		.1		100.0
X	.0	39.2	60.8		.0		100.0
U			100.0				100.0
T	35.0	9.3	51.4		4.3		100.0

Labour Force by Sector and Status 1916 [a)]

Absolute figures in thousands

Sector			Employ-ers	Self-employed	Employ-ees	Workers	Apprent-ices	Family-workers	Un-known	Total	%
			EM	SE	EE	WO [b)]	AP	FW	U	T	
I	Agriculture	Total	185.1	19.4	237.1			(69.8)		441.5	38.2
		males	175.3	19.0	145.4			(34.1)		339.7	42.6
II	Mining	Total	.3	.0	1.8					2.1	.2
		males	.3	.0	1.8					2.1	.3
III	Manufacturing	Total	52.7	16.1	192.9					261.7	22.6
		males	44.8	10.6	149.3					204.8	25.7
IV	Construction	Total	19.1	.6	34.5					54.3	4.7
		males	19.0	.4	34.3					53.8	6.8
V	Utilities	Total	.2	.3	2.2					2.8	.2
		males	.2	.3	2.2					2.7	.3
VI	Commerce	Total	37.7	48.7	24.6					111.1	9.6
		males	31.4	27.2	21.5					80.1	10.1
VII	Transport	Total	6.1	22.3	23.5					51.8	4.5
		males	5.7	18.7	23.3					47.6	6.0
VIII	Banking	Total	.7	6.0	.5					7.3	.6
		males	.7	4.7	.5					5.9	.7
IX	Services	Total	22.4	33.3	148.8					204.5	17.7
		males	15.4	14.7	12.7					42.8	5.4
X	Public admin.	Total	.0	10.3	8.2					18.4	1.6
		males	.0	9.7	7.5					17.2	2.2
U	Unknown	Total									
		males									
T	All sectors	Total	324.4	157.1	674.0					1 155.5	100.0
		males	292.8	105.4	398.6					796.8	100.0

Percent distributions

Total labour force

	EM	SE	EE	WO	AP	FW	U	T
I	41.9	4.4	53.7			(15.8)		100.0
II	12.0	2.3	85.7					100.0
III	20.1	6.2	73.7					100.0
IV	35.3	1.1	63.6					100.0
V	8.6	12.3	79.1					100.0
VI	34.0	43.9	22.1					100.0
VII	11.7	43.0	45.3					100.0
VIII	10.0	82.6	7.4					100.0
IX	11.0	16.3	72.7					100.0
X	.0	55.8	44.2					100.0
U								
T	28.1	13.6	58.3					100.0

Male labour force

	EM	SE	EE	WO	AP	FW	U	T
I	51.6	5.6	42.8			(10.0)		100.0
II	11.8	1.8	86.4					100.0
III	21.9	5.2	72.9					100.0
IV	35.4	.8	63.8					100.0
V	8.6	11.0	80.4					100.0
VI	39.2	34.0	26.8					100.0
VII	11.9	39.2	48.9					100.0
VIII	11.7	79.5	8.8					100.0
IX	35.9	34.3	29.8					100.0
X	.0	56.3	43.7					100.0
U								
T	36.8	13.2	50.0					100.0

Labour Force by Sector and Status 1921 [a]

Absolute figures in thousands

Sector			Employ- ers	Self- employed	Employ- ees	Workers	Apprent- ices	Family- workers	Un- known	Total	%
			EM	SE	EE	WO [b]	AP	FW	U	T	
I	Agriculture	Total	196.6	16.2		261.8		(107.1)		474.6	35.2
		males	185.7	16.0		203.6		(54.9)		405.3	42.8
II	Mining	Total	.6	.0		2.6				3.2	.2
		males	.6	.0		2.5				3.2	.3
III	Manufacturing	Total	76.7	29.4		223.6				329.7	24.5
		males	64.2	21.3		182.4				268.0	28.3
IV	Construction	Total	7.3	.0		19.3				26.6	2.0
		males	7.3	.0		19.1				26.4	2.8
V	Utilities	Total	.4	.0		3.1				3.5	.3
		males	.4	.0		3.1				3.5	.4
VI	Commerce	Total	46.6	49.6		15.6				111.8	8.3
		males	39.1	29.9		13.9				82.9	8.8
VII	Transport	Total	16.0	32.6		29.3				77.9	5.8
		males	13.3	27.2		28.7				69.2	7.3
VIII	Banking	Total	1.6	10.1		.9				12.6	.9
		males	1.1	7.2		.8				9.2	1.0
IX	Services	Total	23.7	30.9		216.5				271.2	20.1
		males	17.5	19.3		17.5				54.2	5.7
X	Public admin.	Total	.0	12.0		8.1				20.2	1.5
		males	.0	11.4		8.0				19.4	2.0
U	Unknown	Total							16.2	16.2	1.2
		males							4.8	4.8	.5
T	All sectors	Total	369.6	180.8		781.0			16.2	1 347.6	100.0
		males	329.2	132.3		479.7			4.8	946.1	100.0

Percent distributions

	Total labour force									Male labour force							
	EM	SE	EE	WO	AP	FW	U	T		EM	SE	EE	WO	AP	FW	U	T
I	41.4		3.4	55.2		(22.6)		100.0	I	45.8		4.0	50.2		(13.5)		100.0
II	19.2		.0	80.8				100.0	II	19.2		.0	80.8				100.0
III	23.3		8.9	67.8				100.0	III	24.0		8.0	68.1				100.0
IV	27.5		.0	72.5				100.0	IV	27.5		.0	72.5				100.0
V	11.3		.0	88.7				100.0	V	11.2		.0	88.8				100.0
VI	41.7		44.3	14.0				100.0	VI	47.2		36.1	16.8				100.0
VII	20.5		41.9	37.7				100.0	VII	19.2		39.3	41.4				100.0
VIII	13.0		80.1	6.8				100.0	VIII	12.4		78.4	9.1				100.0
IX	8.7		11.4	79.8				100.0	IX	32.3		35.5	32.2				100.0
X	.0		59.7	40.3				100.0	X	.0		58.9	41.1				100.0
U							100.0	100.0	U							100.0	100.0
T	27.4		13.4	57.9			1.2	100.0	T	34.8		14.0	50.7			.5	100.0

Denmark

Labour Force by Sector and Status 1930

Absolute figures in thousands

Sector			Employers EM	Self-employed SE	Employees EE [a]	Workers WO [b]	Apprentices AP	Family-workers FW [c]	Unknown U	Total T	%
I	Agriculture	Total	212.6		347.1	(216.5)		(105.5)		559.7	35.2
		males	202.2		236.1	(155.2)		(55.9)		438.2	39.7
II	Mining	Total	.4		2.3					2.7	.2
		males	.4		2.3					2.7	.2
III	Manufacturing	Total	85.4		299.7	(265.8)				385.1	24.2
		males	74.3		248.9	(224.5)				323.2	29.3
IV	Construction	Total	9.5		25.6					35.0	2.2
		males	9.4		25.6					35.0	3.2
V	Utilities	Total	.4		3.1					3.5	.2
		males	.4		3.1					3.5	.3
VI	Commerce	Total	58.9		99.5	(22.0)				158.3	10.0
		males	49.5		65.8	(19.8)				115.3	10.4
VII	Transport	Total	20.0		68.7	(38.5)				88.7	5.6
		males	18.5		63.8	(38.3)				82.4	7.5
VIII	Banking	Total	1.6		12.2	(1.0)				13.8	.9
		males	.9		9.6	(1.0)				10.5	1.0
IX	Services	Total	34.0		268.5					302.5	19.0
		males	24.3		41.3					65.6	5.9
X	Public admin.	Total	.0		17.6					17.6	1.1
		males	.0		17.1					17.1	1.6
U	Unknown	Total							21.3	21.3	1.3
		males							10.7	10.7	1.0
T	All sectors	Total	422.7		1 144.4				21.3	1 588.4	100.0
		males	379.9		713.7				10.7	1 104.3	100.0

Percent distributions

Total labour force

	EM	SE	EE	WO	AP	FW	U	T
I	38.0		62.0	(38.7)		(18.8)		100.0
II	14.1		85.9					100.0
III	22.2		77.8	(69.0)				100.0
IV	27.0		73.0					100.0
V	10.9		89.1	(89.1)				100.0
VI	37.2		62.8	(13.9)				100.0
VII	22.5		77.5	(43.4)				100.0
VIII	11.3		88.7	(7.3)				100.0
IX	11.2		88.8					100.0
X	.0		100.0					100.0
U							100.0	100.0
T	26.6		72.0				1.3	100.0

Male labour force

	EM	SE	EE	WO	AP	FW	U	T
I	46.1		53.9	(35.4)		(12.8)		100.0
II	13.9		86.1					100.0
III	23.0		77.0	(69.5)				100.0
IV	27.0		73.0					100.0
V	11.0		89.0	(89.0)				100.0
VI	42.9		57.1	(17.2)				100.0
VII	22.5		77.5	(46.5)				100.0
VIII	8.8		91.2	(9.3)				100.0
IX	37.1		62.9					100.0
X	.0		100.0					100.0
U							100.0	100.0
T	34.4		64.6				1.0	100.0

L a b o u r   F o r c e   b y   S e c t o r   a n d   S t a t u s   1 9 4 0

Absolute figures in thousands

Sector			Employers	Self-employed	Employees	Workers	Apprentices	Family-workers a)	Unknown	Total	%
			EM	SE	EE	WO	AP	FW	U	T	
I	Agriculture	Total	216.5	14.1	246.6		85.0			562.3	29.9
		males	206.9	13.8	214.8					435.4	33.8
II	Mining	Total	.3	.4	3.9		.0			4.6	.2
		males	.3	.3	3.8					4.4	.3
III	Manufacturing	Total	60.7	45.9	357.0		8.5			472.0	25.1
		males	51.6	29.4	267.2					348.3	27.1
IV	Construction	Total	21.1	3.5	95.2		.8			120.5	6.4
		males	21.0	2.9	95.1					118.9	9.2
V	Utilities	Total	.4	3.0	5.9		.0			9.2	.5
		males	.4	2.5	5.8					8.7	.7
VI	Commerce	Total	66.8	105.9	28.7		14.5			215.8	11.5
		males	53.9	59.6	23.7					137.2	10.7
VII	Transport	Total	13.4	46.4	53.7		.7			114.2	6.1
		males	13.2	35.6	51.8					100.6	7.8
VIII	Banking	Total	2.2	17.7	2.3		.0			22.2	1.2
		males	1.4	12.3	1.5					15.3	1.2
IX	Services	Total	37.4	82.5	190.5		3.5			313.8	16.7
		males	22.3	38.7	22.0					83.0	6.4
X	Public admin.	Total	.0	27.1	4.6		.0			31.7	1.7
		males	.0	21.7	3.2					25.0	1.9
U	Unknown	Total			13.6					13.6	.7
		males			9.8					9.8	.8
T	All sectors	Total	418.7	346.4	1 002.1		113.0			1 880.1	100.0
		males	370.9	217.0	698.7					1 286.6	100.0

Percent distributions

	Total labour force									Male labour force							
	EM	SE	EE	WO	AP	FW	U	T		EM	SE	EE	WO	AP	FW	U	T
I	38.5		2.5	43.9		15.1		100.0	I	47.5		3.2	49.3				100.0
II	6.8		8.1	84.7		.4		100.0	II	7.0		7.1	85.9				100.0
III	12.9		9.7	75.6		1.8		100.0	III	14.8		8.4	76.7				100.0
IV	17.5		2.9	79.0		.6		100.0	IV	17.6		2.5	79.9				100.0
V	4.5		31.9	63.5		.1		100.0	V	4.8		29.2	66.1				100.0
VI	30.9		49.1	13.3		6.7		100.0	VI	39.3		43.4	17.3				100.0
VII	11.7		40.6	47.0		.6		100.0	VII	13.3		35.4	51.5				100.0
VIII	9.9		79.5	10.5		.2		100.0	VIII	9.3		80.6	10.1				100.0
IX	11.9		26.3	60.7		1.1		100.0	IX	26.8		46.7	26.5				100.0
X	.0		85.6	14.4		.0		100.0	X	.0		87.0	13.0				100.0
U				100.0				100.0	U				100.0				100.0
T	22.3		18.4	53.3		6.0		100.0	T	28.8		16.9	54.3				100.0

Labour Force by Sector and Status 1950

Absolute figures in thousands

Sector			Employ-ers	Self-employed	Employ-ees	Workers	Apprent-ices	Family-workers	Un-known	Total	%
			EM	SE	EE	WO	AP	FW[a]	U	T	
I	Agriculture	Total	203.7	7.4	12.1	206.0		89.2		518.3	25.6
		males	196.5	7.3	11.7	181.4				396.9	29.0
II	Mining	Total	.2	.2	.2	3.5		.0		4.1	.2
		males	.2	.2	.2	3.4				4.0	.3
III	Manufacturing	Total	65.5	4.1	62.3	399.2		10.9		542.1	26.8
		males	55.4	3.9	40.2	293.1				392.6	28.7
IV	Construction	Total	25.1	.1	4.1	100.4		2.0		131.8	6.5
		males	25.0	.1	3.1	100.0				128.2	9.4
V	Utilities	Total	.0	.4	3.1	8.2		.0		11.8	.6
		males	.0	.4	2.5	8.0				11.0	.8
VI	Commerce	Total	66.2	7.2	110.8	30.0		18.7		232.9	11.5
		males	55.2	5.8	65.3	25.5				151.7	11.1
VII	Transport	Total	16.3	.2	59.7	61.6		1.5		139.5	6.9
		males	16.1	.2	42.5	58.2				117.0	8.5
VIII	Banking	Total	.1	2.3	22.0	2.3		.1		26.8	1.3
		males	.1	1.6	13.6	1.4				16.7	1.2
IX	Services	Total	36.5	2.1	101.7	181.2		5.6		327.0	16.2
		males	24.6	1.2	40.4	28.4				94.7	6.9
X	Public admin.	Total	.0	.0	40.3	8.9		.0		49.2	2.4
		males	.0	.0	29.9	6.4				36.3	2.7
U	Unknown[b]	Total			16.9	23.5				40.3	2.0
		males			4.8	15.0				19.8	1.4
T	All sectors	Total	413.6	24.1	433.2	1 024.8		128.0		2 023.7	100.0
		males	373.0	20.7	254.3	720.9				1 369.0	100.0

Percent distributions

	Total labour force									Male labour force							
	EM	SE	EE	WO	AP	FW	U	T		EM	SE	EE	WO	AP	FW	U	T
I	39.3	1.4	2.3	39.7		17.2		100.0	I	49.5	1.8	3.0	45.7				100.0
II	3.9	5.3	4.7	85.6		.4		100.0	II	3.9	5.4	4.3	86.3				100.0
III	12.1	.8	11.5	73.6		2.0		100.0	III	14.1	1.0	10.2	74.7				100.0
IV	19.1	.1	3.1	76.2		1.5		100.0	IV	19.5	.1	2.4	78.0				100.0
V	.0	3.6	26.4	69.8		.2		100.0	V	.0	3.9	23.2	72.9				100.0
VI	28.4	3.1	47.6	12.9		8.0		100.0	VI	36.4	3.8	43.0	16.8				100.0
VII	11.7	.2	42.8	44.2		1.1		100.0	VII	13.7	.2	36.3	49.7				100.0
VIII	.5	8.7	82.0	8.5		.3		100.0	VIII	.8	9.3	81.5	8.4				100.0
IX	11.2	.6	31.1	55.4		1.7		100.0	IX	26.0	1.3	42.6	30.0				100.0
X	.0	.0	81.9	18.1		.0		100.0	X	.0	.0	82.4	17.6				100.0
U			41.8	58.2				100.0	U			24.2	75.8				100.0
T	20.4	1.2	21.4	50.6		6.3		100.0	T	27.2	1.5	18.6	52.7				100.0

Labour Force by Sector and Status 1960

Absolute figures in thousands

Sector			Employers	Self-employed	Employees	Workers	Apprentices	Family-workers	Unknown	Total	%
			EM	SE	EE	WO	AP	FW[a)]	U	T	
I	Agriculture	Total	199.2	8.9	137.2		21.1			366.9	17.8
		males	191.6	8.4	131.8					331.8	22.9
II	Mining	Total	.4	.2	3.0		.0			3.6	.2
		males	.4	.2	3.0					3.6	.2
III	Manufacturing	Total	55.6	91.7	443.3		6.1			596.7	28.9
		males	49.7	58.9	334.5					443.0	30.6
IV	Construction	Total	26.5	5.7	117.1		1.1			150.3	7.3
		males	26.3	3.8	116.7					146.8	10.1
V	Utilities	Total	.3	3.5	9.0		.0			12.8	.6
		males	.3	2.8	8.9					12.0	.8
VI	Commerce	Total	79.1	123.0	39.1		12.6			253.8	12.3
		males	64.7	65.0	33.6					163.2	11.3
VII	Transport	Total	18.0	67.3	64.7		.7			150.7	7.3
		males	17.6	47.8	61.1					126.5	8.7
VIII	Banking	Total	1.8	30.2	2.2		.0			34.2	1.7
		males	1.8	16.8	1.3					19.9	1.4
IX	Services	Total	47.9	150.2	171.3		3.6			373.1	18.1
		males	31.1	52.8	31.1					115.0	7.9
X	Public admin.	Total	.0	58.8	7.4		.0			66.2	3.2
		males	.0	42.9	4.1					47.0	3.2
U	Unknown[b)]	Total		24.1	31.6					55.7	2.7
		males		10.7	27.9					38.7	2.7
T	All sectors	Total	429.0	563.6	1 026.0		45.1			2 063.6	100.0
		males	383.4	310.2	753.9					1 447.5	100.0

Percent distributions

	Total labour force								Male labour force							
	EM	SE	EE	WO	AP	FW	U	T		EM	SE	EE	WO	AP	FW	U	T
I	54.4	2.4	37.5			5.7		100.0	I	57.7	2.5	39.7					100.0
II	10.1	6.7	83.1			.2		100.0	II	10.0	5.7	84.4					100.0
III	9.3	15.4	74.3			1.0		100.0	III	11.2	13.3	75.5					100.0
IV	17.6	3.8	77.9			.7		100.0	IV	17.9	2.6	79.5					100.0
V	2.6	27.0	70.4			.0		100.0	V	2.7	23.2	74.1					100.0
VI	31.2	48.5	15.4			5.0		100.0	VI	39.6	39.8	20.6					100.0
VII	12.0	44.7	42.9			.5		100.0	VII	13.9	37.8	48.3					100.0
VIII	5.4	88.1	6.5			.0		100.0	VIII	9.0	84.4	6.5					100.0
IX	12.8	40.3	45.9			1.0		100.0	IX	27.0	45.9	27.1					100.0
X	.0	88.8	11.2			.0		100.0	X	.0	91.3	8.7					100.0
U	.1	43.2	56.7					100.0	U	.1	27.8	72.2					100.0
T	20.8	27.3	49.7			2.2		100.0	T	26.5	21.4	52.1					100.0

Labour Force by Sector and Status 1965

Absolute figures in thousands

Sector			Employ-ers	Self-employed	Employ-ees	Workers	Apprent-ices	Family-workers	Un-known	Total	%
			EM	SE	EE	WO	AP	FW[a]	U	T	
I	Agriculture	Total	173.2	2.9	7.7	98.5		44.1		326.4	14.6
		males	166.8	2.9	6.9	93.2				269.8	18.1
II	Mining	Total	.3	.0	.3	2.6		.0		3.2	.1
		males	.3	.0	.3	2.5				3.1	.2
III	Manufacturing	Total	48.3	5.1	117.7	464.6		9.6		645.3	28.9
		males	43.9	4.9	74.9	347.5				471.2	31.7
IV	Construction	Total	29.2	.3	9.5	142.5		2.9		184.3	8.3
		males	29.0	.3	6.2	141.7				177.2	11.9
V	Utilities	Total	.0	.2	4.3	9.6		.0		14.1	.6
		males	.0	.2	3.3	9.4				12.9	.9
VI	Commerce	Total	66.2	8.6	152.2	43.2		17.4		287.6	12.9
		males	54.0	7.0	74.4	35.4				170.8	11.5
VII	Transport	Total	18.4	.4	72.7	61.1		1.3		153.9	6.9
		males	18.0	.3	49.7	57.1				125.1	8.4
VIII	Banking	Total	.1	.4	38.9	2.6		.0		42.0	1.9
		males	.1	.4	20.5	1.3				22.3	1.5
IX	Services	Total	47.7	2.7	203.4	177.5		5.1		436.4	19.5
		males	32.2	1.2	68.4	35.4				137.3	9.2
X	Public admin.	Total	.0	.0	71.7	8.6		.0		80.4	3.7
		males	.0	.0	50.6	4.6				55.2	3.7
U	Unknown[b]	Total			21.4	38.2				59.6	2.7
		males			8.7	33.9				42.7	2.9
T	All sectors	Total	383.4	20.5	699.8	1 049.0		80.4		2 233.1	100.0
		males	344.3	17.2	364.0	762.0				1 487.6	100.0

Percent distributions

Total labour force

	EM	SE	EE	WO	AP	FW	U	T
I	53.1	.9	2.4	30.2		13.5		100.0
II	8.7	.9	10.3	79.5		.6		100.0
III	7.5	.8	18.2	72.0		1.5		100.0
IV	15.8	.2	5.1	77.3		1.5		100.0
V	.1	1.3	30.4	68.2		.0		100.0
VI	23.0	3.0	52.9	15.0		6.0		100.0
VII	12.0	.2	47.2	39.7		.9		100.0
VIII	.3	1.1	92.5	6.1		.0		100.0
IX	10.9	.6	46.6	40.7		1.2		100.0
X	.0	.0	89.3	10.7		.0		100.0
U			35.9	64.1				100.0
T	17.2	.9	31.3	47.0		3.6		100.0

Male labour force

	EM	SE	EE	WO	AP	FW	U	T
I	61.8	1.1	2.6	34.5				100.0
II	8.9	.9	8.5	81.6				100.0
III	9.3	1.0	15.9	73.7				100.0
IV	16.4	.2	3.5	80.0				100.0
V	.2	1.4	25.8	72.6				100.0
VI	31.6	4.1	43.6	20.7				100.0
VII	14.4	.3	39.7	45.6				100.0
VIII	.4	2.0	91.9	5.6				100.0
IX	23.5	.8	49.9	25.8				100.0
X	.0	.0	91.7	8.3				100.0
U			20.4	79.6				100.0
T	23.1	1.2	24.5	51.2				100.0

Labour Force by Sector and Status 1970

Absolute figures in thousands

Sector			Employ-ers	Self-employed	Employ-ees	Workers	Apprent-ices	Family-workers	Un-known	Total	%
			EM	SE	EE	WO	AP	FW[a]	U	T	
I	Agriculture	Total	135.6		6.6	56.5		45.6		244.4	10.6
		males	131.0		5.7	52.2		.2		189.1	12.9
II	Mining	Total	.3		.4	2.4		.0		3.1	.1
		males	.3		.3	2.4		.0		2.9	.2
III	Manufacturing	Total	44.9		131.1	453.2		12.4		641.6	27.8
		males	41.5		83.7	338.4		.1		463.7	31.6
IV	Construction	Total	28.9		15.5	160.4		5.6		210.5	9.1
		males	28.7		10.1	159.5		.0		198.2	13.5
V	Utilities	Total	.2		5.1	9.6		.0		14.9	.6
		males	.2		4.0	9.4		.0		13.6	.9
VI	Commerce	Total	65.2		161.1	46.1		20.6		293.1	12.7
		males	53.9		75.9	36.8		.3		167.0	11.4
VII	Transport	Total	18.9		73.6	58.0		2.7		153.2	6.6
		males	18.4		51.7	54.0		.0		124.1	8.5
VIII	Banking	Total	.3		50.9	2.1		.0		53.2	2.3
		males	.3		25.1	.4		.0		25.8	1.8
IX	Services	Total	47.4		288.3	186.3		8.3		530.2	23.0
		males	32.8		94.9	38.7		.2		166.6	11.4
X	Public admin.	Total	.0		86.9	11.6		.0		98.5	4.3
		males	.0		56.7	7.1		.0		63.8	4.4
U	Unknown[b]	Total			15.4	51.8				67.3	2.9
		males			8.5	42.4				50.9	3.5
T	All sectors	Total	341.6		834.9	1 038.1		95.3		2 310.0	100.0
		males	306.9		416.7	741.2		.8		1 465.7	100.0

Percent distributions

Total labour force

	EM	SE	EE	WO	AP	FW	U	T
I	55.5		2.7	23.1		18.7		100.0
II	8.5		12.7	77.8		1.0		100.0
III	7.0		20.4	70.6		1.9		100.0
IV	13.7		7.4	76.2		2.7		100.0
V	1.2		34.5	64.2		.1		100.0
VI	22.2		55.0	15.7		7.0		100.0
VII	12.3		48.0	37.9		1.8		100.0
VIII	.5		95.6	3.9		.0		100.0
IX	8.9		54.4	35.1		1.6		100.0
X	.0		88.2	11.8		.0		100.0
U			23.0	77.0				100.0
T	14.8		36.1	44.9		4.1		100.0

Male labour force

	EM	SE	EE	WO	AP	FW	U	T
I	69.3		3.0	27.6		.1		100.0
II	8.6		10.0	81.3		.0		100.0
III	8.9		18.1	73.0		.0		100.0
IV	14.5		5.1	80.4		.0		100.0
V	1.3		29.6	69.1		.0		100.0
VI	32.3		45.5	22.1		.2		100.0
VII	14.8		41.7	43.5		.0		100.0
VIII	1.1		97.4	1.5		.0		100.0
IX	19.7		57.0	23.2		.1		100.0
X	.0		88.9	11.1		.0		100.0
U			16.7	83.3				100.0
T	20.9		28.4	50.6		.1		100.0

Notes:

1880–1970   Resident population
1880–1930   Status classification in Services and Public Administration not directly available; classification
             partially inferred from the nature of the respective occupation/sector

1880   a) Including the Faeroe Islands
             b) Servants engaged in domestic services and/or production activities
             c) Included in the labour force (except for assisting married females), but classification unknown
             d) Included in Manufacturing
             e) Mainly day-labourers

1890   a) Servants engaged in domestic services and/or production activities
             b) Included in the labour force (except for assisting married females), but classification unknown
             c) Included in Manufacturing
             d) Mainly day-labourers

1901   a) Including apprentices
             b) Included in the labour force, but only if living by their own means
             c) Excluding assisting married females

1911   a) Including apprentices
             b) Included in the labour force, but only if living by their own means
             c) Excluding assisting married females

1916   a) Excluding all married females and conscripts; status classification in Agriculture, Banking,
                Services, and Public Administration according to the 1921 classification system
             b) Including family workers

1921   a) Excluding all married females
             b) Including family workers and apprentices

1930   a) Including workers and family workers; distinction between workers and employees available for
                certain sectors only
             b) Including family workers
             c) Excluding assisting married females

1940–1970   a) Including assisting married females, but excluding assisting children
             b) Including conscripts

Finland

The Development of the Labour Force

Year	by Status Independent (IN)	Depend- ent (DE)	Family worker	Un- known	by Sector Agricul- ture (A)	Indus- try (I)	Serv- ices (S)	Un- known	Total labour force	Domestic services	Military personnel	Year
	percent distribution				percent distribution				in thousands			
1970	14.3	78.9	7.4	.3	20.3	34.3	44.1	1.4	2 118.3	31.0	16.4	1970
1960	19.4	65.7	14.9		35.5	31.5	32.8	.3	2 033.3	38.8	15.2	1960
1950	20.2	58.1	21.7		46.0	27.7	24.9	1.4	1 984.3	39.9	16.0	1950
1940			32.5	2.2	57.4	18.5	16.7	7.4	2 017.2	40.3	13.3	1940
1930			35.6	2.2	64.5	14.8	13.4	7.3	1 714.8	38.7	6.6	1930
1920			35.6	1.1	70.4	13.1	11.1	5.3	1 465.7	30.2	3.0	1920
1910			32.3	1.7	71.5	11.1	8.7	8.8	1 253.2	28.3	.8	1910

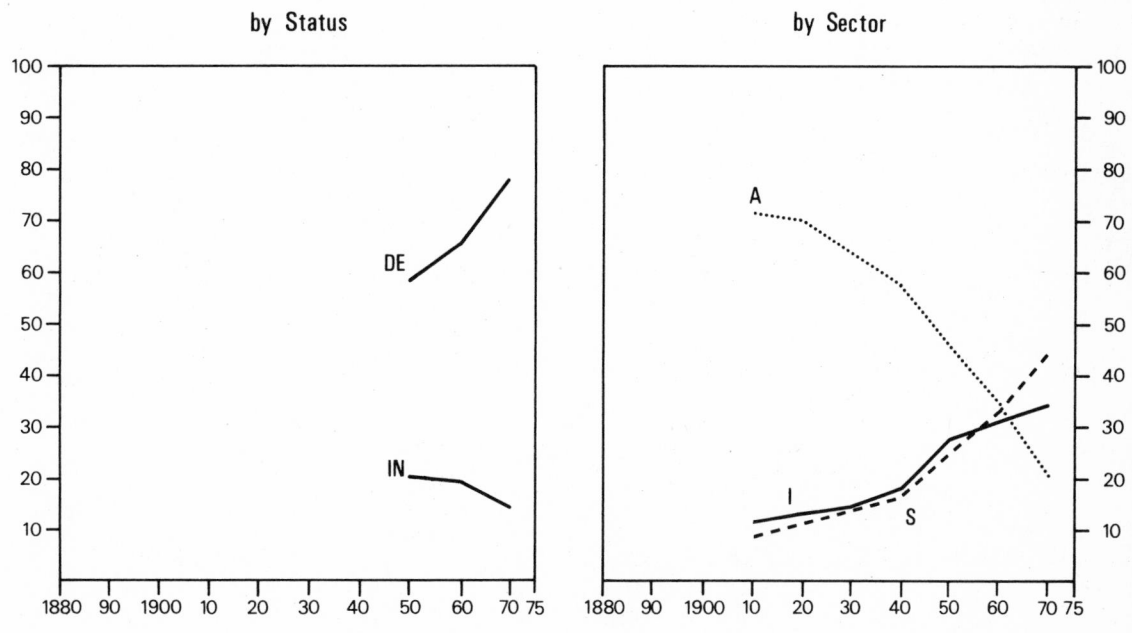

485

Finland

Labour Force by Sector and Status 1910

Absolute figures in thousands

Sector			Employ-ers	Self-employed	Employ-ees	Workers	Apprent-ices	Family-workers	Un-known	Total	%
			EM	SE	EE	WO	AP	FW	U	T	
I	Agriculture	Total		223.0		280.6		392.1		895.7	71.5
		males		202.1		174.4		190.9		567.3	71.0
II	Mining a)	Total		.0		.1		.0		.2	.0
		males		.0		.1		.0		.2	.0
III	Manufacturing a)	Total		13.0		103.2		6.4		122.7	9.8
		males		10.9		73.0		4.4		88.3	11.0
IV	Construction	Total		2.0		11.8		.5		14.4	1.1
		males		2.0		11.4		.4		13.8	1.7
V	Utilities	Total		.1		1.1		.0		1.2	.1
		males		.1		1.0		.0		1.1	.1
VI	Commerce	Total		11.5		10.0		1.1		22.5	1.8
		males		8.5		4.7		.6		13.8	1.7
VII	Transport	Total		7.8		20.0		.9		28.7	2.3
		males		6.7		19.0		.6		26.3	3.3
VIII	Banking	Total		.3		1.0		.0		1.3	.1
		males		.3		.4		.0		.8	.1
IX	Services	Total		17.0		32.3		.2		49.6	4.0
		males		8.2		3.9		.1		12.1	1.5
X	Public admin.	Total		2.4		4.7		.1		7.2	.6
		males		2.3		4.6		.1		7.0	.9
U	Unknown	Total				84.4		4.0	21.3	109.7	8.8
		males				52.5		2.3	13.9	68.8	8.6
T	All sectors	Total		277.2		549.3		405.4	21.3	1 253.2	100.0
		males		241.0		345.1		199.4	13.9	799.5	100.0

Percent distributions

	Total labour force									Male labour force							
	EM	SE	EE	WO	AP	FW	U	T		EM	SE	EE	WO	AP	FW	U	T
I		24.9		31.3		43.8		100.0	I		35.6		30.7		33.6		100.0
II		11.4		84.8		3.8		100.0	II		11.0		86.4		2.6		100.0
III		10.6		84.1		5.2		100.0	III		12.3		82.6		5.0		100.0
IV		14.1		82.5		3.4		100.0	IV		14.5		82.4		3.2		100.0
V		9.2		90.0		.8		100.0	V		9.1		90.3		.6		100.0
VI		50.8		44.3		4.9		100.0	VI		61.3		34.4		4.3		100.0
VII		27.1		69.7		3.2		100.0	VII		25.5		72.1		2.5		100.0
VIII		24.7		73.6		1.7		100.0	VIII		38.9		59.5		1.6		100.0
IX		34.4		65.3		.4		100.0	IX		67.2		32.2		.6		100.0
X		33.4		65.3		1.3		100.0	X		33.4		65.8		.8		100.0
U				76.9		3.7	19.4	100.0	U				76.4		3.4	20.2	100.0
T		22.1		43.8		32.3	1.7	100.0	T		30.1		43.2		24.9	1.7	100.0

486

Labour Force by Sector and Status 1920

Absolute figures in thousands

Sector			Employers EM	Self-employed SE	Employees EE	Workers WO	Apprentices AP	Family-workers FW a)	Unknown U	Total T	%
I	Agriculture	Total		249.1		282.9		500.4		1 032.3	70.4
		males		220.7		166.3		216.0		603.0	69.0
II	Mining b)	Total		.0		.4		.0		.5	.0
		males		.0		.4		.0		.4	.1
III	Manufacturing b)	Total		29.4		130.8		11.0		171.2	11.7
		males		22.0		91.6		7.7		121.3	13.9
IV	Construction	Total		2.2		14.0		.6		16.7	1.1
		males		2.1		13.3		.5		15.8	1.8
V	Utilities	Total		.7		2.8		.0		3.6	.2
		males		.6		2.7		.0		3.2	.4
VI	Commerce	Total		21.4		16.2		1.7		39.3	2.7
		males		14.9		8.1		.8		23.8	2.7
VII	Transport	Total		9.5		29.1		1.2		39.9	2.7
		males		7.3		26.2		.9		34.5	3.9
VIII	Banking	Total		3.6		.7		.0		4.3	.3
		males		1.5		.4		.0		2.0	.2
IX	Services	Total		21.6		42.5		.4		64.4	4.4
		males		10.1		4.7		.1		14.9	1.7
X	Public admin.	Total		6.6		8.7		.1		15.5	1.1
		males		4.7		8.1		.0		12.8	1.5
U	Unknown	Total				56.6		5.9	15.6	78.0	5.3
		males				33.3		2.8	6.6	42.6	4.9
T	All sectors	Total		344.2		584.7		521.3	15.6	1 465.7	100.0
		males		284.1		354.9		228.8	6.6	874.4	100.0

Percent distributions

Total labour force

	EM	SE	EE	WO	AP	FW	U	T
I		24.1		27.4		48.5		100.0
II		7.0		82.5		10.6		100.0
III		17.2		76.4		6.4		100.0
IV		13.0		83.6		3.4		100.0
V		20.5		78.6		.9		100.0
VI		54.4		41.3		4.3		100.0
VII		23.9		73.0		3.1		100.0
VIII		82.7		16.8		.5		100.0
IX		33.5		65.9		.6		100.0
X		43.0		56.3		.7		100.0
U				72.5		7.5	19.9	100.0
T		23.5		39.9		35.6	1.1	100.0

Male labour force

	EM	SE	EE	WO	AP	FW	U	T
I		36.6		27.6		35.8		100.0
II		5.8		84.4		9.8		100.0
III		18.2		75.5		6.3		100.0
IV		13.1		83.8		3.1		100.0
V		17.1		82.1		.8		100.0
VI		62.9		33.9		3.3		100.0
VII		21.3		76.1		2.7		100.0
VIII		77.9		21.8		.3		100.0
IX		68.0		31.3		.7		100.0
X		36.7		63.0		.3		100.0
U				78.0		6.5	15.5	100.0
T		32.5		40.6		26.2	.8	100.0

Finland

Labour Force by Sector and Status 1930

Absolute figures in thousands

Sector			Employers	Self-employed	Employees	Workers	Apprentices	Family-workers	Unknown	Total	%
			EM	SE	EE	WO	AP	FW a)	U	T	
I	Agriculture	Total		287.8		237.4		580.2		1 105.4	64.5
		males		247.8		131.9		253.5		633.2	62.7
II	Mining b)	Total		.1		.5		.0		.6	.0
		males		.1		.5		.0		.6	.1
III	Manufacturing b)	Total		35.8		167.9		14.8		218.4	12.7
		males		26.0		119.0		9.3		154.3	15.3
IV	Construction	Total		3.9		25.1		1.1		30.1	1.8
		males		3.8		23.6		.9		28.2	2.8
V	Utilities	Total		1.0		3.6		.1		4.7	.3
		males		.8		3.5		.1		4.4	.4
VI	Commerce	Total		24.3		25.7		2.6		52.6	3.1
		males		15.9		11.5		1.0		28.3	2.8
VII	Transport	Total		13.9		36.1		1.7		51.7	3.0
		males		11.3		31.9		1.1		44.3	4.4
VIII	Banking	Total		6.1		.9		.0		7.0	.4
		males		2.6		.6		.0		3.2	.3
IX	Services	Total		31.1		56.9		.8	8.5	97.3	5.7
		males		13.2		5.8		.2	5.0	24.3	2.4
X	Public admin.	Total		9.9		11.0		.1		21.0	1.2
		males		7.1		10.5		.0		17.6	1.7
U	Unknown	Total				88.4		8.2	29.3	126.0	7.3
		males				56.6		4.1	10.3	71.0	7.0
T	All sectors	Total		413.9		653.5		609.6	37.8	1 714.8	100.0
		males		328.5		395.4		270.2	15.3	1 009.4	100.0

Percent distributions

Total labour force

	EM	SE	EE	WO	AP	FW	U	T
I		26.0		21.5		52.5		100.0
II		11.3		82.9		5.8		100.0
III		16.4		76.9		6.8		100.0
IV		13.1		83.3		3.7		100.0
V		20.8		77.2		2.0		100.0
VI		46.2		48.8		5.0		100.0
VII		27.0		69.8		3.2		100.0
VIII		86.4		13.0		.7		100.0
IX		32.0		58.5		.8	8.7	100.0
X		46.9		52.5		.6		100.0
U				70.2		6.5	23.3	100.0
T		24.1		38.1		35.6	2.2	100.0

Male labour force

	EM	SE	EE	WO	AP	FW	U	T
I		39.1		20.8		40.0		100.0
II		10.4		84.4		5.2		100.0
III		16.8		77.1		6.0		100.0
IV		13.3		83.6		3.0		100.0
V		17.3		81.2		1.4		100.0
VI		56.0		40.4		3.6		100.0
VII		25.5		71.9		2.5		100.0
VIII		81.4		18.3		.3		100.0
IX		54.4		23.9		1.0	20.7	100.0
X		40.1		59.7		.3		100.0
U				79.8		5.7	14.5	100.0
T		32.5		39.2		26.8	1.5	100.0

Labour Force by Sector and Status 1940

Absolute figures in thousands

Sector			Employ-ers	Self-employed	Employ-ees	Workers	Apprent-ices	Family-workers	Un-known	Total	%
			EM	SE	EE	WO	AP	FW	U	T	
I	Agriculture	Total		324.1		213.3		620.0		1 157.4	57.4
		males		268.4		115.0		245.1		628.6	54.6
II	Mining	Total		1.1		8.2		.9		10.2	.5
		males		.9		7.6		.4		8.9	.8
III	Manufacturing	Total		40.5		254.4		15.5		310.4	15.4
		males		29.5		169.8		9.4		208.7	18.1
IV	Construction	Total		5.5		36.7		1.8		44.0	2.2
		males		5.2		33.0		1.2		39.4	3.4
V	Utilities	Total		1.6		7.7		.2		9.5	.5
		males		1.3		7.3		.1		8.7	.8
VI	Commerce	Total		36.9		38.9		4.9		80.8	4.0
		males		23.3		16.2		1.6		41.2	3.6
VII	Transport	Total		17.3		52.7		1.6		71.6	3.6
		males		13.3		45.9		.9		60.1	5.2
VIII	Banking	Total		7.1		1.5		.2		8.8	.4
		males		2.9		68.8		.0		3.7	.3
IX	Services	Total		71.4		.6		2.2		142.2	7.0
		males		25.8		5.6		.5		31.8	2.8
X	Public admin.	Total		17.1		16.8		.1		34.0	1.7
		males		11.2		14.9		.0		26.1	2.3
U	Unknown	Total				96.8		8.1	43.5	148.3	7.4
		males				61.9		3.4	27.8	93.2	8.1
T	All sectors	Total		522.8		795.6		655.4	43.5	2 017.2	100.0
		males		381.8		478.2		262.7	27.8	1 150.5	100.0

Percent distributions

	Total labour force									Male labour force							
	EM	SE	EE	WO	AP	FW	U	T		EM	SE	EE	WO	AP	FW	U	T
I		28.0		18.4		53.6		100.0	I		42.7		18.3		39.0		100.0
II		10.5		81.0		8.5		100.0	II		10.2		85.5		4.3		100.0
III		13.1		81.9		5.0		100.0	III		14.1		81.4		4.5		100.0
IV		12.6		83.4		4.0		100.0	IV		13.1		83.7		3.2		100.0
V		17.2		80.6		2.2		100.0	V		14.9		83.9		1.2		100.0
VI		45.7		48.2		6.1		100.0	VI		56.7		39.5		3.9		100.0
VII		24.2		73.6		2.3		100.0	VII		22.1		76.4		1.5		100.0
VIII		81.1		16.7		2.2		100.0	VIII		77.6		21.2		1.2		100.0
IX		50.2		48.3		1.5		100.0	IX		81.0		17.6		1.5		100.0
X		50.3		49.4		.3		100.0	X		42.8		57.1		.1		100.0
U				65.3		5.4	29.3	100.0	U				66.5		3.7	29.9	100.0
T		25.9		39.4		32.5	2.2	100.0	T		33.2		41.6		22.8	2.4	100.0

Finland

Labour Force by Sector and Status 1950

Absolute figures in thousands

Sector			Employ-ers	Self-employed	Employ-ees	Workers	Apprent-ices	Family-workers	Un-known	Total	%
			EM	SE	EE	WO	AP	FW a)	U	T	
I	Agriculture	Total	36.7	255.7	14.6	184.7		420.3		912.0	46.0
		males	31.1	220.1	13.7	153.0		124.9		542.7	46.1
II	Mining	Total	.0	.1	.9	5.0		.0		6.0	.3
		males	.0	.1	.7	4.6		.0		5.4	.5
III	Manufacturing	Total	7.7	40.9	53.5	305.7		2.8		410.7	20.7
		males	6.2	18.6	32.9	190.9		1.2		249.8	21.2
IV	Construction	Total	1.6	8.3	8.4	104.0		.4		122.7	6.2
		males	1.6	8.2	7.2	99.5		.3		116.8	9.9
V	Utilities	Total	.0	.0	2.7	7.7		.0		10.4	.5
		males	.0	.0	1.9	7.3		.0		9.2	.8
VI	Commerce	Total	7.6	12.1	84.3	32.1		5.9		142.0	7.2
		males	4.9	8.0	30.6	23.4		.8		67.7	5.8
VII	Transport	Total	2.8	11.3	26.6	65.5		.5		106.8	5.4
		males	2.8	11.2	12.7	57.6		.4		84.6	7.2
VIII	Banking	Total	.0	.0	13.0	1.4		.0		14.5	.7
		males	.0	.0	4.9	.6		.0		5.5	.5
IX	Services	Total	3.7	11.7	76.5	93.9		.8		186.6	9.4
		males	1.4	4.0	23.2	13.5		.1		42.2	3.6
X	Public admin.	Total	.0		34.1	10.2		.0		44.3	2.2
		males	.0		23.0	7.5		.0		30.4	2.6
U	Unknown	Total	.0	.5	3.9	23.9		.0		28.4	1.4
		males	.0	.4	1.4	19.7		.0		21.6	1.8
T	All sectors	Total	60.3	340.6	318.5	834.2		430.7		1 984.3	100.0
		males	48.0	270.7	152.1	577.6		127.7		1 176.1	100.0

Percent distributions

Total labour force

	EM	SE	EE	WO	AP	FW	U	T
I	4.0	28.0	1.6	20.3		46.1		100.0
II	.5	1.0	15.2	83.2		.1		100.0
III	1.9	10.0	13.0	74.4		.7		100.0
IV	1.3	6.8	6.9	84.7		.3		100.0
V	.0	.0	25.9	74.1		.0		100.0
VI	5.4	8.5	59.4	22.6		4.1		100.0
VII	2.7	10.6	25.0	61.3		.5		100.0
VIII	.0	.0	77.0	23.0		.0		100.0
IX	2.0	6.3	41.0	50.4		.4		100.0
X	.0	.0	77.0	23.0		.0		100.0
U	.1	1.7	13.8	84.3		.1		100.0
T	3.0	17.2	16.1	42.0		21.7		100.0

Male labour force

	EM	SE	EE	WO	AP	FW	U	T
I	5.7	40.5	2.5	28.2		23.0		100.0
II	.5	1.1	13.1	85.2		.0		100.0
III	2.5	7.5	13.2	76.4		.5		100.0
IV	1.4	7.1	6.2	85.1		.2		100.0
V	.0	.0	20.5	79.5		.0		100.0
VI	7.2	11.8	45.1	34.6		1.2		100.0
VII	3.3	13.3	15.0	68.0		.5		100.0
VIII	.1	.0	88.6	11.3		.0		100.0
IX	3.3	9.4	55.0	32.1		.2		100.0
X	.0	.0	75.5	24.5		.0		100.0
U	.1	2.0	6.5	91.4		.0		100.0
T	4.1	23.0	12.9	49.1		10.9		100.0

Finland

Labour Force by Sector and Status 1960

Absolute figures in thousands

Sector			Employers EM a)	Self-employed SE	Employees EE	Workers WO	Apprentices AP	Family-workers FW	Unknown U	Total T	%
I	Agriculture	Total	282.1	(252.1)	13.6	137.8		287.4		720.8	35.5
		males	243.4	(219.2)	12.6	122.9		87.3		466.2	37.8
II	Mining	Total	.2		1.2	5.2		.0		6.5	.3
		males	.2		.9	4.8		.0		5.8	.5
III	Manufacturing	Total	31.2		69.8	334.0		3.0		438.0	21.5
		males	19.8		41.8	212.8		1.4		275.8	22.4
IV	Construction	Total	10.6		18.6	146.5		.6		176.2	8.7
		males	10.5		15.4	139.6		.4		165.9	13.5
V	Utilities	Total	.0		4.6	14.2		.0		18.9	.9
		males	.0		3.2	13.1		.0		16.3	1.3
VI	Commerce	Total	28.9	55.6)	132.9	39.9		8.7		210.3	10.3
		males	17.7		45.5	30.3		1.5		95.0	7.7
VII	Transport	Total	23.9	79.0)	35.0	68.6		1.2		128.8	6.3
		males	23.6		15.3	62.2		1.1		102.3	8.3
VIII	Banking	Total	.0		21.6	2.6		.0		24.2	1.2
		males	.0		7.2	.9		.0		8.1	.7
IX	Services	Total	18.2		114.0	117.6		1.4		251.2	12.4
		males	8.3		33.3	16.6		.2		58.5	4.7
X	Public admin.	Total	.0		42.8	9.3		.0		52.1	2.6
		males	.0		27.9	6.0		.0		33.8	2.7
U	Unknown	Total	.1		.8	5.3		.1		6.2	.3
		males	.1		.3	4.3		.0		4.7	.4
T	All sectors	Total	395.1	(331.1)	454.9	880.9		302.3		2 033.3	100.0
		males	323.7	(274.7)	203.4	613.5		91.9		1 232.4	100.0

Percent distributions

Total labour force

	EM	SE	EE	WO	AP	FW	U	T
I	39.1	(35.0)	1.9	19.1		39.9		100.0
II	2.4		18.0	79.2		.3		100.0
III	7.1		15.9	76.3		.7		100.0
IV	6.0		10.5	83.1		.3		100.0
V	.1		24.5	75.4		.0		100.0
VI	13.7		63.2	19.0		4.1		100.0
VII	18.6	61.3)	27.2	53.3		1.0		100.0
VIII	.0		89.2	10.8		.0		100.0
IX	7.3		45.4	46.8		.5		100.0
X	.0		82.1	17.9		.0		100.0
U	1.2		13.2	84.6		1.0		100.0
T	19.4	(16.3)	22.4	43.3		14.9		100.0

Male labour force

	EM	SE	EE	WO	AP	FW	U	T
I	52.2	(47.0)	2.7	26.4		18.7		100.0
II	2.7		14.8	82.2		.3		100.0
III	7.2		15.2	77.2		.5		100.0
IV	6.4		9.3	84.1		.2		100.0
V	.1		19.6	80.2		.0		100.0
VI	18.6	58.5)	47.9	31.9		1.6		100.0
VII	23.1		15.0	60.9		1.1		100.0
VIII	.1		88.9	11.0		.0		100.0
IX	14.3		56.9	28.5		.4		100.0
X	.0		82.4	17.6		.0		100.0
U	1.1		7.4	90.9		.6		100.0
T	26.3	(22.3)	16.5	49.8		7.5		100.0

Labour Force by Sector and Status 1970

Absolute figures in thousands

Sector			Employ-ers	Self-employed	Employ-ees	Workers [a]	Apprent-ices [a]	Family-workers	Un-known	Total	%
			EM	SE	EE	WO	AP	FW	U	T	
I	Agriculture	Total	16.6	192.3	13.4	66.5		140.2	.1	429.0	20.3
		males	14.2	163.0	11.3	60.0		38.3	.0	286.7	23.4
II	Mining	Total	.1	0.1	1.5	5.4		.0	.0	7.0	.3
		males	.1	.1	1.0	4.9		.0	.0	6.1	.5
III	Manufacturing	Total	4.3	9.8	99.2	407.5		2.6	.7	524.1	24.7
		males	3.8	5.3	56.3	260.6		1.0	.4	327.3	26.7
IV	Construction	Total	3.5	5.4	20.5	146.5		.8	.1	176.8	8.4
		males	3.5	5.4	15.7	139.3		.5	.1	164.4	13.4
V	Utilities	Total	.0	.0	5.5	12.9		.0	.0	18.4	1.0
		males	.0	.0	3.6	11.8		.0	.0	15.4	1.3
VI	Commerce	Total	13.0	11.8	175.9	50.4		8.8	.2	260.0	12.3
		males	8.3	7.0	60.2	36.1		1.6	.1	113.3	9.3
VII	Transport	Total	6.1	15.2	42.9	84.2		1.8	.1	150.2	7.1
		males	5.9	15.0	18.6	74.9		1.3	.1	115.7	9.4
VIII	Banking	Total	.0	.0	35.3	3.7		.0	.0	39.0	1.8
		males	.0	.0	9.6	1.2		.0	.0	10.8	.9
IX	Services	Total	8.5	14.8	200.9	175.8		2.6	.3	402.8	19.0
		males	3.6	7.1	58.0	47.8		.6	.1	117.2	9.6
X	Public admin.	Total	.0	.0	65.6	16.2		.0	.1	81.8	3.9
		males	.0	.0	37.3	10.6		.0	.0	47.9	3.9
U	Unknown	Total	.1	.7	5.1	17.7		.1	5.3	29.0	1.4
		males	.1	.6	1.8	14.8		.1	3.6	20.9	1.7
T	All sectors	Total	52.2	250.0	665.6	986.9		156.9	6.7	2 118.3	100.0
		males	39.3	203.4	273.4	662.0		43.2	4.5	1 225.7	100.0

Percent distributions

Total labour force

	EM	SE	EE	WO	AP	FW	U	T
I	3.9	44.8	3.1	15.5		32.7	.0	100.0
II	.7	.7	21.2	76.8		.5	.1	100.0
III	.8	1.9	18.9	77.8		.5	.1	100.0
IV	2.0	3.1	11.6	82.9		.4	.1	100.0
V	.0	.0	29.7	70.1		.0	.2	100.0
VI	5.0	4.5	67.6	19.4		3.4	.1	100.0
VII	4.1	10.1	28.5	56.0		1.2	.1	100.0
VIII	.0	.0	90.4	9.6		.0	.0	100.0
IX	2.1	3.7	49.9	43.6		.6	.1	100.0
X	.0	.0	80.1	19.8		.0	.1	100.0
U	.5	2.5	17.5	61.0		.3	18.2	100.0
T	2.5	11.8	31.4	46.6		7.4	.3	100.0

Male labour force

	EM	SE	EE	WO	AP	FW	U	T
I	4.9	56.8	3.9	20.9		13.3	.0	100.0
II	.8	.9	17.1	80.9		.3	.1	100.0
III	1.1	1.6	17.2	79.6		.3	.1	100.0
IV	2.1	3.3	9.6	84.7		.3	.1	100.0
V	.0	.0	23.1	76.8		.0	.2	100.0
VI	7.3	6.2	53.2	31.9		1.4	.1	100.0
VII	5.1	13.0	16.1	64.7		1.1	.1	100.0
VIII	.0	.0	88.9	11.1		.0	.0	100.0
IX	3.1	6.1	49.5	40.8		.5	.1	100.0
X	.0	.0	77.9	22.0		.0	.1	100.0
U	.5	3.7	8.7	70.7		.2	17.2	100.0
T	3.2	16.6	22.3	54.0		3.5	.4	100.0

Notes:

1910-1940   Skilled employees included among the independent labour force, unskilled employees among Workers

1910   a) Quarrying included under Manufacturing

1920-1930   a) Extensive definition of agricultural family workers as compared to 1910
             b) Quarrying included under Manufacturing

1950   a) Definition not comparable to previous and later censuses

1960   a) Including Self-employed

1970   a) Apprentices included among Workers

France

The Development of the Labour Force

Year	by Status				by Sector				Total labour force	Domestic services	Military personnel	Year
	Independent (IN)	Dependent (DE)	Family worker	Unknown	Agriculture (A)	Industry (I)	Services (S)	Unknown				
	percent distribution				percent distribution				in thousands			
1975	13.9	78.9	3.4	3.8	12.2	34.7	49.3	3.8	21 774.9	360.8	274.3	1975
1968	15.7	75.2	7.0	2.1	15.3	38.9	43.7	2.1	20 439.2	539.8	317.9	1968
1962	18.4	71.7	8.8	1.1	20.3	38.5	40.1	1.1	19 164.5	561.2	398.4	1962
1954	20.6	64.5	13.2	1.7	27.2	35.7	34.1	3.0	19 151.4	560.4	274.4	1954
1946	24.3	57.2	18.5		36.5	29.2	30.3	4.0	20 520.5	671.0	315.6	1946
1936	27.2	55.9	12.6	4.3	35.6	30.8	33.6		20 260.5	759.2	508.0	1936
1931	26.3	59.2	12.4	2.1	35.6	33.5	30.9		21 611.8	794.0	410.2	1931
1926	27.0	59.7	12.2	1.1	38.3	33.0	28.7		21 394.1	780.2	350.6	1926
1921	27.7	57.3	12.5	2.5	41.5	29.6	28.9		21 720.6	787.4	425.5	1921
1906	31.8	54.6	12.4	1.2	42.7	29.5	27.8		20 720.9	946.3	593.9	1906
1901	27.2	62.7	8.5	1.6	41.8	30.0	28.2		19 715.1	956.2	597.5	1901
1896	38.4	53.2	6.9	1.5	44.9	28.8	26.3		18 942.0	969.1	550.0	1896
1891	35.0	65.0			40.3	28.1	31.6		16 209.1	1 609.4	511.3	1891
1886	37.0	63.0			41.4	25.8	32.8		16 709.8	1 950.2	436.4	1886
1881	40.1	59.9			39.1	26.9	34.0		16 490.2	2 557.3	385.0	1881

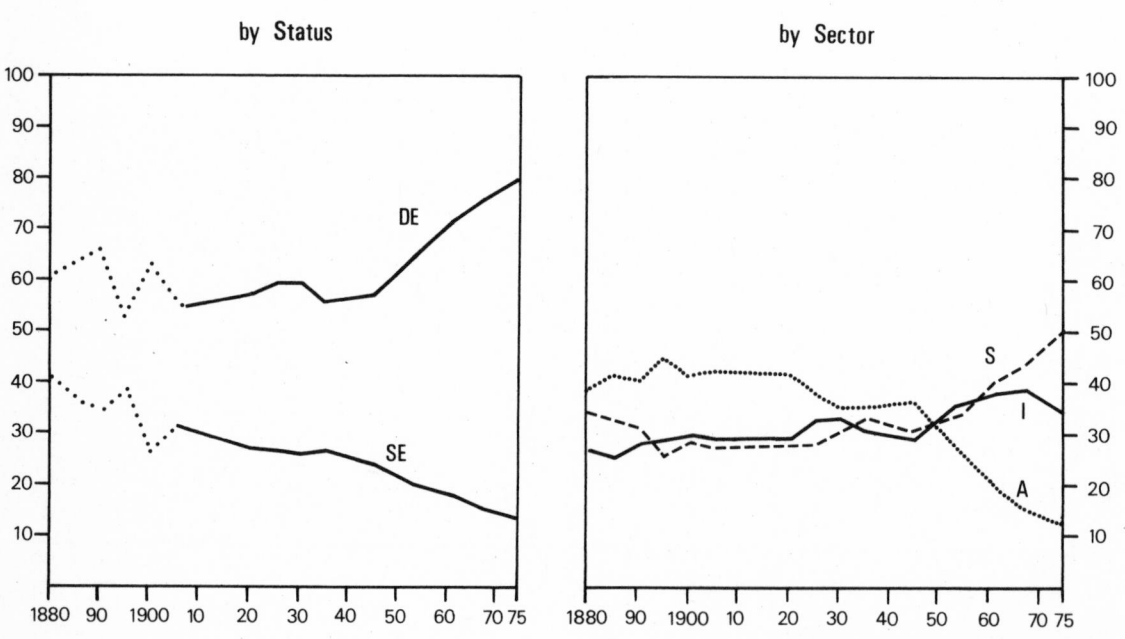

by Status   by Sector

France

L a b o u r   F o r c e   b y   S e c t o r   a n d   S t a t u s   1 8 8 1

Absolute figures in thousands

Sector			Employ-ers	Self-employed	Employ-ees	Workers	Apprent-ices	Family-workers	Un-known	Total	%
			EM	SE	EE	WO	AP	FW	U	T	
I	Agriculture	Total	4 321.0		134.5	1 999.9				6 455.4	39.1
		males	3 523.6		82.4	1 151.8				4 757.9	42.8
II	Mining	Total	32.6		28.9	402.1				463.5	2.8
		males	28.9		25.0	333.2				387.0	3.5
III	Manufacturing	Total	1 137.0		213.7	2 629.5				3 980.2	24.1
		males	907.0		145.3	1 536.5				2 588.7	23.3
IV	Construction[a]	Total									
		males									
V	Utilities[a]	Total									
		males									
VI	Commerce	Total	617.7		328.7	216.4				1 162.8	7.1
		males	435.0		244.4	138.0				817.4	7.3
VII	Transport	Total	62.9		94.0	149.3				306.2	1.9
		males	59.5		88.9	135.9				284.2	2.6
VIII	Banking[b]	Total									
		males									
IX	Services	Total	442.1		300.5	2 633.8				3 376.4	20.5
		males	333.7		170.8	1 091.9				1 596.4	14.3
X	Public admin.[c]	Total			283.3	462.3[d]				745.6	4.5
		males			240.0	456.7[d]				696.7	6.3
U	Unknown	Total									
		males									
T	All sectors	Total	6 613.2		1 383.7	8 493.3				16 490.2	100.0
		males	5 287.6		996.7	4 844.0				11 128.4	100.0

Percent distributions

	Total labour force									Male labour force							
	EM	SE	EE	WO	AP	FW	U	T		EM	SE	EE	WO	AP	FW	U	T
I	66.9		2.1	31.0				100.0	I	74.1		1.7	24.2				100.0
II	7.0		6.2	86.7				100.0	II	7.5		6.5	86.1				100.0
III	28.6		5.4	66.1				100.0	III	35.0		5.6	59.4				100.0
IV									IV								
V									V								
VI	53.1		28.3	18.6				100.0	VI	53.2		29.9	16.9				100.0
VII	20.5		30.7	48.8				100.0	VII	20.9		31.3	47.8				100.0
VIII									VIII								
IX	13.1		8.9	78.0				100.0	IX	20.9		10.7	68.4				100.0
X			38.0	62.0				100.0	X			34.4	65.6				100.0
U									U								
T	40.1		8.4	51.5				100.0	T	47.5		9.0	43.5				100.0

495

Labour Force by Sector and Status 1886

Absolute figures in thousands

Sector			Employ-ers	Self-employed	Employ-ees	Workers	Apprent-ices	Family-workers	Un-known	Total	%
			EM	SE	EE	WO	AP	FW	U	T	
I	Agriculture	Total	4 046.2		97.8	2 772.0				6 916.0	41.4
		males	3 108.6		55.4	1 613.7				4 777.7	43.2
II	Mining	Total	22.0		10.3	220.6				252.8	1.5
		males	20.6		9.6	193.5				223.6	2.0
III	Manufacturing	Total	804.1		198.3	2 359.1				3 361.5	20.1
		males	606.8		140.3	1 344.1				2 091.2	18.9
IV	Construction	Total	169.0		22.4	448.8				640.2	3.8
		males	160.8		21.0	422.7				604.6	5.5
V	Utilities	Total	9.9		5.6	27.7				43.1	0.3
		males	8.7		5.2	22.7				36.6	0.3
VI	Commerce	Total	603.2		302.6	450.3				1 356.0	8.1
		males	405.1		211.3	240.3				856.7	7.1
VII	Transport	Total	53.9		119.5	225.0				398.4	2.4
		males	48.3		107.5	206.7				362.5	3.3
VIII	Banking	Total	10.8		38.0	7.5				56.2	0.3
		males	10.2		35.8	6.4				52.4	0.5
IX	Services [a]	Total	465.0		400.8	2 077.9				2 943.7	17.6
		males	343.8		236.2	752.2				1 332.3	12.0
X	Public admin. [b]	Total			221.2	520.6 [c]				741.8	4.4
		males			205.2	516.1 [c]				721.3	6.5
U	Unknown	Total									
		males									
T	All sectors	Total	6 183.9		1 416.4	9 109.4				16 709.8	100.0
		males	4 713.0		1 027.5	5 318.4				11 058.9	100.0

Percent distributions

	Total labour force									Male labour force							
	EM	SE	EE	WO	AP	FW	U	T		EM	SE	EE	WO	AP	FW	U	T
I	58.5		1.4	40.1				100.0	I	65.1		1.2	33.8				100.0
II	8.7		4.1	87.2				100.0	II	9.2		4.3	86.5				100.0
III	23.9		5.9	70.2				100.0	III	29.0		6.7	64.3				100.0
IV	26.4		3.5	70.1				100.0	IV	26.6		3.5	69.9				100.0
V	22.9		13.0	64.2				100.0	V	23.8		14.2	62.0				100.0
VI	44.5		22.3	33.2				100.0	VI	47.3		24.7	28.0				100.0
VII	13.5		30.0	56.5				100.0	VII	13.3		29.7	57.0				100.0
VIII	19.1		67.5	13.3				100.0	VIII	19.6		68.3	12.1				100.0
IX	15.8		13.6	70.6				100.0	IX	25.8		17.7	56.5				100.0
X			29.8	70.2				100.0	X			28.5	71.5				100.0
U									U								
T	37.0		8.5	54.5				100.0	T	42.6		9.3	48.1				100.0

Labour Force by Sector and Status 1891

Absolute figures in thousands

Sector			Employ-ers	Self-employed	Employ-ees	Workers	Apprent-ices	Family-workers	Un-known	Total	%
			EM	SE	EE	WO	AP	FW	U	T	
I	Agriculture	Total	3 570.0		75.4	2 890.2				6 535.6	40.3
		males	2 869.5		45.6	1 779.6				4 694.7	42.4
II	Mining	Total	24.1		8.8	207.2				240.1	1.5
		males	23.1		8.4	192.5				224.0	2.0
III	Manufacturing	Total	819.8		176.8	2 659.9				3 656.6	22.6
		males	617.4		132.4	1 514.2				2 264.0	20.4
IV	Construction	Total	173.5		16.3	430.5				620.3	3.8
		males	169.3		15.3	421.0				605.5	5.5
V	Utilities	Total	4.3		5.3	21.5				31.1	0.2
		males	3.8		5.0	18.4				27.2	0.2
VI	Commerce	Total	566.6		304.0	394.9				1 265.5	7.8
		males	392.8		228.0	226.8				847.7	7.6
VII	Transport	Total	62.5		138.7	246.0				447.2	2.8
		males	57.4		128.5	226.3				412.3	3.7
VIII	Banking	Total	7.9		30.5	4.2				42.6	0.3
		males	7.7		29.3	3.3				40.4	0.4
IX	Services [a]	Total	447.3		400.1	1 720.5				2 568.0	15.8
		males	325.0		230.4	625.6 [c]				1 181.0	10.7
X	Public admin. [b]	Total			210.6	591.5 [c]				802.1	4.9
		males			201.2	585.0 [c]				786.3	7.1
U	Unknown	Total									
		males									
T	All sectors	Total	5 676.1	1 366.5	9 166.5					16 209.1	100.0
		males	4 466.1	1 024.1	5 592.9					11 083.1	100.0

Percent distributions

Total labour force

	EM	SE	EE	WO	AP	FW	U	T
I	54.6		1.2	44.2				100.0
II	10.0		3.7	86.3				100.0
III	22.4		4.8	72.7				100.0
IV	28.0		2.6	69.4				100.0
V	13.9		16.9	69.2				100.0
VI	44.8		24.0	31.2				100.0
VII	14.0		31.0	55.0				100.0
VIII	18.6		71.6	9.8				100.0
IX	17.4		15.6	67.0				100.0
X			26.3	73.7				100.0
U								
T	35.0		8.4	56.6				100.0

Male labour force

	EM	SE	EE	WO	AP	FW	U	T
I	61.1		1.0	37.9				100.0
II	10.3		3.8	85.9				100.0
III	27.3		5.8	66.9				100.0
IV	28.0		2.5	69.5				100.0
V	13.9		18.4	67.7				100.0
VI	46.3		26.9	26.8				100.0
VII	13.9		31.2	54.9				100.0
VIII	19.1		72.7	8.2				100.0
IX	27.5		19.5	53.0				100.0
X			25.6	74.4				100.0
U								
T	40.3		9.2	50.5				100.0

Labour Force by Sector and Status 1896 [a]

Absolute figures in thousands

Sector			Employers	Self-employed	Employees	Workers	Out of work	Family-workers	Unknown	Total	%
			EM	SE [b]	EE	WO	OW [c]	FW [d]	U	T	
I	Agriculture	Total	3 086.2	2 046.0	3 283.6		38.6		46.6	8 500.9	44.9
		males	1 833.1	1 632.5	2 208.0		27.5		39.9	5 741.1	45.7
II	Mining	Total	6.4	8.6	209.0		1.9		.8	226.8	1.2
		males	6.1	8.6	204.6		1.9		.8	222.0	1.8
III	Manufacturing	Total	590.5	1 273.2	2 609.5		103.7		96.0	4 672.8	24.7
		males	417.7	599.9	1 821.9		71.0		48.4	2 958.9	23.6
IV	Construction	Total	70.9	122.7	315.2		23.9		16.2	548.8	2.9
		males	70.1	122.6	313.7		23.9		16.1	546.3	4.3
V	Utilities	Total	.2	.0	3.5		.0		.0	3.8	.0
		males	.2	.0	3.5		.0		.0	3.7	.0
VI	Commerce	Total	271.1	332.7	442.6		18.5		6.3	1 071.3	5.7
		males	173.1	193.2	353.9		16.4		5.1	741.7	5.9
VII	Transport	Total	21.0	45.3	660.5		37.3		21.4	785.5	4.1
		males	18.4	43.9	497.1		29.4		21.1	609.9	4.9
VIII	Banking	Total	4.4	5.2	41.5		.4		.1	51.5	.3
		males	4.3	5.1	39.2		.3		.1	49.1	.4
IX	Services	Total	230.6	453.0	1 347.3		33.6		103.1	2 167.6	11.4
		males	127.4	165.7	485.2		12.6		10.5	801.4	6.4
X	Public admin.	Total			870.2		.2			870.4	4.6
		males			858.7		.2			858.8	6.8
U	Unknown	Total	.3	4.2	21.6		8.9		7.5	42.6	.2
		males	.2	1.6	14.5		6.7		3.4	26.3	.2
T	All sectors	Total	4 281.6	4 291.0	9 804.6		266.9	(1 298.6)	297.9	18 942.0	100.0
		males	2 650.8	2 773.3	6 800.2		189.8		145.4	12 559.4	100.0

Percent distributions

	Total labour force								Male labour force							
	EM	SE	EE	WO	OW	FW	U	T		EM	SE	EE	WO	OW	FW	U	T
I	36.3	24.1	38.6		.5		.5	100.0	I	31.9	28.4	38.5		.5		.7	100.0
II	2.8	3.8	92.2		.8		.4	100.0	II	2.8	3.9	92.2		.8		.4	100.0
III	12.6	27.2	55.8		2.2		2.1	100.0	III	14.1	20.3	61.6		2.4		1.6	100.0
IV	12.9	22.4	57.4		4.4		2.9	100.0	IV	12.8	22.4	57.4		4.4		2.9	100.0
V	6.1	.6	93.2		.1		.1	100.0	V	6.1	.6	93.1		.1		.1	100.0
VI	25.3	31.1	41.3		1.7		.6	100.0	VI	23.3	26.1	47.7		2.2		.7	100.0
VII	2.7	5.8	84.1		4.7		2.7	100.0	VII	3.0	7.2	81.5		4.8		3.5	100.0
VIII	8.6	10.1	80.4		.7		.2	100.0	VIII	8.8	10.4	80.0		.7		.2	100.0
IX	10.6	20.9	62.2		1.5		4.8	100.0	IX	15.9	20.7	60.5		1.6		1.3	100.0
X			100.0					100.0	X			100.0					100.0
U	.8	9.9	50.7		21.0		17.6	100.0	U	.6	6.2	55.0		25.3		12.9	100.0
T	22.6	22.7	51.8		1.4	(6.9)	1.6	100.0	T	21.1	22.1	54.1		1.5		1.2	100.0

Labour Force by Sector and Status 1901

Absolute figures in thousands

Sector			Employers EM[a]	Self-employed SE[b]	Employees EE[c]	Casual workers CW[d]	Home-workers HW[e]	Family-workers FW[f]	Out of work OW[g]	Total T	%
I	Agriculture	Total	3 469.3	1 080.6	2 918.5	727.9			48.0	8 244.3	41.8
		males	2 029.0	918.7	2 114.4	481.7			37.2	5 581.0	43.2
II	Mining	Total	7.4	.7	250.2	6.3			1.8	266.4	1.4
		males	7.0	.7	245.6	6.3			1.8	261.3	2.0
III	Manufacturing	Total	673.6	406.2	2 929.4	381.9	575.0		120.6	5 086.6	25.8
		males	450.8	158.6	2 044.1	209.1	213.3		82.8	3 158.9	24.5
IV	Construction	Total	76.9	21.7	342.1	95.6			28.5	564.8	2.9
		males	76.0	21.7	341.4	95.6			28.5	563.1	4.4
V	Utilities	Total	.4		8.4	.0			.0	8.8	.0
		males	.4		8.3	.0			.0	8.7	.1
VI	Commerce	Total	439.4	321.9	390.2	9.1			21.5	1 182.1	6.0
		males	250.4	157.3	283.7	9.1			16.5	717.0	5.6
VII	Transport	Total	26.5	7.7	703.4	50.0			43.1	830.6	4.2
		males	21.6	7.5	504.5	49.3			35.0	617.8	4.8
VIII	Banking	Total	5.7	7.5	51.2				.4	64.8	.3
		males	5.5	7.4	48.6				.4	61.9	.5
IX	Services	Total	166.7	314.0	1 849.6	111.3	57.4		39.8	2 538.7	12.9
		males	91.6	140.5	720.4	54.0			17.0	1 023.5	7.9
X	Public admin.	Total			909.1					909.1	4.6
		males			902.9					902.9	7.0
U	Unknown	Total			7.7	.3			10.8	18.8	.1
		males			5.7	.3			8.3	14.3	.1
T	All sectors	Total	4 865.8	2 160.3	10 359.7	1 382.5	632.3	(1 681.4)	314.5	19 715.1	100.0
		males	2 932.4	1 412.3	7 219.6	905.5	213.3		227.6	12 910.6	100.0

Percent distributions

Total labour force

	EM	SE	EE	CW	HW	FW	OW	T
I	42.1	13.1	35.4	8.8			.6	100.0
II	2.8	.3	93.9	2.4			.7	100.0
III	13.2	8.0	57.6	7.5	11.3		2.4	100.0
IV	13.6	3.8	60.6	16.9			5.0	100.0
V	4.7		95.1	.2			.0	100.0
VI	37.2	27.2	33.0	.8			1.8	100.0
VII	3.2	.9	84.7	6.0			5.2	100.0
VIII	8.8	11.6	79.0				.6	100.0
IX	6.6	12.4	72.9	4.4	2.3		1.6	100.0
X			100.0				.0	100.0
U			40.9	1.6			57.5	100.0
T	24.7	11.0	52.5	7.0	3.2	(8.5)	1.6	100.0

Male labour force

	EM	SE	EE	CW	HW	FW	OW	T
I	36.4	16.5	37.9	8.6			.7	100.0
II	2.7	.3	94.0	2.4			.7	100.0
III	14.3	5.0	64.7	6.6	6.8		2.6	100.0
IV	13.5	3.8	60.6	17.0			5.1	100.0
V	4.8		95.0	.2			.0	100.0
VI	34.9	21.9	39.6	1.3			2.3	100.0
VII	3.5	1.2	81.6	8.0			5.7	100.0
VIII	8.9	12.0	78.5	.0			.6	100.0
IX	9.0	13.7	70.4	5.3			1.7	100.0
X			100.0					100.0
U			39.9	2.1			58.0	100.0
T	22.7	10.9	55.9	7.0	1.7		1.8	100.0

France

Labour Force by Sector and Status 1906

Absolute figures in thousands

Sector			Employers EM[a)	Self-employed SE[b)	Employees EE	Workers WO	Casual workers CW[c)	Family-workers FW[d)	Out of work OW[e)	Total T	%
I	Agriculture	Total	4 794.6	644.8	6.0	2 685.5	711.4		12.7	8 855.1	42.7
		males	2 542.6	516.8	5.6	1 996.0	452.9		11.1	5 525.0	42.4
II	Mining	Total	8.1	5.5	8.2	256.5	.7		2.0	281.0	1.4
		males	7.7	5.5	8.1	251.4	.7		1.9	275.4	2.1
III	Manufacturing	Total	694.9	1 300.3	204.3	2 840.9	120.3		99.1	5 259.8	25.4
		males	460.2	541.3	165.1	1 962.3	7.7		68.6	3 205.4	24.6
IV	Construction	Total	77.1	92.5	9.6	324.6	12.1		24.4	540.4	2.6
		males	76.1	92.5	9.3	324.2	12.1		24.4	538.6	4.1
V	Utilities	Total	.8	.0	2.4	8.7	.0		.0	11.9	.1
		males	.8	.0	2.4	8.6	.0		.0	11.8	.1
VI	Commerce	Total	367.0	325.5	432.7	161.9	5.5		27.0	1 319.5	6.4
		males	221.5	176.1	343.6	121.0	5.5		22.4	890.1	6.8
VII	Transport	Total	31.0	24.3	210.4	315.1	365.0		37.0	982.8	4.7
		males	24.2	24.0	182.0	293.2	166.5		30.3	720.3	5.5
VIII	Banking	Total	6.8	9.2	56.2	2.5	.0		.4	75.0	.4
		males	6.6	9.0	52.7	2.3	.0		.4	70.9	.5
IX	Services	Total	306.2	469.0	453.2	1 134.7	85.2		36.2	2 484.4	12.0
		males	164.2	204.9	261.3	243.5	.0		13.6	887.5	6.8
X	Public admin.	Total			734.3	176.5				910.9	4.4
		males			731.0	171.3				902.3	6.9
U	Unknown	Total									
		males									
T	All sectors	Total	6 286.5	2 871.1	2 117.5	7 907.0	1 300.1	(2 565.9)	238.7	20 720.9	100.0
		males	3 503.8	1 570.2	1 761.4	5 374.0	645.4		172.7	13 027.5	100.0

Percent distributions

Total labour force

	EM	SE	EE	WO	CW	FW	OW	T
I	54.1	7.3	.1	30.3	8.0		.1	100.0
II	2.9	2.0	2.9	91.3	.2		.7	100.0
III	13.2	24.7	3.9	54.0	2.3		1.9	100.0
IV	14.3	17.1	1.8	60.1	2.2		4.5	100.0
V	6.4	.3	20.5	72.8	.0		.0	100.0
VI	27.8	24.7	32.8	12.3	.4		2.0	100.0
VII	3.2	2.5	21.4	32.1	37.1		3.8	100.0
VIII	9.0	12.2	74.9	3.3	.0		.5	100.0
IX	12.3	18.9	18.2	45.7	3.4		1.5	100.0
X			80.6	19.4				100.0
U								
T	30.3	13.9	10.2	38.2	6.3	(12.4)	1.2	100.0

Male labour force

	EM	SE	EE	WO	CW	FW	OW	T
I	46.0	9.4	.1	36.1	8.2		.2	100.0
II	2.8	2.0	3.0	91.3	.2		.7	100.0
III	14.4	16.9	5.2	61.2	.2		2.1	100.0
IV	14.1	17.2	1.7	60.2	2.3		4.5	100.0
V	6.4	.3	20.3	73.0	.0		.0	100.0
VI	24.9	19.8	38.6	13.6	.6		2.5	100.0
VII	3.4	3.3	25.3	40.7	23.1		4.2	100.0
VIII	9.2	12.7	74.3	3.2	.0		.5	100.0
IX	18.5	23.1	29.4	27.4	.0		1.5	100.0
X			81.0	19.0				100.0
U								
T	26.9	12.1	13.5	41.3	5.0		1.3	100.0

Labour Force by Sector and Status 1921

Absolute figures in thousands

Sector		Employers EM[a]	Self-employed SE[b]	Employees EE	Workers WO	Casual workers CW[c]	Family workers FW[d]	Out of work OW[e]	Total T	%
I	Agriculture Total	5 017.2	565.2	5.7	2 834.1	576.1		25.3	9 023.5	41.5
	males	2 541.1	337.2	4.9	1 846.7	311.3		19.9	5 061.2	38.6
II	Mining Total	4.7	2.1	13.2	294.2	.0		3.4	317.6	1.5
	males	4.5	2.1	12.3	287.6	.0		3.4	309.9	2.4
III	Manufacturing Total	590.4	926.7	367.3	3 193.0	81.2		287.6	5 446.3	25.1
	males	399.7	393.1	243.2	2 221.7	2.2		159.6	3 419.6	26.1
IV	Construction Total	71.6	70.1	23.5	428.0	2.6		30.2	625.9	2.9
	males	70.2	70.1	20.2	426.6	2.6		30.2	619.8	4.7
V	Utilities Total	1.5	.0	7.8	27.1	.1		.0	36.5	.2
	males	1.4	.0	6.5	26.8	.1		.0	34.9	.3
VI	Commerce Total	410.4	305.7	534.4	182.6	35.0		30.9	1 498.9	6.9
	males	242.8	170.0	321.1	144.3	1.6		19.5	899.2	6.9
VII	Transport Total	33.0	29.4	323.8	578.5	274.3		99.5	1 338.5	6.2
	males	27.1	28.4	252.2	541.8	101.2		72.1	1 022.8	7.8
VIII	Banking Total	9.6	9.1	150.8	7.4	.0		1.2	178.1	.8
	males	9.4	8.8	103.0	6.4	.0		.9	128.5	1.0
IX	Services Total	273.2	414.4	633.2	946.3	19.7		59.0	2 345.9	10.8
	males	140.3	147.7	290.1	174.4	.0		18.9	771.4	5.9
X	Public admin. Total			638.9	270.6				909.5	4.2
	males			589.3	258.0				847.3	6.5
U	Unknown Total									
	males									
T	All sectors Total	6 411.5	2 322.6	2 698.6	8 761.7	989.1	(2 717.0)	537.1	21 720.6	100.0
	males	3 436.5	1 157.3	1 842.8	5 934.3	419.0		324.6	13 114.5	100.0

Percent distributions

Total labour force

	EM	SE	EE	WO	CW	FW	OW	T
I	55.6	6.3	.1	31.4	6.4		.3	100.0
II	1.5	.7	4.1	92.6	.0		1.1	100.0
III	10.8	17.0	6.7	58.6	1.5		5.3	100.0
IV	11.4	11.2	3.7	68.4	.4		4.8	100.0
V	4.0	.0	21.5	74.3	.2		.0	100.0
VI	27.4	20.4	35.7	12.2	2.3		2.1	100.0
VII	2.5	2.2	24.2	43.2	20.5		7.4	100.0
VIII	5.4	5.1	84.7	4.2	.0		.7	100.0
IX	11.6	17.7	27.0	40.3	.8		2.5	100.0
X			70.3	29.7				100.0
U								
T	29.5	10.7	12.4	40.3	4.6	(12.5)	2.5	100.0

Male labour force

	EM	SE	EE	WO	CW	FW	OW	T
I	50.2	6.7	.1	36.5	6.2		.4	100.0
II	1.4	.7	4.0	92.8	.0		1.1	100.0
III	11.7	11.5	7.1	65.0	.1		4.7	100.0
IV	11.3	11.3	3.3	68.8	.4		4.9	100.0
V	4.1	.0	18.7	77.0	.2		.0	100.0
VI	27.0	18.9	35.7	16.0	.2		2.2	100.0
VII	2.6	2.8	24.7	53.0	9.9		7.1	100.0
VIII	7.3	6.9	80.1	5.0	.0		.7	100.0
IX	18.2	19.1	37.6	22.6	.0		2.5	100.0
X			69.6	30.4				100.0
U								
T	26.2	8.8	14.1	45.2	3.2		2.5	100.0

Labour Force by Sector and Status 1926

Absolute figures in thousands

Sector			Employers EM[a]	Self-employed SE[b]	Employees EE	Workers WO	Casual workers CW[c]	Family-workers FW[d]	Out of work OW[e]	Total T	%
I	Agriculture	Total	4 839.2	478.4	5.6	2 375.2	484.2		17.4	8 199.9	38.3
		males	2 464.6	322.4	4.7	1 707.2	295.1		14.7	4 808.8	35.5
II	Mining	Total	5.6	2.6	16.3	407.2	.0		2.2	434.0	2.0
		males	5.5	2.6	15.3	396.8	.0		2.2	422.3	3.1
III	Manufacturing	Total	612.8	761.0	443.3	3 908.5	57.8		98.0	5 881.5	27.5
		males	433.1	379.8	290.8	2 706.9	2.5		66.2	3 879.3	28.6
IV	Construction	Total	94.8	72.0	23.4	490.2	2.9		19.8	703.1	3.3
		males	93.1	72.0	19.8	489.1	2.9		19.8	696.8	5.1
V	Utilities	Total	1.8	.1	10.8	34.8	.0		.0	47.4	.2
		males	1.8	.1	9.0	34.5	.0		.0	45.3	.3
VI	Commerce	Total	499.4	479.3	631.2	237.4	1.9		20.3	1 869.5	8.7
		males	299.9	244.4	376.9	185.3	1.9		13.7	1 122.0	8.3
VII	Transport	Total	28.9	31.3	281.4	622.5	182.8		45.3	1 192.2	5.6
		males	24.1	30.6	213.1	586.2	91.4		37.8	983.3	7.3
VIII	Banking	Total	12.0	12.6	173.2	15.9	.0		1.2	215.0	1.0
		males	11.7	12.3	114.9	14.7	.0		.9	154.5	1.1
IX	Services	Total	181.1	250.6	618.3	955.8	50.9		39.2	2 095.9	9.8
		males	102.9	138.1	288.6	192.2	.0		13.6	735.4	5.4
X	Public admin.	Total			529.1	226.4				755.6	3.5
		males			493.3	215.4				708.7	5.2
U	Unknown	Total									
		males									
T	All sectors	Total	6 275.6	2 088.0	2 732.8	9 273.8	780.6	(2 615.0)	243.4	21 394.1	100.0
		males	3 436.6	1 202.4	1 826.3	6 528.3	393.9		168.9	13 556.3	100.0

Percent distributions

Total labour force

	EM	SE	EE	WO	CW	FW	OW	T
I	59.0	5.8	.1	29.0	5.9		.2	100.0
II	1.3	.6	3.8	93.8	.0		.5	100.0
III	10.4	12.9	7.5	66.5	1.0		1.7	100.0
IV	13.5	10.2	3.3	69.7	.4		2.8	100.0
V	3.8	.1	22.7	73.3	.0		.0	100.0
VI	26.7	25.6	33.8	12.7	.1		1.1	100.0
VII	2.4	2.6	23.6	52.2	15.3		3.8	100.0
VIII	5.6	5.9	80.6	7.4	.0		.6	100.0
IX	8.6	12.0	29.5	45.6	2.4		1.9	100.0
X			70.0	30.0				100.0
U								
T	29.3	9.8	12.8	43.3	3.6	(12.2)	1.1	100.0

Male labour force

	EM	SE	EE	WO	CW	FW	OW	T
I	51.3	6.7	.1	35.5	6.1		.3	100.0
II	1.3	.6	3.6	94.0	.0		.5	100.0
III	11.2	9.8	7.5	69.8	.1		1.7	100.0
IV	13.4	10.3	2.8	70.2	.4		2.8	100.0
V	3.9	.2	19.8	76.1	.0		.0	100.0
VI	26.7	21.8	33.6	16.5	.2		1.2	100.0
VII	2.4	3.1	21.7	59.6	9.3		3.8	100.0
VIII	7.6	8.0	74.4	9.5	.0		.6	100.0
IX	14.0	18.8	39.2	26.1	.0		1.9	100.0
X			69.6	30.4				100.0
U								
T	25.4	8.9	13.5	48.2	2.9		1.2	100.0

France

Labour Force by Sector and Status 1931

Absolute figures in thousands

Sector			Employ-ers EM[a)]	Self-employed SE[b)]	Employ-ees EE	Workers WO	Casual workers CW[c)]	Family-workers FW[d)]	Out of work OW[e)]	Total T	%
I	Agriculture	Total	4 678.8	482.1	6.5	2 140.6	371.2		24.9	7 704.2	35.6
		males	2 374.5	322.2	5.3	1 562.2	224.9		21.3	4 510.4	32.9
II	Mining	Total	5.4	2.1	17.7	411.2	.6		3.7	440.7	2.0
		males	5.2	2.1	16.4	401.3	.5		3.7	429.3	3.1
III	Manufacturing	Total	599.8	737.9	505.5	3 819.4	55.9		196.4	5 914.9	27.4
		males	423.4	368.0	321.6	2 645.3	8.3		124.5	3 891.1	28.4
IV	Construction	Total	93.1	78.9	29.5	574.8	13.0		40.4	829.7	3.8
		males	91.2	78.9	24.4	573.4	13.0		40.4	821.4	6.0
V	Utilities	Total	2.0	.0	15.4	44.9	.4		.0	62.7	.3
		males	2.0	.0	12.3	44.5	.4		.0	59.2	.4
VI	Commerce	Total	596.1	442.4	684.1	264.3	20.3		31.2	2 038.4	9.4
		males	338.7	214.2	389.2	206.9	2.1		20.8	1 172.0	8.5
VII	Transport	Total	30.7	36.4	279.7	660.3	161.2		85.8	1 254.2	5.8
		males	24.6	35.9	199.8	622.8	103.9		71.9	1 059.0	7.7
VIII	Banking	Total	14.1	16.3	199.3	18.1	.0		2.4	250.2	1.2
		males	13.7	15.8	124.9	16.5	.0		1.8	172.7	1.3
IX	Services	Total	216.6	329.6	683.0	955.9	5.8		67.9	2 258.8	10.5
		males	119.0	170.9	303.8	176.9	.0		23.7	794.4	5.8
X	Public admin.	Total			604.1	254.0				858.1	4.0
		males			560.2	241.7				801.9	5.8
U	Unknown	Total									
		males									
T	All sectors	Total	6 236.6	2 125.6	3 024.9	9 143.5	628.4	(2 679.8)	452.8	21 611.8	100.0
		males	3 392.4	1 208.0	1 958.0	6 491.7	353.3		308.1	13 711.5	100.0

Percent distributions

Total labour force

	EM	SE	EE	WO	CW	FW	OW	T
I	60.7	6.3	.1	27.8	4.8		.3	100.0
II	1.2	.5	4.0	93.3	.1		.9	100.0
III	10.1	12.5	8.5	64.6	.9		3.3	100.0
IV	11.2	9.5	3.6	69.3	1.6		4.9	100.0
V	3.2	.0	24.6	71.6	.6		.1	100.0
VI	29.2	21.7	33.6	13.0	1.0		1.5	100.0
VII	2.5	2.9	22.3	52.7	12.9		6.8	100.0
VIII	5.6	6.5	79.7	7.2	.0		1.0	100.0
IX	9.6	14.6	30.2	42.3	.3		3.0	100.0
X			70.4	29.6				100.0
U								
T	28.9	9.8	14.0	42.3	2.9	(12.4)	2.1	100.0

Male labour force

	EM	SE	EE	WO	CW	FW	OW	T
I	52.6	7.1	.1	34.6	5.0		.5	100.0
II	1.2	.5	3.8	93.5	.1		.9	100.0
III	10.9	9.5	8.3	68.0	.2		3.2	100.0
IV	11.1	9.6	3.0	69.8	1.6		4.9	100.0
V	3.3	.0	20.7	75.2	.6		.1	100.0
VI	28.9	18.3	33.2	17.7	.2		1.8	100.0
VII	2.3	3.4	18.9	58.8	9.8		6.8	100.0
VIII	7.9	9.1	72.3	9.6	.0		1.1	100.0
IX	15.0	21.5	38.2	22.3	.0		3.0	100.0
X			69.9	30.1				100.0
U								
T	24.7	8.8	14.3	47.3	2.6		2.2	100.0

France

Labour Force by Sector and Status 1936

Absolute figures in thousands

Sector		Employers EM a)	Self-employed SE b)	Employees EE	Workers WO	Casual workers CW c)	Family-workers FW d)	Out of work OW e)	Total T	%
I	Agriculture Total	4 429.4	473.5	4.9	1 892.9	357.5		45.6	7 203.7	35.6
	males	2 250.0	317.1	3.8	1 437.9	232.9		40.6	4 282.3	33.1
II	Mining Total	5.1	3.2	14.1	312.2	.4		5.3	340.3	1.7
	males	5.0	3.2	12.9	307.6	.4		5.3	334.3	2.6
III	Manufacturing Total	535.7	709.3	428.2	3 041.3	47.4		387.0	5 148.9	25.4
	males	376.4	398.0	274.7	2 124.0	9.5		269.0	3 451.6	26.7
IV	Construction Total	82.8	101.6	23.5	381.4	7.9		89.6	686.8	3.4
	males	80.9	101.6	19.4	379.6	7.9		89.6	679.0	5.2
V	Utilities Total	2.3	.0	16.6	44.2	.5		.3	63.9	.3
	males	2.3	.0	13.1	43.7	.5		.3	60.0	.5
VI	Commerce Total	495.9	389.7	631.6	251.3	8.1		53.0	1 829.5	9.0
	males	292.2	208.9	370.5	205.1	3.0		36.3	1 116.0	8.6
VII	Transport Total	30.4	37.1	226.6	602.7	166.2		150.5	1 213.6	6.0
	males	24.5	36.4	157.5	564.7	112.6		129.8	1 025.6	7.9
VIII	Banking Total	14.3	19.6	176.4	15.8	.0		3.4	229.5	1.1
	males	13.8	18.9	109.2	14.0	.0		2.7	158.7	1.2
IX	Services Total	325.5	411.7	752.9	913.2	43.2		129.4	2 575.9	12.7
	males	171.7	180.9	324.7	166.7	28.4		51.1	923.6	7.1
X	Public admin. Total			702.8	265.6				968.4	4.8
	males			656.4	252.8				909.2	7.0
U	Unknown Total									
	males									
T	All sectors Total	5 921.4	2 145.8	2 977.5	7 720.4	631.2	(2 552.8)	864.2	20 260.5	100.0
	males	3 216.9	1 265.0	1 942.3	5 496.1	395.2		624.7	12 940.3	100.0

Percent distributions

Total labour force

	EM	SE	EE	WO	CW	FW	OW	T
I	61.5	6.6	.1	26.3	5.0		.6	100.0
II	1.5	.9	4.1	91.7	.1		1.6	100.0
III	10.4	13.8	8.3	59.1	.9		7.5	100.0
IV	12.1	14.8	3.4	55.5	1.1		13.0	100.0
V	3.7	.0	25.9	69.1	.8		.5	100.0
VI	27.1	21.3	34.5	13.7	.4		2.9	100.0
VII	2.5	3.1	18.7	49.7	13.7		12.4	100.0
VIII	6.2	8.6	76.9	6.9	.0		1.5	100.0
IX	12.6	16.0	29.2	35.5	1.7		5.0	100.0
X			72.6	27.4				100.0
U								
T	29.2	10.6	14.7	38.1	3.1	(12.6)	4.3	100.0

Male labour force

	EM	SE	EE	WO	CW	FW	OW	T
I	52.5	7.4	.1	33.6	5.4		.9	100.0
II	1.5	1.0	3.8	92.0	.1		1.6	100.0
III	10.9	11.5	8.0	61.5	.3		7.8	100.0
IV	11.9	15.0	2.9	55.9	1.2		13.2	100.0
V	3.8	.0	21.8	72.9	.9		.6	100.0
VI	26.2	18.7	33.2	18.4	.3		3.3	100.0
VII	2.4	3.5	15.4	55.1	11.0		12.7	100.0
VIII	8.7	11.9	68.8	8.8	.0		1.7	100.0
IX	18.6	19.6	35.2	18.1	3.1		5.5	100.0
X			72.2	27.8				100.0
U								
T	24.9	9.8	15.0	42.5	3.1		4.8	100.0

Labour Force by Sector and Status 1946 [a]

Absolute figures in thousands

Sector			Employers	Self-employed	Employees	Workers	Apprentices	Family-workers	Unknown	Total	%
			EM	SE[b]	EE[c]	WO[e]	AP	FW[d]	U	T	
I	Agriculture	Total	2 442.7			5 041.1		(3 804.8)		7 483.8	36.5
		males	2 111.4			2 109.4		(1 153.9)		4 220.8	33.3
II	Mining	Total	8.6			351.1				359.7	1.8
		males	8.3			338.8				347.1	2.7
III	Manufacturing	Total	785.9			3 748.1				4 534.1	22.1
		males	604.2			2 394.3				2 998.4	23.7
IV	Construction	Total	228.4			756.2				984.6	4.8
		males	225.9			741.8				967.7	7.6
V	Utilities	Total	8.9			106.1				114.9	.6
		males	8.7			95.3				104.0	.8
VI	Commerce	Total	921.0			650.4				1 571.4	7.7
		males	505.2			394.6				899.7	7.1
VII	Transport	Total	110.1			1 059.3				1 169.4	5.7
		males	99.5			897.9				997.5	7.9
VIII	Banking	Total	70.1			317.5				387.6	1.9
		males	67.1			141.1				208.2	1.6
IX	Services [f]	Total	385.9		(392.0)	1 385.6				1 771.5	8.6
		males	180.7		(178.1)	408.3				589.1	4.7
X	Public admin. [g]	Total			(227.5)	1 334.6				1 334.6	6.5
		males			(178.9)	895.6				895.6	7.1
U	Unknown [h]	Total	16.0			792.7				808.7	3.9
		males	11.8			427.6				439.5	3.5
T	All sectors	Total	4 977.8		(619.5)	15 542.7				20 520.5	100.0
		males	3 822.8		(357.0)	8 844.8				12 667.6	100.0

Percent distributions

	Total labour force									Male labour force							
	EM	SE	EE	WO	AP	FW	U	T		EM	SE	EE	WO	AP	FW	U	T
I	32.6			67.3		(50.8)		100.0	I	50.0			50.0		(27.3)		100.0
II	2.4			97.6				100.0	II	2.4			97.6				100.0
III	17.3			82.7				100.0	III	20.1			79.9				100.0
IV	23.2			76.8				100.0	IV	23.3			76.7				100.0
V	7.7			92.3				100.0	V	8.3			91.7				100.0
VI	58.6			41.4				100.0	VI	56.1			43.9				100.0
VII	9.4			90.6				100.0	VII	10.0			90.0				100.0
VIII	18.1			81.9				100.0	VIII	32.2			67.8				100.0
IX	21.8		(22.1)	78.2				100.0	IX	30.7		(30.2)	69.3				100.0
X			(17.0)	100.0				100.0	X			(20.0)	100.0				100.0
U	2.0			98.0				100.0	U	2.7			97.3				100.0
T	24.3			75.7				100.0	T	30.2			69.8				100.0

France

Labour Force by Sector and Status 1954 [a]

Absolute figures in thousands

Sector			Employers EM[b]	Self-employed SE	Employees EE	Workers WO[c]	Apprentices AP	Family-workers FW	Unemployed UE	Total T	%
I	Agriculture	Total	412.3	1 533.8	1 177.1		19.9	2 069.7		5 212.8	27.2
		males	357.7	1 311.2	1 003.6		16.2	699.2		3 387.9	27.1
II	Mining	Total	2.9	1.9	375.8		2.1	.4		383.1	2.0
		males	2.8	1.8	366.7		2.1	.3		373.8	3.0
III	Manufacturing	Total	210.2	353.6	4 158.5		133.6	109.6		4 965.4	25.9
		males	181.8	267.9	2 799.5		95.9	31.5		3 376.6	27.0
IV	Construction	Total	99.8	130.4	1 060.7		45.6	20.7		1 357.2	7.1
		males	97.2	127.8	1 018.6		45.3	14.6		1 303.6	10.4
V	Utilities	Total	.0	.0	135.0		.0	.0		135.0	.7
		males	.0	.0	119.1		.0	.0		119.1	1.0
VI	Commerce	Total	147.8	451.3	887.8		28.5	198.0		1 713.5	8.9
		males	119.9	275.0	548.7		21.7	32.8		998.2	8.0
VII	Transport	Total	12.4	35.6	943.5		1.3	5.9		998.7	5.2
		males	11.1	34.4	777.4		1.3	2.1		826.2	6.6
VIII	Banking	Total	5.1	10.1	229.5		.1	1.0		245.8	1.3
		males	4.8	9.4	126.3		.1	.2		140.7	1.1
IX	Services	Total	118.1	390.3	2 117.7		13.6	110.5		2 750.2	14.4
		males	84.9	211.9	670.1		6.3	12.8		985.9	7.9
X	Public admin.[d]	Total	11.4	12.3	796.0		.1	.9		820.7	4.3
		males	11.3	11.5	616.5		.1	.2		639.6	5.1
U	Unknown	Total	3.3	8.5	215.4		10.3	4.2	327.4	569.1	3.0
		males	2.6	5.7	150.2		7.0	.7	187.3	353.5	2.8
T	All sectors	Total	1 023.2	2 928.0	12 096.9		255.0	2 520.9	327.4	19 151.4	100.0
		males	874.1	2 256.7	8 196.7		195.8	794.4	187.3	12 505.1	100.0

Percent distributions

Total labour force

	EM	SE	EE	WO	AP	FW	UE	T
I	7.9	29.4	22.6		.4	39.7		100.0
II	.8	.5	98.1		.6	.1		100.0
III	4.2	7.1	83.7		2.7	2.2		100.0
IV	7.4	9.6	78.2		3.4	1.5		100.0
V	.0	.0	100.0		.0	.0		100.0
VI	8.6	26.3	51.8		1.7	11.6		100.0
VII	1.2	3.6	94.5		.1	.6		100.0
VIII	2.1	4.1	93.4		.0	.4		100.0
IX	4.3	14.2	77.0		.5	4.0		100.0
X	1.4	1.5	97.0		.0	.1		100.0
U	.6	1.5	37.9		1.8	.7	57.5	100.0
T	5.3	15.3	63.2		1.3	13.2	1.7	100.0

Male labour force

	EM	SE	EE	WO	AP	FW	UE	T
I	10.6	38.7	29.6		.5	20.6		100.0
II	.7	.5	98.1		.6	.1		100.0
III	5.4	7.9	82.9		2.8	.9		100.0
IV	7.5	9.8	78.1		3.5	1.1		100.0
V	.0	.0	100.0		.0	.0		100.0
VI	12.0	27.6	55.0		2.2	3.3		100.0
VII	1.3	4.2	94.1		.2	.3		100.0
VIII	3.4	6.7	89.7		.1	.1		100.0
IX	8.6	21.5	68.0		.6	1.3		100.0
X	1.8	1.8	96.4		.0	.0		100.0
U	.7	1.6	42.5		2.0	.2	53.0	100.0
T	7.0	18.0	65.5		1.6	6.4	.5	100.0

France

Labour Force by Sector and Status 1962 [a]

Absolute figures in thousands

Sector			Employ-ers EM [b]	Self-employed SE	Employees / Workers EE WO [c]	Apprent-ices AP	Family-workers FW	Unemp-loyed	Total T	%
I	Agriculture	Total	264.0	1 424.9	830.0	31.9	1 338.4		3 889.3	20.3
		males	232.5	1 233.9	732.3	24.6	394.5		2 617.8	20.8
II	Mining	Total	2.3	2.2	304.1	2.1	.2		310.9	1.6
		males	2.1	2.2	296.3	2.1	.2		302.9	2.4
III	Manufacturing	Total	156.0	263.5	4 664.7	141.2	72.4		5 297.8	27.6
		males	136.9	206.8	3 191.5	106.8	14.2		3 656.1	29.1
IV	Construction	Total	102.7	133.2	1 290.1	73.9	12.8		1 612.7	8.4
		males	99.8	131.2	1 240.7	73.3	7.3		1 552.3	12.3
V	Utilities	Total	.1	.3	148.5	.2	.0		149.1	.8
		males	.1	.2	125.5	.2	.0		126.1	1.0
VI	Commerce	Total	145.4	445.4	1 215.4	64.2	163.4		2 033.8	10.6
		males	117.6	279.4	740.0	50.6	22.2		1 209.8	9.6
VII	Transport	Total	13.3	37.5	1 024.3	3.4	4.5		1 083.0	5.7
		males	12.1	35.6	820.8	3.3	1.7		873.5	6.9
VIII	Banking	Total	6.5	11.5	300.8	.5	.8		320.2	1.7
		males	6.1	10.3	153.4	.3	.1		170.1	1.4
IX	Services	Total	111.5	382.6	2 594.3	39.6	91.5		3 219.5	16.8
		males	77.7	213.7	847.6	20.5	10.8		1 170.2	9.3
X	Public admin. [d]	Total	10.8	12.7	1 008.8	.7	1.0		1 034.0	5.4
		males	10.4	11.0	762.0	.6	.1		784.1	6.2
U	Unknown	Total	.2	.2	5.6		.1	208.1	214.1	1.1
		males	.1	.1	4.1		.0	112.0	116.3	.9
T	All sectors	Total	812.7	2 714.1	13 386.7	357.8	1 685.1	208.1	19 164.5	100.0
		males	695.3	2 124.2	8 914.2	282.4	451.1	112.0	12 579.2	100.0

Percent distributions

	Total labour force								Male labour force						
	EM	SE	EE WO	AP	FW	UE	T		EM	SE	EE WO	AP	FW	UE	T
I	6.8	36.6	21.3	.8	34.4		100.0	I	8.9	47.1	28.0	.9	15.1		100.0
II	.7	.7	97.8	.7	.1		100.0	II	.7	.7	97.8	.7	.1		100.0
III	2.9	5.0	88.0	2.7	1.4		100.0	III	3.7	5.7	87.3	2.9	.4		100.0
IV	6.4	8.3	80.0	4.6	.8		100.0	IV	6.4	8.5	79.9	4.7	.5		100.0
V	.0	.2	99.6	.1	.0		100.0	V	.0	.2	99.6	.2	.0		100.0
VI	7.1	21.9	59.8	3.2	8.0		100.0	VI	9.7	23.1	61.2	4.2	1.8		100.0
VII	1.2	3.5	94.6	.3	.4		100.0	VII	1.4	4.1	94.0	.4	.2		100.0
VIII	2.0	3.6	94.0	.2	.3		100.0	VIII	3.6	6.1	90.1	.2	.0		100.0
IX	3.5	11.9	80.6	1.2	2.8		100.0	IX	6.6	18.3	72.4	1.8	.9		100.0
X	1.0	1.2	97.6	.1	.1		100.0	X	1.3	1.4	97.2	.1	.0		100.0
U	.1	.1	2.6		.0	97.2	100.0	U	.1	.1	3.5		.0	96.3	100.0
T	4.2	14.2	69.9	1.9	8.8	1.1	100.0	T	5.5	16.9	70.9	2.2	3.6	.9	100.0

L a b o u r   F o r c e   b y   S e c t o r   a n d   S t a t u s   1 9 6 8 [a]

Absolute figures in thousands

Sector			Employers EM [b]	Self-employed SE	Employees EE	Workers WO [c]	Apprentices AP	Family-workers FW	Unemployed UE	Total T	%
I	Agriculture	Total	192.5	1 222.2	644.7		28.4	1 066.1		3 125.5	15.3
		males	172.1	1 073.3	566.8		22.6	300.2		2 112.4	15.9
II	Mining	Total	1.8	1.7	291.1		1.5	.5		295.2	1.4
		males	1.7	1.7	276.3		1.4	.3		280.0	2.1
III	Manufacturing	Total	147.6	210.3	5 022.9		119.6	76.4		5 457.2	26.7
		males	133.0	171.3	3 490.4		96.3	13.6		3 808.3	28.6
IV	Construction	Total	141.9	136.1	1 740.0		88.8	16.6		2 034.6	10.0
		males	138.5	133.9	1 665.3		88.2	7.5		1 945.2	14.6
V	Utilities	Total	.3	.3	159.3		.4	.1		160.1	.8
		males	.3	.2	133.2		.4	.1		133.8	1.0
VI	Commerce	Total	176.0	357.1	1 808.4		73.1	150.5		2 491.9	12.2
		males	144.5	228.1	1 102.3		53.5	16.2		1 491.2	11.2
VII	Transport	Total	17.1	44.9	1 128.1		3.0	7.4		1 197.4	5.9
		males	15.6	42.8	892.2		2.9	2.2		952.8	7.2
VIII	Banking	Total	8.8	12.5	391.8		.3	2.0		415.2	2.0
		males	8.2	11.3	195.4		.1	.3		215.2	1.6
IX	Services	Total	143.8	381.1	2 766.7		51.7	116.0		3 407.6	16.7
		males	100.6	225.3	899.4		25.2	17.1		1 242.4	9.3
X	Public admin. [d]	Total	13.1	11.7	1 390.4		1.2	2.3		1 417.5	6.9
		males	12.5	9.5	874.4		.9	.4		896.7	6.7
U	Unknown	Total							436.9	436.9	2.1
		males							237.6	237.6	1.8
T	All sectors	Total	843.0	2 378.0	15 343.4		368.0	1 437.9	436.9	20 439.2	100.0
		males	727.0	1 897.6	10 095.7		291.6	357.9	237.6	13 315.6	100.0

Percent distributions

Total labour force

	EM	SE	EE	WO	AP	FW	UE	T
I	6.2	39.1	20.6		.9	34.1		100.0
II	.6	.6	98.6		.5	.2		100.0
III	2.7	3.9	92.0		2.2	1.4		100.0
IV	7.0	6.7	85.5		4.4	.8		100.0
V	.2	.2	99.5		.2	.1		100.0
VI	7.1	14.3	72.6		2.9	6.0		100.0
VII	1.4	3.7	94.2		.3	.6		100.0
VIII	2.1	3.0	94.4		.1	.5		100.0
IX	4.2	11.2	81.2		1.5	3.4		100.0
X	.9	.8	98.1		.1	.2		100.0
U							100.0	100.0
T	4.1	11.6	75.1		1.8	7.0	2.1	100.0

Male labour force

	EM	SE	EE	WO	AP	FW	UE	T
I	8.1	50.8	26.8		1.1	14.2		100.0
II	.6	.6	98.7		.5	.1		100.0
III	3.5	4.5	91.7		2.5	.4		100.0
IV	7.1	6.9	85.6		4.5	.4		100.0
V	.2	.2	99.6		.3	.0		100.0
VI	9.7	15.3	73.9		3.6	1.1		100.0
VII	1.6	4.5	93.6		.3	.2		100.0
VIII	3.8	5.3	90.8		.1	.2		100.0
IX	8.1	18.1	72.4		2.0	1.4		100.0
X	1.4	1.1	97.5		.1	.0		100.0
U							100.0	100.0
T	5.5	14.3	75.8		2.2	2.7	1.8	100.0

Labour Force by Sector and Status 1975 [a)]

Absolute figures in thousands

Sector			Employers EM[b)]	Self-employed SE[c)]	Employees EE	Workers WO	Apprentices AP	Family-workers FW	Unemployed UE	Total T	%
I	Agriculture	Total	150.2	1 074.7	879.1		15.0	532.0		2 651.0	12.2
		males	132.5	889.6	658.7		13.4	128.1		1 822.2	13.4
II	Mining	Total	.5	.9	154.5		.1	.2		156.3	.7
		males	.5	.8	139.1		.1	.1		140.5	1.0
III	Manufacturing	Total	67.0	114.5	5 110.9		19.0	17.3		5 328.8	24.5
		males	58.7	90.5	3 541.6		15.3	4.8		3 710.9	27.2
IV	Construction	Total	133.8	143.7	1 570.7		33.6	14.7		1 896.4	8.7
		males	131.0	141.0	1 483.3		33.3	4.4		1 793.0	13.1
V	Utilities	Total	.1	.5	170.2		.1	.2		171.1	.8
		males	.1	.4	140.6		.1	.1		141.3	1.0
VI	Commerce	Total	159.4	341.5	1 772.9		31.8	90.3		2 395.9	11.0
		males	116.1	204.2	987.1		19.6	9.9		1 337.0	9.8
VII	Transport	Total	16.3	41.3	1 174.3		.9	6.0		1 238.9	5.7
		males	14.8	38.4	910.3		.8	1.4		965.7	7.1
VIII	Banking	Total	1.0	4.2	490.0		.1	.4		495.8	2.3
		males	.9	3.3	244.2		.0	.0		248.5	1.8
IX	Services	Total	218.3	557.1	3 261.3		40.5	77.3		4 154.6	19.1
		males	167.0	325.6	1 239.9		27.5	12.1		1 772.1	13.0
X	Public admin.[d)]	Total	1.2	8.9	2 439.1		1.4	1.2		2 451.8	11.3
		males	.9	4.9	1 327.3		1.3	.6		1 335.0	9.8
U	Unknown	Total			3.2				831.0	834.3	3.8
		males			1.9				374.5	376.4	2.8
T	All sectors	Total	748.0	2 287.4	17 026.3		142.7	739.5	831.0	21 774.9	100.0
		males	622.4	1 698.7	10 674.0		111.5	161.5	374.5	13 642.7	100.0

Percent distributions

	Total labour force								Male labour force							
	EM	SE	EE	WO	AP	FW	UE	T		EM	SE	EE	WO	AP	FW	UE	T
I	5.7	40.5	33.2		.6	20.1		100.0	I	7.3	48.8	36.1		.7	7.0		100.0
II	.3	.6	98.9		.1	.1		100.0	II	.3	.6	99.0		.1	.0		100.0
III	1.3	2.1	95.9		.4	.3		100.0	III	1.6	2.4	95.4		.4	.1		100.0
IV	7.1	7.6	82.8		1.8	.8		100.0	IV	7.3	7.9	82.7		1.9	.2		100.0
V	.1	.3	99.5		.1	.1		100.0	V	.1	.3	99.5		.1	.1		100.0
VI	6.7	14.3	74.0		1.3	3.8		100.0	VI	8.7	15.3	73.8		1.5	.7		100.0
VII	1.3	3.3	94.8		.1	.5		100.0	VII	1.5	4.0	94.3		.1	.1		100.0
VIII	.2	.8	98.8		.0	.1		100.0	VIII	.4	1.3	98.3		.0	.0		100.0
IX	5.3	13.4	78.5		1.0	1.9		100.0	IX	9.4	18.4	70.0		1.6	.7		100.0
X	.0	.4	99.5		.1	.0		100.0	X	.1	.4	99.4		.1	.0		100.0
U			.4				99.6	100.0	U			.5				99.5	100.0
T	3.4	10.5	78.2		.7	3.4	3.8	100.0	T	4.6	12.5	78.2		.8	1.2	2.7	100.0

Notes:

1886–1891   Excluding persons classified as having no profession, non-classified persons and profession unknown

1896–1968   Services public généraux, i.e. enterprises under state control, here classified under the appropriate sector, if they employ a sizeable work force

1896–1906   Present population without specific age limit

1921–1975   Present population, excluding persons working abroad but with residence in France, and persons working in France but with residence abroad

1881   a) Included under Manufacturing
       b) Included unter Commerce
       c) Persons classified in the census as independent have been included among Employees, except for military forces
       d) Including military forces

1886   a) Including priests and teachers in public schools re-classified as Employees
       b) Civil servants have been re-classified as Employees
       c) Military forces classified as Workers

1891   a) Status classification of some liberal professions inferred from the nature of occupation
       b) Persons classified in the census as independent re-classified as Employees, except for military forces
       c) Including military forces

1896   a) First special occupational census; change in the method of enumeration largely accounting for the increase in the total labour force; excluding 23,559 persons of unknown sex
       b) Travailleurs isolés: self-employed, casual workers, and home-workers
       c) Chomêurs: persons out of work due to unemployment, sickness and invalidity
       d) Estimated minimum number calculated by subtracting from the total number of employers the number of establishments with employees; the true number of family workers is higher since many have been classified as employees or workers

1901   a) Including family workers classified as employers
       b) Travailleurs indépendants, partially estimated from the census category travailleurs isolés
       c) Including workers
       d) Salariés à emploi irrégulier, partially estimated from the census category travailleurs isolés
       e) Ouvriers à domicile, partially estimated from the census category travailleurs isolés
       f) see 1896 note (d)
       g) Persons out of work due to unemployment, sickness and invalidity

1906–1936   a) Including family workers classified as employers
       b) Travailleurs indépendants, partially estimated from the census category travailleurs isolés
       c) Salariés à emploi irrégulier, partially estimated from the census category travailleurs isolés
       d) see 1896 note (d)
       e) Persons out of work due to unemployment, sickness and invalidity

1946   a) Combination of a highly aggregate table and more detailed tables for some sectors; classification by sector not strictly comparable to previous censuses
       b) Including managers and high ranking civil servants
       c) Only certain activities under Services and Public Administration (teachers, civil servants) could be classified as Employees; in other sectors they had to be classified as Workers
       d) Only family workers in Agriculture could be classified; they are included among Workers
       e) Including employees and family workers
       f) Excluding some activities classified in the Public Administration sector

g) Including some activities which should be classified under Services or under Manufacturing (enterprises under state control)

h) Including some activities previously classified under Services and Transport

1954   a) Excluding conscripts (ca 200,000); work force in Agriculture more strictly defined than in previous censuses; according to the older enumeration method the work force would be higher by 1.2 million

b) Including managers and high ranking civil servants

c) Including priests classified as independent in the census

d) Including some liberal professions classified under Services in previous censuses

1962-1968   a) Excluding conscripts (1962: ca 581,000, 1968: ca 243,000)

b) Including managers and high ranking civil servants

c) Including priests classified as independent in the census

d) Including some liberal professions classified under Services in previous censuses

1975   a) Excluding conscripts whose exact number is unknown; classification by sector inferred from a relatively aggregate table; sectors VI-X not strictly comparable to previous censuses

b) Including managers and high ranking civil servants

c) Including priests classified as independent in the census

d) Including certain activities which should be classified under Services (education) or Manufacturing (enterprises under state control)

The Development of the Labour Force

Year	by Status					by Sector				Total labour force	Domestic services	Military personnel	Year
	Inde-pendent (IN)	Depend-ent (DE)	Family worker	Un-known		Agricul-ture (A)	Indus-try (I)	Serv-ices (S)	Un-known				
	percent distribution					percent distribution				in thousands			
1970	9.7	84.0	6.3			7.5	48.9	43.6		26 493.5	116.4		1970
1961	12.2	77.6	10.0	0.2		13.5	48.2	37.8	0.4	26 527.3	341.8		1961
1950	14.8	70.8	14.4			23.2	42.3	32.3	2.2	22 074.0	597.4		1950
1939	13.9	69.7	16.4			26.0	42.1	31.9	.0	34 616.6	1 358.8	464.0	1939
1933	16.1	67.4	16.4			28.9	39.8	30.7	.6	32 296.1	1 086.7	118.7	1933
1925	15.7	67.4	17.0			30.5	41.2	27.6	.8	32 009.3	1 394.0	108.6	1925
1907	18.4	65.0	15.3	1.2		35.2	39.0	25.1	.7	28 092.1	1 580.8	651.1	1907
1895	23.7	66.6	9.4	.4		37.5	36.5	25.0	1.0	22 110.4	1 571.0	630.9	1895
1882	25.7	59.2	10.2	4.9		43.4	32.9	22.3	1.4	18 956.9	1 487.0	451.8	1882

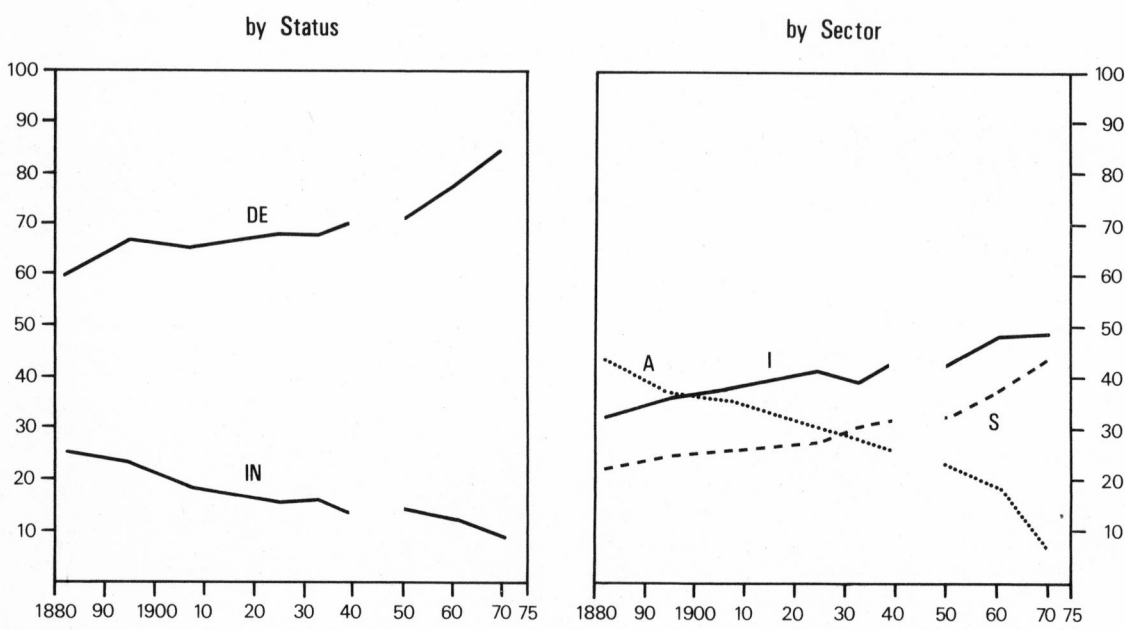

by Status   by Sector

Labour Force by Sector and Status 1882 [a]

Absolute figures in thousands

Sector			Employers EM	Self-employed SE [b]	Employees EE	Workers WO [c]	Apprentices AP [d]	Family-workers FW [e]	Unknown U [f]	Total T	%
I	Agriculture	Total	2 288.0		66.6	5 015.3		(1 934.6)	866.5	8 236.5	43.4
		males	2 010.9		60.8	2 881.7		(1 011.8)	748.2	5 701.6	42.5
II	Mining	Total	2.6		5.7	311.3				319.6	1.7
		males	2.5		5.6	300.4				308.5	2.3
III	Manufacturing	Total	1 576.7		68.3	3 301.7				4 946.7	26.1
		males	1 247.6		66.3	2 627.7				3 941.6	29.4
IV	Construction	Total	171.0		21.6	772.8				965.4	5.1
		males	169.2		21.5	767.8				958.5	7.1
V	Utilities	Total	.5		1.0	7.8				9.3	.0
		males	.5		1.0	7.7				9.2	.1
VI	Commerce	Total	471.4		63.1	277.4				811.9	4.3
		males	357.5		61.5	220.2				639.2	4.8
VII	Transport	Total	42.3		88.8	288.0				419.0	2.2
		males	40.6		87.4	285.5				413.6	3.1
VIII	Banking	Total	9.5		17.8	7.0				34.3	.2
		males	9.4		17.7	7.0				34.0	.3
IX	Services	Total	301.6		240.2	1 683.2			65.9	2 290.8	12.1
		males	159.5		168.2	177.3			59.4	564.5	4.2
X	Public admin. [g]	Total	.0		171.7	492.9				664.5	3.5
		males	.0		169.9	489.9				659.7	4.9
U	Unknown [h]	Total			.9	258.0				258.9	1.4
		males			.6	184.5				185.2	1.4
T	All sectors	Total	4 863.5		745.7	12 415.3			932.4	18 956.9	100.0
		males	3 997.7		660.5	7 949.6			807.7	13 415.4	100.0

Percent distributions

Total labour force

	EM	SE	EE	WO	AP	FW	U	T
I	27.8	.8	60.9			(23.5)	10.5	100.0
II	.8	1.8	97.4					100.0
III	31.9	1.4	66.7					100.0
IV	17.7	2.2	80.0					100.0
V	5.6	11.0	83.4					100.0
VI	58.1	7.8	34.2					100.0
VII	10.1	21.2	68.7					100.0
VIII	27.7	51.8	20.5					100.0
IX	13.2	10.5	73.5				2.9	100.0
X	.0	25.8	74.2					100.0
U		.4	99.6					100.0
T	25.7	3.9	65.5				4.9	100.0

Male labour force

	EM	SE	EE	WO	AP	FW	U	T
I	35.3	1.1	50.5			(17.7)	13.1	100.0
II	.8	1.8	97.4					100.0
III	31.7	1.7	66.7					100.0
IV	17.6	2.2	80.1					100.0
V	5.5	11.1	83.4					100.0
VI	55.9	9.6	34.5					100.0
VII	9.8	21.1	69.0					100.0
VIII	27.6	51.9	20.5					100.0
IX	28.3	29.8	31.4				10.5	100.0
X	.0	25.7	74.3					100.0
U		.3	99.7					100.0
T	29.8	4.9	59.3				6.0	100.0

Labour Force by Sector and Status 1895[a]

Absolute figures in thousands

	Sector		Employers EM	Self-employed SE[b]	Employees EE[c]	Workers WO[d]	Apprentices AP[e]	Family-workers FW	Unknown U	Total T	%
I	Agriculture	Total	2 568.7	96.2		3 724.1		1 903.6		8 292.7	37.5
		males	2 221.8	78.1		2 356.4		883.2		5 539.5	35.7
II	Mining	Total	9.7	16.5		478.1		.3		504.6	2.3
		males	9.5	16.5		466.7		.2		492.9	3.2
III	Manufacturing	Total	1 455.4	191.7		4 500.0		53.2		6 200.3	28.0
		males	1 138.7	182.9		3 497.5		10.7		4 829.8	31.1
IV	Construction	Total	201.8	50.9		1 099.9		1.0		1 353.6	6.1
		males	199.8	50.8		1 088.3		.9		1 339.8	8.6
V	Utilities	Total	.4	1.9		12.1		.0		14.4	.1
		males	.4	1.9		12.0		.0		14.3	.1
VI	Commerce	Total	569.2	118.8		435.1		51.2		1 174.4	5.3
		males	426.7	111.3		333.4		8.0		879.5	5.7
VII	Transport	Total	67.0	101.1		417.3		2.0		587.4	2.7
		males	64.8	98.2		414.3		1.6		578.9	3.7
VIII	Banking	Total	13.1	39.3		6.5		.1		59.1	.3
		males	12.9	38.5		6.4		.1		57.8	.4
IX	Services	Total	343.6	284.3		2 011.1		58.0	80.2	2 777.2	12.6
		males	194.3	203.5		241.8		6.0	70.4	716.0	4.6
X	Public admin.[f]	Total	.0	243.0		680.9		.0		923.9	4.2
		males	.0	241.2		677.3		.0		918.4	5.9
U	Unknown	Total	11.6	.1		211.0		.1		222.8	1.0
		males	7.2	.1		157.8		.0		165.1	1.1
T	All sectors	Total	5 240.5	1 143.9		13 576.2		2 069.6	80.2	22 110.4	100.0
		males	4 276.2	1 022.9		9 251.9		910.6	70.4	15 532.0	100.0

Percent distributions

Total labour force

	EM	SE	EE	WO	AP	FW	U	T
I	31.0	1.2		44.9		23.0		100.0
II	1.9	3.3		94.7		.1		100.0
III	23.5	3.1		72.6		.9		100.0
IV	14.9	3.8		81.3		.1		100.0
V	3.0	12.9		84.1		.0		100.0
VI	48.5	10.1		37.1		4.4		100.0
VII	11.4	17.2		71.0		.3		100.0
VIII	22.2	66.6		11.0		.2		100.0
IX	12.4	10.2		72.4		2.1	2.9	100.0
X	.0	26.3		73.7		.0		100.0
U	5.2	.1		94.7		.0		100.0
T	23.7	5.2		61.4		9.4	.4	100.0

Male labour force

	EM	SE	EE	WO	AP	FW	U	T
I	40.1	1.4		42.5		15.9		100.0
II	1.9	3.3		94.7		.0		100.0
III	23.6	3.8		72.4		.2		100.0
IV	14.9	3.8		81.2		.1		100.0
V	3.0	13.0		84.0		.0		100.0
VI	48.5	12.7		37.9		.9		100.0
VII	11.2	17.0		71.6		.3		100.0
VIII	22.3	66.5		11.0		.1		100.0
IX	27.1	28.4		33.8		.8	9.8	100.0
X	.0	26.3		73.7		.0		100.0
U	4.3	.1		95.6		.0		100.0
T	27.5	6.6		59.6		5.9	.5	100.0

Labour Force by Sector and Status 1907 [a]

Absolute figures in thousands

Sector			Employ-ers EM[b]	Manag-ers MA[c]	Employ-ees EE[d]	Workers WO[e]	Apprent-ices AP[f]	Family-workers FW	Un-known U[g]	Total T	%
I	Agriculture	Total	2 481.6	19.2	98.8	3 129.6		3 894.6	259.4	9 883.3	35.2
		males	2 155.9	16.7	82.5	1 761.6		1 053.7	213.7	5 284.3	28.4
II	Mining	Total	1.6	2.3	35.7	691.0		.4		731.0	2.6
		males	1.5	2.3	35.5	677.1		.2		716.7	3.9
III	Manufacturing	Total	1 342.3	40.1	515.8	6 268.0		121.9		8 288.1	29.5
		males	1 077.2	38.1	457.0	4 784.7		23.7		6 380.7	34.3
IV	Construction	Total	201.8	13.2	119.8	1 568.1		3.1		1 906.0	6.8
		males	199.0	13.2	117.4	1 555.0		2.5		1 887.1	10.1
V	Utilities	Total	.2	.8	7.9	33.7		.0		42.6	.2
		males	.2	.8	7.7	33.4		.0		42.2	.2
VI	Commerce	Total	624.3	20.6	174.6	665.1		134.4		1 619.0	5.8
		males	465.4	14.5	133.0	456.5		16.5		1 085.8	5.8
VII	Transport	Total	78.3	4.3	186.0	706.7		5.4		980.8	3.5
		males	74.5	4.3	161.6	700.7		3.8		944.9	5.1
VIII	Banking	Total	6.2	29.3	134.8	16.6		.4		187.4	.7
		males	6.1	28.9	125.4	16.1		.2		176.7	.9
IX	Services	Total	437.6	334.6	146.0	2 089.9		127.4	90.2	3 225.7	11.5
		males	259.6	242.7	42.7	289.0		9.5	68.8	912.4	4.9
X	Public admin.[h]	Total	.0	88.1	257.3	695.7		.0		1 041.2	3.7
		males	.0	87.8	249.7	690.8		.0		1 028.3	5.5
U	Unknown[i]	Total	7.0	.2	11.1	168.5		.2		187.0	.7
		males	5.2	.2	9.0	125.9		.1		140.3	.8
T	All sectors	Total	5 180.9	552.8	1 687.9	16 033.1		4 287.9	349.6	28 092.1	100.0
		males	4 244.6	449.5	1 421.6	11 090.8		1 110.1	282.5	18 599.2	100.0

Percent distributions

Total labour force

	EM	MA	EE	WO	AP	FW	U	T
I	25.1	.2	1.0	31.7		39.4	2.6	100.0
II	.2	.3	4.9	94.5		.1		100.0
III	16.2	.5	6.2	75.6		1.5		100.0
IV	10.6	.7	6.3	82.3		.2		100.0
V	.5	2.0	18.5	79.0		.0		100.0
VI	38.6	1.3	10.8	41.1		8.3		100.0
VII	8.0	.4	19.0	72.1		.6		100.0
VIII	3.3	15.7	72.0	8.9		.2		100.0
IX	13.6	10.4	4.5	64.8		3.9	2.8	100.0
X	.0	8.5	24.7	66.8		.0		100.0
U	3.7	.1	5.9	90.2		.1		100.0
T	18.4	2.0	6.0	57.1		15.3	1.2	100.0

Male labour force

	EM	MA	EE	WO	AP	FW	U	T
I	40.8	.3	1.6	33.3		19.9	4.0	100.0
II	.2	.3	5.0	94.5		.0		100.0
III	16.9	.6	7.2	75.0		.4		100.0
IV	10.5	.7	6.2	82.4		.1		100.0
V	.4	2.0	18.3	79.3		.0		100.0
VI	42.9	1.3	12.3	42.0		1.5		100.0
VII	7.9	.5	17.1	74.2		.4		100.0
VIII	3.4	16.4	71.0	9.1		.1		100.0
IX	28.5	26.6	4.7	31.7		1.0	7.5	100.0
X	.0	8.5	24.3	67.2		.0		100.0
U	3.7	.1	6.4	89.7		.0		100.0
T	22.8	2.4	7.6	59.6		6.0	1.5	100.0

Labour Force by Sector and Status 1925 [a]

Absolute figures in thousands

Sector		Employers EM [b]	Managers MA [c]	Employees EE	Workers WO [d]	Unskilled workers UW	Family-workers FW	Unknown U	Total T	%
I	Agriculture Total	2 189.8	13.0	161.8	2 607.3	(143.8)	4 790.5		9 762.4	30.5
	males	1 865.9	11.4	149.8	1 553.4	(109.2)	1 212.6		4 793.1	23.3
II	Mining Total	13.2	3.1	70.7	949.0	(219.3)	.8		1 036.7	3.2
	males	12.7	3.1	66.5	935.4	(206.7)	.5		1 018.2	5.0
III	Manufacturing Total	1 185.5	51.8	1 194.0	7 599.0	(2 538.0)	209.3		10 239.6	32.0
	males	965.0	50.5	888.6	5 506.9	(1 549.2)	32.9		7 443.9	36.3
IV	Construction Total	226.5	6.5	136.1	1 342.6	(465.5)	6.0		1 717.6	5.4
	males	223.8	6.4	120.6	1 331.3	(455.1)	3.5		1 685.7	8.2
V	Utilities Total	.3	2.7	46.1	129.3	(55.9)	.0		178.4	.6
	males	.3	2.7	39.5	126.6	(53.3)	.0		169.1	.8
VI	Commerce Total	869.6	21.5	1 047.3	384.8	(276.1)	253.5		2 576.6	8.0
	males	674.7	19.1	561.0	289.7	(203.5)	34.3		1 578.8	7.7
VII	Transport Total	53.7	10.3	759.1	781.5	(461.4)	7.2		1 611.9	5.0
	males	51.2	10.3	679.9	760.4	(440.9)	4.3		1 506.0	7.3
VIII	Banking Total	12.0	16.2	291.1	20.9	(17.5)	.5		340.6	1.1
	males	11.4	16.1	226.7	15.1	(11.8)	.1		269.4	1.3
IX	Services Total	460.8	79.9	896.2	1 900.4	(304.9)	169.4		3 506.6	11.0
	males	316.1	73.3	483.8	278.3	(101.2)	16.1		1 167.6	5.7
X	Public admin. [e] Total	.0	45.2	538.7	205.9	(78.0)	.0		789.8	2.5
	males	.0	44.9	497.9	189.1	(62.3)	.0		731.9	3.6
U	Unknown Total	1.7	.3	28.8	218.1	(217.1)	.1		249.0	.8
	males	1.0	.2	18.0	148.3	(148.1)	.0		167.6	.8
T	All sectors Total	5 012.9	250.3	5 170.0	16 138.8	(4 777.7)	5 437.2		32.009.3	100.0
	males	4 122.2	238.0	3 732.3	11 134.5	(3 341.3)	1 304.3		20 531.3	100.0

Percent distributions

Total labour force

	EM	MA	EE	WO	UW	FW	U	T
I	22.4	.1	1.7	26.7	(1.5)	49.1		100.0
II	1.3	.3	6.8	91.5	(21.2)	.1		100.0
III	11.6	.5	11.7	74.2	(24.8)	2.0		100.0
IV	13.2	.4	7.9	78.2	(27.1)	.3		100.0
V	.1	1.5	25.8	72.5	(31.3)	.0		100.0
VI	33.7	.8	40.6	14.9	(10.7)	9.8		100.0
VII	3.3	.6	47.1	48.5	(28.6)	.4		100.0
VIII	3.5	4.8	85.5	6.1	(5.1)	.1		100.0
IX	13.1	2.3	25.6	54.2	(8.7)	4.8		100.0
X	.0	5.7	68.2	26.1	(9.9)	.0		100.0
U	.7	.1	11.6	87.6	(87.2)	.0		100.0
T	15.7	.8	16.2	50.4	(14.9)	17.0		100.0

Male labour force

	EM	MA	EE	WO	UW	FW	U	T
I	38.9	.2	3.1	32.4	(2.3)	25.3		100.0
II	1.2	.3	6.5	91.9	(20.3)	.0		100.0
III	13.0	.7	11.9	74.0	(20.8)	.4		100.0
IV	13.3	.4	7.2	79.0	(27.0)	.2		100.0
V	.1	1.6	23.4	74.9	(31.5)	.0		100.0
VI	42.7	1.2	35.5	18.3	(12.9)	2.2		100.0
VII	3.4	.7	45.1	50.5	(29.3)	.3		100.0
VIII	4.2	6.0	84.1	5.6	(4.4)	.0		100.0
IX	27.1	6.3	41.4	23.8	(8.7)	1.4		100.0
X	.0	6.1	68.0	25.8	(8.5)	.0		100.0
U	.6	.1	10.8	88.5	(88.4)	.0		100.0
T	20.1	1.2	18.2	54.2	(16.3)	6.4		100.0

Germany

Labour Force by Sector and Status 1933 [a]

Absolute figures in thousands

Sector			Employers EM [b]	Civil servants CS [c]	Employees EE [d]	Workers WO	Apprentices AP	Family-workers FW	Unemployed UE	Total T	%
I	Agriculture	Total	2 177.8	17.0	88.9	2 233.7		4 516.2	309.2	9 342.8	28.9
		males	1 875.9	16.9	71.5	1 420.3		1 046.6	262.8	4 694.0	22.5
II	Mining	Total	13.0	.4	48.4	530.6		.9	292.8	886.0	2.7
		males	12.3	.4	45.4	522.7		.5	289.0	870.3	4.2
III	Manufacturing	Total	1 224.8	2.1	849.2	4 595.9	262.7		2 851.4	9 786.2	30.3
		males	984.4	2.1	609.3	3 191.9	41.1		2 314.4	7 143.3	34.3
IV	Construction	Total	236.0	13.0	59.1	763.6		9.2	890.1	1 971.0	6.1
		males	231.3	12.9	50.4	754.2		5.0	880.0	1 933.8	9.3
V	Utilities	Total	.4	7.8	45.9	112.3		.0	28.2	194.6	.6
		males	.3	7.5	39.3	108.5		.0	26.8	182.4	.9
VI	Commerce	Total	859.6	1.4	951.5	410.0		316.2	533.6	3 072.2	9.5
		males	614.9	1.3	466.6	287.2		47.6	352.7	1 770.2	8.5
VII	Transport	Total	61.0	513.3	109.4	652.4		5.8	210.1	1 552.0	4.8
		males	57.9	475.8	89.1	630.3		2.8	204.0	1 459.9	7.0
VIII	Banking	Total	14.5	20.2	214.1	19.6		.8	38.1	307.4	1.0
		males	13.5	19.4	160.4	11.5		.1	29.2	234.2	1.1
IX	Services	Total	625.7	378.7	705.9	1 720.9	200.2		525.6	4 157.0	12.9
		males	490.8	299.5	303.4	297.9	19.3		222.9	1 633.3	7.8
X	Public admin.	Total	.0	555.0	137.2	102.6			48.7	843.5	2.6
		males	.0	544.5	97.8	77.1			40.1	760.0	3.7
U	Unknown	Total	.8		5.6	49.8		.1	127.2	183.4	.6
		males	.7		4.5	39.9		.0	90.5	135.7	.7
T	All sectors	Total	5 213.6	1 508.9	3 215.1	11 191.4		5 312.1	5 855.0	32 296.1	100.0
		males	4 282.0	1 380.2	1 937.9	7 341.5		1 163.1	4 712.4	20 817.0	100.0

Percent distributions

Total labour force

	EM	CS	EE	WO	AP	FW	UE	T
I	23.3	.2	1.0	23.9		48.3	3.3	100.0
II	1.5	.0	5.5	59.9		.1	33.0	100.0
III	12.5	.0	8.7	47.0	2.7		29.1	100.0
IV	12.0	.7	3.0	38.7		.5	45.2	100.0
V	.2	4.0	23.6	57.7		.0	14.5	100.0
VI	28.0	.0	31.0	13.3		10.3	17.4	100.0
VII	3.9	33.1	7.0	42.0		.4	13.5	100.0
VIII	4.7	6.6	69.6	6.4		.3	12.4	100.0
IX	15.1	9.1	17.0	41.4	4.8		12.6	100.0
X		65.8	16.3	12.2			5.8	100.0
U	.4		3.0	27.1			69.4	100.0
T	16.1	4.7	10.0	34.7		16.4	18.1	100.0

Male labour force

	EM	CS	EE	WO	AP	FW	UE	T
I	40.0	.4	1.5	30.3		22.3	5.6	100.0
II	1.4	.0	5.2	60.1		.1	33.2	100.0
III	13.8	.0	8.5	44.7	.6		32.4	100.0
IV	12.0	.7	2.6	39.0		.3	45.5	100.0
V	.2	4.1	21.5	59.5		.0	14.7	100.0
VI	34.7	.1	26.4	16.2		2.7	19.9	100.0
VII	4.0	32.6	6.1	43.2		.2	14.0	100.0
VIII	5.8	8.3	68.5	4.9		.1	12.5	100.0
IX	30.1	18.3	18.6	18.2	1.2		13.6	100.0
X		71.7	12.9	10.1			5.3	100.0
U	.5		3.3	29.4			66.7	100.0
T	20.6	6.6	9.3	35.3		5.6	22.6	100.0

Labour Force by Sector and Status 1939 [a]

Absolute figures in thousands

Sector			Employers EM [b]	Civil cervants CS [c]	Employees EE [d]	Workers WO	Apprentices AP	Family-workers FW	Unknown U	Total T	%
I	Agriculture	Total	1 965.1	17.8	75.5	2 115.2		4 811.4		8 984.9	26.0
		males	1 719.5	17.8	65.1	1 316.9		945.8		4 065.2	18.6
II	Mining	Total	25.1	.7	109.9	1 249.0		3.2		1 388.0	4.0
		males	23.8	.7	94.0	1 171.6		.7		1 290.8	5.9
III	Manufacturing	Total	1 119.6	2.4	1 345.8	7 866.3		276.8		10 610.8	30.7
		males	900.3	2.3	927.4	5 621.7		21.0		7 472.7	34.3
IV	Construction	Total	232.7	15.2	146.6	1 966.2		14.6		2 375.2	6.9
		males	228.6	15.1	116.3	1 944.8		2.3		2 307.1	10.6
V	Utilities	Total	.3	8.6	63.3	140.9		.1		213.1	.6
		males	.3	8.3	53.1	135.8		.0		197.5	.9
VI	Commerce	Total	850.1	.1	1 075.3	503.7		349.2		2 778.4	8.0
		males	640.0	.1	463.6	352.6		26.4		1 482.8	6.8
VII	Transport	Total	91.9	538.0	223.2	1 033.6		9.9		1 896.6	5.5
		males	88.3	505.3	163.9	999.3		2.8		1 759.5	8.1
VIII	Banking	Total	17.8	42.5	329.4	29.1		1.4		420.2	1.2
		males	16.8	41.1	236.7	13.2		.1		307.9	1.4
IX	Services	Total	513.2	280.9	874.1	2 157.0		208.6		4 033.8	11.7
		males	380.2	255.0	316.0	344.3 [f]		13.5		1 309.0	6.0
X	Public admin. [g]	Total	.0	932.0 [e]	463.5	504.4 [f]		.0		1 899.9	5.5
		males	.0	868.7 [e]	380.1	365.6 [f]		.0		1 614.3	7.4
U	Unknown	Total	.1		3.9	11.5				15.6	.0
		males	.1		1.5	6.2				7.9	.0
T	All sectors	Total	4 816.0	1 838.1	4 710.4	17 577.0		5 675.1		34 616.6	100.0
		males	3 998.0	1 714.4	2 817.7	12 272.1		1 012.6		21 814.7	100.0

Percent distributions

	Total labour force								Male labour force							
	EM	CS	EE	WO	AP	FW	U	T	EM	CS	EE	WO	AP	FW	U	T
I	21.9	.2	.8	23.5		53.5		100.0	42.3	.4	1.6	32.4		23.3		100.0
II	1.8	.1	7.9	90.0		.2		100.0	1.8	.1	7.3	90.8		.1		100.0
III	10.6	.0	12.7	74.1		2.6		100.0	12.0	.0	12.4	75.2		.3		100.0
IV	9.8	.6	6.2	82.8		.6		100.0	9.9	.7	5.0	84.3		.1		100.0
V	.1	4.0	29.7	66.1		.0		100.0	.1	4.2	26.9	68.8		.0		100.0
VI	30.6	.0	38.7	18.1		12.6		100.0	43.2	.0	31.3	23.8		1.8		100.0
VII	4.8	28.4	11.8	54.5		.5		100.0	5.0	28.7	9.3	56.8		.2		100.0
VIII	4.2	10.1	78.4	6.9		.3		100.0	5.5	13.3	76.9	4.3		.0		100.0
IX	12.7	7.0	21.7	53.5		5.2		100.0	29.0	19.5	24.1	26.3		1.0		100.0
X	.0	49.1	24.4	26.5		.0		100.0	.0	53.8	23.5	22.6		.0		100.0
U	.9		25.2	73.9				100.0	1.4		19.6	79.0				100.0
T	13.9	5.3	13.6	50.8		16.4		100.0	18.3	7.9	12.9	56.3		4.6		100.0

Labour Force by Sector and Status 1950 [a]

Absolute figures in thousands

Sector		Total/males	Employers EM [b]	Civil servants CS [c]	Employees EE	Workers WO	Apprentices AP	Family-workers FW	Unknown U	Total T	%
I	Agriculture	Total	1 252.4	7.4	32.4	1 088.7		2 732.7		5 113.7	23.2
		males	1 037.7	7.4	27.3	707.6		536.1		2 316.2	16.4
II	Mining	Total	14.9	.1	69.4	775.7		2.2		862.3	3.9
		males	14.2	.1	60.0	759.7		1.3		835.3	5.9
III	Manufacturing	Total	713.3	.3	879.8	4 839.6		142.8		6 575.8	29.8
		males	569.2	.3	598.5	3 472.9		47.8		4 688.7	33.2
IV	Construction	Total	209.7		110.4	1 411.6		19.6		1 751.2	7.9
		males	205.4		85.5	1 402.0		10.6		1 703.5	12.1
V	Utilities	Total	.1	2.5	46.6	101.0		.1		150.2	.7
		males	.1	2.4	38.6	97.6		.0		138.7	1.0
VI	Commerce	Total	635.6		835.5	357.1		175.5		2 003.7	9.1
		males	487.2		385.1	243.0		29.0		1 144.3	8.1
VII	Transport	Total	76.0	339.3	186.4	611.4		9.0		1 222.0	5.5
		males	72.7	317.0	123.8	576.7		5.0		1 095.2	7.8
VIII	Banking	Total	14.3	10.6	182.1	9.5		.7		217.2	1.0
		males	13.4	10.1	119.1	4.0		.1		146.7	1.0
IX	Services	Total	341.1	233.2	668.7	1 146.8		102.0		2 491.7	11.3
		males	251.7	168.6	238.0	213.5		12.4		884.2	6.3
X	Public admin.	Total	.0	285.1	467.0	450.1		.0		1 202.2	5.4
		males	.0	278.7	314.1	347.4		.0		940.3	6.7
U	Unknown	Total	.8		45.3	437.7				483.8	2.2
		males	.7		21.3	210.3				232.3	1.6
T	All sectors	Total	3 258.3	878.5	3 523.5	11 229.3		3 184.4		22 074.0	100.0
		males	2 652.3	784.7	2 011.5	8 034.6		642.3		14 125.4	100.0

Percent distributions

Total labour force

	EM	CS	EE	WO	AP	FW	U	T
I	24.5	.1	.6	21.3		53.4		100.0
II	1.7	.0	8.0	90.0		.3		100.0
III	10.8	.0	13.4	73.6		2.2		100.0
IV	12.0		6.3	80.6		1.1		100.0
V	.1	1.7	31.0	67.2		.0		100.0
VI	31.7		41.7	17.8		8.8		100.0
VII	6.2	27.8	15.3	50.0		.7		100.0
VIII	6.6	4.9	83.8	4.4		.3		100.0
IX	13.7	9.4	26.8	46.0		4.1		100.0
X	.0	23.7	38.8	37.4		.0		100.0
U	.2		9.4	90.5				100.0
T	14.8	4.0	16.0	50.9		14.4		100.0

Male labour force

	EM	CS	EE	WO	AP	FW	U	T
I	44.8	.3	1.2	30.6		23.1		100.0
II	1.7	.0	7.2	90.9		.2		100.0
III	12.1	.0	12.8	74.1		1.0		100.0
IV	12.1		5.0	82.3		.6		100.0
V	.1	1.7	27.8	70.4		.0		100.0
VI	42.6		33.7	21.2		2.5		100.0
VII	6.6	28.9	11.3	52.7		.5		100.0
VIII	9.1	6.9	81.2	2.7		.0		100.0
IX	28.5	19.1	26.9	24.1		1.4		100.0
X	.0	29.6	33.4	36.9		.0		100.0
U	.3		9.2	90.5				100.0
T	18.8	5.6	14.2	56.9		4.5		100.0

Germany

Labour Force by Sector and Status 1961 [a]

Absolute figures in thousands

Sector			Employers EM [b]	Civil servants CS [c]	Employees EE	Workers WO	Apprentices AP [d]	Family-workers FW	Un-known U	Total T	%
I	Agriculture	Total	1 141.9	5.5	32.6	394.2	21.9	1 990.5		3 586.8	13.5
		males	914.3	5.5	24.8	284.5	17.1	379.0		1 625.3	9.8
II	Mining	Total	.1	.1	71.6	514.7	18.1	.0		604.2	2.3
		males	.1	.1	64.4	507.7	17.7	.0		590.0	3.6
III	Manufacturing	Total	553.0	.6	1 840.2	6 773.7	611.6	178.3	1.1	9 958.3	37.5
		males	464.5	.6	1 176.3	4 695.5	479.4	26.9	.6	6 843.9	41.2
IV	Construction	Total	169.2	.0	150.8	1 553.8	132.2	27.5	.1	2 033.8	7.7
		males	164.8	.0	110.4	1 542.8	126.4	6.4	.0	1 950.8	11.8
V	Utilities	Total	.1	1.9	74.1	117.1	5.8	.0		199.0	.8
		males	.1	1.9	59.7	109.9	5.1	.0		176.7	1.1
VI	Commerce	Total	617.2	.0	1 259.9	478.0	329.0	241.2	.2	2 925.5	11.0
		males	394.7	.0	453.4	329.2	114.5	32.6	.1	1 324.9	8.0
VII	Transport	Total	73.6	467.9	247.2	637.2	39.4	13.5	.3	1 479.1	5.6
		males	68.5	431.0	148.3	571.3	34.2	4.4	.3	1 258.0	7.6
VIII	Banking	Total	23.0	12.7	357.3	23.4	42.5	2.1		461.0	1.7
		males	19.6	12.2	193.8	5.4	24.5	.2		255.7	1.5
IX	Services	Total	658.8	311.0	1 275.2	1 170.1	200.9	204.0	.7	3 820.9	14.4
		males	482.6	212.3	452.0	276.9	51.5	22.0	.2	1 497.1	9.0
X	Public admin.	Total	.0	445.4	531.6	350.1	18.8	.0	.0	1 346.5	5.1
		males	.0	428.5	303.3	258.9	11.2	.0	.5	1 002.6	6.0
U	Unknown	Total	1.0		11.9	48.3	3.6	.4	46.8	112.0	.4
		males	.7		4.9	36.1	1.8	.0	27.4	71.1	.4
T	All sectors	Total	3 237.7	1 245.5	5 852.5	12 060.3	1 423.7	2 657.6	49.9	26 527.3	100.0
		males	2 510.2	1 092.1	2 991.3	8 618.4	883.0	471.5	29.3	16 595.7	100.0

Percent distributions

	Total labour force									Male labour force							
	EM	CS	EE	WO	AP	FW	U	T		EM	CS	EE	WO	AP	FW	U	T
I	31.8	.2	.9	11.0	.6	55.5		100.0	I	56.3	.3	1.5	17.5	1.1	23.3		100.0
II	.0	.0	11.9	85.2	3.0	.0		100.0	II	.0	.0	10.9	86.1	3.0	.0		100.0
III	5.6	.0	18.5	68.0	6.1	1.8	.0	100.0	III	6.8	.0	17.2	68.6	7.0	.4	.0	100.0
IV	8.3	.0	7.4	76.4	6.5	1.4	.0	100.0	IV	8.4	.0	5.7	79.1	6.5	.3	.0	100.0
V	.1	1.0	37.2	58.8	2.9	.0		100.0	V	.1	1.1	33.8	62.2	2.9	.0		100.0
VI	21.1	.0	43.1	16.3	11.2	8.2	.0	100.0	VI	29.8	.0	34.2	24.8	8.6	2.5	.0	100.0
VII	5.0	31.6	16.7	43.1	2.7	.9	.0	100.0	VII	5.4	34.3	11.8	45.4	2.7	.3	.0	100.0
VIII	5.0	2.8	77.5	5.1	9.2	.5		100.0	VIII	7.7	4.8	75.8	2.1	9.6	.1		100.0
IX	17.2	8.1	33.4	30.6	5.3	5.3	.0	100.0	IX	32.2	14.2	30.2	18.5	3.4	1.5	.0	100.0
X	.0	33.1	39.5	26.0	1.4	.0	.0	100.0	X	.0	42.7	30.3	25.8	1.1	.0	.0	100.0
U	.9		10.6	43.1	3.2	.4	41.8	100.0	U	1.0		6.9	50.8	2.5	.0	38.5	100.0
T	12.2	4.7	22.1	45.5	5.4	10.0	.2	100.0	T	15.1	6.6	18.0	51.9	5.3	2.8	.2	100.0

Labour Force by Sector and Status 1970 [a]

Absolute figures in thousands

Sector			Employers	Self-employed	Civil servants [b]	Employees	Workers	Family-workers	Un-known	Total	%
			EM	SE	CS	EE	WO	FW	U	T	
I	Agriculture	Total	663.1		6.6	50.9	261.9	1 008.0		1 990.5	7.5
		males	578.5		5.6	29.7	191.7	219.0		1 024.5	6.0
II	Mining	Total	.4		1.0	56.2	265.3	.0		322.9	1.2
		males	.4		.9	49.3	260.8	.0		311.4	1.8
III	Manufacturing	Total	467.9		2.0	2 713.8	7 019.4	183.4		10 386.5	39.2
		males	405.2		1.5	1 784.6	5 009.8	26.9		7 228.1	42.5
IV	Construction	Total	166.4			263.3	1 563.3	39.6		2 032.5	7.7
		males	161.2			190.5	1 541.8	7.5		1 901.1	11.2
V	Utilities	Total	1.0		2.5	93.7	117.6	.0		214.8	.8
		males	.8		2.4	74.7	108.8	.0		186.6	1.1
VI	Commerce	Total	592.9			1 716.5	789.3	205.8		3 304.5	12.5
		males	407.3			680.1	464.5	24.1		1 576.1	9.3
VII	Transport	Total	77.4		461.9	321.2	565.9	16.7		1 443.0	5.4
		males	70.5		417.6	196.8	494.2	3.7		1 182.7	7.0
VIII	Banking	Total	32.3		17.1	585.9	39.9	6.5		681.8	2.6
		males	27.9		15.8	310.6	13.5	.4		368.2	2.2
IX	Services	Total	570.0		434.8	1 798.9	1 064.9	195.9		4 064.4	15.3
		males	388.3		277.7 [c]	615.9	316.0	22.8		1 620.7	9.5
X	Public admin.	Total	.0		1 002.7 [c]	648.3	401.6	.0		2 052.6	7.7
		males	.0		962.0	351.1	291.7	.0		1 604.8	9.4
U	Unknown	Total									
		males									
T	All sectors	Total	2 571.4		1 928.6	8 248.5	12 089.1	1 655.8		26 493.5	100.0
		males	2 040.0		1 683.6	4 283.5	8 692.8	304.4		17 004.2	100.0

Percent distributions

Total labour force

	EM	CS	EE	WO	AP	FW	U	T
I	33.3	.3	2.6	13.2		50.6		100.0
II	.1	.3	17.4	82.2		.0		100.0
III	4.5	.0	26.1	67.6		1.8		100.0
IV	8.2	.0	13.0	76.9		1.9		100.0
V	.5	1.2	43.6	54.8		.0		100.0
VI	17.9	.0	51.9	23.9		6.2		100.0
VII	5.4	32.0	22.3	39.2		1.2		100.0
VIII	4.7	2.5	85.9	5.9		1.0		100.0
IX	14.0	10.7	44.3	26.2		4.8		100.0
X	.0	48.8	31.6	19.6		.0		100.0
U								
T	9.7	7.3	31.1	45.6		6.3		100.0

Male labour force

	EM	CS	EE	WO	AP	FW	U	T
I	56.5	.5	2.9	18.7		21.4		100.0
II	.1	.3	15.8	83.7		.0		100.0
III	5.6	.0	24.7	69.3		.4		100.0
IV	8.5	.0	10.0	81.1		.4		100.0
V	.4	1.3	40.0	58.3		.0		100.0
VI	25.8	.0	43.2	29.5		1.5		100.0
VII	6.0	35.3	16.6	41.8		.3		100.0
VIII	7.6	4.3	84.4	3.7		.1		100.0
IX	24.0	17.1	38.0	19.5		1.4		100.0
X	.0	59.9	21.9	18.2		.0		100.0
U								
T	12.0	9.9	25.2	51.1		1.8		100.0

Notes:

1882-1907 Present population beyond compulsory education (about 14 years and over); occupational classification for skilled workers and some liberal professions; otherwise industrial classification
1927-1970 Resident population; pure industrial classification
1933-1961 Including unemployed

1882   a) Status distribution for Commerce, Services, Transport, and above all Public Administration
partially based on a re-classification of status categories according to nature of occupation
b) Including directors
c) Including apprentices, family workers, and home-workers
d) Included among Workers
e) Separate figures available for Agriculture only
f) In Agriculture: small peasants working also as agricultural day labourers; in Services: some
liberal professions for which a status classification according to the nature of occupation
would have been too arbitrary (e.g. musicians)
g) Including conscripts
h) Mainly day labourers

1895   a) Status distribution for Services partially based on classification according to nature of occupation; in Public Administration those originally classified as Employers have been re-classified
as Employees or Workers according to the nature of occupation
b) Including directors
c) Including some apprentices
d) Including some apprentices and all home-workers
e) In Agriculture classified as employees; in the other sectors distributed among employees and
workers
f) Including conscripts

1907   a) see 1895 note (a)
b) Including self-employed
c) Including high ranking officials
d) Including some apprentices
e) Including some apprentices and all home-workers, originally classified as self-employed
f) Distributed among employees and workers
g) In Agriculture: small peasants working also as agricultural day labourers; in Services: some
liberal professions for which a status classification according to the nature of occupation would
have been to arbitrary
h) Including conscripts
i) Mainly day labourers without main occupation

1925   a) Change in territory
b) Including self-employed
c) Including high ranking officials
d) Including skilled and unskilled workers as well as home-workers, originally classified as
self-employed
e) Excluding conscripts who were classified according to their previous occupation

1933   a) Excluding the Saar
b) Including self-employed but excluding managers and high ranking officials classified as
independents in the census
c) Civil servants including high ranking officials
d) Including managers
e) Including conscripts and commissioned officers

1939   a) Including the Saar, but excluding Austria and the Sudetenland
      b) Including self-employed
      c) Civil servants including high ranking officials
      d) Including managers
      e) Including commissioned and non-commissioned officers, and volunteers
      f) Including conscripts
      g) Including enterprises under military control

1950   a) Excluding West Berlin and the Saar; excluding foreign military forces in West Germany
      b) Including self-employed
      c) Civil servants

1961   a) Including West Berlin and the Saar; since original data are rounded, rounding errors may occur
      b) Including self-employed
      c) Civil servants
      d) Commercial and industrial apprentices

1970   a) Excluding the unemployed; excluding foreign military forces in West Germany and their families;
       including part-time work
      b) Civil servants
      c) Including all military personnel (officers and conscripts)

The Development of the Labour Force

Year	by Status				by Sector				Total labour force	Domestic services	Military personnel	Year
	Inde-pendent (IN)	Depend-ent (DE)	Family worker	Un-known	Agricul-ture (A)	Indus-try (I)	Serv-ices (S)	Un-known				
	percent distribution				percent distribution				in thousands			
1971	7.2	85.3	0.5	7.0	2.5	42.2	49.4	5.8	25 014.3	239.1	405.7	1971
1961	7.1	89.3	0.7	2.8	3.6	47.4	48.1	0.8	24 014.3	371.5	299.4	1961
1951	7.3	90.4	0.2	2.1	5.1	49.2	45.3	0.5	22 610.0	393.7	762.8	1951
1931	10.1	77.9		12.0	6.0	46.1	47.1	0.9	21 074.8	1 626.3	251.0	1931
1921	10.0	89.4	0.5	0.1	7.6	42.0	35.9	14.4	19 348.3	1 335.4	221.4	1921
1911	11.2	84.1	1.0	3.7	8.1	44.6	42.9	4.4	18 350.5	1 698.0	219.0	1911
1901	12.5	86.1		1.4	7.7	45.6	41.0	5.6	16 174.0	1 678.6	176.3	1901
1891	12.8	83.7		3.5	10.4	44.5	37.3	7.8	14 417.2	1 616.9	134.1	1891

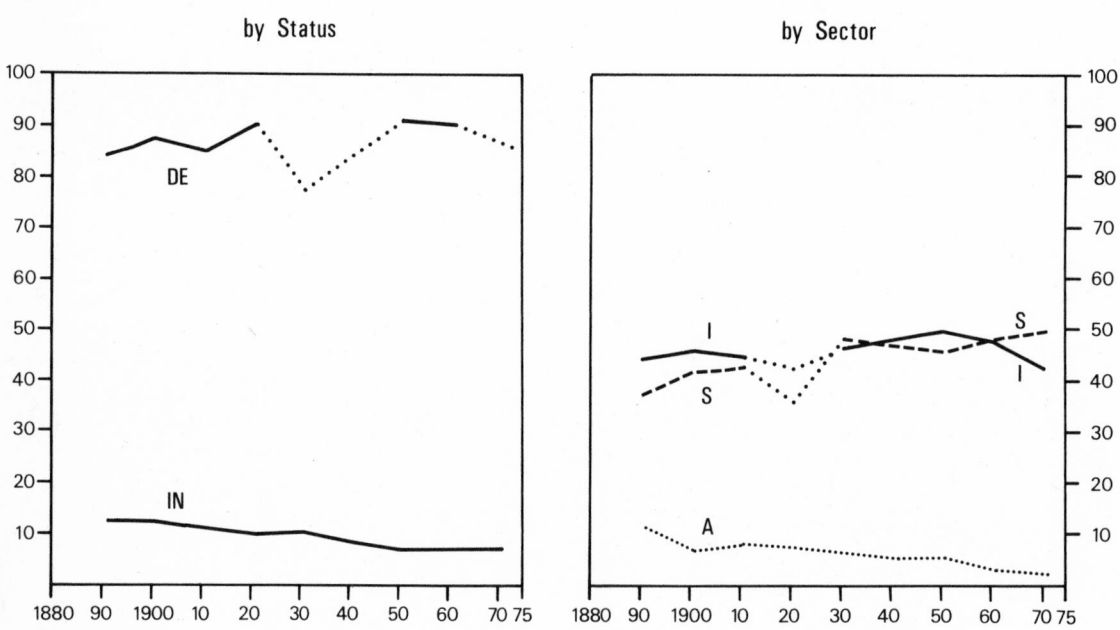

by Status   by Sector

Labour Force by Sector and Status 1891

Absolute figures in thousands

Sector			Employers EM[b]	Self-employed SE	Employees EE	Workers WO	Apprentices AP[c]	Family-workers FW[d]	Unknown U	Total T	%
I	Agriculture	Total	267.5		925.2				76.9	1 269.7	10.0
		males	244.2		897.4				76.0	1 217.6	13.9
II	Mining	Total	0.2	(0.1)	619.0				0.1	619.2	4.9
		males	0.2	(0.1)	614.3				0.1	614.5	7.0
III	Manufacturing	Total	571.3	(348.8)	3 375.1				195.3	4 141.6	32.7
		males	344.2	(158.6)	2 167.1				102.7	2 614.0	29.3
IV	Construction	Total	105.6	(45.4)	669.7				33.7	809.0	6.4
		males	104.8	(45.2)	668.2				33.4	806.5	9.2
V	Utilities	Total	0.3	(0.1)	33.1				1.4	34.8	0.3
		males	0.3	(0.1)	33.1				1.4	34.8	0.4
VI	Commerce	Total	412.9	(238.0)	642.5				64.2	1 119.6	8.8
		males	343.8	(184.0)	532.1				34.5	910.4	10.4
VII	Transport	Total	36.0	(20.1)	742.5				25.8	804.3	6.3
		males	35.0	(19.7)	733.3				24.9	793.3	9.1
VIII	Banking	Total	1.9		51.4					53.3	0.4
		males	1.9		50.7					52.6	0.6
IX	Services	Total	207.6		2 278.0				58.2	2 543.7	20.1
		males	149.0		297.8				18.4	465.2	5.3
X	Public admin.	Total	0.0		270.8					270.8	2.1
		males	0.0		255.7					255.7	2.9
U	Unknown	Total	2.7		991.9				24.1	1 018.7	8.0
		males	2.6		947.8				24.0	974.4	11.1
T	All sectors	Total	1 606.0		10 599.0				479.7	12 684.7	100.0
		males	1 225.9		7 197.6				315.6	8 739.1	100.0

Percent distributions

Total labour force

	EM	SE	EE	WO	AP	FW	U	T
I	21.1		72.9				6.1	100.0
II	0.0		100.0				0.0	100.0
III	13.8	(8.4)	81.5				4.7	100.0
IV	13.1	(5.6)	82.2				4.2	100.0
V	1.0	(0.4)	95.0				4.0	100.0
VI	36.9	(21.3)	57.4				5.7	100.0
VII	4.5	(2.5)	92.3				3.2	100.0
VIII	3.6		96.4				0.0	100.0
IX	8.2		89.6				2.3	100.0
X	0.0		100.0				0.0	100.0
U	0.3		97.4				2.4	100.0
T	12.7		83.6				3.8	100.0

Male labour force

	EM	SE	EE	WO	AP	FW	U	T
I	20.1		73.7				6.2	100.0
II	0.0		100.0				0.0	100.0
III	13.2	(6.1)	82.9				3.9	100.0
IV	13.0	(5.6)	82.9				4.1	100.0
V	1.0	(0.3)	95.0				4.0	100.0
VI	37.8	(20.2)	58.4				3.8	100.0
VII	4.4	(2.5)	92.4				3.1	100.0
VIII	3.6		96.4				0.0	100.0
IX	32.0		64.0				4.0	100.0
X	0.0		100.0				0.0	100.0
U	0.3		97.3				2.5	100.0
T	14.0		82.4				3.6	100.0

Labour Force by Sector and Status 1891

Absolute figures in thousands

Sector			Employers EM[a]	Self-employed SE	Employees EE	Workers WO	Apprentices AP[b]	Family-workers FW[c]	Unknown U	Total T	%
I	Agriculture	Total	89.7		138.0				3.3	231.0	13.3
		males	82.3		115.0				3.2	200.5	16.9
II	Mining	Total	0.1		98.2					98.3	5.7
		males	0.1		97.6					97.7	8.2
III	Manufacturing	Total	63.3	(36.4)	532.7				7.8	603.8	34.9
		males	34.7	(11.8)	323.4				4.8	363.0	30.6
IV	Construction	Total	11.6	(3.5)	88.9				1.4	101.9	5.9
		males	11.6	(3.5)	88.7				1.4	101.6	8.6
V	Utilities	Total	0.0		3.8				0.1	3.9	0.2
		males	0.0		3.8				0.1	3.9	0.3
VI	Commerce	Total	47.1	(22.2)	112.7				2.8	162.5	9.4
		males	35.2	(12.6)	86.6				1.7	123.5	10.4
VII	Transport	Total	4.0	(1.8)	116.9				1.4	122.4	7.1
		males	4.0	(1.8)	111.7				1.4	117.1	9.9
VIII	Banking	Total	0.2	(0.1)	7.6					7.8	0.5
		males	0.2	(0.1)	7.6					7.8	0.7
IX	Services	Total	24.2	(16.2)	246.4				2.9	273.6	15.8
		males	17.3	(10.2)	35.6				1.6	54.4	4.6
X	Public admin.	Total	0.0		26.1					26.1	1.5
		males	0.0		24.2					24.2	2.0
U	Unknown	Total	0.9	(0.2)	98.8				1.6	101.3	5.8
		males	0.9	(0.2)	90.6				1.6	93.1	7.8
T	All sectors	Total	241.1		1 470.1				21.3	1 732.5	100.0
		males	186.3		984.9				15.7	1 186.8	100.0

Percent distributions

Total labour force

	EM	SE	EE	WO	AP	FW	U	T
I	38.8		59.7				1.4	100.0
II	0.1		99.9					100.0
III	10.5	(6.0)	88.2				1.3	100.0
IV	11.4	(3.4)	87.3				1.3	100.0
V	0.8	(0.2)	97.8				1.5	100.0
VI	29.0	(13.7)	69.3				1.7	100.0
VII	3.3	(1.5)	95.5				1.2	100.0
VIII	3.0	(0.9)	97.0					100.0
IX	8.9	(5.9)	90.1				1.1	100.0
X	0.0		100.0					100.0
U	0.9	(0.2)	97.5				1.6	100.0
T	13.9		84.9				1.2	100.0

Male labour force

	EM	SE	EE	WO	AP	FW	U	T
I	41.1		57.4				1.6	100.0
II	0.1		99.9					100.0
III	9.6	(3.3)	89.1				1.3	100.0
IV	11.4	(3.4)	87.3				1.3	100.0
V	0.8	(0.2)	97.8				1.4	100.0
VI	28.5	(10.2)	70.1				1.4	100.0
VII	3.4	(1.6)	95.4				1.2	100.0
VIII	3.0	(0.9)	97.0					100.0
IX	31.7	(18.8)	65.4				2.9	100.0
X	0.0		100.0					100.0
U	0.9	(0.2)	97.4				1.7	100.0
T	15.7		83.0				1.3	100.0

Labour Force by Sector and Status 1901

Absolute figures in thousands

Sector			Employ- ers EM[a)	Self- employed SE	Employ- ees EE	Workers WO	Apprent- ices AP[b)	Family- workers FW[c)	Un- known U	Total T	%
I	Agriculture	Total	293.6		748.6				2.4	1 044.7	7.3
		males	270.4		732.9				2.3	1 005.6	10.0
II	Mining	Total	1.3		753.2				.1	754.6	5.3
		males	1.2		750.1				.1	751.5	7.5
III	Manufacturing	Total	535.4	(387.3)	3 998.8				28.7	4 562.8	32.1
		males	316.0	(186.2)	2 623.3				13.0	2 952.4	29.3
IV	Construction	Total	112.2	(53.8)	932.0				6.3	1 050.4	7.4
		males	111.5	(53.8)	931.9				6.3	1 049.7	10.4
V	Utilities	Total	.1	(.0)	55.4				.2	55.6	.4
		males	.1	(.0)	55.4				.2	55.6	.6
VI	Commerce	Total	572.8		984.8				17.9	1 575.5	11.1
		males	459.8		771.5				11.2	1 242.5	12.3
VII	Transport	Total	41.0		994.8				4.4	1 040.2	7.3
		males	40.0		983.3				4.3	1 027.5	10.2
VIII	Banking	Total	1.5		86.2					87.7	.6
		males	1.5		84.5					86.1	.9
IX	Services	Total	253.2		2 540.3				88.9	2 882.3	20.3
		males	158.4		563.7				51.5	773.6	7.7
X	Public admin.	Total			366.4					366.4	2.6
		males			339.9					339.9	3.4
U	Unknown	Total	.3		800.3				.3	800.9	5.6
		males	.3		783.1				.3	783.6	7.8
T	All sectors	Total	1 811.4		12 260.7				149.1	14 221.3	100.0
		males	1 359.2		8 619.6				89.1	10 067.9	100.0

Percent distributions

	Total labour force									Male labour force							
	EM	SE	EE	WO	AP	FW	U	T		EM	SE	EE	WO	AP	FW	U	T
I	28.1		71.7				.2	100.0	I	26.9		72.9				.2	100.0
II	.2		99.8				.0	100.0	II	.2		99.8				.0	100.0
III	11.7	(8.5)	87.6				.6	100.0	III	10.7	(6.3)	88.9				.4	100.0
IV	10.7	(5.1)	88.7				.6	100.0	IV	10.6	(5.1)	88.8				.6	100.0
V	.1	(.0)	99.6				.3	100.0	V	.1	(.0)	99.6				.3	100.0
VI	36.4		62.5				1.1	100.0	VI	37.0		62.1				.9	100.0
VII	3.9		95.6				.4	100.0	VII	3.9		95.7				.4	100.0
VIII	1.8		98.2					100.0	VIII	1.8		98.2					100.0
IX	8.8		88.1				3.1	100.0	IX	20.5		72.9				6.7	100.0
X			100.0					100.0	X			100.0					100.0
U			99.9				.0	100.0	U			99.9				.0	100.0
T	12.7		86.2				1.0	100.0	T	13.5		85.6				.9	100.0

Scotland

Labour Force by Sector and Status 1901

Absolute figures in thousands

Sector			Employers EM[a)]	Self-employed SE	Employees EE	Workers WO[b)]	Apprentices AP	Family-workers FW[c)]	Unknown U	Total T	%
I	Agriculture	Total	68.1		129.0			30.0	10.2	237.3	12.0
		males	60.1		108.7			17.5	10.2	196.6	14.1
II	Mining	Total	.3	(.1)	128.0				.0	128.3	6.5
		males	.2	(.0)	126.8				.0	127.0	9.1
III	Manufacturing	Total	64.2	(40.6)	610.6				.5	675.3	34.1
		males	33.7	(12.8)	384.9				.2	418.8	30.1
IV	Construction	Total	12.5	(3.1)	124.1				.1	136.6	6.9
		males	12.4	(3.1)	123.9				.1	136.4	9.8
V	Utilities	Total	.0	(.0)	6.7				.0	6.8	.3
		males	.0	(.0)	6.7				.0	6.8	.5
VI	Commerce	Total	51.7	(31.6)	151.7				10.6	214.0	10.8
		males	37.5	(19.5)	101.6				10.4	149.6	10.8
VII	Transport	Total	4.2	(2.0)	118.3				9.8	132.3	6.7
		males	4.2	(2.0)	116.1				9.8	130.1	9.4
VIII	Banking	Total	.0	(.0)	10.6				.0	10.6	.5
		males	.0	(.0)	10.6				.0	10.6	.8
IX	Services	Total	12.9	(4.7)	251.9				36.0	300.8	15.2
		males	9.3	(1.8)	60.8				14.0	84.1	6.0
X	Public admin.	Total	.0	(.0	29.5				.0	29.5	1.5
		males	.0	(.0)	27.3				.0	27.3	2.0
U	Unknown	Total	.5	(.2)	108.2				2.5	111.3	5.6
		males	.5	(.1)	101.1				2.5	104.1	7.5
T	All sectors	Total	214.3		1 668.7			30.0	69.8	1 982.8	100.0
		males	157.9		1 168.5			17.5	47.3	1 391.2	100.0

Percent distributions

	Total labour force									Male labour force							
	EM	SE	EE	WO	AP	FW	U	T		EM	SE	EE	WO	AP	FW	U	T
I	28.7		54.4			12.6	4.3	100.0	I	30.6		55.3			8.9	5.2	100.0
II	.2	(.1)	99.8				.0	100.0	II	.1	(.0)	99.8				.0	100.0
III	9.5	(6.0)	90.4				.1	100.0	III	8.1	(3.1)	91.9				.0	100.0
IV	9.1	(2.3)	90.8				.1	100.0	IV	9.1	(2.3)	90.9				.1	100.0
V	.5	(.1)	99.5				.0	100.0	V	.5	(.1)	99.5				.0	100.0
VI	24.2	(14.7)	70.9				4.9	100.0	VI	25.1	(13.1)	67.9				7.0	100.0
VII	3.2	(1.5)	89.4				7.4	100.0	VII	3.2	(1.5)	89.2				7.6	100.0
VIII	.0	(.0)	100.0				.0	100.0	VIII	.0	(.0)	100.0				.0	100.0
IX	4.3	(1.6)	83.7				12.0	100.0	IX	11.0	(2.2)	72.4				16.6	100.0
X	.0	(.0)	100.0				.0	100.0	X	.0	(.0)	100.0				.0	100.0
U	.0	(.1)	97.3				2.3	100.0	U	.4	(.1)	97.1				2.4	100.0
T	10.8		84.2			1.5	3.5	100.0	T	11.4		84.0			1.3	3.4	100.0

Labour Force by Sector and Status 1911 [a)]

Absolute figures in thousands

Sector			Employ-ers EM[b)]	Self-employed SE	Employ-ees EE	Workers WO	Apprent-ices AP	Family-workers FW[c)]	Un-known U	Total T	%
I	Agriculture	Total	272.8	(114.3)		801.3		154.5	31.9	1 260.5	7.7
		males	254.8	(109.1)		784.9		97.7	28.3	1 165.7	10.2
II	Mining	Total	2.5	(0.5)		971.3			0.9	974.6	6.0
		males	2.5	(0.5)		968.3			0.9	971.6	8.5
III	Manufacturing	Total	467.9	(297.6)		4 589.6			141.3	5 198.8	31.9
		males	296.9	(149.4)		3 030.3			54.7	3 381.8	29.5
IV	Construction	Total	116.5	(54.7)		813.8			24.2	954.4	5.9
		males	115.9	(54.7)		813.7			24.2	953.8	8.3
V	Utilities	Total	0.1			77.2			0.7	78.0	0.5
		males	0.1			77.1			0.7	77.9	0.7
VI	Commerce	Total	628.7			1 291.3			120.3	2 040.3	12.5
		males	522.8			946.2			42.1	1 511.0	13.2
VII	Transport	Total	38.4			1 217.5			18.6	1 274.5	7.8
		males	37.4			1 176.2			17.7	1 231.4	10.8
VIII	Banking	Total	5.2			138.7			0.0	143.9	0.9
		males	5.2			133.2			0.0	138.4	1.2
IX	Services	Total	312.3			2 784.8			164.1	3 261.2	20.0
		males	196.3			701.8			69.6	967.7	8.4
X	Public admin.	Total	0.0			377.4			0.0	377.4	2.3
		males	0.0			354.8			0.0	354.8	3.1
U	Unknown [d)]	Total	3.3	(1.7)		714.4			2.3	719.9	4.4
		males	3.1	(1.6)		693.6			1.8	698.5	6.1
T	All sectors	Total	1 847.7			13 777.2		154.5	504.2	16 283.5	100.0
		males	1 435.0			9 680.1		97.7	240.0	11 452.8	100.0

Percent distributions

Total labour force

	EM	SE	EE	WO	AP	FW	U	T
I	21.6	(9.1)	63.6			12.3	2.5	100.0
II	0.3	(0.0)	99.7				0.1	100.0
III	9.0	(5.7)	88.3				2.7	100.0
IV	12.2	(5.7)	85.3				2.5	100.0
V	0.1		99.0				0.9	100.0
VI	30.8		63.3				5.9	100.0
VII	3.0		95.5				1.5	100.0
VIII	3.6		96.4				0.0	100.0
IX	9.6		85.4				5.0	100.0
X	0.0		100.0				0.0	100.0
U	0.5	(0.2)	99.2				0.3	100.0
T	11.3		84.6			0.9	3.1	100.0

Male labour force

	EM	SE	EE	WO	AP	FW	U	T
I	21.9	(9.4)	67.3			8.4	2.4	100.0
II	0.3	(0.0)	99.7				0.1	100.0
III	8.8	(4.4)	89.6				1.6	100.0
IV	12.2	(5.7)	85.3				2.5	100.0
V	0.1		99.0				0.9	100.0
VI	34.6		62.6				2.8	100.0
VII	3.0		95.5				1.4	100.0
VIII	3.7		96.3				0.0	100.0
IX	20.3		72.5				7.2	100.0
X	0.0		100.0				0.0	100.0
U	0.4	(0.2)	99.3				0.3	100.0
T	12.5		84.5			0.9	2.1	100.0

Labour Force by Sector and Status 1911 [a]

Absolute figures in thousands

Sector			Employ-ers	Self-employed	Employ-ees	Workers	Apprent-ices	Family-workers	Un-known	Total	%
			EM	SE	EE	WO	AP	FW[b]	U	T	
I	Agriculture	Total	28.3	27.2	120.1			27.3	24.1	227.1	11.0
		males	26.1	26.0	104.3			16.6	20.7	193.7	13.1
II	Mining	Total	0.7	0.2	144.3				15.0	160.1	7.7
		males	0.7	0.2	142.0				14.8	157.7	10.7
III	Manufacturing	Total	22.6	33.8	603.0				51.6	711.1	34.4
		males	20.1	13.1	398.9				34.9	467.0	31.7
IV	Construction	Total	9.4	3.8	83.9				9.5	106.5	5.2
		males	9.3	3.8	83.8				9.5	106.4	7.2
V	Utilities	Total	0.0	0.0	4.3				3.9	8.3	0.4
		males	0.0	0.0	4.3				3.9	8.2	0.6
VI	Commerce	Total	26.0	30.7	178.4				14.6	249.7	12.1
		males	23.1	19.3	112.4				9.5	164.2	11.1
VII	Transport	Total	2.2	2.1	143.2				14.5	161.9	7.8
		males	2.1	2.1	137.7				14.2	156.0	10.6
VIII	Banking	Total	0.2	0.1	9.9				4.8	15.0	0.7
		males	0.2	0.1	9.7				4.7	14.7	1.0
IX	Services	Total	15.7	9.5	270.7				18.1	314.0	15.2
		males	14.1	4.6	72.2				10.5	101.4	6.9
X	Public admin.	Total			31.0				0.0	31.0	1.5
		males			30.0				0.0	30.0	2.0
U	Unknown	Total	0.4	0.4	60.6				20.9	82.2	4.0
		males	0.4	0.3	53.7				19.8	74.3	5.0
T	All sectors	Total	105.6	107.8	1 649.5			27.3	176.8	2 067.0	100.0
		males	96.0	69.5	1 149.2			16.6	142.4	1 473.8	100.0

Percent distributions

Total labour force

	EM	SE	EE	WO	AP	FW	U	T
I	12.5	12.0	52.9			12.0	10.6	100.0
II	0.4	0.1	90.1				9.4	100.0
III	3.2	4.8	84.8				7.3	100.0
IV	8.8	3.6	78.8				8.9	100.0
V	0.3	0.3	52.4				47.0	100.0
VI	10.4	12.3	71.4				5.8	100.0
VII	1.3	1.3	88.4				9.0	100.0
VIII	1.4	0.9	65.8				31.9	100.0
IX	5.0	3.0	86.2				5.7	100.0
X			100.0				0.0	100.0
U	0.5	0.4	73.8				25.3	100.0
T	5.1	5.2	79.8			1.3	8.6	100.0

Male labour force

	EM	SE	EE	WO	AP	FW	U	T
I	13.5	13.4	53.8			8.6	10.7	100.0
II	0.4	0.1	90.1				9.4	100.0
III	4.3	2.8	85.4				7.5	100.0
IV	8.7	3.6	78.8				8.9	100.0
V	0.3	0.3	52.4				47.1	100.0
VI	14.0	11.8	68.4				5.8	100.0
VII	1.3	1.3	88.3				9.1	100.0
VIII	1.5	0.9	65.7				32.0	100.0
IX	13.9	4.5	71.2				10.3	100.0
X			100.0				0.0	100.0
U	0.6	0.4	72.4				26.7	100.0
T	6.5	4.7	78.0			1.1	9.7	100.0

England and Wales

Labour Force by Sector and Status 1921[a)]

Absolute figures in thousands

Sector			Employers	Self-employed	Employees	Workers	Apprentices	Family-workers[b)]	Unknown	Total	%
			EM	SE	EE	WO	AP	FW	U	T	
I	Agriculture	Total	149.4	155.5	882.8			95.6		1 283.3	7.5
		males	139.4	145.8	834.6			80.3		1 200.1	9.9
II	Mining	Total	1.2	.1	1 063.8					1 065.1	6.2
		males	1.2	.1	1 060.5					1 061.7	8.8
III	Manufacturing	Total	164.7	265.3	5 063.6					5 493.7	32.0
		males	148.9	176.0	3 494.8					3 819.6	31.6
IV	Construction	Total	27.4	16.5	461.3					505.3	2.9
		males	27.2	16.5	459.8					503.5	4.2
V	Utilities	Total	.0	.0	48.6					48.6	.3
		males	.0	.0	48.2					48.3	.4
VI	Commerce	Total	176.8	326.5	954.8					1 458.1	8.5
		males	155.3	237.7	574.5					967.4	8.0
VII	Transport	Total	16.0	41.4	1 426.8					1 484.2	8.6
		males	15.6	40.9	1 364.2					1 420.6	11.7
VIII	Banking	Total	10.6	7.8	82.7					101.1	.6
		males	10.4	7.4	77.8					95.7	.8
IX	Services	Total	82.6	252.6	2 340.3					2 675.6	15.6
		males	57.3	114.7	452.0					624.0	5.2
X	Public admin.	Total	.0	.0	514.2					514.2	3.0
		males	.0	.0	442.3					442.3	3.7
U	Unknown	Total	8.0	10.4	2 521.5					2 539.8	14.8
		males	7.9	10.1	1 902.4					1 920.3	15.9
T	All sectors	Total	636.9	1 076.2	15 360.3			95.6		17 169.0	100.0
		males	563.2	749.2	10 711.0			80.3		12 103.6	100.0

Percent distributions

	Total labour force								Male labour force							
	EM	SE	EE	WO	AP	FW	U	T		EM	SE	EE	WO	AP	FW	U	T
I	11.6	12.1	68.8			7.5		100.0	I	11.6	12.1	69.5			6.7		100.0
II	.1	.0	99.9					100.0	II	.1	.0	99.9					100.0
III	3.0	4.8	92.2					100.0	III	3.9	4.6	91.5					100.0
IV	5.4	3.3	91.3					100.0	IV	5.4	3.3	91.3					100.0
V	.1	.0	99.9					100.0	V	.1	.0	99.9					100.0
VI	12.1	22.4	65.5					100.0	VI	16.0	24.6	59.4					100.0
VII	1.1	2.8	96.1					100.0	VII	1.1	2.9	96.0					100.0
VIII	10.5	7.7	81.8					100.0	VIII	10.9	7.8	81.3					100.0
IX	3.1	9.4	87.5					100.0	IX	9.2	18.4	72.4					100.0
X	.0	.0	100.0					100.0	X	.0	.0	100.0					100.0
U	.3	0.4	99.3					100.0	U	.4	.5	99.1					100.0
T	3.7	6.3	89.5			0.6		100.0	T	4.7	6.2	88.5			0.7		100.0

Labour Force by Sector and Status 1921 [a]

Absolute figures in thousands

Sector			Employers	Self-employed	Employees	Workers	Apprentices	Family-workers [b]	Unknown	Total	%
			EM	SE	EE	WO	AP	FW	U	T	
I	Agriculture	Total	30.7	39.9	140.8			4.8	.7	216.9	10.0
		males	28.4	37.1	122.5			3.8	.7	192.5	12.5
II	Mining	Total	.2	.1	154.9				.0	155.3	7.1
		males	.2	.1	151.6				.0	151.9	9.8
III	Manufacturing	Total	23.6	25.9	727.8				.2	777.5	35.7
		males	21.8	15.1	531.6				.2	568.8	36.9
IV	Construction	Total	2.9	1.5	60.9				.0	65.3	3.0
		males	2.9	1.5	60.8				.0	65.2	4.2
V	Utilities	Total	.0	.0	8.7				.0	8.7	.4
		males	.0	.0	8.6				.0	8.6	.6
VI	Commerce	Total	25.7	36.0	127.3				.1	189.1	8.7
		males	22.0	23.2	61.4				.1	106.6	6.9
VII	Transport	Total	2.5	3.4	175.0				.1	181.0	8.3
		males	2.4	3.4	164.1				.1	169.9	11.0
VIII	Banking	Total	1.2	.5	8.7				.0	10.4	.5
		males	1.2	.5	8.2				.0	9.8	.6
IX	Services	Total	9.5	21.6	245.0				.7	276.7	12.7
		males	7.8	8.9	47.8				.1	64.7	4.2
X	Public admin.	Total	.0	.0	46.2				.0	46.2	2.1
		males	.0	.0	40.1				.0	40.1	2.6
U	Unknown	Total	1.9	2.4	238.1				9.8	252.2	11.6
		males	1.9	2.3	153.7				7.2	165.1	10.7
T	All sectors	Total	98.1	131.3	1 933.4			4.8	11.7	2 179.3	100.0
		males	88.7	92.0	1 350.3			3.8	8.4	1 543.2	100.0

Percent distributions

Total labour force

	EM	SE	EE	WO	AP	FW	U	T
I	14.1	18.4	64.9			2.2	.3	100.0
II	.2	.0	99.8				.0	100.0
III	3.0	3.3	93.6				.0	100.0
IV	4.5	2.3	93.2				.0	100.0
V	.1	.0	99.9				.0	100.0
VI	13.6	19.0	67.3				.0	100.0
VII	1.4	1.9	96.7				.0	100.0
VIII	11.5	5.1	83.3				.1	100.0
IX	3.4	7.8	88.5				.2	100.0
X	.0	.0	100.0				.0	100.0
U	.8	.9	94.4				3.9	100.0
T	4.5	6.0	88.7			0.2	.5	100.0

Male labour force

	EM	SE	EE	WO	AP	FW	U	T
I	14.7	19.3	63.6			2.0	.4	100.0
II	.2	.0	99.8				.0	100.0
III	3.8	2.7	93.5				.0	100.0
IV	4.5	2.3	93.2				.0	100.0
V	.1	.0	99.9				.0	100.0
VI	20.6	21.7	57.6				.1	100.0
VII	1.4	2.0	96.6				.0	100.0
VIII	11.9	5.0	83.1				.1	100.0
IX	12.1	13.8	73.9				.2	100.0
X	.0	.0	100.0				.0	100.0
U	1.1	1.4	93.1				4.4	100.0
T	5.7	6.0	87.5			0.2	.5	100.0

England and Wales

Labour Force by Sector and Status 1931

Absolute figures in thousands

Sector			Employ-ers EM[a)]	Self-employed SE	Managers MA[b)]	Workers WO[c)]	Apprent-ices AP	Family-workers FW[d)]	Out of work OW[e)]	Total T	%
I	Agriculture	Total	162.5	150.2	7.3	676.8			62.2	1 059.1	5.6
		males	150.5	142.0	7.1	639.7			60.0	999.4	7.5
II	Mining	Total	3.0	.3	5.4	975.2			213.6	1 197.6	6.4
		males	3.0	.3	5.4	966.2			212.6	1 187.5	9.0
III	Manufacturing	Total	158.7	202.6	79.8	4 907.6			920.6	6 269.3	33.3
		males	144.4	142.7	73.1	3 123.7			668.3	4 152.2	31.3
IV	Construction	Total	61.6	42.8	4.3	738.1			174.3	1 021.1	5.4
		males	61.0	42.7	4.2	728.5			173.6	1 010.0	7.6
V	Utilities	Total	.3	.1	2.8	206.5			18.2	227.9	1.2
		males	.3	.1	2.7	199.7			18.0	220.9	1.7
VI	Commerce	Total	198.6	420.6	112.1	1 680.9			186.9	2 599.1	13.8
		males	170.6	304.0	96.9	1 087.6			137.4	1 796.5	13.6
VII	Transport	Total	28.8	41.3	18.3	1 265.4			141.5	1 495.4	7.9
		males	27.9	41.0	14.5	1 178.6			138.4	1 400.3	10.6
VIII	Banking	Total	7.9	3.9	20.6	242.1			9.1	283.7	1.5
		males	7.6	3.5	20.3	183.3			7.6	222.4	1.7
IX	Services	Total	126.7	293.1	56.0	2 807.7			238.7	3 522.2	18.7
		males	90.9	157.9	37.6	874.8			95.8	1 257.1	9.5
X	Public admin.	Total	.0	.0	3.3	936.0			91.5	1 030.7	5.5
		males	.0	.0	2.6	796.6			87.2	886.4	6.7
U	Unknown	Total	1.4	1.4	.1	34.2			110.1	147.3	.8
		males	1.3	1.2	.1	27.2			84.8	114.6	.9
T	All sectors	Total	749.7	1 156.5	309.9	14 470.5			2 166.8	18 853.4	100.0
		males	657.4	835.4	264.6	9 806.1			1 683.7	13 247.3	100.0

Percent distributions

Total labour force

	EM	SE	MA	WO	AP	FW	OW	T
I	15.3	14.2	.7	63.9			5.9	100.0
II	.3	.0	.5	81.4			17.8	100.0
III	2.5	3.2	1.3	78.3			14.7	100.0
IV	6.0	4.2	.4	72.3			17.1	100.0
V	.1	.1	1.2	90.6			8.0	100.0
VI	7.6	16.2	4.3	64.7			7.2	100.0
VII	1.9	2.8	1.2	84.6			9.5	100.0
VIII	2.8	1.4	7.3	85.3			3.2	100.0
IX	3.6	8.3	1.6	79.7			6.8	100.0
X	.0	.0	.3	90.8			8.9	100.0
U	1.0	1.0	.1	23.2			74.8	100.0
T	4.0	6.1	1.6	76.8			11.5	100.0

Male labour force

	EM	SE	MA	WO	AP	FW	OW	T
I	15.1	14.2	.7	64.0			6.0	100.0
II	.3	.0	.5	81.4			17.9	100.0
III	3.5	3.4	1.8	75.2			16.1	100.0
IV	6.0	4.2	.4	72.1			17.2	100.0
V	.1	.1	1.2	90.4			8.2	100.0
VI	9.5	16.9	5.4	60.5			7.6	100.0
VII	2.0	2.9	1.0	84.2			9.9	100.0
VIII	3.4	1.6	9.1	82.4			3.4	100.0
IX	7.2	12.6	3.0	69.6			7.6	100.0
X	.0	.0	.3	89.9			9.8	100.0
U	1.1	1.0	.1	23.8			74.0	100.0
T	5.0	6.3	2.0	74.0			12.7	100.0

Scotland

Labour Force by Sector and Status 1931

Absolute figures in thousands

Sector			Employ-ers EM[a]	Managers MA[b]	Self employed SE	Workers WO[c]	Apprent-ices AP	Family-workers FW[d]	Out of work OW	Total T	%
I	Agriculture	Total	28.6	1.3	31.6	124.7			12.3	198.6	8.9
		males	26.5	1.3	29.7	113.3			11.4	182.1	11.7
II	Mining	Total	.4	.6	.1	109.0			34.2	144.3	6.5
		males	.4	.6	.1	107.3			33.8	142.2	9.1
III	Manufacturing	Total	18.7	4.4	18.3	518.8			177.3	737.5	33.2
		males	17.4	4.0	12.3	338.0			138.8	510.5	32.8
IV	Construction	Total	6.0	.2	2.4	70.4			22.8	101.7	4.6
		males	5.9	.2	2.4	67.3			22.5	98.4	6.3
V	Utilities	Total	.1	.2	.0	15.0			2.2	17.5	.8
		males	.1	.2	.0	14.3			2.2	16.8	1.1
VI	Commerce	Total	28.1	5.0	39.0	226.2			31.5	329.9	14.8
		males	23.6	4.3	26.3	126.8			21.8	202.8	13.1
VII	Transport	Total	2.9	3.0	3.6	144.7			22.6	176.8	8.0
		males	2.8	2.3	3.6	131.5			21.5	161.6	10.4
VIII	Banking	Total	.5	2.8	.2	22.1			1.0	26.7	1.2
		males	.5	2.8	.2	16.4			.8	20.6	1.3
IX	Services	Total	14.4	2.6	19.8	294.6			30.8	362.2	16.3
		males	11.4	1.5	11.3	85.6			10.7	120.6	7.8
X	Public admin.	Total	.4	.4	.1	83.5			9.4	93.7	4.2
		males	.2	.2	.1	67.4			8.8	76.7	4.9
U	Unknown	Total	.3	.1	1.0	17.5			13.7	32.5	1.5
		males	.3	.1	.7	9.5			11.2	21.8	1.4
T	All sectors	Total	100.3	20.7	116.1	1 626.4			357.9	2 221.4	100.0
		males	89.1	17.4	86.6	1 077.4			283.6	1 554.0	100.0

Percent distributions

	Total labour force									Male labour force							
	EM	MA	SE	WO	AP	FW	OW	T		EM	MA	SE	WO	AP	FW	OW	T
I	14.4	.7	15.9	62.8			6.2	100.0	I	14.6	.7	16.3	62.2			6.2	100.0
II	.3	.4	.0	75.5			23.7	100.0	II	.3	.4	.0	75.4			23.8	100.0
III	2.5	.6	2.5	70.3			24.0	100.0	III	3.4	.8	2.4	66.2			27.2	100.0
IV	5.9	.2	2.4	69.2			22.4	100.0	IV	6.0	.2	2.4	68.5			22.9	100.0
V	.5	1.2	.1	85.7			12.6	100.0	V	.5	1.2	.1	85.3			13.0	100.0
VI	8.5	1.5	11.8	68.6			9.6	100.0	VI	11.6	2.1	13.0	62.5			10.8	100.0
VII	1.6	1.7	2.0	81.8			12.8	100.0	VII	1.7	1.4	2.2	81.4			13.3	100.0
VIII	1.9	10.6	.7	82.8			3.9	100.0	VIII	2.3	13.6	.8	79.3			4.0	100.0
IX	4.0	.7	5.5	81.3			8.5	100.0	IX	9.5	1.2	9.4	71.0			8.9	100.0
X	.4	.4	.1	89.1			10.0	100.0	X	.3	.3	.1	87.8			11.5	100.0
U	.9	.2	3.0	53.7			42.2	100.0	U	1.2	.3	3.3	43.6			51.5	100.0
T	4.5	.9	5.2	73.2			16.1	100.0	T	5.7	1.1	5.6	69.3			18.2	100.0

Labour Force by Sector and Status 1951 [a]

Absolute figures in thousands

Sector			Employ-ers	Self-employed	Managers	Workers	Apprent-ices	Family-workers	Out of work	Total	%
			EM	SE	MA[b]	WO[c]	AP[d]	FW[e]	OW	T	
I	Agriculture	Total	107.4	197.1	14.3	645.0	(1.7)	(19.4)	12.9	976.6	4.8
		males	100.4	184.2	13.6	565.6	(1.6)	(6.6)	10.8	874.5	6.2
II	Mining	Total	.5	.2	5.5	735.4	(6.9)	(.0)	16.4	757.9	3.7
		males	.5	.2	5.4	723.3	(6.9)	(.0)	16.3	745.6	5.3
III	Manufacturing	Total	59.1	142.2	245.6	7 085.9	(213.2)	(3.1)	104.3	7 637.2	37.6
		males	54.4	114.4	230.9	4 770.9	(202.8)	(1.2)	77.3	5 247.9	37.3
IV	Construction	Total	40.5	83.6	34.8	1 078.1	(88.5)	(.6)	35.4	1 272.3	6.3
		males	40.1	83.4	33.9	1 045.9	(88.4)	(.3)	34.9	1 238.3	8.8
V	Utilities	Total			3.6	327.0	(8.7)		2.7	333.4	1.6
		males			3.5	298.0	(8.7)		2.6	304.2	2.2
VI	Commerce	Total	117.8	339.5	230.3	1 713.8	(16.3)	(16.2)	32.9	2 434.2	12.0
		males	98.4	240.8	191.8	848.3	(12.4)	(2.3)	20.2	1 399.6	10.0
VII	Transport	Total	10.6	34.8	36.6	1 441.6	(5.7)	(.7)	24.5	1 548.1	7.6
		males	9.7	32.3	31.8	1 263.3	(5.7)	(.3)	22.6	1 359.7	9.7
VIII	Banking	Total	2.2	3.1	29.1	309.9	(.1)	(.1)	2.1	346.5	1.7
		males	2.2	2.9	28.4	189.9	(.1)	(.0)	1.4	224.7	1.6
IX	Services	Total	89.8	270.7	154.3	2 759.3	(27.5)	(7.4)	71.8	3 345.9	16.5
		males	69.9	182.0	81.9	902.7	(20.6)	(1.0)	28.9	1 265.4	9.0
X	Public admin.	Total			5.2	1 568.7	(4.1)		18.1	1 592.0	7.8
		males			3.7	1 322.6	(4.1)		15.3	1 341.6	9.5
U	Unknown	Total	.1	1.9	.3	14.8	(.1)	(.1)	75.2	92.2	.5
		males	.0	1.7	.2	9.2	(.1)	(.0)	50.9	62.0	.4
T	All sectors	Total	428.0	1 073.0	759.6	17 679.3	(372.9)	(47.7)	396.4	20 336.4	100.0
		males	375.6	841.9	625.1	11 939.8	(351.3)	(11.8)	281.3	14 063.5	100.0

Percent distributions

Total labour force

	EM	SE	MA	WO	AP	FW	OW	T
I	11.0	20.2	1.5	66.0	(.2)	(2.0)	1.3	100.0
II	.1	.0	.7	97.0	(.9)	(.0)	2.2	100.0
III	.8	1.9	3.2	92.8	(2.8)	(.0)	1.4	100.0
IV	3.2	6.6	2.7	84.7	(7.0)	(.0)	2.8	100.0
V		.0	1.1	98.1	(2.6)		.8	100.0
VI	4.8	13.9	9.5	70.4	(.7)	(.7)	1.4	100.0
VII	.7	2.2	2.4	93.1	(.4)	(.0)	1.6	100.0
VIII	.6	.9	8.4	89.4	(.0)	(.0)	.6	100.0
IX	2.7	8.1	4.6	82.5	(.8)	(.2)	2.1	100.0
X			.3	98.5	(.3)		1.1	100.0
U	.1	2.1	.3	16.0	(.1)	(.1)	81.6	100.0
T	2.1	5.3	3.7	86.9	(1.8)	(.2)	1.9	100.0

Male labour force

	EM	SE	MA	WO	AP	FW	OW	T
I	11.5	21.1	1.6	64.7	(.2)	(.8)	1.2	100.0
II	.1	.0	.7	97.0	(.9)	(.0)	2.2	100.0
III	1.0	2.2	4.4	90.9	(3.9)	(.0)	1.5	100.0
IV	3.2	6.7	2.7	84.5	(7.1)	(.0)	2.8	100.0
V		.0	1.2	98.0	(2.9)		.9	100.0
VI	7.0	17.2	13.7	60.6	(.9)	(.2)	1.4	100.0
VII	.7	2.4	2.3	92.9	(.4)	(.0)	1.7	100.0
VIII	1.0	1.3	12.6	84.5	(.0)	(.0)	.6	100.0
IX	5.5	14.4	6.5	71.3	(1.6)	(.1)	2.3	100.0
X			.3	98.6	(.3)		1.1	100.0
U	.1	2.7	.3	14.9	(.1)	(.0)	82.0	100.0
T	2.7	6.0	4.4	84.9	(2.5)	(.1)	2.0	100.0

Scotland

Labour Force by Sector and Status 1951 [a]

Absolute figures in thousands

Sector			Employ-ers	Self-employed	Employ-ees	Workers	Apprent-ices	Family-workers	Out of work	Total	%
			EM	SE	EE [b]	WO [c]	AP	FW	OW	T	
I	Agriculture	Total	26.6	19.3	13.2	101.3	.7	1.2	3.5	165.8	7.3
		males	25.1	18.0	11.9	91.1	.7	.5	3.2	150.4	9.5
II	Mining	Total	.1	.0	2.7	95.1	1.6	.0	3.1	102.6	4.5
		males	.1	.0	2.4	93.7	1.6	.0	3.1	101.0	6.4
III	Manufacturing	Total	8.0	9.0	51.8	686.1	49.2	.1	24.6	828.8	36.5
		males	7.5	7.6	41.1	468.7	44.4	.0	19.4	588.7	37.1
IV	Construction	Total	5.5	3.1	7.2	115.3	20.0	.0	7.0	158.1	7.0
		males	5.4	3.1	5.9	110.3	20.0	.0	6.9	151.5	9.6
V	Utilities	Total		.0	2.2	23.7	.6		.6	27.1	1.2
		males		.0	2.0	21.6	.6		.5	24.7	1.6
VI	Commerce	Total	18.1	25.7	33.7	187.7	6.3	.9	6.1	278.5	12.3
		males	14.8	18.2	19.7	84.1	5.2	.2	3.7	145.8	9.2
VII	Transport	Total	1.6	2.3	12.1	163.3	1.3	.1	5.1	185.7	8.2
		males	1.5	2.2	9.7	137.4	1.3	.0	4.7	156.9	9.9
VIII	Banking	Total	.4	.2	14.9	16.3	.7	.0	.3	32.9	1.4
		males	.4	.2	11.8	8.7	.6	.0	.2	21.9	1.4
IX	Services	Total	12.4	15.0	96.2	202.5	6.0	.8	10.3	343.1	15.1
		males	9.9	10.6	41.8	51.7	4.8	.2	3.8	122.8	7.7
X	Public admin.	Total		.1	18.2	101.6	11.1		3.0	134.0	5.9
		males		.0	15.1	81.2	11.0		2.7	110.1	6.9
U	Unknown	Total	.0	.2	.1	1.3	.0	.0	15.4	17.0	.7
		males	.0	.1	.1	.9	.0	.0	10.4	11.5	.7
T	All sectors	Total	72.6	74.9	252.1	1 694.3	97.7	3.1	79.0	2 273.6	100.0
		males	64.7	60.1	161.5	1 149.3	90.1	.9	58.6	1 585.3	100.0

Percent distributions

Total labour force

	EM	SE	EE	WO	AP	FW	OW	T
I	16.0	11.6	8.0	61.1	.4	.7	2.1	100.0
II	.1	.0	2.6	92.7	1.5	.0	3.0	100.0
III	1.0	1.1	6.2	82.8	5.9	.0	3.0	100.0
IV	3.5	2.0	4.6	72.9	12.7	.0	4.4	100.0
V		.0	8.2	87.7	2.1		2.1	100.0
VI	6.5	9.2	12.1	67.4	2.3	.3	2.2	100.0
VII	.8	1.2	6.5	87.9	.7	.0	2.8	100.0
VIII	1.3	.7	45.2	49.6	2.2	.0	.9	100.0
IX	3.6	4.4	28.0	59.0	1.8	.2	3.0	100.0
X		.0	13.6	75.9	8.3		2.2	100.0
U	.1	1.0	.7	7.4	.2	.1	90.6	100.0
T	3.2	3.3	11.1	74.5	4.3	.1	3.5	100.0

Male labour force

	EM	SE	EE	WO	AP	FW	OW	T
I	16.7	12.0	7.9	60.5	.5	.3	2.1	100.0
II	.1	.0	2.4	92.8	1.6	.0	3.1	100.0
III	1.3	1.3	7.0	79.6	7.5	.0	3.3	100.0
IV	3.6	2.0	3.9	72.8	13.2	.0	4.5	100.0
V		.0	8.0	87.6	2.3		2.2	100.0
VI	10.1	12.5	13.5	57.7	3.5	.1	2.5	100.0
VII	.9	1.4	6.2	87.6	.8	.0	3.0	100.0
VIII	1.9	.9	54.0	39.6	2.5	.0	1.0	100.0
IX	8.1	8.6	34.0	42.1	3.9	.1	3.1	100.0
X			13.7	73.8	10.0		2.4	100.0
U	.1	1.3	.6	7.4	.2	.0	90.3	100.0
T	4.1	3.8	10.2	72.5	5.7	.1	3.7	100.0

Labour Force by Sector and Status 1961 [a)]

Absolute figures in thousands

Sector			Employ-ers	Self-employed	Employ-ees	Workers	Apprent-ices	Family-workers	Un-known	Total	%
			EM	SE	EE[b)]	WO[c)]	AP	FW[d)]	U[e)]	T	
I	Agriculture	Total	131.9	158.8	39.3	386.6	10.3	(41.8)	14.6	741.5	3.4
		males	122.8	144.9	37.0	329.2	9.3	(29.7)	12.9	656.1	4.5
II	Mining	Total	.5	.2	63.7	551.3	20.3	(.1)	22.6	658.5	3.0
		males	.5	.2	62.6	533.7	20.2	(.0)	22.4	639.5	4.4
III	Manufacturing	Total	35.5	53.0	792.5	6 466.4	320.6	(6.2)	172.8	7 840.8	36.1
		males	32.6	35.1	723.0	4 218.2	304.5	(2.7)	120.3	5 433.8	37.1
IV	Construction	Total	69.5	92.8	155.4	997.9	110.1	(10.5)	53.0	1 478.7	6.8
		males	69.0	92.6	151.3	943.2	110.0	(7.5)	52.2	1 418.3	9.7
V	Utilities	Total			43.5	290.9	13.2		6.2	353.7	1.6
		males			42.1	254.2	13.1		5.8	315.2	2.2
VI	Commerce	Total	158.8	302.5	398.1	1 927.9	56.8	(60.3)	63.0	2 934.1	13.5
		males	144.0	195.7	309.7	826.0	47.2	(15.3)	37.5	1 560.2	10.7
VII	Transport	Total	14.1	28.5	160.8	1 280.5	13.0	(2.4)	35.2	1 532.1	7.1
		males	13.4	27.8	152.2	1 091.3	12.8	(1.5)	32.1	1 329.5	9.1
VIII	Banking	Total	9.5	6.3	92.5	419.8	1.2	(.9)	4.9	534.3	2.5
		males	8.9	5.3	86.1	208.9	1.2	(.3)	3.1	313.6	2.1
IX	Services	Total	171.5	280.5	482.5	2 888.4	196.0	(34.9)	90.1	4 109.0	18.9
		males	133.8	211.3	306.5	1 003.0	94.4	(8.2)	42.1	1 791.3	12.2
X	Public admin.	Total			187.5	1 109.8	8.5		24.5	1 330.3	6.1
		males			165.0	875.7	7.8		21.5	1 070.0	7.3
U	Unknown	Total	2.4	12.2	14.4	64.7	2.4	(.1)	85.3	181.4	.8
		males	2.0	9.1	12.8	40.6	2.2	(.0)	54.9	121.6	.8
T	All sectors	Total	620.8	934.8	2 430.2	16 384.2	752.3	(157.2)	572.1	21 694.5	100.0
		males	527.2	721.9	2 048.4	10 323.9	622.8	(65.2)	404.8	14 649.1	100.0

Percent distributions

Total labour force

	EM	SE	EE	WO	AP	FW	U	T
I	17.8	21.4	5.3	52.1	1.4	(5.6)	2.0	100.0
II	.1	.0	9.7	83.7	3.1	(.0)	3.4	100.0
III	.5	.7	10.1	82.5	4.1	(.1)	2.2	100.0
IV	4.7	6.3	10.5	67.5	7.4	(.7)	3.6	100.0
V			12.3	82.2	3.7		1.7	100.0
VI	6.3	10.3	13.6	65.7	1.9	(2.1)	2.1	100.0
VII	.9	1.9	10.5	83.6	.9	(.2)	2.3	100.0
VIII	1.8	1.2	17.3	78.6	.2	(.2)	.9	100.0
IX	4.2	6.8	11.7	70.3	4.8	(.8)	2.2	100.0
X			14.1	83.4	.6		1.8	100.0
U	1.3	6.7	7.9	35.7	1.3	(.0)	47.0	100.0
T	2.9	4.3	11.2	75.5	3.5	(.7)	2.6	100.0

Male labour force

	EM	SE	EE	WO	AP	FW	U	T
I	18.7	22.1	5.6	50.2	1.4	(4.5)	2.0	100.0
II	.1	.0	9.8	83.4	3.2	(.0)	3.5	100.0
III	.6	.6	13.3	77.6	5.6	(.0)	2.2	100.0
IV	4.9	6.5	10.7	66.5	7.8	(.5)	3.7	100.0
V			13.4	80.7	4.1		1.8	100.0
VI	9.2	12.5	19.8	52.9	3.0	(1.0)	2.4	100.0
VII	1.0	2.1	11.4	82.1	1.0	(.1)	2.4	100.0
VIII	2.9	1.7	27.5	66.6	.4	(.1)	1.0	100.0
IX	7.5	11.8	17.1	56.0	5.3	(.5)	2.4	100.0
X			15.4	81.8	.7		2.0	100.0
U	1.7	7.5	10.5	33.3	1.8	(.0)	45.1	100.0
T	3.6	4.9	14.0	70.5	4.3	(.4)	2.8	100.0

Labour Force by Sector and Status 1961 [a)]

Absolute figures in thousands

Sector			Employers	Self-employed	Employees [b)]	Workers [c)]	Apprentices	Family-workers	Out of work	Total	%
			EM	SE	EE	WO	AP	FW	OW	T	
I	Agriculture	Total	29.3	19.2	7.7	64.0	.4	7.8	3.9	132.3	5.7
		males	27.0	18.0	7.7	58.1	.4	6.0	3.5	120.8	7.6
II	Mining	Total	.1	.0	8.3	75.6	2.1	.0	4.0	90.0	3.9
		males	.1	.0	8.2	74.0	2.1	.0	4.0	88.3	5.6
III	Manufacturing	Total	3.9	3.5	55.8	614.7	36.1	.6	34.5	749.1	32.3
		males	3.7	3.2	51.6	412.8	33.9	.4	26.1	531.8	33.6
IV	Construction	Total	6.8	2.7	15.0	130.3	18.3	1.1	12.9	187.0	8.1
		males	6.8	2.7	14.7	122.3	18.3	.8	12.7	178.3	11.3
V	Utilities	Total	.0	.0	3.3	25.9	.5	.0	1.0	30.8	1.3
		males	.0	.0	3.2	22.6	.5	.0	.9	27.3	1.7
VI	Commerce	Total	28.9	20.1	28.4	227.2	7.2	5.8	10.9	328.4	14.2
		males	22.8	13.8	20.1	94.1	6.6	1.9	6.9	166.3	10.5
VII	Transport	Total	1.8	2.3	16.2	154.4	1.1	.2	8.0	184.0	7.9
		males	1.7	2.3	15.4	128.4	1.1	.1	7.1	156.2	9.9
VIII	Banking	Total	.6	.2	7.5	33.9	.1	.0	.4	42.8	1.8
		males	.5	.2	7.4	17.8	.1	.0	.3	26.3	1.7
IX	Services	Total	21.9	18.8	44.4	312.0	19.0	2.2	14.4	432.8	18.7
		males	17.3	15.6	28.7	95.7	10.1	.9	6.7	175.0	11.0
X	Public admin.	Total	.0	.0	16.9	103.6	.5	.0	4.8	125.7	5.4
		males	.0	.0	15.2	80.2	.4	.0	4.3	100.1	6.3
U	Unknown	Total	.1	.5	1.2	6.2	.1		8.9	16.9	.7
		males	.1	.4	1.1	4.7	.1		6.6	13.0	.8
T	All sectors	Total	93.4	67.4	204.7	1 747.8	85.3	17.7	103.5	2 319.8	100.0
		males	80.1	56.2	173.4	1 110.8	73.6	10.1	79.2	1 583.4	100.0

Percent distributions

Total labour force

	EM	SE	EE	WO	AP	FW	OW	T
I	22.2	14.5	5.8	48.4	.3	5.9	2.9	100.0
II	.1	.0	9.2	84.0	2.3	.0	4.4	100.0
III	.5	.5	7.4	82.1	4.8	.1	4.6	100.0
IV	3.6	1.4	8.0	69.7	9.8	.6	6.9	100.0
V	.0	.0	10.9	84.2	1.8	.0	3.1	100.0
VI	8.8	6.1	8.6	69.2	2.2	1.8	3.3	100.0
VII	1.0	1.3	8.8	83.9	.6	.1	4.3	100.0
VIII	1.4	.6	17.7	79.3	.1	.1	.9	100.0
IX	5.1	4.3	10.3	72.1	4.4	.5	3.3	100.0
X	.0	.0	13.4	82.4	.4	.0	3.8	100.0
U	.4	2.9	7.2	36.6	.5		52.3	100.0
T	4.0	2.9	8.8	75.3	3.7	.8	4.5	100.0

Male labour force

	EM	SE	EE	WO	AP	FW	OW	T
I	22.4	14.9	6.3	48.1	.3	5.0	2.9	100.0
II	.1	.0	9.3	83.8	2.3	.0	4.5	100.0
III	.7	.6	9.7	77.6	6.4	.1	4.9	100.0
IV	3.8	1.5	8.2	68.6	10.2	.4	7.1	100.0
V	.0	.0	11.7	82.8	2.0	.0	3.4	100.0
VI	13.7	8.3	12.1	56.6	4.0	1.1	4.1	100.0
VII	1.1	1.5	9.9	82.2	.7	.1	4.6	100.0
VIII	2.1	.8	28.1	67.8	.2	.0	1.0	100.0
IX	9.9	8.9	16.4	54.7	5.8	.5	3.8	100.0
X	.0	.0	15.1	80.1	.4	.0	4.3	100.0
U	.5	2.9	8.7	36.1	.6		51.2	100.0
T	5.1	3.5	11.0	70.2	4.7	.6	5.0	100.0

Labour Force by Sector and Status 1971 [a]

Absolute figures in thousands

Sector			Employ-ers EM	Self-employed SE	Managers MA	Employ-ees EE[b]	Workers WO	Family-workers FW[c]	Un-known U[d]	Total T	%
I	Agriculture	Total	136.7	156.0	3.8	21.2	315.7	(19.0)	1.4	634.8	2.5
		males	122.5	136.6	3.5	8.0	253.4	(1.2)	0.5	524.6	3.3
II	Mining	Total	0.3	0.2	8.7	71.5	310.0	(.0)	0.7	391.5	1.6
		males	0.3	0.2	8.2	59.9	305.5	(.0)	0.7	374.7	2.4
III	Manufacturing	Total	45.0	74.5	488.6	2 052.6	5 443.5	(7.6)	31.6	8 135.8	32.5
		males	39.8	59.1	451.5	1 281.7	3 868.8	(1.3)	19.6	5 720.5	36.0
IV	Construction	Total	76.0	245.9	102.7	271.6	969.7	(7.4)	3.2	1 669.1	6.7
		males	74.9	244.7	98.4	193.6	957.4	(2.1)	2.9	1 572.0	9.9
V	Utilities	Total	0.0	0.0	15.9	155.8	189.6	(.0)	0.9	362.3	1.5
		males	0.0	0.0	15.3	105.3	179.5	(.0)	0.8	300.9	1.9
VI	Commerce	Total	201.0	263.8	404.1	1 472.4	667.7	(48.0)	6.9	3 016.0	12.1
		males	140.0	175.4	304.5	352.2	478.9	(5.2)	2.9	1 453.9	9.2
VII	Transport	Total	19.2	50.4	91.2	462.9	935.3	(2.9)	4.8	1 563.9	6.3
		males	17.9	48.6	84.8	273.3	869.6	(0.6)	3.9	1 298.2	8.2
VIII	Banking	Total	17.5	26.9	124.4	679.7	101.3	(0.6)	2.3	952.2	3.8
		males	15.0	15.4	111.4	287.1	44.4	(.0)	1.3	474.7	3.0
IX	Services	Total	154.1	330.5	333.4	2 357.3	2 042.5	(50.8)	18.7	5 236.5	20.9
		males	101.3	264.1	222.3	849.4	644.1	(14.2)	6.1	2 087.3	13.1
X	Public admin.	Total	0.2	0.0	106.9	810.9	416.6	(.0)	258.6	1 593.2	6.4
		males	0.1	0.0	92.4	479.6	324.0	(.0)	244.1	1 140.3	7.2
U	Unknown	Total	0.3	1.7	1.2	11.0	26.8	(.2)	1 417.9	1 459.0	5.8
		males	0.3	1.4	1.0	3.4	17.3	(.0)	907.0	930.3	5.9
T	All sectors	Total	650.3	1 150.0	1 680.9	8 367.0	11 418.8	(136.5)	1 747.1	25 014.2	100.0
		males	512.2	945.5	1 393.4	3 893.6	7 943.0	(24.6)	1 189.7	15 877.5	100.0

Percent distributions

Total labour force

	EM	SE	MA	EE	WO	FW	U	T
I	21.5	24.6	0.6	3.3	49.7	(3.0)	0.2	100.0
II	0.1	0.1	2.2	18.3	79.2	(.0)	0.2	100.0
III	0.6	0.9	6.0	25.2	66.9	(.1)	0.4	100.0
IV	4.6	14.7	6.2	16.3	58.1	(.4)	0.2	100.0
V	0.0	0.0	4.4	43.0	52.3	(.0)	0.3	100.0
VI	6.7	8.7	13.4	48.8	22.1	(1.6)	0.2	100.0
VII	1.2	3.2	5.8	29.6	59.8	(0.2)	0.3	100.0
VIII	1.8	2.8	13.1	71.4	10.6	(0.1)	0.2	100.0
IX	2.9	6.3	6.4	45.0	39.0	(1.0)	0.4	100.0
X	0.0	0.0	6.7	50.9	26.1	(.0)	16.2	100.0
U	0.0	0.1	0.1	0.8	1.8)	(.0)	97.2	100.0
T	2.6	4.6	6.7	33.4	45.6)	(.5)	7.0	100.0

Male labour force

	EM	SE	MA	EE	WO	FW	U	T
I	23.4	26.0	0.7	1.5	48.3	(0.2)	0.1	100.0
II	0.1	0.1	2.2	16.0	81.5	(.0)	0.2	100.0
III	0.7	1.0	7.9	22.4	67.6	(.0)	0.3	100.0
IV	4.8	15.6	6.3	12.3	60.9	(0.1)	0.2	100.0
V	0.0	0.0	5.1	35.0	59.6	(.0)	0.3	100.0
VI	9.6	12.1	20.9	24.2	32.9	(0.4)	0.2	100.0
VII	1.4	3.7	6.5	21.1	67.0	(.0)	0.3	100.0
VIII	3.2	3.3	23.5	60.5	9.4	(.0)	0.3	100.0
IX	4.9	12.7	10.7	40.7	30.9	(0.7)	0.3	100.0
X	0.0	0.0	8.1	42.1	28.4	(.0)	21.4	100.0
U	.0	0.2	0.1	0.4	1.9	(.0)	97.5	100.0
T	3.2	6.0	8.8	24.5	50.0.	(0.2)	7.5	100.0

Notes:

Great Britain

Population of age 10 and over (1891-1911), age 12 and over (1921), age 14 and over (1931), age 15 and over (1951-1971)

1891-1901   Mixed industrial-occupational classification; most people classified by industry; persons who are classified according to their occupation only (the most important cases being: 'clerks in business'; 'engine drivers'; porters and messengers) are usually included under 'sector unknown'
1911   Different classification for England/Wales and Scotland; see notes below
1921   Mainly occupational classification
1931-1971   Purely industrial classification

1971   a) Resident population; including part-time workers; figures calculated on the basis of the reported 10% sample of census returns, by simply multiplying the reported figures by 10
             b) Foremen, supervisors, professional employees and apprentices
             c) Included in the labour force, but classification unknown
             d) Mainly persons out of work whose previous status/sector is unknown (total: 1,288.9, males: 852.3)

England and Wales

1891   a) First census with classification by status; low quality of returns
             b) Including self-employed
             c) Included in the labour force, but classification unknown
             d) Excluded from the labour force because of inadequate coverage

1901   a) Including self-employed
             b) Included in the labour force, but classification unknown
             c) Excluded from the labour force because of inadequate coverage

1911   a) Mixed industrial-occupational classification; see general notes
             b) Including self-employed
             c) Assisting children and other relatives in Agriculture only; other family workers not included in the labour force
             d) Mainly porters, messengers and warehousemen

1921   a) Occupational classification used, because only this classification is cross-tabulated with classification by status
             b) Assisting children and other relatives in Agriculture only; other family workers are not included in the labour force

1931   a) Including directors and higher management
             b) Branch and departmental managers, originally included among Employers; all other employees included among Workers
             c) Workers and employees; see note (b)
             d) Unknown whether included in the labour force
             e) Unemployed and temporarily ill persons, previously not included in the labour force

1951   a) Including part-time work (ca 747,000 persons)
             b) Directors, higher and middle management only; all other employees included among Workers
             c) Workers and employees; see note (b)
             d) Included among workers
             e) Included among workers; separate figures are low, because assisting housewives are probably included among part-time workers

540

1961   a) Including part-time work (ca. 1.9 million persons)

b) Managers, foremen and supervisors (manual and non-manual), professional employees; all other employees included among Workers

c) Workers and employees; see note (b)

d) Probably included among Workers

e) Including persons out of work due to unemployment and illness

Scotland

1891   a) Including self-employed

b) Included in the labour force, but classification unknown

c) Not included in the labour force

1901   a) Including self-employed

b) Including home-workers (domestic industrial work)

c) Assisting children and other relatives in Agriculture only; other family workers are not included in the labour force

1911   a) New industrial classification principle, not used in England and Wales; distribution by sector fairly comparable with previous censuses, but very limited comparability with 1921 occupational census

b) Assisting children and other relatives in Agriculture only; other family workers not included in the labour force

1921   a) Occupational classification used in order to make a comparison with England and Wales possible; however, in contrast to England and Wales, a cross-tabulation of the classifications by industry and status also exists

b) Assisting children and other relatives in Agriculture only; other family workers are not included in the labour force

1931   a) Including directors and higher management

b) Branch and departmental managers, originally included among Employers; all other employees included among Workers

c) Workers and employees; see note (b)

d) Unknown whether included in the labour force

1951   a) Including part-time work (130,540 persons)

b) Managers, foremen and supervisors, professional employees; all other employees included among Workers

c) Workers and employees; see note (b)

The Development of the Labour Force

Year	by Status				by Sector				Total labour force	Domestic services	Military personnel	Year
	Independent (IN)	Dependent (DE)	Family worker	Unknown	Agriculture (A)	Industry (I)	Services (S)	Unknown				
	percent distribution				percent distribution				in thousands			
1971	23.1	65.8	5.3	5.8	25.4	31.5	42.3	0.8	1 119.5	17.4	10.2	1971
1966	24.4	62.8	8.2	4.7	30.7	28.3	40.3	0.7	1 118.2	27.3	9.0	1966
1961	25.8	58.6	10.6	5.0	35.2	25.5	38.8	0.5	1 108.1	34.7	10.0	1961
1951	25.7	56.0	14.2	4.1	39.6	24.4	34.9	1.1	1 272.0	60.2		1951
1946	26.7	51.4	16.5	5.4	45.3	18.3	35.3	1.0	1 298.4	73.2	14.8	1946
1936	27.0	46.1	19.8	7.1	47.6	17.9	34.0	0.4	1 330.5	87.0	6.6	1936
1926	28.8	44.5	20.7	6.0	51.3	14.5	33.3	0.9	1 301.1	90.3	16.1	1926

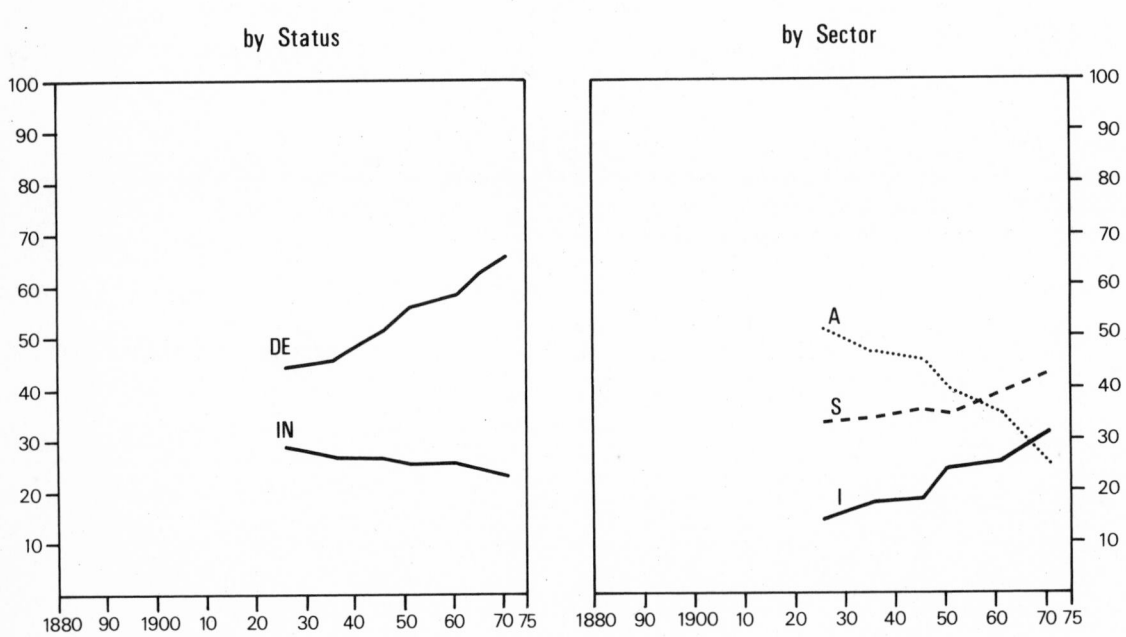

Ireland

Labour Force by Sector and Status 1926

Absolute figures in thousands

Sector			Employers	Self-employed	Employees	Workers	Apprentices	Family-workers	Out of work	Total	%
			EM	SE	EE	WO	AP	FW	OW a)	T	
I	Agriculture	Total	52.2	222.0	115.8			264.1	13.8	667.9	51.3
		males	41.9	183.8	114.0			192.4	13.5	545.5	56.8
II	Mining	Total	.0	.0	1.6			.0	.3	2.0	.2
		males	.0	.0	1.6			.0	.3	2.0	.2
III	Manufacturing	Total	6.0	27.7	83.0			1.5	15.0	133.2	10.2
		males	5.4	18.8	61.2			1.4	12.1	98.8	10.3
IV	Construction	Total	1.5	3.4	31.3			.3	13.6	50.0	3.8
		males	1.4	3.4	31.0			.3	13.5	49.6	5.2
V	Utilities	Total	.0	.0	2.5			.0	.4	2.9	.2
		males	.0	.0	2.4			.0	.4	2.8	.3
VI	Commerce	Total	10.8	21.6	68.7			2.3	9.5	112.9	8.7
		males	8.0	14.5	47.1			1.3	7.6	78.4	8.2
VII	Transport	Total	.6	4.2	46.1			.2	5.4	56.6	4.3
		males	.6	4.2	41.7			.2	5.3	52.0	5.4
VIII	Banking	Total	.1	.1	8.6			.0	.4	9.3	.7
		males	.1	.1	7.3			.0	.3	7.9	.8
IX	Services	Total	7.7	15.9	165.4			1.1	9.0	199.0	15.3
		males	5.1	7.2	47.8			.5	3.6	64.2	6.7
X	Public admin.	Total			49.8				6.1	55.9	4.3
		males			43.7				5.7	49.5	5.2
U	Unknown	Total	.2	.2	6.2			.1	4.7	11.4	.9
		males	.1	.2	4.9			.1	4.0	9.3	1.0
T	All sectors	Total	79.1	295.3	579.0			269.6	78.1	1 301.1	100.0
		males	62.6	232.3	402.6			196.0	66.4	960.0	100.0

Percent distributions

	Total labour force									Male labour force							
	EM	SE	EE	WO	AP	FW	OW	T		EM	SE	EE	WO	AP	FW	OW	T
I	7.8	33.2	17.3			39.5	2.1	100.0	I	7.7	33.7	20.9			35.3	2.5	100.0
II	2.1	1.3	79.6			.5	16.6	100.0	II	2.0	1.3	79.6			.5	16.6	100.0
III	4.5	20.8	62.3			1.1	11.2	100.0	III	5.5	19.0	61.9			1.4	12.2	100.0
IV	2.9	6.8	62.5			.6	27.1	100.0	IV	2.9	6.9	62.4			.6	27.2	100.0
V	.2	.0	85.8			.0	14.0	100.0	V	.2	.0	85.5			.0	14.3	100.0
VI	9.6	19.1	60.8			2.1	8.4	100.0	VI	10.2	18.5	60.0			1.6	9.6	100.0
VII	1.1	7.5	81.5			.4	9.6	100.0	VII	1.2	8.1	80.2			.4	10.1	100.0
VIII	1.4	1.4	93.0			.1	4.2	100.0	VIII	1.6	1.4	92.8			.1	4.2	100.0
IX	3.9	8.0	83.1			.5	4.5	100.0	IX	7.9	11.3	74.5			.7	5.7	100.0
X			89.2				10.8	100.0	X			88.4				11.6	100.0
U	1.6	2.2	54.5			.7	41.0	100.0	U	.8	2.5	53.1			.7	43.0	100.0
T	6.1	22.7	44.5			20.7	6.0	100.0	T	6.5	24.2	41.9			20.4	6.9	100.0

Labour Force by Sector and Status 1936

Absolute figures in thousands

Sector			Employ-ers	Self-employed	Employ-ees	Workers	Apprent-ices	Family-workers	Out of work	Total	%
			EM	SE	EE	WO	AP	FW	OW	T	
I	Agriculture	Total	50.5	212.1	106.1			244.6	20.1	633.5	47.6
		males	40.5	175.5	105.3			185.6	19.9	526.8	53.6
II	Mining	Total	.1	.1	2.5			.1	.4	3.1	.2
		males	.1	.1	2.5			.1	.4	3.1	.3
III	Manufacturing	Total	3.7	24.2	106.4			3.9	14.1	152.2	11.4
		males	3.3	17.7	70.5			3.3	11.4	106.3	10.8
IV	Construction	Total	1.9	4.0	48.8			1.1	22.1	77.8	5.8
		males	1.9	4.0	48.5			1.0	22.0	77.5	7.9
V	Utilities	Total	.0	.0	4.8			.0	.7	5.5	.4
		males	.0	.0	4.5			.0	.7	5.3	.5
VI	Commerce	Total	10.2	23.4	68.5			8.9	10.6	121.7	9.1
		males	7.9	15.3	46.9			4.6	8.7	83.5	8.5
VII	Transport	Total	.9	4.1	44.3			.6	6.0	55.8	4.2
		males	.8	4.0	40.1			.6	5.9	51.5	5.2
VIII	Banking	Total	.2	.1	14.0			.1	.8	15.1	1.1
		males	.1	.1	9.5			.1	.6	10.3	1.1
IX	Services	Total	7.3	16.3	165.1			4.2	10.8	203.7	15.3
		males	4.8	8.2	46.6			1.9	4.4	65.9	6.7
X	Public admin. a)	Total			49.3				6.8	56.1	4.2
		males			40.6				6.7	47.3	4.8
U	Unknown	Total	.0	.1	3.1			.0	2.6	5.9	.4
		males	.0	.1	2.1			.0	2.4	4.6	.5
T	All sectors	Total	74.8	284.4	612.8			263.5	95.1	1 330.5	100.0
		males	59.5	225.1	417.1			197.2	83.2	982.2	100.0

Percent distributions

	Total labour force									Male labour force							
	EM	SE	EE	WO	AP	FW	OW	T		EM	SE	EE	WO	AP	FW	OW	T
I	8.0	33.5	16.7			38.6	3.2	100.0	I	7.7	33.3	20.0			35.2	3.8	100.0
II	3.3	2.7	79.3			1.8	12.8	100.0	II	3.3	2.7	79.4			1.7	12.9	100.0
III	2.4	15.9	69.9			2.5	9.3	100.0	III	3.1	16.7	66.3			3.1	10.8	100.0
IV	2.4	5.1	62.7			1.4	28.3	100.0	IV	2.4	5.1	62.6			1.4	28.4	100.0
V	.1	.2	86.7			.1	12.9	100.0	V	.1	.2	86.1			.1	13.5	100.0
VI	8.4	19.3	56.3			7.3	8.7	100.0	VI	9.4	18.4	56.2			5.6	10.4	100.0
VII	1.6	7.3	79.4			1.1	10.8	100.0	VII	1.6	7.8	78.0			1.1	11.5	100.0
VIII	1.0	.8	92.4			.5	5.3	100.0	VIII	1.4	1.0	91.4			.6	5.6	100.0
IX	3.6	8.0	81.0			2.1	5.3	100.0	IX	7.2	12.4	70.7			2.9	6.7	100.0
X			87.8				12.1	100.0	X			85.8				14.1	100.0
U	.4	2.4	52.1			.2	45.0	100.0	U	.4	2.7	44.2			.2	52.5	100.0
T	5.6	21.4	46.1			19.8	7.1	100.0	T	6.1	22.9	42.5			20.1	8.5	100.0

Ireland

Labour Force by Sector and Status 1946

Absolute figures in thousands

Sector			Employers EM[a)]	Self-employed SE	Employees EE	Workers WO	Apprentices AP	Family-workers FW	Out of work OW	Total T	%
I	Agriculture	Total	47.5	207.4	116.7			203.5	13.7	588.7	45.3
		males	39.0	173.9	115.6			165.4	13.4	507.2	52.6
II	Mining	Total	.1	.1	8.3			.0	.5	9.0	.7
		males	.0	.1	8.0			.0	.5	8.7	.9
III	Manufacturing	Total	4.4	20.3	121.2			1.8	10.8	158.5	12.2
		males	3.9	16.1	79.0			1.6	8.0	108.5	11.3
IV	Construction	Total	1.7	3.6	45.7			.4	12.5	63.9	4.9
		males	1.7	3.6	45.3			.3	12.4	63.4	6.6
V	Utilities	Total	.0	.0	5.7			.0	.3	6.0	.5
		males	.0	.0	5.3			.0	.3	5.7	.6
VI	Commerce	Total	11.7	21.0	76.9			5.4	7.2	122.1	9.4
		males	9.1	14.2	49.0			2.9	5.6	80.8	8.4
VII	Transport	Total	1.1	4.3	50.6			.3	5.1	61.4	4.7
		males	1.1	4.3	45.3			.3	4.9	55.9	5.8
VIII	Banking	Total	.2	.1	11.1			.0	.3	11.8	.9
		males	.2	.1	8.7			.0	.3	9.3	1.0
IX	Services	Total	7.2	15.0	167.0			2.4	10.9	202.5	15.6
		males	5.2	7.8	47.7			1.3	3.2	65.2	6.8
X	Public admin.	Total			57.9				3.1	61.0	4.7
		males			45.4				2.8	48.2	5.0
U	Unknown	Total	.1	.3	6.8			.0	6.2	13.4	1.0
		males	.1	.2	4.4			.0	5.7	10.5	1.1
T	All sectors	Total	74.0	272.1	667.8			213.8	70.6	1 298.4	100.0
		males	60.4	220.2	453.8			171.9	57.2	963.5	100.0

Percent distributions

Total labour force

	EM	SE	EE	WO	AP	FW	OW	T
I	8.1	35.2	19.8			34.6	2.3	100.0
II	.6	.9	92.3			.2	6.0	100.0
III	2.8	12.8	76.5			1.1	6.8	100.0
IV	2.7	5.7	71.5			.6	19.5	100.0
V	.1	.1	94.0			.0	5.7	100.0
VI	9.6	17.2	62.9			4.4	5.9	100.0
VII	1.8	7.0	82.4			.6	8.2	100.0
VIII	1.6	1.2	94.2			.2	2.8	100.0
IX	3.6	7.4	82.5			1.2	5.4	100.0
X			94.9				5.1	100.0
U	.9	2.0	50.7			.1	46.2	100.0
T	5.7	21.0	51.4			16.5	5.4	100.0

Male labour force

	EM	SE	EE	WO	AP	FW	OW	T
I	7.7	34.3	22.8			32.6	2.6	100.0
II	.6	.9	92.2			.2	6.1	100.0
III	3.6	14.8	72.7			1.4	7.4	100.0
IV	2.7	5.7	71.4			.5	19.6	100.0
V	.1	.1	93.7			.1	6.0	100.0
VI	11.3	17.6	60.7			3.5	6.9	100.0
VII	1.9	7.7	81.1			.6	8.8	100.0
VIII	1.9	1.3	93.5			.2	3.2	100.0
IX	8.0	11.9	73.1			2.0	4.9	100.0
X			94.1				5.9	100.0
U	1.0	2.4	42.4			.1	54.1	100.0
T	6.3	22.9	47.1			17.8	5.9	100.0

545

Ireland

Labour Force by Sector and Status 1951

Absolute figures in thousands

Sector			Employ- ers EM	Self- employed SE	Employ- ees EE a)	Workers WO a)	Apprent- ices AP	Family- workers FW	Out of work OW b)	Total T	%
I	Agriculture	Total	33.6	205.0	85.8		.6	171.1	7.8	503.8	39.6
		males	28.0	174.6	85.2		.5	140.2	7.7	436.2	46.0
II	Mining	Total	.1	.4	9.3		.0	.1	.5	10.4	.8
		males	.1	.4	9.2		.0	.1	.5	10.3	1.1
III	Manufacturing	Total	4.0	17.9	148.5		12.3	1.5	8.6	192.8	15.2
		males	3.7	14.3	95.5		9.2	1.3	6.4	130.3	13.8
IV	Construction	Total	2.4	4.8	73.0		4.4	.4	11.3	96.3	7.6
		males	2.4	4.8	72.1		4.4	.4	11.3	95.4	10.1
V	Utilities	Total	.0	.0	9.8		.3	.0	.6	10.7	.8
		males	.0	.0	9.3		.3	.0	.6	10.2	1.1
VI	Commerce	Total	12.8	24.8	89.8		3.9	6.5	6.0	143.7	11.3
		males	9.9	16.8	56.9		2.4	3.7	4.5	94.1	9.9
VII	Transport	Total	.5	4.3	51.1		.5	.2	3.0	59.8	4.7
		males	.5	4.3	45.8		.5	.2	2.9	54.2	5.7
VIII	Banking	Total	.1	.1	11.9		.0	.0	.2	12.4	1.0
		males	.1	.1	8.9		.0	.0	.2	9.3	1.0
IX	Services	Total	4.1	10.9	149.2		13.0	.8	7.8	185.8	14.6
		males	2.9	5.6	43.2		8.2	.4	2.5	62.7	6.6
X	Public admin.	Total			40.4		.2		1.2	41.8	3.3
		males			32.8		.2		1.1	34.1	3.6
U	Unknown	Total	.1	.4	8.6		.1	.0	5.2	14.5	1.1
		males	.1	.3	5.5		.1	.0	4.4	10.4	1.1
T	All sectors	Total	57.8	268.6	677.4		35.4	180.6	52.3	1 272.0	100.0
		males	47.6	221.2	464.3		25.8	146.2	42.1	947.2	100.0

Percent distributions

Total labour force

	EM	SE	EE	WO	AP	FW	OW	T
I	6.7	40.7	17.0		.1	34.0	1.5	100.0
II	.9	3.7	89.3		.5	.7	4.9	100.0
III	2.1	9.3	77.0		6.4	.8	4.5	100.0
IV	2.5	5.0	75.7		4.6	.4	11.7	100.0
V	.1	.1	91.1		2.9	.0	5.8	100.0
VI	8.9	17.2	62.5		2.7	4.5	4.1	100.0
VII	.9	7.3	85.5		.9	.3	5.1	100.0
VIII	1.1	.8	95.8		.2	.1	2.0	100.0
IX	2.2	5.9	80.3		7.0	.4	4.2	100.0
X			96.7		.4	.0	2.9	100.0
U	.9	2.7	59.6		.6	.2	36.0	100.0
T	4.5	21.1	53.3		2.8	14.2	4.1	100.0

Male labour force

	EM	SE	EE	WO	AP	FW	OW	T
I	6.4	40.0	19.5		.1	32.1	1.8	100.0
II	.9	3.8	89.2		.5	.7	5.0	100.0
III	2.8	11.0	73.3		7.1	1.0	4.9	100.0
IV	2.5	5.0	75.6		4.7	.4	11.8	100.0
V	.1	.1	90.8		3.0	.0	6.0	100.0
VI	10.5	17.8	60.5		2.5	3.9	4.8	100.0
VII	.9	8.0	84.5		.9	.4	5.4	100.0
VIII	1.4	.9	95.1		.3	.2	2.0	100.0
IX	4.6	8.9	68.9		13.0	.6	4.0	100.0
X			96.3		.5		3.3	100.0
U	1.0	3.2	52.8		.5	.2	42.2	100.0
T	5.0	23.4	49.0		2.7	15.4	4.4	100.0

L a b o u r   F o r c e   b y   S e c t o r   a n d   S t a t u s   1 9 6 1

Absolute figures in thousands

Sector			Employers	Self-employed	Employees	Workers	Apprentices	Family-workers	Out of work	Total	%
			EM	SE	EE	WO	AP	FW	OW [a)]	T	
I	Agriculture	Total	16.9	195.8	57.8		.0	108.1	11.0	389.0	35.2
		males	14.0	169.6	57.3		.0	95.7	11.0	347.6	42.3
II	Mining	Total	.1	.2	9.2		.2	.0	.8	10.4	.9
		males	.1	.2	9.1		.2	.0	.8	10.2	1.2
III	Manufacturing	Total	1.3	9.7	159.7		7.8	.9	8.4	187.8	17.0
		males	1.2	8.4	103.3		5.8	.7	6.6	126.0	15.3
IV	Construction	Total	1.8	4.7	50.2		2.5	.5	14.1	73.7	6.6
		males	1.8	4.7	49.2		2.5	.4	14.1	72.7	8.8
V	Utilities	Total	.0	.0	9.8		.3	.0	.7	10.8	1.0
		males	.0	.0	9.2		.3	.0	.7	10.2	1.2
VI	Commerce	Total	8.8	29.0	91.1		5.7	6.4	5.9	146.9	13.3
		males	6.8	20.1	58.1		4.6	3.6	4.6	97.8	11.9
VII	Transport	Total	.4	4.1	49.1		.3	.2	3.6	57.8	5.2
		males	.3	3.1	43.3		.3	.2	3.5	50.8	6.2
VIII	Banking	Total	.1	.1	14.0		.0	.0	.2	14.4	1.3
		males	.1	.1	9.4		.0	.0	.1	9.7	1.2
IX	Services	Total	3.2	9.6	143.3		5.5	.9	6.8	169.3	15.3
		males	2.3	6.0	46.0		1.4	.4	2.2	58.3	7.1
X	Public admin.	Total			40.7		.1		1.0	41.8	3.8
		males			32.7		.1		.9	33.8	4.1
U	Unknown	Total	.0	.1	2.1		.0	.0	3.1	5.4	.5
		males	.0	.1	1.6		.0	.0	2.6	4.3	.5
T	All sectors	Total	32.7	253.3	627.1		22.5	117.0	55.6	1 108.1	100.0
		males	26.6	212.3	419.3		15.2	101.2	47.0	821.5	100.0

Percent distributions

	Total labour force								Male labour force							
	EM	SE	EE	WO	AP	FW	OW	T		EM	SE	EE	WO	AP	FW	OW	T
I	4.3	50.2	14.8		.0	27.7	2.8	100.0	I	4.0	48.8	16.5		.0	27.5	3.2	100.0
II	.6	1.5	88.9		1.5	.2	7.3	100.0	II	.7	1.5	88.7		1.6	.2	7.4	100.0
III	.7	5.2	85.0		4.1	.5	4.5	100.0	III	1.0	6.7	81.9		4.6	.6	5.2	100.0
IV	2.5	6.3	68.1		3.3	.6	19.1	100.0	IV	2.5	6.4	67.7		3.4	.6	19.3	100.0
V	.0	.0	90.6		3.1	.0	6.2	100.0	V	.0	.0	90.2		3.3	.0	6.5	100.0
VI	6.0	19.7	62.0		3.9	4.4	4.0	100.0	VI	7.0	20.5	59.4		4.7	3.7	4.7	100.0
VII	.7	7.0	85.0		.5	.4	6.3	100.0	VII	.6	6.2	85.4		.6	.4	6.9	100.0
VIII	.7	.9	97.2		.1	.1	1.1	100.0	VIII	1.0	1.3	96.4		.1	.0	.1	100.0
IX	1.9	5.7	84.6		3.2	.5	4.0	100.0	IX	3.9	10.3	78.9		2.4	.7	3.8	100.0
X			97.3		.3		2.4	100.0	X			96.9		.4		2.7	100.0
U	.1	1.6	40.0		.8	.2	57.4	100.0	U	.1	1.7	36.7		.8	.2	60.5	100.0
T	2.9	22.9	56.6		2.0	10.6	5.0	100.0	T	3.2	25.8	51.0		1.9	12.3	5.7	100.0

Ireland

Labour Force by Sector and Status 1966

Absolute figures in thousands

Sector			Employ-ers	Self-employed	Employ-ees	Workers	Apprent-ices	Family-workers	Out of work	Total	%
			EM	SE	EE	WO	AP	FW	OW	T	
I	Agriculture	Total	11.6	191.2	47.4		.0	83.4	10.0	343.5	30.7
		males	9.7	169.9	46.7		.0	74.1	10.0	310.3	37.4
II	Mining	Total	.0	.1	8.9		.3	.0	.9	10.2	.9
		males	.0	.1	8.6		.3	.0	.9	10.0	1.2
III	Manufacturing	Total	1.3	7.5	181.2		7.7	.6	8.8	207.2	18.5
		males	1.2	6.5	120.5		6.5	.5	6.5	141.8	17.1
IV	Construction	Total	2.4	5.5	60.6		5.1	.5	12.9	87.0	7.8
		males	2.4	5.5	59.3		5.1	.5	12.8	85.7	10.3
V	Utilities	Total	.0	.0	11.2		.8	.0	.6	12.5	1.1
		males	.0	.0	10.4		.7	.0	.5	11.7	1.4
VI	Commerce	Total	7.9	27.1	100.6		6.5	5.5	5.3	153.0	13.7
		males	6.3	19.6	64.2		5.5	3.1	4.1	102.8	12.4
VII	Transport	Total	.5	4.1	51.9		.5	.3	2.8	60.1	5.4
		males	.3	3.2	44.6		.5	.2	2.7	51.7	6.2
VIII	Banking	Total	.1	.2	15.7		.0	.0	.1	16.1	1.4
		males	.1	.2	10.1		.0	.0	.1	10.5	1.3
IX	Services	Total	3.4	9.8	149.4		7.1	.8	6.0	176.5	15.8
		males	2.4	6.2	50.7		1.8	.3	2.0	63.5	7.7
X	Public admin.	Total			43.2		.2		1.3	44.8	4.0
		males			33.7		.2		1.2	35.1	4.2
U	Unknown	Total		.1	3.7		.1		3.5	7.4	.7
		males		.1	2.8		.1		3.0	5.9	.7
T	All sectors	Total	27.3	245.5	673.7		28.3	91.2	52.2	1 118.2	100.0
		males	22.6	211.4	451.6		20.8	78.8	43.9	829.1	100.0

Percent distributions

	Total labour force								Male labour force							
	EM	SE	EE	WO	AP	FW	OW	T		EM	SE	EE	WO	AP	FW	OW	T
I	3.4	55.6	13.8		.0	24.3	2.9	100.0	I	3.1	54.8	15.0		.0	23.9	3.2	100.0
II	.4	.9	86.8		2.8	.2	8.8	100.0	II	.4	.9	86.8		2.9	.2	9.0	100.0
III	.6	3.6	87.5		3.7	.3	4.2	100.0	III	.9	4.6	85.0		4.6	.4	4.6	100.0
IV	2.8	6.3	69.6		5.9	.6	14.8	100.0	IV	2.8	6.4	69.2		6.0	.6	15.0	100.0
V	.0	.0	89.5		6.0	.0	4.5	100.0	V	.0	.0	88.9		6.4	.0	4.7	100.0
VI	5.2	17.7	65.8		4.2	3.6	3.5	100.0	VI	6.1	19.1	62.5		5.4	3.0	3.9	100.0
VII	.8	6.8	86.4		.9	.5	4.7	100.0	VII	.7	6.3	86.3		1.0	.4	5.3	100.0
VIII	.8	1.1	97.2		.0	.1	.8	100.0	VIII	1.2	1.6	96.2		.0	.1	.9	100.0
IX	1.9	5.6	84.7		4.0	.5	3.4	100.0	IX	3.8	9.8	79.8		2.8	.5	3.2	100.0
X			96.6		.5		2.8	100.0	X			95.9		.7		3.4	100.0
U		1.1	49.9		1.1		47.9	100.0	U		1.1	47.5		1.1		50.1	100.0
T	2.4	22.0	60.3		2.5	8.2	4.7	100.0	T	2.7	25.5	54.5		2.5	9.5	5.3	100.0

Labour Force by Sector and Status 1971

Absolute figures in thousands

Sector			Employers	Self-employed	Employees	Workers	Apprentices	Family-workers	Out of work	Total	%
			EM	SE	EE	WO	AP	FW	OW	T	
I	Agriculture	Total	184.4		35.5			53.1	11.5	284.0	25.4
		males	165.7		34.7			47.2	11.4	259.0	31.1
II	Mining	Total	.1		10.3			.0	1.1	11.5	1.0
		males	.1		10.0			.0	1.1	11.2	1.3
III	Manufacturing	Total	8.7		204.5			.4	12.1	225.8	20.2
		males	7.8		140.4			.4	9.7	158.3	19.0
IV	Construction	Total	11.4		72.5			.6	15.5	100.0	8.9
		males	11.4		70.9			.6	15.4	98.3	11.8
V	Utilities	Total	.0		14.2			.0	.6	14.8	1.3
		males	.0		13.1			.0	.6	13.7	1.6
VI	Commerce	Total	34.2		110.2			3.9	6.3	154.6	13.8
		males	26.6		73.0			2.2	5.2	107.0	12.9
VII	Transport	Total	5.5		54.4			.2	3.4	63.5	5.7
		males	4.5		45.9			.1	3.3	53.9	6.5
VIII	Banking	Total	.5		19.0			.0	.2	19.7	1.8
		males	.4		11.2			.0	.1	11.7	1.4
IX	Services	Total	13.9		164.3			.7	7.2	186.0	16.6
		males	10.1		60.3			.3	2.6	73.3	8.8
X	Public admin.	Total			48.9				1.2	50.1	4.5
		males			37.3				1.1	38.4	4.6
U	Unknown	Total	.2		3.2			.0	5.6	8.9	.8
		males	.2		2.0			.0	4.6	6.8	.8
T	All sectors	Total	258.9		737.0			58.9	64.7	1 119.5	100.0
		males	226.9		498.8			50.8	55.2	831.7	100.0

Percent distributions

Total labour force

	EM	SE	EE	WO	AP	FW	OW	T
I	64.8		12.5			18.7	4.0	100.0
II	.9		89.5			.0	9.6	100.0
III	3.9		90.6			.2	5.4	100.0
IV	11.4		72.5			.6	15.5	100.0
V	.0		96.0			.0	4.0	100.0
VI	22.1		71.3			2.5	4.1	100.0
VII	8.7		85.6			.3	5.4	100.0
VIII	2.3		96.6			.1	1.0	100.0
IX	7.5		88.3			.4	3.9	100.0
X			97.6				2.4	100.0
U	2.1		35.5			.2	62.3	100.0
T	23.1		65.8			5.3	5.8	100.0

Male labour force

	EM	SE	EE	WO	AP	FW	OW	T
I	64.0		13.4			18.2	4.4	100.0
II	.9		89.2			.0	9.8	100.0
III	5.0		88.7			.2	6.1	100.0
IV	11.6		72.1			.6	15.7	100.0
V	.0		95.7			.0	4.3	100.0
VI	24.9		68.2			2.1	4.8	100.0
VII	8.4		85.2			.3	6.1	100.0
VIII	3.8		95.3			.0	.9	100.0
IX	13.8		82.2			.4	3.6	100.0
X			97.1				2.9	100.0
U	2.3		29.6			.1	68.0	100.0
T	27.3		60.0			6.1	6.6	100.0

1926-1971	Present population of age 12 and over (1926) and of age 14 and over (1936-1971)
1926-1949	Including persons classified as Out of Work (unemployed, ill at home, etc.) but excluding persons in hospitals, etc.
1951-1971	Including persons classified as Out of Work (unemployed, ill at home, etc.) and persons temporarily in hospitals and similar institutions
1926	a) Including ca. 1,200 persons who were too old to work (age 70 and above) and some retired persons
1936	a) Including some central government employees; probably, unclarified error in source
1946	a) Including company directors, but excluding other persons classified as managers who are included among Employees
1951	a) Including all managers b) Including persons temporarily in hospitals and similar institutions
1961	a) Excluding persons temporarily in hospitals and similar institutions who are allocated to their respective status category

Italy

The Development of the Labour Force

Year	Independent (IN)	Dependent (DE)	Family worker	Unknown	Agriculture (A)	Industry (I)	Services (S)	Unknown	Total labour force	Domestic services	Military personnel	Year
	by Status				by Sector				Total			
	percent distribution				percent distribution				in thousands			
1971	20.5	70.0	4.6	4.9	16.3	42.2	36.6	4.9	19 807.3	229.8	373.9	1971
1961	20.5	66.4	10.2	2.9	28.2	39.4	29.5	2.9	20 172.9	412.1	363.6	1961
1951	22.2	56.0	16.5	5.3	40.0	30.4	24.3	5.3	20 671.8	377.3	141.3	1951
1936	26.0	50.3	21.2	2.6	47.0	27.3	23.2	2.5	18 823.8	660.7	80.9	1936
1931	27.5	53.7	18.9		47.3	29.4	23.3		17 262.5	498.0	77.4	1931
1921	42.5	57.5			55.7	23.9	20.4		18 431.2	445.6	213.5	1921
1911	38.7	61.3			55.5	26.8	17.7		16 370.5	483.0	184.8	1911
1901	45.9	53.1		1.0	59.4	23.7	16.9		16 272.5	482.1	204.0	1901
1881	44.1	51.0		4.8	56.7	26.9	16.2	.2	15 152.7	522.9	160.2	1881

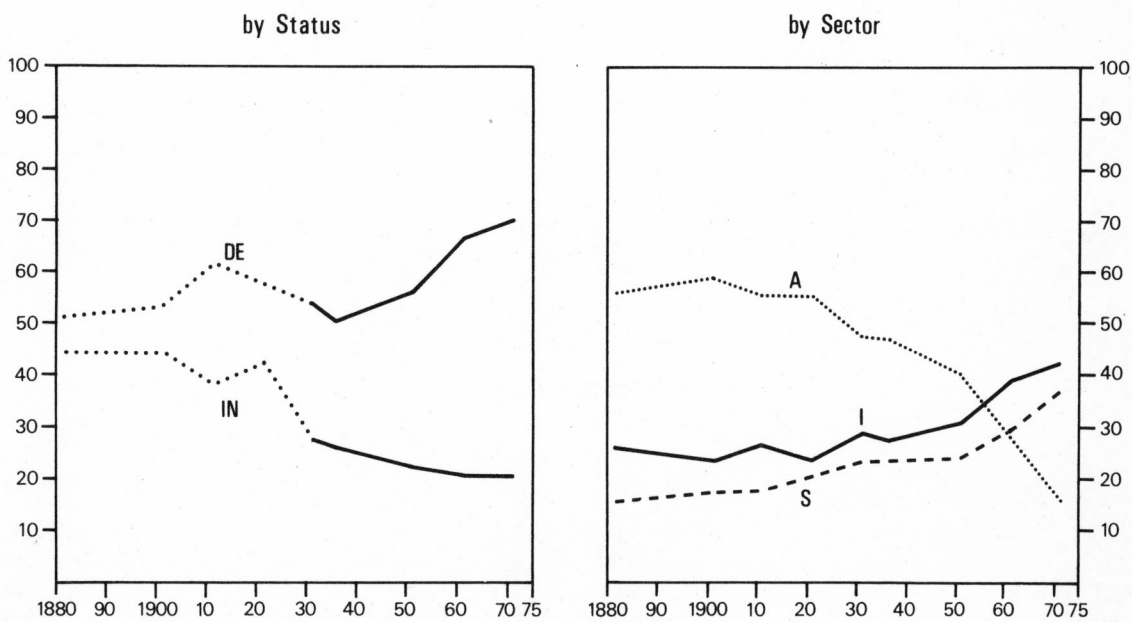

by Status   by Sector

551

Labour Force by Sector and Status 1881 [a]

Absolute figures in thousands

Sector			Employ-ers	Self-employed	Employ-ees	Workers	Apprent-ices	Family-workers	Un-known	Total	%
			EM	SE	EE	WO	AP	FW [b]	U	T	
I	Agriculture	Total	5 644.2		2 789.9				165.0	8 599.1	56.7
		males	3 479.4		1 873.9				144.8	5 498.0	58.2
II	Mining	Total	.0		.7				59.5	60.3	.4
		males	.0		.7				58.9	59.7	.6
III	Manufacturing	Total	492.7		2 402.0				240.6	3 135.3	20.7
		males	365.1		963.9				29.4	1 358.4	14.4
IV	Construction	Total	77.2		794.8					872.0	5.8
		males	77.2		726.7					803.9	8.5
V	Utilities [c]	Total									
		males									
VI	Commerce	Total	161.7		83.9				115.6	361.2	2.4
		males	132.3		72.0				74.7	279.0	3.0
VII	Transport	Total	115.2		197.8					313.0	2.1
		males	114.8		195.5					310.3	3.3
VIII	Banking	Total	36.8		3.7					40.5	.3
		males	36.3		3.7					40.0	.4
IX	Services	Total	162.0		1 092.2				152.1	1 406.3	9.3
		males	129.7		559.7				56.6	745.9	7.9
X	Public admin.	Total			333.5					333.5	2.2
		males			330.1					330.1	3.5
U	Unknown	Total			31.6					31.6	.2
		males			25.1					25.1	.3
T	All sectors	Total	6 689.9		7 730.0				732.8	15 152.7	100.0
		males	4 325.7		4 751.4				364.4	9 450.5	100.0

Percent distributions

	Total labour force									Male labour force							
	EM	SE	EE	WO	AP	FW	U	T		EM	SE	EE	WO	AP	FW	U	T
I	65.6		32.4				1.9	100.0	I	63.3		34.0				2.6	100.0
II	.0		1.2				98.7	100.0	II	.0		1.3				98.7	100.0
III	15.7		76.6				7.7	100.0	III	26.9		71.0				2.2	100.0
IV	8.9		91.1					100.0	IV	9.6		90.4					100.0
V									V								
VI	44.8		23.2				32.0	100.0	VI	47.4		25.8				26.8	100.0
VII	36.8		63.2					100.0	VII	37.0		63.0					100.0
VIII	90.9		9.1					100.0	VIII	90.8		9.2					100.0
IX	11.5		77.7				10.8	100.0	IX	17.4		75.0				7.6	100.0
X			100.0					100.0	X			100.0					100.0
U			100.0					100.0	U			100.0					100.0
T	44.1		51.0				4.8	100.0	T	45.7		50.3				3.9	100.0

Italy

Labour Force by Sector and Status 1901 [a]

Absolute figures in thousands

Sector			Employers EM[b]	Selfemployed SE[c]	Employees EE	Workers WO	Employees/ Workers EW[d]	Familyworkers FW[e]	Unknown U	Total T	%
I	Agriculture	Total	5 391.6		29.1	4 116.9	71.6		57.2	9 666.5	59.4
		males	3 405.4		27.7	2 917.8	59.8		55.4	6 466.2	58.8
II	Mining	Total	4.7		1.0	85.9				91.7	.6
		males	4.7		1.0	84.9				90.7	.8
III	Manufacturing	Total	933.8	297.5	39.1	1 875.8			19.8	3 166.0	19.5
		males	654.9	13.2	31.7	1 191.2			4.8	1 895.8	17.3
IV	Construction	Total	9.1		.2	527.7			29.4	566.4	3.5
		males	9.1		.1	521.9			29.4	560.5	5.1
V	Utilities	Total	.7		1.0	7.5			.0	9.2	.1
		males	.7		1.0	7.1			.0	8.9	.1
VI	Commerce	Total	344.0		140.7	.0			16.8	501.4	3.1
		males	255.2		120.1	.0			16.6	392.0	3.6
VII	Transport	Total	146.0		141.6	21.1	109.7		5.3	423.8	2.6
		males	145.6		138.0	21.0	106.3		5.3	416.2	3.8
VIII	Banking	Total	2.3		11.7					14.0	.1
		males	2.1		11.6					13.7	.1
IX	Services	Total	343.6		25.7	732.0	312.1		38.0	1 451.4	8.9
		males	225.7		25.3	280.5	199.4		36.6	767.5	7.0
X	Public admin.	Total					382.3			382.3	2.3
		males					377.2			377.2	3.4
U	Unknown	Total									
		males									
T	All sectors	Total	7 175.9	297.5	390.2	7 366.8	875.7		166.4	16 272.5	100.0
		males	4 703.5	13.2	356.6	5 024.4	742.7		148.1	10 988.5	100.0

Percent distributions

Total labour force

	EM	SE	EE	WO	EW	FW	U	T
I	55.8		.3	42.6	.7		.6	100.0
II	5.2		1.1	93.7				100.0
III	29.5	9.4	1.2	59.2			.6	100.0
IV	1.6		.0	93.2			5.2	100.0
V	7.8		11.2	81.0				100.0
VI	68.6		28.1				3.3	100.0
VII	34.5		33.4	5.0	25.9		1.2	100.0
VIII	16.3		83.7					100.0
IX	23.7		1.8	50.4	21.5		2.6	100.0
X					100.0			100.0
U								
T	44.1	1.8	2.4	45.3	5.4		1.0	100.0

Male labour force

	EM	SE	EE	WO	EW	FW	U	T
I	52.7		.4	45.1	.9		.9	100.0
II	5.2		1.1	93.7				100.0
III	34.5	.7	1.7	62.8			.3	100.0
IV	1.6		.0	93.1			5.2	100.0
V	8.1		11.4	80.5				100.0
VI	65.1		30.6				4.2	100.0
VII	35.0		33.2	5.0	25.5		1.3	100.0
VIII	15.5		84.5					100.0
IX	29.4		3.3	36.5	26.0		4.8	100.0
X					100.0			100.0
U								
T	42.8	.1	3.2	45.7	6.8		1.3	100.0

L a b o u r   F o r c e   b y   S e c t o r   a n d   S t a t u s   1 9 1 1 [a]

Absolute figures in thousands

Sector			Employers	Self-employed	Employees	Workers	Servants	Family-workers	Un-known	Total	%
			EM	SE	EE	WO	SV [b]	FW [c]	U	T	
I	Agriculture	Total	1 715.7	2 434.0	27.1	4 908.8				9 085.6	55.5
		males	1 109.0	1 792.1	25.9	3 185.3				6 112.2	54.3
II	Mining	Total	7.6	.0	2.7	99.5				109.8	.7
		males	7.4	.0	2.7	96.9				106.9	1.0
III	Manufacturing	Total	898.1	285.5	72.9	2 269.7	1.7			3 527.9	21.6
		males	665.6	57.4	59.3	1 378.5	.6			2 161.4	19.2
IV	Construction	Total	52.1	127.3	.0	518.2				697.6	4.3
		males	52.1	127.3	.0	507.2				686.5	6.1
V	Utilities	Total	2.6	.0	4.0	26.2				32.8	.2
		males	2.6	.0	3.8	25.7				32.1	.3
VI	Commerce	Total	319.9	16.2	105.4	68.7	69.9			580.1	3.5
		males	235.8	15.9	87.0	58.4	51.9			449.0	4.0
VII	Transport	Total	32.7	88.1	74.5	349.0				544.2	3.3
		males	32.5	87.6	69.4	340.4				530.0	4.7
VIII	Banking	Total	2.8	.0	26.4	2.2				31.4	.2
		males	2.7	.0	26.0	1.6				30.3	.3
IX	Services	Total	178.3	182.8	242.9	703.7				1 307.8	8.0
		males	131.2	159.8	116.7	287.9				695.7	6.2
X	Public admin.	Total			115.0	338.3				453.3	2.8
		males			112.8	332.3				445.2	4.0
U	Unknown	Total									
		males									
T	All sectors	Total	3 209.9	3 133.9	670.9	9 284.2	71.6			16 370.5	100.0
		males	2 238.9	2 240.0	503.7	6 214.3	52.4			11 249.4	100.0

Percent distributions

Total labour force

	EM	SE	EE	WO	SV	FW	U	T
I	18.9	26.8	.3	54.0				100.0
II	6.9	.0	2.5	90.6				100.0
III	25.5	8.1	2.1	64.3				100.0
IV	7.5	18.2	.0	74.3				100.0
V	8.0	.0	12.1	79.8				100.0
VI	55.1	2.8	18.2	11.8	12.0			100.0
VII	6.0	16.2	13.7	64.1				100.0
VIII	8.9	.0	83.9	7.2				100.0
IX	13.6	14.0	18.6	53.8				100.0
X			25.4	74.6				100.0
U								
T	19.6	19.1	4.1	56.7	.4			100.0

Male labour force

	EM	SE	EE	WO	SV	FW	U	T
I	18.1	29.3	.4	52.1				100.0
II	6.9	.0	2.5	90.6				100.0
III	30.8	2.7	2.7	63.8				100.0
IV	7.6	18.5	.0	73.9				100.0
V	7.9	.0	11.9	80.1				100.0
VI	52.5	3.5	19.4	13.0	11.5			100.0
VII	6.1	16.5	13.1	64.2				100.0
VIII	8.9	.0	85.9	5.3				100.0
IX	18.9	23.0	16.8	41.4				100.0
X			25.3	74.7				100.0
U								
T	19.9	19.9	4.5	55.2	.5			100.0

Italy

Labour Force by Sector and Status 1921

Absolute figures in thousands

Sector			Employers EM [a]	Self-employed SE	Employees EE	Workers WO	Apprentices AP	Family-workers FW [b]	Unknown U	Total T	%
I	Agriculture [c]	Total	3 427.5	2 416.8	33.6	4 386.2				10 264.1	55.7
		males	2 292.3	1 715.6	30.9	3 108.1				7 146.9	54.3
II	Mining	Total	.8	.0	.7	98.3				99.9	.5
		males	.8	.0	.7	97.5				99.0	.8
III	Manufacturing	Total	48.2	881.2	25.4	2 588.6				3 543.3	19.2
		males	44.9	623.7	21.1	1 667.0				2 356.8	17.9
IV	Construction	Total	17.1	6.0	.0	703.9				727.0	3.9
		males	17.1	6.0	.0	701.3				724.3	5.5
V	Utilities	Total	1.0	3.1	4.6	52.5				61.2	.3
		males	1.0	3.1	4.3	52.0				60.3	.5
VI	Commerce	Total	573.5	.0	174.1	45.1				792.8	4.3
		males	462.1	.0	130.0	39.6				631.8	4.8
VII	Transport	Total	3.5	84.4	120.5	530.2				738.6	4.0
		males	3.3	84.4	104.0	524.9				716.7	5.4
VIII	Banking	Total	3.7		43.0					46.8	.3
		males	3.5		37.9					41.4	.3
IX	Services [d]	Total	209.0	154.6	595.8	623.7				1 583.2	8.6
		males	161.2	110.4	346.2	203.2				821.0	6.2
X	Public admin. [d]	Total			197.1	377.4				574.5	3.1
		males			188.0	368.5				556.5	4.2
U	Unknown	Total									
		males									
T	All sectors	Total	4 284.4	3 546.1	1 194.8	9 406.0				18 431.2	100.0
		males	2 986.3	2 543.1	863.1	6 762.2				13 154.6	100.0

Percent distributions

Total labour force

	EM	SE	EE	WO	AP	FW	U	T
I	33.4	23.5	.3	42.7				100.0
II	.8	.0	.7	98.4				100.0
III	1.4	24.9	.7	73.1				100.0
IV	2.3	.8	.0	96.8				100.0
V	1.6	5.0	7.5	85.8				100.0
VI	72.3	.0	22.0	5.7				100.0
VII	.5	11.4	16.3	71.8				100.0
VIII	8.0	.0	92.0	.0				100.0
IX	13.2	9.8	37.6	39.4				100.0
X			34.3	65.7				100.0
U								
T	23.2	19.2	6.5	51.0				100.0

Male labour force

	EM	SE	EE	WO	AP	FW	U	T
I	32.1	24.0	.4	43.5				100.0
II	.8	.0	.7	98.5				100.0
III	1.9	26.5	.9	70.7				100.0
IV	2.4	.8	.0	96.8				100.0
V	1.7	5.1	7.1	86.2				100.0
VI	73.1	.0	20.6	6.3				100.0
VII	.5	11.8	14.5	73.2				100.0
VIII	8.6		91.4					100.0
IX	19.6	13.4	42.2	24.8				100.0
X			33.8	66.2				100.0
U								
T	22.7	19.3	6.6	51.4				100.0

I t a l y

L a b o u r   F o r c e   b y   S e c t o r   a n d   S t a t u s   1 9 3 1

Absolute figures in thousands

Sector			Employ-ers EM [a]	Self-employed SE	Employ-ees EE	Workers WO	Apprent-ices AP	Family-workers FW [b]	Un-known U	Total T	%
I	Agriculture [c]	Total	1 719.5	1 164.1	41.5	2 376.0		2 867.8		8 168.9	47.3
		males	1 586.4	1 122.4	40.0	1 965.5		1 915.5		6 629.9	49.6
II	Mining	Total	3.8	2.6	3.3	109.9		1.2		120.7	.7
		males	3.7	2.4	3.0	108.8		1.2		119.2	.9
III	Manufacturing	Total	374.0	331.9	153.0	2 784.8		163.9		3 807.6	22.1
		males	343.1	193.3	113.2	1 822.9		127.3		2 599.8	19.5
IV	Construction	Total	39.8	29.5	19.4	925.4		14.0		1 028.1	6.0
		males	39.7	29.4	17.9	920.6		13.9		1 021.5	7.6
V	Utilities	Total	4.6	1.5	12.7	91.3		.7		110.7	.6
		males	4.6	1.5	11.0	90.7		.6		108.5	.8
VI	Commerce	Total	527.7	.0	207.2	78.1		132.4		945.4	5.5
		males	435.4	.0	149.7	72.6		92.8		750.5	5.6
VII	Transport	Total	140.3	.0	164.0	467.4		22.9		794.7	4.6
		males	137.3	.0	143.9	463.8		22.4		767.3	5.7
VIII	Banking	Total			84.8	13.6				98.5	.6
		males			74.3	13.2				87.5	.7
IX	Services [d]	Total	235.8	172.3	539.7	718.1		51.9		1 717.8	10.0
		males	191.9	137.3	275.4	195.9		29.9		830.5	6.2
X	Public admin. [d]	Total			199.3	270.8				470.0	2.7
		males			185.1	259.3				444.4	3.3
U	Unknown	Total									
		males									
T	All sectors	Total	3 045.4	1 701.8	1 424.8	7 835.4		3 254.9		17 262.5	100.0
		males	2 743.2	1 486.3	1 013.6	5 913.3		2 203.7		13 358.9	100.0

Percent distributions

Total labour force

	EM	SE	EE	WO	AP	FW	U	T
I	21.0	14.3	.5	29.1		35.1		100.0
II	3.1	2.1	2.7	91.0		1.0		100.0
III	9.8	8.7	4.0	73.1		4.3		100.0
IV	3.9	2.9	1.9	90.0		1.4		100.0
V	4.2	1.3	11.5	82.4		.6		100.0
VI	55.8		21.9	8.3		14.0		100.0
VII	17.7		20.6	58.8		2.9		100.0
VIII			86.1	13.9				100.0
IX	13.7	10.0	31.4	41.8		3.0		100.0
X			42.4	57.6				100.0
U								
T	17.6	9.9	8.3	45.4		18.9		100.0

Male labour force

	EM	SE	EE	WO	AP	FW	U	T
I	23.9	16.9	.6	29.6		28.9		100.0
II	3.1	2.0	2.6	91.3		1.0		100.0
III	13.2	7.4	4.4	70.1		4.9		100.0
IV	3.9	2.9	1.7	90.1		1.4		100.0
V	4.2	1.3	10.2	83.6		.6		100.0
VI	58.0		20.0	9.7		12.4		100.0
VII	17.9		18.8	60.4		2.9		100.0
VIII			85.0	15.0				100.0
IX	23.1	16.5	33.2	23.6		3.6		100.0
X			41.6	58.4				100.0
U								
T	20.5	11.1	7.6	44.3		16.5		100.0

Italy

Labour Force by Sector and Status 1936

Absolute figures in thousands

Sector			Employers	Self-employed	Employees EE a)	Workers WO b)	Servants SV c)	Family-workers	Unknown	Total	%
			EM	SE				FW	U	T	
I	Agriculture	Total	200.3	2 674.3	21.9	2 431.5	1.6	3 507.2	6.0	8 842.8	47.0
		males	153.6	2 436.0	21.2	1 867.8	1.6	1 925.8	5.8	6 411.7	47.8
II	Mining	Total	3.0	1.7	3.8	117.5	1.3	1.2		128.4	.7
		males	2.9	1.7	3.5	115.8	1.2	1.2		126.3	.9
III	Manufacturing	Total	178.8	614.3	202.7	2 744.2	38.1	168.4		3 946.5	21.0
		males	158.2	463.3	151.1	1 717.4	34.9	117.5		2 642.5	19.7
IV	Construction	Total	37.2	65.6	24.8	835.2	3.0	13.3		979.1	5.2
		males	37.1	65.5	23.1	832.6	2.9	12.8		974.0	7.3
V	Utilities	Total	.6	.0	17.5	46.4	3.8	.1		68.4	.4
		males	.6	.0	15.2	46.1	3.7	.1		65.8	.5
VI	Commerce	Total	606.4	.0	232.6	60.0	44.7	196.3		1 140.0	6.1
		males	467.6	.0	174.5	49.4	43.2	95.6		830.4	6.2
VII	Transport	Total	68.0	87.0	125.0	346.6	57.3	18.4		702.2	3.7
		males	66.0	86.8	100.2	342.9	53.9	17.2		667.0	5.0
VIII	Banking	Total	.9	.0	85.5	1.7	12.3	.1		100.5	.5
		males	.9	.0	74.1	1.4	11.9	.1		88.2	.7
IX	Services	Total	183.8	173.5	521.8	273.2	719.5	78.7		1 950.3	10.4
		males	132.2	130.7	229.3	209.8	107.6	28.7		838.2	6.3
X	Public admin.	Total			244.4	153.6	89.2			487.2	2.6
		males			221.2	149.1	83.9			454.2	3.4
U	Unknown d)	Total			.4	1.3	.1		476.6	478.4	2.5
		males			.3	1.3	.1		304.2	306.0	2.3
T	All sectors	Total	1 279.0	3 616.3	1 480.4	7 011.1	970.8	3 983.7	482.5	18 823.8	100.0
		males	1 019.0	3 184.0	1 013.6	5 333.7	344.9	2 199.1	310.0	13 404.4	100.0

Percent distributions

Total labour force

	EM	SE	EE	WO	SV	FW	U	T
I	2.3	30.2	.2	27.5	.0	39.7	.1	100.0
II	2.3	1.3	2.9	91.5	1.0	1.0		100.0
III	4.5	15.6	5.1	69.5	1.0	4.3		100.0
IV	3.8	6.7	2.5	85.3	.3	1.4		100.0
V	.9	.0	25.6	67.8	5.5	.2		100.0
VI	53.2	.0	20.4	5.3	3.9	17.2		100.0
VII	9.7	12.4	17.8	49.4	8.2	2.6		100.0
VIII	.9	.0	85.0	1.7	12.3	.1		100.0
IX	9.4	8.9	26.8	14.0	36.9	4.0		100.0
X			50.2	31.5	18.3	.0		100.0
U			.1	.3			99.6	100.0
T	6.8	19.2	7.9	37.2	5.2	21.2	2.6	100.0

Male labour force

	EM	SE	EE	WO	SV	FW	U	T
I	2.4	38.0	.3	29.1	.0	30.0	.1	100.0
II	2.3	1.3	2.7	91.7	1.0	1.0		100.0
III	6.0	17.5	5.7	65.0	1.3	4.4		100.0
IV	3.8	6.7	2.4	85.5	.3	1.3		100.0
V	.9	.0	23.1	70.1	5.7	.2		100.0
VI	56.3	.0	21.0	6.0	5.2	11.5		100.0
VII	9.9	13.0	15.0	51.4	8.1	2.6		100.0
VIII	1.0	.0	83.9	1.5	13.4	.1		100.0
IX	15.8	15.6	27.3	25.0	12.8	3.4		100.0
X			48.7	32.8	18.5			100.0
U			.1	.4			99.4	100.0
T	7.6	23.8	7.6	39.8	2.6	16.4	2.3	100.0

Italy

Labour Force by Sector and Status 1951

Absolute figures in thousands

Sector			Employers EM [a]	Self-employed SE	Employees EE	Workers WO [b]	Apprentices AP	Family-workers FW	Unemployed U [c]	Total T	%
I	Agriculture	Total	95.6	2 476.5	27.1	2 660.2		3 001.8		8 261.2	40.0
		males	76.8	2 275.4	25.9	2 005.2		1 844.4		6 227.7	40.4
II	Mining	Total	1.2	4.0	6.2	166.8		1.3		179.5	0.9
		males	1.2	4.0	5.5	164.5		1.3		176.5	1.1
III	Manufacturing	Total	48.2	671.8	318.6	3 370.2		131.8		4 540.7	22.0
		males	46.4	557.1	232.1	2 235.7		112.1		3 183.4	20.7
IV	Construction	Total	19.6	67.3	39.0	1 334.1		12.7		1 472.7	7.1
		males	19.5	67.2	34.5	1 327.7		12.6		1 461.5	9.5
V	Utilities	Total	.5	.0	27.4	68.8		.1		96.8	.5
		males	.4	.0	23.0	68.1		.1		91.7	.6
VI	Commerce	Total	48.2	669.3	109.4	286.2		186.8		1 299.9	6.3
		males	46.8	500.2	79.9	221.0		115.9		963.9	6.3
VII	Transport	Total	7.3	114.8	168.4	480.9		13.8		785.3	3.8
		males	6.9	113.6	126.8	470.2		13.5		731.0	4.7
VIII	Banking	Total	6.3	.0	148.3	21.4		.3		176.2	.9
		males	6.0	.0	123.8	19.9		.2		149.9	1.0
IX	Services	Total	195.0	179.7	636.3	899.8		57.3		1 968.2	9.5
		males	175.8	127.4	294.0	324.0		30.1		951.3	6.2
X	Public admin. [d]	Total			377.5	419.3				796.8	3.9
		males			325.0	401.6				726.6	4.7
U	Unknown	Total							1 094.5	1 094.5	5.3
		males							737.1	737.1	4.8
T	All sectors	Total	421.9	4 183.4	1 858.0	9 707.9		3 406.0	1 094.5	20 671.8	100.0
		males	380.0	3 645.0	1 270.5	7 238.0		2 130.1	737.1	15 400.6	100.0

Percent distributions

Total labour force

	EM	SE	EE	WO	AP	FW	U	T
I	1.2	30.0	.3	32.2		36.3		100.0
II	.7	2.2	3.4	92.9		.7		100.0
III	1.1	14.8	7.0	74.2		2.9		100.0
IV	1.3	4.6	2.6	90.6		.9		100.0
V	.5	.0	28.3	71.1		.1		100.0
VI	3.7	51.5	8.4	22.0		14.4		100.0
VII	.9	14.6	21.4	61.2		1.8		100.0
VIII	3.5	.0	84.1	12.2		.2		100.0
IX	9.9	9.1	32.3	45.7		2.9		100.0
X			47.4	52.6				100.0
U							100.0	100.0
T	2.0	20.2	9.0	47.0		16.5	5.3	100.0

Male labour force

	EM	SE	EE	WO	AP	FW	U	T
I	1.2	36.5	.4	32.2		29.6		100.0
II	.7	2.2	3.1	93.2		.7		100.0
III	1.5	17.5	7.3	70.2		3.5		100.0
IV	1.3	4.6	2.4	90.8		.9		100.0
V	.5	.0	25.1	74.3		.1		100.0
VI	4.9	51.9	8.3	22.9		12.0		100.0
VII	.9	15.5	17.3	64.3		1.8		100.0
VIII	4.0	.0	82.6	13.3		.1		100.0
IX	18.5	13.4	30.9	34.1		3.2		100.0
X			44.7	55.3				100.0
U							100.0	100.0
T	2.5	23.7	8.2	47.0		13.8	4.8	100.0

Labour Force by Sector and Status 1961

Absolute figures in thousands

Sector			Employ-ers EM a)	Self-employed SE	Execu-tives EX	Employ-ees EE	Workers WO b)	Family-workers FW	Un-employed U c)	Total T	%
I	Agriculture	Total	11.7	1 946.2	4.1	32.9	2 074.5	1 623.6		5 693.0	28.2
		males	11.2	1 755.2	4.0	28.9	1 477.3	917.6		4 194.2	27.7
II	Mining	Total	1.5	3.2	.8	7.4	131.3	.9		145.1	.7
		males	1.4	3.2	.8	6.2	130.5	.9		143.0	.9
III	Manufacturing	Total	43.3	644.8	27.6	472.1	4 042.0	124.7		5 354.5	26.5
		males	41.5	530.3	27.0	320.8	2 854.4	91.0		3 865.0	25.5
IV	Construction	Total	26.4	90.7	4.2	55.1	2 152.6	16.5		2 345.5	11.6
		males	26.3	90.5	4.2	45.5	2 140.3	16.1		2 322.8	15.3
V	Utilities	Total	.2	.0	1.9	33.8	82.5	.0		118.4	.6
		males	.2	.0	1.9	28.0	81.4	.0		111.5	.7
VI	Commerce	Total	9.7	764.4	4.9	210.2	328.2	200.3		1 517.7	7.5
		males	9.2	562.8	4.7	133.6	242.9	108.4		1 061.7	7.0
VII	Transport	Total	3.4	117.6	12.4	189.8	631.8	11.7		966.6	4.8
		males	3.2	116.7	11.8	137.7	614.5	11.0		894.9	5.9
VIII	Banking	Total	1.0	1.6	12.8	177.7	24.9	.3		218.4	1.1
		males	.9	1.6	12.7	145.1	23.5	.2		184.0	1.2
IX	Services	Total	170.5	296.5	63.2	733.4	1 105.8	79.9		2 449.2	12.1
		males	151.7	216.3	50.3	314.5	468.3	36.5		1 237.7	8.2
X	Public admin. d)	Total	1.8		32.7	403.8	345.5			783.8	3.9
		males	1.8		32.1	346.1	333.2			713.2	4.7
U	Unknown	Total							580.8	580.8	2.9
		males							417.4	417.4	2.8
T	All sectors	Total	269.4	3 865.0	164.6	2 316.3	10 919.0	2 057.8	580.8	20 172.9	100.0
		males	247.5	3 276.5	149.5	1 506.5	8 366.3	1 181.7	417.4	15 145.3	100.0

Percent distributions

Total labour force

	EM	SE			FW	U	T
I	.2	34.2	.1	.6	36.4	28.5	100.0
II	1.0	2.2	.5	5.1	90.5	.6	100.0
III	.8	12.0	.5	8.8	75.5	2.3	100.0
IV	1.1	3.9	.2	2.3	91.8	.7	100.0
V	.2	.0	1.6	28.5	69.7	.0	100.0
VI	.6	50.4	.3	13.9	21.6	13.2	100.0
VII	.3	12.2	1.3	19.6	65.4	1.2	100.0
VIII	.4	.8	5.9	81.4	11.4	.1	100.0
IX	7.0	12.1	2.6	29.9	45.1	3.3	100.0
X	.2		4.1	51.5	44.1		100.0
U						100.0	100.0
T	1.3	19.2	.8	11.5	54.1	10.2	2.9	100.0

Male labour force

	EM	SE			FW	U	T
I	.3	41.8	.1	.7	35.2	21.9	100.0
II	1.0	2.2	.5	4.3	91.3	.6	100.0
III	1.1	13.7	.7	8.3	73.9	2.4	100.0
IV	1.1	3.9	.2	2.0	92.1	.7	100.0
V	.2	.0	1.7	25.1	73.0	.0	100.0
VI	.9	53.0	.4	12.6	22.9	10.2	100.0
VII	.4	13.0	1.3	15.4	68.7	1.2	100.0
VIII	.5	.9	6.9	78.9	12.8	.1	100.0
IX	12.3	17.5	4.1	25.4	37.8	3.0	100.0
X	.3		4.5	48.5	46.7		100.0
U						100.0	100.0
T	1.6	21.6	1.0	9.9	55.2	7.8	2.8	100.0

Labour Force by Sector and Status 1971

Absolute figures in thousands

Sector			Employers EM a)	Self-employed SE	Employees EE	Workers WO b)	Apprentices AP	Family-workers FW	Un-employed U c)	Total T	%
I	Agriculture	Total	12.5	1 447.9	41.7	1 309.4		423.2		3 234.7	16.3
		males	11.5	1 194.7	33.9	880.3		175.8		2 296.2	16.0
II	Mining	Total	1.7	3.6	11.2	66.2		.7		83.2	.4
		males	1.6	3.5	9.4	65.7		.6		80.9	.6
III	Manufacturing	Total	66.9	711.0	879.5	4 296.6		97.2		6 051.2	30.6
		males	58.9	590.5	625.1	3 102.7		57.2		4 434.3	30.8
IV	Construction	Total	52.5	203.0	110.8	1 681.4		15.6		2 063.3	10.4
		males	51.9	201.2	91.7	1 671.4		14.0		2 030.1	14.1
V	Utilities	Total	.3	.0	62.3	90.9		.1		153.6	.8
		males	.3	.0	53.1	89.7		.1		143.2	1.0
VI	Commerce	Total	39.8	856.5	316.8	486.8		248.7		1 948.5	9.8
		males	32.4	574.0	188.0	346.2		85.5		1 226.1	8.5
VII	Transport	Total	11.6	122.7	310.3	549.0		8.7		1 002.2	5.1
		males	11.2	120.4	244.9	530.9		7.1		914.6	6.4
VIII	Banking	Total	2.2	1.9	259.2	19.4		.9		283.7	1.4
		males	2.0	1.7	210.7	15.1		.5		230.0	1.6
IX	Services	Total	174.7	357.8	1 211.1	1 155.6		112.9		3 012.1	15.2
		males	155.8	225.2	566.8	560.4		43.1		1 551.2	10.8
X	Public admin. d)	Total			650.4	349.5				999.9	5.0
		males			524.7	322.5				847.2	5.9
U	Unknown	Total							974.8	974.8	4.9
		males							626.9	626.9	4.4
T	All sectors	Total	362.1	3 704.4	3 853.3	10 004.8		907.9	974.8	19 807.3	100.0
		males	325.6	2 911.3	2 548.1	7 584.9		383.9	626.9	14 380.6	100.0

Percent distributions

Total labour force

	EM	SE	EE	WO	AP	FW	U	T
I	.4	44.8	1.3	40.5		13.1		100.0
II	2.0	4.3	13.4	79.5		.8		100.0
III	1.1	11.7	14.5	71.0		1.6		100.0
IV	2.5	9.8	5.4	81.5		.8		100.0
V	.2	.0	40.6	59.2		.1		100.0
VI	2.0	44.0	16.3	25.0		12.8		100.0
VII	1.2	12.2	31.0	54.8		.9		100.0
VIII	.8	.7	91.4	6.8		.3		100.0
IX	5.8	11.9	40.2	38.4		3.7		100.0
X			65.0	35.0				100.0
U							100.0	100.0
T	1.8	18.7	19.5	50.5		4.6		100.0

Male labour force

	EM	SE	EE	WO	AP	FW	U	T
I	.5	52.0	1.5	38.3		7.7		100.0
II	2.0	4.4	11.6	81.2		.7		100.0
III	1.3	13.3	14.1	70.0		1.3		100.0
IV	2.6	9.9	4.5	82.3		.7		100.0
V	.2	.0	37.1	62.7		.1		100.0
VI	2.6	46.8	15.3	28.2		7.0		100.0
VII	1.2	13.2	26.8	58.1		.8		100.0
VIII	.9	.7	91.6	6.6		.2		100.0
IX	10.0	14.5	36.5	36.1		2.8		100.0
X			61.9	38.1				100.0
U							100.0	100.0
T	2.3	20.2	17.7	52.7		2.7	4.4	100.0

Notes:

1881–1901	Present population of 9 years of age and over
1911–1936	Present population of 10 years of age and over
1951	Resident population of 10 years of age and over
1961–1971	Resident population of 14 years of age and over
1881–1921	Conscripts included in the public sector
1931–1971	Conscripts distributed according to their previous occupation
1881–1921	Unemployed probably classified according to their previous occupation
1931–1971	Unemployed classified according to their previous occupation

1881
    a) Status classification in Agriculture and sectors VI–X partially inferred from the nature of occupation
    b) Unknown whether included in the labour force
    c) Included under Manufacturing and Construction

1901
    a) Status classification in Agriculture and sectors VI–X partially inferred from the nature of occupation
    b) Including managers
    c) Craftsmen; may also be dependent labourers
    d) No distinction possible between employees and workers
    e) Probably included among Employers

1911
    a) Status classification outside Manufacturing partially inferred from the nature of occupation; partially estimated in Transport and Construction
    b) Domestic servants active in production
    c) Probably included among the independent labour force

1921
    a) Including managers
    b) Probably included among the independent labour force
    c) Status classification in Agriculture inferred from the type of activity performed
    d) Status classification inferred from the nature of occupation

1931
    a) Including managers
    b) Originally included in the various status categories; calculated using a table with fewer, aggregated sectors, but a separate category of family workers
    c) Status classification in Agriculture inferred from the type of activity performed
    d) Status classification inferred from the nature of occupation

1936
    a) Including managers and high ranking civil servants
    b) Including home–workers
    c) Mainly domestic servants, including those active in production
    d) Mainly persons seeking work for the first time

1951, 1971
    a) Including self-employed liberal professionals
    b) Including home–workers
    c) Only persons seeking work for the first time
    d) Excluding state-run firm holdings

1961
    a) Including self-employed liberal professionals, directors of business firms and high ranking civil servants
    b) Including home–workers
    c) Only persons seeking work for the first time
    d) Excluding state-run firm holdings

The Development of the Labour Force

Year	by Status				by Sector				Total labour force	Domestic services	Military personnel	Year
	Inde-pendent (IN)	Depend-ent (DE)	Family worker	Un-known	Agricul-ture (A)	Indus-try (I)	Serv-ices (S)	Un-known				
	percent distribution				percent distribution				in thousands			
1971	11.1	85.2	2.6	1.1	6.1	36.2	49.4	8.4	4 789.6	47.2	30.3	1971
1960	15.4	79.4	4.7	.4	10.7	42.6	46.2	.5	4 168.6	116.4	77.4	1960
1947	18.6	70.9	10.4		18.8	35.0	45.1	1.0	3 866.4	189.0	157.6	1947
1930	21.4	78.6			20.6	36.2	42.2	1.0	3 179.2	243.6		1930
1920	20.0	80.0			23.6	35.6	39.7	1.1	2 719.2	221.1		1920
1909	25.4	74.6			28.4	32.8	37.9	1.0	2 259.1	214.1		1909
1899	26.0	74.0			30.8	31.6	35.8	1.8	1 920.9	197.6		1899

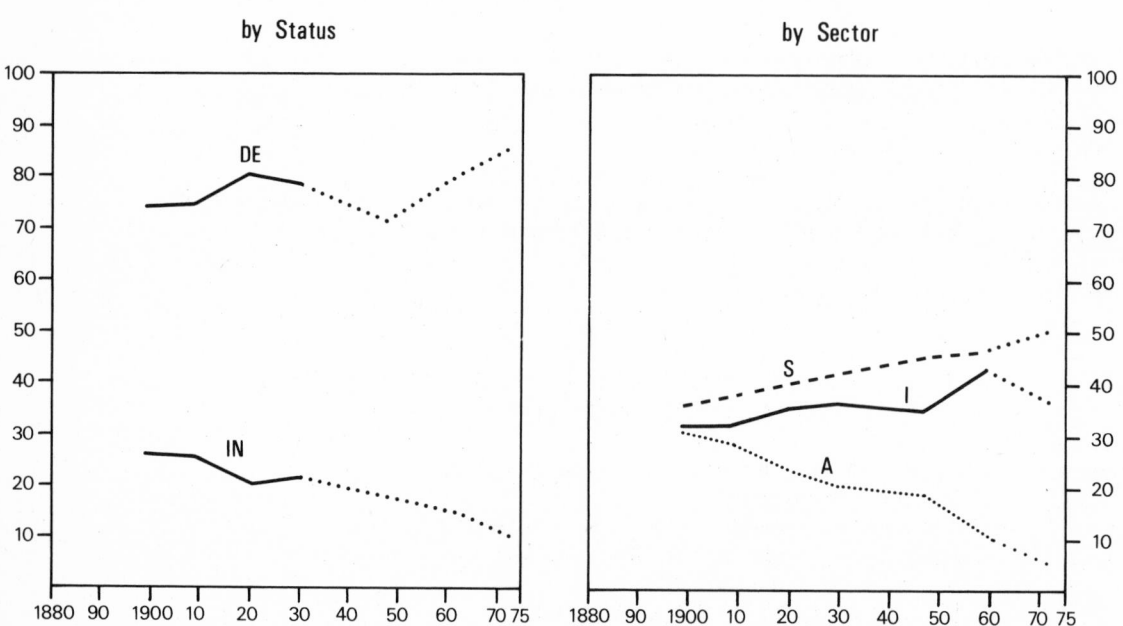

by Status   by Sector

Labour Force by Sector and Status 1899[a]

Absolute figures in thousands

Sector			Employ- ers	Self- employed	Employ- ees	Workers	Apprent- ices	Family- workers	Un- known	Total	%
			EM	SE[b]	EE	WO	AP	FW[c]	U	T	
I	Agriculture	Total	186.6	6.5	399.3					592.3	30.8
		males	165.6	6.3	340.3					512.2	34.4
II	Mining	Total	1.1	.3	14.6					16.0	.8
		males	1.1	.3	13.1					14.5	1.0
III	Manufacturing	Total	101.6	18.2	331.8					451.6	23.5
		males	81.3	17.5	280.5					379.4	25.5
IV	Construction	Total	30.4	1.7	98.3					130.4	6.8
		males	30.0	1.7	98.3					130.0	8.7
V	Utilities	Total	.1	1.1	8.0					9.2	.5
		males	.1	1.1	8.0					9.2	.6
VI	Commerce	Total	117.4	39.2	52.1					208.7	10.9
		males	88.6	30.0	50.0					168.6	11.3
VII	Transport	Total	20.2	12.1	73.0					105.3	5.5
		males	19.6	11.5	71.7					102.8	6.9
VIII	Banking	Total	1.3	7.4	1.4					10.0	.5
		males	1.3	7.3	1.4					9.9	.7
IX	Services	Total	40.2	62.2	215.5					317.9	16.5
		males	25.6	41.2	16.9					83.8	5.6
X	Public admin.[d]	Total	.0	35.3	10.1					45.5	2.4
		males	.0	37.2	8.0					45.2	3.0
U	Unknown	Total			34.0					34.0	1.8
		males			33.9					33.9	2.3
T	All sectors	Total	498.9	183.9	1 238.1					1 920.9	100.0
		males	413.3	154.0	922.1					1 489.4	100.0

Percent distributions

Total labour force

	EM	SE	EE	WO	AP	FW	U	T
I	31.5	1.1	67.4					100.0
II	7.0	2.0	91.1					100.0
III	22.5	4.0	73.5					100.0
IV	23.3	1.3	75.4					100.0
V	1.0	12.2	86.8					100.0
VI	56.2	18.8	25.0					100.0
VII	19.2	11.5	69.3					100.0
VIII	12.8	73.5	13.7					100.0
IX	12.7	19.6	67.8					100.0
X	.0	77.7	22.3					100.0
U			100.0					100.0
T	26.0	9.6	64.5					100.0

Male labour force

	EM	SE	EE	WO	AP	FW	U	T
I	32.3	1.2	66.4					100.0
II	7.5	2.2	90.3					100.0
III	21.4	4.6	73.9					100.0
IV	23.1	1.3	75.6					100.0
V	1.0	12.3	86.8					100.0
VI	52.5	17.8	29.7					100.0
VII	19.1	11.2	69.7					100.0
VIII	12.8	73.5	13.7					100.0
IX	30.6	49.2	20.2					100.0
X	.0	82.2	17.8					100.0
U			100.0					100.0
T	27.7	10.3	61.9					100.0

Labour Force by Sector and Status 1909 [a]

Absolute figures in thousands

Sector			Employers EM	Self-employed SE [b]	Employees EE	Workers WO	Apprentices AP	Family-workers FW [c]	Unknown U	Total T	%
I	Agriculture	Total	239.8		9.7	391.2				640.8	28.4
		males	190.5		9.4	328.5				528.4	30.7
II	Mining	Total	1.6		.5	20.9				23.0	1.0
		males	1.5		.4	18.4				20.4	1.2
III	Manufacturing	Total	100.9		31.4	414.4				546.8	24.2
		males	79.5		29.4	343.7				452.6	26.3
IV	Construction	Total	31.8		4.8	117.3				153.9	6.8
		males	31.5		4.7	117.3				153.6	8.9
V	Utilities	Total	.2		2.0	14.1				16.2	.7
		males	.2		2.0	14.0				16.2	.9
VI	Commerce	Total	126.7		62.3	62.0				251.1	11.1
		males	98.6		45.1	59.7				203.4	11.8
VII	Transport	Total	22.9		21.5	113.3				157.7	7.0
		males	22.3		19.5	111.9				153.8	8.9
VIII	Banking	Total	1.9		14.0	2.2				18.1	.8
		males	1.8		13.2	2.1				17.2	1.0
IX	Services	Total	48.6		85.9	244.5				378.9	16.8
		males	28.5		51.4	22.3				102.2	5.9
X	Public admin. [d]	Total	.0		36.5	13.0				49.5	2.2
		males	.0		38.8	10.3				49.1	2.9
U	Unknown	Total				23.2				23.2	1.0
		males				23.2				23.2	1.3
T	All sectors	Total	574.4		268.6	1 416.1				2 259.1	100.0
		males	454.4		213.9	1 051.5				1 719.9	100.0

Percent distributions

Total labour force

	EM	SE	EE	WO	AP	FW	U	T
I	37.4		1.5	61.1				100.0
II	7.0		2.0	91.0				100.0
III	18.5		5.7	75.8				100.0
IV	20.7		3.1	76.2				100.0
V	1.0		12.3	86.7				100.0
VI	50.5		24.8	24.7				100.0
VII	14.5		13.6	71.9				100.0
VIII	10.4		77.5	12.0				100.0
IX	12.8		22.7	64.5				100.0
X	.0		73.8	26.2				100.0
U				100.0				100.0
T	25.4		11.9	62.7				100.0

Male labour force

	EM	SE	EE	WO	AP	FW	U	T
I	36.1		1.8	62.2				100.0
II	7.5		2.2	90.3				100.0
III	17.6		6.5	75.9				100.0
IV	20.5		3.1	76.4				100.0
V	1.0		12.3	86.7				100.0
VI	48.5		22.2	29.4				100.0
VII	14.5		12.7	72.8				100.0
VIII	10.7		76.8	12.4				100.0
IX	27.9		50.3	21.9				100.0
X	.0		79.0	21.0				100.0
U				100.0				100.0
T	26.4		12.4	61.1				100.0

L a b o u r   F o r c e   b y   S e c t o r   a n d   S t a t u s   1 9 2 0 [a]

Absolute figures in thousands

Sector			Employ-ers	Self-employed [b]	Employ-ees	Workers	Apprent-ices	Family-workers [c]	Un-known	Total	%
			EM	SE	EE	WO	AP	FW	U	T	
I	Agriculture	Total	220.8	6.9	413.2					640.8	23.6
		males	190.9	6.7	353.1					550.8	26.4
II	Mining	Total	.6	2.4	42.6					45.7	1.7
		males	.6	2.3	39.5					42.4	2.0
III	Manufacturing	Total	92.0	51.4	562.9					706.2	26.0
		males	80.8	42.9	455.6					579.3	27.7
IV	Construction	Total	32.2	9.7	143.3					185.3	6.8
		males	31.9	9.3	143.2					184.4	8.8
V	Utilities	Total	.0	8.7	22.8					31.5	1.2
		males	.0	8.4	22.3					30.7	1.5
VI	Commerce	Total	122.0	109.9	69.7					301.6	11.1
		males	99.1	70.3	65.4					234.8	11.2
VII	Transport	Total	22.1	36.0	160.4					218.5	8.0
		males	21.6	28.9	157.9					208.4	10.0
VIII	Banking	Total	1.9	40.0	4.4					46.3	1.7
		males	1.8	32.2	3.4					37.4	1.8
IX	Services	Total	51.8	115.3	278.9					446.0	16.4
		males	32.1	65.5	31.8					129.3	6.2
X	Public admin. [d]	Total	.0	49.8	17.8					67.5	2.5
		males	.0	47.2	15.9					63.1	3.0
U	Unknown	Total			29.8					29.8	1.1
		males			28.9					28.9	1.4
T	All sectors	Total	543.4	430.0	1 745.7					2 719.2	100.0
		males	458.8	313.7	1 317.0					2 089.6	100.0

Percent distributions

	Total labour force									Male labour force							
	EM	SE	EE	WO	AP	FW	U	T		EM	SE	EE	WO	AP	FW	U	T
I	34.5		1.1	64.5				100.0	I	34.7		1.2	64.1				100.0
II	1.4		5.3	93.4				100.0	II	1.4		5.5	93.1				100.0
III	13.0		7.3	79.7				100.0	III	13.9		7.4	78.7				100.0
IV	17.4		5.3	77.4				100.0	IV	17.3		5.0	77.6				100.0
V	.1		27.6	72.3				100.0	V	.1		27.4	72.5				100.0
VI	40.4		36.5	23.1				100.0	VI	42.2		29.9	27.9				100.0
VII	10.1		16.5	73.4				100.0	VII	10.4		13.9	75.8				100.0
VIII	4.0		86.5	9.5				100.0	VIII	4.9		86.0	9.1				100.0
IX	11.6		25.8	62.5				100.0	IX	24.8		50.7	24.6				100.0
X	.0		73.7	26.3				100.0	X	.0		74.8	25.2				100.0
U				100.0				100.0	U				100.0				100.0
T	20.0		15.8	64.2				100.0	T	22.0		15.0	63.0				100.0

Netherlands

Labour Force by Sector and Status 1930 [a]

Absolute figures in thousands

Sector			Employers EM	Self-employed SE [b]	Employees EE	Workers WO	Apprentices AP	Family-workers FW [c]	Unknown U	Total T	%
I	Agriculture	Total	266.0	4.4	385.0					655.4	20.6
		males	215.0	4.2	326.6					545.8	22.6
II	Mining	Total	.7	2.7	46.2					49.5	1.6
		males	.7	2.6	44.4					47.7	2.0
III	Manufacturing	Total	99.6	74.3	648.3					822.1	25.9
		males	88.1	59.7	529.7					677.6	28.1
IV	Construction	Total	39.0	11.7	203.4					254.0	8.0
		males	38.8	11.0	203.1					252.9	10.5
V	Utilities	Total	.0	6.7	17.6					24.4	.8
		males	.0	6.5	17.2					23.7	1.0
VI	Commerce	Total	176.2	146.4	101.2					423.9	13.3
		males	141.3	83.5	95.0					319.7	13.2
VII	Transport	Total	27.2	41.5	171.0					239.6	7.5
		males	26.5	35.1	168.5					230.1	9.5
VIII	Banking	Total	2.2	40.4	5.6					48.2	1.5
		males	2.1	33.5	4.3					39.9	1.7
IX	Services	Total	70.8	157.0	339.8					567.5	17.9
		males	45.3	90.3	52.1					187.7	7.8
X	Public admin. [d]	Total	.0	42.6	18.8					61.4	1.9
		males	.0	40.4	17.0					57.4	2.4
U	Unknown	Total			33.2					33.2	1.0
		males			33.0					33.0	1.4
T	All sectors	Total	681.6	527.6	1 970.0					3 179.2	100.0
		males	557.8	366.8	1 490.8					2 415.4	100.0

Percent distributions

	Total labour force								Male labour force							
	EM	SE	EE	WO	AP	FW	U	T		EM	SE	EE	WO	AP	FW	U	T
I	40.6	.7	58.7					100.0	I	39.4	.8	59.8					100.0
II	1.4	5.4	93.2					100.0	II	1.4	5.5	93.1					100.0
III	12.1	9.0	78.9					100.0	III	13.0	8.8	78.2					100.0
IV	15.3	4.6	80.1					100.0	IV	15.3	4.4	80.3					100.0
V	.1	27.6	72.3					100.0	V	.1	27.4	72.5					100.0
VI	41.6	34.6	23.9					100.0	VI	44.2	26.1	29.7					100.0
VII	11.3	17.3	71.4					100.0	VII	11.5	15.2	73.2					100.0
VIII	4.5	83.9	11.6					100.0	VIII	5.3	83.9	10.8					100.0
IX	12.5	27.7	59.9					100.0	IX	24.1	48.1	27.8					100.0
X	.0	69.4	30.6					100.0	X	.0	70.4	29.6					100.0
U			100.0					100.0	U			100.0					100.0
T	21.4	16.6	62.0					100.0	T	23.1	15.2	61.7					100.0

Labour Force by Sector and Status 1947 [a]

Absolute figures in thousands

Sector			Employers EM [b]	Self-employed SE	Employees EE	Workers WO	Apprentices AP	Family-workers FW	Unemployed UE	Total T	%
I	Agriculture	Total	252.3		5.5	211.1		253.5	5.3	727.7	18.8
		males	238.5		5.1	198.5		111.4	5.2	558.8	19.1
II	Mining	Total	1.0	(.3)	4.8	45.3		.4	.7	52.1	1.3
		males	1.0	(.3)	4.6	44.4		.3	.6	50.8	1.7
III	Manufacturing	Total	121.9	(50.4)	124.6	690.3		22.3	17.7	976.8	25.3
		males	109.4	(41.0)	97.6	576.1		18.1	15.8	817.0	28.0
IV	Construction	Total	51.9	(17.9)	14.9	213.4		9.1	6.7	296.1	7.7
		males	51.6	(17.9)	13.5	213.2		8.6	6.7	293.5	10.0
V	Utilities	Total	.0		10.8	19.3		.0	.0	30.1	.8
		males	.0		9.8	19.0		.0	.0	28.9	1.0
VI	Commerce	Total	163.7		131.2	65.1		88.1	5.6	453.7	11.7
		males	147.8		68.1	61.8		17.4	4.2	299.4	10.2
VII	Transport	Total	33.5		55.9	134.9		8.3	10.9	243.5	6.3
		males	33.0		43.4	132.1		6.9	10.3	225.8	7.7
VIII	Banking	Total	2.9		58.6	5.1		.2	1.9	68.7	1.8
		males	2.9		43.2	4.3		.1	1.5	52.1	1.8
IX	Services	Total	92.5		200.5	309.0		21.5	20.4	643.9	16.7
		males	66.9		101.8	73.8		3.1	10.5	256.0	8.8
X	Public admin. [c]	Total	.0		166.2	169.0		.0		335.1	8.7
		males	.0		142.0	164.8		.0		306.8	10.5
U	Unknown	Total	.1		5.8	5.6		.0	27.4	38.9	1.0
		males	.1		3.7	5.2		.0	24.8	33.8	1.2
T	All sectors	Total	719.8		778.8	1 867.9		403.5	96.5	3 866.4	100.0
		males	651.1		532.9	1 493.3		165.9	79.6	2 922.8	100.0

Percent distributions

Total labour force

	EM	SE	EE	WO	AP	FW	UE	T
I	34.7		.8	29.0		34.8	.7	100.0
II	1.9	(.7)	9.3	86.9		.7	1.3	100.0
III	12.5	(5.2)	12.8	70.7		2.3	1.8	100.0
IV	17.5	(6.1)	5.0	72.1		3.1	2.3	100.0
V	.0		35.9	64.1		.0	.0	100.0
VI	36.1		28.9	14.3		19.4	1.2	100.0
VII	13.8		23.0	55.4		3.4	4.5	100.0
VIII	4.3		85.3	7.4		.3	2.7	100.0
IX	14.4		31.1	48.0		3.3	3.2	100.0
X	.0		49.6	50.4		.0		100.0
U	.2		15.0	14.4		.1	70.4	100.0
T	18.6		20.1	48.3		10.4	2.5	100.0

Male labour force

	EM	SE	EE	WO	AP	FW	UE	T
I	42.7		.9	35.5		19.9	.9	100.0
II	1.9	(.7)	9.0	87.3		.6	1.3	100.0
III	13.4	(5.0)	12.0	70.5		2.2	1.9	100.0
IV	17.6	(6.1)	4.6	72.6		2.9	2.3	100.0
V	.0		34.1	65.9		.0	.0	100.0
VI	49.4		22.8	20.6		5.8	1.4	100.0
VII	14.6		19.2	58.5		3.0	4.6	100.0
VIII	5.5		83.0	8.3		.2	3.0	100.0
IX	26.1		39.7	28.8		1.2	4.1	100.0
X	.0		46.3	53.7		.0		100.0
U	.2		10.9	15.5		.0	73.4	100.0
T	22.3		18.2	51.1		5.7	2.7	100.0

Netherlands

Labour Force by Sector and Status 1960

Absolute figures in thousands

Sector			Employ-ers	Self-employed	Employ-ees	Workers	Apprent-ices	Family-workers	Unem-ployed	Total	%
			EM	SE	EE	WO	AP	FW	UE	T	
I	Agriculture	Total	118.5	106.0	5.6	122.9		92.5	1.6	446.9	10.7
		males	114.7	104.2	4.9	119.2		61.8	1.6	406.4	12.5
II	Mining	Total	.2	.1	9.6	50.6		.1	.1	60.7	1.5
		males	.2	.1	8.9	50.1		.1	.1	59.5	1.8
III	Manufacturing	Total	53.5	40.3	271.7	887.2		15.4	2.3	1 270.4	30.5
		males	52.2	35.1	212.8	750.8		12.4	2.1	1 065.3	32.9
IV	Construction	Total	37.0	11.0	31.9	315.1		8.1	2.2	405.3	9.7
		males	36.8	11.0	28.2	313.9		7.8	2.2	399.9	12.3
V	Utilities	Total	.0	.0	16.7	23.8		.0	.0	40.4	1.0
		males	.0	.0	15.0	23.3		.0	.0	38.4	1.2
VI	Commerce	Total	74.0	82.1	240.3	84.4		59.4	1.6	541.8	13.0
		males	67.2	71.8	118.3	77.5		14.3	1.3	350.3	10.8
VII	Transport	Total	12.7	12.0	91.1	164.9		6.4	1.7	288.9	6.9
		males	12.4	11.9	75.9	161.5		4.3	1.7	267.7	8.3
VIII	Banking	Total	1.5	3.0	91.4	4.0		.2	.1	100.2	2.4
		males	1.5	2.9	65.8	2.2		.1	.1	72.6	2.2
IX	Services	Total	36.9	54.8	323.0	286.7		15.6	2.5	719.5	17.3
		males	32.5	38.8	152.4	84.1		3.0	1.2	312.0	9.6
X	Public admin. a)	Total	.0	.0	159.1	116.3		.0	.3	275.7	6.6
		males	.0	.0	139.4	112.1		.0	.2	251.7	7.8
U	Unknown	Total	.0	.1	1.8	11.5			5.4	18.8	.5
		males	.0	.1	1.1	10.6			4.8	16.6	.5
T	All sectors	Total	334.4	309.4	1 242.2	2 067.3		197.7	17.7	4 168.6	100.0
		males	317.6	275.8	822.6	1 705.4		103.9	15.3	3 240.5	100.0

Percent distributions

Total labour force

	EM	SE	EE	WO	AP	FW	UE	T
I	26.5	23.7	1.2	27.5		20.7	.4	100.0
II	.3	.1	15.8	83.4		.1	.2	100.0
III	4.2	3.2	21.4	69.8		1.2	.2	100.0
IV	9.1	2.7	7.9	77.7		2.0	.5	100.0
V	.0	.0	41.2	58.8		.0	.0	100.0
VI	13.7	15.2	44.3	15.6		11.0	.3	100.0
VII	4.4	4.2	31.5	57.1		2.2	.6	100.0
VIII	1.5	3.0	91.2	4.0		.2	.1	100.0
IX	5.1	7.6	44.9	39.8		2.2	.4	100.0
X	.0	.0	57.7	42.2		.0	.1	100.0
U	.2	.6	9.5	61.2			28.4	100.0
T	8.0	7.4	29.8	49.6		4.7	.4	100.0

Male labour force

	EM	SE	EE	WO	AP	FW	UE	T
I	28.2	25.6	1.2	29.3		15.2	.4	100.0
II	.3	.1	15.0	84.2		.1	.2	100.0
III	4.9	3.3	20.0	70.5		1.2	.2	100.0
IV	9.2	2.7	7.0	78.5		2.0	.5	100.0
V	.0	.0	39.2	60.8		.0	.0	100.0
VI	19.2	20.5	33.8	22.1		4.1	.4	100.0
VII	4.6	4.4	28.4	60.3		1.6	.6	100.0
VIII	2.0	4.0	90.6	3.0		.2	.1	100.0
IX	10.4	12.4	48.8	26.9		1.0	.4	100.0
X	.0	.0	55.4	44.5		.0	.1	100.0
U	.2	.6	6.3	64.1			28.7	100.0
T	9.8	8.5	25.4	52.6		3.2	.5	100.0

Labour Force by Sector and Status 1971

Absolute figures in thousands

Sector			Employers	Self-employed	Employees	Workers	Apprentices	Family-workers	Un-known	Total	%
			EM	SE	EE	WO	AP	FW	U	T	
I	Agriculture	Total	34.1	129.7	6.0	71.7		48.9		290.4	6.1
		males	33.4	127.3	5.1	67.9		17.9		251.6	7.1
II	Mining	Total	.0	.0	5.9	13.9		.0		19.9	.4
		males	.0	.0	5.1	13.8		.0		18.9	.5
III	Manufacturing	Total	20.8	14.4	348.2	758.2		9.8		1 151.4	24.0
		males	20.3	12.7	275.6	644.0		2.1		954.8	26.9
IV	Construction	Total	29.3	13.9	83.2	392.2		3.7		522.2	10.9
		males	29.2	13.8	74.4	389.1		2.1		508.5	14.3
V	Utilities	Total	.0	.0	19.8	21.2		.0		40.9	.9
		males	.0	.0	17.4	20.7		.0		38.1	1.1
VI	Commerce	Total	60.2	81.5	339.5	129.6		40.3		651.1	13.6
		males	54.9	70.5	183.4	113.3		5.3		427.3	12.0
VII	Transport	Total	9.0	12.0	126.4	129.3		3.0		279.7	5.8
		males	8.8	11.7	104.1	126.3		1.3		252.2	7.1
VIII	Banking	Total	1.5	3.8	116.0	4.7		.5		126.6	2.6
		males	1.5	3.5	75.5	2.4		.0		82.9	2.3
IX	Services	Total	42.9	60.4	592.1	316.4		16.7		1 028.6	21.5
		males	38.9	44.6	277.2	155.7		1.9		518.3	14.6
X	Public admin. a)	Total	.0	.0	224.0	54.0		.0		278.0	5.8
		males	.0	.0	189.6	48.4		.0		238.0	6.7
U	Unknown	Total	3.9	12.2	66.3	260.7		3.0	54.5	400.7	8.4
		males	3.6	10.2	35.7	168.3		.4	41.5	259.8	7.3
T	All sectors	Total	201.7	328.1	1 927.5	2 152.0		125.8	54.5	4 789.6	100.0
		males	190.5	294.4	1 243.1	1 749.8		31.1	41.5	3 550.4	100.0

Percent distributions

	Total labour force									Male labour force							
	EM	SE	EE	WO	AP	FW	U	T		EM	SE	EE	WO	AP	FW	U	T
I	11.7	44.7	2.1	24.7		16.8		100.0	I	13.3	50.6	2.0	27.0		7.1		100.0
II	.2	.1	29.7	70.0		.1		100.0	II	.2	.1	27.0	72.7		.0		100.0
III	1.8	1.3	30.2	65.9		.8		100.0	III	2.1	1.3	28.9	67.5		.2		100.0
IV	5.6	2.7	15.9	75.1		.7		100.0	IV	5.7	2.7	14.6	76.5		.4		100.0
V	.0	.0	48.2	51.8		.0		100.0	V	.0	.0	45.7	54.3		.0		100.0
VI	9.2	12.5	52.1	19.9		6.2		100.0	VI	12.8	16.5	42.9	26.5		1.2		100.0
VII	3.2	4.3	45.2	46.2		1.1		100.0	VII	3.5	4.6	41.3	50.1		.5		100.0
VIII	1.2	3.0	91.7	3.7		.4		100.0	VIII	1.8	4.3	91.1	2.8		.0		100.0
IX	4.2	5.9	57.6	30.8		1.6		100.0	IX	7.5	8.6	53.5	30.0		.4		100.0
X	.0	.0	80.6	19.4		.0		100.0	X	.0	.0	79.6	20.4		.0		100.0
U	1.0	3.0	16.5	65.1		.8	13.6	100.0	U	1.4	3.9	13.7	64.8		.2	16.0	100.0
T	4.2	6.8	40.2	44.9		2.6	1.1	100.0	T	5.4	8.3	35.0	49.3		.9	1.2	100.0

Notes:

1899–1971   Present population; unemployed classified according to previous occupation

1899   a) The status distribution of Public Administration is a crude estimate based on a given status
           distribution of the aggregate sectors IX and X, after excluding domestic servants
        b) Including assisting spouses
        c) All family workers included in the labour force, but classification of unmarried family workers
           unknown; see note (b)
        d) Excluding conscripts (who are classified according to their previous occupation)

1909   a) The status distributions of Mining, Utilities, and Public Administration are crude estimates based
           on the proportions in the 1899 census; see also note (a) for 1899
        b) Including assisting spouses
        c) All family workers included in the labour force, but classification of unmarried family workers
           unknown; see note (b)
        d) Excluding conscripts (who are classified according to their previous occupation)

1920   a) The status distributions of Mining, Utilities, and Public Administration are crude estimates based
           on the proportions in the 1930 census; see note (a) for 1930
        b) Including assisting spouses
        c) All family workers included in the labour force, but classification of unmarried family workers
           unknown; see note (b)
        d) Excluding conscripts (who are classified according to their previous occupation)

1930   a) The status distribution of Public Administration is a crude estimate based on a given status
           distribution of the aggregate sectors IX and X, after excluding domestic servants
        b) Including assisting spouses
        c) All family workers included in the labour force, but classification of unmarried family workers
           unknown; see note (b)
        d) Excluding conscripts (who are classified according to their previous occupation)

1947   a) Profound changes in classification as compared to previous censuses
        b) Including self-employed
        c) Including conscripts

1960–1971   a) Including conscripts

Norway

The Development of the Labour Force

Year	by Status				by Sector				Total labour force	Domestic services	Military personnel	Year
	Inde-pendent (IN)	Depend-ent (DE)	Family worker	Un-known	Agricul-ture (A)	Indus-try (I)	Serv-ices (S)	Un-known				
	percent distribution				percent distribution				in thousands			
1970	13.6	83.3	3.1	.0	11.6	37.3	50.9	.2	1 462.2	12.3	86.0	1970
1960	19.4	80.6			19.5	36.5	43.6	.4	1 406.4	34.7		1960
1950	24.7	71.1	4.1		25.9	36.5	37.1	.5	1 388.1	52.4	12.3	1950
1946	26.3	64.2	9.5		29.5	32.3	37.2	1.0	1 368.4	82.1	12.2	1946
1930	27.6	59.9	12.4		35.3	26.6	37.8	.3	1 166.5	120.3	3.3	1930
1920	25.9	66.2	7.8		36.8	27.0	30.6	5.7	1 069.9	97.0	3.4	1920
1910	31.4	61.3	7.3		39.2	26.0	32.0	3.1	914.7	112.5	4.9	1910
1900	32.4	58.9	8.7		41.3	26.9	29.8	2.0	870.0	91.7	6.0	1900
1890	33.2	57.6	9.2		49.6	22.9	26.4	.9	774.9	86.3	2.9	1890

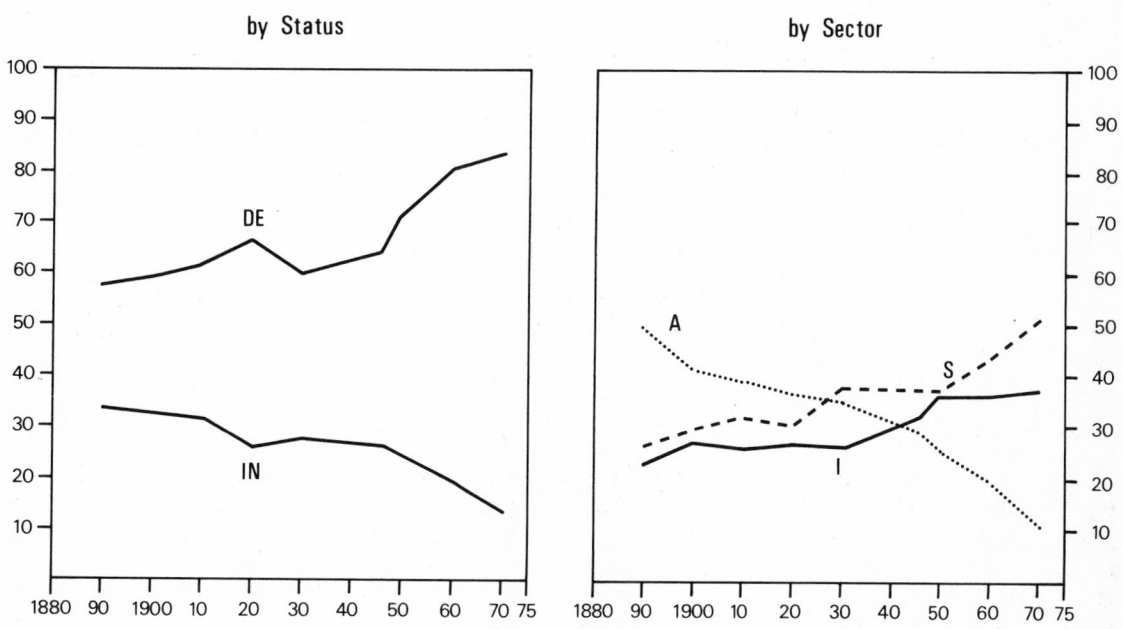

by Status   by Sector

Norway

Labour Force by Sector and Status 1890

Absolute figures in thousands

Sector			Employers EM	Selfemployed SE	Employees EE a)	Workers WO	Apprentices AP	Familyworkers FW b)	Unknown U	Total T	%
I	Agriculture	Total	164.7		3.9	144.6		71.2		384.4	49.6
		males	153.2		3.4	96.6		44.1		297.3	56.0
II	Mining	Total	.0		.3	4.0				4.4	.6
		males	.0		.3	3.9				4.3	.8
III	Manufacturing	Total	60.3		5.2	90.0				155.6	20.1
		males	30.6		4.9	70.0				105.6	19.9
IV	Construction	Total	4.3		.0	12.9				17.3	2.2
		males	4.3		.0	12.9				17.2	3.3
V	Utilities c)	Total	.0		.0	.3				.3	.0
		males	.0		.0	.3				.3	.1
VI	Commerce	Total	17.0		14.1	10.1				41.1	5.3
		males	13.2		9.6	9.3				32.1	6.1
VII	Transport	Total	3.9		12.1	26.7				42.8	5.5
		males	3.6		11.7	26.3				41.5	7.8
VIII	Banking	Total	.0		1.0	.1				1.2	.2
		males	.0		.9	.1				1.1	.2
IX	Services	Total	6.8		24.7	78.8				110.3	14.2
		males	2.7		7.6	7.2				17.4	3.3
X	Public admin. d)	Total	.0		7.3	1.8				9.1	1.2
		males	.0		7.2	1.7				8.9	1.7
U	Unknown	Total			.1	8.4				8.6	1.1
		males			.1	4.8				4.9	.9
T	All sectors	Total	257.1		68.9	377.7		71.2		774.9	100.0
		males	207.7		45.7	233.0		44.1		530.6	100.0

Percent distributions

Total labour force

	EM SE	EE	WO	AP	FW	U	T
I	42.9	1.0	37.6		18.5		100.0
II	1.0	7.6	91.4				100.0
III	38.8	3.4	57.8				100.0
IV	25.2	.0	74.8				100.0
V	.0	.0	100.0				100.0
VI	41.3	34.2	24.5				100.0
VII	9.1	28.4	62.5				100.0
VIII	3.6	84.5	11.9				100.0
IX	6.1	22.4	71.4				100.0
X	.0	80.6	19.4				100.0
U		1.4	98.6				100.0
T	33.2	8.9	48.7		9.2		100.0

Male labour force

	EM SE	EE	WO	AP	FW	U	T
I	51.5	1.1	32.5		14.8		100.0
II	.9	7.8	91.3				100.0
III	29.0	4.7	66.3				100.0
IV	25.1	.0	74.9				100.0
V	.0	.0	100.0				100.0
VI	41.1	29.9	29.0				100.0
VII	8.6	28.1	63.3				100.0
VIII	3.4	84.7	11.9				100.0
IX	15.3	43.6	41.1				100.0
X	.0	80.8	19.2				100.0
U		1.6	98.4				100.0
T	39.1	8.6	43.9		8.3		100.0

Labour Force by Sector and Status 1900

Absolute figures in thousands

Sector			Employ- ers	Self- employed	Employ- ees [a]	Workers	Apprent- ices	Family- workers [b]	Un- known	Total	%
			EM	SE	EE	WO	AP	FW	U	T	
I	Agriculture	Total	124.4	41.0	4.6	113.9		75.6		359.6	41.3
		males	112.9	40.4	3.4	80.9		50.0		287.6	48.0
II	Mining	Total	0.1	0.0	0.2	4.6				4.8	0.6
		males	0.0	0.0	0.2	4.6				4.8	0.6
III	Manufacturing	Total	34.9	33.0	6.7	113.5				188.1	21.6
		males	32.3	2.4	5.9	90.7				131.3	21.9
IV	Construction	Total	4.6	0.0	0.5	35.5				40.7	4.7
		males	4.6	0.0	0.5	35.5				40.6	6.8
V	Utilities [c]	Total									
		males									
VI	Commerce	Total	17.7	5.1	23.7	13.1				59.5	6.8
		males	13.9	3.2	12.9	11.9				41.9	7.0
VII	Transport	Total	2.1	2.0	14.3	32.2				50.7	5.8
		males	2.0	1.9	12.5	32.0				48.5	8.1
VIII	Banking	Total	0.0	0.0	1.4	0.2				1.6	0.2
		males	0.0	0.0	1.3	0.2				1.4	0.2
IX	Services	Total	8.3	8.7	23.5	93.6				134.1	15.4
		males	3.3	0.2	9.2	6.0				18.6	3.1
X	Public admin. [d]	Total	0.0	0.0	10.3	2.9				13.2	1.5
		males	0.0	0.0	9.7	2.9				12.6	2.1
U	Unknown	Total	0.0		1.0	16.7				17.7	2.0
		males	0.0		0.7	11.0				11.7	2.0
T	All sectors	Total	192.1	89.8	86.2	426.3		75.6		870.0	100.0
		males	169.0	48.2	56.3	275.6		50.0		599.0	100.0

Percent distributions

	Total labour force								Male labour force							
	EM	SE	EE	WO	AP	FW	U	T		EM	SE	EE	WO	AP	FW	U	T
I	34.6	11.4	1.3	31.7		21.0		100.0	I	39.3	14.0	1.2	28.1		17.4		100.0
II	1.1	0.6	3.7	94.6				100.0	II	1.0	0.6	3.7	94.7				100.0
III	18.5	17.6	3.6	60.3				100.0	III	24.6	1.8	4.5	69.1				100.0
IV	11.3	0.0	1.2	87.4				100.0	IV	11.3	0.0	1.2	87.5				100.0
V									V								
VI	29.7	8.5	39.8	22.0				100.0	VI	33.2	7.7	30.7	28.5				100.0
VII	4.2	3.9	28.3	63.6				100.0	VII	4.1	4.0	25.9	66.0				100.0
VIII	1.4	0.0	87.6	11.0				100.0	VIII	1.5	0.0	87.2	11.4				100.0
IX	6.2	6.5	17.5	69.8				100.0	IX	17.6	1.2	49.3	32.0				100.0
X	0.0	0.0	77.9	22.1				100.0	X	0.0	0.0	77.2	22.8				100.0
U	0.1		5.4	94.5				100.0	U	0.1		6.4	93.5				100.0
T	22.1	10.3	9.9	49.0		8.7		100.0	T	28.2	8.0	9.4	46.0		8.3		100.0

Norway

Labour Force by Sector and Status 1910

Absolute figures in thousands

Sector			Employers EM	Self-employed SE	Employees EE a)	Workers WO	Apprentices AP	Family-workers FW b)	Unknown U	Total T	%
I	Agriculture	Total	143.7	41.8	4.7	101.7		66.8		358.6	39.2
		males	130.1	40.8	3.6	79.7		51.2		305.4	48.5
II	Mining c)	Total	.0	.0	.4	7.7				8.1	.9
		males	.0	.0	.4	7.5				7.9	1.3
III	Manufacturing	Total	22.7	36.1	7.7	130.5				196.9	21.5
		males	21.9	2.0	6.5	101.9				132.4	21.0
IV	Construction	Total	5.9	.0	.8	25.8				32.5	3.6
		males	5.8	.0	.8	25.7				32.3	5.1
V	Utilities c)	Total	.0	.0	.1	.5				.5	.1
		males	.0	.0	.1	.5				.5	.1
VI	Commerce	Total	19.9	4.7	28.8	14.9				68.2	7.5
		males	14.9	3.4	14.0	13.0				45.3	7.2
VII	Transport	Total	2.3	.9	17.6	34.4				55.3	6.0
		males	2.2	.9	14.8	34.1				52.0	8.2
VIII	Banking	Total	.0	.0	.4	2.2				2.6	.3
		males	.0	.0	.4	1.8				2.2	.4
IX	Services	Total	8.4	1.2	42.0	101.7				153.3	16.8
		males	3.8	.3	10.7	5.5				20.3	3.2
X	Public admin. d)	Total	.0	.0	11.0	2.2				13.1	1.4
		males	.0	.0	10.1	2.1				12.2	1.9
U	Unknown	Total			2.8	22.6				25.4	2.8
		males			1.9	17.6				19.5	3.1
T	All sectors	Total	202.9	84.7	116.3	444.0		66.8		914.7	100.0
		males	178.9	47.4	63.1	289.5		51.2		630.0	100.0

Percent distributions

Total labour force

	EM	SE	EE	WO	AP	FW	U	T
I	40.1	11.7	1.3	28.4		18.6		100.0
II	.5	.2	5.0	94.2				100.0
III	11.5	18.3	3.9	66.3				100.0
IV	18.1	.1	2.5	79.3				100.0
V	.0	.0	12.9	87.1				100.0
VI	29.1	6.8	42.2	21.8				100.0
VII	4.2	1.6	31.9	62.3				100.0
VIII	.5	.0	16.1	83.4				100.0
IX	5.5	.8	27.4	66.3				100.0
X	.0	.0	83.4	16.6				100.0
U			10.9	89.0				100.0
T	22.2	9.3	12.7	48.5		7.3		100.0

Male labour force

	EM	SE	EE	WO	AP	FW	U	T
I	42.6	13.4	1.2	26.1		16.8		100.0
II	.5	.3	5.0	94.2				100.0
III	16.6	1.5	4.9	77.0				100.0
IV	18.1	.1	2.4	79.5				100.0
V	.0	.0	11.6	88.4				100.0
VI	32.9	7.5	30.9	28.6				100.0
VII	4.3	1.7	28.4	65.6				100.0
VIII	.6	.0	17.9	81.5				100.0
IX	18.8	1.3	52.6	27.3				100.0
X	.0	.0	82.8	17.2				100.0
U			9.5	90.5				100.0
T	28.4	7.5	10.0	45.9		8.1		100.0

L a b o u r   F o r c e   b y   S e c t o r   a n d   S t a t u s   1 9 2 0

Absolute figures in thousands

Sector			Employers EM	Self-employed SE	Employees EE a)	Workers WO	Apprentices AP	Family-workers FW b)	Unknown U	Total T	%
I	Agriculture	Total	184.3	4.3	121.4			83.7		393.6	36.8
	c)	males	169.2	4.2	97.5			65.3		336.2	43.5
II	Mining	Total	.0	.0	7.4					7.4	.7
		males	.0	.0	7.4					7.4	1.0
III	Manufacturing	Total	40.7	1.1	188.1					230.0	21.5
		males	34.6	.5	139.7					174.8	22.6
IV	Construction	Total	7.1	.0	42.5					49.6	4.6
		males	7.1	.0	42.5					49.6	6.4
V	Utilities c)	Total	.0	.0	1.5					1.5	.1
		males	.0	.0	1.5					1.5	.2
VI	Commerce	Total	25.9	32.5	13.8					72.2	6.8
		males	19.0	12.9	13.1					45.0	5.8
VII	Transport	Total	7.1	22.4	56.9					86.5	8.1
		males	7.0	16.3	56.6					79.9	10.3
VIII	Banking	Total	3.1	.1	1.0					4.2	.4
		males	1.8	.1	.9					2.8	.4
IX	Services	Total	9.1	22.5	120.9					152.4	14.2
		males	4.1	13.0	6.0					23.1	3.0
X	Public admin. d)	Total	.0	4.0	7.4					11.4	1.1
		males	.0	4.0	7.2					11.2	1.5
U	Unknown	Total		57.4	3.6					61.0	5.7
		males		37.3	3.6					40.8	5.3
T	All sectors	Total	277.4	144.3	564.5			83.7		1 069.9	100.0
		males	242.8	88.2	375.9			65.3		772.3	100.0

Percent distributions

	Total labour force								Male labour force							
	EM	SE	EE	WO	AP	FW	U	T		EM	SE	EE	WO	AP	FW	U	T
I	46.8		1.1	52.1		21.2		100.0	I	50.3		1.2	48.4		19.4		100.0
II	.0		.0	100.0				100.0	II	.0		.0	100.0				100.0
III	17.7		.5	81.8				100.0	III	19.8		.3	79.9				100.0
IV	14.3		.0	85.7				100.0	IV	14.3		.0	85.7				100.0
V	.0		.0	100.0				100.0	V	.0		.0	100.0				100.0
VI	35.9		45.0	19.1				100.0	VI	42.2		28.7	29.2				100.0
VII	8.3		25.9	65.8				100.0	VII	8.8		20.4	70.8				100.0
VIII	73.3		2.5	24.3				100.0	VIII	64.2		3.8	32.0				100.0
IX	6.0		14.7	79.3				100.0	IX	17.8		56.3	25.9				100.0
X	.0		35.3	64.7				100.0	X	.0		35.6	64.4				100.0
U			94.0	6.0				100.0	U			91.2	8.8				100.0
T	25.9		13.5	52.8		7.8		100.0	T	31.4		11.4	48.7		8.4		100.0

Labour Force by Sector and Status 1930

Absolute figures in thousands

Sector			Employ-ers EM	Self-employed SE	Employ-ees EE[a]	Workers WO[b]	Apprent-ices AP	Family-workers FW[c]	Un-known U	Total T	%
I	Agriculture	Total	213.2	5.0	194.1			(144.5)		412.3	35.3
		males	194.1	4.8	172.8			(72.5)		371.7	43.7
II	Mining	Total	.2	.5	13.0					13.8	1.2
		males	.1	.4	12.9					13.3	1.6
III	Manufacturing	Total	40.4	14.2	182.7					237.4	20.3
		males	33.1	10.3	134.4					177.7	20.9
IV	Construction	Total	12.0	1.5	39.2					52.7	4.5
		males	12.0	1.2	39.1					52.3	6.1
V	Utilities	Total	.0	1.2	4.8					6.0	.5
		males	.0	.9	4.8					5.7	.7
VI	Commerce	Total	32.5	55.6	21.4					109.6	9.4
		males	24.7	24.8	18.6					68.2	8.0
VII	Transport	Total	9.3	27.9	71.2					108.4	9.3
		males	9.1	22.0	70.8					101.9	12.0
VIII	Banking	Total	.1	7.9	.4					8.4	.7
		males	.0	6.0	.4					6.5	.8
IX	Services	Total	14.4	33.1	148.5			(.6)		196.1	16.8
		males	6.2	18.9	8.3			(.1)		33.5	3.9
X	Public admin.	Total	.0	12.3	6.1					18.4	1.6
		males	.0	9.7	5.9					15.6	1.8
U	Unknown	Total	.0	.5	3.1					3.5	.3
		males	.0	.4	3.0					3.4	.4
T	All sectors	Total	322.2	159.6	684.7					1 166.5	100.0
		males	279.4	99.4	470.9					849.7	100.0

Percent distributions

Total labour force

	EM	SE	EE	WO	AP	FW	U	T
I	51.7	1.2	47.1			(35.0)		100.0
II	1.7	3.7	94.7					100.0
III	17.0	6.0	77.0					100.0
IV	22.8	2.8	74.3					100.0
V	.2	19.5	80.4					100.0
VI	29.7	50.8	19.5					100.0
VII	8.6	25.7	65.7					100.0
VIII	.7	94.2	5.2					100.0
IX	7.4	16.9	75.8			(.3)		100.0
X	.0	66.7	33.3					100.0
U	.1	13.0	87.0					100.0
T	27.6	13.7	58.7					100.0

Male labour force

	EM	SE	EE	WO	AP	FW	U	T
I	52.2	1.3	46.5			(19.5)		100.0
II	.4	2.7	96.8					100.0
III	18.6	5.8	75.6					100.0
IV	22.9	2.3	74.8					100.0
V	.2	16.0	83.8					100.0
VI	36.3	36.4	27.3					100.0
VII	9.0	21.6	69.4					100.0
VIII	.8	93.3	5.9					100.0
IX	18.6	56.6	24.8			(.3)		100.0
X	.0	62.3	37.7					100.0
U	.1	10.4	89.5					100.0
T	32.9	11.7	55.4					100.0

Labour Force by Sector and Status 1946

Absolute figures in thousands

Sector			Employers	Self-employed	Employees a)	Workers b)	Apprentices	Family-workers c)	Unknown	Total	%
			EM	SE	EE	WO	AP	FW	U	T	
I	Agriculture	Total	164.8	66.3	7.0	166.2		(130.2)		404.3	29.5
		males	146.3	66.3	6.7	145.1		(63.0)		364.4	35.3
II	Mining	Total	.2	.1	.5	8.0				8.9	.7
		males	.2	.1	.5	7.9				8.7	.8
III	Manufacturing	Total	16.0	19.0	27.0	240.3				302.4	22.1
		males	14.9	14.9	19.7	182.2				231.7	22.5
IV	Construction	Total	8.0	18.9	4.0	91.4				122.4	8.9
		males	8.0	18.9	3.1	91.1				121.0	11.7
V	Utilities	Total	.0	.0	2.5	6.4				8.9	.7
		males	.0	.0	1.9	6.3				8.2	.8
VI	Commerce	Total	32.2	.0	70.6	20.0				122.8	9.0
		males	24.5	.0	33.0	16.7				74.3	7.2
VII	Transport	Total	6.2	8.5	39.6	76.4				130.8	9.6
		males	6.0	8.5	29.0	74.6				118.1	11.5
VIII	Banking	Total	.1	.9	10.2	.7				12.0	.9
		males	.1	.9	6.8	.4				8.2	.8
IX	Services	Total	13.6	4.2	47.6	135.0		(.2)		200.3	14.6
		males	9.0	1.8	26.3	15.1		(.0)		52.2	5.1
X	Public admin.	Total	.0	.0	27.2	15.3				42.5	3.1
		males	.0	.0	19.7	14.2				33.9	3.3
U	Unknown	Total			3.2	9.8				13.0	1.0
		males			1.9	9.0				10.9	1.1
T	All sectors	Total	241.3	118.0	239.5	769.7				1 368.4	100.0
		males	209.1	111.4	148.5	562.7				1 031.6	100.0

Percent distributions

	Total labour force									Male labour force							
	EM	SE	EE	WO	AP	FW	U	T		EM	SE	EE	WO	AP	FW	U	T
I	40.8	16.4	1.7	41.1		(32.2)		100.0	I	40.1	18.2	1.8	39.8		(17.3)		100.0
II	2.5	1.2	6.1	90.1				100.0	II	2.5	1.2	5.3	90.9				100.0
III	5.3	6.3	8.9	79.5				100.0	III	6.4	6.4	8.5	78.6				100.0
IV	6.6	15.5	3.3	74.7				100.0	IV	6.6	15.6	2.5	75.3				100.0
V	.0	.0	28.1	71.9				100.0	V	.0	.0	23.6	76.4				100.0
VI	26.2	.0	57.5	16.3				100.0	VI	33.0	.0	44.5	22.5				100.0
VII	4.8	6.5	30.3	58.4				100.0	VII	5.1	7.2	24.5	63.2				100.0
VIII	1.2	7.7	85.2	5.9				100.0	VIII	1.6	10.5	83.4	4.4				100.0
IX	6.8	2.1	23.7	67.4		(.1)		100.0	IX	17.3	3.4	50.3	29.0		(.0)		100.0
X	.0	.0	63.9	36.1				100.0	X	.0	.0	58.1	41.9				100.0
U			24.9	75.1				100.0	U			17.3	82.7				100.0
T	17.6	8.6	17.5	56.2				100.0	T	20.3	10.8	14.4	54.5				100.0

Labour Force by Sector and Status 1950

Absolute figures in thousands

Sector			Employers EM	Self-employed SE	Employees EE	Workers WO[a]	Apprentices AP	Family-workers FW[b]	Un-known U	Total T	%
I	Agriculture	Total	70.7	142.0	8.7	138.2		(57.3)		359.6	25.9
		males	62.5	136.3	8.3	125.5		(49.3)		332.7	31.4
II	Mining	Total	.1	.1	.6	8.4				9.3	.7
		males	.1	.1	.6	8.3				9.1	.9
III	Manufacturing	Total	17.2	25.3	40.3	275.0				357.7	25.8
		males	16.1	14.0	28.6	216.6				275.3	26.0
IV	Construction	Total	8.1	15.0	5.1	100.4				128.6	9.3
		males	8.0	15.0	3.9	99.6				126.6	11.9
V	Utilities	Total	.0	.0	2.8	8.2				11.0	.8
		males	.0	.0	2.2	8.0				10.2	1.0
VI	Commerce	Total	20.4	11.3	79.3	21.4				132.3	9.5
		males	15.9	8.3	37.3	16.9				78.4	7.4
VII	Transport	Total	5.7	8.4	44.7	81.4				140.3	10.1
		males	5.4	8.4	32.4	77.8				124.0	11.7
VIII	Banking	Total	.1	.1	15.0	1.0				16.1	1.2
		males	.1	.1	9.7	.5				10.3	1.0
IX	Services	Total	7.9	11.0	49.3	117.5				185.8	13.4
		males	5.3	6.1	27.3	17.5				56.2	5.3
X	Public admin.	Total	.0	.0	28.8	11.1				39.9	2.9
		males	.0	.0	21.0	9.5				30.5	2.9
U	Unknown	Total	.0	.0	.8	6.5				7.5	.5
		males	.0	.0	.5	6.1				6.6	.6
T	All sectors	Total	130.2	213.2	275.4	769.3				1 388.1	100.0
		males	113.6	188.3	171.6	586.4				1 059.9	100.0

Percent distributions

Total labour force

	EM	SE	EE	WO	AP	FW	U	T
I	19.7	39.5	2.4	38.4		(15.9)		100.0
II	1.4	1.1	7.0	90.5				100.0
III	4.8	7.1	11.3	76.9				100.0
IV	6.3	11.7	3.9	78.1				100.0
V	.1	.1	25.3	74.5				100.0
VI	15.4	8.5	59.9	16.2				100.0
VII	4.1	6.0	31.9	58.1				100.0
VIII	.6	.4	92.9	6.1				100.0
IX	4.3	5.9	26.5	63.3				100.0
X	.0	.0	72.2	27.8				100.0
U	.1	.5	11.3	87.6				100.0
T	9.4	15.4	19.8	55.4				100.0

Male labour force

	EM	SE	EE	WO	AP	FW	U	T
I	18.8	41.0	2.5	37.7		(14.8)		100.0
II	1.4	1.1	6.3	91.1				100.0
III	5.8	5.1	10.4	78.7				100.0
IV	6.4	11.9	3.1	78.7				100.0
V	.1	.1	21.2	78.6				100.0
VI	20.3	10.5	47.5	21.6				100.0
VII	4.4	6.8	26.1	62.8				100.0
VIII	1.0	.6	94.0	4.5				100.0
IX	9.5	10.8	48.5	31.2				100.0
X	.0	.0	68.8	31.2				100.0
U	.1	.5	6.8	92.1				100.0
T	10.7	17.8	16.2	55.3				100.0

L a b o u r   F o r c e   b y   S e c t o r   a n d   S t a t u s   1 9 6 0

Absolute figures in thousands

Sector			Employ- ers	Self- employed	Employ- ees	Workers	Apprent- ices	Family- workers	Un- known	Total	%
			EM	SE	EE	WO[a]	AP	FW	U	T	
I	Agriculture	Total	48.6	113.2	112.4					274.1	19.5
		males	44.5	107.9	109.0					261.4	24.1
II	Mining	Total	.2	.2	8.7					9.1	.6
		males	.2	.2	8.4					8.9	.8
III	Manufacturing	Total	13.8	11.9	332.5					358.2	25.5
		males	13.1	8.7	268.7					290.5	26.8
IV	Construction	Total	9.6	10.9	112.8					133.2	9.5
		males	9.5	10.9	110.6					131.0	12.1
V	Utilities	Total	.0	.0	12.8					12.8	.9
		males	.0	.0	11.8					11.8	1.1
VI	Commerce	Total	22.6	10.5	130.4					163.5	11.6
		males	18.1	8.2	72.6					98.9	9.1
VII	Transport	Total	6.0	7.6	153.8					167.5	11.9
		males	5.7	7.6	134.1					147.4	13.6
VIII	Banking	Total	.1	.0	21.6					21.7	1.5
		males	.1	.0	12.7					12.8	1.2
IX	Services	Total	9.0	8.8	189.2					206.9	14.7
		males	6.6	5.8	63.0					75.4	7.0
X	Public admin.	Total	.0	.0	54.0					54.0	3.8
		males	.0	.0	41.8					41.8	3.9
U	Unknown	Total	.0	.0	5.2					5.3	.4
		males	.0	.0	5.0					5.0	.5
T	All sectors	Total	109.8	163.3	1 133.3					1 406.4	100.0
		males	97.9	149.4	837.6					1 084.9	100.0

Percent distributions

	Total labour force									Male labour force							
	EM	SE	EE	WO	AP	FW	U	T		EM	SE	EE	WO	AP	FW	U	T
I	17.7	41.3	41.0					100.0	I	17.0	41.3	41.7					100.0
II	2.0	2.6	95.4					100.0	II	2.1	2.6	95.3					100.0
III	3.8	3.3	92.8					100.0	III	4.5	3.0	92.5					100.0
IV	7.2	8.2	84.6					100.0	IV	7.3	8.3	84.4					100.0
V	.0	.0	99.9					100.0	V	.0	.0	99.9					100.0
VI	13.8	6.4	79.7					100.0	VI	18.3	8.3	73.4					100.0
VII	3.6	4.5	91.9					100.0	VII	3.9	5.1	91.0					100.0
VIII	.4	.2	99.4					100.0	VIII	.7	.3	99.0					100.0
IX	4.4	4.2	91.4					100.0	IX	8.8	7.7	83.5					100.0
X	.0	.0	100.0					100.0	X	.0	.0	100.0					100.0
U	.1	.4	99.5					100.0	U	.1	.4	99.5					100.0
T	7.8	11.6	80.6					100.0	T	9.0	13.8	77.2					100.0

Labour Force by Sector and Status 1970

Absolute figures in thousands

Sector			Employ-ers	Self-employed	Employ-ees	Workers	Apprent-ices	Family-workers a)	Un-known	Total	%
			EM	SE	EE	WO	AP	FW	U	T	
I	Agriculture	Total	16.2	80.4	37.7			35.6		170.0	11.6
		males	15.2	78.2	35.4			10.7		139.6	13.2
II	Mining	Total	.2	.1	9.0			.0		9.3	.6
		males	.2	.1	8.6			.0		8.9	.8
III	Manufacturing	Total	9.7	7.8	372.3			1.1		390.9	26.7
		males	9.4	6.9	302.8			.3		319.4	30.2
IV	Construction	Total	9.1	14.1	105.4			.4		129.1	8.8
		males	9.1	14.1	102.3			.2		125.8	11.9
V	Utilities	Total	.0	.0	15.8			.0		15.8	1.1
		males	.0	.0	14.4			.0		14.5	1.4
VI	Commerce	Total	17.0	9.3	165.8			6.4		198.5	13.6
		males	13.9	7.4	92.9			.6		114.8	10.9
VII	Transport	Total	4.8	10.6	141.2			.4		156.9	10.7
		males	4.7	10.5	117.0			.2		132.3	12.5
VIII	Banking	Total	.0	.0	31.6			.0		31.7	2.2
		males	.0	.0	16.9			.0		16.9	1.6
IX	Services	Total	9.7	9.2	248.2			1.7		268.8	18.4
		males	7.6	6.1	98.8			.2		112.7	10.7
X	Public admin.	Total	.0	.0	88.0			.0		88.0	6.0
		males	.0	.0	70.4			.0		70.4	6.7
U	Unknown	Total	.0	.2	2.5			.0	.2	2.9	.2
		males	.0	.2	2.0			.0	.1	2.3	.2
T	All sectors	Total	66.9	131.8	1 217.6			45.7	.2	1 462.2	100.0
		males	60.3	123.6	861.5			12.2	.2	1 057.8	100.0

Percent distributions

Total labour force

	EM	SE	EE	WO	AP	FW	U	T
I	9.5	47.3	22.2			21.0		100.0
II	2.2	1.6	96.1			.1		100.0
III	2.5	2.0	95.2			.3		100.0
IV	7.1	10.9	81.6			.3		100.0
V	.2	.2	99.6			.0		100.0
VI	8.6	4.7	83.5			3.2		100.0
VII	3.1	6.7	90.0			.2		100.0
VIII	.1	.1	99.7			.0		100.0
IX	3.6	3.4	92.3			.6		100.0
X	.0	.0	100.0			.0		100.0
U	.6	5.6	86.9			.2	6.8	100.0
T	4.6	9.0	83.3			3.1	.0	100.0

Male labour force

	EM	SE	EE	WO	AP	FW	U	T
I	10.9	56.0	25.4			7.7		100.0
II	2.3	1.7	96.0			.1		100.0
III	2.9	2.2	94.8			.1		100.0
IV	7.2	11.2	81.3			.2		100.0
V	.2	.2	99.6			.0		100.0
VI	12.1	6.5	80.9			.5		100.0
VII	3.5	7.9	88.4			.1		100.0
VIII	.3	.2	99.5			.0		100.0
IX	6.8	5.4	87.7			.1		100.0
X	.0	.0	100.0			.0		100.0
U	.7	6.8	86.2			.2	6.1	100.0
T	5.7	11.7	81.4			1.2	.0	100.0

Notes:

1890–1930	Present population aged 15 years and over
1946–1970	Resident population aged 15 years and over (1946–1960) or 16 years and over (1970)

1890–1920   a) Including directors and high ranking officials
                    b) Adult children and other relatives in Agriculture; assisting married females not included in the labour force
                    c) Partially included in Manufacturing
                    d) Excluding conscripts (who are classified according to their previous occupation)

1930–1946   a) Including directors and high ranking officials as well as part of the family workers in Agriculture and hotels in sector IX
                    b) Including part of the family workers
                    c) Higher reporting as compared to earlier censuses due to changes in enumeration procedure

1950–1960   a) Including family workers
                    b) Assisting children in Agriculture only; assisting married females not included in the labour force

1970   a) Assisting spouses and children

Sweden

The Development of the Labour Force

Year	by Status				by Sector				Total labour force	Domestic services	Military personnel	Year
	Inde-pendent (IN)	Depend-ent (DE)	Family worker	Un-known	Agricul-ture (A)	Indus-try (I)	Serv-ices (S)	Un-known				
	percent distribution				percent distribution				in thousands			
1975	7.3	91.6	1.0	.1	6.4	37.8	55.5	.2	3 547.4	10.5	44.9	1975
1970	8.9	88.8	2.3	.0	8.1	40.3	51.4	.3	3 412.7	20.2	45.0	1970
1965	11.2	85.1	3.8	.0	11.8	43.1	44.7	.4	3 449.9	49.3	43.9	1965
1960	13.9	83.3	2.8	.0	13.8	45.1	40.8	.3	3 244.1	70.7	39.2	1960
1950	19.3	76.8	3.9	.0	20.3	40.6	38.3	.7	3 104.8	90.3	35.0	1950
1945	20.2	74.9	4.9		24.5	38.2	35.9	1.4	2 987.9	120.0	49.6	1945
1940	21.7	70.2	8.1		28.8	35.7	34.4	1.1	2 999.5	158.1	35.1	1940
1930	20.9	65.4	12.0	1.7	35.4	30.9	31.3	2.4	2 942.5	208.8	19.6	1930
1920	21.1	64.4	13.8	.7	40.4	30.4	27.5	1.7	2 620.6	194.4	19.2	1920
1910	26.4	55.4	16.8	1.4	45.6	24.7	26.6	3.1	2 229.3	221.0	28.3	1910
1900	30.5	48.0	21.5		49.8	19.7	23.2	7.3	1 974.0	212.7	38.8	1900
1890	32.7	44.3	23.0		53.9	14.4	24.5	7.2	1 750.4	237.9	40.3	1890
1880	32.4	44.9	22.7		51.5	9.9	28.0	10.6	1 656.7	313.4	40.0	1880

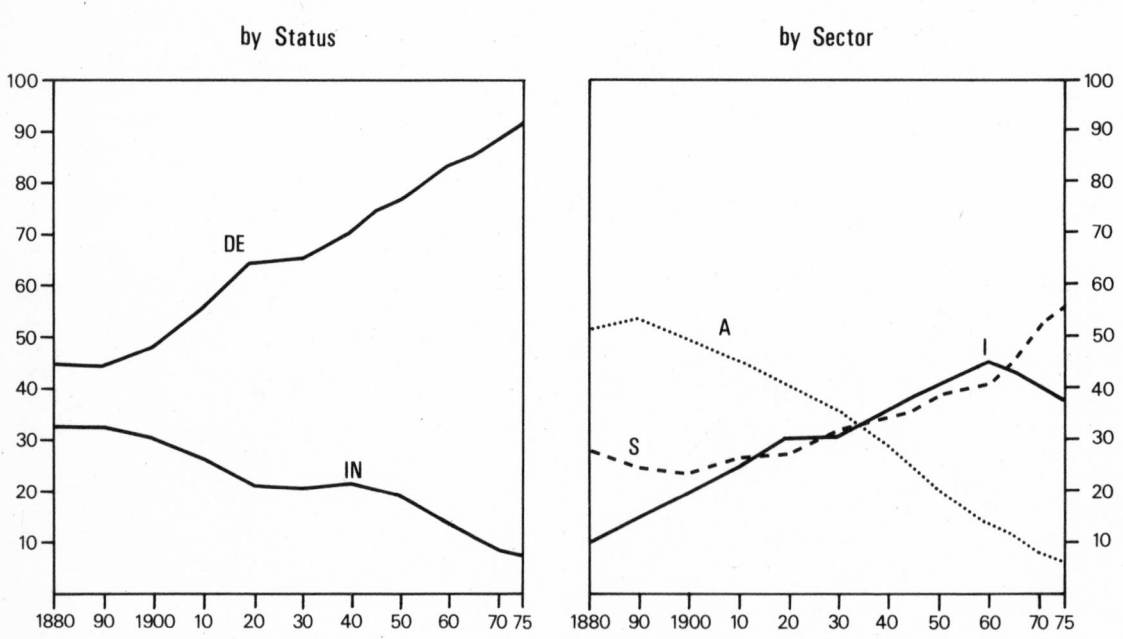

by Status   by Sector

Labour Force by Sector and Status 1880

Absolute figures in thousands

Sector			Employers EM	Self-employed SE	Employees EE	Workers WO[a]	Apprentices AP	Family-workers FW[b]	Servants SV[c]	Total T	%
I	Agriculture	Total	431.5	7.5	414.3			(376.3)	(217.2)	853.3	51.5
		males	395.6	7.5	239.7			(202.1)	(96.8)	642.9	54.4
II	Mining	Total	.4	.9	17.1				(4.3)	18.4	1.1
		males	.3	.9	17.0				(1.1)	18.3	1.6
III	Manufacturing	Total	68.2	.8	59.9				(18.2)	128.9	7.8
		males	67.2	.7	47.7				(4.8)	115.6	9.8
IV	Construction	Total	8.0	1.1	7.8				(2.4)	16.9	1.0
		males	8.0	1.1	7.6				(.3)	16.7	1.4
V	Utilities	Total	.0	.0	.4				(.0)	.4	.0
		males	.0	.0	.4				(.0)	.4	.0
VI	Commerce	Total	18.0	10.6	.5				(16.7)	29.1	1.8
		males	15.6	9.5	.5				(2.5)	25.5	2.2
VII	Transport	Total	2.1	11.3	27.9				(4.5)	41.2	2.5
		males	2.0	11.1	27.6				(.4)	40.8	3.5
VIII	Banking	Total	.0	.7	.1				(.7)	.8	.0
		males	.0	.7	.1				(.0)	.8	.1
IX	Services[d]	Total	8.1	13.2	321.7				(17.7)	343.0	20.7
		males	4.1	8.6	117.1				(2.9)	129.8	11.0
X	Public admin.	Total	.0	7.0	42.3				(11.0)	49.3	3.0
		males	.0	7.0	42.3				(1.4)	49.2	4.2
U	Unknown	Total	.3	.2	174.9				(3.6)	175.5	10.6
		males	.3	.2	140.8				(.4)	141.4	12.0
T	All sectors	Total	536.4	53.4	1 066.8				(296.3)	1 656.7	100.0
		males	493.1	47.4	640.8				(110.6)	1 181.3	100.0

Percent distributions

Total labour force

	EM	SE	EE	WO	AP	FW	SV	T
I	50.6		.9	48.6		(44.1)	(25.5)	100.0
II	1.9		5.1	92.9			(23.2)	100.0
III	52.9		.6	46.5			(14.1)	100.0
IV	47.4		6.6	46.0			(14.5)	100.0
V	.0		6.1	93.9			(10.6)	100.0
VI	61.9		36.3	1.8			(57.4)	100.0
VII	5.0		27.4	67.6			(10.9)	100.0
VIII	.0		91.9	8.1			(87.2)	100.0
IX	2.3		3.9	93.8			(5.2)	100.0
X	.0		14.2	85.8			(22.3)	100.0
U	.2		.1	99.7			(2.0)	100.0
T	32.4		3.2	64.4			(17.9)	100.0

Male labour force

	EM	SE	EE	WO	AP	FW	SV	T
I	61.5		1.2	37.3		(31.4)	(15.1)	100.0
II	1.9		5.1	93.0			(6.0)	100.0
III	58.1		.6	41.3			(4.2)	100.0
IV	47.7		6.6	45.7			(1.6)	100.0
V	.0		6.1	93.9			(.0)	100.0
VI	60.9		37.0	2.1			(9.9)	100.0
VII	5.0		27.2	67.8			(.9)	100.0
VIII	.0		91.5	8.5			(2.6)	100.0
IX	3.1		6.6	90.2			(2.2)	100.0
X	.0		14.2	85.8			(2.9)	100.0
U	.2		.2	99.6			(.3)	100.0
T	41.7		4.0	54.2			(9.4)	100.0

Sweden

Labour Force by Sector and Status 1890

Absolute figures in thousands

Sector			Employers EM	Self-employed SE	Employees EE	Workers WO a)	Apprentices AP	Family-workers FW b)	Unknown U	Total T	%
I	Agriculture	Total	438.3		8.5	496.1		(402.6)		943.0	53.9
		males	391.9		8.5	302.2		(211.7)		702.6	55.6
II	Mining	Total	.4		1.1	24.6				26.1	1.5
		males	.4		1.0	24.6				26.1	2.1
III	Manufacturing	Total	86.5		1.2	114.9				202.6	11.6
		males	84.5		1.2	89.7				175.3	13.9
IV	Construction	Total	7.4		.8	14.7				23.0	1.3
		males	7.4		.8	14.6				22.8	1.8
V	Utilities	Total	.0		.1	.8				.8	.0
		males	.0		.1	.8				.8	.1
VI	Commerce	Total	24.2	15.3	.7					40.1	2.3
		males	20.4	12.1	.7					33.2	2.6
VII	Transport	Total	4.9		12.1	38.1				55.1	3.1
		males	4.8		11.4	37.7				53.9	4.3
VIII	Banking	Total	.0		1.3	.1				1.5	.1
		males	.0		1.2	.1				1.4	.1
IX	Services c)	Total	9.9		18.5	251.8				280.3	16.0
		males	5.1		10.5	80.2				95.8	7.6
X	Public admin.	Total	.0		8.0	44.3				52.3	3.0
		males	.0		7.9	44.2				52.1	4.1
U	Unknown	Total	.2		.7	124.7				125.6	7.2
		males	.2		.7	98.6				99.5	7.9
T	All sectors	Total	571.9		67.6	1 110.9				1 750.4	100.0
		males	514.8		55.4	693.4				1 263.5	100.0

Percent distributions

Total labour force

	EM SE	EE	WO	AP	FW	U	T
I	46.5	.9	52.6		(42.7)		100.0
II	1.7	4.0	94.3				100.0
III	42.7	.6	56.7				100.0
IV	32.4	3.5	64.1				100.0
V	.0	7.0	93.0				100.0
VI	60.3	38.1	1.6				100.0
VII	8.8	21.9	69.2				100.0
VIII	.0	90.2	9.8				100.0
IX	3.6	6.6	89.8				100.0
X	.0	15.4	84.6				100.0
U	.1	.6	99.3				100.0
T	32.7	3.9	63.5				100.0

Male labour force

	EM SE	EE	WO	AP	FW	U	T
I	55.8	1.2	43.0		(30.1)		100.0
II	1.6	4.0	94.3				100.0
III	48.2	.7	51.1				100.0
IV	32.6	3.4	64.0				100.0
V	.0	7.0	93.0				100.0
VI	61.6	36.5	2.0				100.0
VII	8.8	21.1	70.0				100.0
VIII	.0	89.6	10.4				100.0
IX	5.3	10.9	83.7				100.0
X	.0	15.2	84.8				100.0
U	.2	.7	99.1				100.0
T	40.7	4.4	54.9				100.0

Sweden

Labour Force by Sector and Status 1900

Absolute figures in thousands

Sector			Employers	Self-employed	Employees	Workers [a]	Apprentices	Family-workers [b]	Unknown	Total	%
			EM	SE	EE	WO	AP	FW	U	T	
I	Agriculture	Total	432.2		8.1	542.3		(425.3)		982.6	49.8
		males	379.1		8.1	335.7		(224.6)		722.8	50.8
II	Mining	Total	.4		1.4	43.0				44.8	2.3
		males	.4		1.3	43.0				44.7	3.1
III	Manufacturing	Total	106.8		1.9	202.3				311.1	15.8
		males	101.6		1.9	158.9				262.3	18.4
IV	Construction	Total	7.9		3.3	20.5				31.8	1.6
		males	7.9		3.3	20.4				31.6	2.2
V	Utilities	Total	.0		.1	1.8				2.0	.1
		males	.0		.1	1.8				2.0	.1
VI	Commerce	Total	33.4		26.4	.6				60.4	3.1
		males	27.5		18.4	.6				46.5	3.3
VII	Transport	Total	1.8		18.2	47.4				67.4	3.4
		males	1.8		16.6	47.1				65.4	4.6
VIII	Banking	Total	.0		2.6	.0				2.6	.1
		males	.0		2.3	.0				2.3	.2
IX	Services [c]	Total	18.7		25.3	229.8				273.8	13.9
		males	13.7		12.0	65.1				90.8	6.4
X	Public admin.	Total	.0		9.0	44.0				53.1	2.7
		males	.0		8.8	43.9				52.6	3.7
U	Unknown	Total	.7		2.3	141.5				144.5	7.3
		males	.7		2.3	98.7				101.8	7.2
T	All sectors	Total	602.0		98.7	1 273.3				1 974.0	100.0
		males	532.7		75.1	815.2				1 423.0	100.0

Percent distributions

Total labour force

	EM SE	EE	WO	AP	FW	U	T
I	44.0	.8	55.2		(43.3)		100.0
II	.9	3.1	96.1				100.0
III	34.3	.6	65.0				100.0
IV	25.0	10.5	64.6				100.0
V	.0	5.9	94.1				100.0
VI	55.2	43.7	1.0				100.0
VII	2.7	27.0	70.4				100.0
VIII	.0	100.0	.0				100.0
IX	6.8	9.2	83.9				100.0
X	.0	17.0	83.0				100.0
U	.5	1.6	97.9				100.0
T	30.5	5.0	64.5				100.0

Male labour force

	EM SE	EE	WO	AP	FW	U	T
I	52.4	1.1	46.5		(31.1)		100.0
II	.8	3.0	96.1				100.0
III	38.7	.7	60.6				100.0
IV	25.0	10.5	64.5				100.0
V	.0	5.8	94.2				100.0
VI	59.2	39.5	1.3				100.0
VII	2.7	25.3	72.0				100.0
VIII	.0	100.0	.0				100.0
IX	15.1	13.2	71.7				100.0
X	.0	16.6	83.4				100.0
U	.7	2.3	97.0				100.0
T	37.4	5.3	57.3				100.0

S w e d e n

L a b o u r   F o r c e   b y   S e c t o r   a n d   S t a t u s   1 9 1 0

Absolute figures in thousands

Sector		Employ-ers	Self-employed	Employ-ees	Workers	Apprent-ices	Family-workers	Un-known	Total	%
		EM	SE	EE	WO a)	AP	FW b)	U	T	
I	Agriculture	Total	409.0	10.2	596.6		(374.1)		1 015.9	45.6
		males	366.7	10.0	381.0		(192.7)		757.7	47.6
II	Mining	Total	.5		1.3	51.2			52.9	2.4
		males	.5		1.3	51.2			52.9	3.3
III	Manufacturing	Total	89.5	13.7	331.5				434.7	19.5
		males	77.2	13.1	260.9				351.2	22.1
IV	Construction	Total	16.7	.4	42.5				59.5	2.7
		males	16.6	.4	42.4				59.4	3.7
V	Utilities	Total	.1	.2	3.9				4.3	.2
		males	.1	.2	3.9				4.3	.3
VI	Commerce	Total	46.5	58.6	7.9				113.0	5.1
		males	35.2	33.7	7.2				76.1	4.8
VII	Transport	Total	5.5	51.8	54.5				111.9	5.0
		males	5.5	46.2	54.5				106.2	6.7
VIII	Banking	Total	.0	6.5	.5				7.0	.3
		males	.0	5.3	.5				5.8	.4
IX	Services c)	Total	21.2	42.1	248.9				312.3	14.0
		males	10.9	16.8	63.1				90.8	5.7
X	Public admin.	Total	.0	14.3	34.1				48.4	2.2
		males	.0	14.0	33.1				47.2	3.0
U	Unknown	Total			37.5			31.9	69.4	3.1
		males			34.2			6.4	40.7	2.6
T	All sectors	Total	589.0	199.1	1 409.3			31.9	2 229.3	100.0
		males	512.7	141.1	932.0			6.4	1 592.2	100.0

Percent distributions

Total labour force

	EM	SE	EE	WO	AP	FW	U	T
I	40.3	1.0	58.7		(36.8)			100.0
II	1.0	2.4	96.6					100.0
III	20.6	3.1	76.3					100.0
IV	28.0	.6	71.4					100.0
V	2.3	5.6	92.1					100.0
VI	41.2	51.9	7.0					100.0
VII	4.9	46.3	48.8					100.0
VIII	.0	92.5	7.5					100.0
IX	6.8	13.5	79.7					100.0
X	.0	29.5	70.5					100.0
U			54.1				45.9	100.0
T	26.4	8.9	63.2				1.4	100.0

Male labour force

	EM	SE	EE	WO	AP	FW	U	T
I	48.4	1.3	50.3		(25.4)			100.0
II	.9	2.4	96.7					100.0
III	22.0	3.7	74.3					100.0
IV	28.0	.6	71.4					100.0
V	2.3	5.6	92.1					100.0
VI	46.2	44.3	9.5					100.0
VII	5.2	43.5	51.3					100.0
VIII	.0	91.3	8.7					100.0
IX	12.0	18.5	69.5					100.0
X	.0	29.8	70.2					100.0
U			84.2				15.8	100.0
T	32.2	8.9	58.5				.4	100.0

Sweden

Labour Force by Sector and Status 1920

Absolute figures in thousands

Sector			Employers EM	Self-employed SE	Employees EE	Workers WO a)	Apprentices AP	Family-workers FW b)	Unknown U	Total T	%
I	Agriculture	Total	391.7		9.3	657.4		(360.5)		1 058.4	40.4
		males	354.5		8.8	444.4		(168.8)		807.7	44.0
II	Mining	Total	.6		1.5	37.4				39.6	1.5
		males	.6		1.4	37.1				39.1	2.1
III	Manufacturing	Total	57.7		41.8	544.8				644.3	24.6
		males	48.5		34.2	413.2				495.9	27.0
IV	Construction	Total	9.1		3.4	80.3				92.8	3.5
		males	9.1		3.0	80.3				92.4	5.0
V	Utilities	Total	.4		2.7	17.6				20.7	.8
		males	.4		2.3	17.5				20.2	1.1
VI	Commerce	Total	54.1		86.1	28.7				169.0	6.4
		males	40.4		42.3	24.4				107.0	5.8
VII	Transport	Total	11.7		89.6	52.2				153.6	5.9
		males	11.6		74.2	49.9				135.7	7.4
VIII	Banking	Total	.0		16.0	2.0				18.0	.7
		males	.0		10.6	1.6				12.2	.7
IX	Services c)	Total	27.5		66.8	239.3				333.6	12.7
		males	14.4		23.5	18.2				56.1	3.1
X	Public admin.	Total	.0		20.1	26.8				47.0	1.8
		males	.0		16.8	25.5				42.4	2.3
U	Unknown	Total				24.6			19.0	43.6	1.7
		males				18.6			7.6	26.2	1.4
T	All sectors	Total	552.9		337.5	1 711.2			19.0	2 620.6	100.0
		males	479.6		217.1	1 130.7			7.6	1 835.0	100.0

Percent distributions

Total labour force

	EM	SE	EE	WO	AP	FW	U	T
I	37.0		.9	62.1		(34.1)		100.0
II	1.6		3.9	94.6				100.0
III	9.0		6.5	84.5				100.0
IV	9.9		3.6	86.5				100.0
V	2.1		13.0	84.8				100.0
VI	32.0		51.0	17.0				100.0
VII	7.6		58.4	34.0				100.0
VIII	.0		88.7	11.3				100.0
IX	8.2		20.0	71.7				100.0
X	.0		42.9	57.1				100.0
U				56.5			43.5	100.0
T	21.1		12.9	65.3			.7	100.0

Male labour force

	EM	SE	EE	WO	AP	FW	U	T
I	43.9		1.1	52.0		(20.9)		100.0
II	1.6		3.5	94.9				100.0
III	9.8		6.9	83.3				100.0
IV	9.9		3.3	86.9				100.0
V	2.2		11.3	86.5				100.0
VI	37.8		39.5	22.8				100.0
VII	8.6		54.7	36.7				100.0
VIII	.0		87.0	13.0				100.0
IX	25.7		41.9	32.4				100.0
X	.0		39.7	60.3				100.0
U				70.9			29.1	100.0
T	26.1		11.8	61.6			.4	100.0

Sweden

Labour Force by Sector and Status 1930 [a]

Absolute figures in thousands

Sector			Employers EM	Self-employed SE	Employees EE	Workers WO	Apprentices AP	Family-workers FW [b]	Unknown U	Total T	%
I	Agriculture	Total	2.2	389.8	9.3	313.5		326.0		1 040.8	35.4
		males	1.8	348.2	8.7	280.6		159.9		799.3	39.4
II	Mining	Total	.3	.8	1.5	40.9		.2		43.7	1.5
		males	.3	.8	1.4	40.7		.2		43.3	2.1
III	Manufacturing	Total	8.6	82.1	50.4	545.4		12.0		698.4	23.7
		males	8.0	54.6	38.8	409.8		10.0		521.3	25.7
IV	Construction	Total	2.0	11.5	4.9	131.0		2.4		151.8	5.2
		males	2.0	11.4	4.3	130.4		2.3		150.5	7.4
V	Utilities	Total	.1	.1	2.5	12.4		.0		15.0	.5
		males	.1	.1	2.0	12.2		.0		14.4	.7
VI	Commerce	Total	5.7	64.2	114.9	48.6		8.6		241.9	8.2
		males	5.5	44.6	52.9	39.4		4.4		146.9	7.2
VII	Transport	Total	.3	14.2	29.5	146.5		1.2		191.6	6.5
		males	.3	13.9	21.5	132.3		1.2		169.2	8.3
VIII	Banking	Total	.8	.1	17.6	3.0		.0		21.6	.7
		males	.8	.1	10.8	2.1		.0		13.8	.7
IX	Services	Total	.3	33.0	85.3	294.7		3.1		416.3	14.1
		males	.3	16.5	28.7	29.1		.7		75.3	3.7
X	Public admin.	Total	.0	.0	21.1	29.7		.0		50.8	1.7
		males	.0	.0	16.8	27.7		.0		44.5	2.2
U	Unknown	Total				20.5			50.2	70.7	2.4
		males				18.1			31.2	49.3	2.4
T	All sectors	Total	20.2	595.6	337.0	1 586.2		353.4	50.2	2 942.5	100.0
		males	19.0	490.2	186.1	1 122.4		178.8	31.2	2 027.8	100.0

Percent distributions

	Total labour force									Male labour force							
	EM	SE	EE	WO	AP	FW	U	T		EM	SE	EE	WO	AP	FW	U	T
I	.2	37.5	.9	30.1		31.3	.0	100.0	I	.2	43.6	1.1	35.1		20.0		100.0
II	.7	1.7	3.5	93.7		.4	.0	100.0	II	.7	1.7	3.2	94.0		.4		100.0
III	1.2	11.8	7.2	78.1		1.7	.0	100.0	III	1.5	10.5	7.5	78.6		1.9		100.0
IV	1.3	7.6	3.2	86.3		1.5	.0	100.0	IV	1.3	7.6	2.8	86.7		1.6		100.0
V	.8	.4	16.3	82.4		.0	.0	100.0	V	.9	.4	14.0	84.8		.0		100.0
VI	2.4	26.5	47.5	20.1		3.6	.0	100.0	VI	3.8	30.4	36.0	26.8		3.0		100.0
VII	.1	7.4	15.4	76.4		.6	.0	100.0	VII	.2	8.2	12.7	78.2		.7		100.0
VIII	3.8	.7	81.5	14.0		.0	.0	100.0	VIII	5.9	.8	78.5	14.9		.0		100.0
IX	.1	7.9	20.5	70.8		.7	.0	100.0	IX	.3	21.9	38.2	38.7		.9		100.0
X	.0	.0	41.5	58.5		.0	.0	100.0	X	.0	.0	37.8	62.2		.0		100.0
U				29.0			71.0	100.0	U				36.7			63.3	100.0
T	.7	20.2	11.5	53.9		12.0	1.7	100.0	T	.9	24.2	9.2	55.4		8.8	1.5	100.0

Sweden

Labour Force by Sector and Status 1940

Absolute figures in thousands

Sector			Employers EM	Self-employed SE	Employees EE	Workers WO	Apprentices AP	Family-workers FW a)	Unknown U	Total T	%
I	Agriculture	Total	391.3		21.3	246.4		205.1		864.0	28.8
		males	349.9		20.5	239.8		151.8		762.0	34.8
II	Mining	Total	1.3		2.6	30.3		.2		34.4	1.1
		males	1.3		2.4	30.1		.2		34.0	1.6
III	Manufacturing	Total	98.1		91.6	618.1		14.3		822.0	27.4
		males	67.4		71.4	478.0		11.0		628.0	28.7
IV	Construction	Total	28.2		10.6	148.1		5.3		192.3	6.4
		males	28.1		9.5	147.8		5.1		190.5	8.7
V	Utilities	Total	.1		5.1	16.2		.0		21.5	.7
		males	.1		4.2	16.0		.0		20.4	.9
VI	Commerce	Total	66.1		154.6	53.0		13.0		286.7	9.6
		males	48.5		74.2	43.4		6.5		172.6	7.9
VII	Transport	Total	20.0		55.8	123.5		2.3		201.7	6.7
		males	19.7		33.5	120.1		2.2		175.5	8.0
VIII	Banking	Total	.3		23.9	1.7		.0		25.9	.9
		males	.2		14.2	.6		.0		15.1	.7
IX	Services	Total	44.3		171.3	225.3		3.4		444.3	14.8
		males	23.3		60.5	20.5		1.1		105.3	4.8
X	Public admin.	Total	.0		58.0	14.7		.0		72.6	2.4
		males	.0		47.0	11.9		.0		58.9	2.7
U	Unknown	Total	.1		8.0	26.0				34.1	1.1
		males	.1		4.8	22.6				27.4	1.3
T	All sectors	Total	649.7		602.8	1 503.3		243.7		2 999.5	100.0
		males	538.7		342.3	1 130.9		177.9		2 189.7	100.0

Percent distributions

Total labour force

	EM	SE	EE	WO	AP	FW	U	T
I	45.3		2.5	28.5		23.7		100.0
II	3.9		7.4	88.0		.7		100.0
III	11.9		11.1	75.2		1.7		100.0
IV	14.7		5.5	77.1		2.8		100.0
V	.5		23.9	75.5		.1		100.0
VI	23.0		53.9	18.5		4.5		100.0
VII	9.9		27.7	61.2		1.2		100.0
VIII	1.0		92.4	6.4		.1		100.0
IX	10.0		38.6	50.7		.8		100.0
X	.0		79.8	20.2		.0		100.0
U	.2		23.5	76.3				100.0
T	21.7		20.1	50.1		8.1		100.0

Male labour force

	EM	SE	EE	WO	AP	FW	U	T
I	45.9		2.7	31.5		19.9		100.0
II	3.9		6.9	88.5		.7		100.0
III	10.7		11.4	76.1		1.8		100.0
IV	14.8		5.0	77.6		2.7		100.0
V	.5		20.8	78.6		.1		100.0
VI	28.1		43.0	25.2		3.7		100.0
VII	11.2		19.1	68.4		1.2		100.0
VIII	1.6		94.1	4.1		.1		100.0
IX	22.1		57.4	19.5		1.0		100.0
X	.0		79.8	20.2		.0		100.0
U	.3		17.5	82.3				100.0
T	24.6		15.6	51.6		8.1		100.0

Labour Force by Sector and Status 1945

Absolute figures in thousands

Sector			Employers	Self-employed	Employees	Workers	Apprentices	Family-workers	Unknown	Total	%
			EM	SE	EE	WO	AP	FW[a]	U	T	
I	Agriculture	Total	375.4	22.8	213.1			121.5		732.8	24.5
		males	339.9	21.6	207.4			118.8		687.7	30.7
II	Mining	Total	1.2	3.1	27.7			.2		32.2	1.1
		males	1.2	2.8	27.5			.2		31.6	1.4
III	Manufacturing	Total	81.3	125.9	653.8			9.0		870.0	29.1
		males	59.6	93.1	522.0			7.6		682.3	30.4
IV	Construction	Total	23.7	14.5	175.2			3.4		216.8	7.3
		males	23.6	12.5	174.7			3.2		214.1	9.6
V	Utilities	Total	.1	6.1	16.9			.0		23.1	.8
		males	.1	4.8	16.6			.0		21.5	1.0
VI	Commerce	Total	65.2	182.2	57.5			9.4		314.3	10.5
		males	48.9	84.1	45.4			4.7		183.1	8.2
VII	Transport	Total	19.6	65.1	133.4			1.9		220.1	7.4
		males	19.3	36.8	129.3			1.9		187.2	8.4
VIII	Banking	Total	.4	24.8	1.7			.0		26.9	.9
		males	.4	13.7	.5			.0		14.6	.7
IX	Services	Total	36.2	160.8	210.7			1.9		409.6	13.7
		males	20.5	58.8	29.2			.7		109.2	4.9
X	Public admin.	Total	.0	79.7	20.7			.0		100.4	3.4
		males	.0	59.5	16.6			.0		76.2	3.4
U	Unknown	Total	.0	2.6	39.0			.0		41.7	1.4
		males	.0	1.5	31.9			.0		33.5	1.5
T	All sectors	Total	603.2	687.6	1 549.9			147.3		2 987.9	100.0
		males	513.5	389.4	1 201.0			137.1		2 241.0	100.0

Percent distributions

Total labour force

	EM	SE	EE	WO	AP	FW	U	T
I	51.2		3.1	29.1		16.6		100.0
II	3.7		9.6	86.1		.5		100.0
III	9.3		14.5	75.2		1.0		100.0
IV	10.9		6.7	80.8		1.6		100.0
V	.5		26.2	73.1		.1		100.0
VI	20.7		58.0	18.3		3.0		100.0
VII	8.9		29.6	60.6		.9		100.0
VIII	1.6		92.2	6.2		.0		100.0
IX	8.8		39.3	51.4		.5		100.0
X	.0		79.4	20.6		.0		100.0
U	.1		6.2	93.6		.1		100.0
T	20.2		23.0	51.9		4.9		100.0

Male labour force

	EM	SE	EE	WO	AP	FW	U	T
I	49.4		3.1	30.2		17.3		100.0
II	3.8		8.9	86.9		.5		100.0
III	8.7		13.7	76.5		1.1		100.0
IV	11.0		5.9	81.6		1.5		100.0
V	.5		22.2	77.1		.1		100.0
VI	26.7		45.9	24.8		2.6		100.0
VII	10.3		19.6	69.1		1.0		100.0
VIII	2.6		93.6	3.7		.0		100.0
IX	18.8		53.9	26.7		.6		100.0
X	.0		78.2	21.8		.0		100.0
U	.1		4.5	95.3		.1		100.0
T	22.9		17.4	53.6		6.1		100.0

Sweden

Labour Force by Sector and Status 1950

Absolute figures in thousands

Sector			Employers EM	Self-employed SE	Employees EE	Workers WO	Apprentices AP	Family-workers FW a)	Unknown U	Total T	%
I	Agriculture	Total	347.3		24.3	164.0		96.0		631.5	20.3
		males	315.5		22.9	158.0		82.3		578.7	25.3
II	Mining	Total	1.4		3.0	23.3		.1		27.8	.9
		males	1.3		2.6	23.1		.1		27.2	1.2
III	Manufacturing	Total	83.0		159.6	711.9		7.2		961.7	31.0
		males	64.3		118.6	568.7		5.8		757.4	33.1
IV	Construction	Total	27.9		19.6	193.9		2.8		244.3	7.9
		males	27.9		17.0	193.1		2.6		240.6	10.5
V	Utilities	Total	.0		8.1	17.9		.0		26.0	.8
		males	.0		6.4	17.6		.0		24.0	1.1
VI	Commerce	Total	74.4		216.1	64.7		10.1		365.2	11.8
		males	57.4		99.1	51.4		4.3		212.2	9.3
VII	Transport	Total	22.8		81.2	144.6		1.9		250.6	8.1
		males	22.5		43.9	139.4		1.8		207.6	9.1
VIII	Banking	Total	.4		29.0	1.7		.0		31.2	1.0
		males	.4		15.0	.5		.0		15.8	.7
IX	Services	Total	43.2		201.8	199.2		2.1		446.3	14.4
		males	26.1		73.3	35.0		.7		135.1	5.9
X	Public admin.	Total	.0		81.0	16.0		.0		97.0	3.1
		males	.0		58.5	12.3		.0		70.8	3.1
U	Unknown	Total	.1		7.8	15.3				23.2	.7
		males	.0		4.0	12.2				16.2	.7
T	All sectors	Total	600.6		831.4	1 552.6		120.2		3 104.8	100.0
		males	515.5		461.3	1 211.3		97.6		2 285.7	100.0

Percent distributions

Total labour force

	EM SE	EE	WO	AP	FW	U	T
I	55.0	3.8	26.0		15.2		100.0
II	4.9	10.7	84.0		.4		100.0
III	8.6	16.6	74.0		.7		100.0
IV	11.4	8.0	79.4		1.1		100.0
V	.1	31.0	68.9		.0		100.0
VI	20.4	59.2	17.7		2.8		100.0
VII	9.1	32.4	57.7		.8		100.0
VIII	1.4	93.0	5.6		.0		100.0
IX	9.7	45.2	44.6		.5		100.0
X	.0	83.5	16.5		.0		100.0
U	.2	33.6	66.1				100.0
T	19.3	26.8	50.0		3.9		100.0

Male labour force

	EM SE	EE	WO	AP	FW	U	T
I	54.5	4.0	27.3		14.2		100.0
II	4.9	9.7	85.0		.4		100.0
III	8.5	15.7	75.1		.8		100.0
IV	11.6	7.1	80.2		1.1		100.0
V	.1	26.6	73.3		.0		100.0
VI	27.1	46.7	24.2		2.0		100.0
VII	10.8	21.2	67.2		.9		100.0
VIII	2.5	94.6	2.9		.0		100.0
IX	19.3	54.3	25.9		.5		100.0
X	.0	82.6	17.4		.0		100.0
U	.3	24.5	75.1				100.0
T	22.6	20.2	53.0		4.3		100.0

Labour Force by Sector and Status 1960[a]

Absolute figures in thousands

Sector			Employers	Selfemployed	Employees	Workers	Apprentices	Familyworkers	Unknown	Total	%
			EM	SE	EE	WO	AP	FW	U	T	
I	Agriculture	Total	18.5	209.6	22.8	134.3		61.8		447.0	13.8
		males	17.5	201.9	20.3	125.0		43.5		408.1	17.9
II	Mining	Total	.3	.2	4.3	18.7		.1		23.6	.7
		males	.3	.2	3.5	18.2		.1		22.3	1.0
III	Manufacturing	Total	23.4	34.7	277.5	765.6		7.7		1 108.9	34.2
		males	21.7	29.2	193.6	612.6		4.0		861.2	37.8
IV	Construction	Total	9.3	23.2	36.9	223.0		2.6		295.0	9.1
		males	9.3	23.2	30.5	220.1		2.3		285.4	12.5
V	Utilities	Total	.2	.1	11.7	23.3		.0		35.3	1.1
		males	.2	.1	9.1	22.9		.0		32.2	1.4
VI	Commerce	Total	22.0	44.1	239.9	59.0		13.8		378.7	11.7
		males	17.0	33.6	98.9	45.4		3.4		198.3	8.7
VII	Transport	Total	6.8	15.5	102.0	115.3		2.2		241.9	7.5
		males	6.6	15.4	65.6	109.0		1.9		198.5	8.7
VIII	Banking	Total	.1	.2	42.9	2.0		.0		45.1	1.4
		males	.1	.1	19.9	.4		.0		20.6	.9
IX	Services	Total	14.2	27.7	283.7	218.9		3.7		548.2	16.9
		males	9.2	17.9	97.5	43.1		.9		168.6	7.4
X	Public admin.	Total	.0	.0	91.9	18.0		.0		109.9	3.4
		males	.0	.0	62.3	12.6		.0		74.9	3.3
U	Unknown	Total	.0	.4	2.3	7.8		.0		10.6	.3
		males	.0	.4	1.3	6.3		.0		8.0	.4
T	All sectors	Total	94.7	355.8	1 115.9	1 585.9		91.9		3 244.1	100.0
		males	81.8	322.0	602.5	1 215.6		56.1		2 278.1	100.0

Percent distributions

Total labour force

	EM	SE	EE	WO	AP	FW	U	T
I	4.1	46.9	5.1	30.0		13.8		100.0
II	1.1	1.0	18.2	79.4		.3		100.0
III	2.1	3.1	25.0	69.0		.7		100.0
IV	3.2	7.9	12.5	75.6		.9		100.0
V	.4	.3	33.2	65.9		.1		100.0
VI	5.8	11.6	63.3	15.6		3.6		100.0
VII	2.8	6.4	42.2	47.7		.9		100.0
VIII	.1	.3	95.2	4.3		.0		100.0
IX	2.6	5.1	51.7	39.9		.7		100.0
X	.0	.0	83.6	16.4		.0		100.0
U	.2	3.6	22.1	73.9		.1		100.0
T	2.9	11.0	34.4	48.9		2.8		100.0

Male labour force

	EM	SE	EE	WO	AP	FW	U	T
I	4.3	49.5	5.0	30.6		10.6		100.0
II	1.1	1.1	15.8	81.7		.3		100.0
III	2.5	3.4	22.5	71.1		.5		100.0
IV	3.2	8.1	10.7	77.1		.8		100.0
V	.5	.3	28.2	71.0		.1		100.0
VI	8.6	16.9	49.9	22.9		1.7		100.0
VII	3.3	7.8	33.0	54.9		1.0		100.0
VIII	.3	.7	96.9	2.1		.0		100.0
IX	5.5	10.6	57.8	25.6		.5		100.0
X	.0	.0	83.2	16.8		.0		100.0
U	.3	4.5	16.1	79.0		.1		100.0
T	3.6	14.1	26.4	53.4		2.5		100.0

Sweden

Labour Force by Sector and Status 1965 [a]

Absolute figures in thousands

Sector			Employers EM [b]	Self-employed SE [b]	Employees EE	Workers WO	Apprentices AP	Family-workers FW [c]	Unknown U	Total T	%
I	Agriculture	Total	12.6	171.0	124.8			99.2		407.6	11.8
		males	175.6		111.6			27.9		315.0	13.8
II	Mining	Total	.2	.3	19.9			.1		20.4	.6
		males	.5		18.4			.0		18.9	.8
III	Manufacturing	Total	18.7	28.9	1 047.0			7.3		1 101.9	31.9
		males	42.5		796.1			3.1		841.7	36.7
IV	Construction	Total	9.9	23.6	294.1			2.8		330.3	9.6
		males	33.3		281.6			2.1		317.1	13.8
V	Utilities	Total	.1	.2	33.2			.0		33.6	1.0
		males	.3		29.7			.0		30.1	1.3
VI	Commerce	Total	20.9	34.1	385.3			14.3		454.6	13.2
		males	42.9		194.3			2.5		239.7	10.5
VII	Transport	Total	7.1	16.0	221.2			2.3		246.6	7.1
		males	22.9		175.2			1.6		199.7	8.7
VIII	Banking	Total	.1	.1	59.8			.0		60.0	1.7
		males	.2		24.1			.0		24.3	1.1
IX	Services	Total	15.0	25.6	602.9			4.0		647.5	18.8
		males	26.6		179.3			.8		206.7	9.0
X	Public admin.	Total	.0	.0	134.1			.0		134.1	3.9
		males	.0		87.1			.0		87.1	3.8
U	Unknown	Total	.0	.8	12.4			.0		13.3	.4
		males	.8		9.3			.0		10.1	.4
T	All sectors	Total	84.6	300.6	2 934.7			130.0		3 449.9	100.0
		males	345.5		1 906.8			38.1		2 290.4	100.0

Percent distributions

Total labour force

	EM	SE	EE	WO	AP	FW	U	T
I	3.1	42.0	30.6			24.3		100.0
II	.9	1.3	97.5			.3		100.0
III	1.7	2.6	95.0			.7		100.0
IV	3.0	7.1	89.0			.8		100.0
V	.4	.6	98.9			.1		100.0
VI	4.6	7.5	84.8			3.1		100.0
VII	2.9	6.5	89.7			.9		100.0
VIII	.1	.2	99.6			.0		100.0
IX	2.3	4.0	93.1			.6		100.0
X	.0	.0	100.0			.0		100.0
U	.3	6.0	93.5			.2		100.0
T	2.5	8.7	85.1			3.8		100.0

Male labour force

	EM	SE	EE	WO	AP	FW	U	T
I	55.7		35.4			8.9		100.0
II	2.4		97.4			.2		100.0
III	5.1		94.6			.4		100.0
IV	10.5		88.8			.7		100.0
V	1.1		98.8			.1		100.0
VI	17.9		81.1			1.0		100.0
VII	11.4		87.7			.8		100.0
VIII	.7		99.2			.0		100.0
IX	12.9		86.8			.4		100.0
X	.0		100.0			.0		100.0
U	7.8		92.1			.1		100.0
T	15.1		83.3			1.7		100.0

Sweden

Labour Force by Sector and Status 1970 [a]

Absolute figures in thousands

Sector			Employers	Self-employed	Employees	Workers	Apprentices	Family-workers	Un-known	Total	%
			EM	SE	EE	WO	AP	FW	U	T	
I	Agriculture	Total	125.9		95.4			55.1		276.5	8.1
		males	121.6		85.4			14.0		221.0	10.0
II	Mining	Total	.4		19.1			.1		19.6	.6
		males	.4		17.6			.0		18.1	.8
III	Manufacturing	Total	25.1		966.3			4.0		995.4	29.2
		males	22.3		730.2			1.2		753.7	34.2
IV	Construction	Total	32.5		297.9			2.0		332.5	9.7
		males	32.5		285.4			1.3		319.1	14.5
V	Utilities	Total	.0		26.5			.0		26.5	.8
		males	.0		23.1			.0		23.1	1.0
VI	Commerce	Total	45.8		377.6			11.8		435.2	12.8
		males	34.8		190.5			1.8		227.0	10.3
VII	Transport	Total	23.8		221.5			1.8		247.1	7.2
		males	23.5		174.7			.9		199.0	9.0
VIII	Banking	Total	.0		65.0			.0		65.1	1.9
		males	.0		26.4			.0		26.5	1.2
IX	Services	Total	49.0		789.6			4.5		843.1	24.7
		males	35.7		274.1			1.1		310.8	14.1
X	Public admin.	Total	.0		163.0			.0		163.0	4.8
		males	.0		100.9			.0		100.9	4.6
U	Unknown	Total	.7		8.0			.0		8.7	.3
		males	.7		5.8			.0		6.5	.3
T	All sectors	Total	303.4		3 030.0			79.3		3 412.7	100.0
		males	271.4		1 914.1			20.2		2 205.8	100.0

Percent distributions

Total labour force

	EM	SE	EE	WO	AP	FW	U	T
I	45.5		34.5			19.9		100.0
II	2.2		97.6			.3		100.0
III	2.5		97.1			.4		100.0
IV	9.8		89.6			.6		100.0
V	.0		100.0			.0		100.0
VI	10.5		86.8			2.7		100.0
VII	9.6		89.6			.7		100.0
VIII	.1		99.9			.0		100.0
IX	5.8		93.7			.5		100.0
X	.0		100.0			.0		100.0
U	8.3		91.5			.1		100.0
T	8.9		88.8			2.3		100.0

Male labour force

	EM	SE	EE	WO	AP	FW	U	T
I	55.0		38.6			6.3		100.0
II	2.3		97.5			.2		100.0
III	3.0		96.9			.2		100.0
IV	10.2		89.4			.4		100.0
V	.0		100.0			.0		100.0
VI	15.3		83.9			.8		100.0
VII	11.8		87.8			.4		100.0
VIII	.1		99.9			.0		100.0
IX	11.5		88.2			.3		100.0
X	.0		100.0			.0		100.0
U	10.3		89.6			.1		100.0
T	12.3		86.8			.9		100.0

Sweden

Labour Force by Sector and Status 1975 [a]

Absolute figures in thousands

Sector			Employers	Self-employed	Employees	Workers	Apprentices	Family-workers	Unknown	Total	%
			EM	SE	EE	WO	AP	FW	U	T	
I	Agriculture	Total	104.2		97.3			26.2		227.8	6.4
		males	91.7		82.2			3.9		177.8	8.2
II	Mining	Total	.3		18.7			.0		19.1	.5
		males	.3		17.0			.0		17.3	.8
III	Manufacturing	Total	19.3		992.3			1.4		1 013.0	28.6
		males	16.6		746.3			.2		763.1	35.1
IV	Construction	Total	28.0		252.9			.7		281.6	7.9
		males	27.7		237.6			.3		265.6	12.2
V	Utilities	Total	.0		28.6			.0		28.6	.8
		males	.0		24.7			.0		24.7	1.1
VI	Commerce	Total	39.7		405.9			4.7		450.2	12.7
		males	26.3		213.5			.7		240.5	11.1
VII	Transport	Total	20.7		232.8			.8		254.4	7.2
		males	19.9		177.6			.1		197.7	9.1
VIII	Banking	Total	.0		73.8			.0		73.8	2.1
		males	.0		29.5			.0		29.6	1.4
IX	Services	Total	45.8		957.6			1.9		1 005.3	28.3
		males	31.5		311.5			.4		343.4	15.8
X	Public admin.	Total	.0		185.7			.0		185.7	5.2
		males	.0		109.8			.0		109.8	5.1
U	Unknown	Total	.6		4.5			.1	2.7	7.9	.2
		males	.5		3.1			.0	1.6	5.2	.2
T	All sectors	Total	258.7		3 250.1			35.8	2.8	3 547.4	100.0
		males	214.5		1 953.0			5.6	1.7	2 174.8	100.0

Percent distributions

Total labour force

	EM	SE	EE	WO	AP	FW	U	T
I	45.8		42.7			11.5		100.0
II	1.7		98.2			.1		100.0
III	1.9		98.0			.1		100.0
IV	10.0		89.8			.2		100.0
V	.0		100.0			.0		100.0
VI	8.8		90.2			1.0		100.0
VII	8.2		91.5			.3		100.0
VIII	.0		100.0			.0		100.0
IX	4.6		95.2			.2		100.0
X	.0		100.0			.0		100.0
U	7.1		57.0			1.4	34.5	100.0
T	7.3		91.6			1.0	.1	100.0

Male labour force

	EM	SE	EE	WO	AP	FW	U	T
I	51.6		46.2			2.2		100.0
II	1.8		98.2			.0		100.0
III	2.2		97.8			.0		100.0
IV	10.4		89.5			.1		100.0
V	.0		100.0			.0		100.0
VI	10.9		88.8			.3		100.0
VII	10.1		89.9			.1		100.0
VIII	.1		99.9			.0		100.0
IX	9.2		90.7			.1		100.0
X	.0		100.0			.0		100.0
U	9.4		59.7			.4	30.5	100.0
T	9.9		89.8			.3	.1	100.0

Notes:

1880–1910	Predominantly industrial classification
1920–1970	Pure industrial classification
1880–1920	Status distributions in Agriculture, Services, and Public Administration partially estimated according to the nature of the respective occupation/sector
1880–1950	Conscripts included in the labour force and classified according to their previous occupation
1965–1975	Inclusion of conscripts unknown

1880
   a) Including family workers
   b) Children over 15 years of age and other relatives; extensive enumeration in Agriculture
   c) The Swedish census category 'tjenstehjon' mainly includes domestic servants, but also servants active in production; male servants in handicrafts (part of sector III), however, are classified as workers; figures are given in brackets because they are not included in the respective totals; see also note (d)
   d) Including, among Workers, all servants

1890–1900
   a) Including family workers
   b) Children over 15 years of age and other relatives; extensive enumeration in Agriculture
   c) Including, among Workers, all servants (see note c) of 1880), except male servants in handicrafts classified as workers in Manufacturing

1910–1920
   a) Including family workers
   b) Assisting spouses and children over 15 years of age; more extensive enumeration in Agriculture and rural handicrafts; number of family workers in Agriculture not comparable to previous censuses
   c) Including, among Workers, all servants (see note c) of 1880), except male servants in handicrafts classified as workers in Manufacturing

1930
   a) Status distributions in Agriculture and Transport partially estimated according to the nature of the respective occupation/sector and the classification system of the 1940 census
   b) Assisting spouses and children over 15 years of age; extensive enumeration in Agriculture

1940
   a) Assisting spouses and children over 15 years of age; major break in comparability to previous censuses due to a more restrictive enumeration procedure in Agriculture

1945
   a) Assisting spouses and children over 15 years of age; number of family workers in Agriculture not comparable to previous census due to a further restriction in the enumeration

1950
   a) Mainly assisting children; largely excluding assisting married females

1960
   a) Conscripts not included in the labour force

1965
   a) Persons working at least 2o hours during the census week
   b) No separate figures by sex available
   c) Extended enumeration in Agriculture

1970–1975
   a) Persons working at least 2o hours during the census week

Switzerland

The Development of the Labour Force

Year	by Status				by Sector				Total labour force	Domestic services	Military personnel	Year
	Inde-pendent (IN)	Depend-ent (DE)	Family worker	Un-known	Agricul-ture (A)	Indus-try (I)	Serv-ices (S)	Un-known				
	percent distribution				percent distribution				in thousands			
1970	10.5	84.9	4.6		7.7	48.2	43.8	.3	2 995.8	46.9		1970
1960	14.5	80.8	4.7		11.2	50.4	38.0	.4	2 155.7	82.6		1960
1950	19.0	74.9	6.1		16.5	46.2	36.5	.8	2 155.7	111.7		1950
1941	21.1	71.3	7.6		20.8	43.6	33.6	2.0	1 992.5	116.4		1941
1930	22.1	69.7	8.2		21.3	43.8	34.1	.7	1 942.6	133.9		1930
1920	25.1	63.8	11.1		27.1	45.1	26.9	.8	1 871.7	114.6		1920
1910	28.8	59.0	12.2		26.8	44.2	28.5	.5	1 783.2	105.9		1910
1900	27.4	60.2	11.8	.6	31.0	43.7	24.8	.5	1 555.2	92.5		1900
1888	30.5	49.2	12.9	7.3	37.4	40.2	21.4	.9	1 304.8	82.6		1888

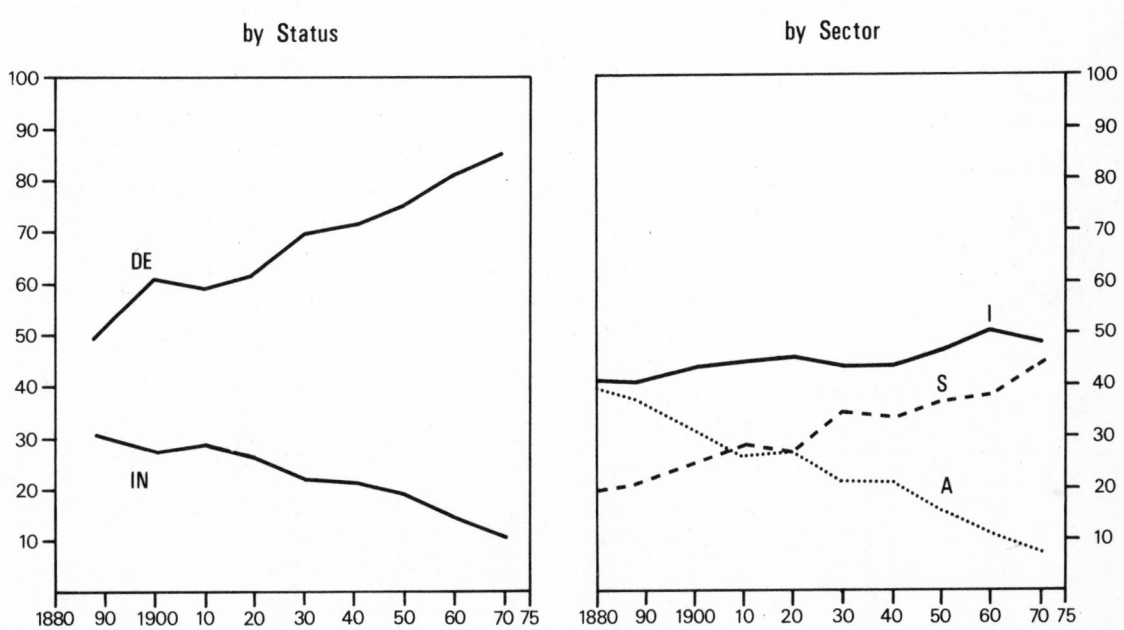

by Status   by Sector

Labour Force by Sector and Status 1888 [a]

Absolute figures in thousands

Sector			Employ-ers EM	Self-employed SE	Employ-ees EE	Workers WO	Apprent-ices AP[b]	Family-workers FW	Un-known U	Total T	%
I	Agriculture	Total	213.2		123.6			139.3	12.4	488.5	37.4
		males	190.0		104.6			93.1	8.3	395.9	45.5
II	Mining	Total	.4		2.5			.1	.2	3.2	.2
		males	.4		2.5			.1	.2	3.2	.4
III	Manufacturing	Total	106.8		295.4			12.4	60.1	474.8	36.4
		males	81.5		174.7			9.1	22.0	287.2	33.0
IV	Construction	Total	14.1		28.1			1.5	2.1	45.8	3.5
		males	14.1		28.1			1.5	2.1	45.8	5.3
V	Utilities	Total	.0		1.2			.0	.0	1.3	.1
		males	.0		1.2			.0	.0	1.3	.1
VI	Commerce	Total	29.4		17.5			6.7	1.0	54.5	4.2
		males	19.6		13.2			1.9	.7	35.4	4.1
VII	Transport	Total	3.2		30.8			.5	1.0	35.4	2.7
		males	3.1		28.7			.5	.9	33.1	3.8
VIII	Banking	Total	1.6		4.7			.1	.1	6.4	.5
		males	1.5		4.5			.1	.1	6.2	.7
IX	Services	Total	29.4		127.9			8.0	7.5	172.8	13.2
		males	17.3		26.3			1.0	1.5	46.2	5.3
X	Public admin.	Total			10.2					10.2	.8
		males			10.1					10.1	1.2
U	Unknown	Total			.4				11.4	11.8	.9
		males			.3				5.7	6.0	.7
T	All sectors	Total	398.0		642.4			168.5	95.8	1 304.8	100.0
		males	327.5		394.3			107.1	41.5	870.4	100.0

Percent distributions

	Total labour force								Male labour force							
	EM	SE	EE	WO	AP	FW	U	T		EM	SE	EE	WO	AP	FW	U	T
I	43.6		25.3			28.5	2.5	100.0	I	48.0		26.4			23.5	2.1	100.0
II	12.3		78.5			2.3	6.9	100.0	II	12.1		78.6			2.3	6.9	100.0
III	22.5		62.2			2.6	12.7	100.0	III	28.4		60.8			3.2	7.6	100.0
IV	30.8		61.3			3.2	4.6	100.0	IV	30.8		61.4			3.2	4.6	100.0
V	2.7		96.6			.2	.6	100.0	V	2.6		96.6			.2	.6	100.0
VI	53.9		32.1			12.2	1.8	100.0	VI	55.5		37.2			5.2	2.1	100.0
VII	8.9		86.9			1.5	2.8	100.0	VII	9.2		86.5			1.5	2.7	100.0
VIII	24.7		72.7			1.3	1.3	100.0	VIII	24.1		73.7			1.0	1.3	100.0
IX	17.0		74.0			4.6	4.4	100.0	IX	37.5		57.0			2.1	3.4	100.0
X			100.0					100.0	X			100.0					100.0
U			3.1				96.9	100.0	U			4.9				95.1	100.0
T	30.5		49.2			12.9	7.3	100.0	T	37.6		45.3			12.3	4.8	100.0

Labour Force by Sector and Status 1900

Absolute figures in thousands

Sector			Employers	Self-employed	Employees	Workers	Apprentices	Family-workers	Unknown	Total	%
			EM	SE	EE	WO b)	AP	FW a)	U	T	
I	Agriculture	Total	215.3		1.4	260.1	1.0	(139.1)	3.9	481.6	31.0
		males	191.2		1.3	204.9	.9	(99.1)	3.0	401.3	37.9
II	Mining	Total	.4		.3	4.7	.0	(.1)	.0	5.5	.4
		males	.4		.3	4.7	.0	(.1)	.0	5.5	.5
III	Manufacturing	Total	115.7	32.5		375.6	39.3	(20.1)	4.1	567.3	36.5
		males	80.1	25.2		217.3	26.8	(13.2)	2.7	352.0	33.3
IV	Construction	Total	15.9	5.8		74.7	3.6	(2.9)	.3	100.3	6.5
		males	15.9	5.7		74.7	3.6	(2.9)	.3	100.1	9.5
V	Utilities	Total	.2	1.1		5.3	.3	(.0)	.0	6.9	.4
		males	.2	1.1		5.2	.3	(.0)	.0	6.8	.6
VI	Commerce	Total	32.5	26.9		11.5	3.5	(7.7)	.3	74.7	4.8
		males	22.5	14.6		10.2	2.9	(2.6)	.2	50.5	4.8
VII	Transport	Total	4.4	13.9		41.7	.9	(.8)	.1	61.1	3.9
		males	4.3	12.0		40.2	.9	(.8)	.1	57.4	5.4
VIII	Banking	Total	2.1	6.7		.6	1.4	(.1)	.0	10.7	.7
		males	1.9	6.2		.6	1.3	(.1)	.0	10.0	.9
IX	Services	Total	38.9	38.1		144.7	2.7	(12.0)	.6	224.9	14.5
		males	19.5	19.2		16.5	1.1	(1.0)	.2	56.5	5.3
X	Public admin.	Total			7.6	7.2	.2		.0	15.1	1.0
		males			7.4	7.0	.2		.0	14.6	1.4
U	Unknown	Total				7.1				7.1	.5
		males				2.9				2.9	.3
T	All sectors	Total	425.5	134.2		933.4	52.9	(182.8)	9.3	1 555.2	100.0
		males	336.0	92.9		584.1	38.0	(119.7)	6.6	1 057.5	100.0

Percent distributions

Total labour force

	EM	SE	EE	WO	AP	FW	U	T
I	44.7		.3	54.0	.2	(28.9)	.8	100.0
II	7.9		5.1	85.8	.5	(1.3)	.6	100.0
III	20.4		5.7	66.2	6.9	(3.5)	.7	100.0
IV	15.9		5.8	74.5	3.5	(2.9)	.3	100.0
V	2.5		16.0	76.9	4.6	(.2)	.0	100.0
VI	43.5		36.0	15.4	4.7	(10.3)	.4	100.0
VII	7.3		22.8	68.3	1.5	(1.3)	.1	100.0
VIII	19.2		62.2	5.8	12.7	(1.2)	.2	100.0
IX	17.3		16.9	64.3	1.2	(5.3)	.3	100.0
X			50.6	48.1	1.3		.0	100.0
U			100.0					100.0
T	27.4		8.6	60.0	3.4	(11.8)	.6	100.0

Male labour force

	EM	SE	EE	WO	AP	FW	U	T
I	47.6		.3	51.0	.2	(24.7)	.7	100.0
II	7.7		5.1	86.0	.5	(1.2)	.6	100.0
III	22.7		7.2	61.7	7.6	(3.7)	.8	100.0
IV	15.9		5.7	74.6	3.5	(2.9)	.3	100.0
V	2.5		15.7	77.1	4.6	(.2)	.0	100.0
VI	44.7		29.0	20.2	5.7	(5.1)	.5	100.0
VII	7.4		20.8	70.1	1.5	(1.4)	.1	100.0
VIII	19.4		61.3	5.7	13.4	(1.0)	.2	100.0
IX	34.5		34.1	29.2	1.9	(1.8)	.4	100.0
X			50.8	47.8	1.3		.0	100.0
U			100.0					100.0
T	31.8		8.8	55.2	3.6	(11.3)	.6	100.0

Switzerland

Labour Force by Sector and Status 1910

Absolute figures in thousands

Sector			Employers EM[a]	Self-employed SE[a]	Employees EE	Workers WO	Apprentices AP[b]	Family-workers FW[b]	Unknown U	Total T	%
I	Agriculture	Total	213.3	2.7	261.1	(.9)	(154.7)			477.1	26.8
		males	187.4	2.6	185.7	(.9)	(91.6)			375.7	31.9
II	Mining	Total	.5	.3	5.3	(.1)	(.1)			6.1	.3
		males	.5	.3	5.3	(.1)	(.1)			6.0	.5
III	Manufacturing	Total	182.2	46.5	429.2	(41.7)	(33.0)			657.8	36.9
		males	101.7	35.4	274.2	(28.1)	(15.2)			411.3	34.9
IV	Construction	Total	15.2	8.6	93.3	(4.0)	(2.2)			117.2	6.6
		males	15.1	8.1	93.3	(3.9)	(2.1)			116.5	9.9
V	Utilities	Total	.0	2.0	6.2	(.2)	(.0)			8.2	.5
		males	.0	1.9	6.2	(.2)	(.0)			8.1	.7
VI	Commerce	Total	37.0	45.8	18.0	(4.5)	(10.1)			100.8	5.7
		males	26.0	23.3	16.7	(3.2)	(2.9)			66.0	5.6
VII	Transport	Total	5.2	25.1	54.4	(1.2)	(.9)			84.7	4.8
		males	5.1	21.5	52.7	(1.0)	(.8)			79.2	6.7
VIII	Banking	Total	.4	11.4	.5	(1.8)	(.0)			12.3	.7
		males	.4	10.1	.5	(1.8)	(.0)			11.0	.9
IX	Services	Total	60.6	58.6	173.1	(3.9)	(16.5)			292.2	16.4
		males	26.9	28.8	26.0	(2.0)	(1.4)			81.7	6.9
X	Public admin.	Total		15.6	2.4	(.2)				18.1	1.0
		males		15.2	2.2	(.2)				17.4	1.5
U	Unknown	Total			8.6					8.6	.5
		males			5.7					5.7	.5
T	All sectors	Total	514.4	216.6	1 052.2	(58.3)	(217.5)			1 783.2	100.0
		males	363.1	147.2	668.4	(41.5)	(114.1)			1 178.8	100.0

Percent distributions

Total labour force

	EM	SE	EE	WO	AP	FW	U	T
I	44.7		.6	54.7	(.2)	(32.4)		100.0
II	7.8		4.9	87.4	(1.4)	(1.9)		100.0
III	27.7		7.1	65.2	(6.3)	(5.0)		100.0
IV	13.0		7.4	79.6	(3.4)	(1.9)		100.0
V	.3		24.4	75.3	(2.2)	(.0)		100.0
VI	36.7		45.4	17.9	(4.5)	(10.0)		100.0
VII	6.2		29.7	64.2	(1.4)	(1.0)		100.0
VIII	3.3		92.3	4.3	(14.7)	(.4)		100.0
IX	20.7		20.0	59.2	(1.3)	(5.6)		100.0
X			86.5	13.5	(1.2)			100.0
U				100.0				100.0
T	28.8		12.1	59.0	(3.3)	(12.2)		100.0

Male labour force

	EM	SE	EE	WO	AP	FW	U	T
I	49.9		.7	49.4	(.2)	(24.4)		100.0
II	7.6		4.8	87.6	(1.4)	(1.9)		100.0
III	24.7		8.6	66.7	(6.8)	(3.7)		100.0
IV	13.0		7.0	80.0	(3.4)	(1.8)		100.0
V	.3		23.3	76.4	(2.2)	(.0)		100.0
VI	39.4		35.3	25.2	(4.9)	(4.3)		100.0
VII	6.4		27.1	66.5	(1.3)	(1.1)		100.0
VIII	3.7		91.9	4.5	(16.1)	(.4)		100.0
IX	32.9		35.2	31.8	(2.5)	(1.8)		100.0
X			87.2	12.8	(1.1)			100.0
U				100.0				100.0
T	30.8		12.5	56.7	(3.5)	(9.7)		100.0

L a b o u r   F o r c e   b y   S e c t o r   a n d   S t a t u s   1 9 2 0

Absolute figures in thousands

Sector			Employ-ers EM[a]	Self-employed SE[a]	Employ-ees EE	Workers WO	Apprent-ices AP	Family-workers FW[b]	Un-known U	Total T	%
I	Agriculture	Total	212.3	3.3	265.5	1.7	(156.6)		482.8	25.8
		males	185.8	3.2	195.0	1.7	(97.2)		385.6	31.2
II	Mining	Total	.4	.4	5.1	.1	(.1)		5.9	.3
		males	.4	.4	5.0	.1	(.1)		5.8	.5
III	Manufacturing	Total	141.6	62.6	429.1	52.3	(25.7)		685.6	36.6
		males	85.5	45.8	271.5	36.8	(13.8)		439.6	35.6
IV	Construction	Total	14.4	6.8	73.7	3.8	(2.5)		98.7	5.3
		males	14.2	6.3	73.5	3.7	(2.4)		97.7	7.9
V	Utilities	Total	.0	3.7	8.5	.3	(.0)		12.6	.7
		males	.0	3.3	8.5	.3	(.0)		12.1	1.0
VI	Commerce	Total	37.9	49.9	19.8	6.3	(8.9)		113.9	6.1
		males	27.5	22.4	18.1	3.5	(2.7)		71.5	5.8
VII	Transport	Total	3.9	27.2	58.1	2.1	(.7)		91.3	4.9
		males	3.8	21.2	56.6	1.7	(.7)		83.3	6.7
VIII	Banking	Total	.4	19.3	.8	2.5	(.0)		23.0	1.2
		males	.4	15.1	.8	2.3	(.0)		18.5	1.5
IX	Services	Total	59.5	66.5	187.1	4.2	(13.6)		317.3	17.0
		males	27.9	33.6	24.8	2.3	(1.3)		88.6	7.2
X	Public admin.	Total		23.0	3.4	.3			26.8	1.4
		males		21.0	3.0	.3			24.3	2.0
U	Unknown[c]	Total		2.0	11.3	.6	(.2)		13.9	.7
		males		.7	8.6	.2	(.2)		9.4	.8
T	All sectors	Total	470.4	264.6	1 062.5	74.2	(208.4)		1 871.7	100.0
		males	345.4	172.8	665.2	52.8	(118.5)		1 236.3	100.0

Percent distributions

Total labour force

	EM	SE	EE	WO	AP	FW	U	T
I	44.0		.7	55.0	.4	(32.4)		100.0
II	6.4		7.5	85.2	.9	(1.9)		100.0
III	20.7		9.1	62.6	7.6	(3.7)		100.0
IV	14.6		6.9	74.7	3.9	(2.5)		100.0
V	.1		29.7	67.7	2.6	(.0)		100.0
VI	33.3		43.8	17.4	5.5	(7.8)		100.0
VII	4.3		29.8	63.7	2.3	(.7)		100.0
VIII	1.6		84.0	3.6	10.8	(.2)		100.0
IX	18.8		21.0	59.0	1.3	(4.3)		100.0
X			86.0	12.9	1.1			100.0
U			14.1	81.6	4.3	(1.8)		100.0
T	25.1		14.1	56.8	4.0	(11.1)		100.0

Male labour force

	EM	SE	EE	WO	AP	FW	U	T
I	48.2		.8	50.6	.4	(25.2)		100.0
II	6.4		7.2	85.5	.9	(1.9)		100.0
III	19.4		10.4	61.8	8.4	(3.1)		100.0
IV	14.5		6.4	75.2	3.8	(2.4)		100.0
V	.1		27.3	70.0	2.6	(.0)		100.0
VI	38.5		31.3	25.3	4.9	(3.8)		100.0
VII	4.6		25.5	68.0	2.0	(.8)		100.0
VIII	2.0		81.7	4.1	12.3	(.2)		100.0
IX	31.5		37.9	27.9	2.6	(1.5)		100.0
X			86.6	12.4	1.1			100.0
U			7.1	90.9	2.0	(2.6)		100.0
T	27.9		14.0	53.8	4.3	(9.6)		100.0

Labour Force by Sector and Status 1930

Absolute figures in thousands

Sector			Employ-ers	Self-employed	Employ-ees	Workers	Apprent-ices	Family-workers	Un-known	Total	%
			EM	SE	EE	WO[a]	AP	FW	U	T	
I	Agriculture	Total	193.4		3.0	97.7	1.7	117.6		413.3	21.3
		males	177.1		2.9	92.4	1.6	88.0		362.0	27.2
II	Mining	Total	.5		.4	6.3	.1	.2		7.5	.4
		males	.5		.4	6.2	.1	.1		7.4	.6
III	Manufacturing	Total	106.7		77.0	439.2	50.9	15.2		688.9	35.5
		males	75.2		55.3	294.0	41.1	10.2		475.8	35.7
IV	Construction	Total	17.1		9.6	102.0	6.7	3.0		138.5	7.1
		males	16.7		8.6	101.8	6.5	2.8		136.4	10.2
V	Utilities	Total	.0		3.9	9.6	.3	.0		13.9	.7
		males	.0		3.5	9.6	.3	.0		13.5	1.0
VI	Commerce	Total	45.3		68.0	21.3	9.0	10.0		153.6	7.9
		males	33.2		37.5	16.0	3.8	3.5		94.2	7.1
VII	Transport	Total	4.3		30.7	47.9	1.5	.6		85.0	4.4
		males	4.2		24.8	46.7	1.2	.6		77.5	5.8
VIII	Banking	Total	.6		24.8	1.4	2.6	.1		29.5	1.5
		males	.6		19.1	1.3	2.3	.0		23.5	1.8
IX	Services	Total	60.7		68.7	225.0	4.5	12.0		370.9	19.1
		males	32.1		35.7	30.4	1.8	4.2		104.1	7.8
X	Public admin.	Total			23.1	3.7	.3			27.1	1.4
		males			20.7	3.3	.2			24.3	1.8
U	Unknown [b]	Total				14.0	.3			14.4	.7
		males				12.5	.3			12.7	1.0
T	All sectors	Total	428.6		309.2	968.1	78.0	158.7		1 942.6	100.0
		males	339.6		208.5	614.3	59.3	109.6		1 331.4	100.0

Percent distributions

Total labour force

	EM	SE	EE	WO	AP	FW	U	T
I	46.8		.7	23.6	.4	28.4		100.0
II	6.8		5.5	83.8	1.8	2.1		100.0
III	15.5		11.2	63.8	7.4	2.2		100.0
IV	12.4		7.0	73.7	4.8	2.2		100.0
V	.1		28.2	69.3	2.5	.0		100.0
VI	29.5		44.3	13.9	5.9	6.5		100.0
VII	5.1		36.1	56.3	1.7	.7		100.0
VIII	2.2		83.9	4.8	8.9	.2		100.0
IX	16.4		18.5	60.6	1.2	3.2		100.0
X			85.3	13.6	1.1			100.0
U				97.6	2.4			100.0
T	22.1		15.9	49.8	4.0	8.2		100.0

Male labour force

	EM	SE	EE	WO	AP	FW	U	T
I	48.9		.8	25.5	.4	24.3		100.0
II	6.8		5.1	84.3	1.8	2.0		100.0
III	15.8		11.6	61.8	8.6	2.2		100.0
IV	12.2		6.3	74.7	4.8	2.1		100.0
V	.1		26.0	71.4	2.5	.0		100.0
VI	35.3		39.9	17.0	4.1	3.7		100.0
VII	5.5		32.0	60.2	1.6	.8		100.0
VIII	2.7		81.4	5.7	10.0	.2		100.0
IX	30.8		34.2	29.2	1.7	4.1		100.0
X			85.2	13.8	1.0			100.0
U				98.0	2.0			100.0
T	25.5		15.7	46.1	4.5	8.2		100.0

Labour Force by Sector and Status 1941

Absolute figures in thousands

Sector			Employ-ers	Self-employed	Employ-ees	Workers	Apprent-ices	Family-workers	Un-known	Total	%
			EM	SE	EE	WO a)	AP	FW	U	T	
I	Agriculture	Total	189.6	2.5	104.4	1.3	117.2		414.9	20.8	
		males	175.7	2.5	100.9	1.2	104.5		384.8	27.1	
II	Mining	Total	.5	.5	6.4	.0	.1		7.5	.4	
		males	.5	.5	6.3	.0	.1		7.3	.5	
III	Manufacturing	Total	101.4	90.6	454.4	46.1	15.0		707.5	35.5	
		males	74.8	66.8	317.5	36.4	10.1		505.5	35.5	
IV	Construction	Total	19.3	11.8	100.6	3.6	2.2		137.6	6.9	
		males	19.0	10.9	100.1	3.5	2.0		135.6	9.5	
V	Utilities	Total	.0	4.7	10.5	.3	.0		15.4	.8	
		males	.0	4.2	10.4	.2	.0		14.9	1.0	
VI	Commerce	Total	46.2	63.4	30.5	8.1	8.6		156.8	7.9	
		males	33.5	28.7	26.5	3.1	3.0		94.9	6.7	
VII	Transport	Total	4.1	29.7	40.8	1.5	.6		76.7	3.9	
		males	4.0	24.9	39.7	1.2	.6		70.4	5.0	
VIII	Banking	Total	.9	27.7	1.4	1.9	.0		32.0	1.6	
		males	.9	22.0	1.2	1.6	.0		25.8	1.8	
IX	Services	Total	58.9	71.6	214.8	6.7	7.1		359.1	18.0	
		males	33.6	40.0	31.8	2.4	1.6		109.4	7.7	
X	Public admin.	Total		36.8	8.7	.4			45.9	2.3	
		males		32.2	8.0	.4			40.6	2.9	
U	Unknown b)	Total		8.8	29.5	.7			39.0	2.0	
		males		6.5	26.0	.6			33.0	2.3	
T	All sectors	Total	420.9	348.2	1 002.0	70.6	150.8		1 992.5	100.0	
		males	342.1	239.2	668.5	50.6	121.9		1 422.3	100.0	

Percent distributions

	Total labour force								Male labour force							
	EM	SE	EE	WO	AP	FW	U	T		EM	SE	EE	WO	AP	FW	U	T
I	45.7		.6	25.2	.3	28.2		100.0	I	45.7		.6	26.2	.3	27.2		100.0
II	6.2		6.8	85.3	.5	1.2		100.0	II	6.2		6.4	85.8	.4	1.2		100.0
III	14.3		12.8	64.2	6.5	2.1		100.0	III	14.8		13.2	62.8	7.2	2.0		100.0
IV	14.0		8.6	73.1	2.7	1.6		100.0	IV	14.0		8.1	73.9	2.6	1.5		100.0
V	.1		30.5	67.8	1.6	.0		100.0	V	.1		28.4	69.9	1.6	.0		100.0
VI	29.5		40.4	19.5	5.1	5.5		100.0	VI	35.3		30.3	28.0	3.2	3.2		100.0
VII	5.4		38.7	53.2	1.9	.8		100.0	VII	5.7		35.4	56.4	1.7	.8		100.0
VIII	2.8		86.7	4.4	5.9	.1		100.0	VIII	3.5		85.3	4.8	6.4	.1		100.0
IX	16.4		19.9	59.8	1.9	2.0		100.0	IX	30.7		36.5	29.1	2.2	1.4		100.0
X			80.2	18.8	1.0			100.0	X			79.4	19.7	.9			100.0
U			22.5	75.8	1.7			100.0	U			19.6	78.7	1.7			100.0
T	21.1		17.5	50.3	3.5	7.6		100.0	T	24.1		16.8	47.0	3.6	8.6		100.0

Labour Force by Sector and Status 1950

Absolute figures in thousands

Sector			Employers	Self-employed	Employees	Workers	Apprentices	Family-workers	Unknown	Total	%
			EM	SE	EE	WO[a]	AP	FW	U	T	
I	Agriculture	Total	171.3		3.0	80.4	1.0	99.8		355.4	16.5
		males	159.9		2.9	77.9	.8	83.9		325.3	21.5
II	Mining	Total	.5		.4	5.2	.0	.1		6.3	.3
		males	.5		.4	5.2	.0	.1		6.2	.4
III	Manufacturing	Total	96.1		129.2	511.2	54.1	12.7		803.3	37.3
		males	76.7		94.0	355.3	45.0	7.8		578.8	38.2
IV	Construction	Total	22.0		17.7	119.3	6.6	2.0		167.6	7.8
		males	21.8		16.1	119.3	6.5	1.8		165.5	10.9
V	Utilities	Total	.0		5.8	11.9	.6	.0		18.3	.8
		males	.0		5.1	11.9	.5	.0		17.6	1.2
VI	Commerce	Total	51.6		92.8	37.2	11.8	8.5		201.9	9.4
		males	38.8		42.1	31.1	3.9	2.6		118.5	7.8
VII	Transport	Total	4.2		41.8	49.6	2.0	.5		98.0	4.5
		males	4.1		33.8	48.2	1.5	.4		88.0	5.8
VIII	Banking	Total	.7		35.6	1.5	2.3	.0		40.0	1.9
		males	.7		26.8	1.2	1.6	.0		30.3	2.0
IX	Services	Total	62.4		86.1	225.8	8.1	7.3		389.7	18.1
		males	38.4		46.5	35.4	2.9	1.1		124.3	8.2
X	Public admin. [b]	Total	.1		42.0	14.9	.8	.4		58.2	2.7
		males	.0		34.8	11.8	.1	.4		47.2	3.1
U	Unknown [c]	Total			4.5	11.8	.6			17.0	.8
		males			2.9	10.3	.3			13.6	.9
T	All sectors	Total	408.9		458.9	1 068.8	87.8	131.3		2 155.7	100.0
		males	341.0		305.3	707.5	63.3	98.2		1 515.2	100.0

Percent distributions

Total labour force

	EM	SE	EE	WO	AP	FW	U	T
I	48.2		.8	22.6	.3	28.1		100.0
II	8.6		6.8	82.6	.8	1.2		100.0
III	12.0		16.1	63.6	6.7	1.6		100.0
IV	13.1		10.6	71.2	3.9	1.2		100.0
V	.0		31.8	65.2	3.1	.0		100.0
VI	25.5		46.0	18.4	5.8	4.2		100.0
VII	4.3		42.6	50.6	2.0	.5		100.0
VIII	1.8		88.9	3.7	5.6	.0		100.0
IX	16.0		22.1	57.9	2.1	1.9		100.0
X	.1		72.2	25.6	1.4	.8		100.0
U			26.8	69.8	3.4			100.0
T	19.0		21.3	49.6	4.1	6.1		100.0

Male labour force

	EM	SE	EE	WO	AP	FW	U	T
I	49.1		.9	23.9	.3	25.8		100.0
II	8.6		6.4	83.2	.8	1.0		100.0
III	13.3		16.2	61.4	7.8	1.4		100.0
IV	13.2		9.7	72.1	3.9	1.1		100.0
V	.0		29.3	67.6	3.0	.0		100.0
VI	32.7		35.5	26.3	3.3	2.2		100.0
VII	4.7		38.4	54.7	1.7	.5		100.0
VIII	2.3		88.3	3.9	5.4	.0		100.0
IX	30.9		37.4	28.5	2.3	.9		100.0
X	.0		73.7	25.0	.3	.9		100.0
U			21.2	76.2	2.6			100.0
T	22.5		20.1	46.7	4.2	6.5		100.0

Labour Force by Sector and Status 1960

Absolute figures in thousands

Sector			Employ-ers	Self-employed	Employ-ees	Workers	Apprent-ices	Family-workers	Un-known	Total	%
			EM	SE	EE	WO[a]	AP	FW	U	T	
I	Agriculture	Total	112.4	27.8	3.2	60.8	1.1	75.0		280.2	11.2
		males	108.7	25.4	3.0	58.7	.8	60.7		257.3	14.7
II	Mining	Total	.4	.1	.6	5.3	.1	.1		6.5	.3
		males	.4	.1	.5	5.2	.0	.1		6.4	.4
III	Manufacturing	Total	52.3	29.8	195.5	638.1	68.0	15.9		999.6	39.8
		males	48.7	21.6	140.9	448.8	58.1	7.6		725.7	41.3
IV	Construction	Total	17.6	6.4	32.1	170.1	10.5	2.7		239.5	9.5
		males	17.5	6.4	28.9	169.3	10.0	2.2		234.3	13.3
V	Utilities	Total	.0	.0	7.4	13.4	1.0	.0		21.8	.9
		males	.0	.0	6.4	13.3	.9	.0		20.6	1.2
VI	Commerce	Total	28.7	17.8	124.8	57.8	18.3	10.5		257.9	10.3
		males	23.0	11.5	51.8	44.8	5.7	2.5		139.3	7.9
VII	Transport	Total	3.1	3.1	53.3	70.5	4.4	.7		135.1	5.4
		males	2.9	3.1	41.1	68.3	3.0	.6		119.0	6.8
VIII	Banking	Total	.8	.2	47.7	2.0	4.1	.1		54.9	2.2
		males	.8	.2	32.9	1.4	2.5	.0		37.9	2.2
IX	Services	Total	36.4	28.6	115.3	233.1	14.5	12.2		440.1	17.5
		males	28.0	11.3	60.1	50.8	5.2	1.8		157.3	9.0
X	Public admin.[b]	Total	.1	.0	51.4	14.5	1.8			67.8	2.7
		males	.0	.0	40.9	10.7	.8			52.5	3.0
U	Unknown[c]	Total				2.2	6.4	.6		9.3	.4
		males				.6	4.6	.4		5.6	.3
T	All sectors	Total	251.7	113.8	633.5	1 272.0	124.3	117.2		2 512.4	100.0
		males	230.1	79.6	407.3	876.0	87.4	75.5		1 756.0	100.0

Percent distributions

Total labour force

	EM	SE	EE	WO	AP	FW	U	T
I	40.1	9.9	1.1	21.7	.4	26.8		100.0
II	6.7	1.0	9.3	81.0	.8	1.3		100.0
III	5.2	3.0	19.6	63.8	6.8	1.6		100.0
IV	7.4	2.7	13.4	71.1	4.4	1.1		100.0
V	.0	.0	33.9	61.6	4.5	.0		100.0
VI	11.1	6.9	48.4	22.4	7.1	4.1		100.0
VII	2.3	2.3	39.4	52.2	3.2	.5		100.0
VIII	1.4	.4	87.0	3.6	7.5	.1		100.0
IX	8.3	6.5	26.2	53.0	3.3	2.8		100.0
X	.1	.0	75.8	21.4	2.7			100.0
U			24.3	69.3	6.5			100.0
T	10.0	4.5	25.2	50.6	4.9	4.7		100.0

Male labour force

	EM	SE	EE	WO	AP	FW	U	T
I	42.2	9.9	1.2	22.8	.3	23.6		100.0
II	6.7	1.0	8.4	82.2	.7	1.1		100.0
III	6.7	3.0	19.4	61.8	8.0	1.0		100.0
IV	7.5	2.7	12.3	72.3	4.3	1.0		100.0
V	.0	.0	31.1	64.5	4.4	.0		100.0
VI	16.5	8.3	37.2	32.1	4.1	1.8		100.0
VII	2.5	2.6	34.5	57.4	2.5	.5		100.0
VIII	2.0	.5	86.9	3.8	6.7	.1		100.0
IX	17.8	7.2	38.2	32.3	3.3	1.1		100.0
X	.0	.0	78.0	20.5	1.5			100.0
U			10.8	82.0	7.2			100.0
T	13.1	4.5	23.2	49.9	5.0	4.3		100.0

Labour Force by Sector and Status 1970

Absolute figures in thousands

Sector			Employ-ers	Self-employed	Employ-ees	Workers	Apprent-ices	Family-workers	Un-known	Total	%
			EM	SE	EE	WO[a]	AP	FW	U	T	
I	Agriculture	Total	81.2	22.8	5.4	39.2	3.5	78.6		230.7	7.7
		males	79.1	21.2	5.0	34.3	3.0	35.2		177.8	9.0
II	Mining	Total	.3	.0	1.3	5.1	.0	.1		6.8	.2
		males	.3	.0	1.0	5.0	.0	.0		6.5	.3
III	Manufacturing	Total	45.3	23.0	308.8	666.6	66.3	19.7		1 129.8	37.7
		males	43.4	17.6	224.2	457.6	56.5	5.0		804.4	40.8
IV	Construction	Total	19.3	6.6	66.6	177.1	12.2	3.3		285.2	9.5
		males	19.2	6.6	58.0	175.4	11.1	1.5		271.7	13.8
V	Utilities	Total	.0	.0	10.0	12.2	1.2	.0		23.4	.8
		males	.0	.0	8.5	11.9	1.1	.0		21.5	1.1
VI	Commerce	Total	27.0	15.5	217.2	92.9	22.4	15.0		390.0	13.0
		males	22.1	9.7	92.4	68.9	9.3	2.3		204.6	10.4
VII	Transport	Total	3.6	4.0	79.4	76.5	5.3	1.1		169.9	5.7
		males	3.5	3.9	56.2	72.0	3.0	.5		139.1	7.0
VIII	Banking	Total	.7	.2	83.2	4.3	6.5	.1		95.0	3.2
		males	.7	.2	50.7	2.4	3.4	.0		57.4	2.9
IX	Services	Total	40.2	22.9	203.8	256.1	21.9	19.5		564.4	18.8
		males	31.0	13.3	99.4	64.5	6.0	1.9		216.0	10.9
X	Public admin.	Total			73.1	16.3	2.2			91.6	3.1
		males			54.9	12.6	1.3			68.8	3.5
U	Unknown[b]	Total			2.1	6.4	.5			9.0	.3
		males			.9	4.3	.2			5.4	.3
T	All sectors	Total	217.7	95.0	1 050.9	1 352.7	142.2	137.3		2 995.8	100.0
		males	199.2	72.5	651.1	909.0	95.1	46.4		1 973.3	100.0

Percent distributions

Total labour force

	EM	SE	EE	WO	AP	FW	U	T
I	35.2	9.9	2.3	17.0	1.5	34.1		100.0
II	4.4	.7	18.7	74.6	.7	.9		100.0
III	4.0	2.0	27.3	59.0	5.9	1.7		100.0
IV	6.8	2.3	23.4	62.1	4.3	1.2		100.0
V	.0	.0	42.6	52.2	5.2	.0		100.0
VI	6.9	4.0	55.7	23.8	5.8	3.8		100.0
VII	2.1	2.3	46.7	45.1	3.1	.7		100.0
VIII	.8	.2	87.5	4.5	6.9	.1		100.0
IX	7.1	4.1	36.1	45.4	3.9	3.5		100.0
X			79.8	17.8	2.4			100.0
U			23.2	71.3	5.4			100.0
T	7.3	3.2	35.1	45.2	4.7	4.6		100.0

Male labour force

	EM	SE	EE	WO	AP	FW	U	T
I	44.5	11.9	2.8	19.3	1.7	19.8		100.0
II	4.5	.7	16.1	77.6	.6	.4		100.0
III	5.4	2.2	27.9	56.9	7.0	.6		100.0
IV	7.1	2.4	21.3	64.5	4.1	.5		100.0
V	.0	.0	39.6	55.2	5.1	.0		100.0
VI	10.8	4.7	45.1	33.7	4.6	1.1		100.0
VII	2.5	2.8	40.4	51.8	2.2	.4		100.0
VIII	1.2	.3	88.2	4.2	6.0	.0		100.0
IX	14.3	6.1	46.0	29.8	2.8	.9		100.0
X			79.7	18.4	1.9			100.0
U			16.7	79.7	3.5			100.0
T	10.1	3.7	33.0	46.1	4.8	2.4		100.0

Notes:

1880-1970	Resident population of age 14 and over
1900-1960	Excluding part-time employment
1900-1930	Including unemployed, classified according to their previous occupation
1941-1970	Including unemployed as a separate category
1970	Including part-time employment

1880
a) Excluding unemployed
b) Apprentices partially included among the dependent labour force, partially excluded from the labour force due to enumeration problems

1900
a) Included in the figures for Employees, Workers and Apprentices
b) Including home-workers

1910
a) Including self-employed home-workers
b) Included among Employees and Workers

1920
a) Including self-employed home-workers
b) Included in the figures for Employees, Workers and Apprentices
c) Including persons in public institutional households working at the time of the census

1930
a) Including home-workers
b) Including persons in public institutional households working at the time of the census

1941
a) Including home-workers
b) Including persons in public institutional households working at the time of the census; including unemployed, in earlier censuses distributed according to their previous occupation

1950-1960
a) Including home-workers
b) Including some private, state-approved reform schools
c) see 1941 note (b)

1970
a) Including home-workers
b) Including unemployed

Labour Force excluding Family Workers

Year	AU	BE	DE	FI	FR	GE	IR	IT	NE	NO	SW	SZ	UK	Year
1975	2 940	3 675	2 368	2 163	21 094	24 790	1 114	18 189	4 932	1 444	3 505	2 967	27 495	1975
1974	2 991	3 669	2 361	2 152	20 796	24 986	1 100	18 128	4 875	1 440	3 466	2 975	27 469	1974
1973	3 033	3 661	2 350	2 140	20 579	25 061	1 086	18 064	4 824	1 434	3 432	2 960	27 424	1973
1972	3 065	3 653	2 336	2 127	20 277	25 044	1 073	17 958	4 771	1 427	3 401	2 930	27 320	1972
1971	3 094	3 643	2 323	2 113	19 967	24 998	1 060	17 872	4 710	1 419	3 367	2 892	27 204	1971
1970	3 127	3 640	2 307	2 110	19 649	24 837	1 050	17 864	4 642	1 413	3 319	2 857	27 072	1970
1969	3 158	3 642	2 289	2 117	19 345	24 700	1 042	17 848	4 573	1 406	3 312	2 823	26 960	1969
1968	3 189	3 637	2 278	2 118	19 062	24 569	1 037	17 835	4 508	1 397	3 312	2 778	28 816	1968
1967	3 218	3 628	2 265	2 108	18 876	24 582	1 033	17 827	4 447	1 388	3 317	2 737	26 668	1967
1966	3 248	3 613	2 245	2 096	18 684	24 626	1 027	17 793	4 387	1 379	3 315	2 698	26 493	1966
1965	3 276	3 594	2 227	2 088	18 484	24 506	1 022	17 762	4 318	1 371	3 306	2 666	26 313	1965
1964	3 302	3 567	2 192	2 080	18 307	24 334	1 015	17 736	4 248	1 363	3 265	2 626	26 104	1964
1963	3 326	3 538	2 158	2 068	18 051	24 186	1 007	17 634	4 180	1 355	3 230	2 571	25 886	1963
1962	3 350	3 525	2 125	2 053	17 686	24 053	998	17 547	4 112	1 348	3 201	2 514	25 693	1962
1961	3 373	3 518	2 091	2 039	17 439	23 869	991	17 536	4 043	1 340	3 173	2 433	25 411	1961
1960	3 360	3 516	2 061	2 024	17 325	23 310	1 001	17 402	3 979	1 332	3 146	2 366	25 165	1960
1959	3 348	3 517	2 057	2 023	17 226	22 834	1 011	17 260	3 943	1 332	3 134	2 314	24 927	1959
1958	3 340	3 516	2 053	2 023	17 121	22 352	1 018	17 108	3 898	1 332	3 121	2 282	24 745	1958
1957	3 335	3 511	2 051	2 021	17 003	21 854	1 034	16 962	3 854	1 330	3 104	2 243	24 602	1957
1956	3 333	3 505	2 051	2 017	16 888	21 357	1 044	16 826	3 817	1 329	3 086	2 202	24 448	1956
1955	3 336	3 502	2 049	2 009	16 795	20 874	1 057	16 691	3 779	1 326	3 066	2 168	24 298	1955
1954	3 337	3 501	2 044	2 001	16 716	20 446	1 069	16 547	3 743	1 324	3 048	2 140	24 176	1954
1953	3 339	3 504	2 036	1 993	16 745	20 011	1 077	16 404	3 711	1 321	3 032	2 112	24 058	1953
1952	3 341	3 503	2 030	1 984	16 780	19 596	1 083	16 275	3 682	1 318	3 015	2 079	23 945	1952
1951	3 350	3 501	2 026	1 977	16 809	19 246	1 091	16 148	3 651	1 315	2 995	2 045	23 842	1951
1950	3 355	3 504	2 020	1 972	16 824	18 890	1 093	15 997	3 608	1 313	2 973	2 016	23 937	1950
1949	3 364			1 964		18 307				1 289	2 950	1 994	23 781	1949
1948	3 375			1 952		17 742				1 265	2 922	1 970	23 605	1948
1947	3 365			1 939		17 072				1 240	2 890	1 946	23 336	1947
1946	3 409			1 926		16 578				1 214	2 857	1 923	23 159	1946
1945				1 950						1 194	2 824	1 900		1945
1944				1 938						1 176	2 801	1 881		1944
1943				1 931						1 159	2 780	1 864		1943
1942				1 925						1 144	2 764	1 849		1942
1941				1 921						1 131	2 754	1 836		1941
1940				1 919						1 118	2 749	1 827	24 229	1940
1939	3 526			1 894		28 835				1 105	2 729	1 821	23 855	1939
1938	3 493			1 943		28 438				1 092	2 710	1 818	23 581	1938
1937	3 407			1 925		28 166				1 080	2 694	1 815	23 339	1937
1936	3 322			1 893		27 940				1 068	2 679	1 813	23 097	1936
1935	3 237			1 863		27 716				1 057	2 665	1 810	22 854	1935
1934	3 148			1 832		27 162				1 046	2 650	1 806	22 618	1934
1933	3 143			1 803		26 981				1 034	2 634	1 800	22 409	1933
1932	3 134			1 774		26 952				1 023	2 617	1 794	22 183	1932
1931	3 124			1 742		26 933				1 010	2 600	1 787	21 922	1931
1930	3 115			1 710		26 890				999	2 584	1 777	21 735	1930
1929	3 105			1 687		26 846						1 760	21 554	1929
1928	3 096			1 664		26 800						1 742	21 422	1928
1927	3 086			1 639		26 741						1 724	21 246	1927
1926	3 077			1 615		26 673						1 709	21 085	1926
1925	3 067			1 589		26 575						1 696	20 917	1925
1924	3 058			1 564		26 473						1 686	20 764	1924
1923	3 049			1 539		26 406							20 530	1923
1922	3 042			1 513		26 330							20 341	1922
1921	3 031			1 486		26 979							20 119	1921

Appendix to Table 1

Labour Force excluding Family Workers

Year	AU	BE	DE	FI	FR	GE	IR	IT	NE	NO	SW	SZ	UK	Year
1920	3 008			1 460		26 779							21 283	1920
1919	2 992			1 442		27 352							21 063	1919
1918				1 342										1918
1917				1 340										1917
1916				1 331										1916
1915				1 320									22 138	1915
1914				1 306									21 684	1914
1913	2 260			1 292		25 609							21 184	1913
1912						25 308							20 775	1912
1911						25 024							20 389	1911
1910						24 738							19 923	1910
1909						24 428							19 711	1909
1908						24 117							19 499	1908
1907						23 807							19 292	1907
1906						23 492							19 090	1906
1905						23 186							18 887	1905
1904						22 879							18 689	1904
1903						22 568							18 494	1903
1902						22 251							18 304	1902
1901						21 922							18 115	1901
1900						21 617							17 944	1900
1899						21 324							17 775	1899
1898						21 013							17 600	1898
1897						20 704							17 426	1897
1896						20 402							17 253	1896
1895						20 124							17 085	1895
1894						19 813							16 925	1894
1893						19 541							16 761	1893
1892						19 294							16 603	1892
1891						19 044							16 455	1891
1890						18 788							16 314	1890
1889						18 458							16 178	1889
1888						18 219							16 045	1888
1887						17 985							15 919	1887
1886						17 769							15 793	1886
1885						17 568							15 660	1885
1884						17 379							15 531	1884
1883						17 209							15 409	1883
1882						17 048							15 300	1882
1881						16 890							15 179	1881
1880						16 717							15 041	1880
1879						16 501								1879
1878						16 264								1878
1877						16 025								1877
1876						15 776								1876
1875						15 529								1875
1874						15 291								1874
1873						15 082								1873
1872						14 911								1872
1871						14 798								1871

Chapter 8

INCOME DISTRIBUTION

This chapter provides data on the distribution of national income by factor shares and on the distribution of personal income by size of income. Data on the distribution of national income come from national account statistics. Data on the distribution of personal income are mainly derived from income tax statistics; in a few cases, they are taken from country studies.

For the classical economists, the most important inequalities of income were those originating from the division of the national product between land and capital on the one hand, and labour on the other. For these economists, the community was correspondingly composed of three classes: landowners, capitalists, and labourers. Compared with the high incomes coming from property (first from land and then increasingly from commercial and industrial capital), income differences within the propertyless labour class seemed negligible. Marx even expected that income differences within classes would diminish and those between them would increase.

This expectation was misleading in several respects. As a long-term trend, the proportion of property income in national income has fallen. Correspondingly, the share of income from work has increased, not only as a consequence of the rise in the share of employees in the total labour force, but also because of the greater investment in maintaining and increasing the quality of labour. In addition, the spread between higher and lower earnings from labour has become wider due to the relative growth of technical and professional labour, and the increase in number of managers and officials in large-scale publice and private enterprise. Thus, in general the variance of personal income today is more attributable to inequalities of earnings than to the inequality of property-holding.

The chapter contains two tables for most countries. The first gives data on the distribution of net domestic product at factor cost (by economic institution, type of income, and income position). Net domestic product is defined as gross domestic product minus capital consumption (depreciation) and minus the net balance of indirect taxes and subsidies or — equivalently — as the sum of all factor incomes (for the absolute figures, see chapter 5). For the purpose of this chapter, the difference between the net domestic product at factor cost and the national income, which includes the net balance of factor payments to and from abroad, is negligible.

The first table shows the percentage distribution of net domestic product among the three categories of 'factor cost': compensation of employees, income of entrepreneurs, and income from property. Whereas the first category is relatively clear, the distinction between the two others is problematic. Income from property usually includes property income of households (dividends, interest, money rents, and rents imputed on owner-occupied housing), net profits of corporations (after payment of dividends but before payment of direct taxes), and property and entrepreneurial income of government. It does not include, however, the capital component of the total income of unincorporated entrepreneurs and self-employed persons. Any allocation of this total income between a compensation of entrepreneurial work and a return on capital is necessarily arbitrary to a large extent.

Several indicators of income inequality can be calculated on the basis of the distribution of national income by factor costs. All of them are based on an assumed identity of functional categories with social classes: the 'compensation of employees' is equalized with the total income of the dependent labour force, and the income from entrepreneurial labour and from property is equalized with the total income of employers and self-employed. This procedure is problematic for two reasons both of which refer to the category of 'property income'. Firstly, workers and employees may also have income from property, and this is increasingly true at least since World War II. Secondly, this category also includes retained profits of corporations and property income of government which are not distributed to private households.

For both reasons, there is a tendency to overestimate the total income of employers and self-employed, especially in more recent periods. No attempt has been made to divide up the property income between entrepreneurs and the dependent labour force, because only slightly different assumptions lead to widely discrepant estimates. We have excluded, however, the property income of government as far as possible (see notes to tables) and then calculated two series: the first by excluding retained profits of corporations, the second by allocating them to the independent labour force. The first table therefore gives the distribution of net domestic product at factor cost by group of recipients (private households, corporations, government).

The relative shares of the two 'social classes' in national income are of course dependent on their relative size. Any meaningful indicator has to take this into account. The first table therefore includes the percentage shares of the dependent labour force in the total labour force (excluding for the sake of greater comparability the category of 'family workers'). For census years these percentages are based on the census figures given in the preceding chapter. For the intercensus years they have been simply interpolated (except for the years around World War I and II for which they have been extrapolated forwards and backwards).

Two principal indicators of inequality have been calculated: the 'wage-profit ratio' and the 'standardized labour's share' (which is more adequately known also as the 'standardized share of compensation'). Both indicators attempt to separate distributional changes from changes in the status composition of the labour force.

The 'wage-profit ratio' compares the 'average dependent income' (compensation of employees divided by the dependent labour force) with the 'average independent income' (income from entrepreneurship and property divided by the number of employers and self-employed). The 'standardized labour's share' instead compares the 'average dependent income' with the 'average national income' (national income divided by the total labour force) and is simply calculated by dividing the share of the compensation of employees in national income (the so-called labour's share) by the share of the dependent labour force in the total labour force (both shares given in the first table). Instead of comparing average incomes one may exclude the status effects by assuming constancy of the status composition. Such an index of the 'hypothetical labour's share' is calculated by multiplying the 'standardized labour's share' by the share of the dependent labour force in the total labour force of a common reference year (here 1970).

These measures (which may point in different directions) give a general indication of the relative income position of the two major 'social classes', workers and employees on the one hand, and employers and self-employed on the other. This is true at least for the period prior to World War II when the property income of the dependent labour force and the retained profits of corporations as well as government property income were relatively insignificant. For a more realistic picture of income inequality, however, the internal heterogeneity of the two 'classes' is too great. This heterogeneity has certainly increased within the dependent labour force due to the relative growth of white-collar occupations. It has probably decreased among employers and self-employed due to the relative decline of agriculture and the concentration process in trade and commerce.

For a more comprehensive and detailed account of the distribution of personal income one has to turn to income tax statistics. These are the only source for an analysis of long-term changes, because the other major source, sample surveys, only covers more recent periods. Income tax statistics usually provide the following information for a varying number of nominal income classes: the number of income tax units, the income, and the assessed taxes (or class specific tax rates). Much less information can be found in these statistics on the distribution of income by occupation and/or economic status or other criteria. In a more systematic way, such information is available only for Austria, Germany, and the Scandinavian countries. These data are not given here, but will be included in a separate handbook (see below).

The second table therefore gives data only on the distribution of pre-tax income among individuals (or other income units) without reference to their socio-economic characteristics. In principle, the data should refer to the incomes that flow directly out of participation in the production process, but in practice they do this only approximately. Especially in earlier times, tax statistics do not provide figures on gross income but only on taxable or even taxed income. The variations in tax exemption levels, deductible items and tax allowances pose a problem of comparability, at least prior to World War II. But even if gross income figures are given, they usually do not include income equivalents such as fringe benefits or retained profits. On the other hand, they may include taxable transfer payments. Among these transfer elements we have generally excluded pensions.

Other problems of cross-national and intertemporal comparability of tax-derived income distribution data arise from differences in the definition of income units and from the varying coverage of income taxation.

It is, individuals who participate in the production process, but in tax statistics the reported income units may be individuals, married couples, or even a mixture of both. This is due to variations in tax legislation (above all in the definition of the tax unit) and differences in publication practices of the statistical offices. The traditional unit of income taxation was the economic household with its aggregate income. In former times a very broad household concept was frequently used which included not only the income of children, but also of other relatives living within the household. More restricted variants of household taxation which confine taxation to the nuclear family have been in existence in France, Italy, and above all in Belgium until the 1970s. In other Western European countries joint taxation (of earned income) has been restricted to married couples for some time now. In the last two decades, however, the individual is increasingly taken as the unit of taxation (in some countries compulsory, in others still optional).

No comparison can be made between income distribution data based on the extended household concept and those based on the individual and/or married couple as tax unit. For this reason the former data have not been included, and Belgium had to be excluded altogether. But even then the problems of comparing the incomes of individuals and couples remain. Fortunately, since World War II, tax returns are increasingly given not only for the respective 'tax units' but also for individuals, and this information may be used for an evaluation of 'mixed' distributions. The synopsis on the following page therefore shows for the relevant countries the respective units of taxation, the units for which statistics are reported, and the share of joint assessments.

A historical analysis of the distribution of personal income requires income tax statistics, but not all income tax systems are equally suitable. The modern European income taxes developed from two types: scheduled taxes and lump-sum taxes (see the following historical synopsis). The scheduled income tax is a set of taxes on different types of income which are not added together to form a person's total income. Very often only certain types of incomes were taxed (partial scheduled income tax). Pure scheduled taxes no longer exist. They have either been supplemented by a personal income tax or replaced by a general personal income tax. The lump-sum income tax, on the other hand, was from the very beginning a tax on an individual's income, although it was often confined to earned income (partial income tax). Only supplementary income taxes and general personal income taxes cover the incomes from all sources and thus provide sufficient information on the size distribution of personal income.

The Introduction of Income Tax Systems

| COUNTRY | SCHEDULE TAXES | | LUMP-SUM TAXES | | |
	Partial Schedule Tax	Schedule Tax	Partial Personal Income Tax	Supplementary Personal Income Tax	General Personal Income Tax
Austria	1849—1896				
Belgium		1919/20—1962		1919/20—1962	
Denmark					1810—44, 70—72, 1903—
Finland					1865—81, 1929—
France	1872—1917	1918—1959			1960—
Germany					1920—
Prussia			1812—14, 51—72		1873—1919
Saxony					1877—1919
Ireland		1923/24—		1923/24—	
Italy	1877—1923			1918—23	1923—
Netherlands			1892/93—1914		1914—
Norway					1892—
Sweden			1861—1903		1810—11, 1903—
Switzerland			1916—32		1933— (Milit.Tax)
U.K.		1803—16, 42—1918		1910—18, 52—	1799—1802, 1918—

The different timing of the introduction of modern income tax systems sets historical limits to a comparative study of income inequality and the different treatment of married couples creates considerable conceptual problems, but the greatest impediment to comparability lies in the varying coverage of income taxation. The synopsis on the following page shows the percentages of taxed persons in the total labour force (in cases of joint taxation of couples the number of single persons has been estimated). It shows that prior to World War II high coverage was the exception rather than the rule. For the interwar period, income distribution can be compared cross-nationally for the upper 50 percent of income recipients at most, while prior to World War I only the upper 10 percent (or even less) can be compared. The major exception from this general trend is Ireland, where the recently introduced super-tax covers only a few top recipients.

It is obvious that income distributions can only be compared for comparable segments of the — often unknown — complete distribution. An attempt has therefore been made to improve the comparability by estimating the total number of tax units on the basis of the labour force statistics in Chapter 7. Excluding family workers and domestic servants from the total labour force, the remaining number of economically active persons has been adjusted to the definition of the units in income tax statistics (for explanations, see notes to the second table). On the basis of the estimated total number of tax units, so-called quantile ratios (see below) have then been calculated.

The second table presents indicators of the structure and degree of income inequality. This is the only section of the handbook where the coverage is limited to less than 13 countries: Belgium had to be excluded because it uses the extended household concept, Ireland because of its pre-modern income tax system, Italy (where data have only been published in recent years) and France because of the low and strongly biased income coverage. Of the remaining nine countries, the structure of income inequality is measured in terms of quantile ratios and fractile shares, and the degree of income inequality in terms of the Gini index and the maximum equalization percentage. The table also provides information on the type of tax unit, the types of reported income units, and the share of couples as well as of economically active married females in the total labour force.

Quantile ratios and fractile shares are both based on a ranking of 'income units' (individuals or couples) by the size of their income. If one takes an income at a certain point of this income hierarchy (e.g. the income of the recipient which marks 75 percent of the ranked recipients) and relates it to a 'typical income' such as the median (i.e. the income of the recipient which divides the distribution of all recipients in half) or the average income, one arrives at quantile ratios (e.g. the percentile ratio 75). If one takes instead a certain segment of the income hierarchy (e.g. the top 10 percent income earners) and relates it to the total income, one arrives at fractile shares (e.g. the income share of the top decile). Fractile shares are superior in the sense that they incorporate more information, whereas quantile ratios have the advantage that they can be calculated on the basis of incomplete information.

The Gini index (known also as the normalized relative mean difference) is derived from a cumulative income distribution which is based on a ranking of all individuals (or other tax units) according to their income. Starting from those with the lowest income, a line is drawn representing the total percentage of income received by increasingly larger percentages of all income receivers: the so-called Lorenz curve. In the case of complete equality, this curve would be a 45-degree line. The area between this hypothetical line and the actual Lorenz curve may be used as an indication of income inequality. Dividing this 'area of inequality' by its maximum size (defined by the case where one person receives the total income) gives the Gini index which ranges between 0 (complete equality) and 1 (maximum inequality).

The maximum equalization percentage (also known as the normalized relative mean deviation) is based on a division of all (ranked) income recipients into two groups (of usually varying size) so that each of them receives half of the total income. It gives the share of total income which would have to be redistributed from the top to the bottom group in order to obtain perfect equality. It therefore is only sensitive to distributional changes between two groups, whereas the Gini index is sensitive to distributional changes over the whole income range. On the other hand, an interpretation of changes in income inequality in terms of Gini indexes may be problematic when Lorenz curves cross-cut each other.

All the indicators of the structure and degree of income inequality had to be calculated on the basis of grouped data. Income tax statistics provide the number of income recipients and their total income only for a limited (and varying) number of income classes (usually, however, for many more than ten and sometimes even more than 100 classes). For the computation of quantile ratios and fractile shares (here in form of deciles) one has to group income classes together, and — in order to get specific quantiles/fractiles — to split up some of them.

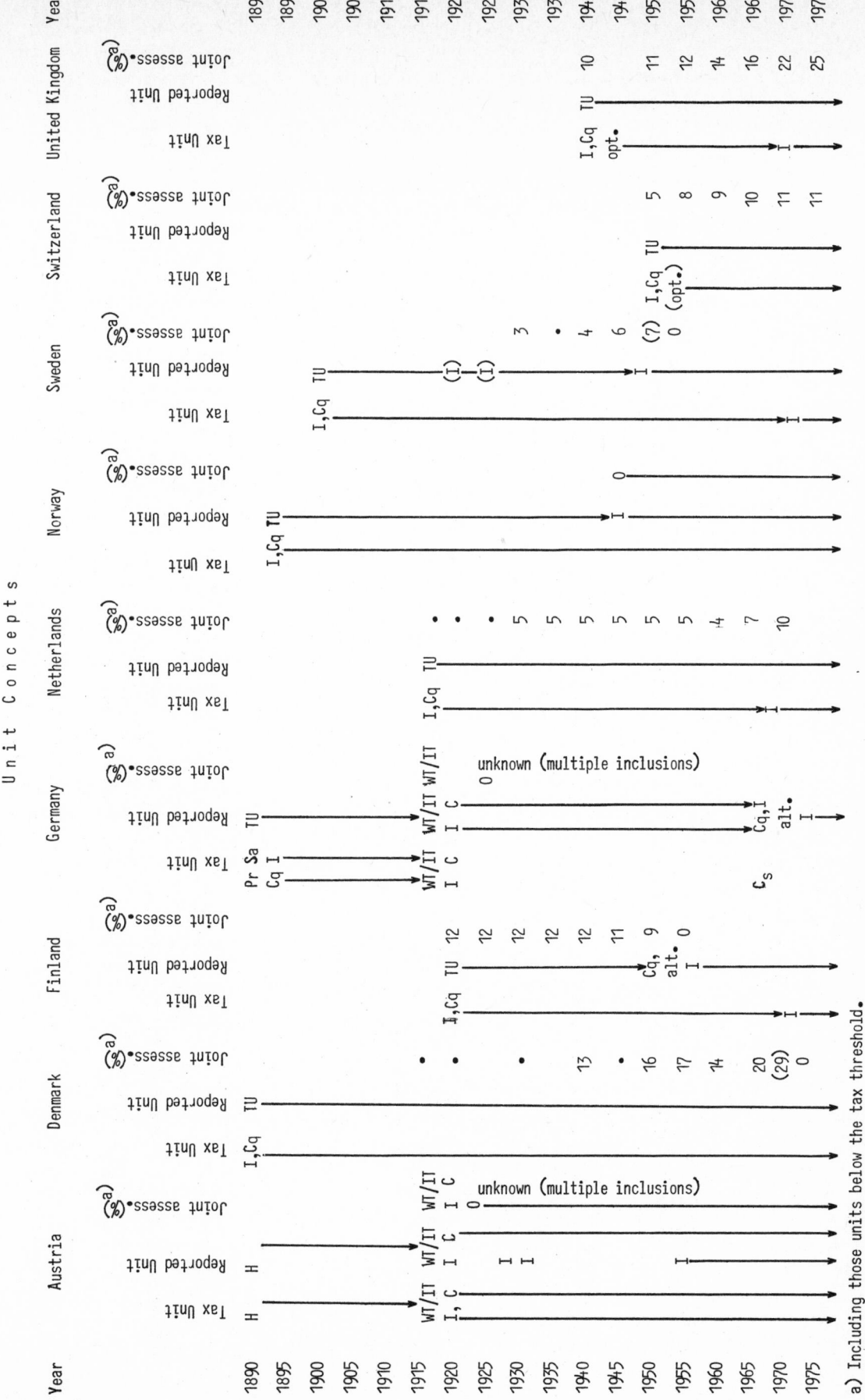

Coverage Ratios of Recipients

Year	Austria	Denmark	Finland	Germany	Pr.	Sax.	Netherlands	Norway	Sweden	Switzerland	United Kingdom[a]	Year
1975	87[b]		106[k]	106[n]			103[p]	10	128	98	108[q]	1975
1970	81	99	108	100			101	98	127	81	144	1970
1965	82[c]	99[h]	112	105			110	93	109	63	130	1965
1960	74[d]	98	104	100[o]				93	108	51	123	1960
1955	76[e]	101	96	91				92	107	63		1955
1950		99	84	66				69	97	46	126[r]	1950
1945		99	56						96	92		1945
1940		97	37[l]	92							46[s]	1940
1935	58[f]	78	23[m]	82								1935
1930	81[g]	78	42	92					89			1930
1925		84										1925
1920		89	35						79			1920
1915		55[i]		41								1915
1910					41	99						1910
1905		32			31	97						1905
1900					26	97						1900

a) Coverage ratios refer to Blue Book tables.   b) 1986   c) 1964   d) 1957   e) 1953   f) 1933   g) 1928   h) 1963   i) 1916   k) 1974   l) 1942   m) 1931
n) 1974   o) 1961   p) 1973   q) Coverage ratio according to Survey of Personal Incomes: 108
r) Coverage ratio according to Survey of Personal Incomes: 97   s) Survey of Personal Incomes

616

For those income classes which had to be divided, the internal distribution was estimated by logarithmic interpolation. The Gini coefficients have been calculated on the basis of these (partly estimated) income deciles — under the conservative assumption of perfect income equality within the deciles. Therefore, they represent lower limits of inequality which are fairly comparable across countries and over time.

Income distribution data certainly belong to the most complex and problematic statistics. Even a cautious interpretation would require more information and additional data. These will be provided in a separate handbook by Franz Kraus, to be published in 1986. It will contain a systematic discussion of sources (tax statistics as well as surveys), a survey of basic measures (including a historical summary of measurement approaches), and additional series of disaggregated and more sophisticated data on income inequality.

Austria

Distribution of National Income

| Year | NDP (f) by economic institution | | | NDP (f) by category of factor cost | | | Dependent labour force | Income positions of two major classes Adjusted labour's shares | | Average compensation to average profit of | | Year |
| | Households | Corporations | Government | Compensation | Entre-preneurship | Property | excl. family workers | Standardized | Hypothetical (1970=100) | (1) Non-government | (2) Private households | |
	%	%	%	%	%	%	%	%	%	ratio	ratio	
1975	94.7	7.0	-1.7	73.5	26.5		86.3	85.1	72.2	0.41	0.55	1975
1974	92.1	9.2	-1.3	68.4	31.6		86.0	79.5	67.4	0.34	0.47	1974
1973	93.6	7.6	-1.2	68.6	21.2	10.2	85.7	80.1	67.9	0.35	0.46	1973
1972	92.8	8.2	-1.0	66.7	22.3	11.1	85.4	78.0	66.2	0.33	0.44	1972
1971	93.4	7.7	-1.1	66.6	23.0	10.5	85.1	78.2	66.3	0.34	0.43	1971
1970	92.0	8.8	-0.8	64.1	24.3	11.7	84.8	75.6	64.1	0.31	0.41	1970
1969	93.2	7.9	-1.0	65.7	24.3	10.0	84.5	77.7	65.9	0.34	0.44	1969
1968	94.5	5.9	-0.5	68.6	23.3	8.0	84.1	81.5	69.1	0.41	0.50	1968
1967	94.0	6.2	-0.2	67.3	24.3	8.4	83.8	80.3	68.1	0.40	0.49	1967
1966	93.3	6.9	-0.2	66.2	24.8	9.0	83.5	79.3	67.3	0.39	0.48	1966
1965	93.0	7.2	-0.2	64.9	25.9	9.2	83.1	78.0	66.2	0.37	0.47	1965
1964	92.7	7.6	-0.2	63.8	26.6	9.7	82.8	77.0	65.3	0.36	0.46	1964
1963	92.4	7.5	0.1	63.3	26.9	9.9	82.5	76.7	65.0	0.37	0.46	1963
1962	91.6	8.3	0.1	63.2	26.3	10.5	82.1	77.0	65.3	0.38	0.49	1962
1961	92.0	7.7	0.3	60.7	29.4	9.9	81.7	74.3	63.0	0.35	0.43	1961
1960	90.0	9.9	0.0	59.5	28.8	11.7	81.5	73.1	61.9	0.33	0.44	1960
1959	91.5	8.7	-0.2	61.5	28.6	9.9	81.2	75.8	64.3	0.37	0.48	1959
1958	92.3	7.9	-0.2	60.1	31.3	8.6	80.8	74.3	63.0	0.36	0.44	1958
1957	92.1	7.9	0.1	60.2	31.2	8.6	80.5	74.7	63.4	0.37	0.46	1957
1956	92.2	7.7	0.2	60.2	31.5	8.3	80.2	75.0	63.6	0.37	0.46	1956
1955	92.1	8.3	-0.4	58.4	33.2	8.4	79.9	73.1	62.0	0.35	0.44	1955
1954	91.4	8.3	0.2	59.0	32.0	9.0	79.6	74.2	62.9	0.37	0.47	1954
1953	92.4	7.4	0.2	60.2	31.8	8.0	79.3	76.0	64.4	0.40	0.49	1953
1952	93.3	6.9	-0.2	58.9	34.1	7.0	78.9	74.6	63.3	0.38	0.46	1952
1951	90.0	9.3	0.7	56.8	33.2	10.0	78.7	72.2	61.2	0.36	0.46	1951
1939							78.3					1939
1938							78.0					1938
1937				54.6			77.6	70.3	59.6			1937
1936				56.3			77.3	72.9	61.8			1936
1935				57.0			76.9	74.1	62.8			1935
1934				57.0			76.5	74.5	63.1			1934
1933				58.7			76.2	77.1	65.3			1933
1932				60.6			75.8	80.0	67.8			1932
1931				61.6			75.5	81.6	69.1			1931

D i s t r i b u t i o n   o f   N a t i o n a l   I n c o m e

Year	NDP (f) by economic institution			NDP (f) by category of factor cost			Dependent labour force	Income positions of two major classes Adjusted labour's shares		Average compensation to average profit of (a)	(2)	Year
	Households	Corporations	Government	Compensation	Entrepreneurship	Property	excl. family workers	Standardized	Hypothetical (1970=100)	Non-government	Private households	
	%	%	%	%	%	%	%	%	%	ratio	ratio	
1930				59.4			75.1	79.1	67.0			1930
1929				57.5			74.8	77.0	65.2			1929
1928				56.8			74.4	76.3	64.6			1928
1927				55.3			74.1	74.6	63.3			1927
1926				56.8			73.7	77.1	65.3			1926
1925				55.6			73.3	75.9	64.3			1925
1924				57.2			73.0	78.3	66.4			1924
1923							72.6					1923
1922							72.3					1922
1921							71.9					1921
1920							71.6					1920

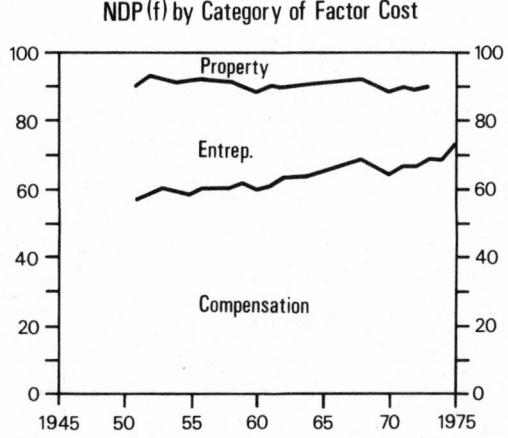

NDP (f) by Category of Factor Cost

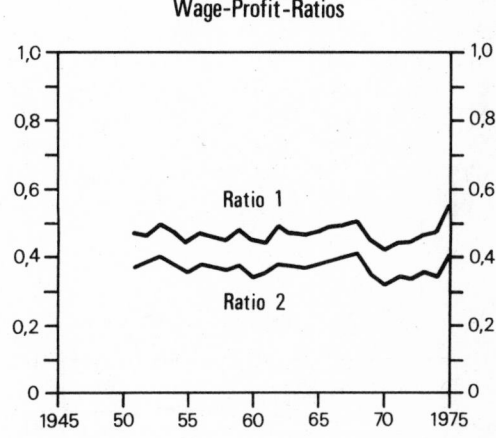

Wage-Profit-Ratios

Distribution of National Income

Year	NDP (f) by economic institution			NDP (f) by category of factor cost			Dependent labour force	Income positions of two major classes Adjusted labour's shares		Average compensation to average profit of (1)	(2)	Year
	Households	Corporations	Government	Compensation	Entrepreneurship	Property	excl. family workers	Standardized	Hypothetical (1970=100)	Non-government	Private households	
	%	%	%	%	%	%	%	%	%	ratio	ratio	
1975	99.4	4.6	-4.0	70.0	16.2	13.9	87.2	80.2	67.8	0.30	0.35	1975
1974	97.6	6.4	-3.9	67.4	16.6	16.0	86.7	77.8	65.7	0.28	0.34	1974
1973	97.2	6.7	-4.0	65.9	18.6	15.5	86.2	76.4	64.6	0.28	0.34	1973
1972	97.8	6.0	-3.8	65.5	19.4	15.1	85.6	76.5	64.7	0.29	0.34	1972
1971	97.9	5.5	-3.4	64.6	19.5	15.9	85.1	75.9	64.2	0.29	0.34	1971
1970	97.0	6.1	-3.1	62.4	20.7	16.9	84.5	73.8	62.4	0.28	0.33	1970
1969	97.4	5.7	-3.1	61.9	22.2	15.9	84.0	73.7	62.3	0.29	0.33	1969
1968	98.2	4.9	-3.1	63.0	22.4	14.6	83.5	75.5	63.8	0.31	0.36	1968
1967	98.2	4.6	-2.9	62.9	22.8	14.3	82.9	75.9	64.2	0.32	0.37	1967
1966	98.9	4.2	-3.1	62.8	23.6	13.6	82.4	76.3	64.5	0.33	0.37	1966
1965	97.8	5.0	-2.8	61.2	24.4	14.4	81.8	74.8	63.2	0.33	0.37	1965
1964	97.7	5.0	-2.7	60.4	24.8	14.8	81.3	74.4	62.9	0.33	0.37	1964
1963	98.4	4.5	-2.9	60.3	24.8	14.9	80.7	74.7	63.2	0.34	0.38	1963
1962	98.1	4.5	-2.6	58.5	25.3	16.2	80.1	73.0	61.7	0.33	0.37	1962
1961	97.8	4.8	-2.7	56.9	26.4	16.7	79.6	71.5	60.5	0.32	0.36	1961
1960	97.8	4.5	-2.3	57.1	26.1	16.7	79.3	72.0	60.9	0.33	0.37	1960
1959	97.9	4.2	-2.1	56.8	26.5	16.7	79.1	71.7	60.6	0.33	0.36	1959
1958	98.2	3.5	-1.8	57.4	26.1	16.5	78.9	72.8	61.5	0.35	0.38	1958
1957	97.0	4.5	-1.5	55.9	26.4	17.7	78.7	71.0	60.0	0.33	0.37	1957
1956	96.2	5.4	-1.6	54.1	27.1	18.8	78.5	69.0	58.3	0.31	0.35	1956
1955	96.5	5.1	-1.6	53.3	28.1	18.7	78.2	68.1	57.6	0.31	0.34	1955
1954	96.8	4.6	-1.4	53.0	28.8	18.3	78.0	67.9	57.4	0.31	0.34	1954
1953	97.2	4.1	-1.4	53.7	29.1	17.2	77.8	69.1	58.4	0.32	0.35	1953

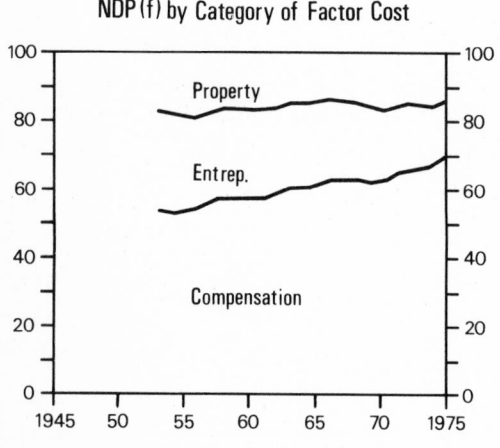

NDP (f) by Category of Factor Cost

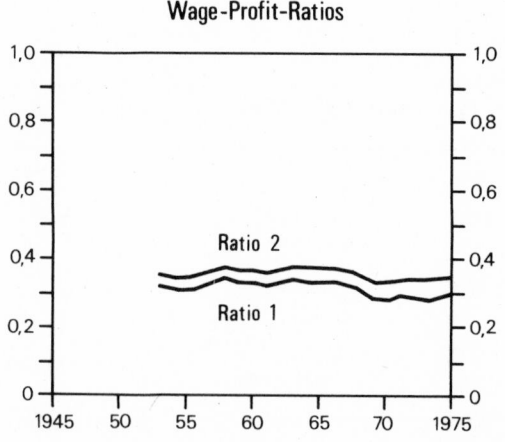

Wage-Profit-Ratios

Distribution of National Income

Year	Households %	Corporations %	Government %	Compensation %	Entre-preneurship %	Property %	excl. family workers %	Standardized %	Hypothetical (1970=100) %	Non-government ratio	Private households ratio	Year
	NDP (f) by economic institution			NDP (f) by category of factor cost			Dependent labour force	Income positions of two major classes Adjusted labour's shares		Average compensation to average profit of (1)	(2)	
1975	92.8	6.1	1.1	78.3		21.7	87.9	89.0	75.3	0.52	0.74	1975
1974	92.2	7.1	0.7	75.4		24.6	87.3	86.5	73.1	0.46	0.66	1974
1973	91.1	8.4	0.5	71.1		28.9	86.6	82.2	69.5	0.39	0.55	1973
1972	91.0	8.7	0.3	70.4		29.6	85.9	81.9	69.3	0.39	0.56	1972
1971	91.1	8.7	0.1	70.5		29.5	85.2	82.7	69.9	0.42	0.59	1971
1970	90.9	8.7	0.4	63.1		36.9	84.6	74.7	63.1	0.32	0.42	1970
1969	89.4	9.9	0.7	66.5		33.5	83.9	79.3	67.0	0.39	0.56	1969
1968	88.4	11.1	0.5	67.1		32.9	83.2	80.6	68.2	0.42	0.64	1968
1967	88.8	10.1	1.1	64.9		35.1	82.6	78.6	66.4	0.40	0.57	1967
1966	89.7	9.4	0.9	64.5		35.5	81.9	78.8	66.6	0.41	0.57	1966
1965	86.8	12.2	1.0	63.1		36.9	81.2	77.7	65.7	0.41	0.62	1965
1964	87.7	11.5	0.8	60.8		39.2	80.7	75.4	63.7	0.38	0.54	1964
1963	88.8	10.3	0.9	61.5		38.5	80.2	76.6	64.8	0.40	0.56	1963
1962	87.5	11.6	0.9	60.7		39.3	79.7	76.1	64.4	0.40	0.58	1962
1961	86.5	12.8	0.7	59.8		40.2	79.2	75.5	63.9	0.40	0.59	1961
1960	87.6	11.6	0.9	57.9		42.1	78.7	73.6	62.2	0.38	0.53	1960
1959	87.6	11.8	0.6	57.6		42.4	78.6	73.3	62.0	0.38	0.52	1959
1958	89.6	9.9	0.5	58.3		41.7	78.4	74.3	62.9	0.39	0.51	1958
1957	88.4	11.3	0.3	57.4		42.6	78.2	73.4	62.1	0.38	0.52	1957
1956	91.6	8.3	0.1	57.1		42.9	78.0	73.2	61.9	0.38	0.47	1956
1955	92.2	7.7	0.0	57.6		42.4	77.8	74.0	62.6	0.39	0.47	1955
1954	91.0	9.0	0.1	57.1		42.9	77.7	73.5	62.2	0.38	0.48	1954
1953	87.7	12.2	0.0	55.4		44.6	77.5	71.4	60.4	0.36	0.50	1953
1952	89.0	11.1	-0.1	55.3		44.7	77.3	71.6	60.5	0.36	0.48	1952
1951	91.2	8.8	-0.0	55.1		44.9	77.1	71.5	60.4	0.36	0.45	1951
1950							76.9					1950
1949							76.8					1949
1948							76.7					1948
1947							76.5					1947
1946							76.4					1946
1945							76.3					1945

NDP(f) by Category of Factor Cost

Wage-Profit-Ratios

Distribution of National Income

Year	NDP (f) by economic institution			NDP (f) by category of factor cost			Dependent labour force	Income positions of two major classes Adjusted labour's shares		Average compensation to average profit of (1)	(2)	Year
	Households	Corporations	Government	Compensation	Entre- preneurship	Property	excl. family workers	Standardized	Hypothetical (1970=100)	Non- government	Private households	
	%	%	%	%	%	%	%	%	%	ratio	ratio	
1975	90.9	6.8	2.3	68.9	13.1	17.9	87.8	78.5	66.4	0.33	0.44	1975
1974	88.6	9.0	2.3	65.6	13.0	21.4	87.1	75.3	63.6	0.30	0.42	1974
1973	89.9	7.9	2.2	66.9	12.9	20.2	86.5	77.3	65.4	0.34	0.45	1973
1972	91.0	6.5	2.4	67.1	13.4	19.5	85.8	78.1	66.0	0.36	0.46	1972
1971	91.6	6.0	2.4	66.5	14.4	19.2	85.2	78.0	66.0	0.37	0.46	1971
1970	89.1	8.4	2.5	63.7	14.5	21.7	84.5	75.4	63.7	0.35	0.46	1970
1969	89.3	8.4	2.3	63.0	14.9	22.1	83.8	75.1	63.5	0.35	0.46	1969
1968	91.9	5.6	2.5	64.4	15.1	20.5	83.1	77.4	65.4	0.39	0.47	1968
1967	91.9	5.4	2.7	64.4	15.1	20.5	82.4	78.1	66.1	0.42	0.50	1967
1966	91.6	5.6	2.8	63.3	16.0	20.8	81.7	77.4	65.4	0.42	0.50	1966
1965	91.6	5.6	2.8	61.8	17.5	20.7	81.0	76.2	64.5	0.41	0.49	1965
1964	91.1	6.1	2.9	60.6	18.1	21.3	80.3	75.5	63.8	0.41	0.49	1964
1963	90.6	6.6	2.8	59.5	18.6	21.9	79.5	74.8	63.2	0.41	0.49	1963
1962	90.0	6.7	3.3	58.7	18.9	22.4	78.8	74.6	63.1	0.42	0.51	1962
1961	89.5	7.2	3.3	56.9	20.5	22.6	78.0	73.0	61.7	0.40	0.49	1961
1960	88.4	8.2	3.4	56.7	20.2	23.1	77.2	73.4	62.1	0.42	0.53	1960
1959	88.6	8.4	3.0	56.7	19.9	23.4	76.9	73.7	62.3	0.42	0.53	1959
1958	90.0	7.0	3.0	57.3	20.7	22.0	76.6	74.7	63.2	0.44	0.53	1958
1957	89.4	7.9	2.7	58.1	19.9	22.0	76.4	76.1	64.3	0.46	0.57	1957
1956	88.3	9.2	2.5	57.9	20.4	21.7	76.1	76.2	64.4	0.46	0.60	1956
1955	87.1	10.3	2.6	55.9	21.8	22.3	75.8	73.8	62.4	0.43	0.57	1955
1954	87.6	10.0	2.4	56.3	22.2	21.4	75.5	74.7	63.1	0.44	0.59	1954
1953	90.5	7.3	2.3	59.0	23.1	17.8	75.2	78.6	66.4	0.50	0.62	1953
1952	91.3	6.9	1.8	57.9	25.9	16.2	74.8	77.4	65.4	0.48	0.58	1952
1951	86.0	13.1	0.8	55.6	23.3	21.1	74.5	74.6	63.1	0.44	0.62	1951

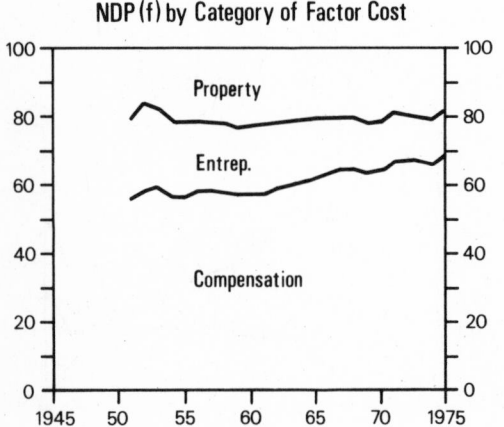

NDP (f) by Category of Factor Cost

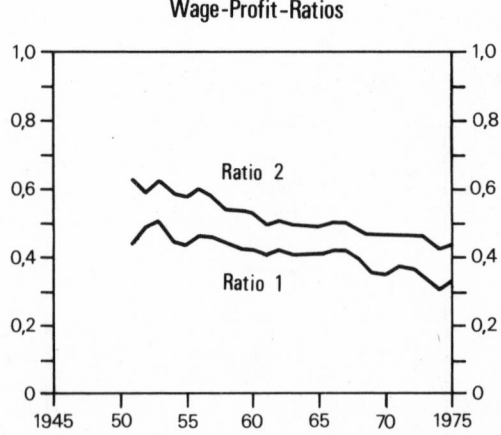

Wage-Profit-Ratios

France

Distribution of National Income

Year	NDP (f) by economic institution			NDP (f) by category of factor cost			Dependent labour force	Income positions of two major classes Adjusted labour's shares		Average compensation to average profit of		Year
	Households	Corporations	Government	Compensation	Entre-preneurship	Property	excl. family workers	Standardized	Hypothetical (1970=100)	(1) Non-government	(2) Private households	
	%	%	%	%	%	%	%	%	%	ratio	ratio	
1975	97.5	2.9	-0.4	70.0	21.5	8.5	85.6	81.8	69.7	0.39	0.43	1975
1974	94.8	5.0	0.2	67.7	21.0	11.3	85.5	79.2	67.5	0.36	0.43	1974
1973	93.0	6.9	0.1	64.6	23.2	12.2	85.4	75.7	64.4	0.33	0.40	1973
1972	93.2	6.8	-0.0	63.8	24.0	12.2	85.3	74.7	63.6	0.32	0.39	1972
1971	93.4	6.7	-0.1	64.0	24.0	11.9	85.2	75.1	64.0	0.33	0.41	1971
1970	92.9	7.3	-0.3	63.4	24.5	12.2	85.2	74.4	63.4	0.33	0.41	1970
1969							85.1					1969
1968	94.1	6.9	-0.9	62.2	23.3	14.5	85.0	73.2	62.3	0.32	0.39	1968
1967	94.0	6.7	-0.7	61.8	23.9	14.2	84.1	73.5	62.6	0.33	0.40	1967
1966	93.4	7.2	-0.6	61.9	23.9	14.2	83.3	74.4	63.3	0.35	0.43	1966
1965	93.8	6.7	-0.6	62.1	24.4	13.5	82.4	75.4	64.2	0.36	0.44	1965
1964	93.1	7.4	-0.5	61.7	24.5	13.8	81.5	75.7	64.5	0.37	0.46	1964
1963	93.5	7.0	-0.5	61.0	25.5	13.4	80.7	75.7	64.4	0.38	0.46	1963
1962	93.4	7.4	-0.8	59.6	26.6	13.8	79.8	74.7	63.6	0.37	0.45	1962
1961	92.2	8.6	-0.8	58.8	26.3	14.9	79.4	74.0	63.0	0.36	0.46	1961
1960	91.5	9.3	-0.9	57.1	27.4	15.5	78.9	72.3	61.6	0.35	0.44	1960
1959	92.3	8.7	-1.0	58.3	27.1	14.6	78.5	74.2	63.2	0.37	0.47	1959
1958	94.7	6.4	-1.1	58.9	29.7	11.3	78.0	75.5	64.3	0.39	0.46	1958
1957	95.1	5.9	-1.0	59.0	29.7	11.3	77.6	76.1	64.8	0.41	0.47	1957
1956	95.3	5.7	-1.0	59.0	29.8	11.2	77.1	76.5	65.1	0.42	0.48	1956
1955	95.4	5.5	-0.9	58.2	30.4	11.5	76.7	75.9	64.6	0.41	0.47	1955
1954	95.9	5.1	-0.9	58.2	30.7	11.1	76.2	76.3	65.0	0.42	0.48	1954
1953	94.8	6.0	-0.8	57.3	31.0	11.6	75.5	76.0	64.7	0.43	0.50	1953
1952	96.2	4.8	-1.0	57.5	32.5	10.0	74.7	77.0	65.6	0.45	0.51	1952
1951							73.9					1951
1950							73.1					1950
1949							72.3					1949
1948							71.5					1948
1947							70.8					1947
1946							70.0					1946

NDP (f) by Category of Factor Cost

Wage-Profit-Ratios

Distribution of National Income

Year	NDP (f) by economic institution			NDP (f) by category of factor cost			Dependent labour force	Income positions of two major classes — Adjusted labour's shares		Average compensation to average profit of (1)	(2)	Year
	Households	Corporations	Government	Compensation	Entre-preneurship	Property	excl. family workers	Standardized	Hypothetical (1970=100)	Non-government	Private households	
	%	%	%	%	%	%	%	%	%	ratio	ratio	
1975	97.0	3.5	-0.6	72.8	20.1	7.2	91.4	79.6	71.3	0.25	0.28	1975
1974	96.8	3.4	-0.2	72.6	20.0	7.4	91.1	79.7	71.5	0.26	0.29	1974
1973	96.0	3.9	0.1	70.7	21.3	8.1	90.7	77.9	69.8	0.25	0.29	1973
1972	96.4	3.6	0.0	69.5	23.2	7.3	90.4	76.9	69.0	0.24	0.28	1972
1971	97.6	2.1	0.3	69.1	24.9	6.1	90.0	76.7	68.8	0.25	0.27	1971
1970	96.9	2.7	0.4	67.8	25.5	6.7	89.6	75.6	67.8	0.25	0.27	1970
1969	95.0	4.6	0.4	66.1	25.5	8.4	89.3	74.0	66.4	0.24	0.27	1969
1968	95.0	4.5	0.5	64.8	27.0	8.2	88.9	72.8	65.3	0.23	0.27	1968
1967	95.8	3.8	0.4	66.4	26.1	7.4	88.6	75.0	67.3	0.26	0.29	1967
1966	95.3	4.1	0.6	66.6	25.7	7.7	88.2	75.5	67.7	0.27	0.31	1966
1965	95.0	4.3	0.7	65.6	26.8	7.6	87.9	74.6	66.9	0.27	0.31	1965
1964	93.1	5.2	1.7	64.6			87.5	73.8	66.1	0.27	0.32	1964
1963	93.1	5.2	1.7	64.5			87.2	74.0	66.4	0.28	0.33	1963
1962	92.8	5.6	1.7	63.9			86.8	73.7	66.0	0.28	0.34	1962
1961	92.2	6.1	1.7	62.5			86.4	72.3	64.8	0.27	0.33	1961
1960	91.7	6.7	1.6	60.8			86.1	70.6	63.3	0.26	0.32	1960
1959	91.9	6.6	1.5	60.2			85.8	70.2	63.0	0.26	0.32	1959
1958	91.9	6.3	1.8	60.5			85.4	70.8	63.5	0.27	0.33	1958
1957	91.6	6.5	1.9	59.7			85.1	70.2	62.9	0.27	0.33	1957
1956	91.9	6.4	1.7	59.5			84.8	70.2	62.9	0.28	0.33	1956
1955	91.7	6.5	1.8	58.8			84.4	69.6	62.4	0.27	0.33	1955
1954	92.1	6.3	1.5	59.4			84.1	70.6	63.3	0.29	0.34	1954
1953	91.8	6.6	1.6	58.7			83.8	70.0	62.8	0.29	0.34	1953
1952	92.0	6.5	1.6	57.4			83.4	68.8	61.7	0.28	0.33	1952
1951				56.7			83.1	68.3	61.2			1951
1950				57.7			82.8	69.7	62.5			1950
1949							82.4					1949
1948							82.1					1948
1947							81.7					1947
1946							81.4					1946
1939				60.0			83.4	72.0	64.5			1939
1938				60.6			82.9	73.1	65.6			1938
1937				61.7			82.5	74.8	67.0			1937
1936				63.1			82.0	76.9	69.0			1936
1935				65.1			81.6	79.9	71.6			1935
1934				66.6			81.1	82.1	73.6			1934
1933				68.2			80.7	84.6	75.8			1933
1932				70.0			80.7	86.7	77.7			1932
1931				71.0			80.8	87.9	78.8			1931
1930				67.7			80.8	83.8	75.1			1930

Distribution of National Income

Year	NDP (f) by economic institution			NDP (f) by category of factor cost			Dependent labour force	Income positions of two major classes Adjusted labour's shares		Average compensation to average profit of		Year
										(1)	(2)	
	Households	Corporations	Government	Compensation	Entre-preneurship	Property	excl. family workers	Standardized	Hypothetical (1970=100)	Non-government	Private households	
	%	%	%	%	%	%	%	%	%	ratio	ratio	
1929				66.2			80.9	81.9	73.4			1929
1928				65.1			81.0	80.4	72.1			1928
1927				63.7			81.0	78.6	70.5			1927
1926				63.8			81.1	78.7	70.6			1926
1925				63.6			81.1	78.4	70.3			1925
1924							81.2					1924
1923							81.2					1923
1922							81.3					1922
1921							81.4					1921
1920							81.4					1920
1919							81.5					1919
1913				48.8			79.7	61.2	54.9			1913
1912				48.4			79.3	61.0	54.6			1912
1911				48.8			79.0	61.8	55.4			1911
1910				48.4			78.7	61.4	55.1			1910
1909				48.5			78.4	61.8	55.4			1909
1908				48.6			78.0	62.3	55.9			1908
1907				48.3			77.7	62.1	55.7			1907
1906				47.6			77.4	61.5	55.1			1906
1905				47.2			77.1	61.2	54.9			1905
1904				47.9			76.7	62.5	56.0			1904
1903				47.8			76.4	62.5	56.1			1903
1902				47.6			76.1	62.5	56.1			1902
1901				48.1			75.8	63.5	56.9			1901
1900				46.7			75.4	61.9	55.5			1900
1899				46.8			75.1	62.4	55.9			1899
1898				46.2			74.8	61.8	55.4			1898
1897				46.8			74.5	62.9	56.4			1897
1896				47.8			74.1	64.4	57.8			1896
1895				47.6			73.8	64.5	57.9			1895
1894				47.2			73.6	64.1	57.5			1894
1893				46.5			73.4	63.3	56.8			1893
1892				46.2			73.2	63.1	56.6			1892
1891				46.9			73.0	64.2	57.6			1891
1890				45.2			72.8	62.1	55.7			1890
1889				46.7			72.6	64.3	57.6			1889
1888				45.7			72.4	63.1	56.6			1888
1887				45.2			72.2	62.6	56.1			1887
1886				45.6			72.0	63.4	56.8			1886
1885				44.7			71.8	62.3	55.8			1885

Distribution of National Income

Year	NDP (f) by economic institution			NDP (f) by category of factor cost			Dependent labour force	Income positions of two major classes Adjusted labour's shares		Average compensation to average profit of (1) (2)		Year
	Households	Corporations	Government	Compensation	Entre-preneurship	Property	excl. family workers	Standardized	Hypothetical (1970=100)	Non-government	Private households	
	%	%	%	%	%	%	%	%	%	ratio	ratio	
1884				44.3			71.6	61.9	55.5			1884
1883				43.7			71.4	61.2	54.9			1883
1882				44.2			71.2	62.2	55.7			1882
1881				43.6			71.0	61.4	55.0			1881
1880				43.2			70.8	61.1	54.7			1880
1879				44.6			70.6	63.2	56.7			1879
1878				43.8			70.3	62.2	55.8			1878
1877				43.6			70.1	62.2	55.7			1877
1876				44.6			69.9	63.8	57.2			1876
1875				44.6			69.7	64.0	57.4			1875
1874				42.0			69.5	60.4	54.2			1874
1873				42.6			69.3	61.4	55.1			1873
1872				42.0			69.1	60.7	54.4			1872
1871				42.7			68.9	61.9	55.5			1871

Germany

Wage - Profit - Ratio

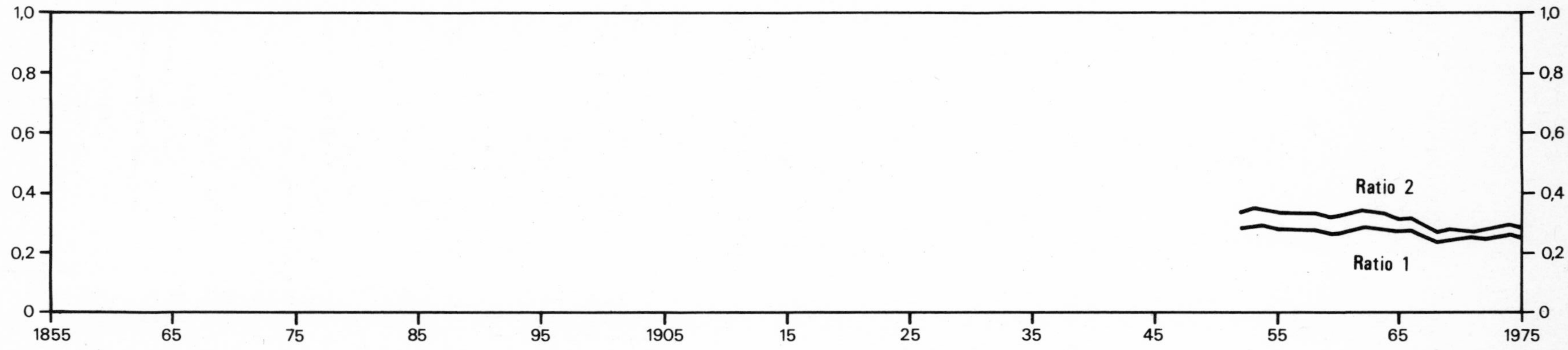

Ratio 2

Ratio 1

NDP (f) by Category of Factor Cost

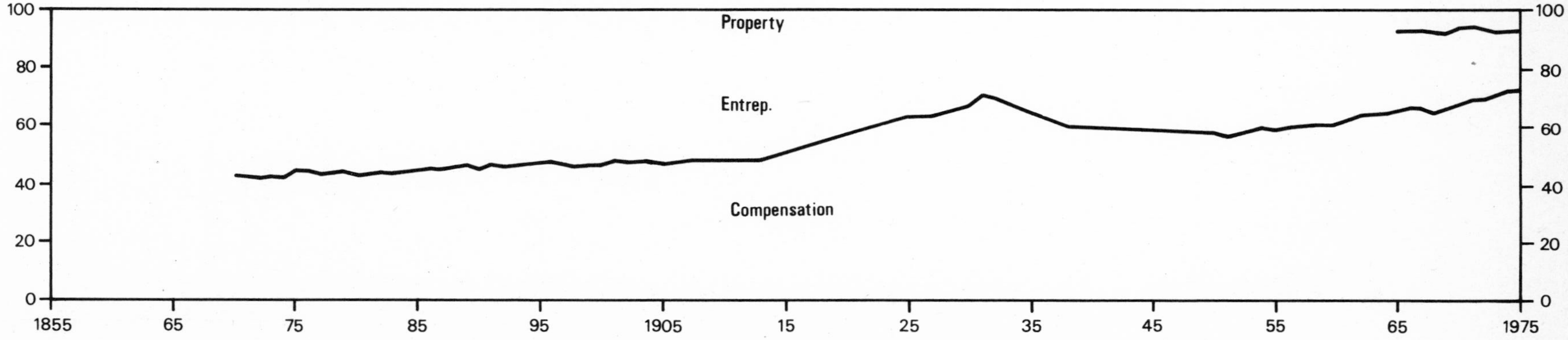

Property

Entrep.

Compensation

627

Distribution of National Income

Year	NDP (f) by economic institution			NDP (f) by category of factor cost			Dependent labour force	Income positions of two major classes Adjusted labour's shares		Average compensation to average profit of		Year
										(1)	(2)	
	Households	Corporations	Government	Compensation	Entre-preneurship	Property	excl. family workers	Standardized	Hypothetical (1970=100)	Non-government	Private households	
	%	%	%	%	%	%	%	%	%	ratio	ratio	
1975							77.3					1975
1974							76.9					1974
1973							76.5					1973
1972							76.0					1972
1971							75.6					1971
1970							75.2					1970
1969							74.7					1969
1968							74.3					1968
1967	96.4	5.5	-1.9	61.3	23.5	15.2	73.9	83.0	62.4	0.53	0.62	1967
1966	96.1	5.4	-1.5	61.3	23.2	15.5	73.4	83.5	62.7	0.55	0.64	1966
1965	94.9	6.4	-1.3	59.0	25.0	16.1	73.0	80.8	60.7	0.52	0.61	1965
1964	95.2	6.0	-1.2	58.6	26.3	15.1	72.5	80.8	60.7	0.52	0.61	1964
1963	94.4	6.5	-0.9	57.6	25.9	16.5	72.1	79.9	60.1	0.52	0.61	1963
1962	95.0	5.8	-0.8	56.7	27.1	16.1	71.6	79.2	59.5	0.51	0.59	1962
1961	94.8	5.9	-0.8	55.3	28.2	16.5	71.1	77.7	58.4	0.49	0.57	1961
1960	94.7	5.9	-0.6	55.0	28.5	16.5	71.0	77.4	58.2	0.49	0.56	1960
1959	96.2	4.3	-0.4	54.8	29.4	15.8	70.9	77.2	58.0	0.49	0.54	1959
1958	95.9	4.4	-0.3	55.6	28.6	15.7	70.8	78.5	59.0	0.51	0.57	1958
1957	96.0	4.4	-0.4	54.4	30.9	14.7	70.7	77.0	57.9	0.49	0.54	1957
1956	95.0	5.4	-0.4	56.2	28.9	14.8	70.6	79.6	59.9	0.53	0.60	1956
1955	94.6	5.6	-0.2	53.7	31.6	14.8	70.5	76.1	57.2	0.48	0.55	1955
1954	94.1	5.9	0.0	54.2	30.5	15.3	70.4	77.0	57.8	0.50	0.57	1954
1953	94.5	5.5	0.1	52.7	32.6	14.7	70.3	75.0	56.3	0.47	0.53	1953
1952	94.1	5.7	0.1	52.9	32.4	14.6	70.2	75.4	56.7	0.48	0.55	1952
1951	93.2	6.4	0.4	53.4	30.5	16.1	70.1	76.2	57.3	0.49	0.57	1951
1950	92.8	6.7	0.5	53.1	30.6	16.3	69.7	76.2	57.3	0.50	0.58	1950

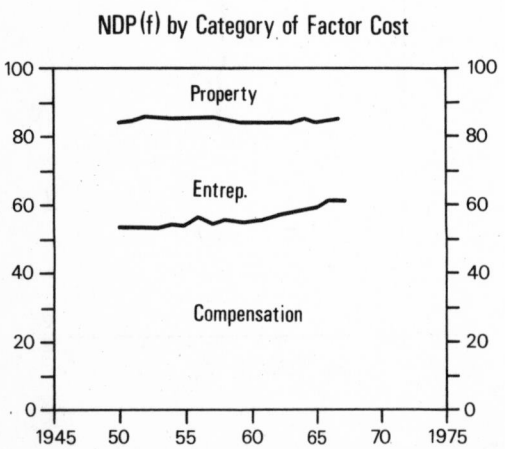

NDP(f) by Category of Factor Cost

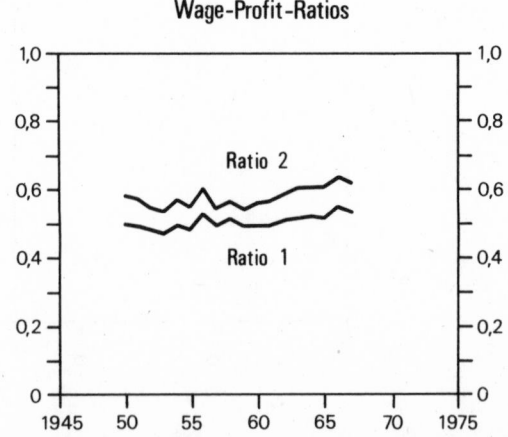

Wage-Profit-Ratios

Distribution of National Income

Year	NDP (f) by economic institution			NDP (f) by category of factor cost			Dependent labour force	Income positions of two major classes Adjusted labour's shares		Average compensation to average profit of (1)	(2)	Year
	Households	Corporations	Government	Compensation	Entrepreneurship	Property	excl. family workers	Standardized	Hypothetical (1970=100)	Non-government	Private households	
	%	%	%	%	%	%	%	%	%	ratio	ratio	
1975	105.4	-1.4	-4.0	70.4	33.5	-3.9	77.7	90.7	70.0	0.60	0.58	1975
1974	101.6	0.8	-2.4	66.8	34.1	-0.9	77.6	86.1	66.5	0.54	0.55	1974
1973	99.7	2.3	-1.9	64.4	34.9	0.7	77.5	83.1	64.1	0.50	0.53	1973
1972	99.6	2.0	-1.6	63.1	35.7	1.1	77.4	81.6	63.0	0.48	0.51	1972
1971	99.6	1.7	-1.3	63.0	35.7	1.3	77.3	81.5	62.9	0.48	0.50	1971
1970	98.5	2.6	-1.0	60.3	37.5	2.2	77.2	78.0	60.3	0.44	0.46	1970
1969				57.4			77.1	74.5	57.5			1969
1968	94.9	5.4	-0.3	56.6	28.9	14.6	77.0	73.4	56.7	0.39	0.44	1968
1967	95.5	4.6	-0.0	56.6	29.9	13.5	77.0	73.6	56.8	0.39	0.44	1967
1966	95.1	4.7	0.2	56.3	30.2	13.6	76.9	73.2	56.5	0.39	0.44	1966
1965	95.7	4.1	0.2	57.1	30.2	12.6	76.8	74.4	57.5	0.40	0.45	1965
1964	96.8	3.1	0.1	58.1	30.5	11.5	76.7	75.7	58.5	0.42	0.46	1964
1963	96.7	3.3	0.0	56.8	31.5	11.7	76.6	74.1	57.2	0.40	0.43	1963
1962	95.8	4.4	-0.2	53.6	33.2	13.2	76.5	70.1	54.1	0.35	0.39	1962
1961	95.1	5.2	-0.3	51.9	33.8	14.3	76.4	68.0	52.5	0.33	0.37	1961
1960			-0.3	51.8			75.9	68.3	52.7			1960
1959			-0.5	50.6			75.4	67.1	51.8			1959
1958			-0.1	50.2			74.9	67.0	51.8			1958
1957			-0.5	50.5			74.5	67.8	52.3			1957
1956			-0.6	49.7			74.0	67.2	51.9			1956
1955			-0.6	49.3			73.5	67.1	51.8			1955
1954			-0.7	49.8			73.0	68.2	52.7			1954
1953			-0.2	48.2			72.5	66.4	51.3			1953
1952			-0.5	48.6			72.0	67.5	52.2			1952
1951				47.1			71.5	65.9	50.9			1951
1950							71.0					1950

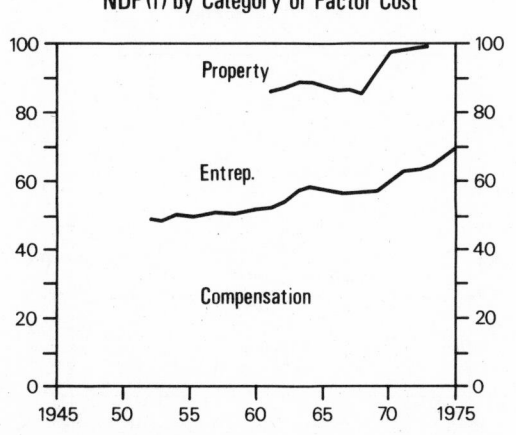

NDP(f) by Category of Factor Cost

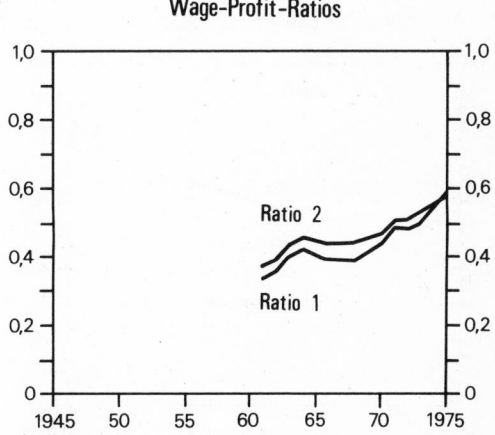

Wage-Profit-Ratios

Distribution of National Income

| Year | NDP (f) by economic institution | | | NDP (f) by category of factor cost | | | Dependent labour force | Income positions of two major classes — Adjusted labour's shares | | Average compensation to average profit of | | Year |
| | Households | Corporations | Government | Compensation | Entre-preneurship | Property | excl. family workers | Standardized | Hypothetical (1970=100) | (1) Non-government | (2) Private households | |
	%	%	%	%	%	%	%	%	%	ratio	ratio	
1975	94.0	5.6	0.4	75.7	6.8	17.5	90.3	83.8	73.8	0.34	0.44	1975
1974	92.3	8.4	-0.8	71.9	6.2	21.9	89.9	80.0	70.5	0.28	0.39	1974
1973	92.9	8.2	-1.1	70.3	7.4	22.3	89.5	78.6	69.3	0.27	0.37	1973
1972	92.9	8.1	-1.0	70.6	7.4	22.0	89.0	79.3	69.9	0.28	0.39	1972
1971	93.5	7.9	-1.4	71.3	7.1	21.6	88.6	80.5	71.0	0.30	0.41	1971
1970	92.3	8.9	-1.2	69.5	7.3	23.2	88.1	78.9	69.5	0.29	0.41	1970
1969	91.9	9.1	-1.1	67.5	8.0	24.5	87.7	76.9	67.8	0.28	0.39	1969
1968	91.8	9.1	-0.9	65.1	7.9	25.6	87.3	74.6	65.7	0.26	0.35	1968
1967	92.3	8.6	-0.9	65.1	7.9	25.8	86.8	75.0	66.1	0.27	0.36	1967
1966	92.8	7.8	-0.7	66.1	7.8	25.1	86.4	76.6	67.5	0.30	0.39	1966
1965	92.0	8.5	-0.5	63.6	8.4	27.1	86.0	73.9	65.2	0.28	0.36	1965
1964	92.0	8.6	-0.6	62.6			85.5	73.2	64.5	0.28	0.36	1964
1963	92.2	8.2	-0.4	62.1			85.1	73.0	64.4	0.28	0.36	1963
1962	90.9	9.5	-0.4	60.7			84.7	71.7	63.2	0.28	0.36	1962
1961	90.5	10.0	-0.5	59.0			84.2	70.0	61.7	0.27	0.35	1961
1960	89.4	11.0	-0.4	56.6			83.8	67.5	59.5	0.25	0.33	1960
1959	89.4	11.0	-0.4	56.7			83.4	68.0	59.9	0.26	0.34	1959
1958	91.2	9.6	-0.8	57.9			83.1	69.6	61.4	0.27	0.35	1958
1957	90.0	10.7	-0.6	56.8			82.7	68.6	60.5	0.27	0.36	1957
1956	90.1	10.8	-0.9	55.4			82.4	67.2	59.2	0.26	0.34	1956
1955	89.1	11.7	-0.8	53.6			82.0	65.4	57.6	0.25	0.33	1955
1954	89.8	11.2	-0.9	54.3			81.7	66.5	58.6	0.26	0.34	1954
1953	89.2	11.8	-1.0	53.9			81.3	66.3	58.4	0.26	0.34	1953
1952	89.5	11.6	-1.1	54.6			81.0	67.4	59.4	0.28	0.37	1952
1951	89.2	12.4	-1.6	55.0			80.6	68.2	60.1			1951
1950	90.0	11.7	-1.7	55.4			80.3	69.0	60.8			1950
1949							79.9					1949
1948							79.6					1948
1947							79.2					1947
1946							78.9					1946

NDP(f) by Category of Factor Cost

Wage-Profit-Ratios

Distribution of National Income

| Year | NDP (f) by economic institution | | | NDP (f) by category of factor cost | | | Dependent labour force | Income positions of two major classes — Adjusted labour's shares | | Average compensation to average profit of | | Year |
| | Households | Corporations | Government | Compensation | Entre-preneurship | Property | excl. family workers | Standardized | Hypothetical (1970=100) | (1) Non-government | (2) Private households | |
	%	%	%	%	%	%	%	%	%	ratio	ratio	
1975	79.5	20.1	0.4	79.5		20.5	89.2	89.2	76.7			1975
1974	76.8	22.7	0.5	76.8		23.2	88.5	86.8	74.6	0.44		1974
1973	76.9	22.9	0.2	76.9		23.1	87.9	87.5	75.3	0.46		1973
1972	77.7	22.1	0.2	77.7		22.3	87.3	89.1	76.6	0.51		1972
1971	76.3	23.6	0.1	76.3		23.7	86.6	88.1	75.7	0.50		1971
1970	72.6	26.7	0.7	72.6		27.4	86.0	84.4	72.6	0.44		1970
1969	72.6	26.6	0.8	72.6		27.4	85.3	85.1	73.1	0.47		1969
1968	80.2	19.1	0.6	68.2	8.7	23.5	84.7	80.5	69.2	0.40		1968
1967	80.6	18.9	0.5	67.9	9.2	23.2	84.0	80.8	69.5	0.41		1967
1966	79.9	19.5	0.5	66.5	10.0	23.9	83.4	79.7	68.5	0.40		1966
1965	79.0	20.5	0.5	65.1	10.4	24.8	82.8	78.7	67.6	0.39		1965
1964	79.7	20.1	0.2	65.8	9.8	24.7	82.1	80.1	68.9	0.42		1964
1963	80.3	18.9	0.8	66.7	9.5	24.1	81.5	81.9	70.4	0.47		1963
1962	81.5	17.5	1.0	67.5	9.8	23.1	80.8	83.5	71.8	0.51		1962
1961	79.6	19.5	0.9	65.1	10.9	24.3	80.2	81.2	69.8	0.47		1961
1960	80.0	19.7	0.3	65.2	11.0	24.1	79.6	81.9	70.4	0.48		1960
1959	81.6	18.3	0.1	65.8	12.1	22.3	79.0	83.2	71.6	0.51		1959
1958	79.6	20.3	0.2	64.6	11.4	24.2	78.4	82.4	70.8	0.50		1958
1957	74.0	25.9	0.1	59.2	11.7	29.3	77.9	76.0	65.4	0.41		1957
1956	73.5	26.5	-0.0	58.0	12.8	29.4	77.3	75.0	64.4	0.40		1956
1955	75.1	24.9	-0.1	59.8	12.5	27.9	76.8	77.9	67.0	0.45		1955
1954	74.6	25.4	0.0	59.1	13.1	27.9	76.2	77.6	66.7	0.45		1954
1953	74.5	25.6	-0.1	59.5	12.9	27.7	75.6	78.7	67.7	0.47		1953
1952	71.5	28.7	-0.2	56.7	13.1	30.4	75.1	75.5	64.9	0.43		1952
1951	67.6	32.6	-0.1	53.7	12.1	34.4	74.5	72.0	61.9	0.39		1951
1950				55.7		44.3	73.9	75.3	64.7			1950
1949				56.2		43.8	73.1	76.8	66.1			1949
1948				55.1		44.9	72.3	76.1	65.4			1948
1947				55.5		44.5	71.5	77.6	66.7			1947
1946				56.6		43.4	70.7	80.1	68.9			1946
1945							70.5					1945
1944							70.3					1944
1943							70.2					1943
1942							70.0					1942
1941							69.8					1941
1940							69.6					1940
1939				49.2		50.8	69.4	70.8	60.9			1939
1938				48.7		51.3	69.3	70.4	60.5			1938
1937				46.1		53.9	69.1	66.7	57.3			1937
1936				46.9		53.1	68.9	68.1	58.6			1936

Distribution of National Income

Year	NDP (f) by economic institution			NDP (f) by category of factor cost			Dependent labour force	Income positions of two major classes Adjusted labour's shares		Average compensation to average profit of (1)	(2)	Year
	Households	Corporations	Government	Compensation	Entre-preneurship	Property	excl. family workers	Standardized	Hypothetical (1970=100)	Non-government	Private households	
	%	%	%	%	%	%	%	%	%	ratio	ratio	
1935				47.4	52.6		68.7	69.0	59.3			1935
1934				48.1	51.9		68.5	70.2	60.4			1934
1933				48.9	51.1		68.4	71.6	61.6			1933
1932				49.1	50.9		68.2	72.0	61.9			1932
1931				49.4	50.6		68.0	72.7	62.5			1931
1930				47.4	52.6		67.8	70.0	60.1			

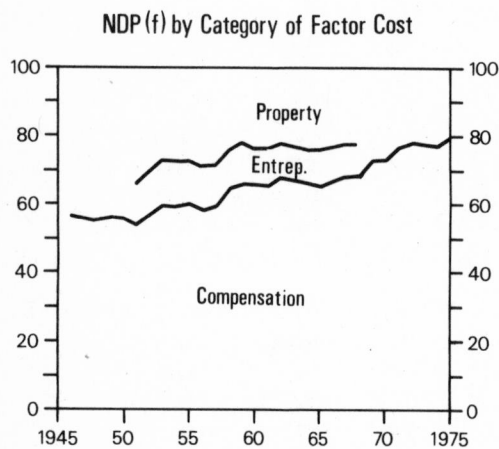

NDP (f) by Category of Factor Cost

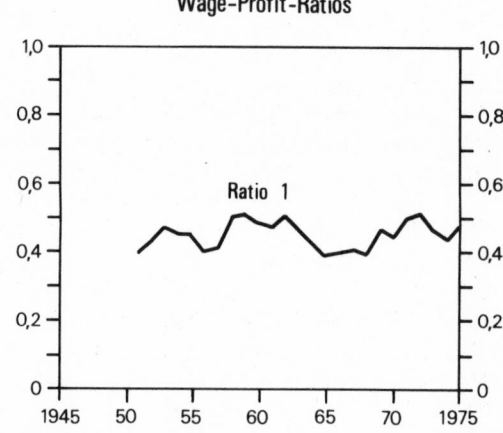

Wage-Profit-Ratios

Distribution of National Income

Year	NDP (f) by economic institution			NDP (f) by category of factor cost			Dependent labour force	Income positions of two major classes Adjusted labour's shares		Average compensation to average profit of (1) (2)		Year
	Households	Corporations	Government	Compensation	Entre-preneurship	Property	excl. family workers	Standardized	Hypothetical (1970=100)	Non-government	Private households	
	%	%	%	%	%	%	%	%	%	ratio	ratio	
1975	96.7	0.2	3.2	83.0	9.5	7.5	92.6	89.6	81.4	0.48	0.48	1975
1974	93.9	3.2	2.9	79.7	10.1	10.3	92.3	86.3	78.5	0.38	0.47	1974
1973	92.5	4.2	3.3	78.7	10.0	11.3	91.9	85.6	77.8	0.38	0.50	1973
1972	94.9	2.2	3.0	80.4	10.8	8.8	91.6	87.8	79.8	0.44	0.51	1972
1971	95.7	1.9	2.4	79.6	11.9	8.5	91.2	87.2	79.3	0.42	0.47	1971
1970	93.2	4.8	2.0	76.1	12.9	11.0	90.9	83.7	76.1	0.35	0.44	1970
1969	93.4	4.2	2.4	75.7	13.6	10.7	90.4	83.7	76.1	0.37	0.45	1969
1968	88.8	8.4	2.9	72.1	5.7	22.2	89.9	80.2	72.9	0.32	0.49	1968
1967	87.6	9.9	2.5	70.5	6.0	23.5	89.4	78.8	71.6	0.31	0.49	1967
1966	86.9	10.9	2.1	69.6	6.0	24.4	88.9	78.3	71.2	0.31	0.50	1966
1965	86.1	11.8	2.1	67.7	6.8	25.4	88.4	76.6	69.6	0.29	0.48	1965
1964	86.0	12.2	1.8	67.2	7.3	25.5	87.9	76.5	69.5	0.30	0.49	1964
1963	86.4	11.7	1.9	67.4	7.2	25.4	87.3	77.2	70.1	0.32	0.51	1963
1962	86.4	11.9	1.6	66.3	7.5	26.2	86.8	76.4	69.4	0.31	0.50	1962
1961	84.6	13.9	1.5	63.5	8.1	28.4	86.2	73.6	66.9	0.29	0.48	1961
1960	84.8	14.1	1.2	62.8	8.4	28.8	85.7	73.2	66.6	0.29	0.48	1960
1959	82.2	16.3	1.5	60.6	8.5	31.0	85.1	71.2	64.7	0.28	0.49	1959
1958	84.1	14.4	1.5	61.5	8.8	29.7	84.5	72.8	66.2	0.30	0.50	1958
1957	84.1	14.6	1.3	61.6	9.2	29.2	84.0	73.3	66.7	0.32	0.52	1957
1956	85.4	13.6	1.1	61.7	10.0	28.3	83.4	74.0	67.3	0.33	0.52	1956
1955	86.0	12.5	1.6	62.4	10.1	27.5	82.8	75.4	68.5	0.36	0.55	1955
1954	84.4	14.2	1.3	60.4	10.8	28.7	82.3	73.5	66.8	0.34	0.54	1954
1953	85.0	13.6	1.4	60.9	11.0	28.1	81.6	74.6	67.8	0.36	0.57	1953
1952	83.4	15.6	1.0	59.2	11.6	29.2	81.0	73.0	66.4	0.35	0.57	1952
1951	79.6	19.5	0.9	55.7	11.6	32.7	80.5	69.2	62.9	0.31	0.57	1951
1950	81.0	18.1	0.9	56.6	11.3	32.1	79.9	70.9	64.4	0.34	0.59	1950
1949				53.3			79.7	66.9	60.8	0.29		1949
1948				53.7			79.4	67.6	61.4	0.30		1948
1947				53.8			79.2	67.9	61.8	0.31		1947
1946				51.9			79.0	65.7	59.7	0.29		1946
1945				51.3			78.8	65.1	59.2	0.28		1945
1944				52.3			78.3	66.7	60.7	0.30		1944
1943				52.5			77.8	67.5	61.4	0.32		1943
1942				52.8			77.4	68.3	62.0	0.33		1942
1941				50.6			76.9	65.9	59.9	0.31		1941
1940				51.7			76.4	67.7	61.6	0.33		1940
1939				54.5			76.4	71.4	64.9	0.37		1939
1938				54.2			76.3	71.0	64.6	0.37		1938
1937				54.2			76.2	71.1	64.7	0.37		1937
1936				55.7			76.2	73.1	66.5	0.39		1936

Distribution of National Income

Year	NDP (f) by economic institution			NDP (f) by category of factor cost			Dependent labour force	Income positions of two major classes Adjusted labour's shares		Average compensation to average profit of		Year
	Households	Corporations	Government	Compensation	Entre-preneurship	Property	excl. family workers	Standardized	Hypothetical (1970=100)	(1) Non-government	(2) Private households	
	%	%	%	%	%	%	%	%	%	ratio	ratio	
1935				57.2			76.1	75.2	68.3	0.42		1935
1934				57.6			76.0	75.8	68.9	0.43		1934
1933				60.1			76.0	79.1	71.9	0.48		1933
1932				63.1			75.9	83.2	75.6	0.54		1932
1931				62.2			75.8	82.1	74.6	0.53		1931
1930				56.2			75.7	74.2	67.5	0.41		1930

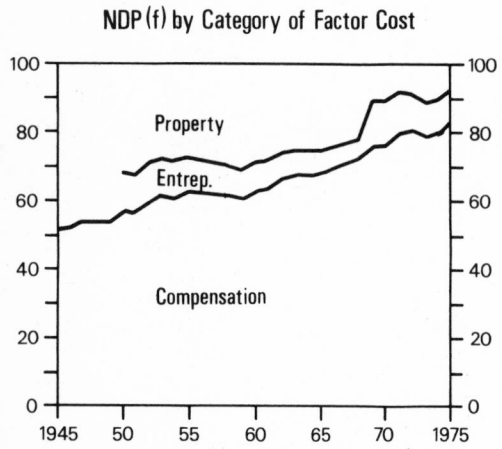

NDP (f) by Category of Factor Cost

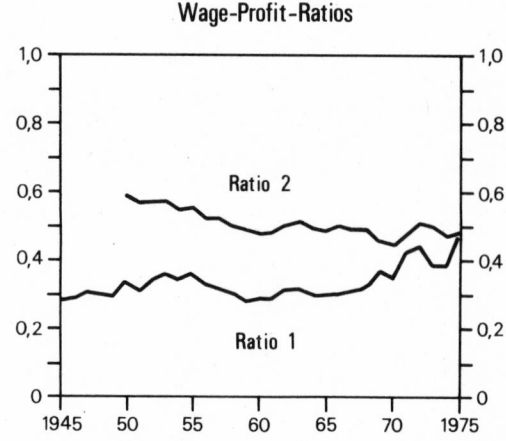

Wage-Profit-Ratios

Distribution of National Income

Year	NDP (f) by economic institution			NDP (f) by category of factor cost			Dependent labour force	Adjusted labour's shares		Income positions of two major classes. Average compensation to average profit of		Year
	Households	Corporations	Government	Compensation	Entre-preneurship	Property	excl. family workers	Standardized	Hypothetical (1970=100)	(1) Non-government	(2) Private households	
	%	%	%	%	%	%	%	%	%	ratio	ratio	
1975				68.5			91.2	75.1	66.8			1975
1974				66.2			90.8	73.0	65.0			1974
1973				65.6			90.4	72.6	64.7			1973
1972				64.7			89.9	72.0	64.1			1972
1971				64.3			89.5	71.9	64.0			1971
1970				63.1			89.1	70.9	63.1			1970
1969				62.6			88.6	70.6	62.9			1969
1968	90.7	8.0	1.4	62.8	28.0	20.6	88.2	71.2	63.4	0.23	0.30	1968
1967	91.3	7.3	1.3	63.5	27.9	19.5	87.8	72.4	64.5	0.25	0.32	1967
1966	91.1	7.6	1.3	63.5	27.7	19.2	87.3	72.7	64.8	0.26	0.33	1966
1965	91.4	7.3	1.3	64.0	27.5	18.5	86.9	73.6	65.6	0.28	0.35	1965
1964	90.7	7.8	1.5	63.2	27.6	18.7	86.5	73.0	65.1	0.28	0.36	1964
1963	90.7	7.7	1.6	63.1	27.7	18.7	86.0	73.3	65.3	0.29	0.37	1963
1962	89.9	8.2	1.9	61.7	28.3	19.6	85.6	72.1	64.2	0.28	0.37	1962
1961	90.0	8.1	1.9	61.3	28.8	19.8	85.2	72.0	64.1	0.29	0.37	1961
1960	90.0	8.2	1.9	60.7	29.4	20.3	84.7	71.6	63.8	0.29	0.37	1960
1959	90.3	7.8	2.0	60.5	29.9	20.2	84.2	71.8	63.9	0.30	0.38	1959
1958	90.0	8.2	1.8	59.5	30.6	20.8	83.8	71.0	63.3	0.30	0.38	1958
1957	89.9	8.1	2.0	60.5	29.6	20.4	83.3	72.6	64.7	0.32	0.41	1957
1956	90.0	8.2	1.9	60.8	29.3	20.4	82.8	73.5	65.4	0.34	0.43	1956
1955	90.5	7.7	1.7	60.3	30.4	20.1	82.3	73.2	65.2	0.34	0.43	1955
1954	91.1	7.3	1.5	60.2	31.0	19.6	81.8	73.7	65.6	0.35	0.43	1954
1953	91.7	6.9	1.4	61.2	30.5	19.3	81.3	75.3	67.1	0.38	0.46	1953
1952	91.8	6.8	1.4	61.2	30.7	19.0	80.8	75.7	67.4	0.39	0.47	1952
1951	92.4	6.4	1.2	60.6	31.8	18.4	80.3	75.5	67.2	0.39	0.47	1951
1950				60.8			79.8	76.2	67.8			1950
1949				62.1			79.5	78.2	69.6			1949
1948				60.2			79.2	76.0	67.7			1948
1947				58.5			78.9	74.2	66.1			1947
1946				56.5			78.6	71.9	64.1			1946
1945				55.8			78.3	71.2	63.4			1945
1944				53.9			78.0	69.1	61.6			1944
1943				52.8			77.7	67.9	60.5			1943
1942				51.5			77.4	66.5	59.2			1942
1941				50.4			77.1	65.4	58.2			1941
1940				51.1			77.0	66.4	59.1			1940
1939				50.0			76.9	65.0	57.9			1939
1938				50.4			76.8	65.6	58.4			1938
1937				49.7			76.7	64.8	57.7			1937
1936				51.0			76.6	66.6	59.3			1936

Switzerland

Distribution of National Income

Year	NDP (f) by economic institution			NDP (f) by category of factor cost			Dependent labour force	Income positions of two major classes — Adjusted labour's shares		Average compensation to average profit of		Year
	Households	Corporations	Government	Compensation	Entre-preneurship	Property	excl. family workers	Standardized	Hypothetical (1970=100)	(1) Non-government	(2) Private households	
	%	%	%	%	%	%	%	%	%	ratio	ratio	
1935				52.9			76.5	69.1	61.5			1935
1934				54.0			76.4	70.7	63.0			1934
1933				54.2			76.3	71.1	63.3			1933
1932				55.8			76.2	73.3	65.2			1932
1931				52.9			76.1	69.5	61.9			1931
1930				50.2			76.0	66.1	58.8			1930
1929				49.3			75.7	65.2	58.0			1929
1928							75.5					1928
1927							75.2					1927
1926							75.0					1926
1925							74.8					1925
1924				51.6			74.5	69.3	61.7			1924
1910				44.6			66.8	66.7	59.4			1910

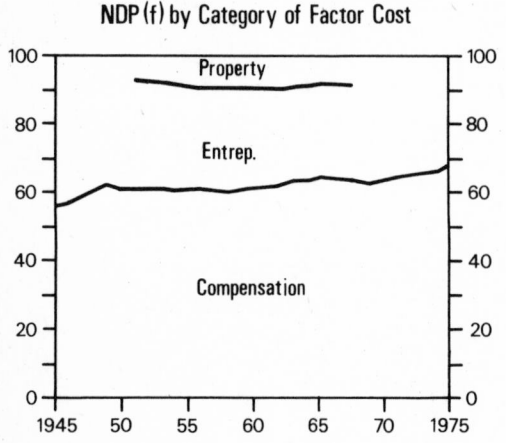

NDP (f) by Category of Factor Cost

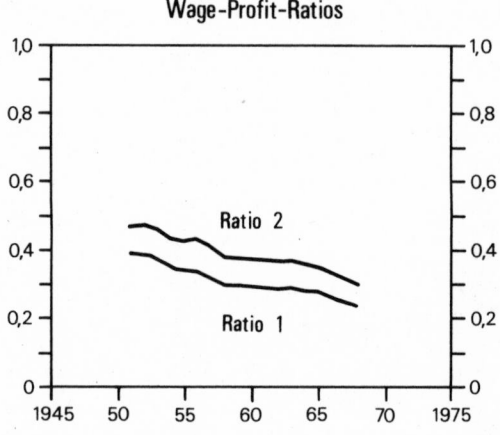

Wage-Profit-Ratios

Distribution of National Income

Year	NDP (f) by economic institution			NDP (f) by category of factor cost			Dependent labour force	Income positions of two major classes Adjusted labour's shares		Average compensation to average profit of		Year
	Households	Corporations	Government	Compensation	Entre-preneurship	Property	excl. family workers	Standardized	Hypothetical (1970=100)	(1) Non-government	(2) Private households	
	%	%	%	%	%	%	%	%	%	ratio	ratio	
1975							93.9					1975
1974	98.6	2.9	-1.5	80.2	13.0	6.8	93.9	85.5	80.0	0.25	0.29	1974
1973	93.7	7.7	-1.3	75.4	12.8	11.8	93.8	80.4	75.3	0.19	0.27	1973
1972	94.0	7.2	-1.2	75.5	12.4	12.1	93.8	80.5	75.4	0.20	0.27	1972
1971	94.2	6.8	-1.0	75.6	11.6	12.7	93.7	80.7	75.6	0.20	0.27	1971
1970	94.6	6.8	-1.4	76.0	11.2	12.9	93.6	81.1	76.0	0.20	0.28	1970
1969	93.7	7.9	-1.6	74.4	10.9	14.7	93.6	79.5	74.4	0.19	0.26	1969
1968	94.7	7.0	-1.8	75.5	7.1	17.6	93.5	80.8	75.6	0.20	0.27	1968
1967	94.3	7.4	-1.7	74.3	7.5	17.8	93.4	79.5	74.5	0.19	0.27	1967
1966	94.9	6.8	-1.7	75.4	7.6	17.3	93.4	80.7	75.6	0.20	0.27	1966
1965	93.1	8.7	-1.8	74.0	7.6	19.3	93.3	79.3	74.3	0.18	0.26	1965
1964	92.4	9.5	-1.9	73.2	7.5	19.7	93.3	78.4	73.4	0.18	0.27	1964
1963	92.5	9.8	-2.2	72.8	7.7	19.4	93.2	78.1	73.2	0.18	0.27	1963
1962	93.4	8.5	-1.9	73.9	7.9	18.0	93.1	79.3	74.2	0.20	0.28	1962
1961	93.2	9.2	-2.5	73.3	8.2	18.3	93.1	78.7	73.7	0.19	0.28	1961
1960	91.2	11.4	-2.6	72.6	8.4	19.8	93.0	78.0	73.0	0.18	0.28	1960
1960	85.3	15.5	-0.8	72.1	8.7	25.1	93.0	77.5	72.6	0.14	0.26	1960
1959	84.8	15.9	-0.7	72.9	8.9	24.8	92.9	78.5	73.5	0.15	0.27	1959
1958	85.1	16.0	-1.1	73.6	8.9	24.1	92.9	79.3	74.2	0.15	0.28	1958
1957	84.3	16.9	-1.2	73.9	9.1	24.1	92.8	79.6	74.5	0.15	0.29	1957
1956	84.1	17.3	-1.4	73.6	9.3	24.3	92.8	79.3	74.3	0.15	0.29	1956
1955	84.0	17.7	-1.7	72.4	9.7	24.9	92.7	78.1	73.1	0.14	0.28	1955
1954	83.8	17.9	-1.6	71.1	9.9	25.3	92.6	76.7	71.8	0.14	0.27	1954
1953	85.1	17.2	-2.3	71.1	10.4	24.4	92.6	76.8	71.9	0.14	0.26	1953
1952	85.2	17.3	-2.6	71.4	10.7	24.0	92.5	77.2	72.3	0.14	0.27	1952
1951	81.8	20.0	-1.8	71.8	10.5	27.4	92.4	77.7	72.7	0.13	0.26	1951
1950	82.9	19.0	-1.9	70.6	11.2	27.4	92.4	76.4	71.5	0.13	0.24	1950
1949	86.2	16.2	-2.4	70.3	12.1	24.4	92.3	76.1	71.3	0.14	0.23	1949
1948	86.2	16.6	-2.8	70.5	12.1	25.1	92.3	76.4	71.6	0.13	0.23	1948
1947	88.8	15.2	-4.0	71.7	12.2	24.9	92.2	77.7	72.8	0.13	0.21	1947
1946	90.8	13.5	-4.4	70.5	12.5	23.3	92.1	76.5	71.7	0.14	0.20	1946
1945			-3.7	71.6	12.0	21.9						1945
1944			-2.7	70.9	11.2	23.5						1944
1943			-2.0	69.1	11.4	24.9						1943
1942			-1.8	67.7	11.7	25.8						1942
1941			-2.0	67.5	12.1	26.4						1941
1940			-2.1	69.5	12.2	28.4	90.9	76.5	71.6	0.14		1940
1939			-2.3	65.5	12.7	28.9	90.8	72.2	67.6	0.14		1939
1938	94.9	7.7	-2.6	62.9	12.3	28.1	90.7	69.3	64.9	0.14	0.17	1938
1937	93.2	9.4	-2.6	63.8	12.7	28.9	90.7	70.4	65.9	0.14	0.17	1937
1936	94.4	8.2	-2.6	63.7	14.0	27.9	90.6	70.3	65.8	0.13	0.17	1936

Distribution of National Income

Year	NDP (f) by economic institution			NDP (f) by category of factor cost			Dependent labour force	Income positions of two major classes Adjusted labour's shares		Average compensation to average profit of (1)	(2)	Year
	Households	Corporations	Government	Compensation	Entre-preneurship	Property	excl. family workers	Standardized	Hypothetical (1970=100)	Non-government	Private households	
	%	%	%	%	%	%	%	%	%	ratio	ratio	
1935	95.8	7.2	-3.0	63.7	14.3	26.7	90.6	70.3	65.8	0.14	0.17	1935
1934	96.4	6.7	-3.2	64.1	14.2	26.1	90.5	70.8	66.3	0.14	0.17	1934
1933	99.1	4.8	-3.9	65.8	14.8	24.8	90.5	72.7	68.1	0.15	0.16	1933
1932	102.1	2.9	-5.0	66.4	14.4	23.5	90.4	73.4	68.7	0.15	0.16	1932
1931	102.1	2.8	-4.8	65.1	14.2	24.5	90.4	72.1	67.5	0.15	0.16	1931
1930	100.8	4.0	-4.8	61.1	14.9	25.2	90.3	67.7	63.4	0.14	0.16	1930
1929	98.3	6.7	-5.0	61.7	15.4	26.0	90.3	68.3	64.0	0.14	0.16	1929
1928	98.6	6.5	-5.1	62.5	15.7	25.7	90.2	69.3	64.8	0.14	0.16	1928
1927	98.3	6.7	-5.1	62.9	15.4	25.4	90.2	69.7	65.3	0.14	0.16	1927
1926	100.5	5.8	-6.3	62.3	16.2	25.0	90.1	69.2	64.8	0.14	0.15	1926
1925	99.7	6.2	-5.9	61.1	16.0	24.5	90.1	67.8	63.5	0.14	0.16	1925
1924	99.4	6.8	-6.3	64.6	15.9	24.4	90.0	71.8	67.2	0.14	0.17	1924
1923	98.9	7.5	-6.3	65.4	15.8	24.4	90.0	72.7	68.1	0.14	0.17	1923
1922	98.9	7.2	-6.1	64.9	15.8	23.4	90.0	72.2	67.6	0.15	0.18	1922
1921	101.4	4.5	-5.9	66.7	14.3	20.1	89.9	74.2	69.5	0.18	0.21	1921
1920	96.4	8.9	-5.2	67.9	14.1	21.0	89.9	75.6	70.8	0.18	0.23	1920
1919			-4.9	65.9			89.8	73.3	68.6	0.15		1919
1918			-3.3	63.9								1918
1917			-2.5	62.9								1917
1916			-1.9	62.2								1916
1915			-0.7	61.8			88.9	69.6	65.1	0.15		1915
1914			0.1	56.5			88.7	63.6	59.6	0.14		1914
1913			0.1	52.6	15.8	34.2	88.6	59.4	55.6	0.13		1913
1912			0.2	52.3	16.3	34.0	88.4	59.1	55.3	0.13		1912
1911			0.0	52.6	16.6	33.4	88.3	59.6	55.8	0.13		1911
1910			0.0	52.9	16.1	33.6	88.1	60.0	56.2	0.14		1910
1909			-0.1	53.0	16.0	33.6	88.0	60.2	56.4	0.14		1909
1908			-0.1	53.2	16.1	33.4	87.9	60.5	56.7	0.14		1908
1907			-0.1	52.5	17.2	32.8	87.9	59.7	55.9	0.14		1907
1906			-0.3	52.1	17.3	33.1	87.8	59.4	55.6	0.14		1906
1905			-0.4	52.9	17.1	32.6	87.7	60.4	56.5	0.14		1905
1904			-0.4	54.2	16.4	32.1	87.6	61.9	58.0	0.15		1904
1903			-0.6	54.7	16.4	31.6	87.5	62.5	58.5	0.15		1903
1902			-0.6	53.3	17.7	31.5	87.4	61.0	57.1	0.15		1902
1901			-0.6	54.4	17.3	30.9	87.3	62.3	58.4	0.15		1901
1900			-0.6	53.6	18.1	30.9	87.3	61.5	57.5	0.15		1900
1899				52.0	19.1	31.3	87.2	59.6	55.8			1899
1898				52.7	18.5	31.1	87.1	60.5	56.6			1898
1897				53.0	18.8	30.6	87.1	60.9	57.0			1897
1896				53.5	18.6	30.2	87.0	61.5	57.6			1896

Distribution of National Income

Year	NDP (f) by economic institution			NDP (f) by category of factor cost			Dependent labour force	Income positions of two major classes Adjusted labour's shares		Average compensation to average profit of (1)	(2)	Year
	Households	Corporations	Government	Compensation	Entre-preneurship	Property	excl. family workers	Standardized	Hypothetical (1970=100)	Non-government	Private households	
	%	%	%	%	%	%	%	%	%	ratio	ratio	
1895				52.8	19.3	30.2	87.0	60.8	56.9			1895
1894				53.0	19.5	29.9	86.9	61.0	57.1			1894
1893				55.3	18.0	29.4	86.8	63.6	59.6			1893
1892				55.3	18.8	28.7	86.8	63.7	59.6			1892
1891				53.9	20.5	28.2	86.7	62.2	58.2			1891
1890				53.1	21.1	28.4	86.7	61.3	57.4			1890
1889				52.0	21.8	28.6	86.6	60.0	56.2			1889
1888				51.0			86.6	58.9	55.2			1888
1887				51.4			86.5	59.4	55.6			1887
1886				50.9			86.4	58.9	55.2			1886
1885				52.5			86.4	60.7	56.9			1885
1884				52.9			86.3	61.3	57.4			1884
1883				53.3			86.3	61.7	57.8			1883
1882				52.0			86.2	60.3	56.4			1882
1881				50.8			86.1	59.0	55.2			1881
1880				51.0			86.1	59.3	55.5			1880
1879				52.1								1879
1878				51.8								1878
1877				52.1								1877
1876				51.3								1876
1875				50.7								1875
1874				50.5								1874
1873				50.3								1873
1872				49.4								1872
1871				47.0								1871
1870				47.9								1870
1869				49.7								1869
1868				49.7								1868
1867				50.9								1867
1866				50.2								1866
1865				50.1								1865
1864				49.1								1864
1863				49.3								1863
1862				49.6								1862
1861				50.7								1861
1860				53.3								1860
1859				53.3								1859
1858				50.9								1858
1857				52.3								1857
1856				53.8								1856
1855				55.1								1855

United Kingdom

Wage-Profit-Ratio

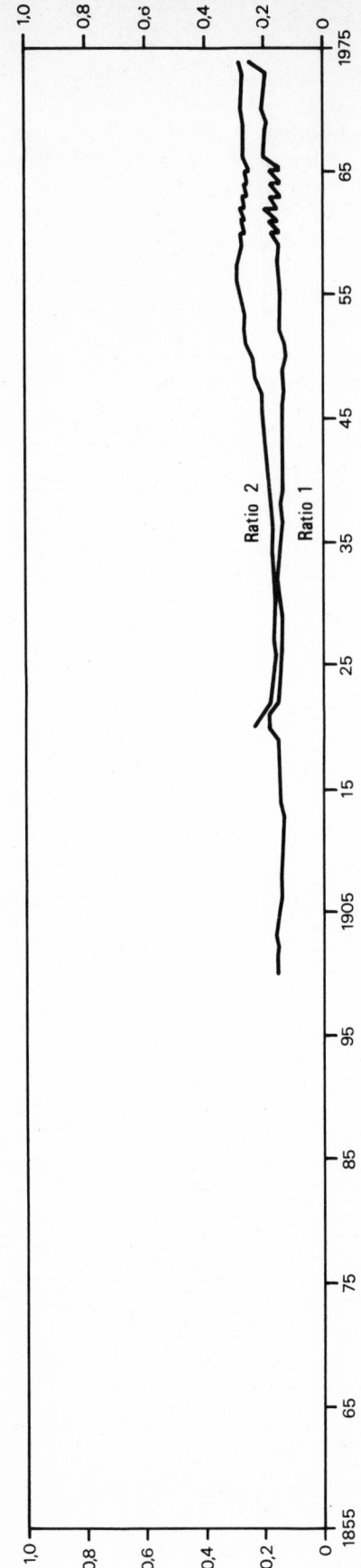

Ratio 2

Ratio 1

NDP (f) by Category of Factor Cost

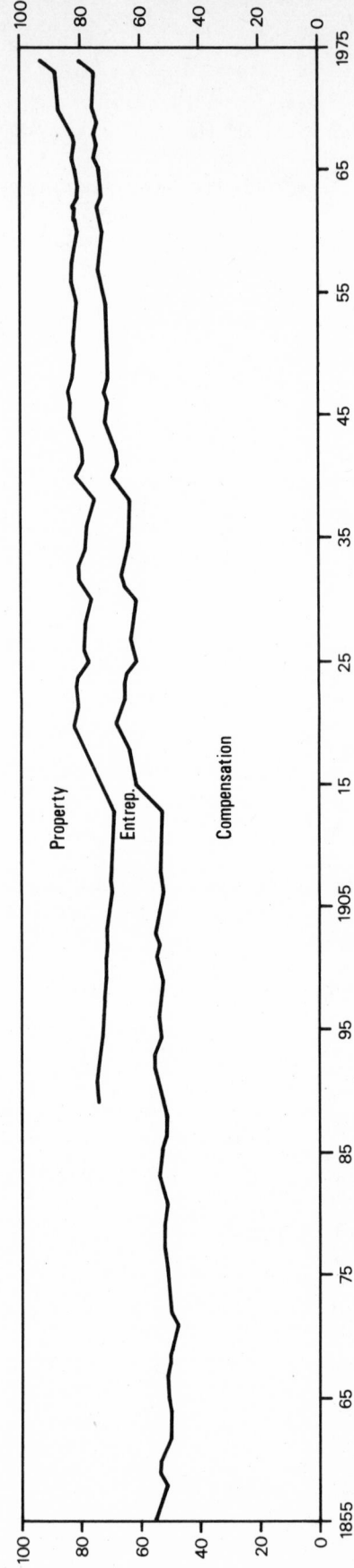

Property

Entrep.

Compensation

A u s t r i a

Distribution of Personal Income before Tax

Structure of Inequality

Year	No of income units in 1,000s	as % of labour force	Fractile Shares — Income of quantile groups as % of total income										Median income	Quantile Ratios — Income level of percentile points as % of the median income								Degree of Inequality Gini coefficient %	Rel. mean dev. %	Year
			Top 10%	90–80	80–70	70–60	60–50	50–40	40–30	30–20	20–10	10–0		Top 95	90	80	75	60	40	25	20			
1976	2600.4	87.2	25.2	15.4	12.8	11.1	9.7	8.5	7.2	5.6	3.6	0.9	106 740	2.4	1.9	1.5	1.4	1.1	0.9	0.6	0.5	34.9	24.5	1976
1973	2408.0	84.2	25.3	15.5	12.9	11.2	9.8	8.5	7.2	5.7	3.5	0.4	76 944	2.4	1.9	1.5	1.4	1.1	0.9	0.6	0.5	35.7	25.0	1973
1970 a)	2164.8	80.6	24.7	15.1	12.7	11.1	9.8	8.6	7.3	5.9	3.9	1.0	55 255	2.3	1.9	1.5	1.4	1.1	0.9	0.6	0.5	33.8	23.7	1970
1970	1953.9	79.0	25.2	15.3	12.9	11.3	10.0	8.7	7.4	6.0	3.3	0.0	56 266	2.3	1.8	1.5	1.4	1.1	0.9	0.6	0.5	35.8	24.7	1970
1967	2225.2	82.3	24.3	15.0	12.6	11.1	9.8	8.6	7.5	6.0	4.1	1.1	43 783	2.3	1.8	1.5	1.4	1.1	0.9	0.7	0.6	33.0	23.0	1967
1964	2172.7	81.8	24.9	15.2	12.7	11.2	9.9	8.6	7.4	5.9	3.9	0.3	33 823	2.3	1.9	1.5	1.4	1.1	0.9	0.6	0.5	34.7	24.1	1964
1957 b)	1885.1	73.7	24.9	15.0	12.6	11.1	9.7	8.5	7.2	5.8	4.0	1.2	21 267	2.4	1.9	1.5	1.4	1.1	0.9	0.6	0.6	33.8	23.0	1957
1957 c)	1715.8	71.8	24.3	14.9	12.6	11.1	9.8	8.6	7.3	6.0	4.2	1.2	21 569	2.3	1.8	1.5	1.4	1.1	0.9	0.7	0.6	32.8	23.0	1957
1953 d)	1869.6	75.7	22.6	14.5	12.7	11.1	10.1	9.1	7.9	6.3	5.7 (20–10 & 10–0)		14 449	2.1	1.7	1.4	1.3	1.1	0.9					1953
1933 e)	1795.7		31.4	17.5	14.1	11.8	25.6 (60–50 to 10–0)						1 931	2.8	2.2	1.7	1.5	1.2	0.8					1933
1933 d)	1869.6	57.5	24.6	13.9	11.3	9.9	8.8	7.8	7.0	6.3	5.4	4.9	2 519											1933
1928 d)	1998.1		28.4	15.4	12.7	11.0	9.5	8.3	7.3	6.3	1.1	0.0	2 209	2.5	2.0	1.5	1.4	1.1	0.9	0.7	0.6	39.9	27.4	1928
1928 e)	1613.2	80.7	25.0	13.5	11.2	9.8	8.7	7.8	7.0	6.3	5.7	5.0	2 515	2.4	1.9	1.5	1.4	1.1	0.9	0.8	0.7	26.9	19.8	1928

Sources:

1976–1953	Statistics on wage-tax.
1933, 1928	Special investigation of the Austrian Statistical Bureau, published in Statistische Nachrichten, Vienna 1953.

Population: The series only refers to employment incomes of employees and workers (largely excl. of family workers). Data include a small amount of double countings.

Income:

1976–1953	Gross income.
1933, 1928	Estimated full-time gross incomes.

Coverage: Tax units as % of employees and workers (excl. family workers).

Adjustment to improper coverage:

1976–1953	No adjustment because improper coverage is not due to the existence of an income threshold.
1933, 1928	Estimate for units below the reported income limit of 1400 Austrian Shillings.

a) Different population concept: employees and workers after exclusion of pensioners. Cf. note 2).
b) Different population concept: employees and workers after the exclusion of substantial parts of pensioners and recipients of old-age benefits.
c) Break in comparability. Cf. general note on income concepts.
d) After adjustment for improper coverage of employees and workers (1933: 588 000 units, 1928: 385 000 units).
   Figures tend to overestimate inequality.
e) Employees and workers incl. of pensioners with an income of Austrian Shillings 1400 and over.

AUSTRIA

Fractile Shares

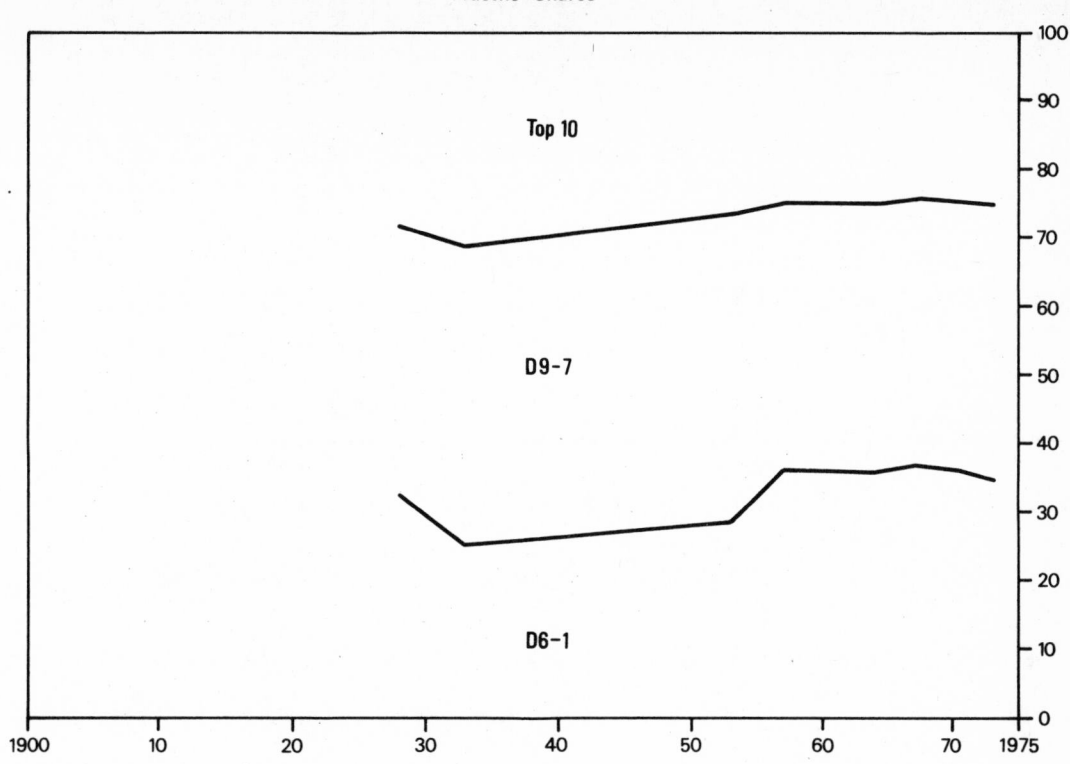

Top 10

D9-7

D6-1

Quantile Ratios

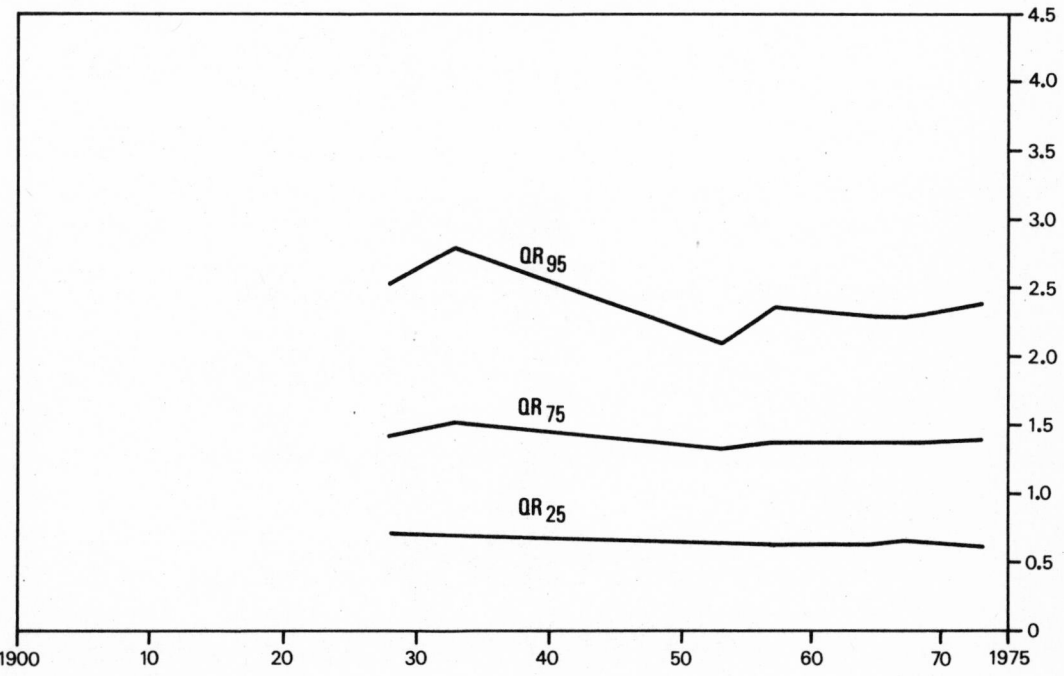

QR 95

QR 75

QR 25

Denmark

Distribution of Personal Income before Tax

Structure of Inequality

Year	No of income units in 1,000s	as % of labour force	Top 10%	90-80	80-70	70-60	60-50	50-40	40-30	30-20	20-10	10-0	Median income in 1,000s	Top 95	90	80	75	60	40	25	20	Gini co-efficient	Rel. mean dev.	Year
1976d)	2334.5		28.4	16.0	13.2	11.7	10.4	8.5	7.2	4.6	0.1	0.0	60 913f)	2.5	2.0	1.5	1.4	1.2	0.8	0.7	0.1	42.5	29.7	1976
1970	1754.2	99.7	32.0	15.6	12.8	11.1	9.7	8.3	6.4	3.7	0.2	0.0	25 032	2.7	2.0	1.5	1.4	1.2	0.8	0.4	0.2	45.8	31.7	1970
1962	1772.4	99.1	26.7	15.6	12.9	11.0	9.5	8.0	6.6	5.0	3.3	1.3	11 755	2.5	2.0	1.6	1.5	1.2	0.8	0.6	0.5	36.8	26.2	1962
1961	1723.7	98.1	27.6	15.7	12.4	10.6	9.5	8.3	6.7	5.0	3.2	1.0	10 215	2.6	2.0	1.5	1.4	1.1	0.8	0.6	0.5	37.6	26.2	1961
1960	1744.2	97.8	27.3	15.3	12.5	11.0	9.8	8.2	6.8	5.0	3.2	1.0	8 970	2.5	2.0	1.5	1.4	1.2	0.8	0.6	0.4	37.3	26.0	1960
1959	1732.6	98.3	27.2	15.2	12.6	11.1	9.6	8.2	6.8	5.0	3.3	1.1	8 320	2.5	2.0	1.5	1.4	1.2	0.9	0.6	0.5	37.1	26.1	1959
1958	1691.7	97.1	26.9	15.3	12.9	11.3	9.6	8.3	6.7	4.9	3.2	0.8	7 730	2.5	1.9	1.6	1.4	1.2	0.8	0.5	0.4	37.5	26.5	1958
1957	1692.3	98.4	26.3	15.3	12.9	11.2	9.6	8.3	6.7	5.1	3.4	1.1	7 528	2.4	1.9	1.5	1.4	1.2	0.8	0.6	0.5	36.4	25.7	1957
1956	1694.3	99.8	26.5	15.1	12.8	11.0	9.5	8.3	6.7	5.1	3.5	1.4	7 376	2.4	1.9	1.5	1.4	1.1	0.8	0.6	0.5	36.0	25.4	1956
1955	1701.5	101.4	26.2	15.1	12.8	10.9	9.5	8.2	6.8	5.2	3.6	1.7	7 114	2.3	1.9	1.5	1.4	1.1	0.8	0.6	0.5	35.3	24.9	1955
1954	1697.3	100.7	26.5	15.2	12.8	10.9	9.6	8.2	6.8	5.1	3.6	1.5	6 869	2.4	1.9	1.5	1.4	1.1	0.8	0.6	0.5	35.8	25.2	1954
1953	1696.1	100.2	27.0	15.4	12.7	10.9	9.6	8.0	6.6	4.9	3.5	1.4	6 337	2.5	2.0	1.6	1.4	1.2	0.8	0.6	0.5	36.7	25.9	1953
1952	1687.3	99.3	27.4	15.5	12.7	11.0	9.5	8.0	6.5	4.9	3.4	1.2	5 951	2.5	2.0	1.6	1.5	1.2	0.9	0.6	0.5	37.4	26.5	1952
1951	1681.5	98.5	27.8	15.5	12.7	11.0	9.3	8.0	6.3	4.9	3.4	1.1	5 550	2.6	2.0	1.6	1.5	1.2	0.8	0.6	0.5	37.9	26.9	1951
1950	1692.7	98.8	28.6	15.3	12.6	10.7	9.2	7.8	6.2	5.0	3.5	1.1	5 228	2.6	2.1	1.6	1.5	1.2	0.8	0.6	0.5	38.3	27.2	1950
1949	1684.3	98.8	29.1	15.3	12.6	10.6	9.2	7.6	6.2	5.0	3.5	1.0	4 713	2.7	2.1	1.6	1.5	1.2	0.8	0.6	0.5	38.7	27.4	1949
1948e)	2045.2		29.3	15.2	12.5	10.5	9.1	7.5	6.3	5.1	3.5	1.1	4 373	2.7	2.1	1.7	1.5	1.2	0.8	0.6	0.5	38.7	27.5	1948
1947	1663.5	98.8	30.1	15.1	12.2	10.5	8.9	7.4	6.4	5.1	3.5	0.9	4 064	2.8	2.1	1.7	1.5	1.2	0.8	0.6	0.5	39.4	27.9	1947
1946	1673.7	99.9	30.3	15.0	12.2	10.4	8.6	7.4	6.4	5.1	3.6	1.1	3 763	2.8	2.2	1.7	1.5	1.2	0.9	0.6	0.6	39.2	27.9	1946
1945	1645.6	98.8	32.7	15.2	12.2	9.9	8.4	7.3	6.0	4.7	3.1	0.5	3 291	3.0	2.3	1.7	1.6	1.2	0.9	0.6	0.5	42.6	30.3	1945
1944	1623.7	98.0	32.5	15.4	12.3	10.0	8.6	7.4	5.9	4.6	3.1	0.3	3 113	3.0	2.2	1.7	1.5	1.1	0.8	0.6	0.5	42.7	30.3	1944
1943	1620.1	98.3	33.6	15.5	12.1	10.1	8.7	7.1	5.7	4.2	3.0	0.0	2 740	3.0	2.3	1.7	1.5	1.2	0.8	0.5	0.5	44.4	31.4	1943
1942	1601.2	97.8	35.4	15.6	12.1	10.2	8.3	6.8	5.3	4.1	2.3	0.0	2 281	3.3	2.5	1.8	1.6	1.2	0.8	0.6	0.5	46.8	33.3	1942
1941	1583.2	97.2	36.4	15.7	12.3	10.2	8.2	6.6	5.1	4.2	1.3	0.0	2 044	3.4	2.5	1.8	1.7	1.2	0.8	0.6	0.5	48.6	34.8	1941
1940	1566.1	96.7	36.8	16.3	12.8	10.1	8.1	6.4	5.3	4.0	0.1	0.0	1 698	3.5	2.7	2.0	1.8	1.3	0.8	0.6	0.1	50.5	36.2	1940

Information on Coverage — Fractile Shares a): Income of quantile groups as % of total income — Quantile Ratios b): Income level of percentile points as % of the median income — Degree of Inequality c)

Denmark

Distribution of Personal Income before Tax

Structure of Inequality

Year	No of income units in 1,000s	as % of labour force	Top 10%	90–80	80–70	70–60	60–50	50–40	40–30	30–20	20–10	10–0	Median income in 1,000s	Top 95	90	80	75	60	40	25	20	Gini co-efficient	Rel. mean dev.	Year
							Income of quantile groups as % of total income (Fractile Shares a)							Income level of percentile points as % of the median income (Quantile Ratios b)								Degree of Inequality c)		
1939	1587.2	96.1	37.3	16.6	13.0	10.1	8.1	6.4	5.3	3.2	0.0	0.0	1 611	3.6	2.7	2.0	1.8	1.3	0.8	0.6	0.0	51.7	37.2	1939
1938	1807.4	95.8	35.3	16.0	12.3	9.7	7.6	6.2	5.3	4.4	3.1	0.0	1 567	3.6	2.8	2.0	1.8	1.3	0.8	0.7	0.6	46.2	33.8	1938
1937	1377.7	80.9	36.0	15.8	12.1	9.5	7.6	6.2	5.2	4.4	3.2	0.0	1 547	3.6	2.7	2.0	1.8	1.3	0.8	0.7	0.6	46.6	34.0	1937
1936	1328.1	88.5	37.6	15.9	12.0	9.4	7.4	6.0	5.1	4.3	2.2	0.0	1 456	3.8	2.8	2.1	1.8	1.3	0.8	0.6	0.6	48.7	35.5	1936
1935	1286.6	77.3	37.8	16.1	12.3	9.5	7.5	6.1	5.0	4.2	1.5	0.0	1 427	3.8	2.8	2.1	1.8	1.3	0.8	0.6	0.6	49.8	36.2	1935
1934	1224.5	82.1	39.0	16.5	12.2	9.5	7.4	6.0	5.0	4.1	0.3	0.0	1 331	4.0	3.0	2.1	1.8	1.3	0.8	0.6	0.3	52.0	37.7	1934
1933	1148.2	70.7	39.0	17.1	12.7	9.7	7.5	6.1	5.1	2.7	0.0	0.0	1 255	4.0	3.0	2.2	1.9	1.2	0.8	0.5	0.0	53.6	39.0	1933
1932	1088.8	74.0	40.0	17.7	12.7	9.6	7.5	6.1	5.1	1.3	0.0	0.0	1 159	4.2	3.2	2.2	1.9	1.2	0.8	0.1	0.0	55.5	40.5	1932
1931	1153.0	73.9	38.7	17.1	12.8	9.7	7.5	6.1	5.1	3.0	0.0	0.0	1 308	4.2	3.0	2.2	1.9	1.3	0.8	0.6	0.0	53.1	38.7	1931
1930 g)	1079.4	74.2	37.8	16.7	12.7	9.9	7.7	6.2	5.1	3.8	0.2	0.0	1 444	3.8	2.9	2.1	1.9	1.3	0.8	0.6	0.2	51.6	37.4	1930
1930	1188.5	78.6	39.9	18.0	13.4	10.4	8.0	6.4	3.8	0.1	0.0	0.0	1 354	4.0	3.0	2.2	1.9	1.3	0.8	0.0	0.0	57.3	41.8	1930
1930 h)	1245.8	85.6	37.8	16.7	12.7	9.8	7.7	6.2	5.1	3.8	0.2	0.0	1 444	3.9	2.9	2.1	1.9	1.3	0.8	0.6	0.2	51.6	37.4	1930
1929	1162.5	78.1	37.9	16.8	12.7	9.8	7.7	6.2	5.0	3.7	0.1	0.0	1 450	3.9	2.9	2.1	1.9	1.3	0.8	0.6	0.1	51.8	37.6	1929
1928	1127.6	77.0	38.6	16.7	12.6	9.8	7.6	6.2	5.1	3.5	0.1	0.0	1 408	3.9	2.9	2.1	1.8	1.3	0.8	0.6	0.1	52.5	38.0	1928
1927	1125.9	78.3	37.4	16.7	12.7	9.8	7.7	6.3	5.2	3.9	0.2	0.0	1 440	3.8	2.8	2.1	1.8	1.3	0.8	0.6	0.2	51.1	37.0	1927
1926	1149.1	81.5	35.7	16.7	12.8	10.0	7.9	6.4	5.3	4.3	1.0	0.0	1 576	3.7	2.8	2.0	1.8	1.3	0.8	0.6	0.5	48.9	35.4	1926
1925	1165.7	84.3	35.8	16.3	12.6	9.9	7.8	6.3	5.2	4.2	1.8	0.0	1 798	3.7	2.7	2.0	1.8	1.2	0.8	0.6	0.5	48.2	34.9	1925
1924	1138.7	83.8	37.0	16.1	12.4	9.8	7.8	6.2	5.1	4.1	1.6	0.0	1 835	3.7	2.8	2.0	1.8	1.3	0.8	0.6	0.5	49.2	35.7	1924
1923	1083.4	81.0	37.5	16.3	12.5	9.8	7.9	6.2	5.1	4.0	0.9	0.0	1 722	3.8	2.8	2.0	1.8	1.3	0.8	0.6	0.5	50.4	36.5	1923
1922	1050.5	79.9	36.7	16.6	12.7	9.9	7.9	6.3	5.2	4.1	0.6	0.0	1 676	3.8	2.8	2.0	1.8	1.3	0.8	0.6	0.5	50.1	36.2	1922
1921	1037.3	80.4	36.3	16.9	13.0	10.1	7.9	6.2	5.0	3.8	0.7	0.0	1 934	3.7	2.8	2.0	1.9	1.3	0.8	0.5	0.4	50.3	36.6	1921
1920 h)	1042.7	89.5	38.9	15.7	12.2	9.8	7.7	6.0	4.7	3.6	1.4	0.0	2 245	3.7	2.7	2.0	1.8	1.3	0.8	0.5	0.5	51.0	37.0	1920
1920 g)	894.9	76.9	39.0	16.6	12.8	10.1	7.8	6.1	4.6	2.8	0.1	0.0	2 175	3.8	2.8	2.1	1.8	1.3	0.8	0.5	0.1			1920
1919	916.2	81.2											1 814	4.0	2.8	2.0	1.8	1.3	0.8	0.5	0.0			1919
1918	694.4	63.6											1 187	5.2	3.3	2.2	1.9	1.3	0.7					1918
1917	611.9	58.0											944	5.3	3.4	2.2	2.0	1.3						1917
1916	560.2	55.0											852	5.5	3.5	2.2	1.9	1.3						1916

Denmark

Sources: Tax statistics and population censuses.

Population:
1976-1939   Labour force excl. of the category 'Unknown'.
1938-1916   Labour force plus renters and parts of the pensioners.

Income:
1976   Gross income.
Prev. years   Taxable income.

Coverage: Coverage ratios show the total number of economically active income recipients as % of
                  the conceptually adjusted labour force (previous to 1939 incl. renters).

Adjustment for   In the case of insufficient coverage inclusion of the missing units within the lowest
improper cov.:   income class and adjustment of the lowest income limit to Kr. 1.

a) For fractiles below the coverage ratio estimates are crude.
b) For quantiles below the coverage ratio estimates are crude.
c) Prior to 1938 estimates are strongly dependend on method of interpolation.
d) Individual taxation; conceptually not comparable to previous years.
e) Inclusive of economically inactive tax units.
f) Refers to gross income; conceptually not comparable to previous years.
g) Population census after exclusion of economically inactive income recipients.
h) Population census before exclusion of economically inactive income recipients.

DENMARK

Fractile Shares

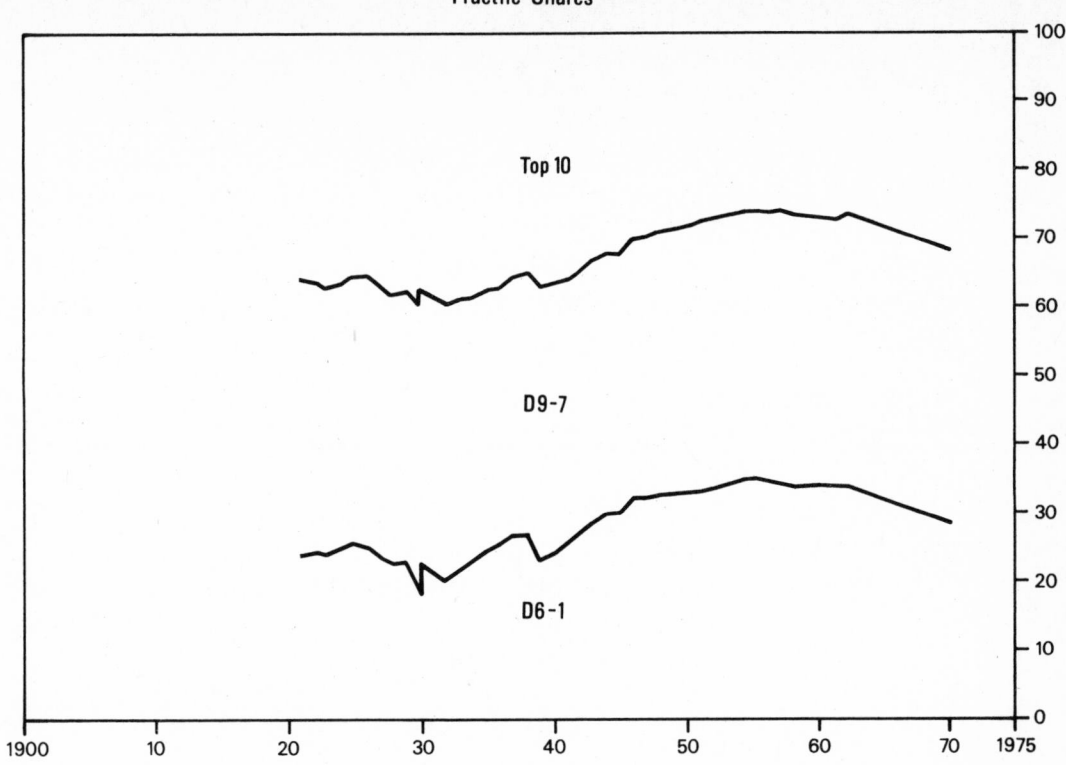

Quantile Ratios

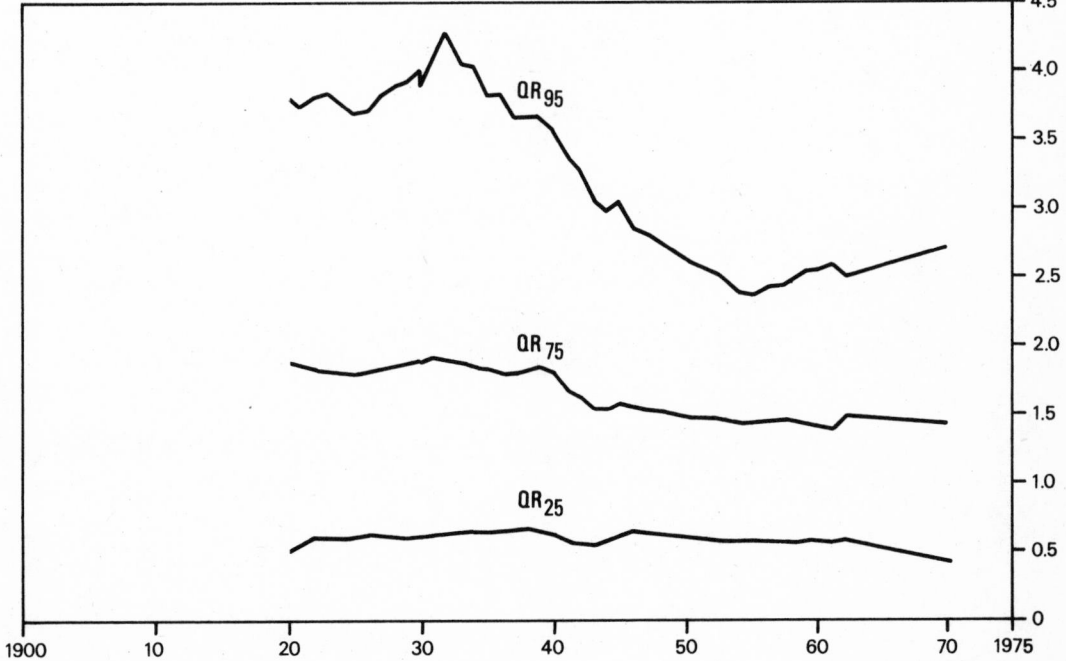

Finland

Distribution of Personal Income before Tax

Structure of Inequality

Year	No of income units in 1,000s	as % of labour force	Top 10%	90-80	80-70	70-60	60-50	50-40	40-30	30-20	20-10	10-0	Median income in 1,000s	Top 95	90	80	75	60	40	25	20	Gini co-efficient	Rel. mean dev.	Year
1974 e)	2760.9	128.3	25.0	14.7	12.1	10.5	9.2	8.0	6.9	5.8	6.3	3.0	17 762	2.5	2.0	1.5	1.4	1.1	0.9	0.7	0.6	27.9	22.4	1974
1974 f)	2279.0	105.9	21.0	15.5	12.7	11.0	9.9	8.6	7.5	6.3	4.7	2.8	18 733	2.3	1.9	1.5	1.4	1.1	0.9	0.7	0.6	30.1	20.3	1974
1973 e)	2643.8	123.3	26.0	15.0	12.3	10.6	9.2	8.0	6.8	5.6	4.0	2.5	14 163	2.5	2.0	1.6	1.4	1.2	0.9	0.6	0.6	33.4	23.9	1973
1973 f)	2184.5	101.8	25.1	15.1	12.5	10.8	9.5	8.2	7.0	5.6	3.9	2.3	14 611	2.4	1.9	1.5	1.4	1.2	0.9	0.6	0.6	33.1	23.6	1973
1972 e)	2587.1	121.2	26.9	15.2	12.4	10.6	9.2	7.8	6.6	5.3	3.7	2.3	11 878	2.6	2.1	1.6	1.5	1.2	0.9	0.6	0.5	35.1	25.1	1972
1972 f)	2161.7	101.2	26.0	15.1	12.4	10.6	9.2	7.9	6.7	5.5	3.8	2.8	12 143	2.6	2.0	1.6	1.4	1.2	0.9	0.6	0.5	33.5	24.0	1972
1971	2215.5	104.2	29.1	15.9	12.8	10.9	9.3	7.8	6.5	4.9	2.4	0.3	10 054	2.8	2.2	1.6	1.5	1.2	0.8	0.6	0.5	40.8	28.8	1971
1971 e)	2525.9	118.8	27.9	15.4	12.4	10.6	9.1	7.7	6.4	5.0	3.5	2.0	10 182	2.7	2.1	1.6	1.5	1.2	0.8	0.6	0.5	36.7	26.3	1971
1971 f)	1907.6	89.7	27.4	15.6	12.7	10.8	9.3	8.0	6.7	5.2	3.2	1.0	10 375	2.7	2.1	1.6	1.5	1.2	0.8	0.6	0.5	37.6	26.6	1971
1970	2296.1	108.4	30.2	16.1	12.9	10.9	9.2	7.7	6.2	4.6	1.8	0.3	8 705	2.9	2.2	1.7	1.5	1.2	0.8	0.5	0.5	42.7	30.2	1970
1968	2326.4	110.7	15.4	19.9	15.7	13.0	11.1	8.6	6.8	5.4	3.4	0.7	6 905	0.0	2.4	1.8	1.6	1.2	0.8	0.6	0.4	41.3	25.1	1968
1967	2388.2	114.1	28.1	16.8	13.2	11.1	9.0	7.2	6.0	4.7	3.2	0.9	6 005	3.2	2.5	1.8	1.6	1.3	0.8	0.6	0.5	41.7	29.2	1967
1966	2361.0	113.3	27.5	17.0	13.4	11.2	8.9	7.3	6.1	4.6	3.2	0.7	5 529	3.2	2.5	1.9	1.7	1.2	0.8	0.6	0.5	41.6	29.2	1966
1965	2315.9	111.6	27.4	17.2	13.7	11.1	8.9	7.4	6.3	4.6	3.0	0.5	5 097	3.3	2.5	1.9	1.7	1.2	0.9	0.6	0.5	41.9	29.4	1965
1964	2273.4	110.0	27.5	17.5	13.9	10.9	9.0	7.7	6.2	4.5	2.5	0.4	4 651	3.2	2.5	1.8	1.7	1.2	0.9	0.5	0.5	42.8	29.8	1964
1963	2243.7	109.0	27.5	17.9	13.6	10.9	9.3	8.0	6.0	4.7	1.8	0.3	4 210	3.1	2.4	1.8	1.5	1.2	0.8	0.5	0.5	43.5	29.9	1963
1962	2194.1	107.0	27.4	18.2	13.7	11.2	9.7	7.8	6.0	4.5	1.2	0.2	3 923	3.1	2.4	1.7	1.5	1.2	0.8	0.5	0.3	44.4	30.6	1962
1961	2166.7	106.1	25.6	17.9	14.2	11.5	9.6	7.4	5.8	4.4	2.3	1.3	352 139	3.3	2.5	1.9	1.7	1.2	0.8	0.5	0.4	41.3	29.3	1961
1960	2106.9	103.6	30.5	16.5	13.0	10.7	8.9	7.3	5.6	4.0	2.5	1.0	327 833	3.0	2.4	1.8	1.6	1.2	0.8	0.5	0.4	42.5	30.7	1960
1959	2052.7	101.2	31.3	16.8	13.1	10.9	8.9	7.1	5.5	3.8	2.1	0.5	294 988	3.1	2.4	1.8	1.6	1.2	0.8	0.5	0.4	44.4	32.0	1959
1958	2026.5	100.1	31.2	16.8	13.2	11.0	9.0	7.2	5.7	3.9	1.7	0.2	275 766	3.1	2.4	1.8	1.6	1.2	0.8	0.5	0.4	44.9	32.2	1958
1957	1989.2	98.5	30.9	16.7	13.3	11.0	9.1	7.3	5.8	4.0	1.7	0.1	265 012	3.0	2.4	1.8	1.6	1.2	0.8	0.5	0.4	44.6	31.9	1957
1956	1974.2	98.0	31.0	16.6	13.4	11.0	9.1	7.4	5.8	4.0	1.5	0.1	251 585	3.0	2.4	1.9	1.6	1.2	0.8	0.5	0.4	44.8	32.0	1956
1955	1935.1	96.3	31.0	17.0	13.7	11.2	9.1	7.4	5.5	4.1	0.9	0.1	220 389	3.0	2.4	1.8	1.7	1.2	0.8	0.5	0.3	45.8	32.9	1955
1954	1874.7	93.6	31.3	17.5	13.9	11.3	9.2	7.4	5.5	3.6	0.5	0.0	205 546	3.0	2.4	1.8	1.6	1.2	0.7	0.5	0.2	47.1	33.9	1954
1953	1796.0	89.8	31.4	17.8	14.2	11.4	9.3	7.2	5.5	3.0	0.2	0.0	191 459	3.0	2.4	1.9	1.7	1.2	0.7	0.4	0.1	48.2	34.8	1953
1952	1767.1	88.6	31.6	18.2	14.3	11.4	9.3	7.1	5.5	2.5	0.2	0.0	177 690	3.2	2.5	1.9	1.8	1.3	0.8	0.3	0.1	48.9	35.5	1952

Information on Coverage — Fractile Shares a): Income of quantile groups as % of total income — Median b) income in 1,000s — Quantile Ratios c): Income level of percentile points as % of the median income — Degree of Inequality d)

Finland

Distribution of Personal Income before Tax

Structure of Inequality

Year	No of income units in 1,000s	as % of labour force	Top 10%	90-80	80-70	70-60	60-50	50-40	40-30	30-20	20-10	10-0	Median income in 1,000s	Top 95	90	80	75	60	40	25	20	Gini coefficient	Rel. mean dev.
1951	1545.7	85.5	32.5	18.4	13.9	10.8	8.6	7.0	5.3	3.3	0.2	0.0	174 797	3.6	2.8	2.1	1.8	1.2	0.8	0.4	0.2	49.1	35.7
1950	1520.4	83.7	32.8	18.4	13.9	10.9	8.8	7.0	5.4	2.7	0.1	0.0	131 475	3.5	2.8	2.0	1.8	1.2	0.8	0.4	0.1	49.7	36.0
1949	1470.1	81.0	32.8	18.6	14.3	11.3	9.1	7.2	5.0	1.6	0.0	0.0	106 246	3.4	2.7	2.0	1.7	1.2	0.7	0.1			
1948	1011.4	55.8	37.0	21.4	16.0	12.0	{13.7}						80 390	4.1	3.2	2.3	2.0	1.3	0.1				
1947	1206.1	66.6	33.9	19.3	14.5	11.7	{20.6}						67 910	3.4	2.7	2.0	1.7	1.2	0.7				
1945	1007.6	55.7	38.3	21.0	15.9	12.0	{12.7}						21 960	4.8	3.8	2.8	2.4	1.6	0.1				
1942	669.4	37.1																					
1938	445.8	25.5																					
1937	400.1	23.3																					
1935	316.9																						
1932	653.2	41.3																					
1931	659.0	42.4																					
1929	737.2	49.0	48.3	18.8	13.0	10.2	{9.7}						3 795	6.4	4.5	2.9	2.5	1.8					
1926	662.3																						
1924	611.6																						
1922	667.2	49.4	50.9	19.8	13.1	9.0	{6.2}						2 368	8.4	5.8	3.8	3.1	1.7					
1921	611.3	46.1																					
1920	457.5	35.1																					

Information on Coverage

Fractile Shares a) — Income of quantile groups as % of total income

Quantile Ratios c) — Income level of percentile points as % of the median income

Degree of Inequality d)

{ } = value given as a combined figure spanning the bracketed fractile columns.

Finland

Sources: Tax statistics.

Population:
1974^e)–1971^e)   Income recipients up to age 64.
1974^f)–1971^f)   Employees and workers.
1971 – 1945   Labour force (excl. of the category 'Unknown'). Post to 1971 distribution data by status
                  of employment have not been available to us.

Income: Assessed income.

Coverage: Coverage ratios show the total number of income recipients as % of the respective
                  population concepts.

Adjustment for   In the case of **insufficient** coverage inclusion of the missing units within the lowest
improper cov.:   income class and adjustment of the lowest income limit to Mk. 1;
                  in the case of excessive coverage exclusion of the excessive units from the lowest income
                  class and corresponding adjustment of the lowest income limit.

a) For fractiles below the coverage ratio estimates are crude. Estimates for 1929 and 1922 are very crude
   and certainly exaggerate inequality.
b) 1974–1962 in new Finnish Marks.
c) For quantiles below the coverage ratio estimates are crude.
d) Prior to 1955 estimates are strongly dependend on the method of interpolation. Cf. note a)
e) Income recipients up to age 64.
f) Employees and workers only.

FINLAND

Fractile Shares

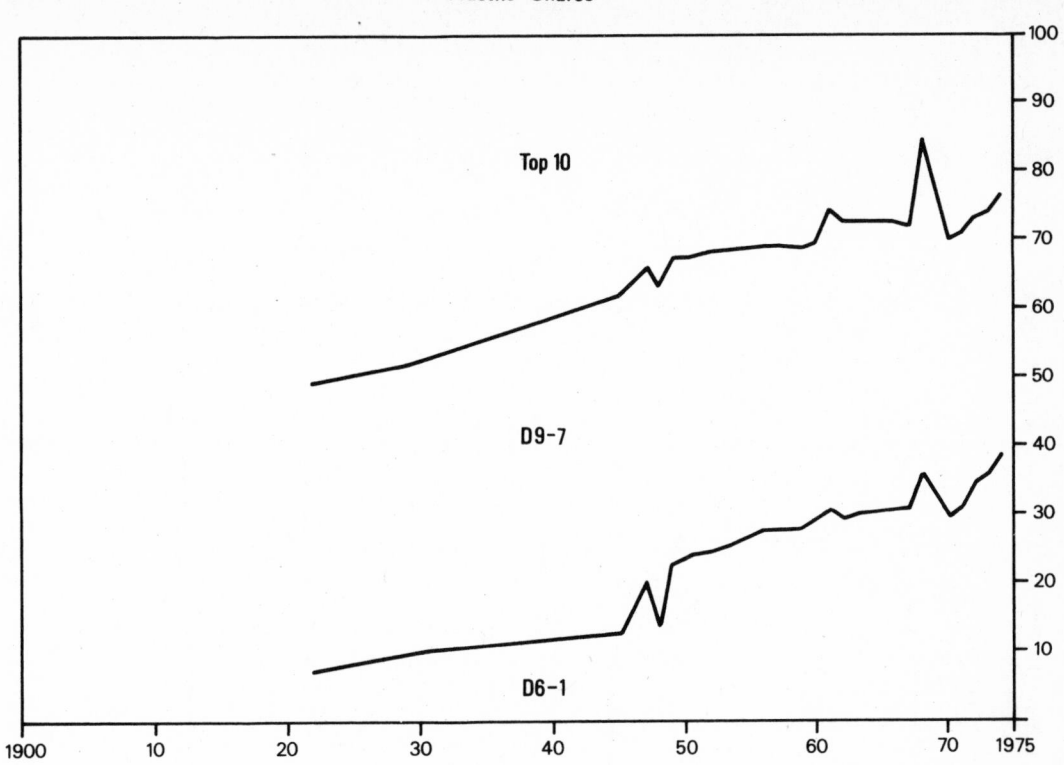

Quantile Ratios

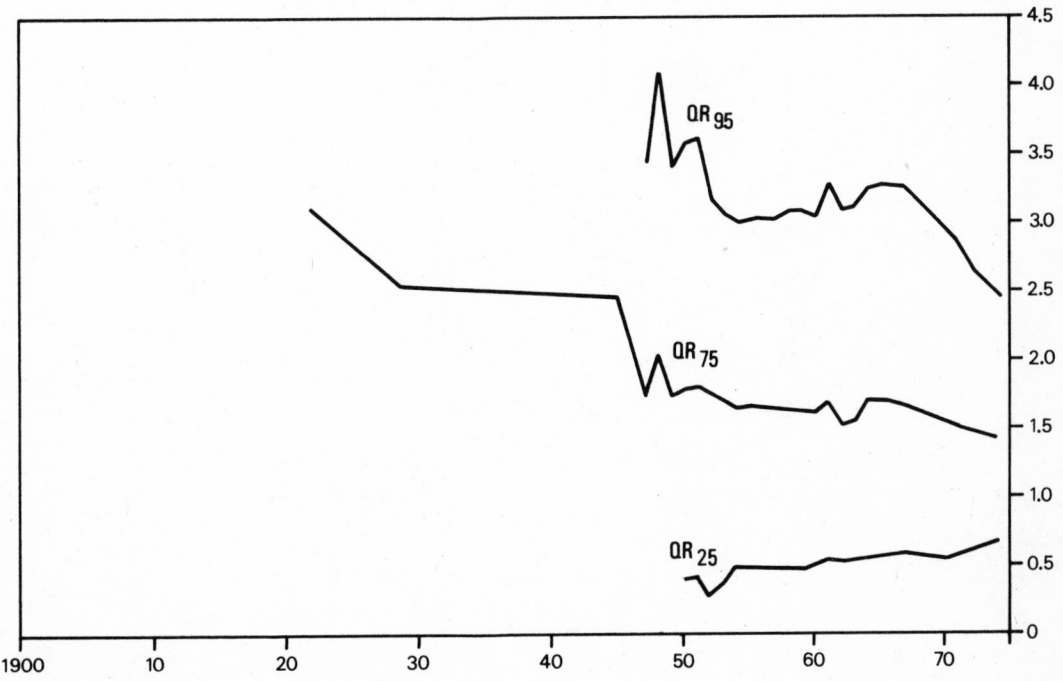

Germany

Distribution of Personal Income before Tax

Structure of Inequality

Year	No of income units in 1,000s	as % of labour force	Top 10%	90–80	80–70	70–60	60–50	50–40	40–30	30–20	20–10	10–0	Median income	Top 95	90	80	75	60	40	25	20	Gini coefficient %	Rel. mean dev. %	Year
1974	21690.9	105.6	31.7	14.6	12.0	10.5	8.8	7.5	6.4	4.9	2.9	0.7	19 757	2.7	2.1	1.6	1.5	1.2	0.9	0.6	0.5	40.9	28.7	1974
1971	21077.3	100.4	33.7	14.4	11.4	9.7	8.6	7.4	6.2	4.8	3.1	0.8	15 078	2.7	2.1	1.6	1.4	1.1	0.9	0.6	0.5	42.0	29.5	1971
1968	19317.3	91.0	35.0	14.0	11.3	9.7	8.3	7.1	6.1	4.7	3.1	0.6	10 039	2.8	2.1	1.6	1.5	1.2	0.9	0.6	0.5	43.1	30.4	1968
1965	23264.2		38.6	14.0	11.1	9.5	8.4	6.9	5.7	4.1	1.8	0.0	7 368	3.0	2.1	1.6	1.4	1.2	0.8	0.5	0.4	48.1	33.7	1965
1961	22218.6		39.4	14.0	11.1	9.2	7.9	7.0	5.5	4.1	1.8	0.0	5 373	3.1	2.2	1.6	1.5	1.1	0.8	0.6	0.4	48.7	34.5	1961
1950a)			36.0			39.0				26.0														1950
1950			33.5			36.5				30.0														1950

Distribution of Employment Incomes before Tax

Year	No of income units in 1,000s	as % of labour force	Top 10%	90–80	80–70	70–60	60–50	50–40	40–30	30–20	20–10	10–0	Median income	Top 95	90	80	75	60	40	25	20	Gini coefficient %	Rel. mean dev. %	Year
1974	25311.7	114.3	21.6	14.5	12.5	11.1	10.0	8.9	7.7	6.2	4.6	2.8	19 911	2.0	1.7	1.4	1.3	1.1	0.9	0.6	0.6	28.1	19.9	1974
1971	24634.1	109.9	22.1	14.8	12.7	11.3	10.1	8.8	7.6	6.0	4.2	2.2	14 030	2.1	1.8	1.5	1.4	1.2	0.9	0.6	0.5	30.0	21.3	1971
1968	21982.8	100.4	24.5	15.9	13.6	12.0	10.6	9.0	7.3	5.1	2.2	0.0	9 527	2.2	1.8	1.5	1.4	1.1	0.8	0.5	0.4	37.4	26.5	1968
1965	22362.0	104.8	22.9	14.9	12.8	11.4	10.2	8.9	7.5	5.8	3.8	1.6	8 484	2.1	1.7	1.4	1.3	1.1	0.9	0.6	0.5	31.7	22.4	1965
1961	20669.5	100.4	24.8	15.4	13.1	11.5	10.2	8.7	7.2	5.5	3.3	0.3	5 844	2.2	1.8	1.5	1.4	1.1	0.8	0.6	0.5	35.7	25.0	1961
1957	17496.0	93.2	25.8	15.9	13.5	11.8	10.4	8.9	7.3	5.6	0.7	0.0	4 240	2.3	1.9	1.5	1.4	1.2	0.9	0.6	0.5	39.4	27.6	1957
1955	16292.8	91.1	22.5	16.7	14.2	12.5	10.8	9.4	7.5	5.9	0.6	0.0	3 763	2.3	1.8	1.5	1.4	1.1	0.8	0.6	0.5	39.1	26.6	1955

Distribution of Personal Income before Tax

Year	No of income units in 1,000s	as % of labour force	Top 10%	90–80	80–70	70–60	60–50	50–40	40–30	30–20	20–10	10–0	Median income	Top 95	90	80	75	60	40	25	20	Gini coefficient %	Rel. mean dev. %	Year
1936b)			37.8			34.5			27.7															1936
1936	31031.0	92.1	36.0			34.5			29.5															1936
1934	29270.0	90.3	34.2			38.2			27.6															1934
1932	25964.0	82.2	33.7			37.2			29.1															1932
1928	29011.0	94.3	36.5			30.3			33.2															1928
1926	27793.0	91.5	35.1			27.0			37.9															1926
1913	23550.0	87.0	40.5			26.3			33.2				1 230	3.8	2.4	1.6	1.5	1.1						1913

P r u s s i a

D i s t r i b u t i o n   o f   P e r s o n a l   I n c o m e   b e f o r e   T a x

Structure of Inequality

Year	No of income units in 1,000s	as % of labour force c)	Fractile Shares — Income of quantile groups as % of total income — Top 10% d) 90–80	80–70	70–60	60–50	50–40	40–30	30–20	20–10	10–0	Median income	Quantile Ratios — Income level of percentile points as % of the median income — Top 95	90	80	75	60	40	25	20	Degree of Inequality — Gini coefficient %	Rel. mean dev. %
1913	7318.4	46	31.1																				
1912	6906.5	44	30.5																				
1911	6551.7	42	30.6																				
1910	6241.5	41	31.1																				
1909	5121.4	34	30.9																				
1908	5876.7	40	30.8																				
1907	5384.5	37	31.2																				
1906	4672.5	33	31.7																				
1905	4390.6	31	31.7																				
1904	4131.0	30	32.0																				
1903	3895.2	28	31.9																				
1902	3759.4	28	32.1																				
1901	3646.5	28	32.7																				
1900	3378.9	26	32.9																				
1899	3092.2	24	32.9																				
1898	2907.3	22	32.7																				
1897	2762.5	22	32.2																				
1896	2652.5	22	31.7																				
1895	2603.3	22	31.4																				
1894	2519.0	21	31.3																				
1893	2479.2	21	31.3																				
1892	2435.9	21	31.5																				
1891	6292.6	55	32.3																				

Saxony

Distribution of Personal Income before Tax

Year	No of income units in 1,000s	as % of labour force	Top 10%	90-80	80-70	70-60	60-50	50-40	40-30	30-20	20-10	10-0	Median income	Top 95	90	80	75	60	40	25	20	Gini coefficient %	Rel. mean dev. %	Year
1913	2323.8	102.2	42.9	17.6		19.8				19.7														1913
1911	2234.5	101.3	42.2	18.0		19.7				20.1														1911
1909	2105.2	98.5	43.1	17.6		19.3				20.0														1909
1907	2038.2	98.5	42.8	17.5		19.4				20.3														1907
1905	1941.4	97.0	43.1	17.5		19.1				20.3														1905
1903	1864.6	96.5	43.1	17.6		19.0				20.3														1903
1901	1780.7	95.5	43.9	17.3		18.7				20.1														1901
1899	1739.5	96.8	43.8	17.2		18.8				20.2														1899
1897	1660.7	96.1	44.0	17.1		18.5				20.4														1897
1895	1575.0	95.0	43.9	17.2		18.3				20.6														1895
1893	1490.6	92.8	44.2	17.2		18.2				20.4														1893
1891	1438.1	92.7	44.0	17.2		18.3				20.5														1891
1889	1398.7	93.5	43.7	17.1		18.4				20.8														1889
1887	1322.7	91.7	43.3	17.2		18.3				21.2														1887
1885	1263.2	91.0	43.5	17.3		18.0				21.2														1885
1883	1209.0	90.7	43.3	17.2		18.1				21.4														1883
1881	1158.9	89.8	42.9	17.7		17.8				21.6														1881
1879	1116.0	88.7	42.7	18.0		17.5				21.8														1879
1878	1084.8	87.3	42.3	18.0		18.0				21.7														1878
1877	1007.5	82.2	42.0	18.0		18.2				21.4														1877
1876	995.8	82.2	42.7	17.7		18.2				21.4														1876
1874	966.4	82.0	44.8	16.7		18.1				20.4														1874

654

West Germany (1974-1950)

Sources:	Wage-statistics, income assessment statistics and various articles in Wirtschaft und Statistik, ed. by Statistisches Bundesamt.
Population:	a) The series on employment incomes in principle refers to employees and workers, largely exclusive of family workers. Cf. notes on improper coverage. b) The series on personal incomes in principle refers to the total labour force, including renters and most of the pensioners. Recipients of old-age pensions are included only to a small degree. Cf. notes on improper coverage.
Income:	Gross incomes.
Coverage:	Coverage ratios show the total number of income recipients on which reported distributions are based as % of employees and workers excl. of family workers, resp. as % of total labour force.
Adjustment for improper cov.:	No adjustments, since improper coverage is not due to the existence of an income limit, but to insufficient coverage of tax returns (especially with respect to low incomes in general and agricultural incomes in particular).

German Empire

Sources:	Wirtschaft und Statistik, 1939, published by Statistisches Reichsamt.
Population:	Total labour force exclusive of family workers and unemployed plus pensioners. Multiple inclusions as a result of the particular taxation system (separate assessment of labour incomes and incomes from other sources) have been excluded by the Statistical Office.
Income: 1932-1938 1930-1913	Gross incomes before any deductions and allowances; mixed definitions (wage-earners in principle are included with their incomes after basic allowances; persons subject to the assessment tax are included with their gross incomes).
Coverage:	Coverage ratios show the total of income recipients on which the reported distributions are based as % of total labour force exclusive of family workers.
Adjustment for improper cov.:	No adjustment could be made to include the unemployed. Agricultural incomes are included also for periods during which they had not been liable to tax.

Prussia

Sources:	J. Müller and S. Geisendörfer, Die Einkommensstruktur in verschiedenen deutschen Ländern 1874-1912, Berlin 1971. Tax statistics published by the Prussian Statistical Bureau.
Population:	Labour force and renters.
Income:	Gross incomes.
Coverage:	The coverage ratios show the total number of taxed units as % of the total labour force after exclusion of family workers. The Prussian labour force has roughly been estimated by applying the activity rates for the German Empire (after exclusion of family workers) to the Prussian population figures. Family workers have been excluded because they form the major part of joint taxations.
Adjustment for improper cov.:	Because of the imprecise and varying assessment rules and administrative procedures no adjustments possible.

Germany contd.

Saxony

Sources: A. Jeck, Wachstum und Verteilung des Volkseinkommens, Tübingen 1970. Coverage ratios own calculations.

Population: Labour force.

Income: Gross income.

Coverage: The coverage ratios show the total number of assessed persons (incl. those below the tax threshold) as % of the labour force of Saxony.

Adjustment for improper cov.: None (insufficient coverage not due to the existence of an income limit).

a) Conceptually comparable to the 1939-distribution. Respective distributions refer, however, to different territories.
b) Including unemployed and excluding pensioners and recipients of old-age benefits. Conceptually comparable to 1950.
c) Crude estimate. Cf note on coverage.
d) Income shares of the top 5% only.

GERMANY

Fractile Shares

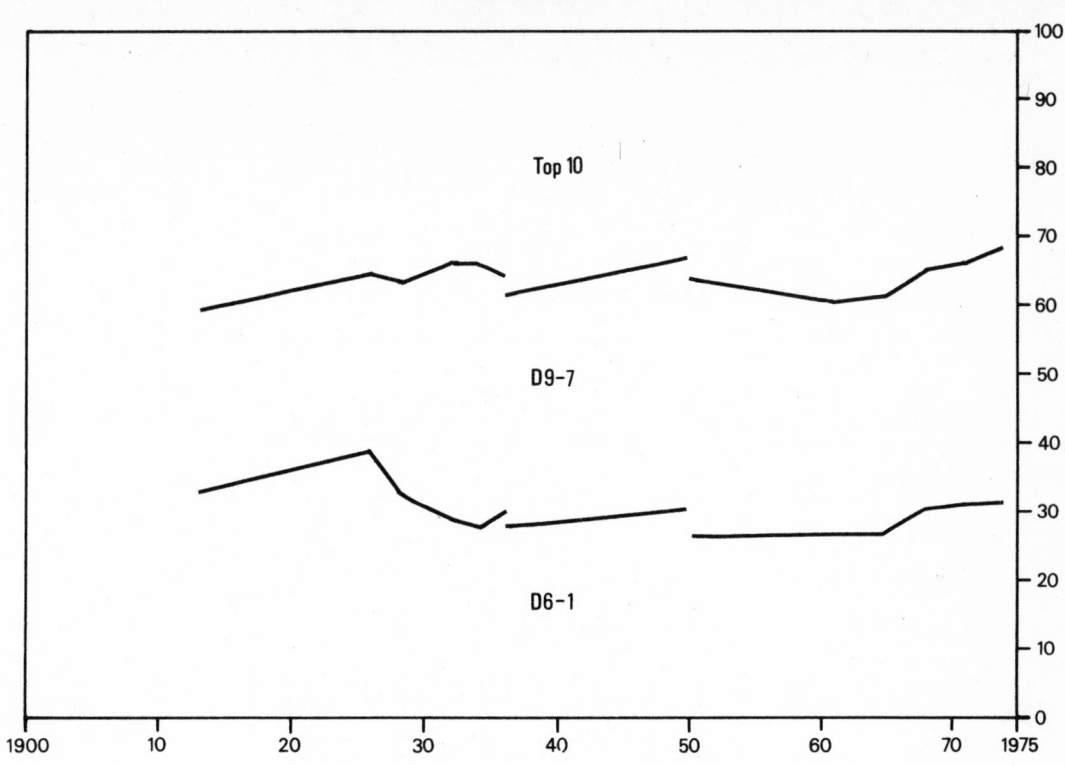

Quantile Ratios

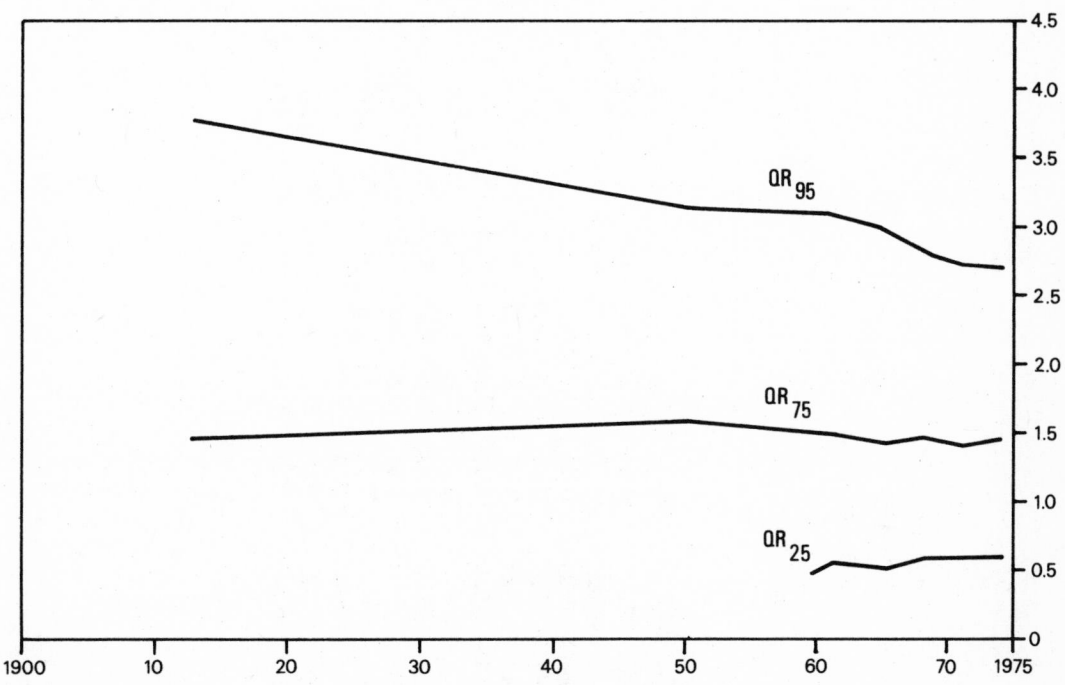

Netherlands

Distribution of Personal Income before Tax

Year	No of income units in 1,000s	as % of labour force	Top 10%	90–80	80–70	70–60	60–50	50–40	40–30	30–20	20–10	10–0	Median income in 1,000s	Top 95	90	80	75	60	40	25	20	Gini co-efficient	Rel. mean dev.	Year
	Information on Coverage		**Fractile Shares** (Income of quantile groups as % of total income)											**Structure of Inequality** — Quantile Ratios (Income level of percentile points)								**Degree of Inequality**		
1973	4489.6	102.5	27.8	14.2	11.5	10.0	8.8	7.9	6.9	5.8	4.4	2.6	17 402	2.6	2.0	1.5	1.4	1.1	0.9	0.7	0.6	33.5	23.7	1973
1970	4340.8	101.1	29.5	14.2	11.4	9.8	8.7	7.7	6.7	5.5	4.1	2.4	12 267	2.8	2.0	1.5	1.4	1.1	0.9	0.7	0.6	35.4	25.2	1970
1967	4696.0	111.6	31.5	14.2	11.2	9.6	8.5	7.5	6.5	5.2	3.6	2.2	9 152	2.9	2.1	1.5	1.4	1.1	0.9	0.7	0.6	37.8	26.9	1967
1966	4808.2	115.1	31.5	14.1	11.1	9.6	8.5	7.5	6.5	5.2	3.7	2.3	8 571	2.9	2.1	1.5	1.4	1.1	0.9	0.7	0.6	37.5	26.7	1966
1964	4534.2	110.0	31.1	13.9	11.1	9.6	8.5	7.6	6.6	5.3	3.8	2.5	7 574	2.8	2.1	1.5	1.4	1.1	0.9	0.7	0.6	36.7	26.2	1964
1962	4430.8	109.1	31.4	13.7	11.0	9.6	8.6	7.6	6.6	5.3	3.7	2.4	6 027	2.8	2.0	1.5	1.3	1.1	0.9	0.7	0.5	37.0	26.1	1962
1959	4095.7	102.9	31.8	14.0	11.1	9.6	8.6	7.6	6.6	5.1	3.5	2.2	4 650	2.9	2.1	1.5	1.4	1.1	0.9	0.6	0.5	38.0	26.9	1959
1958	4049.8	102.4	31.6	14.1	11.2	9.7	8.6	7.6	6.6	5.0	3.4	2.1	4 478	2.8	2.1	1.5	1.4	1.1	0.9	0.6	0.5	38.1	26.9	1958
1957	4074.9	103.7	31.5	13.9	11.2	9.7	8.6	7.6	6.6	5.1	3.6	2.2	4 328	2.8	2.0	1.5	1.4	1.1	0.9	0.6	0.5	37.6	26.6	1957
1954	3794.2	98.4	33.5	14.5	11.5	9.9	8.6	7.6	6.2	4.8	3.1	0.2	3 221	3.0	2.1	1.6	1.4	1.1	0.9	0.6	0.5	42.5	29.7	1954
1953	3611.1	94.3	35.4	15.2	12.0	10.2	8.9	7.3	5.9	4.0	1.1	0.0	2 616	3.1	2.2	1.6	1.5	1.2	0.8	0.5	0.4	47.2	32.9	1953
1952	3611.1	94.9	35.3	15.1	12.0	10.2	8.9	7.3	5.9	4.1	1.2	0.0	2 634	3.1	2.2	1.6	1.5	1.2	0.8	0.5	0.4	46.9	32.7	1952
1950	3579.5	95.4	36.1	15.1	11.9	10.2	8.5	7.4	5.8	4.1	0.8	0.0	2 314	3.2	2.3	1.7	1.5	1.2	0.9	0.5	0.4	47.8	33.4	1950
1946	3605.4	99.1	37.4	15.0	11.3	9.5	8.1	6.7	5.2	3.7	2.3	0.7	1 645	3.6	2.5	1.7	1.5	1.2	0.8	0.5	0.4	47.2	33.8	1946
1940	1536.4	45.1																						1940
1939	1409.1	41.8																						1939
1938	1364.4	40.9																						1938
1937	1304.2	39.6																						1937
1936	1284.5	39.4																						1936
1935	1355.0	42.1																						1935
1934	1445.0	45.4																						1934
1933	1484.6	47.3																						1933

Netherlands

Sources: Tax statistics.

Population: Labour force (excl. of category 'unknown').

Income: Total taxable income.

Coverage: Coverage ratios show the total number of economically active income recipients as % of
                    the conceptually adjusted labour force.

Adjustments for   Exclusion of all economically inactive income recipients.
improper cov.:

NETHERLANDS

Fractile Shares

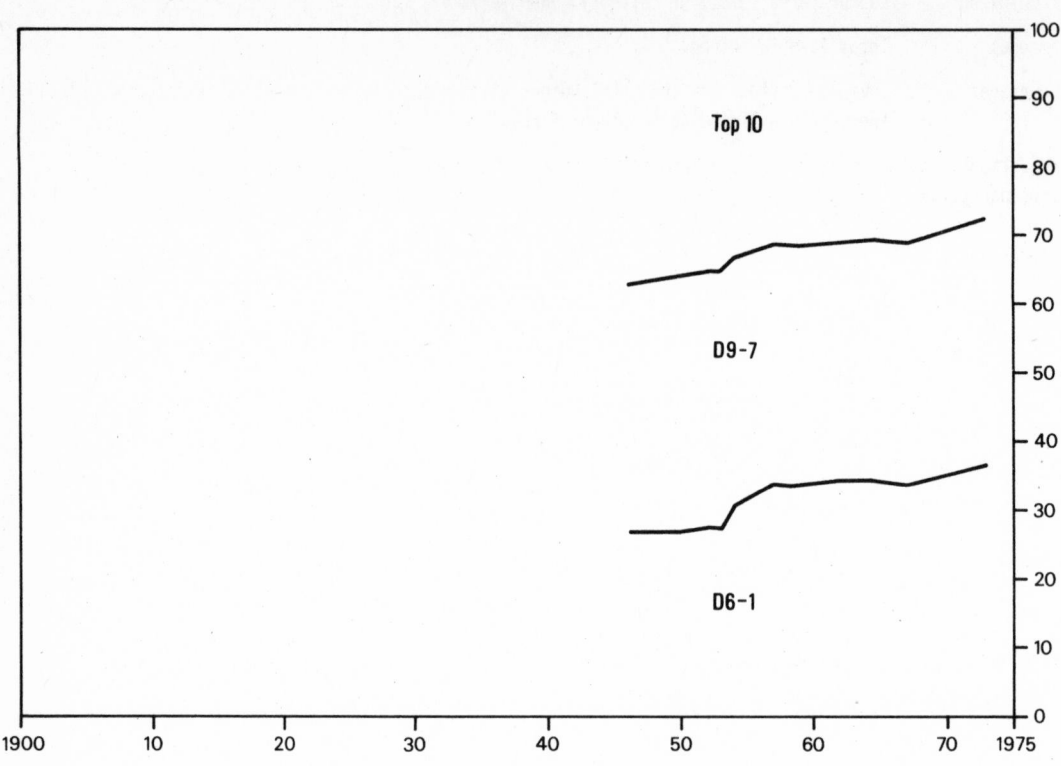

Top 10

D9-7

D6-1

Quantile Ratios

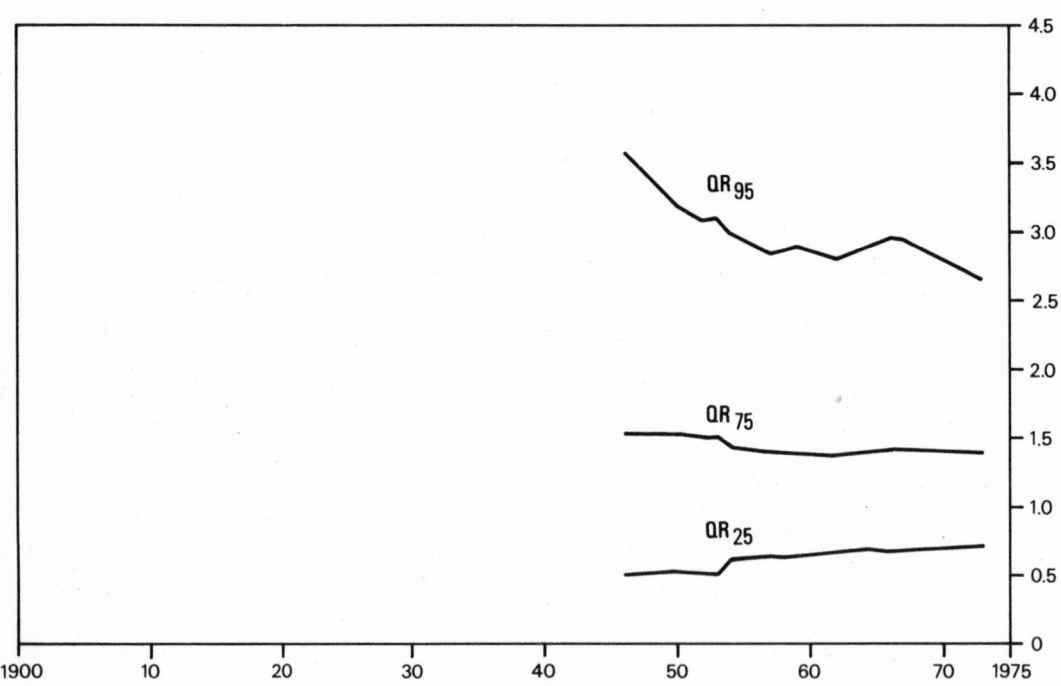

QR 95

QR 75

QR 25

Norway

Distribution of Personal Income before Tax

	Information on Coverage		Fractile Shares — Income of quantile groups as % of total income										Median income in 1,000s	Quantile Ratios — Income level of percentile points as % of the median income								Degree of Inequality	
Year	No of income units in 1,000s	as % of labour force	Top 10%	90-80	80-70	70-60	60-50	50-40	40-30	30-20	20-10	10-0		Top 95	90	80	75	60	40	25	20	Gini co-efficient	Rel. mean dev.
1975	1947.4	105.6	22.9	15.1	12.9	11.3	9.9	8.5	7.0	5.5	4.2	2.7	40 054	2.2	1.8	1.5	1.4	1.2	0.8	0.6	0.5	31.4	22.6
1974	1910.4	104.5	24.1	15.6	13.2	11.5	10.0	8.4	6.8	5.3	3.8	1.4	32 174	2.3	1.9	1.5	1.4	1.2	0.8	0.6	0.5	34.2	24.5
1973	1901.7	104.8	24.4	15.6	13.1	11.4	9.9	8.3	6.7	5.3	3.8	1.5	28 355	2.3	1.9	1.6	1.4	1.2	0.8	0.6	0.5	34.4	24.6
1972	1854.8	103.1	24.3	15.4	13.2	11.3	9.8	8.4	6.8	5.4	3.8	1.6	26 758	2.3	1.9	1.5	1.4	1.2	0.8	0.6	0.5	34.1	24.4
1971	1787.7	100.1	24.3	15.4	13.0	11.3	9.8	8.3	6.9	5.4	3.9	1.6	24 580	2.3	1.9	1.5	1.4	1.2	0.8	0.6	0.5	33.8	24.1
1970	1738.4	98.2	24.7	15.6	13.1	11.3	9.8	8.4	6.9	5.4	3.7	1.1	21 521	2.4	1.9	1.6	1.4	1.2	0.8	0.6	0.5	34.9	24.8
1969	1815.9	103.4	24.4	15.5	13.0	11.3	9.8	8.3	6.8	5.2	3.8	2.0	19 994	2.3	1.9	1.5	1.4	1.1	0.8	0.6	0.5	33.7	24.2
1968	1771.2	101.7	24.5	15.7	13.2	11.4	9.9	8.4	6.8	5.2	3.6	1.4	18 553	2.3	1.9	1.5	1.4	1.2	0.8	0.6	0.5	34.7	24.8
1967	1697.8	98.3	24.6	15.8	13.3	11.5	10.0	8.4	6.8	5.2	3.5	0.9	17 476	2.3	1.9	1.5	1.4	1.2	0.8	0.6	0.5	35.6	25.4
1966	1543.0	94.7	25.0	16.0	13.5	11.8	10.2	8.6	6.8	5.1	2.9	0.0	16 210	2.3	1.9	1.6	1.4	1.2	0.8	0.5	0.4	37.6	26.7
1965	1504.4	93.2	25.3	16.2	13.6	11.9	10.3	8.6	6.6	5.0	2.2	0.0	14 974	2.3	1.9	1.6	1.4	1.2	0.8	0.5	0.4	38.6	27.5
1964	1530.2	95.7	25.5	16.0	13.5	11.7	10.1	8.4	6.6	4.9	3.0	0.3	13 653	2.4	1.9	1.6	1.5	1.2	0.8	0.5	0.4	37.6	26.9
1963	1477.6	93.2	26.2	16.4	13.7	11.8	10.1	8.3	6.5	4.7	2.3	0.0	12 352	2.4	2.0	1.6	1.5	1.2	0.8	0.5	0.4	39.7	28.4
1962	1488.7	94.7	26.3	16.3	13.6	11.8	10.1	8.3	6.4	4.6	2.6	0.1	11 524	2.4	2.0	1.6	1.5	1.2	0.8	0.5	0.4	39.5	28.2
1961	1456.2	93.4	26.9	16.3	13.7	11.8	10.1	8.2	6.3	4.4	2.3	0.0	10 410	2.5	2.0	1.6	1.5	1.2	0.8	0.5	0.4	40.6	29.1
1960	1439.8	93.1	27.2	16.5	13.8	11.9	10.0	8.1	6.2	4.3	2.0	0.0	9 684	2.5	2.0	1.6	1.5	1.2	0.8	0.5	0.4	41.3	29.6
1959	1372.3	88.8	29.0	17.0	13.9	11.9	9.9	7.9	5.8	3.7	0.9	0.0	8 909	2.7	2.2	1.7	1.6	1.2	0.8	0.4	0.3	44.4	32.0
1958	1385.8	89.8	29.0	17.0	14.0	11.8	9.8	7.7	5.7	3.8	1.2	0.0	8 433	2.7	2.2	1.7	1.6	1.2	0.8	0.4	0.3	44.3	31.9
1957	1396.7	90.6	29.7	16.7	13.8	11.7	9.7	7.7	5.7	3.8	1.3	0.0	8 107	2.7	2.2	1.7	1.6	1.2	0.8	0.4	0.3	44.5	32.0
1955	1417.8	92.2	28.3	17.0	14.1	11.9	9.9	7.8	5.8	3.9	1.3	0.0	7 060	2.7	2.2	1.7	1.6	1.2	0.8	0.4	0.3	43.5	31.4
1954	1425.1	92.9	28.1	17.0	14.2	11.9	9.9	7.8	5.8	3.9	1.3	0.0	6 616	2.7	2.2	1.7	1.6	1.2	0.8	0.4	0.4	43.5	31.5
1953	1439.7	94.2	27.8	17.0	14.2	12.0	9.9	7.9	5.9	4.0	1.3	0.0	6 382	2.6	2.1	1.7	1.6	1.3	0.8	0.4	0.4	43.2	31.3
1952	1412.8	92.7	28.6	17.3	14.3	12.1	9.9	7.7	5.8	3.8	0.6	0.0	5 824	2.7	2.2	1.8	1.6	1.2	0.8	0.4	0.4	44.8	32.5
1951	947.8	62.4											4 574	3.1	2.5	2.0	1.8	1.4					
1950	1047.0	69.2											4 010	3.1	2.5	2.0	1.8	1.3					
1949	1010.7	67.3											3 527	3.2	2.6	2.0	1.8	1.3					
1948	954.5	64.2											3 078	3.5	2.8	2.2	2.0	1.4					

Structure of Inequality

Norway

Distribution of Personal Income before Tax

Year	No of income units in 1,000s	as % of labour force	Top 10%	90–80	80–70	70–60	60–50	50–40	40–30	30–20	20–10	10–0	Median income	Top 95	90	80	75	60	40	25	20	Gini co-efficient %	Rel. mean dev. %	Year
	Information on Coverage		Fractile Shares — Income of quantile groups as % of total income											Quantile Ratios — Income level of percentile points as % of the median income											
1929a)	894.6	89.1	38.2	17.2	12.7	9.4	7.0	5.3	4.1	3.1	2.3	0.8	1 280	4.4	3.4	2.4	2.1	1.3				51	38	1929
1913a)	774.1	87.0	31.0	16.2	12.4	10.2	8.4	6.9	5.6	4.6	3.3	1.4	647	3.7	2.6	1.8	1.6					43	30	1913
1911b)	1187.3	127.4	42.3	16.1	12.0	9.3	7.3	5.7	4.5	2.7	0.1	0.0	352	4.1	3.0	2.1	1.8	1.3				56	40	1911
1910a)	520.1	61.3	29.8	16.7	12.9	10.6	8.6	7.1	5.9	4.5	3.3	0.5	555	3.8	2.6	1.8	1.6					43	30	1910
1891c)	13.8	100.0	42.1	14.7	11.0	8.9	7.2	6.0	4.7	3.8	1.8	0.0	419	4.2	2.7	1.9	1.7					52	38	1891

Sources: Kiaer, A. et al, Socialstatistik, Kristiania 1898;
Population censuees (1930, 1910);
Tax statistics.

Population:
1975-1967   All income recipients irrespective of source/size of income.
1967-1948   Total labour force exclusive of seamen.
1929, 1913, 1910 All taxpayers listed in tax enrollments.
1911   All income recipients irrespective of source/size of income.
1891   Representative sample of male labour force (cf. Kiaer).

Income: Income after allowable deductions, reliefs and personal allowances (taxed income).

Coverage: Coverage ratios show the total number of tax units as % of the labour force adjusted
to the prevailing tax unit concepts.

Adjustments for improper coverage:
1929-1891   No adjustments.
1975-1943   Exclusion of excessive units from lowest income class and corresponding adjustment of the
lowest income limit; inclusion of missing units withing the lowest income class and
adjustment of the lowest income limit to 1 Kr.

a) Unadjusted tay data covering recipients with taxed income of 1 Kr and over.
b) Population census.
c) Representative sample for active males.

NORWAY

Fractile Shares

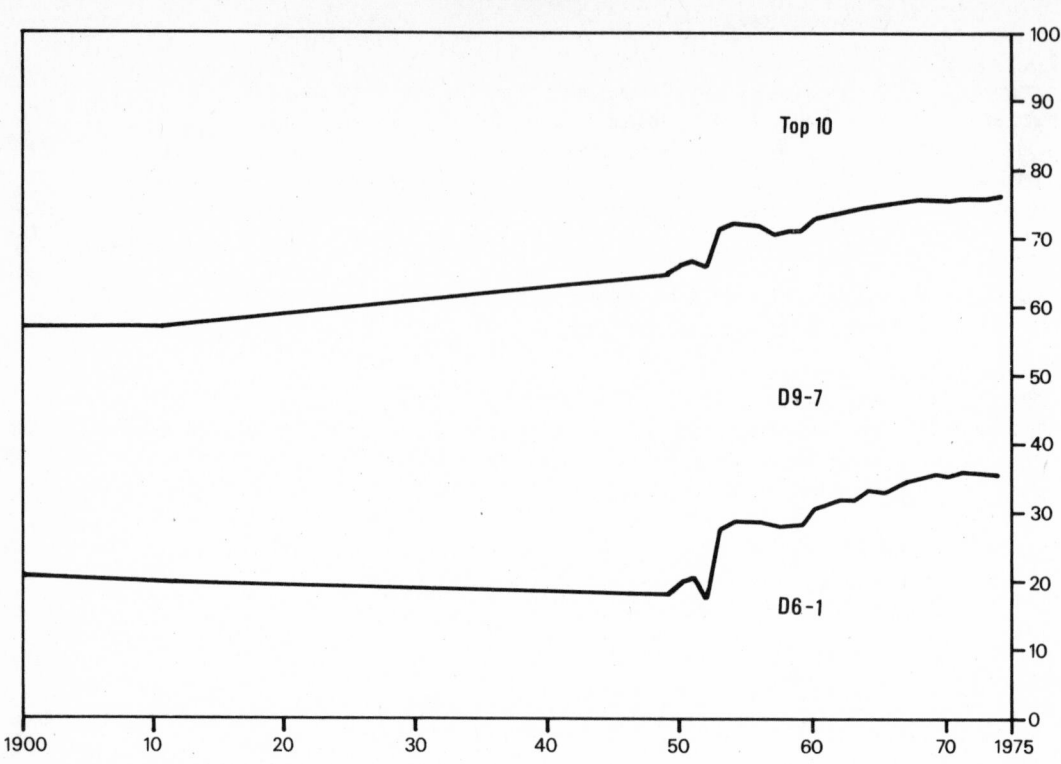

Quantile Ratios

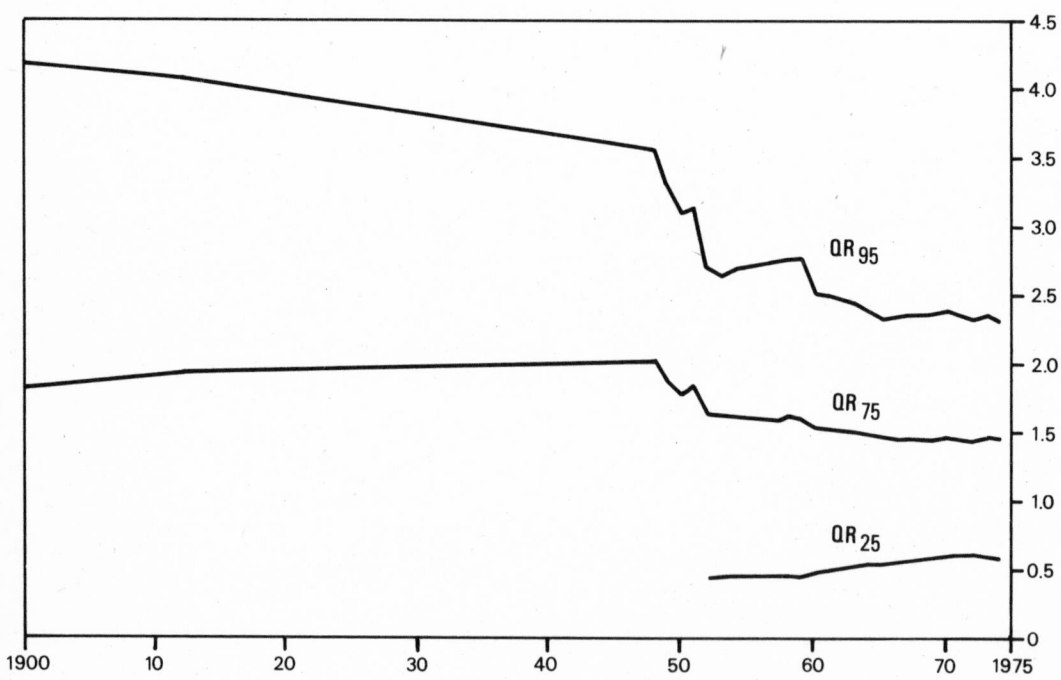

Distribution of Personal Income before Tax.

Structure of Inequality

Year	Information on Coverage: No of income units[a] — in 1,000s	as % of labour force	Fractile Shares: Income of quantile groups as % of total income — Top 10%	90–80	80–70	70–60	60–50	50–40	40–30	30–20	20–10	10–0	Median income in 1,000s	Quantile Ratios: Income level of percentile points as % of the median income — Top 95	90	80	75	60	40	25	20	Degree of Inequality: Gini co-efficient	Rel. mean dev.	Year
1974	5272.4	149.8	20.3	14.5	12.4	11.1	9.4	8.1	7.1	6.4	5.8	4.9	31 180	2.3	1.9	1.5	1.4	1.2	0.9	0.7	0.7	26.0	18.3	1974
1973	4395.0	127.8	19.3	14.6	12.4	11.0	10.0	9.0	7.7	6.7	5.3	4.0	30 508	2.1	1.7	1.4	1.3	1.1	0.9	0.7	0.6	25.9	17.3	1973
1972	4370.8	126.1	19.4	14.8	12.5	11.2	10.2	8.8	7.7	6.6	5.0	3.8	27 540	2.2	1.8	1.4	1.3	1.1	0.9	0.7	0.6	26.8	18.2	1972
1971	4387.2	127.5	23.7	14.2	12.0	10.8	9.4	8.2	7.4	6.1	4.7	3.6	25 030	2.3	1.8	1.5	1.4	1.2	0.9	0.7	0.6	28.8	20.6	1971
1970	4340.6	127.2	24.0	14.2	12.1	10.5	9.2	8.3	7.4	5.8	4.7	3.7	22 721	2.3	1.8	1.5	1.4	1.1	0.9	0.7	0.6	29.1	20.9	1970
1969	4236.8	123.9	24.8	14.6	12.1	10.5	9.4	8.4	6.8	5.5	4.6	3.3	21 047	2.3	1.8	1.5	1.4	1.1	0.9	0.6	0.6	30.8	22.0	1969
1968	4147.0	121.0	25.4	14.8	12.2	10.6	9.6	8.2	6.5	5.4	4.4	2.9	20 081	2.3	1.8	1.5	1.3	1.1	0.8	0.6	0.5	32.2	23.0	1968
1967	4098.2	119.3	25.4	14.9	12.2	10.8	9.7	7.9	6.5	5.5	4.4	2.8	18 316	2.4	1.9	1.5	1.4	1.2	0.8	0.6	0.6	32.6	23.3	1967
1966	3782.0	109.9	24.6	14.7	12.3	10.8	9.6	8.4	7.1	5.6	4.2	2.7	17 471	2.3	1.8	1.5	1.4	1.1	0.9	0.6	0.5	31.7	22.5	1966
1965	3768.3	109.2	25.0	14.7	12.3	10.9	9.6	8.3	7.0	5.5	4.0	2.6	15 903	2.3	1.9	1.5	1.4	1.1	0.9	0.6	0.5	32.3	23.0	1965
1964	3689.5	108.1	25.2	14.8	12.4	10.9	9.6	8.3	6.9	5.5	4.0	2.5	14 594	2.3	1.9	1.5	1.4	1.1	0.8	0.6	0.5	32.7	23.3	1964
1963	3616.4	107.1	25.4	14.8	12.4	10.9	9.6	8.2	6.9	5.4	3.9	2.5	13 341	2.4	1.9	1.5	1.4	1.1	0.8	0.6	0.5	33.1	23.5	1963
1962	3559.9	106.5	25.4	14.8	12.4	10.9	9.6	8.2	6.8	5.4	3.9	2.5	12 460	2.4	1.9	1.5	1.4	1.1	0.8	0.6	0.5	33.1	23.6	1962
1961	3607.4	109.1	25.7	14.8	12.4	10.9	9.5	8.2	6.8	5.3	3.9	2.5	11 439	2.4	1.9	1.5	1.4	1.2	0.8	0.6	0.5	33.4	23.8	1961
1960	3549.8	108.6	25.9	14.8	12.4	10.8	9.5	8.2	6.8	5.3	3.9	2.4	10 574	2.4	1.9	1.5	1.4	1.2	0.9	0.6	0.5	33.7	24.0	1960
1959	3466.8	106.6	25.9	14.8	12.4	10.9	9.5	8.2	6.8	5.3	3.8	2.4	9 717	2.4	1.9	1.5	1.4	1.1	0.8	0.6	0.5	33.8	24.0	1959
1958	3442.8	106.4	25.5	14.8	12.4	10.9	9.6	8.3	6.8	5.3	3.9	2.5	9 366	2.3	1.9	1.5	1.4	1.1	0.8	0.6	0.5	33.2	23.6	1958
1956	3410.5	106.5	25.2	14.6	12.4	10.9	9.6	8.3	6.9	5.5	4.0	2.6	8 625	2.3	1.8	1.5	1.4	1.1	0.8	0.6	0.5	32.5	23.0	1956
1955	3398.1	106.6	25.1	14.5	12.3	11.0	9.7	8.4	6.9	5.5	4.0	2.6	8 175	2.3	1.8	1.5	1.4	1.1	0.8	0.6	0.5	32.4	23.0	1955
1954	3334.8	105.2	25.4	14.5	12.3	10.9	9.6	8.3	6.9	5.5	4.0	2.6	7 493	2.3	1.8	1.5	1.4	1.1	0.8	0.6	0.5	32.6	23.1	1954
1953	3285.9	104.2	25.6	14.6	12.3	10.8	9.6	8.3	6.9	5.4	4.0	2.5	7 072	2.3	1.8	1.5	1.4	1.1	0.8	0.6	0.5	33.0	23.4	1953
1952	3301.2	105.2	25.3	14.5	12.3	10.9	9.6	8.3	6.9	5.5	4.0	2.6	6 969	2.3	1.8	1.5	1.4	1.1	0.8	0.6	0.5	32.5	23.0	1952
1951	3334.9	106.8	26.2	14.4	12.2	10.7	9.4	8.1	6.8	5.4	4.0	2.6	5 914	2.4	1.8	1.5	1.4	1.1	0.9	0.6	0.5	33.2	23.6	1951
1950	3007.2	96.9	28.8	15.4	12.5	10.7	9.2	7.8	6.3	4.8	3.3	1.3	4 943	2.7	2.1	1.6	1.5	1.2	0.8	0.6	0.5	38.5	27.3	1950
1949	3003.3	97.5	28.7	15.3	12.4	10.6	9.2	7.8	6.3	4.9	3.4	1.5	4 723	2.7	2.1	1.6	1.5	1.2	0.8	0.6	0.5	38.0	27.0	1949
1948	3012.9	98.5	28.9	15.2	12.3	10.6	9.1	7.7	6.3	4.8	3.4	1.7	4 576	2.7	2.1	1.6	1.5	1.2	0.8	0.6	0.5	37.9	27.0	1948

Sweden

Distribution of Personal Income before Tax

Year	No of income units in 1,000s labour force	as % of labour force	Top 10%	90–80	80–70	70–60	60–50	50–40	40–30	30–20	20–10	10–0	Median income in 1,000s	Top 95	90	80	75	60	40	25	20	Gini coefficient	Rel. mean dev.	Year
	Information on Coverage		Structure of Inequality — Fractile Shares (Income of quantile groups as % of total income)										Median income in 1,000s	Quantile Ratios (Income level of percentile points as % of the median income)								Degree of Inequality		
1947	2993.0	98.6	29.9	15.2	12.2	10.4	9.0	7.6	6.1	4.7	3.3	1.7	4 113	2.8	2.1	1.6	1.5	1.2	0.8	0.6	0.5	38.9	27.7	1947
1946	2904.1	96.4	32.2	15.1	12.0	10.2	8.7	7.3	5.8	4.4	3.0	1.2	3 598	3.0	2.2	1.7	1.5	1.2	0.8	0.6	0.5	41.6	29.7	1946
1945	2854.7	95.5	32.2	15.3	12.2	10.2	8.6	7.1	5.7	4.4	3.1	1.1	3 071	3.0	2.3	1.7	1.5	1.2	0.8	0.6	0.5	41.9	30.0	1945
1944	2802.1	93.7	32.8	15.6	12.4	10.3	8.5	7.0	5.5	4.2	2.9	0.8	2 776	3.2	2.4	1.8	1.6	1.2	0.8	0.5	0.5	43.4	31.2	1944
1943	2759.1	92.2	33.7	15.8	12.5	10.2	9.4	6.8	5.3	4.0	2.7	0.5	2 567	3.3	2.4	1.8	1.6	1.2	0.8	0.5	0.4	44.9	32.4	1943
1935 a)			39.6	16.6	12.2	9.0	6.7	16.0																1935
1930 b)	2629.6		44.5	17.5	13.0	10.0	7.8	6.3	7.2				1 181	4.2	3.0	2.1	1.9	1.3	0.6			50	36	1930
1920 c)	2066.1		39.2	15.0	11.7	9.5	7.7	6.2	5.0	4.1	1.7	0.0	1 959	3.4	2.5	1.9	1.7	1.2	0.8	0.6	0.5			1920

Sweden

Sources: R. Bentzel, Inkomsfördelningen i Severige, Uppsala 1953;
                 Tax statistics;
                 Population censuses (1920, 1930).

Population: Labour force (excl. activity unknown).

Income:
1974–1943   Taxable income.
1935–1920   Unknown.

Coverage: Coverage ratios show the total number of income recipients (including the category
                 'inactive') as % of the labour force.

Adjustments for Economically non-active income recipients have been excluded.
improper cov.:

a) Coverage data refer to the entire sample of income recipients.
b) Data are from R. Bentzel.
c) Population censuses.

SWEDEN

Fractile Shares

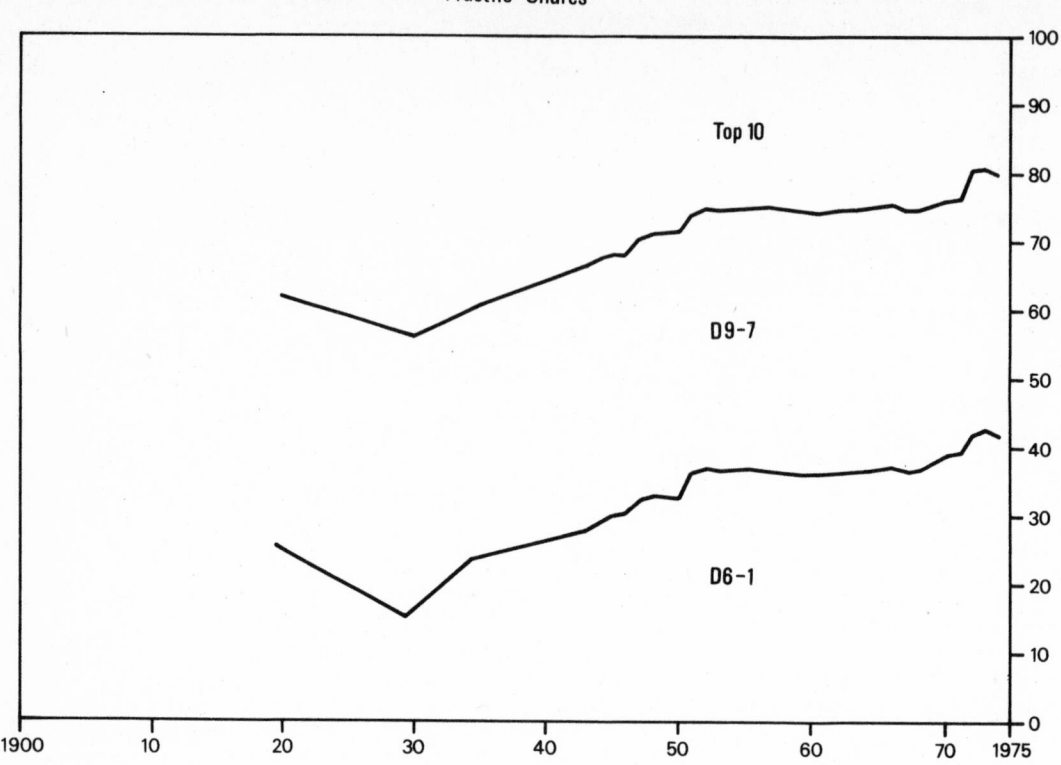

Quantile Ratios

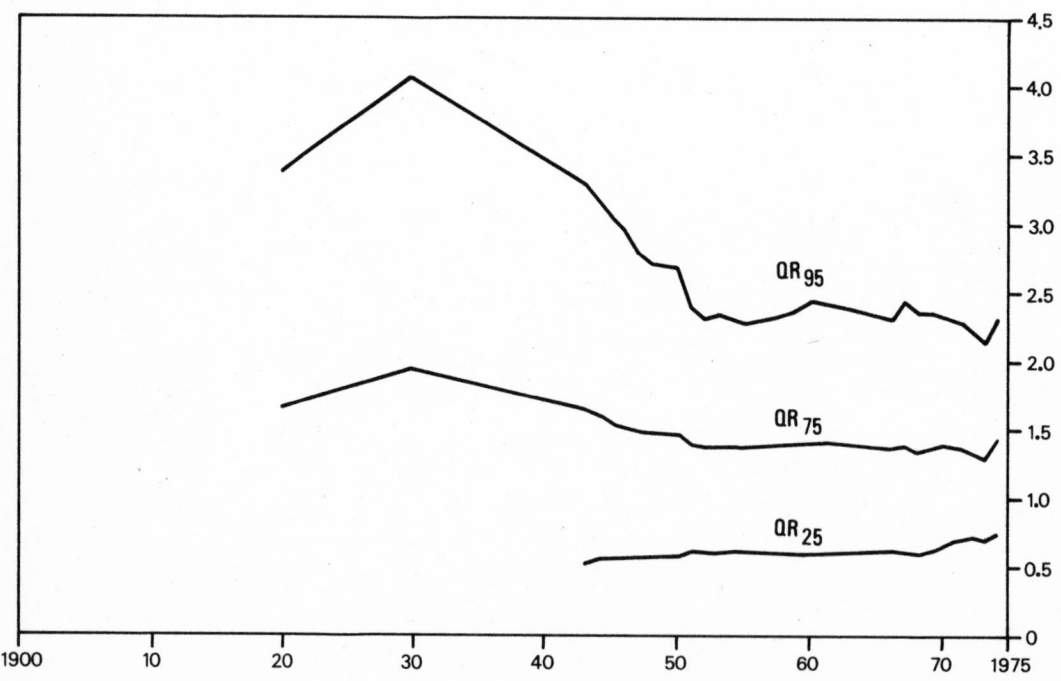

S w i t z e r l a n d

Distribution of Personal Income before Tax

Structure of Inequality

Year	No of income units in 1,000s [a]	as % of labour force [a]	Fractile Shares [b] — Income of quantile groups as % of total income										Median income	Quantile Ratios [c] — Income level of percentile points as % of the median income								Gini co-efficient %	Rel. mean dev. %	Year
			Top 10%	90-80	80-70	70-60	60-50	50-40	40-30	30-20	20-10	10-0		Top 95	90	80	75	60	40	25	20			
1975	2010.6	98.0	29.0	13.9	11.2	9.6	8.4	7.5	6.5	5.6	4.6	3.6	25 596	2.7	2.0	1.6	1.4	1.1	0.9	0.7	0.6	33.2	24.2	1975
1973	1899.4	92.1	30.8	13.4	10.7	9.2	8.1	7.2	6.4	5.6	4.7	3.8	23 382	2.8	2.1	1.5	1.4	1.1	0.9	0.7	0.7	33.9	25.0	1973
1971	1690.5	81.5	32.7	13.0	10.2	8.8	7.7	6.9	6.2	5.5	4.9	4.1	19 183	3.0	2.1	1.5	1.4	1.1	0.9	0.8	0.7	34.6	26.1	1971
1969	1534.4	73.6	32.3	12.9	10.2	8.7	7.7	6.9	6.2	5.6	5.1	4.4	17 052	2.9	2.1	1.5	1.4	1.1	0.9	0.8	0.7	33.6	25.5	1969
1967	1527.5	72.9	32.6	13.0	10.2	8.7	7.7	6.9	6.2	5.5	4.9	4.2	14 266	3.0	2.1	1.6	1.4	1.1	0.9	0.8	0.7	34.4	26.0	1967
1967 [d]	1527.5	72.9	35.1	14.5	11.4	9.6	8.2	7.1	5.9	4.4	2.9	1.0	11 684	3.1	2.2	1.6	1.5	1.2	0.9	0.6	0.4	43.5	31.0	1967
1965	1329.8	63.1	36.6	14.6	11.4	9.5	8.1	6.9	5.4	3.8	2.9	0.8	9 652	3.2	2.3	1.7	1.5	1.2	0.8	0.5	0.5	45.6	32.6	1965
1963	1113.2	53.7	37.7	14.5	11.3	9.4	8.0	6.5	4.9	4.1	3.0	0.6	8 157	3.3	2.3	1.7	1.5	1.2	0.8	0.5	0.5	46.5	33.5	1963
1961	1101.7	50.5	38.4	15.2	11.7	9.7	7.6	5.7	4.9	4.1	2.7	0.1	5 755	3.9	2.8	2.0	1.8	1.4	0.8	0.6	0.5	48.6	35.3	1961
1959	1028.9	49.5	37.8	15.3	11.9	9.5	7.3	6.1	5.5	4.2	2.4	0.0	4 970	3.9	2.8	2.0	1.8	1.3	0.9	0.6	0.5	48.1	35.1	1959
1957	869.1	44.0	35.3	15.5	12.0	9.4	7.8	7.0	6.3	4.5	2.1	0.0	4 639	3.3	2.5	1.8	1.6	1.1	0.9	0.6	0.5	45.9	32.9	1957
1955	1280.1	62.8	36.2	15.9	12.5	9.6	7.6	6.5	5.7	4.1	1.9	0.0	4 761	3.5	2.7	2.0	1.8	1.2	0.9	0.6	0.5	47.8	34.7	1955
1953	1146.6	55.2	37.1	16.4	12.4	9.3	7.8	6.9	5.4	4.0	0.8	0.0	4 341	3.5	2.6	1.9	1.7	1.1	0.9	0.5	0.5	49.7	35.9	1953
1951	1092.0	52.4	36.9	16.6	12.3	9.3	8.0	7.0	5.3	4.0	0.4	0.0	4 230	3.4	2.6	1.9	1.6	1.1	0.8	0.5	0.4	50.0	35.9	1951
1949	963.1	46.2	37.3	17.0	11.9	9.5	8.4	6.9	5.3	3.6	0.1	0.0	3 969	3.3	2.5	1.8	1.5	1.1	0.8	0.5	0.1	50.9	36.2	1949

Sources:
1975-1967   Tax statistics (Eidgen. Wehrsteuer);
1967-1949   Raw data from A. Noth, Die personelle Einkommensverteilung in der Schweiz 1949 bis 1968,
              Freiburg 1975; income estimates and measures derived from own calculations.

Population: All domestic income recipients irrespective of source and size of income.

Income concept: Taxable income (for a series based on an estimate of gross incomes see A. Noth).

Coverage: Total income recipients after inclusion of units below the income limit of tax statistics
              as % of labour force plus pensioners and recipients of old-age benefits.

Adjustment for improper coverage:
1975-1967   Linear extrapolation of total recipients based on the trend 1965 to 1967.
              Income estimated by assuming Pareto-distribution below the tax threshold.
1967-1949   Distribution of the units below the threshold across three income intervals as indicated
              by some provincial income statistics (estimate provided by A. Noth).

a) Series in addition to the labour force includes pensioners and recipients of old-age benefits as well.
   See also note on population.
b) Figures for the individual shares of fractiles below the coverage ratio limited in reliability (strong
   sensitivity to particular estimation methods).
c) Figures for quantiles below the threshold limited in reliability. Cf. notes 2) and 4).
d) Break in comparability due to a change in the method of estimating the incomes below the tax threshold.

SWITZERLAND

Fractile Shares

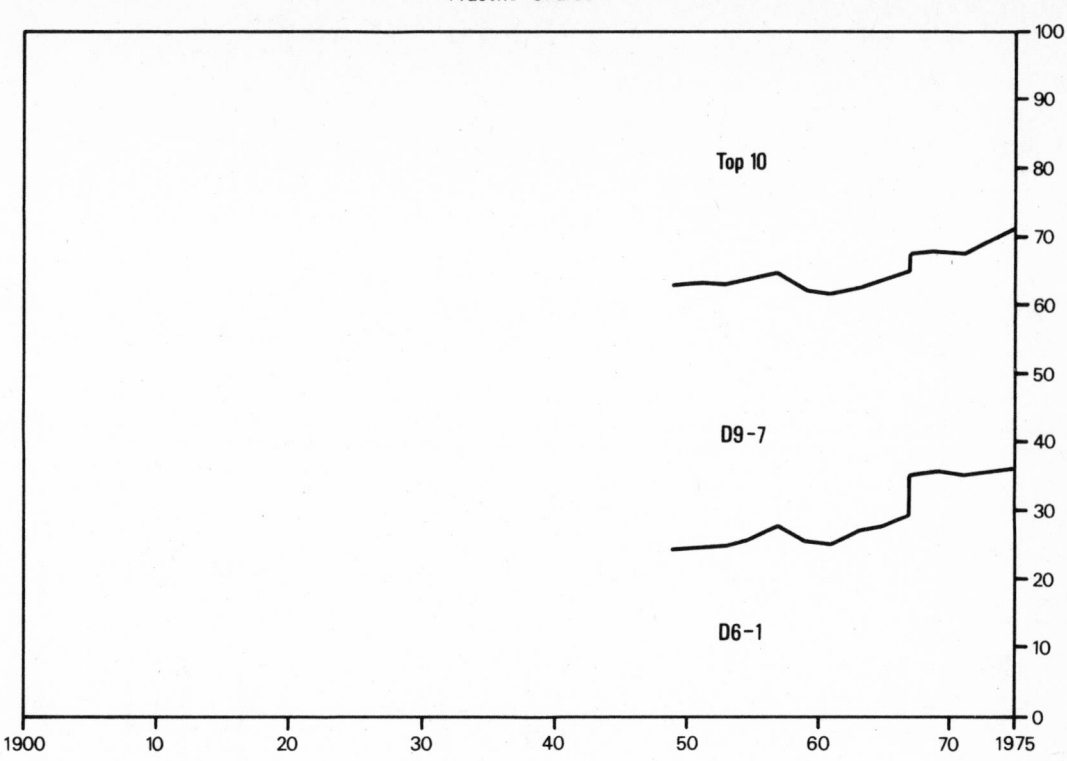

Top 10

D9-7

D6-1

Quantile Ratios

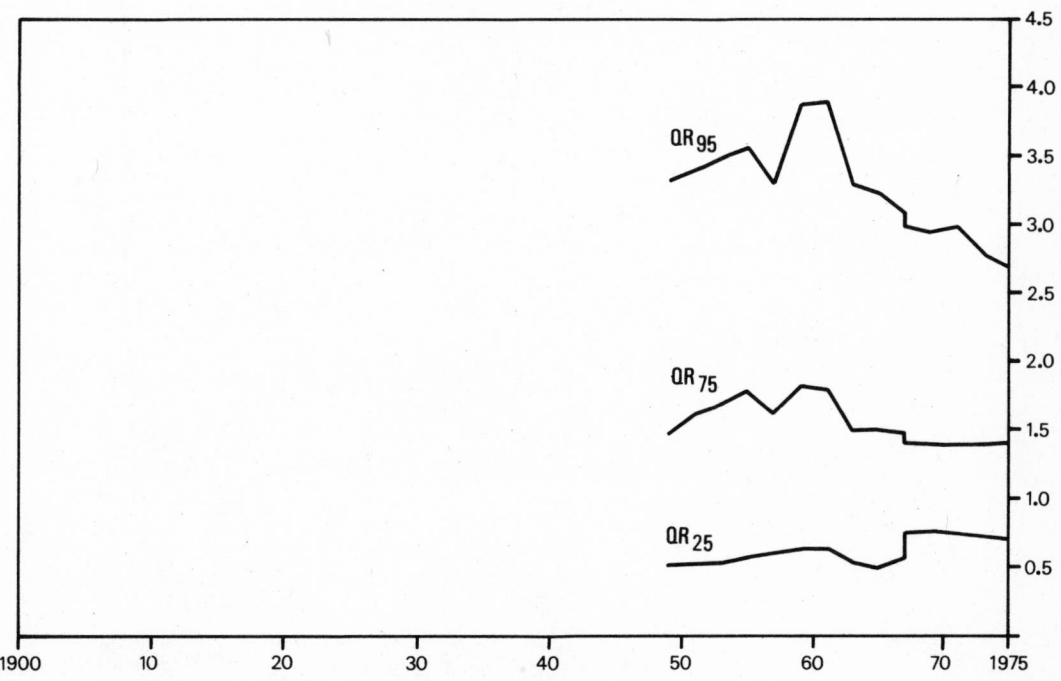

QR₉₅

QR₇₅

QR₂₅

United Kingdom

Distribution of Personal Income before Tax: Population 16 years

Structure of Inequality

Year a)	No of income units in 1,000s	as % of labour force	Top 10%	90-80	80-70	70-60	60-50	50-40	40-30	30-20	20-10	10-0	Median income in 1,000s	Top 95	90	80	75	60	40	25	20	Gini co-efficient	Rel. mean dev.	Year
1976	28500	147.8	25.8	16.1	13.3	11.1	9.2	7.5	6.0	4.7	3.8	2.5	2 615									36.5		1976
1975	28300	147.2	25.8	16.1	13.1	11.4	9.3	7.6	5.9	4.6	3.6	2.6	2 319									36.6		1975
1974	28300	147.2	26.6	15.8	13.1	11.0	9.3	7.6	5.8	4.6	3.6	2.6	1 913									37.1		1974
1973	28100	145.3	26.8	15.6	12.9	11.2	9.3	7.5	5.8	4.7	3.5	2.7	1 550									37.0		1973
1972	28400	147.7	26.9	15.8	13.1	11.0	9.2	7.5	5.9	4.8	{5.8}		1 338		2.1		1.6			0.6		37.4		1972
1970	28200	143.6	27.5	15.9	13.2	10.9	9.0	7.4	5.9	4.6	3.1	2.5	1 050									38.5		1970
1967	27800	136.5	28.0	15.2	12.6	11.1	9.1	7.7	6.0	4.8	3.4	2.2	843		2.1		1.5			0.6		38.2		1967
1966			28.5	15.2	12.6	10.9	9.1	7.4	6.0	4.7	{5.6}		797		2.1		1.5			0.6		38.6		1966
1965			29.0	15.2	12.5	10.7	9.3	7.5	5.8	4.5	5.5		739		2.1		1.5			0.5		39.0		1965
1964	27500	129.4	29.1	15.5	12.6	10.9	9.2	7.4	5.8	4.3	5.2		679		2.1		1.5			0.5		39.9		1964
1963			28.9	15.4	12.6	10.9	9.1	7.5	5.9	4.4	5.3		643		2.1		1.5			0.5		39.5		1963
1962			29.2	15.2	12.6	10.9	9.2	7.6	6.0	4.4	4.9		623		2.1		1.5			0.5		39.7		1962
1961			28.9	14.8	12.5	10.8	9.3	7.8	6.0	4.6	5.3		611		2.0		1.4			0.5		38.8		1961
1959	26500	123.1	29.4	15.1	12.6	10.7	9.1	7.5	5.9	4.4	5.3		514		2.1		1.5			0.5		39.8		1959
1954 b)	26300	123.2	30.1	15.1	12.4	10.5	8.9	7.4	5.3	{10.3}			374		2.1		1.6			0.4		40.3		1954
1949 b)	20050	96.8	32.1	13.2	10.6	9.0	8.0	7.0	6.3	{13.8}			308									36.4		1949
1949 b)	26100	126.0	33.2	14.1	11.2	9.6	8.2	{23.7}					259		2.2		1.5					41.1		1949
1938 c)	9800	45.9	40.5	11.9	8.8	7.3	6.5	5.8	5.3	{13.9}			184									42.3		1938
1938	20050	93.9	38.8	{61.2}																		46.4		1938

Sources: Royal Commission on the Distribution of Income and Wealth, various reports. Data refer
                to Blue Book tables.

Population: All persons receiving income of Pound 50 and over, irrespective of source of income.

Coverage: Incomes liable to tax: taxable income before reliefs and allowances.
                Incomes below the tax threshold: Gross income.

Adjustment for Provided by the CSO.
improper cov.:

a) Beginning of fiscal year.
b) Break in comparability: Figures refer to unadjusted data of the Inland Revenue Survey.
c) After adjustment for incomplete coverage by the Royal Commission of Income and Wealth.

Fractile Shares

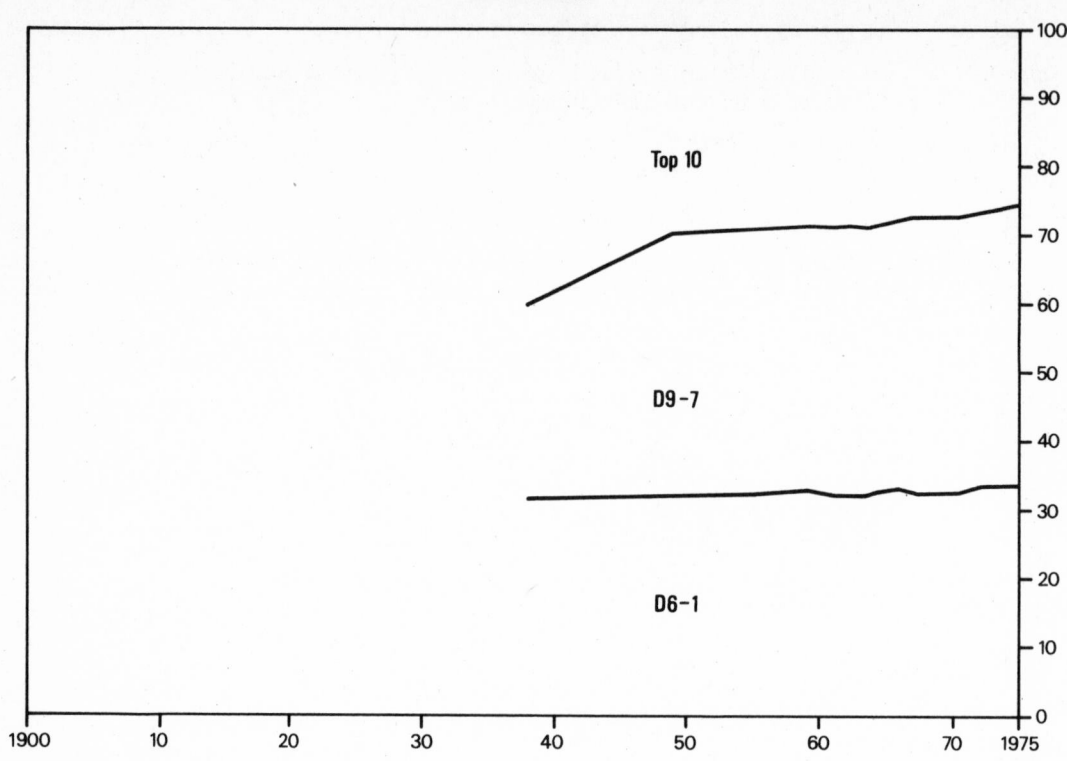

Quantile Ratios

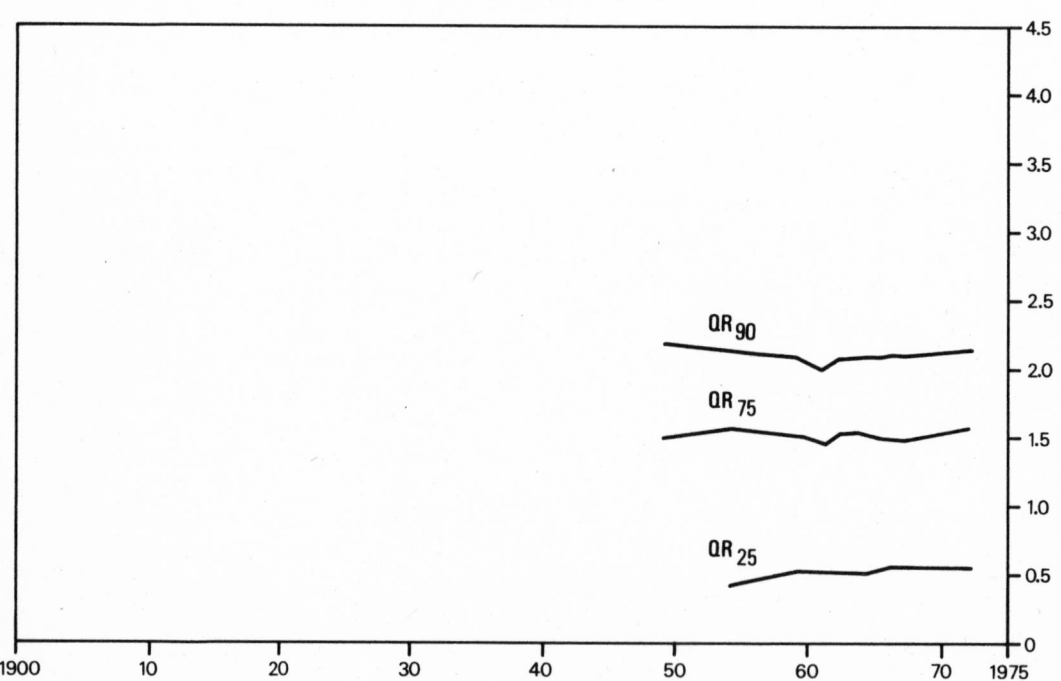

X

Trade Unions and Strikes

Chapter 9

TRADE UNIONS

(missing)

Chapter 10

LABOUR DISPUTES

This chapter presents basic data on the development of labour conflicts in terms of their frequency, size and duration. Time series are given for the following three main indicators: the number of labour conflicts, the number of workers participating in them, and the number of man-days lost due to them. These statistics are presented in the form of national aggregate data, as absolute figures and relative to the dependent labour force.

In most European countries, official statistics on labour conflicts became available around the turn of the century. This must be seen in the context of an increasing incidence of strikes at that time which in turn was largely the result of an improving organization of the working class. Frequently, it was a parliamentary commission which initiated the regular collection of official strike data. In some countries, non-official strike statistics, usually collected by trade unions or employers' associations, exist alongside the official ones. We have utilized these 'private' statistics only in exceptional cases, and when government-produced data are not available.

In the initial phase strike statistics developed rapidly, reaching the highest level of sophistication around World War I. Many of the detailed series on specific characteristics of labour conflicts end in the 1930s, at a time when the Great Depression led to a reduction of trade union power and strike incidence. After World War II strike statistics remained comparatively poor. This may be explained to some extent by the decreasing strike activity in most European countries, a development which led many observers to speak of a 'withering away of the strike'. Since the late 1960s, we know that this view of industrial relations was premature, but the widespread increase in labour conflicts has not led so far to any decisive improvement in strike statistics.

In dealing with these statistiscs, attention must be paid to the difference in the definition of labour conflicts adopted by the statistical agencies: how a single conflict is identified, how its participants are counted and how its duration is measured.

In principle, a strike is any collective work stoppage of dependent workers/employees. A first problem of this definition refers to the status of 'dependence'. There are cases of formally independent, self-employed persons (e.g. tenants of petrol stations or small shopkeepers) who use collective work stoppages as a weapon against private enterprises or public agencies upon which, in practice, they may be very much dependent. For the sake of conceptual clarity, these collective conflicts have not been included. They are also a relatively new phenomenon and not very relevant in terms of national strike statistics.

A second problem is whether collective work stoppages, in order to be called strikes, must have strictly 'economic' goals, i.e. goals which can be attained in negotiations with employers. As we know, many strikes contain a 'political' element in the sense that they are used to influence government action. This political element is more important in some countries/periods than in others, and exclusion of 'political strikes' would seriously reduce comparability. Furthermore, there is no possibility, on the basis of official statistics, to consistently distinguish between 'economic' and 'political' objectives of work stoppage. We have therefore included all strikes, even when their political character was openly declared.

A third more general poblem refers to the distinction between strikes and lock-outs. First of all, there is a practical problem to draw a clear line between these two forms/sides of labour conflicts, because one may easily lead to the other. In addition, data on lock-outs are often not collected or they are not given separately in official statistics. Furthermore, in more recent times lock-outs may also be prohibited. At present, no distinction is usually made between strikes and lock-outs, both being counted as labour conflicts.

If a conflict involves a number of different establishments, is it identified as one strike or several? Disputes affecting several establishments may be counted as one case if they break out simultaneously, if they have a common purpose or if they are organized by one person or one organization. Apart from cases vary greatly, leading to rather different aggregate numbers of strikes. Some countries therefore try to avoid these difficulties by counting only establishments involved in strikes and not the strikes themselves.

The aggregate number of strikes may be influenced by two further variations in operational criteria. One of them refers to the question of whether a minimum number of strikers and/or working-days lost is required. In more recent periods, this is a frequent procedure. Usually, a collective work stoppage is only counted as a strike if at least 100 workers are involved and/or 100 working-days are lost. This leads to a considerable underestimation of the frequency of strikes, as shown in empirical studies, especially in countries/periods in which small-scale and short-term strikes are relatively more frequent. Annual aggregate figures may furthermore be influenced by the method of counting strikes which begin in one year and end in the next. They may be counted only once, in the year when they start or end, or they may be counted in each year that disputes are in progress.

The number of strikes is an important measure of strike activity, but of course the number of strikers involved in each conflict may vary greatly. In counting participants one is confronted with two problems. The first concerns the distinction between workers who are directly involved in strikes, and those only indirectly involved who are much more difficult to enumerate. Usually, these are only included for establishments where conflicts took place. A second problem is whether the average or the maximum number of participants in a labour conflict is taken.

There is no general pattern in the long-term development of strikes except in their duration: strikes tend to last for shorter periods of time. Duration is an indicator of both the intensity of conflicts and the organizational capacity of workers to maintain solidarity. The simplest overall measure of duration is the number of working-days lost in conflicts. Caution must be applied when interpreting these data because of two problems. First, some big conflicts may distort the picture. Second, the method by which the number of working-days lost is obtained varies across countries and periods. They may be counted for each day and participant or calculated by multiplying the duration of the conflicts in terms of working-days by the number of participants. In the latter case, a strike may be said to last from its official declaration to its official end. However, the duration may also be measured from the time when the first workers lay down their tools to the time when the first workers go back on the job.

Major variations in the definition and measurement of labour conflicts are documented in the footnotes to the following tables. For each country, in alphabetical order, two tables are given, one with raw data and one with indicators. The first table contains (1) the number of conflicts (strikes, lock-outs, and total conflicts), (2) the number of participants (strikers, lock-outers, indirectly involved persons, and total participants), and (3) the number of working-days lost (by strikers, lock-outers, indirectly involved persons, and by total participants).

In the second table two types of indicators are given: firstly, indicators which define the shape of the typical strike in a given year, average size (strikers per strike) and average duration (working-days lost per strike and striker); secondly, indicators of the aggregate strike activity which take into account the great variations in the 'potential strike population', namely the dependent labour force. They give the number of conflicts, participants, and working-days lost per 100,000 non-agricultural wage-earners. Figures of the dependent labour force have been derived from the census data in Chapter 7. Census figures of the dependent labour force, expressed as percentage of the total population, have been interpolated for the inter-census years (except for the years around World War I and II for which the percentages have been extrapolated forwards and backwards). The percentages then have been multiplied by the total population figures given in Chapter 1. The tables are preceded by 13 graphs which show the development of the volume of labour disputes.

AUSTRIA

Volume of Labour Disputes

Man – days lost per 100,000 non – agricultural wage - earners (logarithmic scale)

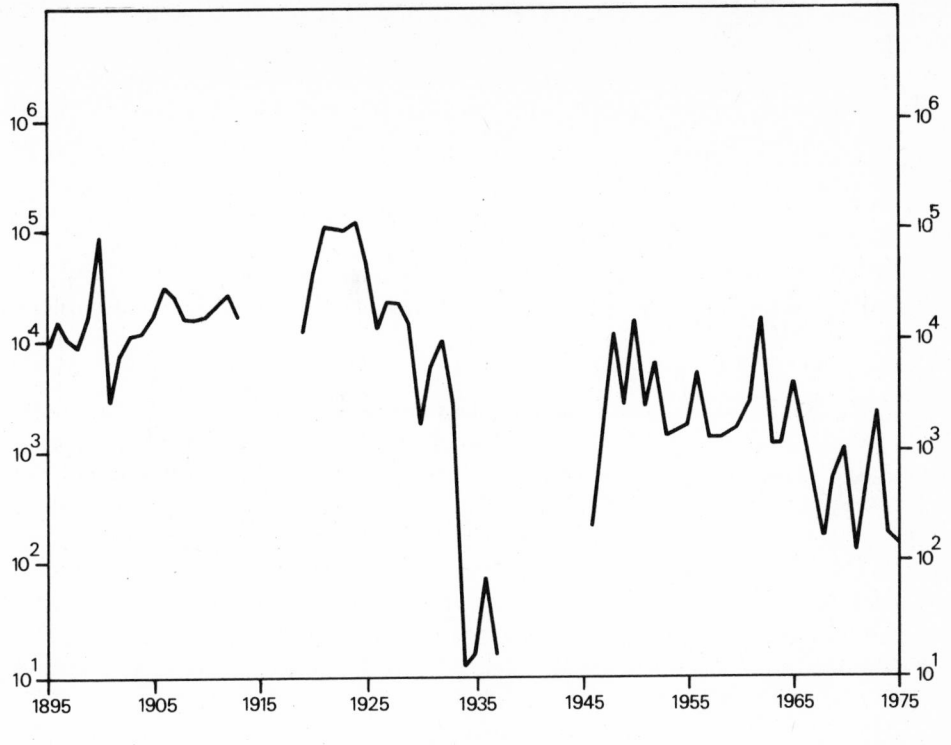

BELGIUM

Volume of Labour Disputes

Man – days lost per 100,000 non – agricultural wage - earners (logarithmic scale)

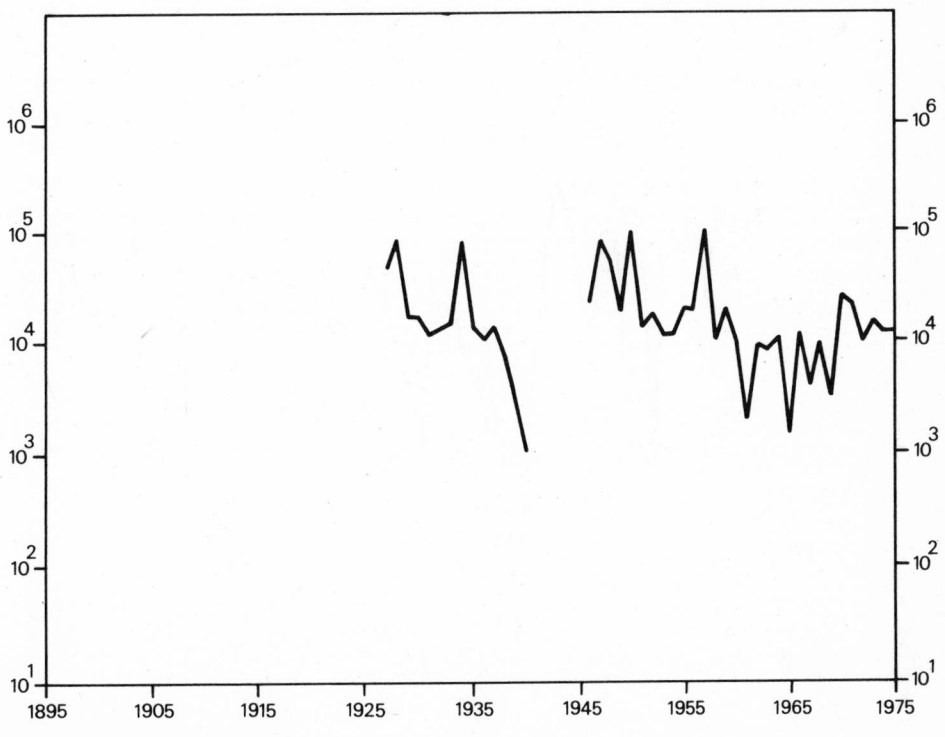

DENMARK

Volume of Labour Disputes
Man – days lost per 100,000 non – agricultural wage – earners (logarithmic scale)

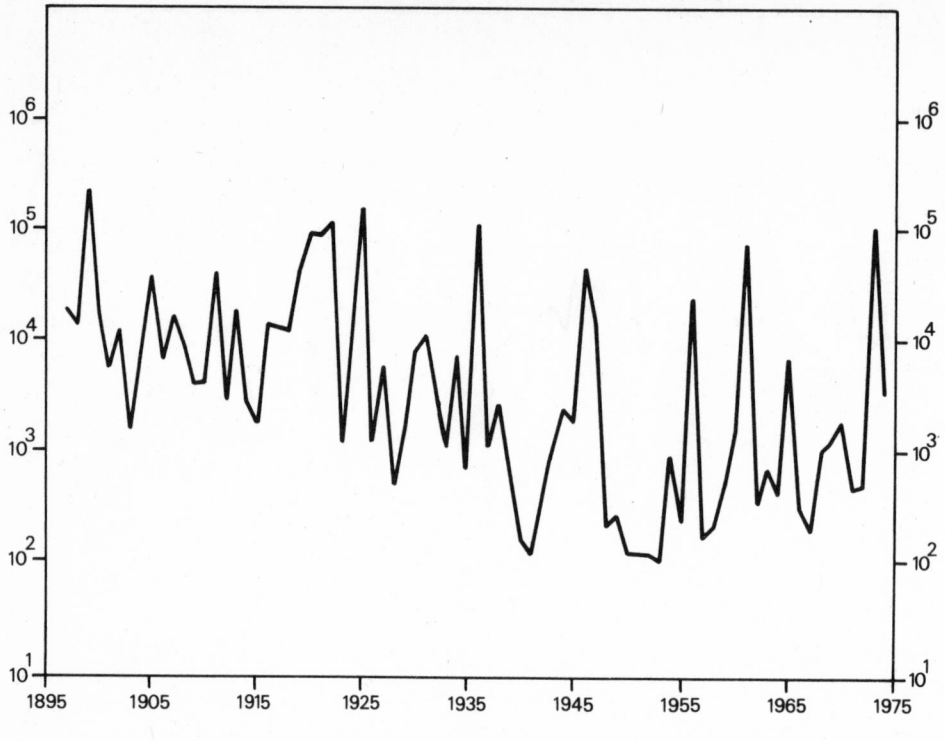

FINLAND

Volume of Labour Disputes
Man – days lost per 100,000 non – agricultural wage – earners (logarithmic scale)

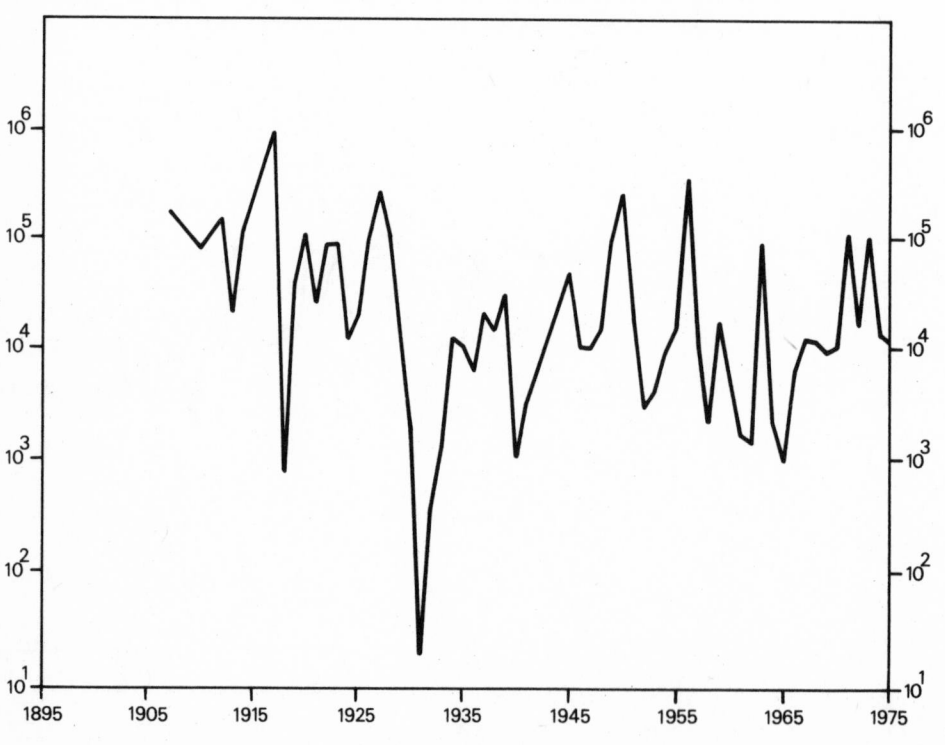

FRANCE

Volume of Labour Disputes

Man – days lost per 100,000 non – agricultural wage – earners (logarithmic scale)

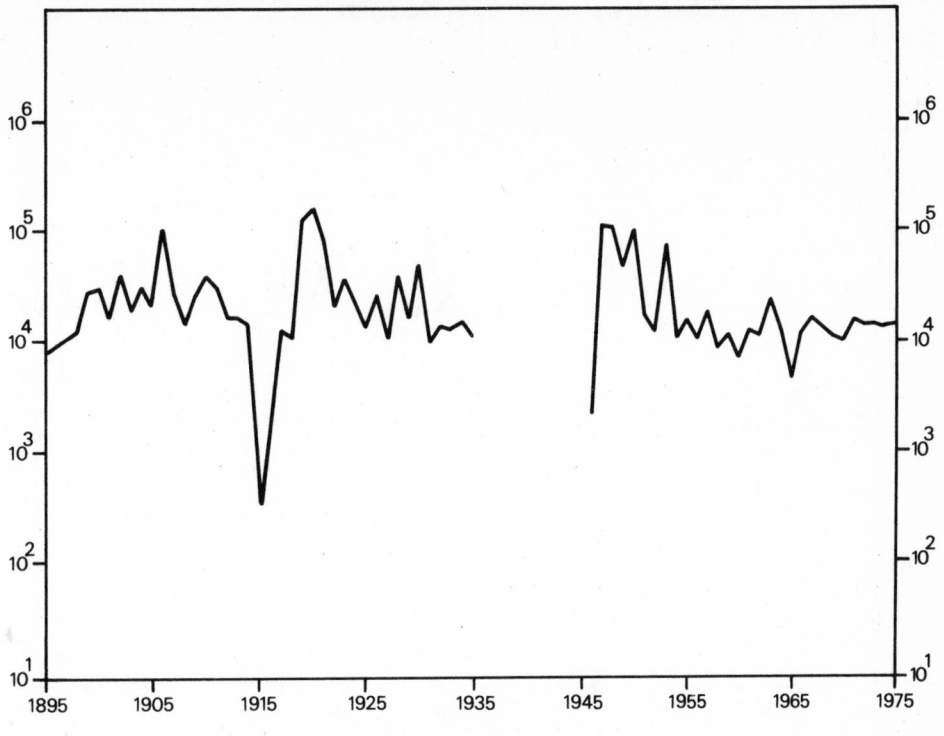

GERMANY

Volume of Labour Disputes

Man – days lost per 100,000 non – agricultural wage – earners (logarithmic scale)

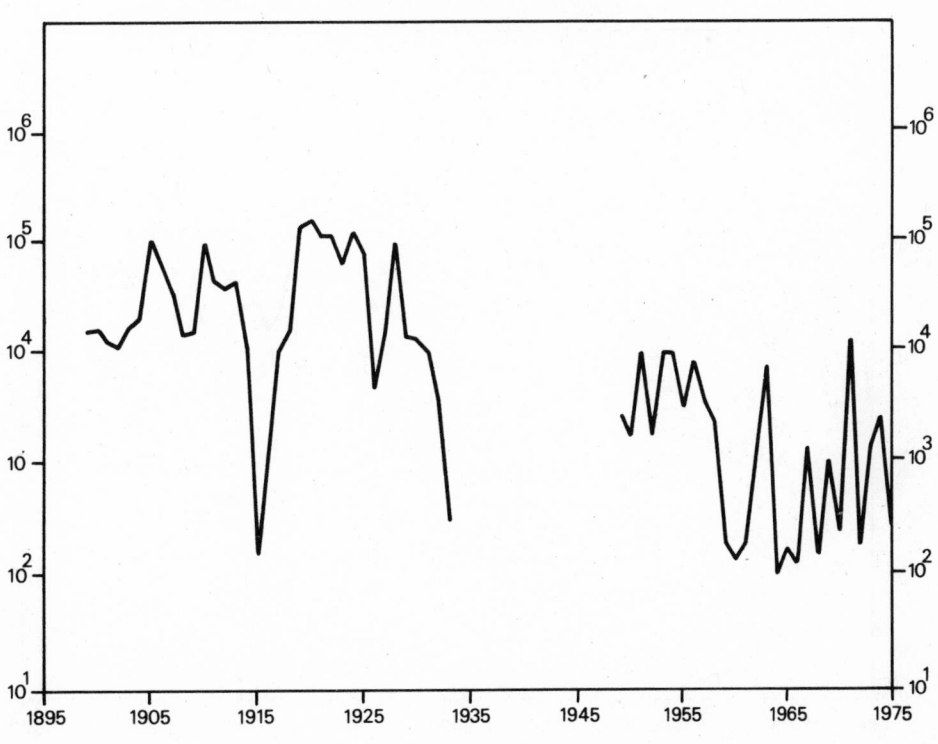

IRELAND

Volume of Labour Disputes

Man - days lost per 100,000 non - agricultural wage - earners (logarithmic scale)

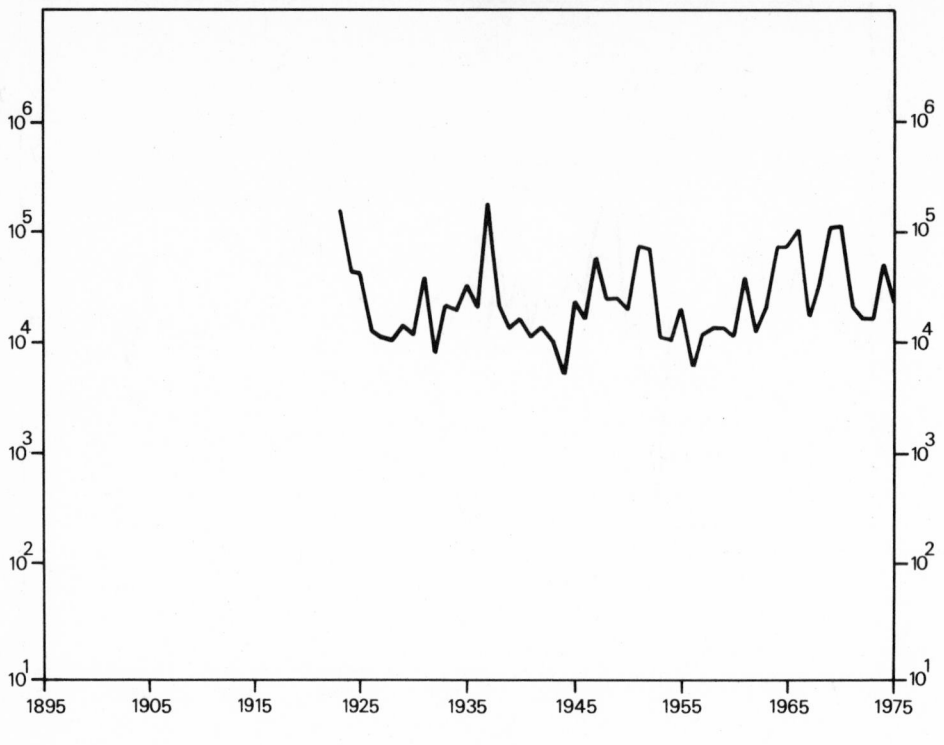

ITALY

Volume of Labour Disputes

Man - days lost per 100,000 non - agricultural wage - earners (logarithmic scale)

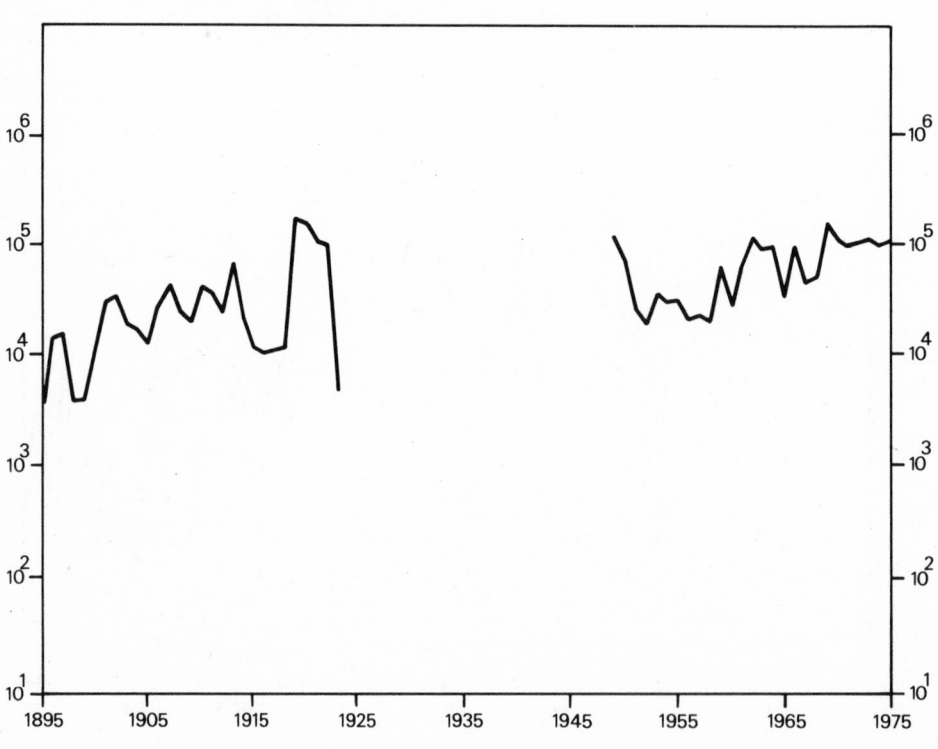

NETHERLANDS

Volume of Labour Disputes

Man - days lost per 100,000 non - agricultural wage - earners (logarithmic scale)

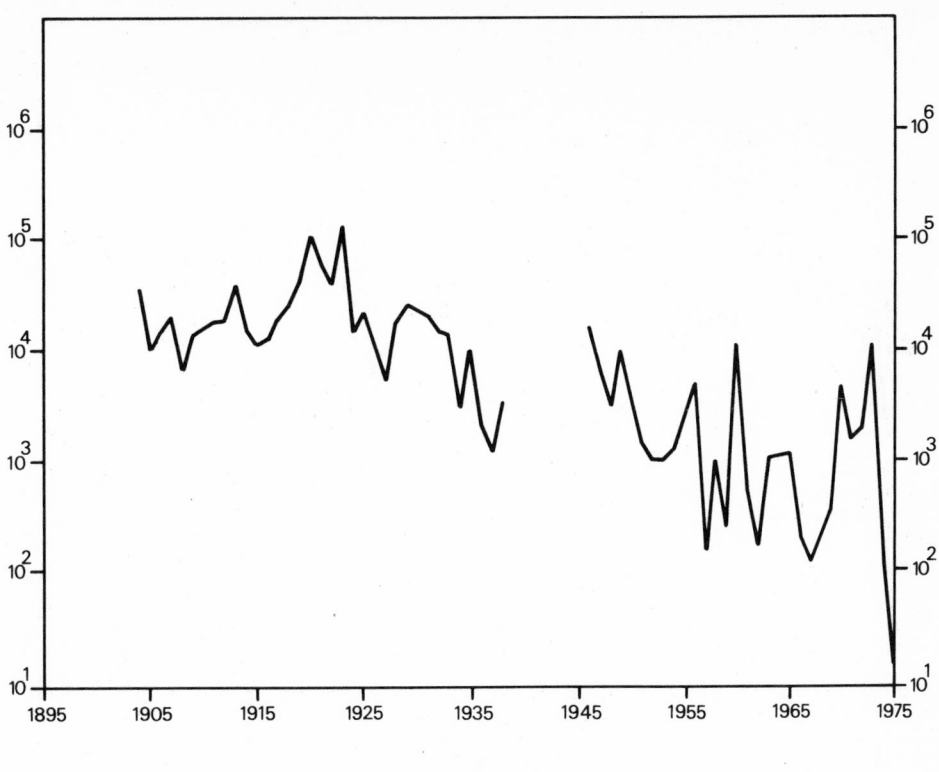

NORWAY

Volume of Labour Disputes

Man - days lost per 100,000 non - agricultural wage - earners (logarithmic scale)

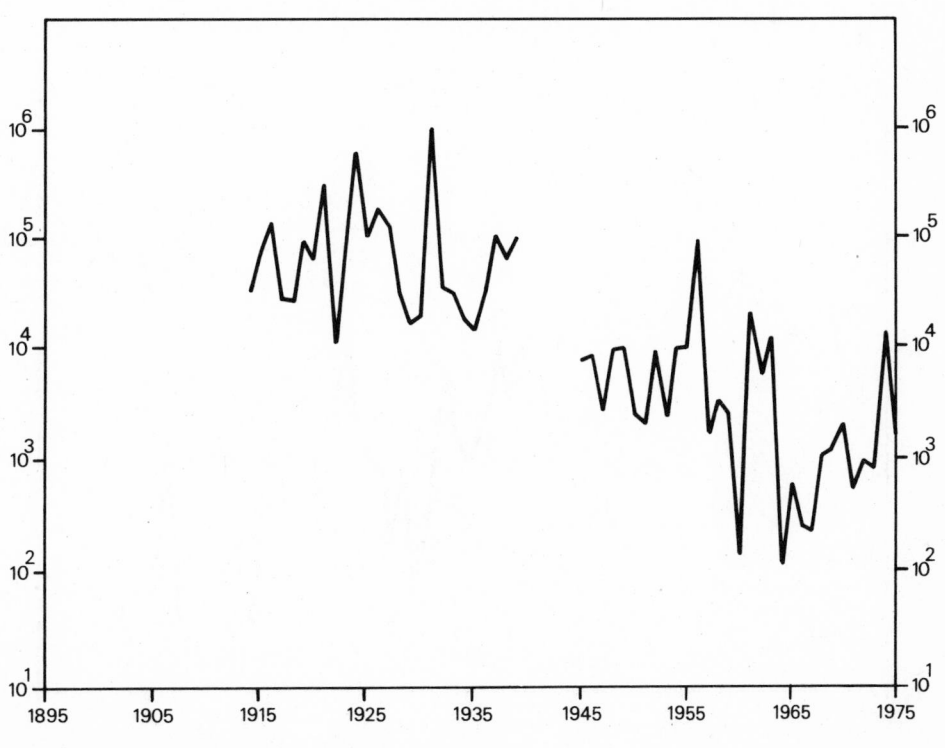

SWEDEN

Volume of Labour Disputes

Man - days lost per 100,000 non - agricultural wage - earners (logarithmic scale)

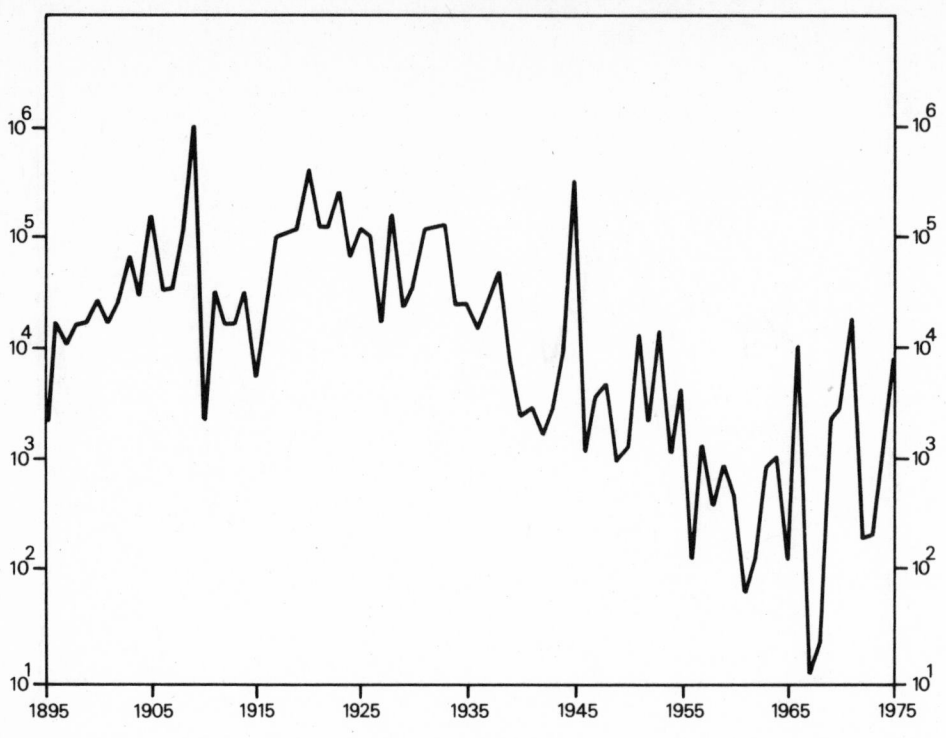

SWITZERLAND

Volume of Labour Disputes

Man - days lost er 100,000 non - agricultural wage - earners (logarithmic scale)

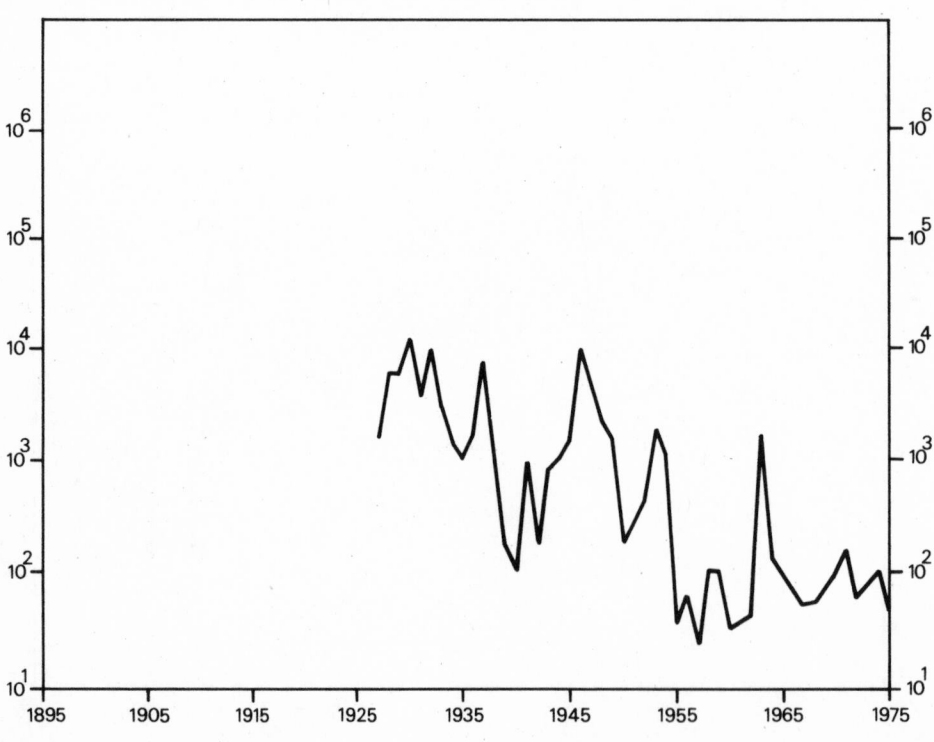

UNITED KINGDOM

Volume of Labour Disputes

Man - days lost per 100,000 non - agricultural wage - earners (logarithmic scale)

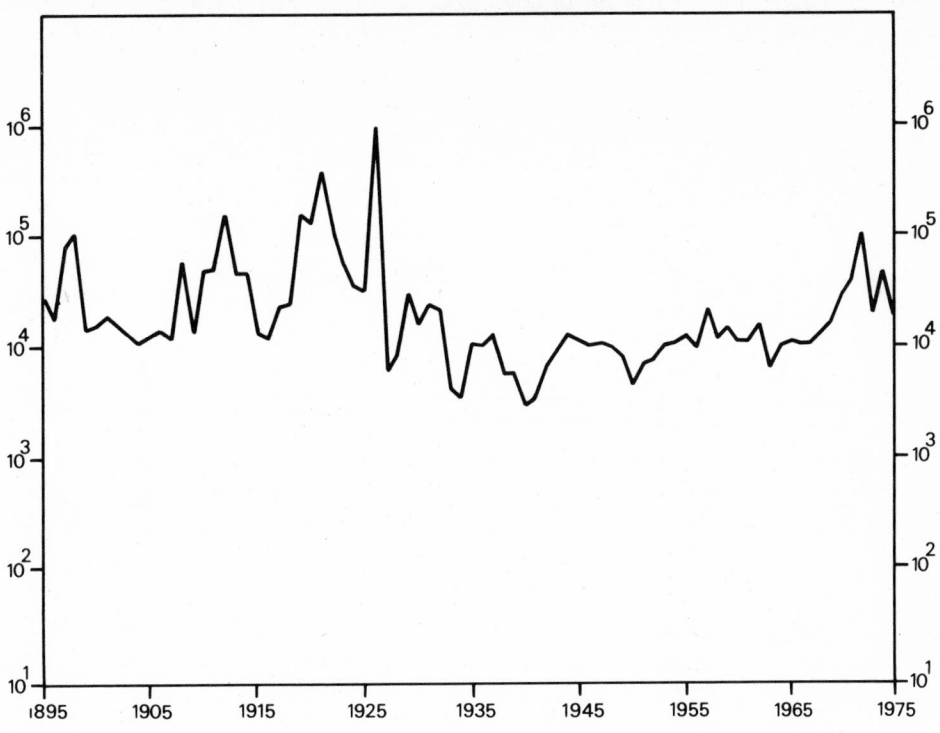

Austria

Labour Disputes [a]

Year	Labour disputes [b]			Persons involved in labour disputes				Man–days lost in labour disputes [c]				Year
	Total	Strikes	Lock–outs	Total	Strikes	Lock–outs	Indirectly	Total	Strikes	Lock–outs	Indirectly	
1975				3 783				5 511				1975
1974				7 295				7 244				1974
1973				78 251				99 265				1973
1972				7 096				15 117				1972
1971				2 431				3 702				1971
1970				7 547				26 616				1970
1969				17 449				18 517				1969
1968				3 129				6 617				1968
1967				7 496				16 411				1967
1966				120 922				71 356				1966
1965				146 009				423 474				1965
1964				40 843				35 448				1964
1963				16 501				34 017				1963
1962				207 459				647 720				1962
1961				38 338				113 878				1961
1960				30 654				68 823				1960
1959				47 007				50 536				1959
1958				28 745				43 726				1958
1957				19 555				45 606				1957
1956				43 249				153 412				1956
1955				26 011				58 021				1955
1954				21 140				51 314				1954
1953				12 695				38 021				1953
1952				31 942				75 345				1952
1951				31 555				84 683				1951
1950				28 095				500 296				1950
1949				25 157				86 389				1949
1948				5 120				305 040				1948
1947				9 175				36 775				1947
1946				4 366				6 960				1946
1945				300				950				1945

a) From 1951 data from the Austrian Trade Union Federation.
b) Data on number of labour disputes not available.
c) Only data on man–hours lost available; number of man–days lost estimated on the assumption of an eight hours working day.

Austria

Labour Disputes

Year	Size	Man-days lost	Duration	Total non-agr. wage earners in 1,000s	Labour disputes	Persons involved	Man-days lost	Year
1975			1.5	2 326		163	237	1975
1974			1.0	2 338		312	310	1974
1973			1.3	2 343		3 340	4 237	1973
1972			2.1	2 340		303	646	1972
1971			1.5	2 333		104	159	1971
1970			3.5	2 329		324	1 143	1970
1969			1.1	2 323		751	797	1969
1968			2.1	2 316		135	286	1968
1967			2.2	2 306		325	712	1967
1966			0.6	2 298		5 263	3 105	1966
1965			1.0	2 288		6 383	6 612	1965
1964			0.9	2 275		1 795	1 558	1964
1963			2.1	2 261		730	1 505	1963
1962			3.1	2 246		9 238	28 842	1962
1961			3.0	2 230		1 719	5 107	1961
1960			2.2	2 189		1 400	3 144	1960
1959			1.1	2 150		2 186	2 350	1959
1958			1.5	2 114		1 360	2 069	1958
1957			2.3	2 079		940	2 193	1957
1956			3.5	2 047		2 113	7 495	1956
1955			2.2	2 017		1 290	2 877	1955
1954			2.4	1 986		1 064	2 583	1954
1953			3.0	1 956		649	1 944	1953
1952			5.0	1 926		1 658	8 328	1952
1951			2.7	1 899		1 661	4 458	1951
1950			17.8	1 865		1 507	26 828	1950
1949			3.4	1 832		1 373	4 715	1949
1948			59.6	1 800		284	16 945	1948
1947			4.0	1 757		522	2 093	1947
1946			1.6	1 742		251	400	1946
1945			3.2	1 720		17	55	1945

Austria

Labour Disputes

Year	Labour disputes[a]			Persons involved in labour disputes				Man-days lost in labour disputes				Year
	Total	Strikes	Lock-outs	Total	Strikes	Lock-outs	Indirectly	Total	Strikes	Lock-outs	Indirectly	
1944												1944
1943												1943
1942												1942
1941												1941
1940												1940
1939												1939
1938												1938
1937	6	6	0	2 606	2 606	0		408	408	0		1937
1936	5	5	0	1 180	1 180	0		1 521	1 521	0		1936
1935	3	2	1	89	65	24		414	174	240		1935
1934	4	4	0	349	349	0		220	220	0		1934
1933	27	23	4	5 657	5 034	623		79 061	64 624	14 437		1933
1932	35	32	3	6 646	5 429	1 217		190 163	79 942	110 221		1932
1931	69	57	12	10 264	8 502	1 762		132 757	100 465	32 292		1931
1930	92	87	5	7 173	6 170	1 003		49 343	40 885	8 488		1930
1929	229	205	24	30 446	23 799	6 647		388 336	286 505	101 831		1929
1928	275	251	24	38 290	32 948	5 342		658 024	562 992	95 032		1928
1927	223	202	21	35 300	28 769	6 531		686 560	476 709	209 851		1927
1926	206	183	18	21 943	18 624	3 319		297 684	232 944	64 740		1926
1925	330	292	38	66 948	46 743	20 205		1 166 817	666 373	500 444		1925
1924	459	413	46	296 878	268 696	28 182		2 815 937	2 295 493	520 616		1924
1923	321	269	52	155 668	116 669	38 999		1 314 156	1 074 377	539 779		1923
1922	423	384	39	228 425	211 429	16 996		1 836 086	1 635 443	200 643		1922
1921	467	442	25	221 482	207 974	13 508		1 904 628	1 762 892	141 736		1921
1920	350	344	6	185 070	179 352	5 718		1 020 800	927 402	93 398		1920
1919	156	156	0	63 703	63 703	0		220 815	220 815	0		1919

a) Including so-called political strikes for which data on participants and man-days lost are not available.

Austria

Labour Disputes

Year	Indicators of average labour dispute			Total non-agr. wage earners in 1,000s	Indicators per 100,000 non-agricultural wage earners			Year
	Size	Man-days lost	Duration		Labour disputes	Persons involved	Man-days lost	
1944								1944
1943								1943
1942								1942
1941								1941
1940								1940
1939								1939
1938								1938
1937	434	68	0.2	1 766	0.3	148	23	1937
1936	236	304	1.3	1 734	0.3	68	88	1936
1935	30	138	4.7	1 701	0.2	5	24	1935
1934	87	55	0.6	1 665	0.2	21	13	1934
1933	210	2 928	14.0	1 663	1.6	340	4 755	1933
1932	190	5 433	28.6	1 658	2.1	401	11 471	1932
1931	149	1 924	12.9	1 653	4.2	621	8 032	1931
1930	78	537	6.9	1 648	5.6	435	2 996	1930
1929	133	1 696	12.8	1 643	13.9	1 853	23 640	1929
1928	139	2 393	17.2	1 638	16.8	2 338	40 180	1928
1927	158	3 079	19.4	1 633	13.7	2 162	42 052	1927
1926	107	1 445	13.6	1 628	12.7	1 348	18 290	1926
1925	203	3 536	17.4	1 623	20.3	4 126	71 911	1925
1924	647	6 135	9.5	1 618	28.4	18 347	174 098	1924
1923	485	5 029	10.4	1 613	19.9	9 651	100 070	1923
1922	540	4 341	8.0	1 609	26.3	14 195	114 101	1922
1921	474	4 078	8.6	1 603	29.1	13 815	118 800	1921
1920	529	2 917	5.5	1 591	22.0	11 631	64 153	1920
1919	408	1 415	3.5	1 583	9.9	4 025	13 953	1919

L a b o u r   D i s p u t e s

Year	Labour disputes			Persons involved in labour disputes				Man-days lost in labour disputes[a]				Year
	Total	Strikes	Lock-outs	Total	Strikes	Lock-outs	Indirectly	Total	Strikes	Lock-outs	Indirectly	
1918	60	60	0	84 024	84 024	0		437 939	437 939	0		1918
1917	131	131	0	161 234	161 234	0		469 014	469 014	0		1917
1916	41	41	0	15 927	14 841	0	1 086	23 012	21 871	0	1 141	1916
1915	40	39	1	8 493	7 951	159	383	18 291	17 638	318	335	1915
1914	278	260	18	43 240	33 412	6 917	2 911	398 647	264 354	115 591	18 702	1914
1913	461	438	23	66 183	39 814	22 258	4 111	1 537 258	409 353	1 071 916	55 989	1913
1912	801	761	40	155 470	120 953	24 295	10 222	2 468 037	1 862 027	471 267	134 743	1912
1911	728	706	22	138 831	122 001	6 375	11 455	1 961 004	1 710 277	112 219	138 508	1911
1910	676	657	19	83 406	55 474	19 292	8 640	1 425 086	1 129 460	208 730	86 896	1910
1909	609	580	29	84 696	61 978	18 165	4 553	1 269 438	729 309	504 621	35 508	1909
1908	756	721	35	95 960	78 562	9 588	7 810	1 273 038	1 011 036	262 002		1908
1907	1 112	1 086	26	204 163	176 789	14 539	12 835	2 087 523	2 087 523			1907
1906	1 133	1 083	50	234 658	153 688	67 872	13 098	2 426 815	2 191 815		235 000	1906
1905	703	686	17	122 128	99 591	11 197	11 340	1 238 458	1 151 310		87 148	1905
1904	420	414	6	97 270	64 227	23 742	9 301	666 658	606 629		60 029	1904
1903	332	324	8	52 794	46 215	1 334	5 245	572 811	500 567		72 244	1903
1902	271	264	8	44 875	37 471	1 050	6 354	363 214	284 046		79 168	1902
1901	273	270	3	28 018	24 870	302	2 846	189 759	157 744		32 015	1901
1900	313	303	10	116 901	105 128	4 036	7 737	3 675 716	3 483 963		191 753	1900
1899	316	311	5	63 594	54 763	3 457	5 374	1 136 185	1 029 937		106 248	1899
1898	255	255	0	45 116	39 658	0	5 458	352 873	323 619		29 254	1898
1897	257	246	11	43 037	38 467	1 712	2 858	401 388	368 096		33 292	1897
1896	315	305	10	75 152	66 234	5 445	3 473	937 884	899 939		37 945	1896
1895	217	209	8	33 031	28 652	2 317	2 062	325 609	300 348		25 261	1895
1894	172	172	0	74 713	67 061	0	7 652	895 728	795 416		100 312	1894
1893		172			28 120				518 511			1893
1892		101			14 123				150 992			1892
1891		104			14 025				247 086			1891

a) Up to 1907 data on man-days lost in lock-outs not available; for 1907 and 1908, data on man-days lost indirectly not available.

Austria

Labour Disputes [y]

Year	Indicators of average labour dispute			Total non-agr. wage earners in 1,000s [z]	Indicators per 100,000 non-agricultural wage earners			Year
	Size	Man-days lost	Duration		Labour disputes	Persons involved	Man-days lost	
1918	1 400	7 299	5.2					1918
1917	1 231	3 580	2.9					1917
1916	388	561	1.4					1916
1915	212	457	2.2					1915
1914	156	1 434	9.2					1914
1913	144	3 335	23.2	5 209	8.9	1 271	29 514	1913
1912	194	3 081	15.9	5 098	15.7	3 049	48 407	1912
1911	191	2 694	14.1	4 990	14.6	2 782	39 297	1911
1910	123	2 108	17.1	4 881	13.8	1 709	29 194	1910
1909	139	2 084	15.0	4 771	12.8	1 775	26 607	1909
1908	127	1 684	13.3	4 663	16.2	2 058	27 302	1908
1907	184	1 877	10.2	4 555	24.4	4 483	45 834	1907
1906	207	2 142	10.3	4 445	25.5	5 279	54 591	1906
1905	174	1 762	10.1	4 344	16.2	2 811	28 510	1905
1904	232	1 587	6.9	4 246	9.9	2 291	15 702	1904
1903	159	1 725	10.8	4 143	8.0	1 274	13 825	1903
1902	166	1 340	8.1	4 042	6.7	1 110	8 987	1902
1901	103	695	6.8	3 904	6.9	711	4 817	1901
1900	373	11 744	31.4	3 838	8.2	3 046	95 766	1900
1899	201	3 596	17.9	3 799	8.3	1 674	29 904	1899
1898	177	1 384	7.8	3 762	6.8	1 199	9 380	1898
1897	167	1 562	9.3	3 724	6.9	1 156	10 778	1897
1896	239	2 977	12.5	3 686	8.5	2 039	25 446	1896
1895	152	1 501	9.9	3 650	5.9	905	8 921	1895
1894	434	5 208	12.0	3 620	4.8	2 064	24 747	1894
1893	163	3 015	18.4	3 588	4.8	784	14 451	1893
1892	140	1 495	10.7	3 559	2.8	397	4 242	1892
1891	135	2 376	17.6	3 532	2.9	397	6 996	1891

y) Up to 1894 refering to strikes only.
z) Not available during World War I.

Labour Disputes [a]

Year	Labour disputes			Persons involved in labour disputes				Man-days lost in labour disputes				Year
	Total	Strikes	Lock-outs	Total	Strikes	Lock-outs	Indirectly	Total	Strikes	Lock-outs	Indirectly	
1975	243			89 359	85 001		4 358	558 676				1975
1974	235			60 764	55 747		5 017	579 663				1974
1973	172			70 134	62 281		7 853	866 023				1973
1972	191			70 570	66 622		3 948	353 790				1972
1971	184			100 066	86 979		13 087	1 240 884				1971
1970	151			111 002	107 670		3 332	1 431 574				1970
1969	88			36 547	24 691		11 856	161 999				1969
1968	72			109 855	109 338		517	363 915				1968
1967	58			38 465	37 627		838	181 713				1967
1966	74			45 523	41 629		3 894	533 239				1966
1965	43			19 631	18 774		857	70 131				1965
1964	41			41 762	40 682		1 080	443 835				1964
1963	48			18 550	17 722		828	247 381				1963
1962	40			22 793	21 995		798	270 975				1962
1961	38			19 214	12 622		6 592	92 092				1961
1960	61			26 576	19 140		7 436	334 446				1960
1959	57			124 188	123 473		715	983 147				1959
1958	43			64 448	62 803		1 645	293 767				1958
1957	114			274 024	267 055		6 969	2 993 738				1957
1956	148			176 140	133 292		42 848	948 170				1956
1955	143			118 578	112 526		6 052	1 001 769				1955
1954	107			60 618	57 133		3 485	443 706				1954
1953	115			116 724	109 931		6 793	411 903				1953
1952	122			278 064	269 123		8 941	863 377				1952
1951	163			121 240	114 528		6 712	593 164				1951
1950	122			149 936	148 080		1 856	2 768 555				1950
1949	99			50 134	47 742		2 392	829 850				1949
1948	155			341 422	334 337		7 085	1 858 190				1948
1947	473			353 732	300 535		53 197	2 211 786				1947
1946	287			183 231	170 135		13 096	1 052 594				1946
1945	160			147 417	139 706		7 711	563 173				1945
1940	43			25 519	22 024		3 495	36 451				1940
1939	126	68	0	46 193	42 598	0	3 595	157 242				1939
1938	126	126	0	32 900	32 338	0	562	240 937				1938
1937 [b]	209	209	0	84 472	81 544	0	2 928	647 647				1937
1936 [b]	111	111	0	564 837	560 716	0	4 121	365 998				1936
1935	150	150	0	104 013	98 543	0	5 470	623 002				1935
1934	79	79	0	36 525	33 628	0	2 897	2 441 335				1934
1933	87	86	1	39 136	34 509	155	4 472	664 044				1933
1932	63	63	0	162 693	161 442	0	1 251	520 674				1932
1931	74	73	1	23 010	19 886	138	2 986	399 037				1931
1930	93	93	0	64 718	54 149	0	10 569	781 646				1930
1929	168	165	3	60 557	45 773	3 463	11 321	789 117				1929
1928	192	191	1	77 780	72 207	2 500	3 073	2 254 424				1928
1927	136	131	5	45 071	35 576	4 297	5 198	1 658 836				1927

Labour Disputes

Year	Indicators of average labour dispute			Total non-agr. wage earners in 1,000s	Indicators per 100,000 non-agricultural wage earners			Year
	Size	Man-days lost	Duration		Labour disputes	Persons involved	Man-days lost	
1975	368	2 511	6.8	2 977	8.2	3 002	20 497	1975
1974	259	2 467	9.5	2 947	8.0	2 062	19 672	1974
1973	408	5 035	12.3	2 916	5.9	2 405	29 703	1973
1972	369	1 852	5.0	2 885	6.6	2 446	12 265	1972
1971	544	6 744	12.4	2 852	6.5	3 509	43 514	1971
1970	735	9 481	12.9	2 825	5.3	3 930	50 680	1970
1969	415	1 841	4.4	2 804	3.1	1 303	5 778	1969
1968	1 526	5 054	3.3	2 778	2.6	3 955	13 101	1968
1967	663	3 133	4.7	2 749	2.1	1 399	6 611	1967
1966	615	7 206	11.7	2 715	2.7	1 676	19 637	1966
1965	457	1 631	3.6	2 679	1.6	733	2 618	1965
1964	1 019	10 825	10.6	2 637	1.6	1 584	16 831	1964
1963	386	5 154	13.3	2 594	1.9	715	9 535	1963
1962	570	6 774	11.9	2 563	1.6	889	10 574	1962
1961	506	2 423	4.8	2 536	1.5	758	3 631	1961
1960	436	5 483	12.6	2 523	2.4	1 053	13 258	1960
1959	2 179	17 248	7.9	2 510	2.3	4 947	39 163	1959
1958	1 499	6 832	4.6	2 498	1.7	2 580	11 762	1958
1957	2 404	26 261	10.9	2 481	4.6	11 044	120 657	1957
1956	1 190	6 407	5.4	2 464	6.0	7 148	38 478	1956
1955	829	7 005	8.4	2 450	5.8	4 840	40 893	1955
1954	567	4 147	7.3	2 437	4.4	2 488	18 208	1954
1953	1 015	3 582	3.5	2 426	4.7	4 811	16 979	1953
1952	2 279	7 077	3.1	2 413	5.1	11 522	35 775	1952
1951	744	3 639	4.9	2 399	6.8	5 053	24 723	1951
1950	1 229	22 693	18.5	2 389	5.1	6 277	115 905	1950
1949	506	8 382	16.6	2 382	4.2	2 105	34 844	1949
1948	2 203	11 988	5.4	2 366	6.6	14 431	78 539	1948
1947	748	4 676	6.3	2 336	20.2	15 142	94 678	1947
1946	638	3 668	5.7	2 310	12.4	7 931	45 561	1946
1945	921	3 520	3.8	2 705	5.9	5 450	20 819	1945
1940	593	848	1.4	2 707	1.6	943	1 346	1940
1939	679	2 312	3.4	2 722	2.5	1 697	5 777	1939
1938	261	1 912	7.3	2 694	4.7	1 221	8 943	1938
1937	404	3 099	7.7	2 663	7.8	3 172	24 317	1937
1936	5 089	3 297	0.6	2 632	4.2	21 462	13 907	1936
1935	693	4 153	6.0	2 601	5.8	3 998	23 949	1935
1934	462	30 903	66.8	2 572	3.1	1 420	94 929	1934
1933	450	7 633	17.0	2 541	3.4	1 540	26 136	1933
1932	2 582	8 265	3.2	2 506	2.5	6 493	20 778	1932
1931	311	5 392	17.3	2 466	3.0	933	16 180	1931
1930	696	8 405	12.1	2 431	3.8	2 663	32 160	1930
1929	360	4 697	13.0	2 397	7.0	2 527	32 925	1929
1928	405	11 742	29.0	2 357	8.1	3 299	95 635	1928
1927	331	12 197	36.8	2 318	5.9	1 944	71 555	1927

Labour Disputes [a]

Year	Labour disputes [c]			Persons involved in labour disputes				Man-days lost in labour disputes [d]				Year
	Total	Strikes	Lock-outs	Total	Strikes	Lock-outs	Indirectly	Total	Strikes	Lock-outs	Indirectly	
1926	140	137	3	82 266	69 912	7 456	4 898					1926
1925	112	108	4	84 783	81 422	566	2 795					1925
1924	188	186	2	90 155	82 747	1 700	5 708					1924
1923	168	164	4	132 518	104 980	21 298	6 240					1923
1922	172	169	3	110 618	85 002	603	25 013					1922
1921	258	252	6	143 383	112 185	5 108	26 643					1921
1920	517	506	11	336 383	289 190	7 002	40 191					1920
1919	372	366	6	184 555	158 253	5 777	20 525					1919
1913	167	162	5	29 447	15 939	7 813	5 695					1913
1912	206	202	4	76 815	60 570	3 202	13 043					1912
1911	162	156	6	62 927	54 947	2 256	5 724					1911
1910	110	108	2	32 047	26 289	968	4 790					1910
1909	123	119	4	19 344	10 867	4 602	3 875					1909
1908	108	101	7	22 700	14 098	2 987	5 615					1908
1907	224	221	3	80 413	45 001	6 184	29 228					1907
1906	212	207	5	59 938	24 892	23 621	11 425					1906
1905	133			117 157	75 672		41 485					1905
1904	81			15 119	12 375		2 744					1904
1903	70			10 394	7 649		2 745					1903
1902	73			15 462	10 477		4 985					1902
1901	117			58 375	43 814		14 561					1901
1900	146			38 087	32 443		5 644					1900
1899	104			68 721	57 931		10 790					1899
1898	91			16 041	13 101		2 940					1898
1897	130			42 057	35 958		6 069					1897
1896	139			30 564	23 204		7 360					1896
1895		43 [e]										1895
1894		11										1894
1893		30			200 000							1893
1892		72										1892
1891		19										1891
1890		13			22 000							1890

a) From 1945 data on disputes and persons involved are reported for the given year, whereas data on man-days lost refer to 'labour disputes in progress'; up to 1940 all data refer to labour disputes terminated in the given year.

b) Excluding 888 strikes against social policy legislation; no data on man-days lost collected during a three-month period.

c) Data on lock-outs not available prior to 1906.

d) Data on man-days lost not available prior to 1927.

e) Very incomplete data for 1890-95 collected by the General Council of the Belgian Labour Party.

Labour Disputes

Year	Indicators of average labour dispute			Total non-agr. wage earners in 1,000s	Indicators per 100,000 non-agricultural wage earners			Year
	Size	Man-days lost	Duration		Labour disputes	Persons involved	Man-days lost	
1926	588			2 281	6.1	3 607		1926
1925	757			2 234	5.0	3 796		1925
1924	480			2 185	8.6	4 126		1924
1923	789			2 145	7.8	6 177		1923
1922	643			2 109	8.2	5 245		1922
1921	597			2 072	12.5	7 431		1921
1920	651			2 066	25.0	16 280		1920
1919	496			2 069	18.0	8 919		1919
1913	176			2 153	7.8	1 368		1913
1912	373			2 112	9.8	3 638		1912
1911	388			2 071	7.8	3 039		1911
1910	291			2 045	5.4	1 567		1910
1909	157			2 020	6.1	958		1909
1908	210			1 981	5.5	1 146		1908
1907	359			1 941	11.5	4 143		1907
1906	283			1 900	11.2	3 154		1906
1905	881			1 859	7.2	6 303		1905
1904	187			1 816	4.5	832		1904
1903	148			1 774	3.9	586		1903
1902	212			1 731	4.2	893		1902
1901	499			1 686	6.9	3 462		1901
1900	261			1 660	8.8	2 294		1900
1899	661			1 640	6.3	4 190		1899
1898	176			1 604	5.7	1 000		1898
1897	323			1 566	8.3	2 684		1897
1896	220			1 529	9.1	1 999		1896

Labour Disputes[a)]

Year	Labour disputes		Persons involved in labour disputes				Man-days lost in labour disputes		Year
	Total I	Total II	Total I	Strikes	Lock-outs	Total II	Total I	Total II	
1975	147		59 128				100 000		1975
1974	134		142 352				184 000		1974
1973	205		327 100				3 901 200		1973
1972	35		7 601				21 800		1972
1971	31		6 379				20 600		1971
1970	77		55 585				102 000		1970
1969	48		35 856				56 200		1969
1968	17		28 772				33 600		1968
1967	22		10 442				9 900		1967
1966	22		10 369				15 400		1966
1965	37		14 194				242 100		1965
1964	40		7 530				17 500		1964
1963	19		6 527				23 600		1963
1962	26		9 518				14 600		1962
1961	34		153 304				2 308 200		1961
1960	82		19 787				60 900		1960
1959	23		5 859				18 100		1959
1958	15		9 474				9 400		1958
1957	14		2 540				7 210		1957
1956	98		66 306				1 086 600		1956
1955	13		6 527				9 900		1955
1954	20		7 673				22 700		1954
1953	8		403				2 300		1953
1952	9		2 397				3 600		1952
1951	12		1 701				3 700		1951
1950	18		2 849				3 700		1950
1949	17		2 654				10 400		1949
1948	24	85	2 722			4 448	8 200	10 000	1948
1947	29	116	7 542			16 174	467 000	473 000	1947
1946	59	108	54 241			56 304	1 389 000	1 386 000	1946
1945	35	85	8 526	8 526	0	9 656	66 000	66 000	1945
1944	34	62	7 690	7 690	0	8 885	88 000	89 000	1944
1943	17	91	6 483	6 315	168	14 795	24 000	31 000	1943
1942		7		3 153	0	3 152		11 000	1942
1941		2		65	0	65		3 000	1941
1940		9		257	0	257		5 000	1940
1939		19		523	0	523		16 000	1939
1938		22		3 645	5	3 650		90 000	1938
1937		22		1 367	5	1 372		21 000	1937
1936		12		403	96 459	96 862		2 946 000	1936
1935		14		827	0	827		14 000	1935
1934		38		10 816	730	11 546		146 000	1934
1933		26		448	44	448		18 000	1933
1932		18		520	5 240	5 760		87 000	1932
1931		16		997	2 695	3 692		246 000	1931

Labour Disputes [y]

Year	Indicators of average labour dispute			Total non-agr. wage earners in 1,000s	Indicators per 100,000 non-agricultural wage earners				Year
	Size	Man-days lost	Duration		Labour disputes	Persons involved	Man-days lost		
1975	402	680	1.7	3 147	4.7	1 879	3 178		1975
1974	1 062	1 373	1.3	3 101	4.3	4 590	5 933		1974
1973	1 596	19 030	11.9	3 059	6.7	10 691	127 513		1973
1972	217	623	2.9	3 021	1.2	252	722		1972
1971	206	665	3.2	2 980	1.0	214	691		1971
1970	722	1 325	1.8	2 928	2.6	1 898	3 484		1970
1969	747	1 171	1.6	2 898	1.7	1 237	1 939		1969
1968	1 692	1 976	1.2	2 875	0.6	1 001	1 169		1968
1967	475	450	0.9	2 855	0.8	366	347		1967
1966	471	700	1.5	2 829	0.8	367	544		1966
1965	384	6 543	17.1	2 797	1.3	507	8 655		1965
1964	188	438	2.3	2 735	1.5	275	640		1964
1963	344	1 242	3.6	2 680	0.7	244	881		1963
1962	366	562	1.5	2 630	1.0	362	555		1962
1961	4 509	67 888	15.1	2 581	1.3	5 939	89 420		1961
1960	241	743	3.1	2 534	3.2	781	2 404		1960
1959	255	787	3.1	2 501	0.9	234	724		1959
1958	632	627	1.0	2 468	0.6	384	381		1958
1957	181	515	2.8	2 432	0.6	104	296		1957
1956	677	11 088	16.4	2 395	4.1	2 769	45 379		1956
1955	502	762	1.5	2 357	0.6	277	420		1955
1954	384	1 135	3.0	2 320	0.9	331	979		1954
1953	50	288	5.7	2 285	0.4	18	101		1953
1952	266	400	1.5	2 250	0.4	107	160		1952
1951	142	308	2.2	2 213	0.5	77	167		1951
1950	158	206	1.3	2 174	0.8	131	170		1950
1949	156	612	3.9	2 136	0.8	124	487		1949
1948	113	342	3.0	2 094	1.1	130	392		1948
1947	260	16 103	61.9	2 050	1.4	368	22 786		1947
1946	919	23 542	25.6	2 005	2.9	2 706	69 293		1946
1945	244	1 886	7.7	1 960	1.8	435	3 367		1945
1944	226	2 588	11.4	1 924	1.8	400	4 573		1944
1943	381	1 412	3.7	1 890	0.9	343	1 270		1943
1942	450	1 571	3.5	1 858	0.4	170	592		1942
1941	33	1 500	46.2	1 831	0.1	4	164		1941
1940	29	556	19.5	1 806	0.5	14	277		1940
1939	28	842	30.6	1 781	1.1	29	899		1939
1938	166	4 091	24.7	1 756	1.3	208	5 124		1938
1937	62	955	15.3	1 734	1.3	79	1 211		1937
1936	8 072	245 500	30.4	1 713	0.7	5 655	172 005		1936
1935	59	1 000	16.9	1 692	0.8	49	828		1935
1934	304	3 842	12.6	1 670	2.3	691	8 743		1934
1933	19	692	36.6	1 648	1.6	30	1 092		1933
1932	320	4 833	15.1	1 625	1.1	355	5 355		1932
1931	231	15 375	66.6	1 602	1.0	230	15 356		1931

Denmark

Labour Disputes

Year	Labour disputes				Persons involved in labour disputes b)					Man-days lost in labour disputes b)							
	Total	Strikes	Lock-outs	Mixed c)	Total	N	Strikes	Lock-outs	Indirectly	Total	N	Strikes	N	Lock-outs	N	Indirectly	N
1930	37	37	0	0	5 349		5 349	0	0	143 774		143 774		0		0	
1929	22	21	1	0	1 040		1 040	0	0	41 283		40 803		480		0	
1928	11	11	0	0	469		469	0	0	10 831		10 831		0		0	
1927	17	14	3	0	2 851		537	2 314	0	118 827		4 552		114 295		0	
1926	32	31	1	0	1 050		975	75	0	23 025		21 225		1 800		0	
1925	49	48	0	1	102 331	47	7 241	0	95 090	4 138 500	47	116 600	46	0	0	4 021 900	1
1924	71	68	1	2	9 758	71	8 993	765	0	175 000	71	133 500	68	200	1	41 300	2
1923	58	57	0	1	1 981	57	1 941	0	40	19 700	57	19 600	56	0	0	100	1
1922	31	28	2	1	48 859	31	640	48 219	0	2 272 000	29	5 100	26	1 400	2	2 265 500	1
1921	110	97	9	4	48 147	107	13 356	34 791	0	1 321 200	103	41 700	90	1 139 000	9	140 500	4
1920	243	234	2	7	21 965	202	19 129	2 836	0	1 306 200	169	1 203 300	167	97 700	2	5 200	6
1919	472	460	3	9	35 575	393	31 210	857	3 508	915 900	157	525 700	128	272 900	3	117 300	2
1918	253	249	1	3	8 819	218	8 078	3	738	182 400	69	103 200	67			79 200	1
1917	215	202	11	2	10 081	209	9 776	296	9	211 000	205	207 800	194	3 000	10	200	1
1916	66	65	0	1	12 803	41	12 795	0	8	241 400	63	241 200	62	0	0	200	1
1915	43	40	2	1	1 914	36	1 662	252	0	31 900	40	23 600	37	7 600	2	700	0
1914	44	41	3	0	3 373	73	3 354	19	0	56 100	35	48 400	32	7 700	3	0	2
1913	76	73	3	3	9 714	58	9 714	0	0	381 500	70	381 400	68	0	0	100	0
1912	60	57	3	0	4 101	50	2 048	2 053	0	49 600	59	26 200	56	23 400	3	0	0
1911	51	43	8	0	28 484	60	5 694	22 790	0	647 800	50	263 500	42	384 300	8	0	0
1910	71	61	3	7	2 478	50	1 681	797	0	60 681	53						
1909	65	40	7	18	2 360	100	769	1 591	0	57 928	47						
1908	122	98	2	22	7 600	86	3 481	4 119	0	85 088	79						
1907	105	79	4	22	8 157	75	5 617	2 457	83	255 195	66						
1906	90	70	5	15	4 441	63	3 237	654	550	68 414	62						
1905	75	61	3	11	5 741		5 677	64	0	499 225	51						

Labour Disputes

Year	Indicators of average labour dispute[z]			Total non-agr. wage earners in 1,000s	Indicators per 100,000 non-agricultural wage earners			Year
	Size	Man-days lost	Duration		Labour disputes	Persons involved	Man-days lost	
1930	145	3 885	26.9	1 580	2.3	339	9 097	1930
1929	47	1 877	39.7	1 559	1.4	67	2 649	1929
1928	43.	985	23.1	1 538	0.7	30	704	1928
1927	168	6 990	41.7	1 518	1.1	188	7 830	1927
1926	33	720	21.9	1 497	2.1	70	1 538	1926
1925	2 177	88 053	40.4	1 476	3.3	6 932	280 351	1925
1924	137	2 465	17.9	1 454	4.9	671	12 033	1924
1923	35	36	1.0	1 433	4.0	138	1 375	1923
1922	1 576	78 345	49.7	1 411	2.2	3 463	161 056	1922
1921	450	12 827	28.5	1 385	7.9	3 475	95 371	1921
1920	109	7 729	71.1	1 357	17.9	1 618	96 223	1920
1919	91	6 685	73.9	1 339	35.3	2 657	68 413	1919
1918	40	2 643	65.3	1 121	22.6	787	16 270	1918
1917	48	1 029	21.3	1 116	19.3	904	18 912	1917
1916	194	3 832	19.8	1 107	6.0	1 156	21 803	1916
1915	47	862	18.5	1 100	3.9	174	2 901	1915
1914	94	1 753	18.7	1 092	4.0	309	5 135	1914
1913	133	5 450	41.0	1 060	7.2	917	35 999	1913
1912	71	841	11.9	1 027	5.8	399	4 828	1912
1911	570	12 956	22.7	995	5.1	2 862	65 095	1911
1910	41	1 145	27.7	963	7.4	257	6 301	1910
1909	47	1 233	26.1	931	7.0	254	6 223	1909
1908	76	1 077	14.2	899	13.6	846	9 469	1908
1907	95	3 867	40.8	867	12.1	940	29 417	1907
1906	59	1 103	18.6	838	10.7	530	8 166	1906
1905	91	9 789	107.4	809	9.3	710	61 704	1905
1904	35	1 129	32.3	781	11.0	327	8 815	1904
1903	27	545	20.4	754	8.1	152	2 457	1903
1902	65	3 029	46.5	729	9.3	527	18 271	1902
1901	83	1 288	15.5	704	8.1	577	7 324	1901
1900	112	3 969	35.5	677	12.1	1 123	32 236	1900
1899	427	48 766	114.1	663	14.8	5 735	426 620	1899
1898	55	1 139	20.5	648	22.7	1 070	18 977	1898
1897	106	5 502	51.9	633	17.5	1 157	33 912	1897

y) From 1931 to 1941 Total I, thereafter Total II.
z) Up to 1925 indicators calculated only for disputes for which data available (see N).

Denmark

Labour Disputes

Year	Labour disputes				Persons involved in labour disputes b)						Man-days lost in labour disputes b)								Year
	Total	Strikes	Lock-outs	Mixed	Total	N	Strikes	Lock-outs	Indirectly	N	Total	N	Strikes	N	Lock-outs	N	Indirectly	N	
1904	86	69	3	14	2 553	73	1 855	698			68 852	61							1904
1903	61	39	4	18	1 148	43	958	190			18 535	34							1903
1902	68	54	6	8	3 842	59	2 345	97	1 400		133 262	44							1902
1901	57	40	11	6	4 061	49	3 574	487			51 525	40							1901
1900	82	62	5	15	7 606	68	7 126	480	3		218 271	55							1900
1899	98	81	3	14	38 025	89	6 366	29 739	1 929		2 828 447	58							1899
1898	147	136	5	6	6 933	125	5 931	856	146		123 000	108							1898
1897	111	77	11	23	7 320	69	3 591	3 559	170		214 564	39							1897

a) From 1943 data on labour disputes collected only in cases with more than 100 man-days aggregate loss; method of collection changed in 1943; for purpose of comparison, additional data, collected according to the old method, provided for several years after this change.

b) Up to 1925 data on participation and man-days not reported for all labour disputes (see N); separate figures for strikes and lock-outs not available prior to 1911.

c) Labour disputes changing from strikes to lock-outs, or vice versa.

Labour Disputes[a)]

Year	Labour disputes			Persons involved in labour disputes[b)]			Man-days lost in labour disputes				Year
	Total	Strikes	Lock-outs	Total	Strikes and lock-outs	Indirectly	Total	Strikes	Lock-outs	Indirectly	
1975	1 530			215 140	213 790	1 350	284 200				1975
1974	1 778			370 700	365 540	5 160	434 800				1974
1973	1 009			678 173	674 446	3 727	2 496 900				1973
1972	849			239 732	232 488	7 244	473 100				1972
1971	838			403 297	400 681	2 616	2 711 100				1971
1970	240				201 556		233 173				1970
1969	158				83 207		161 083				1969
1968	68				26 843		282 287				1968
1967	43				26 591		320 665				1967
1966	150				66 051		122 902				1966
1965	29				6 959		16 047				1965
1964	76				26 929		58 381				1964
1963	66				104 646		1 380 274				1963
1962	46				6 963		33 052				1962
1961	51				45 247		41 437				1961
1960	44				19 285		96 209				1960
1959	49				19 764		429 639				1959
1958	50				14 365		45 185				1958
1957	88				58 716		222 672				1957
1956	43				451 280		6 970 506				1956
1955	72				42 402		344 195				1955
1954	36				19 154		115 810				1954
1953	104				15 521		63 894				1953
1952	43				9 370		54 440				1952
1951	67				10 962		323 985				1951
1950	78				107 515		4 644 367				1950
1949	48				53 642		1 195 404				1949
1948	84				15 057		243 544				1948
1947	228				113 359		479 496				1947
1946	42				18 913		115 984				1946
1945	102				35 762		357 664				1945
1941	12			4 002	2 164	1 838	27 078				1941
1940	4			575	513	62	5 397				1940
1939	29			10 636	6 120	4 516	256 628				1939
1938	31			6 661	4 087	2 574	110 456				1938
1937	37			12 167	6 168	5 999	183 401				1937
1936	29			5 825	2 935	2 890	35 360				1936
1935	23			4 491	2 274	2 217	60 843				1935
1934	46			9 848	5 883	3 965	89 727				1934
1933	4			1 619	1 274	345	9 526				1933
1932	3			284	284	0	2 301				1932
1931	1			106	53	53	106				1931
1930	11			3 066	1 673	1 393	12 120				1930
1929	26			5 361	2 443	1 918	74 887				1929
1928	71			50 908	27 266	23 642	502 236				1928
1927	79			23 699	13 368	10 331	1 528 182				1927

Finland

Labour Disputes [y)]

Year	Indicators of average labour dispute			Total non-agr. wage earners in 1,000s	Indicators per 100,000 non-agricultural wage earners			Year
	Size	Man-days lost	Duration		Labour disputes	Persons involved	Man-days lost	
1975	141	186	1.3	1 726	88.7	12 467	16 469	1975
1974	208	245	1.2	1 689	105.3	21 949	25 744	1974
1973	672	2 475	3.7	1 651	61.1	41 075	151 224	1973
1972	282	557	2.0	1 613	52.6	14 863	29 331	1972
1971	481	3 235	6.7	1 575	53.2	25 609	172 155	1971
1970	840	972	1.2	1 544	15.5	13 052	15 099	1970
1969	527	1 020	1.9	1 522	10.4	5 467	10 585	1969
1968	395	4 151	10.5	1 494	4.6	1 796	18 889	1968
1967	618	7 457	12.1	1 460	2.9	1 822	21 969	1967
1966	440	819	1.9	1 424	10.5	4 639	8 632	1966
1965	240	553	2.3	1 391	2.1	500	1 154	1965
1964	354	768	2.2	1 358	5.6	1 983	4 299	1964
1963	1 586	20 913	13.2	1 323	5.0	7 910	104 335	1963
1962	151	719	4.7	1 286	3.6	541	2 570	1962
1961	887	812	0.9	1 250	4.1	3 619	3 314	1961
1960	438	2 187	5.0	1 215	3.6	1 588	7 921	1960
1959	403	8 768	21.7	1 187	4.1	1 665	36 197	1959
1958	287	904	3.1	1 159	4.3	1 239	3 897	1958
1957	667	2 530	3.8	1 132	7.8	5 189	19 677	1957
1956	10 495	162 105	15.4	1 102	3.9	40 954	632 581	1956
1955	589	4 780	8.1	1 071	6.7	3 959	32 136	1955
1954	532	3 217	6.0	1 040	3.5	1 842	11 137	1954
1953	149	672	4.5	1 009	10.3	1 538	6 928	1953
1952	218	1 266	5.8	978	4.4	958	5 568	1952
1951	170	4 836	28.4	948	7.1	1 203	34 182	1951
1950	1 378	59 543	43.2	919	8.5	11 697	505 301	1950
1949	1 118	24 904	22.3	889	5.4	6 037	134 536	1949
1948	179	2 899	16.2	857	9.8	1 757	28 422	1948
1947	2 103	497	0.2	825	27.6	58 110	13 738	1947
1946	447	2 762	6.2	793	5.3	2 365	14 618	1946
1945	351	3 507	10.0	470	21.7	7 608	76 091	1945
1941	334	2 257	6.8	463	2.6	864	5 848	1941
1940	144	1 349	9.4	463	0.9	124	1 167	1940
1939	367	8 849	24.1	447	6.5	2 379	57 408	1939
1938	215	3 563	16.6	449	6.9	1 484	24 607	1938
1937	329	4 957	15.1	435	8.5	2 797	42 165	1937
1936	201	1 219	6.1	418	6.9	1 392	8 451	1936
1935	195	2 645	13.5	402	5.7	1 116	15 122	1935
1934	214	1 951	9.1	386	11.9	2 548	23 217	1934
1933	405	2 382	5.9	371	1.1	436	2 565	1933
1932	95	767	8.1	357	0.8	80	645	1932
1931	106	106	1.0	341	0.3	31	31	1931
1930	688	1 102	1.6	327	3.4	2 316	3 710	1930
1929	168	2 880	17.2	318	8.2	1 370	23 530	1929
1928	717	7 074	9.9	310	22.9	16 435	162 144	1928
1927	300	19 344	64.5	301	26.2	7 866	507 192	1927

Finland

Labour Disputes [c]

Year	Labour disputes			Persons involved in labour disputes				Man-days lost in labour disputes				Year
	Total	Strikes	Lock-outs	Total	Strikes and lock-outs	N	Indirectly	Total	Strikes	Lock-outs	Indirectly	
1926	72			17 558	10 230		7 328	386 355				1926
1925	38			5 649	2 921		2 728	113 024				1925
1924	31			5 117	3 051		2 066	51 049				1924
1923	50			14 099	7 588		6 511	261 474				1923
1922	53			14 573	9 840		4 733	252 374				1922
1921	76			9 557	6 251		3 306	119 868				1921
1920	146			28 461	21 001		7 460	455 588				1920
1919	39			5 935	4 065		1 870	160 130				1919
1918 [d]	6			312	312		0	1 740				1918
1917 [d]	484				224 074			1 997 190				1917
1916												1916
1915												1915
1914	37			9 983	6 217		3 766	376 260				1914
1913	70			8 623	5 557		3 066	74 400				1913
1912	59			20 442	11 281		9 161	529 340				1912
1911	51			7 906	5 822		2 084	290 570				1911
1910	54			7 456	4 361		3 095	170 950				1910
1909	51			6 820	3 903		2 917	251 960				1909
1908	128			18 725	11 425		7 300	435 970				1908
1907	176			36 737	20 700		16 037	595 860				1907
1906	174				17 592	56						1906
1905	93				3 601	34						1905
1904	36				3 171	16						1904
1903	65				1 644	22						1903
1902	24				581	9						1902
1901	16				458	7						1901
1900	19				1 099	7						1900
1899	33				1 116	10						1899
1898	22				796	7						1898
1897	14				1 130	6						1897
1896	19				1 919	12						1896
1895	3											1895
1894	1											1894
1893	2				74	2						1893
1892	3											1892
1891	7				1 234	5						1891
1890	1				200	1						1890

a) From 1971 new method of collection; data for previous years not strictly comparable.

b) No data on 'persons indirectly involved' available between 1945 and 1970; however, total man-days lost reported for directly and indirectly involved.

c) Up to 1906 data are based on private collection; data on participants not available for all disputes (see N).

d) Including the general strike in 1917.

Finland

Labour Disputes

Year	Indicators of average labour dispute			Total non-agr. wage earners in 1,000s	Indicators per 100,000 non-agricultural wage earners			Year
	Size z)	Man-days lost	Duration		Labour disputes	Persons involved	Man-days lost	
1926	244	5 366	22.0	293	24.6	5 994	131 905	1926
1925	149	2 974	20.0	284	13.4	1 986	39 745	1925
1924	165	1 647	10.0	276	11.2	1 852	18 479	1924
1923	282	5 229	18.5	268	18.6	5 258	97 508	1923
1922	275	4 762	17.3	260	20.4	5 606	97 084	1922
1921	126	1 577	12.5	252	30.2	3 796	47 608	1921
1920	195	3 120	16.0	244	59.9	11 672	186 845	1920
1919	152	4 106	27.0	238	16.4	2 494	67 282	1919
1918	52	290	5.6	197	3.0	158	882	1918
1917	463	4 126	8.9	197	245.6	209 389	1 013 547	1917
1916								1916
1915								1915
1914	270	10 169	37.7	192	19.3	5 198	195 928	1914
1913	123	1 063	8.6	190	36.9	4 541	39 179	1913
1912	346	8 972	25.9	188	31.4	10 894	282 095	1912
1911	155	5 697	36.8	185	27.5	4 267	156 841	1911
1910	138	3 166	22.9	183	29.5	4 079	93 522	1910
1909	134	4 940	36.9	180	28.3	3 782	139 731	1909
1908	146	3 406	23.3	178	72.0	10 529	245 140	1908
1907	209	3 386	16.2	175	100.4	20 948	339 769	1907
1906	314							1906
1905	106							1905
1904	198							1904
1903	75							1903
1902	65							1902
1901	65							1901
1900	157							1900
1899	112							1899
1898	114							1898
1897	188							1897
1896	160							1896
1895								1895
1894								1894
1893	37							1893
1892								1892
1891	247							1891
1890	200							1890

y) From 1945 to 1970 excluding persons indirectly involved, but including man-days lost indirectly.
z) Up to 1906 size calculated by number of disputes for which data on participants are available.

L a b o u r   D i s p u t e s [a)]

Year	Labour disputes			Persons involved in labour disputes				Man-days lost in labour disputes				Year
	Total	Strikes	Lock-outs	Total	Strikes	Lock-outs	Indirectly	Total	Strikes	Lock-outs	Indirectly	
1975	3 888			1 827 142				3 868 926				1975
1974	3 381			1 563 540				3 379 977				1974
1973	3 731			2 245 973				3 914 598				1973
1972	3 464			2 721 348				3 755 343				1972
1971	4 358			3 234 500				4 387 781				1971
1970	3 319			1 159 619				1 742 175				1970
1969 [b)]	2 480			1 433 600				2 223 568				1969
1968												1968
1967	1 675			2 823 619				4 203 509				1967
1966	1 711			3 341 003				2 523 488				1966
1965	1 674			1 237 071				979 861				1965
1964	2 281			1 047 300				2 496 800				1964
1963	2 382			1 147 800				5 991 500				1963
1962	1 884			833 500				1 901 500				1962
1961	1 963			1 269 500				2 600 600				1961
1960	1 494			839 000				1 070 000				1960
1959	1 512			581 000				1 938 400				1959
1958	954			858 000				1 137 700				1958
1957	2 623			2 161 000				4 121 300				1957
1956	2 440			666 000				1 422 500				1956
1955	2 672			792 000				3 078 700				1955
1954	1 479			1 269 000				1 440 100				1954
1953	1 761			1 783 700				9 722 100				1953
1952	1 749			1 155 200				1 752 600				1952
1951	2 514			1 754 000				3 294 000				1951
1950	2 585			1 527 293				11 710 100				1950
1949	1 413			4 329 959				7 229 300				1949
1948	1 374			6 561 176				11 918 900				1948
1947	3 598							12 918 900 [c)]				1947
1946	523							374 000				1946
1938		1 220			1 333 000							1938
1937		2 616			323 800							1937
1936		16 907			2 422 800							1936
1935	384	376	8	110 332	108 884	1 448		1 182 159	1 182 159			1935
1934	390	385	5	100 934	100 584	350		2 393 463	2 393 463			1934
1933	346	343	3	109 108	87 091	22 017		1 923 070	1 199 334	723 736		1933
1932	362	362		71 561	71 561			2 244 281	2 244 281			1932
1931	288	286	2	54 250	48 275	5 975		1 059 939	949 564	110 375		1931
1930	1 097	1 093	4	584 579	581 927	2 652		7 398 253	7 209 343	188 910		1930
1929	1 217	1 213	4	241 040	239 878	1 162		2 772 266	2 764 606	7 660		1929
1928	823	816	7	210 488	204 116	6 372		6 388 225	6 376 675	11 550		1928
1927	405	396	9	112 648	110 458	2 190		1 076 398	1 046 019	30 379		1927
1926	1 678	1 660	18	366 142	349 309	16 833		4 715 572	4 072 163	643 409		1926

Labour Disputes

Year	Indicators of average labour dispute			Total non-agr. wage earners in 1,000s	Indicators per 100,000 non-agricultural wage earners			Year
	Size	Man-days lost	Duration		Labour disputes	Persons involved	Man-days lost	
1975	470	995	2.1	16 313	23.8	11 201	23 717	1975
1974	462	1 000	2.2	16 136	21.0	9 690	20 947	1974
1973	602	1 049	1.7	16 021	23.3	14 019	24 434	1973
1972	786	1 084	1.4	15 839	21.9	17 181	23 709	1972
1971	742	1 007	1.4	15 651	27.8	20 667	28 036	1971
1970	349	525	1.5	15 455	21.5	7 503	11 273	1970
1969	578	897	1.6	15 268	16.2	9 389	14 563	1969
1968								1968
1967	1 686	2 510	1.5	14 783	11.3	19 101	28 435	1967
1966	1 953	1 475	0.8	14 464	11.8	23 098	17 446	1966
1965	739	585	0.8	14 142	11.8	8 747	6 929	1965
1964	459	1 095	2.4	13 840	16.5	7 567	18 041	1964
1963	482	2 515	5.2	13 480	17.7	8 515	44 447	1963
1962	442	1 009	2.3	13 044	14.4	6 390	14 577	1962
1961	647	1 325	2.0	12 700	15.5	9 996	20 478	1961
1960	562	716	1.3	12 453	12.0	6 738	8 593	1960
1959	384	1 282	3.3	12 214	12.4	4 757	15 871	1959
1958	899	1 193	1.3	11 970	8.0	7 168	9 505	1958
1957	824	1 571	1.9	11 716	22.4	18 445	35 177	1957
1956	273	583	2.1	11 462	21.3	5 810	12 410	1956
1955	296	1 152	3.9	11 222	23.8	7 057	27 434	1955
1954	858	974	1.1	10 991	13.5	11 546	13 103	1954
1953	1 013	5 521	5.5	10 880	16.2	16 394	89 355	1953
1952	660	1 002	1.5	10 767	16.2	10 729	16 278	1952
1951	698	1 310	1.9	10 643	23.6	16 481	30 951	1951
1950	591	4 530	7.7	10 503	24.6	14 542	111 495	1950
1949	3 064	5 116	1.7	10 350	13.7	41 835	69 847	1949
1948	4 775	8 675	1.8	10 185	13.5	64 419	117 022	1948
1947		3 591		9 910	36.3		130 365	1947
1946		715		9 814	5.3		3 811	1946
1938	1 093			8 488	14.4	15 705		1938
1937	124			8 716	30.4	3 715		1937
1936	143			8 949	188.9	27 074		1936
1935	287	3 079	10.7	9 197	4.2	1 200	12 853	1935
1934	259	6 137	23.7	9 445	4.1	1 069	25 342	1934
1933	315	5 558	17.6	9 679	3.6	1 127	19 868	1933
1932	198	6 200	31.4	9 923	3.6	721	22 616	1932
1931	188	3 680	19.5	10 178	2.8	533	10 414	1931
1930	533	6 744	12.7	10 087	10.9	5 796	73 348	1930
1929	198	2 278	11.5	9 964	12.2	2 419	27 823	1929
1928	256	7 762	30.3	9 890	8.3	2 128	64 594	1928
1927	278	2 658	9.6	9 832	4.1	1 146	10 948	1927
1926	218	2 810	12.9	9 784	17.1	3 742	48 195	1926

France

Labour Disputes [a]

Year	Labour disputes			Persons involved in labour disputes				Man-days lost in labour disputes				Year
	Total	Strikes	Lock-outs	Total	Strikes	Lock-outs	Indirectly	Total	Strikes	Lock-outs	Indirectly	
1925	936	931	5	250 305	249 198	1 107		2 054 118	2 046 563	7 555		1925
1924	1 090	1 083	7	279 633	274 865	4 768		3 945 803	3 863 182	82 621		1924
1923	1 123	1 114	9	372 870	365 868	7 002		5 680 119	5 488 507	191 612		1923
1922	704	687	17	307 056	300 583	6 473		3 363 992	3 196 419	167 573		1922
1921	576	570	6	453 564	451 854	1 710		8 082 388	8 044 742	37 646		1921
1920	1 915	1 902	13	1 479 801	1 462 133	17 668		24 563 527	24 261 132	302 395		1920
1919	2 138	2 111	27	1 285 690	1 221 233	64 457		16 507 391	15 857 071	650 320		1919
1918	501	499	2	176 357	176 187	170		980 314	979 634	680		1918
1917		696			293 810			1 481 621				1917
1916		315			41 409			235 907				1916
1915		98			9 344			44 344				1915
1914	674	672	2	178 662	160 566	536	17 560	1 892 091	1 892 073	18		1914
1913	1 081	1 073	8	242 994	220 448	3 039	19 507	2 223 842	2 223 781	61		1913
1912	1 120	1 116	4	284 880	267 627	603	16 650	2 318 576	2 318 459	117		1912
1911	1 474	1 471	3	252 676	230 646	149	21 881	4 096 418	4 096 393	25		1911
1910	1 511	1 502	9	318 526	281 425	9 474	27 627	4 830 193	4 830 044	149		1910
1909	1 036	1 025	11	182 699	167 492	897	14 310	3 560 003	3 559 880	123		1909
1908	1 104	1 073	31	133 444	99 042	25 206	9 196	1 721 505	1 720 743	762		1908
1907	1 279	1 275	4	228 820	197 961	175	30 684	3 562 254	3 562 220	34		1907
1906	1 314	1 309	5	468 135	438 466	364	29 305	9 438 778	9 438 594	184		1906
1905	835	830	5	196 398	177 666	586	18 146	2 746 976	2 746 684	292		1905
1904	1 028	1 026	2	309 210	271 097	170	37 943	3 934 905	3 934 884	21		1904
1903	571	567	4	135 225	123 151	806	11 268	2 441 960	2 441 944	16		1903
1902	512	512		222 165	212 704		9 461	4 675 081	4 675 081			1902
1901	523	523		121 561	111 414		10 147	1 862 050	1 862 050			1901
1900	903	902	1	249 526	222 714	55	26 757	3 760 592	3 760 577	15		1900
1899	749	739	10	213 591	176 772	1 243	35 576	3 550 796	3 550 734	62		1899
1898	368	368		82 065	82 065			1 216 306	1 216 306			1898
1897	357	356	1	69 275	68 875	400		780 947	780 944	3		1897
1896	480	476	4	50 020	49 851	169		644 288	644 168	120		1896
1895	407	405	2	46 089	45 801	288		617 484	617 469	15		1895
1894		391			54 576			1 062 480				1894
1893		634			170 123			3 174 900				1893
1892		261			47 903			917 600				1892
1891		267			108 944			1 717 200				1891
1890		313			118 929			1 340 000				1890
1889		199			89 100							1889
1888		188			51 500							1888
1887		194			38 100							1887
1886		195			35 500							1886

710

Labour Disputes [y)]

Year	Indicators of average labour dispute			Total non-agr. wage earners in 1,000s [z)]	Indicators per 100,000 non-agricultural wage earners			Year
	Size	Man-days lost	Duration		Labour disputes	Persons involved	Man-days lost	
1925	267	2 195	8.2	9 593	9.8	2 609	21 413	1925
1924	257	3 620	14.1	9 389	11.6	2 978	42 025	1924
1923	332	5 058	15.2	9 153	12.3	4 074	62 059	1923
1922	436	4 778	11.0	8 908	7.9	3 447	37 764	1922
1921	787	14 032	17.8	8 724	6.6	5 199	92 647	1921
1920	773	12 827	16.6	8 569	22.3	17 269	286 646	1920
1919	601	7 721	12.8	8 396	25.5	15 313	196 609	1919
1918	352	1 957	5.6	7 527	6.7	2 343	13 024	1918
1917	422	2 129	5.0	7 673	9.1	3 829	19 310	1917
1916	131	749	5.7	7 789	4.0	532	3 029	1916
1915	95	452	4.7	7 906	1.2	118	561	1915
1914	265	2 807	10.6	8 100	8.3	2 206	23 358	1914
1913	225	2 057	9.2	7 691	14.1	3 159	28 915	1913
1912	254	2 070	8.1	7 637	14.7	3 730	30 358	1912
1911	171	2 779	16.2	7 593	19.4	3 328	53 947	1911
1910	211	3 197	15.2	7 544	20.0	4 222	64 030	1910
1909	176	3 436	19.5	7 488	13.8	2 440	47 542	1909
1908	121	1 559	12.9	7 442	14.8	1 793	23 132	1908
1907	179	2 785	15.6	7 389	17.3	3 097	48 212	1907
1906	356	7 183	20.2	7 354	17.9	6 366	128 350	1906
1905	235	3 290	14.0	7 313	11.4	2 686	37 565	1905
1904	301	3 828	12.7	7 275	14.1	4 250	54 090	1904
1903	237	4 277	18.1	7 229	7.9	1 870	33 778	1903
1902	434	9 131	21.0	7 184	7.1	3 092	65 075	1902
1901	232	3 560	15.3	7 139	7.3	1 703	26 083	1901
1900	276	4 165	15.1	7 077	12.8	3 526	53 134	1900
1899	285	4 741	16.6	7 015	10.7	3 045	50 621	1899
1898	223	3 305	14.8	6 948	5.3	1 181	17 505	1898
1897	194	2 188	11.3	6 873	5.2	1 008	11 362	1897
1896	104	1 342	12.9	6 793	7.1	736	9 484	1896
1895	113	1 517	13.4	6 996	5.8	659	8 826	1895
1894	140	2 717	19.5	7 184	5.4	760	14 789	1894
1893	268	5 008	18.7	7 347	8.6	2 315	43 211	1893
1892	184	3 516	19.2	7 490	3.5	640	12 250	1892
1891	408	6 431	15.8	7 612	3.5	1 431	22 561	1891
1890	380	4 281	11.3	7 645	4.1	1 556	17 527	1890
1889	448			7 671	2.6	1 162		1889
1888	274			7 681	2.4	670		1888
1887	196			7 707	2.5	495		1887
1886	181			7 722	2.5	457		1886

France

Labour Disputes [a]

Year	Labour disputes			Persons involved in labour disputes				Man-days lost in labour disputes				Year
	Total	Strikes	Lock-outs	Total	Strikes	Lock-outs	Indirectly	Total	Strikes	Lock-outs	Indirectly	
1885	123			20 800								1885
1884	112			33 900								1884
1883	181			42 000								1883
1882	271			65 500								1882
1881	209			68 000								1881
1880	190			110 400								1880
1879	88			54 400								1879
1878	73			38 500								1878
1877	55			12 900								1877
1876	102			21 200								1876
1875	101			16 600								1875
1874	58			7 800								1874
1873	44			4 900								1873
1872	151			21 100								1872
1871	52			14 100								1871
1870	116			88 200								1870
1869	72			40 600								1869
1868	58			20 300								1868
1867	76			32 100								1867
1866	52			14 000								1866
1865	58			27 600								1865

a) Including Algeria from 1890 to 1962, and Alsace-Lorraine from 1919; data up to 1889 drawn from Edward Shorter and Charles Tilly, Strikes in France. Cambridge, Cambridge University Press, 1974.

b) No data collected.

c) Including ca. 1,000,000 man-days lost in a general strike.

France

Labour Disputes [y]

Year	Indicators of average labour dispute			Total non-agr. wage earners in 1,000s [z]	Indicators per 100,000 non-agricultural wage earners			Year
	Size	Man-days lost	Duration		Labour disputes	Persons involved	Man-days lost	
1885	169			7 738	1.6	269		1885
1884	303			7 758	1.4	437		1884
1883	232			7 767	2.3	541		1883
1882	242			7 780	3.5	842		1882
1881	325			7 791	2.7	873		1881
1880	581			7 762	2.4	1 422		1880
1879	618			7 735	1.1	703		1879
1878	527			7 706	0.9	500		1878
1877	235			7 669	0.7	168		1877
1876	208			7 634	1.3	278		1876
1875	164			7 599	1.3	218		1875
1874	134			7 563	0.8	103		1874
1873	111			7 532	0.6	65		1873
1872	140			7 491	2.0	282		1872
1871	271			7 501	0.7	188		1871
1870	760			7 967	1.5	1 107		1870
1869	564			7 957	0.9	510		1869
1868	350			7 945	0.7	256		1868
1867	422			7 924	1.0	405		1867
1866	269			7 893	0.7	177		1866
1865	476			7 880	0.7	350		1865

y) Only strikes up to 1894, from 1915 to 1917, and from 1936 to 1938.

z) Share of labour force was held constant at 1914 level for 1915 to 1918, and at 1881 level for years prior to 1881.

Labour Disputes [a]

Year	Labour disputes			Persons involved in labour disputes				Man-days lost in labour disputes				Year
	Total	Strikes	Lock-outs	Total	Strikes	Lock-outs	Indirectly	Total	Strikes	Lock-outs	Indirectly	
1975				35 814				68 680				1975
1974				250 352				1 051 290				1974
1973				185 010				563 051				1973
1972				22 908				66 045				1972
1971				536 303				4 483 740				1971
1970				184 269				93 203				1970
1969				89 571				249 184				1969
1968	61			57 151				47 480				1968
1967	68			99 641				489 601				1967
1966	28			304 425				36 688				1966
1965	20			7 593				65 427				1965
1964	19			13 726				20 094				1964
1963	19			316 796				1 850 245				1963
1962	34			83 045				457 262				1962
1961	56			25 656				67 875				1961
1960	27			18 551				38 905				1960
1959	31			23 510				65 233				1959
1958	39			207 059				782 929				1958
1957	39			47 487				1 075 474				1957
1956	32			53 020				1 579 966				1956
1955	57			619 391				878 444				1955
1954	44			113 773				1 594 251				1954
1953	41			51 235				1 564 404				1953
1952	56			265 995				517 630				1952
1951	99			178 128				1 652 081				1951
1950	84			247 245				407 703				1950
1949	72			194 843				643 905				1949

a) Up to 1968 drawn from a data collection based on a re-analysis of archive-material in the Federal Statistical Office. These figures are by and large one third higher than the official data, since the official definition excluded labour disputes with less than 100 participants or less than 100 aggregate man-days lost. From 1969 data drawn from official statistics; number of disputes not available.

Labour Disputes

Year	Indicators of average labour dispute			Total non-agr. wage earners in 1,000s	Indicators per 100,000 non-agricultural wage earners			Year
	Size	Man-days lost	Duration		Labour disputes	Persons involved	Man-days lost	
1975			1.9	22 433		160	306	1975
1974			4.2	22 510		1 112	4 670	1974
1973			3.0	22 473		823	2 505	1973
1972			2.9	22 351		102	295	1972
1971			8.4	22 201		2 416	20 196	1971
1970			0.5	21 946		840	425	1970
1969			2.8	21 716		412	1 147	1969
1968	937	778	0.8	21 489	0.3	266	221	1968
1967	1 465	7 200	4.9	21 386	0.3	466	2 289	1967
1966	10 872	1 310	0.1	21 307	0.1	1 429	172	1966
1965	380	3 271	8.6	21 084	0.1	36	310	1965
1964	722	1 058	1.5	20 815	0.1	66	97	1964
1963	16 673	97 381	5.8	20 565	0.1	1 540	8 997	1963
1962	2 443	13 449	5.5	20 327	0.2	409	2 250	1962
1961	458	1 212	2.6	20 045	0.3	128	339	1961
1960	687	1 441	2.1	19 372	0.1	96	201	1960
1959	758	2 104	2.8	18 777	0.2	125	347	1959
1958	5 309	20 075	3.8	18 185	0.2	1 139	4 305	1958
1957	1 218	27 576	22.6	17 587	0.2	270	6 115	1957
1956	1 657	49 374	29.8	16 998	0.2	312	9 295	1956
1955	10 867	15 411	1.4	16 429	0.3	3 770	5 347	1955
1954	2 586	36 233	14.0	15 910	0.3	715	10 021	1954
1953	1 250	38 156	30.5	15 392	0.3	333	10 164	1953
1952	4 750	9 243	1.9	14 897	0.4	1 786	3 475	1952
1951	1 799	16 688	9.3	14 457	0.7	1 232	11 428	1951
1950	2 943	4 854	1.6	14 018	0.6	1 764	2 908	1950
1949	2 706	8 943	3.3	13 416	0.5	1 452	4 800	1949

Germany

Labour Disputes

Year	Labour disputes			Persons involved in labour disputes				Man-days lost in labour disputes[a]				Year
	Total	Strikes	Lock-outs	Total	Strikes	Lock-outs	Indirectly	Total	Strikes	Lock-outs	Indirectly	
1933	69	61	4	10 238	5 176	4 810	252	95 608	69 939	25 669		1933
1932	680	665	17	136 969	132 136	1 796	3 016	1 138 687	1 126 419	10 675		1932
1931	564	493	41	178 223	131 218	41 505	5 500	2 001 978	1 572 030	429 946		1931
1930	366	345	29	224 983	197 459	16 472	11 052	3 935 977	3 602 022	333 955		1930
1929	441	431	19	234 543	140 459	83 565	10 665	4 489 870	1 852 370	2 637 500		1929
1928	763	691	72	780 396	272 382	451 033	56 981	20 288 211	8 519 713	11 768 498		1928
1927	871	759	112	503 217	224 519	269 161	9 537	6 043 698	2 945 815	3 097 883		1927
1926[b]	383	339	44	104 711	55 172	44 055	5 511	1 325 309	869 297	456 012		1926
1925	1 766	1 541	225	777 897	492 729	265 342	19 826	17 113 886	11 267 943	5 845 943		1925
1924	2 012	1 614	398	1 663 521	675 122	977 195	29 204	36 360 134	13 584 360	22 775 774		1924
1923	2 209	2 035	174	2 145 059	1 977 169	120 753	47 137	15 171 773	13 829 996	1 341 777		1923
1922	5 361	4 924	437	2 404 493	2 101 926	219 671	82 896	29 240 740	24 889 500	4 351 240		1922
1921	5 223	4 861	362	2 193 047	1 840 441	201 931	150 675	30 067 894	26 789 411	3 278 483		1921
1920	8 800	8 686	114	8 490 835	8 232 900	91 097	166 838	54 206 962	52 837 409	1 369 553		1920
1919	4 770	4 932	38	4 947 199	4 673 835	32 434	240 930	48 067 180	47 447 156	620 024		1919
1918	773	772	1	1 316 897	1 304 236	12	12 649	5 219 290	5 217 982	1 308		1918
1917	562	561	1	668 032	650 658	803	16 571	1 862 302	1 859 893	2 409		1917
1916	240	240	0	128 881	124 188	0	4 693	245 404	245 404	0		1916
1915	141	137	4	15 238	11 639	1 227	2 372	45 511	41 838	3 673		1915
1914	1 223	1 115	108	98 339	58 682	36 458	3 199	2 843 895	1 714 790	1 129 105		1914
1913	2 464	2 127	337	323 394	254 206	56 842	12 346	11 761 754	8 819 351	2 942 403		1913
1912	2 834	2 510	324	493 749	406 314	74 780	12 655	10 723 782	7 711 764	3 012 018		1912
1911	2 798	2 566	232	385 216	217 809	138 354	29 053	11 466 727	7 731 334	3 735 393		1911
1910	3 228	2 133	1 115	390 706	155 680	214 129	20 897	17 848 440	4 582 036	13 266 404		1910
1909	1 652	1 537	115	130 883	96 925	22 924	11 034	4 151 766	2 812 876	1 338 890		1909
1908	1 524	1 347	177	119 781	68 392	43 718	7 671	3 665 607	2 258 944	1 406 663		1908
1907	2 512	2 266	246	286 016	192 430	81 167	12 419	9 016 856	6 204 558	2 812 298		1907
1906	3 626	3 328	298	376 325	272 218	77 109	27 088	11 567 618	8 176 337	3 391 281		1906
1905	2 657	2 403	254	542 564	408 145	118 665	15 754	18 984 553	14 536 223	4 448 320		1905
1904	1 990	1 870	120	145 480	113 480	23 760	8 240	5 285 125	3 622 998	1 662 127		1904
1903	1 444	1 374	70	135 522	85 603	35 273	14 646	4 158 519	2 815 491	1 343 028		1903
1902	1 106	1 060	46	70 696	53 912	10 305	6 479	1 950 847	1 326 833	624 014		1902
1901	1 091	1 056	35	68 191	55 262	5 414	7 515	2 426 952	2 311 573	115 379		1901
1900	1 468	1 433	35	141 121	122 803	9 085	9 233	3 711 994	3 188 654	523 340		1900
1899	1 311	1 288	23	116 486	99 338	5 298	11 850	3 381 319	3 265 881	115 438		1899
1898[c]		705		72 767								1898
1897		686		63 084								1897
1896		1 082		108 495								1896
1895		846		30 825								1895
1894		305		20 591								1894
1893		242		50 339								1893
1892		323		60 798								1892
1891		326		49 913								1891
1890		630		133 002								1890
1889		1 272		443 835								1889

Labour Disputes[y)]

Year	Indicators of average labour dispute			Total non-agr. wage earners in 1,000s[z)]	Indicators per 100,000 non-agricultural wage earners			Year
	Size	Man-days lost	Duration		Labour disputes	Persons involved	Man-days lost	
1933	148	1 386	9.3	18 918	0.4	54	505	1933
1932	201	1 670	8.3	18 894	3.6	725	6 027	1932
1931	316	3 550	11.2	18 878	3.0	944	10 605	1931
1930	602	10 524	17.5	18 844	2.0	1 194	20 888	1930
1929	522	9 977	19.1	18 809	2.4	1 248	23 871	1929
1928	1 023	26 590	26.0	18 772	4.1	4 157	108 075	1928
1927	578	6 939	12.0	18 727	4.7	2 687	32 272	1927
1926	273	3 460	12.7	18 675	2.1	561	7 097	1926
1925	440	9 691	22.0	18 602	9.5	4 182	92 001	1925
1924	836	18 072	21.6	18 496	10.9	9 091	196 583	1924
1923	971	6 868	7.1	18 414	12.0	11 649	82 393	1923
1922	449	5 454	12.2	18 326	29.3	13 121	159 558	1922
1921	420	5 757	13.7	18 741	27.9	11 702	160 435	1921
1920	965	6 160	6.4	18 567	47.4	45 732	291 960	1920
1919	995	9 671	9.7	18 927	26.3	26 139	253 964	1919
1918	1 704	6 752	4.0	17 433	4.4	7 554	29 939	1918
1917	1 189	3 314	2.8	17 579	3.2	3 800	10 594	1917
1916	537	1 023	1.9	17 669	1.4	729	1 389	1916
1915	108	323	3.0	17 713	0.8	86	257	1915
1914	80	2 325	28.9	17 689	6.9	556	16 077	1914
1913	131	4 773	36.4	17 275	14.3	1 872	68 084	1913
1912	174	3 784	21.7	16 863	16.8	2 928	63 593	1912
1911	138	4 098	29.8	16 468	17.0	2 339	69 630	1911
1910	120	5 495	45.7	16 078	20.2	2 430	111 012	1910
1909	79	2 513	31.7	15 679	10.5	835	26 480	1909
1908	79	2 405	30.6	15 285	10.0	784	23 982	1908
1907	114	3 590	31.5	14 898	16.9	1 920	60 524	1907
1906	104	3 190	30.7	14 512	25.0	2 594	79 709	1906
1905	204	7 145	35.0	14 138	18.8	3 838	134 285	1905
1904	73	2 656	36.3	13 769	14.5	1 057	38 385	1904
1903	94	2 880	30.7	13 404	10.8	1 011	31 024	1903
1902	64	1 764	27.6	13 042	8.5	542	14 958	1902
1901	63	2 225	35.6	12 679	8.6	538	19 142	1901
1900	96	2 529	26.3	12 336	11.9	1 144	30 091	1900
1899	89	2 579	29.0	12 005	10.9	970	28 166	1899
1898	103							1898
1897	92							1897
1896	100							1896
1895	36							1895
1894	68							1894
1893	208							1893
1892	188							1892
1891	153							1891
1890	211							1890
1889	349							1889

Labour Disputes [d)]

Year	Labour disputes			Persons involved in labour disputes				Man-days lost in labour disputes				Year
	Total	Strikes	Lock-outs	Total	Strikes	Lock-outs	Indirectly	Total	Strikes	Lock-outs	Indirectly	
1880	9			1 750								1880
1879	3											1879
1878	12			240								1878
1877	6			500								1877
1876	41			4 550								1876
1875	43			929								1875
1874	103			3 025								1874
1873	224			12 873								1873
1872	218			57 832								1872
1871	186			67 409								1871
1870	79			43 719								1870
1869	106			28 957								1869
1868	14			2 873								1868
1867	14			4 040								1867
1866	8			25								1866
1865	31			2 830								1865
1864	23			1 345								1864

a) Including man-days lost indirectly in strikes and lock-outs.
b) Including political strikes from 1919 to 1925.
c) Up to 1898 data for Prussia and Bavaria only; from two statistical sources differing in method.
d) Data drawn from private data collection by Walter Steglich, based on newspapers.

Labour Disputes[y]

Year	Indicators of average labour dispute			Total non-agr. wage earners in 1,000s [z]	Indicators per 100,000 non-agricultural wage earners			Year
	Size	Man-days lost	Duration		Labour disputes	Persons involved	Man-days lost	
1880	194			7 803	0.1	22		1880
1879				7 725	0.0			1879
1878	20			7 636	0.2	3		1878
1877	83			7 546	0.1	7		1877
1876	111			7 451	0.6	61		1876
1875	22			7 356	0.6	13		1875
1874	29			7 265	1.4	42		1874
1873	57			7 187	3.1	179		1873
1872	265			7 127	3.1	811		1872
1871	362			7 094	2.6	950		1871
1870	553			7 061	1.1	619		1870
1869	273			7 007	1.5	413		1869
1868	205			6 960	0.2	41		1868
1867	289			6 927	0.2	58		1867
1866	3			6 881	0.1	0		1866
1865	91			6 843	0.5	41		1865
1864	58			6 781	0.3	20		1864

y) Up to 1898 strikes only.

z) Share of labour force was held constant at 1914 level for 1915 to 1918, and at 1882 level for the years prior to 1882.

Ireland

Labour Disputes [a]

Year	Labour disputes [b]			Persons involved in labour disputes [c]				Man-days lost in labour disputes [c]				Year
	Total	Strikes	Lock-outs	Total	Strikes	Lock-outs	Indirectly	Total	Strikes	Lock-outs	Indirectly	
1975	151			29 124				295 716				1975
1974	219			43 459				551 833				1974
1973	182			31 761				206 725				1973
1972	181			22 274				206 955				1972
1971				43 783				273 770				1971
1970	134			28 752				1 007 714				1970
1969	134			61 760				935 900				1969
1968	126			38 880				406 686				1968
1967	79			20 925				182 645				1967
1966	112			52 238				783 635				1966
1965	89			39 745				556 475				1965
1964	87			25 245				545 384				1964
1963	70			16 607				233 617				1963
1962	60			9 017				104 024				1962
1961	96			27 437				377 264				1961
1960	49			5 865				80 349				1960
1959	58			9 305				124 479				1959
1958	51			12 043				126 143				1958
1957	45			4 059				92 040				1957
1956	67			4 420				48 069				1956
1955	96			11 241				236 324				1955
1954	81			8 294				66 734				1954
1953	75			7 244				82 046				1953
1952	82			14 851				529 089				1952
1951	138			24 777				545 133				1951
1950	154			18 559				216 505				1950
1949	153			9 837				273 151				1949
1948	147			16 567				258 166				1948
1947	194			22 253				449 438				1947
1946	105			10 896				150 108				1946
1945	87			8 785				243 932				1945
1944	84			4 387				38 308				1944
1943	81			5 921				61 809				1943
1942	69			5 132				115 039				1942
1941	71			4 895				77 133				1941
1940	89			7 715				152 076				1940
1939	99			6 697				106 476				1939
1938	137			13 726				208 784				1938
1937	145			26 734				1 754 949				1937
1936	107			9 443				185 623				1936
1935	99			9 513				288 077				1935
1934	99			9 288				180 080				1934
1933	88			9 059				200 126				1933
1932	70			4 222				42 152				1932
1931	60			5 431				310 199				1931
1930	83			3 410				77 417				1930
1929	53			4 533				109 397				1929

Labour Disputes

Year	Indicators of average labour dispute			Total non-agr. wage earners in 1,000s y)	Indicators per 100,000 non-agricultural wage earners			Year
	Size	Man-days lost	Duration		Labour disputes	Persons involved	Man-days lost	
1975	193	1 958	10.2	753	20.1	3 867	39 268	1975
1974	198	2 520	12.7	740	29.6	5 876	74 616	1974
1973	175	1 136	6.5	726	25.1	4 377	28 492	1973
1972	123	1 143	9.3	712	25.4	3 128	29 066	1972
1971	329	2 058	6.3	699	19.0	6 266	39 182	1971
1970	215	7 520	35.0	687	19.5	4 184	146 644	1970
1969	461	6 984	15.2	677	19.8	9 129	138 333	1969
1968	309	3 228	10.5	668	18.9	5 817	60 843	1968
1967	265	2 312	8.7	660	12.0	3 169	27 665	1967
1966	466	6 997	15.0	651	17.2	8 021	120 327	1966
1965	447	6 253	14.0	640	13.9	6 211	86 958	1965
1964	290	6 269	21.6	628	13.9	4 022	86 882	1964
1963	230	3 337	14.5	615	11.4	2 612	37 979	1963
1962	150	1 734	11.5	601	10.0	1 500	17 301	1962
1961	286	3 930	13.8	589	16.3	4 657	64 032	1961
1960	120	1 640	13.7	593	8.3	990	13 561	1960
1959	160	2 146	13.4	596	9.7	1 562	20 894	1959
1958	236	2 473	10.5	597	8.5	2 016	21 114	1958
1957	90	2 045	22.7	604	7.4	672	15 232	1957
1956	66	717	10.9	607	11.0	728	7 919	1956
1955	117	2 462	21.0	612	15.7	1 838	38 632	1955
1954	102	824	8.0	616	13.2	1 347	10 838	1954
1953	97	1 094	11.3	617	12.2	1 174	13 295	1953
1952	181	6 452	35.6	618	13.3	2 405	85 669	1952
1951	180	3 950	22.0	619	22.3	4 004	88 097	1951
1950	121	1 406	11.7	606	25.4	3 063	35 734	1950
1949	64	1 785	27.8	594	25.8	1 657	46 020	1949
1948	113	1 756	15.6	579	25.4	2 859	44 558	1948
1947	115	2 317	20.2	562	34.5	3 958	79 940	1947
1946	104	1 430	13.8	544	19.3	2 003	27 598	1946
1945	101	2 804	27.8	539	16.1	1 630	45 264	1945
1944	52	456	8.7	533	15.7	823	7 182	1944
1943	73	763	10.4	530	15.3	1 118	11 671	1943
1942	74	1 667	22.4	529	13.1	971	21 767	1942
1941	69	1 086	15.8	530	13.4	924	14 564	1941
1940	87	1 709	19.7	519	17.1	1 486	29 288	1940
1939	68	1 076	15.9	511	19.4	1 311	20 843	1939
1938	100	1 524	15.2	507	27.0	2 706	41 167	1938
1937	184	12 103	65.6	505	28.7	5 296	347 643	1937
1936	88	1 735	19.7	504	21.2	1 874	36 847	1936
1935	96	2 910	30.3	500	19.8	1 904	57 661	1935
1934	94	1 819	19.4	495	20.0	1 877	36 396	1934
1933	103	2 274	22.1	488	18.0	1 855	40 969	1933
1932	60	602	10.0	482	14.5	877	8 753	1932
1931	91	5 170	57.1	474	12.7	1 145	65 408	1931
1930	41	933	22.7	469	17.7	728	16 521	1930
1929	86	2 064	24.1	466	11.4	974	23 501	1929

Ireland

Labour Disputes [a]

Year	Labour disputes [b]			Persons involved in labour disputes [c]				Man-days lost in labour disputes [c]				Year
	Total	Strikes	Lock-outs	Total	Strikes	Lock-outs	Indirectly	Total	Strikes	Lock-outs	Indirectly	
1928	57			2 190				54 202				1928
1927	53			2 312				64 020				1927
1926	57			3 455				85 345				1926
1925	86			6 855				293 792				1925
1924	104			16 403				301 705				1924
1923	131			20 635				1 208 734				1923

a) Excluding labour disputes lasting for less than one day or with less than ten man-days aggregate loss.

b) Labour disputes beginning in the given year; separate figures for strikes and lock-outs not available.

c) Data on participation and man-days lost refer to disputes in progress during the given year; up to 1963 man-days lost have been estimated.

L a b o u r   D i s p u t e s

Year	Indicators of average labour dispute			Total non-agr. wage earners in 1,000s	Indicators per 100,000 non-agricultural wage earners			Year
	Size	Man-days lost	Duration		Labour disputes	Persons involved	Man-days lost	
1928	42	1 042	24.7	462	11.3	474	11 734	1928
1927	44	1 208	27.7	459	11.5	503	13 939	1927
1926	61	1 497	24.7	457	12.5	756	18 685	1926
1925	80	3 416	42.9	454	18.9	1 509	64 682	1925
1924	158	2 901	18.4	453	23.0	3 625	66 670	1924
1923	158	9 227	58.6	449	29.2	4 594	269 098	1923
1922				446	20.9			1922

y) Share of labour force was interpolated between 1936 and 1946.

Italy

Labour Disputes

Year	Labour disputes [a]			Persons involved in labour disputes				Man-days lost in labour disputes [b]				Year
	Total	Strikes	Lock-outs	Total	Strikes	Lock-outs	Indirectly	Total	Strikes	Lock-outs	Indirectly	
1975	3 658			10 717 000				22 672 625				1975
1974	5 174			7 824 000				17 033 375				1974
1973	3 769			6 132 747				23 419 285				1973
1972	4 765			4 405 251				19 497 143				1972
1971	5 598			3 891 253				14 798 589				1971
1970	4 162			3 721 919				20 887 459				1970
1969	3 785			7 506 983				37 824 573				1969
1968	3 777			4 862 201				9 239 793				1968
1967	2 658			2 244 203				8 568 433				1967
1966	2 387			1 887 992				14 473 551				1966
1965	3 191			2 309 800				6 992 856				1965
1964	3 841			3 245 500				13 088 609				1964
1963	4 145			3 693 715				11 394 635				1963
1962	3 652			2 909 831				22 716 540				1962
1961	3 502			2 697 770				9 890 856				1961
1960	2 471			2 337 906				5 786 182				1960
1959	1 925			1 900 321				9 190 360				1959
1958	1 937			1 283 301				4 171 877				1958
1957	1 731			1 226 787				4 618 796				1957
1956	1 904			1 677 750				4 136 672				1956
1955	1 981			1 403 217				5 622 250				1955
1954	1 990			2 045 268				5 376 743				1954
1953	1 412			4 679 091				5 827 620				1953
1952	1 717			1 580 336				3 530 630				1952
1951	1 345			2 257 491				4 514 536				1951
1950	1 491			3 705 859				7 760 849				1950
1949	1 350			3 504 543				16 578 081				1949

a) Excluding political strikes; separate figures for strikes and lock-outs not available.
b) Man-days lost estimated by dividing reported man-hours lost by 8 hours, on the assumption of an average 8 hours-working day.

Italy

Labour Disputes

Year	Indicators of average labour dispute			Total non-agr. wage earners in 1,000s	Indicators per 100,000 non-agricultural wage earners			Year
	Size	Man-days lost	Duration		Labour disputes	Persons involved	Man-days lost	
1975	2 930	6 198	2.1	13 039	28.1	82 189	173 878	1975
1974	1 512	3 292	2.2	12 914	40.1	60 587	131 901	1974
1973	1 627	6 214	3.8	12 784	29.5	47 972	183 192	1973
1972	925	4 092	4.4	12 624	37.7	34 896	154 445	1972
1971	695	2 644	3.8	12 477	44.9	31 187	118 604	1971
1970	894	5 019	5.6	12 382	33.6	30 059	168 689	1970
1969	1 983	9 993	5.0	12 280	30.8	61 132	308 016	1969
1968	1 287	2 446	1.9	12 178	31.0	39 926	75 873	1968
1967	844	3 224	3.8	12 077	22.0	18 582	70 945	1967
1966	791	6 063	7.7	11 959	20.0	15 788	121 030	1966
1965	724	2 191	3.0	11 841	26.9	19 507	59 057	1965
1964	845	3 408	4.0	11 725	32.8	27 681	111 635	1964
1963	891	2 749	3.1	11 557	35.9	31 961	98 596	1963
1962	797	6 220	7.8	11 399	32.0	25 526	199 278	1962
1961	770	2 824	3.7	11 290	31.0	23 895	87 608	1961
1960	946	2 342	2.5	11 062	22.3	21 134	52 304	1960
1959	987	4 774	4.8	10 827	17.8	17 552	84 883	1959
1958	663	2 154	3.3	10 583	18.3	12 126	39 421	1958
1957	709	2 668	3.8	10 340	16.7	11 864	44 668	1957
1956	881	2 173	2.5	10 101	18.9	16 610	40 955	1956
1955	708	2 838	4.0	9 860	20.1	14 232	57 022	1955
1954	1 028	2 702	2.6	9 610	20.7	21 282	55 948	1954
1953	3 314	4 127	1.2	9 360	15.1	49 989	62 259	1953
1952	920	2 056	2.2	9 115	18.8	17 337	38 734	1952
1951	1 678	3 357	2.0	8 869	15.2	25 453	50 901	1951
1950	2 485	5 205	2.1	8 608	17.3	43 049	90 154	1950
1949	2 596	12 280	4.7	8 338	16.2	42 032	198 829	1949

Italy

Labour Disputes [a]

Year	Labour disputes			Persons involved in labour disputes [b]				Man-days lost in labour disputes [c]				Year
	Total	Strikes	Lock-outs	Total	Strikes	Lock-outs	Indirectly	Total	Strikes	Lock-outs	Indirectly	
1924	361	361	0	165 216	165 216							1924
1923	215	201	14	73 358	66 213	7 145		447 977	296 469	151 508		1923
1922	612	575	37	466 748	447 919	18 829		7 295 121	6 916 914	378 207		1922
1921	1 200	1 134	66	784 141	723 862	60 279		8 962 602	8 180 263	782 339		1921
1920	2 086	2 070	16	2 331 798	2 313 685	18 113		30 780 550	30 569 218	211 332		1920
1919	1 879	1 871	8	1 602 786	1 554 566	48 220		22 435 065	22 324 746	110 319		1919
1918	316	313	3	159 451	158 711	740		913 701	909 741	3 960		1918
1917	472	470	2	174 997	174 817	180		850 284	849 444	840		1917
1916	580	577	3	138 932	138 508	424		841 418	837 955	3 463		1916
1915	609	607	2	179 990	179 934	56		1 155 335	1 155 200	135		1915
1914	876	864	12	231 849	222 482	9 367		2 693 020	2 567 602	89 748	89 748	1914
1913	929	907	22	486 165	464 567	21 598		5 320 606	4 542 636	638 777	139 193	1913
1912	1 116	1 090	26	253 186	239 965	13 221		3 318 667	2 889 415	319 729	109 523	1912
1911	1 276	1 255	21	403 840	385 591	18 249		5 073 045	4 341 272	586 174	145 599	1911
1910	1 132	1 118	14	204 759	198 774	5 985		3 827 465	3 299 825	465 908	61 732	1910
1909	1 095	1 062	33	200 989	187 021	13 968		2 257 522	1 846 610	248 794	162 118	1909
1908	1 745	1 745	0	371 383	371 383	0		4 979 594	4 864 327	0	115 267	1908
1907	2 273	2 258	15	581 646	575 630	6 016		5 750 740	5 541 377	75 000	134 363	1907
1906	1 656	1 641	15	387 185	381 091	6 091		3 196 537	2 921 508	120 000	155 029	1906
1905	730	715	15	157 827	154 527	3 300		987 825	827 058	75 000	85 767	1905
1904	846	839	7	221 245	219 590	1 655		1 486 544	1 368 181	17 683	100 680	1904
1903	617	596	21	136 117	131 834	4 283		2 012 817	1 881 145	60 152	71 520	1903
1902	1 054	1 032	22	350 503	344 220	6 283		4 713 840	4 564 164	25 956	123 720	1902
1901	1 701	1 671	30	444 725	419 223	10 828	14 674	5 336 483	5 077 950	55 231	203 302	1901
1900	424	410	14	104 231	93 375	1 508	9 348	643 822	565 150	6 190	72 482	1900
1899	279	268	11	53 904	45 089	628	8 187	291 579	239 065	4 215	48 299	1899
1898	310	292	18	54 054	44 200	2 920	6 934	367 601	322 125	3 434	42 042	1898
1897	243	229	14	111 992	100 705	3 684	7 603	1 671 014	1 435 555	54 350	181 109	1897
1896	217	211	6	102 670	96 151	2 267	4 252	1 201 745	1 152 603	18 243	30 899	1896
1895	140	133	7	24 683	21 072	3 611		260 545	146 533	73 763	40 249	1895
1894	128	117	11	33 869	32 343	1 526		412 959	366 319	37 419	9 221	1894
1893	154	149	5	44 756	44 499	257		1 954 631	1 952 693	1 938		1893
1892	129	129	0	34 304	34 304	0		224 030	224 030	0		1892
1891	164	156	8	43 592	42 528	1 064		293 267	291 936	1 331		1891
1890	152	147	5	43 462	40 352	3 110		183 562	176 077	7 485		1890
1889	133	130	3	24 510	24 409	101		219 122	218 760	362		1889
1888	107	106	1	30 410	30 340	70		193 060	192 570	490		1888
1887	79	78	1	27 362	27 302	60		222 512	222 392	120		1887
1886	114	113	1	20 867	20 797	70		66 395	66 395			1886
1885	154	151	3	43 607	43 017	590		304 854	298 054	6 800		1885

L a b o u r   D i s p u t e s

Year	Indicators of average labour dispute			Total non-agr. wage earners in 1,000s y)	Indicators per 100,000 non-agricultural wage earners z)			Year
	Size	Man-days lost	Duration		Labour disputes	Persons involved	Man-days lost	
1924	458			6 311	5.7	2 618		1924
1923	341	2 084	6.1	6 222	3.4	1 177	7 191	1923
1922	763	11 920	15.6	6 127	9.6	7 207	113 661	1922
1921	653	7 469	11.4	5 900	18.8	11 947	145 005	1921
1920	1 118	14 756	13.2	5 687	33.4	22 614	292 060	1920
1919	853	11 940	14.0	5 618	29.7	19 537	338 153	1919
1918	505	2 891	5.7	5 372	5.7	2 956	16 947	1918
1917	371	1 801	4.9	5 435	8.2	3 106	15 309	1917
1916	240	1 451	6.1	5 456	9.5	2 274	13 580	1916
1915	296	1 897	6.4	5 424	10.0	2 437	17 623	1915
1914	265	3 074	11.6	5 339	14.9	3 418	41 421	1914
1913	523	5 727	10.9	5 255	15.8	7 732	87 863	1913
1912	227	2 974	13.1	5 207	18.1	3 022	46 042	1912
1911	316	3 976	12.6	5 142	21.9	5 272	62 411	1911
1910	181	3 381	18.7	5 066	20.4	3 532	68 791	1910
1909	184	2 062	11.2	4 988	19.3	3 096	38 630	1909
1908	213	2 854	13.4	4 915	29.7	4 027	46 270	1908
1907	256	2 530	9.9	4 844	39.1	6 762	68 924	1907
1906	234	1 930	8.3	4 774	27.5	5 659	53 297	1906
1905	216	1 353	6.3	4 704	15.5	3 355	21 001	1905
1904	262	1 757	6.7	4 631	18.3	4 778	32 103	1904
1903	221	3 262	14.8	4 560	12.5	2 492	36 645	1903
1902	333	4 472	13.4	4 491	18.5	4 538	59 874	1902
1901	261	3 137	12.0	4 419	24.3	5 024	54 413	1901
1900	246	1 518	6.2	4 453	8.9	2 060	12 841	1900
1899	193	1 045	5.4	4 487	6.0	1 159	6 332	1899
1898	174	1 186	6.8	4 518	6.1	1 008	6 303	1898
1897	461	6 877	14.9	4 546	5.1	1 933	29 677	1897
1896	473	5 538	11.7	4 571	4.7	2 244	26 288	1896
1895	176	1 861	10.6	4 602	2.9	498	5 215	1895
1894	265	3 226	12.2	4 631	2.6	629	7 988	1894
1893	291	12 692	43.7	4 655	2.9	695	5 076	1893
1892	266	1 737	6.5	4 680	2.5	658	4 635	1892
1891	266	1 788	6.7	4 705	3.0	761	5 513	1891
1890	286	1 208	4.2	4 730	3.0	878	3 702	1890
1889	184	1 648	8.9	4 750	2.7	493	4 553	1889
1888	284	1 804	6.3	4 768	2.1	609	4 021	1888
1887	346	2 817	8.1	4 789	1.5	524	4 568	1887
1886	183	582	3.2	4 811	2.0	354	1 180	1886
1885	283	1 980	7.0	4 831	1.9	719	5 198	1885

Italy

Labour Disputes

Year	Labour disputes			Persons involved in labour disputes				Man-days lost in labour disputes				Year
	Total	Strikes	Lock-outs	Total	Strikes	Lock-outs	Indirectly	Total	Strikes	Lock-outs	Indirectly	
1884	95	91	4	24 267	24 212	55		149 919	149 460	459		1884
1883	77	76	1	13 167	13 162	5		113 519	113 509	10		1883
1882	51	49	2	8 138	8 054	84		30 053	29 519	534		1882
1881	49	45	4	8 776	8 372	404		99 808	95 778	4 030		1881
1880	29	27	2	5 931	5 900	31		91 930	91 899	31		1880
1879	32	32	0	4 011	4 011	0		21 896	21 896	0		1879
1878	37	34	3	2 992	2 963	29		10 311	10 274	37		1878
1877	55	55										
1876		58										
1875		62										
1874		94										
1873		103										
1872		64										
1871		26										
1870		25										

a) Labour disputes prohibited after 1924; from 1881 including strikes in the agricultural sector which account for a large portion of the total strike activity.

b) Data on persons indirectly involved only collected from 1886 to 1901.

c) Data on man-days lost collected only from 1894 to 1914. Data on man-days lost in agricultural strikes not available for 1904 and 1905.

Italy

Labour Disputes

Year	Indicators of average labour dispute			Total non-agr. wage earners in 1,000s [y]	Indicators per 100,000 non-agricultural wage earners [z]			Year
	Size	Man-days lost	Duration		Labour disputes	Persons involved	Man-days lost	
1884	255	1 578	6.2	4 840	1.8	496	3 093	1884
1883	171	1 474	8.6	4 852	1.5	266	2 302	1883
1882	160	589	3.7	4 870	1.0	122	527	1882
1881	179	2 037	11.4	4 884	1.0	178	2 039	1881
1880	205	3 170	15.5	4 899	0.6	121	1 877	1880
1879	125	684	5.5	4 913	0.7	82	446	1879
1878	81	279	3.4	4 928	0.8	61	209	1878

y) Share of labour force was held constant at 1914 level for 1915 to 1918, and at 1881 level for the years prior to 1881.

z) Excluding agricultural strikes from 1881 to 1924.

Labour Disputes [a]

Year	Labour disputes			Persons involved in labour disputes				Man–days lost in labour disputes				Year
	Total	Strikes	Lock-outs	Total	Strikes	Lock-outs	Indirectly	Total	Strikes	Lock-outs	Indirectly	
1975	5			268				480				1975
1974	14			2 979				6 854				1974
1973	5			58 113				583 783				1973
1972	31			19 548				134 187				1972
1971	15			35 560				96 846				1971
1970	99			52 233				262 810				1970
1969	28			12 403				21 697				1969
1968	11			4 599	4 599			13 698				1968
1967	8			1 836	1 836			6 165				1967
1966	20			11 442	11 442			12 647				1966
1965	60			25 125	25 125			54 607				1965
1964	53			8 679	8 679			43 862				1964
1963	104			30 406	30 406		0	37 757				1963
1962	24			2 383	2 383		0	9 084				1962
1961	43			9 500	9 500		0	24 656				1961
1960	121			84 810	84 810		0	467 391				1960
1959	48			8 091	8 091		0	13 997				1959
1958	73			5 310	5 310		0	37 300				1958
1957	37			1 629	1 629		0	7 214				1957
1956	80			38 102	38 102		0	212 805				1956
1955	63			24 018	24 018		0	132 994				1955
1954	91			21 233	21 103		130	53 283				1954
1953	58			11 383	11 326		57	29 852				1953
1952	40			3 806	3 794		12	31 237				1952
1951	85			15 324	15 260		64	66 740				1951
1950	79			20 944	20 822		122	166 433				1950
1949	116			15 402	14 932		467	289 353				1949
1948	183			19 030	18 660		370	131 400				1948
1947	272			64 440	62 590		1 850	203 400				1947
1946	270			79 750	74 800		4 950	681 600				1946
1940	18			2 894	2 801		93	38 282				1940
1939	86			6 407	6 235		172	93 787				1939
1938	139	138	1	8 641	8 532	19	90	134 400	134 305	95		1938
1937	89	89	0	6 222	5 512	0	710	35 500	35 500	0		1937
1936	92	92	0	12 180	10 880	0	1 300	87 400	87 400	0		1936
1935	142	89	3	12 739	12 430	309		252 300	248 630	3 670		1935
1934	148	140	2	6 121	6 032	89		112 800	112 620	180		1934
1933	168	168	0	18 833	18 833	0	830	498 600	498 600	0		1933
1932	204	201	3	16 792	16 695	97		539 700	538 740	960		1932
1931	200	198	2	27 428	27 290	138		766 800	764 510	2 290		1931
1930	204	201	3	10 197	9 818	399		866 010	844 200	3 450	18 360	1930

Labour Disputes

Year	Indicators of average labour dispute			Total non-agr. wage earners in 1,000s	Indicators per 100,000 non-agricultural wage earners			Year
	Size	Man-days lost	Duration		Labour disputes	Persons involved	Man-days lost	
1975	54	96	1.8	3 872	0.1	7	12	1975
1974	213	490	2.3	3 832	0.4	78	179	1974
1973	11 623	116 757	10.0	3 796	0.1	1 531	15 381	1973
1972	631	4 329	6.9	3 758	0.8	520	3 571	1972
1971	2 371	6 456	2.7	3 714	0.4	957	2 608	1971
1970	528	2 655	5.0	3 664	2.7	1 425	7 172	1970
1969	443	775	1.7	3 614	0.8	343	600	1969
1968	418	1 245	3.0	3 566	0.3	129	384	1968
1967	230	771	3.4	3 522	0.2	52	175	1967
1966	572	632	1.1	3 479	0.6	329	364	1966
1965	419	910	2.2	3 428	1.8	733	1 593	1965
1964	164	828	5.1	3 376	1.6	257	1 299	1964
1963	292	363	1.2	3 326	3.1	914	1 135	1963
1962	99	379	3.8	3 276	0.7	73	277	1962
1961	221	573	2.6	3 225	1.3	295	765	1961
1960	701	3 863	5.5	3 178	3.8	2 669	14 709	1960
1959	169	292	1.7	3 122	1.5	259	448	1959
1958	73	511	7.0	3 059	2.4	174	1 219	1958
1957	44	195	4.4	2 997	1.2	54	241	1957
1956	476	2 660	5.6	2 941	2.7	1 296	7 237	1956
1955	381	2 111	5.5	2 884	2.2	833	4 612	1955
1954	233	586	2.5	2 828	3.2	751	1 884	1954
1953	196	515	2.6	2 775	2.1	410	1 076	1953
1952	95	781	8.2	2 725	1.5	140	1 146	1952
1951	180	785	4.4	2 673	3.2	573	2 497	1951
1950	265	2 107	7.9	2 613	3.0	802	6 371	1950
1949	133	2 494	18.8	2 550	4.5	604	11 346	1949
1948	104	718	6.9	2 489	7.4	765	5 280	1948
1947	237	748	3.2	2 423	11.2	2 659	8 394	1947
1946	295	2 524	8.5	2 351	11.5	3 392	28 992	1946
1940	161			2 412	0.7	120		1940
1939	75			2 385	3.6	269		1939
1938	62	967	15.6	2 349	5.9	368	5 721	1938
1937	70	399	5.7	2 317	3.8	269	1 532	1937
1936	132	950	7.2	2 285	4.0	533	3 825	1936
1935	90	1 777	19.8	2 254	6.3	565	11 194	1935
1934	41	762	18.4	2 220	6.7	276	5 081	1934
1933	117	2 968	25.4	2 184	7.7	901	22 835	1933
1932	82	2 646	32.1	2 144	9.5	783	25 168	1932
1931	137	3 834	28.0	2 103	9.5	1 304	36 461	1931
1930	50	4 245	84.8	2 064	9.9	495	41 949	1930

N e t h e r l a n d s

Labour Disputes a)

Year	Labour disputes			Persons involved in labour disputes b)							Man-days lost in labour disputes b)							Year
	Total	Strikes	Lock-outs	Total	N	Strikes	N	Lock-outs	N	Indirectly	Total	N	Strikes	N	Lock-outs	N	Indirectly	
1929	214	214	0	20 329	213	19 467	213	0	0	862	938 960	210	919 427	210	0	0	19 533	1929
1928	195	191	4	16 765	185	14 009	181	1 207	4	1 549	664 440	185	627 989	181	19 464	4	16 987	1928
1927	216	209	7	13 267	208	11 727	201	243	7	1 297	143 209	201	121 848	194	5 231	7	16 130	1927
1926	212	209	3	9 937	204	8 963	201	88	3	886	236 688	201	217 629	198	2 612	3	16 447	1926
1925	262	250	12	33 559	254	28 998	242	2 697	12	1 864	786 578	253	631 665	241	129 231	12	25 682	1925
1924	239	235	4	27 677	224	26 840	220	251	4	586	427 120	217	410 341	214	3 796	3	12 983	1924
1923	289	274	15	58 140	277	28 620	262	27 774	15	1 746	3 986 523	271	700 493	256	3 244 992	15	41 038	1923
1922	325	304	21	46 282	310	32 092	289	11 890	21	2 300	1 108 325	307	778 184	286	279 316	21	50 825	1922
1921	299	290	9	48 673	287	43 064	278	4 125	9	1 484	1 383 694	277	1 293 095	268	77 251	9	13 348	1921
1920	481	456	25	70 222	471	47 027	446	19 437	25	3 758	2 333 945	453	1 679 909	428	608 644	25	45 392	1920
1919	649	622	27	65 927	635	55 857	608	5 810	27	4 260	1 094 695	630	962 639	603	89 245	27	42 811	1919
1918	325	305	20	44 117	317	35 777	297	3 861	20	4 479	707 264	313	560 069	294	47 167	19	100 028	1918
1917	344	324	20	32 296	328	25 879	308	5 438	20	979	541 446	326	304 221	306	222 286	20	14 939	1917
1916	377	356	21	19 865	365	17 146	345	981	20	1 738	273 626	361	206 287	341	43 155	20	24 184	1916
1915	269	259	10	16 513	254	14 373	244	806	10	1 334	188 041	252	147 618	242	17 629	10	22 794	1915
1914	271	250	21	16 898	262	13 953	241	1 706	21	1 239	369 592	262	302 386	241	59 014	21	8 192	1914
1913	427	400	27	55 326	410	23 990	383	6 171	27	25 165	902 157	409	428 827	382	359 049	27	114 281	1913
1912	283	265	18	26 258	278	19 620	260	2 052	18	4 586	466 546	276	301 762	258	65 789	18	98 995	1912
1911	217	205	12	20 916	209	19 122	197	883	12	911	441 641	208	421 859	196	14 133	12	5 649	1911
1910	146	133	13	14 687	144	4 507	131	8 731	13	1 449	366 312	142	88 581	129	246 014	13	31 717	1910
1909	189	142	47	8 937	181	6 332	134	2 123	47	482	297 061	181	199 515	134	72 498	47	25 048	1909

Labour Disputes

Year	Indicators of average labour dispute [y]			Total non-agr. wage earners in 1,000s	Indicators per 100,000 non-agricultural wage earners			Year
	Size	Man-days lost	Duration		Labour disputes	Persons involved	Man-days lost	
1929	95	4 471	46.8	2 029	10.5	1 002	46 267	1929
1928	91	3 592	39.6	1 994	9.8	841	33 314	1928
1927	64	712	11.2	1 960	11.0	677	7 306	1927
1926	49	1 178	24.2	1 925	11.0	516	12 294	1926
1925	132	3 109	23.5	1 890	13.9	1 775	41 611	1925
1924	124	1 968	15.9	1 857	12.9	1 491	23 005	1924
1923	210	14 710	70.1	1 820	15.9	3 194	219 033	1923
1922	149	3 610	24.2	1 783	18.2	2 596	62 167	1922
1921	170	4 995	29.5	1 748	17.1	2 785	79 178	1921
1920	149	5 152	34.6	1 715	28.0	4 094	136 086	1920
1919	104	1 738	16.7	1 693	38.3	3 895	64 677	1919
1918	139	2 260	16.2	1 526	21.3	2 892	46 356	1918
1917	98	1 661	16.9	1 505	22.9	2 146	35 983	1917
1916	54	758	13.9	1 475	25.6	1 347	18 556	1916
1915	65	746	11.5	1 448	18.6	1 140	12 985	1915
1914	64	1 411	21.9	1 423	19.1	1 188	25 981	1914
1913	135	2 206	16.3	1 383	30.9	4 000	65 222	1913
1912	94	1 690	17.9	1 348	21.0	1 948	34 607	1912
1911	100	2 123	21.2	1 316	16.5	1 589	33 559	1911
1910	102	2 580	25.3	1 285	11.4	1 143	28 511	1910
1909	49	1 641	33.2	1 263	15.0	708	23 528	1909
1908	54	774	14.4	1 233	11.0	581	8 284	1908
1907	98	2 977	30.3	1 203	12.8	1 260	38 113	1907
1906	107	1 697	15.8	1 173	15.4	1 607	25 173	1906
1905	56	977	17.4	1 143	11.5	644	10 764	1905
1904	112	6 713	60.0	1 114	13.6	1 004	59 056	1904
1903	230			1 085	15.0	3 181		1903
1902	113			1 056	13.4	1 424		1902
1901	71			1 027	11.9	442		1901

y) Indicators calculated only for disputes for which data available (see N).

Netherlands

Labour Disputes a)

Year	Labour disputes			Persons involved in labour disputes b)							Man-days lost in labour disputes b)							Year
	Total	Strikes	Lock-outs	Total	N	Strikes	N	Lock-outs	N	Indirectly	Total	N	Strikes	N	Lock-outs	N	Indirectly	
1908	135	108	27	7 165	133	5 650	106	1 515	27		102 107	132	56 882	105	34 978	27	10 247	1908
1907	154	138	16	15 154	154	11 646	138	3 508	16		458 429	154	330 289	138	106 402	16	21 738	1907
1906	181	164	17	18 858	176	11 069	160	7 789	16		295 330	174	208 038	158	66 931	16	20 361	1906
1905	132	126	6	7 364	131	4 657	125	2 707	6		123 059	126	53 439	120	25 123	6	44 497	1905
1904	152	85	17	11 186	100	4 432	84	6 754	16		657 877	96	86 820	82	490 046	14	81 011	1904
1903	163	149	14	34 508	150	33 487	136	1 021	14									1903
1902	142	128	14	15 033	133	12 652	119	2 381	14									1902
1901	122	115	7	4 543	64	4 182	58	361	6									1901

a) From 1945 data refer to labour disputes in progress, up to 1940 to labour disputes beginning in the given year.
b) Up to 1929 data on participation and man-days lost not available for all labour disputes (see N).

Norway

Labour Disputes [a]

Year	Labour disputes		Persons involved in labour disputes	Man-days lost in labour disputes	Year
	Total[b]	Total[c]	Total	Total	
1975	22	20	3 282	12 473	1975
1974	13	13	22 149	318 433	1974
1973	12	11	2 380	11 382	1973
1972	9	9	1 185	12 402	1972
1971	10	10	2 519	9 105	1971
1970	15	15	3 133	47 204	1970
1969	4	4	824	21 636	1969
1968	6	5	486	13 514	1968
1967	7	7	436	4 720	1967
1966	7	7	1 392	5 207	1966
1965	7	6	591	8 927	1965
1964	3	2	230	1 310	1964
1963	8	8	10 588	226 394	1963
1962	8	7	1 069	81 121	1962
1961	19	19	22 910	423 082	1961
1960	12	11	656	2 417	1960
1959	18	17	2 113	47 616	1959
1958	16	15	12 541	59 798	1958
1957	18	18	2 792	27 082	1957
1956	27	26	56 173	964 440	1956
1955	22	19	9 971	108 087	1955
1954	27	24	2 865	104 507	1954
1953	55	45	4 917	40 531	1953
1952	40	38	6 399	124 054	1952
1951	28	27	4 255	35 699	1951
1950	30	30	4 399	42 310	1950
1949	47	46	9 010	104 759	1949
1948	58		5 919	92 278	1948
1947	47		8 250	41 294	1947
1946	39		4 658	79 019	1946
1945	16		4 074	65 145	1945
1939	81		15 978	859 808	1939
1938	248		24 045	567 300	1938
1937	195		28 785	1 013 509	1937
1936	175		15 286	396 487	1936
1935	103		3 548	168 307	1935
1934	85		6 364	235 075	1934
1933	93		6 306	364 240	1933
1932	91		6 360	394 002	1932
1931	82		59 524	7 585 832	1931
1930	94		4 652	240 454	1930
1929	73		4 796	196 704	1929
1928	63		8 042	363 844	1928
1927	96		22 456	1 374 089	1927
1926	113		51 487	2 205 365	1926

L a b o u r   D i s p u t e s

Year	Indicators of average labour dispute			Total non-agr. wage earners in 1,000s	Indicators per 100,000 non-agricultural wage earners			Year
	Size	Man-days lost	Duration		Labour disputes	Persons involved	Man-days lost	
1975	149	567	3.8	1 249	1.8	263	999	1975
1974	1 704	24 495	14.4	1 235	1.1	1 793	25 780	1974
1973	198	949	4.8	1 221	1.0	195	933	1973
1972	132	1 378	10.5	1 205	0.7	98	1 029	1972
1971	252	911	3.6	1 189	0.8	212	766	1971
1970	209	3 147	15.1	1 174	1.3	267	4 022	1970
1969	206	5 409	26.3	1 159	0.3	71	1 868	1969
1968	81	2 252	27.8	1 142	0.5	43	1 184	1968
1967	62	674	10.8	1 124	0.6	39	420	1967
1966	199	744	3.7	1 108	0.6	126	470	1966
1965	84	1 275	15.1	1 092	0.6	54	818	1965
1964	77	437	5.7	1 076	0.3	21	122	1964
1963	1 324	28 299	21.4	1 060	0.8	999	21 351	1963
1962	134	10 140	75.9	1 045	0.8	102	7 763	1962
1961	1 206	22 267	18.5	1 029	1.8	2 226	41 108	1961
1960	55	201	3.7	1 014	1.2	65	238	1960
1959	117	2 645	22.5	1 002	1.8	211	4 751	1959
1958	784	3 737	4.8	990	1.6	1 266	6 038	1958
1957	155	1 505	9.7	978	1.8	285	2 769	1957
1956	2 080	35 720	17.2	965	2.8	5 818	99 894	1956
1955	453	4 913	10.8	953	2.3	1 047	11 347	1955
1954	106	3 871	36.5	939	2.9	305	11 126	1954
1953	89	737	8.2	926	5.9	531	4 377	1953
1952	160	3 101	19.4	913	4.4	701	13 593	1952
1951	152	1 275	8.4	900	3.1	473	3 969	1951
1950	147	1 410	9.6	887	3.4	496	4 772	1950
1949	192	2 229	11.6	869	5.4	1 036	12 050	1949
1948	102	1 591	15.6	851	6.8	695	10 837	1948
1947	176	879	5.0	833	5.6	991	4 958	1947
1946	119	2 026	17.0	814	4.8	572	9 711	1946
1945	255	4 072	16.0	704	2.3	579	9 251	1945
1939	197	10 615	53.8	673	12.0	2 374	127 755	1939
1938	97	2 288	23.6	669	37.1	3 594	84 803	1938
1937	148	5 197	35.2	665	29.3	4 327	152 350	1937
1936	87	2 266	25.9	662	26.4	2 309	59 897	1936
1935	34	1 634	47.4	659	15.6	539	25 546	1935
1934	75	2 766	36.9	656	13.0	971	35 859	1934
1933	68	3 917	57.8	652	14.3	967	55 858	1933
1932	70	4 330	61.9	648	14.0	981	60 769	1932
1931	726	92 510	127.4	644	12.7	9 236	1 177 104	1931
1930	49	2 558	51.7	641	14.7	726	37 524	1930
1929	66	2 695	41.0	638	11.4	752	30 824	1929
1928	128	5 775	45.2	636	9.9	1 265	57 216	1928
1927	234	14 313	61.2	634	15.1	3 543	216 798	1927
1926	456	19 517	42.8	631	17.9	8 156	349 363	1926

L a b o u r   D i s p u t e s [a]

Year	Labour disputes			Persons involved in labour disputes			Man-days lost in labour disputes			Year
	Total[b]	Total[d]	Total[e]	Total	Total[d]	Total[e]	Total	Total[d]	Total[e]	
1925	84			13 752			666 650			1925
1924	61			63 117			5 152 386			1924
1923	57			24 965			796 274			1923
1922	26	89	9	2 168	1 653	553	91 380	99 932	16 461	1922
1921	89	207	169	154 421	41 752	15 236	3 583 742	2 217 786	598 416	1921
1920		383	198	8 629	31 831	8 627	498 299	1 198 733	440 882	1920
1919		341	168	11 146	25 121	10 860	615 780	622 584	554 371	1919
1918		170	108	4 449	7 399	4 465	240 127	187 280	219 599	1918
1917		89	78	6 276	5 445	5 550	246 317	108 709	209 816	1917
1916		85	224	69 000	24 540	24 247	1 200 000	719 909	847 530	1916
1915		102	413	11 100	9 741	6 154	415 000	315 109	396 885	1915
1914		98	47	8 200	5 314	3 724	270 000	155 592	148 605	1914
1913		99	64	6 700	4 941	2 057	150 000	122 126	50 582	1913
1912				14 300			446 000			1912
1911				44 000			1 115 000			1911
1910				4 100			179 000			1910
1909				3 800			185 000			1909
1908				12 000			380 000			1908
1907				10 000			340 000			1907
1906				3 000			95 000			1906
1905				2 000			30 000			1905
1904				1 200			45 000			1904
1903				3 000			130 000			1903

a) Up to 1920 data on participants and man-days lost estimated by the Statistical Office, partially based on private collections; from 1921 data collected by the Statistical Office.

b) Including labour disputes counted in both years when they begin in one year and are still in progress the following year.

c) Labour disputes beginning in the given year.

d) Data collected by the Norwegian Trade Union Federation.

e) Data collected by the Norwegian Federation of Employers' Associations.

Labour Disputes

Year	Indicators of average labour dispute			Total non-agr. wage earners in 1,000s y)	Indicators per 100,000 non-agricultural wage earners			Year
	Size	Man-days lost	Duration		Labour disputes	Persons involved	Man-days lost	
1925	164	7 936	48.5	628	13.4	2 191	106 214	1925
1924	1 035	84 465	81.6	624	9.8	10 121	826 188	1924
1923	438'	13 970	31.9	620	9.2	4 026	128 399	1923
1922	83	3 515	42.1	616	4.2	352	14 833	1922
1921	1 735	40 267	23.2	610	14.6	25 316	587 521	1921
1920			57.7	602		1 432	82 712	1920
1919			55.2	596		1 871	103 352	1919
1918			54.0	480		928	50 069	1918
1917			39.2	475		1 323	51 907	1917
1916			17.4	469		14 704	255 724	1916
1915			37.4	465		2 389	89 302	1915
1914			32.9	460		1 783	58 696	1914
1913			22.4	453		1 481	33 147	1913
1912			31.2	445		3 210	100 125	1912
1911			25.3	439		10 031	254 195	1911
1910			43.7	433		947	41 355	1910
1909			48.7	427		890	43 313	1909
1908			31.7	420		2 854	90 388	1908
1907			34.0	415		2 411	81 988	1907
1906			31.7	410		731	23 159	1906
1905			15.0	406		493	7 396	1905
1904			37.5	401		299	11 224	1904
1903			43.3	397		757	32 786	1903

y) Share of labour force was held constant at 1914 level for 1915 to 1918.

L a b o u r   D i s p u t e s [a)]

Year	Labour disputes				Persons involved in labour disputes				Man-days lost in labour disputes				Year
	Total	Strikes	Lock-outs	Mixed	Total	Strikes	Lock-outs	Mixed	Total	Strikes	Lock-outs	Mixed	
1975	290	289	1		37 511	36 644	867		357 966	357 099	867		1975
1974	237	237	0		27 047	27 047	0		57 514	57 514	0		1974
1973	48	48	0		4 252	4 252	0		11 802	11 802	0		1973
1972	44	44	0		7 145	7 145	0		10 507	10 507	0		1972
1971	60	59	1		96 648	62 848	33 800		1 071 751	838 751	233 000		1971
1970	134	134	0		26 669	26 669	0		155 700				1970
1969	41	40	1		9 023				122 400				1969
1968	7	7	0		379	379	0		1 200	1 200	0		1968
1967	7	7	0		90	90	0		400	400	0		1967
1966	26	25	1		29 436				351 600				1966
1965	8	8	0		248		0		4 100	4 100	0		1965
1964	14	14	0		1 992	1 992	0		34 000	34 000	0		1964
1963	24	23	1		2 841				25 000				1963
1962	10	10	0		3 529	3 529	0		5 000	5 000	0		1962
1961	12	12	0		1 400	1 400	0		2 000	2 000	0		1961
1960	31	29	2		1 479				18 000				1960
1959	17	16	1		1 236				24 000				1959
1958	10	9	1		84				15 000				1958
1957	20	19	1		1 630				53 000				1957
1956	12	12	0		1 570	1 570	0		4 000	4 000	0		1956
1955	18	18	0		3 855	3 855	0		159 000	3 855	0		1955
1954	45	44	1		7 718				25 000				1954
1953	20	17	3		26 198				582 000				1953
1952	32	31	1		2 144				79 000				1952
1951	28	27	1		15 127				531 000				1951
1950	23	21	0	2	2 436	2 375	0	61	41 000	40 000		700	1950
1949	31	31	0	0	1 008	1 008	0	0	21 000	21 000	0	0	1949
1948	47	47	0	0	6 061	6 061	0	0	151 000	151 000	0	0	1948
1947	81	81	0	0	56 851	56 851	0	0	125 000	125 000	0	0	1947
1946	137	136	1	0	1 277	1 272	5	0	27 000	27 000	0	0	1946
1945	163	163	0	0	133 171	133 171	0	0	11 321 000	11 321 000	0	0	1945
1944	214	190	0	24	7 021	6 311	0	710	228 000	223 000	0	5 000	1944
1943	167	167	0	0	6 926	6 926	0	0	94 000	94 000	0	0	1943
1942	139	138	0	1	1 337	1 334	0	3	53 000	53 000	0	0	1942
1941	34	33	1	0	1 929	1 916	13	0	94 000	92 000	2 000	0	1941
1940	38	34	3	1	3 936	3 854	78	4	78 000	70 000	8 000	0	1940
1939	45	44	0	1	2 194	2 131	0	63	159 000	157 000	0	2 000	1939
1938	85	83	1	1	28 951	5 814	12 900	10 237	1 284 200	228 000	635 000	421 000	1938
1937	67	64	0	3	30 904	6 743	0	24 161	861 200	256 000	0	605 000	1937
1936	60	55	3	2	3 474	3 395	49	30	437 500	435 000	1 000	2 000	1936
1935	98	92	4	2	17 189	11 896	41	5 252	788 000	336 000	2 000	450 000	1935
1934	103	103	0	0	13 588	13 588	0	0	760 200	760 000	0	0	1934
1933	140	135	1	4	31 980	27 583	60	4 337	3 434 300	3 219 000	2 000	213 000	1933
1932	182	166	12	4	50 147	17 797	107	2 243	3 094 600	2 931 000	1 000	163 000	1932
1931	193	179	6	8	40 899	40 300	346	253	2 627 400	2 613 000	7 000	7 000	1931
1930	261	238	10	13	20 751	19 675	262	814	1 021 100	976 000	29 000	16 000	1930
1929	180	155	9	16	12 676	12 176	138	362	666 900	635 000	5 000	27 000	1929

Labour Disputes

Year	Indicators of average labour dispute			Total non-agr. wage earners in 1,000s y)	Indicators per 100,000 non-agricultural wage earners			Year
	Size	Man-days lost	Duration		Labour disputes	Persons involved	Man-days lost	
1975	129	1 234	9.5	3 147	9.2	1 192	11 377	1975
1974	114	243	2.1	3 101	7.6	872	1 855	1974
1973	89	246	2.8	3 059	1.6	139	386	1973
1972	162	239	1.5	3 021	1.5	236	348	1972
1971	1 611	17 863	11.1	2 980	2.0	3 243	35 961	1971
1970	199	1 162	5.8	2 928	4.6	911	5 318	1970
1969	220	2 985	13.6	2 898	1.4	311	4 223	1969
1968	54	171	3.2	2 875	0.2	13	42	1968
1967	13	57	4.4	2 855	0.2	3	14	1967
1966	1 132	13 523	11.9	2 829	0.9	1 040	12 428	1966
1965	31	513	16.5	2 797	0.3	9	147	1965
1964	142	2 429	17.1	2 735	0.5	73	1 243	1964
1963	118	1 042	8.8	2 680	0.9	106	933	1963
1962	353	500	1.4	2 630	0.4	134	190	1962
1961	117	167	1.4	2 581	0.5	54	77	1961
1960	48	581	12.2	2 534	1.2	58	710	1960
1959	73	1 412	19.4	2 501	0.7	49	960	1959
1958	8	1 500	178.6	2 468	0.4	3	608	1958
1957	82	2 650	32.5	2 432	0.8	67	2 180	1957
1956	131	333	2.5	2 395	0.5	66	167	1956
1955	214	8 833	41.2	2 357	0.8	164	6 747	1955
1954	172	556	3.2	2 320	1.9	333	1 078	1954
1953	1 310	29 100	22.2	2 285	0.9	1 146	25 465	1953
1952	67	2 469	36.8	2 250	1.4	95	3 511	1952
1951	540	18 964	35.1	2 213	1.3	684	23 998	1951
1950	106	1 770	16.7	2 174	1.1	112	1 872	1950
1949	33	677	20.8	2 136	1.5	47	983	1949
1948	129	3 213	24.9	2 094	2.2	289	7 212	1948
1947	702	1 543	2.2	2 050	4.0	2 774	6 099	1947
1946	9	197	21.1	2 005	6.8	64	1 347	1946
1945	817	69 454	85.0	1 960	8.3	6 794	577 567	1945
1944	33	1 065	32.5	1 924	11.1	365	11 849	1944
1943	41	563	13.6	1 890	8.8	367	4 974	1943
1942	10	381	39.6	1 858	7.5	72	2 852	1942
1941	57	2 765	48.7	1 831	1.9	105	5 135	1941
1940	104	2 053	19.8	1 806	2.1	218	4 320	1940
1939	49	3 533	72.5	1 781	2.5	123	8 929	1939
1938	341	15 106	44.4	1 756	4.8	1 648	73 108	1938
1937	461	12 851	27.9	1 734	3.9	1 782	49 657	1937
1936	58	7 300	126.1	1 713	3.5	203	25 573	1936
1935	175	8 041	45.8	1 692	5.8	1 016	46 581	1935
1934	132	7 379	55.9	1 670	6.2	814	45 510	1934
1933	228	24 529	107.4	1 648	8.5	1 941	208 402	1933
1932	276	17 005	61.7	1 625	11.2	3 086	190 485	1932
1931	212	13 611	64.2	1 602	12.0	2 553	163 982	1931
1930	80	3 912	49.2	1 580	16.5	1 313	64 619	1930
1929	70	3 706	52.6	1 559	11.5	813	42 795	1929

Labour Disputes[a]

Year	Labour disputes				Persons involved in labour disputes				Man-days lost in labour disputes (in 1,000s)				Year
	Total	Strikes	Lock-outs	Mixed	Total	Strikes	Lock-outs	Mixed	Total	Strikes	Lock-outs	Mixed	
1928	201	173	12	16	71 461	18 055	48 748	4 658	4 835	1 006	3 558	271	1928
1927	189	164	15	10	9 477	7 634	1 142	701	400	350	28	22	1927
1926	206	191	4	11	52 891	28 046	24 116	729	1 711	1 622	62	27	1926
1925	239	211	15	13	145 778	20 438	117 772	7 568	2 560	937	1 295	328	1925
1924	251	238	11	12	23 976	19 495	1 545	2 936	1 205	884	89	232	1924
1923	205	192	6	8	102 896	42 995	21 506	38 395	6 907	1 791	661	4 455	1923
1922	392	354	11	27	75 679	43 547	287	31 845	2 675	1 713	11	951	1922
1921	347	302	22	23	49 712	44 053	742	4 917	2 663	2 336	83	244	1921
1920	486	455	9	22	139 039	42 657	37 988	58 394	8 944	1 928	3 225	3 790	1920
1919	440	414	10	16	81 041	69 980	727	10 334	2 296	1 859	15	422	1919
1918	708	668	10	30	61 223	50 377	756	10 090	1 436	1 078	18	340	1918
1917	475	458	8	9	46 701	45 019	1 016	666	1 109	1 075	27	7	1917
1916	227	218	2	7	20 711	19 287	41	1 383	475	401	1	73	1916
1915	80	70	7	3	5 119	4 277	813	29	83	49	33	1	1915
1914	115	105	8	2	14 385	8 832	5 368	185	620	294	324	3	1914
1913	119	118	1	0	9 591	9 574	17	0	303	301	2	0	1913
1912	116	108	4	4	9 980	5 797	2 166	2 017	292	118	15	159	1912
1911	98	85	9	4	20 576	4 940	15 145	491	570	39	519	12	1911
1910	76	66	5	5	3 671	3 420	101	150	39	36	2	1	1910
1909	138	102	22	14	301 749	229 248	71 364	1 137	11 800	7 714	4 052	34	1909
1908	302	229	38	35	40 357	17 187	2 672	20 498	1 842	469	320	1 053	1908
1907	312	243	23	46	23 540	11 278	5 669	6 593	514	207	95	212	1907
1906	290	239	8	43	18 655	15 050	560	3 045	479	275	53	151	1906
1905	189	152	12	25	32 906	13 186	456	19 264	2 390	123	42	2 225	1905
1904	215	169	12	34	12 248	8 299	1 218	2 731	386	140	140	106	1904
1903	142	109	16	17	24 571	5 970	982	17 619	642	128	22	492	1903

a) From 1951 data on participants and man-days lost not broken down by strikes and lock-outs, except in 1971;
up to 1950 data broken down by strikes, lock-outs and mixed disputes (i.e. strikes turning into lock-outs
or vice versa).

L a b o u r   D i s p u t e s

Year	Indicators of average labour dispute			Total non-agr. wage earners in 1,000s y)	Indicators per 100,000 non-agricultural wage earners			Year
	Size	Man-days lost	Duration		Labour disputes	Persons involved	Man-days lost	
1928	356	24 055	67.7	1 538	13.1	4 646	314 377	1928
1927	50	2 116	42.2	1 518	12.5	624	26 356	1927
1926	257	8 306	32.3	1 497	13.8	3 533	114 290	1926
1925	610	10 711	17.6	1 476	16.2	9 875	173 420	1925
1924	92	4 617	50.3	1 454	17.9	1 649	82 856	1924
1923	499	33 529	67.1	1 433	14.4	7 183	482 139	1923
1922	193	6 824	35.3	1 411	27.8	5 365	189 623	1922
1921	143	7 674	53.6	1 385	25.0	3 588	192 228	1921
1920	286	18 401	64.3	1 357	35.8	10 243	658 801	1920
1919	184	5 218	28.3	1 339	32.9	6 053	171 499	1919
1918	86	2 028	23.5	1 121	63.2	5 461	128 087	1918
1917	98	2 335	23.7	1 116	42.6	4 186	99 402	1917
1916	91	2 093	22.9	1 107	20.5	1 871	42 902	1916
1915	64	1 038	16.2	1 100	7.3	466	7 548	1915
1914	125	5 400	43.2	1 092	10.5	1 317	56 843	1914
1913	81	2 546	31.6	1 060	11.2	905	28 591	1913
1912	86	2 517	29.3	1 027	11.3	971	28 421	1912
1911	210	5 816	27.7	995	9.8	2 068	57 277	1911
1910	48	513	10.6	963	7.9	381	4 049	1910
1909	2 187	85 507	39.1	931	14.8	32 418	1 267 719	1909
1908	134	6 099	45.6	899	33.6	4 491	204 988	1908
1907	75	1 647	21.8	867	36.0	2 714	59 251	1907
1906	64	1 652	25.7	838	34.6	2 227	57 176	1906
1905	174	12 646	72.6	809	23.4	4 067	295 402	1905
1904	57	1 795	31.5	781	27.5	1 568	49 418	1904
1903	173	4 521	26.1	754	18.8	3 257	85 097	1903

y) Share of labour force was held constant at 1914 level for 1915 to 1918, and was interpolated between 1940 and 1945.

Labour Disputes

Year	Labour disputes		Persons involved in labour disputes			Man-days lost in labour disputes	Year
	Total a)	Total b)	Total a)	Total b)	N	Total a)	
1902	123	139	9 600	8 587	59	350 000	1902
1901	127	118	6 200	4 633	50	210 000	1901
1900	104	135	10 290	13 880	77	331 600	1900
1899	62	105	8 667	9 399	48	205 900	1899
1898	134	163	16 700	7 185	82	184 000	1898
1897	90	114	5 930	5 478	45	80 100	1897
1896	50	102	4 600	5 916	38	195 200	1896
1895	46	65	2 929	2 529	30	16 110	1895
1894	18	44	768	878	15	4 790	1894
1893	32	53	2 269	2 559	20	201 350	1893
1892	16	26	1 346	683	8	105 900	1892
1891	37	63	2 317	4 680	18	74 120	1891
1890	107	105	3 900	9 039	32	126 100	1890
1889	22	38	2 379	3 031	13	36 190	1889
1888	12	41	2 200	1 440	16	5 350	1888
1887	4	16	300	1 508	11	4 300	1887
1886	12	29	1 185	1 810	8	15 700	1886
1885		10		137	2		1885
1884		6		341	3		1884
1883		5		800	1		1883
1882		4					1882
1881		10		1 740	5		1881
1880		3		490	2		1880
1879		7		4 500	2		1879
1878		1		300	1		1878
1877		3		313	3		1877
1876		1		150	1		1876
1875		3		400	1		1875
1874		9		60	1		1874
1873		11		1 200	3		1873
1872		8		1 170	4		1872
1871		5					1871
1870		1					1870
1869		4					1869
1868		3					1868
1867		2					1867

a) Data drawn from a private collection by O. Dahlqvist.

b) Data drawn from a private colection by A. Raphael; number of persons involved not available for all disputes (see N).

Labour Disputes [z)]

Year	Indicators of average labour dispute			Total non-agr. wage earners in 1,000s	Indicators per 100,000 non-agricultural wage earners			Year
	Size	Man-days lost	Duration		Labour disputes	Persons involved	Man-days lost	
1902	78	2 846	36.5	729	16.9	1 316	47 988	1902
1901	49	1 654	33.9	704	18.1	881	29 850	1901
1900	99	3 188	32.2	677	15.4	1 520	48 974	1900
1899	140	3 321	23.8	663	9.4	1 307	31 056	1899
1898	125	1 373	11.0	648	20.7	2 577	28 389	1898
1897	66	890	13.5	633	14.2	937	12 660	1897
1896	92	3 904	42.4	618	8.1	744	31 579	1896
1895	64	350	5.5	604	7.6	485	2 668	1895
1894	43	266	6.2	589	3.1	130	813	1894
1893	71	6 292	88.7	577	5.5	393	34 899	1893
1892	84	6 619	78.7	567	2.8	237	18 668	1892
1891	63	2 003	32.0	558	6.6	415	13 290	1891
1890	36	1 179	32.3	548	19.5	712	23 017	1890
1889	108	1 645	15.2	546	4.0	436	6 632	1889
1888	183	446	2.4	543	2.2	405	985	1888
1887	75	1 075	14.3	542	0.7	55	794	1887
1886	99	1 308	13.2	538	2.2	220	2 916	1886

z) Labour disputes reported by O. Dahlqvist.

Switzerland

Labour Disputes [a]

Year	Labour disputes			Persons involved in labour disputes				Man-days lost in labour disputes				Year
	Total	Strikes	Lock-outs	Total	Strikes	Lock-outs	Indirectly	Total	Strikes	Lock-outs	Indirectly	
1975	6			323				1 733				1975
1974	3			299				2 777				1974
1973	0			0				0				1973
1972	5			526				2 002				1972
1971	11			2 267				7 491				1971
1970	3			320				2 623				1970
1969	1			33				231				1969
1968	1			70				1 785				1968
1967	1			65				1 690				1967
1966	2			38				62				1966
1965	2			23				163				1965
1964	1			350				4 550				1964
1963	4			1 120				70 698				1963
1962	2			163				1 386				1962
1961	0			0				0				1961
1960	8			214				1 016				1960
1959	4			126				1 987				1959
1958	3			815				2 127				1958
1957	2			71				740				1957
1956	5			286				1 439				1956
1955	4			430				1 036				1955
1954	6			2 997				25 963				1954
1953	6			2 079				61 124				1953
1952	8			1 207				11 588				1952
1951	8			985				8 469				1951
1950	6			288				5 477				1950
1949	12			853				41 113				1949
1948	28			4 277				61 408				1948
1947	29			6 963				102 209				1947
1946	55			15 173				184 483				1946
1945	35			3 686				37 187				1945
1944	18			1 324				17 690				1944
1943	19			1 069				12 050				1943
1942	19			822				4 030				1942
1941	15			722				14 311				1941
1940	6			578				1 480				1940
1939	7			238				4 046				1939
1938	17			706				16 299				1938
1937	37	38	1	6 043	6 035	8		115 648	115 392	256		1937
1936	41	45	4	3 612	3 275	337		38 789	25 673	13 116		1936
1935	17	16	1	874	866	8		15 143	15 135	8		1935
1934	20	20	0	2 763	2 763	0		33 309	33 309	0		1934
1933	35	34	1	2 705	2 642	63		69 065	64 403	4 662		1933
1932	38	36	2	5 083	5 027	56		159 154	157 893	1 256		1932
1931	25	25	0	4 746	4 746	0		73 975	73 975	0		1931
1930	31	30	1	6 397	6 362	35		265 695	265 625	70		1930

Switzerland

Labour Disputes [y)]

Year	Indicators of average labour dispute			Total non-agr. wage earners in 1,000s [z)]	Indicators per 100,000 non-agricultural wage earners			Year
	Size	Man-days lost	Duration		Labour disputes	Persons involved	Man-days lost	
1975	54	289	5.4	2 604	0.2	12	67	1975
1974	100	926	9.3	2 600	0.1	12	107	1974
1973	0	0	0	2 576	0	0	0	1973
1972	105	400	3.8	2 538	0.2	21	79	1972
1971	206	681	3.3	2 494	0.4	91	300	1971
1970	107	874	8.2	2 453	0.1	13	107	1970
1969	33	231	7.0	2 412	0.0	1	10	1969
1968	70	1 785	25.5	2 361	0.0	3	76	1968
1967	65	1 690	26.0	2 316	0.0	3	73	1967
1966	19	31	1.6	2 271	0.1	2	3	1966
1965	12	82	7.1	2 233	0.1	1	7	1965
1964	350	4 550	13.0	2 189	0.0	16	208	1964
1963	280	17 675	63.1	2 132	0.2	53	3 316	1963
1962	82	693	8.5	2 074	0.1	8	67	1962
1961	0	0	0	1 997	0	0	0	1961
1960	27	127	4.7	1 931	0.4	11	53	1960
1959	32	497	15.8	1 873	0.2	7	106	1959
1958	272	709	2.6	1 831	0.2	45	116	1958
1957	36	370	10.4	1 785	0.1	4	41	1957
1956	57	288	5.0	1 737	0.3	16	83	1956
1955	108	259	2.4	1 695	0.2	25	61	1955
1954	500	4 327	8.7	1 658	0.4	181	1 566	1954
1953	347	10 187	29.4	1 622	0.4	128	3 768	1953
1952	151	1 449	9.6	1 582	0.5	76	732	1952
1951	123	1 059	8.6	1 542	0.5	64	549	1951
1950	48	913	19.0	1 506	0.4	19	364	1950
1949	71	3 426	48.2	1 469	0.8	58	2 799	1949
1948	153	2 193	14.4	1 431	2.0	299	4 291	1948
1947	240	3 524	14.7	1 394	2.1	499	7 332	1947
1946	276	3 354	12.2	1 358	4.1	1 118	13 588	1946
1945	105	1 062	10.1	1 305	2.7	282	2 849	1945
1944	74	983	13.4	1 294	1.4	102	1 367	1944
1943	56	634	11.3	1 285	1.5	83	938	1943
1942	43	212	4.9	1 276	1.5	64	316	1942
1941	48	954	19.8	1 269	1.2	57	1 127	1941
1940	96	247	2.6	1 264	0.5	46	117	1940
1939	34	578	17.0	1 260	0.6	19	321	1939
1938	42	959	23.1	1 258	1.4	56	1 295	1938
1937	163	3 126	19.1	1 257	2.9	481	9 198	1937
1936	88	946	10.7	1 256	3.3	288	3 088	1936
1935	51	891	17.3	1 255	1.4	70	1 207	1935
1934	138	1 665	12.1	1 253	1.6	221	2 659	1934
1933	77	1 973	25.5	1 250	2.8	216	5 527	1933
1932	134	4 188	31.3	1 246	3.0	408	12 772	1932
1931	190	2 959	15.6	1 242	2.0	382	5 957	1931
1930	206	8 571	41.5	1 236	2.5	518	21 505	1930

Switzerland

Labour Disputes [a]

Year	Labour disputes			Persons involved in labour disputes				Man-days lost in labour disputes				Year
	Total	Strikes	Lock-outs	Total	Strikes	Lock-outs	Indirectly	Total	Strikes	Lock-outs	Indirectly	
1929	39	37	2	4 661	4 644	17		99 608	99 211	397		1929
1928	45	44	1	5 474	5 339	135		98 015	95 855	2 160		1928
1927	26	23	3	2 058	2 023	35		34 260	33 929	231		1927
1926	35	34	1	2 745	2 721	24						1926
1925	42	42	0	3 299	3 299	0						1925
1924	70	67	3	8 642	6 741	1 901						1924
1923	44	43	1	3 602	3 567	35						1923
1922	104	100	4	12 100	10 340	1 760						1922
1921	55	46	9	3 705	2 786	919						1921
1920	184	174	10	20 803	13 989	6 814						1920
1919	237	233	4	22 137	21 294	843						1919
1918	268	264	4	24 173	24 109	64						1918
1917	140	136	4	13 459	13 109	350						1917
1916	35	34	1	3 330	3 328	2						1916
1915	12	9	3	1 547	1 234	313						1915
1914	31	27	4	3 138	1 353	1 785						1914
1913	64	57	7	5 980	5 707	273						1913
1912	65	54	11	5 007	4 002	1 005						1912
1911	85	79	6	4 020	3 735	285						1911
1910	89	78	11		5 796							1910
1909	72	68	4		11 010							1909
1908	99	88	11		7 847							1908

a) From 1927 data collected by the Statistical Office; prior to 1927 data collected by the trade unions, but number of man-days lost not available.

Labour Disputes [y)]

Year	Indicators of average labour dispute			Total non-agr. wage earners in 1,000s [z)]	Indicators per 100,000 non-agricultural wage earners			Year
	Size	Man-days lost	Duration		Labour disputes	Persons involved	Man-days lost	
1929	120	2 554	21.4	1 214	3.2	384	8 204	1929
1928	122	2 178	17.9	1 192	3.8	459	8 223	1928
1927	79	1 314	16.6	1 170	2.2	176	2 919	1927
1926	78			1 151	3.0	238		1926
1925	79			1 133	3.7	291		1925
1924	123			1 116	6.3	774		1924
1923	82			1 101	4.0	327		1923
1922	116			1 086	9.6	1 114		1922
1921	67			1 075	5.1	345		1921
1920	113			1 063	17.3	1 957		1920
1919	93			1 048	22.6	2 112		1919
1918	90			973	27.5	2 483		1918
1917	96			975	14.4	1 380		1917
1916	95			974	3.6	342		1916
1915	129			974	1.2	159		1915
1914	101			978	3.2	321		1914
1913	93			968	6.6	618		1913
1912	77			954	6.8	525		1912
1911	47			942	9.0	427		1911
1910	65			930	9.6	623		1910
1909	153			917	7.9	1 201		1909
1908	79			904	11.0	868		1908

y) Up to 1910 strikes only.
z) Share of labour force was held constant at 1914 level for 1915 to 1918, and was interpolated between 1941 and 1945.

Labour Disputes [a)]

Year	Labour disputes [b)]	Persons involved in labour disputes [c)] (in 1,000s)			Man-days lost in labour disputes [b)] (in 1,000s)	Year
	Total	Total	Strikes and lock-outs	Indirectly	Total	
1975	2 282	789	570	219	6 012	1975
1974	2 922	1 622	1 161	461	14 750	1974
1973	2 873	1 513	1 103	410	7 197	1973
1972	2 497	1 722	1 148	274	23 909	1972
1971	2 228	1 171	863	308	13 551	1971
1970	3 906	1 793	1 460	333	10 980	1970
1969	3 116	1 654	1 426	228	6 846	1969
1968	2 378	2 255	2 073	182	4 690	1968
1967	2 116	731	551	180	2 787	1967
1966	1 937	530	414	116	2 398	1966
1965	2 354	868	673	195	2 925	1965
1964	2 524	872	700	172	2 277	1964
1963	2 068	590	455	135	1 755	1963
1962	2 449	4 420	4 297	123	5 798	1962
1961	2 686	771	673	98	3 046	1961
1960	2 832	814	698	116	3 024	1960
1959	2 093	645	522	123	5 270	1959
1958	2 629	523	456	67	3 462	1958
1957	2 859	1 356	1 275	81	8 412	1957
1956	2 648	507	464	43	2 083	1956
1955	2 419	659	599	60	3 781	1955
1954	1 989	448	402	46	2 457	1954
1953	1 746	1 370	1 329	41	2 184	1953
1952	1 714	415	303	112	1 792	1952
1951	1 719	379	336	43	1 694	1951
1950	1 339	302	269	33	1 389	1950
1949	1 426	433	313	120	1 807	1949
1948	1 759	424	324	100	1 944	1948
1947	1 721	620	489	131	2 433	1947
1946	2 205	526	405	121	2 158	1946
1945	2 293	531	447	84	2 835	1945
1944	2 194	821	716	105	3 714	1944
1943	1 785	557	454	103	1 808	1943
1942	1 303	456	349	107	1 527	1942
1941	1 251	360	297	63	1 079	1941
1940	922	299	225	74	940	1940
1939	940	337	246	91	1 356	1939
1938	875	274	211	63	1 334	1938
1937	1 129	597	388	209	3 413	1937
1936	818	316	241	75	1 829	1936
1935	553	271	230	41	1 955	1935
1934	471	134	109	25	959	1934
1933	357	136	114	220	1 072	1933
1932	389	379	337	42	6 488	1932
1931	420	490	424	66	6 983	1931
1930	422	307	286	21	4 399	1930
1929	431	533	493	40	8 287	1929

Labour Disputes

Year	Indicators of average labour dispute			Total non-agr. wage earners in 1,000s y)	Indicators per 100,000 non-agricultural wage earners			Year
	Size	Man-days lost	Duration		Labour disputes	Persons involved	Man-days lost	
1975	346	2 635	7.6	20 817	11.0	3 790	28 880	1975
1974	555	5 048	9.1	20 930	14.0	7 750	70 474	1974
1973	527	2 505	4.8	21 019	13.7	7 198	34 241	1973
1972	690	9 575	13.9	21 069	11.9	8 173	113 479	1972
1971	526	6 082	11.6	21 104	10.6	5 549	64 209	1971
1970	459	2 811	6.1	21 138	18.5	8 482	51 944	1970
1969	531	2 197	4.1	21 184	14.7	7 808	32 317	1969
1968	948	1 972	2.1	21 206	11.2	10 634	22 116	1968
1967	345	1 317	3.8	21 215	10.0	3 446	13 137	1967
1966	274	1 238	4.5	21 203	9.1	2 500	11 310	1966
1965	369	1 243	3.4	21 194	11.1	4 095	13 801	1965
1964	345	902	2.6	21 166	11.9	4 120	10 758	1964
1963	285	849	3.0	21 136	9.8	2 791	8 303	1963
1962	1 805	2 367	1.3	21 127	11.6	20 921	27 443	1962
1961	287	1 134	4.0	21 040	12.8	3 664	14 477	1961
1960	287	1 068	3.7	20 833	13.6	3 907	14 515	1960
1959	308	2 518	8.2	20 637	10.1	3 125	25 537	1959
1958	199	1 317	6.6	20 483	12.8	2 553	16 902	1958
1957	474	2 942	6.2	20 363	14.0	6 659	41 310	1957
1956	191	787	4.1	20 233	13.1	2 506	10 295	1956
1955	272	1 563	5.7	20 106	12.0	3 278	18 805	1955
1954	225	1 235	5.5	20 005	9.9	2 239	12 282	1954
1953	785	1 251	1.6	19 906	8.8	6 882	10 972	1953
1952	242	1 046	4.3	19 813	8.7	2 095	9 044	1952
1951	220	985	4.5	19 727	8.7	1 921	8 587	1951
1950	226	1 037	4.6	19 810	6.8	1 524	7 012	1950
1949	304	1 267	4.2	19 684	7.2	2 200	9 180	1949
1948	241	1 105	4.6	19 542	9.0	2 170	9 948	1948
1947	360	1 414	3.9	19 323	8.9	3 209	12 591	1947
1946	239	979	4.1	19 176	11.5	2 743	11 254	1946
1945	232	1 236	5.3	18 992	12.1	2 796	14 927	1945
1944	374	1 693	4.5	18 761	11.7	4 376	19 797	1944
1943	312	1 013	3.2	18 511	9.6	3 009	9 767	1943
1942	350	1 172	3.3	18 199	7.2	2 506	8 391	1942
1941	288	863	3.0	17 971	7.0	2 003	6 004	1941
1940	324	1 020	3.1	17 812	5.2	1 679	5 277	1940
1939	359	1 443	4.0	17 473	5.4	1 929	7 760	1939
1938	313	1 525	4.9	17 212	5.1	1 592	7 751	1938
1937	529	3 023	5.7	16 973	6.7	3 517	20 108	1937
1936	386	2 236	5.8	16 735	4.9	1 888	10 929	1936
1935	490	3 535	7.2	16 496	3.4	1 643	11 851	1935
1934	285	2 036	7.2	16 261	2.9	824	5 897	1934
1933	381	3 003	7.9	16 049	2.2	847	6 680	1933
1932	974	16 679	17.1	15 822	2.5	2 395	41 005	1932
1931	1 167	16 626	14.3	15 571	2.7	3 147	44 846	1931
1930	727	10 424	14.3	15 356	2.7	1 999	28 647	1930
1929	1 237	19 227	15.5	15 144	2.8	3 519	54 720	1929

Labour Disputes [a]

Year	Labour disputes [b] Total	Persons involved in labour disputes [c] (in 1,000s)			Man-days lost in labour disputes [b] (in 1,000s) Total	Year
		Total	Strikes and lock-outs	Indirectly		
1928	302	124	80	44	1 388	1928
1927	308	108	90	18	1 174	1927
1926	323	2 734	2 724	10	162 233	1926
1925	603	441	401	40	7 952	1925
1924	710	613	558	55	8 424	1924
1923	628	405	343	62	10 672	1923
1922	576	552	512	40	19 850	1922
1921	763	1 801	1 770	31	85 872	1921
1920	1 607	1 932	1 779	153	26 568	1920
1919	1 352	2 591	2 401	190	34 969	1919
1918	1 165	1 116	923	193	5 875	1918
1917	730	872	575	297	5 647	1917
1916	532	276	235	41	2 446	1916
1915	672	448	401	47	2 953	1915
1914	972	447	326	121	9 878	1914
1913	1 459	664	497	167	9 804	1913
1912	834	1 462	1 232	230	40 890	1912
1911	872	952	824	128	10 155	1911
1910	521	514	384	130	9 867	1910
1909	422	297	168	129	2 687	1909
1908	389	293	221	72	10 785	1908
1907	585	146	100	46	2 148	1907
1906	479	218	158	60	3 019	1906
1905	349	92	67	25	2 368	1905
1904	346	87	56	31	1 464	1904
1903	380	116	93	23	2 320	1903
1902	432	255	115	140	3 438	1902
1901	631	179	111	68	4 130	1901
1900	633	185	132	53	3 088	1900
1899	710	179	137	42	2 503	1899
1898	695	252	199	53	15 257	1898
1897	848	229	166	63	10 327	1897
1896	906	192	142	50	3 565	1896
1895	728	259	205	54	5 701	1895
1894	903	322	254	68	9 506	1894
1893	599	634	597	37	30 439	1893

a) Labour disputes involving more than 10 participants or lasting more than one day, or which exceed 100 aggregate man-days lost.
b) Labour disputes beginning in the given year.
c) Labour disputes in progress in the given year.

Labour Disputes

Year	Indicators of average labour dispute			Total non-agr. wage earners in 1,000s y)	Indicators per 100,000 non-agricultural wage earners			Year
	Size	Man-days lost	Duration		Labour disputes	Persons involved	Man-days lost	
1928	411	4 596	11.2	14 967	2.0	828	9 274	1928
1927	351	3 812	10.9	14 761	2.1	732	7 953	1927
1926	8 464	502 269	59.3	14 567	2.2	18 769	1 113 720	1926
1925	731	13 187	18.0	14 369	4.2	3 069	55 340	1925
1924	863	11 865	13.7	14 184	5.0	4 322	59 392	1924
1923	645	16 994	26.4	13 943	4.5	2 905	76 538	1923
1922	958	34 462	36.0	13 733	4.2	4 019	144 540	1922
1921	2 360	112 545	47.7	13 508	5.6	13 333	635 729	1921
1920	1 202	16 533	13.8	13 151	12.2	14 691	202 019	1920
1919	1 916	25 865	13.5	12 441	10.9	20 826	281 075	1919
1918	958	5 043	5.3	13 130	8.9	8 499	44 744	1918
1917	1 195	7 736	6.5	13 188	5.5	6 612	42 819	1917
1916	519	4 598	8.9	13 333	4.0	2 070	18 345	1916
1915	667	4 394	6.6	13 542	5.0	3 308	21 806	1915
1914	460	10 163	22.1	14 103	6.9	3 169	70 040	1914
1913	455	6 720	14.8	13 933	10.5	4 766	70 365	1913
1912	1 753	49 029	28.0	13 823	6.0	10 576	295 801	1912
1911	1 092	11 646	10.7	13 732	6.4	6 933	73 951	1911
1910	987	18 939	19.2	13 581	3.8	3 785	72 654	1910
1909	704	6 367	9.0	13 416	3.1	2 214	20 028	1909
1908	753	27 725	36.8	13 254	2.9	2 211	81 374	1908
1907	250	3 672	14.7	13 093	4.5	1 115	16 406	1907
1906	455	6 303	13.8	12 934	3.7	1 685	23 341	1906
1905	264	6 785	25.7	12 778	2.7	720	18 532	1905
1904	251	4 231	16.8	12 622	2.7	689	11 599	1904
1903	305	6 105	20.0	12 469	3.0	930	18 606	1903
1902	590	7 958	13.5	12 306	3.5	2 072	27 938	1902
1901	284	6 545	23.1	12 168	5.2	1 471	33 941	1901
1900	292	4 878	16.7	11 970	5.3	1 546	25 798	1900
1899	252	3 525	14.0	11 770	6.0	1 521	21 266	1899
1898	363	21 953	60.5	11 572	6.0	2 178	131 842	1898
1897	270	12 178	45.1	11 376	7.5	2 013	90 775	1897
1896	212	3 935	18.6	11 184	8.1	1 717	31 877	1896
1895	358	7 885	22.0	10 993	6.6	2 356	51 860	1895
1894	442	13 058	29.5	10 805	6.7	2 980	87 977	1894
1893	1 058	50 816	48.0	10 619	5.6	5 970	286 640	1893

y) Northern Ireland excluded from total labour force; share of labour force was held constant at 1914 level for 1915 to 1918, and was interpolated between 1931 and 1946.

A full documentation of all data presented in our handbook would certainly go beyond the limits even of two bulky volumes — and beyond the reasonable limits of a commercial publishing house. Without documentation, however, a data collection of this kind would of course be much less useful. In the analysis of the long-term changes of the European societies, we need a broad data basis which can be improved step by step. And this means documentation. Given the limits of space, it must be a separate documentation.

In the preface to the first volume, I promised a „separate documentation which will be available through the ICPSR at Ann Arbor for the American user and through the Zentralarchiv in Cologne for Europe". We hold to our promise even though this service for a wider public is a thankless task for persons working on a project basis.

In the course of 1986, altogether eleven data sets will become available including either a machine-readable or typed documentation.

No. of data set	Name of data set	Type of documentation
1	Population structure	machine-readable
2	Labourforce	machine-readable
3	National product	machine-readable
4	Income inequality	machine-readable
5	Labour disputes	machine-readable
6	Public revenues	typed
7	Public expenditure	typed
8	Governmental personnel	typed
9	Public eduation	typed
10	Income maintenance	typed
11	Population movements	typed

With these eleven data sets, 12 out of 19 chapters of the two volumes will be fully documented, i.e. Chapters 5 and 7—10 in Volume I and Chapter 1—2 and 5—9 in Volume II. The remaining 7 chapters contain only a small proportion of all data. These data will not be made available in machine-readable form nor will they be documented in a form which could be distributed.

The data in Chapters 1 and 2 of Volume I and Chapters 3 and 4 of Volume II have all been drawn from official population census publications and are documented in handwritten form. This documentation will not be generally made available, but we hope to publish a bibliography of census publication in the near future.

For Chapter 3 and 4 in Volume I, we have relied mainly on two sources: Tom Mackie and Richard Rose, *The International Almanach of Electoral History*. London, Macmillan, 1974, and Klaus von Beyme, *Die parlamentarischen Regierungssysteme Europas*. München, Piper, 1973. There is a separate typed documentation of the data on the extension of the suffrage by Jürgen Kohl, but the documentation of the other sources as well as of our classifications, calculations and estimates is only in handwritten form and will not generally be made available.

The data in Chapter 6 of Volume I are from David Singer at the University of Michigan, Ann Arbor. For a documentation see: Correlates of War Project, 'Instructions for Collecting Military Personnel Data', Mental Health Research Institute, University of Michigan, July 1971.

In general, we have relied almost exclusively on published official statistics. These sources will be found in the typed or machine-readable documentation of the eleven data sets. A history and bibliography of European official statistics has been published by Peter Flora in Current Sociology 23, 1975, No. 2. In some cases, however, we have used secondary sources for more important parts of our data collection. These sources are given here. They in which they have been used can be found in the documentations.

Government personnel (Vol. I, Chapter 5)

France

Julien Cahen, 'Evolution de la population active en France depuis cent ans', *Etudes et Conjoctures*, 3, (May-June 1953), pp. 230–288.

Germany

Walter Hoffmann, *Das Wachstum der Deutschen Wirtschaft seit der Mitte des 19. Jahrhunderts*. Berlin, Springer, 1953.

Great Britain

Charles Booth, 'Occupations of the people of the United Kingdom, 1801–1881', *Journal of the Royal Statistical Society*, 49, 1886, pp. 314–435.

Moses Abramovitz and Vera Eliasberg, *The Growth of Public Employment in Great Britain*. Princeton, Princeton University Press, 1957.

Italy

Ornello Vitali, *Aspetti dello Sviluppo Economico Italiano alla Luce della Ricostruzione della Populazione Attiva*. University of Rome, Institute of Demography, 1970.

Public expenditure (Vol. I, Chapter 8)

Belgium

Institut Belge de Finances Publiques, *Histoire de Finances Publiques en Belgique*. Bruxelles, Vol. 1: 1950, Vol. 2: 1954, Vol. 3: 1955.

Denmark

Rolf Norstrand, *De offentlige udgifters vaekst i Danmark*. Kobenhavens Universitets Okonomiske Institut, manuscript. Kobenhaven, 1975.

France

Christine Andre/Robert Delorme/G. Terny, 'Les depenses publiques francaises depuis un siecle', *Economie et Statistique*, No. 43, 1973, p. 3–14.

Jacques Edmond-Grangel, *Le Budget Fonctionnel en France*. Paris 1963.

Germany

Suphan Andic/Jindrich Veverka, *'The growth of government expenditure in Germany since the unification'*, Finanzarchiv, N.F., Vol. 33, pp. 169–278.

Otto Weizel, *Die Entwicklung der Staatsausgaben in Deutschland. Eine Analyse der öffentlichen Aktivität in ihrer Abhängigkeit vom wirtschaftlichen Wachstum*. Erlangen-Nürnberg, dissertation, 1968.

Great Britain

Alan T. Peacock, Jack Wiseman, *The Growth of Public Expenditure in the United Kingdom.* 2nd ed., London, 1967.

Ireland

Martin D'Donoghue and Allan A. Tait, 'The growth of public revenue and expenditure in Ireland'. *In* J. Bristol and A. Tait (eds.), *Economic Policy in Ireland.* Dublin, 1968, pp. 267—301.

Italy

Francesco A. Repaci, *La finanza pubblica italiana nel secolo 1861—1960.* Bologna, 1962.

Sweden

Erik Hook, *Den offentliga sektorns expansion. En studie av de offentliga civila utgifternas utveckeling åren 1913—1958.* Stockholm-Goteborg-Uppsala, 1962.

National Product (Vol. II, Chapter 5 and 6)

A) *Comparative Sources*

OECD, *National Accounts Statistics, 1950—1968.*
OECD, *National Accounts Statistics, 1965—1976.*

B) *Country Studies*

Austria

A. Kausel, N. Nemeth, and H. Seidel, 'Österreichs Volkseinkommen 1913—1963', *Monatsberichte des österreichischen Instituts für Wirtschaftsforschung,* 14. Sonderheft. Wien, 1965.

Österreichisches Statistisches Zentralamt und Österreichisches Institut für Wirtschaftsforschung, Österreichs Volkseinkommen 1954—1968', Neuberechnung, *15. Sonderheft des Österreichischen Instituts für Wirtschaftsforschung.* Wien, 1971.

Belgium

Claude Carbonelle, 'Recherches sur la evolution de la production en Belgique de 1900 a 1957, *Cahiers economiques de Bruxelles,* Vol. I, No. 3, April 1959.

Denmark

Svend Aage Hansen, *Oekonomisk vaekst i Danmark,* Vol. I: 1720—1914, Copenhagen 1972: Vol. II: 1914—1975, Copenhagen, 1977.

Finland

Eino H. Laurila, 'Suomen kansantulo vuosina 1926—1949. Ennakkoarviointien tuloskia', *Tilastokatsauksia.* No. 11—12, 1956.

Germany

Albert Jeck, *Wachstum und Verteilung des Volkseinkommens in Deutschland 1870—1913.* Tübingen, 1970.

Walter Hoffmann, *Das Wachstum der deutschen Wirtschaft seit der Mitte des 19. Jahrhunderts.* Berlin, 1965.

Ireland

G. A. Duncan, 'National Income of the Irish Free State', *Majority Report of the Commission of Inquiry into Banking, Currency, and Credit*. Dublin, 1938.

Italy

Giorgio Fuà, *Notes on Italian Economic Growth 1861–1964*. Milano, 1966.

Sweden

Karl G. Jungenfelt, *Loneandelen och den ekonomiska utvecklingen*. Stockholm 1966. Olle Krantz and Carl-Axel Nilsson, *Swedish National Product 1861–1970*. Lund, 1975.

Östen Johansson, *The Gross Domestic Product of Sweden and its Composition 1861–1955,* Stockholm University Studies, New Series VIII. Stockholm, 1967.

Olle Krantz and Carl-Axel Nilsson, *Swedish National Product 1861–1970*. Lund, 1975.

Switzerland

Ulrich Zwingli and Edgar Ducret, 'Das Sozialprodukt als Wertmesser des langfristigen Wirtschaftswachstums', *Schweizerische Zeitschrift für Volkswirtschaft und Statistik*, Nr. 3, 100. Jahrgang, September, 1964.

United Kingdom

Phyllis Deane and W. A. Cole, *British Economic Growth 1688–1959*. Cambridge, 1969.

Phyllis Deane, 'New Estimates of Gross National Product for the United Kingdom 1830–1914', *The Review of Income and Wealth*, Series 14, 1968:2.

C. H. Feinstein, *National Income, Expenditure and Output of the United Kingdom 1855–1965*. Cambridge, 1972.

SAS® System for Regression, Third Edition
by **Rudolf J. Freund**
and **Ramon C. Littell**

SAS® System for Statistical Graphics, First Edition
by **Michael Friendly**

The SAS® Workbook and Solutions Set
(books in this set also sold separately)
by **Ron Cody**

Selecting Statistical Techniques for Social Science Data:
A Guide for SAS® Users
by **Frank M. Andrews, Laura Klem, Patrick M. O'Malley,
Willard L. Rodgers, Kathleen B. Welch,**
and **Terrence N. Davidson**

Statistical Quality Control Using the SAS® System
by **Dennis W. King**

Statistics Using SAS® Enterprise Guide®
by **James B. Davis**

A Step-by-Step Approach to Using the SAS® System
for Factor Analysis and Structural Equation Modeling
by **Larry Hatcher**

A Step-by-Step Approach to Using SAS® for Univariate and
Multivariate Statistics, Second Edition
by **Norm O'Rourke, Larry Hatcher,**
and **Edward J. Stepanski**

Step-by-Step Basic Statistics Using SAS®: Student Guide
and Exercises
(books in this set also sold separately)
by **Larry Hatcher**

Survival Analysis Using SAS®:
A Practical Guide
by **Paul D. Allison**

Tuning SAS® Applications in the OS/390 and z/OS
Environments, Second Edition
by **Michael A. Raithel**

Univariate and Multivariate General Linear Models:
Theory and Applications Using SAS® Software
by **Neil H. Timm**
and **Tammy A. Mieczkowski**

Using SAS® in Financial Research
by **Ekkehart Boehmer, John Paul Broussard,**
and **Juha-Pekka Kallunki**

Using the SAS® Windowing Environment: A Quick Tutorial
by **Larry Hatcher**

Visualizing Categorical Data
by **Michael Friendly**

Web Development with SAS® by Example, Second Edition
by **Frederick E. Pratter**

Your Guide to Survey Research Using the SAS® System
by **Archer Gravely**

JMP® Books

JMP® for Basic Univariate and Multivariate Statistics: A Step-by-
Step Guide
by **Ann Lehman, Norm O'Rourke, Larry Hatcher,**
and **Edward J. Stepanski**

JMP® Start Statistics, Third Edition
by **John Sall, Ann Lehman,**
and **Lee Creighton**

Regression Using JMP®
by **Rudolf J. Freund, Ramon C. Littell,**
and **Lee Creighton**